SANTAL FOLK TALES

SANTAL FOLK TALES

(IN THREE VOLUMES)

P.O. Bodding

VOL. III

GYAN PUBLISHING HOUSE
NEW DELHI

Santal Folk Tales
(Anthropology Culture, Literature)

ISBN : 81-212-0344-9 (Set)

ISBN : 81-212-0347-3 (Vol-III)

Published in 2007 in India by
Gyan Publishing House
5, Ansari Road,
New Delhi-110 002

CONTENTS

STORIES CONCERNING JUGIS

68. Bar dhaoe rajena.[1]

Mitṭaṅ raje tahẹkana. Uni dọ rẹṅgẹć ọrẹć kọejoṅko jāhā khonko hijuḱa, uni raj dọ mitṭaṅ kicrić ar jọmaḱe emakoa are bidạ gọtkakoa.

Khange mit́ din dọ mitṭaṅ jugiye hẹćena, ar raj dọ mitṭaṅ kicriće emae kana, ar caole, dạl, buluṅ sunumko daka jọm lạgit́e emae kana. Adọ uni jugi dọe mẹnkeṭa, Cet́ noa dọm danaṅ kana? Ẹkkalte jọtọ amaḱ oṛaḱ duạr ar tinạḱ dhọn durib menaḱtam, ona jọtọge danaṅme.

Khange uni raj dọe bhabnayena, Cekatebon ạsuloḱa? Ẹnte jugi dọ noako jọtọ oṛaḱ duạr ar dhọn duribe ńam kana. Ar unkin raj ar rạnikin bujhạu baṛayena. Ar unkin rajren barea koṛa gidrạkin tahẹkana. Adọ unkin gidrạ hõkin kuliket́kina. Adọ unkin gidrạkin mẹnkeṭa, baṅma, Ạliṅ dọ cet́liṅ baḍaea? Ma abengeben jāhā lekaege.

Khange uni raj dọ uni jugiye kọelet́ leka jọtọ oṛaḱ duạr dhọn durib sẹ metaḱme disom hõ danadete aćren gidrạ ar oṛaḱ hoṛ, ponon hoṛgeko oḍok calaoena. Cet́ hõ baṅko idi toraleṭa. Kọe kọetegeko jọma, ẹnte jọm lạgit́ dọ kọetegeko ńam, mẹnkhan kicrić dọ ọrẹć cabayentakoa. Adọ rạni raje metaea, Ńẹlme, raja, aboaḱ unạḱ dhọn durib tahẹkan tulućem danketa. Nõḱọe nunạḱ harkhet nitoḱ dọ gidrạ ar alaṅ bana hoṛgebon jọmet́ kana.

Tọbẹ calaḱ calaḱte mitṭaṅ atoko tioḱketa. Adọ ona atote kọejoṅko bọlọyena. Adọ ona atoren hoṛko kuliket́koa, baṅma, Okaren

---

[1] This story was taken down by Gupinat Kisku, at the time a school-teacher at Benagaria, now employed as a kind of school-inspector in the Santal Colony, Goalpara district, Assam. The language is fluent, but shows certain peculiarities in the use of certain conjunctions and expletives (especially the use of ẹnte and metaḱme).

68. TWICE A KING[1].

THERE once lived a king; when poor people came from anywhere to beg, this king always gave them a cloth and food, before he sent them away.

Then one day a jugi[2] came, and the king was giving him a cloth; and rice, split peas, salt and oil he also gave him for his food; but the jugi said: "What is this that you are presenting me with? All your house and home, and whatever you have of goods and property, give it all to me."

The king was grieved: "How shall we support ourselves, seeing that the jugi wants all my house and home and goods and property?" The king and the queen then consulted together; and the king and the queen had two sons; so they asked these two also; but the two children said: "What do we two know? You must do whatever you like."

The king then gave the jugi in accordance with what he wanted, all his house and home, goods and property, and, you understand, his country also, whereupon he with his children and wife, all four of them, went away. They did not take a single thing with them. They got their food by begging; in this way they got what they needed; but their clothes were worn to rags. Then the queen spoke to the king: "See, O king, having so much goods and property, you gave it all away. Now you see what an amount of distress our children and we two are all suffering."

As they passed along, they reached a village and went in there to beg. The villagers asked them: "Wherefrom are you, children?

---

[2] The same as yogin, one who practises yoga, a class of acetics and religious mendicants, supposed to have obtained supernatural powers.

kanape, bacha? Ape do kicrić hõ bạnuḱtapea. Phalna naṅgrahare miṭṭaṅ sodagor menaea. Uni do reṅgeć oreć horko kicrić ar jomaḱgeye danako kana. Ma ape hõ oṇḍe calaḱpe.

Ado ona ato khon koe baṛakateko calaoena. Khange uni sodagor menae ato ạuriko tiogrege rạni do raje metae kana, baṅma, Ape do noṇḍe horrege daka hataṛtabonpe, ar iń do uni sodagor kisạ̃ṛ ṭhen iń calaḱa ar abon joto hoṛ lạgit́ jomaḱ ar kicrić iń koe ạguitabona. Ente ona atoren hoṛko lại akawat́bona, baṅma, uni sodagor kisạ̃ṛ do reṅgeć orećko ạḍi hoṛe danako kana. Onate iń hõń senlen khan, jạnić khạṭigeye emańa abon lạgit́ kicrić ar jomaḱ do.

Ona menkate rạni do uni sodagor kisạ̃ṛ ṭhen kokoeye calaoena. Ado uni sodagor uni rạni kokoeye calaoen khan, uni sodagor do uni rạni bae heć ocoae kana. Metae kanae, baṅma, Bań sen ocoama; ińgeń dohomea.

Khange uni rạni do uni sodagor ṭhen tireye saṕ ocoyen khan, uni rạni doe menkeťa, baṅma, Mit́ eṅgat apat hopon kanań menkhan, nitge ińaḱ hoṛmore emanteaḱ rog bighin janamoḱ ma! Ado uni rạniaḱ hoṛmore rog bighinge janamena.

Khange uni raj ar unkin barea gidrạ uni rạni ńel horteko mokońen khan, dakako jom baṛakate uni rạni paḱńjako calaḱ kana. Calaḱ calaḱte miṭṭaṅ gaḍage horreko ńamkeťa pereć akan. Ado ona gaḍareko paromoḱ kana. Khange unkin gidrạ do mit́ dhaote bae parom daṛeakin kana, ado miṭṭaṅkateye parometkina. Khange unkin gidrạ do mit́ dhaote bana hoṛge parom ocoḱkin ńam kana. Khange miṭṭaṅ gidrạ doe tolkedea, ar miṭṭan do ać sãoteye parom idikedea. Ado uni gidrạ hõ ona sare bae tahen kana. Khange uni gidrạ hõ ona sareye tol oṭokadea, ar uni noa sareye tol oṭo akade uni gidrạ parom idiye lạgiťe hijuḱ kan tahẽkana.

---

3 The word sodagor (from Pers. saudāgar) to a Santal stands for a kind of merchant prince.

4 So lit. It is not uncommon for a Santal to add such a qualification to a definite statement.

You have not even clothes. In such and such a town there is a merchant[3]; he is in the habit of giving poor people clothes and food. You too go there."

After having begged they left this village. Then before they reached the village where the merchant was living, the queen said to the king: "You stay here at the roadside, and prepare food in the meanwhile, while I go to the rich merchant and beg and bring food and clothes for us all. You remember, the village people have told us that this wealthy merchant gives to very many poor people. Therefore, if I too go there, he will probably surely[4] give me clothes and food for us."

With this in mind the queen went to this wealthy merchant to beg. When she had gone there to beg, the merchant would not let her come away[5]. He was saying to her: "I shall not let you go; I shall keep you."

When the queen was caught in the arm by the merchant, she said: "If am the child of faithful parents[6], now this instant may all kinds of disease break out in my body!" And several diseases broke out in the queen's body[7].

When the king and the two children became tired of waiting for the queen, they started, after they had had their food, to follow and find her. As they walked along, they came to a river, running full, and they were trying to cross this river. The father was unable to carry both children across at one time; so he was going to carry them across one by one. But the two children wanted to be carried across both at the same time. So he tied one child up, and carried the other across with him. Then this child would not stay alone on the other side either. So he tied the child up there also and was returning to carry across the child he had left tied up on the other side. Just then the king was

[5] An occurrence like this is supposed to be natural in the 'good old times'.

[6] Lit. the child of one mother-father.

[7] Cf. what the Ramayana tells of Sita.

Unrege uni raj dọe ạtuyena. Khange unkin gidrạ dọ tọlgekin tahẽyena.

. Adọ miťťaṅ mahra ạimại, uni metaḱme ato ato daheye ạkriṅ baṛaea. Khange gaḍa daḱ aṅjẹťen khan, aćaḱ atote uni mahra ạimại dọe ruạṛ hijuḱ kan tahẽkana. Khange gaḍae parọmoḱ kan tahẽkan jọkhẹn unkin gidrại ṅẹlkeťkina. Adọ unkin gidrạ hõ raḱatekin metadea, Okaren kanam, ayo? Ma raṛa idiliṅme.

Adọ uni mahra ạimại dọ unkin gidrạre mãyã hẹćadete aćaḱ oṛaḱteye raṛa idikeťkina. Ẹnte uni mahra maejiuren họpọn dọ baṅko tahẽkantaea, ona iạte unkin barea gidrạ ạḍi napaeteye dọhọyeťkin tahẽkana. Ar unkin gidrạ hõ eṅgat lekakin manaoede kan tahẽkana. Ar unkin gidrạ dọ gẹlbar sẹ gẹlpẹ bọchọr gan ọṇḍẹgekin tahẽkana.

Ar apattẹť dọ gaḍa daḱteye ạtuyen jọkhẹn latar ạḍi utạr gadel hoṛko jarwa akan tahẽkana. Ẹnte oka disomre onko gadel hoṛko jarwa akan tahẽkan, ona disomren raj dọ tisre cọe gọć akan tahẽkan. Adọ ona disomre miťťaṅ raj adọko teṅgoye lạgiť onko gadel hoṛko jarwa akan tahẽkana. Uniye gọćen disomren rajren dọ cele hõ oaris dọ baṅko tahẽkantaea, ẹkẹn uniren rạni ar barea hạtikin tahẽkantaea.

Khange uni rạni dọ aćaḱ disomren jọtọ jạtgeye họhọ ạgu ocokeťkoa, ar nonka lekae metaťkoa, baṅma, Abote raj dọ baṅbon bachaokoa. Nukin hạtige sona reaḱ sikṛibon emakina. Unkin ạkin khusite jãhãegekin horọḱae, unige raj sẹ metaḱme iṅren jãwãe hõ unigeye hoeyoḱa.

Khange aćaḱ disom jọtọ jạtkoko jarwayena ar panteteko duṛuṕena. Ono takre uni cetanrene ạtu akan raj hõ ọṇḍẹye ạtu rakaṕena. Khange uni dọ pharakreye duṛuṕena. Ẹnte gọṭa hoṛmọge emanteaḱ

[8] During the rainy season it often happens that quite small rivers are turned into raging torrents, dangerous to pass. After some hours they may again subside into peaceful streams.

[9] A woman of the Hindu caste generally called Goala, whose principal caste-occupation is the tending of cattle.

carried away by the river[8], and the two children were left there both tied up.

Now there was a cowherd-woman[9], she was selling curds in the villages. When the flooded river dried up, this cowherd-woman was coming on her way back to her village, and, when she was passing the river, she caught sight of the two children. The children also said to her crying: "Where do you belong to, mother? Please unbind us and take us away."

So the cowherd-woman felt pity on the two children, unbound them and took them along to her home. You see, the cowherd-woman had no children of her own; therefore she kept these two and took very good care of them. And the two children also honoured her, as if she were their mother. The two children stayed there for about twelve or thirteen years.

At the time when the father was carried away by the flooded river, somewhere further down a very large crowd of people had come together, the cause being that the king of the country where these crowds of people had come together, had died some time previously; and these crowds of people had come together to appoint[10] a king in this country. The deceased king of the country had absolutely no heir; he had left a queen and two elephants.

The queen ordered all the different castes of her country to come and spoke to them in this way: "We shall not ourselves choose a king; we shall give these two elephants the golden chain; on whomsoever these two of their own accord put it, he shall be king, that is to say, he shall also be my husband"[11].

So all the castes of her country came together and sat down in rows. Just at that moment the king who had been carried away by the flood higher up was also thrown up there by the flood. He sat down away from the others, because, as he was

10 Lit. (make) stand. There is no thought of choosing by vote; the choice muts depend on something outside man's will.

11 This detail is against Hindu rule. It would not be objectionable with the Santals.

dhirikore sẹ metaḱme hurutḱoregeye ạtu huruṛ akan tahẽkana. Ona iạte uni dọ pharakreye duṛuṕ akan tahẽkana.

Khange rạniye hukumketa, baṅma, Ma, hạti sona reaḱ sikṛi emakinpe. Nukin jāhāegekin hor̥oḱae, unige raje hoeyoḱa.

Khange ạṇḍiạ hạti sona reaḱ sikṛiko emadea. Khange uni dọ panteko duṛuṕ hoṛko ṭhen goṭae asẹnketa, mẹnkhan ọkọe hõ bae hor̥oḱatḱoa. Mẹnkhan jọtọ ṭạṇḍi pante akan bhor dāṛākate bae ńamletḱo khan, uni eskare duṛuṕ akan, metaḱme, ọkọe gaḍa daḱ khone rakaṕ akan, uni ṭhen sẹnkate uni hoṛgeye hor̥oḱadea.

Khange disom hoṛ ạḍi āṭko mọn dukena. Ẹnte uni hoṛ ma adọe oka disomren kan cọṅ, ar nitge gaḍa daḱ khone rakaṕ hijuḱ kana. Uni cekate adọ raje hoeyoḱa? Ona mẹnkate uni hoṛ dọ, ọnẹ hạtiye hor̥oḱade tahẽkan sona reaḱ sikṛi adọ onageko rẹć ạgukedea.

Khange mitṭaṅ haṛam hoṛe mẹnketa, baṅma, Cedaḱpe rẹje kana? Ẹnte pasẹć nui kangetabon cọe raj dọ. Alope rẹjea sona sikṛi dọ.

Khange ona tayọm uni rạniye hukumketa, Ma, adọ eṅga hạti emaepe. Nui bhala adọ ọkọe hoṛe hor̥oḱaea.

Khange uni eṅga hạtiko emadea. Khange uni eṅga hạti hõ hoṛko duṛuṕ pante akan bhor goṭae asẹn ạcurketa, mẹnkhan ọkọe hõ bae hor̥oḱatḱoa. Khange goṭa dāṛā sẹskate pạhil leka uni pharakreye duṛuṕ akan hoṛgeye hor̥oḱadea, ar suṇḍte deareye rakaṕkedea. Ar okaṭaḱ siṅghạsọnre gọćen raje duṛuṕ kan tahẽkan, ona siṅghạsọnreye duṛuṕkedea.

Khange siṅghạsọnre duṛuṕ torage uni hõṛ dọe judạ bor̥ọnena; jọtọge cabayentaea, tinạḱ gaḍare ạtuḱ jọkhẹne ghaolen tahẽkan, ar mẽṭāhā hõ judạ bor̥ọnentaea. Adọe rajena.

carried along by the flood, his whole body had been mangled and gashed on stones and roots and the like. Therefore he was sitting at a distance.

The queen then gave the order: "Now give the golden chain to the elephants. Whomsoever these put it on, he shall be king."

They gave the golden chain to the male elephant; he carried it along in front of the people sitting in rows, but he did not put it on anyone there. But when he had walked past all those sitting in rows without finding the right one, he went to him who was sitting by himself, the one who had been thrown up from the river flood, and put it on him.

The people became very grieved, seeing that this man was from who knew where, and just now he had been thrown up from the flooded river. How then should he become king? With these thoughts they forcibly took away from him the golden chain that the elephant had put on him.

Then an old man said: "Why are you taking it forcibly away from him? Who knows, perhaps this one is our king? Do not take the chain away from him."

After this the queen gave the order: "Now give it to the female elephant. Let us see on whom she will put it."

So they gave it to the female elephant. The female elephant also carried it along in front of all the people sitting in rows, but did not put it on anybody. After having walked past all, just as it happened the first time, she put it on the man who was sitting at a distance from the others, and with her trunk she lifted him up on to her back, and she put him down on the throne on which the deceased king used to sit.

The moment the man sat down on the throne, his appearance was changed; all disappeared, all the sores he had got while he was being carried along in the river; his face also was altered. So he became king.

Khangeye rajen khan, disom hoṛe neṇḍawatkoa, baṅma, Phalna dinre iṅak disomre tinạk hoṛ menakpea, jọtọge adọpe jarwaka. .Ẹnte ẹn hilok dọ mittaṅ maraṅ khelọḍge adọ hoyoka.

Adọ uni gaḍa dakteye ạtuyen uni rajren unkin koṛa gidrạ dọ uni mahra maejiu ṭhenge adọkin juạnok kana. Ar uni mahra maejiu hõ ạḍi ãṭe rẹṅgẹćgea. Adọ unkin koṛakin juạnen khankin metadea, Ẹ gọ, oṛakre dọ cetliṅ ṅama? Jãhã disomkote nalhaliṅ calaka.

Khange uni mahra maejiuye mẹnketa, Bogege, bạbu, nalhaben calak khan dọ, nalha ạguabonben.

Adọ unkin koṛa gidrạ dọ nalhakin oḍokena. Khange okare uni nawako raj akade, ọṇḍẹgekin calaoena. Khange rajkin kulikedea, Henda raja, judi jãhãn kạmi menaktam khan, ạliṅliṅ kạmikea.

Adọe kuliketkina, Cetben kạmia, sipạhiben kạmi daṛeaka?

Adọkin mẹnketa, Hẽ raja, adọ amem metaliṅ khanliṅ kạmikea.

Khange unkin dọ sipạhi kạmiye ematkina, ẹnte bakin ṅẹl ṭhike kana, nui dọ ạkinren apat kanae mẹnte. Ar uni raj hõ bae ṅẹl ṭhiketkina, aćren họpọn kanakin mẹnte dọ.

Khange oka dinko neṇḍaleta khelọḍ lạgit, ona din tioken khan, aćak disomren jọtọ jạtko ar inạ dhara dhạri disomren hõko jarwayena. Ẹnte nawa raj reak ạḍi maraṅ khelọḍ hoyok kana ẹn hilok dọ.

Khange uni kisạṛ sọdagọr hõ ẹn hilok ọṇḍẹye calak kana. Ẹnte uni jọmak ar kicrić kọkọeye sẹn, uni maejiu adọ kọkọe jọkhẹćge uni sọdagọr dọ tireye saṗkedea are metadea, Kicrić hõ baṅ emama ar sẹn hõ baṅ sẹn ocoama; iṅgeṅ dọhọmea. Ona mẹnkate tiye jọṭẹtlede khange uni maejiu dọe mẹnketa, baṅma, Dohae, Ṭhạkur! mit eṅgat apat họpọn kan khan dọṅ nitge iṅak họṛmọre rọg bighin janamoka. Khange inạ ghạṛite uni maejiuak họṛmọre ạḍi gọṭaṅ rọgge janamena.

---

12 As the ensuing events show, this happens some twelve years after what has been just told.

13 **Sipạhi** is a soldier, private soldier, messenger, watchman.

When he had become king, he fixed a day[12] for the people, viz.: "So many as you are in my country, on such and such a day all of you are to come together, because on that day there will be a great feast."

Now the two sons of the king who was carried away by the flooded river were growing into maturity staying with the cowherd-woman; and this woman was also very poor. When the two boys had grown into maturity, they said to her: "Mother, what can we get here at home? We shall go away to some country or other to earn our living."

"All right, boys," the cowherd-woman replied, "if you will go to earn your living, do so and bring what you earn here."

So the two boys went away to earn their living, and they went to where they had got the new king. They asked the king: "Listen, O king, if you have any work to be done, we should like to do it."

"What can you do?" he asked them; "are you able to do the work of a soldier?"[13]

"Yes, O king", they answered, "if you tell us to do such work, we shall do it."

So he gave them soldier-work; they did not recognize him, that he was their father; and the king did not recognize them either, that they were his own sons.

When the day that had been fixed for the feast arrived, all castes of his own country and also people from the neighbouring countries came together; you see, the new king's big feast was on that day.

Also the wealthy merchant came there this day. Now at the time when the woman had gone to beg food and clothes of him, the merchant had caught her by the hand and said to her: "Neither will I give you clothes nor will I let you go away; I shall keep you myself." When he, saying this, had touched her hand, the woman said: "Help! O Thakur! if I am the child of faithful parents, let diseases break out in my body!" And at the same moment many kinds of diseases broke out in the woman's body.

Adọ uni sọdagọr dọ uni maejiu ran ocoye lạgiťe ạguledea, ẹnte gẹlbar bọchọr khon ona rọg tahẹ̄kantaea. Ẹnte ạḍi họṛ ọṇḍẹko jarwaǩa; pasẹ onko mọtọren jãhãeko baḍae khan, khạṭigeko ran bogeyea. Goṭa disomren họṛko jarwa akan tahẹ̄kana. Adọ uni sọdagọr dọ emantenko hạḍi bạuṛikoe gọǩ idi ocoketǩoa ona khelọḍ jaegate. Khange uni sọdagọre mẹnkeťa, baṅma, Ẹ raja, iṅren miťṭaṅ họṛ menaea; rọg menaǩtaea, ona iạte pharakregeye tahẹn kana. Ma barea sipạhi baṛẹ ẹmoǩme, jẹmọn unikin họrhọye.

Khange raje mẹnkeťa, baṅma, Barea nawa sipạhi menaǩkina. Unkin sipạhi idikinme ar họrhọ ocokinme.

Khangekin calaoena. Calaokate maraṅić dọ huḍiṅiće metae kana, baṅma, Alaṅ dọlaṅ ṭuạrgea, ẹnte baba hǭ gaḍa daǩteye ạtuyena, ar ayo ma sedaerege ọnẹ sọdagọr ṭhen kicrić ar jọmaǩ kọkọeye sẹnlen, ọṇḍẹ khonge bae ruạṛlena.

Khange uni maejiu dọe bujhạuketa ar raraǩe pọrtọnketa. Adọe metaťkina, Aloben raga, ẹnte eṅgam dọṅ iṅ kangea.

Khange kạu mạu aṅjọmte uni sọdagọr dọ ạḍi ãṭe raṅgaoena. Ar raje metae kana, Ceť lekan sipạhim ẹm akawaťlea? Ọtẹ ceť cọṅ hoeyena? Ona rạniye raǩeť kana.

Khange raje mẹnkeťa, baṅma, Saṗ ạgukinpe, adọ nọṇḍẹgeṅ maǩkina.

Khange sipạhiko calaoena arko sạṗ ạguketǩina. Ar uni eṅgattakin hǭe hẹćena. Adọ hẹćkate raje kulikedea, Ceť lạgiťem họhọaťkina?

Adọe mẹnkeťa, Ceť kạu mạu hoeyoǩ kana?

Adọe mẹnketa, Kạu mạu dọ ceť hǭ baṅ. Iṅren jãwãeye tahẹ̄kantiṅa, ar aleaǩ hǭ nonka disom tahẹ̄kana. Mẹnkhan iṅren jãwãege adọ miťṭaṅ jugiye danadea, adọle kọe baṛayeť tahẹ̄kana. Jọm ma jãhã lekatele ńameť tahẹ̄kana, mẹnkhan kicrić dọ okarele

---

[14] Hadis and Bauris are two of the lowest Hindu castes.

[15] A very common way of commencing a statement among the Santals. A man may come in connexion with a matter of the greatest importance and will commence his statement by saying that the matter is of no importance (katha dọ ceť hǭ baṅ kana).

The merchant had brought the woman to be treated by physicians; for she had had these diseases for twelve years; now very many people would gather here; then perhaps some one or other among all these might know what to do, in which case they would be sure to cure her. The people of the whole land had come together, and the merchant had got different kinds of people, Hadis and Bauris[14], to carry them to the place of the feast. The merchant spoke: "O king, I have a person who is diseased; therefore she remains at a distance. Please, give two watchmen, that they may guard her."

The king then answered: "There are two new watchmen here; take these along and let them guard her."

So these two went; when they had gone there, the elder one said to the younger one: "We are orphans; our father was carried away by the flooded river; and as for our mother, when she at that time long ago went to the merchant to beg for clothes and food, she did not come back from there."

Then the woman understood and commenced to cry, whereupon she said to them: "Don't cry, because your mother am I."

Hearing the noise the merchant became very angry and said to the king: "What kind of watchmen is it that you have sent? Listen, something has happened; it is the queen that is crying."

The king then said: "Fetch both here, and I shall cut them down."

So some other watchmen went and brought the two; and their mother also came. Having arrived she asked the king: "For what purpose have you called these two?"

"What is the noise that is going on?" the king asked.

"The noise is nothing"[15], she replied. "I had a husband, and we also had a country like you here. But my husband gave it to a jugi, and we were supporting ourselves by begging. Somehow or other we were getting our food and drink, but where should we get clothes? Therefore I went to this merchant to beg for

ṅama? Ona iąte iñ dǫ nui sǫdagǫr ṭhen kicrić ar jǫmak̕ kǫe iñ sǫnlen tahẽkana. Adǫ nui dǫe sap̕ dǫhǫkidiña. Onko pǫnǫ apa hǫn dǫ hǫrreñ bągiat̕koa. Nukin gidrą dǫñ ṅam akat̕kina. Ar apattǫt̕ dǫkin laiañ kana, baṅma, gaḍareye ątu goćena.

Khange raje bujhąuket̕a, Ho, nukin dǫ iñren gidrą ar am hǫ̃m iñren kana mǫnte.

Khange uni maejiuye mǫnket̕a, baṅma, Am judi iñren jãwãe kanam mǫnkhan, tǫbǫ khan Ṭhąkur ṅutumte mit̕ bąṭi dak̕ dulaṅme, khangeñ saphak̕a.

Adǫ mit̕ bąṭi dak̕e duladea, adǫe saphayena. Adǫko tahẽyena. Mucąt̕.

69. Jugi gosãe reak̕ katha.

Ḍher dinre pąchim disom khon mit̕ jugi gosãeye hǫćlen tahẽkana, adǫ uḍi bąṛić naksae uduk̕ket̕a, hǫṛe hahaṛa ocoket̕koa. Uni dǫ nonka lekate hǫṛe hahaṛa ocoket̕koa.

Pąhil dǫ hǫć tora mit̕ṭąñ mare mat̕ oṛak̕ tahẽkana, onareye ḍerayena. Pǫ pon mãhã dǫ ać eskargeye tahẽkana, ǫṇḍǫge siñ ṅindąi duṛup̕kok̕a, ar jǫm ṅũ dǫ bako ṅǫl tiogea. Adǫ adǫm hǫṛko mǫnket̕a, Ṅindąreye jǫmet̕ cǫñ cet̕ cǫñ. Onka bujhąukate pon hǫṛko cepet̕ena, mǫnket̕ako, Ma aben bar hǫṛ dǫ siñ hǫrhǫyeben ar bar hǫṛ dǫ ṅindą. Onka cepet̕kateko dhurąuena; mǫnket̕ako, Mabon ṅǫlea, bhala tin jǫkhǫne jǫmet̕a.

[1] This story is probably a reminiscence and gives some insight into how the Santals sometimes come into contact with the jugis. It now and then happens that a man of that class comes and settles down in some place, a little distance away from people, and commences to act somewhat like here told. The writer once came across a man of this type; he had come alone, apparently without any means of subsistence, and did no work, but performed some puja daily. Before long he was considered a very holy man; people, more especially women, brought him milk and food. When I saw him, he had a fine brick building, without comparison the finest in the neighbourhood, used as a combined temple and living place. He did not look an ascetic; he had also at least one serving disciple.

clothes and food; then he took and kept me. I left all three, father and two sons, on the road. Now I have found these two children of mine; as regards their father, they tell that he was carried away by the river and died.

So the king understood, "These are my children and you also are mine."

The woman then said: "If you are my husband, then in the name of Thakur pour a cup of water over me, and I shall be cleansed."

So he poured a cup of water over her, and she was cleansed, whereupon they lived there together. The end.

69. THE STORY OF A JUGI GOSAE[1].

Now long ago a jugi gosae had come from a country to the West[2]. He showed a large number of pictures[3]; he made people marvel; this was the way in which he made them marvel.

At first, just when he came, there was an old bamboo-hut there; in this he stayed. For three or four days he lived there alone by himself; there he would sit night and day, and no one ever saw him take food or drink. Some people said: "He takes his food during the night very likely." Having come to this conclusion, four people took counsel together and said: "Now you two watch him during the day and we two during the night." Having consulted together, they set to, saying: "Well, we shall see at what time he is taking his food."

He was very sociable, permitted me to take a photo of himself and his place, and so on. Gosãe is a kind of title, used also in adressing the spirits. It is here used as a kind of honorific surname of the jugi, showing that the higher class of jugis is meant.

2 These people generally come down from up-country, north of the Ganges.

3 It is not uncommon that people of this class have pictures of scenes in the Ramayana or Mahabharata, which they show to the people with explanations.

Ado̱ sạri bạrsiń dinko ho̱rho̱kedea, me̱nkhan daka se̱ jāhānaḱ jo̱jo̱m bako sạbudlede khan, uni ṭhen jarwakate emanteaḱ kuli baṛaye reaḱko e̱ho̱p̍keťa. Ado̱ uniaḱ kathate miť bar biswạsko ńe̱lkeť khan, ado̱ toako ạgu baṛawae kana.

Ado̱ miť din do̱e metaťkoa, Kuli ar reja ńawạńpe, noa oṛaḱ iń benao aro ocokoa.

Ado̱ sạri dosar hiloḱ khange mõ̱ṛẽ turui ho̱ṛ kuliko ńam ạgukeťkoa. Ado̱ barea ḍhińkiye biť ocokeťkoa, ar iṭại halań jarwa ocokeťkoa. Ado̱ ạyup̍ khange kuṛạiko ko̱eye kana. Ado̱ kathaeye oyo po̱ṭo̱m go̱ťena, ar ceťko co̱e bakhẽṛkeť khan, uni ho̱ṛmo̱ khon bhaḍ bhuḍ poesa ńurhạyena; ado̱ onako halań baṛakate onko kuliye emaťkoa. Ado̱ onka din hiloḱ kạmiye ạcukeťkoa, ar o̱ne̱ onkakate kuṛại do̱e emaťkogea. Ar ona mať oṛaḱe jhalkao ruạṛkeťa, o̱ne̱ onkate poesae emaťkoa. — E̱ne̱ inạge habaṛa kạmi do̱; inạtege ho̱ṛ do̱ko mạluń cabayena.

E̱ne̱ ane̱ć katha do̱; ado̱ purạuena.

70. Miťṭań raj ar jugi reań.

Sedae jo̱khe̱n, kathae, miťṭań raje tahẽkana, ar uniren do̱ eae go̱ṭe̱n erako tahẽkantaea; ar onko era do̱ jo̱ṭo̱ge bạńjhigeko tahẽkana, o̱ko̱eṭaḱ hõ bako gidrạyeťkoa.

Ado̱ kathae, miťṭań ko̱ko̱e jugi o̱ṇḍe̱ raj oṛaḱteye calaoena ko̱ejoń lạgiť, ado̱ ko̱e hõko emadea. Ado̱ kathae, unre raj do̱ uni jugiye kuliyede kana, metae kanae, Henda jugi, am do̱ bhala disom daṛan ho̱ṛ kanam ar disom disom reaḱ tola mamla hõ jạnićem baḍaegea. Ado̱ miť kathań kuliyeťmea, pase̱m baḍae jāhān kan.

---

4 Naturally to make people believe that he got money by supernatural help. A pice is a quarter of an anna, one farthing in value.

70 1 The word used generally refers to legal cases, supposed to be natural in the mouth of a 'king', i. e. a big landowner.

So, truth to tell, they watched him for two days; but as they did not catch him eating rice or anything, they went together to him and commenced to ask him about this, that and the other. As they understood from what he spoke that he was trustworthy, they brought him milk.

One day he said to them: "Get me some working people, men and women; I shall let them rebuild this house."

Truth to tell, the next day they brought five or six labourers. Then he made them fix two husking-machines and set them to gather bricks. When it became evening, they asked him for their wages. Then, people tell, he suddenly covered himself up in a cloth[4], and when he had pronounced some invocation or other, who knows what it was, pice fell with a thud from his body; having collected these he gave them to the labourers. In this way he daily engaged people to work, and in this manner he gave them their wages. So he renovated the bamboo-hut and made it shining; and as described, he gave the people pice. This was the marvellous work; seeing this the people were utterly fascinated.

There, this is the story; so it is ended.

70. THE STORY OF A KING AND A JUGI.

In olden times, people tell, there once lived a king, who had seven wives, and these wives were all of them barren; not one of them gave birth to a child.

One day, people tell, a begging jugi went there to the king, to ask for alms, and they gave him also. At the same time, people tell, the king asked the jugi, saying to him: "Look here, jugi, you are a person who wanders all over the land; likely you also know the way matters[1] are managed in the different countries. There is one matter I will ask you about, perhaps you might know."

Adǫ uni jugiye mǝnkeťa, Masę ente lạilem ceť lekan katha cọṅ, adọṅ bạdae khan iṅ lạiaťmege, ar baṅ bạdae khan iṅ metama, noa dọ ọhọṅ lại daṛelema mẹnte.

Adọ raje mẹnkeťa, Acha, aṅjọmtiṅme. Katha dọ noa kana: iṅren dọ eae gọṭẹn era menaǩkotiṅa, adọ ọkọeṭaǩ hõ bako gidrạwaṅ kana, jọtọgeko bạṅjhiyena. Họpọn sãc oṛaǩ dọ menaǩtako baṅdọ baṅ, ar baṅdọ ẹnte iṅaǩ itạge mạndhuạgete baṅ ọmọnoǩ kan. Adọ masẹ noa reaǩ bean lạiaṅme. Iṅ dọ gidrạ bạnuǩkotiṅte bhabna menaǩtiṅa. Iṅ baṅ hiloǩ dọ hapẹn ọkọe rajoǩa? Iṅaǩ disom dọ hapẹn laṭoǩtiṅa. Adọ ona iạte am iṅ kuliyeťmea, oka lekatele gidrạjoṅa sẹ baṅ, sẹ ale mọtọre jãhãn dọs menaǩte bale gidrạjoṅ kana. Masẹ adọ bujkate lạialeme. Ar jọtọ rạniko hõ noakin galmarao kan katha dọko aǩṅjọm kangea.

Adọ unre uni jugiye mẹnkeťa, Noa katha dọṅ bujkeťtapea. Adọ bhẹd iṅ lạiape reaǩ dọ ceťpe emaṅa?

Adọ rajte rạniteko mẹn gọťkeťa, Jãhãnaǩgem metale, onagele ẹm daṛeama. Ale dọ ceťte khaṭọ? sanamaǩge menaǩtalea.

Adọe metaťkoa, Ma ẹṇḍẹkhan noa reaǩ ekraṛ ọlaṅpe.

Adọ kathae, rajge ona reaǩ ekraṛe ọlkeťa, dọstọkhọtaťteye emadea are metadea, Ma lạime.

Adọ unre jugiye mẹnkeťa, Iṅ dọ disom, sẹ hạti sadọm, sẹ ṭaka poesa, noako dọ ceťge baṅ hataoa. Iṅ dọ jãhãeṭaǩ rạnige lahate koṛa gidrạko janamkoa, uni gidrạ dọ ạikhạ iṅpe emaṅa; uni gidrạ dọ iṅgeṅ hataoea, ar tayọmtenko dọ aperenge. Ẹnẹ inạge iṅ dọpe emaṅa. Ma adọ ceťpe metaṅ kana?

Adọ jọtọ rạnikoe bujhạu baṛakeťkoteye metadea, Acha, male emama.

Adọ unre jugiye mẹnkeťa, Acha, ẹṇḍẹkhan gidrạjoṅ reaǩ bhẹd iṅ lạiape kana, onka leka adọpe kạmia. Sunibar hiloǩ dọpe teke sọbọdoǩa, um naṛkanape, ar bere hạsurena mẹnkhan, mạci

² A peculiar kind of soapy clay, used especially for the purpose here mentioned, from which the name (naṛka means to shampoo one's hair with clay).

The jugi replied: "Well, first tell what kind of matter it is; if I know, I shall tell you, and if I don't know, I shall say so to you, that I am unable to tell you."

"Very well", the king said, "hear what I have to ask. The matter is this: .I have seven wives, and none of them is giving me a child; they are all barren. Whether their body is in order or not, or whether the fault is with me, I cannot say, but I get no children. Please explain this matter to me. It is my grief that I have no children. When some future day I shall be no more, who will be king? My country will some day be usurped by strangers. Therefore I am asking you in which way we may get children, or wether there is any fault among us, that we do not get children. Please consider this and let us know." And all the queens were listening, when they had this talk together.

The jugi then answered: "I have understood what is the matter with you. What will you give me for telling you the remedy?"

The king and the queens at once said: "Whatever you say, we shall be able to give you. What are we in want of? we have everything."

"In that case", he said to them, "give me a written agreement of this."

So the king, people tell, wrote him an agreement, signed it, handed it to him and said: "Now tell."

The jugi then said: "Your country, or elephants or horses, or money, — of this kind I am not going to take anything. Whichever of the queens first gives birth to a child, mind, this child you are to give me; I shall take this child away with me, and those who come afterwards they are 'yours. This is what you are to give me. Now what have you to say to me?"

Having explained it to all the queens and heard their opinion, the king said to him: "All right, we shall let you have it."

The jugi then said: "All right, in that case I am now telling you how you are to get children; you must act in the following way. On Saturday you shall boil and wash your clothes, bathe and wash your hair with soap clay[2]; when the sun sets, do not

ar parkomko do alope joteda, ar ńindą hõ en hilok do otrepe gitića. Ar en hilok do era herel alope jopoteta; ona bąrić kąmi khon en hilok ńindą dope pharak akan tahena. Arhõ dosar hilok setak do beretkate ekkalte umokpe calaka joto horge. Ar um rakapkate ul bagwantepe calaka, ado ul jo thopape ńela, okatak thopare eae goten jo menaka, ona thopa do leṅga tite capat topak godme ar gamchare ataṅ godme, otre alom ńũr ocoaka. Ado joto hor orakte hijukpe, ar heckate joto rąniko pantete durup ocokom. Jemonem ńam akatkoa, temonge durupkom; pąhiltenić do lahare, ini tayomić do laha talare, onkam durupkoa, ar huḍiṅ utąrić do tayomre. Ar mimit gotenem cal idiakoa. Ado onage jom pąhilpe, enkhante jãhãnak dope joma. Ar am do one rąnikoko hoyo giḍikak coklaktetem joma; joto bam jomre hõ, sanam horak mimit kuṭrąm jomtakoa. Ado ona jomle aneć mąci se parkomkore dope durupa, ar jãhãnakpe jom ńũia, ar era herel rit motpe kąmia. Ado enḍete eneć ape dope gidrąjoṅa, ar baṅkhan jonomre hõ ohope gidrąlekoa. Ado ma ene anaṅ bhed do. Senak khan gidrąpe ńamkoa, ar bape senak khan do, ohope ńamlekoa. Ado inąge katha do. Iṅ do kalom nonka jokheniṅ hijuka, unreṅ ńel idipea seṅ hiri idipea.

Ado enka menkategeye bereten khan do, raj do ṭakae ńamkette mõṛẽ ṭaka jugiye cupuṭadea, ado uni jugi do onḍe khone calaoena.

Ado ona tayom raj ar rąni doko dhokak kana, menetako, Oko baḍae, baṅdo sąri kan baṅdo baṅ. Ado bąrsiṅ pe mãhã onkako dhokak·kan tahẽkana.

Khange mit din do uni bąṭki rąniye menketa, Mabon onka gelaegea; bhalabon biḍąulege, pasere pase sąri kange; pase gidrąbon ńamkoge.

---

[3] In Santal medicine the left hand is frequently used. See writer's Studies in Santal Medicine and connected Folklore, p. 151. Memoirs, Asiatic Society of Bengal, Vol.X.

[4] A sentence addressed to the 'queens'.

[5] Something against all rules. A wife may eat what has been left by her husband, but not vice versa, not to mention what has been thrown away and no one ever eats.

touch stools or bedsteads, and that night you shall sleep on the ground; and this night you must remain away from each other. Then again next morning, as soon as you get up, you shall all of you at once go and bathe. Coming up from the bath, you shall go to the mango garden and look at the mango fruit clusters; the cluster that has seven fruits, throw something at this with your left hand[3], so that it breaks and comes down; receive the fruits in your cloth; do not let them fall down to the ground. Thereupon all of you go home, and when you have come back, make the queens sit in a row. In the order you have got them, so let them sit; the first one in front, the one thereafter next, and so on you shall let them sit; the youngest one last. Thereupon you shall hand them each one fruit, and this you[4] shall eat first, after this you may eat anything. And as for you, the rind that the queens peel and cast away, this you shall eat[5]; if you do not eat all of it, you must anyhow eat a bit of what each one throws away. Only when you have eaten this, you may sit down on stools or bedsteads, and eat and drink whatever you like, and live as married people. Only by acting in this way you will get children; otherwise you will never get children. Now there you have the explanation. If you follow it, you will get children, and if you don't, you will certainly never get any. This is what there is to it. Next year at this time I shall come here again; then I shall look you up, that is to say, I shall visit you."

When he, after having spoken in this way, stood up to go, the king brought some money and gave the jugi five rupees into his hand, whereupon the jugi went away from there.

Afterwards the king and the queens were in doubts and said: "Who knows whether this is true or not"; and they harboured doubts of this kind for two or three days.

Then one day the first queen said: "Let us anyhow have a try; well, let us test it, perhaps it might be true; perhaps we might get children."

Adọ sạri raj hõ uniaḱ kathae aṅjọmkeṫteko onkakeṫgea. Adọ kathae, uni raj dọ sanam hoṛaḱ hoyọ coklaḱe jọ̃mkeṫa, mẹnkhan uni huḍiṅ utạrić rạni reaḱ coklaḱ dọ bae jọmleda, ẹnte uni dọ ḍher dọ bae dulạṛede tahẽkana.

Adọ kathae, tahẹn tahẹnte inạ mõṛẽ turui cando khangeko ńẹl oromkede dọ, uni huḍiṅ utạrić chuṭki rạnigeye lakhaoena. Khange raj dọ mọnẹ mọnẹteye mẹnkeṫa, Durrẹ! ọkọeṭaḱ nĩhạt iṅ metadea, unige asọle hoeyena. Khange tayọmte dọ jọtọ khon unige bạṛtiye dulạṛkedea.

Khange noko bạṭki rạniko dọ uniko kurudadea arko mẹna, Ceṫ baṅ, raj, uniyem dulạṛede kan? Mẹnkhan uni gidrạ ma hapẹn jugigeye idiyea, unrem kastaoḱa.

Adọ kathae, duṛuṕ din tioḱentae khan dọ, barea utạr koṛa gidrạgeye janamkeṫkina jawatege. Khange raj dọ ạḍiye rạskạyena, mẹnkeṫae, Marańić jugiye idiye khan, huḍińić thọ ińrengeye hoeyoḱa. Adọ onka mẹnkate jọtọ hoṛte uni huḍiṅ gidrạ dọ ạḍiko dulạṛea.

Adọ kathae, bọchọr purạuen khan, uni jugiye hẹćena. Adọ kathae, ạḍiko peṛakedea. Adọ unkin gidrạ hõe ńẹl baṛa idikeṫkinteye ruạṛena. Are mẹn oṭokaṫa, Nukin gidrạkin cacolen khan arhõṅ ruạṛ hijuḱa.

Adọ kathae, unkin gidrạkin ńir kẹṭẹćen khan dọ arhõe hẹćena, adọ unre hõko peṛakedea. Adọ unreye mẹnkeṫa, Cele adọ ińaḱ pạtiạu biswạspe ńẹlkeṫa thọ. Adọ dẹ bhala ceṫpe metaṅ kana? Gidrạ dọpe emaṅ kana sẹ baṅ?

Adọko mẹnkeṫa, Ceṫle mẹna, pạhilre onkagebon katha akaṫ khan? Adọ amaḱ sana.

Adọ uni jugiye mẹnkeṫa, Ińaḱ sana dọ nukin gidrạṅ idikina.

Adọ raje mẹnkeṫa, Banar dọ cedaḱem idikina? Miṭṭaṅge cọm mẹnleṫ.

---

[6] Lit. 'sitting day', the general Santali term for what is here referred to.

[7] Caco is the name for the first attempts of a child to walk or toddle; ńir kẹṭẹć, lit. running (being) strong, is the term used about children that have learnt to move freely about. Both terms are used instead of giving the age.

And, truth to tell, as the king also listened to what she said, they acted accordingly. And the king, people tell, ate the rind that they all had peeled off; but he did not eat the rind peeled off by the youngest queen, because he did not love her much.

As time passed, people tell, after some five six months, they saw the youngest co-queen, she became visible. The king then said to himself: "Strange, the one that I held in contempt, she has become the real one." And thereafter he loved her more than all the others.

Then the elder queens hated her and used to say: "What can it be, O king, that you find to love in her? Why, the jugi will some day carry this child away; then you will be sorry."

When the day of her confinement[6] came, people tell, she gave birth to not one, but two sons, twins. The king became very pleased and said: "If the jugi takes the elder one away, the younger one will, of course, be mine." As they were having such thoughts, they all of them loved the younger one very much.

When the year was completed, people tell, the jugi came; and they treated him very well. He also looked at the two children, whereupon he went away, saying as he left: "When these two children have learnt to walk[7], I shall come again."

When the two children, people tell, had become strong enough to run about[7], he came again; then also they feasted him. This time he said: "Well, now you have seen what it is to believe in me. So then what have you to say to me? Are you going to give me the children or not?"

"What shall we say?" they replied, "seeing that we have previously made such an agreement. It is as you please."

The jugi then said: "It is my wish to take these two children away with me.

"Why will you take both with you?" the king said. "Why, you said only one."

Adǫ jugiye mẹnkeṫa, Baṅ, nukin gidrạ dǫ banar iṅrenge, ẹnte miṫ dhaoregekin janam akan dǫ. Acha, banargeṅ idilekinge. Adǫ nukin mǫtǫre miṫ hǫṛ dǫṅ ạgu ruạṛkakina. Idikate gun iṅ ceṫakina. Ar ape dǫ alope bhabnaḱa. Ńẹlpe, jǫtǫ hǫṛge adǫpe gidrạjoṅa.

Adǫ unre raj dǫe mẹneṫa, Ǫkǫ bạḍae, baṅdǫko hoeyoḱ baṅdǫ baṅ. Mẹnkhan gidrạ ńẹl gǫṫkakin dǫ baṅ jut ạikạuḱ kana. Ma nukin bakhra dǫ bon kol gǫṫakina.

Adǫ kathae, uni jugiaḱ ńutumko kulikedea, celeama mẹnte. Adǫe lạiaṫkoa, Iṅ dǫ Sitạṛi jugi.

Adǫ unkin bakhra mẹrǫm bhiḍi, ũṭ gadha, hạti sadǫm, ṭaka kạuḍi, thạri bạṭi, jǫtǫko kolaṫkina, adǫ uni jugiye idiyeṫkina.

Adǫ kathae, calaḱ calaḱte mẹrǫm bhiḍi dǫ gujuḱko pǫrtǫnkeṫa, ẹnhõ uni jugiaḱ oṛaḱge baṅ tiogoḱ kan. Adǫ unre unkin gidrạkin raḱeṫa:

Chagǫl muri muri jaye, gǫ baba;
Kạti durire, baba, Sitạṛi jugikera des.

Bheṛ muri muri jaye, gǫ baba;
Kạti durire, baba, Sitạṛi jugikera des.

Arhõ calaḱ calaḱte gadhako gujuḱ kana, ar ẹkẹ ẹkẹte jǫtǫgeko gǫć idiḱ kana, ar sẹ uniaḱ oṛaḱge baṅ tiogoḱ kan. Adǫ onkage jǫtǫko õṛhẽ idiḱa; jẹmǫnko gǫć idiḱ kana, tẹmǫngem sereṅ idiyeṫa:

Gadha muri muri jaye, gǫ baba;
Kạti durire, baba, Sitạṛi jugikera des.

Ũṭ muri muri jaye, gǫ baba;
Kạti durire, baba, Sitạṛi jugikera des.

Ghoṛa muri muri jaye, gǫ baba;
Kạti durire, baba, Sitạṛi jugikera des.

Hạti muri muri jaye, gǫ baba;
Kạti durire, baba, Sitạṛi jugikera des.

---

[8] The following verses are in Hindi.

"No", the jugi replied, "both these children are mine, seeing that they were both born at the same time. All right, let me first take both away with me. Afterwards I shall bring one of them back again. Taking them away with me I shall teach them magic. As for you, don't worry. See, now you will all of you get children."

"Who knows", the king said, "whether there will come any or not. But it does not feel well to say good-by to the children. Anyhow, let us send the share belonging to these two children along with them."

Thereupon they asked the jugi what his name was, and he told them: "My name is Sitari jugi."

As the portion of these two children they sent along with them goats and sheep, camels and donkeys, elephants and horses, money, brass-plates and cups, all this; and the jugi took the children away.

As they passed along, people tell, the goats and sheep commenced to die; still they did not reach the jugi's home. The two children then cried[8]:

Die Ziegen sind gestorben, o Mutter, o Vater;
Wie weit weg, o Vater, ist des Jugis Land?

Die Schafe sind gestorben, o Mutter, o Vater;
Wie weit weg, o Vater, ist des Jugis Land?

As they were passing further along, the donkeys were dying; one after the other they were all dying, and they did not reach his home. In the same way they mention them all in song; as they are dying, so you sing:

Die Esel sind gestorben, o Mutter, o Vater;
Wie weit weg, o Vater, ist des Jugis Land?

Die Kamele sind gestorben, o Mutter, o Vater;
Wie weit weg, o Vater, ist des Jugis Land?

Die Pferde sind gestorben, o Mutter, o Vater;
Wie weit weg, o Vater, ist des Jugis Land?

Die Elefanten sind gestorben, o Mutter, o Vater;
Wie weit weg, o Vater, ist des Jugis Land?

Adǫ jẹ kichuko kolaťkin tahẽkana, onko dǫ hǫrrege miť miťte bebakko gǫć cabayena, tǫbẹ anẹć uni jugiaǩ disom ar oṛaǩ dǫko tioǩketa, adǫ ǫṇḍẹko tahẽyena.

Adǫ dinge guni mantare ceťakina. Ar guni mantar dǫ ạṛhạí kạligea, ẹkẹn khaṭǫ khaṭǫgea. Ar mimiť gǫṭẹn kaṇḍaye kiriń akawaťkina. Ạyup jǫkhẹn dǫ mantare ceťakina, ar setaǩ jǫkhẹn dǫe metakina, Do calaǩte sisir daǩ koṭaete noa kaṇḍare dul pẹrẹjben, tǫbẹ ena guni reaǩ bhẹd dǫben ceť daṛeaǩa.

Adǫ dinge setaǩrekin calaǩa, adǫ koṭa baṛaetege bere rakaṗlen khange sanam aṫ cabayenge. Oka dǫ miť bạṭi gan oka dǫ tala bạṭi gan, nenkakin koṭa ńama.

Ar ona disomre dǫ uni jugi kangeae raj dǫ. Ar ona disomren dǫ sanamge guniko ceť akaťa, ar sanam hǫṛgeko metakina, Ma kurumuṭuiben, aloben ạṛisoǩa; aben hõ hapẹn guni dǫben cedgea.

Adǫ kathae, tahẹn tahẹntekin sẽṛãyen khan dǫ, guni mantar dǫ jǫtǫkin ceťketa, mẹnkhan daǩ loge bakin daṛeaǩ kana. Khange, kathae, cekakote cǫń uni huḍińić gidrạ dǫe hudisketa, bańma, Nonkate khan nãhãǩ iń pẹrẹć gǫda. Adǫ kathae, daǩ lokin calaǩ jǫkhẹnge uni huḍiń hǫṛ dǫ miťṭań gẹndrẹće oko idijońa. Adǫ sẹn torage ona gẹndrẹć dǫ sisirreye laṭpaṭao lǫhǫda ar kaṇḍareye bǫḍǫja. Onkate, kathae, uni do miť ghạṛitegeye pẹrẹć gǫda.

Ar uni marańić dǫ noa bhẹd dǫ bae baḍaeyeťtaea, ar uni hõ bae lạiae kana, iń dǫ nonkateń lo pẹrẹć gǫteťa mẹnte dǫ. Adǫ kathae, uni dǫ bae pẹrẹć daṛeaǩ khan dǫ, darha daǩteye dul pẹrẹćketge are idiketge. Adǫ idikate bana hǫṛaǩe ńẹl baṛaetakina, adǫ unregeye metaea, Am dǫ, marań bạbu, jǫtǫ dǫ ǫhǫm ceť

9 Most magic (among the peoples to whom is here referred) is 'performed' or accompanied by mantras. The writer has hundreds of these; they are generally short rigmaroles with invocation of some godling and mentioning the object.

10 Dew plays some rôle in Santal medicine, obviously on account of its mysterious appearance. The instruction here given has apparently the aim to test the wits of the learners. The tenses used in the Santali text here and in several places below show that the narrator refers to a customary practice.

Whatever they had sent along with the children, all the animals, every one of them died; then only they reached the land and home of the jugi; so they remained there.

The jugi was in the habit of teaching them magic mantras[9] daily. Now the magic mantras are two and a half verses, they are all short. He had also bought one waterpot for each of them. In the evening he taught them mantras, and each morning he said to them: "Now, go out and fill this waterpot by shaking dew[10] into it! only by doing this you will be able to master the real meaning of magic."

Every day they went; but in spite of shaking, when the sun rose, it was all lost. Sometimes they had about one brass-cup full, sometimes about one half, so much as they might get by shaking.

Now the jugi was the king of this country; and in this country all people had learnt magic, and all people were saying to them: "Be diligent; don't get tired; you two will also some day learn magic."

As they stayed there and grew into maturity, they learnt all the magic mantras; but they were unable to fill the pot with water. Then, people tell, somehow or other the younger child had a thought, viz. "If I do it in this way I shall be able to fill the pot quickly." So when they, people tell, went to fetch water, the younger one secretly took a cloth-rag with him; and as soon as he had reached the place, he rolled the rag in the dew and soaked it, whereupon he squeezed the water out in the pot. In this way he would fill the pot in a moment.

The elder brother did not know how the other did it, and his brother did not tell him either that he was filling his pot in such a way. And as the elder one was unable to fill his pot, he, people tell, poured it full with water from a pool and took that home. When they had brought it, the jugi looked at what both had; and he would say[11] to him: "As for you, you big boy, you will

11 A daily utterance.

daṛelea, enka thoṛa thuṛi dom cedgea, ente am do bam lo peṛeć daṛeak kan do. Ado uni koṛa do cet hõ bae mena, thirkokgeae.

Ado kathae, tahen tahente uni huḍinić do khube cetketa. Uni jugiak cet cabakate gate koṛako ṭhene cetkette uni jugi khon hõe sorosena. Ado sanam bhedkoe lai baṛawatkinte side atań ocoketkina. Adoe metatkina, Delabon mit dhao abenren ayo babatekobon hiri ạgulekoge.

Ado onka menkate, kathaeye ạguketkina. Ado uni jugi doe ńeletko do, sanam rạnikogeko gidrạ baṛa akawan. Khange ạdi rạskạteko daramketkoa, ado ạdiko peṛaketkoa. Ado unre jugiye menketa, Ma nui marań koṛa doń ạgukadea, ar nui huḍiń koṛa do ińgeń hataoedea.

Adoko metadea, Bań, am do marań koṛage idiyem, ale do huḍińićge.

Adoe menketa, Bań, ińge uni do.

Ado unre uni huḍiń gidrạ do eńgat ṭhene menketa, Acha, ayo, iń khan ińge idi ocoae; arhõ iń doń ruạṛ hijukgea.

Ado kathae, uni huḍiń gidrạgeye idikedea, adokin calaoena arhõ ona jugi disomtege. Ado kathae, disomte guknikin oḍokena ar nui hõe koṛayena. Ado kathae, uni gidrạ doe sadom oco gode kana ar khub bandhar sadome ńelok kana. Ado bajarte idikate mit sae bar sac ṭakateye ạkriń godea, ar ona joṛa baber do bańgeye emakoa. Khange ruạṛkate ać doe ḍerakoka, adoe ceka god coń, kathae, ona joṛage, ado uni koṛa hoṛ lekateye hećenge uni jugi ṭhenge. Ado onka, kathae, uni koṛa doe baro pheṭea; ghane do merom khạsikateye ạkrińea, ghane do bheḍa khạsikateye ạkrińea, ghane do khub gạḍi ḍańgra lekateye ạkrińea, ar ona

[12] When a disciple is deemed sufficiently instructed to be able to act independently, the guru gives him his s i d, initiation, final instruction, generally combined with some kind of sacrificial worship and symbolic act. One kind of s i d, that given by an ojha to his disciple, will be found described in the writer's 'Studies', p. 61 ss.

never be able to learn all; you will learn a little somehow; you see, you are not able to fill the pot." The young man would not say anything; he kept quiet.

"Now, people tell, the younger one, as time passed, learnt a lot. After having learnt all the jugi knew, he also learnt from his companions and became even superior to the jugi. After having told them both the interpretation of all, the jugi made them both receive the final initiation[12], whereupon he said to them: "Come along, let us go and for once pay your parents a visit."

Having decided on this, he brought them there; and the jugi saw the queens had got children. They received them with great joy and feasted them well. On this occasion the jugi said: "Now I have brought the elder boy; but the younger one I shall keep."

"No", they said to him, "you take the elder one with you; we shall keep the younger one."

"No", he replied, "this one is for me."

Then the younger one spoke to his mother: "All right, mother; if me, let him take me away; I shall come here again."

So, people tell, he took the younger boy with him, and they again went to the land of the jugi. Thereupon, people tell, they went out in the land to practise magic, and the jugi also became a young man. Now, people tell, he would turn the child into a horse, and he looked like a fine stallion. Thereupon he would take him to a town and sell him for one or two hundred rupees; but the halter he would never give them. Returned, he would himself camp somewhere; then he would do something or other, people tell, with the halter, and the young man would come in human shape to the jugi. In this way, people tell, he would turn the boy into a dozen[13] different shapes; sometimes he would sell him after having made him into a goat; another time he would sell him after having turned him into a ram; again he would

[13] Lit. 'twelve shapes', the number not to be stressed.

joṛa do̠ baṅgeye emakoa. Khange, kathae, uni koṛa do̠ arhõ̠ uni jugi ṭhengeye he̠ćenge.

Ado̠ onko kikriṅko do̠ko ńe̠l baṛakoa, Durre̠! kiriṅkate ne̠ṇḍe̠geń to̠lledea, ado̠e okayena? Ado̠, kathae, ko ńam baṛako khan do̠, uni jugi hõ̠e eṭak̕ pheṭ go̠dok̕a, bako ńe̠l orom.daṛeaea. Nonkate, kathae, ạḍi baṛićkin ṭakaea, ar dinge onka eṭak̕ eṭak̕ bajarte se̠nkate ho̠ṛkin e̠ṛe̠ mõ̠ńjkoa.

Ado̠ onako bhe̠d ar targhar hõ̠ jo̠to̠e cet̕kettaea. Mit̕ din do̠e me̠nket̕a, Iạ, baba, teheń do̠ bhala am pạriń ḍaṅgrametalaṅa, bhalań ṭhik daṛekea se̠ o̠ho̠. Bań ṭhik daṛeak̕ khan do̠, lại bhe̠daṅme. Iṅiń cet̕le khan, am do̠ pho̠ko̠t o̠ho̠ hoelentama. Iṅiń rojgar ạguitalaṅa; am do̠ cedak̕em haro̠nok̕a? Am do̠ duṛup̕kate jo̠mjoṅme.

Ado̠ sạri onkae metade khan, kathae, uni jugi hõ̠e pạtiạuenteye me̠nket̕a, Acha, ma e̠ṇḍe̠khan nãhãk̕ iṅiń ḍaṅgrak̕ kantalaṅa, ar am do̠ jo̠no̠mre hõ̠ ona joṛa do̠ alom emakoa, ar baṅkhan topak̕ topak̕ak̕te joṛa idiṅme. Arko koeme khan metakom, Noa do̠ topak̕gea, noate do̠ o̠ho̠pe idi daṛelea, se̠ bań emako reak̕ jãhãn ạṇḍuń katha ro̠ṛme, e̠nrehõ̠ joṛa do̠ alogem emakoa. Ado̠ ạkriṅkate ḍeratem calak̕a, ado̠ ona ḍerare joṛa do̠ nonka onkaeme ar nonka bakhe̠ṛme, khangeń ho̠ṛ go̠dok̕a.

Ado̠ kathae, uniye ḍaṅgra ocokedete inạ hõ̠e cet̕ket̕a. Ado̠ arhõ̠e metae kana, Henda baba, pase̠ joṛa do̠ń emat̕koge, ado̠ cekate to̠be̠ń ho̠ṛok̕a? Ar pase̠ iń sãore o̠ko̠e hõ̠ bako tahe̠n, ar unregeń ḍaṅgralen khan, cekateń ho̠ṛ ruạṛok̕a?

Ado̠ uni jugiye me̠nket̕a, Acha, beṭa, ma niạkoge cet̕ hataṛme, ona do̠ tayo̠mreń cet̕ama.

sell him like a fine cart-bullock; but the halter he would never give them. And the boy, people tell, would always again come to the jugi.

And those who bought would look for their animals, saying: "Strange, I tied him up here; what has become of him?" And when they were searching for them, the jugi also would at once take another shape, so that they were unable to recognize him. In this way, people tell, they made a lot of money, and, going daily to different towns, they fooled people.

The boy too learnt all these tricks and methods of his. One day he said: "I say, father, to-day I should like to try to make you into a bullock, I wonder whether I shall be able to do it correctly or not. If I am unable to do it properly, tell me the proper way. If I learn, it should certainly not be without remuneration for you. I shall work and earn money for both of us; why should you be troubled? You sit quiet and enjoy your food."

Truth to tell, when he spoke to him in this way, the jugi also, people tell, was convinced and said: "All right, then I shall presently turn myself into a bullock; but never on any account give them the halter; or else lead me along tied with a torn rope; and when they ask you for this, say to them: 'this is torn; you will not be able to take him along with this,' or tell them any pretext for not giving it to them; in any case don't give it to them. Having sold me, you will go to where you stay; and there do so and so to the halter, and make such and such an incantation; then I shall at once become a man again."

So, people tell, by turning him into a bullock he learnt this also. Again he said to him: "Look here, father, suppose I gave them the halter; in that case how should I become man again? And suppose there should be no one together with me and I then became a bullock, how should I become man again?"

"Well, my son", the jugi replied, "learn these things for the present; afterwards I shall teach you this."

Ado̱ uni gidrạye me̱nket'a, Henda baba, cedak' onka do̱m me̱net'a? Cet', amren gidrạ do̱ń bań kana? Nun din jāhānak' iń kuliket'mea, onagem lạiadińa, bam ạṇḍuńlet'a; ar noań kuliket'me khan do̱m ạṇḍuńket'a. Ado̱ń bujhạuket'a, noa do̱ bań cet'ań reak' katha kana, ar amak' goṭa mo̱nte do̱ bam dulạṛedińkana. .

Ado̱ uni jugiye me̱nket'a, E̱ beṭa, mase̱ am do̱ nịako baṛe̱ kạmi hataṛme. Ma hape̱n ona hõ̱ń cet'amgea.

Ado̱ cet' hõ̱ bae ro̱ṛ ruạṛlet'a uni koṛa do̱, ado̱ mo̱ne̱regeye do̱ho̱kat'a. Ado̱ kathae, inạ dosar tesar khange uni koṛa do̱ ako atoren se̱ uni jugiak' nańgraharen ać'ren gate koṛako ṭhene cet'ket'a, ar onko ṭhenge ona do̱e biḍạu baṛa aṭkarket'a.

Ado̱ arhõ̱ mit' din do̱e metae kana, Ma baba, o̱ne̱ e̱n hilok' iń metat'me, ona bhe̱d do̱ cet'ańme.

Ado̱e metadea, Hape̱ se̱, cet'amge do̱ń. Bejāeyem ạkutok' kan do̱.

Ado̱ onkan co̱rco̱ṭań lekan kathae ańjo̱mket' khan do̱, mo̱nre hasokedeteye me̱nket'a, Baḍaeket'ań, bam dulạṛedińkana me̱nte. Iń do̱ bań tahe̱na am ṭhen do̱. Ińren ayo babateko ṭhen iń ruạṛ calak'a.

Ado̱e metadea, O̱ṇḍe̱m ruạṛ khan do̱lań go̱ć giḍikama.

Ado̱ uni koṛae bo̱to̱rente inrege uni samań khone dạṛ go̱t'ket'a. Ado̱ kathae, uni jugi do̱e tạrup' go̱t'ena are khudạukedea. Khange uni koṛa do̱e baḍae go̱t'kede khan do̱e parwa go̱t'ena. Ado̱ khange uni jugi do̱e ṭirmuṭi go̱t'enteye lagayede kana. Khange uni koṛa do̱e ro̱ go̱t'ena. Khange uni jugi do̱e bakḍulu go̱t'enteye lagayede kana. Khange uni koṛa do̱e lańgayen khan, mit'ṭań rạni dakae jo̱jo̱m kan tahẽ̱kana. Ado̱ uniak' ona thạrireye ap'ena. Khange bakḍulu ma bako sor ocoae kan.

Khange uni jugi do̱ bakḍulu khon do̱e ho̱ṛena, ado̱e ko̱ko̱e jugiyena. Ar uni rạniye metae kana, Ma ona thạri daka do̱ racare e̱rańme.

---

[14] A small hawk, the Tinnunculus alandarius.

[15] Several kinds are fairly common.

"Look here, father", the child said; "why are you speaking thus? How, am I not your child? Any time up to now when I have asked you about anything, you have told me; you have not excused yourself; but when I asked you this, you excused yourself. Consequently I understand that this is a matter that I am not to be taught, and you do not love me with your whole heart."

The jugi then replied: "Son, you do these things in the meanwhile. Some time in the future I shall teach you this also."

The boy did not say a single word, but he kept this in his mind. But a couple of days afterwards the boy learnt the thing from his companions living in the same village, that is to say, in the town of the jugi, and with these he tried and tested it.

Again one day he said to him: "Father, you remember what I said to you that day, teach me how to do that."

"Wait", he replied, "I shall teach you; you are very impatient."

When he heard such a gruff speech, it pained him and he said: "I understand, you do not love me. I shall not stay with you. I shall return to my parents."

"If you return there", he said to him, "I shall kill you and throw you away."

Then the boy became afraid and at that very moment he fled away from him. The jugi, people tell, then took the shape of a leopard and chased him. When the boy became aware of this, he at once changed himself into a pigeon, whereupon the jugi at once changed himself into a hawk[14] and pursued him. So the boy suddenly changed himself into a fly, whereupon the jugi changed himself into a dragon-fly[15] and pursued him. When the boy became tired, there was a queen taking her food, and he alighted on her plate. And you see, they did not let the dragon-fly come near.

Thereupon the jugi changed himself from a dragon-fly into a man and became a begging jugi. He said to the queen: "Please, strew the rice on your plate out for me in the court-yard."

Khange, kathae, uni rąni dǫ dakae ęr jǫkhęn uni rǫ dǫ thąri khon ucąṛente uni rąni hǫṭǫk̓re pãola malae hǫṛǫk̓ akat̓ tahẽkana. Khange uni koṛa dǫe pãola mala gǫt̓ena. Ar uni jugi dǫ bae ńęl ucąṛledea, uni dǫe pãola malayena męnte dǫ. Ać dǫe parwayente rąniye ęrlet̓ak̓ daka dǫe halaṅ jǫmket̓a. Adǫ bae ńamlede khan dǫ, arhǫe jugiyena. Adǫ ǫntę nǫtęye bęṅgęt̓ baṛaket̓ khan dǫe ńęl ńamkede dǫe pãola mala akan. Adǫ uni rąniye metae kana, Ma ona am hǫṭǫk̓re menak̓ pãola mala dǫ racak̓ topak̓kate racare ęraṅme.

Khange rąni dǫe edreyenteye metadea, Ohǫṅ racak̓ topak̓lea. Daka hõm ęr giḍi ocokidiṅa, bam jǫm ocoadiṅa, arhõ noam ńam kana?

Adǫ onkakin rǫpǫṛ kan khan dǫ, raje aṅjǫmket̓ khan dǫ, uni jugiye ruhet̓kedea. Adǫ unre uni jugi dǫ aćak̓ jǫtǫ kathaye ląi aṅjǫmat̓koa. Ar uni koṛa dǫ onakoe ląiako kanregeye męnet̓a, Nit judiye parwalen khan, iṅ dǫṅ pusi gǫdok̓a.

Adǫ kathae, uni jugi dǫ onakoe ląi mucąt̓ket̓ khan, dǫe pątiąu ocoket̓kote ona pãola mala dǫe racak̓ topak̓ ocoket̓koa. Adǫe metat̓koa, Ma sutąm khon bǫjte racare ęr gǫt̓kape.

Adǫ sąri sutąm khon bǫćket̓te raca sęnko ęr jǫkhęnge uni dǫe dǫn ucąṛ gǫt̓enteye pusi ąṇḍią gǫt̓ena. Ar nui dǫ jęmǫnge raca sęnko ęr gǫt̓kat̓a, tęmǫngeye parwa gǫt̓ente ona mala dǫe halaṅ jǫmet̓a.

Adǫ un jǫkhęnge uni pusi dǫ, kathae, piṇḍą latarreye chapkao akan tahẽkana, adǫ ać sęnak̓e halaṅ jǫmet̓ tahẽkan jǫkhęnge, kathaeye ota gǫt̓kedeteye gęr gǫćkedea ar bahreteye ątkir oḍokkedea. Adǫe hǫṛente uni parwa dǫ sap̓kate hǫṭǫk̓e pęṭęr topak̓ket̓taea, ar bǫhǫk̓ dǫe gochaket̓te hǫr hǫrteye hijuk̓ kana.

---

[16] The **pãola mala** is a necklace of beads generally made from lac, used only by women.

When the queen was strewing out the rice, people tell, the fly flitted from the plate; now the queen had on her neck a necklace of coral-beads[16], and the boy turned himself into a coral-bead. The jugi did not observe that he flitted and became a coral-bead; and he himself changed into a pigeon and picked up and ate the rice that the queen had strewed out. As he did not find him, he again became a jugi. Looking round here and there, he caught sight of him, that he had changed into a coral-bead, and said to the queen: "Please tear off the coral-bead necklace that you have on your neck and strew the beads out for me in the court-yard."

But the queen became angry and said to him: "I shall certainly not tear it off. You made me strew away my food; you did not let me eat; and again you want this."

When they were having words together in this way and the king heard it, he scolded the jugi, whereupon the jugi told them his whole story. While he was telling them this, the boy said: "If he turns himself into a pigeon, I shall now at once become a cat."

When the jugi, people tell, had finished telling his story, he made them believe it and made them tear off the coral-bead necklace; he said to them: "Pull the beads off the string and strew them at once out in the court-yard."

Then, truth to tell, when they had pulled the beads off the string and were strewing them out in the court-yard, the boy at once flitted away and became a tom-cat; and no sooner did they strew the beads out in the court-yard, at the same moment the jugi turned himself into a pigeon and commenced to pick up and eat the beads.

At this time, people tell, the cat was quietly crouching below the veranda; and when he was eating the beads that had fallen in the boy's direction, he suddenly, people tell, pounced upon him, bit him and killed him, whereupon he ran outside with him. Thereupon he changed into a man and catching the pigeon he twisted its neck and tore the head off; and putting this in a fold of his cloth he was coming along the road.

Adǫ kathae, hijuk̕ hijuk̕te tin sạṅgiṅ hǫr cǫe hẹćen, adǫ kathae, tayǫm sẹne bẹṅgẹt̕let̕ dǫe ńẹlket̕, uni jugi bǫhǫk̕ dǫ hǫr hǫrte ać sẹn guḍrạu hijuk̕ kan. Khange adǫe dạṛ idiyet̕a.

Adǫ kathae, cekakote cǫe hudisket̕, mẹnket̕ae, Pasẹ noa bǫhǫk̕ iń gocha akat̕tege jugi bǫhǫk̕ dǫ guḍrạu hijuk̕.kan. Adǫ kathae, mit̕ṭaṅ kamar hǫr aṛerege kuilạye jẹrẹt̕ akat̕ tahẽkana. Khange ona parwa bǫhǫk̕ dǫ, kathae, ona sẹṅgẹlreye capat̕ khadle gǫt̕kat̕a. Adǫ kathae, ona jugi bǫhǫk̕ hõ ona sẹṅgẹlrege guḍrạu bǫlǫyente lǫ rǫṅgǫyena. Ar uni kọṛa dǫ eṅgat apat oṛak̕te calaoente noako jǫtǫ kathae lạiket̕a. Adǫ bogeyena.

Ẹnẹ cabayena.

71. Jugi bhǫr reaṅ.

Sedae jugre, kathae, mit̕ṭaṅ ạḍi dhǫrǫm maejiue tahẽkana, ar uni maejiu ṭhen dǫ cet̕ko lạgit̕ cǫṅ hǫṛ hõ uḍiko jaorak̕a ar ajare hǫṛ hõ uni ṭhen ạḍiko sẹnok̕a, ar hǫṛko hõ sẹ deko pusi hõ uni dǫ ạḍi bhage maejiuko metaea. Ar uni maejiu reak̕ gun dǫ nonka tahẽkantaea, kǫe teṅgonkoe emako anẹć ać dǫe ǫn jǫlǫk̕ kan tahẽkana. Adǫ din hilok̕ kǫe emankoe ẹm pạhilakoa, adǫ ẹṇḍẹkhan khulạsate ać hõe jǫma.

Adǫ onakate tahẹn tahẹnte tin din badre cǫṅ mit̕ din dǫ nonka, kathae, hoeyena, baṅma, ẹn hilok̕ dǫ kǫe teṅgon cele hõ onko oṛak̕te dǫ bako sẹnok̕ kana. Adǫ khange uni maejiu dǫ ńẹl hǫrteye mǫkǫṅok̕ kana; rẹṅgẹćedete ghạṛi ghạṛi ǫntẹ nǫṭẹye bẹṅgẹt̕ baṛayet̕a; adǫ oka sẹn khon hõ bako ńẹlok̕ kan. Adǫ tikinok̕ kan khać, kathae, ṭukućre taben tahẽkana; adǫ bar aṅjle gan, kathaeye gochaket̕a, ar dạṭạuni ńamkate kaṇḍae hẹrmẹt̕kẹt̕a, adǫ ać mǫnẹreye mẹnket̕a, Dak̕ lo ghaṭre noa taben dǫ nãhãk̕ jãhãe iṅ emakoa, adǫ

---

[1] A common name with the Santals for the Hindus, not very respectful.

Then, people tell, as he was coming along, who knows how far he had come, he looked behind and saw, the jugi's head was coming rolling along the road towards him. And he started running.

Then, people tell, somehow or other a thought struck him; he said: "Perhaps it is because I have put this head in a fold of my clothes that the jugi's head comes rolling along." Now, people tell, a blacksmith had made a charcoal-fire at the roadside, and he threw the pigeon's head at once into this fire; whereupon the jugi's head also rolled into this fire and was burnt to cinders. The boy then went to his parents' home and told all this. And all was well.

So there it is ended.

71. THE JUGI'S BLESSING.

Once upon a time in a former age, people tell, there lived a very righteous woman; for some purpose or other, who knows what, lots of people were in the habit of coming together at this woman's place, and people who go about gossiping also constantly went to her; and both Santals and Deko cats[1] called her a very good woman. Now this woman had this quality: only when she had first given those who stood there begging, she would herself take food and drink. Every day she would first give beggars and others; thereupon she herself would take her food cheerfully.

As time passed, who knows how long a time had passed, then, people tell, it one day happened that not a single person that day came and stood begging at their house. The woman was just giving up waiting; she felt hungry and was again and again looking in all directions; but nowhere was anybody to be seen. When it was becoming midday, — there was some flattened rice in an earthen pot, — she took, people tell, about two double handfuls in a fold of her cloth, and having found a tooth-brush twig, she took a water-pot under her arm and said to herself: "At the place from where they fetch water I shall presently give onko ẹmkateń dạṭạuni hijuk̕te iń hǫ̃ń jǫma, ar bańkhan dǫ cekateń jǫma?

Adǫ onka hudiskate dak̕ ghaṭṭeye calaoena; adǫ kaṇḍae dǫhǫe jǫkhange miṭṭań jugi gosãe ać sẹnge hijuk̕ kane ńẹl ńam gǫt̕kedea. Khange adǫ ạḍiye rạskạ gǫt̕ena. Adǫ hẹć sẹṭẹr torae mẹn gǫt̕ket̕a, Enan khon, gosãe, amgeń ńẹl hǫret̕mea; hẹćge bam hẹć hǫdok̕ kan.

Adǫ uni gosãeye mẹnket̕a, Iń hǫ̃ teheń dǫ am ṭhenge hijuk̕ reak̕ iń paetar akat̕a; onate teheń dǫ setak̕ khon iń hijuk̕ kana, adǫ tiok̕ge bań tiok̕ hǫt̕ daṛeam kana.

Adǫ uni maejiue mẹnket̕a, Acha bogege, iń ṭhenem hijuk̕ kante iń hǫ̃ ạḍiń khusiyena. Adǫ nǫ̃k̕ǫ̃e am lạgit̕ taben iń ạgu dara akawat̕mea, adǫ nẹ iń emama.

Adǫ kicrińe aṭẹt̕ket̕a, adǫ onareye raṛawadea. Adǫ unre uni jugi gosãeye mẹnket̕a, Ẹ gǫ, kathae, iń dǫ am bhǫram lạgit̕ iń hẹć akana; adǫ nǫṇḍẹgelań ńapamena. Adǫ ma bhǫr kǫeyeńme. Okaṭak̕em ńam kana, onageń emama — ạikạ miṭṭańge kǫeyeńme, hajar gǫṭẹn dǫ alo.

Adǫ unre uni maejiue mẹnket̕a, Iń dǫ nonkan bhǫr emańme, gǫćkate jivi dǫ okate calak̕ kantabona, ar gujuk̕ jǫkhẹć cet̕ lekate oḍokok̕ kana, ar oka hǫrte, mũ khon sẹ moca khon, ar oḍokkate oka sẹn gǫdok̕ kana — ona ńẹl orom reak̕ bhǫr iń dǫ emańme. Ar iń tis iń gujuk̕a, ar unre ińak̕ jivi dǫ okate calak̕a, ona lạiańme; inạge bhǫr dǫ, ar bạṛti dǫ bań ńam kana.

Adǫ khange uni jugiye mẹnket̕a, Kǫe dǫm kǫekidińa, ar bhǫr hǫ̃ń bhǫramgea; mẹnkhan ạikạ ǫkǫe ṭhen hǫ̃ alom lạị baṛaea; arem lạile khan dǫ noa bhǫr am ṭhen bań tahẹna.

Adǫ unre uniye rǫṛ ruạṛket̕a, Ǫhǫń lạia.

Adǫ uni jugi aćak̕ thạilạk̕ khon miṭṭań cele il kan cǫń, bań ńẹl ṭhikok̕a, onkan ile oḍońket̕a, ar ona ilte uni maejiu reak̕ mẹ̃ṭe gasaoket̕taea, ar dak̕teye ap̣ ocokedea. Khange adǫ uni maejiuak̕ somebody this flattened rice; and after having given them this I shall brush my teeth and have some food I too; otherwise how shall I be able to take food?"

Having thought this, she went to the water-place; then, just as she was putting her water-pot down, she suddenly saw a jugi gosae coming towards herself, and she at once became very glad. As soon as he reached there, she said: "For a long while I have been waiting for you, my lord; you are very late coming."

The gosae said: "As for me, I have been advised by the oracle that I should come to you to-day; therefore I have been on my way to-day since morning; but I have been unable to reach you earlier."

"All right", the woman replied, "since you are coming to me, I am very pleased. And see, I have brought flattened rice with me for you; here, I shall give you."

He spread out his cloth on the ground, and she let the rice fall down on the cloth. Then the jugi gosae, people tell, said: "Mother, I have come to bless you; now we have met here, so ask me for a blessing. What you ask for, I shall give you; however, mind, ask me for one thing, not for a thousand."

Then the woman said: "Give me a blessing like this: after death where our souls go, and how the soul passes out at the time of death, and by which way, through the nose or through the mouth, and where the soul straightway goes after it has passed out, — give me the blessing to be able to see this. And tell me when I shall die and where my soul then will go; this is the boon, anything more I do not want."

The jugi then replied: "You have asked me, and I shall certainly also grant you the blessing; but mind, don't tell it to anybody; if you tell, this blessing will not remain yours."

"I shall certainly not tell," she said.

The jugi then took a feather out of his bag, some kind or other, it was not to be quite identified, such a feather it was; with this feather he brushed the woman's eyes and made her wash them with

mę̃t marsal gǫṭentaea, adǫ boṅga, bhut, ḍạn, cuṛin, gǫć hǫṛko, saname ńęl ńamketko.

Adǫ uni jugiye mẹnkeṭa, Nǫ̃kǫ̃e, adǫm ńęl ńamketkoa; mẹnkhan alom bǫtǫroḱa ar onko tuluć dǫ alom galmaraoa, baṅkhan hǫṛko bheao bǫtẹćkema; ar onko tulućem galmarao khan, nãhãḱ kuṅkiko metama, adǫ onka mẹnkate jǫtǫko bǫsṭǫetama. Ma, adǫ inạḱgeń galmaraoam kana. Noako katha disạ dǫhǫeme, adǫlaṅ apan ạpinoḱa.

Adǫ uni maejiue mẹnkeṭa, Dela teheń dǫ ale ṭhenge tahẹnme, peṛalemgele.

Adǫ uni jugiye mẹnkeṭa, Baṅa, calaḱ kanań. Arhǫ̃ teheṅge miṭ hǫṛ ṭhen calaḱ hukum menaḱtiṅa, onate ape ṭhen dǫ bań peṛaḱ kana. Ma hapẹn jãhã hiloḱ peṛaḱ dǫń hẹćapegea.

Adǫ enka galmaraokatekin apan ạpinena. Adǫ uni maejiu dǫ daḱe lokeṭte oṛaḱteye hẹćena. Ar uni maejiu dǫ pẹ pon gẹlẹ gidrạ eṅgat hǫṛ kanae, ar metaḱme cij bạsut hǫ̃ besge menaḱtakoa, ar hǫṛ hǫ̃ khubko saṅgegea, ar jǫtǫ bhạyạdi ńatea miṭrege menaḱkoa, ar ać hǫńhar hanhartikin hǫ̃ menaḱkingea.

Adǫ khange tahẹn tahẹnte tin din cǫṅ hoeyen, ona dǫ ǫhǫń mẹn daṛelea; mẹnkhan miṭ din dǫ nonka hoeyena, baṅma, ona ako atorege miṭṭań rẹṅgẹć hǫṛe tahẽkana. Adǫ unkin haṛam buḍhi dǫ din hiloḱge hǫṛ ṭhenkin kạmi nalhajǫṅa, ar hǫṛ hǫ̃ dinge unkin dǫ ceṭko cǫṅ kạmi lạgiṭko ạcukina, ar unkin hǫ̃ ạcu toragekin rẹbẹn gǫdoḱa, huć hućkin chuṭạuḱa, bakin kẹṭẹćaḱa. Adǫ onkate unkin hǫṛ dǫ ạḍiko khusiakina, ar jãhãnaḱ reaḱ hǫ̃ unkin dǫ bakin oṭ itạṭaḱa. Onka lekate unkin kuṛạì hǫ̃ oka hiloḱ oka hiloḱ dǫ bạṛtigeko emakina, ar oka dǫ bin sǫṅtege haṭaḱteko uṗ gǫṭakina; adǫ onkate onko dǫko ǫn jǫloḱ kan tahẽkana.

---

[2] The beings here mentioned are, besides the spirits of dead people, boṅga, a spirit or godling, bhut, the spirits of children who have died without having had chạṭiạr performed with them, i. e., without having been given the full rights of a member of the Santal society, and also the spirits of stillborn children; ḍạn, a witch, always a woman; cuṛin, the spirits of women who die pregnant.

water. Then the woman's eyes were opened to see, and she could see bongas, spirits, witches, goblins[2], dead people, all of these.

The jugi then said: "There, now you have seen them; but don't be afraid, and don't talk to them; otherwise people might find you out; and if you talk to them, people will think you mad, and thinking this they will spoil all for you. Now, this is what I have to say to you. Keep these things in remembrance; now we are to part."

The woman said: "Come, stay with us to-day; let us entertain you before you go."

"No", the jugi replied, "I am off; I have an order to go to yet another person to-day; therefore I cannot pay you a visit to-day. But some other day I shall certainly come on a visit to you."

After having had this talk, they parted. The woman drew water and went home. Now the woman was the mother of three or four children; besides they had plenty of food and property; they were also a numerous household; all the brothers with their wives were living together; the woman's parents-in-law were also living there.

Now time passed, who knows how long a time, I am quite unable to tell; then one day the following came to pass. In their village a poor man was living. He and his wife were in the habit of daily working with people to earn some money; and people also every day were employing these two to do some work or other; and they on their part were always at once willing, as soon as they were asked; they set to work energetically; they made no difficulties. In this way all people were very pleased with them; and these two never harboured ill-will for anything. On account of this, people also now and then gave them as wages more than was due to them, and sometimes they would pour rice out to them with a winnowing-fan[3] without measuring. In this way these two were supporting themselves.

---

[3] The Santals use the winnowing-fan as an approximate measure to get a rough idea of the amount of grain that is put in a rice-bundle. To give away like here is to show the opposite of stinginess.

Adọ ceka lekate cọṅ ruạ ńamkedete mit́ din dọe gọć darpoṛena, uni rẹṅgẹć haṛam dọ. Khange adọ unre uni maejiu dọe ńẹlket́koa, uni haṛamak̓ jivi iditae lạgit́ khuṛkhuṛiante bọṛko hẹćena, ar ạḍi rajan bhajanate uniak̓ jiviko idikettaea. Adọ uniak̓ jivi onkako idikettaete uni maejiu dọ ạḍiye khusiyena, ar ać mọnẹreye mẹnwana, sanam hoṛak̓ jivige cele gọćkate dọ nonkageko tul idiyettalea mẹnte. Adọ onka mọnẹre bujhạukate ạḍi khusiye ạikạua. Ar noa jiviko tul idiket́ ghoṭna uniye bhọr akawade maejiu chaḍa cele hõ bako ńẹlleta ar cele hõ bako baḍaeleta sẹko aṅjọmleta; mẹnkhan uni dọ saname ńẹl gọtkata.

Adọ onakate tin din badre cọṅ, kathae, adọ ać họṅhartet́ haṛame gọćena. Adọ, kathae, unre uniye ńẹlkedea, baṅma, ponea sipạhiko hẹć gọtena. Onko dọ mẽṛhẽt́ khạrcạṛi ṭheṅga menak̓takoa, ar goco dọ ạḍi jhạltakoa, ar bọtọrgeko ńẹlok̓ kana.

Adọ, kathae, barea dọ oṛak̓tekin bọlọ gọtena, adọ họṅhartet́ dọ totkare sapkatekin dhaklao oḍokkedea. Adọ racate oḍokkate mẽṛhẽt́ khạrcạṛite bogeteko sọbọk̓kedea, ar tọlkate bogeteko dal idikedea. Adọ uni maejiu dọ onkogeye takao akat́koa, adọ atra dhur sẹn ńõk̓kateye ńẹlet́koa. Khange adọ baṛge mucạt́ko tiok̓ket́ khan dọko dal gitićkedea. Adọ bae calak̓ kante jaṅgareko pạsikedea, adọ sirgạtteko ọr idikedea.

Khange adọ onkae ńẹlkede khan, ạḍi bạṛić bọtọre ạikạuketa, ar ọkọe dalkede leka kạuạ rạuạ kạhu kuṛit́ lekae rak̓keta. Adọ khange uni maejiue mẹnketa, Cedak̓ cọṅ noa bhọr dọṅ hataoket́? Nõk̓õe iṅ ńẹlkedete bạṛićge sanaṅ kana. Adọ onkae rọṛeta are rak̓eta.

Adọ khange onko ako oṛak̓ren hoṛ dọ nui upạrte ạḍi bạṛićko edreyena, arko mẹnketa, Jẹ ṭhen mạṛī menak̓, ọṇḍẹ dọ bae rak̓leta; adọ baṛge latarre sẹnkate dọ cedak̓e rak̓eta? Nuige baba dọe jọmkedea.

---

4 With the Santals it is the fever that catches a person, not the other way that a person catches a fever.

5 The khạrcạṛi is a thick stick used for assuring that the grain is rightly packed in the straw-bundles.

6 'Eat' is the term. techn. for killing by witchcraft.

Then in some unexplained way one day a fever caught him[4] and he died, the poor old man. At this time the woman saw people coming with a palanquin to carry the old man's soul away; and with great pomp and music they carried his soul away. As they carried his soul away in such a style, the woman was very pleased, and she said to herself: "When we die, they likely carry the souls of all of us away in this manner." With this thought in her mind she felt very pleased. But what happened when they carried this soul away, no one saw except the woman who had received this blessing; no one else knew or heard of it; but she saw it all, when it happened.

Some time afterwards, who knows when, people tell, her father-in-law died. On this occassion, people tell, she saw what happened to him, viz., four soldiers suddenly came. These had an iron rammer[5]; they had long beards and were looking appalling.

Two of them, people tell, at once entered the house, and taking her father-in-law by the neck they pushed him out; when they had brought him out to the court-yard, they again and again thrust him with the iron rammer, and, having bound him, they beat him awfully. The woman was watching these, and, following them a short distance, she looked at them. When they reached the end of the homestead-field, they beat him so that he fell down; and as he could not go, they put a noose round his legs and dragged him along, legs first.

When she saw him treated in this way, she felt awfully frightened, and just as if somebody were beating her, she screamed like a crow or a kite. Then the woman said: "Why, O why did I receive such a blessing? Now see, I saw him and am feeling utterly bad." She was speaking in this way and crying.

Then the people of the family became very angry with her and said: "Where the body is, there she did not cry; but why does she go beyond the homestead-field and cry there? She has eaten father."[6]

Adọ ako bhạyạdi ạḍiko kạphạriạuena. Adọ uni maejiuren hẹrẹltẹte mẹnkeťa, Ẹ ya, teheń dọ inạǩge rọṛeńpe, jẹpe rọṛkeťa, inạtegeń bujhạukeťa. Adọ nui gọćen họṛ reaǩbo kaj kọrọmlege, ẹnkhante iń reaǩbo bicạrtińa. Adọ nuiren apat baret hõ nitoǩ dọ nọṇḍẹ bạnuǩkoa; tahẹn khanko nitgebo galmarao gọťkea; galmarao torageń hẹsẹ gọťkea. Adọ bạnuǩkoteń metape kana, ma nitoǩ dọbo thir hataṛoǩa. Nui họṛ thọ nit dọ ọhọe jivẹť daṛelea.

Adọ onkae galmarao baṛawaťkote sanam họṛko thir baṛayente ato họṛko raǩ jaoraketkote adọ sahan sẹṅgẹlae lạgiť apat haṛamko gọǩ oḍoń idikedea. Adọ jalaoe ṭhen idikateko sahan sẹṅgẹladea. Adọ ọṇḍẹ hõ uni maejiu reaǩgeko ẹhọṗkeťa; adọ ọṇḍẹ hõe mana baṛaketkoa. Khange adọko thir baṛayena.

Adọ ạyuṗen khange oṛaǩre hẹćkate ato họṛ lagaete uni ạimạiko kulikedea, Ceť iạte murdạr bạgi oṭokate am dọ baṛge latarre sẹnkate dọm raǩeť tahẽkana, ona lạime; ar bańkhan am dọ khạṭige ḍạnle metam kana. Amge nui haṛam dọm jọmkedea?

Adọ unre maejiu dọ uni jugi ceťkoe lạiadea, ar ceť lekae bhọradea, onako jọtọ kathae lạiaťkoa. Ar nui haṛam reaǩ jivi ceť lekateko idikeťa, onae lạikeť khanko pạtiạuena, adọko ikạkadea. Adọ un khon uni hõ bọsṭọyentaea, adọ bae ńẹl ńamleťa.

Cabayena katha dọ.

---

[7] When a woman is accused, especially of any serious matter like here, it is the custom to call her natural guardians, father and brothers, whoever may be found, to watch her interests.

[8] The word is mostly used about cutting the branches of a tree.

The brothers had a great quarrel, and the husband of this woman said: "I say, you, let it be enough with scolding me to-day. What you have spoken, has been enough to make me understand. Let us now perform the rites and ceremonies in connexion with our dead one; when this is done, we shall investigate my case. Her father and brothers are not here[7] now either; if they were here, we might now at once talk the matter over; and as soon as we had had our talk, I should at once have slashed[8] her head off. But as they are not here, I tell you, let us now keep quiet so long. In any case we are not now able to bring him back to life."

When he had talked to them in this way, they all became quiet, and, having called the village people together, they carried their old father out and away to cremate him; and, having taken him to the place of burning, they cremated him. There also they commenced to talk about this woman, and there also the husband warned them; and they became quiet.

When it became evening and they had come home, they asked the woman with the assistance of the village people: "Why did you leave the corpse and went beyond the homestead-field and were crying there? Tell this; otherwise we are surely calling you a witch. Did you eat this old man?"

Then the woman told them what the jugi had told her, and how he had given her a blessing, all this. And when she had told them how they had carried the old man's soul away, they believed her and let her alone. But from this moment her gift was spoilt; she did not see the spirits any more.

The story is ended.

72. Jhades jugi reaṅ.

Sedaere, kathae, mitṭaṅ haṛamren eae goṭen koṛa hopoṅko tahẽkantaea. Ado unkin haṛam buḍhikin bindaṛen khan, kathae, noko koṛako do bako kạmia, cas basko bạgiketa, mĩhũ merom, sim sukri, bebakko ạkriṅketkoa, ar daka jom hõko bạgiketa. Urni birre oṛakkette dinge noko do sendrako daṛana, ar ona sendrareko goćkoa, inạ jel jomtegeko tahena. Ar joto hoṛko ḍạṅguạgea; ar onkoak do inạ sendragetako dandha do, ar inạ chaḍa-dosra do cet hõ bạnuktakoa.

Ado tahen tahente tinạk serma badre coṅ, kathae, onko ṭhen boṅga kuṛi baṅdo cele kuṛi upeloke portonketa. Joto khon uni huḍiṅ utạrić koṛare noṅjor bajaoentaea. Ar mone monetegeye menketa, Nui koṛa ṭhen doṅ bolokgea. Ar se noko do ona reak nam cintạ cetge bako ror baṛaea, ar noko do uni kuṛi hõ bako ńel akadea.

Khange uni kuṛi do ać monre hudiskate noko gitić oṛakre eae bakhra daka, ạuriko hijukrege, idikateye hạrup oṭokata. Khange ạyubok okte noko koṛako do oṛakteko hećena, ado oṛakre bolokateko ńelket do, eae bakhra dakako utukoko hạrup akat. Adoko meneta, Aboren ma ạimại hõ bạnukkotabon. Celeye dakakette noa doe hạrup akata, ar dạl caole hõ okareye ńamketteye isinketa? Abo ma cetge bạnuktabo. Noa do amdajok kana, aboko goć ocobon lạgit. Alope joteda, pase cekka. Noa katha do marañiće menettakoa.

Arhõ huḍiṅić doe meneta, Bhalaṅ jom gelaea.

Adoko metae kana, Dhut! alom joma; cele reak kan coṅ, ar jojom sanayede kana.

---

[1] The mode of living here described may possibly appeal to the Santals; they are hunters and love hunting.

[2] It is not said so, but the portions must have been placed on separate leaf-plates.

[3] Lit. 'cooked rice'; daka is, however, constantly used for food in general, rice being their principal food at the present day.

72. JHADES JUGI.

In olden times, people tell, there lived an old man, who had seven sons. When the old people died, people tell, these sons did no work; they left off cultivating their fields; their cattle, sheep and goats, their fowls and pigs, they sold all; they also gave up eating rice. They built a house in the primeval forest and every day went hunting, and what they killed while hunting, this flesh and nothing else was their food[1]. All of them were bachelors; their only care was this hunting of theirs, and besides this they did not care for anything.

Then, as time passed, it happened after who knows how many years, people tell, that a bonga girl, or perhaps she was another kind of girl, commenced to show herself to them. Her eyes fell especially on the youngest one of the brothers, and she said to herself: "I shall go in to this young man." Now these brothers had absolutely no knowledge of this and did not speak of such matters at all, and they had not seen this girl either.

The girl then having turned this matter over in her mind carried seven portions[2] of food[3] to the house in which they were sleeping, put it down there, before they returned, covered it up and left. Towards evening the young men returned home, and entering their house they saw that somebody had left and covered up there seven portions of rice and curry. They then commenced to say: "Why, we have no women; whoever then has prepared food and covered it up here? and where did she get split peas and rice, so that she might cook? We have absolutely nothing. It is, may be, that somebody wants to cause our death. Don't touch it; it might perhaps cause harm." The eldest one of them was saying this.

On the other hand the youngest one was saying: "I wonder, I shall like to try to eat it."

The others then said to him: "Faugh! don't eat it; who knows whose it is? and this one wants to eat it!"

Adoe mẹnkeťa, Acha, tọbẹ, họntẹń giḍi dapoṛkaǩa. Adọ onka mẹnkateye samṭaoketa, adọ jọtọ bakhra unigeye jọm cabaketa ọntẹ bahre sẹnre dọ, ar noko ṭhen dọ bae lạiyeťa.

Adọko gitić baṛayen khan, nui huḍińićtako dọ bẹbạṛiće uduret kana. Khangeko mẹneťa, Henda ya, nui dọe cekaǩ kan ba teheń dọ? Khange adọko ḍhakakedege arko ruhet baṛakedege. Adọ inạ ghạṛiye thirenge, arhõ onkageye udura. Khange arhõko ḍhakayea, ona dọ ẹnre hõ bańge cabaǩ kantaea. Bhala uni dọ khube jọm bi akan khan dọ udur bańkhane cekaea? Adọko hudisketa,· Henda ya, bhala pasẹć, ya, ona dakae jọmket? Dhora onageye jọmket cọń cet cọń. Nui dọ eṅgateye gọć utạroǩa. Adọ ṭhelao beretkedeteko kulikedea, Henda ya, pasẹ ona dakam jọm akat? Adọ kathae, cet hõ bae rọṛleťa, arhõe oyo pọṭọmenteye gitićena. Adọko bujhạuketa, jọmketgeae. Adọ onko turui hoṛ dọko bhabnaǩ kana, Nui dọe oka lekaǩ cọń, gujuǩ cọe cet cọń.

Adọ kathae, bestegeko aṅga hạṭińena, bae cekalena. Arhõ sendrako calaoena. Adọ sendra birre khange thọ bogete daǩ tetańede kan. Adọko metae kana, Am dọ ya holanoǩ ona cele daka cọm jọmketa, onatege daǩ dọ tetańetmea.

Adọe mẹneťa, Bań, iń dọ bań jọm akaťa; ona daka ma bahreteń oḍok giḍikat. Tãhã uni dọe amọl akante daǩ dọ tetańede kana. Adọ ẹntẹ besgeko tahẽ ạyuþena.

Adọ oṛaǩre hẹćkateko ńẹlket dọ, tala oṛaǩre eae bakhra dakako hạruþ akat. Adọ uni marań họṛgeye rọṛettakoa, Durrẹ! teheń hõ ya cele hạruþ oṭoatbona. Adọ, kathae, ẹn hiloǩ dọ bar họṛtekin jọmketa, uni huḍińić ar huḍiń talaićtekinge, ar noko dọ bako

[4] The word means any temporary derangement of the stomach combined with acidity.

"All right", he replied, "in that case I shall throw it away over there and have done with it." Saying this he took it up and away, whereupon he ate up and finished all the portions there outside; but he did not tell the others.

When they had lain down to sleep, this youngster of theirs was snoring extraordinarily. So they said: "I say, what ever is the matter with this one to-night?" So they gave him a push and scolded him; then he stopped for a short while, and again he commenced snoring in the same way. Again they pushed him, yet this snoring would not stop. Now you see, when he had eaten so much, what would he do else than snore? So it struck them: "I say, you fellows, I wonder, you, perhaps he has eaten that food? To be sure, he did that, who knows whether he did not. Dash it, he will die utterly." Whereupon they pushed him and made him rise and asked him: "Look here, you, perhaps you have eaten that food?" He did not reply a word, people tell; he only covered himself up in his clothes and went to sleep. They consequently understood that he had really eaten it, and those six ones were anxious, thinking: who knows what will happen to him? he will as likely as not die.

But, people tell, they passed the night well; nothing happened to him. So they again went hunting; but while hunting in the forest the youngster was constantly feeling great thirst, and they said to him: "You fellow, yesterday you ate that food whose ever it was; therefore you are now suffering from thirst."

"No", he replied, "I have not eaten it; why, I threw that food away outside." As a matter of fact, he had a fit of dyspepsia[4] and was suffering from thirst from this cause. Anyhow they stayed well until evening.

When they reached home, they saw, in the middle of the house somebody had left seven portions of food covered up. The eldest one of them said: "Dear me, to-day also, you fellows, somebody has covered this up and left it for us." That day, people tell, jọmleťa ẹn hiloƙ dọ. Khange kathae, iną dosar hiloƙ hõ onkageko hąruṗ akať. Adọ kathae, ẹn hiloƙ dọ pẹ hoṛteko jọmkeťa, enko hupṭićkoge. Khange marańićtako dọe mẹnkeťa, Ią, ya, gapa dọ apege sendra dọ calaƙtabonpe, iń dọ bań calaƙa. Iń dọń tãṛãƙtabona, bhalań ńẹlea, celeye ąguabon kana. Abo dọ bẹgọr kąmi hoṛ ąjgute mãyãwabon kan dọ. Ńamle khan dọń sabetabona, iną dọ sọdọrteye dakawabona. Ar ińaƙ bakhra dọ nãhãƙ ągu daraetińpe.

Adọko mẹnkeťa, Acha, ma ẹṇḍẹkhan tãṛãƙtabonme.

Adọ kathae, ańgayen khan uni dọ bae sẹnlena sendra dọ, enkogeko calaoena. Adọ kathae, tãṛãƙ akan tulućge tinre cọń daka dọe ągu oṭokať, bae ńẹl hẹćledea. Adọ ąyuṗ jọkhẹnko ńẹleť kan dọko hąruṗ akať. Adọko metae kana, Cele dada, saṗledeam sẹ bań?

Adọe mẹnkeťa, Bań yań saṗ daṛeadea; tinre cọe ągu oṭokať, bańgeń ńẹl ńamledea. Ar iń dọń mẹnleťa, Kuṛi kan khane, dọhọkeabo. Onkań mẹnleťa, mẹnkhan iń ṭhen dọ bae sọdọrlena. Adọe mẹnkeťa, Gapa dọ ya phalna, am tãṛąƙtabonme, pasẹye amren kange.

Adọe mẹnkeťa, Acha, ẹṇḍẹkhan gapa dọń tãṛãƙa. Ar ona daka dọ sanam hoṛko jọmkeťa; ini marań hoṛ dọ bae jọmeťtakoa, ẹnẹko ągu darawade tahẽkan, iną jelgeye jọmkeťa. Adọko metae kana, Am dọ, dada, bam jọma?

Adọe mẹnkeťa, Uni ąƙgu hoṛ babon saṗle khan, iń dọ bań jọma. Saṗkate hõ nonka bae ągui sẹ hapẹn, unreń ńamea. Ona dọ edrete onka ãṭa katha dọe mẹnkeťa, noko hõko bujhąukeťgea.

[5] Santali does not distinguish the sexes in the pronouns; but as it is food that is brought, a woman is naturally first thought of. It will have been observed that the narrator has his suspicions what kind of girl this may be. His first thought is that it is a bonga girl, but he seems to have given this idea up; there is no reference to it afterwards.

two of them ate, the youngest one and the one just above him in age; but the others did not eat that day. Next day also, people tell, somebody had left food there, covered up, and that day, they tell, three of them ate, the three youngest ones. Then the eldest one of them said: "I say, you, to-morrow you others go and hunt, I shall not go: I shall lie in wait for us, I want to see who it is who is bringing us this. Whoever it may be, that person is wonderfully kind to us, who have no one to work for us. If I find her[5], I shall catch her; then she may prepare for us openly. And bring my share along with you, when you come."

"All right", they replied, "then you lie in wait for us."

So, people tell, when it dawned of day, he did not go hunting; those others went. Now, while he was lying in wait, some time or other, she brought the food and left it there, but he did not see her come. Then in the evening they saw, somebody had brought food, covered up. So they said to him: "How did you manage, brother, did you catch her or not?"

"No, you fellows", he replied; "I was unable to catch her; some time or other she brought it and left; I did not see her at all. And I was thinking: 'If she is a girl, we may keep her.' This was my thought; but she did not show herself to me." Thereupon he said: "You so-and-so, to-morrow you lie in wait for us; perhaps she is yours."

This one replied: "All right, then I shall lie in wait to-morrow." And all of them ate that food, except the eldest one; he did not eat of this, he ate only the flesh that they had brought along with them for him; and they said to him: "You, brother, will you not eat?"

"If we do not catch the person who is bringing this," he replied, "I shall not eat. Even when she is caught, let her try not to bring anything in this way in the future, then I shall find her." Because he was angry, he spoke such rough words; the others also understood this.

Adǫ kathae, dosar hiloḱ dǫ talaiće tăṛăḱena, adǫ inre hõ enkage daka dǫ tinre cǫe ạgukat́; mẹnkhan hǫṛtẹt́ dǫ bae ńẹl tioḱledea. Ar ạyup̠ jǫkhẹn daka dǫ onkako jǫm idiyet́gea. Adǫ inạkate ini sotoḱiće tăṛăḱena, ẹnrehõ bae ńamlena. Onkage adǫ jẹmǫnko huḍiń idia, tẹmǫngeko tăṛăḱ idiyena, ẹnre hõ bańgeko sap̠ daṛeadea, ar daka dǫ borabor ạḱgutege menaea.

Khange napṛaḱko dǫ jǫtǫko tăṛăḱ purạuena, ẹnre hõ bae ńamlena; adǫ uni huḍińićko metadea, Ma ya, adǫ am pạri tăṛăḱtabonme. Adǫ amre hõ bae sǫdǫrena mẹnkhan, daka hõ babon jǫmtaea. Ar adǫm hǫṛ dǫko mẹnet́a, Nuire dǫ khạṭigeye sǫdǫroḱa; ma hǫnẹćpe ńẹla. Adǫ uniko bạgiadea, ako dǫ sendrako calaoena.

Adǫ kathae, uni dǫ sạṅgiń sẹnre sẹ jăhă danańre dǫ bae tăṛăḱ baṛalena. Uni dǫ oṛaḱrege menaea, aḱe bebenao kana; are mẹnet́a, Nẹṇḍẹń tahẹnteye sǫdǫroḱ khan hẽge, ar bańkhan iạićge. Onka mẹnkate oṛaḱkore menaea.

Ar noko dǫ kichu hǫṛ talare menaḱkoa? Bań, noko dǫ ako eskar urni bir bhitrire onkan ṭhạireko oṛaḱ akana, jẹmǫn cele hõ aloko ńamko; hǫṛ tulućge bako mesaloḱ kana; hǫṛ atoreko tahẹn khan hutẹć, hǫṛko kulikekoa sẹ sǫndhǫte hõko mẹnkea, bańma, Daya ńẹlte ǫkǫe cǫko emabon kana. Noa dǫ sei jǫh thǫ bań kana je hǫṛko ạguako. Hǫṛ reaḱ sae sabad ma jǫnmunige bań ạikạuḱ kan, ona reaḱ nam cintạge bạnuḱ. Onate onko napṛaḱko dadatteko dǫko dhokaḱ kana, noa ṭhạire dǫ ǫkǫeye ạguyet́ kana. Ona iạteko tăṛăḱlen dǫ bako ńamlede, adǫ onate nui pạriko dhurạu akadea, bhala nui hõe sap̠ daṛeaea sẹ bańa. Adǫ uni koṛa dǫ jăhă danań sẹ ạḍre dǫ bae tahẽkana, uni dǫ oṛaḱregeye tahẽyena.

Next day, people tell, the second one lay in wait; then also she brought food in the same way some time or other; but the person herself he did not catch sight of. In the evening they were eating in the same way. Thereupon the next one in age lay in wait; still she was not caught. In this way all of them lay in wait according to age, first the eldest one, then the next in age and so on; still they were utterly unable to catch her; but the food she brought without fail day after day.

Now all the elder ones had done watching; yet she was not caught; so they said to the youngster: "Now you, take your turn to lie in wait. If she does not show herself when you are there either, we shall not eat her food." And some of them said: "She will undoubtedly show herself, while he is there; you will see it." So they left him there and they themselves went hunting.

Now, people tell, he did not lie in wait anywhere at a distance or where he could hide himself. He stayed in the house and was making a bow and was saying: "If she shows herself while I am staying here, well and good, and if not, let her do what she likes, the wretch." With such thoughts he stayed in the house.

Now do you think these brothers were living anywhere near people? Nothing like it; they had built a house for themselves alone in the middle of the primeval forest, in such a place that no one should find them; they did not mix with people; if they had been living in a village with other people, they might have asked people, or else they might have had their suspicions and have said: "Somebody must have taken pity on us and is giving us food." Their situation was naturally not such that anybody would bring them anything. No sound of people or anything like it was ever heard or noticed; such there was no thought of. Therefore the elder brothers were having their doubts as to what kind of people might be bringing anything at this place. Therefore also, when they lay in wait and did not catch anybody, they set the youngster to watch in his turn, wondering whether he would be able to catch her or not. But this young man did not stay anywhere hidden or in cover; he stayed in the house.

Adọ kathae, tikin khange uni kuṛi dọ daka dipilkate hijuḱ kane ńẹlkede khan dọ, nui koṛa dọ oṛaḱteye bọlọyena lajaote. Adọ ạuṛiaḱge ceťko cọe oyoṅ baṛayeť kan. Khange uni kuṛi dọ, kathae, ona racareye sẹtẹr gọťena are rọṛ saḍe gọťkeťa, Ayo, họṛ leka ma nọṇḍẹń ńẹlade, adọ bhalae oka gọťena? Onka uni kuṛi dọe rọṛeťa baṛkaćtege, bhala uni koṛa ceťe mẹna, rọṛa sẹye baṅ; ona biḍạue lagať onka dọe rọṛeťa. Ar sẹ uni koṛa dọe lajao bọtọroḱ kana.

Adọ kathae, dakae dọhọkeťte ọntẹ nọtẹye bẹṅgẹť baṛaketa, cele hõ bạnuḱko; adọe mẹnketa, Hapẹ sẹ, bhala oṛaḱreń ńẹllege; họṛ lekaṅ ńẹladea, adọe oka sẹn gọťena. Adọ kathae, onka mẹnkate oṛaḱe jhićkeť khan dọe ńamkede, adọe mẹnketa, Tọbẹ tẹrọṅ hante pharak khon dọ họṛ lekaṅ ńẹlledea; tãhã tinre cọṅ oṛaḱteye bọlọ akan. Adọ ẹnre hõ uni koṛa dọ ceť hõ bae mẹneťa. Adọ baṅ rọṛ lekae ạikạukede khane kulikedea, apnar haṛam buḍhi lekage, adọe metae kana, Teheń dọ bam sẹnlena sendra dọ?

Adọ unreye mẹnketa, Bạṅ sẹnlena.

Adọ kuṛiye mẹnketa, Cedaḱ? Ruạ ruạgem ạikạueťa?

Adọe mẹnketa, Baṅa.

Tọbẹ cedaḱ bam sẹnlena?

Adọe mẹnketa, Ọkọe cọṅ din hiloḱge daka ạgukate nọṇḍẹ ale oṛaḱreko hạrup̌ oṭokaḱa, ar họṛ ma bale ńẹl tioge, onateko mẹnketa, Ma am dọ tãṛãḱtabonme ar kuliyem, cedaḱe ạguyeťa ar ceť mẹnkate. Ona iạte iṅ dọko bạgi oṭo akawadiṅa.

Adọ onka mẹn tora uni kuṛi dọ oṛaḱte dakae tul ader gọťketa, are mẹn gọťketa, Iṅge cọṅ daka maṅ ạguape kan. Nõḱọe teheń hõṅ ạgu akaťgea. Adọ ma dẹ ạbukoḱme, dakaṅ emama.

6 Ashamed, because it is a girl, afraid, because he does not know what kind she may be.

7 Lit. 'the house'.

8 It is a 'regular' proposal; very likely it may happen in this way in real life, when irregular connexions are entered on. She means marriage.

At noon, people tell, he caught sight of a girl coming carrying the food on her head, and the young man went inside the house out of shame. And on some idle pretext he was looking down as if searching for something. In the meantime the girl reached the court-yard and at once spoke loudly: "O mother, I had a glimpse of somebody like a man here; what has become of him so suddenly, I wonder." The girl was talking in this way feigningly, to find out what the young man would say, whether he would speak or not; it was to test this that she spoke in this way. But as for the young man, he was feeling ashamed and afraid[6].

Then, people tell, she put the food down and looked round in all directions, there was no one there; so she said: "Wait a bit, let me just have a look inside the house; I had a glimpse of somebody like a man; what has become of him so suddenly, I wonder." Saying this, people tell, she opened the door[7] and saw him, whereupon she said: "This is the reason that I saw somebody like a man from a distance over there; naturally, some time or other he has entered the house." Still the young man does not say anything; and as she felt that he was unlikely to speak, she asked him, just as if they had been themselves husband and wife, saying to him: "You did not go hunting to-day?"

Then he replied: "I did not go."

"Why?" the girl asked; "do you feel unwell?"

"No", he said.

"Then why did you not go?"

"Someone or other", he replied, "brings food here every day to our house and leaves it, having covered it up, and we have not succeeded in seeing the person; so they said: 'Lie in wait for us, you, and ask her why she is bringing it, and for what purpose.' Therefore they have gone and left me here."

He just said this, whereupon the girl at once carried the food inside the house and said: "Why, it is I myself who am bringing you the food. See here, to-day I have also brought some. So go and wash your hands[8]; I shall give you food."

Ado uni korae menketa, Okor? Ma seń ńela.

Ado kathae, kicrićteye dapal akat tahẽkana, ado otakkateye udukadea, adoe metadea, Ma abukokme, dakań emama.

Ado korae menketa, Jom doń jomgea, menkhan noa reak asol katha cet kana, ona lailem; cedak ar cet mentem aguyeta? Ale ma apeak cet hõ bale kami kan, ado cedakem aguyeta?

Ado uni kuriye menketa, Kami do ente cet hõ bape kamiale kana; menkhan asol katha do noa kana, am then tahen iń meneta; dohoña sem bań?

Ado uniye menketa, Noko naprakko bako ńam akawan do, cekateń doho dareama?

Ado uni kuriye menketa, Onko do ińem doholiń khan, alańge onko dolań horakoa. One ona menkate iń doń aguape kana. Ado de amge cetem meneta?

Ado uniye menketa, Hape endekhan dadańtekoń kulilekoge. Ado ona ror rortege barić sen ror idikette ona hõkin onkaketa. Khange sanam botor lajao maraoentakina, ado mit then khon alo chapadaok lekakin aikaueta. Khange kora hõe menketa, Judim tahẽyena menkhan doń dohomegea.

Ado uni hõe menketa, Tahengeań. Ado enekin ror gotaketa. Ar mon hõ aditet mitentakina. Ado uni kuriye menketa, Ma daka jomme.

Ado uni korae menketa, Bartim agu akat khan doń joma, ar lekha sumuńge khan, ohoń jomlea.

Ado kuriye menketa, Ape eae horakgeń agu akata, ona khon barti do banukan.

Ado korae menketa, Tobe ohoń jomlea.

9 The expression 'bring for oneself' is commonly used about getting a wife.

10 Against custom. The elder ones provide for the younger ones.

11 Usually the eldest son is first married, then the next one, and so on. This custom may be departed from, if the elder one is unfit or is so far away that he cannot

"Where is it?" the young man said; "let me see."

Now, people tell, she had covered it up with a cloth, and taking this off she showed it to him and said to him: "Please wash your hands; I shall give you food."

The young man then said: "I shall certainly eat; but first tell what the real meaning of this is; why and for what purpose are you bringing this? We do no work for you; why are you bringing it?"

"Quite so," the girl replied, "you do not do any work for us; but the real thing is this: I intend to stay with you; will you have me or not?"

"The big ones," the young man said, "they have not got any for themselves[9], how then shall I be able to take you?"[10]

"As for them," the girl replied, "if you take me, we two shall procure wives for them[11]. It is for the purpose mentioned that I am bringing you food. Now, please what do you say?"

He then said: "Wait then, let me first ask my elder brothers." Continuing to talk in this strain they at last also did what is bad, and they lost all fear and shame and were feeling as if they could never any more be separated. The young man on his side also said: "If you will stay, I shall surely keep you."

Then she also said: "I shall surely stay." So they fixed this, and they became absolutely of one mind. Now the girl said: "Please, take your food."

But the young man replied: "If you have brought anything in excess, I shall eat; but if it is only according to our number one portion for each, I shall not take any."

"I have brought just for the seven of you," the girl said, "there is not more than that."

"Then I shall certainly not eat," the young man said.

be brought. In the case of girls it is customary to give an elder sister one rupee as consolation, in case a younger sister is bespoken and married before her.

Arhõe metadea, Acha, amak' bakhrage ẹnte jọmme, onkoak' dọ tahẽ ocoam.

Adọe mẹnket'a, Ọhọń jọmlea, hẹćkate nãhãk' onako todarota.

Adọe mẹnket'a, Acha, ona bọdọl dọ nãhãk' iń ạgu bhurtia.

Adọe metadea, Baṅ, ẹnḍẹkhan do ạgu pạhillem barẹ, ẹk dọ onage iń dọń jọma.

Adọ onkae mẹnket' khan, kathae, daka ạgui calaoena; arhõ mit' bakhrae ạguket'a, adọ ona dọe jọmket'a. Arhõ jọm barạkate ạḍikin khamḍa kana, adọkin ạkin sạtena. Arhõ uni koṛa rọṛe ẹhọp'ket'a, Iạ, iń mit' katha rọṛ iń mẹnet'a, baṅdọm khusiak' baṅdọ baṅ.

Adọe mẹnket'a, Masẹ ẹnte rọṛlem, khusik' lekanak' dọń khusiak'gea, ar baṅ lekanak' dọ baṅge.

Arhõe mẹnket'a, Rọṛań ẹnḍẹkhan; pasẹm edren?

Adọe mẹnket'a, Ọhọń edrena.

Adọ koṛae mẹnket'a, Iạ, baṅkhan marańić dadań ńutumtege am dọ tahẹnme; inạ dọ sanam họṛ rọṛọṛ hõ ganok'talea. Ar iń dọ huḍiń họṛ kanań, iń ṭhenem tahẽlen khan dọ dak'koko kọeme hõ lajaoge. Onateń mẹnet'a, marań họṛ ṭhenem tahẽlen khan dọ ạḍi bes hoekok'a.

Uni kuṛiye mẹnket'a, Iń dọ am ṭhengeń tahẹna; honko noko dọ alom ńum barạkoa. Ar dak' tanak'ko dọ ẹnteko kọeyeń ma sẹ, onate dọ cet' bạṛić? Mit'ṭan jọpọṭẹt'lem khange baṅ bạṛić dọ? Ẹkẹn rọṛte dọ cet' lajao?

Adọ koṛa hõe hẽat'a, adọ ọnṭẹte hõ kathakin mucạt'ket'a. Khankin thir barạyena, adọ ạkingekin goṭayena. Khange tara sińen khan dọ kuṛiye mẹnket'a, Iạ, ḍher hạbićlaṅ galmaraoket'a, nit dọń calak'a.

12 The boy alludes to the custom that an elder brother has to treat the wife of a younger brother with the greatest possible reverence; on the other hand the wife of an elder brother is the intimate of her husband's younger brothers.

"All right'" she again said, "then eat your portion and let theirs be."

But he replied: "Not at all, I shall not take it. When they presently return, they will enquire into that."

She said: "All right, instead of what you eat I shall presently bring more to fill up."

But he replied: "No, in that case do bring that first; then I shall eat that."

When he had said this, people tell, she went to bring food; she brought one more portion and he ate this. When he had eaten this, they again commenced to flirt, and they became quite united. Then again the young man commenced to talk: "I say, I have one thing to mention; I wonder whether you will be pleased or not."

The girl replied: "Well, out with it; if it is anything to be pleased with, I shall certainly like it, and if not, then surely not."

"I shall mention it then," he again said; "perhaps you will be angry."

"Certainly not," she replied.

The young man then spoke: "I say, if this will not do, you stay in my eldest brother's name; then it will be permissible for all of us to talk. And I am the youngest one; if you stay with me, they will be ashamed even to ask you for a drink of water. Therefore I say, if you stay with the eldest one, it would be very well[12].

"I shall stay with you," the girl replied; "do not mention these or those. And by all means let them ask me for water, what bad is there in that? Only when you touch one another, it becomes bad, is it not so? What is there to be ashamed of in only talking?"

The young man agreed to this, so they finished talking of this proposal. They ceased speaking of this and decided that it should be themselves. When it became the middle of the afternoon, the girl said: "I say, we have been talking for a long while; now I am off."

Adọ koṛae mẹnkeťa, Calak̓ kan khanem, okor tọbẹm sọdọrlena dadaṅteko ṭhen dọ? Tọbẹ am dọ bam tahẹna.

Adọ kuṛiye mẹnkeťa, Teheṅ dọ baṅ tahẹn kana. Ma onko ṭhen noako katha lạilem; adọ onko ceťko mẹna, ona katha gapa lạiaṅme.

Adọe metadea, Acha, ma ẹnḍẹkhan calak̓me. Adọ ẹnẹye calaoena.

Adọ ạyup̓ khange noko sẹṭẹrenteko kulikedea, Cele ya, tebak̓ledeam?

Adọe hẽkeťa, Hẽṅ tebak̓ledegea; dakae ader jọkhẹngeṅ sap̓ gọťkedea.

Adọko kulikedea, Okare am dọm tãṛãk̓ akan tahẽkana?

Adọe mẹnkeťa, Oṛak̓ bhitrireṅ siṅ pọṭọm akan tahẽkana; oṛak̓teye bọlọk̓ jọkhẹngẹṅ sap̓ gọťkedea.

Adọko metadea, Bam kuliledea, ceť mẹnteye ạguyeťa mẹnte?

Adọe mẹnkeťa, Kulikedegeaṅ; mẹnkeťae, Am ṭhen iṅ bạhuk̓ lạgiť, ona iạteṅ ạguape kana; ar noko napṛak̓ko dọ hapẹn alaṅgelaṅ họṛakoa. Onkae mẹnkeťa.

Adọko mẹnkeťa, Bogege, tọbẹ khan ma arhõ miťṭaṅ oṛak̓bon benaoa, are dakawabona. Adọko mẹnkeťa, Ukuric̓ okare?

Adọe metaťkoa, Mẹnkeťae, teheṅ dọ bạṅ tahẹn kana; ma am dọ noako katha lạilem; jọtọ boehako khusiak̓ khan dọ, gapaṅ hijuk̓re lạiaṅme, adọ inregeṅ tahẽyenge; ar bako khusik̓re hõm lạiadiṅge. Uni dọ iṅ ṭhen onkae mẹn oṭokaťa. Adọ masẹ ape ceťpe mẹntabona? iṅạ katha gapaṅ lạiaea.

Adọ jọtọ boeha bujhạ bujhikateko mẹnkeťa, Tahẹne gọrọjen khan dọ, mabon dọhọkaea. Bin katha batratege, ṅẹlme, uni dọ daka ạgum dhuṛạu akan heṛan gọrọj họṛ kanae. Arbo baṅle khan dọ, ạḍiteť mọn khaṭọk̓taea. Ma ẹnḍẹkhan am dọ gapa hõ tahẹnme, ar onka galmaraokate dọhọyem. Ar noa metaeme ạikạ, abo dọ ceť hõ bạnuk̓taboa, jọtọak̓ unige juk̓ṛạu hoyok̓taea. Ona metaeme, ar baṅkhan hẹc̓ eskarkate dọ ceťe cekaea ar ceťe jọma?

"If you are going now," the young man said, "why then, you have not shown yourself to my elder brothers? Are you not going to stay then?"

The girl replied: "I am not staying to-day; please first tell them of these matters; and to-morrow tell me what they have to say."

"All right," he said, "go then." And so she went.

In the evening, when the others had returned, they asked him: "Well, you, did you come across her?"

He said yes to this: "Yes, I certainly came across her; I caught her when she was bringing the food in."

"Where were you lying in wait?" they asked him.

He replied: "I had shut myself up inside the house; I caught her just as she was coming into the house."

"Did you not ask her," they said to him, "what she means by bringing this?"

"I certainly asked her," he replied; "she said: 'I want to become your wife; therefore I am bringing you this; and we two shall later on procure wives for the elder ones.' She spoke in this way."

"Very well," they said; "then we shall build one house more, and she may cook for us." Again they said: "Where then is she?"

He answered: "She said: 'I am not staying to-day; please first tell them of these matters; if all your brothers agree, tell me when I come to-morrow; then I shall stay for good; and if they don't like it, tell me that also.' She spoke in this way to me, before she went away. So now what have you to say? I shall tell her to-morrow."

All the brothers thereupon consulted together and said: "As she wishes to stay, let us keep her. See, without being asked she has set herself to bring food and must be a person with an intense desire; and if we say no to her, she will become utterly down-hearted. So then you stay here also to-morrow, and after having talked to her as we have now said, keep her. But mind, tell her this also: we have absolutely no property, she will have to provide everything. Tell her this; otherwise, coming alone without anything,

Nonka metaeme; noae hẽ khan dọhọyem, ar baṅkhan alogem dọhọyea, jobab chuṭiaeme. Ma ing̣age katha dọ.

Adọ dosar hiloḱ hõ koṛa dọko bạgiadea, ar ako sendrako c̈alaoena. Adọ onkoko sẹnen torage uni kuṛi dọ daka dipilkate arhõe hẹć gọtena, are landa ạguketa. Adọ daka dọhọ torageye kuli gọtkedea, Cele ceṫ leka? Masẹ hola katha lạilem.

Adọe mẹnkeṫa, Hola katha dọ sanam bogegea, mẹnkhan arhõ miṫ kathako metadiṅa, onae khusiaḱ khan dọbon dọhọyegea, ar baṅkhan okorbon dọhọ daṛeae kana?

Adọ uni kuṛiye mẹnkeṫa, Ceṫ katha kana? Ma lạime.

Adọe mẹnkeṫa, Katha dọ noa kana: ale dọ ceṫ hõ bạnuḱtalea, ceṫbo daka ocoyea? Adọ onako hõe ạgui khan dọbon dọhọyegea, ar baṅkhan dọ jobabae ma. Nią kathako metadiṅa.

Adọe mẹnkeṫa, Acha, ona dọń ṅamtabona. Adọ ẹnẹye dọhọkedeteko ṅẹlkedea, khub mõṅj kuṛi kanae. Adọ onko ṭhene tahẽ rophayenteko oṛaḱ duạrkeṫa, gại kaḍaketkoako, jumi jaegaketako. Khange miṭṭaṅ jugi dọ cekakote cọṅ onkoe cialetkote bọchọr onko ṭhen kọkọeye calaḱa. Adọ onko bhạiạdi bạhuako reaḱkin oramkeṫa. Adọ tahẹn tahẹnte jọtọ họṛkin bạhu cabawatkoa. Ar noko koṛako thọ sendra dọ bako bạgiyeṫa, calaḱgeako.

Adọ uni dakae ạguyeṫ tahẽkan, uni kuṛiren dọ balege koṛa gidrại họe akan tahẽkan jọkhẹnge, kathae, uni jugi dọ kọkọeye calaoena. Adọ uniren ma gidrại janam akante ceṫ hõ bae kạmi kana; daka hõ ṅatat eratekogeko dakayeṫ kan. Adọ uni jugiye calaoen khan, kathae, onko kọeko oḍokadea. Adọ bae khusiḱ kana. Adọe metako kana, Uni pạhile emaṅ kan tahẽkan, uni tite khan dọń hataoa, ar baṅkhan dọ baṅ hataoa.

what will she do and what will she have to eat? Speak to her in this way; if she agrees to this, keep her, and, if not, do not keep her; give her a final answer. Well, that is what we have to say."

Also the following day they left the young man behind and went themselves to hunt. No sooner had they gone away, than the girl again came, carrying food on her head; she came smiling. As soon as she had put the food down, she asked him: "Well then, how is it? Tell me at once before anything else the result of yesterday's talk."

He replied: "What we talked about yesterday, that is all in order; but they said one thing more to me: 'If she agrees to this, then we shall keep her; but if not, how shall we be able to keep her'?"

"What is it?" the girl asked. "Please tell."

"It is this," he said; "we have absolutely nothing; what shall we let her have to prepare food? If she will bring also that, we shall keep her, and if not, let her be dismissed. This is what they said to me."

"All right," she replied, "I shall procure this for us." So he married her, and they saw her, that she was an exceedingly beautiful girl. And as she settled down with them, they built houses and acquired property; they acquired cows and buffaloes and broke up land for cultivation.

After this a certain jugi somehow or other found them out and went to them to beg once yearly. The young couple took up the matter of procuring wives for the elder brothers, and as time passed, the two got all of them married; but the young men did not give up hunting, they continued to go.

At the time when the girl who was bringing the food had just got a child, people tell, the jugi came there to beg. Now as her child had been borne, the girl was doing no work; even the food her sisters-in-law were preparing. When the jugi went there, people tell, these women brought out what they had been asked for; but he did not like this and said to them: "If it is given me at the hands of her who formerly used to give me, I shall take it; otherwise I shall not take it."

Adoko metadea, Uniren do gidrai hoe akana, onate bae odokok kana.

Ado uni jugiye menketa, Acha, gidrai hoe akantae khan, uniak ḍuria caurić aguańpe, onań ńelletaege.

Adoko kulikedea, Am do celeama?

Adoe metatkoa, Iń do Jhades jugi.

Ado senkate uni ńatat erako laiadea, bańma, Jhades jugiye hec akana; ado amak ḍuria caurice ńam kana.

Ado onako idiket khan, kathaeye sap gotkette thailakreye bhoraoketa, are beret gotenteye calaoena. Ado kathae, uni kuṛi hõ gidra bagikate unigeye pańja tapkedea, ado ghuria bae ruaṛlena.

Khange ayup jokhen sendra khonko hecen khan doko laiatkoa, bańma, Nui ńatań era do Jhades jugiye atkirkedea.

Khange adiko bhabnayena; menketako, Ape do nui gidra kurumuṭute jotonepe, ale do unile pańjayea arle gojea.

Ado pańja pańjate mitṭań gaḍa aṛe ṭhenko pańja tiokkedea. Khange cekae muhniketko coń, bako tuń ńam daṛeadea; akogeye gocketkote mit ṭhene dhiri cakekatkoa, ar akin dokin calaoente uni jugi gosãe oṛakkin tiokketa.

Ar uni jugi do ona disomren raj kanae, onḍe do rajko metaea. Ar adi baṛić baha koca menaktaea, ar ona baha joton lagit mitṭań malin buḍhi menaetaea. Ar uni buḍhi do dinge baha gutukate rani ṭhene idia, arko tulaitaete damko emaea. Onka uniak dusṭur tahẽkana. Khange uni kuṛi do onḍegeye tahẽyena.

Ado tahen tahente tinak din badre coń kathae, uniye janam oṭolede, uni gidra doko asul harakedea. Ar ona urni bir hõ mak ṭanḍikette goṭako berel tepetketa. Ado uni gidrai harayen khan, kathae,

[13] These two things are used by women setting up their hair. The **caurić** is made from plaited hairs of a cow's tail and is used as a kind of chignon among the hair, when this is tied into a knot (at the back of the head). The **ḍuria** is a tassel of cotton-thread, used in tying the hair knot.

"She has got a child," they said to him; "therefore she is not coming out."

The jugi then said: "Very well, if she has got a child, bring me her tassel and hair-plait[13]; I want to see that before anything else."

"What is your name?" they asked him.

"I am Jhades jugi," he answered them.

So they went and told their sister-in-law: "Jhades jugi has come, and he wants your tassel and hair-plait."

When they had brought this out to him, people tell, he at once took it and put it into his bag, and at once, getting up, he went away. Then, people tell, the girl left her child and followed straight after the jugi, and she did not return any more.

When the men returned in the evening from hunting, they told them, saying: "Jhades jugi has carried off this sister-in-law of ours."

They were very distressed and said: "Nurse this child diligently; we shall track him and kill him,"

They tracked the jugi until they at last reached him at the banks of a river. Somehow or other he bewitched them, so that they were unable to hit him with their arrows; he on the other hand killed them, and turning them into stones, he piled them up in one place, whereupon he and the woman went and reached the house of the jugi lord.

This jugi was the king of that country; people were calling him king there. He had an immense number of flower-beds and a gardener-woman to look after the flowers. This old woman was in the habit of daily making flower-garlands and taking them to the queen; they weighed her flowers and paid her accordingly. Such was her custom. And the girl remained there.

As time passed, who knows how long a time, people tell, they took care of the child whom she had born and gone away from, until he grew up. And people also cleared the primeval forest and settled all over and filled the place. When the child had

kạtiko ẹnẹća; adọ unre ṭhae ṭhui bejhae daoa. Khange sọṅgẹten gidrạ dọko metaea, Bin baper chạlią dao kọrẹ.

Adọ ona katha uni gidrạ dọe añjọm ṭhikkeťa; adọ oṛaǩre hẹćkate goṅgot erateko dọe metako kana, Henda ayo, sạri iñ baba dọ bạnugića?

Adọko metadea, Hẽ beṭa, am ayo Jhades jugiye idikedea; adọ uni pañjako sẹnlena, unregeko okayen cọṅ.

Adọe metaťkoa, Ią, ayo, sạtu sambarañpe, babatekoṅ pañjakoa.

Adọko metae kana, Ią beṭa, alom calaǩa; nõǩõe ạpumtekoko calao aťena, am hõ hapẹn onkagem adoǩa.

Adọ uni gidrại mẹnkeťa, Baṅ, ayo, calaǩgeañ; ńẹlpe nãhãǩ bebak iñ ńam ạgukoa.

Adọ kathae, ạḍiye jidkeť khan dọko sạtu sambaradea. Khangeye sapṛaoenteye mohṇḍayena.

Adọ kathae, calaǩ calaǩte tin din họr cọe calaoen. Adọ họr phẹḍre mẹrọm gupi koṛae ńamkeťkoa, adọ onkoe kuliyeťkoa. Adọko sereńaǩa:

Hã ho chagọl gurkhia,
Ei baṭe Jhades jugi
Dekhalore, guru gurkhia?
Ei baṭe Jhades jugi
Dekhalore, gur gurkhia?

Adọ ẹṇḍẹ khone calaoena. Adọ calaǩ calaǩte bhiḍi gupi gidrại ńamkeťkoa, adọ onkoe kuliyeťkoa. Adọ sereńako:

Hã ho bheṛ gurkhia,
Ei baṭe Jhades jugi
Dekhalore, guru gurkhia?
Ọre bheṛ gurkhia,
Ei baṭe Jhades jugi
Dekhalore, gur gurkhia?

---

14 Kạti is a children's game; there are four kinds. The kind here hinted at is what is generally called cạrlo kạti or kaṭ kạti, in which a small potsherd (made round) or a small flat round stone is placed on the ground and hit by another potsherd, that is propelled by a stick or kicked. The Santal children have a large number of games, played at certain customary times of the year.

15 A rustic Bengali is used. In the verses cowherds seem always supposed to be present.

grown, they were, people tell, constantly playing pitch and toss[14], and then he would always strike vigorously and be victorious. Then his companions would say[15] to him: "Vaterloses Kind, immer gewinnen!"

The child heard this word clearly, and, when he came back home, he asked his aunts: "Listen, mother, is it true that I have no father?"

"Yes, my boy," they answered him, "Jhades jugi carried your mother away; then they went to track him, and who knows what became of them."

"I say, mother," he said to them, "prepare food for a journey for me; I am going to track my father and those with him."

"I say, my boy," they answered him, "don't go; you see, your father and those with him went and were lost; you will also be lost in the same way presently."

But the child said: "No, mother, I shall certainly go; see, I shall presently find them all and bring them back."

Since he was so eager and insistent, people tell, they prepared food for the journey for him, and, when he had made himself ready, he set off.

Now, people tell, as he went along, he walked who knows how many days. Then he happened to see some goat-herd boys near the road, and he asked them. Here they sing:[15]

»Horchet, o Ziegenhirten:
Diesen Weg entlang haben Sie
Jhades jugi gesehen, o Kuhhirten?
Diesen Weg entlang haben Sie
Jhades jugi gesehen, o Kuhhirten?«

So he passed along from there. As he walked along, he happened to see some shepherd children and he asked them. Here they sing:

»Horchet, Schäfer:
Diesen Weg entlang haben Sie
Jhades jugi gesehen, o Kuhhirten?
O Schäfer,
Diesen Weg entlang haben Sie
Jhades jugi gesehen, o Kuhhirten?«

Adǫ ẹṇḍẹ khone calaoena. Adǫ calaḱ calaḱte gạ̣i gupi gidrại ńamketḱoa, adǫ onkoe kuliyetḱoa. Sereńako:

Hā ho guru gurkhia,
Ei baṭe Jhades jugi
Dekhalore, guru gurkhia?
Qre guru gurkhia,
Ei baṭe Jhades jugi
Dekhalore, gur gurkhia?

Adǫ ẹṇḍẹ khone calaoena. Adǫ calaḱ calaḱte kaḍa gupi gidrại ńamketḱoa, adǫ onkoe kuliyetḱoa. Adǫko sereńaḱa:

Hā ho mǫhls gurkhia,
Ei baṭe Jhades jugi
Dekhalore, gur gurkhia?
Qre mǫhls gurkhia,
Ei baṭe Jhades jugi
Dekhalore, gur gurkhia?

Adǫ ẹṇḍẹ khon calaḱ calaḱte mitṭań jạnum dareye ńamketa. Ona jạnum dare dǫ tisre cǫń ǫkǫeaḱ gẹndrẹć cǫko lade akaṭ. Adǫ onae ńẹlket khane mẹnketa, Nui hǫ̃ń kulikaea, pasẹye ńẹllede. Khangeye kuliyede kana. Adǫ sereń:

Hā ho kul gacha,
Ei baṭe Jhades jugi
Dekhalore, gur gurkhia?
Qre kul gacha,
Ei baṭe Jhades jugi
Dekhalore, gur gurkhia?

Adǫ ona jạnum dareye mẹnketa, Nonkatege bạhui calaoena; Jhades jugiye idikedea; ǫr ǫrkadegeań, mẹnkhan bae aṛaḱledea. Nǫ̃ḱǫ̃e nisạna ńẹlme, bam pạtiạuḱ khan. Adǫ ona dare kathaeye capoata, adǫ ǫṇḍẹ khone calaḱ kana.

16 The jujube (or as the Santals call it, the thorn tree), Zizyphus Jujuba, Lam., is a very common bush or small tree, both wild and cultivated. It has thorns, and one may easily tear one's skin or clothes on it.

So he passed along from there. As he walked along, he happened to see some cowherd children and he asked them. Here they sing:

»Horchet, o Kuhhirten:
Diesen Weg entlang haben Sie
Jhades jugi gesehen, o Kuhhirten?
O Kuhhirten,
Diesen Weg entlang haben Sie
Jhades jugi gesehen, o Kuhhirten?«

Se he passed along from there. As he walked along, he happened to see some buffalo-herd children, and he asked them. Here they sing:

»Horchet, o Büffelhirten,
Diesen Weg entlang haben Sie
Jhades jugi gesehen, o Kuhhirten?
O Büffelhirten,
Diesen Weg entlang haben Sie
Jhades jugi gesehen, o Kuhhirten?«

As he walked along from there, he happened to see a jujube[16] tree. Some time or other somebody had put some one's rags on this jujube tree. When he saw this he said: "I shall ask this one, perhaps it saw him." So he asked it. Here they sing:

»Horche, Jujube Baum:
Diesen Weg entlang hast du
Jhades jugi gesehen, o Kuhhirt?
O Jujube Baum,
Diesen Weg entlang hast du
Jhades jugi gesehen, o Kuhhirt?«

The jujube tree then answered: "This way the wife went; Jhades jugi carried her away; I pulled and pulled to keep her back; but he did not let go of her. Here, see the proof, if you do not believe me." So he laid his hand on the tree, people tell, whereupon he went from there.

Adọ calaḱ calaḱte miṭṭaṅ baṛe darere toṛe raraḱ kana. Adọ uniye aṅjọmkede khane mẹnketa, Bhala uni toṛ iṅ kulilege, ceṭ ịateye raḱeṭ kana mẹnte. Adọ kathae, ona baṛe dare ṭhen sẹn sorkate toṛe kuliyede kana.

Hã ho toṛ gurkhia,
Ei baṭe Jhades jugi
Dekhalore, gur gurkhia?
Ọre toṛ gurkhia,
Ei baṭe Jhades jugi
Dekhalore, gur gurkhia?

Adọ uni toṛe mẹnketa, Durrẹ! hola khon, beṭaṅ họḱhọ kana, hẹć bam hẹć họdoḱ kan. Nonkatege, beṭa, Jhades jugi am ayoe idikedea, onate iṅ dọ ạḍi bạṛić iṅ họhọyeṭ kana, hẹćge bam hẹć họdoḱ kan. Ma noa họrte hare phare sẹn họdoḱme, nãhãḱem tioḱkingea. Ar am babateko hõ nonkategeko calao akana.

Khange uni gidrạ koṛa dọ ona katha aṅjọmte ạḍiye rạskạyena, ar tite uni toṛe capo gọṭkedea, are mẹn gọṭketa, Ọh bacha, am dọ ạḍi bhale họṛ kanam; nõḱõe am dọ ṭhikạn ṭhikạnem lạiadiṅa. Adọ kathae, unre uni koṛa reaḱ kạṭup cinhạ dag uni deare ukhṛạuena, onage ọnẹ ọnọl bọnọl cinhạ nit hạbić ṅẹloḱ kantako.

Adọ ẹnḍẹ khone calaḱ kana. Adọ kathae, calaḱ calaḱte miṭṭaṅ gaḍae tioḱketa, adọe mẹnketa, Nịạ gaḍarege sạtuko jọm baṛakate daḱ iṅ ṅũlege. Adọ onka mẹnkate aćaḱ moṭrakoe dọhọketa, ar tãhã ona gaḍarege apatteko dọe kicrić sọbọṭ dhiri akaṭko; ona dọ bae baḍae kan tahẹ̃kana. Khange kathae, jọjọme duṛupen khanko raḱ saḍeketa. Khange uni koṛa reaḱ nọṅjọr khulạuente onkoe ṅẹl ṅamkeṭkote onko hõ jọme emaṭkoa, sẹ ọnḍẹye curućkata.

---

17 The toṛ, Sciurus palmarum, is a very common squirrel; it is striped along its back.

18 Ficus bengalensis, Roxb.

19 Washermen and others washing clothes perform part of their work by dumping the clothes against a flat stone on the water-edge.

As he walked along, it so happened that a squirrel[17] was uttering its call in a banyan[18] tree. When he heard this, he said: "Well, let me ask the squirrel before going further, why it is calling." Whereupon, people tell, he went up to the banyan tree and asked the squirrel:

»Horche, o Eichhörnchen-hirt,
Diesen Weg entlang hast du
Jhades jugi gesehen, o Kuhhirt?
O Eichhörnchen-hirt,
Diesen Weg entlang
Jhades jugi gesehen, o Kuhhirt?«

The squirrel then replied: "O dear! since yesterday, my boy, I have been calling; you are not quick coming. This way, my boy, Jhades jugi carried your mother away; therefore I am calling so awfully; you certainly are not quick coming. Now go along quickly, and you will overtake them presently. Your father and those with him have also passed along this way."

When the boy heard this, he became very glad, and putting his hand on the squirrel he said: "O you dear, you are a splendid fellow; there now, you have told me clues to follow." Then, people tell, the marks of the boy's fingers were imprinted on the squirrel's back; that is the striped marks that are seen on them even now.

So he passed along from there. As he was walking along, people tell, he came to a river and said: "Here in this river I shall eat of my provisions and drink water, before going further." Having said this, he put his bundles down; now it was in this very river that the jugi had turned his father and uncles into stones on which they wash clothes[19]; this he did not know. Then, people tell, when he sat down to eat, they cried and made a sound. The boy's eyes were opened and he saw them, whereupon he gave them also to eat, that is to say, he put some food down with his hand there.

Adọ ọṇḍẹ khon calak̕ calak̕te, kathae, uni jugiak̕ disome tiok̕-keta. Uni jugi dọ, kathae, ona disomre dọe raj akana, ar mit̕ṭaṅ mạlin buḍhi menaetaea. Adọ onakoe kuli ṭhik maṛaṅket̕kote uni mạlin buḍhi oṛak̕teye rakap̕ calaoente uni buḍhi ṭhenge tahẽyen-teye metae kana, Ią, buḍhi, iṅ hõ am ṭhengeṅ tahẹna, bahakoṅ gutuitalaṅa.

Adọ uni buḍhiye mẹnketa, Hẽ ẹṇḍẹkhan, ma tahẹnme.

Adọe tahẽyente baha guk̕tui pọrtọnketa. Adọe gutu purạuket̕ khan dọ adọ ona mucạt̕ sẹnre uni tire tahẽkan mundạme gutu sẹlẹt̕keta; adọe metae kana, Henda gọṛọm ayo, noa baha dọ ọkọe lạgit̕em gutu idiyeta?

Adọ uni buḍhiye mẹnketa, Noa, gọṛọm, uni jugi mit̕ṭaṅ rạniye ạgu akawana, uni lạgit̕ iṅ gutu idiyeta.

Adọe metae kana, Nõk̕õe iṅ gutu akat̕, noa baha hõ uni ṭhenge idime; ṅẹlme nãhãk̕ khub damok̕tama. Ar ona mundạm dọ, kathae, uni jugi ạuriye idiyerege eṅgattẹt̕geye họrọk̕ade tahẽkana.

Adọ ona baha uni buḍhiye idiket̕ khanko tulạket̕taea; adọ nindara khon bạṛti hamal gọt̕entaea. Khange, kathae, uniye ạgu akade uni rạnigeye halaṅ gọt̕keta; adọe mẹn gọt̕keta, Durrẹ! nui buḍhi dọ noa baha dọe dak̕ ạgu akawata. Adọ kathaeye tunum baṛayet̕ dọ, mundạme tunum ṅamket̕. Adọ pharak sẹn họhọ begạrkedete bạṛtige dame emadea, arkin ṅẹlket̕ dọ, mundạm menak̕. Ar uni eṅgattẹt̕ dọe ṅẹl oromketa, baṅma, Noa mundạm dọ họpọniṅ ti reak̕ mundạm kana. Adọe kulikedea, Henda mạlin buḍhi, am oṛak̕re dọ ọkọe hẹć akana?

Adọe mẹnketa, Mit̕ṭaṅ koṛae hẹć akana, unige noa baha dọe gutuleta.

Adọe metadea, Ma tahẽ ocoaeme, alom lại baṛayea, ona reak̕ dọṅ bujhạumea. Ar ma laha hataṛok̕me, iṅ hõ calak̕teṅ ṅẹl ạguyea.

Adọ kathae, inạ mit̕ ghạṛi khange uni kuṛi sẹ rạni dọe calaoen-teye ṅẹlkede, aćren họpọn kane. Adọkin ṅẹpẹl opromena. Adọ

So walking along from there he, people tell, reached the jugi's country. The jugi was, as told, king in that country and he had an old woman as gardener. Having, by asking people, first ascertained this, he went up to the gardener-woman's house, and stopping where she was he said to her: "I say, old lady, I also want to stay with you; I shall make garlands for both of us."

The old woman said: "Well then, stay."

So he stayed and commenced to make a garland; and, when he had finished it, he put a ring he had on his finger in among the flowers at the end of the garland, and said to her: "Look here, granny, whom are you making these garlands for?"

The old woman replied: "This, grandson, — the jugi has brought a queen for himself —, it is for her that I am making this garland."

He then said to her: "Here, I have made a garland, take these flowers also to her; you will see, it will bring you a fine price." The ring, people tell, his mother had put on his finger, before the jugi carried her away.

When the old woman had taken the flowers there, they weighed them, and it was at once found that they were heavier than usual. Then the queen whom he had brought picked them up and said at once: "Dear me, this old woman has kept these flowers watered." Thereupon she felt the flowers with her hand and in this way discovered the ring. Calling the old woman aside away from the others, she gave her a higher price than usual, and they both saw, a ring was there. And the mother recognized it, saying: "This ring is a ring of my own son's finger." An she asked her: "Look here, gardener-woman, who has come to your house?"

She replied: "A boy has come; he made this garland."

"Let him stay with you," she said, "don't tell people of him; I shall show you my appreciation for this. And you go ahead so long; I shall also go and see him."

A short while afterwards, people tell, the girl or the queen went and saw him, that it was her own son. And they saw and

uni koṛae mẹnkeťa, Cele, ayo, am pakńjań hẹć akan dọ, cećem mẹneťa?

Ẹ beṭa, calakgeań, mẹnkhan nuige thọ cekatelań gọjea?

Adọ uni koṛae mẹnkeťa, Ią, ayo, uni dọ kuliyem, Jhades jugi reak jivi dọ okare menakťaea mẹnte.

Adọe mẹnkeťa, Acha, beṭań kuliyea.

Adọ kathae, ẹn hilok khon kukliye pọrtọnkeťa; adọe ạrisea, bańma, Amak jivi dọ cetre menaktama? Adọ ạḍiye ạriskede khane metadea, Ińak jivi dọ kohṇḍa nạṛī ar hẹtọt nạṛīre menaktińa. Khange ona katha dọ uni koṛae lạiadea. Khange ona nạṛī dọe gẹt topakketa; adọ ẹnre hõ bae gọćlen. Khange arhõ uni koṛae mẹnkeťa, Arhõ, ma, ayo, kuliyem, cetre menaktaea mẹnte.

Tọbẹ arhõe ạrisea. Tọbẹ khane lạiadea, bańma, Ińak jivi dọ tarwaṛere menaktińa. Khange inạ katha hõ uni koṛae lạiadea. Khange tarwaṛe hõ gurić mandere idikate onae jẹrẹťaťa, adọ ẹnre hõ bae gọćlen. Khange arhõe metadea, Ma ayo, arhõ kuliyem.

Khange arhõ kukliye pọrtọnkeťa. Adọ din din onkae ạḍiye ạriskede khan dọe lại dapoṛadea, bańma, Ińak jivi dọ, sạmudori talare edel dare menaka, onare barea bok mae cẹ̃ṛẽ menakkina; unkinre ińak jivi dọ menaktińa; unkin cẹ̃ṛẽ jãhãe gọćlekin khan, iń hõń gujuka.

Adọ onkae lạiade khan dọ, arhõ ona katha dọ uni koṛae lạiadea, are metae kana, Henda beṭa, ọṇḍẹ dọm sẹn daṛekoka?

Adọe mẹnkeťa, Calakań. Adọ ọṇḍẹye calak kana.

Adọ calak calakte hẹrre pea buḍhiye ńamketkoa; mit dọ ḍẹkẹre gaṇḍo laṭkao akawade, ar mit dọ bọhọkre sạuṛi biṇḍạ laṭkao

20 Two kinds of pumpkin-vines are mentioned, the one, kohṇḍa, is the Cucurbita moscheta, Duchesne, and the other, hẹtọt, the Cucurbita lagenaria, L., both very extensively cultivated.

21 This word, sạmudori, or sạmuduri, is very seldom heard, and the ideas the Santals combine with it are very vague. It seems to be any stretch of water that cannot be crossed. The word is borrowed.

22 Bombax malabaricum, DC., one of the largest trees seen in these parts.

recognized each other. The young man said: "Well, mother, I have come for you, what do you say?"

"My son, I shall surely go; but how shall we two manage to kill this one?"

The young man replied. "I say, mother, ask him where Jhades jugi has his soul."

"All right, my son," she said, "I shall ask him."

From this day, people tell, she commenced to ask and was worrying him, saying: "Where have you your soul?"

When she had worried him a good deal, he told her: "My soul I have in two kinds of pumpkin-vines."[20] She then told the boy this, and he cut those vines off; yet he did not die. The boy then again spoke: "Ask him again, mother, where he has his soul."

Consequently she commenced again to pester him. Then he told her, saying: "My soul I have in my sword." This she also told the boy. Then he carried the sword to the dung-hill and set fire to this; yet he did not die. Again he said to her: "Do, mother, ask him again."

So she commenced to ask him again; and as she every day constantly worried him in this way, he at last lost patience and told her, saying: "My soul — in the middle of the sea[21] there is a cotton tree[22]; in that tree are two cranes[23]; in those two I have my soul; if any one kills these two birds, I shall also die."

When he had told her this, she again told it to the boy and said to him: "Listen, my son, will you be able to go there?"

"I shall go," he said, and he forthwith started for this place. As he passed along, he met with three old women on the road; one of them had a stool stuck to her back, another had a bundle

[23] This word, b o k m a e, lit. crane-mother, is Bengali; in Santali these birds, of which there are several kinds, are called kŏk̓, a name imitating their call. B o k is, however, also used in Santali for certain species. They are very common, where there is water.

akawade, ar mit' do̱ ḍhiṅkiteye huṛuṅ akan, ona hõ baṅ o̱co̱gok' kan. Khange onko se̱nteye calak' kan khanko kulikedea, Henda bạbu, am do̱ okatem calak' kana?

Ado̱e metat'koa, Iń do̱ sạmudori talare bok mae cẽṛẽ ṭhen do̱rso̱n iń calak' kana.

Ado̱ unreko metae kana, Iạ bạbu, aleak' hõ do̱rso̱n daraeme. No̱k'o̱e noako laṭkao akawat'lea, noa baṅ o̱co̱gok' kana. Noa cekate o̱co̱gok'a, ona do̱rso̱n darakatalem.

Ado̱e me̱nket'a, Achań do̱rso̱nkatapea.

Ado̱ calak' calak'te, bhại, ona sạmudoriye tiok'ket'a. Khangeye guni bhạbik' kana, Cekate unkin cẽṛẽ ṭhen do̱ń se̱n sorok'a? Ado̱ kathae, ona ḍhip aṛe aṛeteye dãṛã baṛae kana. Ado̱ mit'ṭaṅ tayane puti akanteye e̱ṛse̱ń to̱ṛse̱ń baṛae kana; ado̱ nuiye ńe̱lkede khane me̱nket'a, Henda ho, bhala puṭite gujuk' lekań ạikạuet' do̱; cekateń besok'a?

Ado̱ uni koṛae me̱nket'a, Iń noa doreão khon hana edel dare ṭhenem idi ạguliń khanem beskok'a; am reaṅ hõ o̱ṇḍe̱ń do̱rso̱n darakea.

Ado̱e me̱nket'a, Hẽ, idi daṛekemań.

Ado̱e metadea, Delaṅ e̱ṇḍe̱khan idińme.

Khangeye idikedea. Ado̱ ona dare latarreye se̱n go̱t'en khan, cẽṛẽkin comkao go̱t'ena. Ado̱ ona dare phe̱ḍre duṛup'kate uni koṛa do̱e rak'et' kana:

Namo̱, namo̱re bok mae cạṛại,
E̱k ko̱tha do̱rso̱n bulibo.

Ado̱ onkae ro̱ṛlet' khan, kathae, co̱ṭṭekin uḍạu go̱t'ena. Khange uni koṛa do̱e bhabna go̱t'ena. Khange arhõ enkageye rak'et' kana:

Namo̱, namo̱re bok mae cạṛại,
E̱k ko̱tha do̱rso̱n bulibo.

---

24 The Bengali word do̱rso̱n is in Santali used in several ways; e. g. to have a vision of something supernatural, to visit a shrine and worship there, to ask a favour at such a place. The last meaning is obvious here. Pilgrimages to shrines for the purpose of asking favours are common. The writer has often seen crowds of Hindu women passing on their way to a Siva shrine some 60 miles distant to do̱rso̱n there, as the Santals express it.

of thatching-grass stuck to her head, and the third had been pounded by the rice-pounder and could not get this loose. When he was coming in their direction, they asked him: "I say, young man, where are you going?"

"I am going," he replied, "to ask the oracle[24] with some cranes in the middle of the sea."

Then they said to him: "I say, young man, ask the oracle also for us and bring an answer back with you. Here, you see, these things have stuck to us; they cannot be removed. Ask the oracle for us and bring an answer back with you, how these may be removed."

"All right," he said, "I shall ask the oracle for you."

So passing along he at last, friends, reached the sea. Then he was anxiously thinking: "How shall I be able to come near to these two birds?" He wandered, people tell, along the shore. Now an alligator with a swollen stomach was rolling there in pain; when he saw the boy, he said: "Look here you, I feel like dying from a swollen stomach; how shall I get well?"

The boy then answered: "If you take me from this shore over to that cotton-tree and bring me back, you might get well; I might ask the oracle there about you also and bring an answer back with me."

"Yes", the alligator said, "I might be able to take you there."

"Come then," the boy said, "take me there."

So he took him there. But, when he went there below that tree, the two birds were startled; but sitting there at the foot of the tree the boy was crying:

»Kommt herab, o kommt herab, o Kranich-Vögel,
Ich werde um einen Orakelspruch bitten.«

When he spoke in this way, people tell, the two birds flew at once up into the air; and the boy became very distressed. Again he cried in the same way:

»Kommt herab, o kommt herab, o Kranich-Vögel,
Ich werde um einen Orakelspruch bitten.»

Adọ ạḍi hạbić onkae rakket khan dọkin mẹnketa, Ọkọe baṅ alaṅak ṅutum ṅumteye rarak kan? Delaṅlaṅ ṅẹlea. Adọ onka mẹnkatekin ărgoyentekin kuliyede kana, Cedak ạliṅak ṅutum ṅum ṅumte dọm raket kana? Cet duk menaktama?

Adọe mẹnketa, Duk dọ noa kana: pea eṅgaṅtekoko dusko akana, jọnọmre hō ona khon bako besok kana. Onate aben ṭhen dọṅ hẹć akana.

Adọkin mẹnketa, Cet leka dusko?

Kathae, Nẹtẹ ṅōgokben, adọṅ lạiabena. Adọkin sorena. Unreye metakin kana, Mitṭaṅ dọ ḍẹkẹre gaṇḍo laṭkao akawadea, ar mitṭaṅ dọ bọhọkre sạuṛi binḍạ laṭkao akawadea, ar mitṭaṅ dọ ḍhiṅkiteye huṛuṅ akana, ona dọ jọnọmre hō baṅ ọcọgok kantakoa. Onate aben ṭhen dọṅ hẹć akana. Adọ dẹ bhala cekate ona dọ ọcọgok-takoa?

Adọkin mẹneta, Uni pạhil buḍhi dọ jăhăeko calaka, adọ duṛup hō bae metakoa, onate ona dọ laṭkao akana. Do e metako ma, adọ ọcọgoktaea. — Adọ enka hōe galmarao kana are sor idik kana. — Ar uni dosar buḍhi dọ jăhăe bọhọkre jobrae ṅẹla, adọ bae lạiakoa ar bae ọcọgtakoa, onate laṭkao akana. Do e ọcọgtako ma, adọ aćak hō ọcọgoktaea. Ar uni tesar buḍhi dọ rạṇḍi dukhi họṛ, sẹ ṭuạr amar họṛko bae huṛuṅ ocoakoa, onateye tẹn akana. Do e huṛuṅ ocoako ma, adọ ọcọgoktaea.

Adọ inạ hōe lại mucạd jọkhẹnge banar cẹ̃ṛẹ̃ mit dhaoteye sap gọtketkinte phạ̃kṛạke rạput gọtkettạkina. Khange, kathae, nhanḍẹ uni Jhades jugi reak ti sopo rạput gọtentaea. Khangeye baḍae-keta, baṅma, ọkọe cọṅ iṅren bạiriko sẹn akana. Khange arhō jaṅgae coak gọtkettạkina. Adọ kathae, uni jugiak jaṅga rạput gọtena. Adọ unkin cẹ̃ṛẹ̃kin raket khan, kathae, uni jugi hō bogeteye raket kana.

When he had cried in this way for a long while, the two birds said: Who ever is crying mentioning our names? Come, let us have a look at him." Saying this they came down and asked him: "Why are you crying, again and again, mentioning our names? What is your grief?"

He replied: "The grief is this: three mothers of mine have got into great trouble; they are utterly unable to get rid of it; therefore I have come to you."

"What kind of trouble?" they asked.

"Come a little nearer here," he said, "then I shall tell you." So they came near. So he said to them: "One has got a stool sticking to her back, and one has got a bundle of thatching-grass sticking to her head, and one has been pounded by a rice-pounder, and they are utterly unable to get these off. Therefore I have come to you. So do tell, how can it be removed from them?"

So they said: "As for the first old woman, when some one comes there, she does not ask them even to sit down; therefore the stool has stuck to her. Let her say 'Please, sit down' to people, and it will get off from her." — He is talking to them in this way and is getting nearer and nearer. — "And as for the other old woman, when she sees rubbish in anyone's hair, she does not tell them, nor does she pluck it out; therefore this sticks to her. Let her take it away for others; then her own will also be taken away. And as for the third woman, she does not permit poor widows or orphans to use her rice-pounder; therefore she is pressed down. Let her permit them to pound; then it will be removed from her."

Just as the bird finished telling this, he suddenly seized both birds at once and broke their wings. At the same time, people tell, in that other place Jhades jugi's arms were broken; then Jhades knew that some enemy of his had gone there. Again the boy broke off their legs; and, people tell, the jugi's legs were suddenly broken. And when the two birds were crying, the jugi also, people tell, cried awfully.

Ado̱ uni tayane metadea, Delaṅ idi ruạṛkaṅme. Ado̱ kathaeye ạgu ruạṛkede khan do̱, uni tayan hõe khalasena. Ado̱ he̱ćente onko buḍhiko ńamkedea, ado̱ko kulikedea, Cele bạbu, aleak̓em do̱rso̱nlet̓a?

Ado̱e metat̓koa, Hẽ̱ń do̱rso̱n akat̓gea.

Ado̱ko me̱nket̓a, To̱be̱ bạbu?

Ado̱ unre o̱ne̱ cẽ̱ṛẽ̱kin lạiade leka onko buḍhiye galmaraoat̓koa, Ma nonka co̱lo̱npe, ado̱ o̱co̱gok̓tapea.

Ado̱ kathae, o̱ṇḍe̱ khon uni jugi oṛak̓teye he̱ćen khan, unkin cẽ̱ṛẽ̱ reak̓ ho̱ṭo̱k̓e pe̱ṭe̱r topak̓ go̱t̓ket̓tạkina. Khange uni jugi reak̓ ho̱ṭo̱k̓ topak̓ go̱t̓entaea. Khange ado̱ uni eṅgattet̓e oḍok ạgukedea. Khange, kathae, unkin cẽ̱ṛẽ̱ do̱e ạgu darayet̓kingea, ar bo̱ho̱k̓ hõe ạguyet̓gea. Khange, kathae, uni jugiak̓ bo̱ho̱k̓ hõ̱ ạkin tayo̱mte kuṇḍlạṅ hijuk̓ kan. Ado̱ kathae, onakin ńe̱lket̓ khan do̱, ho̱rre kamar kuilạko je̱re̱t̓ akat̓ tahẽ̱kana. Ado̱ ona se̱ṅge̱lre cẽ̱ṛẽ̱ bo̱ho̱k̓ ar ho̱ṛmo̱ sudhạ onarekin khadlekat̓a. Khange uni jugi bo̱ho̱k̓ hõ̱ ona se̱ṅge̱lre kuṇḍlạṅ bo̱lo̱yena. E̱ne̱kin maraokedea.

Ado̱ o̱ne̱ko dhiri cạṭạni akan apattekokin tiok̓ket̓koa. Ado̱ kathae, um he̱ćente gamcha kicrićteye oyo po̱ṭo̱mkat̓koa, ado̱ kathaeko ho̱ṛ ruạṛena. Ado̱ko me̱nket̓a, Durre̱! ạḍi dhạbićbon gitićena.

Ado̱kin me̱nket̓a, Jugiye go̱ćlet̓pe do̱ baṅ? Ape do̱pe me̱net̓a, Ḍher hạbićle gitićena. Ado̱ enkoko e̱ne̱kin samṭao ạguket̓kote e̱ne̱ko tahẽ̱ rophayena.

Ado̱ katha hõ̱ń mucạt̓ket̓a.

---

25 The **gamcha**, a piece of cloth carried loosely over the shoulders, used as a towel, sash, &c.

Now he spoke to the alligator: "Come along, take me back." And, people tell, when he had brought him back, the alligator also was freed of his pain. When he came back, the old women met him and asked him: "Well, young man, have you asked the oracle for us?

"Yes, I have," he answered.

"What is the result then, young man?" they asked.

He thereupon talked to them in accordance with what the birds had told him: "Do behave in such and such a way, and it will be taken away from you."

"When he, people tell, came from there to the jugi's house, he wrung the necks of the two birds off. Then the jugi's neck also was broken off. Thereupon he brought his mother away; and, people tell, he was taking those two birds along with him; he was also taking their heads along. Then, people tell, the jugi's head also was coming rolling after them. When they saw this, people tell, there was a blacksmith who had set fire to his charcoal at the roadside. Into this fire they threw the heads of the birds and their bodies. Then the jugi's head also rolled into the fire. So there they made an end of him.

Thereupon they reached his father and uncles who had been turned into rocks. And, people tell, after having bathed, he wrapped them up in a towel[25], whereupon they, people tell, became human beings again. And they said: "O dear, we have slept for a long while."

They said to them: "The jugi killed you, is it not so? And you say: 'We have slept for a long while'." So they two gathered them and brought them home and there they lived in peace and quiet.

And I too have finished the story.

STORIES CONCERNING THE SOULS IN HUMAN BODIES

73. Mit́ṭaṅ buḍhi ho̱po̱ntet́ gidrại go̱ć bạgiade reaṅ.

Mit́ṭaṅ atoren bar eṅga ho̱nkin tahẽkana, ar unkinren do̱ cele hõ baṅko tahẽkana. Me̱nkhan tahe̱n tahe̱nte uni eṅgattet́ do̱ ạḍitet́e buḍhi tulniyena. Khange uni buḍhi do̱ ruạte jaṛaoenteye go̱ćena.

Khange atoren ho̱ṛ jarwakate uni buḍhi do̱ parko̱mreko sajaokedea; khange pon ho̱ṛte go̱ḱkate kulhi kulhiteko mohṇḍakedea. Me̱nkhan kulhi mucạt́reko do̱ho̱ ńõḱkedea; e̱nte onkage dustur kana, ho̱ṛ ho̱po̱naḱ do̱.

Ar uni huḍiń huḍiń gidrạ do̱ rapage ṭhen do̱ baṅko idi toraledea, me̱nket́ako, Nui do̱ idi torakate cet́ baṅ hoyoḱ. Me̱nkhan uni gidrạ do̱ oṛaḱ khongeye ńe̱l go̱t́kat́koa. Ado̱ atoren ho̱ṛ uni go̱ćić arhõko go̱ḱkedea; ado̱ bir se̱nko mohṇḍakedea, ar bo̱ṛte se̱ṅge̱l hõ, kaṭ mag lạgit́ ṭe̱ṅgo̱ć hõko idi toraket́a. Ado̱ bir aṛereko do̱ho̱kedea.

Ado̱ kaṭko maḱ jarwaket́a, ado̱ onako kuṭrạket́a pon mokakate, ar sarako benaoket́a. Uni buḍhi do̱ ona sarareko do̱ho̱kedea; do̱ho̱kate se̱ṅge̱lko lagaoadea. Khange saname lo̱ ro̱ṅgo̱ khạurạyena. Kạmi baṛakate onko ho̱ṛ do̱ oṛaḱteko calaoena.

Ado̱ uni gidrạ onko ho̱ṛe kuliyet́koa, metako kanae, Henda baba, iń go̱ do̱ oka se̱npe idi oṭo akadea? Khangeko lạiadea,

---

1 As told by Bhuju Murmu of village Dhopahar.

2 So lit. **Buḍhi** may mean an old woman, but is often used about a married woman of middle age, or, as here, apparently a widow.

3 The Santals have naturally a fairly elaborate ceremoniel in connexion with cremation; here all details are left out, except what the child saw. What is told is, so far as it goes, in accordance with their customs.

4 Ordinarly it would have been the duty of this child to set fire to the dead body.

5 Before the introduction of matches the Santals had to resort to some device or other to have a fire. Even now they make use of some of them. Waht is here

73. THE OLD WOMAN WHO DIED AND LEFT HER SON[1].

In a village two people were living, mother and son; they had no relatives at all, and as time passed, the mother became like very old[2], and ultimately she became very ill and died.

Thereupon the village people came together and put the old woman properly on a bedstead, and four people lifted her up on their shoulders and started to carry her away along the street. At the end of the village-street they put her down for a while, because this is the custom with the Santals[3].

Now they did not take the very small child along to the place where they were going to cremate her[4]; they said: "What would it be to take this child along?" The child saw them walking away from the house. Again the village-people lifted her up and carried her on their shoulders, taking her away towards the forest; in a straw-rope[5] they took fire along and also an axe to cut timber with. They put her down at the edge of the forest.

They cut and collected timber and cut it into pieces of four cubits, whereupon they built the funeral pyre and placed the old woman upon this[6]; having placed her there, they set fire to her, and she was burnt to cinders entirely. Having finished their work, the people returned home.

Now the child was asking these people, saying to them: "Listen, sirs, where have you taken my mother away?" They told the

---

hinted at is straw tightly plaited together; when this is set fire to at one end, it will smoulder, and the straw will not be burnt up very quickly. It may, e. g., last over the night. When fire is needed, some hard breathing is sufficient to get a flame.

6 The procedure is as customary; the necessary wood for the funeral pyre is cut when needed.

Am go do hana muṇḍu senrele idi oṭo akadea. Menkhan uni koṛa gidrạ do onageye disạ akaṭa, dinge kulhi mucạtre senkateye raga kuṇḍạl kuṇḍạlte.

Khange, kathae, onka rak rakte, mit din, kathae, Candoe dayayena, coṭ khon adoe phedena, hoṛ leka bheskate. Adoe kuliyede kana, Henda beṭa, cedakem rakjoṅ kana? Ado uni gidrạ rak rakteye lạiketa, Babaṅ lạiam kana bhabna reaṅ katha. Aliṅ do bar eṅga honliṅ tahẽkana; ado tahen tahente uni iṅren iṅgạṅ hoṛ do, mit hapta gan hoyok kana, ruạteye gocena; ado sanam atoren hoṛ jarwayente iṅ go doko idikedea, parkomte gokkate kulhi kulhiteko idikedea. Ado noṇḍeko doholedea, onateṅ rakjoṅ kana noṇḍe kuṇḍạl kuṇḍạlte; enteṅ meneta, pase iṅ goṅ ṅel ruạṛkadege.

Ado ona bhabna katha aṅjomkate uni Cando do ạḍi bhabnae ạikạuketa, menwanae, Uh, nui gidrạ do bạṅ udukae khan, khạṭigeye rak gujuka. Adoe kulikedea, Henda bạbu, enḍekhan do am go dom ṅelegea? Adoe menketa, Hẽ entem udukạṅ khan doṅ ṅelkegea.

Ado uni Candoe menketa, Achaṅ udukamam ṅele khan, ạikhạ alom botoroka, ar alom rak baṛaea. Ado uni gidrại menketa, Acha, ado ohoṅ raga.

Khangeye riạu idikedea nicol sen, jemon okoe hõ dosra hoṛ do aloko ṅelkin. Ado idikateye metadea, Am do noṇḍege duṛup talaṅme, iṅ do am khon thoṛa gan iṅ danaṅlenge; adom ṅelle khan alom hohoea ar alom raga, baṅ khan ekkalteko jommea.

Ado uni gidrạ ma onḍegeye durup akana. Khange thoṛa ghạṛi khange uniren eṅgat ar dosra maejiu peako hecena, uni phed phedtege. Menkhan baṅdo Candoe ạḍkede, baṅdo cele, baṅko ṅel ṅamledea. Ar ac mae ṅel ṅamkedeteye oromkedea, nui do iṅgạṅ kanae mente.

---

7 In several Santal stories Chando (the Supreme Being) is supposed to come down to earth in some shape or other and to have conversation with men. Crying awakens his compassion.

child: "We have taken your mother over to the forest over there." The boy remembered this, and every day went to the end of the village-street and cried there rolling in the dust.

Then, people tell, hearing this crying Chando one day took pity on the child and came down from above[7], having assumed the shape of a Santal. He asked him: "Look here, my child, why are you crying?" Crying, the child told him: "Father, I am telling you my grief. We were we two, mother and son; as time passed, my mother, it is about a week ago, became ill and died; and all the village-people came together and took my mother away; carrying her on their shoulders, they took her away through the village-street. They put her down here; therefore I am crying and rolling in the dust here; because I think perhaps I might see my mother again."

Hearing of this grief, Chando felt great pity and said to himself: "O dear, if I do not show this child, he will cry himself to death." So he asked him: "Look here, my boy, then you want to see your mother?" He said: "Yes, if you will show her to me, I should like to see her."

"Very well," Chando said, "I shall show her to you, as you want to see her; beware, don't become afraid and don't cry." "All right," the child replied, "I shall certainly not cry."

Thereupon he told the child to come along and took him to a lonely place, in order that no other people should be able to see them. Having taken him there, he said to him: "Now you sit here in the meantime; I shall go away just a little from you, so that I am hidden; then if you see anything, don't call out and don't cry, otherwise they will at once eat you."

So the child was sitting there. After a short while his mother and three other women came, passing quite close to him; but whether Chando had screened him or somebody else, they did not catch sight of him. But as for himself, he saw and recognized her, that it was his mother.

Adọ onko ạimạiko galmaraojoṅ kana, Henda na, bhala okare manwa manwage sọ kana? Are ṅẹlkeťkoa, kathae, ḍuluḍuṅ biṅ bogeteko saṕeťkoa; arko mẹneťa, Bhala, họ, sạru aṛaḱ bogete ṅamoḱ kana. Adọ onage bogete biṇṭhiteko gẹť kuṭiyeťkoa. Ar tekekate bogete daka sãoteko jọmeťkoa.

Adọ uni gidrạ onko ṅẹlte bogeteye raḱ baṛajoṅ kana ruạṛkate dọ. Adọ Candoe metadea, Bạbu, adọ teheṅ khon dọ alom raga, baṅ khan am hõko idi aḍomea. Adọ kathae, ẹn hiloḱ khon bọtọrte adọ bae raḱ baṛaca.

Nọṇḍẹ noa kạhni dọ cabayena.

74. Babṛẽ ar gidi reaṅ.

Miťṭaṅ atore miť gọṭẹn babṛẽ kisạṛe tahẽkana; unkinren dọ gidrạ pidrạ dọ baṅko tahẽkan takina; adọ unkin ma dinạmgekin jhogṛaḱa, mẹnkhan jhogṛa dọ uni ạimạigeye ẹhọba. Khange uni dọ ạrisente birạsạli kate bidesteye oḍoṅ calaoena; khange calaḱ calaḱte miťṭen nonkan jaegae ṅamkeťa, ona jaegare dọ aema utạr gọć họṛko giḍi akaťkoa, maraṅ maraṅ bạbu bhạiạ lekanko, ar onko phẹḍrege miťṭaṅ gọć muci hõko giḍi akadea.

Adọ aema utạr gidiko phẹḍena ona mora ṅẹlte; mẹnkhan onko gidi dọ bes sapha gọć họṛ dọ baṅko jọmeťkoa, asọkaete uni

---

8 All dead people are supposed to have become bongas. What is told of these dead women reminds one of the stories of the people of the Netherworld.

9 The ḍuluḍuṅ is a small, very common, non-poisonous snake.

10 The Taro plant (Celocasia antiquorum, Schott.) is very commonly cultivated, the corm being eaten as curry.

11 The biṇṭhi is a cutter, made as a curved kind of knife, but without point; it is either fastened in a small piece of wood, or wholly of iron. When in use, the cutter's edge is turned towards the operator, the whole being held in an upright position by one foot. The stuff is cut by being pressed against the knife. All things that are to be prepared for curry are always cut into small pieces, so as to obviate the need of using any kind of implements at the time of eating.

12 The Santals have certain beliefs that crying intensifies the sufferings of dead relatives; here this is carried to the extreme that those in the other world might take steps to prevent such crying by bringing about the death of the person.

The women were talking together: "Look here, you, I wonder, where is it smelling[8] of man?" He saw them, people tell, eagerly catching grass-snakes[9], while they were saying: "Good for us, a good deal of Taro[10] is to be found." And they were cutting them into small pieces with a cutter[11], and, having boiled them they ate them ravenously together with their rice.

The child seeing them so occupied cried very much after his return. Then Chando said to him: "My boy, from to-day don't cry[12]; else they will take you also." So, from that day, out of fear he did not cry.

Here this story is ended.

74. THE BRAHMIN AND THE VULTURE[1].

In a certain village there was living a brahmin, a wealthy man; he and his wife had no children, and they were daily quarrelling; but it was always the woman who commenced. So he became tired of it all, and in a fit of temper he went away to another country; then, as he walked along, he came to a place, where they had thrown out a very large number of dead people, big big important people and such ones, and near to these they had also thrown a dead shoemaker.

A crowd of vultures[2] came down seeing the dead bodies; but the vultures did not eat the good clean dead ones; they were

74 [1] Told by Bhuju Murmu of Dhopahar.

[2] The vultures, common scavengers in India, are frequently seen circling high up in the air, watching for dead animals and coming down in large numbers, when they have sighted anything. It is rather a sight to see them, when they have collected for devouring a dead body; they apparently have a preparatory consultation; when this is finished, some one leads them on to commence work, the crowd following. It is possibly some such act that has induced the narrator to bring in the 'old vulture'. The collection of dead human bodies is not in accordance with what is customary.

mucigeko jome kana. Adǫ uni babṛę̃ dǫ onko gidi ńęlte mit́ ghạṛiye ţhak utạrena, are hahaṛayena; męnket́ae onko gidi samańre, Bhala noko gidi dǫ ạḍiko lelhagea, noko bes besko jǫmlekope dǫ, nui muci dǫ oka sebelpe jǫme kana. Adǫ ona kathage uni mitţen haṛam gidi dǫe ańjǫm tiok̕ket́a, adǫe metae kana, Henda, babṛę̃, am dǫ nǫṇḍę hęćlenme, adǫń lạiama, ona hahaṛa reań bhędem ńam kan khan.

Adǫ uni babṛę̃ uni haṛam gidi ţhene sęn sorena; adǫe metae kana, Ma sę bhalań ańjǫm tama, cet́ lekan katha kana. Adǫ uni haṛam gidi aćań kanso il mit́ţęne tot́ket́a, ar uniye emadea, are metadea, Ma sę noa am dǫ amak̕ mę̃t́ ţhen cǫsma leka oţkaome ar noko gǫć hǫṛge ńęlkom, bhala cet́ lekako ńęlǫk̕a.

Adǫ uni babṛę̃ ona kanso ilteye ńęlket́koa, onko bes bes gǫć hǫṛ dǫ manwa dǫko bań kana, onko dǫ janwar kanako, metak̕me emantenko, setako, pusiko. Adǫ ńęlkateye kulikedea, Cele, adǫm ńęlket́koa sę? Adǫe męnet́a, Hę̃ń ńęlket́koa. Adǫ uni gidiye metadea, Acha, adǫ do sę amak̕ oṛak̕te calak̕me, adǫ onka kate amren era bhala ńęletam, cele kanae. Adǫ uni babṛę̃ dǫ ǫṇḍę khone ruạṛena aćak̕ oṛak̕te; adǫ ǫṇḍę thoṛa danań khone ńęlkedea, uni aćren oṛak̕ hǫṛ uni hõ manwa dǫe bań kana, uni dǫe seta eńga kana.

Adǫ mǫnę mǫnęreye męnwana, Nui seta ţhen dǫ tahę̃kate cet́ pǫrhǫ bań ńam? Iń dǫ bidesrege bhageń sęnlena. Adǫ arhǫe ruạṛena bidestege.

Khange ona gidi reań kanso il dǫ sǫńgęregeye dǫhǫket́a; adǫ calak̕ calak̕te mit́ ţhen aema utạr hǫṛ muci oṛak̕reko jarwa akana; adǫ onko ńęlte uni babṛę̃ hõ ǫṇḍęye sęn sorena; adǫ ona gidi reań kanso ilteye ńęlket́koa, adǫ onko sanamgeko janwar kana, unkin mucitikin haṛam buḍhi dǫ seta ar pusi kanakin; męnkhan unkinren mit́ţań hǫpǫnerae tahę̃kantạkina, uni dǫe manwa jạt kangea.

[3] The language has a special name (k a n s o i l) for the three or four big feathers of a bird's wing.

especially eating the dead shoemaker. When the brahmin saw these vultures, he was for a moment utterly amazed and was wondering, saying before these vultures: "Well, these vultures are very stupid; eat these good ones first; what savoury do you find in eating this shoemaker?" An old vulture happened to hear this and said to him: "Look here, brahmin, just come over here, then I shall tell you, if you want to know the cause of what you think wonderful."

The brahmin then went up to the old vulture and said to him: 'Well then, I shall like to hear what it is that you can tell." The old vulture thereupon plucked out one of his big wing-feathers[3], and giving it said to him: "Now, you take and place this before your eyes like spectacles, and then look at these dead ones and see how they look."

The brahmin looked at them through the wing-feather and saw that those important people were not human beings at all; they were animals of sorts, dogs, cats, and so on. When he had looked, he asked him: "Well, you have seen them then?" "Yes, I have," the brahmin replied, whereupon the vulture said to him: "Well then, now go home and in this way have a look at your wife and see what kind she is." So the brahmin returned home from there, and, looking at his wife from a hidden place, he saw that she was not a human being either, she was a bitch.

He then considered it in his mind: "What will it possibly profit me to live with this dog? It was good that I went abroad;" whereupon he again went off to another land.

He kept the vulture's wing-feather with him; as he was walking along, he came to a place where a large crowd of people were gathered together in the house of a shoemaker; seeing these, the brahmin went near and looked at them through the wing-feather of the vulture; they were all animals; the shoemaker-couple, husband and wife, were one a dog and the other a cat; but they had a daughter, and she was a human being.

Adọ uni babṛẽ unkin muci haṛam ar buḍhiye metaťkina, Dẹn teheń dọ ape ṭheniń jọm ńũia, imąńpe, iń dọ ąḍi din khon bąń jọm akaťa. Khange unkin muci haṛam ar muci buḍhikin mẹnkeťa, Am dọ babṛẽ, ale dọ muci, metaǩme mora harta karbar họṛ kanale, adọ am dọ cekatele ẹm daṛeama? Adọ uni babṛẽ dọe mẹnkeťa, Bań, teheń dọń jọmgetapea.

Adọkin mẹnkeťa, Acha, ẹntem jọmkhanle emama. Adọko emadea; khangeye daka utukeťa, jọmkeťae; adọ jọm jiṛąu baṛakate adọ galmaraoe pọrtọnkeťa; unkin muci haṛam ar muci buḍhiye metaťkina, Adọ miťṭań iń galmaraoabona, adọben ańjọmkea sẹ bań?

Adọ unkinkin rọṛ ruąṛkeťa, Acha, masẹ ląiąlińme, tọbẹ thọrliń baḍaetama, khusiliń ąikąu khanliń hẽga; bańkhan ọhọliń hẽǩlea. Adọe metaťkina, Katha dọ noa kana. Aben dọ nui họpọneraben ẹmkińa sẹ bań? Onage asọl katha dọ. Adọ unkin muci haṛam ar muci buḍhi ona kathakin ańjọmkeťkhan ąḍitẹťkin hahaṛayena; ẹntekin mẹnwana, Bhala, nui dọ babṛẽ jąt kanae, mẹnkhan alańren họpọnera hataoeye mẹneťa, noa dọ ceť lekan hahaṛa, sẹ nui dọe bąul akana? ma sẹ bes ọkọćtelań kulijọńa, sąri sẹ nasẹ noa katha dọm mẹneťa.

Adọ uni babṛẽye mẹnkeťa, Bań, noa dọ sąri katha kangea; noa dọ ẹṛẹ sẹ phąsiąra katha dọ bań kana; iń dọ abenren họpọnera dọń hataoegea. Adọ unkinkin metadea, Acha, am dọm babṛẽ kana, nui dọ muci kuṛi kanae, mẹnkhan am dọ cekatem hatao daṛeaea? Adọ uni babṛẽye mẹnkeťa, Ona dọ, baba, ińaǩ khusi kana. Adọkin emadea, arkin metadea, Ma ąikhą baḍaekategem hataoede kana. Adọe ągukedea aćaǩ janam oṛaǩte.

Khange uniye adẹrkede khan uni pąhil era dọe dal ńirkedea, ẹnte uni ma manwa mae bań kan, ẹkẹn họṛmọtẹť họṛ andha leka Cando dọe sirjąu akaťa, ọnẹ lahare ọl akan leka, abo manwa dọ,

[4] The word used implies marriage.

[5] Refers to some other stories written down by Bhuju.

The brahmin then said to the shoemaker and his wife: "Let me eat and drink with you to-day; give me something; I have not had anything to eat for a very long time." The shoemaker-couple both of them then replied: "You are a brahmin; we are shoemakers, people who deal in the hides of dead animals; how can we possibly give you anything?" "Not so," the brahmin replied, "to-day I shall eat what you have."

"Very well," they said, "if you will eat, we shall give you." So they gave him, and he prepared rice and curry and ate; after having had his food and a rest, he commenced to talk and said to the shoemaker-couple: "There is one matter I want to have a talk about with you; will you listen to me or not?"

They answered: "Very well, please tell us; then only we shall know what you have in your mind; if we are pleased, we shall say yes, and if not, we are not going to say yes." "The matter is this," he said to them, "would you be willing to give me this daughter of yours? This is what I really mean." When the shoemaker-couple heard this, they became utterly astonished; they thought: "Strange, this man belongs to the brahmin caste; still he says he will take our daughter; what strange thing is this? or perhaps he is crazy? let us enquire carefully, do you really mean this or are you talking fibs?"

The brahmin then said: "No, this is true; this is not false or fraudulent; I want to take[4] your daughter." "Very well," they said to him, "you are a brahmin; she is a girl of the shoemaker-caste; how then can you marry her?" The brahmin replied: "That, sir, is my pleasure." So they gave her to him and said: "Bear in mind, knowingly you are taking her." Thereupon he brought her to his own house.

When he had brought this girl into his house, he gave his first wife a beating and drove her away, because she was not a human being; it was only the body that Chando had created such, as if to deceive people. As it has been previously written[5], as for us

jivi dọ ẹken janwar reak̓ atma kan tabona, ẹnte sedae hapṛamko rọṛ dọhọ akat̓a, baṅma, Abo dọ, kathae, eae dhao bo gujuk̓a ar eae dhao janamok̓ hoyok̓ tabona; unạk̓ dhaobon janamok̓a mẹnkhan jivi unạk̓ dhao purạulen tabon khan adọ, kathae, dhạrti dọ jalao maraok̓a, je leka sedae Cando dọ sẹṅgẹl dak̓re manwakoe jalao maraolet̓koa, ẹkẹn bar haṛam buḍhi dhiri danderreye baṅcaolet̓kina. Onka lekage, kathae, hapṛamkoak̓ katha lekate rọṛ dọhọ akana.

Mẹnkhanko mẹna, kathae, Sedae hapṛamkoak̓ katha dọ baṅ digdhạ akana, ona dọ hoyok̓ kangea. Arhõ mit̓ katha hapṛamko rọṛ dọhọ akat̓a, baṅma, Nãhãk̓ tinạk̓ din tayọmre cọṅ abo manwa dọ beṅgaṛbon banaga nãhãk̓, baṅ dọ beṅgaṛge harak̓, ar baṅ dọ manwagebon rẹṭhẹk̓, ona reaṅ abo dọ ọhọbon mẹn daṛelea. Cabayena noa kạhni dọ.

75. Rajak̓ gujuk̓ ar bọerạṅgi reaṅ gujuk̓.

Mit̓ṭaṅ raj dọ ạḍi họṛ dane emako kan tahẽkana; ẹnte hanapurire suke ṅama mẹnte. Ar mit̓ṭaṅ bọerạṅgi dọ kọekateye jọma, ar dan hõ bae dana. Adọ uni rajren cele hõ baṅko tahẽkantaea, ẹkẹn mit̓ṭaṅ họpọnerae tahẽkantaea, ar uni dọ dolan cọṭregeye tahẽna.

Ar rajak̓ gujuk̓ din sẹṭẹrentaea. Adọ kathae, aema aema Jọm rajako hẹćena. Adọ uniko idiye lạgit̓ko bọlọyena, ar bhageteko

---

6 The use of atma for spirit might be noted; one is reminded of the atman of the Upanishads. Atma is used by some Santals for spirit; but their regular word is jiu.

7 What is here stated as being something handed down by the Santal Ancestors is a curious mixture of Santal traditions and what has been heard from exponents of Hindu teachings.

8 As to the Santal traditions: these tell that all mankind was once destroyed by seven days' fire-rain (or, as some gurus say, by water-rain, they do not profess to be sure which); only one righteous couple (again the tradition is uncertain, whether it was the first human couple or a later one) were saved by Thakur, taking them into a cave in the mountain Harata, and from this couple the present human race is descended. What is here told by the narrator about the world to be destroyed after all human beings having been born seven times, is not regular Santal tradition.

human beings, our soul is only that of an animal[6]; the Ancestors have said[7], viz.: People tell, that we are to die seven times and to be born seven times; so many times we shall be born; but when our souls shall have completed so many times, then, people tell, the world is to be destroyed by fire, in the same way as Chando formerly destroyed all human beings by the fire-rain; he saved only one couple, a man and his wife, in a rock cave[8]. So, people tell, is the word of the Ancestors, that has been handed down.

But, people say, the word of the Ancestors of old is not doubted; that will come to pass. There is another word that has been handed down from the Ancestors: Presently, who can say after how long a time, we human beings shall use a hook to reach the egg-plant[9] fruit; whether the egg-plant will grow, or we human beings shall become stunted, this we are unable to say. This story is ended.

75. THE DEATH OF THE KING AND THE DEATH OF THE BOERANGI[1].

THERE was a king, who was giving gifts to many people, his intention being to secure happiness in the next world. There was a boerangi[2], who got his food by begging; also he did not give any gifts. Now the king had no relatives, he had only a daughter, and this girl was staying in the upper parts of his palace.

So the king's dying day came, and, people tell, a large number of messengers from the netherworld[3] came; they went in to take

---

[9] The egg-plant (Solanum Melongena, L.) is a common vegetable. The tradition referred to is of a very recent growth.

75 [1] As told by Bhuju Murmu of Dhopahar.

[2] A boerangi or boeragi, Sanskrit v a i r ā g i n, lit. passionless, is a religious mendicant, usually a Vishnuite, not a caste.

[3] Jǫm raj or -raja is the regent of the netherworld. The word is the Skr. Y a m a r ā j a, the idea being very hazy with the Santals. Here the messengers of the king of death are also called the same.

dalkedea. Ar mẽṛhẽt́ reaṅ koḍrateko koḍrakedea. Onako sanam uni hopponera do cot khongeye ńeńel kana.

Ar uni boeraṅgi ma ạḍi suk, pạlkire deckateko idiyede kana. Ado ona ńelkate uni raj hopponera do bogeteye rak̀joṅ kana. Ente Jom rajaren sipạhi, uni aćren apat do ạḍi sasetkateko or idikedea. Khange ona reaṅgeye bhabnajoṅa siń ńindạ. Khange mit́ṭaṅ hoṛ uni raj hopponerae kulikedea, metae kanae, Henda raj hopponera, am kulimeń meneta, ente thoṛa thuṛi galmarao katha menak̀tiṅa. Khange uni kuṛi gidrạ do kulikede khane rak̀ mẽtãhãketa. Ado kuṛiye roṛ ruạṛketa, Karon do noa kana, iń baba do ruạteye benḍaoena. Menkhan iń baba do Jom rajae or idikedea. Ar calak̀ bae reben kante, bhagete mẽṛhẽt́ ṭheṅgate bogeteko dalkedea; onate uni mãyãte dingeń raga. Menkhan hạni hana atoren boeraṅgi do ạḍi suk, palak cetanre deckateko idikedea. Ado mase apege bujhạupe, Iń baba do raj lekan hoṛ, ar uni boeraṅgi ma koejoṅ hoṛ kanae. Ado cekate Jom raja do iń baba thoṛa hõ sukte do baṅko idiledea?

Khange uni hoṛ uni kuṛiye metadea, Amren ạpum do, mãi, bedhorom hore tahẽkana. Ente am baba do perjakoren raj rapaje tahẽkana, menkhan perja hoṛ ạḍi harkhete dohoyetko tahẽkana. Onate onko Jom raja do mẽṛhẽt́teko dalkedea. Ar uni boeraṅgi do cele hõ cet́ hõ bae cekalet́takoa.

76. Kisạ̃ṛ haṛam do Jom rajako or idikede reaṅ.

Mit́ṭaṅ atoren mit́ kisạ̃ṛ haṛame tahẽkana, ar uniren do eae goten hopponko tahẽkantaea, ar onkoren bạhuko tahẽkana. Menkhan uni haṛam do, unạk̀ kimintet́ko tahẽkante sanam hoṛ são do katha ma baṅ pantek̀ kan tahẽkana. Maraṅić kimintet́ são do bhage leka katha jurik̀ kan tahẽkantaea.

---

[1] As told by Bhuju Murmu of Dhopahar.

him away and beat him severely; they scourged him with iron scourges. His daughter was seeing all this from her place above.

But the boerangi had great happiness; they put him in a palanquin and carried him away. Seeing this the princess was crying bitterly, because the messengers of the king of the netherworld had carried her father off, giving him hard suffering. She was in constant grief on account of this, both day and night. Then some one asked the princess: "Look here, princess, I want to ask you something; I have a little I wish to talk about." When he asked the girl, her face was flowing with tears. The girl said: "The cause is this, my father got fever and died, and my father the king of the netherworld dragged away, and as he was not willing to go, they beat him severely with an iron stick; therefore I am every day crying, feeling compassion with him. But the boerangi from the village over there had great happiness; they put him on a bedstead and carried him off. Now understand this: my father was a person like a king, and the boerangi a beggar. How is it, then, that the messengers of the netherworld did not let my father have a little ease, when they carried him off?"

The man then said to the girl: "Your father, my girl, was an unrighteous person; you see, your father was a king with subjects; but he kept his subjects in great misery. Therefore the messengers of the netherworld beat him with an iron; but the boerangi had not done anything to anybody.

76. HOW THE MESSENGERS OF THE KING OF THE NETHERWORLD CARRIED A WEALTHY OLD MAN AWAY[1].

In a certain village there lived a wealthy old man; he had seven sons who all were married. But since he had so many daughters-in-law, the old man did not hit it off with all of them; however, he was getting very well along with his eldest daughter-in-law.

Adọ kạmi din jọkhẹn dọ sanam họr kạmiko sẹn cabaḱa. Uni haṛam hõ oka din oka din dọ khẹt sẹngeye sẹnoḱa, onko koṛako bud batlaoakoa mẹnte.

Adọ, kathae, onka onkate miť din dọ uni haṛam nonkan dosa hoeyentaea, maraṅić kimintẹť dọ khẹtte uni haṛamaḱ daka hõe idi toraketa. Mẹnkhan uni haṛam dọ ḍher sạṅgiṅreye kạmi kan tahẽkante daka jọm dọe bilomena. Adọ onko dọ sanamko jọm baṛakette uniaḱ daka dọ khẹt piṇḍhạregeko hạruṗkaťa.

Adọ uni haṛam hẹćkate ona dakae ńẹl baṛaketa, daka ma sanamko mućketa. Adọ uni maraṅić kimintẹte họhọadea, are uduḱadea. Uni kimintẹť dọe mẹnketa, Acha, baba, ma noa dọ aloben jọma; dela oṛaḱre thoṛa daka dọ ṭukućreliń dọhọ akaťa, onaliń emabena.

Adọkin hẹćena, uni kimintẹť dọ ṭukuć reaṅ dakae ńẹlketa, onare hõ muć dọko thopro akana. Adọ uni haṛame mẹnketa, Acha, bạhu, adọ aloben dakaea, ma nãhãḱliń lạiaben kana, Dhinạṅ ạyuṗ daka gọdben, adọ ạḍi usạrate lo baṛa gọdben; ar jọm baṛakate aben dọ kulhi piṇḍạre duṛuṗkoḱben.

Khange kedoḱ jọm baṛakate kulhi piṇḍạreye duṛuṗ akana. Khange bar họṛkin hẹćena cele cọṅ, uni haṛam dọ banar sopokin saṗkedea, arkin idikedea.

Adọ thoṛa ghạṛi khange raraḱko ẹhọṗena. Adọ uni maraṅić kimintẹť dọ sẹnkateye kuliyetkoa, Cedaḱpe raḱjoṅ kana? Adọko lạiae kana, Baba dọe beṇḍaoena. Khange nui dọe mẹnkeťa, Baṅ, bae beṇḍao akana; barea họṛtekin ọr idikedea. Nọṇḍẹ cabayena.

---

[2] The working season is with the Santals the rainy season, when they cultivate their fields; it is one of their names for the rainy season.

[3] When the work is in full swing, the workers do not go home for their food before evening; food is brought out to them by one of the household women, who stays at home as cook.

[4] That ants get into the food is nothing unusual; what is unusual here is that they had also got into the cooking-pot at home. The old man apparently

During the working season[2], all were in the habit of going off to work; the old man would now and then go to the rice-fields in order to instruct the boys.

Then, people tell, it one day so happened with the old man, his eldest daughter-in-law took also the old man's food out to the rice-fields[3]. But, as the old man was working in a very distant place, he was late in coming to eat. When they, all of them, had eaten, they put his food on a rice-field ridge and covered it up.

When the old man came and looked at the food, all the food had become full of ants, whereupon he called his eldest daughter-in-law and showed it to her. She said: "Very well, father, do not eat this; come along home, I have left some rice in the cooking-pot; I shall give you this."

So they returned; the daughter-in-law looked at the rice in the cooking-pot; in this also the ants had come in great numbers. The old man then said: "All right, daughter-in-law, do not prepare any food; I tell you this now: Prepare food in good time this evening, and then be quick and dip the food out; and when you have had your food, go and sit down in the veranda towards the street."[4]

After having had her evening meal she went and sat down in the street-veranda. Then two persons came, who knows who they were; they took the old man, one in each arm, and took him away.

A short while afterwards they commenced to cry, whereupon the eldest daughter-in-law went and asked them: "Why are you crying?" They told her: "Father is dead." "No", she replied, "he is not dead; two persons dragged him away." Here this is ended.

---

takes this as an omen, that his days are over. Incidentally it might be noted that it is of not infrequent occurrence among the Santals that they have a presentiment of coming death and tell even the time when it is to come.

77. Babṛẽ reaḱ katha.

Miṭṭaṅ babṛẽ kisạṛe tahẽkana ar uniren bạhu dọkin bareaḱtaea. Ar uni babṛẽ dọ oka dọe kọe baṛaea, ar kọete hõ besgeye bajhao ạguia. Adọ kathae, miṭ dhao dọ ceṭ cọṅ mọnre hạ̃sade. Adọe mẹnkeṭa, Bhala teheṅ dọ bhagwakate hạṭiạteṅ calaḱa, bhalako manaoiṅa sẹ baṅ. Adọ kathae, onka mẹnkateye bhagwayente hạṭiạteye calaoena. Adọ kathae, ẹn hiloḱ dọ cele hõ bako salamae kana. Adọ ọṇḍẹ hạṭiạ ṭạṇḍire bako salamade khane mẹnkeṭa, Bhala ato sẹn kọkọe iṅ calaḱa, ọntẹre dọko salamaṅa sẹ baṅ, onaṅ biḍạulege. Adọ onka mẹnkate ato sẹn hõe calaoena. Adọ kathae, atoren hõ baṅgeko salamae ar kọe hõ bako emae kan. Khane ạṛisente oṛaḱteye ruạṛ hẹćena.

Adọ arhõ ghuriạ̃ hạṭiạre dọ, kathae, khube dhutiyena, aṅgrọpenae are dạhṛiyena, adọ hạṭiạteye calaḱ kana. Adọ kathae, hor hortege bogeteko salam idiae kana, ar ona hạṭiạ ṭạṇḍire hõ bogeteko salamae kana. Adọ kathae, muluć mulućе landajoṅ kana. Ar onko dokandar hõ, kathae, jãhãnaḱe kọeleko khanko ẹm gọṭae kana.

Adọ inạkateye mẹnkeṭa, Bhala ọnẹ unre bhagwakate kọkọe iṅ sẹnlena, unre bako bạsutadiṅa. Ọkọe tora bhala teheṅ iṅ sẹn gelaḱa, manaoiṅako sẹko baṅ. Adọ onka mẹnkate, kathaeye calaoena. Adọ kathae, ạḍiko salamae kana ar kọe hõ ạḍiko emae kana. Adọ unre hõ muluć mulućе landajoṅ kana.

Adọ ọṇḍẹ khon oṛaḱteye hẹćen khan, kathae, onae idileṭ kicrić dọ dọhọ baṛakate pẹ pon dhaoteye ḍọbọkaṭa. Are mẹneṭa, Dhạni

---

1 As will be seen, the story 'The Brahmin and the Vultures' turns on the same point as the last part of this one. The narrators are different, this tale being one of Sagram's, and there are more than twenty-five years between the taking down of the two stories. It might be noted that the stories do not presuppose the transmigration of human souls into the bodies of animals, but rather the opposite, that the souls of animals may take human shape.

2 The strip of cloth, as the Santali b h a g w a is translated, is a piece of cloth some four feet long and ten to twelve inches broad, taken between the thighs and fixed behind and in front in the ḍ o r a, the waist-string used by all male

77. THE STORY OF A BRAHMIN[1].

THERE once lived a brahmin, who had two wives; this brahmin sometimes went begging, and by begging he also managed to make a good income.

One day, people tell, some fancy or other suddenly took hold of him. He said: "Well, to-day I shall put on only a strip of cloth[2] and go to the market; I wonder whether they will show me respect or not." And with this in mind he put the strip of cloth on and went to the market. That day, people tell, no one greeted him; and as they did not greet him there at the market-place, he said: "Well, I shall go to the village to beg; I shall try whether they will greet me there or not." With this in his mind he went there also. And, they tell, the village people neither greeted him nor gave him any alms. Tired and worried he returned home.

The next time he went to the market, people tell, he clothed himself in fine loin-clothes, donned a jacket and a turban and started for the market. As he went along the road, they tell, people greeted him constantly, and at the market-place also people greeted him everywhere. He was quietly laughing and smiling. The shopkeepers also, people tell, at once gave him whatever he asked them for.

After this he said: "Strange, when I went begging having only a strip of cloth on, they did not heed me. Well, to-day I shall at once go and have a try whether they will show me respect or not. With this in his mind, they tell, he went; and, they tell, everywhere people greeted him and also gave him very much alms. Then also he was quietly laughing and smiling.

When he reached home, people tell, he took off the clothes he had donned and bowed three or four times to them, and said:

Santals, just sufficient to conceal the private parts. Commonly used by all doing work in the rice-fields or mud.

posag! dhạni posag! Tin dhaoe ḍọbọkeťa, un dhaoge onkae rọṛeťa. Are mẹneťa, Pirthimire jọtọ khon manọtanaǩ dọ kicrić kangea, ar noa chaḍa dosra manọtanaǩ dọ ceť hõ bạnuǩan.

Adọ onakate, kathae, arhõ miť dhao dọ disomte kọkọeye oḍok sẹn akana. Adọ unreye ńẹlkeťkoa, miťṭaṅ bajarre maraṅ dukte bẹbạṛić họṛko gujuǩ kana. Ḍọmko, tiliko, kahaṛko, hạḍiko, bạuriko, bhũiạko, jugiko, mahrako, khạtriko, babṛẹ̃ko, kạtko, moerako, tamboliko, jọtọ jạtge bogete gujuǩ kane ńẹlkeťkoa, ar bahreteko giḍikako kana. Ar cọṭren cẽṛẽ ãṛgokate mạṛĩko uṭhạueťa. Adọ onkae ńẹlkeťko khan, uni babṛẽ dọe mẹnkeťa, Durrẹ! noko gidi dọ bhage bhage jạt dọ bako jọmeťkoa. Noko chuṭạliạ jạtgeko jọmeťkoa.

Adọ kathae, unre gidiye mẹnkeťa, Ale dọ họṛaǩ mạṛĩge pạhil dọle uṭhạu maṛaṅeťa, ẹnkhante noko emanten jạtaǩ dọle uṭhạua.

Adọ uni babṛẽye mẹnkeťa, Noko bhale bhale jạt babṛẽ sẹ khạtri, noko dọ bhale jạt dọko baṅ kana?

Adọ gidiye mẹnkeťa, Onko dọko baṅ kana, onko dọko seta pusi kana. Ar judi bam pạtiạuǩ kan khan, nẹ miťṭaṅ il iṅ toťam kana. Kọkọeyem bọlọǩ jọkhẹn noa il dọ bọhọǩre rẹbẹťkam, adọ unrem ńẹl ṭhikkoa, cele cele jạtko họṛ akana mẹnte.

Adọ sạriye emade khan, ona il dọe idi torakeťa. Adọ kọkọe bọlọǩ jọkhẹn, kathae, ona il dọ bọhọǩreye rebeťkeť khan dọ, sạriye ńẹleťkoa, ọkọe dọko pusi kana, ar ọkọe dọko seta kana, ọkọe dọko gạí kana. Nonka emanten jạte ńẹleťkoa. Ar duṛuṕ lạgiť gaṇḍo mạciko hõ mocateko gẹr ạguyeťteko belae kana; ar kọe hõ mocatege gẹr ạguyeťteko emae kana.

---

[3] Lit. 'big grief', one of their names for dangerous epidemics, more especially cholera.

[4] The narrator enumerates the castes most commonly met with in the Santal country. Doms are musicians, Tilis oilmen, Kahars palanquin-bearers, Hadis scavengers, Bauris earth-workers, Bhuyas cultivators (the last three castes, possibly also the Kahars, are semi-hinduized aboriginals), Jugis now cultivators, Goalas (Mahras) cowherds, Khatris up-country traders, Kayasths writers, Moeras confec-

"Lucky raiments! lucky raiments!" Every time he bowed he spoke in this way, and added: "On the earth the most honoured of all are the clothes, and besides them there is nothing honoured at all."

After this, people tell, he had again once gone out in the land to beg. On this occasion he saw that in a certain town an awful number of people were dying from a severe epidemic[3]. Doms, Tilis, Kahars, Hadis, Bauris, Bhuyas, Jugis, Goalas, Khatris, Brahmins, Kayasths, Moeras, Tambolis[4], in fact all castes and races he saw dying, and they were throwing the dead bodies away outside. And the birds of the air[5] were coming down and picking the dead bodies. When he saw them doing this, the brahmin said: "Dear me, these vultures do not eat the better-class bodies; they are eating the bodies of these untouchables."

Then, people tell, a vulture said: "We first pick the bodies of human beings; then only we take the bodies of other kinds."

The brahmin replied: "These better-caste people, Brahmins or Khatris, are not these of better castes?"

The vulture said: "These here are not; they are dogs and cats. If you do not believe it, see, here I am plucking out a feather for you. When you go out to beg, fix this on your head; then you will see right, which castes are human beings."

Truth to tell, when he gave him the feather, he took it along with him; and when he would enter anywhere to beg, and had the feather fixed on his head, he could really see the people, some of them are cats, some are dogs, and some are cows; in this way he could see the different kinds, To sit down, they took seats and stools with their teeth and brought them and placed them before him; their gifts they also brought with their teeth and gave him.

---

tioners and Tambolis traders, to mention their principal occupations. They are all Hindus. It might be noted that they all will, if possible, endeavour to get some cultivation. A plot of land is something to fall back on.

[5] Lit. 'of the high', i. e., air, from where the vultures are seen to come down.

Adǫ kathae, onate bae bataoet'a. Adǫ ać oṛak'teye hęćen khan, kathaeye ńęlet'kin dǫ, ać bạhu hõ mit' dǫe seta kan ar mit' dǫe pusi kan. Khange mǫnre ạḍi hirkhại ạikạuket'a, adǫ ać ǫṛak're hõ bae tahẽ daṛeat'a. Adǫ kathae, daṛan daṛante mit'ṭaṅ mahra kuṛiye ńęlkedea, inige, kathae, hǫṛ jivi dǫ menak'tae. Adǫ kathae, uni kuṛigeye bạhukedea, ar aćren dǫe bạgiket'kina.

Adǫ ǫnę onka emanten jạt reak' jivi hǫṛ manware menak'tabona. Baṅdǫ sạri baṅdǫ nase, ǫnę onka hǫṛko galmaraoa.

Adǫ ęnę niạ katha hõń mucạt'ket'a.

78. Gǫć bạhui ńęl ruạṛkede koṛa reaṅ.

Oka atore cǫṅ, kathae, barea haṛam buḍhikin tahẽkana. Adǫ kathae, erat'tęt' dǫe beṇḍaoena; uni erae beṇḍaoen khan, uni koṛa reak' mǫn dǫ rạput'entaea. Adǫ uni koṛa dǫ siṅ ńindạ bhabna ar rak'tege din dǫ calak'taea. Uni koṛa dǫ oka ṭhen erataeko ḍahǫnledea, ǫṇḍęge sęnkateye raga siṅ hõ ar ńindạ hõ.

Adǫ kathae, uni koṛa reak' rak' aṅjǫmte baṅdǫ Isor baba, baṅdǫ jāhāe ǫkǫe uni samaṅreye teṅgoyena, are kulikedea, Henda bacha, cedak'em rak'joṅ kana? Adǫe rǫṛ ruạṛket'a, baṅma, Ińren juri dǫ Isor babae rẹćkidińa; nǫṇḍęle ḍahǫn akadea, ona bhabnateń rak'joṅ kana.

Adǫe metadea, Alom raga. Uni koṛa dǫe męnket'a, Baṅ, baba, rak' dǫ ǫhǫń bạgilea.

Adǫe metadea, Acha tǫbę khan amren juri dǫm ńęlegea? Adǫe męnket'a, Hẽ ęntem uduk'ạń khan dǫń ńęlkegea. Adǫe metadea, Dela ęṇḍękhan iń uduk'ama.

Adǫ ạḍi sạṅgiṅ hanapuriteye idikedea, are metadea, Am dǫ nǫṇḍę duṛup'kok'me, adǫ nāhāk'em ńęlea. Adǫ kathae, sạrige lagṛẽko ęnęć kane ńęlket'koa. Adǫe kulikedea, Amren juri dǫm ńęl ńamkedea?

---

1 As taken down by Bhuju Murmu of Dhopahar.

2 Isor, from Skr. *iśvara*, master, lord, god, now used all over North India as the name for God, is also used by non-Christians about the Supreme Being.

3 The dance mentioned is the most common of the Santal dances, *lagṛẽ*.

This was not enough, people tell, to make him give in. But when he reached home, he saw his wives, one was a dog and the other a cat. Then he became utterly disgusted in his mind, so that he was unable even to remain in his own home. As he was wandering about, he saw a cowherd girl; she, people tell, had the soul of a human being. So he made this girl his wife, and his first ones he left.

In this way we human beings have souls of different beings in us. Whether it is true or false, anyhow so people say.

So there I have ended also this story.

78. THE YOUNG MAN WHO SAW HIS DEAD WIFE AGAIN[1].

In a certain village, people tell, a couple, a man and his wife, were living. Then the wife died, and when his wife had died, the young man became broken-hearted. Day and night passed for the young man with grief and crying. Where they had cremated his wife, there the young man went and cried both during daytime and at night.

Then, people tell, hearing the young man's crying, whether it was Isor[2] or somebody else, he stood before the young man and asked him: "Listen, my dear youngster, why are you crying?" He replied: "Isor has bereft me of my mate; here we cremated her; on account of this grief I am crying."

"Don't cry," he said to him. The young man then answered: "No, father, I shall certainly not leave off crying."

"Well then," he said to him, "you wish to see your mate?" "Yes", he replied; "if you will show her to me, I should like to see her." Whereupon he said to him: "Come then, I shall show her to you."

Thereupon he took him very far away, right to the other world, and said to him: "You sit down here; presently you will see her." Then, people tell, he really saw people dancing[3], whereupon he

Adoe menketa, Hẹñ ñẹl ñamkedea, mocage thor hendegetaea. Adoe metadea, Onẹ disạime mocarem sẹṅgẹlade tahẽkana, onate moca do hẹndẹyentaea.

Ado uni koṛa do aćren juri ṭhene ñir sẹnenteye hạṛupkedea, unrekin ñapam ruạṛena. Ado ẹnte uni koṛa ma noa disom khon goćkate ma bae sẹn akan, onate bako gateyede kana.

Ado bạhuttẹtgeye metadea, Do ruạṛlenme, culhạ kuḍạmre sakom iñ topa akata, ona ạgu daraeme. Ado uni koṛa doe ruạṛena, ar culhạ kuḍạmre hạtṛạu baṛayet jokhẹnge biñe gẹrkedea; adoe goćena. Ẹnẹkin ñapamena. Noa kạhni do cabayena.

---

[4] When a body is cremated, fire is first set to the mouth of the dead.

asked him: "Have you caught sight of your mate?" "Yes", the young man replied, "I have caught sight of her; her mouth, however, is black." He said to him: "That's so; remember you applied fire to her mouth[4]; therefore her mouth has become black."

The young man then ran up to his mate and embraced her; and so they met again. But the young man had not gone from this land there dead; therefore they did not treat him as their companion.

So his wife said to him: "Do go back at once; behind the fire-place I have buried a wristlet; bring that along with you." So the young man returned, and whilst he was groping with his hand behind the fire-place, a snake bit him, and he died. So in this way they met again. This story is ended.

STORIES ABOUT ANIMALS BORN BY WOMEN

79. Hąṛũ koṛa reaṅ.

Sedae jugre, kathae, mit́ṭaṅ hǫṛ khub kisąṛe tahẹkana, ar uniren dǫ turui gǫṭẹn koṛa gidrą ar barea kuṛi gidrą hoekatege uni hǫṛ dǫ rua̧ ńamkedea; ar uni oṛak̓ hǫṛ dǫ un jǫkhẹn bhąrti hǫṛmǫe tahẹkana. Adǫ uni hǫṛ dǫ ina̧ ruątege bako bes daṛeadete inątegeye gǫćena. Adǫ onko koṛako dǫ uni apat reak̓ dustur leka jǫtǫko kam kajket́teko puruchunkat́a.

Adǫ ona tayǫm uni oṛak̓ hǫṛtaeren dǫ gidrąi hoeyena. Adǫko ńẹlkede dǫ, mit́ṭaṅ hąṛũ gidrąi janam akade; uni hąṛũ hǫ̃e koṛa gidrą kange. Adǫ ona aṅjǫmkate jǫtǫ hǫṛko jarwayena, ar atoren hǫ̃ko jarwayena uni gidrą ńẹle lągit́. Khange adǫ ńẹl baṛakate uni maejiu hǫṛ dǫ ąḍiko landawadea, ar akoren hǫpǫntẹt́ko ar peṛa hǫṛko dǫko metadea, Ma, nui gidrą dǫ gǫć giḍikaeme, alom dǫhǫyea; bogete hǫṛko landawabon kana.

Adǫ unre uni maejiuye mẹnket́a, Baṅa, nui gidrą dǫ ǫhǫń gǫćlea. Candoge cet́ ghoṭnate cǫṅ nonkan gidrą dǫe emadiń, ona dǫ unigeye baḍaea. Iń thǫ hąṛũ sǫṅgẹ lae loṭha dǫ baṅ tahẹkana. Apattẹt́pe ńẹlledegea, ar uni tahẹkanrege hǫṛmǫre hǫ̃ basawadińa. Adǫ Ċando baba nonkan gidrągeye emadiń khan, cet́ iń mẹna? Iń dǫ ǫhǫń giḍilea, ar gǫć hǫ̃ ǫhǫń gǫćlea; ąsul harakaeań. Adǫ Candogeye ja lekayege.

Adǫ onko akoren peṛa ar hǫpǫntẹt́tekoko mẹnket́a, Judi nui gidrą bam giḍiye khan, ẹnḍẹkhan ale dǫ bale sor ocoama; am dǫle begar giḍikama.

Adǫ uni maejiuye mẹnket́a, Ona dǫ apeak̓ khusi; begariṅre hǫ̃pe ar parlek mit́repe dǫhǫń, ona dǫ apeak̓ khusi. Mẹnkhan iń

---

1 The monkey here mentioned, in Santali hąṛũ, is the Langur or Hanuman (Presbytis entellus), common in most parts of North-eastern India, and well known to the Santals.

79. THE STORY OF A HANUMAN BOY[1].

In olden times, people tell, there once lived a very wealthy man. When he had become the father of six sons and two daughters, he got a fever. At this time his wife was with child. As they were unable to make him well from this fever, he died from it; and his sons did all according to custom in connexion with their father and performed the funeral rites.

After this his widow gave birth to a child; when they looked at it, they saw it was a Hanuman child she had given birth to; this Hanuman was also a male. Hearing this, all people there came together, also the village people, to see this child. Having seen it, they laughed very much at the woman, and her sons and relatives said to her: "Do kill this child and throw it away; don't keep it; people are laughing at us a good deal."

The woman then said: "No, I shall certainly not kill this child; who knows what accident it may have been through which Chando has given me such a child; He knows it. I have not been having any liaison with a Hanuman. You saw his father, and I became with child while he was still living. When Father Chando has given me such a child, what can I say? I shall certainly not throw him away, nor am I going to kill him; I shall nurse him, and let him grow up. Afterwards Chando may do with him whatever He likes:"

Her children and their relatives then said: "If you do not throw this child away, we shall not let you come near to us; we shall separate you from us and have nothing more to do with you."

"That is as you please," the woman replied; "whether you separate me from yourselves or you keep me together with yourselves,

do nui gidrạ do ohogeń giḍilea. Jāhā lekateń ạsul harakaegea; ado harakate doe ja lekaḱge. Iń tho jāhāe tuluć do bań gidrạ akadea; apattete tahẽkangea, ar sanam horpe ńelledińgea, un khonge tahẽadińa mente pe baḍaegea. Adope begar giḍiń khan, ceť iń mena? Ona do apeaḱ sana.

Ado khange sạri onkae menkeť khan, ado judạreko kumbạwadea, ar jomaḱ doko emadegea, bako edre sạṅgiń utạradea. Ado sạri murukkate uni ạimại do uni gidrạ doe ạsul harakedegea. Ado tahen tahente sạri uni gidrại hara buruyena, ar onka hoṛ lekage roṛ hõe ceťketa. Khange adoe harayen khan, adoe kạmi baṛaea.

Ado tahen tahente, kathae, tin din badre coń onko napṛaḱko koṛa do birte sahan maḱko calaḱ kana, ar inạ lasāṛhẽte goḍako khetko lạgiťko ṭạṇḍijoń kana. Ado, kathae, uni hāṛū koṛa hõe menketa, Iạ ayo, iń hõ dadańteko sāote birteń calaka. Iń hõ goḍae lạgiť iń maḱ ṭạṇḍialańa.

Adoe metadea, Do eṇḍekhan calaḱme. Ado ṭeṅgoće ńawadea, ado onko sāote birteye calaoena. Adoe metako kana, Henda dada, iń do oka sen iń maga? Ado onko dadatteko do cigạrikate oka sen khub bir gajaṛ menaḱ, onteko udukadea, arko metadea, Hone ya, honte am do maḱ ṭạṇḍijońme. Ado sạri oneko udukade sene calaoena. Ado ńel baṛakate mitṭań darere ṭengoće maḱ biť oṭokata, ado arhõ onko ṭhengeye ruạṛ hećena.

Ado onko dadattekoko maḱ mokońen khanko menketa, Delabo nitoḱ do oṛaḱtebo calaka. Ado ać hõe calaoente ona ṭeṅgoće

2 It might be noted that what has here and in some other places in this story been translated 'human' in Santali may just as well mean Santal or Santali; the narrator has without doubt taken it in this signification. The Santal word hoṛ, by which name they call themselves, means a human being, more especially as represented by the Santal.

3 Goḍa, here translated 'highland-field', is with the Santals a plot of land lying generally some distance away from their houses; these fields are used mainly for cultivating certain jungle corns.

this is as you please; but I am certainly not going to throw this child away. In some way or other I shall nurse him and let him grow up; when he grows up, he may fare as it may happen. I have not got him with anybody; his father was living, and you all were seeing me and know that I was with child from that time. So if you separate me and throw me off, what can I say? That is as you like."

Truth to tell, as she spoke in this way, they made a small hut for her in another place; but they gave her her food; they did not put her utterly away in their anger. So the woman resolutely worked, nursed him and made him grow up. As time passed, the child grew up and became big, he also learnt to speak just like a human being[2]. When he had grown up, he applied himself to work.

As time passed, people tell, who knows after how long a time, the elder boys went to the forest to cut firewood; with this as a pretext they were clearing jungle to make highland-fields[3] and rice-fields. The Hanuman-boy, people tell, then also said; "I say, mother, I also wish to go with my brothers to the forest. I shall also clear jungle[4] to make highland-fields for us two."

"By all means go," she replied, whereupon she found an axe for him, and he went with his brothers to the forest. "Look here, brothers," he said to them, "in which direction shall I clear jungle?" His brothers then sneeringly pointed in the direction where there was thick forest and jungle. "Over there," they said to him; "go over there you and clear the jungle." So he really went in the direction they pointed out to him, and after having had a look round, he drove his axe into a tree, whereupon he again came back to where the others were.

When his brothers had finished cutting trees, they said: "Come along, now we shall all go home." Then he also went and fetched

[4] A genuine Santal trait. To clear jungle is, so to say, an instinct with them.

ạgukeṭṭaea, adọ onko sãote oṛakteye hẹćena. Adọ din hilok onko sãoteye calaka ar onka darere ṭẹṅgọć mak biṭ oṭokate onkoko mamak ṭhengeye hẹćkoka. Adọ tinre oṛakteko hijuk, adọ uni hõ un jọkhẹngeye hijuka.

Adọ tahẹn tahẹnte miṭ din dọko metae kana, Am dọ din hilok nọṇḍẹ ale ṭhengem hẹćkok kana; tin jọkhẹnem makeṭ kana? Dinạm hilok thọ nọṇḍẹgele ńẹleṭmea.

Adọe mẹnkeṭa, Baṅa, dada, iń dọ mak mọkọńkatege cọń ape ṭhen mań hijuk kan.

Adọko mẹnkeṭa, Henda ya, oka batem mak gọṭeṭa? Ẹṛẹyetle cọm ceṭ cọń.

Adọe mẹnkeṭa, Baṅa, dada, bań ẹṛẹyeṭpea, na họnẹć delabon iń udukapea. Inạ dọ ape mẽṭṭepe ńẹl ạguia.

Khange adọko mẹnkeṭa, Delabon sẹ ya, bhalabon ńẹltaea. Behaj khạṭiye rọṛeṭ dọ. Adọ sạri mak mọkọńenteko mẹnkeṭa, Delabon ńẹltaea, adọ henkate oṛaktebon calaka. Adọ sạri jọtọ họṛ sẹnkateko ńẹlkeṭṭae dọ, sạri ạḍi marań ṭạṇḍiye mak akaṭ. Khange adọko mẹnkeṭa, Henda ya, tinkore bhalae makketa? Siń sạṭup thọ abo ṭhengeye sẹnkoka. Nui tuluć dọ eṅgate kạmi dọ ọhọbo daṛelena. Ńẹlpe, abo dọ nunạk kurumuṭutebon makeṭ kanre hõ, nui unạk dọ okorbo ṭạṇḍi akaṭa. Adọ enka rọṛ rọṛtege oṛakteko hẹćena.

Adọ ona mak gitić dareko rọhọṛen khan, ọr jaora baṛakateko jẹrẹṭaṭa, adọ sanam lọ ṭạṇḍiyena. Adọ uni hạ̃ṛũ koṛa họe mẹnkeṭa, Henda ayo, dadańteko dọko atar ṭạṇḍikeṭṭeko siyeṭ kana. Ẹ ayo, iń dọ celeteń sioka? Ḍaṅgra ńam ạguańme.

[5] The manner of clearing jungle here referred to is very primitive. It is now-a-days very seldom resorted to by the Santals; the Paharia tribes living on the hills in the country may still be observed using the method, I am told. The jungle is cut down, the trees and shrubs are left to dry in the sun; just before the rains commence, all is set fire to. The ashes make a kind of manure. The seed, mostly the bajṛa, Sorghum vulgare, Pers., is sown with the help of a primitive wooden bar. What is here told is a little more 'advanced' cultivation, in as much as some ploughing is resorted to.

his axe and went home together with the others. Every day he went together with the others, and acted in the same way; having driven his axe into a tree, he came back to where the others were cutting trees; and when they went home, at that time he also came.

As time passed, they one day said to him: "Every day you come here and stay with us; at what time do you cut trees? Day after day we see you here?"

"No, brothers," he replied, "why, I am coming to you after I have finished cutting."

"Look here," they said, "how is it that you are getting ready so quickly? You are telling us fibs most probably."

"No, brothers," he replied, "I am not telling you fibs; if you don't believe it, come along, I shall show you. Then you will see with your own eyes what it is."

"Come along then, you fellows," they said; "we shall see what he has. He is speaking with an amazing confidence. Having finished cutting, they said: "Come, let us have a look at what he has; then we may go home round that way." So, truth to tell, they all went and looked at his work; really he had cleared a very large piece of land. They said: "Look here, you, at what time, I wonder, has he cleared this? The whole day he has been coming and been with us. We shall certainly not, dash it, be able to work like him. Look, although we have been working so industriously, why, we have not cleared as much as he has." Talking in this way, they reached home.

When the trees they had cut dried, they dragged them together to one place and set fire to them[5]; all was burnt, and it became a bare field. Then the Hanuman boy also said: "Listen, mother, my brothers have set fire to all and cleared their fields and are ploughing. Mother, what shall I have to plough with? Get me some bullocks."

Adọ eṅgattẹt́te mẹnket́a, E beṭa, okareṅ ṅamkoa? Hoṛ hõ iṅ dọ baṅko pạtiạuaṅa. Okarelaṅ ṅamkoa? Ar alaṅ dọ itạ rạnu hõ bạnuḱtalaṅa. Cet́laṅ casa?

Adọ uni hạ̃rũ koṛae mẹnket́a, Dadaṅteko dọ goḍa hoṛoko ẹret́ kana. Alaṅ dọ, ayo, cet́ balaṅ cas?

Adọ uni eṅgattẹt́ arhõe rọṛket́a, Cekayam, beṭa? Onko dọ menaḱtakoteko caset́a. Alaṅ dọ itạ rạnuge bạnuḱ khan, beṭa, cet́laṅ casa?

Adọ uniye mẹnket́a, Henda ayo, cet́ itạ hõ bạnuḱtalaṅa?

Adọe mẹnket́a, Bạnuḱanaṅ, beṭa.

Arhõ uni koṛae mẹnket́a, Henda ayo, adọ jãhãn itạko hõ bạnuḱtalaṅa?

Adọ uni eṅgattẹt́e mẹnket́a, Ona mit́ṭaṅ hotọt́ menaḱa, ar baṅkhan cet́ hõ bạnuḱanaṅ.

Adọ uni koṛae mẹnket́a, Acha, cet́ hõ bạnuḱ khan, dẹn inạge ṅawaṅme; inạge iṅ hõ dadaṅteko sãoteṅ ẹrkaḱa. Adọ sạri ona hotọt́ itạye ṅawadea, adọ ona itạ ghẽṭkate nui hõ ọnẹye maḱ ṭạṇḍilet́ ṭhen sẹnkateye rọhọe baṛaket́a. Adọ dadattekoko kuliyede kana, Henda ya, am dọ tisem sia? Bam ṭạṇḍi baṛayet́ dọ.

Adọe mẹnket́a, Iṅ dọ, dada, bin ṭạṇḍitegeṅ ẹrket́a.

Adọko mẹnket́a, Cet́ yam ẹrket́a?

Adọ ać hõe kuliket́koa, Henda dada, ape dọ cet́pe ẹrket́a?

Adọko mẹnket́a, Ale dọ ya, goḍa hoṛole ẹr akat́a.

Adọ uni hõe mẹnket́a, Iṅ hõ, dada, goḍa hoṛogeṅ ẹr akat́a; ẹr dọ baṅa, rọhọe akat́aṅ.

6 The kind of rice here alluded to is sown broadcast at once and not transplanted. It is very rarely seen in these parts, but is common with the Santals who have migrated to Assam.

7 The pumpkin here mentioned is the Cucurbita lagenaria, very commonly cultivated by the Santals and other races. The fruit may grow to a very large size. It is used for curry. Often the fruit is permitted to remain until it is quite dry with

"Where shall I get them, my son?" his mother replied; "and people will not trust me either. Where shall we get them? And we two have no seed-grain either. What shall we cultivate?"

"My brothers," the Hanuman boy said, "are sowing highland-paddy[6]. What shall we two be able to cultivate, mother?"

His mother then again said: "Son, what can you do? They have what is needed, and so they are cultivating. We two have no seed-grain, so what can we cultivate, my son?"

"Look here, mother," he said, "have we then no seed at all?"

"There is nothing, my son," she replied.

Again the boy asked: "Look here, mother, have we then no seed of any kind at all?"

"There is that pumpkin,"[7] his mother replied; "otherwise there is absolutely nothing."

The boy then said: "Very well, if there is nothing else, bring me that; then I too shall have something to sow together with my brothers." So, truth to tell, she brought him the pumpkin-seed, and, having tied this up in a piece of cloth, he went to where he had cleared the land and planted it. Now his brothers were asking him: "Look here, you, when are you going to plough? You do nothing to clear the ground."

"O brothers," he replied, "I have sown without clearing the ground."

"What have you sown, you fellow?" they asked.

"Look here, brothers," he on his part asked them, "what have you sown?"

"We," they replied, "we have sown highland-paddy."

"I also," he said, "have sown highland-paddy; or rather, I have not sown, I have planted."

a hard rind; when cut through, they use parts of it as cups or ladles; or making a hole at the stalk-end, they empty the rind of everything found inside and use it as a receptacle for seeds of sorts, also as a water-bottle.

Khangeko mẹnkeťa, Henda ya, ceť lekam rọhọeketa? Hoṛo dọ gạchi hoelen bako rọhọea? Am dọ ceť lekam rọhọeketa? Adọ onkako rọreťa arko landawae kana. Adọ uni hąṛũ koṛa dọe thir akangea; ceť hõ bae rọṛ baṛayeťa; landa ocoako kanae.

Adọ sạri tahẹn tahẹnte tin din badre cọṅ, kathae, adọ janamentakoa; adọ onka din hilok ạḍiko hiria, ar uni hąṛũ hõe hiritaea. Adọ miť din dọ onka ńẹl baṛae lạgiťge sanam hoṛ miťtegeko calaoena. Adọ ńẹl baṛakateko mẹnkeťa, Henda ya, bhala delabon sẹ teheń dọ hąṛũakbo ńẹla; bhala ceť leka janam akantaea. Adọ onka mẹnkate jọtọ boehage uni hąṛũak cas ńẹlko calaoena, ar uni hąṛũ hõ onko sãorege menaea.

Adọ jọtọgeko calaoena. Adọko ńẹlkeť khanko metae kana, Okor ya, okakore goḍa hoṛom rọhọe akaťa? Bale ńẹl ńameť dọ. Adọ oka okae rọhọeleť, ona onae uḍuk idiako kana. Adọko ńẹlkeť khanko metae kana, Noa ma ya họtọť kan, hoṛo dọ okor? Pạhil mam mẹnkeť, baṅma, Goḍa hoṛoń rọhọe akaťa. Adọ okoranaṅ? Noa ma họtọť kan.

Adọ unreye mẹnkeťa, Baṅa, dada, pạhil dọń ẹrẹyeťpe tahẽkana. Hoṛoge ẹraṅ mẹnleťa, adọ ayoń kuli baṛakede, adọe mẹnkeťa, Hoṛo itạ dọ bạnukanaṅ. Adọń mẹnkeťa, Ẹnḍẹkhan ceť itạ hõ bạnukan? Adọ unreye mẹnkeťa, Họtọť itạ tin uḍić cọṅ menak. Adọ unreń mẹnkeťa, Dẹn ẹnḍẹkhan, inạgeń rọhọekaka. Adọ eṭak itạ dọ bạnuktalaṅ khan, ceťlaṅ cekaea? Adọ, dada, onka lekate iń dọ noageń cas akaťa.

Adọ miť hoṛe mẹnkeťtakoa, Henda ya, ẹnte itạ bạnuktam khan, cedak ale ṭhen bam hẹćlena? Baṅ hutẹćle ẹmkema?

Adọe mẹnkeťa, Hẽ, baṅ hẹćlen khan, ẹntem cekaea? Acha, noa cas hõ iń dọ besgeń metak kana; ẹnte ape dọ dakape casketťabona ar iń dọ utu. Adọ jọlen khan hapẹn, apeko ṭhen adọ baṅ ạkriń baṛaea? Sẹ jãhãeko ṭhen idikateń ạkriṅte caoleń kiriṅa.

8 The Hanuman says, he has 'planted' the rice, and the brothers hang on to this. Ordinary rice is first sown in a seedling-field, where it remains for a month, more or less, whereupon the seedlings are pulled up and planted in the rice-fields.

"Look here, you," they asked, "how did you plant? Do people not plant paddy, when they have got seedlings and not before?[8] How did you plant?" They talked in this way and were laughing at him; but the Hanuman boy kept quiet; he did not say a word, he let them laugh.

Truth to tell, as time passed, after some days, people tell, what they had sown came up; and they daily went to look at it. The Hanuman boy also went to look at his cultivation. One day they all went together to have a look round. Having looked at their own crop, they said: "Look here, come, let us to-day have a look at what the Hanuman has; I wonder how his has come up." Saying this all the brothers went to see the Hanuman's cultivation; the Hanuman was also together with them.

As said, all went; when they had had a look, they said: "Why, you fellow, where have you sown highland-paddy? We don't see any." He then showed them the places where he had sown; when they had seen all, they said to him: "This is pumpkin, fellow, why, where is the paddy? You have, as you know, formerly said that you have planted highland-paddy. Now where is it? This is pumpkin, as is to be seen."

"Quite so, brothers," he replied; "at first I was telling you fibs. I wanted to sow paddy; so I asked my mother, and she said: 'There is no paddy seed.' Then I said: 'Then is there no seed at all?' She replied: 'There is some pumpkin-seed, who knows how much.' Then I said: 'Give me this then; I shall plant this. As we have no other seed, what can we two do?' This, my brothers, is why I have planted this."

"Look here, you," one of them said, "then since you have no seed, why did you not come to us? Should not we have given you some in that case?"

"Yes", he replied, "but as I did not go to you, what is to be done? Very well, I call this crop also something good; you have cultivated the rice for us and I the curry. When the fruit later on ripens, shall I not sell to you? Or I may take it to somebody else anywhere, sell it and buy rice."

Adoko menketa, Acha, tobe ina hō boge kangea; besgem bud akata.

Ado sari tahen tahente horoko hō besge hoeyentakoa, ar nuiak hotot hō adi barić nārīyena. Ona do jhata leka paraoena se baṅ? Cet baṅ se, gota kurāu nārīyentaea, ado bogete teren goren joyentaea. Ado dingeye hiria.

Ado tahen tahente horoko hō beleyentakoa, adoko menketa, Horo do beleyentabona, ado mabon nāwāitebon ira.

Ado uni hārū kora hōe menketa, Dadaṅteko cet lekako nāwāi, iṅ hō onka lekaṅ nāwāia. Ado sari onkogeye ṅel barakoa, bhala oka lekako nāwāia.

Ado sari mit din do geć guricente horoko ir aguketa, ado boṅgae thenko samaṅketteko nāwāiketa. Ado unre uni eṅgattet ar uni hārū kora bana horko nēotaketkina ona nāwāi bhoj daka jom. Ado sari bana horge ona bhoj jomkin calaoena. Ado unre daka utukette sanam horko jom baraketa, adoko apan apinena.

Ado ina dosar tesar khange uni hārū kora hōe menketa, Ia ayo, gapa do alaṅ hō je cas akat, alaṅ onalaṅ nāwāia. Ado am hō onka geć gurijme, ar alaṅ hō dadaṅteko joto horlaṅ nēotakoa. Geć gurić barakate am do dadaṅteko nēota otokakome. Iṅ do um barakate hotot iṅ got aguia.

Ado eṅgattete menketa, Acha, beta, bogegem menet kana. Ende-khan gapa dolaṅ nāwāia.

---

9 The Hanuman had not burned his cut jungle; the dried trees now function as stakes for the pumpkin climbers.

10 The Santals will not as a rule eat any cultivated stuff, before the firstfruit-offering has been performed. Ordinarily the village priest goes and cuts as much as he can reach standing in one spot; this is then taken to the sacred grove, where spots are cleaned with cow-dung, and offered to the bongas. Milk is also poured out as a libation.

11 Before any offering takes place, a spot is cleared of grass, etc., smoothed and 'cleaned' with cow-dung. When an animal is sacrificed, a handful of rice is put down here, some sindur is stroked on the place; the animal to be sacrificed is made to feed on the rice and thereupon beheaded.

"All right," they said, "then that is quite good also; you have acted sensibly."

Truth to tell, as time passed, the others had a good crop of paddy, and this one's pumpkins also grew luxuriantly; the plants found something like stakes[9] to climb on, don't you see? You have no idea, all over the place he had prepared there were pumpkin climbers, and everywhere it was setting fruit, lots of it. Daily he went to look at it.

As time passed, their paddy also ripened, and they said: "Our paddy has ripened; let us perform the firstfruit-offering[10] and reap it."

Then the Hanuman boy also said: "Just as my brothers perform the firstfruit-offering, in the same way I shall also offer." And he carefully watched them, how they were acting.

Truth to tell, one day they smoothed a small plot of the ground and smeared it with cow-dung[11], whereupon they cut and brought some paddy; and, having offered it at the place of worship, they performed the firstfruit-offering. On this occasion they invited the mother and the Hanuman boy, both of them, to eat the first-fruit-offering festival meal. And both of them went to partake of this feast. At this time they prepared rice and curry and all ate, whereupon they separated, each to their own houses.

A couple of days afterwards the Hanuman boy also said: "I say, mother, what we two have cultivated, in connexion with that we shall perform the firstfruit-offering to-morrow. So you also make a spot smooth and smear it with cow-dung, and we also shall invite my brothers, all of them. After having prepared the spot with cow-dung you go and invite my brothers and their families. I shall bathe[12] and go and bring a pumpkin."

"Very well, my son," his mother replied, "it is good what you are saying. So we shall have the firstfruit-offering to-morrow."

---

[12] Bathing is always preparatory to performing a sacrifice or an offering.

Adǫ sąri dosar hiloḱ khange adǫ ǫnǫkin rǫṛleť lekagekin kajketa Dadatteko hõ jǫtǫgekin nẽotaketkoa; adǫ onko dǫ ako akoko mǫnjoṅ kana, Henda ya, oṛakre ma ceť hõ bąnuktąkin. Cetkin jǫm ocobonte abo dǫkin nẽotayetbona?

Adǫ sąri uni hąṛũ koṛa dǫe umente sǫnkate mitťaṅ hǫtǫť, okaṭak jǫtǫ khǫnak maraṅ jǫ ńǫloḱ kan tahẽkan, onageye gǫtketa, are mǫnketa, Nią̄te khan nãhãk sanam hǫṛbon aṇṭaoka. Onka mǫnkate sẽṛãwakgeye gǫtketa, ar gǫtkate onko dadattekoak oṛak sǫntegeye gǫk ągukeťa; unre onko hõko ńǫlledegea.

Adǫ oṛakte idikate bhitąrteye adǫrketa, adǫ boṅgae ṭhene samaṅketa. Adǫ sim boṅgako leka churite hǫṭǫk ṭhene reta topak gǫtketa; adǫ eṅgattǫť hõ ǫṇḍǫgeye tahẽkana. Adǫe reta topak gǫtkeť khankin ńǫlketa, baṅma, ona hǫtǫť bhitrire dǫ ǫkǫn caolete pǫrǫć akan. Adǫ haṭak ągukate onarekin koṭaketa. Adǫ onare hõ baṅ sahǫṕ cabalente mitťaṅ dąuṛą hǫpǫnrekin uṕketa, adǫ ona hõ thoṛage baṅ pǫrǫćlena; sǫrǫm dąuṛą gan hoeyena. Adǫ ąḍi bąṛićkin rąskąyena; adǫ ona katha dǫ ąkin mǫtǫregekin dǫhǫketa. Bana hǫṛkin mǫnketa, Noa katha dǫ balaṅ ląi baṛaea, baṅkhanko kombṛoetalaṅa.

Adǫ onkakin galmaraokette ąḍi rąskąkate ona caolekin sǫk ągukeťa, ar ona hǫtǫť hartatǫť dǫkin hǫyǫketa, adǫ hǫṛko andhako lągiť ona dǫkin utuketa, ar dąl hõkin utuketa, ar eṅgattǫť dǫe metadea, Ma ayo, am dǫ khub utąr dakaeme, jǫmǫn dadaṅteko ar hiliṅteko sanam hǫṛko aṇṭaok leka. Eṅgate dadaṅtekoko nẽotaletlaṅre dǫ kąṭić kąṭić dakako ematlaṅa. Alaṅ dǫ khub tititlaṅ jǫm ocokoa. Judi noate bako aṇṭaok khan, arhõ mitťaṅ iṅ gǫť ąguia.

13 All sacrifices (except to the Ancestors) are done by the Santals by cutting the head off; the Hanuman boy imitates this by cutting the 'neck' of the pumpkin.

14 One form of the baskets used by the Santals is called dąuṛą; they are flat-bottomed and shallow, but fairly large. At the marriage-ceremony the bride is lifted up sitting in such a basket, when the bridegroom, riding on the shoulder of his relative, applies sindur to the bride's forehead.

15 Before being used for food, the rice is always cleaned by being pounded in a husking-machine. This is different from the first husking.

Truth to tell, the next day they did as they had talked together. They also invited his brothers and their families, all of them. Now these were saying among themselves: "Look here, these two have nothing in their house. What are they going to let us have for food, since they are inviting us?"

Now, truth to tell, the Hanuman boy had his bath and went and plucked a pumpkin, the one that was looking biggest of all, and said: "When I take this, we shall have enough." Thinking this, he plucked the big one, whereupon he carried it home past his brother's houses; at that time they saw him also.

Having brought it home, he put it inside the stall for the Ancestors, and offered it where they offer to the spirits. Just like they do when sacrificing a fowl, he cut it off with a knife at the neck[13]; his mother was also there. When he had cut off the top, they saw: the inside of the pumpkin was full of only rice. Having brought a winnowing-fan, they shook the rice out in this. As this could not hold all, they poured rice out into a small flat basket; it lacked only a little that this also was filled; it was about as much as a three-quarter-full flat basket[14]. They were awfully glad; but this matter they kept to themselves. Both of them said: "We shall tell nothing about this matter; else people will steal from us."

Having talked in this way, they cleaned[15] the rice, whereupon they pared[16] the skin of the pumpkin, and, to mislead the others, they made this into curry; they also prepared curry from split peas. He said to his mother: "Now, mother, prepare a great quantity of rice, so that my brothers and sisters-in-law all may have sufficient. Dash it, when my brothers invited us, they gave us only very small portions. We shall give them large portions to eat. If there is not sufficient for them in this one, I shall go and fetch another."

---

16 Lit. 'shaved'.

Adọ eṅgattẹṭe mẹnkeṭa, Baṅa, bạbu, teheṅ dọ alom ạguia, nią caoletege nāhāk̓ iṅ aṇṭaoabona.

Adọe mẹnkeṭa, Acha bogege ẹṇḍẹkhan.

Adọ sạri daka utu sanam tearenre hō̱, onko dadatteko dọ bako hijuk̓ kan. Adọ uni koṛae mẹnkeṭa, Henda ayo, dadaṅteko dọm lại akawaṭkoa sẹ baṅ? Nit hō̱ bako ṅẹlok̓ kan dọ.

Adọe mẹnkeṭa, Baṅa bạbu, lại akawaṭkogeaṅ.

Adọe mẹnkeṭa, Bako hijuk̓ kana. Ọkọe toraṅ ṅẹl ạgukoa. Adọ onka mẹnkateye calaoena. Adọe metako kana, Cele, dada, bape calak̓ kan dọ? Enaṅ khon iṅ ṅẹl họreṭpea, adọ bape calak̓ kanteṅ paṅjayeṭpea. Jham jhumbo jarwa baṛa gọdok̓a, adọ jọm baṛakatebo apan ạpin baṛayenge.

Khange adọ dadattekoko mẹneṭa, Henda ya, cet̓ nāhāk̓e jọm ocobonte nunạk̓ dọe nẹ̄otayeṭbona? Bejāe khulạsae rọṛet̓ dọ bhala. Acha, delabo ṅẹltaea, cet̓ leka bhalae khawan dawanbona. Adọ onka mẹnkate jọtọge adọ uni oṛak̓teko calaoena. Adọ ạisọ bạisọ ạḍi rẹhlaṅ pẹhlaṅ duṛup̓e metaṭkoa. Adọ khange oṛak̓teye bọlọ gọṭena, adọ eṅgattẹṭe metae kana, Cele ayo, tear akaṭam sẹ baṅ?

Adọ uniye mẹnkeṭa, Hẹ̄, sanamak̓ teargea.

Adọ uniye mẹnkeṭa, Acha, ẹṇḍẹkhan ma dadaṅteko dak̓ taṅ họṭakome.

Adọ uni buḍhią họṛ dọe mẹnkeṭa, Hape bạbu, thoṛa patṛa baṅ hoe akana; inạṅ rọk̓le khange nāhāk̓ kam dọ sạriạuk̓a.

Adọe mẹnkeṭa, Acha bogege ẹṇḍẹkhan ma curemar rọk̓ họdme. Adọ dadattekoe metako kana, Ią dada, hapẹ mit̓ ghạṛi, thoṛa patṛa ọkulạn ṅō̱k̓gea; iną tearlen khange nāhāk̓bo jọm gọda.

Adọ sạri jọtọ hilitteko hō̱ko calaoena ar gidrạko hō̱, adọ jọtọge duṛup̓e metaṭkoa. Adọ maraṅić dadattẹt̓ dọ bae pạtiạuk̓ kante

---

[17] Before eating all wash their hands and rinse their mouths; this is made necessary by their having to use their fingers for eating; in any case a Santal would not think of eating without first having a wash. The water is given out separately in brass jugs (lotas) or something similar, and this serving of water is tantamount to telling that now they are to take their seats for eating.

"No, my boy," his mother replied, "don't bring any to-day; I shall get enough for us with this rice."

"Very well," he said, "that is all right then."

Now, truth to tell, although all was ready, the brothers did not come. So the boy said: "Look here, mother, have you told my brothers or not? There is nothing to be seen of them even now."

"No, my son," she replied, "I have certainly told them."

"They are not coming," he said; "I shall at once go and see what is the matter with them." Saying this he went and said to them: "Well, my brothers, how is it you are not going? I have been expecting you for quite a while; and as you are not coming, I am looking you up. Let us all come together now at once; when we have had our food, we shall go each to our homes."

The brothers were saying among themselves: "Look here, you, what has he to give us to eat that he invites us, so many people? He talks amazingly self-confidently, I wonder. Very well, come along, let us see what he has, how he is going to feed us." After this talk they all went to his house. With exquisite politeness he asked them to sit down, whereupon he went inside and spoke to his mother: "Well, mother, have you everything ready or not?"

"Yes", she replied, "everything is ready."

"Very well then," he said, "be quick then and pour water[17] out for them."

"Wait a little, my son," the old lady said, "some leaf-plates[18] are not ready as yet; as soon as I have stitched them presently, the work will be finished."

"All right," he said, "that is well then; please hurry and stitch the plates." So he spoke to his brothers: "I say, my brothers, have patience one moment; a few leaf-plates are wanting; as soon as they are ready, we shall at once have food."

Truth to tell, all his sisters-in-law also came and their children also, and he asked them all to sit down. The eldest brother did

[18] At feasts most people are served on plates and in cups made from leaves (mostly of the sal tree). Once used, these are thrown away.

sạri oṛakteye bọlọyena; adọe mẹnkeťa, Hape sẹń ńẹl baṛa ạgulege, bhala ceťkoe kulạu julạu akaťa. Adọ sạri bọlọkateye ńẹlkeť dọ, sạri miť dạuṛạkin daka akať. Adọ ạḍi bạṛiće hahaṛayena, adọe mẹnkeťa, Okarekin ńamkeťte nunạk dọkin bhọjkeťa? Ona katha ać mọnẹregeye dọhọkaťa; ceť hõ bae mẹnleťa.

Adọ phuṛuk patṛa tearente daḱe tańaťkoa, adọ sanam họṛ miť dhaoteko ạbukena, adọ daka jọmko duṛupena. Adọ uni eṅgatṭẹťge jọtọ họṛ dakae emaťkoa. Adọe galmaraoako kana, Noa dọ bạbu, họtọťe nạwạikeťtaliṅa, ona reaḱ kana. Adọe mẹnkeťa, Ako hõ nạwạiń jọkhẹnko lạiaťbona, alań hõlań lạiakoa. Adọ ona reań bhọj daka kana.

Adọ unre uni hạṛũ koṛae mẹnkeťa, Ape ma dada, hoṛope nạwạikeťa, unre daka hõ kạṭić kạṭićpe ẹmoḱa, ar iń ṭhen ńẹlpe. Ma arhõ ọkọekope jọm juṭuj khan dọ, ayo kọeyepe; ma jetnape jọm, unạkge nãhãke emapea. Adọ inạko jọm baṛakateko ạpan ạpinena.

Ado unkin eṅga họn dọ ona họtọtre caolekin ńamkeťte ceť bań sẹ, ạḍi rạskạkin ạikạukeťa. Adọ dinge setaḱ ạyuṕ ona kurạu dọ bana họṛtekin hiria, ạḍi cikisạkin lagaokeťa. Adọ onkoaḱ hoṛo hõ beleyentakoa, ar nukinaḱ hõ beleyena. Adọ hoṛoko ir baṛakeť khan, nukin hõkin gọť ạgukeťtakina. Adọ ceť bań sẹ, goṭa oṛaḱ tẹṛẹń gọṛẹńkin dọhọ pẹrẹćkeťa. Adọ khọrca cabalentakin khange, miťṭań gankin posaḱle khange aema caole hoe gọdoḱtakina, adọ onkate unkin dọ goṭa bọchọr reaḱ jọmaḱ hoeyentakina.

Adọ tahẹn tahẹnte, kathae, tin din badre cọń onko dadatteko sadọm kiriṅko calaḱ lạgiťko riạuena. Adọ khange uni hạṛũ koṛa hõe mẹnkeťa, Ią ayo, dadańteko sadọmko kiriṅjoń lạgiť; iń hõ onko sãoteń kiriń ạgujońa.

19 The mother adresses these sons of hers with the word used by an older person to any younger man; a mother may also address her sons in this way, but it is not a term of endearment.

not believe anything, so he really went inside, saying: "Wait, let me first have a look round; I wonder what he has provided." He actually went inside and saw, they had really prepared a flat basket full of rice. He was utterly astonished and said: "Where have they got enough to make such a big feast?" He kept this matter in his mind, he did not say anything.

After having made the leaf-cups and leaf-plates ready, she poured water out for them; all of them washed their hands at the same time, whereupon they sat down to eat. The mother served them all with their food and was talking to them, as she did this: "This, young man[19], is pumpkin of which he has made a firstfruit-offering; it is in connexion with this. He said: 'When they were performing the firstfruit-offering, they told us; we shall also tell them.' This is what there is about this feast."

Then the Hanuman boy said: "You, my brothers, performed the firstfruit-offering of your paddy; on that occasion you were giving only small small portions, and now look how it is here with me. If any of you wants a second helping, ask mother; howsoever much you will eat, she will give you." After having had their food, they separated.

Now mother and son found rice in the pumpkins, you have no idea how pleased they felt. Daily, morning and evening, both of them went to see their clearing; they took great care with it. The others' paddy ripened, and what these two had also ripened. When the others had reaped their paddy, these two also gathered their fruit and brought it home. You have no idea, they filled their house, every corner, and when their foodstuff was finished, if they only broke one or so open, they had at once a lot of rice. In this way these two got food to last them the whole year.

As time passed, people tell, after who knows how long a time, his brothers spoke to each other and agreed to go and buy horses. Then the Hanuman boy also said: "I say, mother, my brothers are going to buy horses; I too want to buy one together with them."

Adǫ eṅgattẹte mẹnkeťa, Ią beṭa, onko dǫ ṭaka poesa menaktakoa, inạteko kiriṅkoa; alaṅ dǫ ceť hǫ̃ bạnuǩtalaṅ; ceťtem kiriṅkoa?

Adǫ uni koṛae mẹnkeťa, Henda ayo, ceť hǫ̃ bạnuǩtalaṅa?

Adǫe mẹnkeťa, Ceť hǫ̃, beṭa, bạnuǩan. Nẹ̃ǩẹ̃ caolege menaǩa ar miť buṛhu baber, ar baṅkhan dǫ ceť hǫ̃ bạnuǩan.

Adǫ uni koṛae mẹnkeťa, Dẹn ẹṇḍẹkhan, inạ buṛhu baberge emaṅme.

Adǫe mẹnkeťa, Henda beṭa, noate dǫ ẹnte sadǫm dǫko emama? Ǫhǫko ẹmleɪna.

Adǫe mẹnkeťa, Dẹn ẹnteṅ idi gelaǩa, adǫko emaṅre hǫ̃ baṅre hǫ̃. Adǫ sạri inạgeye emadea, adǫ onko dadatteko sãote nui hǫ̃e calaǩ kana. Adǫko metae kana, Henda ya, okatem calaǩ kana?

Adǫe mẹnkeťa, Ape sãote iṅ hǫ̃ sadǫm kiriṅ iṅ calaǩa.

Adǫ lajaoko ạikạueťteko metae kana, Am dǫ ale sãote dǫ alom hijuǩa. Adǫ onka dhurmạrko ruheťkede khane tayǫmena.

Adǫ calaǩ calaǩte miť ṭhen ul jǫ akanko ṅamkeťa, adǫko mẹnkeťa, Hạ̃ṛũi tahẹn khan dǫ, noa ul belebo tioǩ ocokea.

Adǫ uni hạ̃ṛũ dǫ tinre cǫe lahayente ona ul dareregeye dẹć akan. Adǫe rǫṛ gǫťkeťa, Menaṅge cǫṅ, dada; adǫ ulpe jǫm khan dǫṅ ṅurhạwapea.

Adǫko mẹnkeťa, Ma ya ẹnte, ṅũraleme. Adǫ sạriye ṅũr baṛawaťkoa. Adǫ arhǫ̃ko calaǩ kana. Atra dhur sẹnkate khange arhǫ̃ko ruheť ṅirkedea. Adǫ ǫntẹrege uni hạ̃ṛũ dǫe tayǫmena. Khange adǫ miťṭaṅ khuiliye ṅamkeťa, ado onkoe sẹn jitạu ṅǫ̃ǩ

[20] Rope is perhaps misleading. What the Santals call b a b e r is some kind of cord or string, manufactured by themselves. A b a b e r made from hemp is used for stringing their bedsteads; it is kept in a kind of hank or bundle. It is probably such a bundle that is here referred to.

"You see, my son," his mother said, "they have money; with money they may buy; we two have nothing; what will you buy them with?"

"Look here, mother," the boy said, "have we absolutely nothing?"

"There is nothing at all, my son," his mother replied. "You see here, we have this rice and one bundle of rope[20], otherwise there is nothing."

"Give me that then," the boy said, "give me the bundle of rope."

"Look here, my son," she said, "do you think they would give you a horse for this? No, be sure they won't."

"Give it me," he said, "anyhow I may have a try, taking it along, whether they will give me or not." Truth to tell, she gave it to him, and he too was starting together with his brothers. But they said to him: "Look here you, where are you off to?"

"I also," he replied, "am going to buy a horse together with you."

They felt ashamed, so they said to him: "Don't you come together with us." As they drove him away with scolding, he lagged behind.

As they went along, they, at some place, found a mango tree full of fruit, and said: "If the Hanuman had been here, we might have made him pluck mango fruits for us."

Now the Hanuman some time or other had come in advance and had climbed this mango tree. So he called out: "Why, I am here, brothers, and if you want to eat mangoes, I shall throw them down to you."

"Well then, since you are here," they said, "throw down to us." And, truth to tell, so he did. So they started again. When they had reached about halfway, they again commenced to scold him and drove him away. Somewhere there the Hanuman lagged behind; then he found a bed-stringer's pin[21], and he let the

[21] A khuili is a pin made of bamboo and especially used when stringing a bedstead to move the strings close together.

ocoat́koa. Khange uni dọ eṭaḱ họrte onko khon lahateye ńir lahayena; adọ ọntẹ khone ńẹl darametkoa.

Arhō̤ko tioḱ ńō̤ḱkedea, mẹnkhan uni dọ lahategeye calao idiḱ kana, onko ṭhen dọ bae ńẹl ocoḱ kana. Adọ onka onkate sadọm palko tioḱkeṭa, ar ạyuṕ hō̤ ạyuṕena. Adọko mẹnkeṭa, Teheń dọ ạyuṕena, babo kirińkoa. Gapa setaḱrebo kirińkoa, adọ dẹćkate ẹkkalte oṛaḱtebo sẹn utạroḱa. Adọ onka bujhạu baṛakateko ḍerayena.

Ar uni hạṛū dọ ẹkkalte onko sadọm goṛaregeye ḍerayena, koale cọṭreye duṛuṕ akana. Adọ un jọkhẹn onko sadọmko galmarao kana, Teheń dọ gahrọkko hẹć akana; ọkoẹko cọń nāhāḱko kirińidibon. Adọ onako galmarao kan khan, uni hạṛū dọ thirkateye añjọmjoń kana. Arhō̤ onko sadọmko mẹpẹn kana, Henda ya, bhalako kirińbona; adọ ọkọe tinạḱbo dạṛ daṛeaḱa? Adọko mẹneṭa, Iń dọ ninạḱ kọs; iń dọ nunạḱ kọs; onka apan ạpinko lạikeṭa. Adọ mitṭań ghuṛiye tahẹ̄kana, adọ uniye mẹnkeṭa, Iń dọ ọtte barọ kọs ar cọṭ cọṭte barọ kọs iń dạṛ daṛeaḱa.

Adọ khange uni hạṛū koṛa dọ onkae añjọmket́ khan dọ, hare phareye āṛgoyente uni ghuṛi sẹ eṅga sadọm, ọkọe barọ kọs siń ńindại dạṛ daṛeaḱe mẹnket́, uni sadọm jaṅgare sẹ khurạ latarre khuciye kuṭạm biṭadea. Khange thọ uni sadọm dọe leḍhayena, adọ khọṛdẹt́ khọṛdẹṭe taṛamet́ kana.

Adọ dosar ńiloḱ khange onko dadatteko dọ sadọm palteko calao gọṭena, adọ uni hạṛū hō̤ ọṇḍẹko ńamkedea. Adọko metae kana, Henda ya, tinrem hẹć akana?

Adọe mẹnkeṭa, Nitge, dada. Adọ sadọmkoko bachao baṛayet́koa, khub moṭa moṭakoko bachaoket́koa. Adọ dọr damkateko kirińket́koa. Ar un jọkhẹn uni hạṛū koṛa dọe thir akana, cet́ hō̤ bae mẹn baṛayeṭa, onkoaḱ dọr damgeye aḱńjọm kana. Khange adọko kirińket́-kote sadọmreko aswarente oṛaḱ sẹn ạguko reaḱko mohṇḍayena.

---

22 Lit. twelve kos, a kos being a distance of about two miles.

23 A khuci is a pointed stick with which holes are made in the ground for putting stakes for beans, &c., in.

others gain a little on himself. Thereupon he ran in advance of his brothers by another road and was looking for their coming.

When they nearly reached him, he again went in advance of the others; he did not let the others catch sight of himself. In this way they reached the place where the horses were; at this time it was also getting dark; and they said: "It is night now, we shall not buy any to-day; we shall buy to-morrow morning; then we shall mount our horses and at once go straight home." Having come to this conclusion, they settled down for the night.

The Hanuman went to the stable and settled down there for the night, sitting aloft on a beam. During the night the horses were talking together: "To-day some buyers have come; who knows which among us they will buy and take away." While they were talking together in this way, the Hanuman was quietly listening. Again the horses were speaking to each other: "Listen, I wonder whether they will buy us; how fast is any one of us able to run?" So they said: "I can run so many miles; I can run so many miles." In this way they told how fast each of them could run. There was a mare there, and she said: "I am able to run twenty-four miles[22] along the ground, and in the air I can run twenty-four miles."

When the Hanuman boy heard this, he got down in a hurry, and in the foot or rather in the hoof of the mare that said that she night and day could run twenty-four miles, on the underside, he drove a dibble[23] in. Consequently this horse became lame and limping.

The next day his brothers at once went to the place where the horses were; here they also met the Hanuman and asked him: "Look here you, when have you come?"

"Just now, my brothers," he replied. So they commenced to select horses; they selected the very fat ones, and, after having agreed on the price, they bought them. At this time the Hanuman boy kept quiet; he did not say a single word, he was listening to their bargaining. When they had bought the horses, they mounted and started to take them home.

Adọ onko sẹnen tayọm uni hạṛũ dọe rọṛ saḍeketa, Henda ho, sadọm kisạṛ, nui sadọm dọe ceka leḍhayentama? Ạḍi harọn dhoṛok dhoṛoke taṛamet dọ. Tis khone leḍha akantama?

Adọ uniye mẹnketa, Hola dọ besgeye tahẽkana; noa ńindạ bhitạrtegeye cekayen cọṅ.

Adọ uni hạṛũi mẹnketa, Nui sadọm dọ ran ocoyem, baṅkhane rọhọṛ gujuktama. Masẹ ńẹleme, tinạk harkhete taṛam kana.

Adọ uni hoṛe mẹnketa, Okọ baḍae, sadọm dọ jãhã rọg ńamketkoa mẹnkhan, ran ocokore hõ bako bańcaoka. Iń dọ ạḍi sedae macha khonge ẹnte sadọm iń ạsul akatkoa. Adọń ńẹletkoa, jãhãn rọg ńamketkoa mẹnkhan, jãhã tinạkem ranako, ẹnrehõ bako bańcaoka, gujukgeako.

Adọ uni hạṛũi mẹnketa, Ẹnḍẹkhan ma nui dọ nenkare ạkrińem nãhãke gujukgea. Nitok dọ ẹnḍẹkhan nui dọe okajentama.

Adọ uni hoṛe mẹnketa, Nui leḍha sadọm dọ ẹnte ọkọe hataoea? Nonka leḍha ńẹlte dọ cele hõ ọhọko hataolea. Adọ dẹ ẹnte, amgem hataoe khan dọń emama. Ar sẹ uni hoṛ dọ bae baḍae kana, nui sadọm dọ nunạke dạṛ daṛeaka mẹnte, ar nuige sadọm dọe leḍha oco akadea mẹnte. Ona katha sẹ bhẹd dọ uni hoṛ dọ bae baḍae kana.

Khange adọ uni hạṛũi mẹnketa, Henda ho, nui sadọm dọ tinạkem damea?

Adọ uni hoṛe mẹnketa, Ẹntem hataoe khan dọń damama.

Adọ hạṛũi mẹnketa, Hatao mań hataokege, mẹnkhan iń dọ bin damteń ńam kana; judim emań khan dọń ran gelakea, adọe beslen khan dọń dẹcaea; ar bae beslen khan, ma ẹnteye gujukge.

Adọ uni hoṛe mẹnketa, Adọ ẹnte nun din iń jọtọnkedea, adọ thoṛa thuṛi hõ bam emańa?

Adọ hạṛũi mẹnketa, Dam tahẹn khan dọ ẹnte, thoṛa thuṛiń ẹmkemgea, adọ dam hõ bạnuktińa. Ar jãhãre rinkatere hõ, thoṛa

[24] It might be noted that the Santali text, except at a couple of places, speaks of a horse that might be supposed to be a male.

After they had left, the Hanuman opened his mouth: "Look here, you horse-owner, how is it that this horse of yours has become lame? She[24] is in great distress limping. Since when has she been lame?"

"Yesterday she was quite well," he replied; "something or other has happened to her during the night."

The Hanuman then said: "Let the horse be treated by a doctor, else she will become emaciated and die for you. Look at her, with what difficulty she is walking."

"Who knows," the man said, "if horses contract some disease, they do not recover, even if you give them medicine. You see, I have for a very long time been rearing horses, and my experience is that, if they get some disease, they do not recover, however much you give them medicine; they die."

The Hanuman then said: "Then sell this one as she is; she will die presently. Now this one has become useless to you."

The man replied: "Who do you think will take this lame horse? When they see how lame she is, surely no one will take her. You then, if you will take her, I shall let you have her." Now the man did not know that this horse was able to run so much, nor that the Hanuman had lamed the horse. The man was in ignorance of it.

"Look here," the Hanuman asked, "what price will you put on this horse?"

"In case you will take him," the man said, "I shall name you a price for her."

"I might take her," the Hanuman replied, "but I want her for nothing; if you will give her to me, I shall try to treat her; and if she recovers, I shall ride on her; and if she does not get well, then she will die."

The man then said: 'Well, you see, I have taken care of her for such a long time; will you not give me just a little?"

"Well, if I had anything to give," the Hanuman replied, "I might have given you a little; but you see, I have nothing. And

thuṛi dam emam khan, bes do bes kangea. Ado noṇḍe iń doń bujhauet́a, sadom jel ma cele hõ bako jomet́, ar harta hõ sadom reaḱ ma cele hõ bako hataoet́. Jel ar harta tanaḱ judi akrińoḱ khan do, dam iń emlere hõe goćlen khan, inakote ona dam iń adaikea. Se hõ tho bań jutoḱ kana. Ar amgem laiyet́a, rog ńamleko khan do, bako besoḱ kana. Ado onatege dam emoḱ do bań sanań kana. Ado nõḱõe buṛhu baber menaḱtińa; judi nia babertem emań khan, iń hataokea.

Ado uni hoṛe menket́a, Mit́ ṭaka gan ente bam em juṭujoḱa?

Ado uni hãṛũi menket́a, Baṅa ho, ina chaḍa jãhãnaḱ do ohoń em daṛelea. Ado amge de khusiḱme. Judi ina buṛhu babertem emań khan do hẽge, ar bańkhan iń calaḱ kana. Enan khon aḍi habić noṇḍegeń duṛupena, ado jãhãnaḱko balań dandha baṛa joṅa?

Ado uni hoṛ bujhau baṛakateye metadea, Acha ho, khusiyenań. Den enḍekhan, ina baberge emańme ar ma idiyem. Menkhan aikha okoe then hõ alom lai baṛaea, nui sadom do buṛhu baberteń hatao akadea mente.

Ado hãṛũi menket́a, Acham emań khan do, okoe then hõ ohoń laia. Ado amgem lai baṛae coń cet́ coń?

Ado uniye menket́a, Cet́ iń doń lai baṛaea?

Adoe menket́a, Hẽ, paset́ okam menket́ge, mit́ṭań sadom do buṛhu baberteń akrińkedea mente.

Ado uni hoṛe menket́a, Cedaḱ onka doń laia? Iń geń emam kana, arhõ ińaḱ bhoromgeń bhańgaoa? Ona do oho hoelena. Iń doń mena, Sadom kiriń gahrokko hećlena; unrege ninaḱ se inaḱ sadom doń akrińket́koa. Inatege iń doń solom loṭoma. Lai bujhi, amgem lai khan.

Ado hãṛũi menket́a, Khusitem emań khan, cedaḱ iń laia?

if I borrowed somewhere and gave you a little for her, it would be all right, quite so. But here in these parts I understand that people do not eat horse-flesh, and no one will buy the hide of a horse either. If the flesh and the hide could be sold, I might get the price back thereby, when she died, even if I had paid for her. Consequently this will not do; and you yourself say, when a horse gets a disease, she will not recover. Therefore I do not wish to pay anything. But you see here, I have a rope bundle; if you will give her to me for this, I may take her."

The man then said: "Could you not then give me as much as one rupee besides?"

"No," the Hanuman replied. "Besides this I am quite unable to give anything. Please yourself; if you let me have her for the rope bundle, well and good; otherwise I am off. I have been sitting here for a long while since early morning; is it not time for both of us to do something?"

After having thought the matter over, the man said: "All right then, I am pleased. Here with it then, give me the rope bundle and take the horse away. But mind, don't tell anybody that you have bought this horse for a bundle of rope."

"Very well," the Hanuman said, "since you are giving her to me, I shall certainly not tell anybody. But you yourself, you will tell perhaps?"

"Why should I tell?" the man said.

"Well," the Hanuman replied, "perhaps you might say: I have sold a horse for a bundle of rope."

"Why should I tell this?" the man said. "I am giving her to you; in addition to this, should I publish my own shame? This would never happen. I shall say: 'Some horsedealers came; at that time I sold so and so many horses'; in this way I shall pass the matter off. There will be a story, if you tell."

"If you give her to me of your own will," the Hanuman said, "why should I tell?"

Adọe mẹnkeṭa, Baṅa, ma khusitegeṅ emam kana. Dẹn ona baber emaṅme.

Adọ sạri uni sadọm reak̕ dam dọ ona buṛhu babere emadea, uni hõe hataokeṭa, adọkin dub danena. Adọe tiạk̕ idikedea. Adọ uni hạṛũ dọ uni hoṛ ṭhen khone danaṅen khan, ona jaṅgare khuciye kuṭạm biṭade tahẽkan, onae ọr toṭkeṭtaea. Khange uni sadọme aosanen khane bes gọṭena, adọ ạḍi sọjhẹye taṛam geṭkeṭa. Adọ khange uni hạṛũ dọ ạḍiye rạskạyena. Khange adọe dẹć gọṭena, adọ ceṭ baṅ sẹye kamsaokedea sẹ, ạḍi tạpis ṭiriṭ lekae dạṛ ocokedea. Adọ onkoe tiok̕ ṅõk̕keṭko khan, ạḍi cọṭteye dạṛ ocokedea. Khange adọ sạri onko dọe parọmkeṭko khan, aćge lahate oṛak̕e tiok̕keṭa. Adọ tiok̕kate chaṭka duạrre tọlkate lobok̕ko, dak̕ko, jọtọe sor akawadea, ar ać dọe um hẹćente daka utu jọmkate adọ onkogeye ṅẹl họreṭkoa.

Adọ inạ miṭ ghạṛi tayọm khange sạri onko dadatteko hõko sẹṭẹrena. Khange sadọm tọl akadeko ṅẹlkede khanko kuliyeṭkoa, Henda ya, uni dọ ọkọeren sadọm kanae?

Adọko lạiaṭkoa, baṅma, Hạṛũi kiriṅ ạgu akadea. Khange adọ sẹn sorkateko ṅẹl baṛa ạgukedetaea. Noko dọ sanam hoṛ ạṇḍiạgeko kiriṅ ạgukeṭkoa, ar uni dọe eṅga kantaea. Khange adọko jirạu baṛayena.

Adọ bạṛsiṅ pẹ mãhã tayọm khangeko mẹnkeṭa, E̱ ya, ma bhala bon kamsao haparaoa, ọkọeren tinạk̕ko dạṛ daṛeak̕tabona. Adọko mẹnkeṭa, Acha bogege, ẹṇḍẹkhan mabon kamsao haparaoa. Adọ sạriko kamsao haparao kana, adọ jọtọ hoṛren khon uni hạṛũrenge bạṛti dọe dạṛ daṛeak̕ kana — ọt ọtte, kathae, barọ kọs, arhõ cọṭ cọṭte, kathae, barọ kọse kamsaokedea. Khange adọko hahaṛayena, adọko metae kana, E̱ ya hạṛũ, dini nui dọ emalem, am dọ alerenle emama, bọdọlkoabo.

---

25 The Santals like symbolic action; it is a common thing with them, on completion of a deal, to show that all is in order, for both parties to give each other a piece of dub (or more commonly by the Santals called dhubi) grass (Cynodon dactylon, Pers.); this grass is common everywhere in the country. It is a kind of receipt and acknowledgment.

"Quite so," the man said, "of my own will I am giving her to you. Please, let me have the rope bundle."

So, truth to tell, he gave the man the bundle of rope to pay for the horse, and he on his side took her, and, as proof of the bargain, they gave each other a piece of dub grass[25]. The Hanuman led the horse away; but when he had reached out of the man's sight, he pulled out the dibble he had driven into the leg. When the horse felt the relief, she at once became well and walked along without limping. The Hanuman became very glad and mounted the horse and galloped her, at top speed straight away he made her run, you cannot imagine how he made her gallop. When he had nearly overtaken his brothers, he made her rise high into the air. And when he had in this way passed the others, he reached home in advance of them. Having arrived there, he tied the horse at the entrance from the street to the court-yard and brought husks, water, all that was necessary to the horse, and himself went and had a bath, and, having had rice and curry, he stayed waiting for the others.

A short while afterwards his brothers also, truth to tell, arrived. When they saw the horse bound there, they asked people: "Look here, you, whose horse is this?"

They told them that the Hanuman had bought and brought her. They came near and looked at the horse. Now they had all of them bought males, and the Hanuman's was a mare. After this they had a rest.

A couple of days afterwards they said: "I say, let us have a race, and find out how each one of ours will be able to run." "All right," they said, "let us do so then." Truth to tell, when they were having the race, the Hanuman's horse beat the others — along the ground, people tell, he made her gallop twenty-four miles, and again through the air twenty-four miles. Then they were astonished and said to the Hanuman: "You Hanuman, come, give us this one, we shall give you one of ours; we shall make a barter."

Adọ uniye mẹnketa, Baṅa, dada, ọhọṅ bọdọllea. Ape dọ lahate hat bachatepe kiriṅ akawana, ar iṅ hõ onkage hat bachateṅ ạgu akawana. Ọhọṅ ẹmlena. Adọko thir baṛayena.

Adọ khange sạri cekakote cọe juṛạu baṛawante dosar tesar serma khange nui hõ bes enka jọm puṛạuk leka dọe arjaoketa; adọe mẹnketa, Iạ ayo, ma nẹs dọ iṅ lạgit bạhulaṅ ṅamkoa.

Adọ khange uni eṅgattẹt dọe hạrịạ busịạyena; adọe mẹnjoṅ kana, Nui lagat bạhu dọ bhala cet lekankoṅ ạguaea? Họṛ ma ọhọko rẹbẹnlen, ar hạṛũ jạt ma họṛ rọṛ bako baḍae. Cet lekankoṅ ạguaea? Adọ onka hudis baṛakateye metadea, Hẽ, bạbu, bạhu dọlaṅ ṅamkogea. Adọ hape ẹnte, raebarkolaṅ saṗleko baṅ?

Adọe mẹnketa, Acha bogege, ma ẹṇḍẹkhan raebarko dhuṛạukom. Bhala onko cetko mẹna, ona katha lạiaṅme.

Adọe mẹnketa, Acha bogege.

Adọ inạ dosar tesar khange sạri uni eṅgattẹt dọe hudis ṭhikketteye metadea, Iạ beṭa, nõkõe ẹn hilok bạhu reak kathalaṅ galmaraoleta; adọ onka lekate raebarkoṅ dhuṛạu gelaketkoa; adọko metadiṅa, kathae, uni họpọnme koṛa dọ aćtege bạhu dọe ṅamkoa; am dọ ẹkẹn gọnọṅ pọn juṛạukakme. Onka, beṭa, raebarko dọko metadiṅa.

Adọe mẹnketa, Acha ayom lạiadiṅ khan dọ besge. Ẹṇḍẹkhan iṅ ṅam ạgukoa. Adọ gọnọṅ pọn dọ tinạk lagaoka?

---

26 A marriage-broker is essential for a regular marriage; the contracting parties are really the two families, the young couple being now-a-days permitted to have the power of refusal. The boy's father or family will engage a man or (more frequently an elderly woman) to find a suitable girl.

27 A man (or his father) buys his bride, that is to say, the legal base of matrimony is the proprietary rights of the husband in the woman, acquired through purchase. The price paid should not be taken as an equivalent, but as a symbol, showing that the girl has passed from one family to another.

"No, my brothers," he replied; "I shall certainly do nothing of the kind. You were the first to choose and buy, and I also in the same way chose and brought mine. I shall certainly not let you have her." So no more was said.

Now, truth to tell, somehow or other the Hanuman gathered property, so after a couple of years he on his part earned well, and had sufficient food to last the whole year, and he said: "I say, mother, this year we shall get a wife for me."

His mother became quite dumbfounded and was saying to herself: "What kind of a wife am I to get for this one, I wonder? No human being will agree, and the Hanumans do not speak a human language. What kind of a wife shall I bring him?" Having thought over the matter in this way, she said to him: "Yes, my son, we shall find a wife. But wait a little, before anything else we must arrange with a marriage-broker"[26].

"Very well," he replied, "engage a marriage-broker then. Tell me what they have to say."

"All right," she said.

Truth to tell, a couple of days afterwards after having turned the matter over in her mind and come to a resolve his mother said to him: "I say, my son, you remember, we talked the other day about a wife for you; in accordance with this I tried to engage a marriage-broker; but they said to me: 'This son of yours will find a wife for himself; as for you, you only collect the bride-price[27] money.' This, my son, is what the marriage-brokers said to me."

"All right, mother," he replied, "as you have told me this, it is good. Consequently I shall myself find and bring one. What is the bride-price charged?"

Adǫ uniye mẹnkeṭa, Henda bạbu, ḍạṅguạko sẹ rạṇḍi chạḍuikom ạgukoa? Rạṇḍi chạḍuiko dǫ thoṛage lagaoḱa, ar ḍạṅguạko khan dǫ, pondro solo ṭaka lagaoḱa.

Adǫe mẹnkeṭa, Ią ayo, ḍạṅguạkoń ạgukoa.

Adǫe mẹnkeṭa, Hẽ beṭa, ḍạṅguạkom ạguleko khan dǫ, ạḍiń khusiḱ kana.

Adǫe mẹnkeṭa, Gapa meań khangeń calao gǫdoḱa.

Adǫ sạri miṭ din dǫ setaḱreye lại oṭoadete ać dǫ bạhu ńame calaoena. Adǫ eṅgattẹṭ dǫe mẹneṭa, Cele bań nãhãḱ am do rẹbẹnam. Seta ṭhen nãhãḱko laga ocome dǫ bań? Onka uni dǫe rǫṛjoń kana.

Adǫ sạri uni hạ̃ṛũ dǫ ḍher sạṅgiṅgeye calaoena; adǫ calaḱ calaḱte miṭṭen bandre kuṛiko dǫ lạṅṭikate umoḱ kane ńẹlkeṭkoa. Adǫ onko ṭhen ńir sẹnkate miṭ hǫṛaḱ khạṇḍi kicrić balańkateye ạtkirkeṭa, adǫ miṭṭań darereye dẹćena. Ar un jǫkhẹn onko kuṛiko dǫ bǫtǫrte ạḍiko kikiạukeṭa, adǫe ạtkirkeṭtae kuṛi dǫ bogeteye raḱ baṛayeṭa.

Adǫ khange uni hạ̃ṛũ dǫ rakap̣kate ona ańcartẹṭ dǫ dare khone ṭạmkur gǫṭ akaṭa. Adǫ onko kuṛi dǫko ńẹlkeṭ khanko mẹnkeṭa, Ǫnẹ cǫń na, darereye rakap̣ oṭo akaṭtam. Adǫ miṭ hǫṛaḱ khạṇḍite bạndiyente ona dare ṭhenko calaoena. Khanko ńẹlkede menaege. Adǫko mẹnkeṭa, Dẹntae, hạ̃ṛũ koṛa, mại reaḱ kicrić ẹmkataeme.

Adǫ uni hạ̃ṛũi mẹnkeṭa, Iń ṭhene rẹbẹn khan, iń ẹmkataea, ar bańkhan bań.

28 When a woman becomes a widow or is divorced, she is free to marry again; but as the marriage of a spinster with a bachelor is valid for the next world also and not influenced there by the remarriage of a widow or divorced person, the bride-price is only half of what is charged for a spinster. The ceremonies gone through with such women are different, and the marriage is for this world only.

29 The bride-price varies; it is three, five or seven rupees (always an uneven number); besides the husband has to give presents (clothes) to a number of female relatives of the bride. It may be from thirteen rupees and upwards all counted, quite apart from all expenses with feasting, &c., previous to and at the time of the marriage.

"Look here, my son," she said, "will you bring a spinster or a widow or a divorced girl? For widows and divorced women[28] the charge is not much, but in case it is a spinster, fifteen to sixteen rupees[29] will have to be paid."

"I say, mother," he replied, "I shall bring a spinster."

"Quite so, my son," she answered. "If you bring a spinster, I shall be very pleased."

"To-morrow or the day after, I shall start," he said.

And, truth to tell, he started one day to find a wife, after having told his mother this in the morning. His mother was saying: "Whoever will agree to become your wife? Won't they set the dogs on you to drive you away?" Such were her thoughts.

Truth to tell, the Hanuman went away to distant parts; as he was passing along, he saw a number of girls bathing naked in a pond. Running up towards these, he took the cloth[30] of one of them, ran away with it and climbed a tree. When this happened, the girls screamed from fear; and the girl whose cloth he had taken was crying sorely.

Having got up, the Hanuman let the border[31] of the cloth hang down from the tree. When the girls saw this, they said: "Look, girl, he has taken your cloth up into the tree." When the girl had taken round herself a cloth belonging to one of the others, they all went up to the tree. They saw him, there he is, whereupon they said: "Down with her cloth, Hanuman boy, give the girl's cloth back to her."

"If she agrees to become my wife," the Hanuman replied, "I shall give it her, otherwise not."

---

30 The Santals do not wear sown cloths (i. e. the old class of Santals who have not been in contact with other races). A woman has one piece of cloth, some nine cubits long, in which she drapes herself. They may sometimes use two separate pieces.

31 The Hanuman does not let the piece of cloth down lengthwise; he simply displays it.

Adǫko mẹnketa, Ǫtẹ na, hǫṛtegeye rǫṛet kana. Adǫ onkae rǫṛket khan dǫ, sạri onko kuṛiko hõ adǫ bako bǫtǫrok kana, adǫ uni tuluć ạḍiko galmarao kana, arko metae kana, Dẹn hạ̃ṛũ, ẹmkataeme.

Adǫ uni dǫ onageye metako kana, Iń thene rẹbẹn khan, dǫń ẹmkataegea.

Adǫ onkae mẹnket khanko ẹgẹr gǫtkedea, Cele baṅ am dǫ jorokam lạgit?

Adǫ onkako mẹnket khane mẹnketa, Nẹtape ẹṇḍẹkhan, mae ǫr tiok gǫd ma. Adǫ ona aṅcar dǫe ṭạmkur ńõketa ar arhõe rakap gǫteta. Adǫ onka onkate sạri cet muhni cǫe lagaoketa, adǫ sạri uni kuṛi dǫ ạḍi garteye jhuṭiạu gǫtkettaea. Khange sạri onae bande akan tahẽkan kicrić dǫe bhạnduṛ gǫtkata, adǫ sạri ona kicrićtegeye ǫr rakapkedea. Adǫ ać ṭhene rakapkede khane hạṛup sãohãkedeteye bande ocokedea. Adǫ baṅdǫ Cando reak likhạ baṅdǫ cet, adǫ uni kuṛi hõe mẹnketa, Do na, ruạṛjoṅpe, iń dǫ nui ṭhengeń tahẹna.

Adǫ khange onko kuṛi dǫko mẹnketa, Delabon na, oṛakrebo lại hǫda. Adǫ khange onko kuṛiko colaoen khan, nui kuṛi dǫe gugukedete curemare ạtkirkedea, okare hõ bae dǫhǫ baṛaledea; ẹkkalte ạkinak oṛakteye ạtkir idikedea.

Adǫ uni kuṛiren eṅgat apatko lạiatko khan, apat baret dǫ ak sarante ar sẹtakoko ạguketkote inạ dhara dhạri goṭako pakre baṛakedea. Ạḍi bạṛić inạ dhara dhạri goṭako sendra baṛakedea. Adǫ bako ńamlede khan, ạḍi bạṛićko rakketa. Adǫ bạrsiń pẹ mãhã dhạbićko sendra baṛakedea, adǫ bako ńamlede khan, rak rakteko ruạṛena. Adǫ onko gate kuṛige bogeteko ruhet baṛaketkoa, metatkoako, Cedak pạhilre dǫ bape lại hǫtleta? Adǫ onko kuṛi dǫ cet hõ bako rǫṛ ruạṛleta, kẹklẹsẹt hapẹyenako. Khange adǫko thir baṛayena.

---

32 Lit. 'warm you', a slang expression; jorok means to warm oneself at a fire.

"Listen girl," they said, "you hear he is speaking our language." As he had spoken in this way, the girls also, truth to tell, did not feel frightened any longer; and they had a long talk with him and were saying to him: "Give it, Hanuman, give her back her cloth."

But he was saying the same thing to them: "If she agrees to become my wife, I shall give her cloth back to her."

When he spoke in this way, they commenced abusing him: "Whoever do you think will be willing to marry you[32]?"

When they had said this, he said: "Here then, take what is yours; let her reach out for it and pull it down." Whereupon he let the border of the cloth a little down and again pulled it up. In this way he, truth to tell, applied some spell or other, and the girl with all her might caught hold of her cloth. So, truth to tell, she threw off the cloth she had taken round her, and he pulled her up by her own cloth. When he had pulled her up to him, he embraced her and let her take her cloth properly on. Now whether it was her fate ordained by Chando or whatever it was, the girl called out: "Girls, go home, I shall stay with this one."

The girls then said: "Come along, girls, we must at once tell this at home." When the girls had gone, he took the girl on his back and ran off with her as fast as he could; he did not put her down anywhere; he took her straight away to their own house.

When the others had told the girl's parents, her father and brothers took their bows and arrows and brought their dogs and searched for the Hanuman all over the neighbourhood; they hunted eagerly all over the vicinity for him, and as they did not find him, they cried sorely. They hunted for him for two or three days; as they did not find him, they returned crying. They scolded her girl companions well and said to them: "Why did you not first tell at once?" The girls did not answer a single word; they were numbed with fright. Ultimately they quieted down.

Ar uni hąṛũ dǫ idikate ạḍiye khusiyena, ar uni kuṛi ńęlte hǫṛ hõ ạḍi bạṛićko hahaṛayena. Adǫ bapla reaḱko nenḍakette bhǫj reaḱ ar hạnḍiko renaḱko tana bhanaketa; jǫmǫn ạḍi hako pako bapla hoe hǫdoḱ lekako usạraketa. Adǫ nenḍa dinre peṛakoko lạiatkote jǫtǫko jaorayena. Adǫ hǫṛ leka onka bapla hoeyena ar hạnḍi mạnḍiko ńũ jǫmketa. Adǫ ǫnǫkin tahẽyena.

Adǫ uni hąṛũ dǫ ǫnǫ onkate oṛaḱ duạre teṅgoketa. Adǫ uni hąṛũ koṛa reaḱ lilạ dǫ cabayena. Adǫ uni bạhu kuṛige daka ṭukućko, oṛaḱ duạrko, jǫtǫko jimạwadea.

Adǫ cabayena katha dǫ.

80. Cǫmǫń koṛa.

Sedae jǫkhǫn, kathae, mitṭań raje tahẽkana, ar uniren dǫ barea rạnikin tahẽkana, chuṭki ar bạṭki, ar nui bạṭki rạniren dǫ turui gǫṭǫnge taeako koṛa hǫpǫn dǫ, ar uni chuṭkiren dǫe mit́ gǫṭǫngea, ar uni hõ hǫṛ manwa muṭhạn dǫ bae janamlena, uni dǫ cǫmǫń-geye janamkedea. Adǫe janamen khan dǫ rajko lạiadea, bańma, nonkan gidrạ uni chuṭki rạni dǫe janamkedea, adǫ cetbo cekaea, giḍikaeabo sǫbo tahẽ ocoaegea?

Adǫ raje mǫnketa, Noa dǫ ạḍi hahaṛa katha hoeyena; manwa kukhi khon sǫ manwa kukhire Cando dǫ mitṭań janwargeye kolkedea, nöa dǫ ạḍi ǫsǫmbhǫg katha hoeyena, uniaḱ cet́ sana

[33] Eating and drinking together is symbolic; the Hanuman is now 'taken into caste' he is not an outsider any longer.

[34] A sign that the bride is now belonging to them, is one of themselves. A stranger would never be permitted to touch the cooking-utensils; and here all is given over to the girl's charge, the fullest degree of honour.

80 [1] As in previous volumes where no narrator is mentioned, Sagram Murmu is the man who has taken the story down.

[2] Bạṭki is the first wife with whom a full marriage ceremony is gone through; chuṭki is the second (or, if there are more wives, the last one). The first wife may be living or dead, it does not alter the designation. Two wives are not

But having brought the girl, the Hanuman was very pleased, and, seeing the girl, the people there also were utterly astonished. Thereupon they fixed a day for the marriage and made all preparations for a feast and for beer and so on; they worked quickly in order that the marriage might take place as soon as possible. On the day fixed they informed the friends, and all came together; and the marriage was gone through as with other people, and they ate the food and drank the beer[33]. Thereupon these two stayed together.

In this way the Hanuman made himself a house and home. The entertainment of the Hanuman boy is at an end; and they gave the bride charge of the cooking-pots, household and properties, in fact all[34].

So the story is ended.

80. THE MONGOOSE BOY[1].

In olden times, people tell, there once lived a king; he had two queens, a second wife and a first wife[2]; the first queen was the mother of six boys, and the second queen was the mother of only one, and this one was not born in human shape; it was a mongoose[3] she gave birth to. When he was born, they informed the king, telling him that the second queen had given birth to such and such a one; "what shall we do? shall we do away with him or shall we let him live?"

"This is a very wonderful thing that has happened," the king replied; "from or in a woman's womb Chando has sent an animal; this is an awful thing that has happened; whatever His will may be, we shall see what this is; we are certainly not superior to

common among the Santals, however more so now than formerly, when the first wife might bring in a second one, in case she did not bear children or was incapable of doing a housewife's work.

3 Fairly common, also in the Santal country.

kana, onagebo ńela; uni khon tho ohobo jadalena, hormo bhitrire garhao ocoko reak do uniak dare ar uniak sana; adoe ematbon khan cetbo menkea; acha, ma tahẽ ocoae, harakaegeabon, ado tayomrebo ńela, bhala nui reak do cet hoeoktaea.

Ado kathae, raj onkaye menket khan, kathaeko tahẽ ocoadegea, nunu harakedegeako. Ado noko bątki hopon korako harayen khan arko buden khan do uni cemeń gidrą doko hirkhąwae kangea, ar uni kąkit eṅgat hõ, baro lekako rorte uni hõko cirhąuea. Ado raj onkaye ańjomketko khan monereye menketa, en kathae, noko do ohoko suluklena, iń baṅ hilok nukin doko dal goć atarkina. Ado onkaye bujhąu barakette nukin eṅga hon do pharakreye orakatkina. Ado onakate noko bątki era hopon do jotoye bąhu cabawatkoa; adoe menketa, Noko maṅ bąhuatko; ado nui lągit bąhu do okareń ńamkoa? Ado bae khoro dareatko khan doe thirena.

Ado jotoko hara juąnena, ar nui hõ hor lekage, kathae, ror doe cetketa, onka lekageye rora, ar uni hõye harayena, ene tin titit cemeńko haraka, in marań doe harayena, ar bąhu do bae bąhuadea.

Khange mit din do raje menketa, aćren joto hopontet korakoye hoho jarwaketkoa, uni chutki hopon hõye hohoadea, adoko jarwayen khane metako kana, Ią beta, bąhu barawatpeań, ar nui do baṅ; adoń metape kana, ma, iń jivet minąṅre jotoń begar barakapea.

Ado unre onko bątki hopon korako menketa, Ią baba, ona katha do thikgem meneta; menkhan ale do noale metam kana, nitre hisą bakhra do bale hataoa, ale do den puńji taka bare emalem, bąnij beparle sen lenge, am jivet menamre disomle

[4] When the sons grow up and marry, it is customary that the father and sons 'separate'; the agricultural land is equally divided between them, the father generally keeping for himself as much as he gives to each son. As a rule the parents will stay with one of the sons, frequently with the younger one. The cause

Him; to let anything take shape in one's body, that depends on His power and His will. And as He has given us this, what can we say? Well then, let him live; we shall keep him and let him grow up; afterwards we shall see what his fate may be."

As the king spoke in this way, they let him live, people tell; they nursed him and let him grow up. Now, when the sons of the first queen grew up and reached the age of discretion, they felt abhorrence towards him; his mother they also constantly mocked, speaking of her in a dozen different ways. When the king heard this, he said to himself: "These children will never live in peace with each other; when I am no more, they will kill these two poor ones." Having come to this conclusion, he built a house for mother and son some distance off. Thereupon he procured wives for all the sons of his first queen and said: "Now I have got wives for these; but where shall I find a wife for this one?" And as he was unable to hear of any, he ceased to try.

Now all of them grew up into maturity, and the mongoose boy also, people tell, learnt to speak like a man; thus, just like the other ones, he was speaking. He also grew into maturity, just as big as a mongoose will grow, so big he became; and his father did not marry him to anybody.

Then one day the king said, — he called all his sons together, the son of his second wife he also called, and when they had come together, he said to them: "I say, my boys, I have got wives for all of you, only not for this one; so now I tell you this, while I am still alive, I shall settle[4] all of you in separate households."

Then the sons of his first wife said: "Quite so, father, it is quite right what you say; but we have this to say to you, at present we shall not take whatever may fall to our share; but please give us some money as capital, and let us before anything

of this setting up separate households very frequently is that the women for some reason or other are unable to hit it off with each other.

dāṛālege, disomle ńel acuranrege, ado ona puńji ṭaka khon bhala okoeko dole lab daṛeaka sele noksana, ado jāhānak gele jāhā cekae disom thole ńeljongea. Ale do puńji ṭaka baṛe emalem.

Ado sari raj hō onkoak kathae bataoket takogea, ar uni cemeń koṛa do Lelsińko ńutum akadea, ar oneko galmarao kan jokhen uni cemeń koṛa Lelsiń do cet hō bae ror baṛayeta, thir akangeae. Ado kathae, enkako galmarao baṛaket khange puńji ṭaka joto horge mimit isiye ematkoa, ar uni Lelsiń do bae emae kana. Khange uni Lelsiń cemeń koṛa doe menketa, Den baba, iń hō imańme, iń hō noko dadańteko sāoteń calaka bạnij bepar.

Ado kathae, enkaye roṛket khange onko dadatteko doko ruhet gotkedea, Dhut, am do ale sāote do alom hijuka, jāhāre seta tanakko ger goć adomea. Khange ado cet hō bae roṛleta, hape hapeteye beret calaoena. Ado oṛakre senkate eńgattete kulikedea, Henda beṭa, cet lagat raj doe khojletmea? Ado unre oneko galmaraolet onako joto kathaye lạiadea, bańma, raj do nonka onkae menleta; ado dadańteko bako khusilente bepar lagat puńji ṭakageko koekedea; ado mimit isi ṭakae ematkoa, ar iń do bae emadińa, ado iń hō onko sāote bepar lagit ṭakań koelede khan do dadańtekoko ruhet gotkidińa, menketako, Ale sāote do alom hijuka, jāhāre seta tanak eńgateko ger goć adomea. Ado onkako menket khan iń doń beret hećena.

Ado eńgattete menketa, Ia beṭa, endekhan eskare tahen jokhen calakte koeyeme. Adoe menketa, Acha, ayoń calaka; are meneta, dadańtekoko meneta, Jāhāre seta tanakko ger goć adomea, cedak ayoko gereńa, iń ki bud do bạnuktińa, onateń ger ocoka? Hape se ṭaka khạjuke imạń, iń hō tayom tayomte doń pańjakogea.

[5] A genuine Santal trait; they are very eager to get an opportunity of 'seeing land', as they call it.

[6] The name is possibly to be derived from the Hindi name for a mongoose, newal or neola. Siń is a common patronymic among Hindus, also heard in Santal names as second part of the nameword.

[7] The small amount of rupees shows the influence of Santal ideas on a story, probably originally borrowed from others.

else do some trading; let us, while you are alive, travel in the country, let us have a look round in the country[5]; and then, with the capital given, probably some of us will be able to make a profit, or else lose it; but whatever happens, we shall in any case see the country. Give us some money for a capital."

Truth to tell, the king agreed to what they said. Now this mongoose boy they had named Lelsiṅ[6], and while they were talking, Lelsiṅ did not speak at all, he kept quiet. Now, when they had had this talk, people tell, the king gave each of them as a capital for trading one score of rupees[7], but he did not give Lelsiṅ. Lelsiṅ, the mongoose boy, then said: "Please, father, give me also; I also want to go with my brothers to trade."

When he said this, his brothers commenced to scold him: "Fie, don't you come together with us; somewhere a dog or some other animal might bite you and kill you." He did not say a word more, but got quietly up and went away. When he reached home, his mother asked him: "Look here, my boy, for what purpose did the king call you?" Then he told her all they had talked together, saying: "The king said so and so; but as my elder brothers were not pleased, they asked him to give them money to trade with, and he gave them twenty rupees each, but me he gave nothing, and when I too asked him for money to go trading together with them, my brothers commenced to scold me and said: 'Don't come with us; somewhere some dog or other animal might bite you and kill you, dash it.' When they spoke in this way, I got up and came here."

His mother then said: "I say, my boy, then go to him while he is alone and ask him." "Very well, mother," he replied, "I shall do so;" and he added: "My brothers say: 'Somewhere a dog or some other animal will bite you and kill you.' Why should they bite me, mother? Have I no sense, that I should let myself be bitten? Wait a bit, provided he gives me some money, I shall follow after them."

Adọ kathae, tin ghuṛire cọñ ńẹl sitte uni dọ sạri ẹnẹye metade lekage eskarre raj ṭhen dọe calao gọtena, adọ ạḍi jide metae kana, Dẹn baba, iń hõm emạńgea; iń hõ bạnij bepar dọń calaḱgea. Adọ kathae, ạḍi jide khọj kan khan dọ gẹl ṭakaye emadea, ar pạtiạu dọ bae pạtiạuḱ kana, nui hõ sạrigeye calaḱa mẹnte dọ; adọe mẹneta, Inạ lasāṛhẽ kateye kọe idijọń kana, nui kiye bepar daṛekea? Nui dọ ọhọe daṛelea. Onka mọnẹre dọe mẹnoaṫa.

Adọ sẹnkate eṅgattẹte udukadea. Khange noko dọ calaḱ lạgitko neṇḍakette sạtu sambarko juṛạu baṛajoń kana; adọ onaye ańjọm ṭhikketkoa, bańma, nią din hiloḱko calaḱa mẹnte. Adọ aćhõ eṅgattẹte lạiadea, bańma, Ma ayo, iń hõ sạtu sambar dọ juṛạuańme, nią inạ dinre dọ bạnij beparko calaḱ lagat, iń hõ tayọm tayọmteń pańja idikoa.

Adọ sạri ẹnẹye juṛạuadea; khange onako dọ jọtọye sapṛao ṭhik ṭhakkata, ar sẹ noko dọ bako baḍaeyede kana, jẹ nui hõ ṭakae ẹm akawadea mẹnte dọ, ar nui hõe calaḱgea mẹnte dọ, arko baḍaele khan hunẹć ńindạre cọko sẹnkoḱ.

Adọ bako baḍaeledete setaḱgeko oḍok calaḱ kana; adọe ńẹl gọtketko khan dọ ać hõye sapṛao gọtena; adọ thoṛae laha ńõḱ ocoatkoa; adọ inạ tayọm ać hõye oḍok gọtena, jẹmọne ńẹl tioḱ idiko enkageye calaḱ kana, ẹkkalte dọ bae sẹn bhiṛạuḱ kana. Adọ ḍher sạṅgiṅgeko calaoena, ar nui dọ bako tuphinede kana; cetko cọko rọṛet arko landa idiyeta, tayọm sẹn dọ bako bẹṅgẹt ruạṛ baṛayeta.

Khange mit́ họṛ dọe mẹnket takoa, Hape ya, tạṅgi hataṛińpe, daḱ sẹćanregeń. Adọ onka mẹnkateko duṛupena, ar uni mit́ họṛ dọ daḱ sẹne calaoena; adọ daḱ sẹn khone hijuḱ kana, ar ọntẹ nọtẹye bẹṅgẹt ạguyeta, ar nui Lelsiń hõko duṛupen khan dọe

[8] People starting on a journey and expecting to be unable to get suitable food on the road generally take some dry eatables with them that may be eaten without the necessity of being cooked. It is generally some kind of cereals, wheat or rice, to which molasses have been added.

So, people tell, some time or other he found an opportunity, and really, as his mother had advised him, he went to the king while he was alone, implored him earnestly, and said to him: "Please, father, give me also, I also shall go trading." Then, people tell, as he implored him so earnestly, he gave him ten rupees; but he did not believe that this son would really go. He thought: "This is a pretext to beg money for himself; should this one be able to trade?" He explained it in this way.

The mongoose boy went and showed it to his mother. Now those others had fixed a day for starting and were preparing the necessary food[8] for the journey; and he heard for certain that they would start on such and such a day. Then he himself also spoke to his mother: "I say, mother, prepare some food for the journey for me too; they are starting on such and such a day; I also shall follow after them."

So, truth to tell, she made up something for him, and he made all necessary preparations; but the others did not know that their father had given money also to this one, and that he also would go. If they had known, they would likely have started some time during the night.

As they did not know, they started in the morning, and when he had seen the others off, he also made himself ready. He let the others get some start, whereupon he himself also went; he kept himself going so that he could just see the others; he did not follow close upon their heels. They went far away, but they did not notice this one; they did not look behind; they constantly were talking and jesting about something or other.

Then one of them said: "Wait a little; wait a bit for me, I must go aside for a moment." After this talk they sat down, and this one went towards water[9]; when he was coming back from there, he was looking round in all directions. Now Lelsiń

9 A common euphemism.

ńẹl aťkeťkote ạḍi dạuṛa dạuṛiye ńir hijuk̓ kana; adọ ọnẹ ọntẹ khone hijuk̓ kan jọkhẹn dọe ńẹl ńamkede dọ dạuṛa dạuṛiye ńir hijuk̓ kan. Adọ miť ghuṛi tengo ńọ̃k̓kateye ńẹle kan dọe ńẹl ṭhikkede, Lelsiń kanae.

Adọ onko duṛup̓ akankoye metako kana, Ea, mase nọtẹ tayọm sẹn bẹńgẹdpe, uni dọ bhala Lelsiń sẹ ọkọeye ńir hijuk̓ kana? Adọko mẹnkeťa, Ukurić ya? Adọe metaťkoa, Nũk̓ũi ya. Khange adọko ńẹl ṭhikkedea, adọko mẹn gọťkeťa, Hapẹ, hẹć ocoae, urni birre nãhãk̓bon ạyur adea; adọ enkako rọṛ hataṛtegeye tiok̓keťkoa.

Adọe sẹṭẹren khanko kulikedea, Henda ya, am hõm hijuk̓ kana? Ale dọle mẹnkeťa, Ṭaka bae emaťmete cele ọhọm hẹćlena; onate bale bẹńgẹť ruạṛ baṛayeťa; miť mohṇḍale hijuk̓ kana; adọ ya, ṭaka dọe emaťmea sẹ bań? Adọe mẹnkeťa, Mahajọn ṭhen iń ńamkeťa; adọ sapṛao baṛak̓tegeń tayọmena; apepe oḍok hijuk̓ dọ jọmak̓koń ńam jarwa ạguyeť tahẽkana, adọ inạk̓tege ạḍi sạṅgińpe jitạu hẹć idiyena, ar un hạbić dọ thoṛań ńẹl tiok̓ ạguyeťpe tahẽkangea. Adọ nọṇḍẹpe duṛup̓en khan dọń ńẹl aťkeťpe khan dọ dạuṛa dạuṛiń ńir hijuk̓ kana, ar alope duṛup̓ khan hutẹć ọhọń tiok̓ daṛelepea. Tãhã baṛkaćtege bae tiok̓eťko tahẽkana.

Adọko metae kana, Dur ya, bale bạḍaeyeť metege, bańkhan hutẹćle tạṅgikemgea; cedak̓ bale tạṅgimea? Miť oṛak̓ren họṛ hõ tọbẹ bale tạṅgikokhan ọkọele tạṅgikoa? Ale dọ bạḍaetege bale bạḍaeleťmea, am hõm hijuk̓ kana mẹnte dọ; ar am hõ un din ma bam lạiyeť tahẽkan, ar bań dọ hijuk̓ jọkhẹn hõm họhọ gọťale kana. Adọe mẹnkeťa, Ghanẹ dọ hijuk̓, ghanẹ dọ bań, onkate bạń họhọaťpea, arhọ̃ń muruk gọťkeťkhan ẹnẹń pańjakeťpea. Adọ inạk̓kategeko thir baṛayena.

lost sight of the others when they sat down, and came running with all his might; and when he was coming from one side, his brother saw him coming along running at top speed. So he stopped for a short while, had a look at him and recognized him, that it was Lelsiń.

He then said to those sitting there: "Hey you, look behind you in this direction, I wonder whether it is Lelsiń or some one else who is coming running." "Why, where is he? we don't see anybody," they said. "Look, here he is," he told them. So they caught sight of him and said: "Wait. let him come; we shall presently guide him to the primeval forest and lose him there." While they were having this talk, he came up to them.

When he reached them, they asked him: "Look here, you, are you also coming along? We thought that, as he did not give you any money, you would be sure not to come; therefore we have not been looking behind us; we have been coming straight along; now did he give you any money or not?" "I got some from a money-lender," he replied, "and, making myself ready, I was delayed; when you were starting, I was occupied getting my food together; and in the meanwhile you came so far more quickly than I could; but up to this I have been able just to keep you in sight. When you sat down here, I lost sight of you, wherefore I am coming running all I can; if you had not sat down, I should certainly not have been able to catch up with you."

"What a pity," they said to him, "we did not know of you, otherwise we might have waited for you, until you could come; why should we not do so? If we who belong to the same house should not wait for each other, whom should we wait for? We had absolutely no knowledge of you, that you too were coming along; and you yourself did not tell all the time either, and when we were starting, you were not calling out to us." "Sometimes," he said, "I wanted to come, then again I did not; in this way I did not call out to you, so again I suddenly decided to come and tracked you, as you see." After this talk they did not say any more on this subject.

Adọ calaoko calaoena sẹ, kathae, ạḍi sạṅgiṅko calaoena, pẹ pon māhā họrko calaoena; adọ miṭṭaṅ maraṅ uṭar urni birko ṅamkeṭa; adọ ona bir phẹḍre miṭ ṅindạko ḍerayena; adọ unreko mẹneṭa, Adọ bhala heć mabon hẹćena, adọ tin din badrebon ruạṛ calaḱa?

Adọ maraṅiće mẹnkeṭ takoa, Turui cando badre; turui cando dọ nọtẹregebon kạmilege, uniye dạṛa, dosra candoye mologoḱa, adọ unrebo mohṇḍa gọdoḱa. Adọ sạri dosar hiloḱ khange ona urni bir talateko mohṇḍayenteko calaḱkana. Adọ kathae, calaḱ calaḱte uni Lelsiṅ dọko ṅir aṭkadea, metaḱme, uni dọko ṅir bạgiae kana; ọṇḍẹgeko bạgiadete ako dọ Lilạm bajarreko rakapena, ar uni dọ Sujạn bajarreye rakapena.

Ar noko dọko sẹṭẹren khan dọ sadọmko bachao baṛayeṭkoa kiriṅko lạgiṭ. Adọ kathae, pạhil dọ pẹa siṅ sadọmko kiriṅ pạhilkeṭkoa; adọ enkotege pẹ cando dọko beparkeṭa; adọko lapha baṛakeṭ khan dọ arhō noko pẹ họṛ lagaṭko kiriṅeṭkoa. Adọ noko lagaṭ hō onko siṅ sadọmgeko kiriṅkeṭkoteko bepar kana.

Ar Lelsiṅ dọ ona Sujạn bajarre rakap kate gutiḱ lagaṭ kisạṛe kuli baṛayeṭkoa. Henda ho, ẹn kathae, gutipe dọhọkiṅa? onkaye kuli baṛayeṭkoa. Adọko metae kana. Hẽ ma hẽge, adọ ceṭ am dọm kạmialea, am thọ jāhān kạmi lek dọ bale ṅẹleṭmea. Adọ goṭa bajar onkaye kuli baṛayeṭko khan dọ inạ kathageko metadea.

---

10 When a Santal wants to show the distance from one place to another, he very commonly does it by telling how long it takes to walk there. E.g. tikin họr, noon-way, means the distance one can walk from early morning to noon, about twenty miles with an ordinary Santal. One day's way will answer to some thirty miles or more.

11 The Santals use the phases of the moon to keep some account of time. The moon is always observable, except just at the time of new moon. In common with a good many other people they also combine superstitions of sorts with the different phases.

12 Lilam Basar, as it is called, literally means 'auction town'; bazar is a name for a town with shops.

Thereupon they went; they went and went, people tell, very far; they went so far as is takes to reach in three or four days[10]; then they reached an immensely big primeval forest and spent one night on the edge of this forest. Then they were saying: "Well, now we have come, after how many days shall we go back again?"

The eldest of them said: "After six months; let us work for six months here in these parts; let that moon change[11] and the next new moon appear; then we shall start for home." Now, truth to tell, the next morning they set out to pass through the primeval forest and were walking along. Then, people tell, as they were passing along, the brothers lost sight of Lelsiń, that is to say, they ran away and left him behind. They left him there and themselves went to a town called Lilam[12]; and Lelsiń found his way to a town called Sujan.

When his brothers reached this place, they commenced to look at horses to buy them. First, people tell, they bought three day-horses[13], and, making use of these, they traded for three months; and when they had gained enough profit, they bought for the remaining three. For these also they bought day-horses and continued to trade.

Now, when Lelsiń reached the town of Sujan, he asked wealthy people there to be taken on as a servant. "Look here," he said, "will you take me on as a servant?" In this way he was asking them. "Well," they would reply, "quite so; but what will you do for us? To us you do not look fit for any kind of work." Everywhere in the whole town they answered him in this way when he asked them for work.

[13] The Santal traditions tell of a day-horse that came down and kicked to pieces the first human beings that Thakur had made from clay, just as Thakur was going to breathe life into them. What is here meant, is not clear.

Adoe guni bhạbik̓ kana, Cet̓ iń cekalere iṅak̓ pọrbạsti dọ calak̓tiṅa; gutik̓iń mẹnetre ma bako dọhọń kan, ar bepar tanak̓ hõ cekatiń calaoa, puńji hõ thoṛagetiń; arhõye mẹnket̓a, Acha, sadọmgiń kuli gelakoa, pasẹ thoṛa damteko ńamok̓ khan dọń kiriṅkoteń bepar gelaea. Adọ sạri kiriṅko lagat̓ sadọme kuli baṛayet̓koa; adọ ạḍi titit̓ko damako kan; adọ arhõko metadea, Nọṇḍẹ dọ sadọm ọhọm hatao daṛelekoa; do Lilạm bajarte calak̓me, ọṇḍẹ dọ sanam lekankoko haṭet̓koa jãhãeṭak̓gem kusik̓, ini baṛẹ kiriṅem.

Adọe metat̓koa, Ona bajar dọ oka sẹnre menak̓a? Adọ mohṇḍateṭ̓ko uduk̓ gọt̓adea; adọ sạri ona mohṇḍateye calaoen khan dọ Lilạm bajare ńamket̓a. Adọ họṛe kuliket̓koa, Henda ho, ẹn kathae, sadọm dọ oka sẹnreko haṭet̓koa? Adọko metadea, Ma am dọ niạ họrte calak̓me, noa bajar hanasa aṛere nãhãk̓ marań utạr baṛe darem ńama, ona ṭhenge hạṭiạ dọ hoeok̓ kana; ọṇḍẹge nãhãk̓ sadọm hõm ńamkoa. Adọ sạri ṭhik ona họrteye calaoen khan dọ baṛe dare ṭhenge hạṭiạ akat̓ko sadọme ńamket̓koa; adọ dame kuli baṛayet̓koa, adọ ạḍi titit̓ko dam akokan. Adọe mẹnket̓a, Sadọm dọ eṅgate ọhọń kiriń daṛelekoa; adọ bhagaoente gadha pal sẹne calaoena.

Adọ onkoye ńẹl baṛayet̓koa, adọko metae kana, Celekom ńẹl baṛayet̓koa? Adọe mẹnket̓a, Gadhań ńẹl baṛayet̓koa, tin titit̓pe damako kana? Adọko metadea, Kiriṅkoam? Adọe mẹnket̓a, Hẽ ẹnte, dọr damreń khusilen khan dọń kiriṅkekoa. Adọko mẹnket̓a, Jẹ jam gadha, onkagele damkoa, bar ṭaka hõ, pẹ ṭaka hõ, ar mõṛẽ turui ṭakaren hõ menak̓koa, sẹ dọs barọ ṭakaren hõ menak̓koa. Adọ onkako mẹnket̓khan dọ mit̓ṭań gadhae bachaokedea, adọe metat̓koa, Ma sẹ nui gadha reak̓ dam lạipe. Adọko mẹnket̓a, Nui dọ mõṛẽ ṭakale dame kana. Khangeye thirena, adọ bae rọṛlet̓

14 The people do much of their selling and buying at market places found in suitable localities and open for business once or twice weekly, or daily.

He was turning this over in his mind: "What shall I do, so that I may have what is necessary to live? When I talk of becoming a servant, they will not take me on; and how should I be able to engage in trade or something of that kind with such a small capital as I have?" Then again he would say: "Very well, I shall try and ask them about horses; if they are to be had for a reasonable price I shall buy one and try to trade." So, truth to tell, he made enquiries about horses, to buy one; but they put a very high price on them; they also said to him: "Here you will not he able to buy any horse; go to the town of Lilam; there they bring all kinds for sale; buy whichever you like."

"In what direction is this town?" he asked them. So they showed him the direction, and when he had proceeded in that direction, he really found his way to the town of Lilam. Here he asked people: "Look here, where are they having a market[14] for selling horses?" "Well, they replied, "follow this way, on the other side of this town, just outside, you will presently find a very big banyan tree; just at that tree a market is on; there you will also find horses." Truth to tell, following this way he found horses for sale in the market at the banyan tree, He asked them the price; but they wanted a very large sum. So he said: "I shall certainly not be able to buy a horse, dash it." So, not being able to do anything here, he went to the donkey flock.

When he was looking at these, they asked him: "What are you looking at?" "I am looking at your donkeys," he replied; "how much do you price them at?" "Will you buy?" they asked him, "Yes," he replied; "if I am pleased with the price, I might buy some." They said: "According to their quality we price the donkeys; some two rupees, some three rupees; there are also those who cost six rupees, or even ten twelve rupees. When they had spoken in this way, he selected a donkey and said to them: "Please tell the price of this donkey." "We fix the price of this at five rupees," they answered. He did not say anything,

khan doko menkeťa, Ma am rorme, tinaktem hataokea? Adoe menkeťa, Adi utargepe dame kan do, ceť iń mena? ma thik dam laipe; judiń khusilen khan doń hataokea. Adoko menkeťa, Thik dam do pon taka, ado uniye menkeťa, Pon taka do bań, pe takań emapea. Adoko menkeťa, Ma arhõ ina talateť jutućaleme. Adoe menkeťa, Bańa ho, ma inaktege imańpe. Adoko cepeť barayen khan sari inaktegeko emadea; ado takae emaťkote gadha do bare dare butateye tiok idikedea.

Adoe menkeťa, Nondegeń deraka. Ado sari bepar lagiť sana phanakoye kirińkeťa; ado un jokhene ńelkeťko do, dadatteko hõ ona bajar reakgeko kiriń akrińeť kan; ado oneko bagiade edrete onko then do bae senlena, ina bare dare then dera kategeye bepar barayeťa. Ar onko hõko ńelkedere hõ ceť hõ bako kuli baraledea. Onka apan apingeko tahẽyena.

Ado ona nenda din purauen khan, kathae, noko do lahatege orakte doko hećena, ar nui hõ ona nenda din mae badae akať tahẽkan, ado nui hõ tayomte orakteye heć seterena. Ado sangiń khonko ńel daramkede khan dadatteko do engat apatkoko laiako kana, Ma se hani ńelepe, Lelsiń do celeye kiriń aguyede kana? Ado onkako laiyeťa, ar bogete khak khakko landayeťa, ar raj do ceť hõ bae menleťa, mone moneteye menkeťa, Nui do thoragiń emadete thora damrengeye kirińkedea. Ar onko korako do bogeteko landa daramadea.

Ado tinake kamaoleťa, ona do engat apate udukaťkina, ar noko ma bako udukleť; ado onate raj do nui Lelsińgeye sarhaokedea, menkeťae, Bańa, nui hoponge engate gun doye manaoa. Ado raj hõ inakgeye rorkaťa. Ado ona katha ańjomkate onko korako do monere edreko dohokaťa.

15 The bargaining is typical. As a rule the seller asks double or treble of what he expects to get. Incidentally it may be remarked that the Santals do not keep donkeys, one of the proofs that the story is originally borrowed.

so they said: "Tell yourself, please, at what price will you take it?" He replied: "You want an excessive price for it, so what can I say? Please tell the proper price; if I think that fair, I may perhaps take it." "The proper price is four rupees, they said, whereupon he replied: "No, not four rupees; I shall give you three." "Well then," they said, "add half a one and give us." "No, you people," he replied, "let me have it at what I said." So they consulted together and really gave it to him for that much, whereupon he gave them the money and led the donkey away to the foot of the banyan tree[15].

So he said: "I shall camp here," whereupon he bought the necessary equipment for trading. At that time he saw that also his brothers were buying and selling goods in this town; but, being angry that they had left him, he did not go to them; camping at this banyan tree, he engaged in trading. They on their part, although they saw him, did not ask him anything either. In this way they kept away from each other.

When the day fixed came, the brothers, people tell, came home before him; he also knew the day agreed on, so he reached home after the others. When the brothers saw him coming, while he was a way off, they spoke to their parents: "Look over there, look at Lelsiṅ, what kind he has bought and is bringing along." They talked in this way and were laughing loudly; but the king did not say a word, he was thinking: "I gave him only a little, so he has bought a low-priced animal." But the boys met him laughing loudly.

Now he showed his father and mother how much he had earned; but his brothers did not do so, wherefore the king praised Lelsiṅ saying: "There is no gainsaying it, this son of mine, dash it, he shows gratitude." The king did not say any more; but when the boys heard this, they became angry and their mind was filled with it.

Adọ tahẹn tahẹnte inạ dosar tesar serma khange, kathaeye akalkeťa; khange nui Lelsiń dọ akal ạikạute ạkinaǩ oṛaǩ dọ ọt latar sẹn goṭaye kholao bhugạǩketa, ar jẹ kichu dhọn tahẽkana, onako dọ miť miťte jọtọ ọt bhitriteye adẹr baeketa, ar ńindạ dọ hoṛkoaǩe kombṛo ạgu aḍoe takoa, adọ onkate nukin eṅga hon dọ bakin rẹṅgẹjoǩ kana, ar gidrạko hõ rẹṅgẹcte bogeteko raǩeť takoa. Khange ona ńẹlte uni Lelsiń dọ eṅgattẹťe metadea, Do, ayo, miť haṭaǩ gan caole idiakome; dadańtekoren gidrạ ạḍiko raǩeť kana, dayageń ạikạueť kana.

Adọ miť khạclạǩ caoleye bhoraoketa, adọe dipil idi oṭoaťkoa; adọ ona ńẹlte onko koṛako dọko mẹnketa, Durre, nukin dọ menaǩgetakina, bakin kọsṭọǩ kana; aboge ạḍibo kọsṭọǩ kana. Adọ rajko metadea, Do baba, Lelsiń tikin ṭhen khon jọmaǩ ạgu abonme.

Adọ sạri onkako metade khan dọe calaoena; adọ rọṛ dọ ceť hõ bae rọṛ saḍeleťa, hape hapete oṛaǩtegeye bọlọyena; adọe mẹnketa, Ńẹl baṛaletakingeń, menaǩ tạkin khan dọń kọekina, ar baṅkhan ceť ạuṛi dọń kọekina.

Adọ sạriye ńẹl baṛakeť dọ ẹkẹn oṛaǩge; adọ onate bae rọṛ saḍeleťa; adọ ruạṛ sẹnkate koṛako dọko kulikedea, Okor babam ạguleťa. Adọe mẹnketa, Unkin hõya bạnuǩtạkina, goṭa bọlọkateń ńẹl baṛaketa, ẹkẹn oṛaǩge. Adọ koṛakoko mẹnketa, Acha bhala, alele ńẹl ạgui tạkina.

Adọ sạri sẹnkateko ńẹl baṛakeť tạkin dọ ẹkẹn oṛaǩge, ẹkẹn inạ haṭaǩ khạclạǩge; adọko thir doroǩena, ar sẹ jọm ńũ ghuṛiko ńẹlkin dọ besgekin jọmeť kan. Adọ ona ńẹlteko mẹnketa, Nukin dọ bakin rẹṅgẹjoǩ kana, besgekin jọmẹta, ma nukin hõbon rẹṅgẹć ocokina, oṛaǩbon jẹrẹťatakina. Khange sạri miť din dọ oṛaǩko

Time went, and the next year or the year after that, people tell, there was a famine; then Lelsiń, feeling that a famine was coming, commenced to burrow and excavated all the ground below their house, and whatever they had of property he brought it all down there and hid it, and at night-time he stole from people and brought it there. In this way these two, mother and son, did not become poor, while even the children of the others were crying from hunger. Seeing this Lelsiń said to his mother: "Please, mother,take about a winnowing-fan full of rice over to them; the children of my brothers are crying very much; I am sorry for them."

So she filled a basket with rice and carried it over to them; seeing this the brothers said: "Strange, these two have something; they are not in want of food, and we are in great distress." So they said to the king: "Listen, father, bring food for us all from Lelsiń and his mother."

Truth to tell, as they said this to him, he went there; he did not utter any sound, but went quietly in, saying: "I shall before anything else see how they are doing; if they have anything, I shall ask them; otherwise, what shall I ask them for, when there is nothing?"

So, truth to tell, he looked round, there was only an empty house; wherefore he did not say anything. When he came back, the boys asked him: "Why, father, you did not bring anything?" "No, boys," he replied, "they have nothing either, I went in and looked everywhere, there was only an empty house." The boys then said: "All right, then we shall go and have a look."

So they really went and looked at what they had, only an empty house, only the winnowing-fan and a basket, whereupon they kept quiet; but they saw those two having their food, they were always eating well. Seeing this they said: "These two do not suffer hunger, they have plenty of food; well, let us make these two also hunger; we shall set fire to their house." And,

jeretat takina, ar hatak khaclakko do joto loyen takina; menkhan dhon do mit tukun hō bań lolena.

Ado kathae, seńgelkokin Irićkette torocko do jotokin har samtaoketa; ado ona torocge bostare bhoraokate akrińe idia. Ado kathae, mit din do dher sańgińgeye idiketa, ado bań akrińlente dahar arere mittań bare dare butareye derayena, bosta doe argoketa, ar uni gadha do ona thenge rehetreye tolkadea, ar se ayupena. Khange kathae, bepariko hecena aema utar chala dańgrawante, ado onko hō ona dare butaregeko derayena. Khange nui do dareteye decena onde gitić lagit; ado dare cot khongeye hohoako kana, Men ho! ińak bostape iditińa sepe kombro botećkea, iń do eken sona, rupa, asarphi menaktińa; bańkhan bes do ohoń menlepea.

Ado sari onkae laikette tinre coń nuiak bosta doko kombroket taea, ar akoak bosta do nuiak thenko agu otokata, ar adi ńindare onde khonko uthauenteko calaoena. Ado setak jokhen bostae ńel tojbijket doko pherao akat. Khange, kathae, hare phareye lade gotkette orakteye hecena.

Ado orakre rarakateye ńelket do, caole ar taka bara bari menak; khange adiye khusiyena; ado eńgattete metadea, Do ayo, dadańteko then khon pai aguime, takalań sońa. Adoe agukette, kathae, mit pai takae bhoraoketa; adoe metadea, Do ayo, dadańteko idiakome, ar noa pai hō idikatakom.

Ado sariye idiatko khan do ona ńelte adiko haharayena; ado joto horko hecente Lelsińko kulikedea, Henda ya, nunak taka do okarem ńamketa?

Adoe metatkoa, Mittań orak reak toroc do tinak bań hoeoktiń, dher ńok orak tahen khan do hutec dhergiń takakea. Ado ona katha ańjomte onko dadattekoko menketa, Ia, ma eńgate abo hō

[16] The banyan tree, Ficus bengalensis, L., sends a number of roots down from its branches; these strike the ground and become fresh trunks. It is such a tree that is here alluded to.

truth to tell, one day they did so, and their winnowing-fan and baskets were all burnt; but of their real property not one bit was burnt.

Now, people tell, when these two had extinguished the fire, they collected all the ashes; and, filling the ashes in a bag, he took it away to sell it. One day he had taken it very far away; but as it could not be sold, be camped at the foot of a banyan tree; taking the bag off, he tied the donkey there to a root of the tree[16]; in the meantime it became evening. Then, people tell, some traders came with a large number of pack-bullocks, and these also camped at the foot of the same tree, whereupon the mongoose boy climbed the tree to sleep up there. From high up in the tree he called out to those others: "Beware, you might take my bag away, or you might even steal it; I have only gold, silver and gold coins; if you do, I shall not call you good people."

Truth to tell, as he had said this, those others some time during the night stole his bag and brought and left a bag of theirs where his had been, whereupon they left, while it was dark night. In the morning he looked at the bag, they had changed it. Whereupon, people tell, he quickly loaded his donkey and went home.

When he opened the bag at home, he saw that it contained rice and money, half and half of each, and he was very pleased and said to his mother: "Please, mother, go and bring a pint measure from my brothers; we shall measure money." When she had brought this, people tell, he filled the pint measure full of rupees and said to her: "Now, mother, take this to my brothers, and give them also their pint measure back."

Truth to tell, when she had taken this back to them, they were very much astonished, and all of them came to Lelsiṅ and asked him: "Look here, you, where did you get so much money?"

"How much," he replied, "should I get for the ashes of one house? if there had been a number of houses, I might have got much money." Hearing this his brothers said: "I say, dash it, we

oṛakbon jeṛetaka ar toṛocbon akriṅa, inạ ṭakatege arhõ nãhãk nenkan oṛak dobon banao adoea. Ado onka menkate sạri ako hõ oṛakko jeṛetata; onkage toṛoc hạrkette bostare bhoraokate akriṅko idiketa. Ado kulhi kulhiteko hoho idiyeta, Chạe libi go, chạe libi go. Ado okoe hõ bako hataoet takoa; ado pe pon atoko dãṛãlet khangeko mokoṅena, okare hõ baṅ akriṅlen tako khan arhõ agu ruạṛ kateko up gidikata; ado bogeteko edreyena, menketako, Nuiak budte oṛake jeṛet ocoketbona, ma nukin do bana hoṛbon gocḱina.

Ado sạri mit din do unkin gogocko calao gotena. Un jokhen Lelsiṅ do oṛakre bae tahẽkana, eṅgattetge eskarko ṅamkedea; uniko goc adokedea. Khange hecḱateye ṅelkede doe goc akan; ado gadhareye ladekedea Gaṅgate idiye lagat. Ado calak calakte tayomteye beṅget ruạṛlet do aema utạr chala daṅgrawante bepari do darako kan. Ado hare phare eṅgattet do uni gadha khon ãṛgokate mitṭaṅ hoṛ aṛe darereye ṭeṇḍarkadea, ar ac do dare cotteye dec gotena; ar onko do adi sạṅgiṅ daṅgra doko tiriạu akatkoa. Adoko hec seṭeren khangeye hohoyeta, Ma ho, eṅgaṅ ruạk hoṛpe lesen ocoyea; baṅkhan boge do ohoṅ menlepea. Ado bako aṅjometa; adoko hec soren khan do adi garte onkageye hohoyeta, khange adoko teṅgoyen khan do ãṛgokateye sapketkoa.

Ado adi bạṛicko botorena, adoe metako kana. ¡Cedakpe lesen goc ocokedea, delabon thanateṅ idipea. Adoko menketa, Alom idilea, ma noko daṅgra ar bostako joto am baṛe hataome, en hõ alom idilea. Khange ini eṅgattet do gadhareye ladekedea, ar onko joto daṅgrae piṭạu agukeṭkoa; ado hoṛre uni eṅgattet doe gidi

[17] In Bengali.

shall also set fire to our houses and sell the ashes; for that money we may again build such houses, forsooth". Thinking this they, truth to tell, set fire to their own houses also, and in the same way, having collected the ashes, they put them in bags and took it all away to sell it. Walking through the streets, they called out[17]: "Wer wird Asche kaufen? wer wird Asche kaufen?" But no one would have any, so, when they had passed through three or four villages, they gave it up; what they had could not be sold anywhere, so they brought it back again home and threw the ashes out and away. They were very angry and said: "Through his craftiness he made us set fire to our houses; come, let us kill these two, both of them."

So, truth to tell, they one day went to kill them. Just at that time Lelsiṅ was not a home; they found only his mother, and her they killed. When Lelsiṅ returned, he saw that she was dead, whereupon he put her on his donkey to take her to the Ganges. As he went along, he happened to look behind and saw traders coming along with an immense number of pack-bullocks. He then quickly took his mother down from the donkey and placed her up against a tree at the roadside, and he himself climbed the tree right up to the top; and the traders had their bullocks coming one behind the other for a very long stretch. When they came up to where he was, he called out: "Have a care, you will let my mother, who is ill, be trampled on; if you do, I shall not call you good." But they did not hear it; when they came quite close, he called out very loudly in the same way, whereupon they stopped, and he came down and caught hold of them.

Now these people got a great fright; he was saying to them: "Why did you let her be trampled to death? Come along, I shall take you to the police station." But they said: "Don't take us there; do take these bullocks and bags, all of them; but don't take us there." So he loaded his mother on his donkey, and, beating the bullocks, he brought them along with him. Somewhere

dapoṛkadea ar onko ḍaṅgrae laga ạguketkoa, adoe hoho ạguyeta, Ma karhaṛ jhijpe, dada, ma karhaṛ jhijpe, dada! Ado ene joto hoṛteko esel adeṛketkoa, ar chala bostako ā̃ṛgokette oṛakteko adeṛketa.

Adoko metaekana, Henda ya, nunạk ḍaṅgra do okarem ńamketkoa? Adoe menketa, Mitṭaṅ iṅgạńren do ente tinạkem ńamkoa? Ado onkoko menketa, Abo khan do aemabo ṭakakea. Ado inạ ńindạ khange sạri onko do akoren joto bạhukoko kuṭạm goc̕ ạdoketkoa, ar setak khange sadomre ladekate ạkriṅko idiketkoa. Ado ato atoko hoho baṛayeta, Mora libi go, mora libi go! Ado bogeteko ruhetketkoa, Mora ke libek re, hai dige nia ja. Ado onka pe pon atoko dā̃ṛālet khangeko ạṛisena; ente goc̕ hoṛ do okoe hataokoa? Ado enko hõ oka horre coko giḍi dapaṛkatkoa, ekenak siṭhạl miṭhạlko ruạṛ hec̕ dapoṛena.

Arhõ uni Lelsiṅ koṛa do, kathae, gadha do ạḍi bariće jotonetae kana; siṅ sạṭup̕ onkoko ńele khangeye jotae jotaea, ar ńindạ do ghā̃s salak ṭakae ajoaea; adoe ij khange ṭaṅgate ḍeke doe kuṭạm kuṭạm godea, ar ona ić doe hoṭor baṛaea, ar ṭaka doe halaṅ begara. Adoko metaea, Henda ya, nui gadha do eṅgate bejae ṭakageye ićet do? Adoe metakoa, Hẽ, dada, ićetgeae, nõkõe ente ńelpe, ape do cet lekanko cope kiriṅ akatkote bako ićet tape, ar iṅ do ij jokhen ḍekeṅ kuṭạm lekhange ṭakageye ićeta. Adoko menketa, Abo hõ bhalabon kuṭạmkoa. Ado sạri onkako kuṭạm baṛaketkoa, ado bako ijtako. Ado arhõko metae kana, Okor yako ićet talea?

along the road he threw his mother away, and the bullocks he drove along home; reaching there, he called out: "Open the bars, brothers, open the bars, brothers!" So all of them surrounded the bullocks and brought them in; and unloading the pack-bags, they took them all into the house.

"Look here, you," they asked him, "where did you get so many bullocks?" "For my mother, for only one, how many will you get?" The others said: "If it had been we, we should have made a lot of money." So, truth to tell, that very night they all of them hammered their wives to death, and in the morning they loaded them on their horses and took them away to sell them. In every village that they passed they called out[17]: "Wer wird Leichen haben? wer wird Leichen haben?" But people scolded them roundly: "Wer wird Leichen haben, nimm es weg!" When they had, in this manner, passed trough three to four villages, they became disgusted; for who is willing to take in dead people? So they also threw the dead bodies away somewhere at the road side and returned home, empty-handed and disgusted, the wretches.

Now the boy Lelsiń, people tell, was taking very great care of his donkey; all day long they saw him stroking and stroking it, and at night he fed it with rupees together with grass; and, when it was voiding excrements, he at once hammered its hind-quarters with an axe, whereupon he picked the excrements with a stick and took the rupees up and kept them separate. They then said to him: "Look here you, this donkey is voiding a lot of money?" "Yes, my brothers," he replied; "it certainly does, as you may see for yourselves here; what kind of animals you have bought, I wonder, since yours do not void the same; as for myself, when it voids excrements and I hammer its hind-quarters, it voids money." "We also," they said, "shall have a try, hammering ours." And, truth to tell, they hammered their horses in the same manner; but they did not void money. So they again said to him: "Why, you fellow, ours do not

Adoe metatkoa, Khub ätte kuṭạmkope. Adọ sạri khub garteko kuṭạmletko, adọ jọtọko kuṭạm gọć aḍoketkoa, ṭaka hõ bako ićleta.

Adọ khange uni upạrteko edreyena, mẹnketako, Nui dọ ya, ạḍi husiạr hor kanae, bạulite mabon gọjea; sanam hor khon eṅgate nuigeye lähätok kana. Abo ma nõkõe jọtọe marao ocoketbon, ẹnre hõ thọ, uni tuluć dọ babon daṛek kana; ma nui dọ bạhuaea mẹnte khuṛkhuṛitebon gọk idiyea, ar Gaṅgarebon bohao gọtkaea; iną dọe unum gọć dapoṛoka. Adọ onako sọlhaketteko metaekana, Ią ya, ḍherem cij bạsutketa, adọle bạhuama, bạhule siṛi akadea. Adọe mẹnketa, Acha besge, dẹbon ńamkoa. Adọko mẹnketa, Ńam akadeale, ma sunum sasaṅ ọjọgme, ar noa khuṛkhuṛire ma dẹjọkme, ọnḍẹ bạhu oṛakrege nähäk ḍhọl ḍhak dọbon ńama.

Adọ onka ạḍi jidko metade khan sạriye ọjọkente khuṛkhuṛireye bọlọyena; adọ khub lekako bọnd urićketa, jẹmọn aloe oḍok daṛeak. Khangeko gọk tapkedea; adọ calak calakte bhại Gaṅgako tiokketa. Adọ ghaṭ ṭhenko dọhọkedete ọkọe dọ ićjọṅko calaoena, ar adọmko dọko mẹnketa, Ghaṭbo cią ṭhiklege, oka ṭhen khạndria, ọnḍẹgebon ṭhelao ńür gọtkaea. Onka mẹnkate apan ạpinko calao baṛayena.

Adọ ona takrege miṭṭaṅ mẹrọm gupi koṛa dọ ona khuṛkhuṛi ṭhengeye hẹć sorena, ar nui dọ khuṛkhuṛi bhitrirege bhabnate khunuk khunuke rakjọṅ 'kana. Adọ uni mẹrọm gupi koṛa dọe mẹneta, Henda ho, cedakem raket kana? Adọe menketa, Iń dọ baṅ bạhujọṅ hor ;jọrmọṭgeko bạhuạń kana, iń bọdọl jähäege nọnḍẹ bọlọlen khan iń bạhu dọ unigeye hataokea.

---

18 The khuṛkhuṛi is a kind of palanquin often used for carrying the bridegroom in.

19 Ghaṭ is here used about the way down to a river or the place on the river bank where people go down to cross, fetch water, bathe.

void money." "Then hammer them hard," he replied. So they, truth to tell, hammered them severely, and in this way they hammered them, so that they all died; and money they did not void.

Now they became very angry with him and said: "This one is a very sly fellow; let us find a pretext and kill him; dash it, he is getting the better of us all; you see, now he has done for all of us; in spite of all we are unable to compete with him. Come, let us carry him away in a palanquin[18], under the pretext of marrying him; then we shall set him adrift in the Ganges; then he will be drowned and killed, the wretch." After having consulted together and come to this decision, they said to him: "Listen you, you have acquired much property, now we shall get you a wife; we have made inquiries and found a wife for you." "Very well," he replied, "that is good, let us get such a one." "We have found her," they said; "anoint yourself with oil and turmeric and sit in this palanquin; there at the bride's home we shall get tomtoms and drums."

As they spoke so earnestly to him, he, truth to tell, anointed himself and entered the palanquin, and his brothers shut it tightly up, so that he should not be able to get out. Then they carried him off, and passing along, my friends, they reached the Ganges. Having put him down at the way down to the river[19], some of them went to pay the call of nature, while others said: "Let us before anything else find out how the place at the river-side is; where there is deep water, we shall push him in." Saying this, they all went in different directions.

Just at this moment a goat-herd boy came up to the palanquin, and the mongoose boy was whimpering from anxiety inside the palanquin. "Look here," the goat-herd boy said, "why are you crying?" "I", he answered, "am a person unwilling to be married, they are marrying me by force; if only some one would come in here in my stead, he might take my bride."

Adọ uni koṛaye mẹnketa, Dẹ tọbẹ iṅiṅ hataoetama. Adọe metadea, Dẹ ẹntẹ jhijte bọlọkme. Adọ sạri rạskạte uni hõye jhić gọtketteye bọlọyena, ar nui dọe oḍok gọtena, adọe metadea, Siṅ urićkokme, am dọm ạnạṛigea, ńẹl ṭhik bọtẹćkemako, jẹmọn họrre dọ aloko ńẹl baṛame.

Adọ onkaye metadea, ać dọ mẹrọm gupıye calaoena. Adọ ạḍi ena noko hõko hẹćlena; adọ khạndri ṭhenko cią ạgukette gọk idikate ẹkkalte ọṇḍẹko ṭhelao ńũr gọtkata; adọ unumen khan dọko ruạṛ hẹćena. Adọ iną pẹ pon mãhã khange nui Lelsiṅ dọ aema mẹrọm bhiḍiye ḍahrao ạguyetkoa, ar baṛge mucạt khone họhọ ạguyeta, Gudṛiko jhijpe, dada! Onka ạḍi dhaoe ḷ ọhọyeta. Adọko ńẹlkede khan dọ jọtọ hoṛteko ẹsẹt adẹrketkoa; adọko mẹneta, Nũkũi ya, oka khone rakap̣ hẹć atarena? abo dọbo mẹnketa, marao atar akadeabon, nũkũi tãhãe hẹć ataren.

Adọ uniye mẹnketa, Ṭẹmẹćrege dadape khadlekadiṅ; adọ onate neko ninạkgeṅ ńamletkoa, arhõ khạndri sẹn ma gại, kaḍako sẹlẹt menakkoa, ọntẹrepe khadleliṅ khan hutẹć ḍhergiṅ ạgukekoa. Adọ onkako mẹnketa, Ea, ale hõ idilem, ạgujọṅale. Adọe mẹnketa, Hẽ ẹnte, mẹnkhan iṅ thọ ọhọṅ gọk idi daṛelepea, dela apetege gọk idikpe, adọ ọṇḍẹ nãhãk iṅ ṭhelao ńũr gọtkapea.

Adọ sạri ona kathageko aṅjọmkette akotege khuṛkhuṛiko gọk idiketa; adọ Gaṅga ḍhipreko dọhọketa, ar onareko bọlọyena arko metaė kana, Iṅ dọ khạndri ńõk sẹn baṛẹ yoi! Adọ jọtọ hoṛ onkako metae kana; adọ sạri mit mitte jọtọye ṭhelao ńũr gọtkatkoa. Adọ khube khusiyena, mẹnketae, Iṅ gọjẹṅpe mẹnleta, adọ

20 The motif of the story is given.

"Well then," the boy said to him, "I shall take your bride." "Come then," he replied, "open this and get in." And, truth to tell, the boy joyfully opened it and got in, and the mongoose boy came out and said to the other: "Shut it up tightly for yourself; you are a stranger; they might see you; be careful that they do not see you while on the road."

Having said this to him, he went off to herd the goats. After a long while the others at last came back; having found out where it was deep water, they took him straight there and at once pushed the whole in there; and when the palanquin had been submerged, they went back home. Some three four days afterwards Lelsiṅ came along with a large number of sheep and goats; when at the end of the homestead land, he called out again and again: "Open the sheep-shed, brothers!" He called out in this way many times. When they saw him, all of them surrounded the animals and brought them in; and they said: "Look at this one here, you; from where did he get up and come here, the wretch? We thought we had done for him utterly; here he is in spite of all."

"Where the water was shallow, my brothers," he said, "you threw me in; so I got only these, so many as you see; out towards the deeper waters there are cows and buffaloes; if you had only thrown me in there, I might have brought a lot". Hearing this they said: "Boy, take us also there; we shall fetch some for ourselves." "Quite so," he replied; "but I shall not be able to carry you; come along, carry yourselves to the place; then I shall push you in there."

Truth to tell, they listened to what he said and themselves carried a palanquin along to the place; and, putting it down on the bank of the Ganges, they entered into it, and each said to him: "Towards fairly deep water with me, you!" All of them spoke to him in this way, and truth to tell, he pushed them all in, one after the other. Then he became very pleased[20] and said: "You

okorpe gọć daṛeadiṅa? Nẹ̃ke apege bạṅ maraoketpea; Cando, mit́ hoṛren dọe baṅkana, sanam hoṛren kangeae. Ape dọ bin ghạṭite iṅgạṅpe gọćkedea, ar tãhã ạliṅ dọliṅ hạṭiṅape kan tahẽ-kangea; ẹn hõpe edreatliṅgea; oṛak̓ hõpe jẹrẹtata, uni hõpe gọć-kedea, ar iṅ hõ phirkạte gọjeṅpe mẹnleta; adọ ona jal aperege baṅ paṛaoena?

Adọ hẹćkate apattẹt́ raj ar uni bạṭki eṅgat ṭhene nẹhõrena, Babaṅ bạṛićketa; dadaṅteko iṅ gọjeṅko mẹnleta, unrege ọnẹ mẹrọm dọṅ laga ạguletko; adọ sẹsre akotegeko gọć ocoyena, mẹnketako, Ma, ḍhaka cạḍo gọtkaleme. Adọ inige ẹnẹ rajọsṭiye ṅamketa.

Adọ cabayena; uni cẹmẹṅ koṛa Lelsiṅgeye rajena.

A variant written down by the same man has some details, lacking in the story rendered above, which, however, has much not found in the other. The introduction with the discussion on the birth of the mongoose boy is wanting. They apparently all start together, but leaving Lel behind in the forest the brothers reach a country with a king's capital, where there is a mart called Lilam Bazar. They agree to trade for one month and then return. Lel also finds his way there, buys a donkey and wants to return with his brothers, but they again leave him behind. But he reaches home, and now the others give him and his mother a separate house to live in. When the famine comes, the others lose all they have, but these two manage to get on, the mongoose hollowing out the ground and always bringing foodstuffs to their subterranean room. Feeling compassion with the others he asks his mother to take a basket full of paddy to his brothers; she does so twice, and on being asked where they have got this, she answers that the boy has collected all by gleaning. The brothers then ask Lel to lend them some rice; but he says that he has nothing, as he has no agriculture. In anger the brothers then set fire to their house; but the mother and Lel are saved, being in the underground room. Next is told of Lel asking his mother to sew him a bag to take the ashes away to sell. Then we have the same story of the traders at the banyan tree, only that we here have one thousand pack-bullocks; the traders leave all to run away with Lel's bag, and Lel drives the bullocks and all the pack home, whereupon he asks his brothers to build pens for the bullocks. When they ask him how he has got so many bullocks, he gives the same answer as in the story. Money is not wanted to kill me; now how did you manage to kill me? Here you see, have I not utterly done for you? Chando is not only for one person, he is the Chando of all. You killed my mother, without her having done anything wrong; on the other hand, we two were sharing what we had with you; in spite of this you were angry with us two; our house you also set fire to; her you also killed, and as for myself, you again wanted to kill me; now did not this net catch yourselves?"

Having returned home, he went to his father the king and his first wife and implored them: "Father, I have done a bad thing; my brothers wanted to kill me; that happened when I brought the goats with me; but now at last they have been killed by their own wish. They said: 'Please, push us out into the water'."

Thereupon this one got the kingdom. Here it is ended. The Mongoose boy Lelsiń became king.

---

mentioned here. The brothers burn down their houses and try to sell the ashes, with the same result, wherefore they decide to kill Lel's mother, while Lel is away. When Lel comes home and finds his mother murdered, he takes her away along a road. Here he sees a flock of bullocks coming, puts his mother against a tree, climbs the tree and commences to call out, as in the above story. They do not understand what he is saying, and the bullocks come and trample on his mother. Lel frightens the traders and gets all their bullocks and goods. When he reaches home with all these, his brothers ask him how he has got them and get the same answer as in the story, whereupon they ask him whether they may not get quite a lot by taking their wives away. To this Lel answers that they naturally will be able to do so; his mother was an old woman, and his brothers' wives are all in prime condition. The brothers kill their wives and try to sell them, with the same result as in the story. Now the others become very poor, while Lel trades and becomes rich. We hear of the same thing in connexion with the donkey voiding rupees, the brothers kill their horses trying to make them do the same. Now they decide to kill Lel, and the story concludes in the same way as the one rendered, except that we are told that the brothers took boxes with them one for each, and in these they were pushed out into the Ganges and were drowned.

MISCELLANEOUS STORIES

81. Mit́ṭań koṛa reak̕ katha.

Sedae jǫkhęn,[1] kathae, mit́ṭań hǫṛren ponea hǫpǫnteṭ́ koṛako tahẽkana; adǫ bạr hǫṛ dǫko bạhu akawat́kin tahẽkana, ar bar hǫṛ dǫ bań. Adǫ un jǫkhęn uni huḍińić koṛa dǫe męnket́a, Iạ baba, iń dǫ bạnij bepar sanayedińa; dęn bar pę isi gan ṭaka emańme, adǫń bepar galaetabona, ar judi ona ṭakań nǫksanle khan, bāṭ bakhra iń dǫ cet́ hõ alope emańa. Adǫ sạri onka ạḍiye jidket́ khan dǫ pę isi ṭakako emadea; adǫ sạri bạnij bepar lạgit́ disomteye oḍok calaoena.

Adǫ calak̕ calak̕te, kathae, bar pę raj disome calaoena. Adǫ mit́ṭań raj atoe tiok̕keta, adǫ ona atoren hǫṛ dǫ mit́ṭań pusi din hilok̕ rajak̕ toae jǫmet́teye hukumat́koa, Ma uni pusi dǫ gǫjępe; uni pusipe gǫćle khan dǫ mit́ isi ṭaka boksis iń emapea.

Adǫ sạri ona atoren hǫṛ dǫ uni pusi gǫje lạgit́ko sendra baṛayede kana, adǫ ona takrege uni bepar koṛae sęṭęrena. Adǫe metako kana, Henda ho, celepe ńam baṛayede kana?

Adǫko męnket́a, Mit́ṭań pusi dinge rajak̕ toae jǫmet́teye metat́lea, Ma uni pusi dǫ gǫjępe, arpe gǫćle khan mit́ isi ṭaka boksis iń emapea, Onate ale dǫ uni pusigele ńam baṛayede kana.

Khange adǫ uni koṛae męnket́a, Iạ hǫń metape kana, uni pusi dǫ ńamle khan, alope gǫjęa, jivęt́te barę sap̕ ạguyepe iń ṭhen; iṅge mit isi ṭaka dǫ uni pusi reak̕ dam iń emapea; ar raj ṭhen sęnkate metaepe, Dęn mit́ isi ṭaka emalem, uni pusi dǫle gǫćkedea. Adǫ nāhāk̕e metape khan, dinih ńęlęa męnte, adǫ

---

1 The ordinary Santal counts in units and scores.

81. A STORY ABOUT A BOY.

ONCE upon a time long, long ago, it is said, there was a man who had four sons. For two of these they had procured wives, but two were not married. So the youngest boy one day said: "I say, father, I have a wish to do some trading. Please give me two or three scores[1] of rupees, then I shall try to do some trading for us, and if in some way I should lose that money, do not give me any part of my inheritance." So, truth to tell, as he was very eager, they gave him three scores of rupees, and then he went out into the world to trade.

As he was walking along, people tell, he passed the countries of two or three kings. Then he reached a village in which a king lived, and in that village a cat was every day eating the king's milk, wherefore the king ordered the people of that village, saying: "Kill this cat, and if you kill this cat, I shall give you twenty rupees as a reward."

So, truth to tell, the people of that village were hunting the cat in order to kill it, and just at that time this young trader came there. He said to them: "Look here, you people, whom are you searching for?"

They answered: "There is a cat, who every day eats the king's milk, therefore he said to us; 'Kill this cat, and if you kill it, I shall give you twenty rupees as a reward.' For that reason we are searching for this cat."

The young man then said: "Look here, I tell you this, if you find this cat, do not kill it; catch it and bring it to me alive. I shall give you twenty rupees as the price of this cat. Then go to the king and say to him; 'Give us the twenty rupees. We have killed the cat.' Now if he then says to you; 'Bring it here, metaepe, Pusile sendraye jọkhẹnge okaren họṛ cọe gatelena; uni salaḱgele sendra kan tahẹ̄kana; adọle gọćkede khan dọe metaťlea, Dini nui pusi dọ alope giḍiyea, nui dọ iñiñ jọmea; toa eskarge thọe jọm akaťa, ar jāhānaḱ ma bae jọm akať. Adọ onkae mẹnkeťte ale dọ sạrige uni họṛle emadea. Onka nāhāḱ ape dọ raj ṭhẹn lạipe.

Khange adọko mẹnkeťa, Acha, ẹnḍẹkhan dọ nẹnḍẹ baṛẹ duṛuṗ hataṛoḱme; nitge nāhāḱ miť ghạṛi khangele saṗ ạgu gọťama.

Adọ sạri onkako mẹn oṭoadete ako dọ uni pusi ńańamko calaoena, ar uni dọ ọnḍẹgeye duṛuṗena. Adọ sạri inạ miť ghạṛi khange uni pusiko ńam gọťkedea; miṭṭań sahan kuṭhạuṛi latarreko ńamkedea. Adọ saṗkedete uni koṛa ṭhẹnko ạgukedea, adọ miť isi ṭakae emaťkoa. Adọe metaťkoa, Ạkriń katha dọ alope lạia, ẹkẹn jọme reaḱge lạipe; ar ạkriñpe lạile khan dọ nāhāḱ ọhọe ẹmlepea.

Adọko mẹnkeťa, Baña, ọhọle lạilea; lạị khan ma nāhāḱ aleaḱge paskaoḱ kantale.

Adọe metaťkoa, Hoi hoi! ọnẹ onka baṛẹ mẹnpe. Adọ pusiye saṗkedete uni koṛa dọe calaoena; ar onko họṛ dọ rajko lạiadete miť isi ṭakae emaťkoa.

Uni koṛa dọ ona disom khon calaḱ calaḱte arhọ̄ miṭṭań raj disome tioḱkeťa, adọ ọnḍẹ họ̄e ńẹleťkoa, miṭṭań pukhrire odam gọje lạgiť ạḍi utạr họṛko jarwa akana, ar ona pukhri dọko sọḍa phoṛ akaťa. Adọ onko họṛ ṭhẹn uni koṛa dọe calaoena, adọe metako kana, Henda ho, nọnḍẹ dọ bhala ceť hoyoḱ kana? Ạḍi utạr họṛpe jarwa akan dọ.

Adọ onko họṛko mẹnkeťa, Hoe dọ ceť họ̄ bań hoeoḱ kana, mẹnkhan rajren ạsul hako odam ạḍi baṛiće jọmeťkoteye metaťlea, Ma uni odam dọ gọjepe; unipe gọćle khan dọ boksis iń emapea. Adọ noa pukhrirele laga ader akadea, onatele phoṛ añjẹťeť kana.

[2] An arrangement as here described would not be considered very improper now a-days. The king represents the state, and anything got from what is styled sọrkari, public property, is considered fair profit.

I want to see it,' then say to him. 'When we were hunting for the cat, a man from who knows where joined us and hunted together with us, and when we had killed it, he said to us: 'Give it to me. Do not throw this cat away, I shall eat it. It has, as you know, eaten only milk and has not eaten anything else.' And as he said so we really gave it to that man.' Speak in this way to the king."

So they said: "Very well; then please sit here in the meantime. In one moment we shall catch it and at once bring it to you."

Then, truth to tell, when they had said this to him, they went to find the cat, and the boy sat down there. And, truth to tell, a short while afterwards they caught the cat. They found him below a pile of fire-wood, and catching the cat they brought it to the young man, and he gave them twenty rupees, whereupon he said to them: "Do not tell anything about the selling, only tell about eating it. If you tell anything about the selling, he will certainly not give you anything."

"Quite so," they said, "we shall certainly not tell. If we tell, our profit will be lost."

Then he said to them: "That is so. Speak in the way agreed on." So the young man took the cat and went away, and these people told the king, and he gave them the twenty rupees[2].

Now the young man went a long way from that country and reached the country of another king, and there also he saw a great crowd of people, who had come together to kill an otter in a tank, and they had dug a ditch to drain the tank. The young man then went to these people and asked them; "I say, you people, I wonder what is going on here? You have collected here, a large crowd of people."

The people answered: "There is nothing happening, but as an otter is eating all the king's preserved fishes, he has said to us: 'Kill this otter. If you kill it, I shall give you a reward.' Now we have chased it into this tank and are draining the tank dry."

Adọ khange uni koṛae mẹnkeṭa, Ią hoṅ metape kana, uni odampe ṅamle khan dọ alope gọjea; uni dọ iṅgeṅ hataoea; jẹ dam lagaoka, ona dọ iṅiṅ emapea.

Adọko mẹnkeṭa, Acha, ẹṇḍẹkhan amgele emama.

Adọ sạriko soḍa aṅjẹṭkeṭa, adọko ṅamkedea; adọ saṕkate uni koṛa ṭhẹnko ạgukedea, adọ tinạk gan cọe emaṭkote uni odam hõe kiriṅkedea; adọ arhõ ọṇḍẹ khon hõe calak kangea.

Arhõ miṭṭaṅ disome tiokkeṭa; adọ ọṇḍẹ hõ onkage ạḍi utạr hoṛ jarwa akane ṅẹlkeṭko khan dọ onko ṭhẹne calaoena; adọe metako kana, Henda ho, bhala nọṇḍẹ dọ ceṭpe cekayeṭa?

Adọko mẹnkeṭa, Miṭṭaṅ goḍole gọje kana.

Adọe metaṭkoa, Cedakpe gọje kana?

Adọko mẹnkeṭa, Rajak kagọjko kọlọmko dinge, kathae, ạḍiye gẹr khaya khucrạ giḍiyeṭa, onate raje hukum akawaṭlea, Ma uni goḍo dọ gọjepe; unipe gọćle khan dọ boksis iṅ emapea. Adọ raj oṛakre gọjea mẹntele laga baṛayede kan tahẽkana, adọ ọṇḍẹ khonge laga ạgukate noa bhugạkrele laga ader akadea.

Adọ uni koṛae mẹnkeṭa, Ią hoṅ metape kana, uni goḍo dọ alope gọjea, saṕkate iṅ emạṅpe; uni goḍo reak dam dọṅ emapea.

Khange adọko mẹnkeṭa, Acha, damem ẹmọk khan, ẹṇḍẹkhan ọhọle gọjea.

Adọe mẹnkeṭa, Hẽ, sạrigeṅ emapea. Nukin ṅẹlkinpe, nukin hõ onka lekaṅ kiriṅ akaṭkina.

Adọ sạri lako lakeṭa sẹ, ẹkkalteko la tiokkedea, adọko saṕkedea; adọ uniye kiriṅkedea, adọ arhõ ọṇḍẹ khone calak kana.

Adọ calak calakte arhõ miṭṭaṅ raj disome tiokkeṭa, adọ ọṇḍẹ hõe ṅẹleṭkoa, raj ato phẹḍre ạḍi utạr hoṛko jarwa akana. Adọ onko ṭhẹn sẹnkateye metako kano, Henda, ape ceṭ lạgiṭ bhala nunạk hoṛ dọpe jarwa akana?

The young man then said: "Listen, I tell you this. If you find this otter, do not kill it, I shall take it, and whatever price is fixed, I shall give you."

"All right," they said, "then we shall give it to you."

And, truth to tell, they drained the tank dry and found the otter, and, having caught it, they brought it to the young man, and he gave them who knows how much; in this way he bought the otter too. Then again he went away from there.

Again he reached another country, and there also in the same way a great crowd of people had collected together, and, when he saw them, he went to them and said to them: "I say, I wonder what it is that you are doing here."

They answered him: "We are killing a rat."

He said to them; "Why are you killing it?"

They replied: "Every day, people tell, the rat is biting the king's papers and pens into small pieces and spoiling them. Therefore the king has ordered us to kill this rat. If we kill it, he will give us a reward. Then we chased the rat in the king's house in order to kill it, but, having chased it away from there, we have driven it into this hole."

The young man then said: "Listen, I say, do not kill this rat, catch it and give it to me. I shall give you the price of the rat."

"All right," they said, "if you give us the price, we shall certainly not kill it."

He said: "Yes, I shall really give it to you. Look at these two here. I have bought these two also in the same way."

So, truth to tell, they dug and dug all they could, and in no time they reached the rat and caught it. So he bought it and again went away from there.

Walking along he reached the country of another king, and there also he saw that a very great crowd of people had collected together close to the king's village. Going up to them he said to them: "I say, I wonder for what purpose have you come together so many people?"

Adoko menketa, Mittan bin oka khon coe hec akan, uni bin do adi hore jometkoa, ado onate raje hukum akawatlea, Ma uni binpe gocle khan do, mit isi takan emapea.

Ado uni korae menketa, Ia hon metape kana, uni binpe namle khan do alope gojea, uni do sap aguanpe; in do mit isi takan emapea.

Adoko menketa, Acha, endekhanle sap aguama.

Ado sariko sendra namkedeteko laga thakaokedea, arko sapkedete uni kora thenko agukedea, ado mit isi takae ematkoa; adoko calaoena. Ar uni kora hõ onde khon doe ruar kana.

Ado hijuk hijukte horrege uni bin do, kathae, rore ehopketa; ado uni korawak nutum numkateye menketa, Ia phalna, am do adi bhage hor kanam; nõkõe in doko gojen kan tahẽkana, amem tahẽkante inak jivi bancaoentina, ar bankhan hutec in do tehenreko mohor metaokina. Ado phalnan metam kana, in do delan ale disomte engan apun then idikanme, ar cetem nam, onagen emama.

Adoe menketa, Cetko menaktapea?

Ado uni bine menketa, Sanamakge menaktalea.

Arhõ uni korae menketa, Durre! ohon idilema; am do ontere nãhãkem jomena.

Ado bine menketa, Bana, phalna, ohon jommea.

Arhõ uni korae menketa, Am bam jomen khan do, engam apum pasekin jomen.

Ado uni bine menketa, Bana, phalna, ohon jom ocomea. Nelme, am do nunak mũhĩn khonem bancaokedina, tobe amak gun do ban manaotama? Albotin manaogetama. Delan in do idikanme bare.

[3] So lit.; 'eat' is the term. techn. for killing or destroying by witches, bongas, etc., also by snakes.

They answered: "A snake has come here from who knows where, and this snake is eating[3] a great many people, therefore the king has ordered us saying: 'If you kill this snake, I shall give you twenty rupees'."

The young man then said: "Listen, I tell you this, if you find the snake, do not kill it, but catch it and bring it to me. I shall give you twenty rupees."

"All right," they said, "then we shall catch it and bring it to you."

Then, truth to tell, they hunted for the snake, found it and chased it until it got tired, whereupon they caught it and brought it to the young man, who gave them twenty rupees; so they went, and the young man also commenced to go back homewards from this place.

As he was coming along the road, the snake, people tell, commenced to talk, and mentioning the name of the young man, he said: "I say, you so and so, you are a very good man. Remember, they were going to kill me; because you were there, I was saved; otherwise they would have made an end of me to-day. Therefore, you so and so. I tell you this, come along, I shall take you to our country to my parents, and whatever you want I shall give you."

"What things have you got?" he asked.

The snake replied: "We have all kinds of things."

The young man again asked: "Strange, I shall certainly not take you there; when we reach there, you will certainly eat me."

The snake replied: "Certainly not, you so and so, I shall surely not eat you."

Again the young man said, "If you yourself won't eat me, perhaps your parents will do so."

Then the snake said: "Certainly not, you so and so, I shall surely not let you be eaten. Look here, you have saved me from so great a danger, then should I not be grateful to you? Come along, please take me there."

Adǫ uni koṛae mǫnketa, Acha, idimegeañ; nokoko ǫṇḍǫkhan oṛakteñ idi oṭolekoge. Adǫ sạri jǫtǫ hǫṛge uni koṛawak oṛakteko calaoena; adǫ onkoko dǫ ǫṇḍǫye jimạ oṭokatkoa, adǫ uni biñtekinkin calaoena.

Adǫ sạri tin dinre cǫñ uni biñ oṛakkin tiok ñǫkketa. Adǫ biñe mǫnketa, Iạ phalna, am dǫ nǫṇḍǫ baṛǫ teṅgo hataṛokme; ǫnǫ ona kana ale oṛak dǫ. Adǫ noam bañcao akadiñ katha unkin eṅgañ ạpuñ iñ lại pạhilạkinrege, inạ dǫ ǫhǫkin jǫmmea, ar am dǫ nāhāk alom bǫtǫrǫka. Ar jāhānakko emam lạgitkin metama, Ma okaṭakem khusiak kan, ma rǫṛme, onagele emama — adǫ nitre am iñ lại ṭhikam kana, am dǫ nāhāk cet hǭ alom khusika; ạpuñ tire mitṭañ mundạm menaka, am dǫ ona chaḍa eṭagak dǫ alom khǫja. Ar ona mundạm reak gun dǫ nonka kana; mit sǫr toare am dǫ ona mundạm caḍoeme, ar un jǫkhǫn cetem mǫna, benaok ma mǫnte, onage benao gǫdoka; sǫ jāhānakgem khǫj, onage hǫć gǫdoka. Ǫnǫ onka kana ona reak gun dǫ. Onate am dǫñ metam kana, ona baṛǫ nāhāk khǫjme.

Adǫe mǫnketa, Acha, ǫṇḍǫkhan onageñ khǫja.

Adǫe metadea, Ma ǫṇḍǫkhan am dǫ nǫṇḍǫ baṛǫ teṅgo hataṛokme, noako kathañ galmarao oṭoakinrege. Adǫ am ikdi nāhāk iñ hǫć ruạṛoka; am dǫ nǫṇḍǫ baṛǫ tahǭ hataṛokme. Dạṛ bǫtǫćkeam, alom dạṛa.

Adǫ uni koṛae mǫnketa, Acha, ǫhǫñ dạṛa; do am dǫ khạtirjoma calakme.

Adǫ sạri onka kạjiạu oṭokadete ać dǫe calaoena. Adǫ oṛake sǫṭǫr gǫṭen khankin ñel gǫtkede khan dǫ, bogete ạḍi bạṛićkin rakketa; adǫkin cǫk baṛawadea, arkin mǫnketa, Durrǫ! ạliñ dǫliñ as chuṭạulen tahǭkana; ạliñ dǫliñ mǫnketa, Nui dǫko gǫćkede cǫñ cet cǫñ. Onka ạliñ dǫliñ bǫbhorsalen tahǭkana. Adǫ nǫkǭe, jāhā lekate arhǫm hǫć ruạṛengea.

The young man then said: "All right, I shall take you there, but let me first take these others home." So, truth to tell, all of them went to the young man's home, and there he gave the others in charge of his people, whereupon he and the snake came away.

Then, truth to tell, after who knows how many days, they reached near to the home of the snake. The snake said: "I say, you so and so, you stand here in the meantime. What you see over there is our house. I shall first tell my parents the story of how you have saved me. When they have heard this, they will surely not eat you; do not you be afraid. They will tell you that they will give you something or other saying: 'Tell us what you see here that you like, and we shall give you that.' I now tell you this, so that you know it. Do not be pleased with anything. There is a ring on my father's hand, do not ask for anything else except that. This ring has this quality. Put this ring in a seer of milk, and whatever you at that time may say is to come into existence, this will at once be there; or whatever you may demand, that will come at once. This is the quality of this ring, therefore I am telling you this; ask for this ring."

"Very well," he said, "I will ask for that."

The snake then said to him: "Then please stand here in the meantime, whilst I speak to them about what has happened. Then I shall presently come back to take you there. You, please remain here in the meantime. You might perhaps run away, do not do so."

The young man then said: "All right, I shall not run away. You go without anxiety as to that."

So, truth to tell, after having earnestly implored him in this way, the snake went, and as soon as he reached home and his relations caught sight of him, they commenced to cry a good deal, whereupon they kissed him and said to him: "O dear, we two had lost all hope. We thought they have surely killed him or something. In this way we had lost all hope, and then here we see, somehow or other you have come back again."

Adọ enka mẹn sãotege uni apattẹt́ dọe mẹn gọt́keta, Okare baṅ eṅgate manwa manwage sọyeṅ kan?

Adọ uni họpọntẹte mẹnketa, Okare, baba, sọyetmea? Ẹṇḍẹkhan iṅge sọyetben cọṅ cet́ cọṅ. Ma ẹṇḍẹkhan iṅge jọm gọt́kaṅben.

Adọkin mẹnketa, Baṅa, am dọ ọhọliṅ jọmlema. Khange adọkin thir baṛayena.

Adọ uni biṅe mẹnketa, Ią, ayo ar baba, iṅ dọ mit́ṭẹć kathaṅ metaben kana, adọ iṅak katha dọben aṅjọmkea sẹ ọhọa? Arben dọhọetiṅa sẹ baṅ?

Adọkin mẹnketa, Ma rọṛme, aṅjọm baṅkhanliṅ cekaea?

Adọe mẹnketa, Iṅ dọ Họṛ disomteṅ sẹnlena ar ạḍi họr iṅ jọmetko tahẽkana. Adọ unre ona disomren raje hukumatkoa, Ma uni biṅ dọ gọjepe, ar unipe gọćle khan dọ boksis iṅ emapea. Adọ, baba, unre iṅ dọ ạḍi bạṛić iṅ bọtọrena; adọ mit́ṭaṅ jhõṛreṅ okoyena, adọ gọṭako sendra baṛayeta.

Adọ apate mẹn gọt́keta, Henda, beṭa, adọ ẹṇḍẹkhan cekatem baṅcaoena?

Adọ uniye mẹnketa, Onko họṛ mọtọrege mit́ họṛe tahẽkana; adọ uni họṛe dayawadiṅte iṅ dọṅ baṅcaoena. Jẹ raj boksis emakoe gọkatko dọ uni họṛge iṅ ṅutumte boksise emat́koa. Tinạk gan ṭaka cọe emat́kote iṅ dọ onko họṛ ṭhẹn khone chaḍaokidiṅa, ar ọṇḍẹ ḳhon pharak disomteye ạtkirkidiṅa. Onkate iṅ dọṅ baṅcao akana; mẹnkhan uni họṛ iṅ dọ khube dayawadiṅa.

Adọ uniren eṅgat apatkin mẹnketa, Henda beṭa, adọ uni họṛ dọ cetem emadea, ar cet́ lekate uni ṭhen khon dọm paskao hẹćena?

Adọe mẹnketa, Iṅ dọ cet́ hõ baṅ emadea, mẹnkhan gọk dọṅ gọkadegea. Adọ cet́ hõ bạnuktiṅte bạṅ emadea.

Adọkin mẹnketa, Henda bạbu, onkae dayawatme khan, cedak uni họṛ dọ bam ạgu daraledea? Nọṇḍẹ hutẹć babon ẹmkea? Cete khọj kan tahẽkan, onagebo ẹmkea.

As they were speaking in this way, his father suddenly said: "Dash it, where can it be? I am feeling the smell of man."

The son then said: "Where, father, do you feel this smell? Then it must be I who am giving you the smell, I think. So please eat me at once."

His parents then said: "Certainly not, we are not going to eat you." Thereupon they did not say anything more about this.

Then the snake said: "I say, mother and father, I am going to tell you something. Will you listen to what I say or not? and will you do what I say or not?"

"Speak then," they said; "what else should we do than listen to you?"

Then he said: "I went to the Santal country, and I was eating a good many people. Then the king of that country gave an order saying: 'Kill this snake, and, if you kill him, I will give you a reward.' Then father, I got a terrible fright and I hid away in a thicket, and they were hunting for me everywhere."

The father asked: "I say, my son, how then were you saved?"

He replied: "Amongst those people there was a man, and I was saved because this man took pity on me. The reward that the king had promised to give, this man gave them in my name. He gave them who knows how many rupees, and in this way he rescued me from those people, and he took me away from there to a distant country. In this way I have been saved, and this man showed me great pity."

Then his parents said: "Look here, son, what have you given this man and how did you get away from him and come here?"

He replied: "I have not given him anything, but I have promised to give him. I had nothing, and therefore I could not give him anything."

Then they said: "Look here, youngster, since he showed you such pity, why did you not bring this man along with you? Should not we give him something here? Whatever he might have asked for, we should have given him."

Adǫ uniye mẹnketa, Hẽ, mẹn dǫ onkageń metade tahẽkana, bańma, Jāhānak nāhākgem khǫj onageń emama.

Adǫ arhǫ̃kin mẹnketa, Durhak! uni dǫ ạḍi bhale hǫṛ kanae. Cedak cọń bam ạgu daralede?

Adǫ uniye mẹnketa, Ạgu darayegeń mẹnet tahẽkana; adǫń mẹnketa, Pasẹ aben ǫhǫben ńẹl sahaole, pasẹben jǫmkedege; adǫ baba, onate bạń ạguledea.

Adǫkin mẹnketa, Bańa, bạbu, am sāotem ạgule khan dǫ ǫhǫliń jǫmlea.

Adǫ uniye mẹnketa, Ẹnḍẹkhan dǫń ạguyea sẹ bań?

Adǫkin mẹnketa, Okare menaea?

Adǫe mẹnketa, Hante khǫn dǫ unigeye ạgu oṭokadińa; adǫ abenben jǫmkea bǫtǫrte nǫnḍẹ dǫ bań ạgu sẹṭẹrledea, hạni hanḍẹń bạgi akawadea.

Adǫkin metadea, Cedakem bạgiadea? Do ạguyem, adǫbo peṛayea ar ṭakabo emaea.

Adǫ arhǫ̃e mẹnketa, Pasẹben jǫme; ạḍi muhim khon uni dǫe bańcao akadińa.

Adǫkin mẹnketa, Ǫhǫliń jǫmea, do am dǫ ạguyem.

Adǫ sạri calaoenteye ạgukedea, adǫ sạri bạrsiń dinko peṛakedea. Adǫ inạ dosar hilok dǫko metae kana, Cele phalna, adǫ nui koṛa nonka muhim khonem bańcaokedea; adǫ dẹ cetem hataoa? Ma ona rǫṛme.

Adǫ uni koṛa dǫ ǫntẹ nǫtẹ oṛakkoe ńẹlettakoa, jhak jhak ńẹlǫk kana, adǫ onkako kuliyedere hǫ̃ bǫtǫrte bae rǫṛ hǫteta.

Adǫ arhǫ̃ uni apattẹte mẹnketa, Ma phalna, rǫṛme, cetem hataoa sẹ ṭakam hataoa.

Adǫ uni koṛae mẹnketa, Iń dǫ cet hǫ̃ bań hataoa ṭaka poesa dǫ, mẹnkhan ǫnẹ am tire mundạm menak, inạgeń hataoa, judipe emań khan; ar bape emań khan, ẹnḍẹkhan cet hǫ̃ bań hataotapea. Iń dẹ muhim khǫn iń bańcaokadea, inạge jǫ jivẹt tǫ disạńtabonpe.

He replied: "Yes, that's so; I also spoke to him in that way saying: 'Whatever you will ask for, I will give you'."

Again they said: "Dear me, he is an excellent man; why did you not bring him along with you?"

Then he replied: "I thought of bringing him along. Then I thought perhaps you two will not stand seeing him, perhaps you might eat him. Therefore father, I did not bring him."

They said: "Certainly not, youngster; if you brought him along, we should surely not eat him."

"Then shall I bring him or not?" he said.

The parents asked: "Where is he?"

He replied: "He brought me along from there and left me here; but, as he was afraid that you two might eat him, I have not brought him right up here. Look, I have left him over there."

"Why did you leave him?" they asked him. "Please bring him here, then we shall give him a feast and give him some money."

Again he said: "Perhaps you will eat him? He has saved me from the greatest danger."

They replied: "We shall surely not eat him. Go and bring him here."

Then, truth to tell, he went and brought him and they treated him for two days. The next day they were saying to him: "Well, you so and so, you saved this boy of ours from such a danger. Then what will you take? Please tell us this."

The young man then looked round their house in all directions. It was looking splendid, but even though they asked him this, he did not answer at once, because he was afraid.

Again the father said: "Please, you so and so, speak. What will you take, or will you take money?"

The young man then replied: "I shall not take anything in the way of money, but I shall take the ring that you have there on your hand, if you will give me that; and if you won't, then I shall take nothing from you. I rescued him from danger. Keep this

Ar ẹnẹń mẹnkeť, inạpe emań khań dọ, iń hõ jivẹť tahẹn bhor iń ńum baṛakepea.

Khange adọ ako akoko bupujhạu baṛayena, Cele adọ noageye khọj kan dọ? Bhalabon emaea sẹ bań? Ar jãhãnaǩ ma bae khọj kan.

Adọ uni eṅgat buḍhiye mẹnkeťa, Ma ẹnte emae ma; adọ onageye khọj kan khać dọbon cekaea?

Adọ sạri ona mundạmko toťkeťa; adọ uni koṛako caladea, ar họrte jọm lạgiť pẹ pon ṭakako emadea.

Adọe ruạṛ hẹćena. Adọ enko pea menaǩko, enkoge kurumuṭuteye ạsulkeťkoa. Adọ kathae, uni koṛa bạhuae lạgiťko ńam baṛayeťkoa. Adọ miťṭań atore, kathae, khub kisạṛ họpọnerako ńamkedea, adọko rẹbẹnengea. Adọ uni kuṛiye mẹnkeťa, Hẹ̃ dọ hẹ̃ge, rẹbẹngeań. Mẹnkhan iń dọ oṛaǩ umul umulte baṛẹ idiyińpe. Jãwãe oṛaǩ khon nọnḍẹ hạbić ọkọe oṛaǩe benaoa, ẹnḍẹkhan uni ṭhẹn iń jãwãeoǩa, ar bań khan dọ bań.

Adọ raebar họṛ ona katha dọ koṛawaǩ oṛaǩte hẹćkate eṅgat apatko lạiaťkina. Khange adọ unkinkin mẹnkeťa, Ọkọe baḍae, ẹnḍẹkhan ọhọle ạgu daṛele cọń ceť cọń. Adọ koṛa hõ okakote cọko sẹn akan, adọ onkolíń kulilekoge. Ma teheń dọ sẹn ruạṛ hataṛoǩme, arhõ nin dinre hẹć ruạṛoǩme, adọ unrege jọtọle lại cabawama.

Adọe calaoena uni dọ. Adọ koṛakoko hẹć jarwa baṛayen khan dọ kukli galmaraokin ẹhọpkeťa. Adọ jọtọ koṛako mẹnkeťa, Ẹnḍẹkhan ọhọbon ạgu daṛelea. Adọ uniko bạhuae kan koṛa dọe thir akangea. Adọ apattẹte mẹnkeťa, Cele ya phalna, am dọ ceť hõ bam mẹneť dọ?

Adọ uni koṛae mẹnkeťa, Bańa, baba, unigebon ạguyea.

Adọ apate mẹnkeťa, Oṛaǩ benaoge thọ ya muskil kana. Nọnḍẹ khọn bạhu oṛaǩ dhạbić dọbon benaokea?

in mind as long as you live, and if you give me just what I mentioned, I shall also praise you as long as I live."

Thereupon they consulted together: "Well, it is this he is asking for. Shall we give it to him or shall we not? You see he does not ask for anything else."

The old mother then said: "Let it be given to him then. As he is asking for this, what can we do?"

So, truth to tell, they took off the ring and handed it to the young man, and they gave him three four rupees for food on his way back.

Thereupon he came back home. Now those three other animals were there, and these he took excellent care of. Now, people tell, they were searching for a wife for the young man, and in a certain village they found the daughter of a very rich man, and these people were agreeable. The girl said: "I am quite willing, I am agreeable, but they must take me there in the shade of houses. Whoever builds a house from my bridegroom's house and up to here, to him I shall be married, otherwise not."

The marriage-broker came to the young man's house and told his parents these conditions. The parents then said: "Who knows, in these circumstances we shall surely not be able to bring her here, we fancy. Our boys are also away somewhere, let us first ask them what they think. Return to-day to them and come back again here after so and so many days; then we shall give you our final word."

So he went; when the young men had all come back, they commenced to talk and ask these. The young men said: "In this case we shall surely not be able to bring her." But the man for whom they were to bring a wife kept quiet. His father then said: "Well, you so and so, you have nothing to say?"

"No, father," the young man replied, "we shall bring this girl."

The father then said: "To build the house, that's the difficulty. Shall we be able to build a house from here and up to the bride's home?"

Adọ uni kọṛae mẹnketa, Hẽ, benao aḍoeabon. Oṛak benao dọ iñ eskarte hõñ benao daṛeakgea.

Adọko mẹnketa, Acha bogege; ẹṇḍẹkhan mẹn ạikhạ tayọmre alom lajao ocobona.

Adọe mẹnketa, Hẽ, menaña; ọhọñ lajao ocobona.

Adọ sạri uni kọṛa dọ dosar hilok ona mundạm dọe biḍạu aṭkareta; jẹmọne lạiadea onkage, kathae, mit sẹr toareye caḍoketa, are mẹnketa, Ma nitge mõṛẽ bhạriạ taben ar bar bhạriạ dahe hẹć gọdọk ma! Khange, kathae, tinạke mẹnlet, unạkge oka khon cọñ hẹć gọtena; adọ oṛakteko tul aderkata. Adọ uni kọṛae mẹnketa, Baña, uni biñ dọać iñ bañcaokede reak dọ khubgeye gun akawadiña. Ar ona kathae rọṛ dọ onkoe ạsul akatko, onko hõko akñjọm kangea.

Adọ inạ dosar hilok khange rạebarićko mañgao gọtkedea ar khub dahe tabenko emadea; arko metadea, Ma ale dọ ni cando mọtọre baṛẹ bapla dọ sạrdi gọdmo; darae cando dọ kọṛawak janam din kana, onate uni cando nãhãk bañ ganok kantalea.

Adọ raebar họṛe mẹnketa, Cele ẹnte, apege jọtọakpe tearena sẹ bañ? Ar ona oṛak benaoko huṛso kan dọ nọṇḍẹ khọn haṇḍẹ hạbić, ona dọpe tear họtkea?

Adọko mẹnketa, Hẽ, ona dọle tear daṛeaka.

Adọ uniye mẹnketa, Mẹn ẹṇḍẹkhan jẹmọn tayọmre iñ alope lajaoiñ.

Adọko mẹnketa, Do ọhọle lajao ocomea; bale benaoketa mẹnkhan, ọṇḍẹle sẹnlen khan, unre ḍaṇḍọmlepe, ar bañkhan kolge alope kolalea. Ma inạge katha dọ. Ọntẹn peṛa ma am dọ lại hotakome.

Adọe mẹnketa, Iñ ma ẹntẹñ lạlại họṛ kange; cedak bañ lạia? Nitge sẹn torañ lạiakoa.

The young man replied: "Yes, we shall build, no fear. As for the housebuilding, I shall be able to build singlehanded."

"Very well then," they replied; "then that's good, but have a care, do not put us to shame afterwards."

"Well, I am here," the young man said, "I shall not put us to shame."

Now, truth to tell, the next day the young man tried to test the quality of the ring. Just as the snake had told him, so, people tell, he put he ring into a seer of milk and said: "May there now at once come five loads of flattened rice and two loads of curds." Then, people tell, just as much as he had said, this quantity at once came from somewhere or other, and they carried it into the house. The young man then said: "Surely, the snake that I saved has shown much gratitude for what I did for him." These words the other animals that he was keeping also heard.

The next day they asked the marriage-broker to come and gave him any amount of curds and flattened rice and said to him: "So far as we are concerned, make all preparations for the marriage to come off inside this month. Next month is the young man's birthday, therefore that month will not be suitable for us."

The marriage-broker then said: "Well then, you are consequently ready with everything now? and as for the house they wish to be built from here up to there, will you be able to get that ready at once?"

They replied: "Yes, we shall be able to get that ready."

"Have a care then," he replied, "that you do not afterwards bring me shame."

"We shall surely not put you to shame," they said. "If we have not built that when we go there, fine us, or else do not send her to us. Well, that's all, you go at once and inform the friends on that side."

He said: "I am the man to take a message. Why should I not tell them? Now I shall at once go straight to them and inform them."

Adọ sạri uni họr dọ sẹn torage onako katha dọe lại gọtkeťa. Adọ uni họrko metadea, Dẹ gapage arhõ sẹn ruạr gọdọkme, metakom, Ma sọntọrọkpe, girạń ạguape kana. Ar metakom, Gẹl din reạk girạń ạguapea.

Adọ sạri dosar hilok sẹn ruạrkate ona katha ọntẹn peṛae lạiatkoa. Adọ noko hõko mẹnkeťa, Acha, ma ạgualeme, khạtirjoma menakʼlea.

Adọ ọṇḍẹ khon ruạr hẹćkate dosar hilok khange girại idi gọtkeťa. Onko peṛa hõko atańkeťa, adọ bapla din tiogok kanre hõ, oṛak dọ bako ńẹleť kan. Adọko mẹneťa, Họ, noko peṛa dọ dhoragebon ḍaṇḍọmkoa. Adọ sạri bạriạt calak hilok ńindạ khange uni koṛa dọ miť sẹr toare ona mundạm dọe cạḍo gọtkeťa, are mẹnkeťa, Ma nọṇḍẹ khọn bạhu oṛak dhạbić oṛak benao gọdọk ma, ar tala talate dọ sọṛọk leka họr tahẹn ma!

Adọ sạri onkage benao gọťena, adọ ona oṛak bhitri bhitrite bạriạtokko calaoena. Khange adọ ọntẹn họṛko hahaṛayena, ar ona oṛak talategeko bapla ạgukedea. Adọ bapla caba baṛayena.

Adọ uni bạhu kuṛi dọ, kathae, ato koṛa sọṅgẹ hõ pạrkạue tahẽkana, ar ḍhertẹť dọ unirege jãwãeok sana menaktaea. Adọ ạkin haṛam buḍhi emanteak reańkin galmarao baṛaea. Adọ miť din dọ uni kuṛiye kukli kana, metae kanae, Henda bhala nọṇḍẹ khọn ale oṛak dhạbić oṛakpe benao idiletre dọ tinạk ganpe khọrọcleťa, ar cekate unạk algate dọpe benao gọťketa?

Adọ uni koṛae mẹnkeťa, Ọkọe baḍae, iń dọ bań baḍaea, ayo babatekinge tinạk cọkin khọrọcleť. Mẹnakin, kathae, ạḍi utạr ṭaka khọrọc akana.

[4] When a day is fixed for a marriage (or other great festivity), small strings are sent out to the parties concerned, with so many knots as there are days coming before the ceremony; each day one knot is untied; when there is no knot left, they know that the day has come. This is Santal custom, quite useful as long as they had no almanacks. It is used even now by people who do not need it.

Truth to tell, the man went straight away and at once told them this, and they said to him: "Please, go back again to them to-morrow and say to them: 'Be careful, I shall bring you the marriage-knots[4]'. And say to them, 'I shall bring you knots for ten days'."

The next day he, truth to tell, went back and informed the other party of this, and these also said: "Very well, please bring it. We are quite satisfied and ready."

Having returned from there, he at once took the marriage-knots with him the next day. The friends also received these, agreeing to the day; but although the day for the marriage was drawing near, they did not see any house, so they said: "Oh, we shall certainly have to fine these friends." Then, truth to tell, the night before the bridegroom's party was timed to go the young man put his ring in a seer of milk and said: "Let there at once be built a house from here to my bride's home, and let there be something like a big road along the middle."

And, truth to tell, in this way it was at once built and the bridegroom's party went along inside this house. The people on the other side naturally became astonished. So they celebrated the marriage and brought the bride away inside this house. The marriage festivities were all finished.

Now this girl, people tell, had been accustomed to be intimate with a village boy, and she wanted more than anything else to be married to him. The young married couple were in the habit of talking together about this, that and the other. One day the girl was asking him saying: "Look here, how was it when you built the house from here up to our home? About how much did you spend, and how was it that you so easily and quickly built it?"

The young man then said: "Who knows, I do not know how much my parents possibly spent. They say, I hear, that a very large sum of money has been spent."

Adọ uni kuṛi dọ ona katha dọe disạ dọhọkaṭa. Adọ dosar hiloḱ khange hanhartẹte kuliyede kana, Henda gọ, nọṇḍẹ khọn ale oṛaḱ dhạbić oṛaḱpe benao idileṭre dọ bhala tinạḱ ganpe khọrọcleṭa?

Adọ uni buḍhiye mẹnkeṭa, Ceṭ hõ, bạhu, baṅ khọrọclena; uni hudiṅićge ceka lekate cọṅ miṭ ṅindạ bhitạrtegeye benao gọṭkeṭa. Adọ onkae mẹnkeṭ khan dọe thirena.

Adọ ạyuṕ khange arhõe kuliyede kana, Otẹ cọṅ, kathae, ceṭ hõ baṅ khọrọclen, ayo onkae lạiaṅ kan; amge, kathae, ceṭ lekate cọṅ miṭ ṅindạ bhitạrtegem benaoleṭ. Adọ masẹ bhala lạiaṅme, ceṭ lekatem benaoleṭa.

Adọ, kathae, ạuṛigeye lại baṛawae kana, adọ bae pạtiạuḱ kana. Adọ uni kuṛiye mẹnkeṭa, Iṅge bam lạiaṅ khan dọ ọkọeyem lạiakoa? Nõkõe laṅ miṭ mọnena, ẹnrehõ am dọ bam lạiaṅ kana, tọbẹ amren hoṛ dọṅ baṅ kana cele; tọbẹrege bam lạiyeṭa.

Adọ, katae, onka ạḍi nindhạne rọṛkeṭ khan dọe metae kana, Acha, ẹṇḍẹkhan iṅ lạiamgea, mẹnkhan ạikhạ, ọkọe ṭhẹn hõ alom lại baṛaea.

Adọe mẹnkeṭa, Ọhọṅ lạia; alaṅ alaṅaḱ katha kana, cedaḱ iṅ lạia? Jọnọmre hõ ọhọṅ lạilea; ar iṅ lạikeṭa mẹnkhan dọ, ẹkkalte am dọ maḱ gọć gọṭkaṅme.

Ar sẹ uni koṛa dọ uni atoren koṛa sọṅgẹ menae dọ bae baḍae kana, adọ onkae ekraṛen khan, kathaeye lạiadea, are mẹnkeṭa, Ạliṅ kanaliṅ ar kiye lạia? Ọhọ jạnićе lạia. Adọ onka bujhạu baṛakate sạri jọtọ katha onka oṛe oṛpaṭ bae lại cabawadea? Adọ uni kuṛi dọ onako katha dọ mọnẹregeye dọhọkaṭa. Adọ onka napaegekin hijuḱ sẹnọḱa.

Adọ tin din badre cọṅ miṭ din dọ uni atoren koṛae riạukedea, metae kanae, Iạ phalna, uni ṭhẹn dọ baṅ tahẹna. Am ṭhẹngeṅ tahẹna, am baṛẹ dọhọṅme.

---

[5] During the first days after a marriage it is customary that the young people go and come from home to home. The young girl is not as a rule previously well acquainted with her new people, and this custom is kept up to help her in her new position.

The girl kept these words in remembrance, and the next day she asked her mother-in-law: "I say, mother, when you built the house from here and up to our house, about how much I wonder did you spend?"

The old woman then replied: "Nothing at all, daughter-in-law, was spent. Our little one somehow or other caused the house to be built within one night." When she had said this, she did not say anything else.

When it became evening, she again asked her husband: "I hear nothing at all was spent. Mother tells me so. She says that you somehow or other built it within one night. So please tell me how you did it."

Then, they say, the young man was telling her fibs; but she did not believe him. The girl then said: "If you do not tell me, whom are you to tell? Here you see, we have become one, still you do not tell me. Then I do not belong to you, I suppose. That's the reason that you do not tell."

Then, when she very humbly spoke in this way, he said to her: "All right, then I shall tell you, but have a care, do not tell it to anybody."

"I shall surely not tell," she said, "it is a matter between us two. Why should I tell? I shall never tell at all, and if I should tell, then at once cut me dead."

Now her husband did not know that the girl was intimate with the village boy, so, when she had given such a solemn promise, he believed her and said: "We are one, and why should she tell?" After having come to this conclusion, did he not tell her everything, from beginning to end? And the girl kept his words in her mind. Everything seemed well, and they were going and coming between the families[5].

Then, after who knows how many days, she spoke to the village boy and said: "I say, you so and so, I shall not stay with him, I will stay with you. You please keep me."

Adọ uni kọṛae mẹnkeṭa, Am dọ jãwãe menaegetama, cet lekate iñ dọñ dọhọmea? Bae mak gọjẹña?

Adọ uni kuṛiye mẹnkeṭa, Nọṇḍẹ dọ balañ tahẹna, jãhã disomtelañ oḍok calaka.

Arhõ kọṛae mẹnkeṭa, Bae pañja ñamlaña?

Adọ uni kuṛiye mẹnkeṭa, Baña, ọhọe pañja daṛelelaña, ona reak bhẹd iñ baḍaea. Adọ ọnẹ jãwãetẹt ṭhẹn mundạm menak, onate cetko hoyok, ona jọtọe lạiadea, are metae kana, Am dọ dọkhọ rẹbẹnme sẹ, jọm ñũ, oṛak duạr, jọtọ iñgeñ benaotalaña. Khange sạriye bulạukedegea, adọe rẹbẹnena, adọ ạñgirok reakkin neṇḍaketa. Are metae kana, Nọṇḍẹ khọn dọ balañ oḍokoka; jãwãe oṛakteñ calaka, adọ ọṇḍẹ khongelañ calaka. Am dọ miṭṭañ kạpi idi toraeme. Adọe metadea, Ma nių din hilok am dọ ona phalna dare buṭạre ñuhum khan baṛẹ sẹṭẹrọkme.

Adọ sạri uni kọṛa dọ kạpiante ẹn hilok dọ ona dare buṭạreye calaoena. Adọ tinkore cọñ sạri uni kọṛatekinkin ñapamena arkin galmaraoketa.

Adọ kathae, uni kuṛi dọ ẹn hilok dọ luṭuk luṭuke bẹñgẹt akatgea, jạpitge bae jạpitet kana. Adọ uni jãwãetẹte jạpitket khan dọ bại bạite ona mundạm dọe totkettaea, adọ bại bạite oṛak khone oḍokena; adọ uni kọṛa ṭhẹne calaoena, adọe metae kana, Dela hijukme, miṭṭañ mẹrọmlañ magea. Adọ sạri gudṛi khọn miṭṭañ mẹrọmkin oḍokkedea, adọkin makkedea, ar mãyãm dọ uni jãwãetẹte gitić akan parkọm latarre gọṭakin jọrọketa, ar uni mẹrọm dọ bọhọk sudhạ okate cọkin idi toraketa.

Adọ tin jọkhẹn cọñ, kathae, uni kọṛae ẹbhẹnena, adọe ạikạuketa, bạhuttẹt dọ bạnugić. Adọe mẹnketa, Pasẹ racateye oḍok akan. Adọ raca sẹn oḍokkateye ñẹl baṛayede dọ bạnugić. Adọ arhõe bọlọ ruạṛente sẹñgẹle jolkette divheye jẹrẹtketa, adọ gọṭae arsal

6 Battle-axes are even now found in many Santal houses; they are chiefly used for sacrificial purposes.

7 The common expression for a natural function.

The boy then said: "You have a husband. How shall I be able to keep you? Will he not kill me?"

The girl then said: "We shall not remain here. We shall go away to some other country."

"Will he not track us and find us?" the young man again asked.

The girl then said: "He will not. He will certainly not be able to track us. I know how to provide for this." Whereupon she told him all about the ring that her husband had and what could be done with that, and she said to him: "You agree to keep me, I shall provide everything for us two, food and drink, house and home."

Then she, truth to tell, prevailed upon him, and he agreed, and they fixed the date for running away together. Then she said to him: "We shall not start from here. I shall go to my husband's home, and from there we shall go away. Remember to take a battle-axe[6] along with you." She further said to him: "This very day, as soon as it becomes twilight, you go to the foot of such and such a tree."

Truth to tell, the young man that day went to the foot of the tree agreed upon, taking the battle-axe with him. Some time during the day she and the young man met and had this talk together.

Then, they say, that day the girl was anxious and kept awake. She did not sleep at all. When her husband had fallen asleep, she quietly took off this ring that he had, and noiselessly she went out from the house and went to the man and said to him: "Come let us kill a goat". And, truth to tell, they took a goat out of the goat-house and killed it and spilled the blood all over under the bedstead on which her husband was lying; but the goat with the head they took away, who knows to where.

Then sometime during the night the young man woke up and felt that his wife was not there. He thought: "Perhaps she has gone out to the courtyard[7]." So going out to the courtyard, he looked for her, but she was not there. Again he went inside, and, baṛayeta. Adọ khange parkọm latarre mãyãm dọ ḍiń ḍạbur jọrọ akane ńẹlketa. Khange adọ ona ńẹlte ạḍi bạṛiće bhabnayena; adọe mẹnketa, Ọkọe bạiri cọko makkedea ar okate cọko idikedea, tọbẹrege bạnugića. Iń dọ nãhãk dhorageko pạsińa. Adọ ona bhabnate uni koṛa dọ cet hõ bae rọṛ saḍeleta, hape hapeteye gitić thirena. Adọ setak aṅga marsalenre hõ uni koṛa dọe gitić akangea, bae oḍokok kana.

Adọ eṅgat apatko mẹneta, Henda, bhala nukin dọkin beret akana sẹ bań? Bakin ạikạuk kan dọ. Adọ eṅgattẹt duạr ṭhẹn sẹnkateye họhọketa. Adọ bakin gọṅlet khan dọ silpińe jhićketteye bọlọyena, adọe ńẹlket dọ, goṭa oṛak mãyãm dọ ḍiń ḍạbur ạtu akan. Adọ ona ńẹlte uni hõ rakkateye oḍok ruạṛena.

Adọ jọtọ họṛko ańjọmket khan dọko ńir jarwayena arko ńẹlketa. Ar uni koṛa dọ parkọmregeye gitić thir akana. Adọko ḍhakakede khane beretena, adọko kulikedea, Noa dọ cele mãyãm kana?

Adọe mẹnketa, Ọkọe baḍae, cele mãyãm kan cọń; iń dọ bań baḍae kana. Adọ arhõko kulikedea, bạhu dọe okayena mẹnte; adọe mẹnketa, Ona hõ bań baḍae kana, uni hõe okayen cọń.

Khange adọ ạḍi bạṛićko bọtọrena; adọ họṛ ar mạńjhi paranik, cạukidar, jọtọko lạiatkoa. Adọ onko hõ jọtọko hẹć jarwayena; adọko ńẹlket dọ, parkom latar sẹnte bogete mãyãm dọ jọrọ akante sạkit akan. Adọ cạukidare kukli kana, uni koṛae kuliye kana, Henda phalna, noa dọ cele mãyãm kana?

Adọe mẹnketa, Ọkọe baḍae, cele mãyãm kan cọń, bań baḍae kana.

Adọ arhõe kulikedea, Am bạhu dọe okayena?

Adọe mẹnketa, Ọkọe baḍae, okayen cọe; ona hõ iń dọ bań baḍae kana. Gitić jạpit akat tahẽkanań, unregeye okayen cọń;

kindling the fire, he lighted a lamp and looked all over with the lamplight. Then he saw that blood had been spilled and was running all over the floor under the bedstead. When he saw this, he became extremely anxious and said: "Some enemy or other has killed her and taken her away somewhere. That is why she is not here. Now they will surely hang me." Being anxious over this, the young man did not call out or say anything. He lay down absolutely quiet, and, even when it became light in the morning, the young man was lying there. He did not come out.

His parents then said: "Look here, I wonder whether these two have got up or not. They are not to be felt." The mother went to the door and called out, but, as they did not answer, she opened the door and went inside and then she saw that the whole house was flowing with blood, and, seeing this, she also commenced to cry and came out again.

Hearing this all the people came running and saw it. And the young man was lying quietly on the bedstead. When they pushed him, he got up, and they asked him: "Whose blood is this?"

He replied: "Who knows whose blood it is? I do not know." Again they asked him what had become of his wife, and he said: "That also I do not know what has become of her."

They became awfully frightened, and they told the village people, the head-man, the deputy head-man and the village watchman, in fact all there. All of them came together and also saw that a great quantity of blood had been spilled on the ground below the bedstead and had coagulated there. The village watchman was asking, that is to say, he was asking the young man: "Look here, you so and so, whose blood is this?"

"Who knows," he replied, "I have no knowledge whose blood this may be."

Again he asked him: "What has become of your wife?"

He replied: 'Who knows where she has gone. This also I do not know. I was lying asleep. Then she disappeared, who knows

adọ beretḱateń ạikạuede kan dọ, bạnugić. Adọń mẹnketa, Pasẹ raca sẹne oḍok akan. Adọ iń hõń oḍokente goṭań aṭkar baṛakede dọ, bạnugić. Khange arhõ oṛaḱteń bọlọyente sẹṅgẹl iń jolkette divhe jẹrẹt marsalkate goṭań arsal baṛaketa. Adọ unrege noa mãyãm iń ńẹlket khan dọ ạḍiń bhabnayena; adọń mẹnketa, Ọkọe bạiri cọko maḱkedete hoṛmọ sudhạ okate cọko idiketa. Ar ạḍi gọṭẹn iń bhabnayente iń dọń gitić thirena, cet hõ bań rọṛ baṛaleta; bhabnate iń dọń gitić thir akangea. Adọe okayen cọń, iń dọ bạń disạledete ọhọń mẹn daṛelea.

Khange adọko mẹnketa, Durrẹ! noa dọ ạḍi hahaṛa reaḱ katha hoeyena. Do sẹ bhala, eṅgat apat oṛaḱte bar hoṛ calaḱtabonpe, pasẹ ọṇḍẹye sẹn akan. Kuli ạgukope, are sẹn akan khan dọ bạhu hõ ạgu darayeben, ar ọṇḍẹn hoṛ ar bạhuren apat baretko hõ ạgu darakoben. Ar bae sẹn akanre hõ ạgu darakoben baṛẹ. Nọṇḍẹ nonka onka hoe akana, onako aben dọ jọtọ katha lạiakoben; andhamạr dọ aloben ạgukoa.

Adọ sạri atoren bar hoṛko ńum begarketkina, arko bhẹj gọtkatkina. Adọ sạri unkin hoṛ dọ sẹnkate onako lạiatkin lekagekin kạmiketa. Adọ bakin ṭewan daṛeade khan ọṇḍẹn hoṛkin ạgu daraketkoa apa bare salaḱ; adọko hẹćena.

Khange onko dọ hẹć torage ẹkkalteko raṅgao gọtente uni jãwãe gomkettako dọko tọl gọtkedea cạukidar pargana lagaete, ar curmar ruḱhetko chuṭạuḱ kana, arko mẹneta, Dinitale họpọnera. Okakedeape? Ạgukaetalepe, ar baṅkhan bes dọ ọhọle mẹnlepea. Judi jãhãnaḱ bae jutlet khan dọ cedaḱ bape jimạkadetalea? Apege

---

[8] When there is anything the matter with a woman who has been brought in as a wife or a servant, custom demands that her male relatives, father and brothers or her natural guardians, should be informed.

whereto. I sat up and was feeling for her; she was not there. Then I thought: 'Perhaps she has gone out to the courtyard'. Then I also went out and sought for her all over, but she was not there. Then I again went inside, made a fire and lighted the lamp, and with this I looked all over the room. Then, when I saw this blood, I became very anxious and said: 'Some enemy or other has killed her and even taken the body away, who knows where.' As I was having many anxious thoughts, I lay down and kept quiet, I did not speak at all on account of my grief. I was lying quiet. What has become of her I am unable to say, as I was not aware of her getting away."

Then they said: "O dear, this is a very strange thing that has happened, so now please let two people among us go to her parents' house, perhaps she has gone there. Ask them and bring word back; and if she has gone there, bring also the wife back with you, and also bring along with you people from there and the wife's father and brothers[8]. Even if she has not gone there, please bring those people along with you here; such and such a thing has happened here, tell them all about it. Do not bring them here in ignorance of what has happened."

Then, truth to tell, they named two village people and at once sent these two on this errand. These went and acted in accordance with what they had told them. As they were unable to get any information about the girl, they brought people from there with them, together with the girl's father and brothers; and so they all came there.

As soon as these people arrived, they flew into a rage, and together with the watchman and overchief they at once bound their son-in-law and commenced to abuse them right and left and said: "Give us our daughter. What have you done to her? Bring her to us, otherwise we shall surely not call you good. If she has, in some respect, not acted properly, why have you not given her into our charge? You yourselves have killed our daughter.

aleren hoponera dope goćkedea. Kạmire sẹ cạl colonre bae jutlet khan, cedakge bape jimạwatlea? Alege hutẹćle sikhạu paṛhaokea. Dini ńam gotalepe, ar bańkhan do bale bạgiape kana.

Khange ẹnte okareko ńamea? Bako ńawatko khan, onko do ẹkkalte hạkim ṭhenko lạiketa, ado doroga capṛasiko hẹć gotente onako todarot baṛakette uni koṛako tol idikedea khũnyạhi mẹnkate.

Ado inạ mit ghạṛi khange cekakote coko suṭik ńam gotketa, bańma, uni kuṛiko ạgulede ona atorenge, kathae, mitṭań koṛa ẹn hilok ńindạge okate coe aten, oṛakre do bạnugić. Ado khange koṛaren apattẹt do inạ ghạṛitege dorkase lagaoketa, bańma, Uni kuṛi do bale goć akadea, mẹnkhan mitṭań koṛa tuluće ạṅgir sẹn akana.

Ado sạri ona katha hạkime ańjomketa; adoe metatkoa, Acha bogege, ma ẹṇḍẹkhan unkin ńamkinpe, oka okakore peṛa menak-kotako, oṇḍẹ oṇḍẹ goṭa dāṛāepe ar hoṛ kuli baṛakope, ar iń hõ huliạ ciṭhiń koleta, adobo ńamkina. Ar mẹnkhan ạuribo ńamkin dhạbić nui koṛa do hajotreye tahẽ hataṛoka.

Ado uni koṛaren apate mẹnketa, Acha bogege, ńamkinale.

Ado enka mẹnkate apat doe hẹćente unkin ńańam ontẹ notẹ hoṛe kolketkoa, ado uni koṛa do hajotteko aderkedea. Ado uni koṛae ujurketa hạkim ṭhen, mẹnketae, Iạ hujur, iń do ạkhirpe gojẹńgea, mẹnkhan pea ạsul janwar menakkotińa; enkotẹt iń do dayakate ạgukakotińpe. Inạge iń doń argojok kana.

Ado hạkime mẹnketa, Cele janwar kanako?

Adoe mẹnketa, Mit do pusi, ar mit do goḍo, ar mit do odam kanae.

Khange sạri hạkim do hoṛe kolketkoteye ạgu ocoketkoa; adoko metadea, Noko dole ạguketkotama. Ado uni koṛa ma hajotre menae; cekateko calaka? Ado pusi ar odamkin mẹnketa, Do ya

If in her work or her behaviour she has not acted properly, why did you not give her in charge to us? Then we might have reprimanded and tutored her. Now find her for us at once, otherwise we are not going to let you off."

Now where should they find her? As they did not find her and bring her to them, they at once informed the magistrate, and police constables at once came, and, after having investigated the matter, they took the young man away bound, charging him with being a murderer.

Now a short while after this somehow or other they found out that a boy belonging to the village from where they had brought the girl had disappeared that very night. He was not at home. The young man's father then at once entered a petition, saying: "We have not killed the girl. She has run away with another man."

Truth to tell, the magistrate listened to this and said to them: "Very well, then, find these two. Wherever they have friends, go to all such places and ask people. I am also sending round a notice, and then we shall find them; but until we find them, this young man will have to stay in prison."

"Very well, that's good," the young man's father said, "we shall find them."

Having said this, the father came home and sent people out in all directions to find these two. The young man they took into the prison. Thereupon the young man made an application to the magistrate, saying: "I say, Sir, afterwards you may kill me. I have three animals that I have tamed. Be merciful and bring these, just these three, to me. That is the only thing I am applying for."

The magistrate then said: "What kind of animals are they?"

He replied: "One is a cat, and one is a rat, and one is an otter."

Then, truth to tell, the magistrate sent people and had them brought, whereupon they said to him: "Here we have brought these ones of yours." Now the young man, as you know, was in prison. How would the animals be able to go? The cat and the

goḍo, am calakme; bhala cetkoe metabona, kuli ạguyem. Am do nãhãkem sen dareaka, ar aliń do cekate onde doliń boloka? Do, amge calaktabonme.

Ado sạri ńindạ jokhen goḍo do uni koṛa ṭhene calaoena; adoe metae kana, De bhala hećen dole; cetem metale kana?

Ado uni koṛae menketa, Ńelpe, iń do tinạk muhim khon apeń bańcao akatpea; ado onkage nitok do iń hõ muhimreń paṛao akana. Ado de noa muhim khon bańcaokańtabonpe. Iń bạhu okoe tuluće ạṅgir sen akana, uni bińe emadiń mundạme idi tora akata, ar okare menakkin, onde do nãhãk khub jhak jhak dolankin benao akatpe ńel ńama. Do, ape do senkate inạ mundạmtet baṛe ạgukatińpe.

Ado goḍoe menketa, Cele, ado inạge se arhõ cetko katha menaka?

Adoe menketa, Inạge katha do.

Ado goḍoe menketa, Hape endekhan, unkin iń lạiakinrege, bhala ado cetkin mena.

Adoe menketa, Acha, do lạiakinme.

Ado sạri senkate onako joto kathae lạiatkina, ado unkinkin menketa, Hẽ, ona mundạm dobon pańja ạguigea. Maye raṛa oco gotkabon ma, mit ghạṛitege nãhãkbon ạgu goda.

Khạnge pusiye menketa, Iń doń ńel got akatkingea; ado noakin idiket hal tho bań badae kana, ar bańkhan hutec unrege ohoń sen ocolekina. Do lạiaeme, odamko raṛa gotkae ma, se jotogeko chuṭi gotkabon ma, adobon pańja ạguia. Do, inạ katha lại oṭoaeme.

Ado sạriye sen ruạṛente onako kathae lạiadea. Ado uniye menketa, Acha bogege, endekhan aṅga ocoak, ado nãhãk iń chuṭi oco gotkapea. Ạikạ ạgu godpe, alope bilomoka.

otter then said: "You rat, you go and ask him what he has to say to us. You are able to go, but we two, how shall we be able to go in there? Please, you go for us."

Then, truth to tell, during the night the rat went to the young man and said to him: "Now we have come. What have you to say to us?"

The young man then said: "Remember from how great a danger I have saved you, and now in the same way I have got into danger. Now then you save me from this danger. My wife has run away with somebody. She has taken away with her the ring that the snake gave me, and where these two are you will be sure to see that they have built a grand splendid palace. Now please, you go and bring this ring back to me."

The rat then said: "Well, is that all, or have you anything else to order us?"

"That's all," he replied.

The rat then said: "Wait a little then. Let me first speak to the other two and hear what they will say."

"All right," he replied, "do tell them."

Then, truth to tell, the rat went and told the two others everything, and they said: "Yes, this ring we must track and bring. Let him at once set us free, and then in a trice we shall bring it."

The cat then said: "I saw the two when they went away; but I do not know the circumstances in which they took this thing away, otherwise I should certainly not have let them go at that time. Please tell him that they at once loose the otter, or rather let them set us all free at once. Then we shall track it and bring it. Please tell him just this and then come."

So, truth to tell, the rat returned and told him this, and the young man said: "All right, that is good. Then let it become morning and I shall at once see that they set you all free, but have a care, be quick and bring it, do not be delayed."

Adoe mẹnketa, Unkinle ńamlekin khangele ạgu goda. Adọ enka galmarao baṛakate uni gọḍo doe ruạṛ hẹćena unkin ṭhẹn, are lạiatkina, Gapa setak nāhāke chuṭi oco gọtkabona.

Adọkin mẹnketa, Acha, bogege.

Adọ setak khange, kathae, uni koṛa pahradare metatkoa, Ma hạkim lạiaepe noko pea janware aṛak gọtkako ma; unkinkin sẹn akan hoṛkinko pańja ạgukina nāhāk.

Adọ sạri hạkim ṭhẹn ona kathako lạiketa, adọ hạkime mẹnketa. Acha ma ẹṇḍẹkhan, ma aṛak gọtkakope.

Adọ sạriko aṛak gọtkatkoa; adọ onko pẹnẹge mittegeko calaoena. Adọ sạri sendrako sendrayetkina dọ, goṭa disomko sendra kana. Adọ, kathae, Ganga parọmre mittań oṛakko ńẹl ńamketa, bańma, khub sona leka jhak jhak ńẹlọk kan. Adọko mẹnketa, Henda ya, ona oṛak kange coń cet coń? Ạkhirge bań ạkhir delabon calakgea.

Adọ pusi ar gọḍokin mẹnketa, Henda ya, noa dakrege thọ cet lekatebon parọmọka?

Adọ odame mẹnketa, Ho, noare dọ ińiń parọmbona.

Adọkin mẹnketa, Acha, ẹṇḍẹkhan dẹ parọmbonme.

Adoe mẹnketa, Ma ińre gugukben.

Adọ sạri odam deare pusi, ar pusi deare gọḍo, onkako guguyena, adoe parọmketkoa. Adọ ona oṛak ṭhenko sẹn sorok kana. Adọ mit hoṛe mẹnketa, Ẹ ya, nitre dọ babon sor utạroka, bańkhan nāhāke ńẹl orombona.

Arhọ̃ mit hoṛ doe mẹnketa, Nitrebo sẹn sẹṭẹrlen nạhībon ńẹl oromea, ar bańkhan cekatebo bạḍaea? Pasẹ unkinak oṛak dọ bań kan.

Adọ arhọ̃ mit hoṛe mẹnketa, Acha ya, ạyup toraregebon calaka, bhalabon ńẹlkoa, ọkọeak oṛak kana mẹnte.

The rat then said: "When we find these two, we shall at once bring it." After having had this talk the rat came back to the two others and told them: "To morrow morning we will at once see that they set us free."

"All right, that's good," the two others said.

As soon as it became morning, people tell, the young man said to the watchman: "Please tell the magistrate that he at once lets these three animals loose. They will presently track the two people who have gone away, and bring them back."

So, truth to tell, they told the magistrate this and he said: "Very well then, set them free at once."

And, truth to tell, so they did, and the three went away together, and they hunted and hunted the run-away. They were hunting all over the country. Then, truth to tell, they caught sight of a house on the other side of the Ganges, glittering like gold. Then they said: "Look here you that must certainly be the house, don't you think? Whatever happens, let us go there."

The cat and the rat then said: "Look here, how are we to get across this water?"

The otter then said: "Oh, here I shall take us across."

The two others then said: "Very well then, take us across."

The otter replied: "Then you two settle on my back."

So, truth to tell, on the back of the otter the cat settled down, and on the back of the cat the rat, and in this way the otter took them across. Now going near to this house one of them said: "Look here, you, we shall not go quite close just now, otherwise she will recognize us."

Again one of them said: "Only if we now go up there, we shall be able to recognize her. Otherwise, how shall we be able to know? Perhaps it is not their house."

Again another of them said: "Very well then, you, let us go as soon as it becomes evening. Then we shall see them, whose house this is."

Adọ sạri ạyup̣ tora khange ona oṛaḱ ṭhẹnko sẹn sẹṭẹr gọṭenteko ńẹlkede dọ, sạrige uni koṛa bạhu kangeae. Adọko mẹnkeṭa, Họbon ńam akaṭkina; adọ dẹsẹ bhala budtabonme ceṭ lekatebon idia ona mundạm dọ. Adọko mẹnkeṭa, Bọlọkatebon ńam baṛaea.

Adọ sạrikin jọm baṛakeṭ khan dọ, oṛaḱ hõ ạḍi kajakkin siṅkeṭa, bọlọḱ họrge bako ńam daṛeaḱ kan.

Adọ pusiye mẹnkeṭa, Ẹ ya goḍo, ma aperen peṛa sẹ am jạt nẽota ạgukom. Nọṇḍẹ khon gẹlẹjpe, hana tala oṛaḱre phuṭpe ar ona mundạm ńam ạguipe; ar bam ạgukeṭkoa mẹnkhan laṅ aḍo ocomea.

Adọ sạriye calaoente aema utạr goḍoe riạu ạgukeṭkoa, adọe metako kana, Ma nọṇḍẹ khonbo gẹlẹja, hana oṛaḱ bhitrirebon phuṭ taba. Ạḍi hako pakobon gẹlẹć họda.

Adọ sạri jọtọ goḍoko chuṭạuente miṭ ghạṛitegeko bhugạḱ parọm gọṭkeṭa. Adọe metako kana, Ma miṭṭaṅ mundạm menaḱa, onabon ńama.

Ar unkin kuṛi koṛa dọ bana họṛ khubkin jạpiṭ akaṭa, ar noko dọ haḍ baḍ ona mundạmgeko ńaṅam kana. Ar uni pusi dọ ọnẹko gẹlẹćleṭ ṭhẹn hẹćkateye durup̣ akana, bae oḍok ocoako kana. Adọ ńam ńamteko bhagaoena. Adọ bako ńam daṛeaṭ khan dọ uni goḍoe mẹnkeṭa, pusiye metae kana, Baṅ yale ńam dareaḱ kana.

Adọ pusiye mẹnkeṭa, Ma kurumuṭute ńampe, ar bape ńamkeṭa mẹnkhan dọ miṭ miṭteń jọm maraopea, am họ̃laṅ jọmmegea.

Khange adọko bọtọrente kurumuṭuteko ńaṅam kana. Adọ bako ńam daṛeaṭ khan, uni sọrdar goḍo dọ unkin parkọmteye dẹćena, adọ unkinaḱ kicrićkore ar ti jaṅga kạṭup̣kore goṭae ńẹl baṛayeṭa. Adọ bae ńam daṛeaṭ khane mẹnkeṭa, Pasẹ mocareye kọpẹṭ akaṭ. Adọ onka mẹnkate sạri uni goḍo dọ kuṛiaḱ koṛamreye ńir dẹć gọṭente caṇḍbọlte mũye gũṛtuć gọṭkedea.

So, truth to tell, as soon as it became evening, they went up to the house and saw her, it was really the young man's wife. Then they said: "Oh, now we have found them, so please think out for us how we shall take this ring away." "We shall enter and search for it," they said.

Now, truth to tell, when the people there had had their food, they shut the house very securely up, and they were unable to find a way inside.

The cat then said: "You rat, invite your friends or your relatives and bring them here. Scratch from here, make an opening out in the middle of the house, and find and bring this ring. And if you do not bring them, we two shall pitch into you."

Now, truth to tell, the rat went and called together, invited and brought an immense number of rats and said to them: "Let us scratch a hole here. Then in the middle of this house we shall make an opening. Let us set to at once, quick."

So, truth to tell, all the rats commenced to scratch, and in one moment they had made a hole right through. Then the rat said to the others: "There is a ring there. We shall find it."

Now the young man and the girl had both fallen fast asleep, and the rats were noisily seeking this ring. Now this cat had come to the place where they had scratched the hole and was sitting there. She would not let them come out, but they could not find it in spite of all searching. As they were unable to find it, the rat spoke and said to the cat: "No, we are unable to find it."

The cat then said: "Search for it with all your might; if you do not find it, I shall eat every one of you. You too I shall eat."

Now they became afraid and were diligently seeking for it, but as they were unable to find it, the chief rat jumped up on the bedstead and looked everywhere in their clothes and on their fingers and toes, and as it was unable to find it, it said: "Perhaps she has taken it into her mouth and kept it there." With this in mind the rat, truth to tell, at once jumped up to the girl's breast and tickled her in her nose with its tail.

Khange, kathae, uni kuṛi doe kopoṭ akaṭ tahẽkana, adoe ạchim pạsir goṭkaṭa. Ado hare phareko ger goṭkeṭteko ạtkirkeṭteko ṅir oḍokena. Ado pusiko metae kana, Ṅamkeṭale; men oḍok ocoaleme.

Ado uni pusiye menkeṭa, Okor? Enḍekhan maseṅ ṅela, udukaṅpe. Ado sạriko udukadea, adoe oḍok ocoaṭkoa.

Ado kathae, ạḍi rạskạkateko hijuk kana; ar ona mundạm do uni goḍogeye ger ạguyeṭtakoa. Ado ona Gaṅgare do, kathae, one calak jokhenko ghõṛã se gugu paromlen leka, onkage ona ruạṛ jokhen hõko paromok kan tahẽkana. Ado un jokhenge, kathae, oka sen khon coṅ miṭṭaṅ kuṛiṭ doe uḍạu heć goṭente goḍoe ạtkirea menteye haloye kan tahẽkana. Ado bae halo ṅamkede khan do phạkṛạkteye thapa goṭkedea. Ado kathae, botorte uni goḍo do ona mundạm doe paskao goṭkeṭa, ona do dakre ṅũrena.

Adoko paromen khan, goḍoe menkeṭa, Mundạm doṅ paskaokeṭa uni kuṛiṭe haloyiṅ jokhen.

Ado pusiye menkeṭa, Sạrige ạḍi muhim khonem baṅcaoena.

Ado odamkin metae kana, De ya odam, ado am pạri nitok do ṅamtabonme. Ạliṅ ma dakre baliṅ bolo daṛeak, baṅkhan do ente jotokotebon ṅamkea, ado onate amliṅ metam kana, De ṅamtabonme.

Ado khange sạri odame boloyena; onako paromlen mohnḍa sente se inạ dhara dhạri goṭae ṅel baṛakeṭa. Ado bae ṅamleṭ khane oḍokena; adoe menkeṭa, Baṅ yaṅ ṅam daṛeak kan do, losoṭkore do.

Ado unkinkin menkeṭa, Enḍekhan hakoge dhorako jom akaṭa; ma hako laćre ṅelme.

Ado khange sạri arhõe boloyena; ado hakoe laga sapeṭkoa are or paṛakeṭkote laćreye ṅel baṛayeṭtakoa, ar onkate ać hõe jom

Now, people tell, the girl had actually taken the ring into her mouth. Then she sneezed and blew it out. Then they in a hurry took the ring between their teeth and, carrying it away, ran out. Whereupon they said to the cat: "Now we have found it. See that you let us get out."

The cat then said: "Why, where is it? Let us have a look at it then. Show it to me." Then, truth to tell, they showed it to the cat, and she let them get out.

Now, truth to tell, they were coming along with great joy, and the rat was bringing the ring between its teeth. Then at the Ganges, as they, when coming there, had been carried across on the shoulder or back of the otter, in the same way they were also crossing on their way back. Just at that time, people tell, a kite suddenly came flying from somewhere and was swooping down to carry the rat away, but as it was unable to catch the rat swooping down, it slapped it with its wing. Then, people tell, from fright the rat lost hold of the ring, and it fell into the water.

When they had crossed, the rat said: "I have lost the ring just at the time when the kite was swooping down on me."

The cat said: "Then really you were saved from a very great danger."

So the other two said to the otter: "You otter, now it is your turn to find the ring for us; do so. We are unable to enter the water, otherwise we should all of us search for it; therefore we are saying to you: Please find it for us."

Then, truth to tell, the otter entered the water, and in the direction where they had passed and in the vicinity all over it searched for it, but as it did not find it, it came out and said: "I am unable to find it in such mud."

Then the two others said: "Then undoubtedly some fish has swallowed it. Look into a fish's stomach."

So, truth to tell, the otter again entered the water and was chasing and catching fishes and tearing them asunder and looking

bik̓ kana ar unkin lạgit̓ hõe capat̓ oḍoket̓koa. Adọ onka onkate, kathae, mit̓ṭẹn hako laćreye ńam gọt̓ket̓a, adọ uni hako sudhạge ghuṭuteye gẹr oḍokkedea, adọe metakin kana, Hẽ, nitok̓ dọń ńamket̓tabona. Adọ onka mẹnkate ạḍiko rạskạjọṅ kana.

Ar hako jelko jọm baṛajọṅ kan tahẽkanrege, kathae, oka sẹn khon cọṅ kuṛit̓ dọe uḍạu hẹć gọt̓ente uni hako dọe ạtkir gọt̓kedea. Khange ạḍiko hae nisạsena, adọ uni kuṛit̓geko kọyọk̓ akadea.

Khange, kathae, Deko ạimại onakorege khạclạk̓ante sahanko halaṅ baṛayet̓ kan tahẽkana; adọ onko ạimại uni kuṛit̓ khon uni hako dọko chaḍaokedea. Adọ pẹnẹ họṛ noko dọko ńẹńẹl kana. Adọ uni hako dọ khạclạk̓reko bhoraokedea, adọ oṛak̓teko idiyede kana.

Adọko mẹnket̓a, Delabon pańjakoa; ona mundạm ma laćrege nãhãk̓ menak̓; lać dọ jạnić ọhọko jọma, ar laćko jọmre hõ, mundạm dọ nãhãk̓ ọhọko jọma. Adọ onka mẹnkate onko ạimại tayọm tayọmteko calak̓ kana.

Adọ odam ar goḍokin mẹnket̓a, Cele ya pusi, dẹ nitok̓ dọ am kạmiletabonme; am bam kạmi daṛeak̓ reak̓ ṭhẹn ma ạliṅliṅ kạmiket̓a. Adọ noko ṭhen sẹ Deko oṛak̓re dọ cekate ạliṅ dọliṅ sorok̓a? Ạliṅ ma nãhãk̓ko dal gọćliṅa, ar am khan dọ nãhãk̓ saṭgem sor gọdọk̓a. Onate amliṅ bharam kana, ma nia dhao dọ amge kạmitabonme. Noa mundạm dọ nãhãk̓ laćrege menak̓a; am dọ ona lać baṛẹ ṭạnkhime, duhạuako sẹko giḍikak̓a, am dọ ona baṛẹ tanin̓an ńẹlme.

Adọe mẹnket̓a, Acha, ẹṇḍẹkhan iṅgeń calak̓tabona; ạikhạ nẹṇḍẹ baṛẹ tahẽ hataṛok̓ben.

Adọkin mẹnket̓a, Ona ik̓dibon hẹć akana, adọ ona chaḍakate ạliṅ dọliṅ calak̓a? Ona katha dọ ọhọ hoelena; adọ aboren kisạ̃ṛ cet̓e mẹnkea? Ma am dọ hako pako sẹn họdok̓me, baṅkhanem ńẹl at̓koa nãhãk̓.

into their stomachs; and in this way it also ate and had its fill, and for the two others it also threw fish out. Carrying on in this way, people tell, it suddenly found the ring in the stomach of a fish, and taking the fish between its teeth it brought both the fish and the ring out to the bank, whereupon it said to the other two: "Yes, now I have found it for us," and when it had said this, they were all awfully glad.

Now while they were occupied eating the fish, from somewhere or other, people tell, a kite suddenly came flying and carried this fish away. Then they became utterly downhearted and were staring up after the kite.

Now, people tell, some Hindu women were picking up firewood in their baskets in these parts, and these women got the fish away from the kite. All three of them were looking at this. The women put the fish in a basket and were taking it away home.

These animals then said, "Come along, let us follow them. The ring is as we know in the fish's stomach. Probably they won't eat the stomach, and even if they do this, they will surely not eat the ring." With this in their thoughts they were following after the women.

The otter and the rat then said: "Well, you cat, now it is your turn to do something for us. Where you were unable to do anything, there we two did our part. Now how shall we two be able to go near to these Hindus' or to a Hindu house? There they will at once strike us dead. But as for you, you may at once be able to go near, therefore we are charging you, this time you must work for us. The ring is certainly in the fish's stomach, and keep your eyes fixed on it. See whether they clean the stomach or throw it away."

"Very well," she replied, "then I shall go, but have a care, you two, stay here in the meantime."

They answered: "We have come to fetch this ring, and should we two go without this? This is surely impossible. Then what would our master say? Now you go quickly, otherwise you will presently lose sight of them."

Adọ sạriye pańja idiketkoa, adọ onakorege meyań meyańateye ạcur baṛae kana. Adọko gẹdẹ kana, ona aṛerege ać hõe ạcur baṛae kana; adọ mit́ bar kuṭrạko capat́ gọt́adea. Adọe ji baṛaketge, jọm dọ bae jọma. Adọ onka onkako mẹnketa, Iạ pusi, cet́ yae ńam kana? Laćtẹt́ tanak capat́ gọt́aepe thọ.

Adọ sạri laćtẹt́ ọr tot́kateko capat́ gọt́adea. Adọ onako capat́ade khan, uni dọ ạḍi rạskạkate onae gẹr gọt́keta, adọ pharak sẹn idikate uni pusi dọ ona laće gẹr boskaokette mucạt́ khọn onae sendra idiyeta. Adọ sạri poṭare khangeye ńam gọt́keta, adọ onae gẹrketa, adọ unkin ṭhẹne idiketa, adọ jọtọko ńapamena.

Adọ mit́ sin mit́ ńindạko calaoena, adọ uni koṛa ṭhẹnko sẹṭẹr gọt́ena. Adọ ona hajọt oṛak ṭhẹnko calao sorena; khanko ńẹlket́koa, adọ goḍo hare phare ona mundạm dọ uni koṛa ṭhẹne idiketa, adọ uni koṛae atań gọt́keta. Adọ onko pakhrakoe metat́koa, Ma ape dọ mit́ sẹr toa ńawańpe; nitge nãhãk unkin họṛ nọṇḍẹń hẹć ocokina.

Adọ sạri onko hõ uniak katha lekage mit́ sẹr toako ńawadea, adọ ona toare ona mundạm dọe caḍoketa, are mẹnketa, Ma niạ ńindạ bhitạrtege jẹmọn parkọmrekin gitić akan onka baṛẹ jẹmọn nọṇḍẹkin sẹṭẹr gọdọk ma!

Adọ sạri jẹmọne rọrlet́, tẹmọnge inạ ńindạ bhitạrtege ạuri ańga hạṭińokrege mit́ parkọmre gitić akan bana họṛkin sẹṭẹr gọt́ena ona hajọt oṛak ṭhẹnge. Adọ sạri sẹṭẹr tora bana họṛko tot́ gọt́ket́kina, adọ hạkimko lạiadea. Adọ uni hõ hẹćkateye ńẹlket́kina, adọe mẹnketa, Do nukinren eńgat apat lạiakope.

Adọ sạri palṭọnko sẹnente unkinren eńgat apatko lạiat́kina, adọ onko hõko hẹćena, adọko ńẹlket́kina, menakkinge. Adọ khange uni koṛa dọko aṛakkadea, adọ unkin kuṛi koṛa bana họṛko hajọtket́kina.

So, truth to tell, the cat followed after them and was turning round there constantly mewing. The women were cutting up the fish; close to where they were doing this the cat also was walking about, and they threw a couple of pieces to her. She smelled at it, but did not eat it. Seeing this the women said: "This wretched cat, what does she want? Please throw the stomach or something of that kind to her."

So, truth to tell, they pulled out the stomach and threw that to her, and when they had done this, the cat with great joy at once took it between her teeth, and, having taken it away some distance, the cat bit the entrails open and searched for the ring from the end of the stomach, and, truth to tell, in the stomach she found it, whereupon she took it between her teeth and carried it to the two others; all of them were now together there.

So they went a whole day and a whole night, whereupon they arrived where the young man was. There they went near to the prison, and they caught sight of them. The rat then in a hurry carried the ring to the young man and he received it, whereupon he said to the watchers: "Please, bring me one seer of milk. Then I shall presently cause those two people to come here."

Truth to tell, they brought him in accordance with his word one seer of milk, and putting the ring into this milk he said: "Now within this night may these two be brought here just as they are lying on their bed."

And, truth to tell, no sooner had he said this than that same night before day dawned those two people arrived there in the prison, lying on one bed; and as soon as they arrived, they pulled both of them out at once, whereupon they informed the magistrate. He also came and saw them and said: "Now inform the parents of these two."

So, truth to tell, soldiers went and told their parents, and they also came and they saw these two, that they were there. So they set the young man free and put the two others, both the girl and

Adọ uni koṛa dọ onko pẹnẹ janwarante oṛakteye calaoena. Adọ unreye kuliyetkoa, Henda ya, cet lekatepe ńamketkina ar noa mundạm dọ cekatepe ńamketa?

Adọ cet lekateko sẹnlena, ar cet lekate ona mundạmko ńamketa, ar họrkore cet ghoṭna hoelena, onako jọtọ oṛ khonak uni koṛako lại ạguadea; ar ọkọeko họṛ ọṇḍẹko tahẹ̃kan, onako jọtọ katha onko hõko aṅjọmketa. Adọ unre, kathae, noa katha dọ pasnaoena, adọ uni kuṛiren eṅgat apatko sapketkina, adọ tinạk baplare khọrọclentakoa, onako hisạbketa, ar ona reak dobṛa khọrọc uni tayọm jãwãe koṛa ṭhẹn khọnko ạdạiketa. Ar ona chaḍa ạḍi utạrko ḍãṇḍ phurạnketkoa, adọko caba baṛaketa.

Adọ uni koṛa arhõ bạhuae reakko bọndọbọsketa, adọ arhõ bạhuko ńamketkoa, adọko baplayena.

Adọ onakate ḍher din hoeyena, uni koṛaren bạhu hõe rophayena. Adọ mit din dọ uni koṛa onko ạsul janware galmaraoako kana, Cele ya, adọ nõkõe ape hõko gọcetpe tahẹ̃kanre iṅiṅ teṅgoyente apnar ṭaka khọrọckateń chaḍaoketpea; ar iń hõko gọjeń kan tahẹ̃kan jọkhẹn apepe ạgukette iń dọń bańcaoena. Adọ ṭaka poesa dọ ape hõ bań ạguyetpea, ar iń hõ bạń ẹm daṛeape kana, Sẹ ẹntepe kọeyeń khan dọń emapea.

Adọko mẹnketa, Bań, ale dọ am ṭhẹn dọ cet hõ bale hataoa. Nõkõe am dọm dayayente amak ṭaka khọrọckate alem bańcaoketlea, ar nõkõe nun din ar nit hạbić hõ amakgele jọmeta; amgem ạsuletlea, arhõ bickọm amgele emam bujhi dọ.

Adọ uni koṛae mẹnketa, Bańa, iń hõ ape ṭhẹn dọ bạń hataoa. Adọ aṛakkape iń dọń mẹneta. Adọ dẹ apege cetpe mẹneta?

Adọko mẹnketa, Acha bogege, ẹnḍẹkhan ale hõle khusik kangea.

---

[9] The story is probably borrowed, but it has many traits peculiar to the Santals. So here. A divorce is to be brought about. Before the final act (when the husband tears three sal leaves asunder and kicks a lota with water) the village council goes carefully into all accounts, to find out how much money may be due from the guilty party. As a rule the injured husband will get the bride-

the boy, in prison, but the young man went home with his three animals, As they were going, he was asking them: "I say, let me know, how did you find them and how did you find this ring?"

Then they told the young man everything from the beginning, how they went, how they found the ring, and what happened to them on the road, and the people who were there they also heard all this. Then, people tell, this story was spread abroad, and they took hold of the girl's parents, whereupon they made up accounts[9] and found out how much had been spent in the marriage, and twice the amount of this they realized from this second husband. Besides this they imposed some very heavy fines on them. In this way they settled the matter.

Thereafter they again arranged to procure a wife for the young man, and when they had found a suitable girl, they were married.

After this a long time passed, and the young man's wife also settled down. So one day the young man had a talk with his tame animals: "Well you," he said, "when they were killing you, I stood up for you and rescued you, spending my own money. At a time when people were on the point of killing me, you also helped me, and I was saved. Then I am not going to take any money from you, and I on my side am also unable to give you any. Else if you ask me for anything, I shall give you."

They replied: "No, we are not going to take anything from you. You see, you took pity on us and, spending your own money, you rescued us, and remember such a long time, even up to now, we have also been eating your food. You are keeping us. So we had rather give you. That would be fair."

The young man then said: "No, I am not going to take anything from you either, and I am thinking of setting you free. What have you to say to this?"

"All right," they replied, "that's good then. We are also pleased."

price refunded, when the woman is the quilty part. In flagrant cases the double amount is often realized (from the corespondent).

Adọ arhõe metaťkoa, Lạiape kanaň, jāhā leka arhõ jāhāeko gọćpe khan, ape dọ ẹkkalte iň ṭhẹn barẹ ňir hẹć gọdọkpe, iňiň baňcaopea; ar baňkhan dọ cekate iň dọň baḍaea?

Adọko mẹnketa, Acha bogege ẹṇḍẹkhan. Adọ amle metam kana, Am hõ judi jāhān gạrrem paṛaolen khan, sẹ noa mundạm aťlen khan, sẹ jāhāeko kombṛoletam khan, saṭ mẹnte kọbher gọťaleme. Jāhāe miť hoṛem lạiale khange, ale alele cepeť gọdọkte am ṭhẹnle calao gọdọka.

Adọe mẹnketa, Acha bogege ẹṇḍẹkhan dọ.

Adọ miťṭaň bajar ato tahẽkana, ona bajarteye idiketkoa. Adọ miťṭaň kisạṛak pukhri tahẽkana, ar ona pukhrire dọ ḍher din khọn ạsul hakoko tahẽkana. Adọ ona pukhrire uni odam dọe aṛakkadea. Adọ uni odame mẹnketa, Am dọ gapa setak ňindạre noa pukhri ṭhẹn hijukme, hako jẹl iň jọm ocomea. Adọ ona pukhri sẹn uni odam dọe bọlọyena.

Ar unkin barea dọ ona ato sẹne aṛak gọťkaťkina, metaťkinae, Ma noa atore aben do ạsulokben ar ape ape alope bapaṛijoka.

Adọ enka mẹnkate ać dọe ruạṛena.

Adọ dosar hiloke hẹćena ona pukhri ṭhẹn, adọ hakoe sap oḍok gọťadea. Ar uni pusi hõ miť din dọ ọkọeak cọň toa kombṛokate uni koṛae gẹr idiadea.

Adọ cabayena katha dọ.

82. Raj ar eae gọṭẹn rạni reaň.

Miťṭẹn rajdọ gidrạ baňko hoyok kantae karọnte eae gọṭẹne eraketkoa. Ẹnte pạhil era bae gidrạjoň karọnte, ar miťṭene ňamkedea. Uni hõ bae gidrạjoň kante ashọ miťṭene ňamkedea; onka lekate eae gọṭẹne purạuketkoa. Mẹnkhan ọkọe rạniren hõ gidrạ dọ baňko hoelena.

[1] The following story was taken down by Bhuju Murmu of Dhopahaṛ. The language is not up to the standard of Sagram's. The story is undoubtedly borrowed. It is of some of interest as showing how Hinduism is affecting the present day Santals.

Again he said to them: "I tell you this, if somehow or other somebody should again try to kill you, then at once come running to me. I shall rescue you; if you don't come, how should I know of it?"

"All right," they said, "that's good then. Then we have this to say to you; if you on your part should get into any difficulty, or if this ring should be lost or somebody should steal it from you, send us word immediately. If you tell any one of us, we shall at once consult together and come to you."

Then he said: "Very well; that is good."

Now there was a market town there. He took them away to this town. Here there was a tank belonging to a wealthy man, and in this tank there had been preserved fish for a long time, and he set the otter free in this. The otter then said: "To morrow morning, while it is still dark, come to this tank. I shall let you have fish to eat." Thereupon the otter went into the tank.

The two others he set free near the town, saying to them: "Now you two support yourselves in this town and do not make trouble for each other."

Having said this he returned home.

The next day he came to this tank, and the otter caught a fish and brought it out to him. And the cat also one day stole some milk from somebody or other and brought it to the young man.

And there the story is ended.

82. A KING AND HIS SEVEN WIVES[1].

THERE ones was a king who took unto himself seven wives, one after the other, because he did not get any children. As his first wife did not bear any children, he again took another. In this way he took in all seven, but none of his queens got any children.

Mẹnkhan uni raj dọ gidrạwak mẹ̃tãhã ńẹl reaṅ ạḍi ạḍi kurumuṭu tahẹ̃kantaea. Uni raj dọ Dibi thanreye manankeṭa, ẹnhõ baṅ hoelena. Inạ tayọm Sib thanreye manankeṭa, ẹnhõ baṅ hoelena. Inạkate Kạli thanreye manankeṭa, mẹnkhan ọkọe boṅga họtẹte hõ baṅ hoelena.

Adọ uni raj dọ nọrọk kuṇḍre sẹnkateye kuṇḍlạṅ baṛae kana, ẹnte ọkọeak biswạs bae ńẹlleṭte.

Unre sermaren Isor baba uni raj kuṇḍlạṅ baṛae kane ńẹlkedeteye phẹḍena; adọe metae kana, Am dọ un maraṅ raj, mẹnkhan cedak am dọ nọrọk kuṇḍre dọm kuṇḍlaṅ baṛae kana? Mẹnkhan Isor baba dọ uni ṭhen gosãe bhẹs lekateye sọdọrena. Ona iạte raj dọ uni Isor baba jugi gosãegeye badkadea.

Adọe metae kana, Baba guru gosãe, iń dọń kuṇḍlạṅok kana, cedak jẹ gidrạwak mẹ̃tãhã bạń ńẹlleṭte, mẹnkhan ona karọnte eae gọṭẹn iń eraketkoa; mẹnkhan ọkọeren hõ gidrạ dọ baṅko hoelena. Ona iạte nọrọk kuṇḍre dọń kuṇḍlạṅ baṛae kana, pasẹ sermaren Isor baba bhọre imạń khan, pasẹ gidrạ reaṅ mẹ̃tãhãń ńẹl daṛekaṭge.

Unre uni gosãe lekate phẹḍ akan, unige raje metae kana, Hã hã, bacha, inạkge kuṇḍlạṅokme nọrọkre dọ, umkate amak oṛakte calakme. Mẹnkhan uni gosãe dọ sermaren Isor baba kanae. Adọe metae kana, Amak ul bagwante calakme, ar ńẹlme okaṭak thoṗare eae gọṭẹn ul jọ menak ona dọ am leṅga tite capadme, ar jọjọm tite ona sanam lokhaeme. Adọ ona ul idikate amren sanam rạni hạṭiṅakotam, miṭṭankate; onako jọmle khan, am dọ gidrạ reaṅ mẹ̃tãhãm ńẹla.

2 Here the king is making vows; it is a very common practice among Hindu women to make vows at shrines in order to get children.

3 Iśvara, or, as adopted by the Santals (from the Bengali Ishọr) Isor, is the Supreme ruler or Lord of the universe. The name is adopted as a name for God by the Christians all over North India. Here it is naturally to be taken in its Hindu significance.

Now this king was very very eager to see the face of a child. He made vows[2] at a Durga temple; still no one was born. Thereupon he made vows at the Shiva temple, but still no one was born. After that he made vows at a Kali temple, but nothing happened through any godling.

Then the king went to a dung-hill, threw himself down and was wallowing there, because he saw he could not put faith in anybody.

Then Father Isor of Heaven[3] seeing the king wallowing came down and said to him: "You are such a big king; why are you wallowing here in this dung-hill?" But Father Isor appeared to him in the guise of a Gosae[4], therefore the king took Father Isor to be a yogi Gosae.

He said to him: "Father Gosae, I am wallowing here, because I have not seen the face of a child. For that reason I have taken to myself seven queens, but none of them has born a child. Therefore I am wallowing in this dung-hill. Perhaps, if Father Isor of Heaven would give me a blessing, perhaps I might be ablo to see the face of a child."

Then he who had come down in the guise of a Gosae said to the king: "Stop, stop, my son. Let it be enough with wallowing in the dung. Have a bath and go home." But this Gosae was Father Isor of Heaven and he said to him: "Go to your mango-grove and look round for a cluster of fruits on which there are seven mangoes. Throw something at these with your left hand and catch all with your right hand[5]. Then take the mangoes and divide them between all your queens, giving them one each. When they have eaten this, you will see the face of a child."

---

[4] Gosae really means 'a master of cows'; it is used as a name for a religious devotee or mendicant.

[5] While the right hand is used for eating, saluting, receiving, etc., and all 'honourable' purposes, the left hand is used for certain ablutions and is not 'honourable'. It is, however, used in medicine and is also, like here, considered fortunate for certain purposes.

Adǫ uniye metade lekage leṅga titeye capaťketa ar jǫjǫm tite dǫe lokhaketa. Adǫ ona ul idikate aćren marańić rąniye emadea, are metadea, Ma sanam hǫṛ hąṭińkate jǫmpe. Adǫ sanamge hąṭińkateko jǫmketa turui gǫṭẹn rąni, ar uni huḍińić rąni dǫ cetko cǫṅe kąmi kan tahẽkana, mẹnkhan uni dǫ baṅko emadea.

Adǫ tayǫmte dąṭąuni hutum baṛayenae, adǫe metako kana, Dẹn dąi enań raj ule ąguleť, adǫń ǫpsǫrena, jǫmąń. Mẹnkhane metae kana, Hąniṭaǩ ṭhen menaǩa. Uni ṭhen sẹnkateye kǫele khan, uni dǫe metaea, Hąni ṭhen menaǩa. Onka apaj apajtege uni dǫ baṅko emadea. Ẹnte cetko emaea, ul ma sanam pąhilregeko jǫm cabaket; mẹnkhan ǫkǫe hõ cet hõ baṅko emadea.

Adǫ ać ona ul reań baklaǩe jǫǩ giḍileta gurić mandere, adǫ onageye halań ągukeťa; ar daǩte ąruṕ saphakate onageye jǫmketa. Mẹnkhan onae jǫmkette unige lahare dǫe hǫṛmǫteyena. Mẹnkhan Isor baba dǫ ẹn hiloǩrege raje mẹn oṭowade tahẽkana, Tǫbẹ khan laharen gidrą dǫ iṅge imąńme.

Adǫ uni gidrą hoyoǩ reań din dǫ sẹṭẹrena. Adǫ raj dǫ barea ghąṇṭiye tǫlketa, miť dǫ nanha ar miť dǫ moṭa saḍeǩ lekanaǩ; are metaťkoa, Koṛa gidrąi hoelen khan moṭa ghąṇṭi ruipe ar kuṛi gidrąi hoelen khan nanhawaǩ ghąṇṭi ruipe. Ar uni ma dinge sendrae daṛana; oṛaǩre dǫ onkae ląi oṭo akawaťkoa.

Khan uni huḍińićren gidrąi hoyoǩ lągidoǩ kana. Khange onko hiromea sikiṛte uni dǫko metae kana, Ma na culhą bhugąǩre bǫhǫǩ dǫ bhoraotam, gidrą hoyoǩ jǫkhẹnko metae kana.

To do so would be most revolting to any one; it shows her great desire for getting children.

Then as he had told him, he threw with his left hand and received with his right hand, and taking the mangoes home he gave them to his senior queen and said to her: "All of you divide these and eat them." Then, having divided them, they all ate, that is to say, six queens ate, but the youngest queen was at the time occupied with something or other, so they did not give her anything.

Afterwards she cleaned her teeth and mouth and said to the others: "Give me, my elder sister, the mango that the king brought a while ago. Now I have leisure and shall eat it"; but she said to her: "It is with her over there." When she went to her and asked her, this one also said to her: "It is with her over there." In this way they were excusing themselves and charging one another, and did not give her anything. You see, what should they give her? They had, you see, already eaten all the mangoes, and no one gave her anything.

Now she herself had swept up the mango rind and thrown it away on the dung-hill, and she picked it up, and having washed it in water she ate this[6]. And as she ate this, she was the first to become with child. But that day Father Isor had said to the king: "The child that is first born you shall give to me."

Now the day for the child's coming arrived, and the king hung up two bells, one that had a tiny sound, and one with a deep sound, and said to the people: "If it is a boy that is born, sound the bell with the deep sound, and if it is a girl, then sound the bell with the tiny sound." He himself was in the habit of daily going out hunting, and before going out he instructed them in this way at home.

Now the youngest queen's child was just going to come. Then her co-wives out of jealousy and hate said to her: "You, young one, put your head into the hole of the fire-place." They said so to her just at that time.

Mẹnkhan gidrạ dọ bareakin janamena. Adọ onko hapṛak̕ rạni dọ unkin gidrạ bọdọl barea ṭhuṭki jọnọk̕ uni sorreko dọhọadea. Adọ banar ghạṇṭiko ruketa. Ar unkin gidrạ dọ kuṅkạl hasako ạgui ona ghaḍlak̕re idikateko bhoraokatkina. Adọ onakin ghạṇṭi saḍe añjọmte uni raj dọe ńir hẹćena; adọe kuliketkoa, Cele gidrại hoeyena? Adọko lạiae kana, Ṭhuṭki jọnọk̕ kana. Adọ ona ńẹlkate raj dọ ạḍiye bhabnayena. Ar unkin gidrạ ma kuṅkạl hasa ghaḍlak̕reko giḍikatkina.

Adọ kuṅkạl haṛam ar kuṅkạl buḍhi bhajan benao lạgit̕ hasa ạgukin sẹnlena, adọkin sẹn sẹṭẹren khan ona hasa ghaḍlak̕re barea gidrạkin ńamketkina. Unkin gidrạ ńẹlte kuṅkạl haṛam dọ aćren buḍhiye metae kana, Hasam idia sẹ gidrạm idikina?

Adọ uni dọe mẹnketa, Iń dọ gidrạgeń idikina. Adọ unkin gidrạgekin idiketkina. Adọ idikate unkin dọ mẹrọm toa ar gại toatekin ạsul haraketkina; enrehọ̃ raj dọ bae baḍaeleta unkin gidrạ reaṅ dọ.

Adọ inạk̕tege arhọ̃ onko turui gọṭẹn rạniren turui gọṭẹn gidrạko hara buruyena; onate raj dọ ạḍiye khusiyena onko turui gọṭẹn era sãote. Mẹnkhan chuṭki era dọ kulhi mucạtre họpọn họpọne kumbạwadea, ar ọṇḍẹgeye kolkadea, ać mọtọgeye tahẹna bạpuṛić ona oṛak̕re.

Ar noko turui gọṭẹn gidrạ họ̃ bại bạiteko hara buruyena. Ar unkin kuṅkạl ṭhenkin gidrạ makin hara juạnen.

Ar onko turui gọṭẹn gidrạ dọ kaṭren sadọmko tahẽkantakoa. Ar unkin kuṅkạl ṭhenkin hara akan unkinren dọ hasaren sadọmkin tahẽkana.

Adọ sadọmante onko turui boeha dọ akoren apat rajak̕ pukhrite sadọm dak̕ ńũko idikoa; adọ nonka sadọmko metakotakoa, Ma kaṭren sadọm mẽṛhẽt̕ reaṅ jhin, adọ baba pukhri reaṅ dak̕ ńũipe. Adọ unkin kuṅkạl ṭhen gidrạ họ̃ uni rajak̕ pukhritegeko idikina dak̕ ńũ, adọko ńapama, mẹnkhan unkin họ̃ unkin sadọm dọ

Two children were born. Then the senior queen put two worn-out brooms near the mother instead of the two children, whereupon they sounded both bells. Thereupon they took the two children away to a pit whence potters were bringing clay, and put them down there. Now, hearing the sound of both bells, the king came running, and asked them what kind of child had been born. They said to him: "It is worn-out brooms." Having seen these, the king became very grieved. As you know, the two children they had thrown away in the potter's clay-pit.

Now two potters, man and wife, had gone to bring clay to make pots, and when they came there to the clay-pit, they found the two children. Seeing these two children the potter said to his wife: "Will you carry clay home, or will you take the two children home?"

She replied: "I shall take the children home." Whereupon they did so, and, having taken them home, they fed them with goat milk and cow's milk and let them grow up. Still the king did not know anything about these two children.

As time passed, the six children that the other six queens had got also grew up, and the king was very pleased and glad together with these six wives. But for the youngest wife he built a tiny hut at the end of the village street, and sent her there, and she, poor one, was living alone by herself in that house.

Now these six children, as told, also gradually grew up, and the two children with the potter grew into maturity.

Now those six children had horses of wood, and the two that had grown up with the potter had horses of clay.

The six brothers took their horses to their father, the king's, tank to let them drink water, and they spoke in this way to their horses: "Wooden horses with iron bridles, drink water from father's tank." And the two children who were with the potter also took their horses to the king's tank to drink, and all of them met there; these two also spoke in the same way to their two

onkagekin metakina, Mạṭi ka ghoṛa loha ka jhin, baba ka pukhrime pạni piolhet'. Ona katha añjo̱mkate onko turui go̱ṭe̱n gidrạ do̱ko me̱na, unkinko ruhet'kina, Noa ma aleren baba reaṅ pukhri kana; abenren kuṅkạl baba reaṅ pukhri ma baṅ kana; cedak'ben me̱net'a, Ạliṅren baba reaṅ pukhri dak' ñũiben me̱nte. Ado̱ dinge onko do̱ onkageko jhogṛak'a.

Ado̱ oṛak're se̱nkateko lạia, apan ạpin akoren eṅgat apat ṭhen se̱nkateko lạia. Me̱nkhan noko gidrạ reaṅ bicạr do̱ o̱ko̱e hõ baṅko phaṇḍao daṛeak' kana. Me̱nkhan unkin kuṅkạl ṭhenkin gidrạ do̱ dinge toakin idia rajak' oṛak'te. Me̱nkhan noko bạṭki erako do̱ko baḍae ñamket'a, Nukin do̱ aboren kangeakin me̱nte.

Ado̱ onko rạni do̱ unkin gidrạ lạḍuko miṭhạikoko emakina onare bis mesalkate. E̱nte unkin do̱ go̱ćkin reaṅ mo̱tlo̱b tahe̱kana.

Me̱nkhan unkin gidrạ ona lạḍuko do̱ baṅkin jo̱ma, ona do̱ oṛak'te-kin ạguia, ado̱ ona laḍu do̱ kuṅkạl buḍhikin emadea. Me̱nkhan uni kuṅkạl buḍhi do̱ ona lạḍu ać hõ bae jo̱mlet'a, mit'ṭaṅ kạhui emadea. Uni kạhu do̱ ona lạḍui jo̱mket', uni kạhu do̱e go̱ćena. Ado̱ uni kạhu ñe̱lte unkin gidrạ do̱ ạḍi ãṭkin bo̱to̱rena.

Ado̱ uni kuṅkạl buḍhikin metae kana, E̱ go̱, ạliṅ do̱ toa do̱ o̱ho̱liṅ idilea, mit' din do̱ ạliṅ do̱ko e̱m go̱ćliṅa nãhãk'. Ado̱e sikhạuket'kina, metat'kinae, Aloben jo̱ma, beṭa, aben do̱, jãhãtinạk'ko metaben, Ne̱ bạhu jo̱mben. Me̱nkhan aben do̱ ona sanam oṛak'te ạguiben.

Khange sermaren Isor baba do̱ jugi gosãe bheskate uni raj ṭhene calaoena. E̱nte pạhile metade tahe̱kana, Laha ho̱po̱n do̱ iñge imạñme. Ado̱ gidrạ ko̱ko̱e me̱nte ado̱ uni raje metae kana, Dini pạhil gidrạ do̱ imạñme.

Ado̱ uni raj bạṭkiren gidrạ ạgukate uni gosãeye samaṅadea; ado̱e metae kana, Nũk'ũi ane̱ć pạhil gidrạ do̱.

Ado̱ unre gosãeye ro̱ṛ ruạṛket'a, Nui gidrạ do̱e baṅ kana.

Khange uni raje me̱nket'a, Nui gidrạ kangeae. Me̱nkhan uni gosãe do̱e me̱nket'a, Nui do̱e baṅ kana.

7 They speak Hindi.

clay horses: "Pferd aus Ton, Sattel aus Eisen, trinkt Wasser in Vaters Teich.[7]" Hearing this, the six others would say, scolding them: "Why, this is our father's tank. This is not a tank belonging to your father, the potter. Why are you saying: 'Drink water from our father's tank?'" Every day the children were quarrelling in this way.

Coming home they would go and tell their parents separately; but no one was able to settle the dispute of the children. Now the two children who were with the potter were daily taking milk to the king's house, and the senior queens somehow got to know, viz., these two belong to us.

Then the queens gave these two children lollipops and sweetmeats, after having mixed poison in them, because they wished to kill both of them.

But the two children did not eat these sweetmeats, but took them with them home and gave them to the potter's wife. But the potter's wife did not eat the sweetmeats herself either. She gave them to a crow, and the crow ate the sweetmeats and died. Seeing what happened to the crow the two children became awfully frightened.

They said to the potter's wife: "Mother, we shall never take milk there any more. They will surely some day give us something and kill us." But she admonished them and said to them: "Do not eat, children, however much they say to you, 'Please eat, youngsters', but bring it all home here."

Now Father Isor of Heaven in this guise of the yogi Gosae went to the king. He had, as you know, previously said to him, "Give me the child first born." Then, in order to demand the child, he said to the king, "Please give me your first child."

Having brought the senior queen's child the king placed him before the Gosae and said to him: "Here he is, the first child."

The Gosae then answered: "It is not this child."

The king then said: "It is this child;" but the Gosae again said: "No, it is not this one."

Khange uni raj doe metadea uni gosãe, Ẹnḍẹkhan dọ ma ńamjoṅme. Adọ uni gosãe dọe mẹnkeťa, Kuṅkạl oṛaǩre amren pạhil gidrạ dọ menaǩkina, do ạgukinpe.

Adọ raj unkin gidrạ ạǩgu sipạhiye kolkeťkoa. Khange sipạhi dọ raj reaṅ hukum lekate kuṅkạl oṛaǩteko calaoena. Adọ sẹnkate sipạhi kuṅkạlko metae kana, Dẹnkin nukin gidrạ dọ ẹmoǩme; ẹnte raje khọjeťkina.

Khange uni kuṅkạl dọe mẹnkeťa, onko sipạhiye metako kana, Nitgẹ gidrạ dọ raj oṛaǩ khonkin hẹć akana; mẹnkhan gidrạ dọ ọhọń sẹn ocolekina; gidrạ sãote jãhãn galmarao rajaǩ menaǩtae khan hẹćkate gidrạ sãoteye galmarao ma.

Ona jobab sipạhiko ńamkeťte hẹćkate rajko lạiadea. Kuṅkạl dọ nonkae mẹneťa, Gidrạ dọ nitgẹ raj oṛaǩ khonkin hẹć akana; adọ raj gidrạ ceť lạgiťe khọjeťkina? Mẹnkhan raj dọ gidrạ sãote galmarao menaǩtae khan nọṇḍẹye hijuǩ ma.

Khange uni raj dọ onako kathae aṅjọmkeť khan uni raj dọ uni gosãe sọṅgẹkate kuṅkạl oṛaǩtekin calaoena. Adọ uni kuṅkạl haṛam dọe ńẹl daramkeťkinte unkin gidrạ dọ awa bhitrireye bhoraokeťkina. Ona aware dọ bhajanko rapaǩeť tahẹ̃kana.

Adọ uni gosãe dọ unkin gidrạ ona awa bhitri khone ọr oḍokkeť-kina. Unre uni gosãe raje lạiae kana, Nukin gidrạ dọ amren chuṭki rạniren pạhil họpọn kanakin. Amren onko turui gọṭẹn rạni menaǩkoa, onko dọ ạḍi badmas kanako; onkoge nukin dọ kuṅkạl hasa ghaḍlaǩreko giḍileťkina. Kuṅkạl dọ emanteaǩ bhajan benao lạgiť kuḍi, ṭạmni ar khạclạǩante hasa ạgukin sẹnlena. Adọ unre unkin gidrạkin idikeťkina, adọkin ạsul hara akaťkina nukin gidrạ dọ.

Unre kuṅkạl haṛam ar buḍhikin unkin gidrạkin metaťkina, Do, gidrạ, calaǩben, abenaǩ jaṅ ar jel dọń rapaǩ isin akaťtabena. Abenben gọćkoa, ar aben dọ baṅko gọć daṛeabena. Adọ unkin gidrạ dọkin mohṇḍayena uni gosãe sãote, adọko sẹn sẹṭẹrena. Adọ uni gosãe unkin gidrại metaťkina, Ma aben dọ sadọm saṗ hataṛeben, iń dọń um hẹćlenge. Adọ uni gosãe umuǩe calaoena.

Then the king said to the Gosae: "Then please find it." The Gosae then said: "Your two first children are in the potter's house. Please bring them."

The king then sent peons to bring these two children, and the peons went in accordance with the king's order to the potter's house. Having arrived there the peons said to the potter: "Please give over these two children. The king is asking for them."

The potter then said, that is to say, he said to the peons: "This moment the two children have come from the king's house; I shall certainly not let the children go there. If the king has anything to say to the children, let him come and talk to them here."

When the peons got this answer, they went to the king and told him: "The potter says: 'The children have just now come from the king's house, then for what purpose is the king asking for them? If the king has anything to say to the children, let him come here'."

When the king heard this, he went together with the Gosae to the potter's house; when the old potter saw them coming, he put the two children inside his kiln. They were burning pots in this kiln.

The Gosae pulled the two children out from the kiln. Then the Gosae told the king: "These two children are your youngest queen's first children. You have those six other queens; they are great rogues. They threw these two in the pit from which the potter fetches his clay. The potter and his wife had gone there with a spade, a hoe and a basket, to bring clay to make pots. Then they brought these two children away; and they have fed and kept these two, so that they have grown up."

The potter and his wife then said to the children: "Please go, children, I have roasted and cured your bones and your flesh. You will kill them; but they will not be able to kill you." Then the two children started together with the Gosae, and reached the king's house. The Gosae then said to the children: "Now you take hold of the horse for a moment. I am just going to have a bath." Whereupon the Gosae went to have his bath.

Unre uni sado̱m unkin gidrạimetakin kana, Cak', bacha, aben do̱ nui sãote do̱ben he̱ćena, nit do̱e mak'bena nãhãk'. Ado̱ sado̱mkin kuli ruạṛkedea, E̱ṇḍe̱khan ạliń do̱ cet'liń upạia?

Unre uni sado̱me metat'kina, Ma ạḍi usạrate ińạk' deare de̱ć ho̱dok'ben. Ado̱kin de̱ćente nonkan jaegateye idiket'kina, are uduk'at'kina, are metat'kina, Noko ńe̱lkoben, tinạk'e mak' akat'koa; tinạk' bo̱ho̱k'e bhorao akat'a kũire.

Unre onko mak' bo̱ho̱k'ko ro̱ṛket'a, Uh bacha, cedak'ben he̱ćena? Aben hõe mak'bena nãhãk'.

Unre unkin gidrạkin ro̱ṛ ruạṛket'a, E̱ṇḍe̱khan ạliń do̱ cekateliń bańcaok'a? Unre onko kũirenko me̱nket'a, Aleben bańcaolele khan aben ho̱le bańcaobena.

Ado̱kin ro̱ṛ ruạṛket'a, E̱ṇḍe̱khan ape do̱ cekateliń bańcaopea? Ado̱ onko pạhil mak' oco akan ho̱ṛko me̱nket'a, Indrạson bhubo̱nre sat ṭi rạni menak'koa dak' bhitrire; onko ṭhenben calaolen khan hawapuri baṅglaben ạguia; ado̱ ruạṛ he̱ćkate aleben bańcao daṛealea. Ar hawapuri baṅgla do̱ chuṭki rạni ṭhen menak'a, dak'ben dalle khan se̱ṅge̱l leka jolok'a, ado̱ unre dak'reben do̱n khadlek'a. Ar nit gosãe caoleye curuja, ado̱ unreye metabena, Ma ikṛumok'ben. Ado̱ unre me̱nben, Ạliń do̱ baliń baḍaea; raj ho̱po̱n kanaliń; uduk' cet' daṛealiń khanem do̱ pase̱liń onka daṛekea. Ado̱ nãhạk'e uduk' cet'abena, ado̱ aben do̱ tarwaṛe sap'kate unige mageben. Mak' o̱ṭokate sado̱mre de̱jok'ben. Ar bar ghaṛa ṭaka menak'a; ona hõ idi toraeben. Ar hawapuri baṅgla ạgukate jạruṛ aleben bańcaolea; baben bańcaolele khan ạḍi marań kạireben ńũruk'a nãhãk'. Nit me̱n, ruạṛben, okare sado̱me do̱ho̱let'bena.

Ado̱ o̱ṇḍe̱gekin ruạṛena, ado̱kin ńe̱lkedea uni gosãe do̱ um rakap'kate bahae sisit' kana. Ado̱ se̱ṭe̱rkate unkin do̱ baha ḍalwak'e

---

8 Indrason, the throne of Indra; as the following shows, the Santal conception is more than hazy on this point.

9 lit. the airworld bungalow. The narrator has evidently no mental picture of what this may be. The story seems to presuppose that it is a small thing that may be easily carried away.

At that moment the horse spoke to the children saying: "Why, my dears, did you come with this man? He will presently cut you down and kill you." Then they asked the horse: "Then what shall we do to save ourselves?"

The horse then said to them: "Please mount my back as quickly as you can," whereupon they got up, and he took them away to a certain place that he showed them saying: "Look at these here how many he has cut down and killed; look how many heads he has thrown into this well."

Then the cut heads spoke: "Alas, my dears, why have you come? Presently he will cut you two down and kill you also."

Then the two children answered: "How then shall we be saved?" Those in the well then replied: "If you will save us we shall save you too."

They answered: "How then shall we save you?" Then the people who had previously been cut down and killed said: "In the Indrason[8] world there are seven queens in the water; if you go to them, you may bring the air-castle[9]; then, having returned thence, you will be able to save us. The air-castle is with the youngest queen. When you beat the water, it will flare up like fire; then jump into the water. Now the Gosae will put some handfuls of rice on the ground and will say to you: 'Kneel down'. Then say: 'We do not know this. We are the children of a king. If you show it to us and teach us, we may perhaps be able to do as you say.' Presently he will show you how; then you take the sword and cut him down. When you have cut him down, mount the horse. There are also two brass-pots full of money. This you must also take away with you; and having brought the air-castle you must be sure to save us. If you do not do so, you will fall into very great sin. Now have a care. Go back to where the horse put you down."

Then they went back there and saw the Gosae, who, after having come up from his bath, was plucking flowers. Having reached calatkina, ar boṅgakin lạgit́e sotok̀ idiket́kina. Uni gosãe dọ siṅjọ sakamko, bahako ar guṛ, gọtọmkoe dhũạket́a; khange siṅjọ sakamre caoleye curućket́ khan unkin hõ bọhọk̀reye sindurat́kina; adọe metakin kana, Ma noa caolere ạtiṅben.

Adọkin metadea, Baba guru gosãe, ạliṅ dọ baliṅ bạḍaea, ạliṅ dọ raj họpọn kanaliṅ; mẹnkhan nonkan bẹbọhar dọ baṅliṅ ńẹl akat́a, ar bạḍae hõ baṅliṅ bạḍaea. Mẹnkhan amem lại cet́aliṅ khan dọliṅ onka daṛekegea pasẹ.

Adọ unre uni gosãeye uduk̀ cet́akin kana. Adọ unre unkin gidrạ dọ ạḍi usạrate tarwaṛe saṕkate uni gosãekin mak̀kedea. Adọ unre ona bar ghaṛa ṭaka sadọmrekin ladeket́te oṛak̀te kin hẹćena. Adọ ona bar ghaṛa ṭaka dọ unkin eṅgatkin hạṭiṅat́kina. Mit́ ghaṛa dọ janam eṅgatkin emadea, ar mit́ ghaṛa dọ ạk̀sul eṅgatkin emadea.

Adọko tahẹna uni janam eṅgat sãotege. Adọkin lại at́kina, uni ạk̀sul eṅgat ar janam eṅgat uni koṛae lại at́kina, Gọ, iṅ dọ hawapuri baṅgla ạguṅ calak̀ kana; adọ mit́ cando reaṅ jọmiṅ khọj kana. Khange mit́ cando reaṅ khorcakin emadete ać janam babae lại adea, Baba, iṅ dọ gapa hawapuri baṅgla ạk̀gu calak̀ iṅ mẹnet́a.

Janam apat dọe mẹnket́a, Beṭa, am eskardọ cekatem calak̀a? Ạḍi kul, tạruṕ ar bana menak̀koa, goe, kumbhiṛ, rakhas, taṛoka emanko janwar menak̀koa. Adọe mẹnket́a uni koṛa dọ, Adọ baba, iṅ dọṅ mẹnket́te dọṅ calak̀gea, iṅak̀ kopalre jage menak̀; onko ako ṭhenge menak̀koa; iṅhõ nãhãk̀ iṅ ṭhengeṅ tahẹna.

Unre onko turui boeha hõko mẹnket́a, Baba, ale hõle calak̀a, dada eskar cedak̀e calak̀a.

---

10 Ægle Marmelos, Correa; the leaves are used in connexion with sacrifices and ceremonies.

11 Sindur is the red lead or vermilion, used for religious purposes, also by the Santals. What is here told is in accordance with the proceedings when an animal is to be sacrificed.

12 The brass-pots here mentioned are large and in the better class of house-holds used for drawing water. It is not uncommon that people bury money in such

there he handed them a basket full of flowers, whereupon he took them along to sacrifice them. The Gosae smoked bael[10] leaves, flowers, molasses and clarified butter; having put handfuls of rice down on the bael leaves, he applied sindur[11] also to the heads of these two, and said to them: "Now feed on this rice."

They said to him: "Father Gosae, we do not know this. We are the children of a king. We have not seen any such performance, nor do we know; but if you will teach us, we may perhaps be able to do as you say."

Then the Gosae was showing them to instruct them. At that moment the two children in great hurry took the sword and beheaded the Gosae. Thereupon they loaded the two brass-pots[12] with money on the horse and went home. These two brass-pots with money they divided between their two mothers, one brass-pot they gave to their real mother, and one brass-pot they gave to their foster mother.

After this they stayed with their real mother. Then they said, that is to say, the boy[13] said to his foster-mother and his real mother: "Mother, I am off to bring the air-castle and want food for one month." Then they gave him this, and he said to his real father: "Father, I intend to go to-morrow to bring the air-castle."

His father then said: "Son, how will you be able to go alone? There are any number of tigers, leopards, bears; wild bisons, alligators, ogres and dragons[14], and various animals live there." The boy then said: "Well, father, as I have said so, I shall go, whatever may be my fate; they live where they are, and as for me, I also shall presently stay with myself."

Then the six other brothers also said: "Father, we will also go. Why shall our eldest brother go alone?"

brass-pots; the Santals tell stories of such having been done, not by Santals, but by Hindus. Mistrust has often caused people to bury money, in stead of e. g. giving it to a banker.

13 The other twin is not mentioned any more.

14 The last mentioned being is supposed to be something like an ogre.

Unre raje metatkoa, Apepe calak khan do songetege tahenpe. Ado ina dosar hilok doko mohndayena. Onko turui boeha do hatireko deċena, adoko mohndayena, Ar kuṅkalkin asul haralede uni ma bania sadomre mitten khatlak parkome tolketa; ado huka condakate deċente ńū ńūteye mohndayena.

Janam eṅgat ar kuṅkal budhi do uni korakin metadea, Beta, am tisem ruara, menkhan aliń do teheń otreliń gitiċ kana; ado am aurim ruar habiċ aliń do baliń beret hataroka. Ado am ruar-kateliń ńelmea, unrege dataunі saphakate dakaliń joma.

Adoko calaoente mitten dosra raj disomteko boloyena, adi marań urni birko seterena. Ado onko turui boeha do birko bolok jokhen, hati cot khon dhiṅki lekan biṅko ńel ńamkedea; uni biń ńelteko botorente ado uniko metae kana, Dada, bam heċ hodok kana, amgele ńel horetmea; baṅkhan bam mena, bagiadińako. Ado baṅko laiae kana, lahare biń menaea mente do.

Ado ako do adiko tayomena, ado pharak khonakgeko ńele kana, bhalae jomea se bań. Uni jomkate bińe darle khan adobon senoka nãhãk. Uni sadomanteye senen kora jome lagitge uni biń do adi cot koyokkate uni sengeye hijuk kana. Unre uni kora do tarware tahẽkantaete uni dhiṅki bińe ńel ńamkede khan do, ona tarwareye or boċketa, adoe mak goċkedea. Ado seṅgele jolkette biń cotrege durupkateye ńūńū kana.

Unre onko turui boeha do pharak khonko ńelkedete uni then bai baiteko sen seterena. Adoko metae kana, Dada, am dom laha gotentabona, ale do hati bae heċ hijuk kana. Unre uni korae

15 The dhiṅki or husking-machine is a piece of timber, some six feet or more long and some six to eight inches thick (square); it has a pestle fixed in one end; an axle through the log near the other end is placed on two pieces of wood fixed in the ground; the whole is worked by the operator stepping on the one end and thereby lifting up the other end with the pestle; stepping down from it the pestle falls down into a mortar in the ground. When the snake is said to be as big as a dhiṅki, the tertium comparationis is not the length of the timber, but its thickness. It is rather strange, when a Santal tries to show the size of a snake he will practically always do it by showing with his fingers how

The king then said to them: "If you go, then stay together." Then, the next day, they started. The six brothers mounted an elephant and started, and the boy that the potters had supported until he grew up tied a small bedstead to his country pony, and, having lighted his hookah, he mounted the horse, and, smoking as he went along, he started.

The real mother and the potter's wife said to the boy: "Son, when will you return? We two are to-day lying down on the ground, and until you return we shall not get up. When we see you return, then only we shall clean our mouth and take food."

Then they went and entered the country of another king; they reached a very large primeval forest. Just when they were entering the forest, the six brothers sitting on the elephant from there caught sight of a snake big as a husking-machine[15]; seeing this snake, they got frightened and called out to the other: "Brother[16], you are slow coming, we are waiting for you; if you do not come, you will say: they left me." But they did not tell him that a snake was there in front.

They themselves kept far behind, and from a distance they were observing him, whether the snake would eat him or not. "If the snake runs away after having eaten him, then we shall go along." Now the young man who went along on horseback, — in order to eat him the snake was coming with its head high up. Then as soon as the young man, who had a sword, caught sight of the huge snake, he drew his sword and cut the snake so that it died. Thereupon he lighted a fire, and, sitting on the snake, he was smoking.

The six brothers saw him from afar, and slowly went up to him and said to him: "Brother, you have got the start of us; as for us, the elephant does not come quickly." The young man then

thick it is, although one may hear them speak of snakes as jeleń hoṛ, long people. To them the size round the body indicates the strength.

16 It might be noted that the text here and further, when this brother is addressed, always has dada, elder brother; in the translation 'brother' is used.

metatkoa, Acha, hạti bae tarạm tarạmet khan, mẹ dela lahaktabonpe; ape tayọm tayọmte iń dọ bạị bạiteń sẹn jarwaka.

Onko turui boeha dọ hạtiko lahakedete ona urni birko parọmkette adọ hạti ạḍi ạṭko lagakedea, mẹnwanako, aboge bon laha hodoka, Ọṇḍẹ khon dọ arhõ dosra[?]raj disomko bọlọyena, ona disomre dọ miṭṭẹn hạtiye bhalok akana.

Uni dọ sadọmante ạḍi sạṅgińreko bạgiadete adọko kọyọk barayede kana, adọ uniye sẹṭẹrente adọ bańko lạiae kana, bhalok hạti menaea mẹnte. Adọko metae kana, Enan khonle kọyọk horetmea. Adọko metae kana, Dada, ma amge lahakme.

Adọ uni dọ sẹṅgẹle jolkette hukạị condaketa, adọ ńũ ńũteye mohṇḍayena; are metatkoa, Ma ape hõ bạị bạite hijukpe. Adọko metae kana, Ma nãhãk dada, mit ghạritegele tiokmea nãhãk.

Adọe lahayen khan uni bhalok hạtiye ńẹlkedea, hor phẹḍregeye burum akana; hạti ṭhene sẹn sẹṭẹrente uni bhalok hạti dọ aḍraoateye ńir beretena. Unre uni kora dọ sadọm cọṭ khone ńir phẹḍena; hạti dọ suṇḍe sapkedea are capat gọtkadea onko turui boeha hana sate.

Unre onko uni bhalok hạtiko ńẹlkedea ako phẹḍre, adọ hako pako uni hạtiko lagakedea akoren dọ. Adọ sẹnkate uniko lạiae kana, Dada, bańdọ cọṭ khon, bańdọ oka khon hạti miṭṭẹne ńurhạyena. Adọe metako kana, Cedak ya bape ạguledea, juri jurikin hoekoktapea. Adọko metae kana, Dada, uni hạti bọtọrgele ńẹle kana bir hạti leka.

Adọe metatkoa, Ma ya, nit dọ apege lahaktabonpe. Adọ onkoko lahayente adọ arhõ onkageko bạgiadea. Adọ calak calakte rakhaspuri disomteko sẹṭẹrena. Mẹnkhan rakhasko ńẹlkedea, horreye teṅgo akana, ar ọt ar sermae cahap akata; uniko ńẹlkedete adọko-

---

17 The word used is the same as is used about animals attacked by rabies. Santals having very little experience of elephants will confound the state of elephants called 'must' with rabies.

18 The hookah or hubble-bubble is lighted by putting a piece of live coal on the tobacco in the bowl.

19 So literally.

said to them: "Well, as the elephant does not walk quickly, come along, you get on ahead; I shall follow you at my leisure gradually."

The six brothers went ahead on the elephant, and got through the primeval forest driving the elephant very hard; they said to themselves: "We shall get ahead in a hurry." From there they entered the country of still another king, and in this country an elephant had become mad[17].

Having left their brother with his horse far behind they were looking out for him; when he came up, they did not tell him that there was a mad elephant there, but said to him: "We have been waiting for you for a long time," and added: "You brother, go ahead."

He lighted a fire and with this his hookah[18], whereupon he started, smoking as he went along, saying to the others: "Now, you too come along at your leisure." "Presently, brother," they answered him, "in a short while we shall catch up with you."

When he had got ahead of the others, he saw the mad elephant, lying down near the road; as he reached him, the mad elephant jumped to his legs trumpeting. The young man then jumped down from his horse; he took hold of the elephant's trunk and flung him away to the other side of his brothers.

Now these suddenly saw this mad elephant near themselves, and they drowe the elephant, that is to say, their own, as quickly as they could. Having reached their brother they said to him: "Brother, whether from above or from who knows where, an elephant fell down." "Why, you fellows," he said to them, "why did you not bring him? then you might have had a pair." "Brother," they answered, "this elephant was fearful to look at, like a wild one."

"Now, you," he said to them, "you get ahead;" whereupon they, doing so, again left him behind in the same way as before. As they passed along, they reached the ogre-world country[19], and they saw the ogre, he was standing on the road, agape so that his mouth reached from the earth to the sky; when they saw

pạc ruạṛena hạtiante; adọ hạti khonakko phẹḍena. Adọko mẹnketa, Hapẹ ya, dada heć ocowae; uniye heclen khan unigebon lahakaea. Adọ dakako jọm baṛaketa.

Adọ thoṛa ghạṛi khange sadọmteye sẹṭẹrena. Adọko metae kana, Dada, daka dọm jọm akata sẹ baṅ? Baṅ khan dela jọmme. Adọ uni hõ sadọm khonake phẹḍena, adọ um baṛakate uni hõe jọmketa. Adọ onkoe metatkoa, Ma usạrate hạti sapṛaoepe, delabon sọṅgẹtege. Adọko mohṇḍayena. Họr họrteko lại idiae kana, Dada, ma sẹ uni ṅẹleme, cele uni dọe cahap akata ọt ar serma.

Adọko metae kana, Ma dada, niạ dhao dọ baṅcaokaleme. Adọe metatkoa, Delabon ya. Adọko mẹneta, Dada, ale dọ ọhọle lahalena. Adọ uni koṛae metako kana, Babae mẹn akata, Alope apan ạpinoka, mittege tahẹnpe. Adọe metako kana, Iṅe jọmeṅ khan ape hõe jọmpea; ar iṅ bae jọmeṅ khan ape hõ bae jọmpea.

Adọko metae kana, Adọ, dada, ma amge lahakme, am tayọm tayọmte ale dọle calaka. Adọ uni dọ ạḍi sạṅgiṅe laha idiyena. Onko turui boeha dọ ạḍi ãṭko bhabna joṅ kana, mẹnjoṅ kanako, Teheṅ dọe jọm ocoketbona nãhãk rakhas ṭhen dọ. Adọko mẹnjoṅ kana, Hapẹ ya bon ṅẹlea, bhalae jọmea sẹ baṅ.

Adọ uni koṛa dọ rakhas ṭhene sẹṭẹrente uni rakhase sapkedea; ar rakhasak jaṅgae pẹṭẹć rạputkettaea; pẹṭẹć rạputkette parkọm baberteye tọlkedea, ar sadọmak caṇḍbọlreye tọlkedea. Adọ inạk-tege onko turui boeha hõko sẹṭẹrena. Adọe metako kana, Nit maṅ kạbu akadea, teheṅ khub jel dakaepe, uni rakhasbon jọm ocoyea.

Adọko calaoena, adọ calak calakte ạḍi maraṅ mitṭẹn naṅgra-hako ṅamketa. Adọko mẹnwana, Ma nọṇḍẹge bon ḍeraka. Adọ ọṇḍẹge mitṭẹn dare buṭạreko ḍerayena. Adọ ona naṅgraharen họṛ sanamko họhọatkoa; arko lạiako kana, Pon mũṛĩ caole

20 The word used may mean either to go ahead, in front, or simply to go along, proceed.

21 The maund, a common unit in India, corresponds to about 40 kg.

him, they turned back with their elephant, and got down from him and said: "Wait, you, let our brother come; when he comes we shall send him ahead." Whereupon they took their food.

Shortly afterwards he came riding, and they said to him: "Brother, have you had your food or not? If not, come and eat." Then he dismounted, and, having had a bath, he also ate, whereupon he said to the others: "Now be quick and make the elephant ready; come, let us get along together." Having started they spoke to him, as they were passing along: "Brother, look, look at him there! What kind can he be he who has opened his mouth so that it reaches from the earth to the sky?"

"This time, brother," they said to him, "do save us." "Come along, you fellows," he answered; but they said: "No, brother, we shall never go further[20]." The young man then said to them: "Father has said: 'Don't separate, stay together';" and he added: "If he eats me, he will eat you too, and if he does not eat me, he will not eat you either."

"Then, brother," they said, "you go in front, we shall follow you;" whereupon he went on a long way in front of the others. The six brothers were very anxious and afraid, saying to themselves: "To-day he will surely let us be eaten by the ogre. Wait," they said, "let us see whether he will eat him or not."

When the young man reached the ogre, he caught hold of him and broke the ogre's leg; having done this, he bound him with some bedstead cord and tied him to the tail of his horse. By this time the six brothers had also come, and he said to them: "Well, now I have subdued him; to-day prepare a large amount of flesh and rice; we shall let the ogre eat."

Then they went, and, as they passed along, they came to a very large town and said: "Let us camp here," whereupon they camped at the foot of a tree. They called out to all the people of this town saying: "Bring four maunds[21] of rice, three castrated goats,

ạguipe, ar pea mẹrọm kạsi ar miṭ ṭin gọtọm ar sasaṅ mọsọla, rakhasle jọm ocoye lạgiṭ. Ar bape ạgui khan noa naṅgrahare nui rakhasle aṛagea, adọ apeye jọm maraopea. Adọ ona bọtọrte sanamko ạgu sorkeṭa, caoleko, mẹrọmko. Adọe metaṭkoa onko turui boeha, Tinaḱpe utu daka daṛeaḱa, adọ nui rakhas hõ emaepe, ar ape hõ jọmpe, ar hạti hõ emaepe.

Adọ mẹrọmko gọćkedea miṭṭen, adọ utu daḱkako ẹhọpena. Ar ać dọ hukại condaketṭe uni rakhas hõ ona parkọmreye tọlkedea, adọ duṛupḱate hukạ ńũńũi ẹhọpena; hukại ńũ bhagaoente adọe kuṇḍlạṅena ona parkọmrege; are metaṭkoa, Ma ya khub jọmpe ńũipe. Enkae mẹnketṭeye jạpiṭ ńọḱketa.

Adọ onko turui boeha dọko mẹnjoṅ kana, Thoṛa ya jạpiṭ ńọḱ ocowae dada dọ; adọ bại bạite raṛa iạ kae ma uni rakhas dọ; iạ rakhasge, ọkọe cọṅ utu daka kate emaea. Ar jãhãnaḱ dadabon edre ocole khan dọe jọm ocobona nãhãḱ.

Unre bại bạite sẹnkate rakhas dọko raṛakadeteko metadea, Mẹn dạṛme hako pako. Rakhas dọ bạpuṛić jaṅga rạpuṭ akadete lẹḍhọḱ lẹḍhọḱe dạṛeṭa; thoṛa gan 'sạṅgińe dạṛkeṭ khan adọko lạiae kana, Dada, hạni tora rakhase dạṛkeṭa.

Adọe metako kana, Pasẹt yape raṛakade? Adọko metae kana, Dada, ale dọ bọtọrte sor hõ bale soroḱ kana. Adọe mẹnketa, Ẹnḍẹkhane dạṛkeṭa. Adọpe daka utukeṭa sẹ baṅ? Adọ jọm baṛakate adọbon uṭhạuḱa. Adọ utu daka jọm baṛakate adọ thoṛako jirạu ńọḱena. Uni koṛa dọ baṛkaćteye jạpiṭketa, adọe udureṭ kana. Onko turui boeha dọko mẹnjoṅ kana, Delabon sẹ ya, dada dọbon bạgi iạwaea.

Adọ onko dọko sapṛaoente hape hapeteko mohṇḍayena. Onkoko sẹnena ạḍi sạṅgiṅ; ona tayọmte nui dọe mohṇḍayena. Adọ ber

[22] Ṭin is the English 'tin'; the tins in which kerosene oil is brought are commonly seen and also used by the people. When such a word is used here, it is something introduced by the narrator. Such a tin takes four-gallons, or a little more.

one tin[22] of clarified butter, turmeric and spices; we are going to let the ogre eat. And if you don't bring, we shall let the ogre loose in the town; then he will eat and make an end of you all." Fearing this they brought it, rice, goats and all, whereupon he said to them, that is to say, to his six brothers: "As much as you are able to prepare of food, make it ready and give the ogre; you also eat and give your elephant also."

Then they killed one goat and commenced to prepare food, and he himself lighted the hookah and also bound the ogre to the bedstead, whereupon he sat down and commenced to smoke; when he had had enough of smoking tobacco, he lay down on the bedstead, saying to the others: "Eat and drink your fill." Having said this he slept a little.

The six brothers said between themselves: "Let our brother sleep a little; let us quietly unloose the ogre; this wretch of an ogre, who is going to give him rice and curry? If we somehow or other should make our brother angry, he will let us be eaten by him."

Thereupon they quietly went and unloosed the ogre, saying to him: "Look out, get away quickly." Now the poor ogre had got his leg broken and was getting away limping; when he had got some distance away, they told their brother: "Brother, look there, the ogre is running away."

"Perhaps," he said to them, "perhaps you set him free?" But they answered him: "We, brother, out of fear we do not even go near to him." "In that case," he said, "he has run away. Have you prepared rice and curry or not? When we have had our food, we shall start." When they had done eating the rice and curry, they rested a while. The young man feigned to sleep and was snoring; the six brothers then said between themselves: "Let us get along, you fellows, let us leave this wretch of a brother here."

Having made themselves ready, they started without making any noise. They went along very far; thereupon he also started,

hasurok jokhen adi marañ birteye boloyena; bir talare mitten adi marañ dolane ńelketa; ado ondeye hohokette rakhasren hoponerae odokena. Uni kora doe menketa, Noa do okoe rajak dolan kana? Ado uni kuri menketa, Noa do rakhaspuri raj reañ dolan kana. Uni kora doe kulikedea, Iñ teheń tahen reañ jaegape em darekiña se bañ? Uni kuri menketa, Em hõle emkema, bañ hõ bañ. Menkhan tahẽ hõm tahẽ dareakgea, tobe iñ go ar iñ baba dokin rakhas kana; pasekin jomme. Ado uni korae menketa, Iñkin jomeń reañ katha do bam badaea. Unre uni rakhas hoponerae menketa, Menkhan manwa hopon do bañkin ńel sahaoetkoa, adokin jometkogea; acha, teheńtet doń oko dohomegea. Ina menkate dolanteye aderkedea. Ar sadom do rakhas hoponerage baekedete jome emadea. Ado ać hõe kulikedea, Am jom lagit cetko jarura se bañ? Uni kora doe menketa, Iñ do jom ńũ bañ jarura; jaegage udukañme.

Ado dolan cotteye rakapkedete ondegeye atetadea. Ado hukai conda ocokedete hukai ńũńũ kana durupkate. Are kukli kana, uni korae kuli ocok kana, metae kanae, Am do okaren mosaphir hor kanam, ar okatem calak kana? Uni kora doe menketa, Iñ doń Satopuri raj hopon kana, ale do eae boehale odok akana; iñren hudiñ boeha do lahateko sen lahayena; hawapuri bañgla aguia mentele senok kana.

Unre uni rakhas hoponerae menketa, Hawapuri bañgla dope agu dareaka ape do? Ado uni korae menketa, Ohole men darelea nitok do ente. Ar rakhas hoponerae menketa, Thakpur nogorpe parom darele nãhĩ tho Hawapuri bañgla dope tioga. Jua enećre onde doko haraoetkoa; okoe jua enećreañ bhede badae khan unigeye jitau dareaka; ar bañ khan bohok hoyo potorkate ghanireko joraoetkoa. Ado raj hopon do uni rakhas hoponerae kuli

23 Dice is very common with certain races; it is not seen practised by the Santals.

24 The oil-mill referred to is that used by the teli caste; it is not a press, but a large receptacle into which the oil seed is put, prepared; to press out the oil, a piece of wood, fixed to an upright, is pulled round; this pulling is done with the help of a bullock. Here men are made to take the bullock's place.

and, at the time of sunset, he entered a very large forest. In the middle of this forest he caught sight of a very large palace, and, as he called out there, a daughter of the ogre came out. "Which king's palace is this?" the young man asked. The girl replied: "This is the palace of the ogre-world king." The young man asked her: "Would you give me a place to stay to-day or how?" The girl replied: "We might give you or we might not; you might certainly stay; but see, my mother and father are ogres; perhaps they might eat you." "You don't know anything about their eating me," the young man said. The daughter of the ogre then said: "But they are not able to stand the look of human beings; they eat them. All right, to-day I shall hide you and let you stay." Having said this she took him into the palace, and the horse the daughter of the ogre also took out of sight, and gave food; thereupon she asked him: "What do you need of food? do you need anything?" The young man replied: "I have no need of food or drink, show me a place to stay."

Then she took him up to the top of the palace, and there she spread something out for him to lie on. Having made her light his hookah for him he sat down and had a smoke. Now she was asking, that is to say, the young man was questioned by her: "You are a wayfarer, where are you from? and where are you going to?" The young man replied: "I am a son of the Satopuri king; seven brothers of us have come away from home; my younger brothers have gone ahead; we are on our way to bring the air-castle."

The ogre girl then said: "Will you be able to bring the air-castle, you?" The young man answered: "We are unable to say as yet, you see." The ogre girl then said: "Only in case you are able to pass the Thakpur Town, you will be able to reach the air-castle. There they beat people by playing at dice[23]; anyone who knows the proper way of playing at dice, he will be able to win; otherwise they shave their heads absolutely bare and yoke them to turn the oil-mill[24]." The prince then asked the ogre girl

nistąkedea, Ẹnḍẹkhan cekateń jitąu parǫm daṛeaka, ona reaṅge lạiąńme.

Unre rakhas hǫpǫnerae lạiadea, Miťṭẹn goḍo baṅkhan cuṭią hǫpǫn tanaḱ am dǫ sabeme, ar mať ṭhoṅgare bhoraokaeme. Adǫ pusiaḱ bǫhǫḱre diąṛa dǫ dǫhǫ ocokom. Adǫ onko tinre jitąuḱ lekam ńẹlkoa, unre am dǫ bąi bąite uni mať ṭhoṅgaren cuṭią dǫ aṛaḱ gǫťkaeme; unre cuṭią sabea mẹnte pusi nãhãḱe dǫna ar diąṛa sẹṅgẹl dǫ ĩṛĩjoḱa; unrege onkoaḱ dan dǫm hatao daṛeaḱa, ẹnḍẹ ẹnẹćem jitąuḱa.

Adǫ enka galmarao galmaraote hukąi ńũńũ kangea, un jǫkhẹn rakhas dǫ kuḍąm sẹnreye hẹć akana; uni rakhas dǫ huką reań saḍeye ańjǫmkeťa, ar thamakur reań base ąikąuketa. Adǫ aćren rakhas buḍhiye lạiae kana, metae kanae, Ẹ rakhas buḍhi, nui menae noa alaṅaḱ dolanre, nuige ińąḱ jaṅga dǫe pẹṭẹć ṛąpuť akaťa; iń dǫ ǫhǫń bǫlǫlena; mẹ dela nǫṇḍẹ khon dǫlań dąṛa; bań khan arhǫe ṛąpuťlaṅa nãhãḱ. Bǫtǫrte adǫkin dąṛketa. Adǫ ẹn hiloḱ dǫ baṅkin bǫlǫlena ona dolante dǫ,

Adǫ thoṛa ghąṛi tayǫmte uni rakhas hǫpǫnera dǫe oḍokena bahrete; adǫe ńẹl baṛayeťkina gǫ ar baba dǫ, teheń dǫ bakin hijuḱ kan dǫ; onage mǫnẹ mǫnẹteye bhabna jǫń kana. Adǫ raj hǫpǫn ṭhengeye ruąṛ calaoena, adǫ raj hǫpǫne metae kana, Iń gǫ baba tikin baṅkin hijuḱ kante iń dǫ bhabnate bąń gitić daṛeaḱ kana; cedaḱ jẹ am hõm jąpida, iń hõń jąpida; ona takrekin sẹṭẹrlen khan bąń disą daramlekin khan am dǫkin gǫćmea; ar phąṛikatekin jǫmmea nãhãḱ.

Unre uni koṛae mẹnketa, uni kuṛiye metadea, Am dǫ am suk leka jąpidme; miť dhao iń dǫ huką condakate imąńme; noa thamakur dǫ ąḍi bas menaḱa; amdaj miť mayel leka calaḱa, noa baste ińkin baḍae daṛeańa. Tinąḱ din dhąbić iń dǫ nǫṇḍẹń

25 The ṭhoṅga, here called 'Bamboo bottle', is a piece of bamboo, a joint, one dividing wall of which forms the bottom of the 'bottle', while the other gets a small or large hole, that may be closed with a piece of wood. Such 'bottles' are fairly common.

further to make sure: "Then how shall I be able to win and pass? Tell me this."

The ogre girl then told him: "Catch a rat or a small mouse, or something like these, and put it into a bamboo bottle[25], and make them put a lamp-stand on a cat's head. Then, when it seems to you as if they are going to win, quietly let out the mouse you have in the bamboo bottle; then the cat will jump to catch the mouse, and the light of the lamp will be extinguished; then you will be able to take their winnings; thus only you will vanquish them."

While they were talking together in this way, he was smoking the hookah; by this time the ogre had come to the back side of the house; he heard the sound of the hookah and felt the smell of the tobacco, whereupon he spoke to his old ogre wife, saying: "Listen, my ogre wife, this one who is now here in our palace, it is he who has broken my leg; I shall certainly not go inside; come, let us get away from here; otherwise he will presently again break both of us." Then they ran away in fear, and that day these two did not enter the palace.

Shortly afterwards the ogre girl went outside; she was looking for her parents, wondering why they were not coming that day; she was feeling anxious on account of this. Then she returned to the prince and said to him: "As my parents are not coming, I am unable to lie down for anxiety; you see you will sleep, I also shall sleep; if they should come at such at time, and I did not become aware of them, they will kill you, and they will cut your limbs off[26] and eat you presently."

The young man then said to the girl: "You sleep and be comfortable; light the hookah once more, and give it to me; this tobacco has a very strong smell; it spreads and is felt a full mile away; smelling this they will be able to know about me. So long as I stay here, all this time your parents will never come near

[26] The expression is the same as is used about cutting the leg and shoulder of an animal.

tahẹna, unạk̕ din dhạbić am gọ am baba nọṇḍẹ dọ ọhọkin hader daṛelena. Unre rakhas họpọnerae mẹnket̕a, Am dọkin bạḍae akat̕mete? Unre uni koṛae mẹnket̕a, Iń hijuk̕ jọkhẹn am baba sãoteń ńapamlena; unreye alae akawadińa noa oṛak̕ dọ; hukạ reaṅ sọbdọe atẹnket̕te uni dọ nitok̕ dọ bae hijuk̕a nọṇḍẹ dọ. Adọkin tahẽyena, bana họṛgekin jaegayena.

Adọ dosar hilok̕ aṅga marsalenteye mẹnket̕a, Nitok̕ dọń calak̕a, iń dọ ẹnte ińren turui boehako sẹn lahayena, ma ẹṇḍẹkhan am dọ tahẹnme. Unre uni rakhas họpọnerae mẹnket̕a, Teheń dọ tahẹnme, teheń dọ tahẹnme baṛẹ, ińhõ iń gọ baba tikinkin hẹćlen khan iń hõ am sãoteń sẹnkok̕a. Unre uni koṛae mẹnket̕a, Iń nọṇḍẹ tinạk̕ din iń tahẹn bhor dọ rakhas ar rakhasni dọ ọhọkin hẹć daṛelena.

Unre uni kuṛi dọ mọnẹ mọnẹteye mẹnwana, Acha, bhala nuigeń biḍạulege. Adọe metadea, Teheń dọ tahẹnme, adọ bhalakin hijuk̕a sẹ baṅ? Ar baṅkin hijuk̕re hõ sẹnkateń lại oṭoakina. Adọ uni kuṛi reaṅ katha lekate ẹn hilok̕ dọe tahẽyena.

Adọ raj họpọne kuli ocok̕ kana, Cekate am bọtọrte dọ baṅkin hijuk̕ kana? Unre uni raj họpọne mẹnket̕a, Iń hijuk̕ jọkhẹn am baba dọ tala họrre ọt ar sermae cahap̕ akat̕ tahẽkana, iń jọmeń lạgit̕; adọ unre iń sãote lạṛhạiye ẹhọp̕ket̕a; unre jaṅgań sap̕ledete jaṅga dọń pẹṭẹć rạput̕ akat̕taea. Unre banar tite jọṛhat-káteye mẹnket̕a, Dayakate ikạkạńme; mẹnkhan ọhọń jọmpea; mẹnkhan jivi dọ alom khotraetińa. Adọ unre mũń bhugạk̕ket̕-taea, ar ona mũ bhugạk̕re baber iń lagaoadea, ar iń ạguyede tahẽkana mit̕ṭaṅ naṅgrahare. Adọ ona naṅgraharen họṛ iń metat̕-koa, Mit̕ ṭin gọṭọm ar pea mẹrọm kạsi ar pon mũṛĩ caole ạguipe; ona dọ bhọjkate nui rakhasle jọm ocoyea; ar bape ạgui khan nui rakhasle aṛak̕kaea, saname jọm ujạṛpea. Adọ jọṭọko ạguket̕a onako jinis. Adọ baṛkaćteń jạpit̕ ńõk̕ket̕a; unre onko ińren turui

---

27 The hands are kept turned up with the palms pressed against each other and before one's face. It is a common Indian way of showing humble supplication.

28 lit. Don't destroy my soul.

here." The ogre girl then asked: "They know you then?" The young man replied: "When I was coming, I met with your father; then he gave this house up to me; he has listened to the noise of the hookah, and will not come here now." Then they stayed, as they were, and both went to bed.

When the next day dawned, he said: "Now I am off; you see, my six brothers have gone ahead; so now you remain here." The ogre girl then said: "Stay to-day, please stay to-day; when my parents come, I wish also to go with you." The young man then said: "As long as I stay here, the ogre and the ogress will never come."

The girl said to herself: "Very well, I shall at once test him;" whereupon she said to him: "Stay to-day; let us see whether they will come or not; and even if they do not come, I shall go and tell them." Then, in accordance with what the girl said, he stayed that day.

Afterwards she asked the prince: "How is it that they, for fear of you, are not coming?" Then the prince said: "When I was coming, your father was in the middle of the road, having opened his mouth so that it reached from the earth to the sky, intending to eat me; then he commenced to fight with me; then I caught hold of his leg, and broke it for him. Keeping his hands pressed together up before his face[27], he implored me saying: "Show mercy and let me off; I shall surely not eat you; whatever you do, don't take my life[28]. Then I made a hole in his nose[29] and put a rope through this, and was bringing him to a town. I said to the people of this town: 'Bring one tin of clarified butter, three castrated goats and four maunds of rice; we will make a feast of this and let the ogre eat; if you do not bring it, we shall set the ogre free, and he will eat and make an end of you all.' Then they brought all this. Then I feigned to sleep a little; at that

29 The septum is perforated, a practice not uncommon with other races, but only rarely seen with Santals.

boehako raṛakadea, adọ unreye dạṛkeťa. Mẹnkhan ona bọtọrte am baba dọ bae hijuǩa.

Adọ uni rakhas họpọnerae calaoena ać gọ baba ṭhen baḍae ńam lạgiť, bhala sạri sẹ naseye mẹneťa; adọ calaoenteye ńẹlkeťa, Sạrige jaṅgae rạpuť akaťtaea, adọ mũ hõe phoṛao akaťtaea. Adọe metakin kana, Henda gọ ar baba, cedaǩ baben sẹnoǩ kana oṛaǩte dọ? Mahnder hiloǩ khon aben lạgiť daka utuń dọhọ akaťa; mẹnkhan iń dọ aben pańjageń hẹć akana.

Adọkin metae kana, Biṭi, cekateliń sẹnoǩa? Am dọ ọkọe cọm dọhọ akadea ona oṛaǩre. Unre uni kuṛiye mẹnkeťa, Baba, tahẽ dọe tahẽkangea, mẹnkhan nitoǩ dọe calaoena; bạnugića. Onkae ẹṛẹkeťkina. Adọkin hẹćena, arkin metadea, Acha, oṛaǩte dọ ạyuṗ jọkhẹnliń bọlọǩa. Kuṛi dọ enka mẹn baṛakateye hẹć lahayena. Adọ hẹćkateye lạiae kana, Sạrigem rạpuť akaťtaea, ar nạthu hõm phoṛao akadegea. Mẹnkhan hijuǩ kin mẹneťa; adọ alom jãhã cekakina, ạḍikin bọtọram kana.

Adọ ạyuṗ ber jọkhẹn uni raj họpọn ar rakhas họpọnera dọ ạḍi pharak sẹnkin sẹnena; unre rakhas ar rakhasnikin hẹć sẹṭẹrena, inạ tayọmte raj họpọn ar rakhas họpọnera; sanamko hẹćena, adọko ńapamena.

Unre rakhas ar rakhasni dọ uni ṭhen banar titekin jọṛhatoǩ kana, metae kanakin, Baba, jivi dọ alom ạguitạlińa, noa rakhas-puri raj dọ tinạǩ hạbić menaǩa, pasẹ aṛẹ dige 16 kọs menaǩa; noa raj dọ amgeliń emama; noa oṛaǩ hõ amaǩge. Ar nui họpọnera menaetalińa, nui hõ amge hataoem. Arkin metadea, Amaǩ udhikar hoeyena.

Adọ onako jimại hataokeťa. Adọ uni koṛa rakhas họpọnerae metae kana, Nẹ̃kẹ̃ iń dọ teheń ńindạ dhạbićge iń dọń tahẹn kana, gapa dọ iń dọ ạḍi setaǩ ńindạre ińren turui boehań pańjakoa. Ar am dọ ọntẹ khon ruạṛ jọkhẹn kusi menaǩtam khan dọń idi toramea. Onae mẹn oṭowadete uni koṛa dọ ạḍi setaǩreye mohṇḍayena.

---

30 lit. Sixteen kos; a kos is equal to two miles.

time my six brothers set him free, and he ran away. It is in fear of this that your father will not come."

The ogre girl then went to find out from her parents whether he was telling the truth or not; and having gone to them she saw, he had really broken his leg and made a hole through his nose. And she said to them: "I say, mother and father, why are you not coming home? Since the day before yesterday I have kept rice and curry for you; now I have come to look for you."

"Daughter," they answered her, "how can we go? You are keeping some one in the house." The girl then said: "Father, he certainly was there, but now he has gone; he is not there." In this way she deceived them; they would come and said to her: "All right, in the evening we shall come in." Having said this, the girl came back in advance and spoke to the man: "You have really broken his leg, and his nose you have also perforated. But they say they will come, so don't harm them in any way; they are very much afraid of you."

In the afternoon the prince and the ogre daughter went away to a considerable distance; then the ogre and the ogress came, and thereafter also the prince and the ogre daughter; they came all and met.

The ogre and the ogress put their hands pressed together up before their faces[27], and implored him saying: "Sir, don't take our lives; so far as this ogre-world kingdom goes — it is about 32 miles[30] each side —, we shall give you this kingdom; this house also is yours. And we have this daughter, take her too." And they added: "Now it has become your lawful property."

Then he took over possession; thereupon the young man said to the ogre daughter: "Look here, I am staying this night and no longer; early to-morrow morning I shall follow after my six brothers. If you, when I return from those parts, are pleased and willing, I shall take you along with me." Having said this to her, the young man left and started very early.

Adọ calak̓ calak̓te ạḍi sạṅgiṅe calaoena; adọ bajare ṅẹl ṅamkette gupi gidrại kuliketkoa, metako kanae, Henda bạbu gupi koṛa, ona dọ oka naṅgraha ṅẹlok̓ kana? Adọko lạiae kana, Ona dọ ạḍi kharap naṅgraha kana. Adọe kuli ruạṛketkoa, Henda bạbu, cekate kharap naṅgraha dọ hoeyena? Unreko lạiadea, Juạko ẹnẹć ocomea, adọm haraolen khan bọhọk̓ko họyọ poṭortama, ar ghạnireko joṛaoetkoa tili ghạnire. Adọ arhõe kuli ruạṛketkoa, Ẹnḍẹkhan bạbu, cekateṅ jitạukok̓a? Adọko lạiae kana, Am jitạuk̓ lạgit dọ nitge ạt dọ menak̓tama; goḍo baṅ khan cuṭiạ tanak̓ mat̓ ṭhoṅgare baekom. Adọ ẹnẹć jọkhẹn onkoak̓ jidem ṅẹlletako khan, ar am haraok̓ lekam ạikạu khan dọ metakom, Pusiak̓ bọhọk̓re diạṛa marsal dọhọepe, adọbon ẹnẹća. Adọ arhõ jitạuk̓ lekam ạikạuko khan, am dọ bại bạite uni goḍo aṛak̓ gọtkaeme; unre pusi dọ uni goḍo sabea mẹnteye dọna nãhãk̓; adọ divhe sẹṅgẹl ĩṛĩjok̓a; unre am dọ onkoak̓ dan sanamem hạr samṭao gọda; adọ amak̓ jitạu hoeok̓a.

Adọ onko' gupi gidrại metatkoa, Ẹnḍẹkhan bạbu koṛa, ma sẹ barea gan goḍo saṗạṅpe, adọ bar ṭaka boksis iṅ emapea. Ona ṭaka lalọcte onko gidrạ dọ ạḍiko chuṭạuena; mẹnkhan pea gidrạte pea goḍoko saṗketkoa; adọ ạgukateko emadete onko gidrạ dọ pea ṭakae ematkoa.

Onko goḍo mat̓ ṭhoṅgareye bhoraoketkote adọ bajarreye sẹṭẹrena; ona bajar kulhiye bọlọyena. Adọko metae kana, Mosaphir, am dọ okaren kanam? Adọ hapẹ teṅgolenme, alom parọmok̓a, juạ ẹnẹćlenme. Adọ unre uni raj họpọne mẹnketa, Cet? juạ ẹnẹć reaṅ dọ mane cet̓ kana? Unre onko họṛko mẹneta, Noa naṅgraha reaṅ onkage dustur kana; juạ bako ẹnẹćlen khan bako parọm daṛeak̓a; jãhãren mosaphir họṛ dọ bako parọm daṛeak̓ kana.

Adọe lạiako kana, Iṅ dọ noa reaṅ mane bape lạiạṅ khan bạṅ ẹnẹća. Adọko lạiae kana, Judi juạ ẹnẹćrem jitạulen khan, amem sẹn parọm daṛeak̓a; ar baṅko jitạulen khan bọhọk̓le họyọetakoa

31 The lamp referred to is a small earthenware cup; for such a lamp some kind of vegetable oil is used; the wick is generally some cotton threads, twisted together, lying in the oil with one end resting on the rim of the cup. For such lamps a stand is frequently used, sometimes quite elaborate in shape.

Passing along, he reached very far; having sighted a town, he asked some cowherd boys there, saying: "I say, you cowherd boys, which is the town that is seen there?" "That is a very wicked town," they told him, whereupon he again asked them: "Look here, youngsters, how has it become a wicked town?" "They will make you play at dice," they told him; "and if you are vanquished, they will shave your head bare and yoke you to an oil-mill, the mill of the oilmen." Again he asked them: "In that case, youngsters, how could I win?" They answered him: "You have even now an opportunity of winning; put some rats, and, if not rats, then mice or some similar ones into the bamboo bottle. Then, when during the play you see their eagerness, and you feel like losing, say to them: 'Put a lampstand[31] with a lighted lamp on the cat's head, then we shall play.' When you again feel that they are winning, let the rat quietly out; then the cat will jump to catch the rat, and the lamplight will be extinguished; then you must gather all their winnings together, and so you will win."

He then spoke to the cowherd boys: "In that case, youngsters, catch me a couple of rats, and I shall give you a present of two rupees." Desiring to get this money, the children commenced eagerly to hunt, and three children caught three rats; and having brought these they gave them to him, and he gave the children three rupees.

He put the rats in his bamboo bottle, and reached the town and entered the bazar street. Here people called out to him: "Wayfarer, where are you from? Wait, stop a little, don't go further; come and play at dice at once." The prince said: "What? Game of dice, what does it mean?" The men replied: "In this town we have such a custom; if they don't play at dice, they are not permitted to pass; no travellers from anywhere can pass."

He then said: "If you don't tell me the meaning of it, I will not play." They answered him: If you win at the game of dice, you may pass; but if people do not win, we shave their heads and yoke them

ar tili ghạnirele joṛaokoa. Adoe metako kana, Iń iń haraolen khan acha ghạnirepe joṛaoińa. Acha, apeń haraolepe khan adope cekaka? Iń doń meneta noa katha, iń iń haraok se apepe haraok, menkhan ona reaṅ ekraṛ olạńpe; adobon eneća. Ińpe haraolin khan do ṭhik iń baḍae kana, ghạnirepe joṛaoińgea bohok hoyo cikạṛkate; ar iń apeń haraolepe khan ape Ṭhakpur naṅgraha tinạk sạṅgińte menaka, unạkteń hataoa.

Ado unre onka mone moneteko menketa, Uh, unạk bon harao akatkoa, ar nui doe cele kana? ma olkate bon emaea. Ado kathae, mitṭen ektiạri khemota kagojre olkateko emadea. Ar paṛhaokateye ńelketa, adoe metatkoa, Enḍekhan tin jokhenbon eneća? Adoko lạiadea, Ayuṕ kedokko jom baṛa tayomte.

Ado mitṭen basako emadete onḍege sadome tolkedea ar ać do aćak jinisko uni sadom khone phedkette basa oṛakreye baekata. Ado bahre sene oḍok calaoena; ado tili ghạni reaṅ saḍe atenkette ona ńeńele calaoena. Unreye ńelketkoa, aćren bokot koṛako hạtire dećkateko lahalen, ńelketkoae ghạnireko joṛao akatkoa; onko ńelte ạḍi tạpise edreyena, metatkoae, Acha, thir hataṛokpe, hape nãhãk iń chuṭipea.

Onḍe khonakge adoe calaoena. Ado ona naṅgraharen hoṛe kuli baṛayetkoa, Okoe ṭhen pusi menakkoa; ado damte imạńpe mitṭen. Adoko ńawadea; uni raj hopon do mitṭen pusi reaṅ dam do mit sae ṭakae ematkoa; kirińkedete adoe ạgukedea.

Ado inạktege tala ńindạyen khan, juạ enećko ehoṕketa. Menkhan eneć enećte bar hel doko bhagaokedea. Adoe metatkoa, Pusi bohokre dịạṛa dohokatebon eneća. Ado pusi bohokreko dohoketa divhe marsal. Ado bar dhaoko haraolede reaṅ ona doe ruạṛketa, inạkate arhõ pe dobṛae jitạuena. Inạkate onkoakge ạḍi ãṭ jitạu hoeok kana.

to the mill of an oilman." "If I should be vanquished, well, then you will yoke me to an oil-mill. All right, then if I vanquish you, what will happen to you? I say this: I may lose or you may lose, write me an agreement concerning this; then we shall play. If you should vanquish me, I know for certain you will yoke me to an oil-mill, after having shaved my head bare; and if I should vanquish you, so far as this Thakpur town of yours goes, I shall take possession of the whole of it."

These people then said to themselves: "Oh, so many we have vanquished, and this fellow, who is he? Let us write, and give it him." Then, people tell, they wrote on a paper a document, giving authority, and gave it to him. He read, and saw what it was, and said to them: "Then at what time shall we play?" "In the evening, after having had our supper," they replied.

Then they gave him a place to stay, and he tied his horse there, and, having himself taken his things down from the horse, he put them aside in his lodgings. Thereupon he went outside, and, listening to hear the sound of the oilman's mill, he went to have a look at it. Then he saw them, his own younger brothers, who had gone ahead riding the elephant, them he saw, they had yoked them to the oil-mill; at the sight of them he became enraged. He said to them: "All right, be quiet for the present; in a short while I shall set you free."

From there he went along; he asked people of the town: "Who has got a cat; I shall pay for it, give me one." Then they found one for him; the prince paid as the price of one cat one hundred rupees; having bought it, he took it along.

By this time it had become midnight, and they commenced to play at dice. As they were playing, they vanquished him twice. Then he said to them: "Let us play after having put the lamp-stand on the cat's head." They did so, put the lighted lamp on the cat's head. Thereupon he got back what they had made him lose twice, and after this he again won thrice; but after this they were winning very much.

Khange unre bạị bạite uni dọ onko goḍoe aṛak gọtkatkoa; unre goḍoe sabea mẹnte pusi dọe dọnketa; adọ pusiak bọhọkre tahẹ̃kan divhe sẹṅgẹl ona dọ ńũrena ar ńũtena. Unre uni koṛa dọ sanam dane hạr samṭaoketa. Onko dọ divhe marsal jọrẹtkette arhõko ẹhọpketa; arhõ onkoak jitạue ńẹlkette arhõ uni dọ mit gọṭẹn goḍoe aṛakkedea; ar pusi dọ uni sabea mẹnte arhõe dọnketa; arhõ divhe dọ iṛićena, arhõ onkage sanam dane hạr samṭaoketa; hatao cabakettakote saname haraoketkoa. Aćren boehako turui gọṭẹn jọtọ tili ghạni khone chaḍaoketkoa.

Adọ tinạk dosra disomrenko tahẹ̃kana, onko hõe metatkoa, Mit hapta din ape dọ tahẽ hataṛokpe; ruạṛ hijukań, unre ape hõń bańcaopea. Adọ dosar hilok setakre dọ ona naṅgrahare ḍhọle piṭạu oṭokata, are họhọ oṭokata, Noa naṅgraha dọ ale eae boeha reań ẹktiạri hoeyena. Inạ mẹn oṭokateko mohṇḍayena hawapuri baṅgla ạgui lagit. Ona raj khonak dọ ạḍi sạṅgińko calaoena.

Adọko calaoente ạḍi marań mitṭań dạriạuko ńamketa; adọ ona dạriạu ńẹlkateko duṛupena. Adọko bhabna joń kana; ẹnte lạukạ jahaj hõ bạnuka; adọ cekatebon parọmoka? Ona takrege mitṭań horọko ńẹl ńamkedea, adọko họhọadea. Uni họrọ dọ onko ṭhene hẹć sorena. Adọko metae kana, Bacha, niạ jalapurim parọmkale khan, ạḍi marań dhọrmọ hoekoktama; mẹnkhan cet hõ bale ẹmama, mitṭań mẹrọm kạsile emama. Adọko emadete uni kạsi dọe jọmkedea.

Adọe metatkoa, Ma ińạk deare dẹjokpe. Adọko dẹćena; adọ họrọ ona jalapuri hanasateye idi parọmketkoa. Adọko mẹn oṭoadea, Ma am dọ nọṇḍẹge tahẽ hataṛokme, adọ nãhãk ruạṛ jọkhẹn arhõm parọmkalea.

Adọko parọmente ạḍi sạṅgińko calaoena. Adọ ạḍi marań jalapuriko ńamketa, ona jalapurirege saṭṭi rạni menakkoa dak bhitrire, ar onko ṭhenge hawapuri baṅgla dọ menaka. Adọ uni marańić boeha dọe metatkoa, aćren kạṭićko turui boehae metatkoa, Ma noa

Then he quietly let the rats out; and to catch a rat the cat made a jump, and the lighted lamp that was on the cat's head fell down, and it became dark. During this the young man collected all the winnings. When the others had lighted the lamp, they again commenced to play; as he saw that they were again winning, he again let one rat out, and, to catch this one, the cat again jumped. Again the lamp was extinguished; again in the same way he collected all the winnings; having taken all they had, he vanquished them all. He also released his six brothers from the oil-mill.

And so many as there were from other countries, them also he spoke to: "You wait for a week's time; I shall come back; then I shall rescue you also." The next morning he let the big drum be beaten as he left, and he called out: "This town has become the property of us seven brothers." Having said this, they set out to bring the air-castle. They went very far from this town.

Having passed along they reached a very large sea; seeing this, they sat down and were in distress, because there was no boat and no ship. "How shall we get across?" Just then they caught sight of a tortoise, and called out to him; the tortoise came up to them, and they said to him: "Dear, if you will take us across this ocean, you will acquire a very great merit; but we shall not give you anything, only a castrated goat we shall give you." Then they gave this to him, and he ate the goat.

Then he said to them: "Please, mount my back." They did so, and the tortoise took them across to the other side. Here they said to the tortoise as they went: "Please stay here for the present; on our way back you must again take us across."

Having reached the other side, they went along very far, and came to a very large ocean; in this ocean the seven queens live in the water, and with them is the air-castle. Now the eldest brother said to them, that is to say, to his six younger brothers:

jalapurire dọnpe; ṭheṅgate miť dhao dalpe daḱ duạr benaoḱa; ar daḱ dọ sẹṅgẹl leka jol rakaṕa sermate; unre dọn gọdpe jalapurire, ọṇḍẹge hawapuri baṅgla dọ menaḱa.

Ona katha añjọmkate onko turui boeha dọko mẹnkeťa, ako akoko galmarao jọñ kana, Henda ya, dada dọ teheñ dọe gọćkeťbona. Adọko apaj kante adọ arhọ̃ko mẹn ruạṛae kana, Dada, amge marañić dọ, amge dọ adọ calaḱtabonme. Unre marañić raj họpọn koṛa daḱe dalkeťte sẹṅgẹl leka jol rakaṕena; ona jol rakaṕ sãoteye dọnkeťa daḱre.

Dạriạu bhitrire eae gọṭẹn rạniko tahẹ̃kana, chuṭki rạni ṭhen hawapuri baṅgla dọ tahẹ̃kana; adọ uniaḱ họbọrrege sẹnkateye ńurhạyena. Adọ landakateko bereťena; jãhã sẹngeko landa idiyeťa, ọntẹge ạḍi mọ̃ńj mọ̃ńj dolan ar oṛaḱ benaoḱ kana; ar sona, rupạ, ṭaka, poesa họ̃ benaoḱ kana. Ar ona chaḍa haṭ bajar họ̃ benao idiḱ kana; jãhã sẹngeko bẹṅgẹťeťa, ọntẹgeko ńẹleťa dokandạri họ̃, cini, moeda emanteaḱko ńẹleťa; onako sanamge daḱ bhitrireye ńẹlkeťa.

Adọe metaťkoa onko satṭi rạni, Delabon bahreḱa. Adọ ona hawapuri baṅgla dọ chuṭki rạni ṭhen tahẹ̃kante uni koṛae jimạwadea; are metadea, Noa dọ sabọdhante dọhọeme. Adọ tire saṕkedete sọṅgẹ sọṅgẹtege ona daḱ khon dọkin bahreyena. Adọ ọṇḍẹ khonaḱ dọ ako oṛaḱ sẹnko mohṇḍayena.

Ạdọ hijuḱ hijuḱte arhọ̃ ona jalapuriko ńamkeťa; uni họrọ họ̃ ona ghaṭregeye tahẹ̃kana. Adọko metae kana, Dẹ arhọ̃ hanasa parọm ruạṛkaleme. Adọ họrọ deareko dẹćena, hawapuri baṅglaren eae gọṭẹn rạni ar onko eae boeha họ̃ sanamge uni họrọreko dẹćena.

Mẹnkhan uni marañić dọ họrọ dea khonko ḍhaka ńurhạkadea; onko turui boehako ḍhaḱkawa, daḱreko ńurhạ gọťkadea. Mẹnkhan ona daḱ bhitrirege miṭṭañ bọṅga kuṛi, uniaḱ ńutum dọ Jọldhạrni, uni kuṛi họ̃ jãwãe ńamkoa mẹnte dinge Isor ṭhene koejoñ kan

"Please jump into this ocean; strike once with your sticks, a water-door will be formed, and the water will flare up to heaven like fire; then you jump into the sea; there is the air-castle."

Hearing this, the six brothers said, that is to say, they were talking between themselves: "I say, you, our brother has killed us to-day." As they were urging each other to set to, they answered him back: "Brother, you are the big one; so you go in for us." The eldest prince then struck the water, and it flared up like fire, and at the moment it flared up he jumped into the water.

Down in the sea there were seven queens living; the air-castle was with the youngest queen; and going down he tumbled into her arms. Laughing they got up again; in whatever direction they turned laughing, everywhere most beautiful palaces and houses came into existence; gold, silver, rupees, pice also came into existence; and besides market-places and towns also came forth; in whatever direction they were looking, there they were also seeing open shops with sugar, flour and such things; all this he saw below in the water.

Then he said to the seven queens: "Come, let us get out." Now as the air-castle was with the youngest queen, she gave it into the charge of the young man, saying to him: "Keep this with care." Then he took her by the hand, and they came out of the water together. From there they started on their way home.

Coming along they again reached the sea mentioned; the tortoise also was there at the landing-place, and they said to him: "Kindly take us again across to the other side." Then they mounted the back of the tortoise, the seven queens of the air-castle and also the seven brothers, all mounted the back of the tortoise.

But the eldest brother they pushed down from the back of the tortoise; the six brothers were pushing him, and made him fall into the water. But down in the water there was a female sprite, her name was Joldharni; this girl was daily praying to the Supreme

tahẹ̄kana. Mẹnkhan uni ma uni ṭhengeye ńurhạyena; adọkin ńapamente dak̕ khonak̕ dọkin oḍok hẹćena. Adọ nonka abo dhạrti daṛan lekage dak̕ khonak̕ dọkin taṛam parọm ạguketa.

Adọ ona jalapuri parọmkate Ṭhakpur naṅgrahakin hẹćena. Adọ ọṇḍẹkin hẹćente adọ onko turui boeha reaṅ katha onkoe kuliyet̕koa, Turui boeha iń sọṅgẹko tahẹ̄kan, onko dọko calaoena? Adọko lạiat̕kina, Hẹ̄, onko dọ eae gọṭẹn kuṛi ar turui gọṭẹn koṛa; calaoenako ḍher sạṅgiṅge. Adọ unre ọṇḍẹ tinạk̕ko ghạnireko dọhọlet̕ko, onko dọ saname chuṭikat̕koa. Ar ać dọ sadọmre dẹćente rakhaspuri rajteye sẹn parọmena; adọ rakhas họpọnera hõe idi torakedea. Adoe ruạṛ calaoena.

Adọ sẹnkate ać janam eṅgate metadea, Onko dọko sẹṭẹrena, gọ? Adọe lạiadea, Onko ma, beṭa, enanre. Adọ uni mit̕ṭẹn kicrićе emadea, are metadea, Gọ, am dọ noa sạri kicrićte bandenme; adọ kulhi duạrte bọlọk̕me mit̕ mohṇḍa; adọ baṛge duạr sẹnte oḍok hijuk̕me mit̕ mohṇḍa; ar alom bẹṅgẹt̕ ruạṛa.

Adọ ać gọ dọ ona kicrić bandeyente adoe calaoena kulhi duạr; adọ baṛge duạr sẹnteye bọlọyen jọkhẹćrege hawapuri ar saṭṭi era doe ńẹl ńamket̕koa. Ar uni hõko ńẹl ńamkedete apan ạpinko ńir oḍok hẹćena uni sọṅgẹ sọṅgẹ; adọko mẹneta, Nuige aboren dọ hanhar gọ kanae. Adọko rọṛeta, landayetako. Onatege oṛak̕, dolan sẹ ṭaka, poesa sẹ haṭ bajar benaok̕ kana jãhã sẹngeko calak̕ kana, ọntẹgeko ńẹleta. Ona lekate ạḍi maraṅ raje hoeyena; ar ạḍi maraṅ hawapuri baṅgla hoeyentaea; gại kaḍa, sona rupạ emanteak̕ uniak̕ purạu menak̕taea.

Ona jokha raj haṛame mẹnketa, onko turui boeha aćren họpọne kuliket̕koa, Ape dọ ya turui boehape sẹnlena, adọ okor cet̕ nisạnape

---

32 In the villages known to the Santals the houses lie on both sides of a street; more well-to-do people often have a wall round their houses, one door in this leading out to the street (there is no door from a dwelling house leading directly out into the street); another door in the enclosing wall leads directly out to the homestead field.

deity to get a husband; and now this man fell down to her. Then they met, and both came out of the water. Just as we walk here in the world, in the same way these two came walking across and out of the water.

Having crossed this sea these two reached Thakpur town; and as they came, they were asking them for news about the six brothers: "My six brothers, who were together with me, have they gone?" They told them: "Yes, they were seven girls and six young men; they have gone and are far away." At this time he set all free, so many as they had yoked to the oil-mill there; and he himself mounted his horse and went through to the ogre-world kingdom, and he took also the ogre daughter along with him and returned home.

Having reached there he asked his own mother: "Have they arrived, mother?" "Oh, they, my son, they came long ago." Then he gave her a cloth and said to her: "Mother, take this piece of cloth on, and enter straight through the street-door, without looking anywhere; and then come straight out through the door that leads to the field[32], and don't look behind you."

Then his mother took this cloth on, and went through the street-door. As she reached the door that leads to the field, she caught sight of the air-castle and the seven queens, and as they also saw her, they came one after the other running out following after her, and were saying: "Here is our mother-in-law." And they were talking and laughing. Thereby houses, palaces and money of silver and copper, and market places, and towns were coming forth in every direction where they were going. In this way he became a very great king, and he got a very large air-castle[33]; cows and buffaloes, gold, silver and so on he had in plenty.

At this time the old king said, he asked the six brothers, his sons: "You youngsters, did you not go you six brothers? then

---

[33] So literally; the narrator's ideas are not clear to himself.

ạguleťa? Unre apat haṛam marañić hopone metae kana, Beṭa, soṅgeteñ kolleťpea eae boeha hawapuri baṅgla ạgui lạgiť, ado okor onkoak̓ do? Unre uni koṛae mẹnkeťa, Baba, onkom hohoako khan doñ lại daṛekema onko samañre.

Unre uni raj haṛam turạtge hoṛe kolkeťkoa onko hoho ạguko lạgiť, metaťkoae, Do se calak̓pe, iñren turui goṭen hopon menak̓koa haṇḍe. Adoko hoho ạguketkote akoren dadat oṛak̓ko boloyente ạḍi rokom nana hunạr jinisko ñelkeťa; ar uni dadat reañ hoṛmore hõ sona, rupạ reañ abhranko ñelkeťa; ado ñelketťe ako monereko menjoñ kana, Abo hõbon senlengea, mẹnkhan okor nonkan jinis dobon ạguleťa. Unre onko turui goṭen hopon uni raj haṛame kuliketkoa, metako kanae, Henda beṭa, ape do eae boehañ kolleťpea hawapuri baṅgla ạguia mente, ar soṅgerepe tahena mente; ado okor ape do ceťpe ceka akaťa? Unre turui boehako mẹnkeťa, Baba, mẹnkhan dadage okore hạṭiñale kana?

Unre marañić koṛae mẹnkeťa, Baba, iñak̓ gamem añjomle khan pase rak̓ hõm raga, pase rạskạ hom rạskạk̓a. Unre raje mẹnkeťa, Noa katha do, beṭa, ạḍi hahaṛagem lạikeťa.

Unre uni koṛae lạikeťa, Baba, mẹnkhan katha do noa kana; entem kolleťlegea, soṅgete ma bale senlen, ar soṅgete ma tahẽ hõ bale tahẽlena. Ente kul ṭhen khoniñ bañcaoketkoa, oṇḍe khonko lahayena. Hor talare mitṭañ ḍhiṅki biñko ñel ñamkedea hạti coṭ khonak̓; mẹnkhan bañko lạiạñ kana, biñ menaea mẹnte do. Adoko mitạñ kana, Dada, ma lahak̓me, am do ạḍim tayomok̓ kana. Ado uni biñ iñ sen tiok̓kedete iñ hõe ñel ñamkidiña; ado ạḍi ãṭge dareko hõe saḍe ocokeťa; ado ạḍi coṭ koyok̓kate thoṛa sạṅgiñe lagakidiña; unre tarwaṛe or boćkeťte biñ do, baba, iñ mak̓ goćkedea. Ar mak̓ goćkate sẹṅgel iñ jolkeťa, ado hukạñ where is any token that you have brought?" About the same time the old father said to his eldest son: "Son, I sent you together all seven to bring the air-castle; now where is what they have?" The young man replied: "Father, if you call them, I might tell you before them."

The old king then at once sent people to fetch these; he ordered them: "Go, my six sons are living over there; bring them." When they had gone and fetched them, they came into the house of their eldest brother, and saw many different kinds of things; and on their brother's person they saw jewelry of gold and silver; seeing this they were saying to themselves: "We also went, but we surely did not bring any such things." The old king then asked these six sons, saying: "Look here, my sons, I sent you seven brothers to bring the air-castle and ordered you to go together; now then what have you done?" The six brothers answered: "Father quite so, but our brother, why, he does not give us any share with him."

The eldest son then said: "Father if you will listen to my story, you may perhaps cry, perhaps you will also be glad." The king then said: "It is a very strange thing, my son, that you there said."

The young man then spoke: "Father, the facts are these: you certainly sent us, but we did not go together, nor did we stay together. I saved them from a tiger; from there they went ahead. Sitting on the elephant they caught sight of a snake in the middle of the road, big as a husking-machine; but they did not tell me that there was a snake there. They said to me: 'Brother, go ahead of us, you are getting so far behind.' When I got up to the snake, he also caught sight of me; he also caused the trees to make a tremendous noise. With his head high up in the air, he chased me for some distance; then I drew my sword and cut the snake, father, so that he died. Having cut and killed the snake, I lighted a fire and made the hookah ready, and called out to condaketa, ar iń hohoatkoa; biń hormore duruṕkate iń do hukạń ńũńũ kana. Adoko hećena, adoko lạiań kana, Dada, nui biń ńel katege ale dole ruạṛlena. Ado, baba, onare hõ iń do cet hõ bạń metatkoa jãhãnak do. Inạkate ado songe songetegele calao idiyena; menkhan sadom cotre iń do thoṛa ganiń jạpit ńokketa; unre ạḍi sạṅgiṅko bạgiadiṅa. Ado arhõ lahare bir hạtiko ńamkedea; ado uni botorte ạḍi sạṅgiń arhõko ruạṛena. Adoko ḍera akana dare buṭạre, adoń sen tiokketkote adoko mitạń kana, Dada, nonḍe do babon ḍerak̕a, me delabon, lahak̕me. Ado, baba, hukạń condakette sadomreń dećena; ado, baba, hukạ ńũ ńũtege sadom doń kamsaokedea, ar iń men otoatkoa, Me delabon ape hõ usạrate. Ado, baba, ạḍi sạṅgiń iń calaoente horregeń ńelkedea bir hạtiye burum akana; ado babań koyok̕ ruạṛkette noko do ạḍi sạṅgińreń ńel ńamketkoa, iṅgeko koyok̕ akadiṅa. Unre, baba, uni bhalok̕ hạti doń ńelkedea, iń sengeye ńir hijuk̕ kana; ado, baba, sadom khon iń pheḍente uni bir hạti do sunḍreń saṕkedea, ariń capat gotkadea.

Ado, baba, uni hạtiko ńelkedete adoko hohoyeta, Hape, dada, ale hõ tạṅgilem. Adoko seṭerente iṅko lạiạń kana, Dada, baṅdo serma khonak̕, baṅdo oka khonak̕ bir hạtiye ńurhạyena. Ado enrehõ iń do cet hõ bạń metatkoa; ado onḍe khon songetegele calaoena; ado baba, rakhaspuri naṅgrahare bir bhitrireko bạgiadiṅa.

Ado babako hec lahayente ạḍi marań rakhasko ńamkedea, serma ar ote cahaṕ akata. Adoko mitạń kana, Dada, enḍekhan cekatebon paromok̕a? Adoń metatkoa, Acha dela iń songetege hijuk̕pe. Onko turui boeha do rakhas botorte bako sen sorok̕ kana. Ar iń doń sen sorente uni rakhas jaṅgań saṕkedete jaṅgań peṭec rạputkettaea. Banar tite joṛhatkateye mitạń kana, Mosaphir, menkhan jivi alom khotraetiṅa. Ado nạthuń phoṛaokedete parkom baberteń tolkedea; ar hukạń condakette sadomreń dećena, adoń them; sitting on the body of the snake, I was smoking the hookah. Then they came; then they said to me: 'Brother, seeing this snake we turned back.' But, father, in connexion with this I did not say anything to them. After this we went along together; but sitting on the horse I fell asleep for a moment; then they left me very far behind. Again somewhere in front they met a wild elepant; fearing him, they again turned back and went a great distance. They camped at the foot of a tree, and when I came up to them, they said to me: 'Brother, we shall not camp here; come along, get ahead of us.' Then, father, I lighted the hookah and mounted my horse; and then, father, smoking the hookah I made the horse gallop, saying to them, as I left them behind: 'Come along, come you also quickly.' Then, father, when I had gone a good distance, I saw the wild elephant lying down there on the road; then, father, when I looked back, I saw these very far behind; they were looking towards me. At this moment, father, I saw the mad elephant, he was coming running towards me; then, father, I got down from the horse, caught the wild elephant by the trunk, and threw him away.

Then, father, when they saw the elephant, they called out: 'Stop, brother, wait for us also.' When they reached me, they told me: 'Brother, whether from the sky or from who knows where a wild elephant fell down.' Still I said nothing to them; then from there we went along together; then, father, they left me in the middle of the forest at the ogre-world city.

Then, father, as they went ahead, they met a very big ogre, who had his mouth agape so that it reached from the earth to the sky. Then they said to me: 'Brother, how then shall we be able to pass?' 'All right,' I said to them, 'come along together with me.' My six brothers did not go near for fear of the ogre. And I went up to the ogre, caught hold of his leg and broke it for him. Keeping his hands pressed together up before his face, he spoke to me: 'Wayfarer, whatever you do, don't take my life.'

mohnḍayena. Mẹnkhan ẹnrehõ bako paṅjalidiṅa. Ạḍi sạṅgiṅ iṅ calaoenre, baba, iṅko sẹn sẹṭẹrkidiṅa. Adọko mitạṅ kana, Cedak̕ nui rakhas dọm ạguyede kana? Adọṅ metako kana, Teheṅ dọ nui dọ khubbon jọm ocoyea. Adọ, baba, mit̕ṭẹn naṅgraharele sẹn sẹṭẹrena; naṅgraharen hoṛle hohoat̕kotele metat̕koa, Pon mũṛĩ caole ar pea mẹrọm kạsi ar mit̕ ṭin gọṭọm ạguipe. Ar bapẹ ạgui khan dọ noa naṅgrahare nui rakhasle aṛak̕kaea, saname jọm ujạṛpea. Adọ bọṭọrte onako jinisko ạguket̕a.

Adọko ạguket̕ khan onko turui boehaṅ metat̕koa, Ma ape hõ jọmpe, ar nui rakhas hõ emaepe, hạti ar sadọm hõ emakinpe, ar iṅ dọ, baba, baṛkaćteṅ jạpit̕ket̕a. Unre onko turui boehako mẹnket̕a, Ea, dada dọe jạpit̕ket̕a; adọ bạı bạite sẹnkatebon raṛakaea; ar baṅ khan jãhãnak̕ bon edre ocole khan dọe jọm ocobona. Adọ, baba, rakhas dọ hape hapeteko raṛakadea. Adọ thoṛa sạṅgiṅe calaoen khan dọ adọko lạiaṅ kana, Dada, hạni tora uni rakhas dọe dạṛket̕a. Adọṅ metako kana, Dhur ya, do sap̕ ạguyepe. Adọko mitạṅ kana, Dada, ale dọ sẹn hõ ọhọle sẹnlena, bọṭọrgele ạikạuet̕a. Adọ rakhas dọe dạṛket̕a. Adọ, baba, jọm ñũ baṛakatele gitić thirena. Adọ iṅ ma gitićgeko bạgiadiṅte ṭinre cọṅko bạgiadiṅa; onko dọko calaoena lahate.

Adọṅ ẹbhẹnenteṅ ñẹl baṛayet̕ko dọ bạnuk̕ko. Adọ ạḍi sạṅgiṅ iṅ calaoente mit̕ṭaṅ ạḍi maraṅ bạsti iṅ ñamket̕a; adọ, baba, gupikoṅ ñamket̕kote onkogeṅ kuliket̕koa, Noa dọ oka naṅgraha kana? Adọko lạiadiṅa, Noa dọ ạḍi bạṛić naṅgraha kana. Adọṅ kuliket̕koa, Cekate bạṛić naṅgraha dọ hoeyena? Adọko lạiạṅ kana, Noa naṅgrahare dọ juạ bam ẹnẹćlen khan ọhọm parọm daṛelena. Adọṅ kuli ruạṛket̕koa, Juạ ẹnẹć reaṅ dọ cet̕ mane kana? Adọko lạiạṅ kana, Noa naṅgraha reak̕ hukumge onkangea; jãhãren bidisiạ

Then I perforated his nose and bound him with some bedstead cord; and having lighted the hookah, I mounted my horse and started. But in spite of this they did not follow me. When I had gone very far, father, they reached me, and said to me: 'Why are you taking this ogre along?' I said to them: 'To-day we shall give this one a good feed.' Then, father, we reached a town; calling out to them we said: 'Bring four maunds of rice, three castrated goats and one tin of clarified butter. If you don't bring it, we shall let the ogre loose here in the town; he will eat and make an end of you all.' Then for fear they brought those things.

When they had brought all, I said to my six brothers: 'Please, eat you, and also give the ogre to eat, and also give the elephant and the horse; and I, father, feigned to fall asleep. Then my six brothers say: 'Look here, you, our brother has fallen asleep; let us go quietly and set him free; otherwise, if we somehow or other should make our brother angry, he will let us be eaten by him.' Then, father, they set him loose, without making any noise; and when he had got away to some distance, they said to me: 'Brother, look there, the ogre is running away.' I said to them: 'Off with you, catch him and bring him back.' But they answered me: 'Brother, we shall never go to fetch him, we are afraid.' Then the ogre escaped. Then, father, after having had food and drink, we lay down quietly. Leaving me lying there, they sometime or other left me behind; they went ahead.

When I woke, I looked for them; none of them was there. Then I went along very far, and came to a very large village; finding some cowherds, father, I asked them: 'What town is this?' 'This,' they replied, ' is a very wicked town.' I asked them: 'How has it become a wicked town?' Then they told me: 'If you don't play at dice in this town, you will be unable to pass.' Then I again asked them: 'The game of dice, what does it mean?' Then they told me: 'Such is the rule of this town; if any stranger passes through the street, they block the way for them, and make

hoṛ kulhiteko paromlen khan esetkoako ar juạko eneć ocokoa; ar aema bidisiạ hoṛ juạ enećreko haraolente tili ghạnireko joṛaoketkoa bohok hoyo potorkate; noko hõko joṛaoletkogea.

Ado, baba, juạ enećre iṅiṅ jitạuente, ado noko hõko joṛaoletkogea, menkhan iṅ doṅ baṅcaoketkoa. Ado, baba, soṅgetege hawapuri baṅgla ạguia mentele mohṇḍayena. Ado ạḍi sạṅgiṅle calaoente ạḍi maraṅ jalapurile ṅamketa; ado, baba, uni horole hohoadea, arle metadea, Ma paromkaleme. Ado mitṭen merom kạsile emadea. Ado uni jomkedete uni dearele dećena; hanasale paromena. Adole men oṭoadea, Teheṅ din bhor hạbić do niạ jaegarege tahẽ hataṛokme.

Ado, baba, ona hanasare maraṅ utạr jalapurile ṅamketa. Adoṅ metako kana, Ma ona jalapuri reaṅ dak dalpe ar ona dakre donpe, ar ona dak do sermate jol rakapa nãhãk. Unre, baba, bar ṭheṅgako dalkette botorte baṅko donleta.

Ado, baba, iṅ senkateṅ boloyena; bolokate hawapuriren satṭi rạniṅ ạguketkoa; ado hawapuri baṅgla do iṅ ṭhen tahẽyena. Ado arhõ uni horrele dećena; unre, baba, iṅ doko ṭhelao ṅurhạkadiṅa. Ado, baba, onage bicạrkatalem; menkhan iṅ do gojeṅko menwan tahẽkana; ado cekateṅ hạṭiṅ daṛeakoa?

Ado onako katha aṅjomkate onko turui boehae metako kana, Bạbu, iṅ hõ ohoṅ em daṛelepea; ente apetegepe bạṛić akata.

Ado uni koṛae menketa, Iṅ mageṅ lạgit gosãeye idilidiṅa; ona jaegare katha menaka. Pạhile makletko, onko senkateṅ jivet oḍokkakoa. Ado senkate onkoe metatkoa, Apeak katha lekateṅ baṅcaolena; ado do ape hõṅ baṅcaoketpea; ado apan ạpin oṛakte senjonpe.

them play at dice; and a large number of strangers that have lost at the game of dice they have yoked to the oilmen's mill, after having shaved their heads absolutely bare.' These here they also yoked.

Then, father, as I won at the game of dice — they had yoked also these — I rescued them. Thereupon, father, we started together to bring the air-castle. Having gone along very far, we reached a very large sea; then, father, we called out to the tortoise, saying to him: 'Please, take us across.' We gave him one castrated goat, and when he had eaten it, we mounted his back, and crossed to the other side. There we said to him: 'Stay the whole day and wait here at this place.'

Then, father, on the other side of this we reached a very large ocean. Then I said to them: 'Please, strike the water of the ocean and jump into the water; the water will presently flare up to the sky.' Then, father, when they had struck twice, they were frightened and did not jump in.

Then, father, I went in; having done so, I brought the seven queens of the air-world out, and the air-castle remained with me. Thereafter we again mounted the tortoise; then, father, they thrust me so that I fell down into the water. Now, father, judge in this matter of ours; they intended to kill me; how can I give them any share?"

When he had heard this tale, the old king said to the six brothers: "Boys, nor am I able to give you anything; you have yourselves spoilt all."

The young man then said: "The Gosae took me away to kill me; at that place there is something to do. I shall go and bring to life again those whom he had formerly killed." Having gone there he said to these: "In accordance with your word I was saved; and now I have rescued you too; go away home to your own all of you."

Ar satṭi rạni haṛam rajrenko tahę̃kantaea; turui gǫṭęn rạni dǫ rajko ęṛęledete uni raj dǫ kũiye la ocokeťa; adǫ onko turui gǫṭęn rạniye metaťkoa, Teheń dǫ kũi baplaepe. Adǫ onko turui gǫṭęn rạni dǫ haṭaḱre adwa caole, dhubi ghãs, sindur ar divhe mạliko haṭaḱreko sajaokeťa, adǫ ti tiko sapaṕente kũi ṭhenko ęnęć ạcuroḱ kana. Uni raj dǫ turui moka ṭheṅga saṕkate, teṅgokateye ńęńęl kana; adǫ mǫ̃ṛę̃ dhao puṛạuḱ sãote saname ḍhaka ńurhạkeťkoa, ar cetanreye hasawaťkoa. Nǫṇḍę noa kạhni dǫ cabayena.

83. Raj ar sadher hǫpǫnteť reań.

Sedae jǫkhęn miťṭań raje tahę̃kana. Uni raj dǫ ạṭkuṛạgeye tahę̃kana. Gidrạ ńamkoa męnte aemaye bạhuana; męnkhan ęnrehǫ̃ ǫkǫeṭaḱ ạimạige bae gidrạ ocoleťkoa. Ar uḍi bạṛiće manan jonanketa are gǫḱ bhạriạketa, ęnre hǫ̃ gidrạ dǫ baṅgeye ńamleťkoa. Khangeye thir doroḱena. Męnkhan Ṭhạkur dǫe hiṛińkedea, uni ṭhen dǫ bae nęhǫ̃rlena, ar bae kǫeledea.

Adǫ ona tayǫm ḍher din badre, kathae, oka sęn khon cǫń miťṭań jugi gosãeye hęćena uni ṭhen. Adǫ uni jugi gosãeye męnketa, Henda raj, amren dǫ miť gǫṭęn hǫ̃ gidrạ dǫ bań ńęleťko dǫ?

Unreye męnketa, Ińren gidrạ dǫ bạnuḱkotińa.

Khange uniye męnketa, Cekate bạnuḱkoa? Amren dǫ nunạḱ rạni menaḱkotama, ęnre hǫ̃ ǫkǫeṭaḱ hǫ̃ bako gidrạwana? Noa dǫ ạḍi hahaṛa leka ńęloḱ kana. Jãhãkore jãhãnaḱko bam ceka baṛaleťa?

---

34 When a tank has been excavated, it is common practice to have an inaugural festivity of a partly religious character; this is called a 'marriage'. Here the same is pretended to be performed in connexion with a well.

35 The things brought are all intended for ceremonial, religious use. The **dhubi** grass, Cynodon dactylon, Pers., is very common and plays some part in Santal life. It was according to the Santal traditions the second grass sown by Ṭhakur, when He had created the earth. When Santals marry, the dhubi grass is used

Now the old king had seven queens; as six of the queens had deceived the king, he had a well dug, and said to the six queens: "To-day perform the well-marriage[34]." Then the six queens arranged sun-dried rice, dhubi grass[35], sindur and lamp-cups in winnowing-fans; and catching hold of each other's hands they were dancing round the well. The king was standing there with a nine feet long stick in his hand, and was looking at them; and just as they were finishing the fifth round, he pushed them all down into the well, and filled earth on top of them. Here this story is ended.

83. THE KING AND HIS ONLY SON.

ONCE upon a time long ago there lived a king, who was childless. In order to get children he married many wives; but in spite of this with none of his wives did he get any children. He made any amount of vows and promises[1]; yet he never got any children. So he ceased doing anything, poor fellow. He forgot Thakur; he did not implore him and did not ask him.

Some day, a long time after this, people tell, a jugi Gosae came to him from who knows where. The jugi Gosae said: "Look here, raja, I do not see a single child of yours."

"I have no children," he replied.

"How is it that you have none?" the other asked. "You have so many queens; yet has none of them borne children? This looks very strange. Have you not tried to do something in some place or other?"

---

at the cumaṛa, the symbolic blessing of the bride; it is also used when performing a similar ceremony over the cattle (during the Santal Sohrae festival); when a Santal sells a head of cattle to another, he gives on delivery a bit of this grass to the other part, who later on will do the same to the seller.

83 [1] It is common, not so much with the Santals as with the Hindus, to make vows in order to obtain their wishes. The Santali text here has two expressions for the same, the last one literally meaning 'carry on the shoulder'.

Adoe menketa, Udi baric iń kurumutu legata; udi then iń manan jonanketa je ińak monre sanakidińak; ar horko hõko batlao barawadińak do joto lekageń kaj akata. Ado enre hõ bako hoelen khan doń thir dorokena.

Ado uniye menketa, Gidra ńamko do sana menaktama se bań?

Adoe menketa, Sana do menakgea, menkhan cekateń ńamkoa?

Ado uniye menketa, Judi sanayetme khan do, ona reak upai hõń laikema, arem senak khan.

Adoe menketa, Mase ente laime, ańjomlegeń.

Adoe metadea, Thakur then dom nehõr akana se bań, ar uni do gidra ńutumte jãhãtisem koe akadea se bań?

Adoe menketa, Uni do nun din hoyok kana bań koe akadea, ar uni then do bań nehõr akana.

Adoe metadea, One ńelme, onde mittań bhul iń ńelettama. Ado ma nehõrokme ar koeyeme, ar kami do nonka leka kami. Amak tinak dhon menaktama, ona reak siki bhag do rengeć oreć danakome. Tobe khan do ńelme hapen kora gidram ńamjońa. Ado mase bhala, noa ińak katha leka kamilem, adobo ńela.

Ado khange sari uni raj do uni jugi gosãeak katha lekae kamiketa. Ado tin din tayom coń, kathae, sarige uniak katha lekage mittań kora gidrai ńamkedea, ar uni gidra do sanam khon hudiń utarić chutki erageye janamkedea. Khange raj do adiye khusiyena. Ar uni gidra do nunak mõńj ar jute ńelok kana do, uni leka dhartire cele manwa hõ bako ńelok kana unak mõńje ńelok kana. Ar uni gidra do mit heogeko dohoyea. Sadher gidrai hoeyena se bań? Onate uni do adi dular.

Ado tahen tahenteye harayen khan, raj doe menketa, Nui gidra lagit do okare bahubon ńamkoa?

Ado ranikoko menketa, De ente ona do amgem badaea. Am jãhãregem men, onde khongebo agukoa.

---

2 The people are very anxious to get children, more especially sons. Incidentally it may be remarked that the goal of every girl is to be married and bear children.

3 The Santals always carry their children riding on the left hip.

He replied: "I have tried my uttermost[2]; I have made vows in many places, whatever wish came into my heart; people have also given me advice, and I have done all in accordance with their instructions. But as in spite of all no children came, I have ceased trying.

The other asked him: "Do you wish to get any children or how?"

"I certainly have the wish," he replied; "but how am I to get any?

"If you have the wish," the jugi said, "I might tell you the way to get them, provided you follow it,"

"Please then, tell," the king said: "let me first hear what it is."

He then asked him: "Have you implored Thakur or not? and have you sometimes asked him to get a child, or have you not?"

The king replied: "So long a time has passed, but I have not asked him, and have not implored him."

"There you see," the jugi said, "there I see one fault of yours. Therefore, implore him and ask him, and what you have to do is this: All you have of property, give one fourth of whatever there is to the poor. Then see, some day you will get a child. Please do this; do as I have told you, then we shall see."

Truth to tell, the king acted in accordance with the jugi Gosae's word; and some time afterwards, people tell, he really, in accordance with his word, got a child; this child was born to the youngest co-wife of them all. The king was very pleased; and this child was so beautifull and fine to look at, no single human being on this earth looks so fine; so beautiful he looked. They were always carrying this child on the hip[3]. He was an only child, you see; therefore he was so beloved.

As time passed and he grew up, the king said: "Where shall we get a wife for this child?"

The queens said: "Well, you know about this. Wherever you say, from there we shall fetch some one."

Khange adọ raebarkoko dhurạuketkoa. Are metatkoa, Ạikhạ jẹmọn nui koṛae mõñja, onkanko baṛẹ nolaokope. Rẹṅgẹć hoṛren hõ sẹ kisạṛ hoṛren hõ, jọtọgeń balakoa, mẹnkhan muṭhạnteṭ nui leka jẹmọnko ńẹlok.

Adọko mẹnketa, Acha, onkankole ńamleko anẹć ạikhạ, ale dọle ruạṛa, ar bańkhan dọ ọhọle ruạṛlena ạuri ńamko dhạbić dọ.

Adọ enka mẹn baṛakate khangeko calaoena. Adọ sạri gọṭa disomko dãṛãyetre hõ, uni muṭhạn lekankoge bako ńam daṛeako kana, onate bako ruạṛ daṛeak kana. Ạḍi din hoeyena; bar pẹ serma khon hõ bickom bạṛtiyena. Lọ dọs bọchọr gan hoeyena, ar inạktege uni gidrạ hõe harayena, gean manenae.

Adọ bạhuko ńam baṛayetko kathaeye añjọmketko khan dọe metatkoa, Iń lagat bạhu dọ alope ńamkoa. Iń dọ alope bạhuańa. Iń dọ bań bạhujońa, nenkategeń tahẽ hataṛoka. Ma hapẹn ińtegeń bạhujońa. Ape dọ bań jalapea.

Khange raj dọ uniak katha añjọmkate bae khusilena. Metadeae, Cedak bale bạhuama? Disom hoṛre cọń am dọm lajao ocoń. Hoṛ bako metańa, Nui raj dọe ciṭạṛgea? Sadherre mitṭań hopọn hõ bae bạhu daṛeadea. Nonka hoṛ dọ bako metańa?

Khange uni koṛa gidrạ dọ cet hõ bae mẹnleta, ar bạhu ocok dọ bańgeye rẹbẹn kana. Khange uni apatteṭ raj dọe rańgaoenteye ruhetkedea. Ar onate hõ bae tirpetlente uni koṛa dọ hajọt oṛakreye bhọraokadea. Are mẹnketa, Am dọ ińak hukum bam añjọmeta. Ạkhir thọ bọdnamińgem mẹneta. Bọdnam khan dọ bọdnamge; enkate hõ bọdnamge, nenkate hõ bọdnamge. Inạ dọ hoṛko mẹna, Raj hopọn koṛa dọ bạhu ocok bae rẹbẹn kanteye hajọtkedea. Ma nọṇḍẹ baṛẹ tahẽ dapoṛokme.

[4] Lit. I shall make all (i. e. anybody) a co-parent-in-law. Bala is the term of relationship applied to the parents of one's son- or daughter-in-law.

Then they engaged marriage brokers, and he said to these: "Beware, select such a one who is just as beautiful as this boy. Whether she is the child of poor people or of wealthy people, I shall become the co-parent-in-law[4] of any class; only that her form and looks are like this one's."

"All right," they said, "only when we find such a one, mind you, we shall return; we shall in no case return until we find some one."

Having spoken in this way they started. But, truth to tell, although they wandered through the whole land, they were unable to find any one with a form and looks like that of the boy; therefore they were unable to return. A long time passed, perhaps two or three years or even more. Nine or ten years passed, and by this time the child also grew up, and came to years of discretion.

When he, people tell, heard that they were seeking a wife for him, he said to them: "Don't seek a wife for me; don't bring me a wife. I am not going to marry; I shall remain as I am for the present. Later some time I shall find a wife for myself; I shall not give you any trouble."

Hearing what he said the king was not pleased. He said to him: "Why are we not to bring you a wife? You will bring shame on me among the people of the land. Will people not say of me: 'This king is a miser. Although he has only one son, he has not been able to get him a wife.' Will not people speak of me in this way?"

The boy did not say anything, but he was absolutely unwilling to be married. Then his father became angry and scolded him; and not being satisfied with this, he put him into jail, and said: "You will not listen to my command. In any case you want to disgrace me. If it is to be disgrace, let it be so; in this way it is disgrace; in the other way it is disgrace. This is what people will now say: 'He has put the prince into jail, because he is unwilling to be married.' So now stay here and enjoy yourself."

Ar pahradarkoe metaťkoa, Khub sontorte pahrayepe. Engatkoko oḍokkea, phuslaukepeako; se jãhãeko phuslaukepea, se daya ńelte ape hõpe aṛakkea. Se do baṅ. Onako katha do alogepe aṅjomtakoa ar alope dayaka. Bahujoṅ se bahuae auriye hẽg habić alope oḍok ocoaea. Ar kuli do dinge kuliyepe, ar bahuaeye hẽle khan seye aṅgocle khan, iń laiaṅpe. Iń hećkate nui doń oḍok idiyea. Ar noko kaidi hoṛ lekage nui hõ khataoepe.

Khange pahradarko menkeťa, Acha, raj, amem meneť lekagele kamia. Amak nun panle jomeťa; amak kathage bale dohoe khan, okoeakle dohoea?

Ado raje menkeťa, Ma tobe ina kathage. Judi iṅak katha bape aṅjom khan se iṅak katha leka bape kamile khan doń goćpea. Uniak edre apereń jhaṛaoa.

Khange pahradarko do raj moca khon ona kathako anjomkeť khan doko botorena, ado khub sontorteko pahrakedea. Ar ako akoko menjoṅa, Ma ya, khub sontortebon pahrawa. Nuj raj doe kurmutahagea. Jokhon aćren sadher hopon bae mãyãwadea, abo dobon cele kanteye mãyãwabona? Aṛakle khanbo, khatigeye goćbona. Abo samaṅre okae roṛkeťa, ona doe puraugea. Ma jãhãeak paliregebo aṛage, tobe abotegebon saboka, Menkhan joto hoṛe cehao akaťbona; sontorbo tahen ma ar alobon ḍhili sili ma.

Khange pahrako do khub kajakteko pahrakedea, ar dingeko kuliae kuliaea. Khange, kathae, miť din do nonka hoeyena, baṅdo Ṭhakur dayate baṅdo aćak nusib jorte, kathae, ńindage boṅga pargana buḍhi ar uni sãote barea boṅga uni koṛa ṭhenko hećenteko hoho bereťkedea, uniak ńutum ńumkateko hohoketa. Khange pahrako doko botorena. Ar kathae, galmarao doko aṅjomeťgea, menkhan ńel tho baṅgeko ńel ńam daṛeako kan.

---

[5] All the wives of the king are included.

[6] Lit. 'salt betel-nut'.

[7] The Pargana (overchief) bonga is one of the more feared bongas; he has a place in the sacred grove. His 'old woman' or wife is not otherwise worshipped or mentioned. The two bongas accompanying her are apparently supposed to be her sons.

To the watchmen he said: "Guard him very carefully; his mothers[5] might get him out; they might coax you; or some other people might coax you; or, feeling pity with him, even you yourselves might set him free. Such things must not happen. Don't listen to words of this kind from them, and don't take pity on him. Until he agrees to take a wife or to a wife being brought to him, don't let him get out. But ask him every day, and if he agrees to get a wife, if he acknowledges this, tell me. I shall myself come and take him out. And let him also work like the other prisoners."

The watchmen then said: " Very well, raja, we shall do as you say. We are eating your salt[6]; if we do not obey you, whom should we obey?"

"Well, that is all," the king said. "If you do not listen to what I say, or if you do not act as I tell you, I shall kill you. My anger with him I shall vent on you."

When the watchmen heard these words from the king's mouth, they became frightened and kept a very careful watch over him. They were saying to each another: "Well, you, let us keep a very careful watch; this king is revengeful. Since he has not shown his only son mercy, then who are we that he should show mercy to us? If we set him free, he will surely kill us. He will fulfil what he spoke before us. If we set him free in any shift of ours, we shall let ourselves be caught. He has warned all of us; let us be careful, and let us not be negligent."

Consequently the watchmen kept a very strict watch on him, and every day they asked him the same question. Then, people tell, one day it so happened, whether it was by the grace of Thakur, or it was on account of his fate, at night, people tell, the Pargana bonga's wife[7], and with her two other bongas, came to the young man, called him and made him get up; they called out, mentioning his name. Then the watchmen became frightened. People tell, they heard them talking, but as for seeing, they were unable to see anybody.

Khangeko mẹnkeťa, Thirkoǩabon. Oeťkoko rọṛa, bhalabon aṅjọmkoa. Ar onka mẹnkateko thir akana ar onkoaǩ rọṛko aǩtẹn kana. Adọ kathae, uni pargana buḍhiye mẹneťa, Iạ beṭa, nui koṛa dọ mabon bạhuaea. Nuiren bạhu dọ manwa họtẹte dọ ọhọ hoelena. Manwa dọ nuiren bạhu ọhọko ńam daṛelekoa, ẹnte dhạrtire nui leka juť ar mọ̃ńj koṛa dọ bạnuǩkoa.

Adọ unkinkin mẹnkeťa, Hẹ̃ ma hẹge, ayo, mẹnkhan, nui koṛa thọ bạhujoṅ dọ bae rẹbẹn kana. Cekatebon bạhuaea?

Adọ uniye mẹnkeťa, Hẹ̃, rẹbẹn ma bae rẹbẹn kan, mẹnkhan bạhuae lek mane harayena. Adọń mẹneťa, uni aboren phalna kuṛige ạguyete nui ṭhen miťrebon gitićkakina, arbo ńẹlkina, dupulạṛa sẹkin baṅa.

Khange unkinkin mẹnkeťa, Acha, tọbẹ amem mẹneť lekaegeabon.

Adọ dosar ńindạ khange sạri miťṭaṅ kuṛiko ạgukedete uni koṛa tulućko gitić miťkadea. Arko mẹnkeťa, Bhala nukin dọkin dupulạṛa sẹ baṅ. Adọ kathae, uni kuṛi họ̃ uni koṛa muṭhạngeye ńẹloǩ kana. Ṭhik ṭhak ona họṛmọ onka ẹsẹl ar ona rupgeye ńẹlena.

Khange uni kuṛi dọ koṛa phẹḍreye duṛuṕ akana, ar koṛa dọe jạpiť akaťa. Uni kuṛiko ạgu oṭokade jọkhẹn dọ bae disạleťkoa, ar uni kuṛiye duṛuṕ akan họ̃ bae disạledea. Khange uni kuri họ̃ koṛae ńẹlkede khan dọe khusiyena. Mọnreye mẹnkeťa, Hẹ̃, nui ṭhen dọń tahẹngea. Are duṛuṕ akangea, ceť họ̃ bae cal bọlẹ kana.

Adọe duṛuṕ bhagaoen khan dọ, kathaeye gitićena. Adọ ona tayọm koṛako ẹbhẹn ocokedea arẹ bujhaukeťa, ọṇḍẹ miťṭen họṛ menaea. Khangeye tunum baṛakedea.

Adọ kathae, ać tire mundạm tahẹ̃kantaea. Adọ ona mundạme toťkeťte uni kuṛiye họrọǩae kana. Adọ un jọkhẹne ạikạukeť dọ, uni tire họ̃ mundạm menaǩtae. Adọ aćaǩ mundạm dọ uniye họrọǩadea ar uniaǩ mundạm dọ aće họrọǩkeťa. Khange bana họṛkiń jạpiťkeťa. Adọ marsal hạbićkin gitić akan. Adọ ạḍi enakin

8 The narrator presupposes that the bonga girl's name is mentioned.

"Let us keep quiet," they said. "Let us hear what they are talking." Saying this they kept quiet, and were listening to what they were speaking. The Pargana woman, people tell, was saying: "I say, my son, let us procure a wife for this young man. Through human beings this one will not get a wife; human beings will never be able to find any wife for him, because on the whole earth there is no young man fine and beautiful like him."

The two others then said: "That is quite so, mother; but you know, this young man is unwilling to marry. How shall we get him a wife?"

"Yes," she replied, "quite so, he is unwilling; but he has grown fit to be married. So I say, let us bring our girl so and so[8], and let us place her here with him, and we shall see whether they will love each other or not."

"All right," the two others said, "we shall do as you say."

Then, truth to tell, next night they brought a girl, and placed her here and said: "Let us see whether they will love each other or not." The girl, people tell, was looking exactly like the young man. Her body was exactly looking fair like his, and the form was the same.

The girl was sitting near the boy, who was asleep. He was not aware of it when they brought her, and he was not aware of the girl sitting there. When the girl saw the boy, she was pleased, and said to herself: "Yes, I shall stay with him." She was sitting there, without speaking or moving.

When she got tired of sitting, she lay down. Afterwards they woke the young man, and he became aware of somebody being there. He felt over her with his hand. Now he had a ring on his finger; taking this off, he put it on the girl's finger. At this time he became aware that she also had a ring on her finger, whereupon he took her ring on his own finger. Afterwards they both slept, until it became daylight. It was late before they woke.

ẹbhẹnoḱ kan. Adọ bereṭ baṛakatekin bẹpẹṅgẹṭjoṅ kana, adọ bana hoṛkin khusiyena.

Adọ rajko lạiadea, koṛa dọ bạhui ạguana mẹnte. Adọ ona katha aṅjọmte jọtọ hoṛge ạḍiko hahaṛayena, ar unkin ńẹńẹl jọtọ hoṛko ńir hẹćena. Adọ kuṛiko ńẹlkedete ạḍiko rạskạyena, adọ ọṇḍẹ khonko oḍok idikeṭkina.

Adọ unkin baplakin reaḱ raj dọe neṇḍa goṇḍakeṭa. Bạjniạko nạṭuạkoe girạwaṭkoa, ar emanten tamasaekoe girạwaṭkoa, metaḱme rasdhạriko, balọk naṭko, sẹ emanten kheloḍia tamasaeko. Ar aćaḱ disomren mạńjhiạḱko, parganako, des mạńjhiko, perjako, miṭ miṭte jọtọgeye girạwaṭkoa, baṅma, Niạ inạ dinre dọ jọtọge iṅ ṭhen bapla bhọj jọmpe hijuḱa. Ar ọkọeko ceṭ ceṭko tamasape baḍaea, onako sapaṕ dọ ạgu daraetape ar nọṇḍẹṅ tamasa ocopea, ar ona reaḱ dọ boskis iṅ emapea.

Khange bhại, disom hoṛ dọ girạko ńamkeṭ khan ar ona kathako aṅjọmkeṭ khan dọko chil bilạuena, ạḍiko rạskạyena, adọ ona neṇḍa dinre ọṇḍẹko sẹnena. Khange uḍi bạṛić bajna tamasateko andoṛ uṭhạukeṭa. Adọ unkinko sindrạdankeṭkina, ar uḍi bạṛiće khelaokeṭa. Ar ọnẹye mẹnleṭ lekageye ẹm baṛawaṭkoa. Ar kathae, mọ̃ṛẽ mãhãe bhọjkeṭa ar un dinge disom hoṛe dọhọleṭkoa. Adọ bhọj jọm baṛakateye bidạkaṭkoa.

Adọ ẹnẹ cabayena katha dọ, ẹṇḍẹge mucạṭena.

9 Lit. 'made knots for them'. See note 4 p. 194.

10 The 'artists' mentioned are those known to Santals: dancers, musicians, and play-actors of sorts.

Having got up they looked at each other, and both of them were pleased.

Then they informed the king that the young man had brought a wife. Hearing this all people were very much astonished, and all came running to see these two. When they saw the girl, they were very glad, and they took them away from there.

Thereupon the king fixed a day for celebrating their marriage. He made appointments for the day[9] with male and female dancers, also with performers of sorts, that is to say, artists, boy dancers, or different festival artists[10]. He invited all the headmen, the overchiefs, the country-headmen, the farmers of his land[11], every one of them, viz. On such and such a day you are all to come to me to partake of the marriage feast. And such of you as know to give exhibitions of some kind, bring your instruments with you, and I shall let you give a show here, and for this I shall give you a present.

Then, my friends, when the people received the invitation and they heard all, they became utterly excited; they became very glad, and on the day fixed they went there, and with all kinds of music and entertainments they raised an awful noise. Also they made these two go through the marriage ceremony, and they spent an awful amount of money. As the king had promised, he gave the people presents. And, people tell, he let them feast for five days; so many days he kept the people there. After they had eaten and done with the feasting, he said good-by to them.

Then there the story is finished; there it is ended.

---

11 All classes are mentioned, village headmen, overchiefs, tenants and country-headmen. These last ones are something between a village headman and an overchief.

84. Tạrup̣ ar raebar hoṛak̓ katha.[1]

Noa katha do̠ nonkako galmarao kana, se̠ nonkako lạia, se̠ noa katha do̠ nonkana. Jāhāe ho̠ṛrenge koṛa gidrạ se̠ kuṛi gidrạkoko haralentako khan, baplakako ane̠ć, kathae, putistạ do̠ hoeok̓ kana. Bam baplale khan, kathae, o̠ne̠m pap akat̓ reak̓ chut do̠ baṅ meṭaok̓ kana. E̠nte era hereltem papket̓te gidrạm janamkedea arem ạsul harakedea se̠m hara burukedea. Ado̠ o̠ne̠m papket̓ reak̓ chut do̠, kathae, baplaleko ane̠ć meṭao cabak̓ kana.

Onate, kathae, adalo̠t duạrre hõ pe̠ tekhaṛko kukli kana, se̠ pe̠a goha ane̠ćko muṅjurok̓ kana, se̠ to̠be̠ ena mamla do̠ cabak̓ kana. Ado̠ onkage noa pap reak̓ hõ, kathae, pe̠ tekhaṛem dho̠ro̠mle ena se̠m putisṭạle ena puruchun do̠ hoeok̓ kana. Pạhilte do̠ narta chạṭiạrko ṅutum akat̓a.[2] Unre do̠ uni ạimại eskargeye o̠ṛhẽ̠yena; ado̠ inre thoṛa thuṛi pap meṭaok̓ kantakina. Arhõ inạkate caco chạṭiạrko ṅutum akat̓a.[3] Unre do̠ ạimại herel se̠ banar haṛam buḍhigeko o̠ṛhẽ̠kina. Binti jo̠khe̠n phe̠nteko ro̠ṛ

---

1 The story itself is a very short one; but it touches on some matters that occupy a large place in the minds of the Santals. The narrator, Sagram, apparently felt himself called upon to furnish the story with a long introduction. The whole is so characteristic of the way of thinking of the ordinary village Santal that it is reproduced. It might be noted that according to Santal theories sexual intercourse is considered as a sin in all cases; one of their most common names for it is bạṛić kạmi, lit. bad work.

2 The narta or janam chạṭiạr is the name-giving (birth-) ceremony, in case a boy is born, five days after birth, and in case a girl, three days after birth. Until this ceremony is gone through, the village is unclean; no sacrifice can be performed in the village, and no outsiders can take any food in the house of birth. This is the first purification, and, having gone through this ceremony, the now-born babe so to say becomes a recognized human being, belonging to a family and sept. In case of change of moon being near, the ceremony may be hastened and even performed on the day of birth; a child must not be named in another month than when it is born, otherwise it will, when grown up and married, soon become a widow or widower.

3 The caco chạṭiạr (lit. walking chạṭiạr) is a ceremony by the performance of which a Santal becomes a full member of the Santal society. It may be performed

84. THE STORY OF THE LEOPARD AND THE MARRIAGE BROKER[1].

People talk about this matter in the following way, or they tell it thus, or this matter is as follows. When anybody's sons or daughters have grown up, then, people say, only when they are married, will there be purification. If you don't marry them, people say, the religious uncleanness due to what you have sinned will not be wiped out. You see, through what you sinned you got a child and you supported it and kept it until it grew big. So the religious uncleanness due to your sin, people say, is fully wiped out only when you marry them.

In accordance with this, people say, they examine people three times also in a court of justice, or accept as true a case, only when there are three witnesses, that is to say, then only a suit is finished. It is the same with this sin also, only when you have three times performed religious duties or purifications, there is propitiation. The first they have named the birth ceremony[2]; on this occasion the woman alone is praised, and then a little sin is wiped off. Again after this there is what they have named the walking ceremony[3]; on this occasion they praise[4] the woman

at any age; and as it involves some expense in feasting, a man will generally go through the ceremony for all his children at one time. A Santal cannot be married without having been through this, wherefore it must be performed before marriage; this is the only limit as to time or age. A Santal cannot be cremated after death if he or she has not been through this; I have heard that the ceremony has been performed with a dead body to ensure its being cremated and the bones being taken to the sacred river. The ceremony is brought to a close by the recitation of the history of mankind (acc. to Santal traditions), brought up to date; the persons concerned from now on belong to Santal history. The recitation is always wound up by an application, that they may now be permitted to be parties to all social events and ordinary life's work, whereupon it is said: 'We implore you Five (i. e. the Santal community), we were like crows (i. e. black), we have become white like paddy-birds, so you Five be witnesses.' Thereupon they drink beer and sing.

[4] The word means mentioning with praise, especially in song.

ạguia, ona herelak̓ khaṇḍa ạimạiak̓ khaṇḍa ar haṛam buḍhi cet̓ lekako kajet̓ kana, cet̓ cetko saḍea, ar gidrạ hoekate okakore uni ạimại hasoledea, onako jọtọko ọ̃ṛhẽtakina. Adọm dọ binti jọkhẹnko rọṛ tiok̓atakina, ar adọm dọ ona jhikạ ẹnẹć jọkhẹn dhại buḍhi cet̓ lekae jọtọnkedea ar cet̓ sakamkoteye sekaoledea, onako phẹnte jọtọko ńum tiogtạkina. Adọ mọ̃ṛẹ̃ họṛ onkako ọ̃ṛhẽte, kathae, unkinak̓ pap dọ kaṭaok̓ kantakina.

Adọ unre hõ jọtọ dọ baṅ kaṭaolentakina. Adọ onate baplare huḍiń huḍiń ghaḍlak̓ko laea; ona dọ pukhriko ńutumet̓ kana. Ona ṭhen barea arā̃ṛko dọhọea; ona cetanre apat họṛ dọ tarwaṛe sap̓kateye teṅgona. Ar ona reak̓ dak̓ baplaye gidrại jọrọwaea. Eṅgat họṛ dọe nunuaea. Toa dọ todok̓re hõ baṅre hõ, ẹnhọ̃e cẹpẹć ńọ̃k̓aegea. Ar koṛa gidrạ dọ bạhu ạgu bạriạtko calak̓ hilok̓e nunu gọt̓aea, ar ona reak̓ eṅgat họṛ dọ mit̓ ṭakae ńama. Adọ ẹnẹ inre, kathae, unkinak̓ pap dọ kaṭao cabayentakina.

Adọ onka jọtọ gidrạkin bapla cabaket̓koa mẹnkhan dọ, ạkinak̓ bhar dọ onko gidrạkore ucạṛena. Unkin buḍhi haṛam ạurikin gujuk̓ hạbić jọk̓tọn ar ạk̓sul reak̓ sir bhar lagaoakoa. Unkinko bạṛićkin khan dọ, Ṭhạkur onkoe sạjạiyet̓koa. Arkin gọćena mẹnkhan, eṅgat apat reak̓ko puruchunkak̓a, adọko chuṭiyena. Adọ Ṭhạkur ona reak̓, kathae, bae sap̓koa.

---

5 The **jhikạ** dance is a kind of ceremonial dance, gone through especially at the **karam** festival. It is danced by men only, who take hold of each other's hands and move from side to side with a swaying motion.

6 The small hole is generally dug close to where the water-pots stand. The two yokes are put one on each side of the 'tank', and the father stands with one foot on each of these, with a sword in his two hands. He keeps the sword above his head (his hands resting on his head), the blade pointing backwards. The person on whom the water is to fall is sitting behind the man. Somebody (a relative) now brings a lota (brass cup) with water, and pours some out over the sword. Running down the sword, it falls on the head of the person sitting behind. She keeps her hands up before her face, and receives some water also in these, licks it, and then wipes it over her head. The man goes through this performance, first with his wife and thereupon with his daughter, who is the bride.

and the man, that is, both the husband and the wife. When the ceremonial recitation is gone through, they allegorically mention the man's and the woman's body and all they do, how they call out, how the woman felt pain when the child was born, all this they praise. Some of it they mention at the time of recitation, part of it again at the time of the jhika[5] dance, when they describe how the midwife took care of the mother and what leaves she fomented her with, all of it allegorically. And when the village people mention all this in their praise, then, people say, the parents' sin is removed.

But not even then all is wiped off. Therefore they, at the time of marriage, dig a small small hole; this is called a tank. Close to this they put two yokes; with a sword in his hands the father stands on these. He lets some water from this[6] fall down on the child he is marrying away. The mother sucks her son. Whether any milk comes out or not, in any case she gives him a little to suck. When the bridegroom's party start to fetch the bride, his mother lets him suck, as he goes off; for this the mother gets one rupee[7]. Just then, people say, is the sin of the parents wiped entirely off.

When they have, in this way, married all their children, the responsibility of the parents is transferred to the children. It becomes the duty of these to take care of, and to support, their father and mother until they die. If they let harm come to these, Thakur punishes them; and when they die, they make propitiation for the parents; then they are free of responsibility, and Thakur will not, people say, hold them responsible for anything in this connexion.

A similar ceremony is gone through with the bridegroom in his village, before the bridal party starts for the bride's village.

[7] The mother of the bridegroom lets her son put his head to her breast, at the same time holding her hand near to his mouth. The young man has a rupee in his mouth, and lets this fall into his mother's right hand.

Adọ ọnẹ onka, kathae, jāhān papge ẹkkalte dọ baṅ kaṭao họdọk kana, dinek dinekte ruti rutite mimiť tilmiṅkate ọcọgok kana. Adọ onka onkate tis ọcọk cabaka, ẹnḍẹ enam nirọpọnok kana, ẹnḍẹ ena, kathae, suk dọm ṅama. Ẹnteko mẹneťa, Solo anabon ghạṭi akaťa, adọ ona mimiť tilmiṅte tis ọcọk cabaka, ẹn hilok khon jivire suk dọm ạikạua. Ar ona hõ nonka kana. Adọ ạikhạ alom ghạṭ bọlọe khan, khaṭaoktama, ar baṅkhan baṅge khaṭaoka. Ọnẹ onkako mẹneťa.

Adọ ona raebar katha dọ nonka kana. Koṛa gidrạko haralen khan, eṅgat apatko rọṛ saḍea, baṅma, Nẹs dọ nui koṛa lagať bạhubon ṅamkoa. Adọ họṛ samaṅre enkako rọṛle khan, ato họṛko uprạ upri baṛaea. Huni hõe mẹna, Bahu dọ iṅiṅ udukapea. Huni hõe mẹna, Iṅiṅ udukapea. Adọ onkako mẹn khan, eṅgat apatokkin dọ jọtọgekin ṅẹl idikoa. Adọ jāhāeṭakrege mọn gaḍaoktakin, adọ inạkin goṭaea. Dẹnẹ banarko kupulia, khusi sẹ baṅ. Adọ duyo dige khusigeko mẹnle khan dọ, sar sạgunko paṅjaea, oṛak duạrko ṅẹla, họpọrọgokteko baplaka.

Ar ona jạt pạrisko ma ṅẹpẹl hilokrege jọtọko phaṇḍaokak. Uni ọkọe ukduk kan, unige onako ma jọtọe ṭhik ṭhak akať are lại laha akawaťkoa, noko dọko noa mạilạ họṛ kana mẹnte. Adọ noa mạila reak hõ sedae dọ ạḍiko paṅjayeť tahẽkangea, mẹnkhan

8 The mustard-seed plays some part in Santal speech, to show smallness. E.g. they say about a disease that it comes on in one night, but abates by the size of one mustard-seed at a time.

9 The parents arrange all; the young pair may now-a-days be asked whether they are pleased, when they are pointed out to each other at a distance. They are not supposed to have any conversation with each other at all before the marriage.

10 Omens play a large role in connexion with the important events in a Santal's life, especially so in connexion with a marriage. Certain things seen or met with inside the boundaries of the villages of the contracting parties, when they go from one village to the other in connexion with any of the several preliminaries and functions, are considered auspicious or the opposite; meeting with what is considered a bad omen they will turn back or even give the whole up. Now-a-days they let people know what they are going to do, so that the village people are careful not to meet the party with anything that is bad. E. g. a full

In this manner, people say, no sin is wiped off at once with one stroke; day by day, gradually it is removed, just as much as the size of a mustard-seed[8] at a time. When, in this way, it has been removed little by little, then only you become well and sound, then only, people say, you become happy. Because, people say, we have sinned one hundred percent; when, little by little, the size of a mustard-seed at a time, it has been entirely removed, from this day only you will feel happy in your soul. And so it actually is. But beware, if you don't let any new sin come in, it will go so with you, otherwise it will not. This is what people say.

Now the matter of the marriage broker is as follows. When a son has grown up, the parents will say, so that people hear it: "This year we must get a wife[9] for this boy." When they say this in the hearing of people, the village people will commence to vie with each other. One will say: "I shall show you a bride." Another will say: "I shall show you." When they speak in this manner, the parents have a look at all, one after the other; and when they feel pleased in their minds with some one they make up their mind. Both sides ask each other whether they are pleased ar not, and when they on both sides say 'pleased', they commence to look out for omens[10], go to see each other's place and circumstances, go through the mutual betrothal ceremonies and celebrate the marriage.

The question relating to septs and subsepts is gone into on the day they let the young ones have a look at each other. He who 'shows' has arranged all these matters, and he has beforehand told them that these people are of such and such a subsept[11].

waterpot, a pack bullock, a cow, the pug marks of a tiger or leopard are all good omens; to see a fire, an axe, some one carrying firewood, a snake or a jackal (especially crossing the road in front from the left side) are bad omens. Except for the snakes or the wild animals all is easily arranged.

11 Lit. dirt, an expression very commonly used when asking for the sept or subsept.

onako nāhāk̕ dǫ bako pańjayeṭa; ǝkǝn nią̣ko pańjayeṭa, mit̕ mạilą utạr khạjuk alo. Jāhā dosrayen dǫ, ona dǫ ganok̕ kangea. Ǝnte nāhāk̕ dǫ disomre hǫṛko sańgeyena, ar hǫṛ ma ǝkǝn barǫ pạrisko tahǝ̣kana. Onakate arhǫ̃ barǫkate pạrisko juṭućaṭa, adǫ jǫtǫre guṭ 144, nunạk̕ pạris hoe akana. Adǫ hǫṛ baḍhaoente onako pạris hǫ̃ tǫl cabayena. Ǫnǝko mǝn leka, Laṛ nạṛī bando nāṛī tǫlen dǫ, mạiri, tǫlen dǫ. Ona sik jǫtǫ ghaṭ ǝsǝt̕ cabayena. Ạḍim pańjaete ma ghaṭge bań ńamok̕ kan; onate unạk̕ hạbić dǫ bako khudạuet̕ kana.

Adǫ koṛa gidrą reak̕ dǫ ǝnǝ enka eńgat apat hǫṛem murukle khange, bạhu dǫm ńamkedetem juri pạrikadea.

Mǝnkhan kuṛi hǫpǫn reak̕ dǫ muskilgea. Eńga apa murukkate hǫ̃ bań jutok̕ kana. Ǝnte jāhāeye hataoetam bań; ǫkǫe ṭhen ạuṛi dǫm jāwāekaea? Hǝ̃, jāhāeko khǫj khan, inre enko ṭhenem ṭhāokadea, ar bańkhan ạuṛi dǫ ǫkǫe ṭhenem jāwāekaea? Hǝ̃, jumi jaege ḍher tahǝntam khan, onako aekate ghạrdi jāwāe dǫm dǫhǫ daṛekekogea. Ar ona hǫ̃ bạnuk̕tam khan, cekatem dǫhǫ daṛeaege? Adǫ kajetege kuṛi hǫpǫn dǫ bae hara jhakak̕tama?

---

12 The old Santal rule is, that if two belonging to the same sept marry, they are outcasted from Santal society. Now-a-days outcasting is done if the parties are of the same sept and subsept, otherwise not. The narrator himself was an example in point. When he came here in the early nineties, he had no wife, and soon wanted to be married to a girl from the village. She belonged to the same sept, but was of another subsept than Sagram Murmu. As we would not like to have anything that should go against the Santal customs, I called some of the leading Santals of these parts and asked their opinion. Their answer was: We do not like it, but we do not outcaste such people. It might be noted that it is only on the father's side that they keep account of the septs. They say gạí ḍahar eńga ḍahar bako pańjaea, i. e. they do not follow a cow's way or a mother's way.

13 This is the theory. The Santals are divided into twelve septs, of which one is lost (i. e. no one belonging to this lost sept is known); each sept is in the same way supposed to be divided into twelve subsepts; as a matter of fact, there are more than twelve subsepts to each of the known septs, some having as many as thirty. But this does not affect the theory.

Formerly they were very careful in following up the question of septs; now-a-days they do not follow this up so carefully[12], they only find out so much that they make sure that they do not belong to the same subsept. If the subsepts are different, it is in order. Now-a-days the inhabitants have multiplied in the country, and the Santals were originally only twelve septs. Therefore they have added twelve[13] subsepts to each, so that now it has in all become 144 subsepts. And as the people have multiplied, these subsepts have also become fixed; as people say: 'The lar climber and the bando climber[14] have been tied, darling, have been tied.' In the same way all opportunities have been blocked up; if you try to follow anything up very closely, no opportunity may be found; therefore they do not pursue this so far.

So far as a son is concerned, when the parents take the matter up as described, then you find a bride for him, and give him a mate.

But as regards daughters it is difficult. It will not do for the parents to take the matter up, because you must have some one who will take your girl; to whom should you marry her away when there is no one? Yes, when somebody asks for a wife, then you settle her with them, otherwise with whom should you marry her at random? Well, if you have much agricultural land, you might, estimating the value of this, get a home-son-in-law[15]. But if you have nothing of the kind, how will you be able to keep one? Undoubtedly will not your daughter grow up and become an old maid?

---

[14] Two large forest climbers, the first being Bauhinia Vahlii, W. & A., the second Spatholabus Roxburghii, Benth., the first represents the man, the second the woman.

[15] The girls are a problem to the Santals in the way stated. They will, in case there are only girls in a family, arrange to get a g h ạ r d i j ã w ã e, a son-in-law who comes and lives with the girl's parents, if there are no other ways; this is fairly common. Old maids are practically unknown, i. e., if a girl has no mental or corporal defect that makes marriage impossible.

Adǫ onkate kuṛi hǫpǫn dǫ disomre hara lambo menaḱkoa. Adǫ onate ǫkǫekoren kuṛi gidrạ menaḱkotako hǫṛ dǫ apnartege jãhãkoren peṛakoko metakoa, Jãhãeko bạhuko ńam baṛako khan dǫ, lại saḍeakope, ar bańkhan ạyur hǫralepe; bogete kuṛi gidrạ menaḱkotalea. Jǫtǫ ṭạṇḍiren peṛako ṭhen sẹ ńẹpẹl oprom hǫṛko ṭhen onkako rǫṛ saḍekaḱa. Adǫ jãhãeko khǫj khan, unre onko peṛako idikoteko uduḱakoa. Adǫko khusi rạji baṛayena mẹnkhan dǫ, uniye ạyur ạguleťko hǫṛge raebar hǫṛ dǫe hoeyena. Unige ǫntẹ nǫtẹnaḱ kathaye idi ạguia; uni dǫ bǫlẹ ciṭhiye hoeyena.

Ar sedae dǫko lạia, bańma, raebar hǫṛ dǫ, kathae, hijuḱ sẹnoḱte barǫ kaṭ bạndi ạuriko jǫm otoṛ dhạbić dǫ bako lǫgǫn hǫda. Adǫ onako jǫm cabakeťa mẹnkhan, baplako sạrdi gǫda. Ar sedae jǫkhẹn dǫ, kathae, raebar hǫṛ dǫ ạḍiko bǫrǫako kan tahẽkana, onateko manaoeťko tahẽkana, bańre mae lại bhiṛkạuko. Adǫ aloe lại bhiṛkạukoa mẹnte bǫtǫrte uni dǫ ạḍiko manaoea.

Onkage, kathae, sedae dǫ bir tahẽkana sẹ bań. Onate un jǫkhẹn dǫ kul tạruṗ hõ ạḍiko jǫjǫm kan tahẽkana. Adǫ un jǫkhẹnge miť hǫṛe raebar kan tahẽkana. Ar ona bir talatege hǫr dǫ sẹn akan tahẽkante onkategeye hijuḱ sẹnoḱ kan tahẽkana. Adǫ tis khon cǫń, kathae, tạruṗ dǫe ciạkedeteye mẹnkeťa, Nui hǫṛ miť din dǫń jǫmegea. Onka tạruṗ dǫ, kathae, mǫnreye mẹnwana.

Adǫ ona takrege uni raebar hǫṛ dǫ bǫṛ ạguko kole kana. Ẹn kathae, Baplaḱ lagať din tiogoḱ kana, inạ peṛa daramko lạgiť miť bar kuṭrạ bǫṛ kǫe ạguabonme.

Adǫ raebarićе mẹnkeťa, Ẹnḍẹkhan teheńgeń calaḱa. Miťṭań bosta ńawańtabonpe.

---

[16] The marriage broker may be either a man or a woman; very frequently it is an old widow.

[17] Rice and other cereals are stored in bundles, fastened by straw-ropes prepared for the purpose. The Santals like to express themselves metaphorically; here straw-rope stands for the contents of such a bundle, viz. rice. The contracting parties will lend rice, etc. to each other, when needed. This is paid back at any convenient time, but no interest is charged.

[18] Bits is euphemistic for maunds (kuṭrạ for kaṭ, as the Santals generally call a maund, a weight corresponding to nearly 40 kg.).

In this way there are girls in the country, grown up and overripe. For this reason people who have daughters will themselves speak to friends or others and say: "If somebody wants a bride, let them hear of us; and if not, prepare the way for us; we have a good many girls with us." They will speak plainly in this way to relatives they may have somewhere or to acquaintances. If then somebody asks for a wife, they will take the relatives there, and let them have a look. If they are satisfied and willing, then the person who brought them becomes the marriage broker[16]. He or she goes and comes between the parties; he, so to say, becomes a letter.

Formerly, they tell, that a marriage broker would not let the final arrangements come to a head until he had finished eating the contents of a rice-bundle taking twelve maunds; but when he had finished this, he would hurry up the marriage. In olden times, people tell, they were in great fear of the marriage brokers, so that they showed them great respect; if they did not do so, he might tell something or other and scare the others away. So in order that he might not tell anything to scare the others away, people were showing him great respect.

In this way, people tell, — formerly there was only forest as you know. In those times tigers and leopards also killed a good many. In those days there was a man who acted as marriage broker. The road was passing through the forest, and he was going and coming there. Then, people tell, a leopard had found out and for some time been aware of the man, and said: "One day I shall eat this man." This was what the leopard had decided.

About this time they were sending the marriage broker to bring straw-rope[17]; they said to him: "The day for celebrating the marriage is coming; go, ask for and bring us a couple of bits[18] of straw-rope to have to meet the friends with in connexion with this."

The marriage broker then replied: "In that case I shall go to-day; get me a sack."

Adọ sạri dakako emadea. Jọm baṛakate mit̕ṭaṅ bostako ṅawadea, adọ onae gọk̕keta̕, adọe calak̕ kana. Ar uni raebarić jọmeye mẹnet̕, uni dọe eṅga tạrup̕ kana. Ar nui họṛ dọ bae baḍae kana, teheṅ dọ nāhāk̕ tạrup̕e jọmeṅa mẹnte dọ. Khange ona hoṛte tumbut̕ tumbut̕ nui hoṛ dọe calak̕ kana, ar tạrup̕ dọ nui hoṛe ṅẹlkede khan dọ lahareye tāṛāk̕ hataṛ akana.

Adọ katha tahẹn reak̕, bhại, ar Candọ reak̕ lilạ, uni tāṛāk̕ akan tạrup̕, bhạiye ṅẹl ṅam gọt̕kedea. Ar un jọkhẹnge, kathae, rọrọṛ sarbharao gọt̕kedeteye rọṛ gọt̕keta̕, Iṅ dọ, tạrup̕, alom jọmeṅa. Iṅ dọ mit̕ hoṛ khon iṅ bar hoṛkako kana.

Khange, kathae, uni tạrup̕ hō̱e bujhạu gọt̕ket̕teye mẹnketa̕, Sạrige mit̕ hoṛ khonem bar hoṛet̕koa?

Adọ uni hoṛe mẹnketa̕, Hẽ̱ sạrige.

Khange tạrup̕e mẹnketa̕, Tọbẹ khan iṅem bar hoṛ daṛekiṅa?

Adọ uni hoṛe mẹnketa̕, Hẽ̱ṅ bar hoṛ daṛekema, ạikạ nẹṇḍẹ khon thoṛa sẹn ṅōgok̕ hoyok̕tama.

Khange tạrup̕e mẹnketa̕, Cedak̕? Nọṇḍẹ dọ ọhọm bar hoṛ daṛeliṅa?

Adọ uni hoṛe mẹnketa̕, Hẽ̱ṅ bar hoṛkemgea; ẹnte nọṇḍẹ dọ hoṛtẹt̕ kana; pasẹn ona takrege jāhāeko heć bọtẹć kange. Onate ona dọṅ metam kana, thoṛa nẹṇḍẹ khon dọlaṅ sa ṅōgok̕a, adọ nāhāk̕ iṅ bar hoṛ gọt̕mea.

Adọ sạri tạrup̕ hō̱ onageye bataoket̕teye mẹnketa̕, Acha, ẹṇḍẹkhan delaṅ iṅ calak̕a.

Adọ mit̕ṭaṅ gaḍa sor ṭhene teṅgoyenteye metae kana, Dela nọṇḍẹ hijuk̕me ar noa bostare ma bọlọk̕me.

Adọ sạriye sẹn sorente ona bostareye bọlọyena. Khangeye pọṭọmkedete khub lekae tọl urićkedea, ar ona bostareye bọlọk̕ khangeye metae kana, Ạikạṅ jāhā lekamege, rọṛtẹt̕ cet̕ hō̱ alom rọṛ baṛaea. Arem rọṛ saḍele khan ạikạ, gun ọhọ lagaolentiṅa

Then, truth to tell, they gave him food, and, when he had done eating, they found a sack for him; he took this on his shoulder and started. Now the leopard who intended to eat the marriage broker was a female; and the man did not know that a leopard would presently eat him that day. The man was walking along the road with his head bent, and when the leopard saw the man, she went ahead, and was lying in wait somewhere in front.

Then as to what is to happen, my friends, and Chando's wonderful work, — the man suddenly caught sight, my friends, of the leopard that was lying in wait. Just at this moment, people tell, he got a sudden impulse to speak and said: "Don't eat me, leopard. I am making one person into two."

Then, people tell, the leopard also suddenly understood what this was and said: "Really, do you make two persons from one?"

"Yes, that's the truth," the man replied.

"Will you then," the leopard asked, "be able to make me into two?"

"Yes," the man answered, "I might be able to make you into two; only you will have to go a short distance away from here."

"Why?" the leopard asked. "Will you not be able to make me into two here on the spot?"

"Yes, I might," the man replied; "but you see, here is the road; just at the moment when I work somebody might come. Therefore I say to you, we shall go a short distance away from here, then I shall make you into two."

Truth to tell, the leopard also saw the reasonableness of this, and said: "All right, come along then, I shall go."

The man stopped near a river, and said to the leopard: "Come here and enter into this sack."

Truth to tell, the leopard went up to the man and entered into the sack. He thereupon cowered her up, and tied her well and fast; and, as she entered into the sack, he said to her: "Have a care, whatever I may do to you, don't in any case utter a word. If you make any sound, know then my magic power will have no

ar ọhọm bar hoṛlena. Arem hape akan tahẹna mẹnkhan, ẹkkaltegem bar hoṛ gọdoka.

Adọ enka mẹnkatege, kathae, khub lekae tọl urićkedete gaḍa ḍhipteye kuṭuṅ idikedete ọṇḍe khon gaḍa daḱreye kuṇḍel ńũr gọťkadea. Adọ Cando reaḱ lilạ, bhại, adọ kathae, daḱre hõ bae unumlena, cetan cetantege ḍọmbọl ḍọmbọle ạtu calaḱ kana.

Adọ latarre miťṭaṅ ạṇḍiạ tạrup̣ dọe tãṛãḱ akan tahẹ̄kana. Adọ uni bostaren tạrup̣e ạtu calaḱ kane ńẹlkede khan dọe mẹnketa, Gại ge celeye ạtu hijuḱ kana. Adọ jẹmọne tioḱ gọťkedea, tẹmọnge uni dọe dọn gọ̄ťkeťte gẹrkateye capať toť gọťkedea. Khange ghuṭure oḍokkate bostae gẹr ọṛẹć gọťket. Khange eṅga tạrup̣ dọ bosta khon buṛiuṅ manteye oḍok gọťen khankin ńapam gọťena. Adọ galmarao baṛakate ẹnẹkin bạhu jãwãeyena. Adọ onkate ẹnẹ miť hoṛ khonkin bar hoṛena.

Adọ unre eṅga tạrup̣ dọe mẹnketa, Sạrige thọ uni hoṛ dọ ṭhikgeye mẹnleťa. Nọ̄ḱọ̄e miť hoṛ khone bar hoṛkadiṅa. Uḍiye maha bhạgkadiṅa.

Adọ unre jọtọ tạrup̣ko ṭhen noa katha dọe lại pasnaoketa, are metaťkoa, Teheń khon raebar hoṛ dọ alope jọmkoa, sẹ babon jọmkoa.

Un khon, kathae, raebar hoṛ dọ jãhã tinạḱ ńindạ ńutạko hijuḱ sẹnoḱ, onko dọ cele hõ baṅ ńamkoa, khạtirjomako hijuḱ sẹnoka. Unrege, kathae, raebar hoṛ dọ Candoe bhọr akawaťkoa. Ọkọe sikṛi mạkṛiko joṛaoeť hoṛ dọe bhọr akawaťkoa, ar ọkọeko topaḱeť hoṛ dọe sarap akawaťkoa. Onate jãhãeye joṛaoeť khan, ona dọ ọkọe hõ bin dọste dọ aloe rạpud ma. Bạṛićaḱ hõ jẹmọn bes baṛẹye lại ma, baṅkhan uni hoṛ dọ aćtegeye sẹn hamaloka; ona reaḱ tayọmre phọle ńama.

Adọ ọnẹ onka kana nukin tạrup̣ ar raebar hoṛ reaḱ katha dọ.

effect, and you will not become two. And if you remain without speaking, you will at once become two."

Speaking in this way, people tell, he tied her up well and fast, and carried her away to the river bank, and from there he tumbled her down into the river. Then, the wonderful doings of Chando, my friends, — she did not, people tell, sink in the water, she was floating along on the surface, heaving up and down.

Lower down a male leopard was lying in wait; when he saw the sack in which the leopard was coming floating, he said: "It is likely a cow coming floating." As soon as she reached him, he at once jumped, and using his teeth he threw her at once out. Having got her out and up to the bank, he bit and tore the sack open. Then the she-leopard with a rush slipped out of the sack, and then the two met, and, after having had some talk together, they became husband and wife. Then in this way from one they became two.

On this occassion the she-leopard said: "Really, this man spoke the truth. As is seen here, from one he made me into two. He has made me entirely happy."

At this time she caused the story of this to be told to all leopards, and she said to them: "From to-day don't eat marriage brokers; we shall not eat them."

From this time, people say, marriage brokers may go and come, however late and dark it may be, nothing will happen to them; they go and come without fear and secure. At that time, people say, Chando blessed the marriage brokers, and the blessing remains. The persons who join people in the bonds of matrimony, them He has blessed, and those who break these He has cursed. Therefore any one who joins people together, let no one break it asunder without fault. If there is anything bad, let him say it is well, otherwise this man will himself have to bear the consequences; afterwards he will get the fruit of his doing.

This is the story of the leopard and the marriage broker.

85. Backo̱m ceť leka janamen.

Oka disomre co̱ṅ, kathae, eae boehako tahẹ̃kana; onkoren do̱ miťṭaṅ miserae tahẹ̃kan takoa. Ado̱ tahẹn tahẹnte miť din, kathae, uni kuṛi do̱ oka khon co̱ṅ aṛaḱe siť ạguketa, ado̱ ona aṛaḱ do̱e ge̱ťketa. Ona aṛaḱ ge̱ge̱ť jo̱khẹnge sić kạṭuṕ do̱e ge̱ťena ar aṛaḱre mãyãm do̱e jo̱ro̱ata; ado̱e teke isinketa, are emaťkoa aćren sanam baretteko, jomketako, ado̱ tayo̱mteko galmarao kana, Henda ya, teheńaḱ aṛaḱ do̱ ạḍi sebel kana base̱? Ado̱ ona reaṅko suṭikketa, baṅma, Aboren misera sić kạṭuṕe ge̱ťlena, ar ona mãyãmge ona aṛaḱreye jo̱ro̱ata, onate ạḍi sebel kana.

Ado̱ko hudisketa, Henda ya, to̱be̱ khan aboren misera reaḱ jel do̱ ạḍi sebeltaea. Ado̱ marańić boeha do̱e me̱nkeť takoa, Acha ma baṅkhanbo jo̱m ạdoyea. Ado̱ jo̱me reaṅ ponthako lagaoketa.

Miťṭaṅ ṭạṇḍire joṇḍrako e̱rketa; joṇḍra do̱ beleyena. Khange miseratko metadea, Iạ mại, am do̱ hana ṭạṇḍi baṛge reaṅ joṇḍra ho̱rho̱e tabonme. Ado̱ko maṛo̱madea. Uni kuṛi do̱ maṛo̱mregeye de̱ćkoḱa, ar o̱ṇḍe̱ khonge kạhu, kisni, toyo ar setakoe lagakoa.

Ado̱ noko eae boeha do̱ aḱ sar anteko calaoena, danaṅ khon uni kuṛi tuńeko po̱rto̱nketa; ado̱ tuń tuńteko ạṛisena. Huḍiń utạrić dadatte̱ť do̱ go̱je reaṅ do̱ bae me̱nan tahẹ̃kana, onate uni se̱ć baṅ tuńkate eṭaḱ se̱ne tuń go̱ťkaḱ kana. Ado̱ onka onkate, ạḍi dhao hoeyena, se̱sre marańić dadatte̱ť do̱e tuń jhaṅkaṛkedea, ar o̱treye so̱ho̱r ńũrena, are go̱ćena.

Khangeko calao jarwayena, jo̱me lagať gaḍa aṛereko idikedea, ar jo̱meko po̱rto̱nketa. Ado̱m ho̱ṛ do̱ ro̱ro̱ ar ado̱m ho̱ṛ do̱ ge̱ge̱ťko

---

1 As told by Bhuju Murmu of Dhopahaṛ.

2 When the Indian corn is ripening, it is very common to erect a 'Machan' in the middle of the field. It is generally a raised platform, fixed to four poles, with or without a 'roof' as a shelter against rain, high enough to enable the watcher to look over the field.

85. HOW THE SABAI GRASS CAME INTO EXISTENCE[1].

In some country, who knows which, people tell, there lived seven brothers. They had one sister. As time was passing, people tell, one day this girl had plucked and brought from somewhere some vegetables, and she cut these into bits. At the time when she was cutting the vegetables, she cut her little finger, and blood trickled down on the vegetables. She cooked these, and gave them to all her brothers, who ate them. Afterwards they were talking together, saying: "I say, the vegetables that we had to-day were extremely savoury, were they not?" Then they tried to find out the reason for this, and learnt that their sister had cut her little finger and had let the blood trickle down on the vegetables. This was the cause of its being so extremely savoury.

Then they considered this matter, saying: "Look here, then our sister's flesh must be extremely savoury." Whereupon the eldest brother said: "Very well then; in that case let us eat her." And they made up a plan how they could manage to do this.

They sowed Indian corn in a field, and the Indian corn was ripening. Then they said to their sister: "Look here, girl, you watch the Indian corn that we have in the field over there." They made a raised platform[2] for her, and the girl would mount this, and, sitting there, she was driving crows, mynas, jackals and dogs away.

These seven brothers then went with bows and arrows, and from some hidden place they commenced to shoot at the girl; they were shooting and shooting, until they became tired of it. Now the youngest of her brothers was not willing to kill her; therefore, instead of shooting at her, he was shooting in some other direction. It went on in this way for a long time. At last the eldest brother hit her, and she tumbled down to the ground and died.

Thereupon they came together and took her away to the bank of a river, to eat her there, and commenced to make ready for

dhuṛauena, hudiṅić dọ dak̓ sẹn mẹnteye gusạuena; ẹnte ạḍi māyāgeye ạikạuketa; mẹnanae, Boeha kan taleae, cekate nuiak̓ jeliṅ jọma? Onako hudis baṛakate gaḍa sẹne gusạuena; ọntẹ khonge kaṭkọm thoṛae gọć ạguketkoa, rapak̓ketkoae.

Inạk̓tege uniak̓ jel hõko tearketa arko hạṭiṅ baṛaketa eae ṭhen, ar apan ạpinko idi baṛawana. Huḍinić dọ ona jel bae jọmleta; ona jel bọdọl kaṭkọm jelgeye jọmketa, ar ona jel dọ ọko okote bunum bhugạk̓reye dọhọkata. Adọe metatkoa, Cabakedaṅ. Jọm baṛakate ako oṛak̓teko calaoena.

Ona jọkhẹn onko dọ ạḍi kisạṛko tahẽkana; uni kuṛiko gọćkede khan ẹkkalteko ḍingrạ cabayena, baṅ dọ unirege kopal dọ tahẽkan baṅ dọ cet, ẹkkalte phukir lekako hoeyena.

Adọ thoṛa din tayọm khange onae dọhọlet jel ona khonge mitṭaṅ ạḍi mõṅj mat kạrlạ janamena. Mitṭaṅ họṛ dọ dāṛā dāṛāte onae dāṛā ṅamketa; adọ uni họṛ onae nolaoketa, baṅma, noa dọ banamiṅ benaoa; adọ ona mẹnkateye ruạṛ calaoena.

Adọ dosar hilok̓ setak̓re uni họṛ dọ ṭẹṅgọć ante ona mat dare ṭhengeye sẹn sẹṭẹrena, are hudis baṛajoṅ kana, oka ṭheniṅ mak̓le khan jut hoekoka? Adọe mẹnketa, Ẹṇḍak̓ge cọṭ machareṅ maga; adọ cọṭre mit ṭẹṅgọćgeye hubạk̓leta; inạk̓ khange ona dare khon aṛaṅ aṅjọmena, baṅma, dekoteye rọṛketa, Hā hā, upọre kaṭis na, namọte kaṭis. Ar hõ phẹḍre mit ṭẹṅgọće hubạk̓keta; arhõ onkage aṛaṅ aṅjọmena, baṅma, Hā hā, namọte kaṭis na, upọre kaṭọ. Ar hõ cetanre mamak̓e dhuṛạuena; arhõ onkage araṅ aṅjọmena, baṅma, Hā hā, upọre kaṭis na, namọte kaṭọ. Adọ inạ dhaore dọ ẹkkalteye mak̓ bindạṛketa; adọe idiketa, ar ona reaṅ baname benaoketa; ona banam dọ tọrhọt hartateye dapketa; adọ ạḍi mõṅj

[3] When an animal is killed, the first thing done in order to prepare it for food is to put it on a low fire, to singe off the hairs, etc. (Incidentally, wonder whether it is not the same that is referred to in the not understood Prov. 12, 27).

[4] Generally flutes are made from bamboo; occasionally a part of the one-stringed fiddle may be of the same.

eating her. Some of them took in hand to singe her[3], some of them to cut her to pieces, but the youngest one slipped away on the pretext of going towards water, because he felt a very great pity. He said to himself: "She is our sister. How shall I be able to eat her flesh?" Thinking this he slipped away, and went to the river. There he caught and brought some crabs and fried these.

While he was doing this, the others made the girl's flesh ready, and divided it into seven portions, and they took it away, each one his own portion. The youngest did not eat his flesh. Instead of this he ate the crab flesh, and the girl's flesh he secrectly put away in a hole in a white-ant's hill, whereupon he said to the others: "I have finished it," When they had eaten, they all went home.

At that time these people were very wealthy; but as soon as they had killed this girl, they at once became utterly poor. Whether their fate was bound up with the girl or whatever it was, they at once became like fakirs.

After a short time a most beautiful bamboo-shoot sprung out from the place where the youngest brother had put the flesh. A man happened to walk past there, and saw this; this man then thought: "I shall make a fiddle[4] from this." With this thought he returned from there.

The next morning this man came with an axe, and went up to this bamboo, thinking to himself: "Where had I better cut this?" Then he said: "Dash it, I shall cut it somewhat high up," whereupon he slashed it once high up with his axe. When he had done this, a voice was heard out of this tree. It said in Bengali: "Stop, stop! Do not cut high up. Cut low down." Again he gave one slash with his axe near the root. Again a voice was heard sobbing in the same way: "Stop, stop! Do not cut at the foot. Cut high up." Again he commenced to cut higher up, and again the same voice was heard: "Stop, stop! Do not cut high up. Cut at the foot," but just then he cut it so that it fell down, whereupon he took it with him and made a fiddle of it. He covered the fiddle with

aṅjo̱mok̓ kana; cet̓ leka uni kuṛiye sereṅet̓ tahe̱kana, sinạm onkage ona banam ho̱ saḍea; e̱nte uni kuṛige ona banamre menaea, ar uni bak̓nam ho̱ṛ do̱ bae baḍaejoṅ kana, noare manwa menaea me̱nte.

Ado̱ onka onkate ạḍi dine banamket̓a. Ado̱ mit̓ din do̱ ona banam khon uni kuṛiye oḍokena, ar ạḍi mõṅje ṅe̱lkedete uniye do̱ho̱ sãohãkedea; ado̱ unkin ho̱ ạḍi ãṭkin kisạ̃ṛena.

Onko barette̱t̓ko re̱ṅge̱ćen khan disom disomko dãṛãna; ado̱ dãṛã dãṛãte uniak̓ oṛak̓ko dãṛã ṅamket̓a; me̱nkhan bako oromledea; uni kuṛi do̱ saname ṅe̱l oromet̓koa. Ado̱ jãwãete̱t̓e metadea, Noko do̱ iṅren bareṅteko kanako, noko do̱ thoṛalaṅ man mạrjạt ṅo̱k̓koa, ko̱e do̱ balaṅ emakoa. Ado̱kin metat̓koa, E̱ho, ma thoṛa gan jirạuanpe, ado̱pe calak̓a nãhãk̓.

Onko do̱ ạḍiko khusiyena; e̱nteko me̱nana, Ho, bhage kopal ạcur akan tabona; teheṅ do̱bon bho̱j marak̓a.

Ado̱ ạḍi din khon sunum ho̱ bako o̱jo̱k̓ akat̓a, ar kicrić ho̱ baṅ, onate uni jãwãete̱t̓ do̱e me̱nket̓a, Sunumiṅ emakoa. Ado̱ mit̓ ṭaka bạṭi sunume emat̓koa; ona sunum ma re̱ṅge̱ćteko ṅũ cabaket̓a. Ado̱ uni jãwãete̱t̓e hudisket̓a, Dhorage noko ho̱ṛ do̱ko ṅũ cabaket̓a. Ado̱ aćge bạṭire sunum sajaokate bandte umok̓e mohṇḍaket̓koa; bandreye um ocoket̓koa ar sunume emat̓koa, to̱be̱ ena ho̱ṛ leka do̱ko ṅe̱lena; pạhil do̱ o̱ne̱ko me̱n leka, gurur parako ṅe̱lok̓ kan tahe̱kana.

Ado̱ um baṛakate oṛak̓teko he̱ćena, ar mit̓ ghạṛi jirạu baṛakate inạk̓tege daka ho̱ isinena. Ado̱ daka jo̱m lạgit̓ dak̓koe taṅ baṛawat̓koa; daka jo̱mko ạbuk bo̱lo̱yena. Jãwãete̱t̓ ho̱ onko sãote daka jojo̱me bo̱lo̱yena; ado̱ jo̱jo̱mko dhurạuena. Mit̓ dhao reaṅ

---

5 Expression that may have a double meaning (like a guru), refers to untidiness.

6 Hands and mouth are always washed before taking a meal.

the skin of an iguana, and the fiddle was sounding extremely beautifully. Just like when the girl was singing, exactly in the same way this fiddle also was sounding, because this girl was inside of this; but the player did not know that a human being was inside.

In this way he was fiddling for a long time. Then one day the girl came out of the fiddle, and, as she looked very beautiful in his eyes, he took her and made her one of his family. From this time these two also became very wealthy.

Now after her brothers had become poor, they were wandering from country to country, and during their wanderings they also happened to come to their sister's house; they did not recognize her, but the girl recognized all of them, whereupon she said to her husband: "These are my brothers. We shall treat these a little. We shall not give them alms." Whereupon they said to them: "Please rest a little. Afterwards you may go."

They were very pleased at this; they said to themselves: "Oh, now our good fortune has come back to us. To-day we shall have a proper feast."

Now for a long time they had never anointed themselves with oil, nor had they any clothes. Therefore the girl's husband said: "I shall give them oil," and he gave them an one-rupee-size cup full of oil, whereupon they out of hunger drank up all this oil. The husband then said to himself: "Surely they have drunk it all up," whereupon he himself took oil in a cup, and guided them to a tank, to have a bath. In the tank he let them bathe and gave them oil, and previously they were looking, as people say, like cows.[5]

After having bathed, they came up to the house, and, when they had rested for a while, the food also was ready prepared by that time. The girl thereupon poured out water for them preparatory[6] to their taking food; they washed themselves, and went inside to eat. The girl's husband also went inside to take food together with these, and then they commenced to eat. When

daka cabakate dosar dhao ar hõe ạṛtiaťkoa, unre onko dọ sedaeaǩ kathakoe lạiako kana, baṅma, Dada, ape dọ iṅpe ṅẹl oromediṅa?

Adọko mẹnkeťa, Baṅ, acha, ma sẹ lạime, ọkọe kanam.

Adọ unre sanam katha lạlạiye pọrtọnkeťa, Abo dọ irạl boehabon tahẽkana, ape eae boeha, ar iṅ dọ aperen misera kanaṅ; adọpe disạyeťa jonḍra baṛge maṛọmrepe tuṅ gọjeṅ dọ? Adọ ẹnte hopọn dada dọ iṅ baṅcaoiṅ reaṅ ạḍi mọnẹ tahẽkantaea; adọ apege ạḍipe murukkeťa; mẹnkhan nit hõ hopọn dada reaṅ budtegeṅ baṅcao akana.

Adọ inạ katha aṅjọm mucạťrege marañić dadattẹť dọ bereťkateye tẹṅgoyena, ar ọte lẹbẹť gọťkeťa. Ọt dọ họṛ sahọṕ leka paṛaǩena, ar onareko ṅir bọlọyena; ẹnte lajaoteko kẹklẹsẹť utạrena; tumbuť khon baṅko kọyọǩ rakaṕ daṛeaťa.

Adọ huḍiṅić dọ tayọm machae bọlọǩ kan tahẽkana; adọ ọr ruạṛea mẹnte bọhọǩreye racaǩ tiọǩledea, mẹnkhan bae ṭarhaoledea, bọhọǩ reaṅ uṕgeye racaǩ toťkeťtaea. Adọ uni kuṛi ona uṕ dọe chitiạu baṛakaťa. Adọ kathae, onageko mẹna backọm dọ. Ona khonge hoe akana; noa pạhilre dọ backom dọ baṅ tahẽkana.

86. Eae boeha ar miťṭaṅ misera.

Miťṭaṅ atore eae boehako tahẽkana, ar miťṭaṅ misera menaetakoa. Onko dọ nonkan họṛ kanako, baṅma, jaejug miť bepargeko tahẹna, kaṭ sẹ ona chaḍa ar ar jinisko bepareť tahẽkana. Sanam boeharenge era dọko tahẽkan takoa, miserattako dọ sanam khon-

---

7 The backọm, Pollinia eriopoda, Hance., is used for making twine (and also for making paper, naturally not by Santals). The plant is found wild and is also cultivated. Twine made from this grass is used for many purposes, more especially for tying down the straw-thatch of roofs.

86 1 As told by Bhuju Murmu of Dhopahar. The story is recorded here as an example of how certain beliefs are creeping in among the people.

2 The Santal word denotes trading done away from home; e. g. a man takes a bullock-cart and goes somewhere to buy timber; having got this, he takes it to

they had finished the first serving of food, she again served them a second time. Then she was telling them what had happened formerly, and she said to them: "Brothers, do you recognize me?"

They said: "No. Well, then please tell us who you are."

Then she commenced to tell all her story. "We were eight brothers and sisters, you seven brothers, and I am your sister. Then do you remember that you were shooting at me and killed me on the raised platform in the Indian-corn field? Then my youngest brother was exceedingly anxious to save me, but you were very eager; but even so I was saved by the wit of my youngest brother."

When they had heard the end of this, the eldest brother stood up and trampled on the ground, and the ground opened as much as to hold a man, and they ran into this, because they were utterly afraid and ashamed, and they were unable to raise their heads and look up.

Now the youngest one was going down somewhat later than the others, and to pull him back she took hold of his hair, but was unable to keep him. She pulled out his hair. Thereupon the girl spread this hair round. This, people tell, became "sabai" grass[7]. It has come from his hair. Previous to this there was no "sabai" grass.

86. SEVEN BROTHERS AND ONE SISTER[1].

In a certain village there were seven brothers; they had one sister. They were people of this class, they were always away trading[2], buying and selling timber or, if not this, some other goods. All the brothers had wives; their sister was the youngest[3] of them all. When her brothers were away from home, the others

---

some place and sells it there at a profit. It is a not uncommon way of earning some money with many Santals.

[3] The girl is apparently very small and unmarried.

geye huḍiṅa. Dadatteko bako tahẽnre uni kuṛi ḍoko posṛayea, metaeako, Do hana, do noa ạguime. Adọ onka ạcu ạcuteko ạṛis cabakedea.

Uni kuṛi dọe birạsạliyente miťṭaṅ rọkọt cọndọn dare ṭhene sẹnena; adọ ona dare buṭạregeye duṛupena. Adọ cetko cọṅ bujhạu baṛa kate ona dareteye dẹcena pạsi gujuk mẹnte; mẹnkhan bae pạsilena, jọ lekae sidhọyena ar ọṇḍẹgeye, tahẽyena. Tahẽn tahẽnte ḍher dinge hoeyena.

Adọ bepar khon acren dadattekoko ruạṛ kana, ar ona dare buṭạregeko ḍerayena; adọ, kathae, ona jọkhẹnge miť ṭhọp mẹť dak jọrọatkoa; adọ miť họṛe mẹnkeť takoa, Henda ya, mạiak mẹť dak lekage jọrọyena? Adọ cọṭ sẹnko kọyọkketa, ar miťṭaṅ jọko ṅẹl ṅamketa, ar tiokkate bạī bạiteko paṛakketa, ar uni kuṛiko ṅamkedea. Adọ sanam kathae lạiatkoa, baṅma, Apepe oḍok sẹnen tayọm hiliṅteko dọ ạḍiko kọsṭọkidiṅa, onate birạsạlikateṅ oḍokena, ar Cando nonkae dọhọkidiṅa; iṅ dọ pạsi gujuk reaṅ mọnẹ tahẽkantiṅa.

Adọ onko akoren era cetanre ạḍiko raṅgaoena; adọko metadea, Am dọ, họpọn mạī, noa bostare bọlọkme, adọ nãhãkle metakoa, Okayenae họpọn mạī dọ? Adọ sạri gạḍireko ladekedea, adọko mohṇḍayena; oṛakko tiokkeť khan onko dadatteko dọ akoren erako họhọ sorketkoa arko kuliketkoa, Henda, bhala okayenae họpọn mạī dọ? Adọ cetge bako rọṛ ruạṛleta. Adọ ạḍi rạṅgaokateko mẹnketa, Dini ṅam họdepe, baṅkhan ṭhik baṅ hoeok kana.

Adọ uni kuṛi un hõ baṅko sọdọrledea; ona bostarege jọmko emadea. Munis ṅamkate miťṭaṅ indạra kũiko la ocoketa; adọ la sạt kateko mẹnketa, Ma hijukpe, kũibon baplaea. Adọ akoren erako hẹcena, khange onko maejiu dọ beṛhaeko ẹnẹc ạcurok kana, koṛako dọko jhũkente apan ạpin era ona kũireko ṭhelao

⁴ Santalum album, L., a not large tree; the strongly smelling heart-wood is used for many religious and medical purposes all over India.

⁵ It is not unknown, even among the Santals, that girls or women commit suicide by hanging.

were bullying the girl, saying to her: "Bring this, bring that." By constantly setting her to do work in this way, they utterly worried her.

Hurt by all this, the girl went away to a sandal-wood tree[4], and sat down at the foot of this tree. Having thought over all, she mounted the tree to hang herself[5]; but she was not hanged, she was transformed into a fruit, and stayed there. A long time passed.

Then one day her brothers were coming back from their trading tour, and camped at the foot of this tree; while there, people tell, a tear-drop fell down on them, and one of them said: "I say, you, something fell down like a tear of our sister's." Then they looked up and caught sight of a fruit; having got this down, they carefully split it open, and found the girl. She told them everything, saying: "After you had gone away, my sisters-in-law plagued me very much, wherefore I came away, hurt and wounded, and Chando kept me like what you see; I was intending to hang myself."

The brothers then became very angry with their wives, and said to their sister: "Our little sister, enter this sack; then we shall presently ask them: 'What has become of our little sister?'" Then, truth to tell, they loaded her on a cart, and started; when they reached home, her brothers called their wives and asked them: "Look here, what has become of our little sister, we wonder?" They did not answer a single word. Then in great anger they said: "Bring her, find her at once, else it will not be well with you."

Even then they did not bring the girl out, they gave her food there in the sack. Hiring labourers they made them dig a well, and, when this was dug ready, they said: "Come, we shall have the well-marriage[6]." Then their wives came, and the women were dancing round the well, then the young men pushed each his own wife into the well, and placed a cart-wheel on the well

---

[6] See note 34 p. 270.

ńūrkatkoa, ar ona kũi duạr dọ sagaṛ cakteko esetketa. Adọ uni miseratakoko rapakedea arko metadea, Am dọ, mãi, noa kũirege jao hilok ijme. Adọ ona kũiregeye ija, jọm hõ bako emakoa, adọ sanam maejiu uni kuṛiak icgeko jọma. Uni kuṛi dọe metakoa, Ạḍi coṅ iṅpe kọsṭọlidiṅ; tọbe terọṅ iṅ hõṅ kọsṭọyetpea. Adọ onko hilitteko dọ kũi bhitri khonko mẹna, Adọ mãi ọhọle kọsṭọmea, ma niạ dhao dọ daya kate baṅcaokaleme. Onko dọ ạḍi din reṅgecte-geko tahẽyena; adọ ạḍi din badre ar hõko rakap ruạṛketkoa.

87. Raj Kumạri reak katha.

Mittaṅ raje tahẽkana ar uni rajren dọ eae boeha koṛa gidrạko tahẽkantaea; ar huḍiṅ utạrić dọe kuṛi gidrạ kantaea. Adọ onko koṛakoe bạhu baṛawatko sermage ạkin dọ banar haṛam buḍhikin gọcena. Uni kuṛi gidrạ dọ bakin ṭhão oṭoledea, un dọ uni kuṛi gidrạ hõ huḍiṅgeye tahẽkana. Adọ onko eae boeha koṛa dọko bepar kan tahẽkana, ar onkoren bạhuko ar uni miserattako dọ oṛakregeko tahẹna.

Adọ mit dhao dọ ạḍi saṅgiṅte bạnij beparko calaoena, bọchọr din hoyok kan hõ, bako ruạṛ kana. Adọ khange onko ńatea dọko riạuena, baṅma, nui miserattako dọko santaoea. Khange adọko metaea, E mãi, nọkọe dadamteko hõ bako ruạṛ kana dọ. Noa bhugạk kanḍate dak ạgualeme; ar bam ạgui khan dọ, daka hõ ọhọle emlema. Onkako metaea. Adọe cekaea, bẹcara? Onkoak kathageye sẹnatakoa. Adọ bhugạk kanḍako ńawaea, adọ ona kanḍa

---

7 This unsavoury part of the story should not be taken as representing anything else than pure imagination.

87 1 As will be seen, this story is the same as the preceding one; but there are so many differences that it is worth while to have both. The differences show how the same story may be developed. This story, written down in the nineties by Sagram Murmu, has many details that have been lost in the first.

2 King means landlord.

and shut it up. Thereupon they let their sister out, and said to her: "You, girl, go every day and ease yourself at this well." She did so[7], and as they did not give them any food, all of them had to eat what fell from the girl. She said to them: "You plagued me very much, therefore I am also plaguing you." From down in the well her sisters-in-law would then say: "We shall never any more plague you; in mercy rescue us this time." They stayed there many days without food; at last, after a long time, they brought them up again.

87. THE STORY OF A PRINCESS[1].

THERE once was a king[2], and this king had seven sons, full brothers, and a girl, who was the youngest of them all. In the year when he had got wives for his sons, he and his wife both of them died. Before this happened, they had not settled the girl anywhere; at this time she was also small. The seven brothers were engaged in trading, while their wives and this sister of theirs stayed at home.

Once they went to very distant parts to trade; even when a full year was coming to an end, they did not return. Then the wives of the brothers consulted together, agreeing[3] that they would harass and plague the sister of their husbands. Then they would say to her: "You girl, now you see, your brothers are not coming back. Bring us water in this holey water-pot; and if you don't bring, we shall certainly not give you any food." In this way they were speaking to her; then, what could she do, poor little one? She had to do what they told her. Then they brought out a holey water-pot for her, and carrying this on her head she

[3] The Santal word means to call upon in order to induce some one to do something, to urge to do. The whole throws a peculiar light on the estimation in which women are held.

dipilkate daḱ ghaṭṭeye calaḱa. Adọ daḱ ghaṭre kaṇḍa dọhọkateye raga. — Adọ ona raḱge sereń leka rạṛko joṛao akaťa.

Sereń.

Bhugạḱ ghạllạ pạni, mại, yanalom,
Bhugạḱ ghạilạ pạni, mại, yanalom,
Kạti durire dada bạnij bepar?

Adọ onka daḱ lo ghaṭre sẹnkate uni kuṛi dọe raḱeť kana; adọ ạḍi hạbić ọṇḍẹgeye raraḱ kana. Adọ ona daḱ khonaḱge, kathae, rọṭẹko oḍokena; adọko metae kana, Henda mại, cedaḱem raḱeťa? Enań khonle ńẹleťmea duṛuṕ akan, ar amaḱ raḱ ańjọm ańjọmte ale họ̃ bạṛićge sanayeťlea. Ma lạime, cedaḱ amem raḱeť kana.

Adọe mẹnkeťa, Dadańtekoko eae boehaḱa, ar kuṛi dọ iń eskargeań. Adọ onko eae gọṭẹn hilińtcko ińko santaoedin kana, bhugạḱ kaṇḍate daḱko lo ocoń kana. Miť ṭhen bhugạḱ tahẹn khan, tite ẹsẹťkate jãhã lekateń idikea. Adọ mọ̃ṛẽ turui ṭhen bhugạḱ menaḱa. Ceť lekateń idia? Arko metań kana, Hasate sẹ lạhite dọ alom ẹsẹda; onkate baṛẹ ạguime. Adọ onage ạḍi bhabnań ạikạueťteń raḱeť kana.

Adọ khange onko rọṭẹko mẹnkeťa, E mại, alom raga; ma hapeḱme ar alom bhabnaḱa. Ma kaṇḍate daḱ bhurạgme; ona bhugạḱ dọ ale nãhãḱle taber ẹsẹda, ar dipil idime, ar sẹṭẹrkate bạị bạite nãhãḱ dọhọeme, ạḍi garte dọ alom giḍi gọťkaḱa. Ma kaṇḍa sabte bhurạgme.

Adọ khangeye hapeyente kaṇḍae saṕkeťa, are bhurạḱkeťa, are dipil idikeťa, adọ gãṛsãodereye dọhọkaťa. Adọ khange onko hilittekoko mẹpẹnwana, Durrẹ! ạgukeťgeae na, babo bhagao daṛeadea.

---

[4] The songs in this story are in a curious mixture of Bengali and Santali; the constructions are mostly Bengali, but pronunciation and some of the words are pure Santali.

[5] So literally.

[6] In more well-to-do houses they always have a stand for the water-pots; it may be of earth, or it may be a heavy piece of wood, resting on poles fixed in the

would go to the place from which they were fetching water. Here she would put the pot down and cry. Now they have made this cry into a song, this[4]:

> Einen löcherigen Wassertopf, Mädchen, brachte ich,
> Einen löcherigen Wassertopf, Mädchen, brachte ich,
> Wie weit weg sind die Brüder Handel treibend?

Having gone to the place from which they were fetching water the girl was crying in this manner; she was crying there for a long while. Then, people tell, frogs came out from the water and said to her: "I say, girl, why are you crying? We have seen you sitting here for a long time, and hearing you continually crying, we also feel very bad. Please, tell why you are crying."

She replied: "My elder brothers are seven, and I am the only girl, and my sisters-in-law, all the seven of them, are tormenting me; they are making me fetch water in a holey water-pot. If there were only one hole, I might stop it with my hand and somehow take it along; but there are holes in five or six places. How shall I take it along? And they say to me: 'Don't stop it with earth or lac; bring it as it is.' It is this that I am grieved for and cry."

Then the frogs said to her: "Don't cry, girl; be quiet and don't grieve. Fill the pot with water; we shall presently lie flat down over the holes and shut them up; then carry it away on your head, and, when you have reached there, put the pot slowly[5] down; don't throw it down with any force. Now take the pot and fill it."

Then she stopped crying, and took the pot and filled it, and carried it along on her head; she put it down on the water-pot stand[6]. Then her sisters-in-law said to each other: "Strange! she has brought it, girls; we were unable to get the better of her."

---

ground. In both cases there are small concavities made to let the pots stand securely. The wooden stand has been the more common one with the Santals; it is fairly high, to keep dogs, etc., away from the pots.

Adọ kaṇḍako ńẹl baṛakeṭtaea, ona kaṇḍa hō̤ enka bhugạkge ńẹlok̕ kana, ar dak̕ dọ bań jọrọk̕ kana.

Adọ inạkate khangeko metadea, Do mạ̃i, bin tọlte sakam hẹć ạguime. Khange sạri adọ birteye calaoena; adọ birre sẹnkate uni kuṛi dọe rak̕eṭ kana.

Sereń.

Bin doṛi pata, mạ̃i, yanalom,
Bin baber pata, mạ̃i, yanalom,
Kạti durire dada bạnij bepar?

Adọ khange onkae rak̕eṭ khan dọ miṭṭań bukạ sọbọk̕ bińe oḍokena; adọe metae kana, Henda mạ̃i, cedak̕ onka dọm rak̕eṭa? Amak̕ rak̕ ańjọmte ińak̕ mọn sanam bikoliyentińa. Masẹ lạiańme, cedak̕ onka dọm rak̕eṭ kana.

Adọ khange uni kuṛiye mẹnkeṭa, Dadańteko bạnij beparko sẹn akana, adọ hilińteko ạḍiko santaoedin̕ kana. Daka dak̕ mạṇḍi hō̤ bako emań kana, ar teheń dọko mẹn akawadińa, Do bin tọlte sakam hẹć ạgualeme, ẹṇḍẹkhan dakale emama; ar bańkhan ọhọle ẹmlema. Onate iń dọń bhabnak̕ kana, ar ona bhabnate iń dọń rak̕eṭa. Nō̤k̕ō̤e sakam mań hẹć jaorak̕eṭ, adọ cekateń idia? Ona ạḍi bhabnań ạikạueṭ kana.

Khange adọ uni bińe mẹnkeṭa, Ho, idi reak̕em bhabnak̕ kana? Idi reak̕ dọ alom bhabnak̕a, khạtirjoma tahẹnme. Ińiń idikatama, ar nãhãk̕ idi sẹṭẹrkate dọ napae bại bạite nãhãk̕ dọhọeme, alom giḍi gọtkak̕a. Adọ onkae lạiadete uni bin̕ dọe tićena, are mẹnkeṭa, Iń cetan cetante bạisạume, ar iń dọ ona sakam iń bedhao binḍạkatama.

Khange sạri miṭ khạclạk̕ sakame hẹć akaṭ tahẽkana; ona sakam dọ jọtọ uni bin̕ cetan cetanteye bạisạu cabakeṭa. Adọ uni bińge

[7] The snake mentioned is a long thin species; the name lit. means 'the navel piercing (or stabbing) snake'; there are two species, Dipsadomorphus trigonatus, or D. gokul, both non-poisonous.

[8] A gruel consisting of rice and water, the poorest food in a household.

Then they looked at the water-pot she had had; this was looking just as holey as previously, and no water was trickling down.

Afterwards they said to her: "Now, girl, pluck and bring leaves without tying them up." Truth to tell, she went to the forest; having reached there she was crying this song[4]:

> Ohne Leine Blätter, Mädchen, brachte ich,
> Ohne Schnur Blätter, Mädchen, brachte ich,
> Wie weit weg sind die Brüder Handel treibend?

Then, as she was crying in this way, a tree-snake[7] came out and said to her: "I say, girl, why are you crying in this manner? Hearing your crying my mind has become wholly troubled. Please, tell me why you are crying in this manner."

The girl then answered: "My brothers have gone away to trade, and their wives are tormenting me. They do not give me even rice-water[8], and to-day they have said to me: 'Now pluck and bring us leaves without tying them up, then we shall give you food; otherwise we shall surely not give you any.' For this reason I am in grief, and grieved by this I am crying. As you see here, I have plucked the leaves together; but how shall I carry them along? This is the reason why I am feeling such grief."

The snake then answered: "Oh, you are in grief as to how you shall carry them along? Don't grieve for this, keep your mind easy. I shall take it along for you; when you have reached home with it, only put it nicely and slowly down, don't throw it down." Having told her this the snake stretched itself out at full length and said: "Lay it all down upon me[9], then I shall wrap myself round the leaves and make a bundle for you."

Truth to tell, she had plucked as much as a basketful of leaves[10]; all these leaves she laid down upon the snake, whereupon

---

9 The Santal words would imply that the girl should put it on the top of the snake's whole length.

10 The basket is meant as a measure. In Santal households leaves are constantly used to make cups and plates; to go to the forest to fetch firewood and leaves is among the duties of Santal women.

ona sakam dọe mẽṛhao biṇḍạketa. Adọ uni kuṛiye dipilkette oṛakteye idiketa. Adọ hilittekoko ńẹl daramkedea, adọko mẹnketa, Masẹ na, ńẹltaepe cetteye tọl akata.

Adọ uni kuṛiye mẹnketa, Hapẹń dọhọlege, adọ ńẹlpe nãhãk. Adọ bạí bạiteye dọhọ gọtlet khange, uni biń dọ oka sẹć cọe lẹń gọten, bako ńẹl gọtledea. Adọko mẹnketa, Bań nabo haṭhao daṛeae kan dọ. Adọko mẹnketa, Gapa dọ, mại, bin tọlte sahan ạgualeme. Adọ khange dosar hilok birteye calaoena, ar sahankoe mak jaora baṛakcta, adọ ọṇḍẹge duṛupenteye rakjọń kana.

Sereń.

Bin bandhal kạṭhi, mại, yanalom,
Bin bandhal kạṭhi, mại, yanalom,
Kạti durire dada bạnij bepar?

Adọ onka ona birrege sahan dọhọ jaorakateye rakjoń kana; ạdi hạbić ọṇḍẹge duṛupkateye raket kana. Adọ uniak rak ańjọmte mittạń jambṛo bińe oḍok hẹćena, adọe metae kana, Henda mại, enan khon cedakem raketa? Dayageń ańjọmetmea. Cedakem raketa? Masẹ lạiańme.

Adọ uni kuṛiye mẹnketa, Rak bańkhan iń cekaea? Ińak jivi dọ carẹć lekayentińa; dadańtekoko bạnij sẹn akana, hilińteko ạḍi bạṛićko santaoedin kana. Bin tọlte sahan ạguko mẹn akawadińa. Adọ nọ̃kọ̃e jaora mań jaoraket; adọń ceka idia? onate iń dọ ạḍi bhabnań ạikạuetteń rakjoń kana.

Adọ uni jambṛo bińe mẹnketa, Ho, onam bhabnak kana? Alom bhabnaka. Ma hapekme, iń nãhãk iń idi ocomea; ar nãhãk idi sẹṭẹrkate bại bạite dọhọeme, alom giḍi gọtkaka. Adọe tićena,

---

11 The women do not take an axe, but a chopper along, just strong enough to enable them to cut branches and shrubs.

12 The rat-snake, Zamenis mucosus, is common and may grow to a very large size, six feet or more in length and fairly thick. It is non-poisonous and eaten by the Santals.

she took it on her head and carried it home. Her brothers' wives saw her as she came, and said: "Look, girls, see what she has tied it up with."

The girl then said: "Wait, let me first put it down, then look." When she thereupon had put it slowly down, the snake crawled away somewhere, they did not see it disappear. Then they said: "No, girls, we are unable to do for her;" whereupon they said: "To-morrow, girl, bring us fire-wood without binding it up."

Then the next day she went to the forest and cut[11] and collected some fire-wood; sitting down there she was crying, singing[4]:

> Ohne Zusammenbindung brachte ich, Mädchen, die Zweige,
> Ohne Zusammenbindung brachte ich, Mädchen, die Zweige.
> Wie weit weg sind die Brüder Handel treibend?

Having collected and put the fire-wood down she was crying in this way there in the forest; she was sitting there for a long time crying. Hearing her crying a rat-snake[12] came out, and said to her: "I say, girl, why have you been crying like this now for a long time? It is pitiful to hear. Why are you crying? Please tell me."

The girl then answered: "What should I do else than crying? My soul has become like a straw[13]; my brothers have gone away to trade; their wives are tormenting me awfully. They have ordered me to fetch firewood without binding it up. As you see here, I have collected it; but how shall I carry it away? It is this I am so grieved over and cry."

The rat-snake then said: "Oh, is it this that you are in grief for? Don't grieve. Please, keep quiet, I shall let you carry it along presently; only when you have reached home with it, put it down slowly." Thereupon the snake stretched itself out to its

[13] The strength is estimated in accordance with the girth; here this same way of estimating is used for the soul; there was very little left of life.

adoe metadea, Ma iń cetan cetante sahan bạisạume, ar nāhāk̕ iṅgeń mẽṛhao urićkatama.

Ado khange sạri uni biń cetanreye bạisạuketa; ado uni biń-geye bedhaoente ona sahane tol urićkettaea.[14] Khange ado uni kuṛiye dipilketa; ado oṛak̕re idi seṭerkate bại bạite jhạṇṭi phedreye dohoketa. Ado doho torage uni biń do jhạṇṭi sene sunduć gotena.

Khange ado hilittekoko odokenteko ńel baṛakettaea. Khange ado jotoak̕rege bako haṭhao daṛeadea. Ạdi leka arhõko santao-ledea, menkhan okaṭak̕re hõ bako harao daṛeadea.

Khange ado mit̕ din do joto ńateako cepetena, bańma, Delabon sanam hoṛ birte sahan ạgubon calak̕a. Ado sạri sanam hoṛ birte sahan ạgui lạgitko calaoena, ar uni erveltet̕ kuṛi hõko idi torakedea. Khange ado birte calak̕ calak̕te horre mit̕ṭań mackundạ[14] baha dareko ńamketa. Arko ńelket̕ do ạdi bạrić baha akan. Adoko menketa, De noa bahabo tiok̕lege, adobo calak̕a nāhāk̕. Khange ado onko hilittekoge pạhil doko deć gelak̕ kana, ado baṛkaćteko hos hosao ńũr godok̕ kana. Adoko meneta, Iń do, na, bań deć daṛeak̕ kana. Ado sanam ńateage onkako menketa. Ado sesre uni kuṛiko metadea, Do mạ̃i, am dejok̕tabonme.

Adoe menketa, Oko badae, iń hõ ohoń deć daṛelena.

Adoko menketa, Mase ente, deć gelak̕me, pasem deć kange.

Ado sạri jormotteko dhaka dećkedegea; adoe dećen khanko metae kana, Ma, nitok̕ dom dećentabona; dher titit̕ ńuṛhạitabonme. Ado noko hilitteko do jạnumko[15] ńam ạguketa, ado ona darereko rampha esetketa, ar baber ńam ạgukateko tolketa; ado ona dare coṭregeko bạgiadea, ado akoko calaoena.

---

14 The machkunda tree, Pterospermum acerifolium, Willd., is a large tree, not common wild.

15 The Zizyphus Jujuba, Lam., very common both wild and planted. The fruit is eaten; the branches are commonly used for making fences. The branches are full of sharp thorns (hence the Santal name, lit. thorn-tree).

full length, and said to her: "Now put the firewood upon me, and I shall presently wind myself round it and fasten it for you."

Then, truth to tell, she laid all upon[9] the snake; and the snake wound itself round the firewood and bound it tight for her. The girl then carried it on her head, and having reached home she put it slowly down near the fence; and as soon as she had put it down, the snake shot away towards the fence.

Then the wives of her brothers came out, and looked at her work. There was nothing they could conquer her with. They also tormented her in many other ways, but were unable to do for her in any way.

Then one day all the wives of her brothers took counsel together, and agreed upon the following, saying: "Come, let all of us go to the forest to fetch firewood." Truth to tell, they all of them did so; they also took their sister-in-law along with them. As they were walking along to the forest, they came to a machkunda tree[14] at the road-side; they saw that it was full of flowers. Then they said: "Come, let us first get down some of these flowers, thereafter we shall go on." Then first the wives of the brothers tried to climb; they only made a pretence of climbing, and were at once slipping down, and every one of them said: "I, girls, am unable to climb." All the wives of the brothers said the same; at last they said to the girl: "Up, girl, you climb up for us."

"Who knows," she replied, "surely I shall not be able to climb either."

"Do," the others said, "try to climb, perhaps you may manage to get up."

Then, truth to tell, they used force and pushed her up; when she had got up, they said to her: "Now you have got up for us, so throw a lot down to us." In the meantime the wives of the brothers brought some thorn-tree[15] branches and fixed these all round the tree, and having brought some string, they tied all fast, whereupon they left the girl there up in the tree and went away.

Adọ onakate tin din badre cọṅ adọ onko dadatteko eae boehako sẹṭẹrena. Adọ hijuk jọkhẹć onko koṛako dọ ona baha dare buṭạregeko duṛupena, arko mẹnketa, Hapẹ, mit ghạṛi noa dare buṭạrebo jirạulenge. Adọ sạri sanam hoṛ ona dare buṭạregeko duṛupena.

Adọ khange uni kuṛi ma rẹṅgećte rọṛ hõ bae rọṛ daṛeak, ar se jivi ma menakgetae. Are ńẹl orometkoge, mẹnkhan rọṛge thọ bae rọṛ daṛeak kan. Adọ onkoko duṛup akan jọkhẹćge uni kuṛiak mẹt dak jọrọ gọtentaea. Ona mẹt dak dọ ẹkkalte marańić dadat dearege paṛao gọtena. Adọe mẹn gọtketa, Mase ya, deare ńẹltińpe, celo bae ićadiń.

Adọko ńẹlket, adọko metadea, Noa dọ, dada, abo họpọn mạiak mẹt dak leka ńẹlok kana. Adọko kọyọk rakapket khanko ńẹl ńam gọtkedea. Adọ khange ona jạnumko ọr ọcọkketa, arko ạrgokedea. Adọ taben khạjạṛiko lọhọtketa ar guṛ tulu\u0107 sipikateko emadea, ar daka dakko condaketa.

Adọ taben khạjạṛiye jọmket khan dọe ṭọnkọ ńõkena, adọe rọṛketa; ar baṅkhan pạhil dọ bae rọṛ daṛeak kan tahẽkana. Arhõko ẹm juṭućadea, adọ jọmkateye gitić jirạuena.

Adọe beretẹn khan dọ ona darere cekateye dẹćlena, ar ọkọeko rampha ẹsẹtledea, onako jọtọe lạiako kana. Ar pạhilte cet lekako santaoledea, onako hõ jọtọe lạiatkoa. Khange adọ onko dadatteko dọ ako akoren bạhutteko upạrte ạḍi bạṛićko edreyena, arko mẹnketa, Durrẹ! nui mit họṛgetabonae misera, cak nonka dọko santaoede kana? Abobo hẹćen tẹrọṅbo bańcaokedea, baṅkhan hutẹć nui dọ nọnḍẹgeye rọhọṛ gọćkoktabona. Abokoren ạimại dọ ạḍiko kumãyãgea; ẹnḍẹkhan abo hõ onko dọ babo mãyãwakoa. Sẹnkate mitṭaṅ kũibo laea, ar ona kũirebo ḍhaka ńũrkoa; nui cet lekako

After who knows how long a time her elder brothers, all seven, came there. As they were coming, the young men sat down at the foot of this flowering tree, saying: "Wait, let us rest a little at the foot of this tree;" and, truth to tell, all of them sat down at the foot of this tree.

Now the girl was unable even to speak on account of hunger, but she was still alive; and she saw and recognized them, but was entirely unable to speak. While they were sitting there, some tears of the girl fell down, and these tears happened to fall right on the back of the eldest of the brothers. "Hey, you chaps," he said, "look at my back, some one dropped something on me."

Having looked at it they said to him: "This, brother, looks like the tears of our little girl." They looked up and caught sight of her; then they pulled the thorn-tree branches away and brought her down, whereupon they moistened some parched and flattened rice, and having mixed this with molasses they gave her, and put rice on the fire to boil.

When she had eaten the parched and flattened rice, she was a little revived, and spoke; otherwise she was at first unable to speak. Then they gave her a little more, and when she had eaten, she lay down and rested.

When she got up again, she told them everything, how she had climbed up into this tree, and who had fixed thorns round the tree, so that she had to stay there. How they had previously tormented her, all this she also told them. Then her brothers became awfully angry with their several wives, and said: "What a pity, this is the only sister we have; why are they tormenting her in this way? Happily we came and rescued her; otherwise she might have shrivelled up and died for us here. Our women are utterly merciless; therefore we shall not show them mercy either. We shall go home and dig a well, and into this well we shall push them down; just as they have tormented this one, in the same

saset akadea, onkage ako hõbo santao halakoa. Bhala, ako do cet́ lekako ạikạua?

Ado joto boeha nonkako cepet́ ṭhikena, sanam horko hẽ hũ baṛaket́a, arko mepenena, Noako katha do aperen ạimạiko ṭhen okoe hõ alope lạia, ar jãhãepe lạiket́a menkhan, endekhan uni doe bhạị phuṭok̇a, ado uni hoṛ do boeha ṭhen khonbo laga ńirea. Ado noako joto katha sanam boehako aṅgocket́a, adoko menket́a, Men bhạị, noa katha endekhan alo eṭagok̇tabon. Ado sanam horko menket́a, Oho eṭagok̇tabona.

Ado dakako jom baṛaket́a ar uni kuṛi hõko emadea, ar barea pea suiko emadea, ado borareko bhoraokedea, arko metadea, Hilimteko tul ak̇der nãhãk̇le metakoa, unre nãhãk̇ am do noa suite khub leka pạṭikom, ar bako tul ader khan nãhãk̇ khuble humạk̇koa. Ado onkako sikhạukadea, ado borare bhoraokedete ḍaṅgrareko ladekedea, ado ondẹ khonko uṭhạuena.

Ado oṛak̇ko tiok̇ket́ khan uni bhorao akade gõrẽ do bạị bạiteko tul ãṛgoket́a. Ado otre dohokate onko bạhutkoko hohoat́koa arko metat́koa, Ma noa bora do ape ạimạị eskarte baṛe oṛak̇te tul aderpe ar bạị bạite dohoepe. Alope giḍi got́kak̇a, baṅkhan nãhãk̇le humạk̇ got́pea.

Ado sạriko hećena, ado tul ader jokhen bogeteye pạṭiyet́koa, khab khabe sobok̇et́koa. Khangeko doho got́et́a. Khange ado beṅget́ urićkateko ruhet́et́koa, metako kanako, Hako pako ader hodpe, horko heć botećkok̇a. Khange ado kurumuṭuteko tul aderket́a, pạṭik̇ hõ bako bataolet́a. Ar onkoak̇ ti do siro sorge sobok̇ mãyãmket́takoa. Adom adomko doko rak̇ utạrket́a.

Ado khange boge judạ duk suk kathako kupulik̇ kana. Ado oka hạbić bạnij beparko senlena, onako joto kathako lạiat́koa.

way we shall also torment them and pay them off. I should like to know how they themselves will feel it."

All the brothers took counsel together and decided this; all of them said yes to it, and said to each other: "Don't any of you mention this to your women, and if any of you tell, he shall not be a brother of ours any more; such a one we shall drive away from being with us as a brother." All the brothers agreed to this, and said: "Have a care then, brothers, this matter must not then be altered among us." And all of them said: "Surely, it shall not be altered."

Then they had their food; they also gave to the girl; and giving her a couple of needles they put her into a sack, and said to her: "We shall presently tell your sisters-in-law to carry this inside; then you prick them to good purpose with these needles; if they don't carry it inside, we shall give them a sound thrashing." In this way they instructed her, whereupon they put her into the sack and loaded her on a bullock; then they started from there.

When they reached home, they lifted the sack in which they had put her carefully down. When they had put it down on the ground, they called their wives, and said to them: "Here, you women, carry this sack alone into the house, and put it carefully down; don't throw it carelessly down, else we shall give you a thrashing."

So, truth to tell, they came, and when they were carrying it inside, she pricked them awfully; she stabbed them deeply, and they would put it down at once; but their husbands looked steadfastly at them and scolded them, saying: "Take it in quickly; people might come." Then they exerted themselves and carried it inside; even though being pricked, they did not heed; and she pricked their hands so that they trickled blood. Some of them downright cried.

After this they asked each other for news, about how they had been going on and fared. The men told them how far they had

Ar ako hõko kuli ruạṛketkoa, adọ ako hõ tin dinko tahẽkana, ar cetkoko kạmi hataṛlaka, onako jọtọ kathako lạiatkoa. Mẹnkhan uni kuṛiko santaolede katha dọ ọkọe hõ bako lạiyeta.

Adọ khangeko kuliketkoa, Họpọn mãi dọe okayena? Bale ńẹlẹ kan dọ. Uni tite dakle ńũia.

Adọko mẹnketa, Gate sọṅgetẹ cele birte sahan ạgui sẹn akana. Adọ onka cetko cọṅ ẹndẹ pẹndẹko lại baṛawako kan; mẹnkhan ṭhik dọ ọkọe hõ bako lạileta.

Adọko mẹnketa, Ape dọ ạuṛiakgepe mẹneta, birteye sen akana mẹnte. Mẹnkhan ale dọ aleren misera dọ mackundạ baha darerele ńamkedetalea. Ape dọ cedak nonka ạuṛiak dọpe lại baṛayeta?

Khange adọ onko ạimại dọ cap cupko thirena, ẹkkalteko kẹklẹset utạrena. Adọ ona bora khonko raṛa ọḍọkkede khan, bogete kạumạuko rak utạrketa. Adọ onakate tayọmte bogeteko ruhet baṛaketkoa. Khange cet hõ bako rọṛ daṛeata. Adọko mẹnketa, Ale dọ beparle sẹnlenre mitṭaṅ muhimrele gọk kạbul akata, baṅma, mitṭaṅ kũibo laea ar ona kũi dọbo baplaea. Inạge katha dọ. Ar onale manankettege cele nui misera hõle ńamkedetalea.

Adọ inạ dosar hilok khange kũi lala adọko ẹhọpena. Khub bar arpa osarko ẹhọpketteko la khạndriketa. Khub pẹ purus amdaj cọṅ kichu dọ bạṛtige cọko laket. Adọ nasenak ọlhantẹtko tiokkata, adọko bạgiata.

Adọ khangeko nenḍaketa, baṅma, Niạ phalna din hilok dọbo baplaea. Adọ sunum sindurkoko juṛạu baṛaketa, adọ ẹn hilok dọ ḍọmko ạguketkoa arko ru ocoyetkoa. Adọ onko koṛako dọ akoren

16 See note 34 p. 270. The cumạuṛa is performed by moving one's hands backwards and forwards above the thing to be blessed or wished luck. When the ceremony is performed at the time of marriage, a flat basket with some rice, etc., is moved over the bridal pair.

17 The arpa is the distance between the finger tips when both arms are stretched horizontally out, the natural fathom, not a fixed measure.

gone trading, and all this. They on their side also asked their wives; and these also told them how they had spent the whole time, and what they had been doing, all this. But that they had tormented the girl none of them told.

Then they asked them: "What has become of our little girl? We don't see her anywhere. We wish to drink water from her hand."

"She has gone to the forest," they replied, "together with her companions to fetch firewood." In this way they were telling them fibs, this, that and the other; but not one of them told the truth.

Then they said: "It is false what you say, that she has gone to the forest. We ourselves found our sister up in the machkunda tree. Why are you telling such falsehoods?"

Then these women became dumb and tongue-tied, they became at once speachless with fright. And when they had released the girl and taken her out of the sack, they made an awful noise and cried outright. Afterwards they scolded them awfully, and the wives were unable to say a single word. The men then said: "When we were away trading and had fallen into a dangerous difficulty, we made a vow and promised, viz., 'We shall dig a well, and we shall perform the ceremony of well-marriage[16] with this well.' This is what it is; and likely because we made this vow, we have also found this sister of ours."

The next day they commenced to dig the well; they commenced to make it two fathoms[17] broad and dug deep down; they dug fully three heights of a man[18] down, or perhaps even a little more; then they just reached moist earth, and stopped digging.

Thereupon they fixed a day, saying: "On such and such a day we shall have the marriage." They collected oil and sindur, and on the day fixed they brought Doms and made them drum. The

[18] To measure height or depth the Santals use as a measure the height of a man standing with arms stretched straight up with fingers extended. It is about the same length as the **arpa**; this is called **purus** (from Hindi or Bengali **purush**, meaning man).

bạhuko metaťkoa, Teheń dọ bae kicrićte bandenpe; ona kũi apan ạpin nãhãk̕ miť dhaote cumạuṛaepe. Inạge apeak̕ kạmi dọ, ar bańkhan ceť hõ bale cumạuṛa ocopea.

Adọ sạri onko ḍọm dọ oṛak̕ khonko ru idiketkoa ona kũi ṭhen dhạbić. Adọ ona kũi ṭhenko tiokkeť khan dọ ona kũi aṛe aṛeteko pante ocoketkoa. Adọko metako kana, Ma apan ạpin nitok̕ dọ cumạuṛaepe. Adọ khangeko cumạuṛayeť jọkhẹnge ako akọren bạhu apan ạpinteko ḍhaka ńũr gọťkaťkoa. Adọko ruạṛ baṛayena, onko dọ ọṇḍẹgeko bạgiaťkoa. Adọ ona kũi kaṭṭeko gaṇḍe ẹsẹťkeťa, adọ tin serma uni kuṛiko santaolede, un serma hạbić onko hõ ona kũiregeko tahẽ ocoaťkoa rẹńgẹćtege, dak̕ daka ceť hõ bako emaťkoa. Adọ ona din purạuen khan dọko ọr rakap̕keťkoa.

Adọ cabayena katha dọ, in marańgea.

88. Akele kirińket koṛa reań.

Sedae jugre, kathae, miťṭań raje tahẽkana, ar uni rajren dọ miť goṭańgetaea koṛa họpọn dọ. Adọ uni koṛa gidrại metaea, Ẹ bạbu, ọlok̕ paṛhao dọ ma sẹ cetjońme. Adọ uni gidrạ dọ bae mọnẹak̕a; dinạmge raj dọ họpọntẹťe metaea, Masẹ bạbu, ọlok̕ dọ cedme, alom kuṛhiạk̕a; iń bań hilok̕ dọ hapẹn cekatem ạsulok̕a? Onka dingeye bintiaea, ẹnrehõ uni gidrạ dọ bae ańjọma.

Khange adọ tahẹn tahẹnte tin din cọń hoeyen, in dintege uni dọe juạnena, ar bạhu dọ gidrạregeko bạhu akawadea. Raj họpọn ma ẹnte gidrạregeko bạhuakoa sẹ bańa? Onkage nui gidrạ hõ huḍiń huḍińregeko bạhu akawade tahẽkana. Adọ khangeye hara juạnenre hõ ọlok̕ paṛhao katha dọ dingeye sikạuea.

---

19 So lit.; the meaning is clothes that are used for festival occasions, but are not in daily use.

20 See above note 16.

88 1 To learn to read and write is deemed highly important by certain classes. The writer remembers to have seen in a First Reader (translated from Bengali) two sentences running something like this: 'If you learn to read and write, you will get eternal bliss;' and 'if you don't learn, you will get eternal misery.'

young men then said to their wives: "To-day dress yourselves in stored[19] clothes; then you shall all of you at the same time perform the blessing ceremony[20] at the well. This is what you have to do; besides this we shall not ask you to perform any other blessing."

Then, truth to tell, the Doms took them with drumming away from the house up to the well. When they had reached the well, they made the women stand beside each other along the brink of the well, and said to them: "Now all of you perform the blessing." Then, when they were swinging their hands in blessing, each man of them pushed his own wife down, whereupon they went home again, leaving the women there. Then they closed this well up, putting timber across; and as many years as they had tormented the girl, so many years they also let these women stay there in this well without food; they did not give them water or food, anything at all. When this time was completed, they pulled them up.

So the story is at an end; it is this much.

88. THE YOUNG MAN WHO BOUGHT WISDOM.

In olden times, people tell, there once lived a king, and this king had only one son. He was always saying to the boy: "My boy, you must learn to read and write;[1] but the boy did not pay any attention to this; every day the king said to his son: "Do, my son, learn to write; don't be lazy; when some day I shall be no more, how will you support yourself?" In this way he daily exhorted him; but in spite of all the boy did not listen.

Then they lived, who knows how long a time it was, but as time passed, the boy grew into maturity; while he was yet a child, they had procured a wife for him. You see, for princes they procure wives while they are yet children, or is it not so? In this way they had married this child also, when he was very small. Now, although he had grown into maturity, his father daily urged him to learn to read and write.

Adọ mit́ din dọ ãt̤ machae rọṛadea, adọe metadea, Henda bạbu, am dọ ọlok̍ paṛhao iń metama, ẹnre hõ bam mọnẹak̍a. Nọ̃k̍ọe nun marań disom iń hatao akat́a. Nonka lelhate dọ hapẹn cekate disom dọm calaoa? Ar am dọm raj họpọn kana; disomren mạńjhi sẹ mapańji, sẹ pargana, dẹs mạńjhi, sẹ jãhãeṭak̍ rayotge, am ṭhen jãhãn katha galmarao lạgit́ko hẹćlen khan dọ cet́ lekam beohara, ar cet́ lekam galmaraoa? Galmarao họ̃ thọ bam cet́ịoń kana, cekatem galmaraoa? Ar jãhãnak̍ lạlis lạgit́ko hẹćlen khan, cet́ lekam bicạrtakoa? Ar iń bań hilok̍ dọ hapẹn noako katha dọ khạṭige hoeok̍gea. Judi bam pạtiạuk̍ kan khać, hapẹn tayọmtem bujhạua.

Khange sạri uni koṛa dọ onako katha dọ mọnẹre gaḍaoadea, are mẹn utạrket́a, Okako katha ạpuńe rọṛadiń, ona dọ sạri kangea. Ọkọe tora katha cet́ disomteń oḍok calak̍a. Adọ onka bujhạu baṛakate uni koṛa dọ mit́ gạńjiạ ṭakae bhoraoket́a ar pẹa sona. Khange adọ disomte katha ced lạgit́e oḍok calaoena; ar ać bạhu dọe lại oṭoadegea.

Khange adọ calak̍ calak̍te ạḍi sạṅgińe calaoena, ẹnre họ̃, kathae, họṛge bae ńamko; ẹnre họ̃e calak̍ kangea. Khange adọ mit́ din dọe laṅga machayena. Ona jọkhẹć, kathae, mit́ họṛ siok̍ kane ńẹl ńamkedea; adọe mẹnket́a, Ọkọe tora uni họṛ ṭhen cun thamakur iń jọmlege. Onka mẹnkate adọ uni họṛ ṭhene calaoena. Adọ cun thamakur họ̃kin jọmet́a, ar galmarao họ̃e ẹhọpket́a; adọe metae kana, Henda ho, bhala noakore ọkọeko katha bạḍohi họṛ menak̍koa?

---

2 lit. the company or collection of village headmen.

3 The narrator enumerates the different men in authority in the country whom he knows. The first is the village headman; above him stands the pargana or overchief, who is supposed to look after a number of villages; between him and the village headman comes the dẹs mạńjhi, lit. country headman, an assistant of the pargana, also having separate authority. The ordinary village people are called rayot or tenants; they hold their land from the 'king' or landlord against paying an annual rent.

4 The gạńjiạ is a knitted purse, long and thin, carried tied round the waist.

5 The Santal way of using tobacco: a bit of a leaf is mixed with unslacked mussel-lime and chewed. Offering or asking for such tobacco is the general way they follow to get into conversation with people.

Then one day he spoke rather hard to him, and said: "Look here, my son, I tell you to learn to read and write; still you do not pay any attention to it. Here you see, I have acquired such a large country. Being such a fool, how will you in time to come administer the country? You are a king's son; if a village headman or all of them[2], or an overchief, a country headman[3], or some tenant or other should come to you to speak of any matter, how would you act? You are not learning to speak either, how will you be able to speak? And if people come with any case, how will you judge their case? And when I shall some day be no more, such matters will come to pass. If you don't believe it, you will understand what it is later on."

Then, truth to tell, these words made a deep impression on the young man, and he said outright: "What my father has said to me, that is all true. I shall without further delay start and visit countries, in order to learn," Having come to this conclusion, the young man filled a net-purse[4] full with money and three gold-pieces. Thereupon he started to visit countries, in order to learn; he told his wife before he left.

Passing along he travelled very far; still, people tell, he did not find anybody; in spite of this he went along. Then one day he felt fairly tired. Just at that time, people tell, he caught sight of a man who was ploughing, and said to himself: "Let me at once before anything else get some lime and tobacco[5] with this man." Saying so he went up to the man; they had lime and tobacco together, and also commenced to talk; he asked the man: "I say, I wonder whether there are any masters of speech[6] here in these parts."

[6] The word katha bạḍohi is generally used about a fluent speaker or also about a fabricator of tales, who spins yarns, the ordinary meaning of bạḍohi being 'carpenter', 'worker in wood'. Here the word is about equivalent to a man of knowledge.

Adoe menketa, Adom cekakoa katha bạḍohi hoṛ do?

Adoe menketa, Iń do phalna disomren raj hopon kanań. Iń do katha bań baḍaete katha ced lạgit nun sạṅgiń disomteń heć akana. Onate katha bạḍohi hoṛ doń khoj kana; se ente, amem baḍae khan do, amge cetańme.

Adoe menketa, Hẽ, baḍae doń baḍaegea, adom khusiak nạhĩ mit bar goṭań iń lạikema, cecet sanayetme khan.

Adoe menketa, Iń ma cedgeń menet kan, ar onate nõkõe nun sạṅgińteń heć akana. Ado amge cetem meneta? Mostetem cetańa, se damem ạguińa? Ona lạime.

Adoe menketa, Mostete do ohoń cetlema, dam iń ạgumea.

Adoe menketa, Acha, dam khan damgeń emama. Tinạk katham cetań, katha piche mimit goṭań sonań emama.

Adoe menketa, Acha, tobe khan iń cetama; ạikhạ khub ańjom ṭhik idime; alom hiṛińa; disạ dohokam. Katha do noa kana: am dom raj hopon kana, am do jãhãe ṭhen peṛa hoṛokem calaka, se jãhãe mạńjhi se pargana ṭhen, se jãhãe rayot ṭhenge, ado unre mạci se parkom, se gaṇḍo, se pạṭiạ, se jãhãn bichạnageko belam, ar oṇḍe duṛupko metam khan, ekkalte do alom duṛupa; oka ṭhenko belam, oṇḍe khon do or ocok ńõgme, ar onare duṛupme. Inạge katha do. Den, sona emańme. Khange ado miṭṭań sonae emadea.

Adoe menketa, Acha, arhõ mit kathań cetam kana. Am dom raj hopon kana; umokem calaka; bandre, se pukhrire, se gaḍare, se jãhãregem umok, menkhan ghaṭre do alom umoka; begor

---

7 lit. the word or story.

8 We have no word for this kind of 'stool'. It is a piece of wood, fashioned a little, just big enough to sit on. It should be remembered that to a Santal (or most Indians) it is just as uncomfortable to sit on a high stool as for us to sit on the floor.

9 A mat of straw.

10 The word signifies something spread to sit on, may be a rug, a thin mattress or the like. The narrator enumerates all things that are used by Santals to sit on.

The other asked: "Then what do you want with masters of speech?"

"I am the son of the king of such and such a country," he replied. "As I do not know anything, I have come to a country so far away to learn. Therefore I ask for masters of speech; or if you yourself know, teach me yourself."

"Yes," he said, "I certainly have knowledge; and in case you are pleased with it, I might tell you one or two things, that is, if you want to learn."

The prince replied: "Naturally I want to learn; therefore, as you see, I have come so far. Then what have you to say? Will you teach me gratis, or will you charge me for it? Tell me."

"Gratis," the other one replied, "I shall certainly not teach you; I shall charge you for it."

"All right," he said, "if there is any charge to pay, I shall give this. As many things[7] as you teach me, I shall give you one gold-piece for each."

"All right," the other replied, "in this case I shall teach you; but mind, listen and pay close attention; don't forget anything; keep it in your remembrance. The matter is this: You are the son of a king; you will pay a visit to somebody, to some village chief or other, or to an overchief, or else to some tenant or other, then, when they place a stool or a bedstead or a piece of board[8], or a mat[9], or a rug[10] before you and ask you to sit down there, don't sit down at once; pull it a little away from where they place it for you to sit down, and then sit down on it. That is all. Out with it, give me the gold-piece." Then he gave him one.

Thereupon he said: "Very well, I shall teach you one thing more. You are the son of a king; you will go to bathe; you may bathe in a reservoir[11], or a tank, or a river, or anywhere, but don't take your bath where people go down to fetch water; bathe

[11] The word translated 'reservoir' means a dam constructed by making an embankment across a depression in the land; a tank is an excavation on flat land.

ghaṭre umokme. Nẽkẽ enec katha do. Den, sona emaṅme. Khane emadea.

Adoe metadea, Arhõ miṭṭaṅ iṅ cetama. Am dom raj hopon kana; am ṭhen jāhānak bicar lagit, se galmarao lagit, se mali mamla lagit am ṭhenko hijuka, se amge onko ṭhenem calaka, unrepe galmaraoa. Ado onko dos se mõrẽ hoṛ oka kathako roṛ goṭae, ona baṛe senakme; am jidre do alom tahena; onkoak katha alom nehõttakoa, ona senakme. Inage katha do. Den, sona emaṅme. Khange adoe emadea.

Ado uni raj hopone menketa, E ho, sona tho joto cabayentiṅa, ado cet iṅ emama?

Ado uni hoṛe menketa, Tobe do cet lekatem ceda, cabayentam khan? Acha endekhan, mostete miṭṭaṅ iṅ cetama.

Adoe menketa, Ma tobe khan cetaṅme.

Adoe metadea, Ia, am do raj hopon kanam; laiam kanaṅ, jāhān ghuri hako pako do alom edre hodoka, edre do jom ruaṛme baṛe; jāhānak ṅelte, se jāhāe lai cal kathate, se roṛ roṛte raṅgaolenre hõ, ekkalte hat do alom calaoa, edre do jom ruaṛ hataṛme; dene banar reak kathage aṅjom pahillem, ar am monere ona do gandon pahilme, enkhante jāhānak roṛme, se hat calaome; kusurem ṅamle khan, hat calaome; ar bam ṅamle khan do, ika daporkam; edrete hat bako calao hoda, edre doko jom ruaṛgea; ek tekhar du tekhar doko ikakogea, baṅte baṅ jutok khan jāhāṭakem bicara. Inage

12 Every landlord has a so-called cutcherry, court-house or office, and it is of very frequent occurrence that people come there with their cases, to let the landlord settle their disputes or judge between them, to get advice, and so on.

13 The village council is sometimes called The Five, sometimes The Ten, it is the same thing. 'The Five', in Santali **mõrẽ hoṛ**, the five men, really means the village community. The name has possibly some connexion with **panchayat**, **panch** meaning five.

14 lit. eat the anger back.

away from this place. There, that's the thing. Out with it, give me the gold-piece. Then he gave it to him.

Thereupon he said to him: "One thing more I shall teach you. You are the son of a king; people will come to you to have some dispute or other decided[12], or to talk, or they will come to you with a lawsuit, or you will go to them; at such occasions you will talk together. Then whatever the council of the ten or of the five[13] will decide, agree to this; do not persist in having your own way; don't disregard their word; follow it. That's all. Out with it, give me the gold-piece." Then he gave it to him.

The prince then said: "Look here, all my gold-pieces have been spent; what shall I then give you?"

The man replied: "In that case how will you learn, when you have spent what you had. All right then, I shall teach you one thing gratis."

"Well," he said, "teach me then."

Then the man said to him: "I say, you are the son of a king; I am telling you this: at any time don't be quickly angry; keep your anger back[14]; if by seeing anything, or by any one's slandering tales[15], or by talking and answering you should become angry, do not at once use force[16]; keep your anger back for a while; first listen to what there may be on both sides, and consider it in your own mind first; afterwards say what you like, or use force[16]; if you find any real fault, use force; if you don't, let the matter rest and don't trouble; people are not quick to use force in anger, they keep the anger back; once, twice they let them off; if there is no possibility at all of a peaceable settlement, then you may decide whatever you like. That is the thing. Now

---

15 The Santals have a proverb: **Lại cal katha aręć cal dak̕, hak̕soa,** a slandering tale (going round), water thrown (at one), pains. They do not approve of slandering gossip.

16 lit. 'let hand go'; if it had been proper for a 'king', 'use one's fists' would have been a fairly literal translation.

katha do. Ma, nią do mosteteń cetatmea, sonage cabayentam khan; ar bańkhan do hutąń arhõń cetkema. Adokin apan ąpinena.

Khange uni raj hopon do mone moneteye guni bhąbik kana, Durre, nui hoṛ do kąṭić kąṭić katharege joto sonae ere cabakidińa, bańdo sąri katha kantae bańdo bań. Arhõ ać monereye menketa, Achań bidąutaea.

Khange ado oṇḍe khongeye ruąṛ kana. Ado hijuk hijukte jomak cabayentaea. Khange adoe menketa, Okoe tora noa bajarre jomak iń kirińanrege. Ado ona miṭṭań bajarreye boloyena; ado huni nhui onte noteko hohoae kana, Dela ho noṇḍe, dela ho noṇḍe kirińmc; ar okoe doko metae kana, Acha bam kiriń khan do, huką thamakur ńũanme. Onkako hohoae kana.

Khange ado miṭṭań dokanreye calao sorena. Khange ado bichąnare duṛupko metadea, ado duṛup lągite rakapena. Adoe duṛup jokhećge uni guruak kathae disą gotketa; ado ona bichąna oṇḍe khone or ocok gotketa. Khangeye ńelketa, kũiko aṭet loṭom akat tahẽkana. Khangeye bujhąuketa, Durre, iń do ądi bąrić iń lelhagea; alon cetle khan hutec, dhorage teheń doń khańjo goćkoka. Ohre, ądi bhage guru kantińae, khub jut kathae cet akawadińa. Ado jol pankoe kirińketa, ado calak tuluć ona katha do mone moneteye hudis idiyeta.

Calak calakte tin sąngiń coe calaoen, ado miṭṭań pukhriyc ńamketa; adoe menketa, Nią pukhrirege um baṛakate jol pan iń jomlege. Khange ado pukhri ṭhene sen sorena, adoe disąketa, bańma, gurui men akawadińa, Ghaṭre do alom umoka, begor ghaṭre umokme. Ado ona disąkate begor ghaṭ sene calaoena; ado oṇḍe kicrićko moṭrako doho baṛaketteye um baṛayena, ado jol pan jom baṛakateye calaoena.

Khange ona gąńjią ṭaka do oṇḍegeye hiṛiń oṭokata; ado tin-sąngiń coe calaoen khange adoe disąketa bańma, gąńjią ṭaka doń

---

17 True to life.

18 Foodstuff that does not need cooking.

this I have taught you gratis, since your gold-pieces are spent; if this were not the case, I might have taught you still more." After this they separated.

The prince was turning this thoughtfully over in his mind: "Dear me, this man has with tiny tiny matters fooled me out of all my gold-pieces; I wonder whether his words were true or not." Again he said to himself: "Very well, I shall test it."

Then he turned back from there. As he was coming along, his food came to an end, and he said: "I shall at once, before going further, buy some food in this town." Then he went into the town; and one here, another there were[17] on all sides calling out to him: "Come here, you, come here you, buy!" And some were saying to him: "All right, if you dont't buy, come and have a smoke of tobacco." In this way they were calling out to him.

Then he went near to a shop; there they told him to sit down on a rug, and he ascended to sit down. Just as he was going to sit down, he suddenly remembered his teacher's words, whereupon he pulled the rug aside a little there. Then he saw that they had covered over and hidden a well there, and he thought: "Dear me, I am awfully foolish; if I had not learnt this, I should surely have fallen in and been killed to-day. Oh, it is a splendid teacher I have; he has taught me excellent things." Then he bought some foodstuff[18], and as he was walking along, he was turning this matter over in his mind, remembering all.

Walking along, he came who knows how far; then he found a tank, and said: "I shall have a bath in this tank and have some food before going further." He went near to the tank; then he remembered: "My teacher has said to me; 'Don't take a bath at the place where all go to fetch water; bathe away from this place'." Remembering this, he went to where there was no such place, and having put down his clothes and bundles there, he had his bath, and after having eaten, he went away.

Now he forgot and left behind the net-purse with his money there; when he had gone some distance, he remembered: "I have

hiriṅket. Adoe menketa, Begor ghaṭregeṅ doholaka; janić okoe hō bako idi akattiṅa. Okoe toraṅ ruaṛ calaka, pase do menakgetiṅ. Khange ado oṇḍe khongeye ruaṛena. Sariye ṅelket do, menakge. Khange aḍiye raskayena, adoe menketa, Khub bhale guru kantiṅae; huteć ghaṭreṅ umlen khan do noa ṭaka do ohoṅ ṅamlea.

Ado khange oṇḍe khon calak calaktegeye ayupketa. Khange ado mitṭaṅ atoteye rakapena, ado gitić ṭhaiye kuli baṛayetkoa. Ado khange joto hoṛgeko metae kana, Ma hanko maṅjhiko ṭhen baṛe calakme, onko ṭhen do nāhāk bestem gitića; aḍi osar piṇḍa hō menaktakoa. Khange sari ado maṅjhiko ṭhengeye calaoena. Adoe metako kana, Henda baba, gitić ṭhāope aṛakkea?

Adoko menketa, Hē do hēge, baba, ado nōkōe piṇḍakorege tho aikha ṭhai do.

Adoe menketa, Ho piṇḍare hōṅ besokgea nāhāk.

Adoko metadea, Am lekan mosaphir hoṛge ona piṇḍareye gitić akana. Ma eṇḍekhan am hō ona piṇḍare baṛe gitićme.

Khange ado ona piṇḍateye rakapena, ar uni pahil hoṛ do busupkoe aṭet akat tahēkana. Ona busupge thoṛa thuṛiye koekedea ar oṇḍeye gitićena. Ar uni pahiltinić do jugiye tahēkana. Adokin gitić baṛayen khange uni jugi do oṇḍegeye goć dapoṛena.

Setak khangeko ṅelkede doe goćen. Khange uni raj hopon hōko metadea, Hape, alom calaka; mitṭaṅbo galmaraolege. Ado khange maṅjhi do atoren sanam hoṛe jaoraketkoa, adoe metako kana, De bhala, cetbo cekaea? Nukin bidisia mosaphir do holanok noṇḍe gitić ṭhāo iṅ aṛakatkina. Adoe cekalen coṅ, nōkōeye goćena. Adobo ceka lekayea?

Ado ato hoṛko menketa, Giḍikae ma, cekayeabo baṅkhać? Adoko menketa, De okoeko mako giḍiye ma. Khange ado bar-

19 The procedure always followed by a village headman; he will act in consultation with the village people.

20 So literally.

left my money in the net-purse." He said: "I put it down away from the place where people fetch water; perhaps no one has taken it. I shall at once go back; perhaps my thing is there." Then he returned from there, and he actually saw: there it was. He became very glad, and said: "It is an excellent teacher I have; if I had bathed at the water-fetching place, I should surely not have recovered this money."

Going away from there, he went until it became evening; then he went up to a village, and asked people for a place to lie down. All people said to him: "Go to the village headman's over there; with them you will be able to lie comfortably; they also have very broad verandas. Then, truth to tell, he went to the headman's people, and spoke to them: "I say, sir, would you let me have a place to lie down?"

"Well, yes, sir," they replied; "but mind, it is here on the veranda there is any place."

He answered: "Yes, I shall be quite well off also on a veranda."

Then they said to him: "A wayfarer like yourself is lying on that veranda. Please, you then also lie down there."

Then he ascended this veranda; the man who was there before had spread some straw out to lie on; he asked him for a little straw and lay down there. The man who was there already was a jugi, and when they had both lain down, the jugi, poor fellow, died there.

When it became morning, they saw that he had died; then they spoke to the prince also: "Wait, don't go away; we must first have a talk," whereupon the headman called all the village people together[19], and said to them: "Let us see, what shall we do? These two wayfaring strangers I yesterday let have a place to lie down here; then something or other happened to him, who knows what, and, as you see, he has died; what shall we do with him?"

The village people then said: "Let him be thrown away[20]; what else shall we do with him?" Then they said: "Let us see,

ho̱ṛkin me̱nket́a, O̱ko̱e eṭaḱ ho̱ṛ do̱ko giḍiyea? Ać so̱ṅge̱rengeye giḍiyea.

Ado̱ inạge sanam ho̱ṛko me̱nket́a, Sạri unigeye giḍiye ma; ar bae giḍiye khanbo aḍo ocoyea.

Khange ado̱ uniye me̱nket́a, Iń do̱ń raj ho̱po̱n kana, o̱ho̱ń giḍilea. Khange onkae me̱nket́ khanko ruhet́ go̱t́kedea. Khangeye thirena; ado̱e disạket́a, gurui me̱n akawadińa, Do̱ṣaḱ katha do̱ alom ne̱ho̱ta. Khange ado̱e gachaoket́a, Acha ho, alope ruhedińa, giḍiyegeań.

Ado̱ sạriye idikedea, ado̱ mit́ṭań so̱ḍo̱ḱreye o̱r khańjo̱ go̱t́kedea. Khange arhõ̱e me̱nket́a, Hapṛamkoko ro̱ṛa, bańma, Ho̱ṛmo̱ reaḱ bo̱sto̱r do̱ko o̱co̱ḱkatakogea. Onka bujhạukate bhagwae o̱r o̱co̱ḱket́taea. Khangeye ńe̱lket́ do̱, beṛhaete mit́ ḍaṇḍa ṭaka menaḱtae. Khange ado̱ inạ ṭakae raṛawana, ado̱e me̱nket́a, Baṅa, guru do̱ khub bhage ho̱ṛ kanae, khub kathageye cet́ akawadińa. Khange ado̱ inạḱtege tikinena, ado̱e um baṛayente ać oṛaḱ se̱ne mohṇḍayena.

Ado̱ calaḱ calaḱtegeye ńindạyena, ar apnar amda hõ e̱n hiloḱ do̱e tioḱket́a. Ghane̱ do̱ calaḱ sanayea, ghane̱ do̱ tahe̱n hõ sanayedea, du mo̱noḱ kantaea jivi do̱. Ado̱ khangeye muruk go̱t́ket́a, ado̱e me̱nket́a, Baṅa, bań tahe̱na; jãhã lekate teheń do̱ oṛaḱgeń se̱n tioga.

Khange sạri ado̱ ńindạ hõ ńindại calaḱ kangea. Ho̱ṛ gitić saṛa sạtiń khangeye tioḱket́a. Ado̱ bae ho̱ho̱ saḍelet́a, hape hapetegeye bo̱lo̱ go̱t́ena. Ado̱ ạkin gitić oṛaḱ duạr ṭhene calaoen khan do̱ mit́ jo̱ṛ panahi ar mit́ṭań tarwaṛe ona duạr ṭhenko do̱ho̱ akat́e ńe̱l ńamket́a. Khange tarwaṛe saṕkateye o̱r bo̱ć go̱t́ket́a are ho̱ho̱ket́a, Henda ya, o̱ko̱e ińaḱ oṛaḱre do̱pe bo̱lo̱ akana? Ar ona oṛaḱre do̱ uni ko̱ṛaren bạhu ar uniren miserat, ạkinge hiliyeakin gitić akan

21 lit. 'make him pass water', a very common term.

22 The **bhagwa** is a narrow piece of cloth passed between the legs and fastened in the waist-string in front and at the back.

who then can throw him away?" Two men then said: "Who else should throw him away? He who was with him shall do this."

All of them said the same: "Surely he will have to throw him away; and if he will not do so, we shall bring him to his bearings."[21]

He then said: "I am the son of a king, I shall not throw him away." When he said this, the others scolded him, whereupon he ceased speaking, and he remembered: "My teacher has said to me. Don't disregard what the council say's." Then he agreed: "All right, you, don't scold me; I shall throw him away."

Truth to tell, he took him away and pulled him down into a river-bed. Then he again said: "The Ancestors say: 'They remove the clothes of their bodies.'" Having come to this understanding, he pulled his waist-strip[22] off; then he saw, he had money all round his waist. Then he loosed it, and took the money and said: "There is no denying it, my teacher is an excellent man; he has taught me excellent things." By this time it had become noon; then he had a bath and started for his home.

As he went along, it became night; this day he also reached his own parts. Now he wants to go home, again he wants also to stay where he is; he was of two minds. Then he made up his mind and said: "No, I shall not remain here; somehow I shall reach home to-day."

Then, truth to tell, he walked along even when it was full night. When people had gone to bed and were fast asleep, he reached home. He did not call out or make any noise, but entered quietly. When he came to the door where he and his wife used to sleep, he saw that they had put a pair of shoes and a sword[23] at the door. Then he took the sword, drew it and called out: "I say, who are you who have entered my house?" Now in this house the young man's wife and his sister, these two sisters-in-law,

---

[23] A supposed precautionary measure; the Santals will mention this as good; the writer has never heard of an actual occurrence.

tahẹkana. Adọ uni kọṛae họhọket́ khan dọkin beret́ena, ar divhekin jẹrẹt́ket́a, adọ uni kuṛiye mẹnket́a, Iạ hili, nitok̕ dọ dadańe hẹćena, iń dọ haṇḍẹń calak̕ kana.

Khange onka mẹnkateye oḍokok̕ kan tahẹkana. Khangeye ńẹlkede dọ, tarwaṛe bọćkateye epel akat́. Adọe pạc ruạṛena are mẹnket́a, Oḍoklen khan nãhãk̕, dhorageye mageńa. Adọe mẹnket́a, E dada, iń kangeań. Am bam tahẹkante gitić gọṛọae lạgit́ iń hẹć akana, ar jãhãe eṭak̕ hoṛ aloko bọlọka mẹnte panahi ar tarwaṛe dọ duạrrele dọhọ akat́a. Eṭak̕ hoṛ dọń bań kana, amren miseram kangeań.

Mẹnkhan uni kọṛa dọ bańgeye pạtiạuk̕ kana, unạk̕e nẹhõrok̕ kanre hõ. Arhõe metae kana, Nọtẹ oḍokok̕me, dada nạhĩ phada, iń dọ bań bataoa.

Khange uni kuṛiye bujhạuket́a, Dhorage nãhãk̕e mageńa. Edreteye bul cabayena. Khange uni kuṛi dọ kicrić bhạnduṛente[24] dadattẹt́e udukadea; tọbẹ enae pạtiạuena.

Adọ khange uni kọṛa dọ guru reak̕ kathae disạ gọt́ket́a ar hũk hũke rak̕ket́a. Ạḍi bạṛiće bhabnayena, adọe mẹnket́a, Guru dọ ṭhikgeye metadińa, edre dọko jọm ruạṛa mẹnte. Nõkõe huṭẹć dhorageń khũnkea. Adọ uni guru reak̕ katha disạ disạte ạḍi hạbiće rak̕ket́a.

Onate ale Hoṛ họpọn dọ daka jọm jọkhẹć ganḍoko belale khan dọ kạṭić talańre hõle ghaskao nõggea.

Cabayena katha dọ, in marańgea.

24 lit. lying down help. When a woman is temporarily alone, it is customary that some related woman goes to her and sleeps in the same room. It is a natural and needed precaution in the circumstances of the Santals.

were sleeping. When the young man called out, they both got up, and lighted a lamp, whereupon the girl said: "Now, my sister-in-law, my brother has come; I am going over to the other place."

Saying this she was on the point of going out. Then she saw him, he had drawn the sword and was keeping it high up ready to cut with it. Then she drew back and said: "If I go out, he will surely cut me." She called out: "My brother, it is I. Because you were not here, I have come to sleep here with her[24]; and to prevent any other people from entering here, we have put shoes and a sword at the door. I am not a stranger, I am your own sister."

But the young man would not believe it, however much she implored him. Again he was saying to her: "Come out here, brother or not, I don't care."

The girl then understood: "He will surely cut me down; he is drunk with anger." Then the girl tore off her cloth and showed it to her brother, then only he believed.

Now the young man remembered the words of his teacher and commenced to cry bitterly; he became full of grief and said: "My teacher told me what is right, that people keep their anger back. Surely I might have committed a murder here." Remembering the words of his teacher he cried for a long while.

What was told above is the reason why we Santals, when people at the time of eating place a board for us to sit on, push it a little, however little, to one side.

The story is at an end; it is thus much.

89. Barea bhaiadi reaṅ.

Sedae jugre, kathae, miṭṭan atore bar boehakin tahẽkana. Ado bana horkin bahu barawana; adokin gidar pidar barawan khan dokin begar barayena.

Ado khange tahen tahente tin din badre coṅ mit́ din do cekate coṅ jhogra kapharìaukin ehopketa; ado adi baric utka patkakin kapharìauena, ar dapal hõkin dapalena.

Khange hudiṅić doe raṅgaoente ato hore jarwaketkoa. Ado ato hor hećkateko galmarao barakattakinteko samjhao barakatkina, Men! teheṅ khon do aloben kapharìaua; nẽkẽle solhokaben kana; arhõ nonkaben jhograk khan dole dandombena. Men! nia kathage disakaben. Ado enka men barakategeko beret́ calao barayena.

Arhõ onakate tin din badre coṅ arhõ onkage kapharìau jhograkin ehopketa; onkage unre hõ adikin jhograyena. Ado hudiṅiće menketa, Cet́ onka dom ruhetediṅ kana? Hor jarwakatelaṅ dandom ocomea.

Khange sariye raṅgao gotente ato hor jarwako lagite calao gotena. Khange atoren joto hore lai idiatkoa. Ado atorenko menketa, Teheṅ do ṅindayena, nitok do bale galmaraoettabena. Ma gapa setakre arhõ hećkate lai bara dohrawaleme. Ado enkako metade khan, uni doe ruar calaoena. Ado onko ato horko meneta, Nukin hor do eṅgate khub lekabon dandomkina, babon bagiakina.

Ado sim rak khange dadattet́ do ać bokot thene calaoena, adoe hoho beretkedea; adoe metae kana, Henda ya, alaṅ alaṅlaṅ larhaiyena,

1 The village people, presided over by the headman, called The Five or sometimes The Ten, sit in council, whenever called on, to settle disputes between the villagers. They can only impose fines; serious cases are supposed to be brought before the ordinary courts of law. The parties concerned are expected to give certain small sums to the villagers for their trouble, generally five four-annas (Re. 1—4—0) each or the double. This money is now-a-days generally spent in beer. Formerly they bought a pig or other animal, and the whole village got a portion for each house.

89. TWO BROTHERS WHO QUARRELLED.

ONCE upon a time long ago, people tell, there were two brothers in a certain village. They had both of them married, and when they got children, they separated and set up separate households.

As time passed one day, who knows how long afterwards, it happened somehow or other that they commenced to wrangle and quarrel; they quarrelled awfully, raking up all kinds of old matters; they even came to blows.

Then the younger became angry, and called the village people[1] together; and these came and talked the matter over, and made peace between them, saying: "Take care, from to-day don't quarrel any more; here now we are reconciling you; if you again wrangle in the same way, we shall fine you. Take care, remember this." Having spoken words to this effect, the village people rose and went their several ways.

Some time afterwards, who knows how long after, they again commenced to wrangle and quarrel in the same way; then also they went beyond all bounds. The younger said: "What are you scolding me for in this manner? We two[2] shall call the people together and have you fined."

And, truth to tell, having become very angry he hurried off to call the village people together. He told all the people of the village from house to house, and the villagers said: "It has become night to-day; we are not going to talk your matter over now. Come again to-morrow morning and give us notice once more." When they spoke to him in this way, he returned home; and the village people were saying: "These two fellows, dash it, we shall fine them effectively; we shall not let them alone."

At cock-crow the elder brother went to the younger one and called him up, and said to him: "Look here, you, we two alone

[2] Inclusive dual in threatening language.

ar am dọ ona kathage ato hoṛ ṭhenem lạlisketa, adọ ato hoṛ nāhāk bako ḍaṇḍọmlaṅa? Adọ ńẹlme, iń hõko ḍaṇḍọmińa, ar ona reak adha am hõko ạgumea. Ar ńẹlme, alaṅak cijge hoṛ nāhāklaṅ emakoa. Masẹ bujhạutalaṅme noa katha dọ ṭhik iń rọṛeta sẹ baṅa. Adọ alaṅtelaṅ cabalc khan, baṅ beskoktalaṅa? Cak eṅgate alaṅak cij hoṛ dọlaṅ emakoa? Inạ hoṛ emako ńutum poesage bana hoṛlaṅ ẹmọka, ar alaṅrenge mitṭaṅ bạdhiạlaṅ kiṛińea inạ poesatege, ar sanam cṅga họpọnbo jọmjoṅa. Adọ nonkale khan baṅ ạdi beskoka? Adọ masẹ bhala, rọṛ ruạṛtalaṅme, bes iń mẹneta sẹ bạṛić.

Adọ uni bọkọttẹṭẹ mẹnketa, Noako rọṛ ma besgem rọṛket; mẹnkhan ato hoṛge thọ holareń lại baṛawatkoa, pasẹ onko cetko metaṅ. Adọ bako metaṅa, Hola ma ạdi jidem mẹnet tahẽkan, adọ okorem jarwayetbona? Adọ bam jarwabon khan, tisre hõ amak katha dọ ọhọle bạsutletama. Onka nāhāk bako metaṅa?

Adọ uni dadattẹṭe mẹnketa, Acha, ona hõ bogcgea; mẹnkhan cet leka ińiń metama, adọ onka nāhāk ato hoṛ dọ metakom, baṅma, katha dọ nonka kana: ato hoṛ dọ ma jarwakom, ar onko jarwakate nāhākko kulimea, Cele phalna, cet lạgitem họhọ jarwa akatlea? Adọ masẹ lạialem. Adọ nāhāk am dọ metakom, Iạ baba, holanok ạliń bhạiạdi ạdi bạṛićliń jhogṛa akana, adọ onateń họhọ jarwa akatbona; adọ masẹ bhala, ona baṛẹ bicạrkataliṅpe. Adọ nāhāk unreko kulimea, Cet lekaben jhogṛalen, ona reak oṛ phẹḍ ma lạime, tọbẹ nạhĩle bujhạutele bicạra. Adọ masẹ bhala lạialeme. Adọ nāhāk unre am dọ metakom, Ọnẹ babaṅ lạiyetge cọṅ, holanok ạlińliń jhogṛa akana. Adọ unreko mẹna, Ma ẹtọhọp khon lạime, cet lekateben ẹhọpleta ar cetkoben rọpọṛ akana, ona lạime. Adọ unre am dọ nāhāk metakom, Ma baba ẹnte, bujhạupe ape mõṛẽ hoṛge, cet lekaliń rọpọṛ akana, bicạrtaliṅpe; bicạr ocoka mẹnte.

---

3 Inclusive plural is used. The parties concerned are not excluded.

had a fight, and you brought this matter before the village people; now will not the village people fine both of us? See, they will fine me, and half of the amount they will fine you too. And observe, our property we shall in this way give to others. Please understand this matter of ours, am I speaking right or not? Now if we settle it between ourselves, would it not be good for both of us? Why shall we, dash it, give other people our property? The money that should be given to the people, let both of us give that, and let us buy a hog for ourselves with that money, and then both our families, all of us, will have a feast. If we did this, would it not be well? So now there, give an answer for us both, am I speaking well or the opposite?"

The younger brother then said: "What you there say is quite good; but yesterday I told the village people; what will these say to me? Will they not say, 'Yesterday you were very eager speaking to us; then why are you not calling us together? If you do not call us together, we shall never again take any notice of any matter of yours.' Will they not speak so to me?"

The elder brother then said: "All right, that is quite so; but speak to the village people just as I shall tell you, in the following way. Call the village people together, and when they have assembled they will presently ask you: 'Well, so and so, for what purpose have you called us together? Please tell us.' Then you say to them: 'Well, sirs, yesterday we two brothers had an awful quarrel; therefore I have called us[3] together; therefore now, please, settle that matter for us two.' Then they will ask you: 'Tell us in detail, from the very beginning, how you quarrelled; then only shall we understand and be able to settle your case. So please tell us.' Then you say to them: 'There, sirs, that is just what I am telling; yesterday we have had a quarrel.' Then they will say: 'Tell, from the very beginning how you commenced, and what you have said to each other, tell this.' Then you say to them: 'Yes, sirs, understand it, you village five, how we have

nõkõe iń ạgu jarwa akaťpea; adọ ceťkoliń rọpọṛlen, ma bicạrpe. Adọ nãhãk̓ onkam mẹnle khan, ceť hõ ọkọko ceka daṛelea. Adọ ruheť baṛakate nãhãk̓ko bereť calak̓a. Adọ inạ tayọm nãhãk̓ alaṅ dọ miťṭaṅ sukrilaṅ gọjea, adọbo jọmea. Adọ ẹnẹ enkaṅ lạiam kana; inạ katha disạkam; inạk̓ khon bạṛti dọ alom lạiakoa. Ma inạk̓ge katha dọ. Do calak̓te lại baṛawakome jarwak̓ lạgiť.

Adọ sạri uni bọkọt koṛa dọ ato họṛko jarwako lạgiť setak̓ jọkhẹć dọe calaoena; adọ sanam họṛe lại baṛawaťkoa. Adọ miť ghạṛi khange ato họṛko hẹć gad gadao gọťena; adọ mạci parkọmko belaťkote duṛuṗ teṅgonko metaťkoa.

Khange adọ onko ato họṛ dọ uni jajaorae sẹnlen họṛko kulikedea, Henda phalna, cele, bạbu, ceť lạgiťem jaora akaťbona? Masẹ bhala, lạile udukletam, tọbẹ nạhĩle baḍaea oroma jẹ kana bhuk duk, onam lạile kathale baṅle bujhạua.

Adọ khange uni họṛe rọṛkeťa, Iạ, baba, apege atoren põc miťṭaṅ bicạra baste iń dọń ạgu jaora akaťpea. Adọ onage bicạrkataliṅpe, ạliń eskarte dọ baliń bicạr ṭhik daṛeak̓ kana; onate ape ato họṛ iń rak̓ akawaťpea.

Adọ ato họṛko mẹnkeťa, Masẹ bhala, lạime ceť lekan katha kana; aṅjọmle nạhĩle rọṛa.

Khange adọ uni họṛe mẹnkeťa, Iạ baba, holanok̓ ạliń bhạiạdige ạḍiliń kạphạriạu akana, adọ onage ma phaṇḍaokataliṅpe; ona lạgiťgeń ạgu jarwa akaťpea.

Adọ ato họṛko mẹnkeťa, Ma ẹnte, lại idilem; ceťkoe ruheť akaťmea, lạime; ạuṛi dọ ceť lekale bicạra?

Adọ uni họṛe mẹnkeťa, Ọnẹ cọń babań lại akawaťpe, ạliń bhạiạdiliń jhogṛa akana. Adọ ceť lekań lạiapea?

had words together, and settle the matter. It is to have the matter settled that I have called you together; so settle what words we had.' When you speak in this way, they will certainly not be able to do anything. Then they will give you a scolding and go away. And afterwards we two shall kill a pig, and all of us have a feed. This is what I am telling you to do; remember it; do not say more to them than this. Well, that is all. Now go and tell them to come together here."

Truth to tell, the younger brother went that morning to call the village people together; he informed all; and a short while afterwards the village people came, crowds of them; they brought out stools and bedsteads for them, and invited them to sit down.

Thereupon the village people asked the man who went to summon them: "Look here, you so and so, well, young man, for what purpose have you called us together? Tell us that before anything else; then only we shall know and understand that such and such is the difficulty; only when you tell, when you state this, we shall be able to understand what it is."

The younger brother then said: "Well, sirs, you village-five, I have brought you together to settle a matter. So settle that for me; we two alone are unable to settle it properly; therefore I have complained to you."

The village people then said: "Well then, please tell what kind of a case it is; only when we hear this, we shall be able to say anything."

The man then said: "Well, sirs, yesterday, we two brothers had an awful quarrel; settle that for us; it is for this purpose that I have brought you together."

The village people then said: "Well then, tell how it went off; tell how he has abused you; how shall we be able to judge at random?"

The man replied: "Well, sirs, it is what I have told you; we two brothers have had a quarrel. How shall I tell you?

Adǫ ato hoṛko mẹnkeṭa, Hẽ sẹ bạbu, jhogṛa mabẹn jhogṛa akange; adǫ ona reak oṛ phẹḍge thǫ bam lạiyeṭa.

Khange adǫ uniye mẹn ruạṛkeṭa, Ma baba, hudis ńampe; ẹnte ceṭ lekalin jhogṛa akana, ona dǫ bape hudis ńameṭa? Onate nõkõe iń ạgu akaṭpea. Arhõ ińgeń lạiape khan, ẹnḍẹkhan okor oka lekape bicạreṭtalińa? Adǫ ghạṛi hõ ghạṛi inạ katharegeko ẹpẹsẹṭ kana.

Khange adǫ ato hoṛko rańgaoente bhageteko ruheṭkẽdea, Iạ hoṛge, oṛ phẹḍ bam lại khan, ạuṛigem jaora akaṭlea.

Are mẹneṭa, Bicạrtińpe.

Ạuṛi dǫ eńgate oka lekale bicạra? Oṛ phẹḍ ńamle bale rǫṛa. Adǫ nun hạbićle tahẽyena, ona reak dẹn mańjan daka ẹmǫkme; ona dǫ ǫhǫle bạgilema. Amem lại baṛawaṭle iạte dǫle hẹćena; ar bańkhan jãhãnak hutẹć bale kạmikea? Dẹn, mańjan daka dǫle ạgumegea arem ẹmǫkgea.

Adǫ uni hoṛe mẹnkeṭa, Cedak iń ẹmǫka, baba? Oka hõ bape galmaraoleṭtińa; ạuṛiakte dǫ ǫhǫń ẹmlepea. Hẽ, judipe galmaraole khan hutẹć, jẹ kana dǫs reak lẹg, ona hutẹć iń ẹmkepea. Ona iạte ạuṛiakte dǫ ǫhǫń ẹmlena, inạte dǫ jagepe metań.

Khange adǫ bhageteko ruheṭkedea, ar ruheṭ ruheṭteko bereṭ calao baṛayena. Adǫ enko sẹn tayǫmge nukin dǫ bạdhiạkin gǫćkedetekin jel dakawaṭkote ako sanam hoṛ ạḍi rạskạteko jǫm ńũkeṭa. Adǫ uni dadaṭtẹṭe mẹnkeṭa, Ńẹlkeṭam ya, bud iń ceṭaṭmete balań baclaoena? Ar bańkhan hutẹć nãhãk hoṛgelań ajǫkekoa.

Adǫ cabayena katha dǫ, in marańgea.

---

4 Lit. thinking find.

5 The motive underlying the supposed action of the elder brother is one that may be heard urged against 'going to law'. The whole proceeding is what the Santals style p h e p ṛ a, perverse and dishonest. They will laugh at such a story; but if a man would attempt such nonsense, he would not fare well and would have to smart for it afterwards.

The village people said: "Quite so, young man, you have had a quarrel."

He answered back: "Please, sirs, think it out; are you not thinking out[4] how we have quarrelled? Therefore, as you see, here I have brought you. If I shall again tell you, why, how are you then judging between us?" Again and again they were arguing this very matter.

Ultimately the village people got angry and scolded him a good deal, saying: "You unspeakable fellow, if you will not tell us the case from the beginning, it is for no purpose at all that you have called us together."

"Judge my case," he said.

"How are we to judge at random, dash it? Only when we have heard the whole from the start, we shall be able to say anything. Now we have stayed here up to now; for that give us our midday meal; we shall not let you off this. We came because you told us; otherwise should we not have been able to do some work? Out with it, we charge you a midday meal, and you will have to give this."

Then the man said: "Why should I give, sirs? You have not decided anything at all for me; I shall certainly not give anything for nothing. Yes, if you had settled anything, I should of course have given you what the council have a right to. Therefore I shall certainly not give you anything for nothing, you may say whatever you like."

Then they scolded him violently, and whilst scolding they got up and went their several ways. After these had gone, the two brothers killed the hog and gave their people meat-curry and rice, and all of them ate and drank with great joy. The elder brother said: "Did you see, young man? I taught you how to act, and were we not rescued thereby? If not, we should now have heen feeding other people."[5]

So the story is ended; it is thus much.

90. Miťťaṅ tili haṛam ar uniren hǫpǫntęťko reaṅ.

Miťťaṅ tili haṛamė tahẽkana, ar uni haṛamren dǫ mõṛẽ gǫtęć hǫpǫnko tahẽkantaea. Adǫ onko jǫtǫ koṛae bąhuaťkoa, adǫ miťre tahęn tahęnte ḍher dinko tahẽyena, ęnre hõ unkin haṛam buḍhi dǫ begaroǩ reaǩ kathage bakin rǫṛ.

Adǫ onkage miťre tahęn tahęntege onko koṛako dǫkǫ chaona paonawana; adǫ uni haṛamren kiminko dǫko ąrisoǩ kana. Adǫ ako akoren hęręlkoko metakoa, Ma, ayo babatekin dǫ galmaraoakinpe, tin din miťre dǫkin dǫhǫboa; adǫ babo bagaroǩ, sę nonka miťregebo tahęna? Ma, noa katha galmaraoakinpe, ayo babatekin dǫ.

Adǫ onko koṛakoǩo męnkeťa, Miťre dǫpe mǫkǫṅente onka dǫpe męneťa?

Adǫko męnkeťa, Hẽ, mǫkǫṅ hõ mǫkǫṅ, baṅ hõ baṅ. Adǫ ęnte miťrege jaejugbo tahęna?

Adǫ onko koṛakoko męnkeťa, Achale galmaraoakina ęṇḍękhan.

Adǫ sąri ąyuṕ jǫkhęć jǫtǫ hǫṛko jarwa baṛayenkhan, adǫ onko koṛako dǫko ęhǫṕkeťa, adǫ apattęťko metae kana, Ę baba, ale dǫ miťťaṅ galmaraole disą akaťa, aṅjǫmkatalem.

Adǫ uni apat haṛam dǫe męnkeťa, Ceť lekan katha kana ya? Ma rǫṛpe.

Adǫ koṛakoko męnkeťa, Bes katha cǫṅ, bąṛić cǫṅ, ęntem aṅjǫmle nąhĩ.

Adǫe męnkeťa, Aṅjǫmeťtapegeaṅ, rǫṛpe.

---

[1] Tili, as the Santals pronounce the Bengali teli, a caste whose principal occupation is to press oil.

[2] The separation of brothers is a great problem also with the Santals. It will be understood from this story that also their ideal is that all should live together so long as the parents are alive. Very frequently this living together leads to much ill-feeling, due to the inability of the strange elements, brought in by the marriage of the sons, being able to hit it off together. The daughters-in-law and their children feel the need of being able to have their own establishment.

It is the father who has to give the permission to separate; he calls in the village people with the village headman; with the assistance of these all lands

90. AN OILMAN AND HIS SONS.

THERE once lived an old oilman[1], who had five sons. He procured wives for all his sons, and, living together in one household, a long time passed; still the old man and his wife never mentioned a word about setting up separate households[2].

Living together in this way the young men had children born to them, and the old man's daughters-in-law were feeling worried, and they spoke to their husbands, saying: "Do speak to mother and father, how long will they keep us in one household? Shall we not be separated, or shall we live on like this together? Do speak to mother and father about this matter."

The young men then asked: "Have you become tired of living together, since you say this?"

"Yes", they replied, "both tired and not tired also. Shall we then eternally live together in one household?"

The young men then said: "All right, we shall speak to them then."

Then, truth to tell, when they had all come together in the evening, the young men took the matter up and said to their father: "Father, we have bethought ourselves of a matter which we must have a talk about; listen to us."

The old father replied: "What kind of matter is it, boys? Out with it."

The young men replied: "May be it is a good thing, may be it is bad; you must hear about it first."

"I am hearing," he said, "speak."

and properties are divided into as many equal shares as there are sons, plus the father. The father keeps one share, the sons get one share each. Daughters do not inherit or get anything, but at the time of marriage a 'calf' is generally given to them; if there are any unmarried girls at the time of separation, they get a 'calf'.

Adọ onko koṛako mẹnketa, Katha dọ cet hõ baṅ; ale dọ begar ocokle ńam kana. Tin din mitre dọle tahẹna? Adọ bam begar baṛakalea? Iną dọ apan ąpinte gidrąkoko dak mąṇḍi baṛawakotakoa. Nẹkẹ nią kathale disą akata, ąḍi utąr dọ baṅ, niąge hujhąume.

Adọ uni haṛame mẹnkettakoa, Henda ya, eṅgam tite dọ bape bik kana sẹ?

Adọko mẹnketa, Bi dọle bik kangea.

Tọbẹ dọ ẹṇḍẹkhan cedak onka dọpe rọṛeta?

Adọko mẹnketa, Ẹnte ẹṇḍẹkhan baṅle rọṛa? Am mọnẹte ma bam begaretle, onatẹle rọṛ saḍeketa. Adọ apan ąpinte bale ghọrkornajoṅa? Onatele rọṛ saḍeketa. Adọ dẹ, amge cetem mẹneta?

Adọ haṛame mẹnketa, Hẹ̃ ya, baḍaeyetgeaṅ: bąhuko ya bako bik kantapea, ẹnre hõ iṅ dọ baṅ begarpea. Adọ onkae mẹn baṛawatko khanko thir baṛayena.

Adọ mọ̃ṛẹ̃ turui mãhã khange arhõ ona begarok kathageko ẹhọpketa. Khange adọ uni haṛame mẹnketa, Acha ya, begarok ąḍi hąspe metak kana. Dẹn ẹṇḍẹkhan bar moka jeleṅ kaṭ ar bar tite tọhọp purąukak ąguipe. Onareṅ biḍąulepege, ẹṇḍẹkhan iṅ begarpea; ar baṅkhan dọ ọhọṅ begarlepea.

Khange sąri in maraṅ kaṭko ągu gọtketa, ar tala racareko dọhọ gọtketa; adọko metadea, Nõkõele ąguketa.

Adọe metatkoa, Ma sẹ bhala, ọkọe tinąkpe daṛea, noa kaṭ judipe rąputketa mẹnkhan, ẹṇḍẹkhan iṅ begarpea. Ar judi baṅpe rąputketa mẹnkhan, ẹṇḍẹkhan dọ ọhọṅ begarlepea.

Adọko mẹnketa, Dẹn thọ ya, ṭẹṅgọc ągui ma, mak rąput gọtka ma.

The young men then said: "It is really nothing; we only want to set up separate households. How long shall we live together? Will you not separate us? In this case they will be able to prepare food for their own children separately. This is what we have bethought ourselves of; it is not much; think this matter over."

The old man then spoke: "I say, boys, don't you get your fill by your mother's hand, or how?"

They replied: "Certainly, we are satisfied."

"Why then are you talking in this manner?"

"Should we not speak then?" they replied, "you do not think yourself of separating us; therefore we have mentioned it. Should we not each one of us separately acquire what we need for the household? It was therefore that we mentioned it. So let us hear, what do you say?"

The old man then said: "Yes, boys, I know what it is; your wives are not getting what they want, boys; still I am not going to separate you." When he had spoken to them in this way, they did not say any more.

When five six days had passed, they again started this matter of being separated. The old man then said: "All right, boys, to be separated you think is great fun. Find and bring then a piece of wood, two cubits long, and so thick that you need both hands to hold round it. I shall first test you with this, and then I may separate you; and if you do not stand the test, I am not going to separate you."

Then, truth to tell, they brought a piece of wood of this size, and said to him: "See here, we have brought it."

"Now then," he said, "I shall like to see what strength each of you has; if you are able to break this piece of wood, I shall separate you; but if you are unable to break it, I shall not do so."

"Come, you fellows," they said, "let an axe be brought; then it may be cut into pieces in a trice."

Adǫ uni haṛame męnket́a, Baṅa, pạhil dǫ pęṭęjte; sę mocṛaote, sę lębędte, sę thạiạte baṛę, sę jãhã lekatege ape daṛete rạpudpe. Adǫ bape rạput́le khan, nãhãḱ ṭęṅgǫćte hõń hukumapegea.

Adǫ khange sạri ękę ękęte ona rạput́ lạgit́ko jhũkena, ęnre hǫ̃ ǫkǫe hǫ̃ bako rạput́ daṛeat́a. Khange adǫ babar hǫṛkateko jhũkena, ęnre hǫ̃ bako lęṭęć dareat́a. Khange adǫko thir doroḱena.

Adǫ haṛame męnket́a, Cele ya, lęṭęćket́a sępę baṅa?

Adǫko męnket́a, Bale lęṭęć daṛeat́a.

Adǫe metat́koa, Apepe mõṛẽ hǫṛa, ar iń lagaete turui hǫṛbo hoeoḱ kana. Ma ęṇḍękhan dǫ turui paṛagpe noa kaṭ dǫ.

Khange sạri adǫ ona kaṭ dǫko turui paṛaḱket́a; adǫ mimit́ goṭaṅ pataṛaḱe hạṭiń baṛawat́koa, ar mit́ṭaṅ dǫ aće hataoket́a. Adǫe metat́koa, Masę bhala, nitoḱ dǫ rạput́ gelaepe, rạput́kea sępe baṅ?

Adǫko męnket́a, Ǫh! rạput́ baṅkhanle cekaea? Enaṅ dǫ moṭa kaṭem metale kan khan, ma rạpudpe męnte, un maraṅaḱ dǫ bhala, caḱ rạpudoḱ? Nit ma mit́ ghạṛitele rạput́ gǫt́kea.

Adǫe męnket́a, Ma sę bhala, rạpudpe. Khange adǫ apan ạpinko pęṭęć coaḱ baṛa gǫt́ket́a. Khange adǫ uni haṛame męnket́a, Cele bạbu, noa kaṭ rạpud iń metat́pea. Adǫ noa kaṭ khon cet́pe bujhạuket́a?

Onkoko męnket́a, Ale dǫ bale bujhạu daṛeaḱ kana, cet́ko cǫń hana nha bhędem lạiyet́. Ale dǫ ma thǫ begarkaleme. Ale dǫ bhęd bhad cet́ hǫ̃ bale baḍaea. Ale dǫ lelha bhucuṅ koṅka bhũiạ kanale. Begar ocoḱle ńam kana: inạgele baḍaea.

Adǫ uni haṛame męnket́a, Ẹ bạbu, noa kaṭ reaḱ bhęd bape bujhạuet́ khan dǫń lạiape kana. Bujhạutabonpe; ńęlpe, ona kaṭ ạuri paṛagre dǫ ǫkǫe hǫ̃ bape rạput́ daṛeat́a; ar paṛaḱ hạṭińket́ khan dǫ algatepe rạput́ baṛa gǫt́ket́a, Onkage abo hǫ̃ goṭa kaṭ

3 The word translated 'rustics' is the name given to a semi-hinduized aboriginal caste, the Bhuyas, whose name means something like 'belonging to the soil'. It is here used in a deprecatory sense.

The old man then said: "Not so; first try to break it by bending, or twisting, or stamping, or kicking, or in any possible way with your own strength. If you are unable to break it, then I shall order you to use also the axe."

Then, truth to tell, they one after the other vigorously tried to break it; but in spite of all exertion none of them was able to manage it; then they gave it up, what else could they do?

"Well, boys," the old man asked, "did you manage it or not?"

"We were unable to do it," they replied.

Then he said to them: "You are five, and when you count me, we become six persons. So now then split this log up into six pieces."

Then, truth to tell, they split the log into six pieces, and he divided the split pieces between them, giving them each one, and one piece he took himself, whereupon he said to them: "Now at it; now try to break it; do you think you will be able to break it or not?"

"Oh," they said, "what should we do else than break it? When you told us a while ago to break the thick log of wood, how would it be possible to break anything so big? Now we shall break this in one moment."

"At it then," he said; "break it." Thereupon each one of them at once snipped their piece off. The old man then said: "Well, young men, I told you to break this piece of wood. What have you now understood from this?"

They replied: "We are unable to understand anything you show us, whatever it may be. In any case, separate us. We know nothing, neither sense nor meaning. We are foolish, stupid, witless rustics[3]. We want to be separated; that is what we know."

The old man then said: "Young men, as you do not understand the inner meaning of this piece of wood, I shall tell you. Understand this: see, before you split the log, none of you was able to break it; and when it had been split up into pieces, you easily all of you broke it. Similarly we too are like the whole

leka mit́ ṭhen dǫ aema jinis ńęloḱ kantabona, ar nãhãḱbo begarle khan dǫ, sanam chir chạturoḱtabona, ublạ ḍublạitepe ręṅgęjoḱa. Ńęlpe, nitoḱ dǫ ǫkǫe nusibte cǫṅ abo oṛaḱre cij basa akan, ona ape dǫ bape bujhạuet́a. Ar ńęlpe, abo jǫtǫ apa hǫn mit́rebo tahęn khan, ęṇḍękhan aboren bạiri sę dusmạn jãhãe abo tuluć ṭhǫkko lagaole khan, onkobo hạr daṛeakoa. Ar judi abobo apan ạpinlen khan, ęṇḍękhan cekatebo hạr daṛeakoa? Ękę ękęte cǫṅ aboko hạrbon. Ma sę bhala, bujhạutabonpe, noa katha dǫ ṭhika sę baṅ.

Adǫko męnket́a, Noako katham rǫṛet́ ma sạri kange, pạtiạuḱ kangealo, ạuṛi dǫ bạm rǫṛet́a; męnkhan do begarkaleme baṛę, na hǫnęć sanam hǫṛ nǫṇḍęgele tahęna. Ar cij bạsut bam hạṭińalere hǫ̃, celaṅtęt́ emalem, inạre aṛaḱ sakamkole teke baṛajoṅa.

Adǫ uni haṛam ać mǫnę mǫnęteye guni bhạbiyena are męnwana, Durrę, noko koṛa dǫ ạḍitęt́ko koṅka cabayena, unạḱ man kathaṅ galmaraoat́kore hǫ̃ bako bujhạulet́a. Achaṅ begarkakogea. Ękęn celaṅ eskar iṅ emako khan nãhãḱ hǫṛko rǫṛa. Metaṅako, Nui haṛam dǫ ạḍiye ciṭạṛgea, unạḱ cij bạsut menaḱre hǫ̃, hǫpǫntęt́ko dǫ ękęn titeye begarkat́koa. Nui dǫ ạḍi pạpi haṛam kanae. Onka nãhãḱ hǫṛko rǫṛa. Acha, jage hoeoḱ, dǫhǫere hǫ̃ baṅre hǫ̃, ęnre hǫ̃ somangeṅ hạṭińakoa.

Onka bujhạu baṛakate adǫ sanamaḱge bara bạriteye hạṭińat́koa, adǫ apan ạpin oṛaḱte cijko idiket́takoa.

Adǫ tahęn tahęnte tin serma badre cǫṅ arhǫ̃ko ręṅgęćena, jǫmaḱ baṅ juṭạuako, kicrić hǫ̃ baṅ, adǫ ạḍiko bhabnayena. Ar unkin haṛam buḍhikin hǫ̃ daḱ mạṇḍi hǫ̃ baṅ juṭạuakin.

4 The word basa is used about temporarily taking up one's abode anywhere.

5 The expression aṛaḱ sakam, lit. vegetables leaves, is commonly used about the stuff from which the Santals make their curry.

log; when we are together in one place, much property is seen belonging to us; if we now set up separate households, all ours will be scattered; you will squander it and become poor. See, by some fortune or other goods have now settled[4] in our house; this you do not understand. And see, when all of us, father and sons, stay together, then if our enemies or any one who hates us should pick a quarrel with us, we shall be able to vanquish them. But if we are separated, how should we be able to vanquish them? They would do for us one after the other separately. So now then, think our case over, is this I say right or not?"

They answered: "All that you say is quite right; we believe so, you do not talk nonsense; but please give us separate households; in any case we shall all remain here; and even if you do not give us our shares of the property, give us the cooking-pots; in this we shall cook vegetables and leaves[5] for ourselves."

The old man then became distressed in his mind, and said to himself: "What a pity, these young fellows have become utterly foolish; words so full of meaning I have spoken to them, still they do not understand. Very well, I shall let them have separate households. If I now give them only the cooking-pots, then people will talk. They will say about me: 'This old man is a great miser; although he has so much property, he has let his sons set up separate households empty-handed. He is a very stingy old man.' In this way people will talk. Well then, whatever it may be, whether they will receive it or not, still I shall divide all and give them equal shares."

Having come to this conclusion he divided all his property into equal shares and gave them, and they took each of them what they got of property home to themselves.

Living on then, after some years, who knows how many, they again became poor; they had not sufficient food, no clothes either, and they became full of anxiety. And the old man and his wife had not enough to support themselves either.

Adọ miṭ din dọ jọtọ koṛako ar bạhuko miṭ miṭteye họhọ jaoraketkoa, adọe metako kana, Cele beṭa, bujhạukeṭtabonape, ceṭ hal hoeyentabona? Haṛam họṛak katha nẹhọt dọ baṅ bogea. Ṅẹlpe, ape dọ apekoren bạhukoak kathape sẹnaṭa; onate nonka harkhet dọbo ṅam akaṭa. Ona baṛẹ ape mọnre bujhạu kandhaotabonpe. Ar miṭṭaṅ iṅ kudumape kana, ọna reak bhẹd bhaṅgaoaṅtabonpe. Adọe kudum gọṭketa: Kudum kuṛiṭ kuṛiṭ, Ponea kũi menaka; pẹa kũi dọ khạligea ar miṭṭaṅ kũire dọ pẹrẹć dak menaka. Adọ ona dak lokate noako pẹnẹ kũirem dulle khan, jọtọ kũige pẹrẹjoka. Ar noa kũi khạli tahẹn ar onako pẹrẹć tahẹn jọkhẹć onako kũi reak dak noarem dul khan dọ baṅ pẹrẹjoka. — Adọ ṁa rọṛpe noa reak bhẹd dọ ceṭ kana. Inạ lạiaṅtabonpe.

Khange thọ adọko as basaoena, ạḍi dhạbićko tirup thirena. Ar uni haṛam dọe metako kana, Ma lại gọṭaṅpe. Khange adọe metako kana, Bape rọṛeṭ khan dọ aṅjọmpe. Iṅiṅ lạiape kana: ponea kũi dọ noa kana, baṅma, miṭṭaṅ haṛamren ponea họpọnko tahẽkantaea; adọ ạuriko begarokre dọ uni haṛam họṛge jọtọ garọsṭi họṛe ạsuleṭko tahẽkana. Adọe begar baṛaketko khan dọ, uni haṛam họṛ dọ onko ponea họpọn menakkotaere hõ, adọ ạḍi bạṛić rẹṅgẹćteye harkhetok kana. Onko họpọntẹṭ ạuriko harakre dọ ona kũi dul pẹrẹj leka onko koṛakoak laće bi ocokeṭtakoa; adọko bhinạ baṛayen khan, uni haṛam reak laćge bako bi daṛeatae kana. Asọl dọ noa kana, baṅma, uni haṛam dọ dak mạṇḍi ọkọe họpọn hõ bako emaea. Onate noa khisạ dọe rọṛketa. Onka leka ṅẹlpe, ape hõ nun din dọ cekakote cọṅ iṅgeṅ dọhọkeṭpetepe hara buruyena, rẹṅgẹćte hõ baṅ kọsṭọ ocoleṭpea. Adọṅ begar baṛakaṭpe khan, ọkọe hõ dak mạṇḍi dọ bape emaṅ kana. Inạge bujhạutabonpe.

---

6 When Santals give out a riddle, they always commence as here. I have never been able to get an explanation of what is really meant by these words. The kite is a constant trouble to the Santals; it comes suddenly, swoops down and carries a chicken away. It may possibly be a way of saying: be quick to tell the meaning, else somebody else may do it before you.

Then one day he called all the young men and their wives together, every one of them, and said to them: "Well, my sons, have you understood our case, what circumstances have become ours? It is not good to disregard the word of an old man. See, you listened to what your wives said; thereby we have got into such difficulties. Now turn this over in your mind, and find out what it means. And I am giving you a riddle to solve, tell me its meaning. Then he named the riddle: "A riddle, the kite, the kite[6]: there are four wells; three wells are empty, and one well is full of water. If you draw water from this and pour it into the three others, all the wells become full. But when this well is empty and the others are full, if you draw water from them and pour it into this one, it does not become full. So now say what this means, tell me."

They became utterly perplexed; for a long time they were sitting quiet with bowed heads. The old man said: "Be quick now and tell me." Then he said to them: "As you do not speak, listen. I am telling you the meaning, this is the four wells: A man had four sons; before they separated, the old man was supporting all the people in the family. Then when the old man had given them separate households, he was suffering awfully from want, although he had these four sons. Before the sons grew up, he filled the stomach of these boys full, just as they filled the wells; but when they parted from each other, they were unable to fill the stomach of the old man. The real thing was this: none of his sons gives the old man any gruel; therefore he spoke such vexatious words. In the same way you see, so long a time I kept you also somehow or other and you grew up; I never let you suffer hardship from hunger either. Now after I have given you separate households, not one of you has been giving me even gruel. Understand what this means to us."

Adọ khange onko koṛako dọ ạḍi lajaoko ạikạuketa. Adọ arhõko mit ruạṛena, arko mọnketa, Ayo babatekin jivẹt tahẹn bhor dọ ọkọe hõ babo begaroka. Ar nukin baṅ hilok dọ apan ạpinbo dandha baṛajona; mẹnkhan unkin jivẹt bhor dọ mitregebo tahẹna.

Inạge katha dọ. Cabayena nitok dọ; in maraṅgea.

91. Mit hoṛ tạrupe bạhuade reaṅ.

Sedae jọkhẹn, kathae, pẹ pon hoṛ mitṭaṅ atore bạhu ṅẹlko sẹn akana. Adọ mitṭaṅ kuṛiko nolaolede tahẽkana. Adọ ona atoren mit hoṛ girhoṛ sapkateko metadea, Delabon ho, uni phalua hopon kuṛibo ṅẹlea,' ar jutlen khan dọ, nãhãk amge ghoṭọkdar dọle sapmea.

Adọ uni hoṛ hõe mẹnketa, Acha, delabon ẹṇḍẹkhanbo kulikoa. Adọ sạri onka mẹnkate uni kuṛitekoak oṛakteko calaoena. Adọ ọkọe kuṛiko mẹnlet, uni kuṛi eskarge oṛakre dọe tahẽkana. Ar onako kuliye jọkhẹnge mitṭaṅ dosra kuṛi hõ ọṇḍẹge ajareye hẹćena; adọ uni kuṛi dọe thir akangea. Adọ uniko mẹnet kuṛigeko kuliyede kana, Henda mại, ạpum dọe okayena?

Adọe metako kana, Apuṅ dọ, baba, dak dakrame sẹn akana.

Ar eṅgam dọ, mạiye okayena?

Adọe metako kana, Eṅgaṅ dọ, baba, mit hoṛ khon bar hoṛko lạgite sẹn akana.

Khange adọ onko hoṛ dọ bako bujhạuette cet hõ bako roṛ ruạṛleta. Adọ un jọkhẹnge uni ajare kuṛi dọe roṛ gọtketa, O

---

1 This story has interpolated a variant of the story of the leopard and the marriage broker; it contains an addition to this and so much other matter, characteristic of the Santals, that it deserves to be rendered.

2 When a marriage is to be arranged, the first thing is naturally to get some idea what the prospective bride may be; they do not, however, as the story reveals, go very deeply into the matter. As a rule it is done as follows: when the marriage broker has found what he thinks is a suitable girl, and has got the consent of the girl's father for a possible union, some people from the boy's village (generally his father included) go to the girl's village and are permitted to see the girl

Then his sons felt greatly ashamed, and they moved together into one household again and said: "So long as mother and father live, we shall none of us separate. The day when they are no more, we shall look out for ourselves; but so long as they live, we shall stay together."

That is the story, it is at an end now; it is this much.

91. ABOUT A MAN WHO PROCURED A WIFE FOR A LEOPARD[1].

In olden times, people tell, three four men had once gone to look at a bride[2] in a certain village. There was a girl whom they had estimated would be suitable. Then, laying hold of a man in the village to act as a guide, they said to him: "Come along with us, you, let us have a look at so and so's daughter, and if it turns out well, we shall lay hold of you to be our marriage broker."

"All right," the man replied; "come along then, and we shall ask them."

Then, truth to tell, after this talk they went to the girl's parents' house. Here the girl whom they had thought of was alone in the house. And at the time when they were asking the girl, another girl came there to gossip; but she was keeping quiet. Then they were asking the girl they had in view: "I say, girl, what has become of your father?"

She replied: "My father, sir, has gone to meet the rain."

"And what has become of your mother, girl?"

"My mother," she answered them, "has gone, sir, to make two persons of one."

As they did not understand the meaning of this, the men did not say anything in reply. Then the girl who had come there

---

moving about in the company of two other girls, she being always between the two others. In this way they 'see the bride'.

hae, bhala nọṇḍẹgeń teṅgo akan, nẹte mit̕ sẹr kaskọm dọń rit̕ pitet̕kea. Adọ enka rọṛ oṭokate khange uni kuṛi dọ ako oṛak̕teye beret̕ calaoena.

Adọ noko hoṛ dọ ako mọtọreko mẹpẹnena, Otẹ, unige ạḍiye kạmia, unigebon idiyea, uni dọ mit̕ ghạṛitege, kathaeye kạmia. Adọ onka mẹnkateko beret̕ calaoena. Adọ uni ajare kuṛige bạhuye reak̕ko goṭaket̕a, ar uni hoṛge raebarko dhuṛạukedea. Adọko mẹnet̕a, Henda ya bhala, uni kuṛi dọ eṅgat apat reak̕bon kulil̕edea, adọ mit̕ hoṛ khon bar hoṛ ar dak̕ dak̕rame metat̕bona. Bhala noa dọ cet̕ katha kana? Adọ ọkọe hõ bako hudis ńam daṛeat̕a.

Adọ ako oṛak̕re sẹnkate akoren ạimại ṭhen ona kathage lahareko lại gọt̕ket̕a, arko mẹnket̕a, Ma sẹ bhala, lạialepe noa dọ cet̕ katha kana. Bạhu ńẹlle sẹnlena, unre noa katha dọ uni bạhu kuṛiye rọṛlet̕a. Adọ bale bujhạulet̕te cet̕ hõ bale rọṛ ruạṛadea.

Adọ uni khạmid ạimạiye mẹnket̕a, Cekate bape bujhạulet̕a? Noa ma ạḍi bhale katha cọe metat̕pe; apat dọ sạuṛi irok̕e sẹn akana, ar eṅgat dọ dạl rit̕. Noa katha cọe lạiat̕pe; cekate bape bujhạulet̕a?

Adọ kathae, onko hẹrẹl dọ onkako rọṛ ocoyen khan, aṛae oṛoeko cahap̕ baṛaket̕a. Khange adọ ẹnẹko landa baṛaket̕a, adọ bạhuko ńẹlkede reak̕ko lại baṛawat̕koa.

Adọ uni raebar hoṛge ọntẹ nọtẹ katha dọe idi ạguyet̕a. Adọ ona horre oka ṭhen cọṅ bir ńõk̕gea. Adọ mit̕ din dọ raebar hõ raebar katha idi lạgit̕ ar ako hõ jọmak̕ bạnuk̕takote uni khạmid hoṛ thoṛa thuṛi joṇḍra ẹmae lạgit̕e bhorsawade tahẽkante, uni raebar hoṛ dọ mit̕ṭaṅ gõṛẽye idi torayet̕ tahẽkana. Adọ kathae, ona bir ṭhenge mit̕ṭaṅ tạrup̕tikinkin ńapam gọt̕ena. Adọ uni hoṛe

3 The first thing to do with cotton is to clean it of the seeds; this is done by letting it pass between the two rollers (wooden) of an implement called cạrkhi (made on the same principle as a clothes-wringer); the cotton passes through, the seeds are pressed out.

to gossip suddenly said: "Dear me, I am standing here; by this time I might have cleaned[3] and carded[4] one seer cotton." Saying this as she left the girl stood up and went to her own house.

These people then talked together among themselves: "You heard that; she must be a good worker; we shall take her; she will apparently do a lot in one moment." Having said this, they got up and went away, whereupon they decided to get the girl who had been there gossiping for a wife, and they engaged the man living there as a marriage broker. They said: "Look here, you fellow, we asked that girl about her parents, and she told us about making one of two and about meeting rain. I wonder, what this means." But none of them was able to think what it might be.

When they reached home, before telling anything else they told this, saying: "Do please tell us what this may mean. We went to look at a bride; then this girl spoke these words; and as we did not understand it, we did not answer her anything."

The lady of the house then said: "How did you not understand this? Of course it was very good what she said to you; her father had gone to cut thatching-grass and her mother to grind split peas. This was what she told you; how is it that you did not understand this?"

Then, people tell, being spoken to in this way the men stood there with wide-open mouths. Afterwards they burst out laughing, and told about how they had been looking for a bride.

Now the marriage broker was going and coming and bringing words from the one side to the other. Somewhere along the road there was a little jungle. One day the marriage broker was going there with some communication in connexion with the marriage, and as they had no food in their house, and the principal on the other side had given him hopes of letting him get some Indian corn, the marriage broker was taking along a sack. Then, people

---

[4] The 'carding' is done with a bow, especially made for this purpose.

mẹn gọtketa, Iạ tạruṕ, iń dọ alom jọmeńa, iń dọ ạḍiń bhageyeta; mit́ hoṛ khon iń bar hoṛkako kana.

Adọ ona katha añjọmkate uni tạruṕ hõe hahaṛayena, are mẹnketa, Eṇḍẹkhan iń hõm bar hoṛ daṛekińa? Judim bar hoṛiń khan dọ ohọń jọmmea; ar bańkhan dọlań jọmmegea.

Adọ uni hoṛe mẹnketa, Disom disomren hoṛ raebarkateń bar hoṛ akatkoa, am bań bar hoṛ daṛeama? Albọt iń bar hoṛkama.

Adọ uni tạruṕ arhõe mẹnketa, Judim bar hoṛliń khan, adọ ale tạruṕ jạt jọtọń lạikekoa, bańma, teheń khon raebar hoṛ dọ alope jọmkoa.

Adọ uni hoṛe mẹnketa, Ho, nitgeń bar hoṛ gọtmea. Ma thọ am dọ noa gõṛẽre bọlọkme, ar ạikhạ cet́ hõ alom rọṛ baṛaea; ar ạikhạm rọṛketa mẹnkhan, ohọm bar hoṛlena.

Adọ uni tạruṕe mẹnketa, Acha, eṇḍẹkhan cet́ hõ bań rọṛ baṛaea. Adọ onkae kablaokedete ona gõṛẽreye bọlọ ocokedeteye tọl esẹtkedea, adọ gaḍa aṛeteye dipil idikedea. Adọ bar pẹ ṭheṅga khube humạḱkedea, adọ gaḍa daḱreye ạtu gọtkadea.

Adọ bhạí, latar sẹnre, kathae, mit́ṭań tạruṕ ona bora ạtu calaḱ kan gạí lekae ńẹlkette gaḍa ḍhip ṭhene tãṛãḱ akana. Ac̀ dọe mẹneta, Dhora gạigeye ạtu hijuḱ kana. Adọ ac̀ sor ṭhen ạtu hẹc̀en khan dọ ẹkkalteye dọn gọtkette gẹrkate ghuṭu sẹne capat́ oḍok gọtkedea. Adọ uni oḱoar tạruṕ dọ eṅgae tahẽkana.

Adọ ghuṭure ona borae gẹr ọrẹc̀ gọtket khange uni tạruṕ ạṇḍiạ ḍọe oḍok gọtena. Adọ uni eṅgae mẹnketa, Durrẹ, am kanam! Nẹge nãhãḱlań jọmetme tahẽkana. Ceka lekate noarem bọlọyentem ạtuḱ kan tahẽkana?

tell, just there in this forest he met a leopard. The man said to the leopard: "I say, you leopard, don't eat me; I am doing some very meritorious work; I am making two persons from one."

Hearing this the leopard also was very much astonished, and said: "In that case you might perhaps also be able to make me into two? If you will do this to me, I shall surely not eat you; but if not, we two shall eat you."

The man answered: "I have arranged marriages for people in many countries and made pairs, should I not be able to make two of you? Of course I shall make you into two."

Again the leopard said: "If you make me into two, then I shall tell all us leopard people, saying: From to-day don't eat any marriage broker."

"Oh", the man said, "just now I shall make you into two. Come, get into this sack, and have a care, don't say a single word; if you speak, you will not become two."

The leopard then said: "All right, in this case I shall not say anything." Having made the leopard agree to this, he made him get into the sack, and tied him securely up, whereupon he carried him on his head to the river bank; and having given him a couple of hard strokes with a stick, he throw him out into the water and let him float down the river.

Now, my friends, somewhere further down the river, people tell, a leopard saw this sack coming floating, and thought it was a cow and was lying await there on the river bank. The leopard thought: "Surely, it is a cow that is coming floating." And when it came near to her, she at once jumped, bit into the sack, and threw it out and up to the bank. But the leopard who pulled the other out of the water was a female.

On the bank she bit and tore the sack, and the male leopard came out. Then the she-leopard said: "Strange, it is you! I was just on the point of commencing to eat you. How did you get into this and come floating?"

Adǫ unre uni ạṇḍiạ tạruṗ dǫ uni raebar hoṛ reaḱ kathae galmaraoadea, baṅma, nonka onka mẹnkate noa boraręṅ bǫlǫ akana. Adǫ sạri ona katha nǫ̃ḱǫ̃e ṭhik gǫṫentaea. Adǫ ẹnte nǫ̃ḱǫ̃elaṅ ńapamena.

Adǫ uni eṅga tạruṗ hǫ̃ ona kathae pạtiạuaṫa. Adǫe rạjiyentekin jǫṛena, adǫ ẹnẹkin haṛam buḍhiyena. Adǫ unkin tạruṗ dǫ ona katha sanam tạruṗkin lạiaṫkoa, ar jǫtǫko lạpại idiyena. Adǫ ona iạte, kathae, nit dhạbić ona katha naṅ leka jug leka tahẽ akangea, baṅ ḍigạu akana nit hạbić; raebar hoṛ dǫ bako jǫm oco akana ar baṅ aṅjǫm akana.

Adǫ uni hoṛ dǫe mẹnkeṫa, Cele nui tạruṗ dǫṅ gǫćkedea. Adǫ ona bujhạukate ạḍi khulạsate uni hoṛ dǫe raebarkeṫteye bạhu jãwãe ocokeṫkoa. Adǫ uni kuṛi dǫ tulạm kaskǫm kạmi dǫ baḍaege bae baḍaea. Jǫtǫaḱ kạmi dǫ besgeye kạmia, mẹnkhan ona kạmi mǫtǫre dǫe kǫmgea.

Adǫ jǫtǫaḱ kạmi cabayen khan, adǫ Mag Phạgun din tioḱena. Adǫ khạmid hǫṛe mẹnkeṫa, Ma nẹtar dǫ tulạm sutạm kạmitabonpe, kicrijoḱabon. Sanam hoṛ eṅgateṅ bạhuaṫpea, adǫ onkoko sutạma, adǫṅ kicrić baṛakapea, ar ǫkǫe bape sutạm khan, ẹnḍẹkhan dǫ baṅ kicrićpea.

Adǫ onka galmaraokate kaskǫme tulạ hạṭiṅ baṛawaṫkoa. Adǫ sanam hoṛko riṫ tulạm baṛakeṫteko piteṫ baṛakeṫa. Adǫ uniye aodaleṫ bạhu kuṛi dǫ taḱkoege bae baḍaea; hoṛ ńẹlte ạḍiye takoe gelaḱ kana, baṅgeye jut ocoyeṫa, adǫ ạḍiko landawae kana. Adǫe

5 Naṅ leka jug leka is an expression very rarely used and is intended to convey the idea of 'ever and always', the time from the remotest antiquity to any future day.

6 Mag Phạgun are the two months corresponding to January-February and February-March. Mag is the month when servants leave and new ones are engaged; certain Santal festivals fall in these months. The festivals here referred to must, however, be really non-Santal, because later on the expression ńẹńẹl, seeing, is used, and this word is used about Santals going to 'look at', i. e. participate in Hindu festivals.

The male leopard then spoke to her about the marriage broker, saying: "With this in mind I entered this sack; and as we see, what he said has really come true; here, as you see, we two have met."

The she-leopard then also believed the story, and as she was willing, they became a pair, and in this way they became husband and wife. Thereupon these two leopards told all leopards, and all of them passed the word to each other, and for this reason, people tell, this has until now remained settled through all ages[5]; until now it has never failed; marriage brokers have not been eaten; it has not even been heard of either.

But the man said: "Likely I have killed this leopard, throwing him in." Thinking this the man was very happy, performed his marriage-broker work, and made people into husband and wife. Now the girl we heard of knew absolutely nothing of working in cotton. All other work she was doing well; but in this she was deficient.

When all work had been finished, the Mag Phagun time[6] came round. The master of the house then said: "Now please at present work the cotton and spin thread, we shall get clothes. I have, dash it, procured wives for all of you[7]; so let them spin thread, then I shall clothe you, and if any one of you will not spin thread, I shall not clothe them either."

Having spoken in this way, he divided the cotton among them by weight, whereupon they all cleaned out the seed and commenced to tease the cotton. Now the girl who had spoken so confidently did not know how to spin; keeping her eyes on the others she attempted to spin, but was unable to do it properly, and the others

[7] At this time new clothes are or may be provided. Formerly the Santals would weave themselves; the women spun the thread, the men wove the cloth Now it is very rare to see a Santal weaving; mill cloth is cheaper, they think, and in any case much nicer to look at.

metako kana, Noa carkha bhala bae ńel oromedińa; eṅgań reak̕ carkha do̠ khube ńel orom akadińa.

Ado̠ko metaea, Ba ho̠m baḍaea ho̠; carkha do̠ cet̕ ṭhen ba̠ṛića? Eṅgamak̕ carkha do̠ me̠t̕anteye ńel orommea? Noa do̠ e̠ke̠n e̠ṛe̠ katha kana.

Ado̠e me̠na, Bańa ho̠, ona carkhare khan, ne̠te̠ suta̠mkate lahare iṅgeko kicrićkińa hute̠ć.

Ado̠ko metadea, E̠ṇḍe̠khan ona baṛe̠ a̠guime se̠; ina̠ do̠ hare pharem suta̠m ho̠dteko kicrićmea.

Ado̠ mit̕ din do̠e calaoente ona eṅgat reak̕ carkhageye dipil a̠guket̕a, ado̠ ona caṛkhare hõ̠e takoe gelak̕ kana, ado̠ bae jut ocoyet̕a. Ado̠ pe̠ pon mãhã badreko metae kana, Okor ho̠, tina̠k̕em takoeket̕a?

Ado̠e metako kana, Noa carkha hõ̠ bhala ho̠, nin din no̠ṇḍe̠bo tahẽ̠yentege bhalae ńe̠l eṭak̕kidińa, bae ńe̠l oromedin kana, ńe̠l eṭak̕ uta̠ṛkidińgeae. Ado̠ landa baṛawadeteko thir baṛayena. Ado̠ dosrako do̠ko suta̠mket̕teye kicrić baṛakat̕koa. Ado̠ uni kha̠mid ho̠ṛe me̠nket̕a, Okor ba̠hu, aben do̠ tisben suta̠ma? Kicrićkabena̠lin.

Ado̠e me̠nket̕a, Carkhage, baba, bae ńe̠l oromet̕lińa, onate balin suta̠m daṛeak̕ kana.

Ado̠ uniye me̠nket̕a, E̠ṇḍe̠khan cekate kicrić do̠ hoeok̕a? Ma e̠ṇḍe̠khan o̠ko̠eko bape suta̠mlet̕ ho̠ṛ do̠ nõ̠k̕õ̠e po̠ro̠b dara kantabona, ape do̠ guṛ o̠jo̠k̕kate tula̠mte baṛe̠ laṭkaojońpe. Ado̠ bape suta̠mlet̕tabon khan, iń hõ̠ nit do̠ cet̕ iń me̠na? Ar bape baḍae khan hute̠ć, pa̠hilre cedak̕ bape la̠ilet̕a? Jãhãe ṭhen babo suta̠m were laughing at her. Then she said to them: "This spinning-wheel probably does not recognize me; my mother's spinning-wheel knows me very well."

But they said to her: "No, girl, you don't know; what is wrong with the spinning-wheel? Has your mother's spinning-wheel eyes to see and know you with? This is only a fib of yours."

She would reply: "Not so, you; if it had been that spinning-wheel, I should have spun thread, and they would have clothed me before you others."

"In that case," the others said to her, "do bring that wheel; with that you will be able to spin thread quickly, then they will give you clothes."

Then one day she went, and brought her mother's spinning wheel, carrying it on her head; she tried to spin with this also, but was unable to do it properly. After three four days the others said to her: "How is it, girl? we see nothing; how much have you spun?"

"This spinning-wheel also," she replied, "must take me to be somebody else, since we have lived here for so long a time; it does not recognize me; it has taken me to be an entirely strange person." Then they laughed at her, and did not say anything more about it. Now the others spun thread, and they gave them clothes. The master of the house then said: "Well, daughter-in-law, I do not see anything; when will you spin thread? I want to give you clothes."

She replied: "The spinning-wheel, father, does not recognize me; therefore I am unable to spin thread."

"In that case," the man said, "how will there be clothes? So you who have not spun thread — you know, a festival of ours is coming — you rub yourselvf in with molasses and take cotton and stick on to you. As you have not spun thread, what shall I say now? If you don't know how to do it, why did you not tell so at once? Should we not have let somebody spin? Dash

ocoea? Ma eṅgate tulạmte baṛe laṭkaojoṅpe. Adọ enka rọṛ baṛakatege uni hõe thirena.

Adọ ceṭ pọrọb cọṅ seṭeren; adọ ṅeṅel calak lạgiṭ nawa nawanak kicrić ṅam oḍokkateko bandek kana. Ar uni bạhu kuṛi ma kicrić bạnuk khan, cete ṅam oḍoka? Adọ kathae, ṭukuće guṛ tahẽkana; tinre cọṅ onae ṅam oḍokkette goṭa hoṛmọreye ojoḱante, oṇeye riṭ tulạmleṭ, ona tulạm dọ goṭa hoṛmọreye laṭkaoana, adọ oṇko sãote nui hõ hạdui hạduiye helaoena. Adọ bogeteko landawae kana.

Adọ uni jãwãeteṭ dọ uniye ṅelkede khan dọ ạḍi bạṛiće edreyena, are meneṭa, Ạyup se ạyuboka, nui ạimại dọ khub lekaṅ dalea. Eṅgate haṛạm dọ cigạri lekae menleṭ khan, nui dọ onageye sạri-keṭa. Nui ạimại dọe dundhigea, bud dọ miṭ hõ bạnuktaea, ar lajao hõ bạnuktaea. Nui dọ baṅ dọhọyea. Adọ kathae, ạyupen khan, oṛakteko hećena, adọ unre bogeteye dalkedea. Are bạgi utạrkedea.

Adọ inạ dosar serma khange, kathae, uni raebar hoṛ dọ arhõ miṭ hoṛ reake raebar kan tahẽkana, adọ ona bir sentegeye hijuk senok kan tahẽkana. Adọ uni pạhile bạhuade uni tạrupṭekinge arhõkin ṅapamena. Khange uni hoṛ dọ bọtọrteye dạṛeṭ tahẽkana. Adọ uni tạrupe menketa, E ho, alom dạṛa, ọhọṅ jọmmea. Hape, teṅgolenme; am tuluć miṭṭaṅ galmarao menaktiṅa.

Adọ khange uni hoṛe teṅgoyena, adoe menketa, Ceṭ katha kana? Ma rọṛme.

Adọ uni tạrupe menketa, Iṅ dọm ṅel oromediṅa se baṅ?

Adoe menketa, Baṅ ṅel orometmea.

Adọ tạrupe menketa, Acha bam ṅel oromediṅ khan iṅ cekaea? Adọ amge ma kọeyeṅme, ceṭ boksisem hataoa? Ọne miṭ dhao borare bhoraokatem bar hoṛ akadiṅa, adọ ona katha reak mọnẹre disạ menaktiṅa. Onate am dọṅ metam kana, ma ceṭ boksisem it, take cotton and stick on to you." Having spoken in this way, he did not say any more either.

Now some festival or other came round; in order to go and amuse themselves the others were taking out their new clothes, and were putting them on; but as there was no cloth for her, what could this daughter-in-law take out? Now, people tell, there were molasses in a pot; some time or other she took this out and rubbed herself in all over her body with this, whereupon she took the cotton she had cleaned of seed, and stuck it on all over her body, whereupon she also went off together with the others, shaggy and bushy. They laughed a good deal at her.

When her husband saw her, he became very angry and said: "Let it only become evening; then I shall give this woman a sound thrashing. Dash it, the old man said this to her as a sarcasm, and she has taken it as if he meant it. This woman is a blockhead; she has no sense, not one bit, nor has she any shame. I shall not keep her." When it became evening, people tell, they came home, and then he gave her a sound thrashing, whereupon he sent her away for good.

The next year, people tell, this marriage broker was again acting as such for somebody, and he was going and coming through this particular forest. Then one day he again met the leopard for whom he had formerly procured a wife. The man was running away for fear, but the leopard called out: "You there, don't run away; I shall not eat you. Wait a bit, stop; I have something to talk about with you."

Then the man stopped and said: "What is it? Please speak."

"Do you recognize me or not?" the leopard asked.

The man replied: "I don't recognize you."

"All right," the leopard said, "if you don't recognize me, what shall I do? Now you please ask me, what gift will you take? Once you put me in a sack and made me into two; I have had this matter in my mind, remembering it. Therefore I am saying

hataoa, onageń emama. Gai jelem joma, se kaḍa jel, se bir janwar jelem joma? Ma ona rorme, adoń goć aguama.

Ado uni hore menkeťa, Acha, bir janwarko motore bare mitťań khub marań murum goć aguańme.

Ado tarupe menkeťa, Acha, gapa endekhan hane hana dare buta then tikin jokhen hijukme, ado idijońme. Ado amem khusi ocokidińa, onate iń hõ am iń khusi ocomea. Ado enka menkategekin apan apinena.

Ado dosar hilok uni hor do horante tikin jokhen ona dare buta thene calaoente sari mitťań murume ńamkedea. Adoko tolkedeteko gok agukedea. Ado unre uni hor noako katha doe galmaraoleťa, ado nõkõe, sarite coń nasete coń, kathateť do nit habić menaka.

Ado cabayena katha do, in marańgea.

92. Boehako baplaleťkin reań.

Sedae jokhen, kathae, eae boeha korako tahẽkana ar huḍiń utarić mitťań miserat; ar miserat do ini miť hor eskargetakoae, ar uni do bako jãwãe akadea, ḍańguageye tahẽkana. Ar kora hõ naprakko doko bahuaťkoa, ar uni huḍińić do ḍańguage menaea. Ado uni hõ bahuae lagiť bahuko ńam barayeťkoa, ado okare hõ jokhage bań hoeok kan — ńamkate hõ bhińgrauk kangea.

Ado bar pe sermako ńam barakeťkoa — onkage okare hõ jokhage bań hoeok. Ado uni korae menkeťa, Ia, ayo ar baba ar sanam boehako, ińiń metape kana, bahu bako ńamok kan khan, ikakakpe. Iń do gapanok mitťań baha bir khon ńam agukate noa aboak gãrsãodere mucať senreń rohoekaka. Ado ona baha do okoe hõ alope bahaea, ar judipe bahakeťa menkhan, endekhan inige ińren

---

8 The murum jel (from which one of the Santal septs, the Murmu, have got their name) is the Nilgae, Portax pictu, now practically exterminated where the Santals live; a couple of generations ago it was not uncommon.

92 1 It is a very common thing with Santal girls to take a flower and put it in their hair or behind the ear, as an ornament. Especially big red flowers are used in this way.

to you: "What gift you will have, this I shall give you. Will you eat cow's meat, or buffalo meat, or the meat of a forest animal? Please tell, and I shall kill and bring you."

"All right," the man said, "kill and bring me from among the forest animals a large Nilgae[8]."

The leopard said: "Very well, then come to-morrow about noon time to the foot of the tree over there, and take it away from there. You made me pleased, therefore I am also going to make you pleased." After having had this talk, they separated.

The next day the man took some people with him and went by noon-time to the foot of this particular tree, and really found a Nilgae there. They bound this up and carried it home. On this occasion the man told these happenings, and as you hear, whether it is true or not, the story is there even up to now.

Now the story is ended, it is this much.

92. WHEN THEY TRIED TO MARRY A BROTHER AND SISTER.

In olden times, people tell, there once lived seven brothers and a sister, who was the youngest of them all, and this sister was the only one they had, and they had not married her away; she was a spinster. The elder ones of the brothers they had all procured wives for, but the youngest one was unmarried. They were seeking a wife for him also; it never anywhere came to anything; even when they had found a girl, it fell through.

They were seeking a wife for him for two three years; it was the same, it never came to anything anywhere. Then the young man said: "I say, mother and father and all my brothers, I tell you this, since no wife is to be found, give it up. To-morrow I shall fetch a flowering plant from the forest, and shall plant it near the one end of this waterpot-stand of ours. And don't any of you adorn herself with the flower[1]; if you do so, she

bạhui hoeok̕a. Adọ onka mẹnkateń rọhọe lạgit̕, ar onate jọtọ họṛ iń lại saḍeape kana, jẹmọn abo oṛak̕ren ọkọe hõ alope bahae ma. Adọ ayo, am iń metam kana, ma noa baha dọ tunkhime, jẹmọn abo oṛak̕ren ọkọe hõ alope bahae ma. Ar atoren hõ judi jãhãeko sid khan, pạhilre noa katha lạiakome, baha dọ alope bahaea mẹnte, arpe bahae khan, ạikhạ uni phalna koṛaren bạhupe hoeok̕a. Nonka pusṭạu lạiakome, noa katha dọ alom okọea; adọ ona baha khub tunkhime.

Adọko mẹnket̕a, Acha bogege, ẹnḍẹkhan ma rọhọeme. Adọ nẹk̕ẹ thọ oṛak̕ren sanam họṛle ak̕ńjọm kange. Ar ki jạnić bańle bujhạuket̕te?

Adọ uni koṛae mẹńket̕a, Hại, inạge thọ, bańkhanpe andhakok̕a. Ar onka lạiako tulućko sid khan, sit̕ ocoakome.

Adọ kathae, dosar hilok̕ khange uni koṛa dọ cet̕ lekan baha cọe ạguket̕te ona gãṛsãoderegeye rọhọeket̕a, ar ọnẹ onkae mẹnlet̕ katha dọ goṭa ato pasnaoena arko baḍaeket̕a. Are rọhọeket̕ khan dọ, ńẹl hõ sanam họṛko ńẹl idiket̕a. Adọ sạri uni koṛa dọ dinge ona baha dọe ńẹlak̕ ńẹlak̕a. Adọ tin din badre cọń ona baha dọ bahayena, adọ ạḍi jut ńẹlok̕ kana, ar sọ hõ ạḍi jut hạsge sọ kana. Adọ kuṛiko hõ hạs ńẹlok̕te dinge ńẹńẹlko hijuk̕a arko ńẹl idia.

Adọ kathae, mit̕ din dọ uni akoren miserat kuṛige dak̕e tatań kan tahẹ̃kana, adọ jut ńẹlteye sap̕ gọt̕ket̕a, bae jivilet̕a. Adọ ẹ̃gattẹt̕e ńẹl tiok̕ gọt̕kedea; adọe metae kana, Henda mại, ona baha dọ cedak̕em jọṭẹt̕et̕a? Cet̕ kichu bam baḍaea?

Adọ uni kuṛiye mẹnket̕a, Iạ ayo, hape sẹń baha gelaea, bhala cet̕ lekań ńẹlok̕a.

who does shall be my wife. It is for this purpose that I am going to plant it; therefore I am saying this to you all, that none of you here in our house may take the flower to adorn herself with. And, mother, I am saying this to you: watch this flower plant, that none here in our house may adorn herself with it. And if any girl from the village will pluck it, tell them in beforehand: you are not to take this flower to adorn yourselves with; and if you do so, know that you will become the wife of so and so. Tell them distinctly; don't keep this back; and keep a careful watch on this plant."

"All right," they said, "this is good; so you plant it. Now naturally all we here in our house hear what you say. Likely we have all understood it, is it not so?"

The young man then said: "Yes, that's just what it is; else you might do something inadvertently. If they being told this pluck it, let them."

The next day, people tell, the young man brought the flower plant, who knows what kind it was, and planted it near the waterpot-stand, and what he had spoken in this connexion was spread out over the whole village, and people got to know it. When he had planted it, all people had a look at it. And, truth to tell, the young man was every day looking and looking at it. After some time the plant blossomed, and it was very beautiful to look at, and the odour of it, it was very delightful. And as it was delightful to look at, the girls used to come every day and have a look at it.

Then one day, people tell, it so happened that this sister of theirs was pouring out some water, and as the flower looked beautiful to her, she suddenly caught hold of it; she could not forbear; her mother saw her doing it, and said to her: "Look here, my girl, why are you touching this flower? Don't you know anything?"

The girl replied: "I say, mother, wait a little, I shall have a try with the flower, I wonder, how I shall look."

Adọ eṅgate mẹnkeť́a, Baṅa, mạ̃i, am dọ alogem bahaea.

Adọ uni kuṛiye mẹnkeťa, Baṅa, ayo, dare sudhạ toťkateń bahaea, arhõ enkageń rọhọekaḱa; sid khange thọe ńẹl oroma, ar dare sudhạ khan dọ, cekateye ńẹl oroma?

Adọ eṅgate mẹnkeťa, Acha, am dọń manayeťmete bam'añjọmeť khan dọń cekamea?

Adọ sạri bae añjọmleťa, dare sudhạ̃i toťkeťte bọhọḱreye bahakeťa; arhõ dọhọkeťte pạhil lekae rọhọekaťa.

Adọ tin ọktẹre cọń sạri dadatteť, sẹ uni rọhọeleť koṛageye hẹćena, adọ nin dara lekage ẹn hiloḱ hõ ona baha, ṭhengeye calaoena. Ar uni kuṛi dọ un jọkhẹn goṛare bọlọkateye ńẹńẹl kana, ar uni eṅgatteť dọ duạr ṭhen piṇḍạreye duṛuṕ akana. Adọ un jọkhẹnge uni koṛa dọe mẹneťa, Henda ayo, noa baha dọ ọkọe bahaleťa?

Adọ uniye mẹnkeťa, Okor, bạbu, ọkọe hõ bako baha akaťa.

Adọ uni koṛae mẹnkeťa, Baṅa, ayo, ọkọe cọko bahaleťge, onkage sọyeń kana. Ma lạime ọkọeko bahaleťa; thoṛa bas dọń bas ṭhikeťgea.

Adọ apattẹťe mẹnkeťa, Ma lạiaeme, ọkọeko bahaleťa mẹnte.

Adọ eṅgattẹťe mẹneťa, Ọkọ baḍae ẹṇḍẹkhan, iń dọ bań ńẹl tioḱleťkoa.

Adọ uni koṛae mẹnkeťa, Nõḱõe ńẹlpe, bape pạtiạuḱ kan khan, noarege uṕ hõ laṭkao akana, ar abo họpọn mạ̃iye bahaleť lekage sọyeń kana.

Adọ apate mẹnkeťa, Henda na, sạri amem bahaleťa?

Khange uni kuṛi dọ ceť hõ bae rọṛleťa. Adọ eṅgattẹťe mẹnkeťa, Nui kuṛi dọ ceť bam metae? Manayede kan tulućgeye baha

"No, my girl," her mother said, "don't adorn yourself with this flower."

"No, mother," the girl replied, "I shall pull out the whole plant and take the flower on; then I shall plant it again, just as it is; if I pluck it, he will see what has been done; but if I take the whole plant, how will he be able to see that anything has been done?"

"Very well," her mother said, "if you don't listen when I am warning you, what shall I do to you?"

Truth to tell, she did not listen to her mother; she pulled the whole plant out, and put it on her head; then putting it down again she planted it as it had been before.

Then some time that day, truth to tell, her elder brother, that is to say, the young man who had planted it came; and as was his habit, he also that day went to the plant. The girl had gone into the cow-stall and was at the time looking out from there, and the mother was sitting on the veranda at the door. At that time the young man said: "I say, mother, who adorned herself with this flover?"

"Why, my boy," his mother replied, "no one has adorned herself with the flower."

"No, mother," the young man said: "somebody did adorn herself with the flower; it smells so to me. Please tell who did so; I also seem to feel a little whose smell it is."

Then his father said: "Do tell him who adorned themselves with the flower."

But the mother said: "Who knows then? I did not see who it was."

The young man then said: "Look here at this then, if you do not believe; some hair has also stuck to this, and it smells to me as if our little girl had adorned herself with this flower."

The father then asked: "Answer, girl, did you really adorn yourself with the flower?"

The girl did not say a single word; then her mother said: "What will you say to a girl like her? Although she was warned,

goťketa, are męneťa, Miť ghąrige, gǫń bahaea, arhǫ̃ń dǫhǫkaǩa. Adǫ sąrigeye bahaleťa.

Khange adǫ uni kuṛi dǫe raǩ gǫťketa. Adǫ apattęťe męnkeťa, Baṅa, noa dǫ nukinge baplakin reaǩ likhą tahę̃kana, onatege bąhu hǫ̃ babo ńam daṛeaťkoa. Ar ńęlpe, nui kuṛi hǫ̃ ląiade ar manaye tulućge noa bahae bahaketa. Adǫ abo hǫ̃ nitoǩ dǫ cetbo męna? Ma nukingebon baplakakina.

Adǫ khange uni kuṛi dǫe raǩketa. Adǫ ęnte cekaeako? Adǫ unkin baplakin reaǩ sǫrǫmjamko juṛąu baṛayeta, ar hoṛokoko teke caole baṛayeta.

Khange uni kuṛi dǫ mǫnę mǫnęteye hudisketa, baṅma, Noko dǫ nãhãǩ dhorage ąliń dǫko baplaliṅgea. Ǫkǫe tora męn, nǫṇḍę khon dǫń dąṛjoṅa, ar baṅkhan dǫ ǫhǫń baṅcaolena. Onkae ȟudis baṛakeťte uni kuṛi dǫ ǫṇḍę khone dąṛketa. Ar miťṭaṅ ąsul mirui tahę̃kantaea, adǫ uni miru hǫ̃e idi torakedea.

Adǫ calaǩ calaǩte tin sąṅgiń cǫe calaoen. Adǫ miťṭaṅ ḍobhaǩ ṭhene umoǩ kan tahę̃kana, adǫ ti jaṅgakoe iskirok kana. Adǫ ona hǫṛmǫ khonge, kathae, mąilą dǫ pĩũri oḍokoǩ kana. Adǫ ḍher ńǫ̃ǩe iskir oḍokkeť khan, miťreye pĩũri miťkeťte ǫtreye dǫhǫkaťa. Adǫ kathae, ona mąilą dǫ tale dare janamena. Adǫe um baṛaǩtege ona tale dare dǫ hara gǫťena.

Adǫe męnkeťa, Hǫ, noa tale daręregeń dęjoǩa; noa dǫ ąḍi algate dare gǫdoǩ kana. Adǫ onka męnkate uni mirui teveṅkedete ona tale darerekin dęćena. Adǫ uni kuṛiye męnkeťa, Ią tale dare, khub cǫṭ haraǩme, jęmǫn ǫkǫe hǫ̃ aloko ńam daṛeaṅ ma. Adǫ sąri onkae męnkeť khan dǫ, kathae, hara harayena sę, ąḍi usul harayena. Ar uni miru dǫe aṛaǩkadete uni dǫ jǫmaǩe ąguitakina. Adǫ onako jǫm baṛaete onkatekin tahę̃yena.

2 The word is the name for the rolls of cotton or wool from which thread is spun.

3 The Palmyra palm, Borassus flabelliformis, L., is the most common palm in the Santal country.

she adorned herself with the flower, saying: 'For one moment only, mother, I shall take the flower on; then I shall put it back again.' In this way she really took the flower on."

The girl then commenced to cry, whereupon her father said: "No, there is nothing else; it was the fate of these two that they should be married; therefore we too were unable to procure a wife for him. And see, although she was told and warned, the girl adorned herself with this flower. Then what can we say now? Well, we shall marry these two."

But the girl again cried. But what should they do? Then they gradually collected what was necessary to celebrate their marriage, and they boiled the paddy and prepared the rice.

The girl considered the matter in her mind, saying: "They will surely marry us presently. Heigh ho, I shall at once run away from here; if I don't, there will be no rescue for me." Having come to this conclusion the girl ran away from there. She had a kept parakeet, and this she also took along with her.

Walking along she went who knows how far; as she was bathing somewhere at a water-pool, she was rubbing her arms and legs; and from her body, people tell, the dirt came out in rolls.[2] And when she had rubbed out quite a quantity, she made it all into one roll, and put it on the ground. Then, people tell, this dirt became a Palmyra palm;[3] and as she was bathing, the palm suddenly grew up.

Then she said: "Oh, I shall mount this palm; this easily and quickly grows big." Saying this she took the parakeet in her hand, and both of them mounted the palm. The girl said: "I say, palmyra palm, grow very high, so that no one may be able to find me." And, truth to tell, when she had spoken thus, the palm, people tell, commenced to grow and grow; it grew to a very great height. Then she let the parakeet loose, and the bird brought food for them, and getting food they both lived in this way.

Ar oṛakren hoṛ do uni bạnugite ãoda ạudiko ńam baṛayede kana, ar se baplakin reak̕ hõko sor akat̕a. Ado bạrsiń pe mãhã dhạbićko ńam baṛakedea, ado bako ńamlede khanko thir dorok̕ena.

Ado tin din badre coń mit̕ṭań mahle kuṛi tikin jokhen ona hoṛtege bhajan ạkrińe calak̕ kan tahẽkana. Ado dak̕ tetańkede khan, ona tale dare buṭạrege ona bhajanko doe dohokat̕a, ado ona ḍobhak̕ reak̕ dak̕e ńũket̕te arhõ ona umulregeye dụṛup̕ena. Ado uni kuṛiye roṛket̕a, Iạ mahle kuṛi, den mit̕ṭań suptić emańme, iń do mit̕ṭań sakom iń emama.

Ado uni mahle kuṛiye menket̕a, Den ente, ńũr got̕ańme. Ado sạri sakome ńũr got̕adea, ado mit̕ṭań suptiće capat̕ rakap̕ got̕adea. Ado ona suptić hõ ẽkkalte uni kuṛi ṭhenge ạpir calao got̕ena, adoe sap̕ got̕ket̕a. Adoe metae kana, Iạ mahle kuṛi, noa sakom do horok̕ dom horok̕ket̕a, menkhan okoe ṭhen hõ alom ńel ocoea; ato sen bhajan ạkrińem calak̕ khan, sakom do oyo poṭomkam, ar bańkhan nãhãk̕ko reć botećkema.

Adoe menket̕a, Acha, atoń botolen khan, noa doń oyo poṭomkak̕a. Ado enka men baṛakate khange uni mahle kuṛi doe beret̕ena. Ado arhõe metae kana, Noṇḍe iń menań reak̕ katha okoe ṭhen hõ alom lạia, arem lạiket̕a menkhan, ạikhạm goć utạrok̕a.

Ado uniye menket̕a, Acha, okoe ṭhen hõ bań lại baṛaea. Ado enka menkate uni hõe calaoena.

Ado uni kuṛiren eńgat apat doko menet̕a, Nui kuṛi do dhik jaṅlateye unum goćen coń cet̕ coń; toberege babon ńame kana, ar bańkhan doe ńamkok̕gea huteć. Ado ńam mokońkate onko doko as chuṭạuenteko thir baṛayena.

---

4 The Mahles are a tribe closely related to the Santals; they are workers in bamboo. The Santals look down upon these people with contempt; they charge the Mahles with being unreliable and untrustworthy; they are generally sharp; I am afraid the Santal estimation of them is near the truth. The story shows how far Santals will take a Mahle's word for good.

5 A **suptić** is a winnowing-fan shaped like the ordinary **haṭak̕**, but much smaller. It is mostly used as a play-thing by small girls.

Now as the girl was not seen, the people of her home were searching for her anxiously, and, you see, the preparations for marrying the two were also nearly ready. They searched for her for two three days, but as they could not find her, they stopped searching, what could they do else?

After some time, who knows how long afterwards, a Mahle[4] girl was at noon time passing along the road to sell basket-ware. As she felt thirsty, she put the baskets down at the foot of this Palmyra palm, and, having drunk some water from the pool, she sat down in the shade there. Then the girl spoke: "I say, you Mahle girl, give me a small winnowing-fan;[5] I shall give you a wristlet."

"Give it me then," the Mahle girl answered, "throw it down to me." Then, truth to tell, she threw it down to her, whereupon the other girl threw a small winnowing-fan up to her; and this winnowing-fan also at once flew straight up to the girl, and she caught hold of it, whereupon she said: "I say, you Mahle girl, you have taken this wristlet on; but don't let anybody see it; when you go to the village to sell baskets, cover the wristlet up; else they might take it from you by force."

"All right," she replied, "when I go into any village, I shall cover this up." Having spoken in this way the Mahle girl stood up, whereupon the other girl again spoke to her: "Don't say a word to anybody about my being here; if you tell, beware, you will utterly die."

"All right," she replied, "I shall not tell anyone." Saying this she went away.

Now the parents of the girl were saying: "This girl of ours must in distress[6] have drowned herself or something; this is the reason why we do not find her; otherwise she would be found." Having searched everywhere they lost hope and ceased searching.

---

[6] The word is used about being tired of life.

Adọ tin dinre cọṅ, kathae, uni kuṛi dọ bhajan ạkriṅ ạkriṅte mit́ din dọ onko oṛak̓tegeye calaoena. Adọ ona ti dọe oyo pọṭọm akat́gea. Adọko ńẹlket́taea; khanko metae kana, Henda mahle kuṛi, ona tire dọm ceka akana?

Adọe mẹnket́a, Noa ti dọń ghao akana.

Adọko mẹnket́a, Masẹle ńẹltama, bhala tin maraṅem ghao akana. Adọ bae uduk̓ako kana. Adọ ạḍiko jidket́ khan dọe mẹnkẹt́a, Baṅa, noa ghao nāhāk̓pe ńẹlletiṅ khan, nitge nāhāk̓ iṅ gọć gọdok̓a.

Adọ khangeko landawadea arko mẹnket́a, Behaj reak̓em rọṛket́ dọ! Ghao udugte kọkhọn hoṛko gọć akana? Ona dọ ọhọle pạtiạulena. Okor, masẹle ńẹltama, bhalam gujuk̓a sẹ nāhāk̓.

Adọ sạri onka ạḍi lekako rọṛket́ khan dọe uduk̓at́koa, bogege. Adọko metae kana, Okor tamaṅ ghao? Ạuṛigeye rọṛet́a. Adọ ona sakọmko ńẹl oromket́ khanko metae kana, Henda mahle kuṛi, noa sakọm dọ okarem ńamket́a?

Adọe mẹnket́a, Ńam akat́aṅ, lại dọ ọhọń lạilepea; lạile khan dọ nāhāk̓ nitgeṅ gọć utạrok̓a.

Adọko mẹnket́a, Am dọ ẹkẹn ẹṛẹ rọṛ kantama. Pạhil hõ ghao udug jọkhẹn onkagem mẹnlet́a ar okorem gọćlena? Ar noa sakọm dọle ńẹl oromket́a, ale họpọn mãi reak̓ sakọm kana; onatele kuliyet́mea okarem ńam akat́a mẹnte.

Adọe mẹnket́a, Ọhọń lạilepea. Mẹn akawadiṅae, ọkọe ṭhen hõ alom lạia mẹnte.

Adọko mẹnket́a, Mage lạialeme. Uni ńam ńamte ale dọle bhagao akana, onatele kuliyet́mea.

Adọe mẹnket́a, Baṅ, ọhọgeṅ lạilea.

Adọ khange eṅgatṭẹt́ dọe mẹnket́a, Ma Mahle kuṛi, lạialeme; mit́ haṭak̓ hoṛo nāhāk̓le emama.

---

7 Haṭak̓, the full-sized winnowing-fan, is inter alia used as a kind of rough measure, and, like here, when one gives paddy away in a very liberal way.

After some time, people tell, the Mahle girl, going round selling baskets, one day came to these people's house; she had her hand covered up. When they saw this, they asked her: "I say, you Mahle girl, what has happened to your hand?"

"I have got a wound on this hand," she replied.

"Come, let us have a look at it," they said; "we should like to know, how big a wound you have got." But she did not show it to them; and as they eagerly persisted, she said: "No, if you see this wound of mine, I shall die here now at once."

Then they laughed at her and said: "It is amazing what you have said! Have people ever died by showing a wound? We shall never believe this. Surely not, come let us have a look at your hand and see whether you will die or not."

Then, truth to tell, when they had spoken in this and many other ways, she showed it to them, the hand was all right. Then they said to her: "Where is your wound? She is telling fibs." And when they saw and recognized the wristlet, they asked her: "Look here, you Mahle girl, where did you find this wristlet?"

"I have found it," she replied; "but I shall never tell you; if I told, I should die now at once here."

Then they said: "You have only lies to tell. At first when you should show the wound, you also said the same, and you see you have not died at all. And we have recognized this wristlet, it is the wristlet of our little girl; therefore we are asking you where you have found it."

"I shall never tell you," she replied. "She has said to me that I must not tell anybody."

"Do, tell us," they said. "Searching and searching for her we have had to give in; it is therefore that we are asking you."

"No", she said, "I shall never tell."

Then the mother said: "Please, you Mahle girl, tell us; we shall now here give you a winnowing-fan[7] full of paddy."

Adoe menketa, Acha, den endekhan em pahilanpe. Ado sari mit hatak horoko emadea, adoe menketa, Hane hankate hor sen akana, ado ona horte calakpe; ado ona phalna dare then mittan tale dare menaka. Ado ona dare cotre menaea, ar mittan miru menaetaea.

Adoko menketa, Ho, khati uni kangeae.

Adoko calaoenteko ńele kan do, sariye uni kange. [8]Ar ona dareko ńeleta, banma, adi usul dare akan. Khanko ceka ãrgoyea? Adoko hohoae kana, Dela mãi, ãrgonme, unire do ohole jãwãemea. Onkako phuslau ãrgoyea menteko metae kana. Ado bae ãrgon kana. Ado kathae, adi lekako galmaraoadea, ado enrehõ bae ãrgolen khan, eńgat apatkin rakketa. Adoko serena:

Maila reak tale darem benaoket,
Onareben dec akan, mai na;
De mãi na, nãrgo hijukme.

Ayo baba, cedakben raket?
Iń do nondege jivi calaktiń;
Do, baba, ruarjońben.

Ado unkin dokin ruar calaoena. Ado hilittekoko hecente; ado onko pariko raketa:

E tale tale dare, de mãi do ãrgoyem;
Bhai bahinak bapla hoeoka.

Khange uni do cet hõ bae rorleta, ar ãrgo hõ bae ãrgolena; ar dare hõ adi usul dare akana, cekateko tiogeteko ãrgoyea? Khangeko sithauenteko ruar calaoena. Ado eke ekete jotoko hecenteko nehõr gelawadea, ado bae ãrgolen khanko edreyena. Ado hoe

---

8 It might be noted that the song is in Santali, not, as so frequently in these folktales, in Bengali or Hindi. The dual naturally refers to the girl and the parakeet.

"Very well then," she said, "give me this first then." Then, truth to tell, they gave her a winnowing-fan full of paddy, whereupon she said: "Along over there a road is passing, as you see; go along this road; near such and such a tree there stands a Palmyra palm. She is up there in the top of the tree, and she has a parakeet."

"Yes", they said, "surely it is she."

Then they went and saw her, it was really she herself. They looked at the tree, it had grown to a very great height. How were they going to get her down? They were calling out to her: "Come, girl, come down; we shall not marry you to him." They were speaking to her in this way to coax her to come down. But she was not coming down. They spoke to her, people tell, in many different ways; but as she still did not come down her parents commenced to cry. Here they sing:[8]

> Of dirt you made a Palmyra palm;
> This you have mounted, you two, our girl.
> Do, our girl, come down.
>
> Mother and father, why are you crying?
> As for me, here my soul will pass away;
> Do, father, go home both of you.

So both went back home. Thereupon the wives of her elder brothers came, and in their turn were crying:

> O Palmyra palm, Palmyra palm, please bring the girl down;
> The marriage of the brother and the sister is to take place.

The girl did not say anything, nor would she come down; the tree had also grown to a very great height; how should they be able to reach her and bring her down? Then they got tired of it, and went home. Thereupon all of them came, one after the other alone, and tried to implore her; and as she did not come

dakko ḍakaoketa; ado sari hoe dak hecena; hoeate halae halaeye daketa. Ado uni kuṛi do dakteye lohoten khan, bogete rabañede kana, ar hoe hõ, kathae, ạḍi ãṭe hoeyeta, ona tale dare do hoete likir likirok kana.

Ado khangeye menketa, Durre! nonḍe do ohoń tahẽ daṛelena; okoe torań ãṛgona. Ado kathae, hoete ona tale dare do otre taberok kana, arhõ rakap kana. Ado ona hoete taberlen jokhenge khać, uni kuṛi do miru sapkateye ãṛgoyena.

Ar ona atoren hoṛko metatkoa, Judi uni kuṛiye hećlen khan, oṛak do okoe hõ alope jhijćaea; arpe jhićadea menkhan, aperen hoponeragele bạhukoṭapea. Ar ako oṛakren hõ joṭoko siń potom-ena. Ado uni koṛa okoe bahae rohoelet, uni doko men akawadea, Am do goṛare sengel jolte khub utạr sahan oropkakme, khub tiṅgi aṅgrakakme; ar parkom belkate onḍe baṛe gitićkokme. Ado aćtege nãhãke hijukte am ṭhene gitića, ado bạhuyem.

Ado sari uni koṛa hõe onkaketgea. Ado kathae, rabañkede khan, uni kuṛi do atoteye hećena. Ado oṛak oṛake hohoako kana, ado okoe hõ bako jhićade khan, ako oṛakteye hećena. Ado onḍe hõe hohoketa, de jhićańpe mente. Ado sari bako jhićadea.

Khange goṛate uni koṛa ṭhene calaoena; adoe jorok sanṭhaoena. Adoe menketa, Nui bototregeń daṛleta, arhõ nokõe nui ṭhengeń hećena. Ạkhirge bań ạkhir iń do dhạrtirege bań tahena. Nokõe iń do sanam hoṛgeko edreadińte oṛak hõ bako bolo ocoadiña. Iń do hoṛ tulućge bań ńepela.

9 Hoe dak, lit. wind rain, is the Santal name for the thunderstorms that occur during the hot season; they may be very violent and often cause accidents; they are accompanied by more or less rain, sometimes hail, and cool the atmosphere to a considerable extent.

down, they became angry, whereupon they called on a rain-storm[9] to come; and the rain-storm really came; it stormed and the rain was beating. When the girl became wet through with the rain, she felt it intensely cold; it was also, people tell, storming heavily, and the palm was swaying to and fro in the wind.

Then she said: "What a pity! I shall never be able to remain here; let me get down at once." Then, people tell, the palm was bending right down to the ground with the wind; again it was righting itself up. And when the palm was just bending itself with the wind, the girl took her parakeet and came down.

The others had spoken to the village people: "If the girl should come, don't any of you open and let her into your house; if you do so, we shall make one of your daughters a wife for us. In their own home they also all shut themselves in; but to him who had planted the flower plant they had said: "You light a fire in the cow-shed and pile up a mass of firewood and put fuel on and get a lot of live coals; place a bedstead there and lie down. Then she will presently come of her own accord and lie down there beside you, and she will become your wife."

Truth to tell, the young man did as they told him. Now, people tell, when the girl felt cold, she came to the village. She called out to people at every house; but as no one opened the door for her to come in, she went to their own house. There she also called out: "Do open for me." But, truth to tell, they did not let her in.

Then she went to the cowshed where the young man was, and warming herself she recovered somewhat, and she said: "For fear of this one I ran away; then again I have come to him, as is to be seen. Happen what may, I shall not stay in this world. As is seen, all people have become angry with me, wherefore they have not let me come into their houses either. I shall not see anybody."

Adoe jorok saṇṭhaoen khan, uni koṛa ṭhen parkomreye duṛuṕena. Ado naharni tahẽkantaea, ado onae raṛaketa, ado ona tuluće gitićena. Ado naharnite aćak nạṛṛiye reta topakketṭaea; adoe goćena.

Adoe phandayet khan, uni koṛa hõe beretenteye ńelẹ kan do, bogete mãyãm do ḍiń ḍạbur ạtuk kan. Ado emenketa, Ho, nui do noa naharnitegeye get goćena, toberege ona doe raṛakettińa. Ado monre ać hõ cetko coe bujhạu baṛakette ać hõ ona naharnitegeye reta goćena.

Ado setaken khan, bana hoṛko ńeletkin do, mit parkomre gitićkatekin goćen. Ado khangeko cekaea? Ado ato hoṛko lạiatkoa, Delabo gok sahan.

Ado unreko menketa, Durre! hola ma besgeko tahẽkan; bhala okoe cekayena? Dhora uni kuṛige coń cet coń.

Ado ato hoṛko heć jarwayenteko ńelketkin do, banar boehakin goćen. Ado mãyãmko ńelkettakina, bańge mitlena, judạ judạge ạtuyentakina, okare hõ mit ṭheć gan hõ bańge mitlena.

Ado rapakkin lạgitko gok idiketkina, ado mit sararegeko ladeketkina. Ado unre hõko ńelketa, bańma, dhũạ do bańge mitlentakina, judạtege calaoentakina. Ado unreko menketa, Boeha boeha baplakinbo menleta, menkhan Cando ona do bae khusiata. Ńelpe, mãyãm hõ mit nalatege ạtuyena, enhõ tho bań mitlena, judạtege ạtuyena. Ar nit hõ ma ńelpe, noa dhũạ okor midok kana? Ado onate baḍaeok kana, bańma, boeha boeha bapla do ohoge ganlena. Ado un khon boeha do bako baplayetkoa.

Ado ene cabayena katha do.

---

10 The naharni is a small instrument of iron, generally consisting of three implements, tweezers (used for pulling out thorns, etc.), a pricker, needlelike (also used for getting thorns out) and a cutter, used for paring nails. The last two implements very frequently are the two ends of the same piece of iron. The whole is carried tied to the waist-string.

11 'Saw', so lit. The word is used about drawing backwards and forwards, e. g. a file or a violin bow.

12 This term is used about assisting at cremation.

13 It is perhaps unnecessary to remark that the Santals, while endogamous as a people, are exogamous in their septs. The writer has heard of one case in which

When she had warmed herself and recovered, she sat down on the bedstead near the young man. Now he had a nail-cutter;[10] this she loosed, and with this she lay down. And with this nail-cutter she sawed her windpipe[11] through and died.

As she was kicking, the young man was also awakened and saw her, that blood was streaming down. Then he said: "Oh, she has killed herself, cutting herself with this nail-cutter; therefore she loosed my cutter." Then having thought matters over, who knows what his thoughts were, he himself also sawed himself with the nail-cutter and died.

When it became morning, they saw them both, lying on the same bed they were both dead. What should they do then? They informed the village people, saying: "Come along with us, to carry fire-wood."[12]

Then people said: "What a pity! yesterday they were well; who is it, we wonder, to whom something has happened? It must surely be the girl, as likely as not."

Then the village people came together, and saw the two, brother and sister were both dead. And they saw the blood that had run down from them, it had not mixed, it had flowed separately; nowhere, not even in one single place, had it run together.

Then they carried them away to cremate them, and put them on the same funeral pyre. Then also they saw this: the smoke from them was not mixed together, it went in different directions. Then they said: "We intended to marry brother and sister, but Chando did not like this. See, their blood flowed in the same ditch, still it was never mixed; it flowed in separate streams. And also now look, why, the smoke is never mixed into one." Then hereby it is to be known, it will never do to marry brother and sister. From that time people do not marry brother and sister together.[13]

So there, the story is ended.

93. Bạhui bañcaokede raj hopon reak katha.

Sedae jokhen, kathae, mitṭañ disomre mitṭen raje tahẽkana, ar uni rajrenge mitṭañ dewan hõe tahẽkantaea. Ado gidrạkoko hoeyen khan, mitṭañ paṭsalkin dohoketa; ado jemonge ạkinren gidrạko harak kana, temonge ona pāṭsal iskulrekin dhurạu horayetkoa. Ar onko gidrạ do kạṭićregekin bạhuako kana, ar onko gidrạ do bako disạia, bañdo bapla hoe akantale bañdo bañ; onkako bujhạua.

Ado sạri raj hopon koṛa ar uni dewan hopon koṛa dokin hara idiyen khan, olok paṛhao hõ beskin cet idiketṭekin pasena; ado eṅgat apat ar uni cecetić guru hoṛ hõ ạdiye khusiyente unkin gidrạ do ạdiye sarhaokina.

Ar unkin koṛa do mitṭegekin tahena, ado ạkin ạkinkin galmaraojoña, menakin, Henda ya, bhala alañ do tisko bạhualaña? Bhalako bạhualaña se bañ? Ar tãhã gidrạreko bạhu akawatkin, ona do

---

a brother and a sister (who had never been living together in their parents' house) commenced to cohabit. When this became known, the horrified people drove the two away.

A variant taken down by Bhuju Murmu some thirty years after Sagram's story was written has some details not found in the other and some slight differences. The story starts by telling that the seven brothers every day went to the forest to hunt; one day the youngest brought an Indian Laburnum plant (Cassia Fistula, L.) and planted this as described, with the same result as in the above story. The boy seeing a hair on the flower asked his mother who had been there, and the mother told. The boy wanted to marry his sister, but his grandmother objected, saying that such a thing was never done anywhere. The girl also objected and left home. Passing a tank she climbed up into a palm-tree there. One day an old Mahle woman passed there; the girl came down and commenced to talk to the woman, asking her: 'what basket are you carrying there?' The woman answered: 'I am going to such and such a village where a brother and sister are to be married, and it is for these that I take this basket along.' The girl told that she was the bride, asked her not to tell of her, and gave her a wristlet to silence her. Thereupon is told how the old woman went to the girl's home and there was induced

93. THE STORY OF THE PRINCE WHOM HIS WIFE SAVED.

In olden times, people tell, there lived in a certain country a king; this king also had a minister. When they had got children, they set up a school[1] with a guru, and, as soon as their children grew big enough, they at once sent them to learn in this school. And they married the children while they were quite small[2], so that the children had no remembrance whether they had been married or not; this was what they had in their mind.

Now, truth to tell, when the king's son and the minister's son had grown up, they learnt to read and write well and passed;[3] and their parents and the teaching guru were also very pleased, and were always praising these two boys.

The two boys were constantly together, and they were talking together, saying: "I say, you, I wonder when they will marry us two? I wonder whether they will marry us or not. Now, as mentioned, they had married them both while they were small

---

to tell, without, however, being paid. The relatives went to the girl and tried to induce her to come down. We have the same song; the elder brothers' wives are not mentioned, but the boy himself sings: 'You have climbed to the top of the Palmyra palm, darling; we are husband and wife, come, come down.' As she did not listen, the boy demanded a big storm to come. All then goes as in the other story, up till the point where the girl comes to the house (not the cowshed) where the young man stays and has made a great fire. When the girl reaches there, the young man is sitting at the door; the girl has a sword, and with this she first beheads the young man and thereupon kills herself. A voice is heard from the head of the man: 'May our blood flow together and our smoke be mixed.' And from the girls head a voice came saying the opposite. And so it happened.

93 [1] The school called paṭsal is a village school with a Hindu guru as a teacher.

[2] A Hindu trait. A few Santals have during the last sixty years or so (i. e. from some time after the rebellion in 1855) under Hindu influence been marrying their children while they are quite small; never, however, in infancy as here. The common rule is that they marry when fully grown up.

[3] The word is adopted from English and is quite recent.

bakin disạyeta. Adọkin mẹna, Bạhu hõ bako bạhualaṅ kana, delaṅ jãhã disomtelaṅ oḍok calaka.

Adọ onkakin mẹn baṛae jọkhẹn, baṅdọ inạ ursiṅ bạrsiṅ jọkhẹn, kathae, okaren sadọm bepariko cọṅ ạkriṅko lạgit khub khub sadọmko ạguketkoa. Adọ unkin koṛakin mẹnketa, E yã, jãhãte dọ balaṅ calaka; noko sadọmko ạgu akatkoa, ma mimit gọṭẹnlaṅ kiriṅ ocokoa, adọ nukin sadọmre khub lekalaṅ dẹć heyalenge, ẹnkhante jãhãte dọlaṅ calaka. Adọ bana hoṛ ona kathage beskin metattekin hẽ hũketa.

Adọ sạri oṛakrekin lại saḍeketa, Ma mimit gọṭen sadọmbon kiriṅkoa; ạḍi bes beṣ sadọmko ạgu akatkoa. Adọ ona katha aṅjọmkate raj ar dewankin mẹnketa, Gidrạkin jidketa; malaṅ kiriṅakina, ar baṅkhan nãhãk nukinak mọn khaṭọktakina; usạt bọṭẹćkokakin.

Adọ sạri onka bujhạukatekin kiriṅatkina, adọ unkin koṛa dọ ạḍikin rạskạyena. Adọ din hilokge unkin sadọmre dẹćkate mimit ghạṛi dọkin ṭahlaoka.

Adọ cekakote cọṅ, kathae, mit din dọ uni raj họpọn koṛa dọ, oka pukhri reak dakko loyet arko umok kan, ona ghaṭ sẹnge ać eskargeye kamsao idikede. Adọ ona ghaṭre kuṛikoko umok kan ṅẹlte uni raj họpọn koṛa dọ, kathae, bạṛić sanakedea. Adọ mocate ma bae rọṛ daṛeak kan. Adọ ona ghaṭ ṭhenge uni sadọm dọ curmare kamsao baṛayede kana. Adọ onko ạimại dọ bọṭọrteko pic picạu baṛae kana. Adọ sanam họṛko mẹneta, Nui dọe koṛayente kuṛi ṭhen ṅẹl ocok lạgit nonka dọe kamsaoede kana.

Adọ dak hõ bae lo ocoako kante mitṭaṅ buḍhi dọ uni koṛa ṭhen sẹnkateye metadea, Henda beṭa, ḍạṅguạ hoṛ leka am dọ nọṇḍẹm ạcur baṛae kan dọ? Am male bạhu akawatme cọn.

[4] From here the son of the minister or chief secretary disappears from the story.

children; but this they had no remembrance of. So they would say: "They are not procuring wives for us either; come let us go away to some foreign country."

When they were talking in this way, perhaps it was just about this time or a couple of days afterwards, some horse-dealers from who knows where, people tell, brought some very fine horses there to sell. The two boys then said: "I say, you, don't let us go anywhere; they have brought these horses; we shall make our people buy one for each of us; then we shall first become experienced riders, and then we shall go somewhere or other." Both of them thought this very good and agreed to it.

Then, truth to tell, they mentioned the matter at home, saying: "Let us buy a horse for each of us; some people have brought excellent horses." Hearing this the king and his minister said: "The two children are very persistent; let us buy horses for them; otherwise they will become despondent; they might begin to sulk."

Having come to this conclusion they, truth to tell, bought horses for these two boys, who naturally became very glad. Every day they both mounted their horses and rode backwards and forwards for a while.[4]

Then, people tell, somehow or other the king's son one day by himself alone galloped his horse towards the place at the tank where they were fetching water and were bathing. Seeing the girls bathing there the king's son, people tell, felt a bad desire. Now he could not say anything; therefore he kept his horse galloping all he could there near the water-fetching place, and the women became terrified, and were running backwards and forwards, and all the people said: "He has become a grown-up boy; therefore he is galloping the horse here to display himself before the girls."

As he prevented them from fetching water also, an old woman went up to the boy, and said to him: "Look here, my son, you are turning round here like an unmarried youngster; why, we have married you, don't you know?"

Ado̱ uni koṛae me̱nket́a, Tispe bạhuadiń a? Iń do̱ baco̱ń disạyet́ kan. Ar bạhu akawadiń khan, e̱ṇḍe̱khan bạhu do̱ okorić? Bań ńe̱le kan do̱.

Ado̱ uni buḍhiye me̱nket́a, Huḍiń huḍińreko bạhu akạwat́mea, onate bam disạyet́a; ar doṅga bań hoe akante no̱ṇḍe̱ do̱ bako ạgu akadea, nạihạrrege menaea. Ado̱ no̱ḱo̱e am ho̱m harayena, ne̱s do̱ pase̱n doṅga hoeoḱ. Nun din do̱ huḍińgem tạhe̱kante doṅgame reaḱ do̱ raj ho̱ bae ro̱ṛ baṛayet́ tahe̱kana. Ado̱m harayena, ne̱s do̱ pase̱n dhorage nāhāḱbon ạguyea.

Ado̱ uni koṛae me̱nket́a, Henda buḍhi, ińaḱ nạihạr do̱ oka atoretiń?

Ado̱ uni buḍhiye me̱nket́a, Phalna disom phalna atoren raj ho̱po̱nera kuṛi am do̱le bạhu akawat́mea.

Ado̱e me̱nket́a, Acha bogege, e̱ṇḍe̱khan ado̱ eṅgań ạpuńiń kulikina, bhala doṅga do̱ hoeoḱa se̱ bań.

Ado̱e me̱nket́a, Acha, ma kulikinme.

Ado̱ enka me̱nkatege uni raj ho̱po̱n koṛa do̱ oṛaḱ se̱n sado̱me kamsao idikedea, ado̱ khulạsate onko maejiu do̱ko um naṛkayena, ar daḱko lo baṛaket́te oṛaḱteko he̱ćena.

Ado̱ uni raj ho̱po̱n koṛa do̱ oṛaḱre he̱ćkate eṅgatte̱t́e kuliyede kana, Henda go̱, ińaḱ baplạ do̱ hoe akana se̱ bań?

Ado̱e me̱nket́a, Hoe akangea.

Ado̱ koṛae me̱nket́a, E̱ṇḍe̱khan cedaḱ babon ạguede kana?

Ado̱ eṅgatte̱t́e me̱nket́a, Iạ beṭa, doṅga bapla bań hoe akante babon ạgu akadea; ado̱ nāhāḱ ne̱s do̱bo ạguyea.

Ado̱ uni koṛae me̱nket́a, Iạ ayo, iṅge o̱ko̱e tora se̱nkateń ńe̱l ạguyea; judiko kolań khan do̱ń ạgu darayea.

Ado̱e metadea, Acha bogege, ma calaḱme.

5 The word **doṅga** is very rarely heard and does not refer to a Santal, but to a Hindu custom. A **doṅga** is a kind of palanquin, more like a bedstead, on which the girl is carried. When infants are married, the bride naturally remains with her parents until she is big enough to come to her husband. It is this home-bringing which is here referred to.

The young man then said: "When did you marry me? As for me I have no remembrance of it. And if they have married me, why, where is my wife? I don't see her."

The old woman replied: "They married you when you were very very small; therefore you don't remember it; and as the bride-bringing[5] has not come to pass, they have not brought her here; she is in her father's home. So now, as we see, you are grown up also, so perhaps the bride-bringing may come to pass this year. So long a time you have been small, therefore the king has not spoken about bringing your bride. You have grown up; perhaps this year we shall bring her undoubtedly."

"I say, old lady," the young man asked, "in what village is my wife's home?"

The old woman replied: "A daughter of the king of such and such a village in such and such a country we have procured for you to be your wife."

"All right," he said, "in this case I shall ask my parents whether the bride-bringing will come to pass or not."

"Very well, ask them," she replied.

Having said so much the king's son galloped his horse towards his home, and now the women without anxiety bathed and washed their hair, drew water and went home.

When the young son of the king reached home, he asked his mother: "I say, mother, have I been married or have I not?"

"You have," she replied.

"Then why do we not bring her?" the young man asked.

"Oh, my son," his mother replied, "the bride-bringing marriage-ceremony has not taken place; therefore we have not brought her; this year we shall bring her presently."

The young man then said: "I say, mother, without further delay I shall go and look her up and bring word back; if they will send her with me, I shall bring her along."

"Very well, that is good," she replied; "please go."

Adọ sạri jọm baṛakateye sapṛaoena, adọ sadọmre dẹćkate bạhu ạguye calaḱ kan tahẽkana. Adọ calaḱ calaḱte, kathae, miṭṭaṅ sạuṛi goḍare sẹṅgẹlko jẹrẹt́ akawaṫe ńẹlkeṫa. Adọ ona sạuṛire dọ beṛhaete sẹṅgẹl dọ lagao akante lọ hijuḱ kana; ar ona sạuṛi goḍarege miṭṭaṅ maraṅ utạr bisan biṅe tahẽkana. Adọ ọntẹ nọtẹ khon sẹṅgẹle ńẹleṫte oḍokoḱe mẹnjoṅ kana; adọ lọḱ bọtọrte bae oḍok daṛeaḱ kana.

Adọ ona takrege uni raj họpọn koṛa dọ nạihạrte bạhu ạgu calaḱ kane ńẹlkede khan dọe họhọkeṫa, Ẹ raj họpọn koṛa, am dọ ạḍi rạskạkate bạhu ạgum calaḱ kana, ar iń dọ noa muhimreń paṛao akana. Dẹ dayạkate noa muhim khon dọ bańcaokańme. Judiyem bańcåokidińa mẹnkhan, miṭṭaṅ bhọr iń emama.

Adọ uni koṛae mẹnkeṫa, Durrẹ! ọhọń bańcaolema. Am dọń bańcaolem khan, nãhãḱem jọmeńa. Biń jạt dọ gun bape manaoa; jãhã tinạḱle dulạṛpe, ẹnre hõpe jọjọmgea.

Adọ uni biṅe mẹnkeṫa, Baṅa, iń dọ bań onkana. Ọkọeko cọń gun bako manaoleṫ; mẹnkhan iń dọ bań onkana. Nitoḱ dọń gujuḱ kana, dẹ dayakate niạ muhim khon dọ bańcaokańme baṛẹ, ạḍi bạṛić iń nẹhõram kana.

Adọ sạri uni koṛae dayayente sadọm khone ãṛgoyena, adọ uni aṛe ṭhenaḱ sẹṅgẹle dal īṛīćkeṫte pạńci kicrićе aṭẹṫadea, adọ uni biń ona kicrić cetanteye lẹń'oḍokena. Adọe metae kana, Dẹ nitoḱ dọń bańcaokeṫmea, adọ ceṫ lekan bhọr emańem mẹnleṫa? Adọ dẹ·bhọrańme.

Adọ uni biṅe mẹnkeṫa, Bhọr dọ ceṫ hõ baṅ kana. Am dọ un maraṅ muhim khonem bańcaokidińa, ạḍim bhagekeṫa. Adọ iń bańcaoiń jọkhẹn cekate bam bọtọrlena? Iń bańcaoiń reaḱ behajem

6 The Santals largely use sạuṛi, Heteropogon contortus, R. & S., for house-thatching; it is much stronger and more lasting than ordinary straw. The plant is wild in the country; although the Santals do not regularly cultivate the sạuṛi, they take care of the fields where the grass grows and keep the cattle away (cattle will eat the straw when the plant is young). When the grass is cut (in Jan.—Febr.), they set fire to the stubble, to clean the field up.

Then, truth to tell, after he had had his food, he made himself ready; and mounting his horse he started to go and bring his wife. As he passed along, people tell, he saw that people had set fire to a field where there had been thatching-grass growing.[6] The fire had got hold in the thatching-grass round everywhere and was spreading burning; and in this grass-field there was a tremendously big poisonous snake; and as the snake saw the fire on every side, it was trying to get out; but fearing that it would be burnt, it was unable to get out.

Just at this moment the snake caught sight of the king's son, who was on his way to his wife's home to fetch her, and called out: "O prince, you are going in great joy to fetch your wife, and I have got into this danger. Do have pity and save me from this danger. If you save me, I shall give you a blessing."

"Fie", the young man replied, "I shall certainly not save you. If I save you, you will at once eat me. You snake beings don't show gratitude; however much we love you, still you eat us."

The snake then said: "No, I am not that kind. Whoever did not show gratitude, — I am not that kind. Now I am dying here; do have pity and save me from this danger; I implore you most earnestly."

Then, truth to tell, the young man took pity on the snake and dismounted from his horse, and beating the fire out near the snake he spread a strip of cloth[7] out for it, and the snake crawled out on this cloth. The man then said to the snake: "Give me, now I have saved you; what kind of blessing did you say you would give me? Then please, give me the blessing."

The snake replied: "The blessing is nothing; you saved me from such a big danger; you did very well. But how is it that you were not afraid, when you were saving me? You showed

---

[7] The pąńci is a piece of cloth narrower than the ordinary.

dilkeť! Nit dǫ amgelaṅ jǫmmea; pharakoḱ khangelaṅ sogaḱ gǫtmea. Ma sẹ bhala, iṅ ṭhen khon ceka lekatem pharakoḱa?

Adǫ uni koṛae mẹnkeťa, Pharakoḱ khange tǫbẹm jǫmeṅa?

Adǫ biṅe mẹnkeťa, Hẽ, jǫmmegeaṅ. Pạhil dǫ bam baḍaeleťa, biṅ dǫko bisana mẹnte? Nit ma iṅ ṭhen khon ǫhǫgem ǫcǫḱ daṛelena.

Khange adǫ uni koṛa dǫe asbasaoena; adǫe mẹnkeťa. Acha, nit ma am ṭhen khon ǫhǫgeṅ paskao daṛelena. Adǫ miť kathaṅ metam kana, adǫm aṅjǫmtiṅa sẹ baṅ?

Adǫ biṅe mẹnkeťa, Acha, ma sẹ rǫṛme; ceť lekan katha kana?

Adǫ uni koṛae mẹnkeťa, Ạkhirem jǫmeṅgea, ẹnḍẹkhan hape, miť bar hǫṛlaṅ jarwaleḳoge; onkoge pɔ̃claṅ badãokoa; judi onko hǫ̃ am sẹn lekạgeko rǫṛ khan, ẹnḍẹkhan dǫ nãhãḱ jǫmeṅme.

Adǫ biṅe mẹnkeťa, Hǫṛ pɔ̃ć dǫ balaṅ ṅamkoa, onko dǫ nãhãḱ am sẹn lekageko rǫṛa. Onko baṅ khusiako kana; eṭaḱ eṭaḱ jạtgelaṅ pɔ̃ckoa.

Adǫ uni koṛae mẹnkeťa, Acha bogege, ma sẹ ẹnḍẹkhan lại idi sẹ ṅum idilekome, bhala cele celekolaṅ pɔ̃ckoa.

Adǫ biṅe mẹnkeťa, Miťṭaṅ dǫ gại, ar miť dǫ dare, ar miť dǫ daḱ, neko pẹ hǫṛge pɔ̃claṅ badạokoa. Adǫ jãhã sẹngeko rǫṛ, inạgelaṅ bataotakoa. Judi am sẹnko rǫṛ khan, iṅ gǫjeṅme; ar iṅ sẹnko rǫṛle khan, am iṅ jǫmmea.

Adǫ uni koṛae mẹnkeťa, Ạcha besge. Delaṅ ẹnḍẹkhan onkolaṅ sendra ṅamkoa.

Adǫ sạrikin calaḱ kana. Adǫ calaḱ calaḱte miťṭaṅ baṛẹ buṭạre ạḍi utạr gại aḍa akankin ṅẹlkeťkoa. Adǫkin mẹnkeťa, Delaṅ onko gại ṭhenlaṅ calaḱa, ar ona baṛe daregelaṅ metaea, ar jạnić daḱ hǫ̃ onko gại phẹḍrege menaḱ bạṛića. Ǫnḍẹge nãhãḱ pẹnẹ hǫṛlaṅ ṅamkoa. Adǫ bana hǫṛkin hẽ hũkeťa.

Adǫ ona baṛe dare buṭạrekin calaoena; adǫ baṛe dare ar gạikin hǫhǫaťkina, adǫ ona daḱ phẹḍ ṭhenko calaoena. Adǫ uni koṛae

8 See note 8, p. 182.

9 Pɔ̃c, lit. the Five.

10 The large Ficus bengalensis, Roxb.

an astonishing courage to save me. Now we two shall eat you;[8] when we get a little away from here, we two shall bite you. Look out, how will you get away from me?"

"If I move away," the young man asked, "then you will eat me?"

"Yes", the snake replied, "I shall surely eat you. Did you not know before that snakes are poisonous? Now you will never be able to get away from me."

The young man became dumbfounded, whereupon he said: "All right, now I am certainly unable to escape from you. Then I have one thing to say to you, will you listen to me or not?"

"All right," the snake said; "let me hear; what kind of a matter is it?"

The young man then said: "Finally you will kill me; then wait a little, let us first call together a couple of people; these we shall make our judges;[9] if these also speak as you do, then you may eat me."

The snake replied: "We shall not get men to be judges; they will presently speak in your favour. I don't like such ones; we shall make other classes judges."

"All right," the young man said, "that is good; now then you tell or name them, which we shall appoint to be judges."

The snake then said: "One is a cow, another is a tree, and a third is water; these three we shall make our judges. And whatever these decide this we two shall obey. If they speak in your favour, kill me; and if they decide in my favour, I shall eat you."

"All right," the young man said, "this is well; come along then, let us hunt these up."

Then, truth to tell, they went along. As they walked along, they saw an immense number of cows resting at the foot of a banyan[10] tree; then they said: "Come, let us go up to these cows, and we shall speak to the banyan tree also, and there is likely also water near these cows. There we shall presently find all three." Both of them agreed to this.

Then they went to the foot of this banyan tree, and called out to the banyan tree and a cow, whereupon they all went near the

mẹnkeťa, Iạ ho, ape pẹnẹ hoṛ iń galmaraoape kana; miťṭań bicạr phaṇḍaokatalińpe.

Adọko mẹnkeťa, Acha bogege; ma sẹ bhala lạilem; ańjọmle nạhile rọṛa.

Adọe mẹnkeťa, Achań rọṛeťa, ańjọmpe.

Adọko mẹnkeťa, Acha, male ańjọmeťa.

Adọe rọṛeťa, Iń dọ nạihạrte bạhu ạguń calaǩ kan tahẽkana, adọ nui bhiń dọ miťṭań sạuṛi gọḍareye tahẽkana, ar ona sạuṛi dọ beṛhaete sẹṅgẹlko lagaoatte lọ idiǩ kana. Adọ lọǩ bọtọrte nui biń dọ ona khon bańcaoǩa mẹnte ńir oḍokoǩe mẹnjoń kan tahẽkana. Adọ ạḍi ăṭ jolọǩ kanto bae oḍok daṛeaǩ kana. Adọ ińe ńẹlkidiń khane hohoadińa, adọe metań kana, E ho, ińaǩ jivi calaǩ kantińa, dayakate dẹ noa muhim khon bańcaokańme; judim bańcaoliń khan dọ miťṭań iń bhọrama. Adọń metadea, Ọkọ baḍae, biń jạt dọ gun bape manaoa; ạsullepere hõpe jọjọmgea. Adọe mẹnkeťa, Onko dọko ceť lekan cọń, iń dọ bań onkana; ma dayakate nią muhim khon bańcaokańme. Adọ onkae mẹnkeť khan dọń dayayente sẹṅgẹl dal īrićkate ińaǩ pạńci kicrić ona lọlọ akan ṭhen iń aṭẹťkeťte nui biń dọe lẹń oḍokena. Adọń metae kana, Nitoǩ dọń bańcaokeťmea, ma adọ bhọrańme. Adọ nui bińe mẹnkeťa, Ceť bhọrem ńam kana? Ińem bańcaokidiń dọ cekate bam bọtọrlena? Iń mań jọjọm janwar kan; nitoǩ dọ dhoragelań jọmmea; ma sẹ bhala, ceť lekate iń ṭhen khon dọm ọcọǩ daṛeaǩa? Adọ onka mẹnkate sạri nui biń dọe teṅgoyenteye saṛ gọťena. Adọ unreń mẹnkeťa, Iạ ho, ạkhirem jọmeńgea; delań põclań bicạr ocolekoge; bhala onko hoṛ oka sẹnko rọṛa; adọ am sẹn lekageko rọṛ khan, ẹṇḍẹkhan dọ jọmeńme; adọń bańcaokeťmea, adọ gun bam manao khan dọń

11 The description fits the cobra, one of the most poisonous of Indian snakes, and also very aggressive. When going to strike, it 'stands up', raises about one third or more of its whole length erect, expands its hood (so that the 'spectacles' become very plainly seen), and watching all in front of it, it may suddenly throw itself forward to bite. When it hisses, one should think one hears a being from the nether regions.

water. The young man then said: "I say, I am speaking to all you three; pass judgement in a case for us two."

"All right," they said; "do tell what it is first; only when we have heard, we shall speak out."

"All right," he said; "I am speaking, listen."

"Well then," they said; "we are listening."

Then he said: "I was on my way to fetch my wife from her father's home; then this snake was in a thatching-grass field; and as they had set fire to this grass on all sides, the fire was coming burning. And fearing that it would be burnt the snake was thinking of running out to be saved from the fire; but as it was burning fiercely, it was unable to get out. When it saw me, it called out to me, and said: 'You there, my soul is passing away; have pity and save me from this danger; if you save me, I shall give you a blessing.' Then I said to the snake: 'Who knows, you snake-beings don't show gratitude; even when you are kept and fed, you eat people.' Then it said: 'Those are who knows of what kind; I am not that kind; do have pity and save me from this danger.' As the snake said this, I took pity on it, beat the fire out and spread my overcloth where it had become hot, and then this snake crawled out. Then I said to it: 'Now I have saved you, so please give me the blessing.' The snake then said: 'What blessing do you want? How was it that you were not afraid to save me? I am a dangerous animal; now we two shall surely eat you; look out, how will you be able to get away from me?' Speaking in this way this snake actually stood up and expanded its hood.[11] Then I said: 'I say, you, finally you will eat me; come let us make the Five judge in our case and hear how these will decide; if they speak in your favour, then eat me; I saved you, and if you don't show any gratitude, what shall I do with you?' Then, having talked in this way, we

cekamea? Adọ onka mẹnkate ape pẹ hoṛliñ ñumñam akaṭpea. Adọ dẹsẹ bhala, noage bicạrkataliñpe. Adọ bhalañ besleṭa sẹñ bạṛić akaṭa?

Adọ baṛe dareye rọṛkeṭa, Bes mam besleṭge; adọ besket reak kuṛạitẹt ma bạṛić kange. Am dọm bañcaokedea, nui dọe gọćmegea; am dọ dhorageye jọmmegea. Noako bicạr dọ ape manwa ṭhengele cet akaṭa. Ńẹlme, iñak umulre dọ jirạu hõpe jirạuk kana, adọñ besketpege. Adọ ñẹlme, ḍạr hõpe pẹṭẹjtiña ar ọnarepe duṛuṗa arpe gạsićaka. Adọ ñẹlme bhala, tinạk pọr mondape kạmiyeṭa! Adọ ona iạte sạri khạṭige am dọe jọmmegea.

Adọ uni koṛae mẹnkeṭa, Ẹ gại, dẹsẹ bhala, adọ am rọṛlem. Amak dọ cet lekan tọjbij kantama?

Adọ uni gạiye mẹnkeṭa, Hẽ, sạrigeye jọmmegea, dareye rọṛket lekage hoeoka. Ẹnte ñẹlme, ale dọ gidrạle janamjoñ kana, adọle nunuako jọkhẹn dọpe rẹćetkoa; onko dọpe laga ñirketkoge, adọ apege toa dọpe hataoeṭa ar dal hõ bogetepe dallea; si arjaoape kanale, arhõ alegepe bạṛićlea. Ona iạte am dọ sạrigeye jọmmegea.

Adọ uni koṛae mẹnkeṭa, Ẹ dak, adọ dẹ am rọṛme; adọ amak tọjbij cet leka?

Adọ dake mẹnkeṭa, Iñak tọjbij hõ nukinkin mẹnket lekage hoeoka; bhạlại bọdọl burạ̣i dọ ṭhika. Ńẹlme, iñ dọ ñũ hõpe ñũyeñ kana, onate apeak jivi bañcaok kantapea. Adọ ñẹlme, iñ dọñ beseṭgea, adọ ape mañwa jạt dọpe burạyet kana: oka dọ dakregepe moelaea, ḍẹkẹ hõpe ạbukoka, tho hõpe thoea ar kharak hõpe kharaga. Adọ ma sẹ bhala bujhạume, bhạlại bọdọlte ape dọpe mọndọyeṭa; noa dọ thọṛẹnpe ọpọmaneṭa. Ona sikte am dọm besket khan, nui dọ bae bạṛija? Hẽ, sạrigeye bạṛijgea, am dọe jọmmegea.

Adọ biñe mẹnkeṭa, Cele ho, adọ cetem mẹneṭa? Nẹkẹ thọ pọc reak katha dọlañ añjọmkeṭa, adọñ jọmmegea.

Adọ uni koṛae mẹnkeṭa, Acha jọmeñgeam; adọ neko pẹ hoṛ goha samañreñ nẹhõrok kana, iñak duk iñ lạilege, añjọmtiñpe; sẹ ẹnte bape añjọmtiñ khan, inạ hõ metañpe.

---

12 It might be noted that the Santals always wash themselves as indicated. To act in any other way is considered disgraceful and awful.

mentioned you three. So now please, please, pass judgement in our case. I should like to know whether I did well or I have done what is bad."

The banyan tree then spoke: "Quite so, you acted well; but the reward of good is what is bad. You saved him; the snake will kill you; it will surely eat you. Such judgements we have learnt from you human beings. See, in my shade you rest, and I act well towards you. Then see, you break my branches, and you sit down on them and break wind there. So see there how unjustly you act. Therefore to be sure the snake will undoubtedly eat you."

The young man then said: "O cow, speak you, please. How is your decision?"

The cow then said: "Yes, really it shall eat you; it must be as the tree spoke. For see, we give birth to young ones, and when we suckle them, you rob them; you drive ours away, and you take the milk, beside this you also beat us awfully; we plough for you and earn for you, again you ruin us. Therefore the snake shall really eat you."

The young man then said: "O water, now you speak, please; what is your decision?"

The water answered: "My decision will also be just as these two spoke; bad for boon, this is right; look here, me you are drinking, thereby your life is saved. Then see, I am doing good; then you human beings act badly: sometimes you ease yourselves in water; you wash your hindquarters also with water;[12] you also spit and expectorate. So understand this, as a recompense for a boon you act basely; this you do very wrongly. In accordance with this, as you acted well, shall not the snake act badly? Yes, surely, it must act badly; the snake will eat you."

The snake then said: "Well then, you, what have you to say? Here we have just heard what the Five have to say; so I shall eat you."

"All right," the young man said, "you will eat me; but before these three witnesses I make an humble request; let me tell my sorrow, listen to me; or if you will not listen, then say so much to me also."

Adǫko mẹnketa, Acha añjǫmgeale; ma rǫṛme.

Adǫ uni koṛae rǫṛeta, Iñ dǫ tinạk huḍiñre cǫko bạhu akawadiñ, ar iñ dǫ bạhu reak mẽtãhã hõ bañ ñẹl akata, uni hõe cet lekan cọñ. Adǫ nẹkge pạhil pạhil nạihạrte bạhu ạguñ calak kana. Adǫ hǫrre nonka ghoṭna hoeok dǫ bañ baḍaeleta. Adǫ ape ṭhen iñ nẹhõrok kana, ma niạ dhao dǫ sẹn ocoañpe, bạhu tuluć iñ ñẹpẹllenge, adǫ nonkategeñ ruạṛa, unreye jǫmeña.

Adǫ baṛe dareye mẹnketa, Cele ya biñ, cetem mẹneta? Nui ma ǫnẹ onkae mẹnet kan dǫ.

Adǫ biñe mẹnketa, Hẽ ma hẽge, adǫ dẹ ẹṇḍẹkhan apege jạmin ar sạkhi tahẹntabonpe. Iñ hõ põc reak katha dǫ bañ nẹhǫtet kana.

Adǫ baṛe dareye mẹnketa, Cele ya, aboge thǫ põc? Dẹ bhala, jạminbon teñgokoka sẹ ǫhǫ?

Adǫ unkinkin mẹnketa, Hẽ ma hẽge, adǫ ẹnte tin dinreye ruạṛa? Adǫ uni koṛako kulikedea, Cele ho, adǫ tin dinrem ruạṛa sẹ ǫhǫm ruạṛlena?

Adǫ uni koṛae mẹnketa, Gapa dǫ bañ, meañ khangeñ ruạṛa. Teheñ khon pẹ mãhã reak iñ nenḍawape kana. Ma inạ din hilok dǫ khạṭigeñ hijuka, ǫhǫñ ẹṛẹpea.

Adǫko mẹnketa, Mẹn ẹṇḍẹkhan alom ẹṛẹlea, ar bañkhan nãhãk nahak alegem lajao ocolea.

Adǫe mẹnketa, Baña, ǫhǫñ lajao ocopea; mañ ruạṛgea.

Adǫ biñko metae kana, Cele ho biñ, ma ẹṇḍẹkhan niạ pẹ mãhã din dǫ aṛakaeme; ale jạminle teñgon kana. Ñẹlme ẹnte, gidrạre bapla hoe akantaea, adǫ mit din hõ uni tuluć bae rǫṛ landa akata. Adǫ nitem jǫmle khan, nahakge ẹṇḍẹkhan nui koṛa dǫko bạhu akawadea. Adǫ onatele metam kana, ma niạ pẹ mãhã din dǫ aṛakaeme; ale jạminle teñgon kana. Adǫ ruạṛ hilok dǫ jǫmeme; ẹn hilok dǫ cet hõ bale metama.

"All right," they said, "we shall listen; please speak."

Then the young man commenced: "I was married, who knows how small I was; and I have not seen the face of my wife either, however she may look. And just now I am for the first time going to my father-in-law's house to fetch my wife; and I had no idea that any misfortune like this should happen on the way. So I am imploring you, please let me go this once, let me meet my wife; then I shall return by this road, and then the snake may eat me."

The banyan tree then said: "Well, you snake, what have you to say? This man speaks as we hear."

The snake replied: "That is quite so, but then please stand surety and be witnesses for us. I am not disregarding what the Five say either."

Then the banyan tree said: "Well you, we are the Five, or how? Then shall we stand surety or shall we not?"

The two others then said: "Yes, that is so, but then in how many days will he return?" Then they asked the young man: "Well, you, in how many days will you return, or perhaps you will not return at all?"

The young man replied: "Not to-morrow, but the day after I shall return. I fix the third day from to-day for you. On that day I shall certainly come; I shall not deceive you."

Then they said: "Beware then, don't deceive us; if you do, you will bring shame on us to no purpose."

"Certainly not," he replied; "I shall not bring shame on you."

Then they said to the snake: "Well, you snake, in this case let him have three days; we are standing surety for him. Think of it, his marriage was gone through when he was a child; he has not spoken and jested with her even one single day. So if you eat him now, it will be to no purpose that they have married this young man. Therefore we say this to you: allow him these three days; we are standing sureties. Then eat him the day he comes back; that day we shall say nothing to you."

Ado uni biñe mẹnketa, Acha, ẹnḍẹkhan iñ hō pōc reak katha do bañ nẹhọteta. Ma ẹnḍẹkhane calak ma.

Adọ enka mẹnkate uni kọṛa dọ sadọmreye dẹćente nạihạrteye calaoena. Adọ ọnḍẹye sẹṭẹren khan parkọmko beladẹa, adọe duṛupḅena. Adọ bako ñẹl oromede kanteko kulikedea, Cele baba, am dọ oka sẹn khon peṛa dọ? Bacọle ñẹl orometme.

Adọe mẹnketa, Hẽ, ñẹl dọ ọhọpe ñẹl oromliña; lạileṅẹnẹćpe ñẹl orom daṛeaña.

Adọko mẹnketa, Okaren kanam?

Adọe mẹnketa, Iñ dọ phalna disomren phalna raj họpọn kanañ. Nọnḍẹ khongẹ, cele, bạhuko idi akawadiña; nui phalna rajren họpọnerage iñ bạhu dọe hoe akana, onate iñ dọ bạhu idiye lạgitgeñ hẹć akana.

Adọko mẹnketa, Hẽ, inạkge rọṛme, nit dọle bujhạuketa. Adọ dakko ạguketa, jaṅgako ạbukkedea; adọ sunum ar dạtạuniko ñamkette umokko idikedea. Um hẹćkate dahe tabenko emadea; jọm baṛa tayọm kạsiko gurkedea, khubko peṛakedea. Adọ ạyuḅen khan mitṭañ oṛakreko jagakedea, ar uni akoren họpọnerat sunumko emadea arko metadea, Do mạ̃i, jãwãe sunum ọjọkaeme ar ti jaṅgako iskir baṛakaeme, ar am hō ọnḍẹ uni tuluć baṛẹ gitićme.

Adọ sạri uni kuṛi hōe jụạn akante hẹrẹlgeye ñam kana, adọ metade chọṭgeye calao gọtena. Adọ sunumkoe ọjọkadete ti jaṅgakoe iskir baṛayede kana ar emanteakkoe kuli baṛayede kana. Adọ uni kọṛa dọ khulạsage bae rọṛeta, ar haṛam buḍhik sẹnak dọ mọnẹge bae mọnẹak kana. Adọ ḍher hạbić uni kuṛi dọe ñẹl họrkedea; adọ bae mọnẹat khan dọ bhại, bae jivileta, kuli gọtkedeae, mẹnketae, Henda bhala, am dọm juạn akana sẹ bañ, landa katha dọ cet hō bam rọṛet kan dọ?

Adọ uni kọṛae mẹnketa, Juạn mañ juạn akange, onatege am ikdi dọñ hẹć akana. Adọ mẹnkhan cele ẹkẹn nia mẽt ñẹpẹlok

"All right," the snake then said, "I am not disregarding what the Five say either. Let him go then."

After this talk the young man mounted his horse and started for his wife's home. When he arrived there, they put a bedstead before him to sit on, and he sat down. As they did not recognize him, they asked him: "Well, sir, you are a friend from what parts? You see, we don't recognize you."

"Quite so," he replied;" you will surely not recognize me; only when it is told, you will be able to know who I am."

"From where are you?" they asked.

Then he said: "I am the son of such and such a king in such and such a country. From here, I understand, they have taken a wife for me; the daughter of this so and so king has become my wife; therefore I have come to take my wife away."

They replied: "Yes, this is enough, don't say anything more; now we understand." Then they brought water, washed his feet, and, bringing oil and a tooth-brush, they took him away to bathe. Returned from the bath they gave him curds and flattened rice; after he had eaten, they killed a castrated goat and feasted him splendidly. When it became night, they gave him a room to sleep in; and they gave their daughter some oil and said to her: "Please, girl, rub your husband in with oil and massage his arms and legs, and you too stay there with him."

Now, truth to tell, the girl was grown up and felt like a grown-up person, so at once when they said so to her, she went. She rubbed him in with oil and was giving him massage to his arms and legs, and was asking him about many different things. Now the young man would not talk freely, and seemed utterly unwilling to have anything to do with her. The girl waited for some time; then she suddenly asked him: "I say, you, you are a grown-up man, is it not so? Is there no fun in you?"

The young man replied: "Of course I am grown up; therefore I have come to take you away; but I suppose, it will for us only

lạgiťge cọń ceť cọń; iń dọ mọnre ạḍi bhabnań ạikạueťa. Ado onatege haṛam buḍhiḱ sẹnaḱ dọ bań mọnẹaḱ kana; ẹkẹn miť din lạgiť dọ ceť iń hewakama? Adọ hewalen khan, am hõ bạṛićem ạikạua. Adọ hapẹnem uihạṛińa, ar bańlań onkalen khan, ẹnḍẹkhan inạ dọ ọhọm uihạra.

Adọ uni kuṛiye mẹnkeťa, Cekate onka dọm mẹneťa? Am dọm okateḱa? Ma ona reaḱ bhẹd baṛẹ iń dọ lạiańme, ar bańkhạn am dọ bạgitẹťge ọhọń bạgilema.

Adọ koṛae mẹnkeťa, Lạile khan ma artẹťge bạṛić sanamea.

Adọ uni kuṛiye mẹnkeťa, Ma lạime, bạṛić sanańre hõ cetre hõ, ẹnhõ lạiańme baṛẹ.

Adọ sạri ọnẹ hijuḱ jọkhẹn bińe lọ gujuḱ khone ẹhọpketa, adọ jọtọ onakoe lại ạguadea. Adọe metae kana, Nẽkẽ iń dọ pẹ mãhãren jạmin teńgokate nọṇḍẹ am ṭhen dọń hẹć akana; nọṇḍẹ khon ruạṛ jọkhẹnge uni bıń dọ nãhãḱe jọmeńa. Adọ onateń metam kana, miť din lạgiť dọ ceť am tuluć dọń rọṛ landaea? Am nãhãḱ bạṛić sanamea.

Adọ uni kuṛiye mẹnkeťa, Tọbẹ iń hõ am tulućgeń gọć sẹlẹdoḱa; ẹnte iń dọń amren họṛ kana jivẹť janam hạbić. Am dọm kirińlidińa, adọ am okarem gujuḱ, ọṇḍẹ iń họ̃ń gujuḱa. Adọń metam kana, jẹ lekaḱgem; ma ẹṇḍẹkhan jivẹť menamre haṛam buḍhi reaḱ rit beohar lekalań kạmilege, adọ calaḱ hiloḱ dọ iń hõ am sãoteń calaḱa. Bhalań ńẹlea, ceť lekateye jọmmea.

Adọ uni koṛae mẹnkeťa, Bańa, am dọ alom calaḱa.

Adọ uni kuṛiye mẹnkeťa, Bańa, am dọ ọhọgeń bạgilema. Nitoḱ iń dọ noa katham lạiadińte bạṛićgeń ạikạueťa. Hẽ, alo hutẹćem lạile khan, ceť ọhọń mẹnlea; adọm lạiadińte bań jut iń ạikạueťa.

Adọ onka ạḍi lekan kathae galmaraoadete uniaḱ jiviye khạtirkeťtaea. Khange adọ mitrekin gitić ańgayente ceťko cọkin bạṛićkeť, adọ ẹnrehõ uni koṛa dọ bhabnageye ạikạueťa.

Adọ inạ neṇḍa din hiloḱ dọ uni koṛae mẹnkeťa, Teheń dọń calaḱa, in dingeń tahẹna.

be this seeing each other; I have a great grief in my mind. Why should I treat you in such a way that you will afterwards feel badly. You would only remember me with longing."

"How is it that you talk in this way?" the girl asked; "where are you off to? Please explain this to me; otherwise I shall certainly not think of leaving you."

"If I tell," the young man replied, "you will only feel still worse."

"Please tell," the girl said; "however I may feel, bad or otherwise, still tell me."

Then, truth to tell, he commenced from the snake on the point of being burnt to death when he was coming, he told her all, as it had happened; then he said: "Here you see, I have come here to you with those standing surety for me for three days; when I return from here, this snake will presently eat me. It is therefore that I speak in this way to you. Why should I enjoy myself with you for one single day? You would only feel it bad."

The girl then said: "Then I too shall go along with you and be killed together with you; for I am yours for my whole life. You bought me, therefore where you are going to die, there I also shall die; and I tell you this, whatever may happen, the day you go I shall go together with you. I shall like to see him, how he is going to eat you."

"No," the young man said, "you must not go."

"No," the girl replied, "I shall certainly not leave you. Since you have told me this, I am feeling very bad. If you only had not told me, I should not have minded; but as you have done so, I do not feel well."

Talking together in this way, the young man felt somewhat more confident; they spent the night there, but in spite of all the young man was feeling grief.

On the day fixed the young man said: "I am leaving to-day; I shall stay only so long."

Adǫko męnkeťa, Acha bogege. Adǫ uni kuṛi hǫ̃ko sapṛāokedea, adǫko bidąkeťkina. Ar ona katha dǫ ǫkǫe ṭhen hǫ̃ bakin ląileťa. Adǫ hǫrre uni koṛae męnkeťa, Ią, am dǫ alom hijuka; ma nęṇḍę khonge ruąṛme.

Adǫ uni kuṛiye męnkeťa, Acha ruąṛgeań. Oka tin sąṅgińreye jǫmmea, ona ląiańme.

Adǫ uni koṛae męnkeťa, Hane hana buru aṛere miťṭąń baṛe dare menaka, ona dare buṭąrege nąhāk iń dǫe jǫmeńa.

Adǫ uni kuṛiye męnkeťa, Acha, ęṇḍękhan dǫ ona dare buṭą hąbić dǫń calakgea; adǫ am ńęl gǫćkate iń dǫń ruąṛa.

Adǫ ąḍi bąṛiće manakedea, adǫe ḍhaka ruąṛ geladea; adǫ bae ruąṛ kan khańe iką ḍapoṛkadea. Adǫ miťtekin calaoena. Adǫ ḍarekin tiok ńǫ̃kkeť khan, uni kuṛiye męnkeťa, Iń dǫ amak māyā ǫhǫń chaḍaolea. Am ma nāhāk sąrigeye jǫmmegea; adǫ onateń metam kana, nit dǫ ińgeń lahaka, ar am dǫ iń tayǫmre tahęnme. Ińge nāhāk uni biń dǫń daramea.

Adǫe metadea, Acha, ęṇḍękhan ma lahakme.

Adǫ sąri uni kuṛigeye lahayena. Adǫ sąri calak calakkin ńęlkede dǫ, hǫrtętre teṅgokateye saṛ akan; adǫ ęnhǫ̃kin calak kangea. Adǫkin sęn tiokkede khan, uni kuṛiye męnkeťa, Ią biń, pąhil dǫ iń baṛę jǫm pąhillińme, ęnkhante nui iń jāwāe dǫm jǫmea; ar nuim jǫmle khan, iń dǫ okaṛeń tahęna?

Adǫ uni bińe męnkeťa, Am dǫ ǫhǫń jǫmlema. Am dǫ am ayo babateko oṛakre baṛę tahęnme.

Adǫ uni kuṛi arhǫ̃e męnkeťa, Ona katha dǫ ǫhǫ hoelena, ęnte eṅgań ąpuń ma nui ṭhenko ąkrin akadiń, ar nui dǫ jań hǫ̃ jań ar tǫrǫć hǫ̃ tǫrǫće kirin akadińa, adǫ nui satategeń ja lekakge. Adǫ onateń metam kana, nuim jǫme khan, ęṇḍękhan dǫ iń hǫ̃ jǫmeńme.

---

13 A quotation from the Santal marriage ritual. When the bride is leaving her old home for her husband's, the headman of the bridegroom's village says, among other matters: 'Both bones and ashes have we bought to-day'. The same authority on the bride's side says the same, the meaning being that living or dead the girl now belongs to those who have bought her. The legal foundation of a Santal marriage is that the bride is bought; a symbolic price is paid.

"All right," they said, "that is good." Then they also made the girl ready, and they saw them off. Now these two had not told any one of this matter. Then on the road the young man said: "I say, don't come any further; do return from here."

The girl then said: "Very well, I shall return. Tell me how far away is the place where the snake will eat you."

"Near the hill you see over there," the young man replied, "there is a banyan tree; at the foot of this tree the snake will eat me."

"All right," the girl said, "then I shall go so far as up to the foot of this tree; and having seen the snake killing you, I shall return."

He tried to persuade her all he could not to go; he tried to push her back; but as she was not returning, he let her be, what else could he do? Then they went along together, and when they had reached nearly up to the tree, the girl said: "I am unable to give up my affection for you. Presently the snake will surely eat you; therefore I say this to you: let me go along in front of you, and you stay behind me. I shall presently have a meeting with the snake."

"All right," he said, "then you go in front."

Then, truth to tell, the girl went in front; and, truth to tell, as they were walking along, they saw the snake, it was standing on the road with expanded hood; still they went along. When they reached it, the girl said: "I say, snake, eat me first; thereafter you may eat this husband of mine; if you eat him, where shall I stay?"

The snake then replied: "You I shall certainly not eat; you stay, please, in the house of your mother and father."

Again the girl said: "This is impossible, because, you see, my parents have sold me to this man. Both bones and ashes he has bought me[13]; therefore, whatever may happen to him, I shall have the same. Therefore I am saying to you, if you are eating him, then eat me too."

Adọ bińe mẹnkeťa, Baṅ, am dọ ọhọgeń jọmlema. Adọ uni bińi dọ nui koṛa jọme lạgiť sojhegeye hijuk kana, adọ uni kuṛige laha lahae teṅgo danaṅ idiyede kana. Adọ uni kuṛiye mẹneťa, Ceť ba bińem mẹneťte iń bam jọmlin khan dọ? Ọhọgeń jọm ocolema. Niki baṛe dare sạkhi menaea. Adọ bhala hẹrẹlińgem jọmle khan, iń dọ cekateń ạsuloka ar cele dọhọńa? Dẹ ẹṇḍẹkhan onage lại pạhilaṅme.

Adọ uni bińe mẹnkeťa, Acha ẹṇḍẹkhan dọń bhọrama, adọ miťṭaṅ gun mantar iń ceťama, adọ onka lekate am dọm ạsuloka.

Adọe mẹnkeťa, Acha ẹṇḍẹkhan ma ceť pạhilaṅme, ẹṇḍẹkhan iń aṛakama, ar baṅkhan dọ ọhọgeń aṛaklema.

Adọe mẹnkeťa, Acha ceťamaṅ. Adọ sạri ceť leka cọṅ kathae bhọradea ar gun mantar hō̃e ceťadea, are metadea, Am dọ nonka mantarkate dhuṛi hạr rakapkate miť satahẹťtẹ ọṅ gọdme, adọ ona dhuṛi jāhāegem ẹrako, ẹkkalteko lọ tọrọć gọdoka.

Adọ uni kuṛiye mẹnkeťa, Onka maṅ onkakoge, adọ ceť lekateko bes ruạṛoka, ona ceťaṅme. Adọ sạri ona hō̃e ceťadea. Adọ arhō̃ uni kuṛiye mẹnkeťa, Hape, ẹṇḍẹkhan iń biḍạulege; pasẹm ẹṛẹyediń kan.

Adọ uni bińe mẹnkeťa, Acha bogege; ma ẹṇḍẹkhan noa tarọp darere biḍạume.

Adọ kuṛiye mẹnkeťa, Acha, ẹṇḍẹkhan iń bidạulege, adọ jọmeme.

Adọ sạri dhuṛi hạr rakapkateye gun mantar gọťkeťteye ọṅ gọťkeťa. Adọ, kathae, uni bińgeye ẹr gọťadea; khange uni bińe dọe tọrọć gọtena; adọ khange uni bińe dọ ọṇḍẹgeye mọhọr meṭao utạrena.

14 We have no name for tarọp, Buchanania latifolia, Roxb., a fairly large forest tree; its fruit is eaten, and the wood is used for several purposes.

"No," the snake replied, "I shall certainly not eat you." Whereupon the snake came straight along to eat the young man; and the girl was standing in front of him shielding him, as the snake moved. Then the girl said: "Why, what are you thinking, you snake, if you will not eat me? I shall certainly not let you eat him. This banyan tree here is my witness. If you eat my husband, I should like to know how I shall support myself, and what kind of people will keep me. So there, tell me this first."

The snake then said: "All right, in this case I shall give you a blessing, and I shall teach you a magic formula; then in this way you will be able to support yourself."

"All right," she replied, "then teach me this first, then I shall let you off; if you don't, I shall certainly not let you off."

Then the snake said: "Very well, I shall teach you." Thereupon, truth to tell, the snake gave her a blessing, whatever it might be; a magic formula it also taught her, saying to her: "Pronouncing this formula pick up some dust and blow it off with one breathing; then on whomsoever you scatter this dust, he will at once be burnt into ashes."

"Quite so," the girl said, "I shall do so to people; then teach me also how they may become well again." And, truth to tell, the snake taught her also this. Then the girl again said: "Wait, I shall have a try first then; perhaps you are deceiving me."

"All right," the snake replied; "then try it on this small tree[14] here."

"Very well," the girl said; "then I shall first have a try; thereupon eat him."

Then, truth to tell, she took up some dust, and pronouncing the magic formula she blew it out; and, people tell, she scattered it on the snake, whereupon the snake was at once turned into ashes; then the snake was utterly made an end of then and there.

Khange unkin kuṛi koṛa dọ khulạsatekin parọm calaoena. Adọe metae kana, Ńẹlketam? Iń iń hẹć darayente am iń rukhiạketmeteń bańcaoketmea. Iń aloń hijuk khan hutẹć, am dọ tehenre dhạrti lẹbẹt dọm bạgi utạrkea. Amak katha ańjọmkate hutẹć iń ruạṛlen khan, amak mẹtãhã dọ tisre hõ ọhọń ńẹl ruạṛlea.

Adọ uni koṛa dọ cet hõ bae mẹnleta; uniak katha ańjọmteye kẹklẹsẹt hapeyena. Adọ ,eṭagak galmarao galmaraotegekin sẹn idiyena.

Adọ uni koṛa reak oṛakkin tiokketa, adọ onako katha jọtọkin lạiketa, adọ ạḍi bạṛićko bhabnayena arko hahaṛayena. Adọ ọnḍẹ hõ khạsiko makketkotẹ khubko bhọjketteko jọm ńũketa arko rạskạyena. Arko mẹnketa, Gọć họṛkin bańcao ruạṛentabona, ar bańkhan hutẹć nukinak mẹtãhã dọ ọhọbon ńẹllea; ạḍi muhim khonkin bańcao ruạṛ akantabona. Adọ enka rọṛ baṛakategeko thir baṛayena. Adọ ọnẹ onkate uni koṛa dọe bańcaoena ona muhim khon.

Adọ cabayena katha dọ, uni koṛa reak katha dọ in marańgea, ẹnḍẹge mucạtena.

After this the boy and the girl passed along without anxiety, and she said to him: "Did you see? Because I came along, I rescued you and saved you. If I had not come, you would to-day have ceased altogether to trample this earth. If I had listened to what you said and had returned, I should surely never have seen your face again."

The young man did not say a single word; hearing what she said he became utterly dumbfounded. Then they started some other talk, and went along.

Then they reached the young man's home, and there they told all this; they became awfully anxious and were wondering. There they also killed some castrated goats, and made a great feast; they ate and drank, and were very merry. They said: "'Dead people have been saved and have returned to us; else we should certainly not have seen their faces again; they have come back, saved from a very great danger." Having spoken in this way they did not say anything more. Then in this way this young man was saved from this danger.

Thus the story is at an end; the story of this young man is this much; there it is finished.

SANTAL FOLK TALES

SANTAL FOLK TALES

(IN THREE VOLUMES)

P.O. Bodding

VOL. I

GYAN

GYAN PUBLISHING HOUSE

NEW DELHI

Santal Folk Tales
(Anthropology Culture, Literature)

ISBN : 9788121203449(Set)

ISBN : 9788121203456(Vol-1)

Published in **2007** in India by
Gyan Publishing House
5, Ansari Road,
New Delhi-110 002

Printed at Goyal Offset Printers Delhi

CONTENTS

PREFACE

It has been my privilege to see Mr. Bodding's Santal Folk Tales through the press, and it has given me great pleasure to do so. That such has been the case is due not only to the intrinsic value of the tales, but also to the light they throw on several interesting questions.

That they are genuine folk tales cannot be doubted. They have been noted down by a Santal, whose horizon was limited to the Santal country and Santal traditions. It is not difficult to detect traces of Aryan folklore in these stories, and sometimes we can point to parallel tales in the well-known collections of Aryan India. It is probable that a not inconsiderable portion of Santal folklore has been derived from Aryan sources, and even from such as are available in printed books. Still we have no right to speak of these tales otherwise than as the property of the Santals, as real folk tales.

We must not forget that the folk tales and popular traditions of a people are nowhere entirely of indigenous growth. Not rarely they have been imported from abroad, as is e. g. the case with more than one Norwegian fairy tale, which to-day makes the impression of having taken its rise on Norwegian soil. They are nevertheless the property of the people, if they have been adapted to its mentality: in folklore as in civilization generally property is not only inherited but also acquired.

If we apply such a test to the Santal folk tales, we will find that every page bears testimony to the angle of vision characteristic of the Santals, the individuals whom we learn to know in the stories are Santals and not Hindus.

Much has been written about the various aboriginal tribes of India, but nevertheless they are still only imperfectly known. It is not easy for a European to become quite familiar with their way of thinking and of looking on the world, and even if he more or less succeeds in doing so, he will experience some difficulty in explaining things to other people. Even the most careful and conscientious observer has his bias and his particular idiosyncrasy, and the picture he draws will bear the stamp of his individual mentality. It will have to be filled up with numerous details and features.

It will be easily seen that there cannot be a better or more reliable guide to the mentality of a strange people than a comprehensive collection of such tales and traditions which live on the lips and in the hearts. Through them the people is able to speak to us without the aid of an interpreter, and we have only to listen and to concentrate our attention on what we hear. Therefore Mr. Bodding's folk tales should be welcomed by everybody who wishes to understand the primitive Kolarian tribe to which they belong.

The social and mental features of the Santals can, however, claim our interest also from another point of view. The Kolarian tribes, of which the Santals are the most important one, are the last Indian remnants of a race which in ancient times seems to have played a considerable rôle in India and in the countries and islands around the Indian ocean. When the Aryans entered India, they were met with the ancestors of the present day Dravidians and Kolarians, and the latter ones seem to have formed the bulk of the population in the northern and central parts of the continent. We would therefore expect to find a Kolarian substratum in the languages and in the civilization of India, and a critical examination of the remnants of the ancient population

which have preserved their ancient speech and mentality till the present day may be apt to throw light on several questions connected with the development of India through the ages. And because we know that the ancient civilization of the Kolarians and also their indigenous languages have to a great extent disappeared, having become inundated by the strong Aryan wave, we may reasonably hope, from a study of what still remains, to be able to draw general conclusions about the laws underlying the growth and expansion of a superior civilization. I shall only mention some few points.

In comparative folklore the traditional tales handed down in Indian literature have always played a prominent rôle, since a solid foundation of this branch of research was laid through Benfey's translation of the Pañcatantra. Now Indian tradition states that the Pañcatantra was composed in the Dekhan, dakshiṇāpathe, and similary another important collection of Indian tales, Guṇāḍhya's Bṛhatkathā, is localized in the Vindhya country. In these parts of India the ancient population was not Aryan, but either Dravidian or Kolarian, or a mixture of both. It therefore seems probable that tribes related to the Santals have contributed to the rich store of Indian traditional tales, and a careful analysis of the folk tales now published may some day lead to important results.

In this connexion I should like to draw attention to the tales about jackals, because the jackal plays such a great rôle in Indian folklore. Even a cursory perusal will show that the jackal is not throughout described and characterized in a uniform way. Usually he is a clever and dexterous animal, which is always prepared to assist those who have suffered wrong in asserting their right. In some tales, however, he acts in a different way. He is malicious and treacherous, but usually he is defeated in the end, just like the foolish devil in European folklore.

This double conception is curious. It is possible that we have to do with two different elements, one originally Kolarian and

the other originally Aryan. It is, however, also possible that the stories about jackals, which are of such importance in ancient Indian folklore, originally belong to the Kolarian tribes, and that they have thence been adopted by the Aryans. The latter ones at an early period made use of tales about animals in order to inculcate certain doctrines, and more especially they were employed for the purpose of teaching political wisdom. The various animals were brought together into an organized state under the rule of the lion as king. The wily and crafty jackal then acted as the minister of the king, and as such he had to find a way out of difficulties. It is possible that this led to the conception of the jackal as the prudent adviser and dexterous helper, which was then reimported into Santal folklore, without the accompaniment of the organized animal state with its king. The crafty and treacherous jackal would then represent the more original type.

I can only point to these explanations as possibilities. The students of comparative folklore will some day be able to solve such questions in a satisfactory way, and the Santal tales here published are likely to be of importance to them in doing so.

They will also prove of interest to the folklorist in other respects. The 22nd story shows e. g. how different tales and motifs can be combined into one, a fact which is well known to every student of popular traditions. The chief interest about this tale rests with the fact that we can watch the process before the different tales have become really melted together, and see how insignificant the connecting idea can be.

The Santal folk tales also throw some light on the process of Aryanization which has been going on through the ages, and which has melted the different Indian races and tribes together in a common civilization. We can to some extent trace some of its different stages.

We can see how the Santals have been influenced by the Aryans in numerous details. Wild animals usually retain their Santali names. Thus the jackal is called toyo, but when the

gender is to be indicated, we find the Aryan word aṇḍia used to indicate the male jackal, and when the Santal narrator wants to speak about the shrewdness of the jackal, he talks about sat siyaler budi, the wit of seven jackals, and uses Aryan words throughout.

Domesticated animals are also largely distinguished by means of indigenous words, but the cow is called gại, which is Aryan, and we should perhaps infer from this fact that the Santals did not originally keep cows. It is also characteristic that Aryan words are largely used in order to denote various things connected with the keeping and watching of domesticated animals. Thus we find goṛa, cattle-shed, sukri, pig-sty, (mẹrọm) gupi, (goat) herd, &c.

Aryan designations are also largely used about articles of food and dress; thus lạḍu, cake, miṭhại, sweets, dạl, beans, caole, rice, panahi, shoes, &c. It will be seen that we are mostly concerned with such objects as bear witness to a certain amount of civilization.

The Santals themselves are skillful at such work which they are accustomed to. Specialized crafts, however, do not seem to belong to them. The shoemaker, muci, the blacksmith, kamar, the carter, gaḍwan, are designated with Aryan words and do not belong to Santal society, which is not differentiated in this way. Also the names of many implements, such as bọtọl, bottle; basta, bag; sui, needle; loṭa, cup; ukhuṛ, mortar; churi, knife; lasẹr, razor, are of foreign origin.

In a similar way trade does not form a regular means of livelihood with the Santals. The trader is called bepari, and Aryan words such as mal, cij, asbab are used about different goods; the market is called bajar; depense is khorca, and even about the exchange of cows in order to cheat a person we find an Aryan term used. No wonder then that a word such as kiriń, to buy, is of Aryan origin. It has, however, been so thoroughly assimilated that it has given rise to new derivatives such as ạkriń, to sell; kikriń họṛ, a selling man, a seller.

Money has evidently been introduced from the Aryans, and several terms of calculation have the same origin. We find ṭaka, rupee; lekha, counting; mit́ hajar gan, one thousand in number, &c.

Also in the calculation of time the influence of Aryan civilization can be felt. Thus we find ghari, a while; tin din, three days; bar cando, two months; bo̱cho̱r purạukate, after a year, and more general terms such as cirokal, a long time; jive̱t bhor, lifelong; jaejug tire jug, for ever, &c. Even a designation of time with reference to the height of the sun such as bar ḍaṅ, two poles, contains an Aryan word for 'pole'.

That the various notions connected with administration and law are of foreign origin is only what we would expect. The complainant goes to the hạkim, to lodge a complaint, lạlis or, with a Santali infix lạḱlis; the judge considers, bicạr, the case and is therefore a biḱcar, and may give an order, hukum, or a decree, ḍigri, or he may dismiss, ḍhismis, the matter. He has at his disposal the police, pulis, messengers and peons, cạukidạr, sipạhi, do̱ro̱ga, &c.

The Santals themselves have their own village organization. Even here, however, we can trace the Aryan influence. The headman is designated as mạṅjhi, and the village council is evidently framed on Aryan patterns, the mõ̱ṛẽ̱ ho̱ṛ, the five men, being an adaptation of the pañcāyat of the Aryan villages.

Even the life in the house and the family shows traces of Aryan influence. The house itself, oṛaḱ, retains its old name, but it has been provided with a bhitạr, an inner appartment, and a door, duạr, and in the fire-place, culhạ, there may be coals, aṅgra. Near the village we further find tanks, pukhri, bande, and watering-places, daḱ ghaṭ, &c.

Even the terms of relationship are to a great extent of Aryan origin. A man takes a wife, bạhu, he has a nạihār or father-in law, and he may become a raṇḍi or widower. We hear of mama sạsur, uncles, and bhạgnạ, nephews, and strangers may

be of pọr jạt, lit. another caste. Even the father may be designated as janamdata, and the son as beṭa or as bacha, and the well-known word bhại, brother, is also met with.

We are expressly told that the Santals have a recollection of having abandoned many of their ancient customs at a certain time and place, after long deliberations, that is to say, they have themselves a vague notion of the fact that they are becoming more and more aryanized. And that such has been the case is, as we have already seen, evident enough. When we are told that a woman is never her own master, but the property of her father or brothers until she is married, that she then belongs to her husband and after his death to her son, we are faced with well-known Aryan notions, though the position of Santal women may have been similar in ancient times.

We arrive at the same conclusions when we examine the terms used about sentiment and human feelings. We hear about mãyã, affection, and daya, compassion, and when somebody has put me to shame it is said that he lajaokidiṅa.

Even the religious notions have not been proof against the Aryan pressure. The worship is still mainly directed towards the old boṅgas, but we also hear of bhuts and of higher gods such as Cando and Ṭhạkur, and the ancient Aryan idea of the jealousy of higher powers is known to the Santals, though here it is possible that the idea is old. Many of the sacrificial customs also make the impression of being Aryan or semi-Aryan, and when the women try to perform a sacrifice, they make themselves pujhạr or priests.

Altogether we can see how the Aryanization is steadily progressing, and it may be foreseen that the day will come when it has thoroughly refashioned Ṣantal society and partly also the mentality of the people. From the point of view of the comparative study of the development of eivilization the Santals of the present day are therefore of exceptional interest, and the folk tales here published offer a rare opportunity for observing the

laws regulating the interchange of conceptions and institutions between peoples on a different stage of civilization.

The time may soon have past for making such observations. The few examples which I have mentioned show that the changes which have already taken place are great and thorough-going. And even the language is, to a great extent, giving way.

We have already seen many examples of this. Numerous common words are borrowed from Aryan vernaculars, and their number is increasing. In a sentence like bicạr pạhiltalinpe, first decide between us two, only the final elements taliṅpe are Santali, the remainder being Aryan.

This sentence also shows how the foreign elements are assimilated. The vocabulary gives way, but the grammar remains, the new words being inflected according to Santali rules. Thus we find Aryan verbs conjugated in the Santali way, e. g. calak'-kan tahẹ̄kana, he was going; bujhạuket'a, he understood, where the bases cal and bujhạu are Aryan, but the terminations indigenous. In other cases Aryan nouns are inflected as verbs in accordance with Santali grammar, where practically every word can be used to denote the predicate. Thus bidạkaea, they sent him off, gave him permission to go; bạhuadea, gave him a wife, &c.

This state of things is of interest, because it shows how the process of Aryanizing un-Aryan languages has apparently always been going on in India. The ancient vocabulary is replaced by an Aryan one, but the grammatical principles of the old language assert themselves and give a peculiar shape to the resulting mixed tongue. In Saṅtali we can see this process going on before our eyes, and the comparative philologist will not fail to see the importance of this feature. He will bear it in mind where he is met with a similar state of things, mixed languages where the vocabulary points in one direction and the grammar in another. He will be inclined to think that the grammar belongs to the

old substratum and the vocabulary to a language which has been subsequently engrafted on the old stock.

There are no doubt some features which are apt to make us cautious in drawing such general conclusions. And such are also found in Santali. We find several Aryan postpositions such as lạgiṫ, for the sake of; ṭhen, at, with; sọṅgẹ, with; upạr, above. And more especially relative idioms seem to be gradually introduced, while relative constructions seem to have been usually expressed in a different way in the old language. Thus we find judi, if; jẹ mọn, so that; jāhānak̇ge jạruram, whatever is necessary for thee, &c.

Here we are met with an introduction of grammatical principles belonging to the language which is gradually superseding Santali, but they do not, in the same way, affect the grammatical framework as the ordinary terminations, and rather bear testimony to an increasing faculty of compound thinking than to a change in grammatical mentality.

That the latter one is still strongly Santali is evident in many ways. I shall only mention the curious use of the inclusive dual in threatening language. Thus we read amgelaṅ gọćmea, which apparently means 'I and thou shall kill thee'. Similarly we read in Nr. 22 that there lived a carpenter in a certain village, and then the story goes on: ar uṅkinren gidrạ dọ miṫtaṅ koṛa họpọne tahẹ̆kantạkina, and of them two a child a boy was of them, and they two, i. e. the carpenter and his wife, had a son.

Such passages are of interest because they throw light on the original meaning of the dual. It does not signify the number two, but one or two who necessarily belong together as a pair. The man who threatens another sees himself in the act which he is to perform as necessarily connected with the other one, and the man who has a son can only have him in necessary connexion with his wife.

The fact that the original significance of the dual is still strongly felt by the present day Santals, in spite of the Aryan admixture in their language, shows that their linguistic mentality is still strongly Santal. Nevertheless it is to be feared that Santali will some day cease to be a living language. Even at the present time most Santals are bilingual, and the Aryan influence will certainly make itself still more felt in future. The more thankful we must be to Mr. Bodding for making his rich treasure of genuine Santal folk tales available to us.

Sten Konow.

STORIES ABOUT JACKALS

1. Toyo ar haṛam buḍhi reaṅ.

Noa dǫ nonka leka kana. Sedae mare hapṛamkoko lại akat́a, adǫ cele nitre hǫ̃ inạ lẹbẹt́ lạṇḍhutege darabon kana. Adǫ onkoge oka dharare cǫṅ lẹg carko bandhaoket́, baṅdǫ duṛup̍kate baṅdǫ teṅgo-kate, jǫtǫak̍ge sire sire paṭhẹ paṭhẹko lẹg akat́ car akat́a. Gam, kạhni, kudum emanteak̍ko joṛao akat́a. Adǫ onkoak̍ sik bidiạtege nit hạbić menak̍ hataṛgea. Nit joṛao akat́ katha dǫ baṅ kana. Ar noko toyo emanteak̍ reak̍ katha hǫ̃ un jǫkhẹn reak̍ kangea. Adǫ ale Hǫṛ hǫpǫn lekha pǫṛha ma bale baḍae, ar nạthi sẹ puthi eman dǫ bạnuk̍talea. Adǫ ẹnre hǫ̃ cekakote cǫṅ nǫ̃k̍ǫ̃e menak̍getalea, baṅ at́ akantalea. Ar noa ǫlok̍ paṛhaok̍ ma neko Saheb hǫpǫn rakap̍kate sẹ noa disom dǫkhǫlkate Hǫṛ hǫpǫnko cet́ akawat́koa. Adǫ ẹnre hǫ̃ unạk̍ hǫṛ ǫlok̍·paṛhaok̍ko cet́ket́a. Adǫ ẹnre hǫ Hǫṛ hǫpǫnak̍ jug reak̍ katha nạthi dǫhǫkak̍ lagat́ dǫ ǫkǫe hǫ̃ baṅ sarbharaoet́koa. Ar iṅ hǫ̃ Sahebe ɲam kante mit́ bar kathaṅ khẹṛẹ khǫṛcẹ baṛakak̍

---

[1] This expression refers to a statement in the Santal traditions according to which their ancestors at a certain time and place, after having deliberated for either twelve years or twelve days — they profess not to remember which —, gave up old customs and settled new usages, many of them certainly under influence from Hindu custom. The traditions proper do not mention anything of the matters here referred to; but that is no hindrance to popular thought suggesting a similar origin to folktales.

[2] There may be one or two very small attempts made by Santals to put down in writing something of their old traditions; but it amounts to practically nothing, and this in spite of the really very extensive oral 'literature' which they have. When a Santal gets sufficiently educated to be able to undertake such a work, his interests are generally drawn elsewhere.

1. THE JACKAL AND HUSBAND AND WIFE.

THIS story is as follows. Our ancestors of old have told it, and now also we are, I presume, following in the same trodden path. In whichever manner our forefathers settled customs and usages, whether they did it sitting or standing[1], they have established and made customary all and everything, rules and forms. They have joined together the stories and tales, riddles and so on, and, being learnt as they have told them, these remain with us until this day. They are not stories which have been composed now-a-days. These stories about the jackals are also from that old time. We Santals do not know to read and write; and written sheets or books and the like we have none. Still, somehow or other, we have these stories, as it is seen; they have not been lost to us. These Sahebs have taught the Santals to read and write, after they arrived here or after they took possesion of the country. But in spite of so many people having learnt to read and write, still no one has felt impelled to make a record in writing of the old-times story of the Santals[2]. As regards myself, the Saheb[3] wants it done, so I am, without any form or method, putting down a few tales, otherwise who knows what I

[3] The Saheb is the present writer. The Santal (Sagram Murmu of Mohulpahari) who here introduces himself has been in the writer's employ for about thirty years, and this story was one of the first which he took down for me. This explains this introductory chapter. It might be noted that the word Saheb is, in these eastern parts, pronounced as here written, and not Sahib.

kana, ar baṅkhan ọkọe baḍae cọṅ. Adọ noa katha ḍher lacharte calaoena toyo reaǩbon lạiakorege. Ona dọ nonka kana.

Sedae jọkhẹn, kathae, miṫṭẹn koṛako bạhuadea. Adọ jọkhẹć jọkhẹćre unkin kuṛi koṛa dọ sẹ haṛam buḍhi dọ nạihạrkin hijuǩ sẹnoǩa. Miṫ din unkin dọ nạihạr khonkin hijuǩ kan tahẹ̃kana. Uni kuṛi dọ taben khạjạṛiko moṭra gọṫ akawadea. Ona dọ ńẹl danaram sandesko metaǩa. Ar sedae jọkhẹn sunum asẹn lagaṫ bọtọl cọlọn ma baṅ tahẹ̃kan; maejiuko lagaṫ dọ kupi sunum ar hẹrẹl họpọnko lagaṫ dọ maṫ ṭhoṅga, noakin cọlọn tahẹ̃kana. Ar nitkate dọ bọtọlko cọlọn akaṫa. Noa dọ saheb họpọn rakaṕkate cọlọn akana. Adọ ona kupi cukạǩ tahẹ̃kan jọkhẹć reaǩ katha kana noa dọ.

Adọ unre uni kuṛi dọ ona taben khạjạṛi moṭra dọe dipil akaṫa, ar kupi sunum cukạǩ dọe teweń akaṫa. Ar nạihạr khon jãwãe oṛaǩte sẹ uni koṛawaǩ oṛaǩtekin calaǩ kana. Unre koṛa dọ laha lahateye calaǩ kana ar kuṛi dọ tayọm tayọmte. Adọ miṫṭan tapọl ṭhen kuṛi dọe ãṛgo akan jọkhẹnge, kathae, bhut dọ oka sẹn khon cọe oḍok gọṫena, onka họṛ chin lekate, ar uni kuṛi tayọm tayọmtegeye sẹn idiǩ kana. Ar kuṛi dọe mẹneṫa, Okate cọṅ nui hõe calaǩ họṛ kangea cele. Onate ceṫ hõ bae metae kana ar bae kuli baṛayede kana. Ar bela dọ hạsuroǩ lagaṫ bar ḍaṅ gan menaea, inạ ọktẹ jọkhẹn.

4 It is in fact a roundabout way of telling the story. This introduction has been kept here, because it gives a good insight into the Santal mind.

5 Two different kinds of parched rice.

6 Oil, especially pressed from the seeds of Bassia latifolia, or from mustard and similar seeds, is much used to keep the skin smooth and is considered a necessity.

7 A kupi is a small earthenware receptacle for oil. Cukạǩ mentioned further on is about the same thing.

8 It has been and still is very common for men to carry oil with them in a bamboo-bottle, i. e., a bamboo-joint so cut that one partition 'wall' forms the bottom, while the other one is perforated, a wooden stopper being used for the small hole. Those carried about are generally quite small, others of the same pattern are used at home as receptacles for oil for any purpose. Sometimes Santals carry with them long bamboo sticks, the upper joint being used as an oil-bottle.

should have done. Now this was a rather roundabout way when we should tell about a jackal[4]. But the story is this way.

Once upon a time, in the old days, people tell, it happened that a young man had been married. From time to time these two, the boy and the girl, or to be correct, husband and wife, used to go visiting the wife's old home. One day they were on their way back from this place, and there they had given the girl some taben and khạjạṛi[5], which she had tied up in a cloth. This people call visitors' food-present. In the old days it was not the custom to carry oil about with oneself in a bottle[6]; for women it was the custom to use a kupi[7], a small bottle of earthenware, and for men a bamboo receptacle[8], these two. Now-a-days people have introduced the use of bottles; this has become the custom after the coming of the Sahebs. This tale refers to the time when the earthenware pot was in use.

At the time the girl was carrying the bundle with taben and khạjạṛi on her head, and the earthenware pot she was carrying in a string hanging down fom her hand. They were on their way to the husband's house, i. e. this young man's home. At the time the boy was walking in front and the girl after him[9]. Once, whilst the girl had gone down into a hollow in the ground, a bhut suddenly came out from somewhere, in the likeness of a human being, and commenced walking behind her. The girl thought by herself: "This is presumably also a man who is on his way somewhere." She did not say anything to him, and he did not ask her any question. The sun was near the horizon, about two poles up[10]; that was the time.

9 It is customary to walk one behind the other in Indian file. When the family is out, the husband generally, but not necessarily walks behind.

10 When the sun is near setting, i. e. after huḍiń dak lo ber, or after about 5 p. m., time is shown by saying, that the sun is one or more poles up. 'A pole' is about so high up as the sun is some fifteen minutes before sunset, two poles about, but perhaps not quite, half an hour before sunset. It might be noted that the sun is setting fairly vertically, not like in our northern latitudes.

Khange uni koṛa dọ cekakote cọe bẹṅgeṭ ruạṛleṭ dọe ńẹlkede dọ, ać bạhu tayọm tayọmte mit họṛe calak̕ kan. Khangeye teṅgoyena. Adọ jẹmọn uni koṛae teṅgoyena, tẹmọn khange bhut dọ uni kuṛiye ọr ruạṛede kana. Khange uni koṛa dọ ṭheṅga epelkateye ńir hẹć gọṭena. Are ruheṭ gọṭkedea, Ińren họṛ ceṭ iạtem jọṭẹṭkedea? Nitgelaṅ dal gọć utạrmea.

Adọ bhute mẹnkeṭa, Nui ma ińren họṛ kane, ar am mam pẹṛa họṛ kan. Onate am ma lahatem calak̕ kan, nui mam bạgiae kan. Judi amren họṛe tahẹntam khan, bam sotok̕kea? Ńẹlme, iń dọ ińren họṛ iạteń sotok̕ akadegea. Adọ ọr baṅkhan iń cekayea? Am dọ okate cọm calak̕ kan, do calak̕me. Nui dọ iń oṛak̕teń idiye lagaṭ.

Adọ onka menkate koṛa hõ miṭ ti sopoye saṗ akadea ar nui bhut hõ miṭ ti sopoye saṗ akadea. Uni hõ ọntẹye ọre kana, nui hõ nọtẹye ọre kana. Adọ un jọkhẹn uni kuṛi dọe họhọkeṭa, Dela baba, họrtenko birtenko, jãhãe menak̕pe khan, hijuk̕te dok̕kaṅpe, ar baṅkhan iń dọkin ciṛạ jọmeń kana.

Adọ un jọkhẹnge, kathae, toyo dọ oka sẹn cọṅ ạtińe calak̕ kan tahẽkana. Adọ uniye họhọkeṭ khan, ona ańjọmte toyo dọe ńir hẹć gọṭena. Adọe mẹn gọṭkeṭa, Cedak̕, cedak̕, cedak̕pe ṭana ṭạnik̕ kana?

Adọ uni họṛ koṛae mẹn gọṭkeṭa, Nui kuṛi dọe iń bạhu kana, iń orak̕teń idiyede kana, nạihạr khonliń hijuk̕ kana. Adọ nui iạ sala dọ oka khoṅ cọe oḍok gọṭente iń bạhu dọe ọr ruạṛede kana.

Khange uni bhute mẹn gọṭkeṭa, Baṅa, nui kuṛi dọe iń bạhu kana, ona iạte iń dọ nui sotok̕kateń hijuk̕ kana, baṅ bạgiae kana. Ar nui iạ salage ạliń laha lahate okate cọe calak̕ kan tahẽkan. Adọ ạlińe ńẹlkeṭliń khan dọ, ṭheṅga epelkateye ńir hẹć gọṭena, adọ ińe dhomkaoediń kana. Ar iń bạhu sopore saṗkateye ọre kana. Adọ cak̕ iń idi ocoaea? Adọ niạ karọntegele ṭana ṭạnik̕ kana.

---

11 When using threatening language about doing something or other to the one spoken to, it is very common to use the inclusive dual form and not the singular.

12 The word translated 'stranger' may mean a relative or a friend. The meaning here seems to be a stranger, but of the Santal race.

Then the young man somehow or other happened to look round and saw a man was coming along walking behind his wife. Then he stopped; but just as the young man stopped, at the same moment the bhut caught hold of the girl and pulled her backwards. The young man then ran up to them, brandishing his stick. "Why did you touch my wife?" he scolded him. "Now this moment we two[11] shall thrash the life out of you entirely."

"Why, this is my wife," the bhut said, "and you are a stranger[12]. That is why you are walking on in front and are leaving this one behind. If she were your wife, would you not follow and look after her? Look, because she is my wife, I am following and looking after her. Then, have I not the right to take hold of her, or how? You go wherever you are going to. I am taking her to my house."

During this talk the young man had taken a firm hold of one hand, and the bhut had done the same with the other hand of the girl. The young man was pulling her in one direction, and the bhut in the other direction. Just at that time the girl called out: "Come, sirs, wayfarers, forest-dwellers, any one who may be near here, come and rescue me; else they are tearing me to pieces and will finish me."

At that time, people tell, a jackal was on his way somewhere to seek food. When the girl called out, the jackal heard it, came running to the spot at once, and said: "Why, why, why are you at variance?"

The young man then spoke out: "This girl is my wife; I am taking her home; we are coming from her parents' home. This unspeakable villain came out from who knows where and is pulling her back."

"Not at all," the bhut then said, "this girl is my wife; therefore I am taking her along, following after her; I am not leaving her behind. And this unspeakable villain was walking in front of us two, who knows whereto; then, when he saw us, he came running up to us, brandishing his stick, and he is using threats towards me. He has caught hold of my wife's hand and is pulling at her. Why should I let him take her away? This is what we are at variance for.

Adǫ khange toyoe mẹnkeťa, Hapẹ, alope ṭana ṭạnika, bicạrlegebon. Adǫ uni toyoe bujhạukeťa, miť dǫe bhut kana mẹnte. Khange toyo dǫ kuṛiye mẹtadea, Ona tire dǫ ceťem teweṅ akaťa? Dẹsẹṅ ṅẹltama. Adǫe emadea. Toyo dǫ ona kupi reaǩ sunume dul giḍikaťte cukạǩ dǫ kuṛigeye emadea. Adǫ toyoe mẹnkeťa, Jãhãege noa cukạǩreben bǫlǫ daṛeaǩ, inige nui kuṛi dǫe hataoyea; ar ǫkǫe bae bǫlǫ daṛeaǩ hǫṛ dǫ bae ṅamea.

Khange bhut dǫe mẹn gǫťkeťa, Acha besge. Dẹ ho, tǫbẹ bǫlǫǩtalaṅme.

Adǫ uni hǫṛ koṛa dǫe mẹnkeťa, Ǫhǫṅ bǫlǫlena.

Ar uni bhut dǫ phuc manteye bǫlǫ gǫťena. Adǫ jẹmǫne bǫlǫ gǫťlena, tẹmǫngekin kilạp ẹsẹť gǫťkedea. Are metaťkina, Noa cukạǩ dǫ aloben idia, nǫṇḍẹ baṛẹ giḍikaben.

Adǫ sạri ǫṇḍẹgekin bạgiaťte ạkin dǫkin calaoena. Adǫ pharak ṅǫ̃ǩ sẹnkate toyokin hǫhǫadete tabenkin emadea.

Adǫ ẹnẹ nią katha hǫ̃ṅ mucạťkeťa.

2. Toyo ar tạrup̣ reaṅ.

Sedae jǫkhẹn, kathae, miťṭan birre tạrup̣ ạḍiye caṅkelen tahẽkana, metaǩme gại ḳaḍa, mẹrǫm bhiḍi, sẹ hǫṛ hõe jǫmeťko tahẽkana. Nonka lekate ạḍi bạṛiće caṅkelen tahẽkana, jãhãege bir bǫlǫ akan sẹye ạtkir gǫťeťko tahẽkana. Iną dhara dhạririen hǫṛ saname bẹrǫstǫ cabakeťkoa, Ar uni gǫje reaǩ ạḍi lekako upạikeťa, mẹnkhan oka lekate hǫ̃ bako dhẹj daṛeae kana. Ḍher hǫṛko sẹnlen khan ṃa ṅamge bako ṅame. Ar miť bar hǫṛ ona bir sẹnko sẹnlen khan, mae kuṭuṅ gǫťkako kana.

Khange adǫ iną dhara dhạririen hǫṛ jarwakateko rǫṛ ṭhikkeťa, Ma arhǫ̃ hǫṛbo lạiakoa, Nui tạrup̣ dǫbon sendra gǫjea, ar baṅkhan

1 It might be mentioned that leopards are very common in the forests of the country where the Santals live.

2 The proceedings mentioned are as the writer has known such to happen. Some villages join together to get rid of a dangerous animal. The proposal to cut down the forest would not, however, be feasible at the present day.

"Please wait," the jackal said, "do not fight one another. Let us first investigate the case." Now the jackal understood that one was a bhut. So he said to the girl: "What is it you have there hanging down from your hand? Please, let me have a look at what you have." She gave it to him, and the jackal poured out the oil that was in the kupi and gave the pot back to the girl. Thereupon the jackal said: "That one of you two who can enter into this pot, he shall have this girl; the one who cannot do that, he shall not have her."

"All right," the bhut said at once; "now then, get in for us."

"I shall never get into that," the young man said.

Then the bhut entered with a swish, and the moment he got in, they at once closed the mouth of the pot and shut the bhut up. And the jackal said to them: "Don't take this pot along with you; throw it away here."

They did so and left it there and went their way. When they were some distance off, they called the jackal and gave him taben.

So there now, I have finished this story also.

2. THE JACKAL AND THE LEOPARD.

Once upon a time in the old days, people tell, a leopard[1] had been haunting a forest, that is, he was eating cows and buffaloes, goats and sheep, and people also. In this way he had become very ravenous; if anybody went into the forest, he would at once carry them off. The people in the vicinity, all of them, he had frightened out of their wits. They planned and tried in many ways to kill him, but were utterly unable to manage it. If many people went in search of him, then, of course, they did not find him. And if one or two went to the forest, then he, of course, carried them off at once.

So the people of the neighbourhood came together[2] and, after some discussion, agreed to the following: "Let us inform people that we are going to kill this leopard, or else, that we shall cut the trees

noa birgebon mak̕ ṭạṇḍi utạra. Adọ nonkako sọlhaket̕teko ḍhạrwạk̕ket̕a, baṅma, Nią phalna din hilok̕ noa birbon sendraea, tạrup̕bon gọjea, ar baṅkhan birgebon mak̕ ujạṛte nui tạrup̕ dọbon laga ṅirea.

Adọ sạri inạ neṇḍa din hilok̕ dọ uḍi utạr phạdko jarwayena. Ar aema ṭamakko jarwaket̕a, arko ruyet̕a, cet̕ baṅ sẹ, ona reak̕ saḍete ọt ulṭạuk̕ leka ạikạuena. Khange ona saḍe aṅjọmte uni tạrup̕ dọe bọtọrente ona bir khon ṅir oḍokente eṭak̕ birteye ucạṛok̕ kan tahẽkana. Nonka ać mọnreye hudisana, Noko họṛ din hilok̕ ma bako sendrayiṅ, ẹken teheṅ mọtọge thọ. Acha, teheṅ din dọ jãhã dosra birteṅ sa hataṛlenge. Adọ okareko ṅameṅteko gọjeṅa? Arhõ gapa dọṅ hẹćkenge. Adọ onka mẹn baṛakateye ucạṛok̕ kan tahẽkana.

Adọ ona bir tala talate dọ mit̕ṭaṅ ḍahar sẹn akana, ar ona ḍahartege ẹn hilok̕ dọ bepari chala ḍaṅgrawanteko calak̕ kan tahẽkana. Adọ jẹmọn nui hõ bọtọrte noa bir khone ucạṛok̕ kan tahẽkana, tẹmọnge onko bepari họṛ tuluće ṅapam gọt̕ena. Khange adọe metat̕koa, Ią ho, bepari họṛ, mit̕ kathaṅ metape kana. Judi iṅak̕ kathape aṅjọmletiṅ khan, ar ona kathape dọhọletiṅ khan, jaejug hạbić reak̕ apeak̕ suk hoeyok̕tapea. Ar bape aṅjọmtiṅ khan, ar ona katha bape dọhọetiṅ khan, apeak̕ dọ ạḍi bạṛić harkhet hoeyok̕tapea. Ẹnte iṅ ma noa birren raj kanaṅ, baḍaepe. Tin dhao iṅ ṅampea, uṇ dhaoge ḍaṅgraṅ jọmkotapea.

Khange adọko metadea, Acha besge, masẹ ẹnte rọṛlem cet̕ lekan katha kantama. Adọle aṅjọmle nạhĩ jãhãṭak̕ dọle rọra.

---

3 When a day for a public function has been fixed, people are notified as described. Somebody is sent with a branch of the sal-tree (Shorea robusta, Gaertn.) to the market-places or similar public places where many people meet, sometimes with a drum. The branch has so many leaves as there are days left before the gathering takes place. This way of notifying may be seen every year in connexion with the tribal hunts. It might be noted that something similar is used to keep count of the occurrence of family gatherings, especially marriages. Here a string is sent to every family invited to be present, with as many knots tied on each as there are days before the celebration. The families untie one knot every evening. When all knots have been removed, the day has arrived.

4 The drums used are what the Santals call ṭamak, a kettle-drum made of iron covered with leather. It is used for making noise and for signalling, also sometimes in connexion with dances. It is a hunting and war-drum. It makes a

down and clear the forest entirely." After having decided on this they sent the branch[3] round with this notice: "On such and such a day we are to hunt in this forest. We must kill the leopard, or else we shall have to cut the forest down to drive this leopard away."

On the day fixed an immense crowd came together. They brought a lot of drums together and were drumming, you can scarcely imagine what a noise; at the din of it it was felt as if the ground were turning upside down[4]. When the leopard heard this noise, he was frightened and ran out of this forest to move over into another. He was thinking by himself: "These people will not hunt me every day; it is surely only to-day. All right, to-day I shall take myself off to some other forest, in the meantime. Then, where will they find me and kill me? To-morrow I shall be coming back." Thinking thus he was on his way to another place.

Now a road is running through the middle of that forest, and that very day traders with their beasts of burden were passing along that road, and just as the leopard, in fear, was moving out of the forest, at that moment he ran across the traders. Then he spoke to them: "I say, you traders, I have one thing to say to you: if you listen to what I have to say and do as I tell you, there will be no end to the happiness you will get. But if you don't listen to me and will not do as I tell you, you will get into awful trouble. For know this, I am the king of this forest[5]. So often as I meet you, every time I shall eat your bullocks."

"All right," they said to him, "speak then and let us first hear what it is you have to say. Only when we have heard that, can we say anything."

---

tremendous noise. When a party like that one here described has a number of drums beaten, it may be heard some five-six kilometres away. It is a terrible din which leaves no room for anything else.

5 It is common in Santali to speak of leopards, and, of course, tigers when such are there, as b u r u r a j, i. e., mountain king. They are lording it and are subject to none. Sometimes expressions are used which might seem to imply that these 'kings' are masters only within certain circumscribed spheres, something like what the leopard here, hints at.

Adǫ unreye mẹnkeťa, Iạ ho, katha dǫ noa kana: teheń dǫ ińko gǫjeń lagať hǫṛko jarwa akana. Ǫtẹ ṭamakko ruyeť kan. Adǫ sendrakate ińko gǫjeń lagať. Adǫ onateń nẹhõrape kana sẹń metape kana, teheń din noko sendra hǫṛ khonpe bańcaolíń khan, ạḍi boge hoekokťapea. Dayakate mage oko bańcaokań tabonpe. Niạ noako bosta reak̉ mal dǫ uṗ giḍikape, ar ińge ona bostare bhorao okokańpe. Adǫ noko sendra hǫṛko parǫm calaolen khan, raṛakańpe. Katha dǫ niạge.

Adǫ khange onko bepari hǫṛko cepeť baṛayenteko mẹnkeťa, Acha besge, ạikạ noa katha jaejug tire juge tahẹntabo ma. Siń kan ńindạ kan, hijuk̉ale sẹnok̉ale, ạikạ nae baṛẹ napae baṛẹ hoeyok̉tale ma; ḍańgra sẹ hǫṛ alom jǫmlea.

Adǫe mẹnkeťa, Hẽ ho ẹnte, ǫnẹ cǫń iń ma lahareń lạiaťpege. Adǫ nonkan muhim khonpe bańcaolíń khan, noa reak̉ cedak̉ gun bạń manaoa? Do, noa dǫ cirokal napaege tahẹntabona. Jãhã tinạk̉ ńũt ńindạpe hijuk̉ sẹnok̉, iń reak̉ dǫ alogepe bǫtǫrok̉a.

Adǫ onkako kiriạ baṛayen khan, kathae, miťṭań bosta reak̉ malko uṗ giḍikaťa, adǫ ona bostare uni ṭạruṗko bǫlǫ ocokedeteko tǫl ẹsẹťkedea, ar chala ḍańgrareko ladekedea. Ar ḍańgrako lagakeťkote ona bir khon dǫko parǫmkedea. Ar onko sendra phạd hõ bako ńam daṛeadete apan ạpin akoak̉ oṛak̉koteko ruạr calaoena.

Adǫ un jǫkhẹnko lạiae kana, bańma, Ona bir khon dǫle parǫm ạgukeťmete eṭak̉ birbon tiok̉ akaťa. Ar onko am sesendrako hõko ruạṛ caba baṛayena, miť hǫṛ gan hõ bạnuk̉koa.

Adǫ khange ṭạruṗe mẹnkeťa, Tǫbẹ khan ma nẹṇḍẹge raṛakańtabonpe. Adǫ khańge bhạgteko raṛa lede ńamlede uni ṭạruṗ dǫe rǫṛ gǫťkeťa, Nit mape bańcaokadiń, jǫm aḍopeań. Ḍańgra hõń jǫmkotapea, ar ape hõń jǫmpegea. Onka adǫe bǫrǫ ocokeťkoa.

[6] There are stories about people going for certain purposes being thought secure against attacks from animals. One of this kind will be translated below.

Then the leopard said: "I say, you good people, it is this: to-day people have come together to kill me. Listen, they are beating the drums: they are hunting and want to kill me. Therefore I implore you, or rather I tell you, if you to-day rescue me from these hunting people, it will be a very good thing for you. Please show kindness and hide and save me. Throw out the goods you have in one of these bags, and then put me into that bag and hide me. When these hunting people have passed away, you may let me out. That is all."

The traders then took counsel together and said: "All right, but understand this: this agreement shall remain between us for ever and always. By day and by night we the traders shall go and come, mind you, no accident or injury shall happen to us. Do not eat our bullocks or our men."

"Yes, surely," he replied, "that is just what I told you beforehand. And if you save me from such a danger, why should I not show my gratitude for it? Be sure, this shall be kept unbroken for all ages between us. Let it be the darkest possible night when you go and come; do not be afraid of me[6] at all."

When they had sworn in this way, they threw the goods out of a bag and let the leopard enter into it and tied him well up, whereupon they loaded him on a pack-bullock, drove the bullocks along and brought the leopard past the forest. The army of hunters, thus, were not able to find him, so they returned home, every one to his own house.

After this they spoke to the leopard saying: "We have now brought you past that forest and have reached another, and those who were hunting for you have also all returned home; there is not a single one left."

"Then let me out here," the leopard said. No sooner had they let him out and set him free than the leopard said: "Now you have saved me, to be sure; I shall eat you in return. I shall eat your bullocks, and you also I shall eat." In this way he frightened them.

Adǫ onko hoṛko mẹnkeťa, Acha besge, jǫmlegeam. Hapẹ tǫbẹ khan noa reaǩbon bicạr ocolege. Judi onko biǩcạr hoṛko hukumle khan, jǫmlem baṛẹ, onate jãhãn hat aḍ dǫ bạnuǩtalea.

Adǫ tạruṗe mẹnkeťa, Acha besge. Ǫkǫe ṭhenpe bicạr ocoea? Delabo idibonpe.

Adǫ inạkore hoṛ ma bako ńẹloǩ kan. Adǫ matkǫm dareko ńẹl ńamkeťa. Adǫko mẹnkeťa, Acha, delabo ona darebo bicạr ocoyea. Adǫ kathae, ona dare ṭhen calaoenteko metae kana, Ią dare, bicạrkatalem. Nui tạruṗ dǫko gǫje kan tahẽkana, adǫ unrele bańcaokedete hõ bań? Ar nit dǫe metale kana, Jǫm aḍopegeań. Pạhil dǫe mẹnkeťa, Nią muhim khonpe bańcaolińkhan dǫ, ǫhǫń jǫmpea; ar nit dǫe metale kana, Jǫmpegeań. Adǫ dẹsẹ bhala noage bicạrkatalem.

Khange dareye mẹn gǫťkeťa, Jǫmreye jǫmpea. Ape manwa jạt dǫ ạḍipe kharapgea. Dare umulre hõpe duṛuṗa, ar dare hõpe maǩaǩa, ar rẹhẹť hõpe maǩaǩa, onate khạṭigeye jǫmpegea.

Khange tạruṗe mẹnkeťa, Ǫtẹ cǫń bicạren, jǫmpegeań.

Adǫ onko hoṛko mẹnkeťa, Hapẹ, ar bar ṭhenbo bicạr ocolege. Adǫ ǫṇḍẹ hõ nonkage hukum hoelen khan, jǫmlem baṛẹ.

Adǫ tạruṗe mẹnkeťa, Acha besge, delabon ạyurbonpe.

Adǫ miťṭań darhako ńẹl ńamkeťa. Adǫko mẹnkeťa, Delabon ona darha daǩbon bicạr ocoyea. Adǫ ǫṇḍẹ sẹnkateko metae kana, Ią darha, bicạrkatalem. Nui tạruṗ dǫko gǫje kan tahẽkana, unreye metaťlea, Noa muhim khonpe bańcaolińkhan dǫ, ǫhǫń jǫmpea. Adǫle bańcaokedete hõ bań? Adǫe metale kana, Jǫm aḍopeań. Adǫ dẹsẹ bhala bicạrkatalem.

[7] The Bassia latifolia, Roxb., a large and very common tree, in Santali called matkom. Here a Hindi name is used, the one commonly used in official documents. The flowers which fall down during the early hours at blossoming time (the commencement of the hot season) are collected and dried and used for sundry purposes, as food for men and cattle, and to distil liquor from. The fruit is eaten, and the kernel is used for pressing oil. It is a most useful tree.

"Very well," they said, "you will eat us surely. But wait then, we must first get somebody to judge in this matter. If the judges pass such an order, please eat us, we shall take no shelter then."

"All right," the leopard said. "With whom are you going to seek judgement? Come, take us all there."

No one was to be seen there in the vicinity. Then they saw a mahua[7] tree and said: "Well, let us ask that tree[8] to judge." Whereupon they went to that tree and said to it: "Look here, you tree, judge in our case. They were trying to kill this leopard. Then we saved him, don't you see? But now he says to us: I shall eat you in return. At first he said: If you save me from this danger, I shall never eat you. And now he says to us: I shall eat you surely; so now, please, judge this matter of ours."

"He shall certainly eat you," the tree said at once. "You human beings are very wicked. You sit in the shadow af a tree, and a tree you also use the axe on, and the roots also you use the axe on. Therefore he shall surely eat you."

"Listen," the leopard said, "listen, there judgement was passed. I shall eat you."

"Wait," the traders said, "let us hear judgement from two more. If there also the same order is passed, please eat us."

"All right," the leopard said, "come along, lead us on."

They next caught sight of a water-pool and said: "Come, let us ask that water-pool to judge." So they went there and said to the water-pool: "Listen, you water-pool, judge in our case. They were trying to kill this leopard. At that time he said to us: If you save me from this danger, I shall surely not eat you. Then we saved him, don't you see? But he says to us: I shall eat you in return. So now please judge our case."

---

[8] It might be noted that trees and other objects may be quoted by Santals as witnesses, or rather, appealed to.

Adọ darhae mẹnkeṭa, Jọmreye jọmpea. Ape manwa jạt dọ ạḍipe kharapgea. Ńẹlpe, iń dọ ńũ hõpe ńũń kana, ar ić hõpe ạbukań kana, onate khạṭigeye jọmpegea.

Adọ tạrupe mẹnkeṭa Ọtẹ cọń, bar ṭhen ma bicạren. Jọmpegeań.

Adọ un khange onko bepari họṛ dọko lukuṭ lukudok kana. Mẹneṭako, Durrẹ! nãhãk khạṭigeye jọmbongea. Arhõko mẹneṭa, Acha, jãhãnakge hoyoktabon, miṭ ṭhenbo bicạr ocolege.

Adọ tạrupe mẹnkeṭa, Acha besge, dela idibonpe.

Adọ calak calakte miṭṭań toyoko ńẹl tiokkedea. Adọko mẹnkeṭa, Acha, delabo uni toyobo bicạr ocolege. Adọ judi uni hõ nonkageye hukumae khan, cetbo mẹnkea? Nonka hudiskate bẹbhọrsakateko calak kana. Adọ tiok ńõkkede khanko họhọadea, Ẹ ho, hapẹ teṅgolenme, miṭṭań bicạrkatalem.

Khangeye teṅgoyena; adọe kuliketkoa, Masẹ lạipe, cetpe bicạr ocok lagaṭ. Onkae kuliyetkoa, ar mẽṭãhã sẹne bẹṅgẹṭ rakapako kan dọ, sanamge ạḍitẹṭ bạpuṛić mẽṭãhãko ńẹlok kan.

Adọ bọtọr bọtọrteko rọṛkeṭa, Nui tạrup dọko gọje kan tahẽkana, adọ unreye metatlea, Dẹ nịạ muhim khon bańcaokańpe. Judi nịạ dhaope bańcaolin khan, ńindạ ńutạ hijuk sẹnok tisre hõ ọhọń jọmpea. Nonka kiriạkate bosta reak mal gidikatte nuigele bhorao okokedea. Onko sendra họṛko ruạṛen khan dọ bosta khonle raṛakadea, arle metạdea, Ma nit dọ sẹnjońme. Adọ khangeye metale kana, Uh! nit mape bańcaokidiń, jọm ạḍopegeań. Adọ dẹ bhala, noage bicạrkatalem. Bańcaokedete hõ bań? Arhõ alegeye jọmle lagaṭ. Ninạkgea kathatale dọ.

Khange toyo dọ tạrupe kulikedea, Cele ho, katha dọ onka leka kana sẹ cet leka? Bańkhanem mẹnkea, Iń dọ miṭ katha gan

---

[9] Santals, after a call of nature, always wash themselves using the left hand, which for this reason must not be used for anything in connexion with food, saluting, handing anything to others, and so on. The left hand is, on this account, often called ić ti, the excrement hand. It might be noted that the Santal ojhas (medicine-men) use their left hand when applying medicine externally, probably to have the right hand undefiled, although the reason given is that the right hand is not propitious for such work.

"He shall certainly eat you," the water-pool said. "You human beings are very wicked. See, me you drink, and me you also use for washing yourself[9] when you have gone to stool. Therefore he shall surely eat you."

"Listen," the leopard said, "listen, at two places judgement has been passed. I shall eat you."

From then the traders were trembling with fear saying: "Alas, in a moment he will surely eat us." Again they said: "Very well, whatever will be our fate, we shall first hear judgement at one place more."

"All right," the leopard said, "come, take us along."

As they were walking along, they caught sight of a jackal and said: "Well then, come let us ask the jackal to judge. If he also passes him such an order, what can we say?" Thinking so and quite without hope, they walked on. When they came near to him, they called out to him: "Hey you there, wait, stop a moment, there is a matter we want you to judge for us."

The jackal stopped and asked them: "Please then, tell what is it you want to have passed judgement on?" As he asked them this and looked up into their faces, he saw that all of them were looking utterly downcast.

Speaking in fear and trembling they said: "This leopard, — they were trying to kill him; then he said to us: Do save me from this danger. If you save me this time, at night and in darkness, when you come and go, I shall not eat you, no, never at all. After he had sworn in this way, we threw away the goods we had in a bag, put him in and hid him. When the hunters had returned home, we released him, and let him out of the bag and said to him: Please now go your way. Then he says to us: Ho, now you have saved me; I shall eat you in return, surely. Do, please, pass judgement in this case for us. We saved him also, don't you see? Now he is on the point of eating us. That is all there is to our case."

Then the jackal asked the leopard: "I say, sir, is the case like that or how? Otherwise, you might say: He did not ask me one

hõ bae kulilidiña. Onateñ kuliyetmea. Ma lạime sẹ, katha dọ enka kangea?

Adọ uni tạrupe mẹnketa, Baña, katha dọ enka kangea.

Adọ noko họṛe kuliyetkoa, Henda baba, oko ma okogepe lạiyet kan, adọ onage thọ bañ bujhạuettapea. Cet lekape okoledea? Udukañpe, iñ mẹtteñ ñẹllege, tọbẹ nạhĩ ṭhik dọñ bicạra.

Adọko metae kana, Bostarele bhorao okoledea.

Arhõ tạrupe kuli gọtkedea, Sạri ho, bostareko bhoraoletmea?

Adọe mẹnketa, Hẽ sạrige.

Adọ onko hoṛe metako kana, Masẹ udukañpe, cet lekaledeape. Onako jọtọge udukañpe.

Khange mit hoṛ dọe bujhạu ṭhik gọtketteye mẹn gọtketa, Dela hijukmeñ okolemge. Khange uni tạrup dọ bostareye bọlọyen khan, uni hoṛ dọ khub lekae tọl urićkedea, are mẹnketa, Nõkõe nonkale okoledea ar ḍañgrarele lade ạgu akadea.

Adọ toyoe mẹnketa, Acha besge. Hapẹ, bes ọkọćte ạri bạndhiñ ñẹllege. Adọ un jọkhẹn uniye bujhạu ñõkket hoṛe isạrat gọtadea. Khange uni hoṛ dọ marañ utạr dhiri hare phareye dipil ạgu gọt-ketté ẹkkalte bọhọkregeye giḍi gọtadea. Adọ jọtọ hoṛte tiñko tiñkedea dọ, ẹkkalteko tiñ gọć utạrkedea.

Khange toyo dọ onko hoṛe metatkoa, Ñẹlketape? Iñ iạte bañkhan nui nimukharami hoṛ dọe jọmkepegea. Adọ unạkpe dayawade reak gun dọ okortae? Iñ alo khan hutẹć khạṭigeye jọmkepegea.

Adọ unreko mẹnketa, Hẽ baba, boge Cando lekam hẹćen, bañkhan sạri utạrgeye jọmkelegea, ona reak digdhạdọ bañ kana.

Adọ noa katha hõ cabayena.

single word. Therefore I am asking you. Please say, is the case like that?"

"Quite so," the leopard answered, "the case is exactly like that."

Then the jackal asked the traders: "I say, sirs, you mention hiding; now that is what I do not quite understand in what you tell. In which way did you hide him? Show it to me. I must see it with my own eyes, then only I shall be able to judge properly."

"We put him into a bag and hid him," they replied.

Again he asked the leopard: "Is that so, sir? Did they put you into a bag?"

"Yes," he replied, "that is what they did."

Then he said to the traders: "Please show me how you treated him. Show me all of it."

One of the men suddenly saw what he was driving at and said: "Come here, let me hide you." When the leopard had entered into the bag, the man tied him up as tightly as he could, and said: "Look here, in this way we hid him and brought him along, loaded on a bullock."

"Very well then," the jackal said, "let me first have a good look and note everything carefully." At the same time he made a sign to the man who had understood what he was driving at, and this man at once fetched a huge stone, carrying it on his head, and straight away threw it at his head. Thereupon all of them started stoning the leopard and stoned him to death then and there.

The jackal then said to the traders: "Do you see? I helped you, otherwise this ungrateful person would have eaten you. Why, where was his gratitude that you had shown him so much kindness? If I had not been here, he would certainly have eaten you."

"Yes, sir," the traders said, "it was fortunate you came like Chando, otherwise he would surely indeed have eaten us; there is no doubt about that."

So this story is also ended.

3. Toyo reak̕ khisạ.

Mit̕ṭaṅ hǫṛ ạkin apa hǫnkin tapamlena. Adǫ haṛamge bae daṛelena, ota ocoyenae. Adǫ bhala uni dǫ koṛa hǫṛ ar nui dǫ haṛam hǫṛ, koṛa tuluć dǫ cak̕e daṛek̕a? Adǫ bae daṛelente haṛam dǫ bicạr ocoe lagat̕ hǫṛe lại baṛawat̕koa. Adǫko metadea, Acha, ma sẹn laha hataṛok̕me, uni koṛa lại hataṛaeme, jẹmǫn jãhãte aloe calak̕. Ma nãhãk̕ ale dǫle calak̕ kana. Adǫ enka mẹnkate uni dǫko kol laha gǫtk̕adea.

Adǫ oṛak̕re sẹnkate uni haṛam dǫ hǫpǫntẹt̕ koṛae metae kana, Iạ ya phalna, lạiam kanaṅ jãhãtem sẹn bǫtẹćkok̕a, alom calak̕a. Ǫnẹ holam ota akadiṅ, ona galmarao ocoko lagat̕ hǫṛ iṅ rak̕ akawat̕koa. Nitgeko hijuk̕ lagat̕, onateṅ lại lahawam kana.

Adǫ unre koṛae mẹnket̕a, Henda baba, alaṅ apa hǫnlaṅ tapamena, adǫ cedak̕ mõṛẽ hǫṛ ṭhen dǫm lạlisket̕a? Onko ma nãhãk̕ alaṅgeko jǫmlaṅa. Alaṅ eskarte dǫ hutẹć ǫhǫlaṅ jutlea?

Adǫ haṛame mẹnket̕a, Ǫkǫ baḍae, jutkok̕ cǫṅ baṅ cǫṅ. Ạḍi ãṭem kurudadiṅte ạḍi bạṛićem otakidiṅa, ona tẹṛǫṅ mõṛẽ hǫṛ ṭhen dǫṅ lạlisket̕a, ar baṅkhan hutẹć cak̕ iṅ lạlisa? Adǫ jage mõṛẽ hǫṛ nisạpre hoyok̕ kan, onalaṅ aṅjǫmlege.

Adǫ koṛae mẹnket̕a, Iạ ba, iṅ mit̕ kathaṅ metam kana, aṅjǫmtiṅme baṛẹ. Iṅ dǫ bạṛtiṅ dǫs akat̕a: holanak̕ edre ma teheṅ dǫ kusiạ̃ dal daleṅme. Onate dǫ cet̕ hõ ǫhǫṅ metama ar baṅ dal ruạṛmea. Ẹnteṅ bujket̕a, hola dǫ bẹbujkate am janamdata hǫṛ iṅ

1 The introduction to this story is an example of how the Santal folktales may be told, and the rôle they may play in the life of the people.

2 The proceedings here described are a good example of how the village council is appealed to and called together. The complainant goes to the village headman, who sends his g o ḍ e t or messenger to call the village people. The council is a kind of court of arbitration.

3 'So and so', in Santali p h a l n a, means that the name of the person in question is used.

4 'To eat one' is a very common expression about doing anything in excess, taking too much, and so on. It is very frequently used about destruction supposed to be caused by bongas or witches. Here the meaning is, that the village council will fine and otherwise make these two pay more than they can afford.

3. THE ASTUTENESS OF THE JACKAL[1].

Two men, father and son, had been fighting with each other, and the old man did not get the better of it, he was thrown down and pressed against the ground. No wonder, the one was a young man and the other an old man, how should he be able to get the better of it with a young man? As it went this way with him, the old man told the village people of it, to get them to judge in the matter. They told him: "Very well, you go home in the meantime and tell the boy, so that he does not go anywhere. We are coming presently." With these words they sent him home in advance[2].

When he reached home, the old man spoke to the boy: "I say, so and so[3], I tell you — you might go somewhere, — don't go. That which happened yesterday when you threw me down, — I have appealed to the village people and asked them to talk the matter over. They are coming just now; therefore I am telling you this beforehand."

Then the young man said: "Look here, father, we two, father and son, had a fight; why should you complain to the village council? They will presently devour[4] both of us. Should we not be able to settle this matter between ourselves, we two alone?"

"Who knows," the old man said, "whether that would do or not. You showed an awful anger and pressed me to the ground something terrible; therefore I have complained to the village people; otherwise, why should I complain? Whatever it may come to in the estimation of the Five, that we shall pay heed to."

"I say, governor," the young man replied, "I have one word to say to you; please listen to me. I am most at fault; in return for yesterday's anger please give me to-day a beating to your heart's content. I shall not say a word to you and I shall not strike back, because I have understood that yesterday I very wickedly laid hands on you, who have given me life; that is my

jǫtǫť gǫťketmea, noa dǫ iṅak bhul kạmi kana. Adǫ enka rǫṛ sãotege haṛamak jaṅgae sap̣kedeteye nẹhõradea are mẹnketa, Baba, ikạkaṅme, ạḍi utạr iṅ dǫs akata.

Adǫ haṛame dayayenteye mẹnketa, Beṭa, nẹhõrenteyem ikạkam kanaṅ. Ar iṅ metam kana, adǫ tisre hõ nonka haṛam hǫṛ sẹ buḍhi hǫṛ sǫṅgẹ dǫ alope ṭhǫka ar alope dabaokoa. Ẹnte onko dǫ ako lagaṫ dǫ bako rǫṛa, ape hǫpǫnko lạgiṫge. Ar ape hǫpǫnko dǫ ạgu pichu bape bujhạute haṛam hǫṛ sẹ buḍhi hǫṛ dǫpe dabao gǫťeťkoa arpe kãṛgo gǫťeťkoa. Adǫ teheṅ khon onkan cǫlǫn dǫ bạgime. Adǫ mõṛẽ hǫṛ iṅ rak akawaťkoa, adǫ khạṭige nãhãkko hijuka. Adǫ un jǫkhẹn am dǫ oṛak bhitri khonge alom oḍokoka, hǫhǫam khan dǫ gǫṅ dǫ gǫṅkom, mẹnkhan alom oḍokoka. Ar jãhãnakko kulime khan, ceť hõ alom lạiakoa. Adǫ enkae sikhạu baṛakadea, adǫkin thir baṛayena.

Adǫ inạ miť ghạṛi khange atoren hǫṛ dǫko hẹć jarwayena, adǫ besge duṛup̣ teṅgone metaťkoa. Duṛup̣ jarwa baṛayenako. Adǫko kupuli baṛayena, Cele ho, jǫtǫbon hẹć cabayena sẹ baṅ?

Adǫko mẹnketa, Hẹ̃, jǫtǫbon jarwa ṭhik baṛayena cele. Adǫ dẹsẹ bhala nui phalna haṛam kuliyetabonpe ceťko lagaťe doať delawaťbona. Adǫ uni khon oṛ babon ṅamle hǫtẹte dǫ, oka lekabon katha oco daṛeaka? Adǫ uni haṛamko kulikedea, Dẹsẹ baba, am phalna, ceťko lagaťem dela jarwaketlea? Ma duk suk dǫ lạialeme.

Adǫ uni haṛame mẹnketa, Ǫnẹ cǫṅ, baba mõṛẽ hǫṛ, iṅ ma enaṅre cǫṅ jǫtǫ kathaṅ lại caba akawaťpe, inạkoge cele katha dǫ.

Khange onkoko mẹnketa, Koṛa dǫ okare menaea?

Adǫe metaťkoa, Oṛakrege menaeả, ǫnẹ enaṅpe mẹn gǫťadiṅte okate hõ baṅ sẹn ǫco akawadea. Adǫ ma apege hǫhǫaepe.

---

5 Also among the Santals it is very common that a person appealing to the mercy and kindness of somebody catches hold of this one's feet, and does not let go until he has got what he wants.

6 i. e. the village council.

7 The whole shows the loose and free manner of getting along. Anyone who feels enough interested may take the lead, always provided that he acts in accordance with the sense of the whole company.

8 He addresses the council as 'father': they represent society.

wrongdoing." As he spoke thus he caught hold of the old man's feet[5] and implored him. "Father," he said, "forgive me, I have sinned very much."

The old man felt pity and said: "Son, you have asked for mercy, so I forgive you. But I tell you this, never at all quarrel in such a way with an old man or an old woman, and don't illtreat them. Because they do not act for themselves, it is you children they are acting for. And as you children do not understand the ins and outs of things, you illtreat the old people, your parents, and bear them down. Quit such behaviour from to-day. Now I have appealed to the Five[6], and they will be sure to come presently. But when they are here, don't you come out from the house; when they call out to you, answer them, but don't come out. And if they ask you any question, do not tell them anything." In this way he instructed him, whereupon they did not say anything more.

A short while afterwards the village people came together, and the old man very politely asked them to sit down. They found seats and then asked one another: "Well, how is it, have we come all of us or how?"

"Yes," they said, "we have all come together all right. Well then, please ask this so and so[3] old man for us for what purpose he has called on us and asked us to come[7]. If we do not hear from him what it really is, how should we be able to take the matter up?" So they asked the old man: "Well then, sir, you so and so, for what purpose is it that you have called us together? Please tell us what is the matter."

The old man replied: "Well look, respected[8] Five, a short while ago this morning I have told you all and everything; that is what there is to it."

"Where is the boy?" the people asked.

"He is at home," he replied; "in accordance with what you told me this morning, I have not let him go away anywhere. Please, you call him."

Adǫko hǫhǫae kana. Khange gǫṅ dǫe gǫṅet́kogea, adǫ oḍok thǫ bae oḍokoḱ kana. Pę pon dhaoko hǫhǫket́re hõ, jǫnǫmge bae oḍoklena. Adǫ haṛamgeko metadea, Ale hǫhǫte dǫ bae oḍokoḱ kana. Ma am baṛę hǫhǫaeme.

Adǫ uni haṛame bǫlǫyena, adǫ cet́ko cǫkin galmarao baṛaket́. Adǫ oḍokkate mõṛẽ hǫṛe metako kana, Ią baba mõṛẽ hǫṛ, cet́ bape galmarao? Ęn kathae onako dǫ jǫtǫliṅ jutket́a. Ma nią dhao dǫ ruąṛjoṅpe; arhõ judiye onkaket́a męnkhan, unre dǫ baṅtęt́gebon bągiaea, ękkaltebon saṕ ḍhumbąḱ utąrea. Ma nią dhao dǫbon ikąkaea.

Adǫ unre mõṛẽ hǫṛ toyo reaḱ khisąko rǫṛket́a. Ona dǫ nonka kana:

Mit́ṭaṅ toyo ąṇḍią hõe rąṇḍi akan tahẽkana ar mit́ṭaṅ toyo eṅga hõe rąṇḍi akan tahẽkana. Adǫ unkin rąṇḍi rąṇḍikinge mit́ din dǫ ątiṅ ątiṅtekin ńapamena. Adǫ khangekin ąkinena. Adǫ unrekin galmaraojoṅ kana, Nit ma alaṅgelaṅ haṛam buḍhiyena. Adǫ hapęn cekalekate gidrą dǫlaṅ ąsulkoa? Adǫ budi balaṅ khaṭaole khan, alaṅ hõ cekate balaṅ ąsuloḱ?

Adǫ unre, kathae, uni ąṇḍią toyo dǫe rǫṛ gǫt́ket́a, Uh! cekate hale balaṅ ąsuloḱa? Iṅ ṭhen dǫ barǫ bhąri sę barǫ gąḍi budi menaḱtiṅa, unąḱre hõ balaṅ ąsuloḱa? Albǫt jąnićlaṅ ąsuloḱgea. Acha, am dǫ tinąḱ budi menaḱtama?

Khange uni eṅga toyo dǫe męnket́a, Iṅ dǫ tinąḱ baṅ menaḱtiṅ? Iną aṛaḱ sit́ ṭuṅkite mit́ ṭuṅki budi menaḱtiṅa.

Adǫ kathae, inąkin galmarao jǫkhęnge tąruṕteko sę tąruṕ tuluć dǫkin ńapam gǫt́ena. Khange, kathae, uni tąruṕ dǫe rǫṛ gǫt́ket́a, Hẽ, teheṅ dǫṅ ńam ąkat́bena. Khange, kathae, unkin dǫ uṛić hǫpǫn lekakin dupąi dupąiyena. Arhõ uni ąṇḍią dǫ ḍhertęt́geye dupąi-

---

[9] The basket here mentioned, in Santąli ṭuṅki, is a small basket with a comparatively narrow mouth, used especially by women for collecting pot-herbs in. The Santals make very extensive use of wild vegetables, leaves, &c. to prepare their curry.

[10] The uṛić is a small bird which plays a rôle in giving omens in certain circumstances.

So they called him, and he answered them, but out he did not come. They called him three or four times; still he did not come out at all. So they said to the old man: "It is of no use, he will not come out at our calling him. Please you call him."

The old man then entered the house, and they had some talk together. When he came out, the old man said to the Five: "I say, respected Five, what is there to talk about? What I spoke to you about this morning, we have settled between us; so this time please go back home. If he should another time attempt the same, then we shall not let him off; we shall catch him at once and bring him to his bearings. Well, this time we shall leave him alone."

Then the Five mentioned the astuteness of the jackal. The story is as follows:

A male jackal had become a widower, and a female jackal had also become a widow. Then it happened one day that these two, the widow and the widower, met whilst they were out seeking food, and they became a pair. Thereupon they were talking together: "Now we two have become husband and wife. How shall we in future be able to support our children? If we two do not use our wits, how should we also be able to support ourselves?"

Then, they tell, the male jackal said: "Ho, how should not we be able to support ourselves? I have myself wit, twelve cartloads or twelve carriages full, with so much should we two not be able to support ourselves? We shall likely be able to support ourselves, I suppose. Well, how much wit have you?"

"I," the she-jackal replied, "how much should I have? If you measure by the basket[9] used for gathering pot-herbs in, I have one basketful of wit."

Whilst they were talking together, they suddenly met a leopard. "Yes," he said, "to-day I have found you two." And those two were trembling like youngs of the urić bird[10]. The male jackal was especially afraid and trembling, his hind-quarters were

yena, linḍhi dǫ bhukuć bhukućentaea, ar rǫṛ hõ bǫtǫrte aṭ́ utạrentakina, ẹkkaltekin kẹklẹsẹṭ́ utạrena.

Adǫ kathae, uni tạrup̣geye rǫṛ saḍeketa. Metaṭ́kinae, Ceṭ́ben galmaraojoṅ kan tahẽkana?

Khange uni ạṇḍiạ dǫ kaṇṭa sudhạ rǫhǫṛentaete bae rǫṛ daṛeata. Adǫ uni eṅgageye rǫṛ gǫṭ́keta, Iạ mama sạsur, nui dǫ tin anẹć cǫe rǫṛ. Noaliṅ galmaraojoṅ kan tahẽkana, ạliṅren dǫ mǫ̃ṛẽ gǫṭẹn hǫpǫn menaḱkotaliṅa. Adǫ din hiloḱ onageliṅ jhogṛaḱ kana. Adǫ onko gidrạgeliṅ rẹpẹć kana. Iṅ dǫṅ mẹneta, Peaṅ hataokoa, am dǫ bareage; ẹnte iṅ dǫṅ nunu baṛa akaṭ́koa. Ar ać dǫe mẹneta, Iṅge pea dǫ, am dǫ bareagelaṅ emama. Nonka dingeliṅ jhogṛaḱa. Ar teheṅ hõ onageliṅ rǫpǫṛ kan jǫkhẹnge nẽḱẽbon ṅapamen. Adǫ mama sạsur, bhagebon ṅapamena; dela am baṛẹ hạṭiṅ oṭokakotaliṅme.

Adǫ ona katha aṅjǫmte uni tạrup̣ dǫ ạḍiye rạskạyena. Mǫnẹ mǫnẹteye mẹnketa, Ho, khub nãhãḱ iṅ besoḱa. Nikin barea ar enko hǫpǫn mǫ̃ṛẽ gǫṭẹn, khub nãhãḱ iṅ jǫm biḱa. Adǫ onkae hudis baṛakeṭ́ khan dǫe mẹn gǫṭ́keta, Acha besge, okare menaḱkotabena? Delabon idiṅben, hạṭiṅkakotabenaṅ.

Adǫ uni eṅgae mẹnketa, Delaliṅ idimea, hana bhugạḱre menaḱkotaliṅa.

Khangekin laha gǫṭ́entekin ạyur idikedea. Adǫ bhạgte ona bhugạḱkin tioḱkẹ̄ta. Uni ạṇḍiạ dǫ hare phareye bǫlǫ gǫṭ́ena are gampatao gǫṭ́ena. Ar uni eṅga dǫ duạr ṭhengeye duṛup̣ akana.

---

[11] All Santals when living in the same village or having anything to do with one another will, if they are not related, construct an artifical relationship with each other. They say it is especially to avoid having to use the proper names in adressing people. Very likely they feel the necessity of belonging to one large family in their daily life. It is their way of visualizing society. They will also enter into the same kind of artificial relationship with others, non-Santals, when living in more or less close contact with them. Probably the supposed necessity for themselves makes them imagine that also the animals of the forest feel it the same way. The relationship generally mentioned in the folktales as existing between animals of different kinds is that between a person and his mother's brother or sister, in Santali m a m ǫ b h ạ g n ạ. Such relatives are always treating

quivering, and out of fear they both lost the power of speech; they became utterly numbed with fright.

Then the leopard spoke and said to them: "What were you two talking together?"

Even the throat of the he-jackal had become dry, so he could not utter a word; the she-jackal then said: "I say, uncle[11], who knows how long a time it will take him here to speak. We were talking about this: we have five young ones, and we are every day quarrelling over them, who of us is to have them. I say: I shall take three, you take two, because I have suckled them. And he himself says: I take the three, and to you we shall give two. In this way we quarrel every day. To-day also we were having words on this subject, and just at that moment we met with you. Well, uncle, it was fortunate we met. Come along, you please divide our young ones between us."

When the leopard heard this, he became very glad. He was saying to himself: "Ho, I shall do exceedingly well presently; these two and those five young ones — I shall presently be well satisfied." Thinking this he said: "All right then, where have you got them? Come along, take me there; I shall divide them for you."

"Come along," the she-jackal said, "we shall take you there. We have them in that cave over there."

The two jackals went in front and led the leopard along. Fortunately the jackals reached the cave; the he-jackal hurriedly entered and rolled over like dead, and the she-jackal was sitting at the door, the leopard also sitting near by. As a long time

---

each other with the greatest respect; anything unseemly between them would be punished with great severity, in certain cases outcasting from Santal society. According to Santal standards, such people cannot intermarry. As is only natural, the bigger, and consequently more dangerous animal is represented as the maternal uncle and the weaker one as the nephew, bhạgnạ. The she-jackal here addresses the leopard as her maternal uncle-father-in-law. The Santals are always very exact in their relationship appellations, having a very large number of such.

Ar uni tạruṗ hō̃ inạ phẹḍregeye duṛuṗ akana. Adọ ḍher hạbić hoeyen khan, eṅga dọe họhọ saḍeketʼa, Okor, tinrem ạguyetʼkoa? Tin hạbićliṅ duṛuṗkokʼa?

Adọ bhitri khonge uni ạṇḍiạ dọe rọṛ gọtʼketʼa, Bogeteko hamal kana, eskarte baṅ idi daṛeako kana. Dela hijukʼme, bana họṛtelaṅ idi họtʼkoa.

Adọ eṅgae rọṛ gọtʼketʼa, Ọtẹ, mama sạsur, hamal iạte eskarte dọ bae ạgu daṛeako kana. Bọlọlengeṅ, inạ dọ bana họṛte hare phareliṅ hẹo oḍok gọtʼkoa.

Adọ tạruṗe mẹnketʼa, Acha besge, ma hako pako ạgu họtʼkoben. Adọ mọnẹ mọnẹte uni tạruṗ dọe mẹnjoṅ kana, Bọlọkʼ jọkhẹn nāhākʼ ẹkkalteṅ gẹr gọdea, baṅkhan nāhākʼ bana họṛkin bọlọ adokʼ kana. Adọ uni toyo eṅga hō̃e budi gọtʼketʼa. Bọlọkʼ jọkhẹn dọ pạclạteye bọlọkʼ kana, liṇḍhigeye lahaketʼtaea. Adọ un jọkhẹn uni tạruṗ dọe rọṛ gọtʼketʼa, Oe oe, oe ki?

Khange toyo eṅgae mẹn gọtʼketʼa, Ọh, mama sạsurke pand dekhabo.

Khange ẹnẹ ini hō̃e bọlọyen dọe bọlọ gusạuena. Khange tạruṗ dọe họhọketʼa, Okor? Tinreben ạguyetʼkoa?

Adọ uni eṅgageye mẹn ruạṛadea, Iạ mama sạsur, ạliṅtegeliṅ hạṭiṅketʼkoa. Iṅ dọ peae emadiṅa, ać dọ bareae hataoketʼkina. Onate baliṅ idiyetʼkoa.

Khange uni tạruṗ dọ ạḍi bạṛiće edreyena. Mẹnketʼae, Lahare hutẹć nonkaṅ baḍaele khan, unrege bana họṛ iṅ jọmkekina. Adọ bhugạkʼtekin bọlọyen khan, cetʼ iṅ cekaea? Ar noa bhugạkʼre iṅ ma baṅ sahọṗ kan, ar baṅkhan nıtge bọlọkateṅ gẹr gọćkekina. Adọ bhugạkʼkoe raḅoṛ baṛaketʼa, ọṅ baṛaketʼkinae. Adọ oka lekate hō̃ bae ạt daṛeatʼkin khan dọe calao dorokʼena.

Adọ baba mō̃ṛẽ họṛ, masẹ bujtabonpe, nukin toyo sikketʼbonakin. Pạhil dọ abo mō̃ṛẽ họṛ ṭhenkin lạiketʼa. Adọ ona katha aṅjom-

[12] The leopard is here introduced as speaking a low kind of Bengali. Especially the jackal is often made to speak either Bengali or Hindi. Here it is only this remark and its answer which is in a foreign language.

passed without their hearing anything, the she-jackal called out: "What's the matter? when are you bringing them? How long are we to sit here?"

The he-jackal then answered from inside: "They are so very heavy, I am not able to carry them out alone. Come, then we shall help each other to take them out."

"You heard, uncle," the she-jackal said, "they are so heavy, he is unable to bring them out alone. Let me get in first, then we shall help each other and carry them out in a moment."

"All right," the leopard replied, "be quick and bring them then." But in his mind the leopard was saying to himself: "When she is entering, I shall at once bite her; otherwise both of them will enter and be lost to me." The she-jackal also used her wits; when she entered, she did it moving backwards, she let her hind-quarters get in first. Then the leopard called out: "Was, was, was ist das[12]?"

The she-jackal then said: "Oh, ich wünsche nur dem Oheim Achtung zu zeigen."

In this way she also got in and out of the way, whereupon the leopard called out: "What is the matter? When are you bringing them?"

"O uncle," the she-jackal answered him, "we have divided them ourselves; he gave me three, and he himself took two. Therefore we are not taking them out."

The leopard now became awfully angry and said: "If I had known anything like this beforehand, I should have eaten both those at once. As they have entered this hole, what can I do? I am too big to get into this hole, else I should enter this instant and bite and kill them." He used his claws on the hole, he hissed at them; but as he could not in any way get at them, he had to go away.

Now, respected Five, please see how these two treated us just like the jackals did the leopard[13]. First they complained to us,

katebon mẹnkeťa, Khubbon ḍaṇḍọmkina. Adọ nọ̃kõebon jarwayen khan dọ unkin toyo leka kathakin miťkeťa. Adọ okorbon dhẹj daṛeaťa? Niạgeko metaǩa, baṅma, Sat siyạler budi, caṇḍbọltegeko ẹǩṛẹa. Adọ nẹ̃ǩẹ̃ caṇḍbọlte bakin ẹṛẹ lipuǩkeťbona? Masẹ bhala uni tạruṗ leka ceťbon cekaea? Inạ miť ṭuṅki buditege un maraṅ dusmạn gẹgẹr janwarkin bhagaokedea.

Adọ ạkin haṛam buḍhikin galmaraojoṅ kana. Eṅgae mẹneťa, Am dọ barọ gạḍi budi dọ nahakgem lạia. Okor jojaolentama? Nahakge hutẹnem jọm ocokelaṅa. Iṅaǩ budi aloṅ oḍokle khan dọ khạṭigeye jọmkelaṅgea. Adọ iṅaǩ budi iạte bana họṛ iṅ baclaokeťlaṅa.

Adọ nukin apa họn hǭ nãhãǩ onka lekakin galmaraojoṅa.

Ar noa kathate abo hǭ miťṭaṅ nomonabon ceťjoṅ kana. Mẹnako, baṅma, Aimạiren jhin dọbon hẹrẹl kana. Jhin jãhã sẹngem ọr, ọntẹge sadọm dọko ạcuroǩa. Sẹ jãhã sẹntege sui parọmoǩ, enkatege sutạm hǭ parọmoǩ kana. Sẹ ạimạI dọ ḍhertẹť dundhibon metako kana. Adọ masẹ bujpe, jọtọ ạimạI dọ bako dundhia. Miť bar dọ bickom hẹrẹl khon hǭ upạrge budi menaǩtakoa. Hẹrẹl họpọn bọrọṅko latar ocoǩ kangea. Ọkọe mẹn sikte ma hẹrẹl họpọn dọ leṅga ti śẹnreko dọhọyeťkoa. Ar niạ miťṭen bujhạupe sẹ, ṭạṇḍire tahẽkan bhorgem mẹneťa, Iṅaǩ cas. Oṛaǩrem aderkeť khan ma ạimạiaǩ cij hoeyentae. Am mam seta baragen. Tinrebo lẹh-ako kana, un utạr jọm dọko ṅameťa. Tọbẹ abo hǭ onkage.

---

13 The story is nearly ended and someone of the village council makes the application.

14 Here the end comes, or, it may be, an addition.

15 The Santal writer gives vent to some opinions of his own, a side-application which did not interest the village council. The position of women among the Santals is theoretically low, see the introductory remarks to the stories about women, below. *De facto* the Santal women have a fairly good and strong position.

16 Especially the last proverb is very commonly heard when a man is told to consult his wife about any matter. He is naturally the lord and absolute ruler.

17 Before eating the Santals will always wash their hands. They do not use spoons or forks or knives, but only their right hand, in all cases when the food is not quite liquid. Then they eat with a 'spoon' made of a leaf.

the village council, and when we had heard the case, we said we should fine them heavily. But see, as soon as we came together, they just like the jackals found something and agreed on that. Then how could we manage? This is what people say: The wit of seven jackals — they take people in by their tail. Did not these two now take us in by their tail? Like that leopard, what shall we do? By the help of that one small basketful of wit those two got the better of such a big dangerous biting animal.

Now those two, husband and wife, were talking together[14]. The she-jackal said: "It is to no purpose your talking about twelve cartloads of wit. Why, what did it help you? For nothing you would have let us both be eaten. If I had not brought my wit out, he would certainly have eaten us both. By my wit I saved us both."

And these two, father and son, will also now talk together in the same way.

This story has something to teach also us[15]. People say: We men are the women's bridle. To whichever side you pull the bridle, to that side the horse will turn. Or, the way the needle goes that way also the thread follows[16]. Or, we men mostly call the women silly. Be sure, all women are not silly. A few of them have intelligence superior even to that of men. The men are rather worsted. In accordance with what some say they put the men to the left. And keep this one thing in mind: As long as the crops are in the field, you say 'my crop'. As soon as you take it into the house, it becomes the woman's goods. You become like a dog. When you call them, then only they get their food. It is just the same with us. When the women pour out water for us[17], then only we get food. Am I then not right

---

The Santali writer rather overdoes the thing. It might be remarked that a woman, who gives birth to girls only, is sometimes said to be a mother of dogs.

These personal remarks of the Santali writer have been retained, because they show how a story told reacts on the minds of the people. A folktale very frequently gives rise to discussions or preachings of a similar kind.

Tinre dak̕ko taṅabon kana, un ut̤ar jom dobo ńamet̕a. Ado kajege babon seta baragena? Ado amak̕ tahentam khan, am sana leka bam jomkea? Ado okorbon daṛeak̕ kana? Ado ona ịate ạimại hõ alope nĩhạt ut̤arkoa. Adom adom ạimại do herel khon bạṛtige bud menak̕takoa.

Ma nui toyo reak̕ kạhni bujhạujoṅpe. Ạimại reak̕ budte bana hoṛe rukhiạket̕kina, baṅkhan huten bana hoṛe jom dorok̕kekina.

Ado nia kạhni doń mucạt̕ket̕a.

4. Toyo bicạr.

Sedaere mit̕t̤aṅ raje tahẽkana, ar uniren mit̕ gọṭeć koṛa gidrại tahẽkantaea. Khange uni gidrại hara ar bud akelen khan, mit̕ din doać apate galmaraoae kana, Ią beṭa, jãhã hilok̕ iṅiṅ goćlen khan do, am do maraṅ hoṛ tuluć baṛe hirlạk̕me; maraṅ hoṛ tuluć hirlạk̕ do bogegea.

Ado tinạk̕ din tayomte coṅ apat hõe goćena. Ado uni koṛa do aće hirlạk̕ lạgit̕ hapṛak̕ hoṛe ńam baṛayet̕koa. Ado khange ona takre mit̕t̤aṅ raj pạlkiteko gok̕ ạguyede kan tahẽkanre khen leka mit̕t̤aṅ toyo leṅga pahṭa khon jojom pahṭate onko lahareye ńir paromena. Raj uni toyoye ńelkede khan, aćak̕ pạlki khon ãṛgo got̕ente uni toyo seć samaṅkate bogeteye salam salamket̕a, jemon oka kạmi lạgit̕e calak̕ kan, ona jemon purạuk̕tae ma; ona ńutumteye salam got̕adea.

Ado khange uni koṛa do uni raj reak̕ dosa mucạt̕ dhạbić tan mane ńelkedea. Ar aćak̕ monereyo menket̕a, Dhorage nui toyo do jạnić maraṅ hudạren kanae, onatege raj hõ raje salamadea.

---

1 Up to not very many years ago the most common way of travelling was to go in a palanquin. The most ordinary form is a box with a curved roof and one opening on each side, which can be shut by sliding panels. It is just long enough for a grown-up person to lie down in, and high enough to sit in without bending; it is carried by generally four persons, two in front and two behind, by the help of two poles, fixed one in front and the other behind. The carriers, often of a certain Hindu caste, generally make use of a kind of sing-song to regulate the stepping, as they carry the palanquin along.

in saying we are like the dogs? If it remained yours, could you not eat at your pleasure? But when are we able to do so? Therefore, do not utterly despise the women. Some women have more intelligence than men.

Understand the story of this jackal. The woman's wit rescued both of them; otherwise, he would have eaten both of them, what could they have done?

So I have finished this story.

4. JACKAL JUDGEMENT.

In the old days there was a king, who had one only son. When that child had grown up and reached the age of sense and discretion, his father one day talked to him saying: "I say, my son, when, some day, I am dead, then find refuge and protection with some big man; it is good to seek protection with such."

Some time afterwards the father died, and the boy commenced to look for great people to seek protection. At that time it so happened, whilst they were carrying a king along in a palanquin [1], that a jackal accidentally ran across the road in front of them, from the left to the right side[2]. When the king saw the jackal, he at once got out of his palanquin, turned towards the jackal and saluted again and again, in order that the business he was out on might prosper and be accomplished. This was why he saluted him.

The boy was looking intently at the king, what he was doing, until it was all finished; then he said to himself: "Surely, this jackal must likely be one in high authority; therefore, even the king[3] saluted him." Having come to this conclusion, the boy

---

[2] If a jackal crosses the road as described, it is considered a bad omen. If e. g. this happens when they are going to arrange some of the preliminaries of a marriage, they will return, and may even give the whole up.

[3] What is here called a king, must not be taken as something necessarily very grand. Any landlord is called a raj, i. e. a king.

Ona niṭante uni koṛa dǫ raje salamadea, ar uni toyogeye pańjakedea. Ar pańja pańjate mit́ṭań bhugąk̓reye pańja aderkedea. Ar uni koṛa hǫ̃ ona bhugąk̓ ṭhengeye duṛuṕena. Ar uni toyoren eṅga hǫpǫn sanamge ona bhugąk̓reko tahẹ̃kana.

Ar bąrsiń pẹ māhāe hǫrhǫket́ko khan, eṅga hǫpǫn kąumąu bogeteko garjaoket́a. Ar hǫpǫn māyāte eṅga ąṇḍiąkin niṭket́a, Ma jāhā lekatelań bidąkaea. Adǫ niṭket́te mit́ṭań gąikin emadea. Adǫ uni gąi reak̓ gun dǫ nonka tahẹ̃kantaea, jāhānak̓gem kǫeye, onageye ulą toda. Uni gąikin emadea, arkin metadea, Ma nui gąiliń emam kana, idijońme; ar jāhānak̓ge jąruṛam, onage kǫeyeme.

Ar uni koṛa dǫ uni gąigeye idikedea. Calak̓ calak̓te mit́ṭań bande tiok̓ket́a, ar rẹṅgẹćkedete ǫṇḍẹge gąi hǫ̃ dak̓e ąńūadea ar ać hǫ̃e dąṭąuniyena. Ar thąri bąṭiko pąhil dǫe kǫekedea; inąkate jǫl pan hǫ̃e kǫekedea. Inąko jǫm baṛakate adǫe kǫekedea caole, dął, buluń sunum ar jǫtǫ jąruṛ jinis cet́ko ać jǫm sanakedea, ona dǫ jǫtǫe kǫekedea.

Ona takre mẹnkhan mit́ṭań maejiu dak̓teye sẹnlen tahẹ̃kana. Ar uni maejiu dǫ ẹtǫhǫṕ khon tan mane ńẹńẹl kan tahẹ̃kana. Sanam onakoe ńẹl mucąt́ket́kin khan, hako pako oṛak̓te ruąṛ sẹnente aćren jāwāetẹt́ jǫtǫ sǫmbate ląiadea. Are metadea, Do calak̓me, jāhā lekate ẹṛẹ ąguyem baṛẹ uni gąi dǫ.

Khan uni jāwāetẹt́ dǫ hako pako ńir sẹn gǫt́ente uni koṛae metadea, Ią ho, peṛa hǫṛ, alom calak̓a nitok̓ dǫ, ẹnte tala birregem ńindąk̓a nāhāk̓, ar bir hǫ̃ ąḍi bagahi akana. Dela

---

4 In Santali eṅga hǫn means 'mother and son', the expression here used eṅga hǫpǫn, lit. 'mother-child' means the whole family, husband included. It is just mentioned here, as it might point towards a former state of matriarchate. It should, however, be noted that other traces are not found among the Santals, but much which points the other way. The whole Santal society is founded on the superiority of man over woman.

5 The climate makes it most desirable, not to say necessary, to have sufficient water, also for bathing purposes, more especially during the hot season. To store water, excavations are made, the 'holes' being square or rectangular in shape. The earth is thrown up on the sides, the embankments being planted with trees,

saluted the king and followed after the jackal. He kept on following him, until he saw him enter a cave, whereupon the boy himself sat down near the entrance. The whole family[4] of the jackal was in that cave.

When the boy had remained watching them for two or three days, the mother and the young ones commenced to howl and cry, and out of compassion with their young ones the jackals, father and mother, determined that, somehow or other, they would send him off. And having determined this, they gave him a cow, and this cow had such a quality: whatever you might ask her for, that she would bring forth out of her mouth. They gave him this cow and said: "See, we are giving you this cow; take her along with you, and whatever you need, ask her for that."

The boy then took the cow with him. As he was walking along, he came to a tank[5], and as he felt hungry, he gave the cow to drink and he himself also cleaned his teeth[6]. First he asked the cow for a brass plate and cup; thereupon he asked her for light refreshments, and having eaten this, he asked her for rice, beans, salt, oil and all other things; whatever he wanted to eat, all that he asked her for.

Just at that time a woman had gone down to the water, and she had from the very first been looking intently on. When she had seen it all, she hurried back home and told her husband everything and said to him: "Do go, under some pretext or other, bring that cow here."

Her husband then at once ran as quickly as he could and said to the boy: "I say, my friend, don't start now; you will in that case be in the middle of the forest by midnight; the forest is also much infested with wild animals. Come back and turn in

especially palm-trees, as the leaves of these do not fall down and rot in the water. Such is the 'tank' found where the country is flat. The size varies very much, some may be small, others may be large, up to an acre or even more. A very common size in the Santal country is something like a fifth to

ruạṛme ale ţhenge, gitić ţhại hǒle emama nãhăk. Adǫe ruạṛ ạgukedea.

Ar ạyup̣en khane metadea, Ma gại dǫ goṛa duạrre tǫlkaeme, ar am dǫ noa piṇḍạte hijukme. Ạḍi noa disom dǫ bǫtǫrgea.

Adǫ sạrige gại dǫ goṛa duạrreye tǫlkadea, ar ać dǫ piṇḍạreye giticena. Ar ạḍi ghạṛi emanteak galmaraoteye bodhao akadea. Ar ona tayǫm ạḍi ăţ dudṛumkedete khube jạpitketa. Ona takre uni hǫṛ dǫ uni gại raṛa ạgukedete aćren gạiko tulućе aderkadea goṛare, ar aćren gại tiạk oḍokkedete ǫṇḍẹye tǫlkadea.

Khan adǫ aṅgayen khan, uni koṛa dǫ gạiye ńẹlkedea, aćren dǫe baṅ kan. Adǫe mẹneta, Henda ho, cedak gại dǫm bǫdǫladiṅa?

Adǫ uni hǫṛe rǫṛ ruạṛadea, Okor baṅ, okareṅ bǫdǫl akawatme? Amge cǫm tǫl akade. Bejãe iṅ dǫ amren gại lạgit iṅ rẹṅgẹjok kan! Iṅren bam ńẹletkotiṅa mit goṛa gại?

Arhǒ uni koṛae rǫṛ ruạṛ gǫtadea, Mit goṛa maṅ ńẹletkotamge, ar onko ma baṅ kǫeyetme; ẹkẹn iṅ dǫ iṅren iṅ ńam kana.

Khange adǫ onka onkate kạphạriạukin sạrdiketa. Khange adǫ ona atoren hǫṛko metatkina, Aloben kạphạriạuka. Bana hǫṛge hǫṛ jarwajoṅben, ǫkǫeko abenren gạiko ńẹl akatko. Ar uni koṛa hǒko metadea, Am hǒ uni gại okarem ńam akadea, onko hǫṛ baṛe ạgukom. Adǫko nẹṇḍaketa. Ar uni koṛa dǫ toyo ţhene sẹnena, ar aćak sanam ḍuke lạiatkina.

Aṛ neṇḍa din sẹţẹren khan, uni koṛa dǫ toyoe ạgukedea; banarge eṅga ạṇḍiạkin hẹćena. Ar uni dosarić dǫ khub moṭa moṭa raj hǫṛkoe bạnijketkoa, ar jǫtǫ hǫṛ ţakae ematkoa, jẹmǫn ać sẹćge sanam hǫṛko rǫṛ. Khange adǫ sạlisko duṛup̣ena.

---

an eigth of an acre. The tanks are generally individual undertakings, but are sometimes given over to public use. Some people wish, in such a way, to make themselves a name to be remembered, or to do something meritorious. Where the country is hilly, the water-storage is very often effected by damming up a sloping depression in the ground. The natural depression is enlarged, the excavated earth being thrown across the 'valley', to form an embankment. This kind is less expensive and is very common in the Santal country. It is called a band, which means an embankment. The Santali text has band here.

with us; we shall give you a place to sleep in." In this way he brought him back and to his house.

When night fell, he said to the boy: "Please tie your cow at the entrance of the cattle-shed, and you come up here to this verandah. It is a dangerous country here."

The boy then tied his cow at the entrance of the cattle-shed and himself lay down in the verandah. Talking to him for a long time about this that and the other, the man put the boy at his ease. Some time afterwards, the boy felt very drowsy and fell fast asleep. At that time the man untied the cow and put her into the cattle-shed together with his own cows; thereupon he led a cow of his own out and tied her where the boy's cow had been.

When it became morning, the young man saw that it was not his cow that was there, and said: "Look here, why have you exchanged cows for me?"

"Why, not at all," the man replied, "where have I made any exchange for you? You yourself have tied your cow here. I am, of course, awfully hungry for your cow, don't you think? Don't you see my cows, one cattle-shed full?"

"To be sure," the boy replied, "I see your cattle-shed full; but I am not asking you for those. I want only my own cow."

In this way they quarrelled violently, so the people of the village said to them: "Don't quarrel. Both of you call people together who have seen your cows." And to the boy they said: "You also bring those people from whom you have got this cow." Thereupon they fixed a time, and the boy went to the jackal and told him all his trouble.

When the day fixed came, the boy brought the jackal; they came both of them, the he- and the she-jackal. The other party brought big big people, landlords[7] and such, and all of them he gave money, to make them all speak up for himself. So they sat down to arbitrate.

---

[6] Preparatory to eating. A twig of the sal tree is used as a tooth-brush.

[7] In Santali 'kings', see p. 33 note 3.

Adọ khange uni toyo ạṇḍiại ẹhọp̍keťtakoa, Ią ho bhala, ạliń bana horge haram buḍhi reaǩ bicạr pạhiltaliṅpe. Bhala bana họṛ miťtegeliń jọm ńũyeťa, ar tahẽ hõ miťtegeliń tahẹnkana. Cekate iń dọ miť dhaogeń ićeťa ar eṅga dọ pẹ dhao?

Khange thọ ọkọe hõ ceť hõ bako rọṛ ruạr daṛeaťa. Adọ khange eṅgako kulikedea, Cekate am dọ pẹ dhaoem ićeťa ar ạṇḍiạ dọ mit dhaoge?

Khange adọ toyo eṅgae lạiako kana, baṅma, Ọkọe bẹdhọrọmko bicạra, onkoren sat gusṭire paṛaoǩa ona bar dhao reaǩ ić dọ; ar miť dhaoaǩ ić dọ ạṇḍiạń juriatae kana.

Khange ona katha ańjọmte biǩcạrko dọko thar bhasaoena, ar mọnẹ mọnẹteko mẹnwana, Ẹrẹ nãhãǩbon rọṛlere ma toyo ić abore paṛaoǩa. Onate ẹrẹ bako rọṛ daṛeaťa. Khange ọkọe oṛaǩreye gitićlen tahẽkan, uni họṛ dọ rajko metadea, Okare gại pal dọ menaǩa?

Khane lạiaťkoa, Phalna ṭạṇḍireko ạtińeťkoa.

Metadeako, Nọṇḍẹ ạgu ocokom.

Ạgukeťkoako. Khangeko metaťkina toyotekin haṛam buḍhi, Ma ẹṇḍẹkhan abenben ẹm akawade gại ma ńẹl oromeben.

Khange toyo ạṇḍiạ dọ unạǩ gại talare bọlọyente uni gại bachao toťkedeteye tiạǩ oḍoṅkedea ar koṛae jimạwadetaea. Khan onko biǩcạrko dọko ṭhakente apan ạpin oṛaǩteko ruạṛ baṛayena. Ar toyo hõ ạkinaǩ danḍertekin ruạṛ calaoena. Ar uni koṛa hõ adọe calao idiyena okạ sẹ̈ć aćaǩ disom menaǩa.

Mucạťena.

5. Toyo ar họṛ koṛa reaṅ.

Sedae jọkhẹn, kathae, miťṭaṅ họṛe tahẽkana, ar miťṭaṅ koṛa họpọne tahẽkantaea, ar uni gidrạ dọ huḍiṅgeye tahẽkanre, eṅgattẹť dọe gọćena. Khange uni gidrạ dọe ṭuạrena, apattẹť dọe rạṇḍiyena. Khange uni họṛ dọ ạḍi bhabnạreye paṛaoena: kạmiae, sẹye daka

[1] This and the following story are the same as the preceding one, which is taken down by the woman mentioned at the end of the story. The language is that of a woman in some places. No.s 5 and 6 are both taken down by Sagram Murmu, but at different times, and from different people.

The he-jackal commenced: "I say, please first decide a case between us two, husband and wife. Both of us eat and drink together, and we stay together. How is it that I go to stool once daily and she thrice?"

No one of them could answer anything to this. Then they asked the she-jackal: "How is it that you go to stool thrice and your husband only once?"

Then the she-jackal said to them: "On those who pass unrighteous judgements, to their seventh generation the twice passed stools will fall; that of the third time I match with that of my husband's."

When the judges heard this, they were terror-struck and were saying to themselves: "If we now speak falsely, the jackal's stools will fall on us." Therefore they did not dare to speak falsely. The landlords then said to the man in whose house the boy had passed the night: "Where is your herd of cows?"

"They are grazing them on such and such a plain," he told them.

"Let them be brought here," they ordered him.

When they had been brought, they said to the two jackals: "Now then, see which cow you have given to the boy."

The he-jackal then ran in among all those cows, found the cow, led her out and gave her over to the boy. The arbitrators were amazed and went home, each one to his own house. The two jackals also returned to their cave, and the young man thereupon went away to where his own country was.

That is the end.

(Told by Sąṅkhi Hąsdak wife of Lothro Murmu, late of Mohulpahari.)

5. THE JACKAL AND THE SANTAL[1].

In the old times, people tell, there once was a man, who had a son. Whilst the child was still quite young, his mother died; the child became motherless and the father a widower. Great trouble befell him: should he do his ordinary work, or should

utuia, sęye gupia, sę gidrąi jǫtǫnea? Nonka ąḍi moskil kąmireye paṛaoena. Khange bhabnateye osok̔ena.

Mit̔ din dǫ ać hǫpǫn gidrąi metae kana, Ią bąbu, iṅ hõṅ gujuk̔ge cǫṅ cet̔ cǫṅ, ęnte baṅ jut mǫnreṅ ąikąuet̔a. Ią bąbu, iṅ metam kana, judiṅ gǫćlen khan dǫ, ląṭu hǫṛ sę napṛak̔ hǫṛ ṭhen baṛę am dǫ gutik̔me, sę onkan hǫṛ ṭhen baṛę am dǫ gitićme.

Ona tayǫm khange sąri uni apat hǫṛ hõe gǫćena. Khange uni gidrą dǫe ṭuąren khan dǫe awa ṭapayena. Adǫ kakattekoko idikedete onko ṭhene hara juąnena, ar sanam tij bostu sę tij durib dǫ onkogeko idi samṭaoket̔taea, ar jǫtǫ tij duribko hatao cabaket̔taea, ar ǫṇḍęge jǫtǫ maraoentaea.

Are juąnen khan dǫko metae kana, Ią bąbu, oṛak̔re hõ cet̔ jǫmak̔ bąnuk̔tabona. Dę baṅkhan am dǫ gutik̔tabonme, kisąṛle siṛiama.

Adǫ uni koṛa dǫ cet̔ hõ bae rǫṛlet̔a, hape akangeye tahẽyena. Adǫ mǫnę mǫnęteye bujhąu baṛajoṅ kana, adǫ ǫnę apate metade tahękan, ona kathae disą ṅamket̔a. Adǫ dosar hiḷok̔ khange onko kakatteko ṭhen khon hõe oḍokena, adǫ ać mǫnęreye męnket̔a, Jãhãe napṛak̔ hǫṛ ṭhengeṅ gutik̔a. Onka męnkateye oḍok calak̔ kana.

Adǫ tin sąṅgiṅ cǫe sęn akan tahękan; khange mit̔ṭaṅ raj dǫ pąlkire ḍahar ḍaharteko gǫk̔ ąguyede kane ṅęlket̔koa. Adǫe męnket̔a, Cele bhalako gǫk̔ ąguyede kana? Khange adǫe kuliket̔koa, Henda ho, celepe gǫk̔ akadea?

Adǫko metadea, Rajle gǫk̔ akadea. Enka męnkatege onko dǫko parǫmena.

Adǫ uni koṛae męnket̔a, Nui kangeae ląṭu hǫṛ dǫ, tǫbę tęṛǫṅko gǫk̔ akadea? Ǫkǫe tora nui ṭhengeṅ tahęna; jãhãrege nuiye calak̔, ǫntęge iṅ hõṅ calak̔a. Adǫ onka męnkate sąri unigeye paṅjakedea, onko tayǫm tayǫmteye calak̔ kana.

---

2 When a man dies and his children are not big enough to look after themselves, the brothers of the deceased are the natural guardians and take charge. The younger brothers — so here — most commonly act; a possible cause for this may be the relationship often found between a man and his h i l i, i. e. elder brother's wife.

he prepare food, should he herd his cattle, or should he nurse his child? In this way, he had fallen into the greatest difficulties, and he wasted away from sorrow and grief.

One day he said to his child: "Listen to me, my boy, I also am very likely going to die, I am feeling very unwell. Listen, my boy, I tell you this: if I should die, take service with big or important people, or pass the night with such people."

Some time after this the father also really died, and as the boy became an orphan, he became destitute. His uncle's family[2] then took him to themselves, and he grew up and reached manhood whilst with them. These people collected and took away all his property and all his goods and took possession of all he had, and there, with them, it was all utterly lost.

When he had grown into manhood, they said to him: "Look here, my boy, we have absolutely nothing to eat in the house. So you take service with somebody; we shall look out for a master for you."

The young man did not say a word, he remained silent and was thinking it over in his mind. Then he remembered what his father had said to him, and the next day he left the family of his uncle, saying to himself: "I shall take service with some big people." With this in his mind he was walking along.

When he had walked some distance, who knows how far it was, he caught sight of some people who were carrying a king in a palanquin along the road towards him. He said to himself: I wonder whom they are carrying along. When they met, he asked them: "I say, whom are you carrying?"

"We are carrying the king," they replied, and as they said this, they passed.

"This is likely a big man," the boy said; "therefore they are carrying him. I shall not wait a moment, I shall stay with him. Wherever he goes, there I shall also go." Having said this, he really commenced to follow him; he walked along behind those people.

Adǫ tin sa̜ṅgiń cǫe pańja idiketko, khange adǫ onko gǫgǫkko laharege mittaṅ toyo a̜ṇḍia̜ dǫe parǫm gǫtena. Khange uni raj dǫ uni toyoe ńe̜lkede khan, gǫgǫkko se̜ kahaṛko dǫe metatkoa, Mase̜ mit gha̜ṛi dǫhǫ ńǫ̃geńpe. Khange sa̜riko dǫhǫkedea; adǫ uni raj dǫ pa̜lki se̜ khuṛkhuṛi khone oḍokente uni toyo a̜ṇḍia̜i ḍǫbǫkadea.

Adǫ ona ḍǫbǫk ńe̜lte uni koṛa dǫ mǫne̜ mǫne̜teye me̜njoṅ kana, Ayo! nuige maraṅ hǫṛ me̜nkateń pańja a̜guyede kana, arhǫ̃ nui dǫ uni toyoe ḍǫbǫkae kana. Tǫbe̜ nui khon dǫ unigeye maraṅa, ona te̜ṛǫṅe ḍǫbǫkadea.Ać khon huḍińgeye tahe̜n khan, hute̜n ǫhǫe ḍǫbǫklea. Onakoe buj baṛaketteye me̜nketa, Baṅ, iń dǫ la̜ṭu hǫṛ iń pańjayea. Adǫ onka me̜nkate sa̜ri uni toyo a̜ṇḍia̜geye pańjakedea.

Khange bha̜i, pańjae pańjakedea se̜, jāhā man tāhāe pańjakedea. Ar uni toyo dǫ gha̜ṛi hǫ̃ gha̜ṛiye be̜ṅge̜t rua̜ṛeta, ar se̜ uni hǫṛ dǫ baṅgeye ba̜giae kana. Khange oka ṭhen dǫ uni toyo dǫe da̜ṛ ńǫ̃ga, khange uni koṛa hǫ̃e da̜ṛ idia; are ńe̜l atkedea me̜nkhan ampa ompoe ńir calaka. Khange uni toyo dǫe bujha̜uketa, Nui hǫṛ dǫ cet cǫṅ iń tuluć galmarao menaktaea. Khangeye ta̜ṅgikedea, adǫe metae kana, Henda beṭa, okatem calaka? Enaṅ khon iń ńe̜letmea, iń tayǫm tayǫmtem hijuk kana.

Adǫ uni koṛae me̜nketa, Am ṭhenge, babaṅ calak kana; e̜nteń baḍaeyeta dha̜rti mǫtǫre dǫ am kangeam ma̜lik dǫ. Am ṭhenge iń dǫ gutiń tahe̜na; e̜nte huḍiń huḍiń iń tahẽ̜kanre iń ayo dǫe gǫćena, unre iń baba dǫe metadińa, Ia̜ ba̜bu, iń baṅ hilok dǫ hape̜n am dǫ la̜ṭu hǫṛ se̜ maraṅ hǫṛ ṭhen baṛe̜ gutikme ar onkan hǫṛ ṭhen baṛe̜ gitićme. Onate, baba, iń dǫ amgeń pańja a̜guyetmea am ṭhen tahe̜na me̜nte.

Adǫ uni toyoe me̜nketa, Cekate am dǫm baḍaekidińa iń dǫń maraṅgea me̜nte?

[3] See p. 33, note 2.

[4] Kahaṛ is the name of a Hindu low-caste man, one of whose occupations is to be a palanquin-bearer.

When he had followed after them for some distance, a male jackal suddenly passed the road in front of the carriers[3]. As soon as the king saw the jackal, he spoke to the carriers or palanquin-bearers[4]: "Put me down a moment." They put him down, and the king got out of the palanquin or litter and bowed deeply to the jackal.

When the young man saw that bow, he said to himself: "Oh mother[5], thinking that this one was the big man, I have been following him, and now he himself bows to the jackal. It must be because this one is bigger than the other that he bowed to him. If the jackal was of less importance than himself, he would surely not bow to him." Having reached this conclusion he said: "No, I shall follow the big one." And, having said this, he started following the jackal.

If you believe it or not, he followed him; wherever he went, he followed after him. The jackal again and again looked backwards, but the man would not leave him alone. When the jackal here and there tried to run a little, the young man also ran along, and if he lost sight of him anywhere, he ran hurriedly here and there to find him. At last the jackal understood that the man had likely something he wanted to talk to him about. He therefore waited for him and spoke to him: "I say, my son, where are you going? I have seen you for a long while, you are coming after me."

"I am coming to you, father," the boy answered, "because I know, that in the whole world you are the master. I want to stay with you as your servant; when I was very young, my mother died, and then my father said to me: "Listen, my boy, some day in future when I am no more, seek service with big or important people, and pass the night with such people. Therefore, father, I have been following you, in order to stay with you."

"How did you know me," the jackal asked him, "that I am the big one?"

Adǫ unreye mǫnkeťa, Iń dǫ nǫtǫge marań hǫṛ ṭhen gutiǩa mǫnte oṛaǩ khon iń oḍok hijuǩ kan tahẽkana. Adǫ unreń ńǫlkedea miťṭań raj dǫ khuṛkhuṛiteko gǫǩ idiyede kan. Adǫ unreń mǫnkeťa, Nui kangeae cele lạṭu hǫṛ dǫ. Adǫ onka mǫnkate iń dǫ uni ṭhenge gutiǩa mǫnte unigeń pańja ạguyede kan tahẽkana. Adǫ un jǫkhǫnge am dǫ uni laharem parǫm gǫťena; adǫ am ńǫlte uni raj dǫ khuṛkhuṛi khon ãṛgoyente ame ḍǫbǫǩaťmea, are mǫnkeťa, Iń khon dǫ nuigeye marańa. Adǫ ona ańjǫmkate iń dǫ mǫnreń bujhạukeťa, tǫbǫ dhạrti mǫtǫre dǫ unigeye marańa mǫnte. Ǫnka bujhạukate iń dǫ amgeń pańja ạgukeťmea am ṭhenge guti tahǫna mǫnte.

Adǫ uni toyo ạṇḍiại mǫnkeťa, Henda bacha, iń ma cas bas hǫ̃ bạnuǩtiń, ceťreń kạmi ocomea? Iạ bacha, ma ruạṛjońme, iń dǫ guti ǫhǫń dǫhǫ daṛelema.

Adǫ uni koṛa dǫ ceť hǫ̃ bae mǫnleťa. Khange uni toyo dǫe calaoena. Khange uni koṛa hǫ̃e pańja idikedegea. Khange uni toyo dǫ miťṭań danderreye bǫlǫyena. Khange uni koṛa hǫ̃ ona dander duạr ṭhen sǫnkateye duṛuṕena, adǫ ǫṇḍǫge ạḍi hạbiće duṛuṕ akangea. Ar uni toyo dǫ ghạṛi ghạṛigeye bǫńgǫťae bǫńgǫťae kangeae. Adǫ ạḍi hạbiće duṛuṕen khan, eńga toyo dǫe mǫnkeťa, Nui hǫṛ dǫ ceť lạgiť nǫṇḍǫ dǫe duṛuṕ akana? Enan khone duṛuṕ akan dǫ. Sǫ alań gǫćlań lạgiťgeye duṛuṕ akana, sǫ amge ceťem mǫn akawadea?

Adǫ ạṇḍiại mǫnkeťa, Ǫkǫ baḍae, bań baḍae kana.

Adǫe metadea, Cekate ǫṇḍǫkhan am dǫe pańja ạgu akaťmea?

Adǫ unreye mǫnkeťa, Hẽ, uni tuluć thoṛa thuṛi dǫ katha menaǩa.

Adǫe mǫnkeťa, Ċeť katha kana? Ma lạiańme.

Adǫ unreye mǫnkeťa, Nui dǫe ṭuạr gidrạ kana, adǫ alań ṭhenge guti tahǫna mǫnteye pańja ạgu akadińa. Mǫneťae, bańma, Dhạrti mǫtǫre toyogeko marańa, toyo khon dǫ celege bako marańa. Onate

5 A very common exclamation to show surprise; if the most common Santali word for mother, g o, or only the emphatic particle g e is added, it is also used to indicate pity and pain.

"I was coming from home," the boy replied, "in this direction, to seek service with some big person; then I caught sight of a king, whom they were carrying in a litter. Then I said to myself: This one is likely to be a big man. Thinking this, I was following after him, to take service with him. Just then you passed across the road in front of him, and, seeing you, the king came down from his litter and bowed to you and said: This one is bigger than myself. Hearing this, I understood that this one then is the biggest in the whole world. With this in my mind, I have been following you to be with you as your servant."

"Look her, my son," the jackal said, "I have no cultivation or farm-work[6] of any kind, so how can I let you work at anything? I say, my son, please return home. I am unable to keep you as my servant."

The boy did not say a word, and the jackal went away. Then the boy again followed after the jackal, until the jackal entered a cave. The boy then went and sat down at the entrance of that cave, and there he remained sitting until late. The jackal again and again looked out at him, and as he remained sitting there until late, the she-jackal said: "What is this man sitting here for? He has been sitting here for a long while. Or perhaps be is sitting here to try to kill us, or has he said anything to you?"

"Who knows," the he-jackal said, "I don't know."

"How is it then," she asked, "that he has followed you here?"

"Well," he replied, "I have something, a very little, to do with him."

"What is it?" the she-jackal asked, "please tell me."

Then the jackal said: "He is an orphan boy and has followed me here to take service with us two. He says: In the whole world the jackals are the biggest; absolutely no one is bigger

[6] It might be noted that other work than farm-work seems to be outside of possibilities. The Santals were formerly in the habit of working at whatever they could; even now there is no innate objection against any work; but under Hindu influence the Santals are becoming something like an agricultural caste; they feel this to be their natural and desirable occupation.

uni dǫ maraṅ hǫṛ ṭhenge gutike mẹnette iṅ dǫe paṅja ạgu akadiṅa.

Adǫ eṅgae mẹnketa, Cekateye baḍaeketa dhạrtire dǫ toyogeko maraṅa mẹnte dǫ?

Adǫ ạṇḍiại mẹnketa, Oka disomren raj cǫṅ pạlkiteko gǫk idiyede tahẹkana, unre iṅ dǫ onko lahareṅ parǫmena, ar raj dǫ iṅe ṅẹlkidiṅ khan dǫ, onko pạlki gǫgǫkkoe metatkoa, Masẹ mit ghạṛi dǫhǫliṅpe. Adǫko dǫhǫkedete pạlki khone oḍokente iṅe ḍǫbǫkadiṅa. Un jǫkhẹn nui gidrạ dǫ onko tayǫm tayǫmteye hijuk kan tahẹkana, unige maraṅ hǫṛ bujhạukate ar uni ṭhenge gutika mẹnteye mẹnjoṅ kan tahẹkana. Adǫ uni raj dǫ iṅe ḍǫbǫkadiṅe ṅẹlkede khan dǫe mẹnketa, Raj khon dǫ tǫbẹ nuigeye maraṅa, tǫbẹ tẹṛǫṅe ḍǫbǫkadea, ar baṅkhan dǫ hutẹć ohoe ḍǫbǫklea; tǫbẹ khan iṅ dǫ nui ṭhengeṅ gutika. Adǫ onka mẹnkate ǫṇḍẹ khonge nui bạpuṛić gidrạ dǫe paṅja ạgu akadiṅa. Hǫrre mit dhao dǫṅ galmaraoadea, ẹn kathae, Bạbu, iṅ dǫ cas bas hõ bạnuktiṅa; cetreṅ kạmi ocomete iṅ dǫ gutiṅ dǫhǫmea? Ma jãhãe kisạṛ baṛẹ ṅẹlkom. Adǫ unre cet hõ bae rǫṛ ruạṛadiṅa. Khangeṅ bạgiadea, ar ṅir adea mẹnte ạḍi ãṭ iṅ dạṛketa, menkhan nui dǫ rukhi paṅjae paṅjakidiṅte nõkõe alaṅ oṛak hạbiće paṅja ạgukidiṅa. Adǫ dẹ bhala nui gidrạ dǫ ạḍi as mǫnkateye hẹćen dǫ, adǫ cetlaṅ metaea, cet kạmirelaṅ dǫhǫyẹa, sẹ cetlaṅ metaea?

Khange toyo ẹṅga dǫ ona kathae aṅjǫm purạukettae khan dǫe oḍokenteye kuliyede kana, Henda bạbu, cet mẹnkate nui dǫm paṅja ạgu akadea, sẹ cet lagatem hẹć akana?

Adǫe mẹnketa, Aben ṭhenge gutika mẹnteṅ hẹć akana.

Adǫe metadea, Ạliṅ ṭhen dǫ kạmi bạnukan, cetliṅ kạmi ocomea?

Adǫe mẹnketa, Jãhãnakgeben kạmi ocoṅ, onageṅ kạmia.

---

7 Note the avoiding of using any kind of name.

8 Loṭa is a brass cup, wide at the bottom, with a narrow neck and fairly broad brim. It is a very common brass vessel of universal use for liquids, especially water for washing purposes. It is not originally a Santal household utensil. It is manufactured by Hindus. Within certain limits, the form varies considerably.

9 It is always an object with them to make sure that a gift is voluntary.

than the jackal. He is seeking service with some big people, therefore he has followed me here."

"How did he know," the she-jackal said, "that the jackals are the biggest in the world?"

The he-jackal then answered: "They were carrying the king of some country or other along in a palanquin; at that time I happened to cross the road in front of them, and when the king saw me, he said to the palanquin-bearers that they should put him down for a moment. They put him down, and he got out of the palanquin and bowed to me. At that time this boy was coming after them, because he had understood that he was the big man, and he intended to take service with him. When he saw that the king bowed to me, he said: Then this one is, of course, bigger than the king; therefore he bowed to him, otherwise he would certainly not have bowed; therefore I shall take service with this one. With this in his mind, this poor child has followed me right here. Whilst coming, I spoke to him once, saying to him these very words: "My boy, I have no cultivation or farm-work of any kind, so what kind of work can I give you, to keep you as my servant? Please find some one else to be your employer! At that time he did not answer a single word. Then I left him, and to put him off my tracks I came running very fast; but this boy tracked me everywhere all along and followed me, as you see, right here to our house. Well, this boy has come with great expectations, what shall we two say to him? in what kind of work can we keep him, or what shall we say to him?"

When the she-jackal had heard all this to the end, she went out and asked the boy: "Look here, boy, for what purpose have you followed this one[7] here, or what have you come for?"

"To you I have come to be in your service," he replied.

"There is no work to be had with us," she said, "what can we let you do?"

"Whatever you give me to do," he replied, "that I shall do."

Adọe metadea, Ma calak̕me, ạliṅ ṭhen dọ kạmige bạnuk̕an.

Enka mẹnkate uni toyo eṅga oṛak̕teye bọlọyena sẹ ona danderteye bọlọyena, adọ ẹnre hõ uni koṛa dọ ọṇḍẹgeye duṛup̕ akangea, bae beret̕ kana. Adọ ḍher dhạbić hoeyen khan, unkin toyo dọ bana hoṛkin mẹnket̕a, Nui gidrạ dọ jãhãnak̕ balaṅ emae khan dọ ọhọe uṭhạulena. Ma jãhãnak̕laṅ emaea. Adọ mit̕ṭaṅ gạiye tahẹ̃kantạkina; adọkin mẹnket̕a, Ma nui gạigelaṅ ẹm dapoṛaea.

Adọ sạri uni gạikin uduk̕adea arkin metadea, Ma bạbu, nui gạiliṅ emam kana, idijoṅme. Guti dọ baliṅ dọhọyet̕mea, arliṅ lạiam kana, nui gạirege jọtọak̕ menak̕a, jegem khọje, onageye emama, metak̕me, thạri bạṭi, loṭa, taben khạjạṛi, miṭhại, kicrić khạṇḍuạk̕, caole, buluṅ sunum, mọsọla, sẹ jọtọak̕geye emama. Arhõ jọm ńũ baṛakate metaeme, ma baekam mẹnte, adọe baekatama.

Adọ onkakin metade khan, uni dọ ạḍi rạskạkateye beret̕ gọt̕enteye mẹnket̕a, Acha baba, khusiteben emaṅ kan khan dọṅ hataoea.

Adọkin mẹnket̕a, Khusitegeliṅ emam kana.

Khange adọ uni gạiye lạga ạguyede kana. Adọ hijuk̕ hijuk̕te belayen khan dọ, dak̕ tetaṅede kana ar rẹṅgẹćede kana. Adọe mẹnket̕a, Okare baṅ dak̕ iṅ ṅam? Bhala nui gạiyiṅ kọe gelakea, sạri sẹ naseye ẹmọk̕a mẹnte. Adọ khange ḍạḍiye ńẹl ńamket̕a; adọ ona ḍạḍi-ṭhene calaoen khan dọ, mit̕ṭẹn maejiu dak̕ lo ọṇḍẹgeye hẹćena. Adọ un jọkhẹnge uni koṛa dọ gạiye metae kana, Dẹn ayo, thạri bạṭi ar jọl pan emaṅme. Khange uni maejiu dọ tan mane ńẹńẹl kana. Adọ sạri thạri ar bạṭiye emadea ar jọl pan, noako jọtọge moca khone ulạ oḍokadea. Arhõ jọm baṛakateye metadea, Ma ayo, baek̕ak̕me. Adọ sạri ona thạri ar bạṭi dọe ut̕ket̕a.

---

10 Addressing as 'mother' shows honour and respect and endearment. The term is frequently used to females with whom no relationship is established, even to girls very much younger than oneself. It may be that this has come in from the Bengalis. Some of the Santal religious sects that have shown themselves sporadically since about 1874 have adopted this form of addressing all females. Our way of addressing children might be compared.

"Please go," she said, "there is no work to be had with us."

Having said this the she-jackal entered the house, or rather, she entered the cave. Still the boy remained sitting there; he did not get up. When a long time had passed, the jackals, both of them, said: "If we do not give this child something, he will surely not move from here. Let us give him something." Now they had a cow, so they said: "Let us give him this cow and have done with him."

Thereupon they showed him that cow and said to him: "Well, my boy, we are giving you this cow; take her along with you. We cannot keep you as a servant, but we tell you this, everything is to be found in this cow; whatever you ask her for, she will give you, that is to say, brass plates and cups and lotas[8], taben and khạjạri, sweets, clothes, rice, salt, oil, spices, in short, everything. Again when you have had your food and drink, tell her to put it away for you; and she will do so."

When they had said this to him, he got up very glad and happy and said: "Very well, father, since you are giving me this with pleasure[9], I shall take her."

"We give her to you with pleasure," they both said.

Thereupon he started driving the cow away. As he was going along and it became late in the afternoon, he felt thirsty and hungry, and said: "Wherever shall I find water? I wonder, I might try to ask this cow whether she really will give or not." He thereupon caught sight of a water-pool; when he went down to that, a woman came there to fetch water. Just at that moment the boy said to the cow: "Please, mother[10], give me a plate and a cup and some light refreshments." The woman was looking on, all she could, and, in very truth, the cow gave him a plate and a cup and some light refreshments; all this she brought out of her mouth. When he had eaten, he again said to her: "Please, mother, put it away." And then, in very truth, she swallowed the plate and the cup.

Adọ enkae ńẹllede khange uni maejiu dọ dak̓e lokett̓e hare phare oṛak̓te sẹnente aćren herel noako jọtọ kathae lạiadea are metadea, Masẹ uni gạ̣i dọ jāhā lekatelaṅ ẹṛẹyegea. Khange sạri phọrpundikin joṛaoket̓a uni gạ̣i ẹṛẹye lạgit̓. Khange uni herel họṛ dọ hare phare calaoente uni koṛae sẹn tiok̓kedea; adọe metadea, Dẹn bạbu, cun thamakur ẹmok̓me, jọmletamgealaṅ. Ar nui gạ̣i dọ okatem idiyea?

Adọe mẹnket̓a, Hana phalna atote.

Arhọ̃e metadea, Oka khonem ạguyede kana?

Hana phalna ato khon.

Arhọ̃e kuliyede kana, Henda bạbum kiriń ạguyede kana sẹ oṛak̓ren gạ̣i kangetamae?

Adọe mẹnket̓a, Oṛak̓renge; ọṇḍẹye tahẽkana, adọń ạgu ruạṛede kana.

Adọ henda bạbu, nui gạ̣i dọm ạkrińkea?

Adọe mẹnket̓a, Baṅ, nui gạ̣i dọ ọhọń ạkrińlea.

Khange adọ uni họṛe mẹnket̓a, Henda bạbu, teheńge nāhāk̓ oṛak̓ dọm tioga sẹ ọhọm tiok̓lea?

Adọe mẹnket̓a, Teheń dọ ọhọń tiok̓ daṛelea, gapa dọ nāhāk̓ iń tioggea ạyup̓ sumuṅkote dọ, ar baṅkhan meaṅ dọ nāhāk̓ ạḍireń tioga.

Adọ bạbu, teheń dọ okarem gitića?

Adọe mẹnket̓a, Jāhārege ạyubok̓, ọṇḍẹgeń gitića.

Adọe metadea, Peṛa jāhān noakore menak̓kotama?

Adọe mẹnket̓a, Peṛa dọ bạnuk̓kotińa.

Adọe metadea, Iạ bạbu, tọbẹ khan dọ dela ale ṭhenge teheń dọ gitić aṅgak̓me; jọm ńū họ̃le emama ar nui gạ̣i lạgit̓ jọm họ̃le emama, cedak̓ ẹnte eskargeń ńẹlet̓meteń metam kana.

---

11 The Santal way of using tobacco is as follows; a bit of a tobacco leaf and some unslaked mussel lime is put in the hollow of the hand and thoroughly mixed by grinding the stuff with the thumb or the end of a stick. A small pinch of the powder is then thrown into the mouth and chewed, the stuff being ultimately spat out. People meeting each other, strangers or not, will stop up and ask for tobacco, the one asking being quite prepared to give. It really means an

When the woman had seen all this, she drew water, hurried back home and told her husband all she had seen, saying to him: "This cow we must somehow or other cheat him for." So they concocted some stratagem for doing this, and the man went hurriedly and overtook the boy and said to him: "Please, my boy, give lime and tobacco[11] and let us taste what you have. Where are you taking this cow?"

"To such and such a village," the boy replied.

"From where are you bringing her?" the man again asked him.

"From such and such a village."

"I say, my boy," the man again asked, "have you bought the cow, or is she a cow from your own house?"

"She is from our house," the boy replied; "she was there, and I am taking her back again."

"Look here, my boy, would you be willing to sell this cow?"

"No," the boy replied, "I am not selling this cow at all."

Then the man said: "Look here, my boy, will you be able to reach home to-day now, or will you not?"

"To-day," he replied, "I shall not be able to reach home, to-morrow I shall arive there at nightfall, or else I shall be home the day after to-morrow very early."

"Where are you going to pass the night then, my boy?"

"Wherever I may be at nightfall, there I shall pass the night," he said.

"Have you relatives or friends of any kind hereabouts?" the man asked him.

"I have no friends," the boy replied.

"I say, my boy," the man said to him, "in that case, come along and pass the night with us. We shall give you food and drink, we shall also give you food for this cow of yours. I say this to you, because I see you are alone."

---

invitation to stop and have a talk. If anybody refuses, it means either that the person is in a great hurry or that he is unwilling to talk with the other party. It is, of course, only men who practise this.

Adoe menketa, Oko badae, bando nondeń tahen, bando atra dhur iń sen ńogok.

Adoe metadea, Ancinre derak do ber tahenregeko deraka, ar ber hasurkate derak do bań besa. Ar ńelme, am do gai menaetama, jãhã atore ńuhumkatem rakaplen khan do kombro hõko men dareama, ar nui gai hõ mit lagate do tinakem idiyea? Uni hõ thora do bam jirau ńõgea? Ina doe atiń barajońa.

Ado onka adi leka najere udukadea. Ar adi lekae galmaraoade khan do mone labitkettaea. Khane menketa, Acha endekhan delań am orakrege teheń doń gitić angalenge.

Ado onkae menket khan doe ayur idikedea ać orakte. Ado seter torage aimaitet doe men gotadea, Den hare phare busup agu godme, nui gaiye joma becara, tin khon coń rengećtegeye laga aguyede kana.

Khange uni aimai do busupe hobor agu gotketa; ado unre uni kora do uni aimaiye ńel oromkedea, dak ghatre jol pan iń jom jokhen do nui maejiugeye tahẽkana mente. Unre nui doe ńellidińa, dhorage nui gai dokin ereń coń cet coń. Ona do moneregeye menwana.

Ado uni herel hore menketa, Ma babu, ona gorare tolkaeme.

Ado sari uniak gorareye tolkadete busupe emadea, dakkoe emadea, ado inaktcge ayupena. Ado kedok okte hoeyen khan do, kedokko isinketa, ado uni hore menketa, Nui pera gidra hõ kedok disayepe. Ado noa kathage uni hor do phenteye rorketa, bańma, Usul buru rakap tarup dharna buru siloda ho?

Ado aimaitet doe utar ruar gotketa, Hoi, hoi! damhã khon dumhẽte doń ãrgo akata.

Adoe lo baraket khan, herel hor do orakteye boloyente ać rinińe metae kana, Aliń do daka emalińme; aliń dakaliń jojom jokhenge

12 The two enigmatic sentences refer in a veiled way to the food. It is ready.

13 Directly from the cooking pot to the plate or cup.

14 Before eating water is always given, and they go aside and wash their hands. The same is repeated after food, but not so carefully.

"Who knows," the boy replied, "whether I should remain here or walk on halfway?"

"To camp where you are unknown," the man said, "may do whilst the sun is up; after sunset, it is not safe to camp in that way. Remember also, you have a cow. If you, after it has become dusk, enter a village, they might call you a thief, and how can you drive this cow along without stopping? Ought you not to let her rest a little also? Then she will be able to graze a little also."

The man tried to persuade him in this way by mentioning several things, and when he had mentioned a great many considerations, he softened him, so he said: "Very well then, come, let me pass the night in your house to-night."

As he said this, the man led him along to his own house; when they reached there, the man at once spoke to his wife: "Do bring some straw quickly, let this cow get something to eat, poor animal; he has been driving her along since who knows when, without her getting any food."

The woman then brought some straw in her arms, and the boy recognized the woman: "It was this same woman who was at the watering-place, when I asked the cow for light refreshments. Then she saw me; surely, now they will cheat me for this cow, it seems." He said this to himself.

"Well, my boy," the man said to him, "tie your cow in the cow-shed."

He did so, tied the cow there, gave her straw and gave her water, and during this it became evening. When the time for supper came, they prepared this; the man said: "Remember this young visitor also with supper." Thereupon the man spoke these words allegorically: "The leopard that ascended the high mountain, is he kept a prisoner, the huge mountain beast?"

And the woman at once answered: "Yes, yes, from the gorge I have brought it down to the foot of the hill[12]."

When she had poured out[13] the food, the husband went into the house and said to his wife: "Give us two food; whilst we

am dọ goṛate bọlọ gọdok̇te nuiren gạ̣i dọ raṛakaeme, ar uni gạ̣i lekaniće aboren gạ̣i ona babertege uni gạ̣iye tọl akade ṭhenge am dọ hare phare tọl họt́kaeme, ar nọṇḍẹ oḍok hijuk̇me.

Adọ sạri dakae lo gọt́ket́te dak̇e taṅat́kina are metat́kina, Ạbukok̇ben, kedok̇bon jọmlege.

Adọ sạri uni herel họṛ dọ bạṭi dak̇e saṕ gọt́ket́teye mẹnket́a, Ma bạbu laṅ ạbukok̇a, kedok̇bo jọm baṛawanrege.

Adọe mẹnket́a, Ma amge jọmme.

Adọe metadea, Baṅ bạbu, ma bana hgṛgelaṅ jọma.

Adọ uni koṛae mẹnket́a, Dẹn ẹṇḍẹkhan iń dọ nọtẹrege ạguạńpe.

Adọ uni họṛe mẹnket́a, Oṛak̇regelaṅ jọma. Hẽ, oṛak̇ baṅ tahẹn khan, niạkore hõ jutok̇gea; adọ oṛak̇ menak̇ tuluć nọtẹre dọ cedak̇? Hẽ, pọr jạtem tahẹn khan, nọtẹregele ẹmkema, mẹnkhan geãt kantem oṛak̇tele aderet́mea.

Khaṇge onkae metade khan, ạbukente oṛak̇tekin bọlọyena. Adọ dakae ẹm baṛawat́kinte uni ạimại dọe oḍokente ọnẹye metade lekaket́ae. Adọ dakakin jọmket́ khankin oḍokena, adọ ạbuk baṛakate cun thamakure emadea; benaoket́tekin jọm baṛaket́a. Adọe metae kana, Iạ bạbu, ma gạ̣i dọ raṛa oḍokete nọtẹre baṛẹ tọletam, rọk̇ bọtẹćketamako.

Adọ sạri raṛa oḍokkedete goṛa duạrreye tọlkadetaea, ar ńũt iạte bae ńẹl ṭhikleḍea. Adọ gitić aṅgayente piạṅ payaṅ jọkhẹne lagakedea, adọ ẹnre hõ bae ńẹl oromedea. Adọ rẹṅgẹćkede khan, dak̇ ghaṭ ṭhene idikedeteye kọeye kana, Dẹn ayo, thạri bạṭi emańme. Adọ bae emae kana. Adọ bar pẹ dhaoe kọekedere hõ bae emade khan dọe bujhạuket́a, nui gạ̣i dọe baṅ kana mẹnte, gạ̣i dọ ọṇḍẹgeko bọdọladińa.

[15] Here not the goḍet, but a person called 'chowkedar', a kind of village constable, who is supposed to walk through the village several times each night, calling out in a loud voice, as he walks along. The idea is to ascertain whether people are at home, and to warn against thieves. There is one chowkedar to each village, or if the village is very small, one to two or even three neighbouring villages. They are paid from certain taxes, and are appointed by the local magistrate. Here the chowkedar is brought in to give an official colouring to the house-search. Ordinary people have no right to such extremes.

are eating, you go to the cattle-shed and untie his cow; then be quick and tie with the same string and where he has tied his cow one of ours, looking like that cow, and then come out here."

She did so. When she had poured out the food, she brought them water and said to them: "Please wash your hands, we shall have supper at once."

The man then took a bowl with water and said: "Please, my friend, let us wash our hands; we shall now have supper before anything else."

"Please, eat yourself," the boy said.

"No, my friend," the man said, "we shall both of us eat together,"

"Please then," the boy said, "bring it to me somewhere here."

But the man said: "We shall eat inside. Well, if we had no house, it would do also hereabouts; but when we have a house, why hereabouts? Yes, if you had been of another race, we should have let you have it hereabouts; but as you are the same as ourselves, we are taking you into the house."

When he had spoken to him thus, they washed[14] and went inside, and the woman put food before them, whereupon she went out and did as the man had told her. When the two had had their meal, they went out and washed their hands, and he gave him lime and tobacco. When he had prepared this, they chewed, whereupon he said to the boy: "I say, my friend, untie your cow and bring her out and tie her somewhere here; the others might but and gore your one."

Then he really did this. He untied her, brought her out, and tied her at the entrance to the cow-shed; but as it was dark, he did not see the cow properly. He slept till dawn, and at daybreak he drove the cow away with him; still he did not recognize her, that it was not his own. When he felt hungry, he took her down to a watering-place and asked her: "Please, mother, give me a plate and a bowl." But she did not give him. As she, although he asked her two three times, did not give him anything, he understood that this one was not his own cow, but that they had exchanged cows for him there.

Khange uni koṛa dọ ọṇḍẹ khonge uni gạidọe laga ruạṛkedete, ọnẹye giticlen ona atotegeye laga ạgukedete ona atoren họṛe jarwaketkoa. Adọ jarwakateko kulikedea, Cele bạbu, cet lạgitem jarwaketlea?

Adọ unreye mẹnketa, Iạ baba, iṅ dọ phalna ato khon mittaṅ gạiiṅ ạgujoṅ kan tahẽkana, adọ nindạyente noa oṛakreṅ gitic kana. Adọ daka jọmko aderkidiṅa, unrege gạidọko bọdọladiṅa; eṭak gạiiṅiṅ ṭọllede ṭhen dọko ṭọlkadea. Mẹnkhan iṅren gạire dọ mit leka gun menaktaea, thạri bạṭi kọele khan dọe emaṅgea. Adọ nui gạiiṅ kọeye kana, adọ bae emaṅ kana; onareṅ baḍaeketa, nui gạidọe baṅ kantiṅa mẹnte. Adọ iṅ eskarte kọeyere ma pasẹte phepṛayiṅ, onate adọ ape ato họṛ dọṅ rak akawatpea. Adọ ṅẹl oromkate gạiye ẹmkaetiṅ ma. Inạge katha dọ.

Khange ato họṛ uniko kulikedea, Cele ho phalna, masẹ lạime, nui koṛae lạiket, ona katha dọ sạri sẹ nase kana?

Khange uni họṛ dọ phepṛae ẹhọpketa, ạḍi lekae rọṛ idiketa; mẹnkhan ato họṛ ona katha dọ bako sẹn ocoattaea, metadeako, Nui bạpuṛic gidrạ alom posṛayea; ẹnte ale dọ atoren họṛ kanale, nui gạile ṅẹl oromedetama; nui mae amren kan, gidrạ pidrạ jọtọ họṛ geko ṅẹl akadetama; ạnạṛi gạima judạgeko ṅẹlok.

Adọ uni họṛe mẹnketa, Ma ẹnte iṅren gạipalre ṅẹlkope, judi ạnạṛi gạipe ṅamketkoa mẹnkhan, sạjạiyiṅpe.

Adọ sạri uniren gạipalteko calaoena; adọ bako ṅamleḍea. Adọ mạṅjhi họṛe mẹnketa, Judi nuiren gạile ṅamkedea mẹnkhan, tinạkem ẹmọka?

Adọ uni họṛe mẹnketa, Ṅamle khanpe, gẹl ṭakaṅ ẹmọka, ar bape ṅamle khan dọ, nui gidrạ tire menae gạiiṅ hataoea.

Adọko mẹnketa, Hẽ, hataoem.

Adọ mạṅjhiye mẹnketa, Do sẹ ghor tolasitaepe.

---

16 Every Santal house in which the head of the family lives has a bhitạr. This is part of the otherwise one-roomed house, in one corner, separated from the rest of the room by a low wall, which runs out from the side-wall and some two to three meters into the compartment. It is a kind of stall, and is sacred to the ancestors. Here food &c., only a very little, is put for the ancestors.

The boy then drove the cow back from there, brought her to the village where he had slept, and called the people of that village together. When they had come together, they asked the boy: "Well, young man, for what purpose have you called us together?"

Then he said: "Well, sirs, I was bringing a cow with me from such and such a village, and as I was benighted, I passed the night here in this house. They took me inside to give me food, and just at that moment they exchanged my cow. They tied another cow where I had tied mine. Now my cow has a certain quality: when I ask her for plates and bowls, she gives me that. But when I ask this one, she does not give me anything. Thereby I understood that this cow is not mine. If I myself alone ask him, perhaps he might be obstinate towards me; therefore I have complained to you village people. Let him find out my cow and give her to me. That is my case."

The village people then asked the man: "Well, so and so, please tell, what this boy has now told, is that true or false?"

Then that man commenced to use falsehood and talked a good deal; but the village people would not let his word pass for good and said to him: "Don't treat this poor child in such an overbearing way. We belong to this village, and we recognize this cow of yours. This one is your cow, that children and grown ups, in fact all people have seen. Strange cows look otherwise."

"Well then," the man said, "look over my cows in my herd; if you find any strange cow there, punish me."

Then they went to the cow-herd of this man and did not find a strange one. The village headman then said: "If we should find this boy's cow, how much will you give?"

"If you find her," the man replied, "I shall give ten rupees, and if you don't find her, I shall take the cow which is in the hands of this boy."

"Yes," they said, "take her."

The headman then said: "Do, search his house."

Khange sạri cạukidar lagaete oṛak̕teko bo̱lo̱yen khan do̱, bhitạrre gạị do̱to̱l akadeko ńamkedea. Ado̱ uni gidrạko metaḍea, Cele bạbu, nui kantamae?

Ado̱e me̱nket̕a, Hẽ̱, nui kangeae.

To̱be̱ ma idiyetam.

Ado̱e idikedea, ar uni ho̱ṛ do̱ ge̱l ṭakako ḍanḍo̱mkedea.

Ado̱ e̱ne̱ cabayena katha do̱, in marańgea.

6. Toyo ar raj ho̱po̱n reań.

Sedae jugre, kathae, mit̕ṭań raje tahẽ̱kana; uni rajren do̱ mit̕ṭań koṛa ho̱po̱n eskargeye tahẽ̱kantaea, ardo̱ cele hõ bako tahẽ̱kantaea.

Ado̱ tahe̱n tahe̱nte, bhạị, cekakote co̱ń ado̱ uni raj do̱e re̱ńge̱ć-ena, ado̱ nunạk̕ ãṭe re̱ńge̱ćena, cet̕ bań se̱, ko̱e baṛae lekenae, ar uni koṛa gidrạ hõ me̱ro̱m gupi leke harayena.

Ado̱ uni raj do̱ ać ho̱po̱nte̱t̕ mit̕ din do̱e sikhạukedea se̱ye galmaraoae kana, Iạ bạbu, amgeń galmaraoam kana, nõk̕õebon re̱ńge̱ć cabayena; sedae do̱ ạḍi bạṛić cij tahẽ̱kantabona, ar disom hõ tahẽ̱kange̱tabona, gạị kaḍa hõko tahẽ̱kangea. Ado̱ nõk̕õe cet̕re co̱ń cekayente sanam dho̱n durib cabayentabona; ado̱ am reań nitok̕ do̱ ạḍi bhabnalíń ạikạuet̕a. Sedae do̱ ạḍi bạṛić toa daheliń jo̱mket̕a, ado̱ am biḍạl do̱ cet̕ hõ bań juṭạuk̕ kana, onate ạḍi bhabnalíń ạikạuet̕a. Ado̱ bạbu, am iń lạị oṭoam kana, noa dhạrtire do̱ ạḍi bạṛić raj menak̕koa, raj cetan raj menak̕koa. Nitok̕ do̱ iń hõń haṛamena ar eńgam hõe buḍhiyena; ạliń do̱ pase̱ oka hilok̕ co̱liń gujuk̕. Am do̱ hapṛak̕ raj ṭhen baṛe̱ hapen hirlạjońme ạliń bań hilok̕ do̱.

Ado̱ oṛak̕re cet̕ upạị hõ bako ạikạulet̕te uni koṛa gidrạ do̱ mit̕ṭań raj ṭhenkin gutikadea;' ado̱ uni gidrạ do̱ me̱ro̱m gupiko

---

No stranger is permitted inside this stall. A married daughter of the house, who in her girl days might go in there, is frequentty not permitted inside. She now belongs to another family and might cause religious pollution.

Then they together with the village watchman[15] entered the house and found the cow tied in the bhiṭar[16], the inner apartment reserved for the ancestors. They asked the boy: "Well, young man, how is it, is this your cow?"

"Yes," he replied, "it is this one."

"Well then, take your cow with you."

So he went away with his cow, and they fined that man ten rupees.

So there this story is at an end. It is thus much.

6. THE JACKAL AND THE PRINCE.

ONCE upon a time in the old days, people tell, there was a king, and this king had a son, an only one, and besides him he had no children.

Well, my dear fellow, as time passed, this king somehow or other became poor, he grew so poor, you can scarcely believe it, he became such as to go round and beg, and his son grew up to be fit to be a goat-herd.

One day the king gave his son some advice, that is, he talked to him: "Listen, my son, I am speaking to you; you see, we have grown poor. Formerly we had any amount of property; we had a kingdom[1], we had also cows and buffaloes. But now, however it has come to pass, all our wealth and goods have come to an end, and we are much concerned about you. Formerly we were having any amount of milk and curds; but in your time nothing at all comes into our hands; and we are feeling very dejected. Now, my son, I tell you this, before I leave you: in this world there is a tremendous number of kings, there are kings upon kings. Now I have become an old man, and your mother also is an old woman; we shall likely die some day, sooner or later. The day when we are no more, seek protection with some big king.

As they did not see any means of help at home, they let their boy take service with a king[2], where they set him to herd

dhuraukedea, ado uni gidra do ondegeye tahẽyena. Ado jom ńũ, kicrić, jotogeko emaea, ar bochor puraukate do bar ṭaka dormahako emaea; nonkate uni gidra doe asulok̕ kan tahẽkana.

Ado tahen tahente, kathae, uni gidraren apattet̕ doe goćena. Khange uni eṅgat buḍhi do aḍi baṛiće rak̕ baṛaea. Ado uni gidra koṛae menketa, Ia raj, apuńe goćena, aḍi uni reak̕ iń kaj korom lagit̕ rinte thoṛa thuṛi ṭaka emańme.

Ado uni raje menketa, Em mań emamge, ado cekatem halaetińa?

Ado uni koṛae menketa, Ona ṭaka auriń halaetam dhabić am baṛe khaṭaoińme.

Ado raj hõ, kathae, uniak̕ roṛe ańjomkettaea, ado mõṛẽ ṭakae emadea. Ado uni gidrai menketa, Noate do oka hõ oho hoelena, arhõ mõṛẽ ṭaka emańme, ar baṅkhan mõṛẽ ṭaka reak̕ caole baṛe emańme.

Ado sari mõṛẽ ṭaka reak̕ caolegeye emadea. Ado onako idikate peṛae nẽotaket̕koa, ado peṛa jarwakateko kaj koromketa. Ado jom ńũ baṛakate onko peṛa doe bida got̕kat̕koa. Ado arhõ uni koṛa do uni kisaṛ ṭhengeye calaoena.

Arhõ dapoṛ akat̕ ina mõṛẽ turui mãhã tayom khange uni eṅgattet̕ hõe goćena. Ado arhõ ona katha uni aćren kisaṛe laiadea, are metadea, Den arhõ rinte ṭaka emańme.

Ado uni kisaṛe menketa, E ya, rinte aḍim tenok̕ kana; ne bar ṭakań emam kana; ma niate baṛe kajkak̕me.

Ado uni koṛae menketa, Baṅa, raj, tinak̕re hõń jãhãnre hõ, pahil· unak̕ baṛe emańme; bań hala daṛeak̕tam khan, jivet̕ bhor am ṭhengeń tahena, enre hõm emańgea.

1 See p. 33, note 3. The Santali text has 'land', here meaning something belonging to a king or landlord.

2 See the same note p. 33.

3 Servants wages have been: food and clothes (two sets) and one rupee per year. Now-a-days they are raised to something more, four or five rupees, or other arrangements are made.

goats, and the boy stayed on there. They gave him his food and drink and clothes, in fact everything, and when a year was past, they gave him two rupees in wages[3]. In this way this child was maintaining himself.

In the course of time the father of the boy died, and his old mother was crying very much. The boy then said: "I say, king, my father has died; as I have much to perform on his behalf[4], please lend me a few rupees."

"I will certainly give you," the king replied; "but how are you going to pay me back?"

"Keep me in your service," the boy said, "until I pay you the money back."

The king listened to him and gave him five rupees; but the boy said: "With this nothing can be done; give me five rupees more, or else give me five rupees worth of rice."

So he gave him five rupees worth of rice; and, taking it all with him, the boy went and invited his friends and relatives, and when these had come together, he performed the usual ceremonies. When the friends had feasted, he bade farewell to them, and again returned to his employer.

Then, what a pity it was, som five or six days afterwards his mother also died. He again told his employer this, and said to him: "Please, lend me some rupees more."

His employer said: "Well, my lad, you are much burdened by debt; look, I am giving you two rupees; do what you have to do with this."

„No, king," the boy replied, "however much it may be and whatever may happen to me, please give me as much as the first time. If I cannot repay you, I shall stay with you my whole life; still you must give me."

[4] The Santals have also a number of ceremonies to perform in connexion with death, the last among these being what is called b h a ṇ ḍ a n, performed after some of the bones of the cremated body have been thrown into the Damuda river.

Adǫ bhạui, ạḍiye nẹhõren khane emadea; adǫ jǫtǫre kuṛi ṭakae hisạbadea are ǫl dǫhǫkaťa. Adǫ ona tayǫm uni rajren hǫpǫntẹťko añjǫmketa, nui mẹrǫm gupi koṛa isi ṭaka rine emadea mẹnte. Khange apattẹťko ruhẹť baṛakedea. Adǫ uni apatťẹťe mẹnketa, Acha cekaeam adǫń emade khan?

Ar uni rajren dǫ eae goṭań koṛa hǫpǫnko tahẽkantaea, adǫ onkoge onka dǫko metae kana. Arko mẹneťa, Ceť ńẹlte unạk ṭaka dǫm emadea? Uni dǫ ceťte ona ṭaka dǫe halaea? Uni dǫ abo ṭhene lade akana, arhõ rinem emae kana? Adǫ raj dǫ inạ kathage arhõe mẹneťa, Acha nit dǫ idi ocoae ma; hapen jãhã hiloke halaea.

Adǫ sạri uni koṛa dǫe idikeťte eńgat reake kaj kǫrǫmketa. Arhõ ruạṛkate uni koṛa dǫ uni kisạṛ ṭhengeye tahẽyena.

Adǫ tahẹn tahẹnte uni koṛa dǫ onko raj hǫpǫn koṛa dingeko ạṛisea, ona ṭaka reakgeko dhirạuea. Khange uni koṛa gidrạ dǫ ǫnẹ [5]apate metade tahẽkan, ona kathae disạketa, bańma, Noa dhạrtire dǫ ạḍi utạr raj menakkoa, raj cetan rajge menakkoa. Nonka khijlạute dǫ noko ṭhen dǫ ǫhǫń tahẽ daṛelena. Ǫkǫe tora nǫṇḍẹ khon dǫń dạṛa.

Adǫ onka mẹnkate uni koṛa dǫ ǫṇḍẹ khone dạṛketa, adǫe mẹnketa, Jãhãrege dhạrti mǫtǫren marań raj iń ńamkoa, onko ṭhengeń tahẹna. Adǫ onkae hudis idiyeta are calao idik kana.

Adǫ calak calạkte, kathae, raj bạriạtkoe ńamkeťkoa, bạhuko idiyede kan. Adǫe kulikeťkoa, Henda ho, okaren bạriạtko kanape?

Adǫko lạiadea, bańma, Phalnaren raj kanae; bạhu ạgule sẹnlena; hǫpǫntẹť koṛa lạgiť bạhule ạguyede kana, ar hạniań haṛam raj dǫ lahareko gǫk akadea khuṛkhuṛire.

---

[5] Marriages are as grand as possible, and a large body of men start from the bridegroom's house to attend the marriage ceremony and bring the bride back. These here are on their way back and are evidently Hindus.

[6] See p. 32, note 1. There are several shapes, the one here referred to is called khuṛkhuṛi. These have a bottom hanging from a long pole, which is curved like a dromedary's back, with a cloth-covering hanging down over the litter on both sides from the pole.

As he implored him very much, he let him have it; he made an account with him for altogether twenty rupees, and wrote it down. Shortly afterwards the king's sons heard that their father had lent twenty rupees to this goat-herd boy, and scolded him on that account. The father only said: "Well, what will you do, since I gave it to him?"

This king had seven sons, and it was they who spoke thus. They said: "What did you see that you gave him so many rupees? What has he to enable him to repay the money? He has been thrown upon us, a burden; on the top of that, you are lending him money?" The king again replied in the same way: "Well, let him have it now; some day in future he will pay it back."

The boy went away with the money and performed the proper ceremonies for his mother, and having come back again, he stayed on with his employer.

As the days passed, those princes worried the boy every day and used threats towards him in connexion with this money. Then the boy remembered the words his father had spoken to him, namely: "In this world there is a tremendous number of kings; there are kings upon kings. When they are tormenting me in this way, I shall certainly not be able to stay. I shall run away from here this instant."

With this in his mind, the boy ran away from there. "Somewhere I shall find the biggest kings on earth and shall stay with them;" saying this to himself, he went along.

As he was walking along, he met with a royal bridal procession[5]; they were carrying the bride along. "I say," he spoke to them, "wherefrom are you with this bride?"

"She belongs to such and such a king," they told him; "we went to bring the bride; we are bringning a bride for his son. Look there in the distance in front of us they are carrying the old king in a litter[6]."

Adǫ uni koṛa dǫe mẹnketa, Ǫkǫe tora iń hõ nui rajgeń pańja idiyea, pasẹťe nui kange marań raj dǫ. Adǫ onka hudiskate uni koṛa dǫ uni raj tayǫm tayǫmtegeye pańja idiyeťkoa.

Adǫ un jǫkhẹnge, kathae, eṅga toyo dǫ onko lahareye ńir parǫm gǫťena. Adǫ khange uni haṛam raj dǫ khuṛkhuṛi khon oḍokkate uni eṅga toyogeye salamadea. Adǫ uni koṛa dǫ onae ńẹlkede khane mẹnkeťa, Nui toyogeye marańa; judi nui raj marańe tahẹn khan, uni toyo dǫ ǫhǫe salamlea. Adǫ onka bujhạu baṛakate uni koṛa dǫ raj bạriạtko bạgikate uni toyogeye pańjakedea; jãhã sẹnge uni toyoe calaǩ, ǫntẹge uni koṛa hõe calaǩ kana, uni toyogeye pańja baṛaye kana.

Ar sẹ uni toyo dǫe hǫpǫn akaťkote hǫpǫn lạgiť jǫmaǩ sendrae sẹnlena. Adǫ uni koṛae pańja baṛayedete okare hõ bae ạt daṛeaťa. Uni toyo dǫ mẹrǫmko sẹ jãhãnko uni koṛa bǫtǫrte bae ạt daṛeaťa. Adǫe ạrisen khan, danderteye ruạṛ calaoena. Khange hǫpǫnko dǫ kẹyǫń mẹyǫṅko raǩ daramadea. Adǫ uni eṅga toyo dǫ haṛamtẹťe lạiae kana, bańma, Teheń dǫ miťṭań manwa gǫṭa ṭạṇḍiye pańja baṛayedińa; jãhã sẹngeń calaǩ, ǫntẹgeye pańjayediń kana. Onate teheń dǫ okare hõ bań ạt daṛeaťa, ẹkẹngeń ruạṛ hẹćena. Iṅgeye khudạu baṛań lekań ạikạukeťte bań gǫćleťkoa, ar uni manwa dǫ nǫṇḍẹ hạbiće pańja ạgukidińa.

Adǫ uni ạṇḍiạ ṭoyoe mẹnkeťa, Adǫ oka sẹn uni manwa dǫe calaoena?

Adǫe mẹnkeťa, Hǫntẹregeń ńẹl oṭokadea, adǫe oka sẹnen cǫń.

Adǫ uni ạṇḍiại mẹnkeťa, Do sẹ ńẹllem, bhalae oka sẹnena.

Adǫ sạri oḍok ńõǩkateye ńẹlkede dǫ, dander duạrreye japaǩ akan. Adǫ pạc ruạṛkateye metadea, Nǫṇḍẹge duạr ṭhene japaǩ akana. Ar uni koṛa dǫ japaǩkate ǫntẹ nǫtẹye bẹṅgẹť baṛayeťa. Adǫ ona dander sẹne bẹṅgẹťkeť dǫ miťṭan gạiye ńẹl ńamkedea; adǫ rǫṛ dǫ ceť hõ bae rǫṛ baṛayeťa, ẹkẹne thir akangea.

7 See p. 33, note 2.

8 The word used by the jackal, manwa, means man, one of the human species, as different from an animal.

The boy then said: "Well then, I also shall now this instant follow this king; perhaps he is the big king." Thinking this, the boy followed after the king's procession.

Just then, people tell, a she-jackal ran across the road[7] in front of them, and the old king got out of the litter and saluted the she-jackal. When the boy saw him do so, he said: "This jackal is the bigger one; if the king were the bigger one, he would surely not have saluted the jackal." Having reached this conclusion, the boy left the royal bridal procession and followed after the jackal. Wherever the jackal went, there also the boy went, he was constantly tracking the jackal.

Now this jackal had got young ones and had been out to hunt for food for them, and as the boy was following her, she could nowhere get a chance to catch anything. Out of fear of the boy, she was unable to find an opportunity to take a goat or anything else. As she got disgusted at this, she returned to her cave, and her young ones met her whining and whimpering. The she-jackal then spoke to her husband and said: "To-day a man[8] has been following me everywhere. In whatever direction I went, there he followed me. Therefore I have not been able to get a chance anywhere to-day; I have come back empty-handed. I felt as if he were pursuing me; therefore I did not kill anything, and this man has followed me right up here."

"And where has the man gone now?" the he-jackal asked.

"I last saw him over there," she replied. "Who knows where he has gone?"

"Do," the he-jackal said, "do look out and see where he has gone."

She consequently peeped out a little, and there he was, leaning against the side of the entrance to the cave. Drawing herself back she said: "He is here, leaning against the side of the entrance." The boy standing there leaning in this way, looked hither and tither. As he looked towards the cave, he saw a cow; but he did not say a single word, he remained silent.

Adọ uni ạṇḍịạ toyoe mẹneťa, Do sẹ kuliyem, bhala uni manwa dọ ceťe ńam kana.

Adọ uni eṅga dọe mẹneťa, Do am baṛẹ kuliyem. Adọ onka bana hoṛkin apaj kana.

Adọ uni ạṇḍịạ dọe mẹnkeťa, Amge enan khone pańja baṛayeťmea, am baṛẹ kuliyem.

Adọ onka uni ạṇḍịại metade khan dọe oḍokenteye metae kana, Henda manwa, ceť nọṇḍẹ dọm ńam kana?

Adọ uni koṛae mẹnkeťa, Aben ṭhenge hirlạjoṅ iń dọń hẹć akana.

Adọ uni eṅga dọ bọlọyente ạṇḍịại lạiadea, baṅma, Uni dọ alaṅ ṭhenge hirlạjoṅe hẹć akana.

Adọ onkae lạiade khan, kathae, bana hoṛkin oḍokena, adọkin metae kana, Ạliń dọliń toyo jạt kana ar am dọm manwa kana; ạliń ṭhen dọ cekatem hirlạ daṛeaǩa? Am lạgiť jọm dọ cekateliń kulạu daṛekema? Do calaǩme. Ar ạliń ṭhen dọ kạmi hõ bạnuǩtaliṅa, ceťliń kạmi ocomea?

Adọ uniye mẹnkeťa, Ọhọgeń sẹnlena; aben jãhãnaǩgeben kạmi ocoń, onageń kạmia. Iń dọ aben ṭhen askateń hẹć akana; nit dọ ọhọgeń sẹnlena.

Adọ onka ạḍi jide ṛọṛkeť khan, unkin toyo dọ mãyã lagaoǩeťkina, adọ ạkin ạkinkin galmaraokeťa, baṅma, Nui manwa dọ alaṅ ṭhen ạḍi askateye hẹć akana; jãhãnaǩ balaṅ bhọrae khan dọ, nọṇḍẹ khon•ọhọgeye sẹnlena. Ma nui gạigelaṅ ẹm dapoṛaea.

Adọ sạri uni gạikin emadea arkin metadea, Adọ manwa, ạliń ṭhen bhorsa mọntem hẹćen khan dọ, acha ẹṇḍẹkhan amaǩ pạtiạu lekaliń emam kana. Nũǩũi miťṭaṅ gạiye tahẽkantaliṅa; adọ uni gạige amliń emaṃ kana, ar nui gại khonge amaǩ dọ sanamaǩ hoyoǩtama. Jãhãnaǩge am jạruṛam, ona dọ nui gại ayo mẹnkate kọeyeme, onako jọtọ nui gại khonem ńama. Ar jãhãnaǩgem

---

[9] The Santal word h i r l ạ means refuge and protection, the protecting party standing between the other and all difficulties. The person seeking hirlạ acknowledges the protector as the one with whom he will deal in his relations to others. A servant is in his master's hirlạ, a wife is in the hirlạ of her husband, children in that of their father and so on.

"Do," the he-jackal said, "do ask him, what can this man possibly want?"

"You ask him, please," the she-jackal said. In this way they were urging each other.

Then the he-jackal said: "It is you he has been following the whole time. You ask him."

As the he-jackal said this, she went out and asked him: "Look here, man, what do you want here?"

"I have come to seek protection[9] with you," the boy said.

The she-jackal then entered the cave and spoke to her husband: "He has come to seek protection with us."

As he spoke in this way, they both went out and said to the boy: "We are of the jackal race and you are a man; how could you possibly find protection with us? How should we be able to provide you with food? Please, go away. There is no work for you with us; what could we let you do?"

"I am not going away," he replied. "Whatever you give me to do, that I shall do. I have come to you with great expectations; I am certainly not going away now."

As he spoke so persistingly, the two jackals felt compassion for him, and had some talk together, saying: "This man has come to us with great expectations; if we do not give him some kind of blessing, he will surely not go away from here. Let us give him this cow and have done with him."

Then, in very truth, they gave him the cow and said to him: „Well, man, as you came to us with expectations in your heart, we are giving you something according to your faith. Look here, we have a cow, and we are giving you this. From this cow you may get everything; whatever you need, ask this cow for that, calling her mother[10], and you will get it all from her. But whatever you ask her for, don't do it in the presence of people; otherwise they will rob you. When you ask her for anything,

---

[10] See p. 48, note 10.

kǫeye, ona do hǫṛko samańre dǫ alom kǫeyea, bańkhanko ṛećmea. Am dǫm kǫeye khan, eskarre kǫeyeme, ar jāhāeko bulạumere hǭ, am dǫ alogem emakoa.

Adǫ uni koṛae mẹnketa, Acha, adǫ niạge bhǫrben emadiń khan, uḍi maha bhạg, ma sarhaokokben, ar Cando aben hǭe bhǫraben ma!

Adǫ kathae, uni koṛa dǫ gạiye tiạkkedea, adǫ oṛak sẹne ruạṛ kana. Adǫ calak calakte mitṭań bajar atoe ńamketa, adǫ ona bajar paṛǫmkate arhǭ mitṭań bajare ńamketa; adǫe mẹnketa, Ạkhir iń calakgea, nẹtẹrege um baṛakate jǫl pankoń jǫm baṛawanrege. Adǫ mitṭań pukhriye ńamketa, adǫe mẹnketa, Niạ pukhrirege um baṛakateń jǫm baṛawanrege. Adǫ ona pukhriregeye um baṛayena.

Adǫ ona pukhrirege pharak sẹnre mitṭań maejiu dǫ kicriće sǫkbǫt kan tahẹ̃kana. Adǫ uni koṛa dǫe mẹneta, Nui ạimại dǫ ǫhǫ jạniće pǫhǫmińa. Adǫ kathae, onka mẹnkate uni koṛa dǫ um rakapkate gại ṭhen sẹnkateye metae kana, Dẹ ayo, palaṭ emańme. Adǫ kathae, kicriće ulạwadea, adǫe ḍeṅga baṛayena, adǫ khub marań bhǫdrǫ hǫṛ lekae ńẹlena. Adǫ onakate thạri bạṭiye kǫekedea, adǫ inạ hǭe emadea; arhǭ piṭhạ tabenkoe koekedea, adǫ ońa hǭe ulạwadea. Adǫe jǫm baṛaket khane metadea, Ẹ ayo, ma noa thạri bạṭiko dǫ baekakme. Adǫ kathae, onako dǫ arhǭ uni gạigeye utketa.

Ar uni ạimại dǫ tan man onakoe ńẹńẹl kana, adǫ hare phare sẹn gǫtente uni ạimại dǫ ać hereltẹte lạiadea bańma, Mitṭań birana hǫṛren gạiyiń ńẹlkedea, onkan gạị dǫ tis hǭ bań ńẹl akatkoa.

[11] Chando is the Santal name for the sun and also for the moon, in the last case generally, or, if necessary, with ńindạ, i. e. 'night' put before. In the course of time, but so far as it is possible to ascertain now, not very long ago, the Supreme Being, called Ṭhạkur by the old gurus, has been to a certain extent identified with the sun. Chando here means the Supreme Being. It might be noted that some missionaries for some time used Chando as their name in Santali for the Christian God. This shows how Santals may be understood to use the word.

do it privately, and if people try to persuade you, you must not on any account give them anything."

"Very well", the boy said, "since you have given me this blessing, it is an exceedingly great luck for me; may praise be yours, and may Chando[11] also bless you two."

Thereupon the boy led the cow away and started for his home. As he walked along, he came to a bazar town[12], and having passed through this he came to another bazar; then he said: "Afterwards I shall go further; let me first have a bath and get some refreshments somewhere here." So he found a tank[13] and said: "Here in this tank I shall take a bath and afterwards take some food." Thereupon he bathed in the tank.

Now a woman was washing clothes in the same tank some distance off, and the boy said to himself: "This woman will likely not be able to see me clearly." So, having come up from his bath, he went to the cow and spoke to her: "Please, mother, give me a change of clothes." She brought clothes out for him. He put the loin-cloth on, and now he looked like a very fine gentleman. Thereupon he asked the cow for brass plates and cups, and she gave him that also. Then he asked her for cakes and *taben*[14], and this also she brought forth for him. When he had had his food, he said to her: "Please, mother, put these plates and cups away." And the cow, people, tell, swallowed those again.

The woman was looking at as much as she could, and hurrying away, she went to her husband and told him, saying: "I have seen a cow belonging to a stranger; cows like her I have never in my life seen. The man bathed in the tank; then he asked the

12 People live in villages; when these are large, with shops and the like, they become bazars or towns. The name presupposes that it is not a Santal village but a Hindu or other town.

13 See p. 84, note 5.

14 See p. 4, note 5.

Uni hoṛ do̠ pukhrireye umena, ado̠ uni gại̤ge palaṭe ko̠ekedea, arhō̠ thạri bạṭiye ko̠ekedea, ona hō̠e emadea; arhō̠ piṭha tabene ko̠ekedea, inạ hō̠e emadea. Arhō̠e metadea, Ma baekam; ado̠ arhō̠ uni gại̤ge ona do̠e ut́ket́a. Ado̠ń metam kana, ma nui gại do̠ jāhā lekatelaṅ e̠ṛe̠yea.

Ado̠ uni herel hoṛ do̠ bae pạtiạuk̓ kan tahē̠kana, me̠nkhan uni ại̤mại do̠ ạḍiye jidket́a. Khange ado̠ uni herele me̠nket́a, Acha, bhalaṅ biḍạulege, ado̠ e̠ṇḍe̠ anaṅ iń pạtiạuk̓a, ar baṅkhan o̠ho̠geń pạtiạulena.

Ado̠ uni ho̠ṛkin ho̠ho̠ ạgukedea, ado̠kin metae kana, Iạ ho peṛa, okatem calak̓a? Teheń do̠ no̠ṇḍe̠ ale ṭhenge gitiće me; gapa do̠ ạḍire beret́katem calak̓a. Am jo̠m ńūi lạgit́ do̠ alele emama, ar nui gại jo̠m lạgit́ ghās hō̠le emama.

Ado̠ uniye me̠net́a, Baṅa, iń do̠ baṅ gitića am ṭhen do̠.

Ado̠ banar haṛam buḍhite ạḍikin jidket́a, ado̠ ạkin oṛak̓tekin idikedea, ar mit́ṭaṅ mela oṛak̓ gitić lạgit́kin aṛak̓adea. Ado̠ jo̠m ńū reaṅko kuli baṛakedea, ado̠e me̠nket́a, Baṅ jo̠ma, nitgeń jo̠m baṛa akat́a. Ar se̠ uni koṛa do̠e me̠net́a, Sanam hoṛ iń jạpit́ ocoakoa, ado̠ unre nạhāk̓ jo̠m lạgit́ do̠ nui gại̤geń ko̠eyea. Ado̠ onka me̠nkate onko ṭhen daka jo̠m do̠ bae re̠be̠nlena.

Khange unkin ona oṛak̓ren haṛam buḍhi do̠ nonka me̠nkate kạphạriạukin e̠ho̠p̓ke̠t́a: uni herele me̠nket́a, Bhala e̠ṛe̠ e̠ṛe̠laṅ kạphạriạua, ado̠ nạhāk̓ iń do̠ usạt́ iń oḍok calak̓a, ado̠ jāhā se̠nreń tāṛāk̓kok̓a; ado̠ bhalaṅ ńe̠lea cet́koe ko̠eyea, ado̠ sạri kana me̠nkhan do̠laṅ e̠ṛe̠yea.

Ado̠ onka galmaraokate ạkin haṛam buḍhi kạphạriạukin e̠ho̠p̓ket́a, ado̠ ạḍi bạṛić cet́ko co̠ṅ uṭkạ paṭkakin kạphạriạuena. Ado̠ khange uni herel hoṛ do̠e usạt́ go̠t́ena; ado̠e me̠n oṭokak̓ kana, Ma ape baṛe̠ tahē̠kok̓pe, iń do̠ baṅ tahe̠na ape ṭhen do̠. Ado̠ onka me̠nkate uni hoṛ do̠e oḍok calaoena. Ado̠ arhō̠ oka se̠nte co̠ṅ ruạṛ he̠ćkate uni hoṛ do̠ uni koṛae ḍera akan tahē̠kan oṛak̓ co̠ṭre

[15] The thing meant is a contrivance to be used with bullock-carts. It is a wooden frame with four uprights, the 'walls' being made from some kind of rough rope or twigs or the like.

cow for a change of clothes; brass plates and cups he also asked her for. That she also gave him. Again he asked her for cakes and *taben*; this she also gave him. Again he said to her: Please, put it away, and then the cow swallowed the things. I tell you this, somehow or other we must cheat him for this cow."

The man, her husband, did not believe this story; but as the woman persisted, her husband said: "All right, I shall put it to the test; then only I shall believe this; otherwise I shall certainly not believe it."

They thereupon called the man and said to him: "I say, my friend, where are you going? Stay the night here with us to-day; then you may get up and go away to-morrow, early in the morning. We shall give you food and drink, and we shall also give you straw for your cow."

"No," he replied, "I shall not stay the night with you."

But both husband and wife were very persistent, and finally took him to their home and let him have an empty house to sleep in. They asked him about food; but he said: "I shall not have any food, I have just had." The boy was thinking: "I shall let all people go to sleep; then I shall presently ask this cow for something to eat." Having this in his mind, he was unwilling to take food with these people.

Then the husband and wife living in that house commenced to quarrel in the following way: the husband said: "I say, let us pretend to quarrel; so I shall go out sulky and lie in wait somewhere; then I shall see what he asks her for, and if it is true, we shall cheat him for that cow."

Having talked together in this way, husband and wife commenced to quarrel; they quarrelled something awful, raking up old and forgotten matters. The husband then suddenly commenced to sulk and said: "Well, you stay on, I am not going to stay with you." Saying this, he went out. Some time afterwards, the man returned by another way — now there was under the roof in the house where the boy was staying a manuring basket[15] —

mitʼṭaṅ gurić caklaoak duli tahẽkana. Adǫ oka sẹnte cǫe dẹćente ona duli cetanreye gitić akana; uni koṛa hõ bae disạ rakapledea.

Adǫ khange mitʼ ghạṛi tayǫm khan uni ạimại dǫe ńam baṛayedea, adǫ uni koṛa ṭhene calaoena; adǫe metae kana, Henda bạbu, pasẹ nọṇḍẹ am ṭhene hẹć akan?

Adǫ uni koṛae mẹnketʼa, Okorić? Nọṇḍẹ dǫ bae hẹć akana. Adǫ uni koṛae mẹnketʼa, Ceka baṛalenaben?

Adǫ uniye mẹnketʼa, Cetʼko cǫliń joṛo baṛawana. Adǫ ńẹlme sẹ, okate cǫe oḍok calaoen; iń dǫń mẹnetʼa, pasẹ nọṇḍẹ am ṭhene hẹć akan.

Adǫ uni koṛae mẹnketʼa, Baṅ, nọṇḍẹ dǫ bae hẹć akana; hećlen khan dǫń lạikema. Adǫ enka mẹnkate uni maejiu hõe ruạṛena.

Adǫ khange uni koṛa dǫe gitićena. Adǫ sać sućsanam hǫṛko thir cabayene aṭkarketʼko khan dǫe mẹnketʼa, Nit dǫ sanam hǫṛko jạpitʼketʼa, ǫhǫ jạnićko disạńa, jǫmak iń kǫeanrege. Adǫ sạri onka mẹnkate uni koṛa dǫ gại ṭhen jǫmake khojkedea, ar emadete jǫm ńũ baṛakate arhõe bae ocokedea, are gitićenteye jạpitʼketʼa.

Ar uni tãṛãk hǫṛ dǫ onako tan mane ńẹlkede khane mẹnketʼa, Baṅa, oka kathae lạiadiń, ona dǫ sạri kangea. Nui gại dǫ phǫr phundikateliń hataoetaegea. Adǫ khub jạpitʼ akatʼe ạikạukede khane ãṛgoyente uni gại dǫe raṛa idikedetaea, ar uni gại muṭhạn lekanićge aćren gại ạgukate uniye tǫllede ṭhene tǫlkadea, ar uniren gại dǫ aćren gại ṭhene ader mitʼkadea.

Adǫ dosar hilok aṅgayen khan, uni koṛa dǫe beretʼena, adǫ gạiye raṛakedeteye tiạge kana. Adǫ kathae, uni gại dǫ bae calak kana. Adǫ uni koṛae mẹnketʼa, Iạ ho peṛa hǫṛ, gại dǫpe bǫdǫladiṅa; nui gại dǫe baṅ kana iṅren dǫ.

Adǫko metae kana, Baṅ, uni gại kantamgeae. Ẹṇḍẹge holam tǫlledea, ar amge teheń hõ ŕaṛakatem tiạk oḍokkedea. Cedak onka dǫm pharebetʼlea? Ma bhala noko ato hǫṛ kulikom, nenkan

---

[16] See p. 46, note 7.

and having mounted up there somehow, he was lying on the top of that basket. The boy was not aware of his mounting up there.

A short while afterwards the woman came looking for her husband; she came to the boy and said to him: "I say, my lad, perhaps he[16] has come here to you?"

"Why, no," the boy replied, "he has not come here. What happened to you two?" he asked.

"Oh," the woman said, "we had some disagreement. Then, you see, he went out somewhere; I am wondering, perhaps he has come here."

"No," the boy replied, "he has not come here; if he had come, I should tell you." After this had been said, the woman went back again.

Thereupon the boy lay down; when he felt that all were resting and all was quiet as the grave, he said: "Now all people have gone to sleep; no one will be likely to be aware of what I do; let me ask for food." Saying this the boy asked the cow for food, and when she had given him and he had eaten, he let her put all away, whereupon he lay down and slept.

When the man who was lying in wait had been looking all he could at this, he said: "No, what she told me, that is the truth. We shall get possession of this cow by some stratagem or other." When he understood that the boy was soundly asleep, he came down, unbound the cow and took her away; thereupon he brought one of his own cows, looking just like the other cow, and tied her where the boy had tied his, and so he took the boy's cow in among his own cows.

When it dawned next morning, the boy got up, unbound the cow and commenced to lead her along; but the cow would not go. The boy then said: "Look here, my friend, you have changed cows with me. This cow is not mine."

"No," they answered him, "the cow is yours. You tied her there yesterday, and you have also yourself unbound her and led her out to-day. Why are you making such false charges

gaige holako ńel agu akatmea. Adǫ cekatem mẹneťa, nui gại dǫe baṅ kantiṅa mẹnte?

Adǫ uni koṛae mẹnkeťa, Iṅren gại dǫ tiạk̓ hewa gại kanae; nun din iṅ dǫ goṭaṅ tiạk̓ baṛayede kana, ar nui gại dǫ tiạk̓te bae calak̓ kana; are baṅ kantiṅa nui gại dǫ, ǫhǫṅ idilea.

Adǫko mẹnkeťa, Bam idiye khanle cekamea?

Adǫ uni koṛae mẹnkeťa, Acha, noa reaṅbon bicạrlege.

Adǫko mẹnkeťa, Acha, do ạgukom.

Adǫ ona atoren mostajir ar atoren hǫṛe riạu ạguketkoa. Adǫ uni hǫṛ dǫ tinre cǫṅ uni mostajir ar ato hǫṛ dǫe ran gǫtketkoa; uni mostajir hǫṛ mit̓ sae ṭakae gǫk̓adea ar onko ato hǫṛ mit̓ saeye gǫk̓atkoa, are metatkoa sanam hǫṛ, Iṅ sẹn baṛe rǫṛpe ar iniye tǫl akade gại baṛẹ ḍigriaepe.

Adǫ onko dǫs jona hō̧ uniak̓ ṭakako jǫmkettae khan, uni sẹn lekageko rǫṛketa, ar uniye bǫdǫl akawade gạigeko ḍigriadea. Adǫ uni koṛae mẹnketa, Iạ baba mō̧ṛȩ̃ hǫṛ, noa bicạrre dǫ baṅ khusilena; hapẹ, uni ǫkǫe hǫṛ ṭhen gạiyiṅ ńam akade, uni hǫṛ iṅ ạgulege; adǫ ǫkǫeṭak̓ gạiye ẹm akawadiṅ, unigeye baḍaea. Nui gạigeye metaṅ khan dǫ, nuigeṅ idiyea; adǫ hapẹ, uni hǫṛ iṅ ạgulege.

Adǫko metadea, Acha, do ạguyem.

Adǫe metatkoa, Ma ẹnḍekhan gại dǫ ape jimạgeṅ bạgiae kana.

Adǫko metaḍea, Acha, do calak̓me, gại dǫ ǫhǫe cekak̓tama.

Adǫ khangeye calaoena, ar unkin toyo dǫ, kathae, cekakote cǫkin baḍae gǫtketa, uni gại dǫe ẹṛẹ ocoyena mẹnte. Adǫ uni koṛae sẹn tiok̓ketkin khangekin kuli gǫtkedea, Cele ya manwa, gại dǫ ẹn kathaeyem ẹṛẹ ocoyena?

---

17 & 18 In the first instance the village authorities are appealed to. Also Hindu villages have a kind of headman or leading man.

19 Now-a-days the Five are frequently called the Ten, (d ǫ s, the ten persons) always using the Bengali word. When speaking of the Five, both Santali — so most commonly — and Bengali are used; but if the Santali word for 'ten' is used, it does not mean anything else than the number.

against us? Well, ask the people of this village whether they have seen such a cow of yours yesterday. How can you then say that this cow is not your cow?"

"My cow," the boy said, "is a cow accustomed to be led; so long a time I have been leading my cow everywhere; but this cow will not be led. She is not my cow this one; I am not taking her away."

"If you don't take her away, what can we do with you?" they said.

"Very well," the boy replied, "we shall first let people judge in this matter."

"All right," they said, "do bring judges."

The boy then called the headman of the village[17] and the village people[18]. The other man in the meantime had found an opportunity of bribing the headman and the village people. He promised the headman one hundred rupees, and the village people one hundred, and said to them: "Speak on my side and decree him the cow he has tied there."

As the Ten[19] had taken his money, they spoke on his side, and decreed the exchanged cow to belong to the boy. The boy then said: "Well, respected Five, I am not satisfied with this judgement; please wait, let me first bring the person from whom I have got the cow. He knows which cow he has given me. If he tells me it is this cow, I shall take her away. Wait then, let me bring that person first."

"Very well," they said, "bring him."

"Then I leave this cow in your charge," he said to them.

"All right," they replied, "do go; nothing shall happen to your cow."

The boy then went. Now the two jackals somehow or other had got to know that he had been cheated out of the cow, and when the boy reached them, they at once asked him: "Well, you man, they tell you have been cheated out of the cow?"

Adǫe mȩnkeťa, Hȩ̃ baba, sạrigeń ȩṛȩ ocoyena.

Adǫkin metadea, Tǫbȩ ceť lạgiťem hȩć akana?

Adǫe mȩnkeťa, Aben iḱdigeń hȩć akana; delabon bicạra.

Adǫ unkinkin mȩnkeťa, Ǫṇḍȩn ato hǫṛ ar mạńjhi dǫ bam saᵽleťkoa?

Adǫe mȩnkeťa, Saᵽ jarwaleťkogeań, mȩnkhan uni sȩn lekage sanam hǫṛko rǫṛkeťte iń dǫ bạń khusilena, adǫ onateń hȩć akawaťbena. Adǫ delabon bicạrkate gạï delaoańben.

Adǫkin mȩnkeťa, Acha, delabon.

Adǫko calaoena; adǫ sȩnkate ȩkkalte uni mostajir mạńjhiko saᵽkedea, adǫko metadea, bańma, Noa atore aleren gạï bǫdǫlte dosra gạiko ȩm akawaťlea. Ma adǫ ato hǫṛ jarwakate uni hǫṛ saᵽaleme, adǫbon galmaraoa, ar bańkhan am upạrtele lạlisa.

Adǫ khange uni mạńjhiyo lǫlǫ gǫťente gọḍete kolkedea ato hǫṛ lạlạï, ar uni kombṛo hǫṛ hǫ̃ko laiadea. Khange adǫ miťṭań hesaḱ buṭạreko jarwayena. Adǫ onko toyoteko hǫ̃ko calaoena, adǫ satrạńgi bichạnakin aṭeťkeťa unkin toyo dǫ, adǫ onare duruᵽkate pankin jǫjǫm kana. Adǫ sanam hǫṛko thir baṛa akana, ǫkǫe hǫ̃ ceť hǫ̃ bako rǫṛeťa.

Adǫ uni toyo ạṇḍịạï mȩneťa, Ǫkǫe ghus jǫmkateye bicạra, tǫbȩ uniren bǫ̃s . dǫ eae pusṭi dhạbić ićko jǫmtaea noa purire hǫ̃ ar hana purire hǫ̃. Ar judi ona ghusaḱ mǫ̃ṛȩ̃ hǫṛ samańre khulạukateye lạï sǫdǫrkeťa mȩnkhan, tǫbȩ ona bidhi dǫ bań lagaoaea. Nonka leka mare hapṛamkoko rǫṛ akaťa. Ar jãhãeaḱ jinis hạuṇḍikate jãhãeye hataoa, uni dǫ nǫrǫk kũṇḍreye ḍubạuḱa. Noa hǫ̃ko rǫṛ akaťa. Adǫ bhala aboge mǫ̃ṛȩ̃ hǫṛ, noa katha dạriạp

---

20 The jackal is acting in proper pleader style.

21 See p. 20, note 2.

22 Ficus religiosa, L.

23 For important people a fine cloth is spread to sit on. What is here mentioned, is a kind of rug with stripes of different colours. It is scarcely ever found with the Santals, but used by the better class of Hindus.

24 Betel nut, commonly chewed by the Hindus, sometimes also by Santals at the present day.

"Yes, father," he replied, "I have really been cheated."

"What have you come for then?" they asked him.

"I have come," he answered, "to take you along with me. Come, we shall judge the case."

"Did you not apply to the village people and the headman there?" they asked him.

"I applied to them and brought them together," he replied: "but as they alle spoke on his side, I was not satisfied, and therefore I have come to you. Please come and judge and help me to get the cow."

"All right," they said, "come along."

So they went; having arrived there, they at once took hold of the headman and spoke to him: "Here in this village they have given us[20] another cow instead of our own. Please gather the village people and bring the man to us: then we shall talk the matter over; otherwise we shall bring a suit against you."

The headman then took the matter up at once and sent the goḍet[21] to tell the village people; the thief he also called. They assembled at the foot of a pipol[22] tree. The jackal-party also went there, and the two jackals spread out a many-coloured durrie[23], and sitting down on this, they were eating pan[24]. All present were quiet; no one said anything.

Then the jackal said: "He who passes judgement after having taken a bribe, his descendants shall for seven generations eat his stools both in this world and in the next. But if he gives information about the bribe before the Five and tells everything, then this fate will not befall him. So the ancestors have told. And if anybody by oppression takes anybody else's property, then that person will be immersed in hell's dung[25]. This they have also told. Now we are the Five, the judges; investigate this matter properly and speak. Let us judge righteously before

---

25 The idea is a place in the nether-world filled with dung. Here those who have committed certain sins are immersed.

ṭhikkate rọṛtabonpe. Cando samaṅre dhọrọmgebon bicạra, ar unkin bạdi ar protibạdi hõ dhọrọmkin rọṛ ma. Oka hike kan, onagebon bicạra. Ma rọṛtabonpe.

Adọ uni mạṅjhiye mẹnkeťa, Noa katha dọ sạri kangea, baba; iṅ dọ nui kombṛo hoṛ miť sae ṭakae ẹm akawadiṅa are metadiṅa, Iṅ sẹn leka baṛẹ rọṛme, onate noa bicạr dọ bale phanḍaoleťa.

Khange ato hoṛ hõko mẹnkeťa, Hẽ, baba, sạrige ale hõ miť sae ṭakae ẹm akawaťlea, onate bicạr dọ oka hõ bale goṭaleťa.

Adọ uni toyoe mẹnkeťa, Ọtẹ, baba mõṛẽ hoṛ, aṅjọmpe sẹ, katha dọ sọdọren dọ. Ma bhala, am protibạdi hoṛ, ceťem mẹneťa?

Adọ uniye mẹnkeťa, Baṅa baba, ini gạị kangetaeyae, iṅ dọ baṅ hatao akadetaea.

Adọ uni toyoe mẹnkeťa, Pasẹ noa katha sạbudlen khan, ceťem ẹmọḱa?

Adọ uni hoṛe mẹnkeťa, Sạbudena mẹnkhan, dobṛa sạjạiyiṅ ẹmọḱa.

Adọ toyoe mẹnkeťa, Ma aṅjọm dọhọkape, baba ape mõṛẽ hoṛ, ar katha hõ bujhạutabonpe. Nui hoṛ dọ aćtegeye ḍanḍọmoḱ kana. Judi bae hatao akade khan, cedaḱ ghus dọe ẹm akawaťkoa? Nui dọ maraṅ ḍạkuren sẹs kanae. Ńẹlpe, hatao akade tuluć bae goḍaoeťa. Ar ape dọ nui hoṛ gai ạguye jọkheć jạnićpe ńẹl akadetaegea, ar ạliṅ dọ baliṅ ńẹl akadetaea? Ar delabon nãhãḱ, gạị paltebon calaḱa; ẹkkalte uni gạigeliṅ udugea sẹ baṅ nãhãḱ, na honẹć iṅ dọ baṅ udugea, nui iṅ bạhugeye udugea, onare biswạs ńẹl-taliṅpe.

Khangeko mẹnkeťa, Acha delabon, bhala onagebon ńẹllege.

Adọ sạri gạị palteko calaoena; ọkọeṭaḱ kane nuiren gạị, unige ẹkkalteye uduḱ goťkedea. Adọ mạṅjhi ar ato hoṛteko kulikedea, Cele bạbu, nui gạị kangetamae?

26 See p. 68, note 11. The Supreme Being is believed to be the final judge.

27 One is here reminded of the proceedings of a regular court. Some expressions used here and also further down are taken from the court language.

Chando[26], and the accused and the complainant[27] let them also speak righteously. What is right, that we shall decide. Please now, speak up."

Then the headman said: "That is a true word, sir; this thief has given me one hundred rupees and said to me: "Please speak on my side;" therefore we did not settle this matter."

Then the village people also said: "Yes, sir, in truth, he has also given us one hundred rupees; therefore we did not come to any decision in connexion with this matter."

"Listen," the jackal said, "do you hear, respected Five; please listen, the whole has been disclosed. Now you defendant, what have you to say?"

"No, sirs," the man answered, "this is his; I have not taken his cow."

"If by any chance," the jackal then said, "this case is proved, what will you give?"

"If it be proved against me," the man answered, "I shall pay double."

"Please remember this," the jackal said, "keep it in mind, respected Five; also understand what he says. This man is being fined by himself. If he has not taken the cow, why has he given bribes to these people? This man is the limit, the very worst type of a robber. Mark this, although he has taken the cow, he does not confess. And you have likely seen his cow when he was bringing it, and we two, have not we seen her? Please come then, let us go to the cow-herd; we shall at once point out the cow, you will see presently. If I should fail in doing so, this wife of mine will point her out. Thereby see our reliability."

"Very well," they said, "come along; let us have a look round first."

They then went to the cow-herd, and the jackal at once pointed out the cow that belonged to the boy. The headman and village people then asked him: "Well, my lad, is this your cow?"

Ado̱ uni koṛae me̱nket́ae, Hẽ̱, baba, nui kangeae.

Ado̱ ona katha ńe̱lkate onko ho̱ṛ do̱ ạḍi bạṛićko hahaṛayena arko me̱nket́a, Baṅa, noa bicạr do̱ sạri kangea, ar baṅkhan nukin toyo jạt abo phạrsi do̱ o̱ho̱kin ro̱ṛlea. Ar ńe̱lpe, nukin do̱kin oka disomren kan co̱ṅ, nui gại do̱ cekatekin ńe̱l oromkedea? Ado̱ khange uni ho̱ṛko kulikedea, Cele phalna, sạrige nui gại do̱m hataoledea se̱ baṅ?

Ado̱ khangeye tirupena, cet́ hō̱ bae ro̱ṛlet́a. Khange ạḍi bạṛićko ro̱ṛkede khane kạbulket́a. Ado̱ko metadea, Cele nit do̱ ho̱rem manaoket́a se̱ baṅ?

Ado̱e me̱nket́a, Hē̱, manaoket́geaṅ.

Ado̱ khange toyoe me̱nket́a, Ado̱ de̱ bhala abo mō̱ṛē̱ ho̱ṛ, ado̱ tinạḱbon ḍaṇḍo̱mede kana?

Ado̱ onko mō̱ṛē̱ ho̱ṛko me̱nket́a, De̱ amge ro̱ṛtabonme.

Ado̱ uni toyoe me̱nket́a, Tinạḱ babon ḍaṇḍo̱me? O̱ne̱ enanre aćtegeye ro̱ṛ akat́, Judi noa katha sạbudena me̱nkhan, dobṛa sạjạiyiń e̱mo̱ḱa. Nonka ać mocategeye ro̱ṛ akat́a se̱ baṅ?

Ado̱ onko mō̱ṛē̱ ho̱ṛko me̱nket́a, Hē̱, noa katha do̱le aṅjo̱m akat́gea.

Ado̱ onage tho̱, baba. De̱n nitoḱ do̱ dobṛa sạjạiye e̱mo̱ḱ ma; ape ato ho̱ṛ mit́ sạe, ar mạṅjhi ho̱ṛ mit́ sae, ar nui gại reaḱ bar sae; ado̱ jo̱to̱re pon sae hoyoḱ kana. Ado̱ pon sae reaḱ dobṛa, irạl saeye e̱mo̱ḱ ma, ar baṅkhan o̱ho̱ń bataolea. Judi baṅ hute̱ć sạbudlen khan, ać hō̱ co̱ṅ dobṛae hataoke. Ado̱ de̱n nitoḱ do̱ irạl sae e̱mo̱ḱme.

Ado̱ sạri jo̱to̱koteko ruhe̱t́kedete irạl sae ṭakako e̱m ocokedea. Ado̱ ona ṭaka do̱ onko mō̱ṛē̱ ho̱ṛge jo̱to̱ ṭakae emat́koa, ar uni gại kisạ̃ṛ koṛa do̱ ge̱l ṭakae emadea, ar uni toyo do̱ cet́ hō̱ bae hataolet́a. Ado̱ ini gạiko tiạḱḱedete onko do̱ko calaoena; ado̱ inạ bajar paṛo̱mkatekin metadea, Me̱n ado̱ nonka ho̱ṛ samaṅre do̱ jãhãnaḱ alom ko̱eyea, baṅkhan arhō̱ko e̱ṛe̱mea. Ado̱ unkin toyo do̱ ạkin oṛaḱtekin calaoena, ar uni koṛa hō̱ ać oṛaḱ mohṇḍa se̱ne calaoena.

"Yes, sirs," the boy replied, "this one it is."

When they saw this, the people were very much astonished and said: "Surely, this is the true judgement; otherwise, these two jackals would not have spoken our language. And mark this, how did these two, who are from who knows which country, recognize the cow?" They then asked the man: "I say, so and so, did you really take this cow or not?"

He sat there with bowed head and did not say a word; when they had given him an awful scolding, he at last confessed. Then they asked him: "Well, did you respect the way or not now?"

"I did so," he replied.

Then the jackal said: "Well, now then, we the Five, how much are we fining him?"

"Please," the Five said, "you speak for us."

The jackal then said: "Why, how much should we fine him? A while ago he himself has spoken: If this case be proved against me, I shall pay double. He has spoken in this way with his own mouth, is it not so?"

The Five then said: "Yes, we have heard that said."

"Just so, sirs. Now then let him give double punishment: You village people one hundred, and the headman one hundred; and for this cow two hundred; that is in all four hundred rupees. Let him so give the double of four hundred, that is eight hundred; otherwise I shall not heed you. If the case had not been proved, he would, of course, himself have taken double. So now then, out with eight hundred rupees."

As they all scolded him, they made him give eight hundred rupees. This money he all gave to the Five, and to the boy, the cow's owner, he gave ten rupees; but the jackal did not take anything. The boy and the jackals led the proper cow away and went along. When they had passed the bazar, the two said to the boy: "Be careful, don't ask her for anything in that way when others are present; otherwise people will cheat you again." The pair of jackals then went home, and the boy also started going towards his home.

Adọ kathae, calaḱ calaḱte uni koṛa dọ arhõ mit́ṭan bajar atoe tioḱket́a, adọ ona bajar ṭhenge ber hõe hạsuroḱ kana. Adọ ona bajar hana sare mit́ṭaṅ maraṅ utạr ul bagwan tahẽkana, ar ona bagwanre dọ haṭ hõ hoyoḱa, ar ọṇḍẹge ạḍi utạr bepari gaḍwanko ḍera akan tahẽkana. Adọ uni koṛa hõe mẹnket́a, Iń hõ noa bagwanregeń ḍeraḱa, adọ gapa setaḱre beret́kate oṛaḱ sẹn iń calaḱa. Adọ kathae, onko gaḍwanko ḍera akan hana sare onko khon tophat ńọ̃kre mit́ṭaṅ dare buṭạre aćhõe duṛup̣ena, ar uni gạị hõ ona dare rẹhẹt́reye tọlkadea.

Adọ inạ mit́ ghạṛi khange, kathae, maraṅ utạr họedaḱe unạuket́a, goṭa, kathae, ńũt cabayena; ar inạ mit́ ghạṛi khange họedaḱ hẹć gọt́ena ar bogeteye daḱet́ kana. Ar onko gaḍwan dọ, kathae, jọtọre mit́ hajar ganko tahẽkana; ar ona họedaḱ jọkhẹn dọ akoaḱ gạḍi latarkoreko bọlọ akana. Ar uni koṛa dọ, kathae, họedaḱ hẹćen khan dọ uni gạige tạmbui kọekedete onae beret́ket́a, ar ona bhitrire bana hoṛkin bọlọ akana; ar mit́ ńindạị daḱketa setaḱ dhạbić.

Khange onko gaḍwan dọko mẹnet́a, Durrẹ! hola ma cet́ hõ baṅ tahẽkantae; adọ okare noa tạmbu dọe ńamket́a? Dhora nui gạị khonge noa dọe ńam akat́a.

Adọ kathae, aṅga marsalen khan, uni koṛa hõe as basaoena, adọe mẹnet́a, Nit nãhãḱ noa tạmbuń bae ocoye khan dọ hoṛko ńẹleńa. Pạhil ṙeka baṅkhan arhõ gạiko ẹṛẹ bọtẹćkińa; teheń dọ nẹṇḍẹgeń tahẹna; ạyup̣ ocoaḱ, adọ unre nãhãḱ iń bae ocoyea, adọ gapa dọ sim raḱre nọṇḍẹ khon iń dạṛa.

Adọ kathae, goṭa sińe tahẽ ạyup̣ena. Adọ ńindạ khange, kathae, ona tạmbu dọe bae ocokedea. Adọ uni koṛae jạpit́ket́ jọkhẹnge onko gaḍwan dọko hẹć gọt́ena, adọ mit́ṭaṅ dhĩṛũ gạị uni ṭhenko tọl oṭokadea, ar ako dọ uniren gạiko idikedetaea. Adọ setaḱ

---

28 In the hot season, the eastern parts of India are very often visited by what is called Nor'westers, sudden and violent thunderstorms. Such a one is meant here.

29 It often does not take so very many to make a thousand.

30 The whole is a good description, so far as it goes. The heavy bullock-carts afford some protection.

As he was passing along, they tell, the boy reached another bazar, and there at this bazar the sun set for him. On the other side of this bazar there was a very large grove of mango trees; in that grove they also had a market, and a very large number of traders with their carts had camped there. Then the boy said to himself: "I shall also camp in this grove; then to-morrow morning I shall get up and start for home." So he himself sat down on the other side of where the carters had camped, some little distance away from them at the foot of a tree; and he also tied his cow to the roots of the same tree.

A short while afterwards the weather became very threatening, a thunder-storm was brewing, it became black all over[28]. A few moments more, and the storm burst, and it rained very heavily. The carters were about one thousand[29] in number, and during the storm they had crept in[30] under their carts. But when the storm came, the boy asked his cow for a tent and put that up, whereupon both of them entered the tent. It rained the whole night incessantly until morning.

Then those carters said: "Strange, yesterday he had nothing; where has he got the tent? Undoubtedly he has got it from this cow of his."

When it became morning, the boy became very perplexed what to do, and said to himself: "Now if I let her put this tent away, people will see me. Then they will try to cheat me out of the cow again, like the first time; I shall remain here to-day, let it become evening, and then I shall let her put it away, and to-morrow at cock-crow I shall run away from here."

So he remained the whole day until evening, and when it became night, they tell, he let her put it away. When the boy had fallen asleep, the carters came, tied a cow in milk[31] near him and came away; they took the boy's cow with them. When it

---

31 A cow in milk means with a Santal always a cow with her calf. They have the idea that a cow will not give milk unless she has her calf to look at or lick during the milking operation.

khange uni koṛa do̠e bhabnak̕ kana, are metako kana onko gaḍwan do̠, Dini uni gạ̣i do̠ e̠mkaetiṅpe.

Ado̠ko metae kana, Cele gạ̣i ale do̠m kho̠jet̕lea? Uni co̠ṅ gạ̣i ma am ṭhenge menae; aleren ma e̠ke̠nko ḍaṅgra kange. Ar se̠ uni gạ̣i do̠ idikate ona gõ̠ṛẽ̠ bostako ạgu jarwaket̕te uni gạ̣i beṛhaeteko cake ạcurket̕a, uni gạ̣i do̠ko aḍ e̠se̠t̕kedea. Arko metae kana, Ukurić amren gạ̣i do̠? Ma e̠nte ale ṭhen menae khan, do ńameme.

Ado̠ uni koṛae me̠net̕a, Baṅ; iṅren gạ̣i do̠ ape ṭhenge menaea.

Ado̠ko metae kana, Uni co̠ṅ gạ̣i ma am ṭhengem to̠l akade. Ado̠ cele gạ̣iyem ńam kana?

Ado̠ uniye me̠net̕a, Nui gạ̣i do̠e baṅ kana iṅren do̠. Iṅren do̠e ṭhạ̣ṭ gạ̣i kana, ar nui ma mĩhũ menaetae.

Ado̠ko metae kana, Pase̠ teheń ńindạ̣geye busạ̣k̕entam. Ado̠ onako kathage ghạ̣ṛi ghạ̣ṛiko ro̠po̠ṛ kana.

Ado̠ uni koṛae me̠nket̕a, Noko gaḍwan do̠ nãhãk̕ko e̠ṛe̠yiṅa. O̠ko̠e tora atoren mạ̣ṅjhiṅ lạ̣iaea. Ado̠e calaoente mạ̣ṅjhi ar cạ̣ukidare ạguket̕kina, ado̠e metat̕kina, Ia̠ baba, iṅren mit̕ṭaṅ 'gạ̣iye tahẽ̠kantiṅa, ar noa dare buṭạ̣reń gitić kan tahẽ̠kana. Uni gạ̣i do̠ nui cạ̣ukidar hõ̠e ńe̠lledetiṅgea. Ado̠ ńindạ̣ jo̠khe̠n nokoge iṅren gạ̣i do̠ko ạtkirkedetiṅa.

Ado̠ uni cạ̣ukidare me̠nket̕a, Hẽ̠ sạ̣rige, iṅ hõ̠ gạ̣i do̠ṅ ńe̠lledegea.

Ado̠ onko gaḍwanko me̠nket̕a, Besge e̠nte gạ̣iyem ńe̠lledea; uni co̠ṅ gạ̣i ma menaegetae.

Ado̠ uni koṛae me̠nket̕a, Baṅa, iṅren do̠e ṭhạ̣ṭ gạ̣i kana, mĩhũ do̠ bạ̣nugića.

Ado̠ mạ̣ṅjhiye me̠nket̕a, Ma nui gạ̣i baṛe̠ idiyem; amren do̠ ṭhạ̣ṭ gạ̣iye tahẽ̠kana, ado̠ mĩhũanić gạ̣iyem ńawana; ado̠ cet̕ bạ̣ṛić? Bhage akange co̠m.

Ado̠ uni koṛae me̠nket̕a, Baṅ, iṅ do̠ iṅren gạ̣igeń hataoea; nui gạ̣i do̠ baṅ hataoea.

---

32 See p. 54, note 15.

became morning, the boy was in great sorrow and said to the carters: "Come with her, give me back my cow."

"Which cow are you demanding from us?" they replied; "why, there you have your own cow with you; we have only bullocks with us." Now the carters had taken the cow, collected a lot of gunny bags and piled these up round the cow, and they had, in this way, hidden her. "Why, where is your cow here? If she is with us, do find her by all means."

"No," the boy said, "my cow is with you."

"There she is," they replied, "you have tied your cow there with you. Which cow are you then looking for?"

"This one is not my cow," the boy said; "my cow is a barren cow, and this one has a calf."

"Perhaps," they said, "perhaps she has given birth to a calf to-night?" Again and again they were quarrelling using the same words.

Then the boy said: "These carters will cheat me presently. I shall go and tell the village-headman this instant." Consequently he went and brought the headman and the watchman[32] and said to them: "Please, sir, I had a cow, and I passed the night here at the foot of this tree. This watchman also saw the cow. Then, during the night, these people have stolen my cow away."

"Yes," the watchman said, "I myself also really saw the cow."

The carters then said: "Very well then; you saw the cow; his cow, why, he has got her there."

"No, not at all," the boy said; "my cow is a barren one; she has no calf."

The headman then said: "Please, take this cow with you; your cow was a barren one, and now you have got a cow with a calf. What bad is there in that? Why, you are very fortunate."

"No," the boy replied, "I will take my cow; this cow I shall not take."

Ado̱ onko gaḍwanko me̱nkeťa, Ma e̱nte ńamepe ale ṭhen menae khan; ale ma oṛaǩ duạr hõ̱ bạnuǩtale; oṛaǩ tahe̱n khanpe me̱nkea, Okare co̱pe oko akade. Nẽ̱ǩẽ̱ tho̱ so̱ṅge̱rege ale do̱ jo̱to̱ menaǩtalea.

Ado̱ sạri goṭako ńe̱l baṛakedea, ado̱ bako ńamledete mạńjhiye me̱nkeťa, Cele bạbu, ceťem me̱neťa? Gạị ńamea me̱ntem ạguleťlińa, ado̱ nõ̱ǩõ̱e ạlíń cạukidartelíń ho̱ṭe̱te do̱ bańlíń ńamledetama. Ado̱ amge de̱ ceťem me̱neťa?

Ado̱ uni koṛae me̱nkeťa, Iạ baba mạńjhi ar cạukidar, aben mạujạre ińren do̱ gạiye ať akana, ar iń do̱ noko gaḍwanreń subhạ akaťkoa. Metaben kanań, noko gaḍwan do̱ rahdạni hataṛkoben, ar nui dhĩṛũ gạị do̱ aben jimạre do̱ho̱ hataṛeben. Iń do̱ noko ńutumteń lạlisa, ar judiben se̱n ocokeťkoa menkhan, aben upạrteń lạlisa.

Ado̱ uni mạńjhi ar cạukidar gaḍwankin metaťkoa, Cele ho gaḍwan, ceťpe me̱neťa? Nui koṛa do̱ ape upạrte lạlise me̱neť do̱. Khange onko gaḍwanko me̱nkeťa, Do ona do̱ khạtirjomae metaǩ ma; arhõ̱ judi kho̱rcako bań kulạuǩ kantae khan, alele emaea.

Ado̱ mạńjhiye me̱nkeťa, Me̱n ado̱ inạ kathage tho̱; ạikạ noa bicạr ạuri ńisputiǩ dhạbić no̱ṇḍe̱ khon o̱ho̱lín se̱n ocolepea. Ar judi noa katha nõ̱ǩõ̱e ańjo̱m torape uṭhạuena me̱nkhan, khạṭi apegepe saboǩa.

Ado̱ onkoko me̱nkeťa, Acha, o̱ho̱le calaǩa; calaoenale me̱nkhan, alege hajo̱trele bo̱lo̱ǩa. Ado̱ onka galmaraokateko apan ạpinena.

Ádo̱ uniren gạị do̱ unkin jimạreye bạgiadete uni koṛa do̱ hạkim ṭhen lạǩlise calaoena. Ado̱ miťṭań Muslạ Badsa hạkime tahẽ̱kana; ado̱ uni ṭhene lạlisketa. Ado̱ kathae, turạ̃tge parwana oḍok go̱ťena. Ar uni hạkim do̱, kathae bhaleye tahẽ̱kana, o̱ko̱eaǩ hõ̱ be̱ho̱k do̱ bae bicạreť tahẽ̱kana, ṭhik ṭhike bicạreť tahẽ̱kana, ghus

33 The introduction of a Mohammedan judge does not make it probable that this story has been borrowed from Mohammedan sources. The law court, as described, is a somewhat misdrawn picture of a modern court, such as Santal imagination may like to think it. A Santal knows, of course, very little of the inner workings

"Please find her then," the carters said, "if she is with us. We have no house or hut either. If we had houses, you might say: you have hidden her somewhere. Look at us, why, we have all we have with us here."

Then they looked for the cow everywhere; but as they could not find her, the headman said: "Well, my lad, what do you say? You brought us to find your cow; and now you see, myself and the watchman being present did not help, we could not find her. What have you then to say?"

"I say, father headman and watchman, in your village my cow has been lost, and I am suspecting these carters. Now I say this to you two: keep these carters here in the meantime, and also keep this cow with calf in your charge for the present. I am going to bring a suit against these people, and if you let them go away, I shall bring a suit against you."

The headman and watchman then said to the carters: "Well, you carters, what have you to say? This boy is going to bring a suit against you."

"By all means," the carters said, "let him be confident as to that, and if he should not have enough money for the purpose, we shall let him have."

The headman then said: "Take care then that is the case. Mind you, until this case is settled, we shall not let you go away from here. And if you, after having heard this, nevertheless depart, you will certainly be caught."

"All right," they said, "we shall not go at all; if we, in spite of this, should go, we go to jail." After having had this talk, they separated.

Having left the cow in the charge of those two, the boy went to bring a suit before the judge. Now a Mussulman Badsha[33] was judge, and he made his complaint before him. A written order was sent out immediately. This judge was a good man; he did not judge anybody's case unjustly; he was judging rightly and truly; he did not take bribes and was not a respecter of persons.

hō̱ bae jo̱meť tahē̱kana, ar ho̱ṛaǩ mē̱ťāhā ńe̱lte do̱ bae bicạra, me̱nkhan jāhā se̱nge ạn calaǩ, onageye pachaea, bańdo̱e re̱ńge̱ć ho̱ṛ kan, bańdo̱e kisạ̄ṛ ho̱ṛ kan. Bicạr darate jāhāegekin haraoǩ, inigeye sạjạiyeťko tahē̱kana. Bạdi ar protibạdi, bana ho̱ṛ reaǩge lạlise hatao maṛańa, e̱nkhanteye bicạrtakina. Nonka ṭhik bicạr karo̱nte uni hạkim do̱ ạḍi bạṛiće namḍak akan tahē̱kana — ar bańkhan o̱ko̱e co̱rpo̱ṭ hạkim do̱ o̱ko̱ege lahateye lạlis maṛań, iniaǩgeye se̱naǩa, ar o̱ko̱e tayo̱mteye lạlis, uniaǩ do̱ ańjo̱mge bae ańjo̱mtaea, ar laha ho̱ṛ do̱ ṭhike lạị akať se̱ be̱ṭhike lạị akať, uniaǩgeye se̱nataea ar uniaǩ kathategeye puṭi cabakoǩa; onko do̱ lelha hạkimko metakoa. Me̱nkhan nui hạkim do̱ bae onkana; bana ho̱ṛ kulikate ane̱će dusikoa se̱ye hajo̱tkoa.

Ado̱ uni koṛae lạliskeť khan, inạ hō̱e atańkeťgea, ar onko gaḍwan hō̱e to̱lo̱pkeťkoa ar unkin mạńjhi caukidar hō̱e to̱lo̱pkeťkina, ado̱ jo̱to̱ ho̱ṛaǩ ijhạre hataokeťa. Ar onko gaḍwan do̱ kiriạkateko me̱nkeťa, Ale do̱ bale hatao akadetaea; judi nuiren gạị ale ṭhene ńamena me̱nkhan, gạị hō̱le e̱mkaetaea ar je kichu dho̱n durib menaǩtale, onako jo̱to̱ nuigele emaea. Onka e̱ktiạri kiriạkateko me̱nkeťa.

Ado̱ khange uni hạkim do̱ do̱ro̱ga pulise metaťkoa, Do se̱nkate ḍera tolasipe.

Ado̱ bhạị, onko do̱ se̱nkate onkoaǩ ḍerako tolasikeťa, ado̱ ona gō̱ṛē̱ bostako cạke akať tahē̱kan, ado̱ onako jo̱to̱ko o̱co̱ǩ ocokeťko khan do̱ sạri uni gạiko ńamkedea. Ado̱ uni gạite ar ho̱ṛte jo̱to̱

---

of a law-court. It may seem strange that a Mohammedan judge should be introduced as here done, when the Santals harbour such feelings as they do towards people of that persuasion. The explanation may be that the present-day Santals have had experiences which they like with Mohammedan judges. These are perhaps less liable to lose themselves in legal technicalities than certain other people, and are appreciated accordingly.

There are several points in this story which seem to make it likely that it has been originally borrowed from outside.

From a certain point of view it is of interest to compare this with the foregoing story. They have both been written by the same man, but at different times, some years lying between the two. The narrator has heard the story from other

Whatever be the law, that he followed, whether it was a poor man or a wealthy person. The one who was defeated according to law, him he punished. Accuser and accused, he listened to what they both had to bring forward; then only he passed judgement. Because he was such a true judge, he had become very famous, — otherwise one who is a corrupt judge will listen to him who comes first with his complaint; one who comes afterwards, him he will not even listen to, and whether the first one has told the truth or he has told what is false, he does what he says, and he permits himself to be filled with his tale, so there is room for nothing else. Such ones people call foolish judges. But this judge was not of that kind; only when he had examined both parties, did he find them guilty or sent them to prison.

When the boy had lodged his complaint, he took it up, and he also summoned the carters and also the headman and watchman, whereupon he recorded the statements of all of them. The carters swore and said: "We have not taken his cow; if his cow be found with us, we shall give him his cow, and whatever property we have, we shall give him all of it." They took their oath and spoke in such a highfalutin way.

The judge then said to the head constable: "Go and search the camp."

The police then went and searched their camping place; now they had piled up the gunny bags, as told, and when they made them take all that away, they found the cow. So they tied the cow and the men and took them all with them. Then

sources than when he first wrote. The last specimen shows more experience and acquaintance with certain sides of life than the first one. Chowkedars were formerly unknown in the Santal country; such vere introduced some twenty years ago. This may throw some light on the way in which stories of this kind develop and, most likely quite unconsciously, are adapted to the circumstances of life or the environments of the narrator. Everything is internal evidence of how near the details of these stories lie to Santal life and ideas, when the folktale flight of imagination is deducted.

miť miťteko tọl idikeťkoa. Adọ hạkime metaťkoa, Ńẹlpe, gại dọ ape ṭhenge menaea, ẹnre hõ ape dọ bape kạbuleťa ar nahakgepe ekraṛena. Adọ dẹ okape mẹnleť, ona purạupe.

Khange adọ ẹmoḱ bako rẹbẹn kante onko gaḍwan dọ miť miťte jọtọe hajọtkeťkoa, ar onkoaḱ dhọn dọ miť miťte uni koṛae ḍigriadea. Gại ar onako dhọn dọ uni koṛae ńawante ać oṛaḱ sẹne mohṇḍayena. Gạḍiko, ḍaṅgrako ar ona jọtọ dhọn uni koṛage hạkime soprot gọťadea.

Adọ khange uni koṛa dọ ać atote, sẹ ọnẹ eṅgat apatkin tahẹ̃kan, ọṇḍẹgeye calaoena. Adọ ona disomren họṛ dọ ọkọe hõ bako ńẹl oromedea. Adọko mẹneťa, Ọkọeaḱ nunạḱ asbab dọ hẹćena? Adọ khangeye lạiaťkoa, Iń dọń phalna họpọn kana. Adọ ạḍiko haharayena.

Adọ oṛaḱko benao baṛakate miť din dọ uniye tahẹ̃kan raj ṭhene calaoena, ar ọnẹ eṅgat apatkin gọćlenre ṭakae rinleť tahẹ̃kan, ona ṭakae idi oṭokaťtaea. Adọ kathae, uni raj hõ bae ńẹl oromledea. Adọe lại ṭhikade khane disạkedea, are metae kana, Durrẹ! am kanam, phalna?

Adọe mẹnkeťa, Hẽ, iń kangeań. Adọ ṭakako ẹm baṛakate duk suk reaḱkin kupuliyena.

Adọ kathae, sedae sedae apat jọkhẹć reaḱ rajọsṭiye pachakeťte onae ńam ruạṛkeťa. Khange uniye tahẹ̃kan kisạ̃ṛge, kathae, miťṭań họpọneṛae gọńadea. Adọ ẹnẹye tahẽyena.

Ar uniye tahẹ̃kan rajren eae gọṭẹn koṛa họpọnko mẹnkeťa, Ale hõ disomte bidesle calaḱa. Ńẹlepe, nui dọ gutiye tahẹ̃kana, adọ disomteye oḍoklente nunạḱ dhọne ạguana. Ale hõle sẹnlen khan pasẹle ạgukaťge.

Adọ apattẹť ṭakako kọekedete bidesko calaoena. Adọ inạko jọtọ ṭakako ublạ ḍublạ oṭokať khan, arhõko ruạṛ hẹćena.

Adọ ẹnẹ cabayena katha dọ; in maraṅgea.

the judge said: "Now look, the cow is with you; nevertheless you did not confess, and you have purposelessly bound yourselves by a promise. So now carry out what you have said."

As the carters refused to give, he put them all in prison, every one of them, and he decreed that all their property, everything, should be given to the boy. When he had got the cow and all the goods, the boy started homewards. The carts, the bullocks and all the goods the judge gave over to the boy.

Thereupon the boy went to his village, or rather to where his father and mother had been. None in that country recognized him, and the people said: "To whom do all the goods that have come belong?" Then he told them: "I am the son of so and so," and they were very much astonished.

After he had built houses, he one day went to the king with whom he had been, and he took with him the money he had borrowed when his father and mother had died, to pay that. The king did not recognize him either. When he told him who he was, he remembered him and said to him: "Strange, is it you, so and so?"

"Yes, it is I," he said, whereupon he paid him his money, and they enquired of each other how everything was going on with them.

Afterwards he took up and made inquiries regarding his father's kingdom of long long ago, and got that back. And the king who was there gave him his daughter in marriage. So he stayed on there.

The seven sons of the king with whom he formerly stayed said: "We will also go to a foreign country. Look, this one was a servant; then he went to a foreign country and brought so much wealth with him. If we also go, perhaps we might bring something."

So they asked their father for money and went to a foreign country. But when they had squandered all their money, they came back again.

There the story is ended; it is thus much.

7. Toyo reak̕ pho̱rphundi.

Mit̕ṭań haṛam ho̱ṛe me̱nket̕a, Gapa do̱ me̱ro̱m bodabon ko̱ṭe̱ćkoa. Ona katha mit̕ṭań me̱ro̱m boda do̱e ańjo̱mket̕te buruteye dạṛket̕a, ado̱ tạrup̕ danderre dhirireye burum akana. Ado̱ tạrup̕ do̱e he̱ćena. Un jo̱khe̱ć me̱ro̱m boda do̱e me̱nket̕a, Hum, pak pak! Un jo̱khe̱ć tạrup̕ do̱ bo̱to̱rteye dạṛket̕a.

Ado̱ mit̕ṭań toyo do̱e ńamkedea. Metae kanae, Ia̱ bhạgnạ, teheń do̱ ińak̕ oṛak̕re cele co̱e he̱ć akan.

Ado̱ toyo do̱e me̱nket̕a, Cet̕ lekanić kanae, mamo̱?

Ado̱e me̱nket̕a, Iạ bhạgnạ, keware so̱bo̱t̕ jạ̃ṛīye to̱l akawana.

Ado̱ toyo do̱e me̱nket̕a, Iạ mamo̱, iń do̱ nonkanko do̱ ko̱to̱ ko̱to̱ń jo̱m hajam akat̕koa.

Ado̱ caṇḍbo̱l caṇḍbo̱lkin joṛao mit̕ akana, ado̱kin calak̕ kana. Tiok̕ket̕akin. Ado̱ me̱ro̱m boda do̱e teṅgoyena. Tạrup̕ do̱e me̱nket̕a, Cet̕ko co̱ń enańe metadiń tahẽ̱kana. Onka me̱nkate ado̱kin dạṛket̕a. Ado̱e o̱ṛ poṭak̕ede kana. Ado̱ toyo do̱e me̱net̕ kana, Iạ mamo̱, mare mare mạilạ, mamo̱m chaḍaoket̕tińa.

Ado̱ mit̕ ṭhen tạrup̕ ar tạrup̕ eṅgakin ho̱po̱n akat̕koa. Unkin do̱ jãhã se̱n jel ạgukin calaokok̕a. Ado̱ toyo do̱e he̱ć go̱dok̕a, ado̱e metakoa, E̱re̱ dhan dibe na? Coṛo moṛo dibe. Ado̱ okako jelkin ạgu jaorakak̕, onageko emadege. Ado̱ tạrup ạṇḍiạ do̱ he̱ćkateye me̱nket̕, Henda ya, unạk̕ jelliń ạguape kana, e̱nhõ̱ cekatepe mo̱ro̱dok̕ kana?

---

[1] This story is one of the few that Phagu of Dhaka village told the writer. The language is very different from that of the stories written by Sagram. Phagu was more accustomed to the style of the gurus; the language reminds one of that found in the Traditions and Institutions, dictated by Kolean guru. See the Foreword.

[2] The operation here referred to is one commonly practised by the Santals. The seminal ducts are destroyed by beating with a stone.

[3] The words used in Santali are likely meant to remind one of the bleating of a goat. I remember Phagu enjoyed this part very much; he told me at the time that if I could only understand the inner meaning of this, I should have a good laugh. H u m is the word used to make bullocks stay quiet or stop, p a k to turn.

7. THE JACKAL'S CRAFTINESS[1].

An old man said: "To-morrow we shall geld[2] the he-goats." A he-goat heard this and ran away to the mountains, where he lay down on a rock in a leopard's cave. When the leopard came, the he-goat said: "Wo, back back[3]." Then the leopard, out of fear, ran away.

Running along, he met a jackal and said to him: "I say, nephew[4], somebody, who knows who, has come to my house to-day."

"What is he like, uncle?" the jackal asked.

"Well, nephew," the leopard replied, "he has tied washed hemp-fibre to his chin."

"Well, you know, uncle," the jackal said, "such ones I have eaten and digested several."

So they tied their tails together[5] and went along and reached the place. Then the he-goat stood up, and the leopard said: "He said something, whatever it was, to me a while ago." As he said this, they ran away, and the leopard dragged the jackal along so his skin was rubbed off. Then the jackal says: "I say, uncle, you are removing my old, old dirt[6], uncle."

Now a pair of leopards had their young ones at a certain place. When the parents went somewhere to bring flesh, the jackal came at once and said to the young ones: "Du da, wirst du nicht den Reis geben? Du mußt augenblicklich etwas geben[7]." So they gave him whatever flesh the parents had brought together. One day the he-leopard coming back said: "Look here, we are bringing you so much flesh, how is it that, nevertheless, you are getting so thin?"

4 See p. 26, note 11.

5 A safeguard to prevent their being separated.

6 A fairly commonly used expression to say that one's skin is being abraded.

7 The jackal is speaking Bengali. The mone-ylenders and shopkeepers always make use of non-Santals to go round and tell debtors to pay.

Adoko menket, Tiskore coṅ toyoak rinben dharao akattae; din hilokgeye koe idilea.

Adokin tãṛãkena. Ado mit ghaṛi khange toyo doe heć gotena: Are dhan dibe na? Coṛo moṛo dibe. Adoe lagae lagakedea se, mittaṅ rehḍa bhugakre toyo doe ṅir tapena. Ar taruṗ hõe ṅir tabok kan tahẽkana, adoe riḍet goćena. Ado toyo doe metae kana, Ai! baṅ ṅeletmea, onḍem tãṛãk akana?

Ado lumam ṭhuyakteye panahi akana ar lumam dhutiteye dhutiyena ar ḍekeye thayakedea. Ado heć ruaṛkate taruṗ hopon ṭhene calaoena. Adoe metako kana, Okoe ṭhenpe tahena? Apum maṅ goćkede.

Taruṗ eṅga doe menketa, Tobe am ṭhengele tahena.

Adoko calaoena urni birte sendra. Ado onko doko sendraea arko jhoṛa agukoa, ar toyo do tãṛãkkoka menteye tahena. Botorte bunum coṭreye dećkoka. Ado jelkoko ṅir hijuka, ado botorte aćgeye ciḍira. Hećkate taruṗ eṅgatekoko metaea, Okorko, tinakem goćketkoa?

Adoe metakoa, Sojhetege bape laga agukoa. Nõkõe nankateṅ laga ciḍir akatkoa.

Ado taruṗ eṅgae tãṛãkena, ado toyo ar taruṗko jhoṛa aguia. Ado khange taruṗ eṅga do mittaṅ jele saṗ gotkedea. Ado toyo doe menketa, Cet.leka sojhe sojheṅ laga aguam kana, onatem goć goletkoa. Ado toyo doe menketa, Hape na, sedae haṛam iṅ boṅgawae lagit. Ger gerkatae, ado bae bhugak daṛeata. Adoe menket, Ma na, ma na, ger bhugakaṅme. Adoe bhugakadea.

---

8 The soil is here and there saline, containing salt. The rains may wash parts of this away, leaving narrow passages.

9 The cocoon of the silkworm generally reared by the Santals (Antheraea mylitta) has a hard cover and is fairly large. The peons mentioned in note 7 always wear some kind of heavy shoes. The cocoon-shoes are supposed to remind one of the noise made by these peons when coming.

10 A very common phenomenon always observed by the Santals; fear will cause it.

11 The jackal makes use of a pretext to secure for himself what is considered the most savoury part. He pretends to offer something of the food to the dead leopard. Ancestors have food offered to them now and then.

"Sometime," the young ones replied, "you have become indebted to the jackal; he demands of us and takes away every day."

Then the parents lay in wait, and a short while afterwards the jackal came and called out: "Du da, wirst du nicht den Reis geben? Du mußt augenblicklich etwas geben." They started chasing the jackal and chased and chased, until the jackal ran through a hole in some saline ground[8], The male leopard also tried to run through; but he stuck and died there. Then the jackal said to him: "Hey, I don't see you. Are you lying in wait?"

The jackal had put on silk-cocoons as shoes[9] and had taken a silk loin-cloth on, and he kicked the leopard in his hind-quarters. Thereupon he went back to the young leopards and said to them: "With whom are you going to stay? I have killed your father, you see."

The she-leopard then said: "In that case we shall stay with you."

Thereupon they went to the jungle-forest to hunt. The leopards hunted and drove the game before them towards the jackal, who stayed in order to lie in wait and kill. Out of fear, he mounted to the top of a white-ants' hill. When the deer came running, the jackal himself purged[10] out of fear. When the leopard mother and the young ones came, they asked him: "Why, where are they? How many did you kill?"

He then answered them: "You do not drive them straight towards me. Look here, along here I have been chasing them, so they have purged."

After this had happened several times, the she-leopard lay in wait, and the jackal and the young leopards drove the game towards her. The she-leopard caught one deer; then the jackal said: "How straight and direct I am driving the game towards you; therefore you are killing them so quickly." "Wait, girl," the jackal then said, "I shall just make a sacrifice[11] to the late old man," whereupon he commenced to bite; but he was unable to bite a hole and said: "Do, girl, do bite a hole for me." She made a hole for him, whereupon the jackal entered and ate the

Adǫ toyo dǫ bǫlǫkate inkoe jǫmkeťa. Jǫm biyenae are oḍokena. Adǫe metako kana, Hę̃ na, ma jǫmpe nitoǩ dǫ. Enko hǭ iną jeltęťkoko jǫm baṛakeťa.

Adǫ jąpuť jąpuťko hijuǩ kana; gaḍa hǭ pęręć akana; adǫko parǫmoǩ kana. Tąruṕ hǫpǫn dǫe męnkeť, Dę babań ghõṛãmea. Ḍuṭ! chąiokań, gidrą ṭhen dǫń ghõṛã ocoǩa.

Adǫko męnkeťa, Mabo parǫmoǩa. Khange tąruṕ eṅga tąruṕ hǫpǫnko dǫn parǫmkeťa. Adǫ toyoe dǫneť tahę̃kana, tala daǩreye ńurhąyena. Adǫko męnkeťa, Ma ya, ma ya, oarepe.

Adǫe męnkeťa, Alope oariṅa, iń puruseťa.

Adǫ gaḍa ḍhipre tayane jęḍęr akan tahę̃kana. Adǫ toyoe męnkeťa, Ma ya, ma ya, oarkańme. Itil itil jel iń ąguama.

Adǫe metadea, Ią ya, jąpiťkate cahaṕkaǩme.

Adǫ toyo dǫ jivęť dhiri ągukate mocareye tiṅkedea, adǫe dąṛkeťa. Adǫe męnkeťa, Hapę ya, ią toyom tiń akadiṅa. Miť dinlań ńammea arlań jǫmmea.

Uni toyo dǫ dinąmge miťṭań pukhri reaǩ kąuhą ręhęť cetan khon daǩe ńũia. Adǫ tayan dǫe cirąkedea. Khange thǫ daǩ bhitrire tayan dǫe unum akana. Adǫ kąuhą ręhęť cetan khon daǩe ńũńũ kana. Adǫ kaṭae ǫrkedea. Khange ǫrkede khane, toyo dǫe męnkeťa, Ią tayange, iṅaǩ kaṭa gęr bągiate kąuhą ręhęťe gęrakaťa. Khange. tayan dǫ toyo jaṅgae aṛaǩ gǫlkaťa ar kąuhą

12 It is commonly observed that certain wild animals when they have killed, start eating from the hind-quarters, the intestines, liver, heart and kidneys.

13 The expression used in Santali really means 'carry on the shoulder', 'riding'.

14 The narrator has apparently forgotten all about the raining. The crocodile is represented as basking in the morning sun. The crocodile is now scarcely ever met with in the Santal country; in the flat low country, the crocodile is fairly common.

15 The narrator has omitted to tell that the crocodile has carried the jackal out of the water, and that the jackal has found the 'fat meat' to pay for the service rendered.

16 See p. 6, note 11.

17 Terminalia Arjuna, Bedd., a large timber tree, frequently growing on the banks of rivers and near water. The roots of the tree are generally much ramified, the earth being often washed away from between the more superficial roots.

liver[12]. When he was satisfied, he came out and said to the others: "Well, girl, now please eat," and then they also ate; they got the flesh.

It was raining continually as they came along; the river was also running full. Whilst they were going to cross, one of the young leopards said: "Come, father, I shall carry you on my back[13]."

"Fie! confound it! I shall never let me be carried on the back of my child."

"Well, let us get across," they said, whereupon the leopard mother and the young ones jumped across. But when the jackal jumped, he fell in the middle of the water, and the other ones called out: "Do, do rescue him."

"Don't pull me out," the jackal said, "I am standing on the bottom."

Now a crocodile was lying on the river bank basking[14], and the jackal said: "Please, please, get me out. I shall bring you some fat, fat meat."

The jackal[15] then said: "I say, you, shut your eyes and open your mouth."

The jackal brought some quartz stones, and threw them, as forcibly as he could, into the crocodile's mouth, whereupon he ran away. The crocodile said: "Wait you fellow, you rascal of a jackal have stoned me. Some day we two[16] shall find you and eat you."

The jackal was in the habit of daily drinking water from a tank, standing on the roots of a k a u h a[17] tree, and the crocodile found this out. The crocodile then dived in the water and was lying so out of sight. When the jackal was drinking water there, standing on the roots of the kauha tree, the crocodile caught him by the leg and pulled. As he pulled him, the jackal said: "That rascal of a crocodile, he has let go of my leg and has bitten the kauha root." The crocodile then let the jackal's leg go at once and bit the kauha root. Then the jackal said:

re̱he̱t́e ge̱rket́a. Unre toyo do̱e me̱nket́a, Iạ tayan, ne̱ yae jo̱meṅ kan tahẽ̱kana.

Ado̱ arhõ̱ mit́ ṭhen janhe̱ busuṕ ṭhene je̱ḍe̱rkoḱa. Tayan do̱e ciạkede khan, janhe̱ busuṕreye topa akana. E̱n hiloḱ do̱ toyo do̱ mit́ṭaṅ me̱ro̱m ṭo̱ṭko̱e ṅam akawan tahẽ̱kana. Ona do̱ ho̱ṭo̱ḱreye to̱l akawana. Ado̱ ṭo̱ko̱r ṭo̱ko̱re do̱n baṛae kana. Khange tayan do̱e me̱nket́a, He̱ḍo̱ḱ! iạ me̱ro̱m. Toyoṅ tãṛãḱ akawade khan aćgeye ṭo̱ko̱r ṭo̱ko̱roḱ kana.

Toyo do̱e me̱nket́a, Iạ tayan, no̱ṇḍe̱ye taṛaḱ akana? Khange se̱ṅge̱l ạgukateye je̱re̱t́at́a, ado̱ e̱ne̱ye lo̱ go̱ćena. Niạ do̱ mucạt́ena.

(Told by Phagu, of Dhaka village.)

8. Mit́ṭen toyo reaṅ.

Mit́ṭan atore bar eṅga ho̱nkin tahẽ̱kana, ho̱po̱nte̱t́ do̱ Ạnuạ aea. Ado̱ uni koṛa do̱e sioḱa ar uni eṅgat buḍhi do̱ baskeaḱe idi baṛawaea. Ado̱ khange mit́ din do̱ baskeaḱ idi jo̱khe̱ćge mit́ṭaṅ toyotekinkin ṅapamena. Ado̱ uni toyoe me̱nket́a, E̱ buḍhi, mase̱ do̱ho̱lem, cet́em idiyet́a? Ar bam do̱ho̱e khan do̱ nãhãḱlaṅ ge̱r gitić go̱t́ mea, ar nãhãḱ bogetelaṅ thạyạmea.

Ado̱ khange 'uni buḍhi do̱ bo̱ṭo̱rteye do̱ho̱ket́a, ado̱ uni ho̱po̱nte̱t Ạnuạ lạgit́e idiyet́ tahẽ̱kan khicṛi daka ado̱ uni toyoge ḍherte̱t́ do̱e jo̱mket́a, ado̱ thoṛa thuṛiye sare̱ćket́a. Inạge uni buḍhi do̱ Ạnuạ

18 Janhe, Paspalum scrobiculatum, L., is a very common cultivated millet. The grain is eaten; beer is made from it. The straw is not suitable for cattle-fodder, but is burnt. The potters use it to burn their earthenware. It is very warm to lie in.

81 During the agricultural season, or whenever the Santals plough, they start ploughing at about sunrise and continue up to nine or ten in the forenoon or, when very busy, perhaps a little longer. The Santal way of ploughing is very superficial, a kind of 'scratching' the soil, possible only when rain has softened the surface, consequently not very heavy and not very tiring. In spite of this

"That rascal of a crocodile, he was just going to eat me, the fellow."

The jackal was in the habit of warming himself in the sun lying in some millet[18] straw. When the crocodile found this out, he buried himself in the straw. That day the jackal had found a goats' wooden bell and had tied that round his neck. He was jumping about making it jingle. The crocodile then said: "Get away, you silly goat. When I am lying in wait for the jackal, she is jingling-jingling here."

"The rascal of a crocodile," the jackal said, "is he lying in wait here?" So he brought fire and set fire to the straw, and the crocodile was burnt to death.

This is ended.

8. THE STORY OF A JACKAL.

In a village there were living two persons, mother and son. The name of the son was Anua. The young man was ploughing[1], and the old mother was in the habit of taking his forenoon meal out to him. One day whilst she was taking this out to him, she met with a jackal. The jackal said: "Old woman, put it down at once; what are you taking along? If you don't put it down, we two[2] shall presently bite you, so you will lie there, and we shall give you a good kicking."

The old woman was frightened and put it down, whereupon the jackal ate most of the mixed rice and dal[3] that she was taking out to her son Anua; he left only a little, which the old woman

---

they do not work their bullocks more than as told, some three to four hours in the morning.

2 See p. 6, note 11.

3 Dąl is the common name in a number of north Indian languages for split peas or beans. The dąl is in daily use for making curry. What is here mentioned is rice and dąl cooked together, sometimes prepared in this way by the Santals, but much more common with other races.

ṭhene idiket́a. Khange uni koṛa hõ iną toyo itąt́geye jo̱mket́a, ar uni koṛa do̱ bae baḍaelet́a, je iń do̱ toyo itąt́e ągu akawadińa me̱nte, bin baḍaeteye jo̱mket́a. Ado̱ uni toyo do̱ din hiloḱge onkae e̱ṛe̱yea uni buḍhi do̱.

Khange ado̱ mit́ din do̱ uni koṛae me̱nket́a, Henda go̱, cekate bań ne̱tar do̱ sigić bigić dakagem ągują́ń kan, nonkagem dakayet́a se̱?

Ado̱ uni buḍhiye me̱nket́a, Bańa bąbu, oṛaḱ khon do̱ bhagegeń daka ąguyet́a; me̱nkhan ągui jo̱khe̱ćge mit́ṭań toyo ho̱rregeye e̱se̱dińa; ado̱e metańa, Ma buḍhi, daka do̱ho̱eme, ar bam do̱ho̱e khan do̱ nãhãḱlań ge̱r gitić go̱t́mea ar bogetelań thąyąmea, Ado̱ bo̱to̱rteń do̱ho̱adege, ado̱ uniye jo̱m itąda, iną dakage ado̱ am ṭheniń ąguyet́a, ado̱ am hõm ruhediń bo̱to̱rte bąń ląi baṛawama.

Ado̱ uni koṛae me̱nket́a, E̱ go̱, gapa do̱ amge sioḱ ṭhen ḍańgra do̱ laga ągukinme, ińge baskeaḱ do̱ń ąguia.

Khange eṅgatte̱t́e me̱nket́a, Acha, beṭa, bogege, gapa do̱ e̱ṇḍe̱khan nahelko so̱ḱ go̱t́ąńme; iń do̱ am leka ḍeṅgakate sioḱ ṭhen ḍańgra laga ągukateń teṅgokakina.

Ado̱ koṛae me̱nket́a, Hąi hąi, onkage iń ąuriń hijuḱ hąbić do̱ no̱ṇḍe̱ baṛe̱ ṭekaokakinme.

Ado̱e me̱nket́a, Acha bogege, beṭa. Sim raḱre ḍańgram aṛaḱkin jo̱khe̱ćrege iń' hõń daka oṭoama; ado̱ nãhãḱ baskeaḱ ber jo̱khe̱ć nãhãḱ am do̱ ąguime. Ado̱e me̱nket́a, Acha besge.

[4] The Santals are very careful not to eat anything left, i. e. touched by others. A woman may eat what is left by her husband and children, a man will never eat what is left by women. Two persons will not, e. g., drink water of the same cup, unless the cup is first scoured. They are very particular in this respect, from a sanitary point of view excellently so. To eat anything touched by an animal would be horrible.

[5] The Santal plough is a very light implement, except for the ploughshare, made entirely from wood. The plough consists of three parts, the plough itself, the handle and the plough-beam, to which the yoke is fastened. To plough is always used a pair of bullocks or buffaloes. When going to or coming from the fields, they fasten the plough to the yoke in such a way that the plough itself hangs

took to Anua. The young man then ate what the jackal had left; but he did not know that he had eaten a jackal's leavings[4]; he did it unknowingly. After this the jackal every day in this way fooled the old woman.

Then, one day, the young man said: "I say, mother, what is the matter, that you now-a-days bring me such small dirty bits of food? do you prepare the food in this way or how?"

"Not at all, my lad," the old woman replied; "the food is quite good when I bring it from home; but whilst I am on the road with it, a jackal blocks the way for me and says to me: "Old woman, put the food down; if you don't put it down, we two shall presently bite you, so you will lie there, and we shall give you a good kicking." So, out of fear, I put it down to him, and he eats and leaves a little; that is the food that I bring you, and, fearing that you also would scold me, I have not told you of it."

"Well, mother," the young man said, "to-morrow you shall drive the bullocks to where I am ploughing; I myself shall bring my forenoon food."

"Very well, my boy," the old woman replied, "that is good; to-morrow then you hang the plough[5] on the yoke for me; I shall take loin-clothes on like you, drive the bullocks to where you are ploughing and let them stand there."

"That is right," the young man said, "keep them here until I shall come."

"Yes, very well, my boy," she replied; "at cock-crow, when you loose the bullocks, I shall prepare the food and leave it for you; then you take the food along at mealtime." "All right, that is good," he said.

down just below the yoke, whilst the plough-beam points upwards. The bullocks then carry the whole along. Sometimes the plough is left in the field, only the iron ploughshare being taken home, sometimes the ploughman may carry it himself. Here the bullocks are to take the plough along.

Adǫ khange sạri, ǫnẹkin galmaraolet́ lekage ḍaṅgrakoe joṛao gǫt́adete uni buḍhi dǫe laga idiket́kina, ar uni Ạnuạ koṛa dǫ kanthateye bandeyena are gǫgǫḱena, ar ḍạlićre dakae sajaoket́a. Adǫ baskeaḱ beren khan dǫ ḍạlić dakae dipilket́a, adǫ uni buḍhi hǫṛ lekage ṭheṅga tirup̠ tirup̠te adǫ baskeaḱe idiyet́ kana.

Khange adǫ uni toyo dǫe oḍok gǫt́ena, adǫe mẹn gǫt́ket́a, Daka dǫhǫeme, buḍhi, baṅkhanlaṅ gẹr gitić gǫt́mea. Adǫ khangeye dǫhǫket́a, adǫ uni toyo dǫe jǫjǫm kana. Un jǫkhẹćge Ạnuạ dǫ ona ṭheṅgate uni toyo dǫe dal bạji gǫt́kedea. Khange uni toyo dǫe ńir beret́ gǫt́enteye dạṛ gǫt́ket́a, are mẹn gǫt́ket́a, Durrẹ, Ạnuạ kanae ya. Adǫe ruhet́ gǫt́kedea, Hape ya, Ạnuạ, cet́em dal akadińte, iạićge, kā̃ṛbalaṅ jikiatama ar nahellaṅ ićatama. Adǫ onkae ruhet́ baṛaket́te uni toyo dǫe dạṛket́a.

Adǫ uni koṛa dǫ eṅgat buḍhi ṭhen sẹnkateye lại baṛawadea. Adǫ khange ạḍi baṛićkin landaket́a; adǫ oṛaḱte ḍaṅgrakin laga ạguket́kina. Adǫ khange dosar hiloḱ khon dǫ uni koṛa dǫ ona kā̃ṛbare holat́e tǫl akat́a.

Adǫ khange mit́ din dǫ ńindạ jǫkhẹć uni toyo dǫe hẹć gǫt́ena, adǫ nahele ić gǫt́at́a ar kā̃ṛbareye jikiḱ kan jǫkhẹćge liṇḍhiye gẹt́ gǫt́ena. Adǫ uni toyoe mẹn gǫt́ket́a, Durrẹ, iạ Ạnuạ ya, liṇḍhiye gẹt́ ocokidiń dǫ. Hape ya Ạnuạ, malhanlaṅ jǫm ạḍoetama.

Adǫ uni Ạnuạ dǫ ona malhan jhaṭa dǫ jạnumte goṭae ram ẹsẹt́ket́a. Adǫ khaṅge ńindạ jǫkhẹć uni toyo dǫe hẹć gǫt́ena, adǫ gǫd lạgit́ mocae idi khangeye rǫgoḱa. Adǫe mẹnet́a, Durrẹ,

---

6 Especially during the rainy season, but also at other times, women may dress not in one piece of cloth covering the breast and doing service for a petticoat, but in two pieces, one just big enough to go round the waist and cover the body below, whilst the other and smaller piece is taken up over the shoulder. It is a poor woman's clothing, but also used by all, when out doing fieldwork during the rainy season and the like.

7 The Santal word means a flat kind of basket. They have a large variety of forms.

8 Among the Santals, men carry on the shoulder, women on their head. When a child is born and people ask for or are told the sex of the new-born, the standard way of telling it is to say 'carrying on the shoulder' or 'carrying on the head', bhạrią or dipil, as the case may be.

Thereupon, in accordance with what they had talked together, he yoked the bullocks for the old woman, and she drove them along, whilst Anua dressed himself up in women's way, with a bit of cloth for a loin-cloth, and a piece over the breast[6], and put the food ready in a basket[7]. When the time for the forenoon meal came, he took the basket on his head[8], and leaning on a stick, like the old woman, he took the food along.

The jackal then all at once appeared and called out: "Put the food down, old woman, otherwise we two shall bite you, so you will lie there." So he put the basket down, and the jackal started eating. Whilst he was doing this, Anua struck the jackal with the stick, so he turned over and over. The jackal got on his legs in a hurry and ran away, saying: "Oh my! it is Anua, the fellow." Then he commenced scolding him: "Wait a bit, you fellow, you Anua; what, you have struck me, you unspeakable fellow, for that we two shall drag our posteriors along your plough-handle and pass stools on your plough." Having railed at him in this way, the jackal ran away.

The young man went to his mother and told her all, and both of them laughed heartily, whereupon they drove the bullocks home; from the next day the young man kept a razor tied to his plough-handle.

Then, one day, it happened at night that the jackal came and passed stool on the plough; when he was dragging his posteriors along the plough-handle, he cut himself in his hind-quarters. "Oh dear me!" the jackal cried, "this Anua has caused me to cut myself in my hind-quarters. Wait a bit, you fellow, you Anua, we two shall eat your beans for you."

Anua then fenced his bean-stakes[9] in entirely with thorn-tree branches. When the jackal came at night and stretched out his snout to pluck beans, the thorns pierced him. "Oh dear me!"

---

[9] This bean (Dolichos Lablab, L.) is generally grown in one small spot, the plant being trailed over the (dried) branches of a bush planted there.

Ạnuạwak̕ malhan dǫ bejãe yae gẹgẹra ya. Adǫ bae jǫm daṛeat̕a. Khangeye mẹnket̕a, Hape ya, Ạnuạ, malhan dǫ bejãeye gẹgẹrtama, iạić̕ge, sim yalaṅ jǫm atarkotama; hape gapa ocoak̕, dhoragelaṅ jǫmkotama.

Adǫ khange uni Ạnuạ dǫ datrǫm saṗkate dosar hilok̕ dǫ sim kundhi ṭhene duṛuṗ akana, adǫ ṅindạ khange uni toyo dǫe hẹć gǫt̕ena; adǫ oṛak̕teye bǫlǫ gǫt̕ena, adǫ sim kundhi ṭhene calao gǫt̕ena, adǫ gẹrko lạgit̕ mocae idi khangeye tobak̕ daram gǫdea. Khange uni toyo dǫe pạc gǫt̕enge; arhõ onka mocae idi khange ona datrǫmte bǫhǫk̕e tobak̕ gǫdea. Adǫ onka onkateye bhagaoen khan dǫe oḍokena, adǫ racare oḍokkateye mẹnet̕a, Cet̕ ya, Ạnuạ simpe tobak̕ akadiṅa, ar Ạnuạ hõ liṇḍhiye gẹt oco akadiṅa; iạ Ạnuạge, eṅgatem gǫć ataroḱa. Adǫ onka ruhet̕ baṛakate uni toyo dǫe calaoena.

Adǫ uni Ạnuạ dǫ ẹṛẹ ẹṛẹ kathaeye gǫćena, adǫ uni eṅgat buḍhi dǫ, kathae, adǫ dosar hilok̕ dǫe rak̕ baṛayet̕a, adǫ ẹṛe ẹṛe, kathaeye rak̕ baṛayet̕a, adǫ rak̕ rak̕te, kathae, adǫ bir sẹn calaokateye rak̕ baṛayet̕a. Adǫ khange uni toyo dǫ, kathaeye oḍok gǫt̕ena, adǫe kuli gǫt̕kedea, Henda buḍhi, cedak̕ adǫm rak̕ baṛayet̕a?

Khange adǫ uni buḍhiye mẹnket̕a, Amge thǫ hǫpǫniṅ dǫm sarapadea, onatege uni Ạnuạ dǫe gǫćentiṅa.

Khange adǫ unị toyoe mẹn gǫtket̕a, kathae, Bhagelenam, iạ Ạnuạge, eṅgate uḍiyem daleṅ kan tahẽkana — bam gǫć atarena? Adǫe mẹnket̕a, Henda buḍhi, adǫ tisem bhaṇḍanea?

---

10 The Santal sickle looks very much the same as the Norwegian implement.

11 The fowls live in the same house as the family. Generally a small part of the floor in a corner is set aside for the fowls. Here the fowls stay from evening to morning. A tiny ridge is often put as a barrier across the floor.

12 It is very common that both men and women in speaking add to the verb a word which is supposed to emphasize the meaning, but is untranslatable, except by something akin to swearing. The men use a word meaning 'to urinate', and the women a word meaning 'to burn up'. The jackal here uses the latter word.

13 The last of the Santal funeral ceremonies, bhaṇḍan, is regularly performed after the bones of the corpse have been thrown into the Damuda river. It is a

the jackal said, "Anua's beans are biting something awful, oh my!" He could not eat and said: "Wait a bit, you fellow, you Anua; your beans are biting something awful, you uspeakable fellow; your fowls, you fellow, we two shall eat up entirely; wait, let it become to-morrow, we two shall surely eat those you have."

The next day Anua took a sickle[10] and sat down near the fowls' corner[11]. At night the jackal appeared, entered the house and went straight to the fowls' corner; then, when he put his mouth out to catch some, Anua met him with the sickle and pecked him. The jackal then drew back, and when he again put his mouth out, he met him with the sickle and pecked him in his head. When he had to give it up after having tried the same several times, he went out. When he came out into the court-yard, he said: "What, you fellow, you Anua-fowls have pecked me, and Anua has also caused me to get my hind-quarters cut. You unspeakable Anua, dash it, you shall die and be done for[12]." Having scolded in this way the jackal went away.

Thereupon, people tell, Anua pretended to die, and his old mother the next day commenced to wail, that is to say, she pretended to wail, and crying she went to the forest and wailed there. Then the jackal came suddenly out from somewhere and asked her: "I say, old woman, what are you crying for?"

"It was yourself," the old woman replied, "who cursed my son; therefore my Anua died for me."

"It served you right," the jackal said; "you rascal of an Anua, dash it, you were beating me very hard, — did you not die, confound you[12]?" "Look here, old woman", he said, "when are you going to have the funeral ceremonies[13]?"

---

circumstantial affair, with offerings to the spirit of the dead and feasting and drinking. What is here called bhaṇḍan is, of course, not the proper thing.

14 The woman is wailing in Bengali, possibly because it is meant to be more impressive, the jackals in the Santal tales being frequently introduced as speaking Bengali.

Adọ uni buḍhi dọe mẹnkeťa, Teheń ńindạgeń bhaṇḍane lạgiť; onate am lạlạige iń dọń hẹć akana. Adọń mẹnkeťa, Ọ hae, bhala họpọniń lekage dakakoń idiae kan tahẽkana, adọ nịạ bhaṇḍanre dọ ọkọe tora uni hõń lạiaegea. Adọ onka mẹnkate, beṭa, nõǩõe am ṭhen lạlại iń dọń hẹćakana. Dakaeań, utuiań, piṭhạiań nãhãǩ, adọ ọkọe iń ẹm pạhilakoteń jọma? Nin dara dọ uniye tahẽkante uniń ẹm pạhilaea, ẹṇḍẹ ẹnẹć iń jọmeť tahẽkana. Adọ uni bạnugićte iń dọ ạḍi bhabnań ạikạueťa.

Adọ khange uni toyoe mẹn gọťkeťa, Alom bhabnaǩa, buḍhi, uni bọdọl dọ iń menańa; ińge nãhãǩ ẹm pạhilạńme.

Adọe mẹnkeťa, Acha, tọbẹ calaǩme nãhãǩ.

Adọe mẹnkeťa, Acha dhinạń ạyuṗge thọ?

Adọe mẹnkeťa, Hẽ, dhinạṅge calao gọdoǩme nãhãǩ, alom ẹṛẹńa.

Adọe mẹnkeťa, Ma, ọhọń ẹṛẹmea.

Adọ uni buḍhi dọe ruạṛena, ar uni toyo dọ ako jạt aemae riạu jarwakeťkoa. Adọ ạyuṗ khangeko calao gọťena. Adọ uni buḍhi dọe mẹn gọťkeťa, Ma beṭa, duṛuṗtabonpe. Khange adọko duṛuṗ baṛayena. Adọ uni buḍhi dọe raǩeťa, kathae, Hae! hae! Ạnuạ beṭa muri gelae, hae! hae! Ạnuạ beṭa muri gelae.

Onka, kathae, uni buḍhi dọe raǩ baṛayeťa. Adọ, kathae, uni toyoe mẹnkeťa, Alom raga, buḍhi. Ma, hapeǩme, inạǩge ragme. Nitoǩ dọ gọćen họṛ dọ ọhọm ńamlea. Nitoǩ dọ hapeǩme, ar ma daka baṛaetabonme.

Khange ṭukućkoe gitil baṛa aderkeťa, sẹṅgẹle jolkeťa; adọ uni toyoe mẹnkeťa, Ẹ buḍhi, tọl hataṛkaleme, baṅkhan nãhãǩle lạṛhại bọtẹćkoǩa.

Adọ uni buḍhiye mẹnkeťa, Sạrige, beṭa, bhagegem mẹnkeťa; tọl pạhilkapegeań. Adọ joteko, barahiko ńamkateye tọlkeťkoa, ar uni pagla toyo dọ khub kajake tọlkedea. Adọe metae kana,

15 The Santali word, karahi, means a kind of shallow cooking vessel, used among other things to cook Santal cakes in; it is usually made from earthenware, but may also be of metal.

"To-day," the old woman replied, "this night I am going to have the funeral ceremonies; therefore I have come to tell you. I said to myself: Alas, I was taking food out to him like to a son of mine; therefore I shall this instant also invite him to the funeral ceremonies. Having this in my mind, my son, I have, as you see, come to you to let you know. I shall cook rice, I shall prepare curry, I shall make cakes presently: but to whom shall I give first, and then eat myself? Formerly, when he was there, I was giving him first; then only I took my food. Now when he is no more, I am feeling exceedingly sorrowful."

"Don't be sorrowful, old woman," the jackal replied, "I am here in his stead; give me first now."

"All right," she said, "come then."

"All right," he replied, "it is later to-day, in the evening, is it not?"

"Yes," she said, "be sure to come in the afternoon; don't fail me."

"Be sure," he replied, "I shall not fail you."

The old woman then returned, and the jackal invited a great crowd of his kind to come along. When it became evening, they went; the old woman met them and said: "Please, my son, be seated all of you," and they sat down. The old woman was crying: "Ach, ach[14], Anua mein Sohn ist gestorben, ach, ach. Anua mein Sohn ist gestorben."

In this way, people tell, the old woman wailed. Then the jackal said: "Don't cry, old woman. Be quiet, stop that, let that be enough crying. Now you will not get the dead one back. Stop now, and please prepare food for us."

She then scoured the cooking pots and took them in; thereupon she lighted a fire. The jackal then said: "Old woman, tie us up for the present, otherwise we might commence fighting presently."

"That's true, my son," the old woman said, "it was well you said that; I shall first tie you all." She then found yoke cords and ropes and tied them all up; and that rascally jackal she tied very firmly. So she said: "First, my son, I shall make cakes

Ẹ beṭa, pạhil dọń piṭhạ maṛańtabona, inạbo jọm hataṛa. Daka dọ ọhọ nãhãk̉ isin họt̉lena: daka dọ tayọmteń isina.

Adọko mẹn gọt̉ket̉a, Acha bogege, ma ẹṇḍẹkhan piṭhạ họdme. Adọ, kathae, karahiye dhipạuket̉a; adọ onare pọhrẹk pọhrẹk dak̉e chiṭkạu gọt̉ak̉ kana, adọ chọń chọń saḍe gọdok̉ kana. Adọ uni toyo dọe mẹnet̉takoa, Ọtẹ ya, cet̉ leka mõ̱ńj saḍe kana! Khub nãhãk̉bo jọma. Adọ onka chọń chọń saḍe torage, kathae, uni pagla toyo dọe dọn gọt̉et̉ tahẽ̱kana.

Khange uni Ạnuạ dọ bhitạrreye gitić akan tahẽ̱kana. Adọ hape hapeteye beret̉ente ṭheṅgae ńamket̉a, adọ ṭheṅga mũṭkateye ńir ọḍok hot̉ena; adọ dale dalket̉koa dọ, andhe mundheye uyuk̉ket̉a. Adọ khange onko dọko gẹr topak̉ baṛaket̉teko dạṛket̉a. Ar nui dọ bae topak̉ daṛeat̉a; khangeye dal jhin jhinạukedea, adọ leṭep̉ leṭep̉e tahẽ̱ aṅgayena.

Adọ dosar hilok̉ dọ dak̉ lo ghaṭteye idikedea, ar ọṇḍẹye khuṇṭạukadea, ar mit̉ṭaṇ guḍnạ benaokate ọṇḍẹye dọhọkat̉a. Adọ jãhãe ạimạige dak̉ loko calak̉, adọ sanam hoṛ mimit̉ guḍnạko piṭạuea. Onka onkate uni toyo dọko dal mõ̱kedea.

Khange adọ mit̉ din dọ ńindạ jọkhẹć dosra toyo dak̉ ńũ ọṇḍẹko hẹćena, adọ dak̉ko ńũ baṛaket̉a, adọko metae kana, Henda ya, cet̉ jọmte bań onka dọ bẹbạṛićem moṭa akan dọ? Bhala cet̉kom jọmet̉a, ar ale dọ okorle moṭak̉ kana?

Adọe mẹnket̉a, Dakań jọmet̉a; tinạk̉ hoṛ nọṇḍẹ dak̉ loko hijuk̉ kan, sanam hoṛ mimit̉ bakhra dakako ạgu darawań kana.

Adọko mẹnket̉a, Ale hõ ẹṇḍẹkhan nọṇḍẹ khuṇṭạulele khanko ạgukelea?

Adọe mẹnket̉a, Hẽ̱ ya, ạikạ sanam hoṛ dọkọ ạgukepe cọń bań cọń, mẹnkhan mit hoṛ dọ khạṭigeko ạgukepea. Ar bam pạṭiạu

---

16 See p. 56, note 16.

17 Ghaṭ in Santali means generally a passage down to, or the place where people fetch water. To have access to such a place means that one belongs to a particular society or caste. In the villages people are often rather strict and hard in respect of this. The ghaṭ may be at a river or a tank.

18 The Santali word is used about a heavy piece of wood, used for beating the rice bundles (bạndi) to tighten the ropes with which these are bound.

for us; we shall eat them for the present. It will take some time for the rice to be cooked; I shall cook the rice afterwards."

"Very well," they said, "please, then, be quick and make cakes." The old woman then put a pan[15] on the fire and let it become hot; now and again she sprinkled a little water on it, so it made a hissing sound. The jackal every time remarked: "Listen, my friends, how beautifully it sounds. We shall get a rich feed presently." And every time he heard that hissing sound, the rascally jackal jumped for joy.

Now Anua had been lying down in the bhitạr[16]. He very quietly got up and found a stick, and taking a firm hold of the stick with his fist, he ran out and commenced to beat the jackals all he could, he struck out in all directions. The jackals then tore the ropes with their teeth and ran away; but this one was not able to tear the cords, and he beat him so he became faint and was lying there utterly exhausted until dawn.

The following day Anua took him down to the place where people fetched water[17] and tied him to a post there; he also made a club[18] and put it there. It then came to pass that, whenever women came to fetch water, every one gave him a blow with the club. In this way they beat the jackal, so that he swelled up.

Then, one day at night time, some other jackals came there to drink water. When they had drunk water, they said to him: "Look here, you fellow, what can you be eating to become so enormously fat? What on earth are you eating? and we others, we do not become fat at all."

"I am eating rice," he replied; "every one who comes here to fetch water, all of them bring some along and give me a portion rice."

"Would they then," one of them said, "bring us also something, if we were tied to a post here?"

"Yes, of course, you fellow," that jackal replied; "now I could not say whether they would bring or not to all of you; but to one they would be sure to bring. If you don't believe it, please release me, and I shall tie you with the same rope that I am

khan do̱ ho̱ne̱ć ma iń rar̤akańme ar ona jor̤atege amiń jor̤akama. Ńe̱lme nãhãk̕ gapa setak̕ khangeko ạguama.

Khange tho̱ uni dosra toyoe me̱nket̕a, Acha bhalań biḍạutama. Ado̱ sạri onka me̱nkate uni do̱e rar̤akedea ar aće to̱l ocoyena. Khange ado̱ aṅgayen khan, sạri ado̱ mõr̤ẽ go̱ṭe̱n ạimại dak̕ loko hijuk̕ kane ńe̱l go̱t̕ket̕koa. Ado̱e me̱nket̕a, Mõr̤ẽ ho̱r̤ko hijuk kana, mõr̤ẽ bakhra nãhãk̕ko ạguyet̕a; khub jo̱m nãhãk̕iń jo̱ma.

Onkae me̱njoṅ kan tahẽkange ado̱ko se̱ṭe̱ren khan do̱ kanḍako do̱ho̱ bar̤akat̕a, ar ona guḍnạ saṕkate sanam ho̱r̤ mimit̕ guḍnạko muker̤kedea. Khange ado̱ ạr̤iste uni toyo do̱ ạḍi bạr̤iće do̱net̕a. Khange arhõ pe̱a ponea ạimạiko he̱ć juṭućena. Khange ado̱e do̱net̕ ńe̱lte dalko dalkedea do̱, e̱kkalte o̱ṇḍe̱geko dal go̱ć utạrkedea. O̱ne̱ onka lekate uni pagla toyo do̱e jitạuena.

Cabayena katha do̱.

9. Turtạ kor̤a ar toyo reaṅ.

Ạḍi sedaere mit̕ṭaṅ rạṇḍi maejiue tahẽkana. Uniren do̱ mit̕ṭaṅgetaeyae ho̱po̱n do̱ sadherre. Unige mit̕ṭaṅ gaḍa ar̤e beḍare eskare siok̕a. Eṅgat buḍhi do̱ baskeak̕ dak̕ mạṇḍiye idiaea. Ar mit̕ṭaṅ toyo do̱ goṭe ciṇḍkạreye tãr̤ãk̕kok̕a.

Ado̱ khange uni buḍhi do̱ kor̤a baskeak̕ dak̕ mạṇḍiye idiaea; ado̱ uni toyo do̱ buḍhiye metaea, De̱n buḍhi, dak̕ mạṇḍi emańme. Baṅdo̱ Turtạ do̱e siok̕ kan? Iṅge co̱ṅ siok̕ kan tahẽkan. Uni buḍhiren ho̱po̱nte̱t̕ kor̤awak̕ ńutum do̱ Turtạwaea.

Ado̱ onkae metade khan, e̱ne̱ye do̱ho̱ket̕ge, ado̱e dul bar̤awadege. Ado̱ uni Turtạ lạgit̕ do̱ dak̕ dak̕e sare̱ć idiadege. Ado̱ Turtạ do̱e me̱na, Henda go̱, cet̕ leka baṅ dak̕ mạṇḍi do̱m ạguạṅ?

---

[1] The name of the man who wrote this story down is Kạnhu Mạrṇḍi of village Chondorpura in the Dumka Damin. He was a well educated man, at one time a school teacher. Died in Mesopotamia during the war. The Santal original is considerably below the standard set by Sagram. It seems to be two stories, dimly remembered and joined together.

[2] The Santali word for food used here is lit. rice-water, a very common dish. The word is, however, often used as a modest name for food in general.

tied with. Be sure, as soon as it becomes morning to-morrow, they will bring you something."

The other jackal then said: "Very well, I shal like to try what you say." And verily, having said this, he released the jackal and let himself be tied up. When it dawned next day, he saw five women coming to fetch water. "Five persons are coming," he said, "they are surely bringing five portions; how well I shall eat!"

Whilst he was saying this to himself, they arrived and put their water-pots down; thereupon they took the club and all of them hit him one blow with the club. The jackal did not feel pleased at this and jumped and leaped all he could to get loose. Then three or four more women came, in addition to the first ones. When they saw how he was jumping, they beat him again and again; they beat him to death then and there. In this way that rascally jackal came away safely.

The story is ended.

9. TURTA AND THE JACKAL[1].

ONCE upon a time long long ago there was a widow. She had one son, an only one. This young man was ploughing some land along the bank of a river, quite alone. His mother was in the habit of taking his forenoon-meal rice-water[2] out to him. And a jackal was lying in wait in a croton thicket[3] near by.

Well, the old woman was carrying the forenoon meal out to the boy, and the jackal says to the woman: "Please, old woman, give me food. Do you think it is Turta who is ploughing? Why, it was I who was ploughing." The name of the son of the old woman was Turta.

When the jackal spoke to her in this way, she put the basket down and poured food out for him, whereupon she took the remainder, just the water, to Turta. Turta asked her: "I say, mother, what kind of stuff is this rice-water you bring me?"

---

[3] The tree or rather bush mentioned is Croton oblongifolius, Roxb., fairly common in the Santal country.

Adọ buḍhi dọe mẹna, Uni toyogeye ẹṛẹṅa. Din hiloḱ metaṅae, Turtạ dọ bacọe sioḱ kan. Onka dinạmgeye ẹṛẹyea ar deakoreye capo baṛaea.

Adọ miť din dọ uni koṛa dọ palkoe toťkeťa, ar ḍaṅgra dọ uni buḍhigeye gupi baṛayeťkoa. Adọ aćge buḍhi lekae bandeyena ar sakọmkoe họṛọḱketa, ar miťṭaṅ potam cupi ṭẹṅgọće gọḱ torakeťa. Adọ daḱ mạṇḍiye dipil idiyeťa. Adọ khange uni toyo dọ gajaṛ khone ṅir oḍokena are metadea, Dẹn buḍhi, daḱ mạṇḍi dul oṭo-aṅme. Iṅge thọr iṅ sioḱ kana.

Khan adọe emadea, adọe jọmjoṅ kana. Ar ać dọ uni dea sẹćreye duṛuṗena, adọ uni eṅgat buḍhi lekage caṇḍbọlkoreye tunum baṛayedea. Toyo dea sẹćre duṛuṗkate tunum baṛayede-khane mẹnkeťa, uni toyo dọ, baṅma, Noa dọ kaca kantiṅa. Khan tunum baṛa tunum baṛa phẹḍ muṇḍre ona potam cupi ṭẹṅgọćte caṇḍbọle samaḱ kuṭṛakeťtaea, adọe dạṛ taṗkeťa.

Ar toyoe mẹnkeťa, Hapẹ ya, Turtạ, 'caṇḍbọlem samaḱ akaťtiṅa, kāṛbalaṅ jikiatama.

Khange Turtạ dọ ona kāṛbare miťṭaṅ lasẹr holaťe tọlkaťa. Adọ toyo dọ kāṛbareye jikiaḱ jọkhẹn liṇḍhi dọ gẹť māyāmentaea. Adọe mẹnkeťa, Bejāe Turtạwaḱ kāṛba dọ lasẹrtaea. Hapẹ, sim iṅ jọm-kotaea. Ạḍi liṇḍhiye gẹť oco akadiṅa.

Onkae mẹnkeť khan, Turtạ dọ ạyuṗ jọkhẹn datrọmante sim kundhi ṭhene duṛuṗ thirkoḱa. Adọ toyo dọ hape hapeteye ṅam baṛayeťko kana. Uni Turtạ dọ mar datrọmte tobage. Khange adọe mẹna, Durrẹ! bạṛić Turtạren sim dọko toḱbaḱtaea.

Adọ arhō̱ Turtạ dọe mẹna, Hapelaṅ batraoeťme kana.

Adọ toyo dọe mẹnkeť, Ọh! Iạ Turtạ, mẹrọmlaṅ jọmkotama.

---

4 Santal women make extensive use of wristlets of sorts, every married woman has some.

5 The Santals have several forms of axes, the one here mentioned, called 'dove-tail' axe, being very small, size and form reminding one of the tail of a dove.

6 What is here translated 'trousers' is a piece of cloth, some 2 1/2 m. long and 1/2 m. broad, taken round the loins and between the legs. It is the old regular form of Santal loin-cloth for men.

7 See p. 6, note 11.

"That jackal," his mother said, "he deceives me. Every day he says to me: Turta, why, he does not plough." In this way the jackal fools her every day, and she pats the jackal on the back.

Then, one day, the young man took the ploughshares off, and the old woman was tending the bullocks, whilst he himself clothed himself like an old woman and put wristlets[4] on; as he went, he took a small axe[5] along, carrying it on his shoulder, and he also carried the food on his head. As he went along, the jackal came running out of the thicket and said to him: "Please, old woman, pour rice-water out for me, before you go further. It is I who plough, you know."

He gave him some, and the jackal commenced eating. He sat down behind the jackal, whilst he, like his old mother, was touching him with his hand over his back and tail. As he was sitting there and touching the jackal, he, i. e. the jackal, said: "That's my trousers[6]." The young man kept on touching him until he suddenly, with his small axe, cut the jackal's tail off at the root, whereupon he ran away.

"Wait a bit, you Turta," the jackal called out, "you have cut my tail; I shall drag my posterior along your plough-handle."

Turta then tied a sharp razor to the plough-handle, and when the jackal dragged his posterior along the plough-handle, his hind-quarters were cut, and the blood flowed out. "Turta's plough-handle," the jackal said, "is awfully sharp. Wait a bit, I shall eat his fowls. He is the cause of my having got my hind-quarters so badly cut."

When he had said this, Turta, in the evening, took a sickle and sat down quietly at the fowls' corner. The jackal came and was trying to catch some without making any noise, and Turta at once pecked him with the sickle. "Oh my," the jackal said, "it is something awful those fowls of Turta's peck."

"Wait," Turta said, "we two[7] are making a fine show of you."

"Oh," the jackal called out, "you unspeakable Turta, we two shall eat your goats."

Adǫ khange Turtą dǫ mẹrǫm gudṛi ṭhene duṛupkoḱa muṅgạrante. Adǫe gẹr baṛako jǫkhẹć mar uni dǫ muṅgạrte kuṭạme. Adǫe mẹna, Turtạren mẹrǫm dǫ bejãeko kuḱṭạmtaea. Hapẹ, Turtại gǫćlen khan, bhaṇḍan iṅ jǫmtaea.

Turtą dǫ ona kathae aṅjǫmkeť khan buḍhiye metadea, Ią gǫ, birte calaḱme, sahan sakamko hẹć baṛaeme, ar iṅ ṅutumte raḱ baṛaeme.

Adǫ sẹnkate nonkae raḱ baṛayeťa: Turtą rẹ, Turtą mori gel rẹ! Turtą rẹ, Turtą mori gel rẹ!

Adǫ khange toyoe hẹćena; adǫe kulikedea, Henda buḍhi, cedaḱem raḱeťa?

Hǫ, Turtại gǫćena, onateṅ raḱeťa, ar bhaṇḍane lạgiť sakamkoṅ hẹć idiyeťa; hǫṛ hõ bạnuḱkoa.

Adǫ toyo dǫe mẹnkeťa, Ho, ma am dǫ jǫtǫ tear hataṛme, iṅ nãhãḱ peṛa dǫṅ nẽota idikoa.

Khan uni buḍhi dǫ oṛaḱteye sẹnena ar mẹrǫme gǫćkeťkoa. Khange toyo dǫ toyokoe riạu jaora ạgukeťkoa. Adǫ onko toyo dǫ bebak poska poska sikol baberteye tǫlkeťkoa jhạṇṭi aṛe aṛete, ar uni bạṇḍią toyo dǫ khub kẹṭẹć baberteye tǫlkedea, jẹmǫn rẹpẹćkate aloko jǫm, adǫe emaťkoa. Nẹko jǫm adha ạdhi akať jǫkhẹn buḍhi dǫe raḱeťa: Turtą rẹ, Turtą kahã gel rẹ? Turtą mutąk lele an.

Adǫ uni bạṇḍią toyo buḍhiye metae kana, Ceť leka bam raḱeť kan?

Adǫe mẹneťa, Ceť leka baṅ raḱeť kan? Turtạwaḱ mutąk tahẽkantaea, ona baṅ kolkaťtaea. Ona disạte ona mutąk iṅ ṅẹleťa ar iṅ raḱeťa.

Ona tayǫm Turtą dǫ mutạkanteye oḍokena, ar uni dǫ mar ona mutạkte ghatrako. Onko toyo dǫ topaḱkateko dạṛkeťa; ar uni bạṇḍią toyo dǫ ukhuṛreye tǫlledea ar khub moṭa baberte. Chại

---

8 The Santal word likely means to convey 'with the hoof'.

9 The old woman is using Bengali.

10 Some of the personal belongings of the deceased are usually 'sent with' him. That is effected through certain symbolical acts.

Turta then sat down at the goat-pen with a wooden mallet, and when the jackal was biting at the goats, he hammered him with the mallet. The jackal then said: "These goats of Turta's are hammering[8] something awful. Wait a bit, when Turta is dead, I shall feast at the funeral ceremonies."

When Turta heard this, he said to his old mother: "I say, mother, go to the forest to fetch firewood and leaves, and wail for me."

The old woman went and cried thus: "Turta oh, Turta ist gestorben[9], oh! Turta oh, Turta ist gestorben oh!"

Then the jackal came and asked her: "I say, old woman, what are you crying for?"

"Oh, Turta is dead; therefore I am crying, and I am finding leaves to prepare for his funeral ceremonies; there are no people either to help."

"O," the jackal replied, "you make everything ready; I shall invite the friends and bring them."

The woman then went home and killed some goats, and the jackal called a crowd of jackals together and came with them. The old woman tied all the jackals with some rotten straw-rope along the fence; but the tailless jackal she tied with a very strong rope; she did all this to prevent them from fighting over the food; thereupon she gave them. When they had half done eating, the old woman wailed: "Turta oh, wohin ist Turta gegangen? Turta, hole den Hammer[9]!"

"How is it you are wailing?" the tailless jackal called out to her.

"How is it I am wailing?" the old woman said; "Turta had a wooden mallet, and I did not send that with him[10]. I remember this when I see the mallet, and wail."

After this, Turta came out with the mallet and slashed at them right and left with the mallet. The other jackals tore their ropes and ran away; but the tailless jackal he tied to the rice mortar[11]

11 A large and heavy wooden implement, used by the Santals and also by many other races for husking rice and other purposes.

daṛeaťae topaǩ daṛeaťae. Mar bhagete mukeṛe. Adọ dal dalteye dal mõkedea. Adọ khange duạr ṭhene tọlkadea, adọ jao hiloǩ oḍokoǩ bọlọǩe dalea, adọ artẹťgeye dal mõkedea.

Khan miť din dọ miťṭaṅ tạruṗ ạṇḍiạụ hẹćena, adọe mẹneťa, Henda bhạgnạ, bejãeyem moṭa akan dọ?

Ọh mamọ, ceť baṅ mẹn? Iṅ dọ baṅ ṅẹlaǩ iṅ ṅẹleťa ar baṅ jọmaǩ iṅ jọmeťa.

Adọ tạruṗe mẹneťa, Tọbẹ iṅ nọṇḍẹṅ tahẽlen khan, iṅ hõṅ moṭakoǩa?

Adọ toyo dọe mẹnkeť, Hẽ, am dọ arhõ bạṛti moṭam ṅẹloǩa; am ma ẹnte napṛaǩ jạt kanem.

Khange adọ toyo dọe mẹneťa, Dẹ ẹṇḍẹkhan raṛakaṅme. Adọe raṛakadea, adọ ać bọdọl uni kul ạṇḍiạgeye tọlkadea.

Adọ Turtạ koṛa dọ racateye oḍokoǩ kan tahẽkana. Adọ maraṅ utạṛe ṅẹlkede khan, mutạk ṭheṅgate bhageteye dalkedea, dal aḍraokedeae. Onka dal dalteye dal mõkedea. Ona dosar tesar khangeye gọćena. Uni Turtạ koṛa dọe khalkedea. Khalkate ona harta dọe rọǩ joṛaokeťa ar busuṗe bhọraokeťa. Ar ona dọ ato atoe gọǩ baṛayeťa, are kọe baṛaca ar poesakoko emaea. Onatekin ạsuloǩa ạkin banar eṅga họn. Ḍher din onka onkateye poesa jaorakeťa.

Adọ miť din eṅgatṭẹťe metadea, Ẹ gọ, iṅ dọ bạnij bepar iṅ calaǩa. Ma sạtu sambaraṅme.

Adọe sạtu sambaradeteye oḍok calaoena miť raj disomte. Adọ raj naṅgrahae ṅamkeťa. Adọ ọṇḍẹye kuli baṛayeťkoa, Ọkọeko sadọmpe ạkriṅkoa? Uni rajrenge ạḍi utạr hạti sadọm menaǩkoa. Adọ ạyuṗente ẹn hiloǩ dọ ona naṅgraha aṛe sadọm oṛaǩ phẹḍregeye ḍerayena.

---

[12] This Santal word is generally used about the tiger, but is also used as a common name for tigers and leopards.

[13] Pice, or in North Indian languages paesa or poesa, is 1/4 anna, about one farthing. In Santali it is very generally used to mean 'money'.

[14] It is very seldom that Santals go about to buy and sell. They may take animals to a distant market to sell, or go to such places to buy; otherwise trading is something Santals have not as yet shown themselves fit for.

with a very heavy rope. He tried, but he was utterly unable to tear himself loose. So Turta laid it thickly on with the mallet. He continued beating him until he swelled up. Then he tied him at the door, and whenever he went out or came in, he gave him a blow every day, so he swelled still more.

Then one day a big leopard came. "I say, nephew," he said, "you have grown exceedingly fat."

"O uncle, what can I say? I see what is not seen, and I eat what is not eaten."

"Then," the leopard said, "if I stayed here, should I also grow fat?"

"Yes," the jackal replied, "you will look still much fatter; for you, you see, are of a big race."

"Please then, unbind me," the jackal said, whereupon the leopard unbound him, and the jackal tied the big leopard[12] there in his stead.

When Turta was coming out into the courtyard and saw that he was so immensely big, he gave him a good hiding with the club; he beat him so that he bellowed. By beating him in this way, he made him swell up, and two three days afterwards the leopard died, and Turta flayed him. When he had done this, he sewed the skin together and filled it with straw. This stuffed thing he carried about from village to village begging, and people gave him p i c e[13]. By these means they supported themselves, both mother and son. A long time they collected money in this way.

One day Turta said to his mother: "Mother, I am going off to trade[14]. Please, make me some provisions for the road."

When she had given him some food to take with him, he started and came to a king's country. When he reached the capital, he asked the people there: "Is there any one here who sells ponies?" Now the king had a large number of elephants and horses, and when it became evening that day, he stopped for the night in the outskirts of the town near the stables.

Ado̱ ạyup̓ jo̱khe̱n onko sado̱mko galmaraojoń kana. Mit̓ṭań sado̱m do̱ jańgare khil menak̓taea. Uni do̱e menet̓a, Noa khil jãhãeye o̱co̱k̓letiń khan, e̱kkalte o̱t ar sermań uḍạukok̓a. Ar mit̓ sado̱m do̱e me̱net̓a, Iń hõ̱ jańga bań murukok̓ kante, bańkhan ge̱l bar ko̱s oṭańok̓ lekań dạṛkea, ar ona oṭańok̓ dhuṛi ạuri cabak̓regeń he̱ć ruạṛkok̓a. Ar ado̱m sado̱m do̱ko me̱net̓a, Hẽ̱, ale do̱ bạr siń pe̱ mãhã ho̱r do̱ mit̓ dintele calaokok̓a. Ar uni Turtạ koṛa do̱ onako jo̱to̱ galmaraoe ańjo̱mket̓takoa.

Ado̱ dosar hilok̓ onko sado̱me bachaoet̓koa. Khan raj sipạhiye lạiat̓koa. Ado̱ rajko lạiadea, Mit̓ṭań ho̱ṛ sado̱me kirińko lạgit̓.

Ado̱ raje me̱nket̓, Ho̱, ma emaepe jãhãeṭak̓geye khusiako.

Ado̱ko he̱ćente uni khe̱ṛdo̱k̓ khe̱ṛdo̱k̓e taṛam, uni sado̱mge hataoe lạgit̓e metat̓koa, Iń do̱ nuigeń hataoea. Eṭak̓ko ma mõ̱ṛẽ̱ ge̱l turui ge̱l dhạbiće damako kan. Ado̱e me̱nket̓a, Iń do̱ re̱ńge̱ć ho̱ṛ, ni khoṛda sado̱mgeń hataoea.

Ado̱ko damadea, Nui do̱m khusik̓ khan, ge̱l bar ṭakale damae kana.

Ado̱ khusiyente ge̱l bar ṭakateye hataokedea. Ado̱ ona disom khon eṭak̓ disomteye calak̓ kana. Ado̱ uni sado̱m do̱ khe̱ṛdo̱k̓ khe̱ṛdo̱k̓e calak̓ kana.

Ado̱ enka calak̓ calak̓ mit̓ṭań eṭak̓ raj disome tiok̓ket̓a. O̱ṇḍe̱ do̱ dinạmge rajko bahalok̓a ar dinạmgeko gujuk̓a. E̱ke̱n rajren era ar ho̱po̱nerage menak̓kina. Ar uni koṛa sado̱mre de̱ćkateye tiok̓ket̓ khan, o̱ṇḍe̱n sipạhiko kuliyedea, Okatem hijuk̓ kana?

Ado̱e metat̓koa, Iń do̱ bạnij bepar iń oḍok̓ he̱ć akana.

Ado̱ko metae kana, No̱ṇḍe̱ rajem tahẽ̱kok̓a?

Ado̱e me̱nket̓a, Iń do̱ re̱ńge̱ć ho̱ṛ, khusiań bańe?

Ado̱ko me̱nket̓a, Ale hõ̱le khusikok̓a ar uni raj era hõ̱e khusikok̓a. Hẽ̱, ado̱m tahẽ̱ daṛeak̓ khan, ona reak̓le lại bujhạu baṛawama, bańma, uniak̓ ho̱ṛmo̱re kal menaea. Uni ado̱e oḍoklen

[15] Twelve is in Santali frequently used to express perfection, maximum etc. One ko̱s in Santali is equivalent to about two English miles.

[16] I. e. rupees. One rupee is about 1 sh. 4 d.

In the evening, the horses were talking together. One of the horses had a splinter in his hoof; he said: "If any one would remove the splinter I have, I should at once fly over earth and heaven." Another horse said: "As for me also, there is no power in my legs, otherwise I should run like twelve[15] miles like dust carried away by the wind, and I should return before the dust ceased to be blown away." And other horses said: "Yes, we should in one day go two three days' way." And Turta heard all this that they were talking together.

The following day he picked out these horses and said so to the king's peons. Then these told the king: "A man wishes to buy horses."

"O," the king said, "let him have any he may like."

When the horses came, he said he wanted to take the horse that was limping. "This one I shall take," he said; "the others he is pricing fifty to sixty[16]. I am a poor man," he said, "I shall take this lame horse."

They told him the price. "If you like this one, we want to have twelve rupees for him."

He was pleased at this price and bought the horse for twelve rupees, whereupon he went from that country to another; and the horse was limping along.

Going along in this way he reached the country of another king. There kings were appointed every day, and were dying daily. Only the queen and a princess were living. When the young man reached there, riding his horse, the soldiers asked him: "Where are you coming?"

"I have come from home," he replied, "to trade."

"Would you like to stay here as our king?" they asked him.

"I am a poor man," he answered; "it depends on whether she would like me."

"We should be pleased," they said, "and the queen would also be pleased. Well, if you are able to stay, we shall tell you and let you know, how the state of matters is. It is this, there is

khan, ạḍi marań janwar uni dọ. Ọt khon serma tuṅgạu dhạbiće cahaba. Uni dọ mũ họrteye oḍokoḱa. Onate raj dọ pasẹć miť hajar ganko gọć akana. Noakole lạiam kana.

Adọ uni kọṛa sadọmre dilte ar aćaḱ dilteye menkeťa, Acha, tahẽ daṛeaḱ khan iń ńẹla.

Adọ enkako galmaraokeťte adọ bapla hoeyena, ar raj ṭika hõko emadea. Khan uni Turtạ kọṛa dọ miťṭań saṇḍasiye ńamkeťa ar miťṭań piṭi khaṇḍa. Onako jọtọe tearante ać ṭhene dọhọkeťa. Ar uni puṅkhi sadọm hõ ać ṭhene dọhọkedea.

Ar ona ńindạtẹťrege uni kal kạrinạṅgin dọe oḍok gọťena uni họṛaḱ mũ họr khon. Ar ọt serma adọe cahaṗeťa, uni raj jọme lạgiťe lagayede kana. Khan sadọmre dẹćente ona khiltẹťe toťkeťtaea, serma tuṅgạue uḍạuḱ lạgiťe ńẹlede kante are lagayedete cọṭrege bar pẹ dhaoe bhuṅgrạukedea, adọe ńũrena. Inạ tayọm sadọme ãṛgo ạgukedea. Kate adọ rạniye dọhọkedea.

Tahẹn tahẹnte raje mẹnkeťa, Ińren buḍhi eṅgạń menaea. Uni ṭhen iń calaḱa, hiri ạguyeań. Adọ bana họṛgekin sapṛaoena, ar bana họṛ sadọmregekin dẹćena, adọ cọṭteye uḍạu calaoena.

Bar raj disom parọmkate uni buḍhi ṭhenkin tioḱkeťa. Adọ jọtọ duk kathae lạikeťte ạḍiye rạskạyena. Adọ boge juḍạ kupuli baṛakate adọko jọm ńũkeťa. Jọm baṛakate adọkin metadea, Iạ gọ, ọntẹregebon taȟẹna. Adọ jọtọ sipạhiko ruạṛ hẹćena. Ar ọṇḍẹge raj oṛaḱre tahẹn tahẹnte ạḍi utạr acel pacelge hoeyentakoa, ar ạḍiko kisạ̃ṛena. Adọ ẹnẹko tahẽyena.

---

17 What is here translated dragon, kal, is used about specially dangerous snakes, such as those kept by snake charmers.

18 Certain rajas get a sindur (red-lead) mark on their forehead as a kind of affirmation or 'coronation'. It is not a present day Santal custom.

19 What is here translated 'coil-sword', piṭi khaṇḍa, is not at present found among the Santals. I have heard told that they used such during the Santal rebellion in 1855, but have never succeeded in getting a reliable description of it. One old man described it as a kind of arrow 'mitrailleuse', another as a kind of boomerang; piṭi means 'coil' and is e. g. used about snakes coiling themselves up.

20 The queen is meant.

a dragon[17] in her body. When he gets out, it is a tremendously big animal. When he opens his mouth, he gapes from the earth to the sky. He comes out through her nose. Therefore perhaps about one thousand kings have died. We tell you these things."

The young man then said, trusting in his horse and in himself and his own courage: "All right, if I can stay, I shall see about this."

After they had talked together as told, the marriage was celebrated; they also put the mark of kingship[18] on his forehead. Turta now got hold of a pair of tongs and a coil-sword[19]. When he had provided himself with all this, he kept it with himself. The lame horse he also kept near himself.

That very night, the black dragon came out from the nose of that person[20]. He opened his mouth so that it reached from the earth to the sky, and he commenced to chase the king. Then the king mounted his horse, removing the splinter, and the dragon saw him about to fly up to the sky, and he was chasing him, when the king cut him through two three times up there in the air, and the dragon fell down. Thereafter he brought his horse down. After this was done, he kept the queen.

After some time the king said: "My old mother is living. I am going to her, I want to see how she is." Both of them then made themselves ready for the journey, and they both mounted the horse, and he flew up into the air.

Having passed the countries of two kings they arrived at his mother's. When he had told of all his vicissitudes, she became very glad, and after having asked each other how all was with them, they ate and drank. After this was done, they said to her: "I say, mother, we shall live there in that country." All the soldiers then returned, and they remained there in the king's palace, and in the course of time they got an immense amount of wealth and property, and they became very rich. And so they lived there.

10. Miťṭaṅ tạnti kọṛa reaṅ.

Sedae jǫkhęn, kathae, Jogesor ńutuman miťṭaṅ tạnti kọṛae tahękana. Uni dǫ ṭuạrgeye tahękana, ać eskargeae. Adǫe hara juạnen khan dǫ, setoṅ din jǫkhęn miťṭaṅ gaḍa beḍare tạrbuj ar khiṛuạkoe rǫhǫeana. Adǫ kathae, ạḍi bạṛić jǫyentaea. Adǫ beleḱ ęhǫṕen khan dǫe ạkriṅa, ar inạtege anaje kiriń ạgujoṅa.

Adǫ ona takrege, kathae, miťṭaṅ toyo dǫ ona khiṛuạ jǫme pạrkạuena, adǫ dingeye jǫmtaea. Adǫe męna, Cele bhala noa dǫko jǫmeťtińa. Adǫe oyoṅ baṛakeť dǫ, toyo pańjae ńęl ńamkeť. Adǫe męnkeťa, Ho, nui toyo dǫń pạsiyea. Adǫ kathae, pạsiye benaokeťte onae oḍaokeťa. Adǫ kathae, miť din dǫe pạsi gǫťena. Adǫ pạsi akane ńęlkede khan, mutạkanteye ńir calao gǫťena. Adǫ daleye męneť tahękan jǫkhęnge uni toyo dǫe męn gǫťkeťa, Hã hã! alom daleńa, raebaramaṅ.

Adǫ uniye męnkeťa, Sạrigem raebaraṅa?

Adǫe metadea, Hę̃, sạrigeń raebarama.

Khange sạri adǫ bae dalledea, pạsi khone chaḍaokadea. Adǫ uni toyoe metadea, Adǫ hǫrreń jǫm lagať miťṭaṅ khiṛuạ emaṅme. Nitge nãhãḱ iń calao gǫdoḱa, Adǫ sạri inại emade khan, unrege uni dǫe calao gǫťena.

Adǫ kathae, calaoe calaoena dǫ, ạḍi sạṅgiń disome calaoena. Adǫ miťṭaṅ raj naṅgrahae ńamkeťa. Adǫ rajaḱ pęa ponea pukhri menaḱtaea. Ar ona pukhri piṇḍhạre dǫ emanteaḱ dareko rǫhǫe akaťa; maťko hõko rǫhǫe akaťa. Adǫ ona mať dạndhi talarege,

---

1 This story shows several traces of being of foreign origin.

2 Tanti is the name of a Hindu weaver caste.

3 The sweet melon is Cucumis Melo, L. The water-melon is very commonly cultivated in the Santal country. For hot-weather cultivation water is essential; consequently it must be near to where water is obtainable, as on river banks.

4 The Santali word means a snare. The Santals have various devices for catching or killing animals, also large ones.

5 It might be noted, that all regular marriages among the Santals are family arrangements. The two most concerned do not meet or fall in love with each other and so get married. Such may sometimes happen among the Santals, but is irregular.

10. THE STORY OF A TANTI BOY[1].

ONCE upon a time in the old days, people tell, there lived a tanti[2] boy called Jogesor. He was an orphan, quite alone by himself. When he had grown up, it so happened that he once, during the hot season, planted sweet melons and water-melons[3] on the bank of the river, and he got an immense amount of fruit. As they commenced to ripen, he sold, and for the money he bought food for himself.

At that time, people tell, a jackal had got into the habit of eating his water-melons; he did so daily. "I wonder who it is," the boy said, "who is eating my fruits." When he looked well below the leaves, he saw the footprints of a jackal and said: "Oh, this jackal I shall snare." So he made a snare and set it. One day the jackal was caught in the snare[4], and when the boy saw this, he quickly ran there with a thick stick. But just as he was going to strike him, the jackal called out to him: "Hold, hold! don't strike me. I shall arrange for you to get married[5]."

"Really," the boy said, "will you really get me a wife?"

"Yes, in very truth," the jackal replied, "I shall arrange for you to be married."

Consequently he did not beat him, but released him from the snare, whereupon the jackal said to him: "Now give me a water-melon that I may have something to eat on the way. I shall start now at once." And when he had given him this, he started.

The jackal went and went, he went until he reached a country very far away, and there he came to the capital. The king had three or four tanks[6], and on the embankments of these tanks they had planted different trees; bamboo they had also planted[7]; and the jackal was sitting in the middle of that clump of bamboos.

---

6 See p. 34, note 5.

7 Bamboo is very commonly planted in the vicinity of tanks, but not close to the water, as the leaves when falling would be liable to fall into the water and pollute it.

kathae, uni toyo do̱e duṛuṕ akana. Ado̱ raj oṛaḱrenko do̱ thạri bạṭi mańjao lạgiťko calaḱ kana, ar rạniko ar ho̱po̱neratko hõ umoḱ lạgiťko calaḱ kana.

Ado̱ un jo̱khe̱n, kathae, uni toyo do̱e ro̱ṛ go̱ťkeťa, Chi! nui do̱ ceť lekan raj kanae? Inạregeko ija, arhõ inạregeko jo̱ma. Chi! nui do̱ ceť lekan raj kanae? Raj do̱ Jogesor rajge sanam khone bogea. Uni do̱ oka thạrireye jo̱ma, ona do̱ e̱kkalteye giḍikaḱa. Sona thạrireye jo̱ma, ona do̱ e̱kkalteye giḍikaḱa. Chi! nui do̱ ceť lekan raj kanae?

Ado̱, kathae, noa kathage ghạṛi ghạṛiye ro̱ṛeťa. Ado̱ thạri bạṭi maḱńjaoko do̱ko me̱nkeťa, O̱ko̱e bań okareye ro̱ṛeť kan? Ado̱ko be̱ṅge̱ť ạcurkeť khan do̱ mať dạndhi talare toyoe ro̱ro̱ṛ kanko ńe̱l ńamkede. Ado̱ko me̱nkeťa, Ayo, nui toyo do̱ bejãe he̱no̱stae ro̱ṛeť do̱! Bhala sạri se̱ naseye ro̱ṛeťa. Noa katha do̱ rajbo lạiaea.

Ado̱ sạri se̱nkate rajko lạiadea, bańma, Okaren toyo co̱ń ona pukhri piṇḍhạ mať dạndhi ṭhene duṛuṕ akana, ar nonkae ro̱ṛeťa, Chi! nui do̱ ceť lekan raj kanae? Inạregeye jo̱ma, inạregeye ija. Raj do̱ Jogesor raj. Sona thạrireye jo̱ma, ar ona do̱ dingeye giḍi horaea. Nonkae ro̱ṛeťa.

Ado̱ uni raje me̱nkeťa, Acha, do ho̱ho̱ ạguyepe.

Ado̱ kathae, ho̱ṛ kolkeťkote uni toyo do̱ raj ṭhenko ho̱ho̱ ạgukedea. Ado̱ rạje me̱nkeťa, Henda ya, toyo, am do̱m oka disomren kana?

Ado̱ uniye me̱nkeťa, Iń do̱ń ạdi sạṅgińren kana.

Ado̱ ceť leka pukhri piṇḍhạ ṭhenem ro̱ṛeť tahẽ̱kana, mase̱ ona ro̱ṛlem. Ańjo̱mtamań. Ado̱ kathae, o̱ṇḍe̱ye ro̱ṛleť lekageye ro̱ṛkeťa. Khange raje me̱nkeťa, Sạrige noa katha do̱ khạṭigem ro̱ṛeťa?

Ado̱e me̱nkeťa, Khạṭigeń ro̱ṛeťa.

Ado̱ raje me̱nkeťa, Am do̱ ceť lagať un sạṅgiń khon no̱te̱ do̱m he̱ć akana?

8 It is very common, that the metal utensils are taken down to a tank or similar place to be cleaned there.

9 The Santals are very particular in the matter here hinted at.

Those belonging to the king's house came to this place to scour[8] their brass plates and cups, and the queen and her daughters also came there to bathe.

At such a time the jackal all at once called out: "Fie, what kind of a king is this? Here in this place they pass stool, and here in the same place they take food[9]. Fie! what kind of a king is this? King Jogesor is a king better than all others, The plate he is eating off he throws away at once. When he eats off a gold-plate, he throws that away at once. Fie! what kind of a king is this?"

He kept saying these words again and again. Those who scoured the plates and cups then said: "Where on earth is he, where is he speaking?" When they looked round, they caught sight of the jackal speaking, and said: "Oh mother, this jackal is speaking in an awfully contumelious way. Wonder whether he is speaking the truth or it is false. We shall tell the king of this."

They thereupon went to the king and told him: "A jackal from somewhere is sitting on the tank embankment near the clump of bamboos and is speaking like this: Fie, what kind of a king is this? They take food in this place, and in the same place they pass stool. King Jogesor is a king. He eats off a gold-plate, and he throws that away every day. So the jackal is speaking."

"Very well," the king said, "send for him, bring him here."

So they sent for the jackal and called him to the king's presence, and the king spoke: "Look here, you jackal, from which country do you come?"

"I am from a country very far away," the jackal replied.

"Please speak now in the same way as you were speaking on the tank embankment. I want to hear what you say." The jackal then spoke in the same way as he had spoken there, whereupon the king said: "Are you really quite sure about this?"

"I am speaking the truth," he replied.

"For what purpose have you come here from such a distance?" the king asked.

Adọ toyoe mẹnkeťa, Uni raj lagaťge iń dọ bạhu ńame kol akadińa.

Adọ raje mẹnkeťa, Adọm ńamkeťkoa sẹ bań?

Adọ toyoe mẹnkeťa, Ạurih ńamkoa.

Adọ rajren hõ pẹ pon gọṭẹn hopọnerako tahẽkantaea. Adọe mẹnkeťa, Bam ńam akaťko khan, ińren hopọnera menaǩkoa. Adọm khusiako khan, ma ńẹl ṭhikkom.

Adọe mẹnkeťa, Mase ẹnte, nọtẹ họhọ oḍokkom.

Adọ sạriko họhọ oḍokkeťko khan dọ talaić kuṛiye bachaokedea. Adọe uduǩkedea, bańma, Nuiṭaǩ kuṛih khusi akana. Adọ, kathae, raebar họṛ iạte ạḍiko peṛakedea. Adọ jọm baṛakateye mẹnkeťa, Acha, ma duṛup̌jońpe. Iń dọ noa katha unih lại oṭoaea.

Adọe calaoente uni tạnti koṛae lạiadea, bańma, Ma sapṛaoǩme. Bạhu dọń ńawaťmea. Adọ ma sapṛaoǩme.

Khange uni dọ ceť menaǩteye sapṛaoǩa? Ạuṛigeye mẹnkeťa, Iń dọń sapṛaogea. Ma ọntẹn peṛa lạiakome, jẹmọn ẹkkalte bapla reaǩbon lọgọn gọda.

Adọ, kathae, ona kathae idi ruạṛkeťa, are metaťkoa, Ma bapla reaǩbon lọgọn gọda.

Khange sạri ọntẹn peṛa hõko mẹnkeťa, Acha besge. Nẹle girạwam kana, ma idime.

Adọe mẹnkeťa, Acha, dẹn emańpe.

Khange sạri giṛạko emadea, adọe idikeťa. Arhõ pẹ pon mãhã khangeye sẹn ruạṛ gọťena. Adọ raje metae kana, Henda raj, bạriạtko dọ tinạǩ ganle hijuǩa, miť isi, sẹ bar isi, sẹ mõṛẽ isi, sẹ tinạǩle hijuǩa? Ona kuǩli iń dọko kol akadińa.

Khange raj dọe mẹnkeťa, Apeaǩ khusi tinạǩ cọpe hijuǩ.

10 See p. 10, note 3.

11 In regular marriages a party will always follow the bridegroom to the house of the bride's parents where the actual ceremonies are performed. When the bride, after the marriage, is taken to her future home she is accompanied by a similar number of her own relatives. All the followers are feasted. When a large party is coming along with the bridegroom, it is understood that the number shows his importance and wealth, and it is also taken as given that the bridegroom is prepared to feast as many of the other side as he is bringing with him.

"The king," the jackal replied, "has sent me to find a wife for himself."

"Have you found any or not?" the king asked.

"Not as yet," the jackal replied.

Now the king had three or four daughters, so he said: "If you have not found any, I have daughters of my own. If you like them, see whom you think suitable."

"Please then," the jackal said, "call them out here."

When they had called them out, he selected the middle one. He pointed to her and said: "I am pleased with this girl." Thereupon they entertained him in grand style on account of his being marriage-broker. When they had feasted, he said: "Very well, you remain, please. I am going to tell him of this."

The jackal then went and told the tanti boy: "Please, make yourself ready. I have found a wife for you. So please make yourself ready."

Now what did he have that he should make himself ready? So he said heedlessly: "I am ready. Please, tell the friends on that side that they at once fix a day for the marriage."

The jackal then took word back to them, saying: "Please, let us fix a day for the marriage now."

The friends on that side then also said: "All right, that is good. See, here we are giving you the marriage-knots[10]; take them along."

"Very well, please give me," the jackal replied.

Then they gave him the marriage-knots and he took them away. After some three or four days he came back again, and said to the king: "Pray, king, about how many shall we come with the bridegroom[11]? one score, or two scores, or five scores, or how many are we to come? They have sent me to inquire about this."

"As many as you please," the king replied, "any number may come."

They are rather particular that the feasting expences should be the same on both sides.

Adọ toyoe mẹnkeťa, Pasẹ ẹnte ạḍi utạrle hẹćlen khan pasẹ bam daram daṛeale, onateń kuli bujhạu idiyeťmea.

Adọe metadea, Acha, unrege nãhãǩ iń tọjbijpea, tinạǩ iń daram daṛeapea mẹnte.

Adọ enka mẹnkatege uni toyo dọe sẹn ruạṛena. Adọ neṇḍa din tioǩen khan, toyo dọ uni koṛae metadea, Ma ḍọmko, kahaṛko, pạlkiko ńamme, bạriạtoǩbon calaǩa.

Khange uni koṛa dọ peṛa hõ bạnuǩkotaete onako họ̃ bae juṛạu daṛeaǩ kana. Khange uni toyoge onako họ̃e ńam juhṛạukeťa. Ar bạriạtko dọ inạ dhara dhạririen toyo ar kõǩe nẽotakeťkoa. Metaťkoae, Ape dọ ma disạkape niạ din hiloǩ dọ hạni phalna disomren raj ṭhen bhọj jọmbon calaǩa.

Khange sạri onko hõ ạḍiko rạskạ gọťena. Adọ inạ din hiloǩ dọ jọtọgeko hạjirena. Ar uni toyoge pạlkiko, kahaṛko jọtọe ńamkeťkote bạriạtoǩko calaǩ kana. Adọ uni raebar toyoe mẹnkeťa, Ape jọtọ kõǩ dọ toyo deare dẹćkate calaǩtabonpe. Nonkakatebo sẹnlen khan, raj dọ nãhãǩ khube manọtbona. Adọ sạri ọnẹye metaťko lekage jọtọ họṛko calaǩ kana.

Adọko tioǩ ńõǩkeť khan, uni toyo dọe ńir lahayena raj lạiae lạgiť. Adọ sẹṭẹrenteye metae kana, Henda raj, tinạǩ ganle hijuǩa? Ma oḍokoǩte bạriạtko dọ ńẹlkom. Unạǩ bam cahao khan dọń ruạṛkoa. Ar hẹć sẹṭẹrlen khanko, ar unre ruạṛko dọ lajao paṛagea. Ma oḍokoǩte ńẹl hoťkom; ẹkẹn aswariạgeko hijuǩ kana.

Adọ sạri raj dọ oḍokenteye kọyọǩkeťko dọ, baṅgeye ńẹl mucạť daṛeaťko. Miť kọs khon hõ bhạṛti sạṅgiń hạbić menaǩko, ar toyo

[12] Ḍọm, a low Hindu caste; one of their occupations is to furnish the music, i. e especially the drumming at marriages. Whenever a marriage party passes a village, they make a tremendous din, beating their drums. During the ceremonies and at the feasting, they also keep the drumming going, often incessantly.

[13] See p. 42, note 4.

[14] See p. 32, note 1.

[15] The Paddy-bird (in Santali kõǩ, a name formed in imitation of the sound of. the call of this bird) is very common. It is a kind of heron, the kind here men-

"You see," the jackal said, "perhaps if we came in a very large number, perhaps you will not be able to receive us; therefore I am asking you to take word to those others."

"Very well," the king replied, "when you come, then I shall estimate you and see how many of you I can receive."

After this talk the jackal returned. When the day fixed came, the jackal said to the boy: "Please get hold of Ḍoms[12], Kahars[13] and palanquins[14]; we shall start for the marriage."

The young man had no friends, so he was unable to provide any. The jackal then procured these also, and to come along in the marriage party he invited the jackals and the paddy-birds[15] of the neighbourhood. He said to them: "Remember, please, that on such and such a day we are to go to the king of that country to partake of a feast."

Then these also became very glad, and on the fixed day they all presented themselves. The jackal provided palanquins and carriers, in fact everything, and they started for the marriage. The marriage-broker jackal then said: "You paddy-birds, all of you mount the backs of the jackals and proceed. If we proceed in this way, the king will presently do much honour to us." Then they really did as the jackal told them, and they all went along.

When they had nearly reached the place, the jackal ran ahead to inform the king. When he arrived, he said to him: "Pray, king, about how many are we to come? Please come out and have a look at the marriage party. If you don't wish for so many, I shall send some back. To send them back after they have come, would be a great shame. Please come out and have a look at them quickly; only mounted people are coming."

The king came out and had a look at them, he was absolutely unable to see the end of them. They filled the place up to more

---

tioned (there are several species) being entirely white, except for its legs and beak. They very frequently follow the cattle, catching grasshoppers and the like that fly up when disturbed by the movements of the cattle. As a rule they are seen in great flocks.

cetanre kǫ̃k̕ko ap̕ akante pondgeko ńęlok̕ kana. Khange raj dǫ ńęltegeye hahaṛayenteye metadea, Do ruạṛ ạdhikakome. Unạk̕ hoṛ dǫ ǫhǫń daram daṛelepea, ar unạk̕ dǫ kulạn hǫ̃ bạnuk̕tińa.

Khange uni toyo dǫ atra hǫrreye ńir daramket̕koteye metat̕koa, Męn, męnge ruạṛpe. Raje męnket̕a, Unạk̕ hoṛ dǫ ǫhǫń daram daṛelepea, mage ruạṛkakome. Onate ape dǫń ruạṛet̕pea. Adǫ kathae, ęndę khonge kǫ̃k̕ aswariạko dǫko ruạṛena; adǫ enko Kahaṛ, Dǫm, enkogeko hęć sętęrena. Adǫ raje męnket̕a, Bạriạtko dǫ jǫtǫgem ruạṛkat̕koa? Thoṛa thuṛi dǫ bam ạgu darakoa?

Adǫ toyoe męnket̕a, Onko dǫko męnket̕a, Calao khan dǫ jǫtǫgele calak̕a, ar bańkhan jǫtǫgele ruạṛa. Adǫm hoṛ dǫle calak̕a ar adǫm hoṛ dǫle ruạṛa, noa dǫ cet̕ leka? Onko ruạṛ hoṛ reak̕ mǫn dǫ nāhāk̕ thǫręn khaṭǫk̕takoa. Adǫ onkako męnket̕te jǫtǫgeko ruạṛena. Ale nę̃kę̃ ninạk̕ hoṛgele hęćena.

Adǫ inạk̕ hoṛgeko daramket̕kote bapla hoeyentakoa. Adǫ ńindạ dǫko bhǫjket̕a. Adǫ khub bhage sebel sebelak̕ko utuket̕a. Adǫ ạuri bhǫj jǫmrege uni tạnti koṛa dǫe sikhạukae kana. Metae kanae, Ę ya, daka jǫm nāhāk̕ko idimea. Unre nāhāk̕ barea pęa utuko ęmok̕a, męnkhan jǫtǫ baṛę jǫmme, hinạ mit̕ dhao, nhiạ mit̕ dhao. Onka mit̕ dhaotege jǫtǫ jǫmme, ar bańkhan am dǫ oṛak̕re mit̕ṭań utu jǫm hewate mit̕ṭańgem jǫmkea, — se dǫ bań, męnkhan mit̕ dhạote jǫtǫgem jǫma. Ar daka jǫm baṛa tayǫm nāhāk̕ pan khiliko emama. Adǫ alom atańa. Tinre ṭakako cuput̕ama, unre ona pan khili dǫm atańa. Ma noako katha disạkam ar onka kạmime, tǫbę ęna raj hǫpǫn dǫko metama.

Adǫ kathae, tisre hǫ̃ onka sebel utu bań jǫm hewa adǫ sebel utui ńamket̕ khan, khub jǫm bae jǫmket̕a? Khange thǫe puṭiyente

---

16 The distance mentioned, one kǫs, is generally equal to two English miles, in other parts it may be less or more.

17 There may be a formal reception, but necessarily not so elaborate as the farewell-bidding.

18 See p. 76, note 24.

19 The Santals buy their wives; it is, of course, no regular sale but something to symbolize that the husband is the lord and proprietor henceforth. Here the husband apparently is to receive money; this is the custom among certain classes of Hindus.

than two miles[16] away, and as the paddy-birds were mounted on the jackals, all were looking white. The king was astonished at the sight and said to the jackal: "Please, send half of them back. I am unable to receive so many of you, and I have not sufficient provisions for so many either."

The jackal then ran to meet them half-way and called out to them: "Stop, stop! turn back! The king has said: 'I am unable to receive so many people; do please, turn them back.' Therefore I am turning you back." The mounted paddy-birds then went back from that place, and the Ḍoms and the Kahars alone came. The king then said: "Did you turn the whole marriage party back? Will you not bring a few along with you?"

The jackal replied: "They said: If we go, we shall go all of us, otherwise we shall all of us return. That some of us should go and others turn back, how would that be? Those who returned would become very downhearted and hurt. Having said this, they all of them returned. We have come as many as you see here."

They then formally received[17] these; the marriage was celebrated, and at night they had a feast. They had prepared some excellent and most savoury curry. Before they sat down to eat, the jackal gave the tanti boy some advice and said to him: "Look here, my lad, they will presently come and take you off to eat. They will certainly give you two three kinds of curry; eat all, now this kind, then that kind alternatively. In this way eat of all at the time; otherwise, as you are accustomed to eat only one course of curry at home, you might eat only one; that is not the way; but you must eat of all at the time. After you have eaten, they will offer you a quid of *pan*[18]. Don't take any. When they put the money into your hand[19], then only you shall take the quid of pan. Please keep these things in your mind and act accordingly; then only they will call you a prince."

Now he had never in his life been accustomed to eat such savoury curry, so when he got this splendid food, didn't he eat?

ńindạ dọe cịdirkeťa; kicrićko saname thọkọ bọkọkeťa. Khange toyo dọ cekate cọe disạkede, cịdirkeťae mẹnte. Adọe mẹnkeťa, Durrẹ! nui dọe lajaokidińa. Ar sẹ jọtọ họṛko jạpiť akaťa. Khange toyo dọ ona narak dọ onko gitić họṛgeye jọť idiaťkoa ḍẹkẹ ḍẹkẹre. Ar uni koṛa dọe um ocokedea are jal saphakeťtaea. Arhọ̃kin gitićena.

Adọ sim raḱ khange, kathae, uni toyo dọ lahategeye bereť họťenteye mẹneťa, Okare bań moela moelage sọ kan? Adọe bas baṛakeť khan dọ onko rajren peṛa geye metako kana, Ape sẹnge sọ kana.

Adọ sạri setaḱ khangeko ńẹlkeť dọ, onkoaḱ ḍẹkẹ ṭhenaḱ kicrićre dọ laṭkao akan. Khange toyo dọ ruḱhẹťe pọrtọnkeťa: Iạko eńgate tisre utu dakako ńẹl akawana? Salasreko ńawan khanko jọm cịdirena! Adọ ẹnẹ boge baṛayena.

Ạyuṕ khange bidạ hoeyente uni tạnti oṛaḱteko calaḱ kana. Adọ calaḱ calaḱte onko lumti baretko dọko lańgayena. Adọ uni toyoko metae kana, Okor tin sạńgińre? Raj oṛaḱ dọbon tioḱeťa?

Adọe metakoa, Hapẹ, ạuribon tioga. Arhọ̃ thoṛa sạńgińko calaoen khan, arhọ̃ko kuliyede kana, Okor tinrebo tioḱeť kana?

Adọ tale bagwane ńẹl ńamkeť khan dọe uduḱako kana, Hanẹ ńẹlpe tale bagwaṇ. Ona dọ nui rajaḱ bagwan kangea. Ona bagwan talarege rajaḱ oṛaḱ dọ menaḱa. Dolanko dọ mareyente hẹndẹgea, onate sạńgiń khon dọ bań ńẹl ṭhikoḱa.

Adọ kathae, calaḱ calaḱte ona tale bagwan họ̃ko tioḱketa, adọ oṛaḱge bako ńẹl ńameť kan. Adọko metae kana, Okor oka ṭhen raj oṛaḱ dọ?

---

20 What is here described, is a fairly common sequence to feasting among the Santals, their daily diet being so plain and poor that any deviation is liable to have disastrous results.

21 See above note 17.

22 See above note 11. When the bride leaves for her husband's home, she is accompanied by a party, among these some old woman, who is to give her some final and formal advice.

Consequently he got indigestion and commenced to purge[20] during the night and dirtied all his clothes. Somehow or other the jackal became aware of his purging and said: "Oh my! this fellow has brought shame on me." Now all people were asleep. The jackal then went and daubed the people lying there with the filth in their hind-quarters. Thereupon he made the boy bathe, and he licked him and cleaned him, and both of them lay down to sleep again.

At cock-crow the jackal got up first and called out: "Where is it smelling so badly?" When he had sniffed round, he said to the guests of the king: "It is your way it's smelling."

Then really, when it became morning, they saw that something stuck to their clothes behind. And the jackal started scolding: "Those unspeakable ones, dash it, have they ever seen curry and rice? When they got it for the first time, they ate so they got diarrhoea." So nothing more was done in this matter.

In the evening, after they had been ceremonially bidden farewell to[21], they started for the tanti boy's house. Walking and walking along, the followers and relatives of the bride[22] became tired and said to the jackal: "Where is it, how far away? Are we reaching the king's palace?"

"Wait a bit," he says, "we are still a little way off." When they had come a little further, they asked him again: "Where is it, when are we reaching there?"

When they caught sight of a palm-tree[23] grove, he pointed it out to them and said: "Look over there, there is a palm-tree grove. That is a grove belonging to this king. The king's palace is in the middle of that grove. The mansions have become dark from age; therefore it is not possible to see them distinctly from afar."

Walking on, they finally reached the palm-tree grove, but did not see any houses anywhere. So they said to the jackal: "Where? why, where is the king's palace?"

---

[23] The most common palm tree in the Santal country is the Palmyra palm, Borassus flabelliformis, L.; it has very large fan-shaped leaves. It is very common on tank embankments.

Ado̱ ona bagwan bhitrirege uni tạnti koṛa do̱ tale ḍhoakoteye oṛak' akat' tahẽ̱kana. Ona oṛak'geye uduk' dapoṛat'koa, Ado̱ ona kumbạ oṛak'ko ńe̱lket' khaṅ do̱, ạḍiko khae khabṛok'ena. Arko me̱pe̱nena, Durre̱! nui toyo do̱ ạḍi bạṛiće e̱ṛe̱ket'bon do̱. Po̱rkartegeye bapla ocoket'bona. Pạhilrebo baḍaele khan hute̱n, o̱ho̱bo re̱be̱n atarlena. Nit do̱ cet'bo ceka daṛeak'a? Ado̱ toyoko metadea, Cedak' nonka do̱m e̱ṛe̱ket'lea? Me̱nket'am, Sona thạrire dakae jo̱ma ar ona sạkṛi thạri do̱e giḍi horaea.

Ado̱ toyoe me̱nket'a, Onka ma ba co̱ń me̱n akat'. Iń do̱ń me̱nlet'a, sakam patṛareye jo̱ma ar ona do̱ dingeye giḍi horaea. Iń do̱ nonkań lại akat'a. Ado̱pe khusiyen khan cet' iń me̱na? Ado̱ e̱ne̱ń baplakat'pea.

Khangeko me̱nket'a, Ma ya, sabete humạge ma! Ado̱ onkako me̱nlet' khange uni toyo do̱e dạṛket'a. Ado̱ lumti baretko hõ e̱n hilok'geko ruạṛena. Uni kuṛi do̱ o̱ṇḍe̱geko bạgi oṭoadea. Ar ruạṛ se̱nkate noako jo̱to̱ katha raj ar rạniko lạiat'kina. Khange unkin hõ ạḍikin bhabnayena, ado̱kin me̱nket'a, Nit do̱ cet'bo cekaea? Chaḍa chạḍikin hõ tho̱ abore do̱ co̱lo̱n bạnuk'an. Mabon ạgu mit'kinte no̱ṇḍe̱gebon do̱ho̱kina.

Ado̱ Kahaṛko pạlkikoko ńamket'kote ar bar pe̱ ho̱ṛko kolket'kote ako ṭhenko ạgu ruạṛkot'kina. Ar ạsulok' lagat' tara nakha disomko emat'kinạ.

Ado̱ o̱ne̱ onkate uni koṛa do̱e bạhuadea. Ado̱ ona khiṛuạko hõ okayen co̱ṅ ṭhikạn bạnuk'an.

Ado̱ e̱ne̱ cabayena katha do̱, in maraṅgea.

24 A distinctly Hindu trait. Divorce is very common among the Santals. Strangely enough, it is valid for this world, but in the next the man who has married a spinster will get this one there to be his partner whether he has divorced her or not.

In the middle of that palm-tree grove the tanti boy had erected a hut of palm-leaves. He showed them that wretch of a house. When they saw that booth, they became very downhearted, and said to each other: "Oh dear, this jackal has deceived us something terrible. He has tricked us into this marriage. If we had known about this beforehand, we should never have agreed to it, no never. But what can we do now?" They then said to the jackal: "Why did you deceive us in this way? You said: He eats rice of a gold plate, and he throws the used plate away every time it is used."

"No," the jackal replied, "I did not say so. I said, that he eats off a leaf plate, and he throws that away every time he has used it. That is what I have said. When you were pleased, what was I to say? So I had you married, you see."

Then they cried: "Do, do catch him and give him a hiding!" As soon as they said this, the jackal ran away, and the followers and relatives of the bride also returned home that same day; they left the girl there. When they reached home, they told the king and the queen all this. Then these also became very grieved and said: "What shall we do now? With us it is not the custom to dissolve a marriage[24] either. Let us bring them here to us, and then we shall keep them both here."

So they fetched carriers and palanquins and sent these with a couple of men and brought the two back to themselves, and to support themselves they gave them a strip of the country.

In this way the jackal procured a wife for the boy. What became of the water-melons there is no report of.

There the story is ended; it is thus much.

11. Mitťaṅ ṭuạr gidrạ reaṅ.

Sedae jugre kathae, mitťaṅ hoṛe tahẽkana; uni hoṛ do̠ miť ge̠le̠kin gidrạwan khangeye begarena, ar uni do̠ kuṛi gidrại tahẽkantakina. Ado̠ besge din nirbhạ do̠ calaḱ kan tahẽkantakina. Ado̠ uni kuṛi gidrạ hõe ńir ke̠ṭe̠ćena.

Ado̠ miť din ạyuṕ jo̠khe̠nkin galmarao kana; ado̠ emanteaḱ ceťko co̠ṅ galmarao galmaraote uni oṛaḱ ho̠ṛte̠ť do̠e me̠nkeťa, Arhõ ho̠ṛmo̠teaḱ do̠ basawadińa.

Ado̠ uni herel hoṛe me̠nkeťa, Cekatem baḍae kana?

Ado̠ uniye me̠nkeťa, E̠nte nõḱõe bar cando din bạń ńe̠l akaťa.

Ado̠ inạkin galmaraokeť tayo̠m jạnić miť hapta gan hoe akan, khange uni herel hoṛ do̠ aco̠kge bih ge̠rteye go̠ćena. Ado̠ khange uni maejiu do̠ ạḍi bạṛiće bhabnayena, siń sạṭuṕgeye raga uni

[1] This story is a vivid picture of life as it may be met with among the Santals, when certain features of pure folktale nature are eliminated. It touches on many sides of Santal customs or rather communal rules and practices.

[2] It is looked upon as good for the members of a family to live together as long as possible; it lends strength to the family. It is, however, fairly common among the people that the property is divided between the male members, when all or some of them have grown up and have married, even before the father's death. They love independence, and it naturally often happens that the strange element brought in through marriage makes it desirable to separate. The division is made in the following way: all land is divided into equal parts, one for the father, if he is living, and one for each son. The cattle is divided in the same way, the only difference being that daughters get a calf each, as it is called, at the time; it is generally a cow. Married daughters do not get anything, as they have already got one at the time of their marriage. Other property is also equally divided between the male members of the family. It is all done with the assistance of the village headman and people, especially as regards the cultivated land. This must be so to give the whole a legal stamp; the village community must be a party to all such transactions. When the division is completed, the parents will generally live with one of the sons, frequently the youngest one, the mother's pet. On the death of the father, his share is again divided between all the sons, although the widow is often permitted to cultivate this land until her death.

11. The Story of an Orphan Boy[1].

ONCE upon a time in the old days, people tell, there was a man; they had got one child, when the property was divided[2], and he set up a separate household. Their child was a girl[3]. Life was going well with them, and the girl also grew to be strong on her legs[4].

One evening they were talking together; they were talking about this, that and the other, and in the course of their conversation the wife said: "It has again temporarily taken up its abode in my body[5]".

"How do you know?" her husband asked.

"Well," she replied, "because I have not seen[6] anything for two months."

About one week after they had had this conversation it so happened, that the husband suddenly died from a snake-bite. The woman felt terrible grief; she wailed[7] all day in affectionate

---

3 Girls are debarred from inheriting land. They are supposed to get married and go to their husbands' homes. In case of a family with daughters only, the Santals have found a way of circumventing the otherwise rigid rules of inheritance. It is also due to them to say that they are trying to better the position of their womenkind. If the first child had been a boy, there would have been no possibility for a story like the present. In that case, he would have been the natural heir. For further information with regard to the position of the Santal woman the reader is referred to the writer's paper in the Journal of the Bihar & Orissa Research Society, 1916, Some Remarks on the Position of Women among the Santals.

4 The Santal expression is used about children some two years old, lit. strong enough to run about.

5 One of several ways of expressing that a woman is with child. The Santali word means to lodge, stay for a time.

6 'See' is the common way of referring to the menses.

7 Women give expression to their grief through wailing and lamentation, some words, more or less stereotype, being sung or chanted to a certain tune. It may be heartrending to hear a woman wailing, generally standing somewhere away from the house, turned towards the fields or the forest.

uihạrte; oka dọ daka hõ bhabnate bae jọma; dine rateye guni bhạbiḱa ar Candogeye ńumea. Mẹnae, Ọ hae! Cando boṅga, ceť baliń ghạṭikeťte ạliń dọm jọṛ bhaṅgakeťliń? Ọ hae Cando, bạrsiń gan lagať ạliń dọm juri pạrileťliń dọ! Ọ hae Cando, iṅgem andaḱ ocokidiń dọ! Ọ hae, Cando boṅga, chatar umul reaḱ rup dọ cekate bạń ńẹl ńamtae?

Nonka uni ạimại dọ ńum ńumteye họmọr halaṅa. Are mẹna, Ẹ Cando boṅga, herelińem idikedetińa; herel bọdọl koṛa gidrạ baṛẹ emańme. Oka ińaḱ kukhire basa akan, koṛa gidrạ baṛẹ hoe ocoetińme; inạ dọ ini gidrạ ńẹlte jiviń tẹntińa. Adọ nonka dinge uni maejiu dọ koṛa gidrạ lạgiť Cando ṭhene arọjoḱa.

Adọ kathae, turui eae cando hoeyen khan, uni maejiu dọ hoṛmọte menaḱtae, ona dọ ńẹlentaea. Ar onko ẹrvẹltẹťteko ar bahọńhartẹťtekoko mẹnkeťa, Nui phalna eṅgat dọ ya, ọkọe tuluć cọń menae. Ńẹlpe, uni phalna apat tahẽkan jọkhẹn dọ besgeye tahẽkana. Adọ uni mae gọćen; adọ okọe nui dọe laćkedea? Dhorage nui dọ ọkọe tuluć cọń menae; onatege herel dọ aćtegeye jọmkedea; nui kangeae jọma dọ. Eṅgate ma noako cij bạsut dọ sanambon rẹjea, ar uni kuṛi gidrạ hõ abo ṭhenbon ạguyea.

Adọ kathae, onka mẹnkate bogeteko ruhẹťkedea, ar jọtọ cij bạsutko rẹćkedea. Ar uni maejiu dọe lại gujuḱ kana, mẹneťae,

---

[8] See p. 68, note 11. The lamentations do not, as a rule, make any appeal, but only state the loss and personal feelings. The appeal here made to Chando is not, however, impossible. The idea af a Supreme Being is always present with the Santals, and there are several examples of Santals making direct invocations to Him. In their most solemn oaths Chando or Ṭhạkur or Siń boṅga, all names for the same, is referred to. Santal women are not permitted to participate directly in religious service; but I do not think that this would affect any proceeding like the one here described.

[9] These words are very commonly heard in lamentations over a dead husband. The husband is the protecting and shadowing shelter.

[10] See above note 3. A boy is supposed to support his mother; her rights rest with him. Even as a babe he is a kind of protector.

[11] See p. 20, note 3.

remembrance of him. Sometimes she could not even take food for grief; day and night she was filled with anxious thoughts, and she called on Chando[8] saying: "Alas! Chando boṅga, what had we two sinned that thou hast separated us by taking him away? Alas! Chando, only for a couple of days didst thou join us together! Alas! Chando, thou hast thrown me into trouble! Alas! Chando boṅga, the form of my shadowing canopy[9], why shall I not see that any more?"

In this way the woman enumerated her griefs and wailed, and she said: "O Chando boṅga, thou tookst my husband away; instead of my husband do give me a boy[10]! What has taken up its temporary abode in my womb, do make that become a boy for me! Then, by seeing this child, I shall keep my soul in patience." Every day the woman in this way implored Chando to get a boy.

When she was in her sixth or seventh month, it was to be seen that she was with child, and her several brothers-in-law said: "This mother of so-and-so[11] must be living with somebody, who knows who. Remember, when the father of so-and-so was living, she was well[12]. Now he is dead, so who has made her pregnant? Surely this woman is living with somebody, who knows who; therefore she herself has eaten her husband; she is the cause of his death. Dash it, we shall take all the goods and property[13] away from her; the girl[14] we shall also take and keep with us."

Having said this, they abused her badly and took all her goods and property away from her by force. The woman assured them

---

12 A common expression for a woman who is not with child, just as the opposite 'to be spoilt' is used about a girl, especially unmarried, who has been impregnated.

13 See above, note 2. The expression especially covers cultivated land and cattle.

14 When a man dies leaving only minors, it is customary for the brothers of the dead person to take these into their houses, at the same time taking over the property and cultivating the land until the minors grow up, when they are to have the whole back. What is here done, would have been in order if they had provided for the widow, i. e., had taken her into their house also. This they absolve themselves from doing by denying the legitimacy of the posthumous child.

Baṅa, baba, jāhāe dosra hoṛaḱ do baṅ kana; apat tahẽkanre bar cando reaḱ tahẽadiń tahẽkana. Adoko metań kana, baṅma, okoe reaḱ kan coṅ; ar baṅkhan dosra hoṛaḱ do baṅ kana. Adoko rejeń kan khać, ceť iń mena? Noa do Candogeye bicạrtabona.

Ado enre hõ bako bataoleť khan do sạriko reć idikedegea; ado inạ oṛaḱteť do bako otoṛleťa, ado inạ oṛaḱrege uni maejiu doe tahẽyena.

Ado kathae, uniaḱ duk saset harkhet Candoe ńelkeťtaete jemone menleťa, koṛa gidrạ baṛe emańme, ado sạri din tioḱen khan, koṛa gidrạgeye hoeyentaea, ado uni maejiu do ạḍiye rạskạyena. Adoe menkeťa, Cando ińaḱ raḱe ańjomkeťtińa, jemon iń menleťa, temonge Cando ińaḱ sanae purạukeťtińa; Candoe sarhaokoḱ ma! E Cando, nitoḱ do ińaḱ jivigem raṛećkeťtińa; arhõ, Cando boṅga, nui gidrạ hara burukaetińme.

Ado kathae, tahen tahente uni gidrạ doe hara buruyena. Ado uni gidrại mena, Henda ayo, iń baba doe okayena?

Khange uni eṅgatteť doe raḱ goťkeťa, are metadea, Am baba do, beṭa, hoṛmorem tahẽkanrege bińe gerkedeteye gocena.

Ado uni gidrại menkeťa, E ayo, alom raga; iṅge am doń ạsulmea; ạpuń bạnugić khan dom cekaea? Iń ńelte am do jivi tentam.

Khange eṅgatteť. uni gidrạ reaḱ bud ańjomkateye hahaṛayena, are menkeťa, Candoge nui gidrạ doe bud ocoyede kana. Ado uni maejiu do siń sạṭuṗ Cando ṭhengeye dohae akae tahena. Ar jāhāeko ṭhen nalha tumạle calaḱa, khubgeye ńama ar nāṛā hõ sanamko uni do khugbeko nāṛāwaea; ar kokoe hõ jāhā sengeye calaḱ, uni do baṅko baṅea, emaegeako; onkate unkin do bakin reṅgejoḱa.

---

15 The literal meaning of the Santali words is something like 'speaking die', often used about persistent assertion of a statement.

16 It might be noted, that the inanimate construction is used in this passage.

17 *Lit.* 'cooled my soul'.

18 The translation is literal. Chando is considered as acting directly.

in the most solemn way[15], saying: "No, sirs, no never; it does not belong to anybody else; when the father was yet alive, I had been with child for two months. And they say it[16] is somebody else's; but it is not anybody else's. If they take all away from me by force, what can I say? Chando will judge between us in this matter."

As they, in spite of all, did not listen to her, they took all away from her by force. They did not pull down her house, though; they left that, and the woman continued to live in the old house.

Now, people tell, Chando looked to her sorrow and misery and affliction, and, in accordance with what she had asked: 'give me a boy', when the time came, she really got a boy and became very glad. She said, "Chando has heard my cry. In accordance with what I asked, just so Chando has fulfilled my wish. Chando be praised! O Chando, thou hast comforted[17] me! Now again, O Chando, make this child grow up[18] for me."

Days passed, and the child grew up. The child sometimes asked: "Mother, what has become of my father?"

His mother then cried and said: "When I was carrying you in my body, my son, a snake bit your father, so he died."

"Don't cry, mother," the child said; "I shall support you. As my father is no more, what will you do? Remember me[19] and control yourself."

When his mother heard how intelligent her son was, she was astonished and said: "Chando it is who is making this child intelligent." The woman was continually and all day invoking Chando. And when she went to somebody or other to work for wages or to glean, she always got good pay, and all left abundant ears for her to glean. Also if she went anywhere to beg, they did not refuse to give her; they were sure to give. In this way these two did not suffer hunger.

---

19 *Lit.* 'seeing me, keep your soul pressed down'.

Ar uni maraṅić kuṛi gidrạ hō̠ nuiye hoeyen torarege no̠ṇḍe̠ge arhō̠e he̠ć ruạṛena. Ado̠ unkin gidrạge oṛak̕re do̠kin tahe̠na, ar eṅgatte̠t̕ do̠ o̠nte̠ no̠te̠ se̠ tumạl tosaṅe daṛana. Ar ạḍi khạṭir mo̠nte̠ko tahe̠na, cet̕ hō̠ bako bhabna baṛak̕a. Ado̠ simko sukrikoko juṛạu baṛaket̕koa, ado̠ enkoko ạkriṅkate me̠ro̠m bhiḍikoko juṛạuket̕koa; ado̠ onkoko bạḍ biritket̕ko khan, sạṇḍi do̠ gayako do̠ho̠ket̕koa, ar me̠ro̠m sukri hō̠ kuḍu do̠ko bạdhiạ ocoket̕koa, ar me̠ro̠m bhiḍi hō̠ boda do̠ khạsiket̕koteko harayen khanko ạkriṅket̕koa.

Ado̠ ṭakako do̠ho̠ jarwaket̕ khan, eṅgatte̠t̕ do̠e me̠nket̕a, Iạ beṭa, noa ṭakate do̠ gạibon kiriṅjoṅa; pheṭạṛ mĩhũbon kiriṅkoa.

Ado̠ uni koṛa gidrạ hō̠, kathaeye, harayen reak̕ katha kana noa do̠. Ado̠ unre uni koṛae me̠nket̕a, Henda ayo, cet̕ lekan pheṭạṛbon kiriṅkoa?

Ado̠ eṅgatte̠t̕e me̠nket̕a, Iạ beṭa, me̠nako, kathae, o̠ko̠eṭak̕ko ạkriṅe, ado̠ kik̕riṅ ho̠ṛe uduk̕am jo̠khe̠n uni pheṭạṛe ić go̠t̕ket̕a me̠nkhan, ona do̠ ạḍi bhạgana; onkanko do̠, kathae, co̠ṛ damte hō̠ko hataokogea; onkanko do̠, kathae, oṛak̕ duạrko rophaea, ạḍiko bạḍ go̠dok̕a. Ar baṅko ijre hō̠, kathae, onkanko do̠ ḍaṭam ṅe̠let̕taea, o̠ko̠eṭak̕re are go̠ṭe̠n ḍaṭa menak̕tae, to̠be̠ onkanko hō̠ko bogegea; enko hō̠ inạ bhe̠d kangea. Ar onkanko ạurim ṅamko dhạbić do̠ bam kiriṅedea; inạ khon dosra lekanko do̠ bam kiriṅede kana.

Ado̠ uni koṛae me̠nket̕a, Iạ ayo, e̠ṇḍe̠khan gạì kiriṅ do̠ iṅgeṅ calak̕a; onkanko ạuriṅ ṅamko dhạbić do̠ bạṅ ruạṛa; tinreṅ ṅamkoa ado̠ onko kiriṅleko e̠ne̠ć iṅ ruạṛ hijuk̕a.

Ado̠ eṅgatte̠t̕e me̠net̕a, Baṅa, beṭa, noakorege hape̠nbo kiriṅkoa.

Ado̠ uni koṛae me̠nket̕a, Baṅa, ayo, gạì kiriṅ do̠ iṅgeṅ calak̕a.

Ado̠ ạḍiye jidket̕ khane metadea, Acha, ma e̠ṇḍe̠khan kiriṅ ạgukom.

Ado̠ khange atoren ho̠ṛe metako kana, Delabon ho, gạì kiriṅ go̠ṛo̠ạṅtabonpe. Ado̠ cet̕ko co̠ko ạṇḍuṅ baṛaket̕ge, o̠ko̠e hō̠ bako

The eldest child, the girl, also came back, when this boy was born. The two children remained at home, and the mother went here and there to glean. They lived with an easy mind; they had no cares at all. They gradually acquired fowls and pigs; when these had grown to a fair size, they sold them and acquired goats and sheep. When these had multiplied, they made the cocks into capons and kept them, and the boars they castrated, and the he-goats and rams they also castrated, and when they had grown sufficiently, they sold them.

When they had got together some money, their mother said: "I say, my lad, for this money we shall buy a cow. We shall buy a heifer."

Now this was something that was said when the boy had grown up. The boy then said: "Listen, mother, what kind of a heifer shall we buy?"

"O, my lad," his mother replied, "people say that, if at the time when the seller shows the buyer the animal, the heifer lets something drop, that is very fortunate; such ones people buy even at a very high price; such ones keep house and property in order; they also quickly multiply, people tell. If they do not let anything drop, you must look at their teeth, such who have nine teeth, they are also good; these also have the same quality. Until you find one of this kind, you are not to buy any; you are not to buy any of another quality."

The boy then said: "Well mother, then I shall go to buy a cow; until I find such a one, I shall not came back; only when I find such a one and buy her, I shall come home."

"No, my son," his mother replied, "not so; we shall some day buy one here in this neighbourhood."

"No mother," the boy said, "I shall go and buy a cow."

But when he persisted, she said: "All right then, buy and bring one."

The boy then spoke to the village people, saying: "Come along with me somebody, help me to buy a cow." But they pleaded some excuse or other; no one was willing to go, Then he spoke

ṛe̱be̱n kana. Ado̱ kakat goṅgottekoe metako kana, Delabon, baba, gạiu kiriń go̱ṛo̱ạńpe, kiriń ạguạńabon. Ado̱ onko hõ̱ bako ṛe̱be̱n kan.

Ado̱ kathae, mit́ oṛak̕ kamarko tahẽ̱kana, ado̱ onkoe metako kana, Delabon ho, gại kiriń go̱ṛo̱ạńpe. Eṅgate ato ho̱ṛ iń riạu baṛayet́koa, o̱ko̱e hõ̱ bako ṛe̱be̱n kana; ar kakań goṅgońtekoń riạuet́koa, onko hõ̱ bako ṛe̱be̱n kana. Jo̱m ńũiak̕ do̱ iṅge nãhãk̕ iń e̱mo̱k̕ do̱, e̱n hõ̱ eṅgate bako ṛe̱be̱n kana. Nit do̱ ho̱ṛ menak̕ bako bạsutań kana; jãhã hilok̕ hape̱n iń ho̱ṛ hartalen khan, unre do̱ ạḍi peṛako todok̕a; nit do̱ cele hõ̱ bako bạsutań kana. Ado̱ kamare metae kana, Cele ho, amem go̱ṛo̱kińa se̱ o̱ho̱?

Ado̱ uni kamare me̱nket́a, Acha, o̱ko̱e hõ̱ bako go̱ṛo̱am kan khan, ińiń go̱ṛo̱ama.

Ado̱e me̱nket́a, Acha bogege, e̱ṇḍe̱khan gapa do̱ jo̱mak̕koń juṛạuletalaṅge; meań do̱ ạikạ ạḍi sim rak̕relań calak̕a.

Ado̱ uniye me̱nket́a, Acha, ma e̱ṇḍe̱khan juṛạulem.

Ado̱ uni koṛae me̱nket́a, Me̱n ạikạ alom e̱ṛe̱ńa.

Ado̱e me̱nket́a, Acha, o̱ho̱ń e̱ṛe̱mea.

Ado̱ kathae, inạ neṇḍa dinre do̱ gại kirińkin calaoena. Ado̱ kathae, gạige bakin ńam ṭhik daṛeako kan. Ado̱ onka kuli kulitege ạḍi sạṅgińkin calao idiyena. Mit́ raj disom paro̱mkin calaoena, ado̱ un sạṅgińre e̱ne̱ć, kathae, mit́ṭạṅkin ńamkedea. Uni gạikin ńe̱le jo̱khe̱n do̱ bae ićlet́a; ado̱ saṗkatekin ńe̱lkede do̱, are go̱ṭe̱n ḍaṭa menak̕tae, ar marań utạr pheṭãṛe ńe̱lok̕ kana. Ado̱ uni koṛae me̱nket́a, Nuigelań hataoea.

Ado̱ kamare me̱net́a, Bań, nui do̱ balań hataoea; nõ̱k̕õ̱eye ḍaṭa purạuena, e̱nhõ̱ bae pal akana. Nui do̱ bạhlạge co̱ń cet́ co̱ń.

Ado̱ uni koṛae me̱nket́a, Acha, bạhlạre hõ̱ cet́re hõ̱ nuigelań hataoea.

20 There is no common word for uncle, and the text here speaks of the younger and elder brothers of the father, who each have separate designations.

21 One rupee is one fifteenth part of a pound sterling. The haggling here described is very much like what daily occurs.

to his uncles[20], saying: "Come with me, father, help me to buy a cow; we want to buy me one." But they would not consent to go either.

Now there was one blacksmith family living there, and he spoke to them: "Please come with me, help me to buy a cow. Dash it, I am calling upon the village people to go with me; but not one of them is willing. And I am calling upon my uncles, and they too, they are not villing. I am, of course, standing the travelling expenses; still they are not willing, dash it. Now they don't estimate me as a human being of any consequence; some day in future, when I behome well-to-do, then a crowd of friends will come out; now not one of them estimates me." So he said to the blacksmith: "Well, would you be willing to help or how?"

"All right," the blacksmith replied, 'when no one else is willing to help you, I shall do so."

"Very well," the boy said, "that is good; then I shall to-morrow make up the necessary food for the journey for us, and the day after to-morrow very early, mind you, we shall start."

"All right," he replied, "then provide the necessary food."

"Take care then," the boy said, "mind you, don't disappoint me."

"All right, I shall not disappoint you," he replied.

On the fixed day they started to go and buy a cow; but they were unable to find a suitable one. They went along, making inquiries as they went, and in this way they got very far off. They went past the country of one king, only when they had reached so far, they found a suitable one. When they saw the cow, she did not drop anything; but when they lay hold of her and looked at her, they saw that she had nine teeth, and she looked an unusually large heifer. The boy then said: "We shall take this one."

"No," the blacksmith said, "don't let us take this one; as you see, she has got all her teeth; still she has not had a calf. She is very likely barren."

"Well," the boy said, "whether she is barren or whatever she is, this one we shall take."

Ado̱ damkin kulikedea, Cele, gạite do̱liń khusi ńõḱ akangea; ado̱ ma bhala dam lạilem, to̱be̱ baliń hatao daṛeae kana.

Ado̱ uni reaḱ dame ro̱ṛkeťa, Are ṭaka. Ado̱ uni koṛae me̱nkeťa, Baṅa, ṭhik dam lạime.

Ado̱e me̱nkeťa, Do hataoe khanben, irạl ṭaka.

Ado̱ uni kamare me̱nkeťa, Nui bạhlạ gạige unạḱem damae kana, arhõ besko khan, tinạḱ co̱m damkekoa?

Ado̱ uni ho̱ṛe me̱nkeťa, Baṅa, bạbu, bae bạhlạwa, miť bihạ̃ṛ hõ ạuriye busạgoḱa; nẽḱẽ sor dingeye pal akana.

Ado̱ kamare me̱nkeťa, Ma ńe̱leme, ḍaṭa purạuen hõ bae busạḱ akana; ar baṅkhan gạị do̱ bar ḍaṭaregeko paloḱa ar pon ḍaṭareko busạgoḱa; ar baṅkhan pon ḍaṭareko paloḱa, turui ḍaṭareko busạgoḱa. Ar nui do̱ ńe̱leme, ḍaṭa purạuenre hõ bae busạḱ akana. Nui do̱ bạhlạ baṅkhane cele kana?

Ado̱ uni ho̱ṛe me̱nkeťa, Acha, mase̱ e̱nte aben ro̱ṛleben, tinạḱte khanben hataokea.

Ado̱ uni kamare me̱nkeťa, Pon ṭakate khanliń hataokea.

Ado̱ uni ho̱ṛe me̱nkeťa, Baṅ, turui ṭaka e̱moḱben.

Ado̱ uni koṛae me̱nkeťa, Turui hõ baṅ ar ponea hõ baṅ; do mõṛẽ ṭakań emama.

Ado̱ uni ho̱ṛe me̱nkeťa, Baṅa, bạbu, ạḍiń maraḱ kana.

Ado̱e metadea, Khusi khan e̱mo̱ḱme, ar baṅkhan jãhã se̱nliń ńe̱lkoa.

Ado̱e me̱nkeťa, Acha, de̱n e̱ṇḍe̱khan e̱mo̱ḱme. Ado̱kin emadea; ado̱ uni gạikin to̱lkedea arkin tiạḱ ạguyede kana.

Ado̱ hijuḱ hijuḱtekin ạyuṗena; ado̱ miťṭań bajar macha atokin ńamkeťa. Ado̱kin me̱nkeťa, Noa ńindạ do̱ okatelań calaḱa? Ma

---

22 What is here stated regarding the teeth and the age of cattle is in accordance with fact and daily practice. When buying a cow or a bullock they always ascertain the age by seeing the number of teeth in the nether jaw; when the calf is about three years the first two appear, then yearly two up to in all eight, according to the Santals. Nine teeth do not occur; that belongs to the folktale.

23 *Lit.* 'a bazar village', i. e. a village with some shops.

Thereupon they asked the owner the price: "Well, we are fairly pleased with the cow; but you must first tell us your price, then we shall know whether we can take her."

The owner then named the price, nine rupees[21]. The boy then said: "Oh no, name the proper price."

"Well," the man said, "if you take her, eight rupees."

"You are prizing this barren cow so much," the blacksmith interposed; "I wonder what price you would ask if they were really good."

"No, my lad," the owner replied," she is not barren; she has not had her first calf; but she has quite recently rutted."

"Please look at her," the blacksmith said, "although she has got her full set of teeth, she has not as yet had a calf. As a rule cows rut when they have got two teeth, and calve when they get four, or else they rut when they have four teeth, and calve when they get six[22]. But look at this one, although she has got all her teeth, she has not calved as yet. She is barren, what else is she?

"Well," the man said, "well then, speak you, then, how much might you be willing to give for her?"

"If we get her for four rupees," the blacksmith said, "we might take her."

"No," the man said, "give six rupees."

The boy then said: "Neither six rupees, nôr four; look here, I shall give you five rupees."

"No, my lad," the owner said, "that won't do, it will be a great loss to me."

"If you will agree to that, give her; otherwise we shall go somewhere else and look for a cow," the boy said.

"All right then," the owner replied, "give me that then." So they paid him, tied a rope round the neck of the cow and started leading her away.

As they were coming along on their way home, they were benighted; they came to a fairly large[23] village and said: "Where shall we go now at night? Let us pass the night on

nią atorege jãhãe pinḍarelaṅ gitić aṅgak̔a. Adọ onka mẹnkate ato sẹnkin rakap̔ena; adọ mit̔ horak̔ pinḍąkin ńẹl ńamket̔takoa, adọkin metako kana, Henda baba, noa pinḍąkore gitić ṭhãokọpe aṛak̔kea?

Adọko mẹnket̔a, Hẽ jąnić, bale aṛaga?

Adọ ọnḍẹkin ḍerayena; adọ taben khąjąṛi jọm baṛaket̔te gąikin tọlkadea, ar ona pinḍąrekin jaegayena. Adọkin jąpit̔ket̔re onko dọ uni gąiko raṛakedetakina; adọ eṭagić mit̔ṭaṅ akoren buḍhi gąi ągukate unkinren gąiye tahẽkan ṭhen ągukateko tọlkadea, arko gitićena.

Adọ dosar hilok̔ aṅga marsalen khankin ńẹle kan dọe baṅ kan ąkinren gąi dọ. Adọ uni hoṛkin metae kana, Ią baba, gąi dọpe bọdọlat̔liṅa, nui gąi dọe baṅ kantaliṅa; ąliṅren dọpe hataokedea, eṭagićpe ẹm akawat̔liṅa.

Adọe metakin kana, Baṅa, nui kangeae abenren dọ; nui gąige holaṅ ńẹl ągu akat̔bena.

Adọ unkinkin mẹnket̔a, Baṅa, ąliṅren gąi dọ hąni goṛarepe ader akadea.

Adọ uniye mẹnket̔a, Baṅ, uni gąi dọe iṅren kana; cedak̔ iṅ emabena? Ọkọe gąiben ągu akade, ini baṛẹ idiyetaben; iṅren dọ cak̔ iṅ ẹmọk̔a? Adọ nonka ądi bąṛićko kąphariąuena.

Khange uni hoṛ dọe mẹnket̔a, Baṅa, nonka jhogṛak̔ dọ baṅ bogea; hapẹ, nọnḍẹn hoṛ iṅ jarwalekoge, nui gąi reak̔bon bicąrlege.

Adọ onka mẹnkate mąṅjhi ṭhene calao gọt̔ena, ar atoren mit̔ bar bhọdrọ porja adọ mąṅjhi oṛak̔reko jarwayena. Adọe ląi bhẹdako kana, baṅma, Mit̔ṭan bidisią hoṛren gąi iṅ dọṅ gabṛe akadea; uniren gąi dọ iṅgeṅ hataokedea ar iṅren buḍhi gąi uni dọṅ em akaawadea. Adọ onaṅ ląiape kana, ape dọ iṅ sẹn leka baṛẹ rọṛpe; ma ona reak̔ dọṅ bujhąupea.

Adọ mit̔ hoṛe mẹnket̔a, Acha, tinąk̔em ẹmọk̔a?

somebody's verandah here in this village." With this intention they went up to the village, and when they saw a house with a verandah, they spoke to the people: "I say, sir, might you be willing to let us have a place to lie down in here somewhere on the verandah?"

"O yes," they said, "most likely; should we not let you have a place?"

So they settled down there for the night: after having eaten t a b e n and k h a j a r i they tied the cow, whereupon they lay down on the verandah. When they were asleep, those other ones untied their cow, brought another, an old cow of their own, and tied her where the cow of these two had been, whereupon they lay down.

When it dawned the next morning, the two saw that is was not their cow, and said to the man: "I say, father, you have changed the cow for us; this one is not our cow; you have taken our one and given us another one."

"Not at all," the man replied, "this one is yours, I saw you two bring this cow yesterday."

"Certainly not," they said, "see there is our cow, you have put her into your cow-shed."

"No," he answered, "that cow is mine; why should I give you that one? Take away with you the cow you brought, please; why should I give you mine?" And they had a hot quarrel over this.

At last the man said: "No, it is no good to quarrel in this way. Wait, let me call the people of this place together; then we shall have this matter judged first."

Saying this he went straight to the headman, whereupon a few of the more respectable inhabitants came together in the headman's house; the man explained the meaning of it all to these: "I have helped myself to a cow belonging to a man from another country; I have taken his cow and have given him an old cow of my own. I tell you this; speak you in my favour, and I shall show you my appreciation of it."

"All right," one man said, "how much will you give?"

Adǫ uni hǫṛe mẹnkeťa, Do jitạukidiṅape mẹnkhan, mõṛẽ ṭaka ṭhan manteṅ ẹm gǫdoḱa.

Adǫko mẹnkeťa, Acha, ẹṇḍẹkhanle jitạu ocomea.

Nonka adǫ sạri ghus ẹmkateko gohayente unkin hǫṛ ṭhenko calaoena, adǫ bicạrre unkin dǫko posṛakeťkina, gạí dǫ ini buḍhi gạigeko metaťkina, idiyeben mẹnte. Adǫ uni ṭuạr koṛae mẹnkeťa, Iạ baba, mạṅjhi paranik ar ape mõṛẽ hǫṛ, ạliṅ dǫ noa bicạrre baliṅ khusilena. Noa dǫ ẹkẹn tǫrǫpdạri bicạr lekageliṅ ạikạukeťa. Hapẹ, ạliṅ hõ miť bar galmarao hǫṛliṅ bạnijanrege.

Adǫko metaťkina, Acha, do ạgukoben. Adǫ onko hǫṛ seko bujhạueťa, baṅma, nukin dǫ bidisiạ hǫṛ, galmarao hǫṛkin ạgukore hõ thǫ niạkorenge; onko dǫ nãhãḱ ẹkkaltebon ran gǫťkoa. Adǫ onka bujhạukateko mẹnkeťa, Acha, do ạgukoben.

Adǫ uni ṭuạr koṛae mẹnkeťa, Iạ ho, ma am dǫ nǫṇḍẹ baṛẹ tahẽ hataṛoḱ talaṅme, noako moṭra hǫrhǫ hataṛme. Iṅ dǫ hinạ ato khon miť bar hǫṛ iṅ riạu ạgulekoge. Adǫ onko hõ ni gạigeko ḍigrialaṅ khan, nigelaṅ idiyea.

Adǫ onka mẹnkate aćdǫe bereť calaoena; adǫ hǫr hõ bae ṅẹl akať iạte ạuṛige bin hǫrtegeye calaḱ kana. Adǫ sạṅgiṅ machare miťṭạṅ atoe ṅẹl ṅamkeťa. Adǫ ona ato ṅẹlkate hǫr dǫe aťkeťa; adǫ pataṛ potoṛ miťṭạṅ bir menaḱa; adǫ ona bir tala talateye calaḱ kan tahẽkana. Adǫ ona bir talarege, kathae, toyotekin haṛam buḍhiye ṅamkeťkina, adǫkin dạreť tahẽkana. Adǫ uni koṛae hǫhǫkeťa, Ẹ ho, hapẹ sẹ, teṅgolenben, abengeṅ ṅam baṛayeťbena.

Adǫ kathaekin teṅgoyena, adǫkin mẹnkeťa, Cedaḱem ṅam baṛayeťliṅa?

Adǫ uni koṛae mẹnkeťa, Iṅ dǫ ṭuạr hǫṛ kanaṅ, eṅgaṅ kukhireṅ tahẽkanrege ạpuṅ dǫe gǫćena, ar okako ạpuṅe cijleť tahẽkan, onako dǫ goṅgoṅ kakaṅteko eṅgaṅko dhomkaokedete sanam cijko idikeťa, ar jumi hõko rẹćkeťlea; adǫ nalha tumạlte poesa jarwa-

24 Ficus bengalensis, Roxb. This tree grows to an immense size; the aerial roots coming down from the branches strike root and form a fresh stem; in this way one tree may become quite a grove.

"If you let me gain the case, I shall at once give five rupees," the man replied.

"Very well," they said, "then we shall let you gain the case."

After he had bribed them to be witnesses for him, they went to those two; in judging they bullied them; they told them that their cow was that old cow, and said that they should take that one with them. The orphan boy then said: "Well, sirs, headman and vice-headman and you Five, we two are not satisfied with this judgment, we feel it to be like a biassed judgement only. Wait, let us also bring a couple of men who can speak."

"All right, do bring some," they said to them; they were, of course, thinking by themselves: "these two are from another country; even if they bring some to speak for them, it must be somebody from hereabouts, and those we shall straight away medicine." It was with this in mind that they said: "All right, do bring some."

The orphan boy then said to his companion: "Look here, my friend, you please remain here for the present, and watch our bundles for us during my absence. I shall go and ask a couple of men from that village over there to come. If those also decree this cow to be ours, we must take this one with us."

Having said this, he got up and went off. As he had not seen the way, he was walking along at random, where there was no road. Some distance away he sighted a village; but when he had sighted it, he lost his bearings. There was some scrubby jungle there, and he was walking along through this. Then he suddenly, in the middle of that jungle, met a pair of jackals; they were running along. The boy called out to them: "I say, wait, stop a moment; it is you two I am looking for."

They stopped and asked him: "Why are you looking for us two?"

"I am an orphan," the boy replied, "whilst I was still in my mother's womb, my father died, and what my father had acquired of goods and property all that the elder and younger brothers of my father took away after having scolded my mother into silence; our land they took from us by force. After having

kate miťṭaṅ mīhũń kiriń idijoṅ kan tahẽkana. Adọ ona bajar atore miť hoṛaḱ piṇḍạreliń gitić kan tahẽkana. Adọliń jạpiťkeť jọkhẹn uni họṛ ińren pheṭãṛ mīhũi kombṛokedete ińiń tọllede ṭhenge miťṭaṅ buḍhi gại ạgukateye tọl oṭokadea. Adọ setaḱ jọkhẹn iń ńẹle kan dọe baṅ kantiń, ar iń ạgu gại dọ aćaḱ goṛareye ader akade. Adọ uni họṛ iń metae kana, Iạ baba, nui gại dọe baṅ kantińa, ińren dọe uni uni kantińa. Adọ uni họṛe mẹnkeťa, Baṅ, nui gạige cọṅ holam ạgu akawan; ińren dọ caḱ iń emama? Adọ ona karọnte bogeteliń kạphạriạuena. Adọ ona karọnte họṛe jarwakeťkoa, adọ jọtọ họṛ uni sẹn tọrọpdạri lekageko rọṛkeťa. Adọ onare bạń khusilente mõṛẽ họṛ iń metaťkoa, Iạ baba, noa bicạrre dọ baṅ khusilena; hapẹ, iń hõ galmarao họṛ iń ạguanrege. Adọ họṛ ńam iń calaḱ kan jọkhẹnge adọ aben iń ńamkeťbena. Adọ dela abenge bicạrkatińben.

Adọ unkin toyokin mẹnkeťa, Bhala ato họṛ ghus tanaḱko jọm akaťa sẹ?

Adọ uniye mẹnkeťa, Ọkọ baḍae, mẽťte dọ baṅ ńẹl akaťkoa.

Adọ unkinkin mẹnkeťa, Acha, delabonliń bicạrkatama; adọ askatem hẹćena, delaliń bicạrkatama.

Adọko hijuḱ kana, adọ unrekin metae kana, Atore ọhọliń sẹnlena, seta nãhãḱko gẹrlińa; ato bahre sẹnre jãhã dare buṭạ tanaḱrebon jarwaḱa; ạr unkin gại dọ banar baṛẹ ạgu darakinpe, ona bicạr ṭhengebon tọl hataṛkakina.

Adọko hẹć sẹṭẹren khan, kulhi mucạťre miťṭaṅ baṛe dareko ńamkeťa; adọkin metadea, Do noa dare buṭạ ṭhen họhọ ạgukom; nọṇḍẹgebon galmaraoa.

Adọ sạri unkin dọ ọṇḍẹge dare buṭạrekin tahẽyena, ar uni koṛa dọ ato sẹne calaoente mạńjhi paranik ar ato họṛ ar uni mudại

---

25 The end of the village street, i. e., the land just outside the last houses lying along the street, is a place very commonly used for sundry purposes. The 'Five' or the village council frequently meet here and not inside the village, because they here feel themselves less liable to interruption and may be sure that women are not listening. The Santals are very particular as to what should be said before women. It is one of their gentlemanly traits.

scraped together some money by working for others and by gleaning, I bought a calf and was taking her with me home. Then we two were passing the night in a man's verandah in that bazar town. When we had fallen asleep, that man stole my heifer, and, bringing an old cow, he tied that where I had tied mine. In the morning I saw that it was not my one, and that he had taken the cow I had brought into his own cow-shed. Then I say to this man: 'I say, father, this cow is not mine; that one there is mine.' Then the man said: 'Why, no it is this cow that you brought yesterday; why should I give you mine?' On account of this we had a hot quarrel, and on account of this he brought people together, and all of them spoke in his favour in a biassed way. As I was not satisfied with this, I said to the Five: 'Well, sirs, I am not satisfied with this judgement; wait, let me also bring some who can speak.' As I was coming along looking for some such people, I met with you. So come along, you two, and be my judges."

The two jackals then said: "I wonder, perhaps those village people have 'eaten' bribes, or how?"

"Who knows?" the boy said, "with my eyes I have not seen it."

"Very well then," the two jackals said, "come along, and we two shall decide your case; you came with confidence, come, we shall judge your case."

Whilst they were on the way, the jackals said to the boy: "We cannot in any case go into the village; the dogs will bite us; let us meet somewhere outside the village, at the foot of some tree or other; and bring the cows, both of them, along with you; we shall tie them in the meanwhile there where we are to have the meeting."

When they reached the place, they came upon a banyan[24] tree at the end of the village street[25]. So the jackals said to him: "Do bring them here to the foot of this tree; we shall have the discussion here."

The jackals then remained there at the foot of that tree, and the boy went to the village and invited the headmann and the

hoṛ, jotoe riạuketkoa, ar unkin gại do soṅgeteko ạgu daraketkina. Ado joto hoṛ ona baṛe dare buṭạreko jarwayena.

Adoko metae kana, Okorkotam oaris do, se galmarao hoṛ do okorkotam?

Ado unkin toyo do pharak ṅōk̕rekin duṛup̕ akan tahēkana. Adoe metako kana, Hankinkin duṛup̕ akan.

Adoko menketa, Unkin makin toyo kan.

Ado uniye menketa, Unkingeṅ ạgu akatkina.

Adoko menketa, Acha besge.

Ado ona dare buṭạreko duṛup̕ena, ado unkin toyo hōkin heć sorente mit̕ aṛe senrekin duṛup̕ena. Ado sanam hoṛko thir baṛa akangea, okoe hō cet̕ hō bako roṛ baṛayeta. Ado mạṅjhiye menketa, Durre! thir baṛayen dobo. De cet̕ katha kana, lại saḍepe.

Ado adom hoṛko menketa, Okoe ente roṛ saḍea? Okoeye jarwaketbon, uni bae lại maṛaṅle khan, dosra hoṛ do cet̕ lekae ehoba?

Adoko menketa, De ho, tobe roṛtabonme, cetko katha kana; cet̕ lạgitem jarwa akatbona, onako dom lạile baṅle baḍaetama?

Ado uni koṛae menketa, Hē, baba, sạri kangea, lạile eneć baḍaeoka. Iạ baba, katha do noa kana, one enanbo galmaraoket̕, ona kathage arhōbon galmarao dohṛaea.

Adoko men gotketa, Ona ma one coṅ enanrebon cabaket̕; ado cetem ṅam kana? Ma uni enanle metatme, uni gại baṛe idiyem.

Ado uni koṛae menketa, Enan do galmaraore bạṅ khusilente baṅ idiledea, ar iṅ sećren oaris okoe hō un do bako tahēkana. Ado bar hoṛ iṅ ạgu akatkina, ado unkin salakrebon galmaraolege; ado uni gạiye ṭhikok̕ khan, inigeṅ idiyea.

Ado onkako ropoṛ kan jokhen do unkin toyo dokin tirup̕ akana. Ado onko hoṛko men gotketa, Dos nạhīkin iạ kana; mit̕ ṅindạ

26 Jackals acc. to Santal observation largely feed on grasshoppers and crabs, these last ones being commonly found in the rice fields during the rainy season.

27 The jackal quotes in a rustic Bengali. The sentence is very likely borrowed from Hindu villagers.

vice-headman and the village people and the opponent, all of them, to come and they also brought the two cows along. The whole party assembled there at the foot of the banyan tree.

"Why, where are your spokesmen?" they said, "where are those who are to speak for you?"

The two jackals were sitting a little distance off, and the boy said: " Look, they are sitting over there."

"Why, those two are jackals," they said.

"It is those two that I have brought," the boy replied.

"All right, it is good," they said.

When they had sat down at the foot of that tree, the two jackals also came near and sat down on one side. All were sitting quietly, no one of them was speaking a single word. The headman then said: "Dear me, we have become quite silent. Please speak out, what is the matter."

Then some one said: "Well, who should speak out? If he who has called us together does not first state his case, how can we other people begin?"

"Well then you," they said, "speak then what it is; for what purpose have you called us together? only when you tell that, we shall know what you mean."

"Yes, sirs," the boy said, "that is quite so; only when a thing is told, it will be known. Well, sirs, it is this; what we talked about a while ago this morning, that matter we must discuss once more."

"Why," they answered, "that we settled this morning; what more do you want then? Do take with you the cow we told you this morning."

"I was not satisfied with the decision this morning," the boy said, "therefore I did not take her away; neither had I then any one to be spokesman for me. Now I have brought two persons, so let us discuss the matter with them present. If then this cow is found to be the right one, I shall take her away with me.

Whilst they were talking together in this way, the two jackals were sitting with bowed heads. The other ones then said: "They

kaṭkǫm sǫsrǫćkokin sendra kan tahẹ̄kana, adǫ dudṛumeťkina. Niṭok̖ dǫ galmarao hǫṛ khan jãhãn katha bakin rǫṛkea? Adǫ okorkin rǫṛeťa?

Adǫ toyo ạṇḍiạye rǫṛ gǫťkeťa, Hẹ̃, baba, galmarao hǫṛ kangealiń. Ape dǫpe mẹneťa, dudṛumeťkina; mẹnkhan dudṛum dǫ baliń dudṛum kana. Miťṭań ạliń mǫtǫrege jhogṛa menaǩtaliña. Adǫ nui koṛa reaǩ bicạr lạgiťbon jarwa akana, ona ma hẹ̃ kange, uniaǩ hǫ̃bon bicạrgetaea, ona hǫ̃ babon bạgiaǩa. Adǫ bhage nǫṇḍẹ ape mǫ̃ṛẹ̃ hǫṛliń ńamkeťpea; mẹnkhan pạhil dǫ ạlińaǩ bicạr maṛańkatalińpe. Ape dǫ biǩcạr hǫṛ kanape, nui koṛa reaǩpe bicạrkeťa; besge ona hǫ̃liń metaǩ kana. Adǫ ạlińaǩ bicạrlepe, tǫbẹliń metapea, noko dǫ nui koṛa reaǩ ṭhikko bicạr akaťa mẹnte. Ar ạlińaǩ bicạr bape phaṇḍaokeťa mẹnkhan, ẹṇḍẹkhan ṭhik biǩcạr hǫṛ dǫpe bań kana.

Adǫ onko mǫ̃ṛẹ̃ hǫṛko mẹnkeťa, Acha, ceť leka kana, masẹ lạitaben.

Adǫ uni toyo ạṇḍiạye mẹnkeťa, Ạliń dǫ miťtegeliń daṛan kana ar miťgeliń jǫmeťa, daǩ hǫ̃ miťgeliń ńũyeťa; adǫ cekate nui dǫ bar dhaoe ićeťa? Ić dǫ din mǫtǫre miť dhaogeń ićeťa ar nui dǫ bar dhao. Adǫ masẹ noa baṛẹ bicạrkatalińpe.

Adǫko mẹnkeťa, Ǫkǫ baḍae ẹnte, cekate cǫń bar dhaoe ićeť kan.

Adǫ uni toyo ạṇḍiạye mẹnkeťa, Adǫ ona baṛẹ ẹnte masẹ kuliyepe, cedaǩ bar dhao dǫe ićeť kana.

Adǫ sạriko kulikedea, Sạri am dǫ bar dhaoem ićeťa, sẹ nui dǫ ạuṛigeye lạiyeťa? Onkako kuliyede kana arko landayeťa.

Adǫ toyo ạṇḍiạye mẹneťa, Hã! hã! alope landaea, landa katha dǫ bań kana. Hapṛamkoko rǫṛakaťa, "Bhalǫ bhalǫ loker sǫńgẹ dǫrbar jachore puṭạ hạ̃si katha na bǫlǫre." Onateń metape kana, landa katha dǫ bań kana, alope landaea.

Adǫ khangeko thirena, adǫko kulikedea, Ma lạime, cedaǩ bar dhao dǫm ićeťa? Sǫńgẹgeben daṛan kana, sǫńgẹgeben jǫm ńũyeťa, adǫ cekate am dǫ bar dhaoem ićeť kana?

28 It is a common expression. When something is done or happens, different from the ordinary, without any observable cause, especially when it is of constant occurrence, it is supposed to be due to the 'command' of the higher powers.

29 *Lit.* 'what is together with', the meaning apparently being that which pairs with that of others, perhaps of her husband's, in other words, what is natural.

are fine judges those two. They spent the whole night hunting for crabs and grashoppers[26], and now they are feeling drowsy. If they were persons who can speak, would they not now say something? Why, they are not speaking a single word."

The he-jackal then said: "Yes, sirs, we are spokesmen. You are saying: they are feeling drowsy; that is not so, we are not feeling drowsy. We two are having a quarrel between ourselves. Now we have come together to decide this boy's case; that is quite so, we shall judge his case, we shall not forget that. It was very fortunate that we two met with you council-people here; but first judge our case. You are people accustomed to judge; you judged this boy's case; we call that quite good. Now first judge our case; then we shall be able to tell you that these people have judged rightly in this boy's case. And if you don't settle our dispute, in that case you are not proper judges."

The Five then said: "All right, state your case, what it is."

The he-jackal then said: "We two are going about together, and we are eating the same food: we are also drinking the same water: how is it then that she voids excrements twice? I myself void once daily and she twice. So please settle this matter for us."

"Well, who can tell," they said, "how it can be that she voids twice daily."

The he-jackal then said: "Then please ask her about this, why she voids excrements twice."

So they really asked her: "Is it true that you void excrements twice, or is he telling fibs?" They asked her and were laughing.

The he-jackal then said: "Hold! hold! don't laugh; it is not a laughing matter. The ancestors[27] have said: 'Wenn man mit vornehmen Leuten im Rate sitzt, kein leichtfertiges Sprechen.' I therefore tell you, it is no laughing matter; don't laugh."

So they stopped laughing and asked her: "Please tell, why are you voiding excrements twice? You two are going about together, you are eating and drinking together: how is it then that you are voiding excrements twice"?

Adǫ uniye mẹnkeťa, Noa dǫ sạri kangea, sǫṅgẹgeliń daṛan kana, ar jǫm ńũ hǫ̃ miťgeliń jǫm ńũyeťa, mẹnkhan sạrige iń dǫ bar dhao iń ićeťgea. Adǫ nonka leka iń dǫ hukum menaǩtińa, baṅma, miť dǫ sǫṅgẹ ić kantińa, ona dǫ dhạrtirege ńũroǩ kante ẹṇḍẹge tahẹn kana; ar miť dhao iń ićeťa, ona dǫ ǫkǫe hǫṛ ghuse jǫmeť ar ona ghus karǫnte rạṇḍi dukhi, ṭuạr amar, guni gurib reaǩ bicạre bẹhǫkeť, adǫ uniren usṭi pusṭikoaǩ mocare ona ić dǫ paṛaoǩ kana, ar uniye jǫm akať mocare hǫ̃ ona ić dǫ hapẹn hana purire paṛaoaea, ona ić dǫ moca ar mocarege hapẹn tahẹna. Ar ǫkǫe hǫṛ ghuse jǫm akaťre hǫ̃, mǫ̃ṛẽ hǫṛ ṭhen aṅgǫckate iń ńutumteye dohaele khan, onako hǫlǫp do sanam kaṭaokoǩtaea; ar bae aṅgǫc khan dǫ, hapẹn ǫnẹ onka onko hǫṛaǩ dosa dǫ hoyoǩtakoa. Adǫ ǫnẹ ona iạte iń dǫ bar dhao ij reaǩ hukum menaǩtińa. Ma adǫ katha bujhạupe.

Adǫ ạṇḍiạye mẹnkeťa, Dẹ baba, ape mǫ̃ṛẽ hǫṛ bujhạupe. Pasẹć ape mǫtǫre nonka leka hoe akan khan dǫ, lạipe ninạǩ mǫ̃ṛẽ hǫṛ samaṅre; ar baṅkhan dǫ hapẹn onka dosa hoyoǩa.

Adǫ ǫkǫeko hǫṛ ghusko hataolaǩa, sẹ hataoko mẹneť tahẽkan, onko hǫṛ dǫ akotege lạlạiko pǫrtǫnkeťa, adǫ jǫtǫ katha ṭhik ṭhikko rǫṛkeťa. Khange uni koṛaren gạiko delaokadetaea, ar uni kombṛo hǫṛge ulṭạute mǫ̃ṛẽ ṭakako ḍãṇḍkedea. Adǫ uni koṛa dǫ gạiye tiạǩkedetaea, adǫe calaoena; ar noko hǫ̃ko bhiṛ bhaṅgaoena; ar nukin toyo hǫ̃ uni koṛa tayǫmtekin pańja idikedea, adǫ birko tioǩkeť khankin mẹnkeťa, Ma bạbu, ẹṇḍẹkhan gạï dǫ idiyeben, ạliń dǫ nẹtẹliń calaǩ kana. Adǫ ẹnẹko apan ạpin baṛayena.

· Adǫ uni gạï dǫkin idi sẹṭẹrkadea, adǫ goṛare baṅ dǫ sate umulre, kathaekin tǫlkadea. Adǫ eṅgattẹť dǫ bạṭiko mańjao baṛakate daǩe taṅaťkina; adǫ ńũ baṛakate jaṅga dhuṛikin ạbukena. Adǫ uni eṅgattẹť dǫ bạṭire daǩ taṅkate uni gạiaǩ jaṅgae ạruṗkeťtaea ar busuṗe ạguadea. Adǫ onakin sẹnlenaǩ duk suke kuli baṛayeť-

30 Bribery as described occurs among the people. It is very common all over India. In the ordinary Santal village-quarrels only one form of bribery is common, that of giving food and drink, especially the latter, to the more important persons.

She then said: "It is quite true. We are going about together, and we are also eating and drinking the same; but in truth I void excrements twice. I have such an order[28], namely, one is my company-dung[29]; this falls down on the earth and remains there; and once more I void, the meaning of that is: he who takes bribes[30] and for that bribe's sake judges unjustly the widow's, the orphan's and the poor and indigent people's case, in the mouth of his offspring for generations upon generations that dung falls; that filth will remain in their mouth for ever. But any person who has 'eaten' bribes, if he confesses it before the council and makes supplication in my name, from him all that curse will be removed; and if he does not confess, then such as stated the fate of those will be. For this reason I have order to void excrements twice. Please understand this."

The he-jackal then said: "Please, sirs, you Five, understand the matter. If by any chance such a thing should have happened among you, tell it before so many councillors; otherwise, such a fate is in store for you."

Then those who had taken bribes or who had intended to take, commenced of their own accord to tell, and they told everything exactly as it was. Thereupon they formally gave the boy's cow over to him and they turned the whole against the thief and fined him five rupees. The boy went away, leading his cow, and those other ones also went, each his own way. The two jackals also went along after the boy until they reached the forest, when they said: "Now, my boy, take the cow with you; we two are going in this direction." So they parted company there.

The two of them then brought the cow home and tied her in the cattle-shed or perhaps it was in the shade of the eaves. The boy's mother scoured and cleaned some cups and poured out water for them; when they had drunk, they washed the dust off their feet. His mother then poured some water into a cup and washed the cow's feet and brought her straw. Thereupon she asked them what had happened to them, good and bad, on their journey, and

kina, tinạk̕teben kiriṅkedea, onakokin lạiae kana, ar o̱ne̱ko kombṛolede tahẽkan ar ceka lekatekin ńam ruạṛkede, onako jo̱to̱ beạn, je kichu hoelenak̕ do̱, jo̱to̱kin lại cabawadea.

Ado̱ uni kamare me̱nket̕a, Iń do̱ unkin toyo ńe̱lte ar unkinak̕ katha ańjo̱mte ạḍiń hahaṛayena. Ńe̱lme se̱ e̱nte, toyo jạt kanakin, ho̱ṛ ro̱ṛ do̱ okarekin cet̕ket̕te onka pusṭạu do̱kin galmarao kana? Ona ańjo̱mte iń do̱ ạḍiń hahaṛayena. Ar bicạr hõ ạikạ khub ṭhikkin bicạrlet̕a, e̱kkalte ro̱ṛ sit̕ utạrena, ona khon do̱ cele hõ baṅko ro̱ṛ daṛeat̕a, e̱kkalteko hẽk̕ utạrket̕a, gại hõko e̱m utạr go̱t̕at̕liṅa, arhõ mõṛẽ ṭakako ḍanḍo̱mkedea.

Ado̱ uni kamare lạiet̕a se̱, cet̕ baṅ ona ro̱ṛ ańjo̱mte ạḍi ho̱ṛko jarwayena, ado̱ cet̕ baṅ se̱ye mạluṅ cabaket̕koa. Ado̱ uni koṛaren eṅgatte̱t̕e menet̕a, Iạ bạbu, unkin do̱ toyo do̱ bakin tahẽkana; unkin do̱ Candogekin tahẽkana, onatege nonka hahaṛa do̱kin ro̱ṛket̕a. Ado̱ko me̱nket̕a, Hẽge co̱ṅ.

Arhõ uni kamare me̱nket̕a, Kakat goṅgotteko nuiak̕ cijko hatao akat̕taea, ona hõ hape̱ne ńam ruạrtaea; e̱nte onko do̱ be̱ho̱kteko hatao akat̕taea.

Ado̱ onko jarwa akan ho̱ṛko me̱nket̕a, Baṅa, noa katha do̱ ṭhikgem me̱net̕a, ar ale hõ ona do̱le bujhạu akat̕gea. Ado̱ cet̕em me̱na? Ado̱ o̱ko̱e onaren dhatkae teṅgolen baṅ. Ar ńe̱lpe, jo̱to̱ko re̱ć caba akat̕kore hõ, noko do Candoe dayawako kante re̱ṅge̱ćte do̱ bako ko̱sṭo̱ akana.

Ado̱ enka galmarao baṛakate khange uni kamar do̱e me̱nket̕a, Acha, ma galmaraotabonpe, iń do̱ oṛak̕teṅ se̱nlenge, dakaṅ jo̱m ạgulege.

---

31 Pại is very nearly half a litre. The size varies with the different localities, the shopkeepers often also have several sizes, one to buy with, another to sell with, and a third used when dealing with those whom it might be inconvenient to try to cheat, *viz.* the standard measure. The standard pại is half a seer, and this is to be equivalent to eighty tolas (one tola is the weight of one rupee, the silver coin unit). It is fairly common to see people in the rural shops testing the size of the measures. One way of doing it is to weigh dried rice grain with rupees. If the amount of rice contained in a pại measure weighs forty rupees,

how much they had paid for the cow; they told her all that, also how people had stolen her, and in which way they got her back, the story of all this, every particular happening, in fact everything they narrated to her.

The blacksmith then said: "I was much astonished seeing those two jackals and hearing their words. For, remember, they are of the jackal race; where had they learnt the Santal language so they could speak so distinctly? By hearing that, I was very much astonished. And think, their judging, that was also excellent; all talk was immediately utterly put a stop to; no one could speak anything further; they at once agreed to all; the cow they also gave over to us immediately, and the man they fined five rupees."

The blacksmith was telling, you can't imagine how fine it was and by hearing his tale very many people came together, and you can't imagine how nicely he told, he absolutely fascinated them. Then the boy's mother said: "I say, my boy, those two were no jackals; they were Chando himself; therefore they spoke so wonderfully." "Yes, perhaps so," the others said.

Again the blacksmith commenced to speak: "His uncles, the younger and elder brothers of his father, have taken the boy's property; this he will also get back some day; for they have taken it from him unjustly."

"Yes," the assembled people said, "that is quite so; you are speaking quite right; we have also understood that. But what can you say? The claimant must, first of all, stand up. But see, although they have robbed them of everything, Chando is taking pity on them, so they do not suffer distress from hunger."

After they had had this talk, the blacksmith said: "Very well, you continue to talk; I must go home and have some food."

it is a correct or standard paị measure. It might be mentioned that the measures in common use are of a local manufacture, some made of wood, others of wood with brass or iron mountings, and others of metal cast by a certain Hindu caste.

Adọ sạri onkae mẹnkeť khan dọ uni koṛaren eṅgattẹť dọ bọlọyente bar pẹ pại gan caoleye ọḍokkeťte uni kamare emadea; adọe metadea, Nẹ ghẹ̃ṭme, gidrạko nãhãǩko ńẹl darammea.

Adọ sạriye ghẹ̃ṭkeťa, arhõ dạl buluṅkoe emadea, adọ inạ ghẹ̃ṭ baṛakate khange uni kamar dọe calaoena. Adọ onko jarwa họṛ hõ cun thamakur jọm baṛakateko apan ạpinena.

Adọ inạ dosar tesar khange, kathae, kakat goṅgotteko dọko aṅjọmkeťa, baṅma, nui koṛa dọ apat reaǩ jumiye pachae lạgiť. Adọ onkoko mẹnkeťa, Acha besge, mase bhala abo hõ nịạ aḍe ṭola họṛko ṭhenbo bujhạu baṛalege; ar baṅkhan bhọrmẹ bhọrmẹtebon ẹm ruạṛkataea.

Adọ sạri okakore cọko bujhạu baṛakeť, ar ọnẹ gại kiriṅkin sẹnlenre toyoe bicạrkeťtakin, adọ ona katha hõ aḍe ṭola họṛ ṭhenko lại saḍekeť khan, onkoko mẹnkeťa, Ma uniaǩ cijko dọ ẹm ruạṛkataepe; ar baṅkhan hapẹn apegepe lajaoǩa. Ńẹlpe, uniren dọ sẹ uni uparte dọ bir janwar hõko teṅgon kana. Abo họṛ họṛre ma jãhã lekatebon ẹṛẹ daṛekekogea; mẹnkhan pasẹ Candoge uniaǩe bicạrtae, ar uni họṛ leka pasẹťe sạbud ape hõ bẹhọktegepe hatao akaťtae, tọbẹ un jọkhẹn moskil hoyoǩa.

Adọ sạri onkako bujhạu baṛawan khanko mẹnkeťa, Mabon ẹm ruạṛkataea, ar ọnẹbon hataotae jọkhẹn hõe mẹn akaťa, apat tahẽkanre bar cando·reaǩ tahẽkategeye gọć akana. Pasẹ ona kathage sạriǩ, tọbe nãhãǩ ceťbon mẹna? Kajetege babon lajaoǩa? Ma nenkare onako dọ jọtọbon ẹmkataea. Inạ dọ abore hõ suluk tahẹna, ar baṅkhan hapẹn jãhã hiloǩ jhogṛa hapẹn hoyoǩa, abore baṅkhan hapẹn gidrạkoko jhogṛaǩtabona.

---

32 See p. 99, note 3.

33 As they have no pockets, it is common to tie things they take along with them in their cloth.

34 The Santals make beer from malted grain, now commonly from rice. The grain of j a n h e, Paspalum scrobiculatum, L., is also much used for the purpose and said to be more intoxicating than other kinds of beer. Beer is very commonly taken, thus at all festivals, and as the final part of any discussion or decision reached in the village council, and so on. The most objectionable thing about

When he said this, the boy's mother entered her house, brought out about two or three *pai*[31] rice and gave the blacksmith, whereupon she said to him: "Here, take this and tie it up in your cloth; your children will be waiting for you now."

He tied the rice up in his cloth; she further gave him *dal*[32] and salt, and having tied it all up[33] the blacksmith went. Thereupon the people who had come together separated, after they had chewed lime and tobacco.

A couple of days after this, his uncles heard it told that the boy was going to inquire into the circumstances of his father's land. They said: "Very well, let us also seek advice with people here in the vicinity; else we shall give it back to him without making any fuss."

They really did so and sought advice here and there, and when they told people in the nearest villages of how the jackal had passed judgement when they had gone to buy a cow, these people said: "Give him back his property; if you don't, you will certainly some day be put to shame. See, on his side or on his behalf even forest animals stood up. We human beings between ourselves, we may somehow or other be able to fool people; but perhaps Chando will judge his case, and perhaps the man also will prove that you have unjustly taken his property; then there will come difficulties."

When they had sought advice in this way, they said: "Well, let us give him back what is his; at the time we took it from him, the woman also said that his father died when she was two months with child from him. Perhaps that will be shown to be true, what shall we then be able to say? Without doubt, shall we not be put to shame? Let us, whilst it is like this, give him all that is his. Thereby there will be peace also between ourselves. If we don't do so, there will some day in future arise quarrels between ourselves, or, if not, then our children will some day quarrel."

Adǫ unąk̓ hąbićko bujhąuket̓ khan, hąṇḍiko dǫhǫket̓a; ona dulkate uni koṛa ar eṅgattẹt̓ ar ato hǫṛ jǫtǫko jarwaket̓koteko galmaraoket̓a. Adǫ gąiko ar jumi baṛgeko jǫtǫko ẹm ruąṛ kat̓taea.

Adǫ cabayena katha dǫ. Qnẹ onkate, kathae, uni koṛa dǫ jumi baṛgeye ńam ruąṛket̓taea. Sąri cǫṅ nase cǫṅ, hǫṛ onkako galmaraoa.

12. Mit̓ṭẹć toyo ar sim reak̓ katha.

Sedae jugre, kathae, mit̓ṭaṅ toyo ar mit̓ṭaṅ sim phulkin pataolet̓ tahẽkana, ar unkin dǫ boehakin sągąilet̓ tahẽkana. Adǫ mit̓ din dǫ manǫtok̓ reak̓kin neṇḍaket̓a; bana hǫṛ hąṇḍikin dǫhǫket̓a; adǫ isinen khan dǫ dul baṛakatekin ńẽotayena. Pąhil dǫ toyo oṛak̓rekin ńũ baṛaket̓a, adǫ onakate sim oṛak̓tekin calaoena.

Santal drinking is that the aim is to get drunk. As to beer itself, it is not very intoxicating; it is always made so by adding vegetable poisons. In the villages, these additions do not lead to more than intoxication. In the beer-shops, it sometimes happens that people die after drinking the drugged beer. They make use of one or more among 23 different kinds of vegetable poisons, so far as I remember. The matter here referred to is a peculiar custom, by which an intimate and lifelong friendship is established between two persons of the same sex. The parties concerned put a flower (frequently of the Plumeria acutifolia, Poiret) in each other's hair and exchange presents of cloth and money. They address each other and speak of each other as p h u l, flower; they feast each other and assist each other in all circumstances. The ceremony gone through when first establishing this friendship is to a certain extent public, relatives and others being present. Persons of different race, i. e., a Santal and a Hindu, may contract this kind of friendship, although such is not often the case. The present story may possibly give a hint that friendship of this latter kind is unnatural and leads to disaster. According to what the Santals tell, they have got this peculiar form from the Hindus. The name p h u l is Hindi (from Sanskrit).

It might be mentioned that the Santals have a similar custom of their own. When two young people of the same sex, especially two girls, not so frequently

When they had got so far in thinking the matter over, they started making beer[34]; when that was ready, they called the boy and his mother and the village people together and talked the matter over. Thereupon they gave him his cows and his rice-lands and fields back, all of it.

Now there this story is ended. In this way that boy got his rice-lands and fields back. Whether it is true or not, people tell the story in this way.

12. THE STORY OF A JACKAL AND A HEN.

ONCE upon a time, in a former age, people tell, a jackal and a hen had engaged themselves to be flower-friends for life[1], and they agreed to stand in the relationship of brother and sister[2] to each other. Thereupon they fixed a day to celebrate their friendship[3]; both of them brewed beer, and when this was ready fermented[4], they drew it off and invited each other. First they had a drink in the jackal's home; thereupon they went to the hen's house.

boys, have become intimate friends, they make this friendship public at a Karam festival. This is celebrated in the Santal villages immediately after the Durga festival. The persons concerned take two leaves of a branch of the karam tree (Adina cordifolia, H. f. & B.) and fix one leaf in each other's hair, whereupon they salute all the villagers there assembled, one after the other. Afterwards they treat the village-people to beer; they also give each other presents of cloth. These also do not use other names (especially of relationship) in calling to one another, but only karam ḍạr (lit. karam branch). It is an idealistic friendship into which they enter, lasting for life. It is told that such friends have given their life to serve each other.

2 This is against the rule; two persons of different sex must not become phul. Santali has here one word for brother and sister.

3 See above note 1. The feast here referred to is not the public ceremony, but the friendly entertainment following afterwards.

4 Beer takes five days to brew. See p. 186, note 3.

Adǫ khange uni sim dǫe bulena, adǫe kǫbǫk̕ kǫbǫgǫk̕ kana, ar uniren hǫpǫn dǫ cia̧p̕ cia̧p̕ bogeteko rak̕et̕ kana; adǫ ǫnre hö̃ uni sim eṅga dǫ bae disa̧yet̕koa. Adǫ uni toyoe mǫnket̕a, Nui sim dǫń jǫmegea. Adǫ sa̧riye bul giticen khan dǫ, gǫrkateye a̧tkirkedea are jǫmkedea. Adǫ khange onko sim hǫpǫn dǫko ṭua̧rena.

Adǫ dosar hilok̕ dǫ cia̧p̕ cia̧p̕ a̧ḍi ba̧ṛicko rak̕ baṛayet̕a. Khange uni toyo dǫ noko hö̃ jǫmko la̧git̕e locor locorok̕ kana; uni eṅga reak̕ a̧ḍi sebele a̧ika̧ukette noko hö̃ jǫm maraokoe mǫnket̕a. Adǫ khangeye hǫć gǫt̕ena; adǫe kuliyet̕koa, Henda bha̧gna̧, cedak̕pe rak̕et̕ kana?

Khange adǫko mǫnket̕a, Hola mahṇḍerre, mamǫ, eṅgańe gǫć ba̧giat̕lea.

Adǫe kuliket̕koa, Okarepe giticа?

Adǫko mǫnket̕a, Ale dǫ pakharele gitić kana.

Adǫ enka kuli baṛakatege uni toyo dǫe calaoena, Adǫ noko sim hǫpǫnko galmarao jǫń kana, Nui toyoge thǫ ya aboren ayo dǫe jǫmkedea; adǫ abo hö̃ jǫmbon la̧git̕e kuli ṭhiket̕bona. Adǫko mǫnket̕a, Teheń dǫ pakhare dǫ babon giticа.

Khange adǫ ona pakhare dǫ holat̕ko, churi binṭhikoko dǫhǫkat̕a. Adǫ ńinda̧yen khan dǫ uni toyo dǫe hǫć gǫt̕ena, adǫ ona pakhageye ha̧tṛa̧u gǫt̕ket̕a. Adǫ khange holat̕ko churikote bhageteye gǫt̕ siro sǫrǫyena. Adǫ hasokede khan a̧ḍiye ãk̕ ũk̕ket̕a. Khange ǫn hilok̕ dǫe rua̧ṛ calaoena.

[5] The Santali word is cia̧p̕ cia̧p̕, onomatopoetic like the English equivalent.

[6] In the Santal folklore the animals make use of artificial relationship, just as the Santals themselves, and address each other accordingly. It is generally the relationship of mother's brother and nephews and nieces of such that is supposed to be established. These relatives are expected, according to the rules of Santal society, to 'honour each other like the Sun'. The bigger or dangerous animal is always the 'uncle'.

[7] In houses with thick mud-walls (probably not originally Santal, but borrowed from the Hindus) small niches are made into the wall, intended for various purposes, such as putting a lamp or small things in.

After a while the hen became drunk; she was continually nodding her head, whilst her chickens were cheeping[5] as much as they could. Still the hen mother did not mind them. The jackal then said: "I shall eat this hen." And when she was lying there drunk, he took her in his mouth, carried her away and ate her. Thus the chickens became orphans.

The day after the chickens were cheeping something awful, and the jackal's mouth was watering to eat these also. The hen had been so savoury that he thought he would eat all these also. So he one day came and asked them: "Look here, nephews and nieces[6], why are you crying?"

"A few days ago, uncle," they replied, "our mother died and left us."

"Where do you sleep?" he asked them.

"We sleep in the wall-niche[7]," they replied.

Having enquired of them in this way the jackal went off. The chickens then had a talk together: "It was this jackal who ate our mother, and now he is making enquiries from us to be able to eat us also," whereupon they said: "We shall not sleep in the wall-niche to-night."

After this talk they put razors[8], knives[9] and carving-knives[10] in the niche. As soon as it had become dark, the jackal came and commenced to grope in the niche with his forelegs, with the result that he cut himself badly on the razors and knives, so that he bled profusely. It pained him and he groaned much. So this time he went away.

---

8 The Santals ordinarily shave; their razors are country-made, small, fixed in a handle. Ancient stone implements, found in the country, are used as hones.

9 Country-made, generally something like kitchen-knives.

10 This implement (b i ṇ ṭ h i) is a curved knife fixed slantingly in a piece of wood at one end, with the edge upwards. A person using it keeps it in position by putting his foot on the wood, the edge being towards the one using it. The biṇṭhi is used for cutting meat and vegetables into bits, and if needed and practicable, also for similar cutting of anything else. It is country-made; now-a-days one may sometimes see such knives entirely made of iron.

Khange arhõ dosar hilok̓ doe heće̜na; arhõ onkageye kuliyet̓koa, Henda bhạgnạ, cedak̓pe rak̓et̓a?

Adoko menket̓a, Hola mahn̩d̩erre, mamo, eṅgań goć bạgiat̓lea.

Adoe menket̓a, Okarepe gitić kana?

Adoko menket̓a, Ale do culhạrele gitić kana.

Ado enka men baṛakatege ać doe ruạṛ calaoena. Ado ạyup̓ khangeye heć got̓ena; ado bako jạpit̓ akat̓teye ruạṛ senena. Ado onko sim do, kathae, culhạre do khubko tiṅgi aṅgra akat̓ tahẽkana; ado ona seṅgel aṅgra do toroćteko topa akat̓ tahẽkana. Ado inạ mit̓ ghạṛi khange uni toyo doe heć got̓ena, ado culhạ duạrreye paṭgaṇḍo got̓ena. Ado laha jaṅgate culhạye ṭamḍao got̓ket̓a; adoe lo got̓en khan do ạḍi garteye gạduć got̓ket̓a. Ado ona seṅgel aṅgra do goṭa lać senteye gạduć rakap̓ got̓ana. Khangeye lo got̓en khan do ạḍi garteye kikiạu got̓ket̓a.

Ado un jokheć khange onko sim hõko landa got̓ket̓a. Onko sim do mit̓tań tumbạre bolokateko gitić kan tahẽkana. Khangeye eset̓ket̓koa; adoe metako kana, Ape do goṭa hoṛmope lo oco akadińa. Ape do mit̓ mit̓teń jom cabapea.

Ado unre onko simko menket̓a, Iạ mamo, ạkhirrem jomlegea; menkhan oṛak̓re do alom jomlea; ente aleren ayo hõ oṛak̓re ma ba

[11] A Santal fire-place is mady of clayish earth. The fire-place is made by women, who all know how to make it; sometimes men may also be seen making it. It is done in the following way: the earth is kneaded or pugged with the feet and formed into a mass some 40 to 50 cm. long, 25 to 30 cm. broad and 20 to 25 cm. high. (The measures given by a Santal woman for a two-holed culhạ are: one cubit long, one span and two fingers broad and one span high). When it becomes somewhat dry, two circular openings are made from above, and the earth is dug out with the hands. The openings are provided with three pommels or knobs; when in use, the cooking-pot rests on these, while there is just room enough beneath to permit of free draft. On the front-side a semicircular opening is made for the fire-wood. The space between the two openings is called the breast (koṛam), i. e., the top side; below the same is the 'stomach' (lać). This is the most common form of culhạ, the two openings enabling the housewife to cook rice and curry at the same time. There are other forms, with one opening, or three or four such, generally made for special purposes.

The next day he came again, and again enquired of the chickens: "Look here, nephews and nieces, why are you crying?"

"A few days ago, uncle," they replied, "our mother died and left us."

"Where do you sleep?" he asked them.

"We sleep in the fire-place[11]," they replied.

When they had talked in this way, he went away. As soon as it became evening, he returned; but as they had not then fallen asleep, he went away again. Now the chickens, people tell, had made a fire and got a lot of live coals, which they covered up with ashes. A short while afterwards the jackal came again and sat down on his haunches in front of the fireplace-opening. Thereupon he put his foreleg into the fire-place, groping about; and when he burnt himself, he withdrew his paw in hurry and haste and at the same time scratched the live embers up over the whole of his stomach. He burnt himself still more and screamed loudly.

When this happened, the chickens commenced to laugh. Now the chickens had entered a gourd[12] and were passing the night there. The jackal then blocked the way for them and said to them: "It is your fault that I have burnt myself all over my body. I shall eat you, every one of you."

The chickens then said: "Look here, uncle, you may eat us afterwards; but please do not eat us here in the house. You

---

12 Santals make, for various purposes, use of the shell of a pumpkin, called h o t o t́, Cucurbita lagenaria, L. There are two kinds, one eatable, much used for curry, another bitter and not fit for eating. These pumpkins have many shapes, some being roundish, others long, like clubs or bottles, and varying in size. Both the eatable and the bitter pumpkins have, when ripe, a shell that hardens like wood. This shell is used for a great many purposes, according to size and form. Of such they make ladles, cups, water-bottles, receptacles of sorts (for mustard-seed, &c.), and so on. They are clean, according to their ideas; water keeps cool in them. These utensils were much more in use formerly than now-a-days, when brass-ware is ousting the old things. The t u m b ạ is mostly used as a water-bottle.

cọm jọmlede; onatele metam kana, ale hõ nọṇḍẹ dọ alom jọmlea. Hana baṛge mucạt́re dhiri cạṭạni menak̕a, ọṇḍẹ idikate jọm marao gọt́kaleme.

Adọ uni toyoe mẹnket́a, Baṅa, bhạgnạ, besgepe metaṅ kana; ọṇḍẹ dọ dhiri cetanre paṭgaṇḍokateṅ jọmpea.

Adọ sạri onka mẹn baṛakate khange ona tumbạ sudhạgeye kuṭuṅ idiket́koa. Adọ ona dhiri ṭhen sẹṭẹrkatege ceka lekate cọe paskao gọt́ket́ khan, ona tumbạ dọ dhirire ạḍi garte ṅurhạ posak̕ gọt́ena. Un jọkhẹn onko sim dọ jọtọko dạṛ baṛa gọt́ket́a, ọntẹ nọtẹ phar phurko uḍạu baṛa gọt́ena.

Khange uni toyo dọe haemoekaṭena, ọntẹ nọtẹye kọyọk̕ gọt́kat́koa. Adọ latar utạrre mit́ṭaṅe tahẽkana; uni dọ jọtọkoteko ić ṭhẹkọm akade tahẽkante bae uḍạu daṛeat́a. Adọ uni toyoe mẹnket́a, Acha, iṅ jọm mọtọ dọ Candoe deao akawadiṅgea; onko dọ bẹhọkko tahẽkana, onate onko dọe dạṛ ocoket́koa; nitege iṅ mọtọ dọṅ besok̕a.

Adọ uni sime mẹnket́a, Ạkhirem jọmeṅgea; nonka ić salak̕ dọ cet́ lekatem jọmeṅa? Ạrup̕ saphaliṅme, adọ jọmeṅme.

Adọ uni toyoe mẹnket́a, Acha, ẹṇḍẹkhan ạrup̕kategeṅ jọmmea.

Adọ khange sạriye ạrup̕kedea. Adọ arhõ uni sime mẹnket́a, Iạ mamọ, ạkhirem jọmeṅgea; thoṛa hawẹt́ ṅõk̕ ocoạṅme; mit́ ghạṛiṅ rọhọṛ ṅõk̕lenge.

Adọ uni toyoe mẹnket́a, Baṅa, rọhọṛlen khan dọ nãhãk̕em dạṛa.

Adọ uni sime mẹnket́a, Baṅa, mamọ, judi unạk̕em ọbiswạsok̕ kan khać, ẹṇḍẹkhan amak̕ luṭire baṛẹ rọhọṛkạṅme, ar iṅ rọhọṛlen khan iṅtegeṅ metama, ma cahabme mẹnte.

Adọ sạri uni simak̕ kathageye aṅjọmket́a; adọ sạri aćak̕ luṭiregeye ap̕kadea. Adọ khube rọhọṛen khane metae kana, Ma cahabme, rọhọṛenaṅ.

---

[13] The house-field, in Santali baṛge, the field on which the Santals have their houses, used for Indian corn and cold-weather crops.

[14] This and several other things mentioned give a local colouring. Large flat rocks belong to the Santal country and the hilly regions.

[15] Cf. p. 68, note 11.

see, you did not eat our mother either here in the house. Therefore we tell you, don't eat us here either. Over there at the other end of the house-field[13] there is a large flat rock[14]; take us there and eat us all there".

"Quite so, nephews and nieces," the jackal replied, "that is a good proposal; there on that large flat rock I shall sit down comfortably and eat you."

Having spoken in this way he really took the gourd up and carried it off with the chickens. When he reached the stone, he somehow or other let the whole slip down; the gourd fell with a loud crash and was broken into pieces. As the opportunity offered itself, the chickens all of them got off in a hurry, flying, flapping and fluttering hither and thither.

The jackal became stiff like wood from astonishment; he looked for them in all directions. Now there was one chicken underneath all the rest; all of them had dropped on this one and plastered it up, so he could not fly. "Very well," the jackal then said, "the needful food for me Chando[15] has stood surety for; those other ones were unrighteous ones; therefore he made them run away. Now I shall do myself very well."

Then the chicken said: "To be sure you will eat me afterwards; but how can you eat me in such a dirty state? Wash me clean first and then eat me."

"All right," the jackal said; "I shall eat you after having washed you."

So he really washed the chicken. Then this one again said to him: "I say, uncle, to be sure you will eat me afterwards; let me get a little dry. Let me first dry myself a little."

"Not so," the jackal replied, "if you get dry, you will run away."

"Not at all, uncle," the chicken said; "if you have so little faith in me, please dry me on your lip; then when I get dry, I shall myself tell you to open your mouth."

Truth to tell, the jackal listened to what the chicken said and perched it on his lip. When the chicken had become quite dry, it said to him: "Please open your mouth wide; I am dry."

Khange adoe cahaṗ ocokedea, adọ mocareye ić gọťadea, adoe uḍạu gọťena. Uḍạue uḍạuena sẹ, ạḍi sạṅgiṅre miťṭaṅ bunum danaṅreye tạpuǩ gọťena.

Adọ uni toyo dọ ićtẹťko mẹlọť baṛakeťteye calaoena ona bunum ṭhen, adọ beṛhae bunume oyoṅ ạcureťa. Adọ miť sẹćre ti bọlọǩ in maraṅ gan bunum bhugạǩe ńamkeťa, adoe mẹnkeťa, Dhora noa bhugạǩregeye bọlọ akana. Adọ cur mar ona bhugạǩgeye soǩeťa; adọ ona hõ bae soǩ tioǩ daṛeaǩ kana. Adọ khange jaṅgateye raboṛ gelaǩ kana; ghanẹ dọ mocate hõe gẹr chaḍao gelaǩ kana. Adọ oka lekate hõ bae daṛeaǩ kana, enre hõ bae bạgiaǩ kana. Ar uni sim dọ tãhã oka sẹn coe calaoen.

Adọ uni toyoe mẹnkeťa, Bhalare, sim, mocare ić oṭokatem dạṛ akaťa; am dọ ạurilaṅ jọmme dhạbić dọ balaṅ bạgiam kana. Adọ bae tioǩ daṛeae khane mẹnkeťa, Iạ simge, tin hạbićem bọlọkoǩa? Bhalalaṅ ńẹlmea; bhugạǩ iń duṛuṗ ẹsẹda; amtege nãhãǩem ghul ghulạu gọć aḍoǩa.

Adọ sạri onka mẹnkate ona bhugạǩ doe duṛuṗ ẹsẹťkeťa. Adọ, kathae, tin hạbić cọṅ ọṇḍẹgeye duṛuṗen khan bhuku dọ gọṭa liṇḍhiko jọm khalkedea. Adoe duṛuṗ ạṛisen khan dọ rẹṅgẹćkedea. Adoe bereťen khan doe mẹnkeťa, Amar muher mas gẹlọ; nahakgeń duṛuṗ akana; nui sim dọ ạḍiye ẹṛẹkidińa. Unre baṛẹń jọmle khaṅ dọń beskea; nahakge moca reaǩ jel iń paskaokeťa.

[16] The termites or white ants are met with everywhere; the ant-hills are fairly frequent in the jungle and elsewhere, varying in size from below one up to two or three meters in height and correspondingly large in circumference. The ant-hills seen in this country are generally dark brown in colour (they consist of earth brought up from underneath by the termites and have consequently the same colour as the earth); in shape they are like miniature hills with peaks and pinnacles and steep, often nearly perpendicular 'ravines' or sides. Small holes may be found here and there; whether they are made by the termites or by animals, I cannot say. The ground below such a hill is correspondingly 'excavated' with passages, galleries and termites' nests.

As soon as it, in this way, had made the jackal gape, it eased itself in his mouth, and then at once flew away. It flew, oh, how it flew; far, far away, behind a white-ant hill[16], it alighted on the ground.

The jackal again and again put his tongue out to get the dirt off, whereupon he went to that white-ant hill and looked everywhere round it. Ultimately he found a hole in the ant-hill, about big enough for a hand to get in; he said: "Undoubtedly, it has entered this hole." Then he commenced vigorously to thrust his paw into that hole; but he was not able to reach the bottom of it. Then he tried to scratch the earth away with his foot; now and then he also tried to bite the earth away with his teeth. He was not able to manage it in any way; still he did not leave off. And as for the chicken, it went who knows where in the meantime.

Ultimately the jackal said: "Well and good, chicken, you have run away after having eased yourself in my mouth; we two[17] shall not leave you alone until we have eaten you." And as he was unable to reach it, he said: "You unspeakable chicken, how long are you remaining in there? Well, we two shall have a look at you; I shall sit and block the hole up; presently you will be choked and die by your own doing, you rascal."

Truth to tell, when he had said this, he sat down over the hole and blocked it up. Then when he had been sitting there for who knows how long, the white ants ate the skin off the whole of his hind-quarters. Ultimately he became tired of sitting and felt hungry. Getting up he said: "Das Fleisch meines Maules ist verloren gegangen[18]; I have been sitting here in vain; this chicken has cheated me badly. If I had only eaten it at that time, I should have done well; to no purpose I have let meat in my mouth slip away."

17 Inclusive dual used in threatening language.

18 The jackal makes use of Bengali.

Adọ siṭhạl miṭhạl bereťente bạihạṛ sẹn hako kaṭkọm sendrae bereť calaoena. Khange adọ miťṭaṅ buḍhi hakoe sasap̣ kane ńamkedea; adọe metae kana, Ẹ buḍhi, iń hõ hako sap̣ ocoańme.

Adọ uni buḍhiye mẹnkeťa, Arẹć harọn akanaṅ, ọhọń sap̣ ocolema. Am dọ kichum arẹćlaǩa?

Adọ uni toyoe mẹnkeťa, Ho, iạ buḍhige, bam sap̣ ocoań khan dọlaṅ gẹr aḍomea.

Adọ uni buḍhiye mẹnkeťa, Baṅa, sap̣ ocoamgeań, alom gẹreńa. Dela hijuǩme! Bana họrtelaṅ sap̣ hạṭińkoa.

Khange uni toyoe ằṛgoyena, adọkin sap̣eťkoa. Adọ uni buḍhiye mẹneťa, Ma am hõ leoḍaeme, umjhạukoalaṅ. Adọ uni toyo hõe leoḍayeťa, khẹṇṭẹ pẹṛẹ khẹṇṭẹ pẹṛẹye dọneťa. Adọ khange miťṭaṅ puṭhiye ńam gọťkedea, adọe jọm gọťkedea. Adọ uni buḍhi dọ ghuṭuteye rakap̣ena. Adọ arhõ onka khẹṇṭẹ pẹṛẹ khẹṇṭẹ pẹṛẹye leoḍa gọťkeťa. Adọ uniye jọmlede puṭhi hakoge, kathae, liṇḍhi sẹn khone parọm gọťena. Adọ arhõ inigeye ńam gọťkedea.

Adọ uni toyoe mẹn gọťkeťa, Henda buḍhi, ceť leka bam sap̣keťko? Ẹkṭi khaelọm ẹkṭi paelọm.

Adọ uni buḍhiye mẹnkeťa, Inige cọṅ ghạṛi ghạṛim sabe kan.

19 The Santali word b ạ i h ạ ṛ is the name for the low-lying rice-fields, during the rainy season always more or less full of water. It is their best rice-land.

20 Tiny fish, crabs, and so on, are to be found in these rice-fields, when the rains have lasted for some time. They are in the autumn caught by the Santals in a kind of fish-trap called ṭọrọḍaṅ, put in an opening made in the earth-ridge on the lower side of the field, through which superfluous water is let out. The jackals are said to feed on fish, crabs, grasshoppers, and so on.

21 B u ḍ h i, old woman, is quite proper when speaking of an old lady, but in addressing it is somewhat disrespectful. When not having any relationship, natural or artificial, with a woman, such a one older than oneself is generally addressed as 'mother', g ọ or a y o.

22 The locality in which the woman is catching fish seems to be some place outside, below or between the rice-fields, where there is water standing. In such places the Santals may catch fish in the way described. The water is first baled out sufficiently to make it possible to reach the bottom with one's hand. People then go into the water, moving about to stir up the mud.

He got up rather down in the mouth and went towards the low-lying rice-fields[19] to hunt for fish and crabs[20]. Then he met an old woman who was catching fish and said to her: "You old woman[21], let me also catch fish."

"I have had no end of trouble baling out the water[22]," the old woman replied, "I am not going to let you catch fish. Did you perhaps bale out the least part?"

"Oh," the jackal said, "you rotten old woman, if you don't let me catch any, we two shall bite you."

"No, no," the old woman said, "I shall let you catch; don't bite me. Please come! Let us both catch fish and divide them between us."

Thereupon the jackal came down, and they were both catching fish. The old woman was saying: "Now you also stir up the water and make it muddy; we shall make them exhausted[23]." Thereupon the jackal also stirred up the water and made it muddy; he was floundering and plunging, jumping about. So he caught a small carp[24] and ate it at once. Then the old woman went up to the high ground near by. But the jackal kept on floundering and plunging and making the water muddy. Now, people tell, the carp he had eaten came out of him behind; again he caught this and ate it.

"Look here, old woman," the jackal then called out, "how was it you did not catch any? Wie ich einen gegessen habe, hab' ich einen gefangen[25]."

"It is the same one, don't you see," the old woman said, "that you are catching again and again."

The fish becomes tired and 'confused' in the generally fairly tepid water, and is easily caught with the hand. I have seen this done, and have always thought that fish of a northern climate would not be caught in such an undignified way.

23 See preceding note.

24 The fish mentioned, in Santali p u ṭ h i, said to be the small fry of what is called p o ṭ h a when fullgrown, is a tiny thing, a few inches long.

25 The jackal again makes use of Bengali.

Adọ uniye mẹnkeťa, Baṅa, buḍhi, etaǩkogeń ńameťkoa.

Adọ uni buḍhiye mẹnkeťa, Baṅ, ini kangeae, liṇḍhi tapaṗge tamte inigeye parọm gọdoǩ kana. Bam pạtiạuǩ kan khać, ma nāhāǩ carẹć gutu cinhạwaeme ar jọmeme; ńẹlam nāhāǩ, inigeye parọm gọdoǩa.

Adọ sạri buḍhiaǩ katha lekage carẹće gutuadea, are jọm họťkedea. Adọ arhō̱ onka khẹṇṭẹ pẹrẹye leoḍayeť tahẹ̄kan jọkhẹnge uni puṭhi hako dọe parọm gọťena. Adọe ńẹlkede do, carẹć menaǩtae. Adọ liṇḍhiye tunumlen dọe ạikạukeť, liṇḍhi dọ bhugạǩgetae. Adọe mẹnkeťa, Henda buḍhi, ọkọe ẹsẹdtińa?

Adọ uni buḍhiye metadea, Muci ṭhen calaǩme; uniye daṗkatama.

Adọ toyoe mẹnkeťa, Acha, ẹṇḍẹkhan uni ṭhengeń calaǩa.

Adọ muci ṭhene calaoena; adọe metae kana, E̱ muci, ma liṇḍhi daṗkatińme; miťṭań sim iń ạguama. Adọ sạriye daṗkaťtaea, ar miť aṛere ṭiạle dọhọadea; adọ onate calaǩ jọkhẹn dọ dal calaǩa, adọ ṭẹpẹr ṭẹpẹr saḍe idiǩa. Adọ khange ạḍiye khusiyena. Khange adọ miťṭań sime saṗ idiadea.

Adọ inạ miť ghạṛi tayọm khange uni toyo dọ ṭạṇḍitejoṅ osorkedea, adọ bae lẹṭẹć daṛeaǩ kan khange muci ṭhen arhō̱e ńir calaoena; adọe metae kana, Iạ muci, bań ić daṛeaǩ kan dọ, liṇḍhi dọ cedaǩ bam dọhọadińa?

Adọ muciye mẹnkeťa, Do kamar ṭhen calaǩme, unige nāhāǩ liṇḍhi dọe balkatama.

26 The 'shoemaker', muchi, is the name of a low Hindu caste, working in leather, found here and there in the Santal country.

27 In most Santal villages there are blacksmiths, called k a m a r. If the village is large enough, one kamar is kept; if it is small, two or three villages may have one together. The kamar's, work is to make and repair all iron implements used by the villagers, the iron being paid for in money, but all work done, in kind, e. g., 30 seers paddy yearly for each plough a man has. The kamar is a kind of Hindu; some of them also work in other metals than iron.

28 Although a kind of drill may be seen used by the country carpenters (they have not augers and gimlets except imported ones); the most common way of

"Not at all, old woman," the jackal replied, "I am catching different ones."

"No," the old woman said, "it is the same one; there is a gap in your hind-quarters; therefore this same one comes through. If you don't believe it, just put a straw through the carp and mark it, and eat it; you will see presently, it is the same that will come through."

In accordance with the old woman's advice he put a straw through the fish and ate it. Whilst he was floundering and plunging again to make the water muddy, the carp passed through. He looked at it and saw that the carp had the straw. Then he felt his buttocks with his paw: he had a gap there behind. "Look here, old woman," he said, "who will be able to close this up for me?"

"Go to the shoemaker[26]," the old woman replied; "he will cover it for you."

"Very well," the jackal said, "then I shall go to him."

Thereupon he went to the shoemaker and said to him: "Shoemaker, please cover my buttocks; I shall fetch you a fowl for it." And really and truly, he put a patch on for him, and on one side he fringed it for him, so when he was walking, it was flapping and making a rattling rustling sound as he went along. He felt very pleased at this; thereupon he caught a fowl and took it to the shoemaker.

A short while after this the jackal felt a call to stool, and as he was unable to manage, he again ran back to the shoemaker and said to him: "I say, shoemaker, I am unable to answer the call of nature; why did you not put an opening for that purpose for me?"

The shoemaker replied: "Do go to the blacksmith[27]; he will presently make you an opening for that purpose with a red-hot iron[28]."

making a hole in wood or in leather is to make use of a red-hot iron of the required size. It might be noted that they make use of the same also to open a boil. A blacksmith is naturally the nearest one to help the jackal.

Ado̱ sa̦ri kamar t̤hene calaoena, ado̱e metae kana, E̱ ho kamar, ma linḍhi bal bhuga̦k̕katiṅme, mit̕t̤aṅ sim iṅ a̦guama.

Ado̱ uni kamare me̱nket̕a, Do e̱ṇḍe̱khan a̦gu maṛaṅaṅme, e̱ṇḍe̱khan iṅ balmea; ar baṅkhan do̱ o̱ho̱ṅ ballema. O̱ko̱e baḍae, a̦gua̦ṅ co̱m baṅ co̱ṅ; toyo do̱ a̦ḍipe e̱k̕ṛe̱gea. A̦gu maṛaṅlem, e̱ṇḍe̱khan iṅ balmea; ar baṅkhan do̱ o̱ho̱ṅ ballema.

Khange sa̦riye calaoena, ado̱ ina̦ mit̕ gha̦ṛi khange oka khon co̱ṅ sa̦ri mit̕t̤aṅ maraṅ uta̦r gaya sime ge̱r a̦gu go̱t̕kedea, ado̱e metae kana, Nũk̕ũi ṅe̱leme iṅ a̦guat̕mea; ma bal ho̱deṅme. Am do̱ mit̕t̤aṅ toyoe pha̦sia̦rayentem me̱net̕a, je toyo do̱ sanamko pha̦sia̦ragea me̱nte. Iṅ do̱ ba̦ṅ e̱k̕ṛe̱a, se̱ ado̱m ado̱mko do̱ bale e̱k̕ṛe̱a.

Khange sa̦ri sime hataokedea, ado̱ t̤a̦ku dhipa̦ukate ḍe̱ke̱ye bal bhuga̦k̕ go̱t̕kede khan |got̤a koṛam se̱nteye ciḍir go̱t̕adeteye da̦ṛ uta̦rket̕a; ado̱ ghuriã̦ bae rua̦ṛlena.

Ado̱ tahe̱n tahe̱nte, kathae, tin din badre co̱ṅ ado̱ uni toyo do̱ mit̕t̤aṅ atote sim jo̱me calak̕ kan; ado̱ ona t̤ia̦lte dal calak̕ kana, ado̱ t̤e̱pe̱r t̤e̱pe̱r sa̦ḍe idik̕ kana. Ado̱ a̦ḍi ra̦ska̦i a̦ika̦uket̕ khan do̱, sereṅe disa̦ go̱t̕ket̕a. Ado̱e sereṅ idiyet̕a:

Ne̱te̱ do̱ jo̱jo̱m Tuṛuk darako kan,
Ne̱te̱ do̱ Koeṇḍa rapajko!

Me̱n yoe, da̦ṛjoṅpe, baṅkhanko suma̦r akat̕pea!

---

29 It is very common with Santals to castrate cocks; they perform the operation themselves.

30 The Santals have hand-spindles of sorts, smaller and larger, according to the thickness of the thread or twine to be spun. They consist of a rod, to the lower end of which a small 'wheel' or two cross-bits of a rod are fixed. The smaller hand-spindle, used for spinning yarn, has a rod of iron; this is called t̤a̦ku (like here); the same name is also given to the iron rod on which the yarn is wound in a spinning-wheel.

31 The Musalman, or Mogul, cavalry (in Santali called tuṛuk) is still remembered by the Santals as cruel, depredatory bands. Mentioned together with these are the Koeṇḍa kings. The traditions of the Santals tell that whilst their ancestors were living in a country called Champa (possibly a part of the Chota Nagpur plateau) the Kisku sept were 'kings'; they had a gaṛ, a fort of some kind, called Koeṇḍa. It must be these who are here referred to; it seems

Thereupon the jackal, truth to tell, went to the blacksmith, and said to him: "I say, blacksmith, please burn a hole for me with an iron in my hind-quarters; I shall fetch you a fowl for it."

"Well then," the blacksmith replied, "bring me the fowl first, then I shall burn a hole for you; otherwise I am certainly not going to do it for you. Who knows whether you will bring me any or not; you jackals are awful cheaters. Bring me the fowl first, then I shall make you a hole with a red-hot iron; and if not, I am certainly not going to do it."

Then, truth to tell, the jackal went, and in a moment from somewhere he really came with a tremendously large capon[29] in his mouth, and said to the blacksmith: "Here, look at this one I have brought you. Now be quick and make an opening for me. Because one jackal has been a cheat, you think that all jackals are cheats. As for me, I don't deceive, or, some of us do not deceive people."

The blacksmith then really accepted the fowl, whereupon he made a spindle-rod[30] red-hot, and with this he pierced the jackal's hind-quarters; when he did this, the jackal purged and squirted all over the breast of the blacksmith; thereupon he ran off and did not return there anymore.

Now as time passed, it once happened, who knows how long a time afterwards, that this jackal was going to a village to catch fowls; those fringes were flapping when he moved, and it was making a rattling rustling sound, as he went along. As he felt very pleased, he suddenly remembered a song, and commenced to sing, as he passed along:

"Here the devouring Mogul cavalry[31] are coming,
Here the Koenda kings!"

"Beware[32], look out, run away; else they will utterly destroy you!"

---

strange that the old Santal 'kings' and the Musalman cavalry should be paired together.

32 This does not apparently belong to the 'song', but is a warning shout.

Khange ona atoren hoṛ do̱ onkako aṅjo̱mket́ khan do̱ mit́ mit́teko dạṛket́a. Ado̱ uni toyo do̱ se̱nkate ona atoren sim do̱ cur mare laga sap̔et́koa are jo̱met́koa. Ado̱e jo̱m biyen khane calaoena. Khange onko hoṛ hõ arhõko ruạṛ he̱ćena.

Khange uni toyo do̱ arhõ dosar hilok̔ do̱ ona atotege sim jo̱me calak̔ kana; ado̱ o̱ne̱ pạhile sereṅlet́ lekageye sereń idiyet́a. Khange ona atoren hoṛ do̱ arhõko dạṛket́a. Ado̱ mit́ṭaṅ buḍhi do̱ bae dạṛ daṛeat́a; ado̱e me̱nket́a, Iń do̱ o̱ho̱ń dạṛlea; iń do̱ko go̱ć ataringe. Ado̱ onka me̱nkate uni buḍhi do̱ bae dạṛlet́a, mit́ṭaṅ sukri bãṛãreye bo̱lo̱ okoyena.

Ado̱ uni toyo do̱ ona atore se̱nkate onko sim do̱ lagae lagayet́koa se̱, cure mare lagayet́koa; hapṛak̔koge bachao bachaoteye lagayet́koa. Ado̱ mit́ṭaṅ sạṇḍi do̱ lagae lagakedea se̱, e̱kkalte uni buḍhiye oko akan ṭhengeye laga idi go̱t́kedea. Ado̱ uni sim do̱e paro̱m go̱t́ena. Ado̱ uni toyo do̱ uni buḍhiye ńe̱l ńam go̱t́kedea. Ado̱ uni toyo do̱ buḍhiye metae kana, Ma buḍhi, sim sap̔ạńme; baṅkhan do̱ nãhãk̔ ḍaṭamelaṅ ko̱ṭe̱ć ńũrtama.

Ado̱ uni buḍhi do̱e me̱net́a, Ma, amte baṛe̱ sap̔ jo̱ńme; iń do̱ o̱ho̱ń sap̔ daṛelekoa. Khange ado̱ bae re̱be̱nlen khan, aćtegeye laga sap̔ket́koteye jo̱m biyena. Ado̱ uni buḍhi ṭhene calaoena, ado̱e metae kana, E̱ buḍhi, sim bam sap̔ akawadińa; nitok̔ do̱laṅ ńam akat́mea. E̱ buḍhi, mase̱ me̱nme — Toyo! Ado̱ uni buḍhi hõe me̱nket́a, Toyo!

Khange guṛgute jo̱to̱ ḍaṭae ko̱ṭe̱ć ńũrket́taea. Ado̱ arhõe metae kana, E̱ buḍhi, mase̱ me̱nme, — Toyo! Ado̱ uni buḍhi Toyo me̱nae me̱nlet́a, ado̱ ḍaṭae ńũrket́taete toyo do̱ bae pusṭạulet́a; ado̱e me̱n

[33] The Santals keep pigs; there is no curry they enjoy like that prepared from pig's meat. In appearance the Santal pig very much resembles his wild namesake. As a rule the Santals build a small sty for their pigs at one side of the court-yard, often a little out of sight, a small house, some 2 m. long and 1,50 m. broad, with a thatched roof. At one end there is an entrance that may be shut by means of a few bits of wood hanging down from a cross-bar fixed at the top of the opening. Only a small person would be able to enter such a place.

When the inhabitants of that village heard this, they ran away, every one of them. Hereupon the jackal went, and briskly chasing and catching the fowls in the village he ate them. When he had had his fill, he went away, whereupon the villagers returned.

Now the jackal also the following day went to this village to eat fowls, and whilst passing along he was singing the same song as the first time. Then the inhabitants of the village again ran away. But there was an old woman who did not run away; she said: "I am not running away; they may kill me and do away with me, the rascals." Speaking in this way the old woman did not run away; she entered a pigsty[33] and hid there.

When the jackal reached the village, he chased the fowls for all he was worth, chased and chased, all over; selecting the big ones he chased these. There was a cock he was chasing and chasing; he chased it straight to where the old woman was hiding. The cock passed in there, and the jackal at once caught sight of the old woman. The jackal then said to the old woman: "Hey, old woman, catch the fowl for me; if not, we two shall presently knock your teeth out for you."

"Catch them yourself," the old woman replied, "I am utterly unable to catch them." As she was unwilling, the jackal himself chased and caught fowls and ate until he was satisfied. Thereupon he went to the old woman and said to her: "Old woman, you did not catch any fowls for me; now we have found you, we two. Old woman, say t o y o!" The old woman also said t o y o.

The jackal then with a spice-roller[34] knocked all her teeth out. Then he again said to her: "Old woman, say t o y o." Now the old woman meant to say t o y o; but as he had knocked

[34] As the curry is always prepared with spices of sorts, a spice-roller is a necessary implement in every Santal household. It is a cylindrical stone of a not very large size, called g u ṛ g u. The spices are ground with this; it is also used for other purposes, to crush with; in this case one of the ends is used as a hammer.

go̱ťkeťa, Hoyo! Ado̱ onka bae pusṭạuleť khan, uni toyo do̱ ạḍiye rạskạyena. Arhõe metae kana, Mase̱ buḍhi, toyo me̱nme. Ado̱e me̱nkeťa, Hoyo! Ado̱ uni toyo do̱ landa landatege oka se̱n co̱e calaoen.

Ado̱ ạyuṕ khange onko dạrleť ho̱ṛ do̱ko ruạṛ he̱ćena. Ado̱ unre onko ho̱ṛ uni buḍhiye lạiako kana, Jo̱jo̱m Tuṛuk nạ̃hīko chạ̃i kana, hoyo koṛa kanae! Sanam sime jo̱meťko do̱ bań? Iń hõ̱ sim sasaṕe metadińa; ado̱ bạń saṕadete nõ̱k̃õe ńe̱lpe, jo̱to̱ ḍaṭae ko̱ṭe̱ć ńũr akaťtińa.

Khange ado̱ sanam ho̱ṛko me̱nkeťa, Gapa do̱ babon dạṛa, oṛaǩregebo sić po̱ṭo̱m hataṛkoǩa, ado̱bo dal go̱jea.

Ado̱ miť ho̱ṛe me̱nkeťa, Bańa, onkate do̱ o̱ho̱bon go̱ć daṛelea. Ińiń metabon kana, nui buḍhi lekage miťṭań siteťren ho̱ṛbo benaoea. Ado̱ hana kulhi mucạťrebo idikaea, ar o̱ṇḍe̱ duṛuṕkate ti do̱bo lap lapakataea; ado̱ nãhãǩ uni buḍhiye ruhedea, ado̱ unregebo so̱nto̱ṛ go̱doǩa. Ado̱ sanam ho̱ṛko me̱nkeťa, Bańa, ṭhikgem me̱nkeťtabona; mabon onkaegea.

Ado̱ sạri sanam ho̱ṛ ṭhenaǩ sitạťko jaorakeťa, ado̱ ona ńindạ bhitạrtegeko benao go̱ťkedea. Ado̱ setaǩ khange kulhi mucạťteko idikadea, ar ako do̱ kạpiko, aǩ sarko, ṭe̱ńgo̱ćko, ṭheńgako, onka apan ạpinko hạthiạu akawana; ado̱ onka so̱nto̱rge menaǩkoa.

Ado̱ uni toyo do̱ jo̱m hewa se̱ bań? Ado̱ inạ miť ghạṛi khangeko ańjo̱m go̱ťkedea, bańma, ḍahar ḍaharteye sereń ạguyeťa. Onkage pahil lekae sereńeťa, ar bin bo̱to̱re hijuǩ kana. Ado̱ noko ato ho̱ṛ do̱ so̱nto̱rkateko sić po̱ṭo̱m baṛa akana. Khange uni toyo do̱

---

35 The Santali word for 'jackal' is toyo. They have good ears and enjoy faulty pronunciation of their own language. There are many stories among them, immensely relished, of how foreigners have mispronounced their language. They also have a few stories, the points of which are to tell how Santals have, through false pronunciation, said something very different from what they intended to say.

36 Wax may be found with Santals, although not likely in such quantities as here presupposed. Many kinds of wild bees are found in their country, and the wax is taken from the honeycombs. The Santals use wax for waxing thread; a Hindu caste living in the country use wax for their work as brass-founders.

all her teeth out, she did not pronounce it clearly, and said hoyo[35]. Then, as she was unable to pronounce it clearly, the jackal felt very pleased. Again he said to her: "Old woman, say toyo!" And she said: Hoyo. Thereupon the jackal went away to who knows where, laughing as he went along.

In the evening all those who had run away came back, and the old woman said to them: "Devouring Mogul cavalry! Just so! no, nothing of the kind; it is a jackal fellow! He is eating all the fowls, don't you see? Me he also ordered to catch fowls, and as I did not catch any for him, look here at me, he has knocked all my teeth out."

Then all of them said: "To-morrow we shall not run away; we shall shut ourselves up in our houses, and then we shall beat him to death."

But one of them said: "No, not so; in such a way we shall never be able to kill him. I have a suggestion: let us make a woman of wax looking like this old woman, and take her to the end of the village street over there; there we shall place the wax-woman in a sitting position and make her arms stand out; then he will commence scolding the old woman; at that moment we shall keep ourselves ready." And all of them said: "Quite so, you have made an excellent proposal; let us act accordingly."

Thereupon they, truth to tell, collected all the wax[36] found with them, and spent the night preparing the wax-woman. When it became morning, they took her to the end of the village street, whilst they themselves got hold of battle-axes[37], bows and arrows, axes, sticks, and the like, each of them; in this way they kept themselves ready.

Now the jackal had acquired the habit of eating, as you know. A short while afterwards they heard him, he was coming along the road singing. He was singing just like previously and was coming along without fear. The village people kept themselves ready, having shut themselves up in their houses. When the jackal reached the end of the village street, he caught sight of

kulhi mucạt́reye sẹṭẹren khan dọ uni sitet́ren buḍhiye ńẹlkede tiye lap lapa akat́. Adọe ruhet́ gọt́kedea, Mẹn buḍhi, ọcọk̕anme! Cedak̕em ẹsẹt́ akadińa? Holanok̕ ḍaṭań kọṭẹć ńũrlet́tam dọ bam bọṭọrok̕ kana? Mẹn, họr aṛak̕ họt́ańme, bańkhan nãhãk̕lań thạyạ bit́ gọt́mea.

Adọ bae ọcọk̕ kante sạriye thạyạ gọt́kedea. Adọ sạri ona sitet́rege jańga dọ laṭha ṭarhaoentaea. Adọ uni toyoe mẹnet́a, Mẹn buḍhi, aṛak̕kańme! Ayoge, nui buḍhi dọ jańgae saṗkidiń dọ. Iạ buḍhige, bam aṛagiń khan nãhãk̕lań ceṭak̕ gọt́mea.

Adọ sạri onka ruhet́ ruhet́te bae chaḍao daṛeat́ khane ceṭak̕ gọt́kedea. Adọ ona ti hõ laṭkaoentaea. Adọ uni toyoe mẹnet́a, Ayoge, nui buḍhi dọ ti hõ yae saṗkidiń dọ. Adọ nhoa titeye ceṭak̕lede dọ, ona hõ laṭkaoentae. Adọ jọtọ laṭkaoentae khangeye metae kana, Ayoge, iạ buḍhi, jọtọ ti jańgae saṗkidiń dọ! Mẹn buḍhi, aṛak̕kańme, bańkhan nãhãk̕lań gẹr aḍomea.

Adọ sạri bae paskao daṛeat́ khan dọ bae gẹr gọt́kedete? Adọe gẹrkede khan, ḍaṭa hõ ona sitet́rege laṭha ṭarhaoentaea; adọ rọṛ hõ bae rọṛ daṛeat́a. Adọ ọṇḍẹgeye laṭ paṭao bindạṛena.

Adọ ḍher hạbić hoeyen khan, onko ato họṛko mẹnket́a, Henda ya, enanre hijuk̕ lekabo ạikạuledea; adọe oka sẹćena? Bae ạikạuk̕ kan dọ. Adọ oḍokkate ọntẹ nọṭẹko bẹńgẹt́ baṛayet́a. Adọ khange kulhi mucạt́ sẹnre kha khọk̕ kan bańko ańjọm gọt́kedea? Adọko mẹnket́a, Ọtẹ ya, ọntẹre menaea. Adọ sẹn ńõk̕kateko ńẹlkede dọ, uni sitet́ren buḍhi ṭhene bindạṛ akan. Khange adọ ńir sẹnkate kạpiteko mak̕ gọć gọt́kedea, ar ṭhẹńgakote hõ bogeteko dalkedea luṭhum luṭhum.

Adọ cabayena uni toyo reak̕ katha dọ; ẹṇḍẹgeko mọhọr meṭaokedea.

37 The old battle-axes (of various shapes) are still found in Santal houses, and also manufactured by the above mentioned kamars. They are now used exclusively in sacrifice, and even there they are gradually disappearing.

38 A commonly used ejaculation, signifying astonishment, horror, pain, resentment.

the wax-woman, with arms stretched out, and he commenced scolding: "Have a care, old woman! get out of the way for me! Why have you blocked the road for me? Yesterday I knocked your teeth out, are you not afraid? Beware, get out of my way; if not, we two shall presently kick you and fix you in no time."

As she did not get out of his way, he really gave her a kick. Then, truth to tell, his foot stuck in the wax and was fixed there. The jackal then said: "Take care, old woman, let me go! Oh mother[38], this old woman has caught hold of me. You unspeakable old woman, if you don't let me go, I shall give you a slap now."

And truth to tell, as the jackal could not free himself by scolding in this way, he gave her a slap. Then his paw also stuck, and the jackal said: "Oh mother, this old woman has caught hold of my hand." And as he slapped her with his other paw, that also stuck. And when all his feet had stuck, he said to her: "Oh mother, this unspeakable old woman, she has caught hold of all my hands and feet! Take care, old woman, let me go; otherwise we two shall bite you presently."

And truth to tell, as he was unable to escape, did he not bite her? And when he bit her, his teeth also stuck fast in the wax; then he was not able to speak either. So he fell down there on that spot exhausted.

When a considerable time had passed, the villagers said: "Look here, some time ago we thought that he was coming; then what has become of him? Nothing can be heard any longer." They thereupon went out and looked in all directions; then did they not hear him puffing and panting somewhere at the end of the village street? So they said: "Listen, he is over there in that direction!" Going a little distance they caught sight of him, fallen down beside the wax-woman. So they ran up to him and killed him with a battle-axe, they also struck him blow after blow with sticks, thud upon thud.

Now there the story of the jackal is ended; then and there they utterly finished him.

13. Toyo ar sim hoponko reak katha.

Sedae jugre, kathae, mittań toyo ar sim phulkin pataoketa; ạḍi baṛić unkin dokin gateyena. Ado tahen tahente mit din dokin menketa, Ią phul, alań do ạḍilań gateyena, adolań nẽ-pẽotaka.

Ado sime menketa, Acha bogege, enḍekhanlań nẽpẽotaka.

Ado toyoe menketa, Acha, enḍekhan am jom lạgit iń kulạu julạua, ar am hõ iń jom lạgit kulạu julạume; ar bana hoṛ hạnḍilań dohoea.

Ado sạri onkakin cepeteńte bana hoṛge hạnḍikin dohoketa. Sim do hoṛo, jonḍra, bajṛa, janhe, se okako aće jom, onako

---

[1] This story has many points in common with the preceding one, but is in certain ways essentially different. The jackal is the false friend and the villain; he eats his friend the hen and wants to eat her chickens. In the first story the chickens escape, and the jackal comes to grief, after a good many eventful happenings. Here the chickens take action, engage the help of an egg, a pestle and a mortar, and manage to kill the villain, and end by eating his brain in revenge.

[2] To give parties, or to entertain, except on special occasions such as marriages, certain family gatherings, and similar functions, is not common, but not unknown. To invite friends to drink beer, when such is brewed, is common. 'Flowers', like the two ones here mentioned, entertain each other; this is customary.

[3] The beer manufacture here described is, as will be understood, not the way in which Santals go about doing it. The story may possibly imply that the 'persons' referred to manufacture their own kind of beer, something quite different from what Santals have. In any case Santal humour will enjoy the idea of beer manufactured as here told. As it may be of some interest, a description of how the Santals manufacture their beer is here given. They now-a-days commonly brew beer from rice; and it is this brewing which is here described.

The first thing is to prepare the pot in which the beer is to be manufactured. Any earthenware pot with a fairly large mouth will do, what the Santals call **ṭukuć** or **hanḍia** (the latter is the larger kind), especially the former one. The **ṭukuć** is filled with dry leaves, straw, &c., which is set fire to. This is done in the morning of the day when they are going to start brewing. It takes some hours before everything is burnt. The pot is generally put a short distance away from the house, as there is much smoke. When the pot has cooled down, the ashes are taken out, and the stuff to be used is put in. This is prepared in

13. THE JACKAL AND THE CHICKEN[1].

ONCE upon a time in a former age, people tell, a jackal and a hen engaged themselves to be flower-friends for life; they became very close companions. As the time passed, they one day said: "I say, flower, we two have become very close companions; now we shall invite each other and feast[2]."

"Very well," the hen said, "then let us invite each other and feast."

"All right," the jackal said, "then I shall provide the necessaries for you to eat, and you also must provide for me to eat; and we shall both of us brew beer."

Having consulted together in this way they actually both of them started brewing beer[3]. The hen took paddy, maize, b a j ṛ a

---

the afternoon. They take rice (t e k o c a o l e, rice boiled in the husks before it is husked, what they use for their ordinary food, and not a d w a c a o l e, rice husked after having been dried in the sun, not boiled) and roast this a little. The roasting is said to give a certain flavour to the beer. Thereupon the rice is boiled, and after boiling spread out to dry. The quantity of rice used for one brew varies from four to six p ạ i, or even to ten p ạ i; it all depends on how many may be counted on to drink, and, of course, on the ability of the house to give rice for this purpose. One p ạ i is half a s e e r; this is very nearly equal to one kg.

When the rice is fairly dry, it is mixed with r ạ n u, some vegetable fermenting stuff, which is rolled and ground and prepared. It might be mentioned that the r ạ n u ordinarily consists of some four or five different vegetable ingredients; generally it is bought in the markets prepared, in small white balls; but most Santals know how to prepare it. As the primary object of a Santal drinking is to become drunk, it is very common that certain vegetable poisons are added to the r ạ n u to make the beer intoxicating. I have heard as many as 23 different ingredients mentioned, of course not all used at the same time, only one or two in addition to the fermenting stuff, for the purpose mentioned. Especially the Hindu s u ṇ ḍ i caste, which manufactures and sells beer in the country, makes use of these poisons, to make their clients quickly drunk. When they are drunk and continue to drink, the Suṇḍis are reported to give them practically only water in the last cups sold. It has several times happened that people who have been to such shops and have drunk have died on their way home, from the effects of these poisons.

reaḱe dohoketa. Ar toyo do kakṛa, ghirṛi, sosroć, roṭe, hako emanteaḱ, uni hõ okako aće jom, onako reaḱe dohoketa.

Ado pe pon mãhã khange simaḱ do isinena, ado sime meneta, Cele phul, amaḱ do isinoḱ kana se baṅ? Iṅaḱ do isinena, heṛemge so kana.

When the rice and the r a n u are properly mixed, it is all put into the brewing pot, prepared as described above, generally in the evening. The contents of the pot (the boiled rice has swollen, so that the pot will be fairly full) are covered with a leaf-plate, pressed down on the rice. Another leaf-plate is put over the mouth of the pot, and a ḍ h a k n i ć, an earthenware lid for such pots, or a small cooking pot is put on the top, to keep it all in proper position. There is now nothing more to be done for some days, so the brewing pot is put aside in some place where people do not often go, commonly in the b h i t a r, the 'stall' walled off for the worship of the ancestors. As it must not tumble over, the pot is placed on a b i ṇ ḍ i, a ring of straw made for putting pots on.

The rice takes some five days to ferment (i s i n it is called, the same word as that used for cooking); it can be heard outside the pot when the process is complete. There is an exudation (called j h a r) from the rice, looking like brown water. This stuff is laded out with a leaf-spoon; it is said to be the most intoxicating part of the beer; it is drunk, generally mixed with a little water; this stuff may be kept, they say, up to a month; it does not go bad. As a rule it is finished very soon.

To get the beer proper, hot water is now poured on the rice left without the j h a r in the pot. During fermentation the rice subsides somewhat in the pot. If not sufficient hot water is available, ordinary cold water may be added, until the pot is full. The ready stuff looks like milk-water, a little brownish in colour. It has a peculiar acid-sweet smell; any one who has drunk a little may be detected by the smell from a considerable distance.

Before people drink, libations are made to M a r a ṅ b u r u, the principal national godling, possibly, however, in his capacity of belonging to the ancestors. (The Santal traditions tell that our first parents were taught to brew beer by M a r a ṅ b u r u, who came to them and told them he was their grandfather; by drinking the beer he taught them to brew they became drunk and fell in sin, i. e. had sexual intercourse). Further they libate to the ancestors, one after the other. It is done by pouring a little beer out on the floor inside the house (but not in the b h i t a r) for each.

After this is done, they take a broom (made from the straw of s i r o m, Andropogon muricatus, Retz.) that has not been used to sweep the floor with,

grain[4], millet[5], that is to say, what she herself was in the habit of eating, and started brewing from these. And the jackal found lizards[6], brown lizards[7], grasshoppers, frogs, fish and so on, i. e., he also took what he was in the habit of using for food, and commenced to brew[8] from these things.

Some three or four days afterwards the hen's beer was ready brewed, whereupon she said: "Well, flower, how is it, is your beer getting ready or how? Mine is ready brewed; it has a sweet smell."

---

consequently generally a new one, or one kept for this purpose; this they put into the mouth of the pot with the broom in, the object being to prevent the rice from coming out when they tilt the pot to let the beer run out.

The beer is poured out into brass cups, with rims (this to make it easy to pour out of the cup); if there are enough cups, they drink from these; otherwise the beer is poured from the brass-cup into leaf-cups. Of such they have one kind, called hạṇḍi phuṛuk', beer leaf-cup, as the name shows especially intended for drinking beer, although used for any household purpose that it will suit. The hạṇḍi phuṛuk' is made from one sal (Shorea robusta, Gaertn.) leaf; both ends are plaited (once on each side of the midrib, which the plaits cover), the plaits being kept in position by a pin of stiff straw, a thorn, or the like, stuck through. Filled up to just below the holes made by the pins at each end such a cup will take about two ounces fluid. It should be mentioned that the beer is stirred with a wooden ladle before it is poured out.

The leaf-cups are filled over and over again; it is said that it will take some twenty of these cups to make a person drunk.

When the first 'edition' is finished, fresh hot water is again poured on the rice; this is called doja hạṇḍi, second brew beer; it is, of course, not so strong as the first, tań hạṇḍi, poured out beer, as it is called (tań means to pour out by tilting the container). For the second brew the pot is not filled to the brim.

The same rice must generally also serve for a third brew, called bọḍọć hạṇḍi, lit. squeezed out beer. The rice is taken out of the pot and put into a pạtiạ, a small basket made of bamboo; a little water is poured on, and the rice is squeezed with the hand. Another way is to put the rice inside paddy-straw, a hole being left above for the purpose of putting the right hand in; water is then poured on, and the rice squeezed. The 'beer' that trinkles down is received in a cup and drunk.

The rice, or rather the refuse, is given to pigs to eat; if they eat too much, they get drunk, it is told.

Adọ uni toyo hõe mẹn gọṭketa, Hẽ, phul, iṅak hõ isinena. Adọkin mẹnketa, Ẹṇḍẹkhan dọ malaṅ dula arlaṅ ṅũia.

Khange sạrikin dulketa; ado toyoe mẹnketa, Iạ phul, dela iṅak maṛaṅlaṅ ṅũia.

Khange sime mẹnketa, Acha bogege, ẹṇḍẹkhanlaṅ ṅũia.

Adọ sạri toyo oṛakte bana hoṛkin calaoena; adọ toyoak hạṇḍikin ṅũyeta. Adọ khange sim dọ seage sọye kana, ar ṅũ hõ bae ṅũyeta. Adọ toyoe mẹnketa, Henda phul, am dọ bam ṅũyet kan dọ?

Adọ sime mẹnketa, Ẹ phul, amak hạṇḍi dọ seage sọyeṅ kana; ọhọṅ ṅũ daṛeletama.

Adọ toyo eskargeye ṅũ baṛaketa. Bhala, ona sea jạt dọ baṅhewa hoṛ dọ cekateye ṅũia? Adọ khange sime mẹnketa, Iạ phul, dela adọ iṅaklaṅ ṅũ aṭkara.

As remarked above, Santals drink in order to become drunk; there is no description needed of a drinking bout. According to what has been told to the writer, they pass through all the stages, some becoming hilarious, others melancholy, some scold and vituperate, others sing and tell stories; some become vile, lascivious and pugnacious, others moral, amiable, religious, and so on. The avowed object is to be able to forget for a few hours the miseries of this world and feel like kings, as they say. Drunkenness is one of the great obstacles to Santal developing.

The above description refers to the manufacture of beer from rice. It is manufactured in the same way from janhẹ and other cereals, that are husked. It is also manufactured from maize and bajṛa (Sorghum vulgare, Pers.) in the same manner, only omitting the roasting at the start.

It might further be mentioned, that they prepare a kind of beer from matkọm, the dried flowers of Bassia latifolia, Roxb.; these are steeped for three days in water, thereupon strained off; ranu is then added to the water, which is allowed to stand for five days, when it is fermented, and drunk. This stuff is called duhli, not hạṇḍi. The Santals also know to distil liquor from matkọm; but such distilling is illicit; those doing it are punished when caught. It is not of very frequent occurrence, but it happens.

The beer has to be 'watered' and drunk when fermentation is ready; they say they may let the fermented stuff stand to next day and then pour on water; but if it is left longer, it turns very sour and unsuitable for any use.

[4] See preceding note. Bajṛa is cultivated on high land, hill sides and the like. It is harvested about January. It is more common among other tribes than among the Santals.

They jackal also at once answered: "Yes, flower, mine is also ready brewed." Whereupon they both said: "In that case let us pour water on[9] and drink."

They consequently poured it out, and the jackal said: "I say, flower, come let us first drink mine."

"All right," the hen said, "let us do so then and drink."

Thereupon they really both went to the jackal's house and commenced drinking the jackal's brew. But the hen was feeling the rotten smell and was unable to drink. "Look here, flower," the jackal said, "you are not drinking anything?"

The hen replied: "Oh flower, your beer smells rotten to me; I am utterly unable to drink yours."

The jackal then drank alone. No wonder, how should any one not accustomed to it be able to drink that rotten stuff? Thereupon the hen said: "Listen, flower, come then let us drink and taste how mine is."

---

5 Millet, in Santali janhẹ, is a jungle corn (Paspalum scrobiculatum, L.), fairly common with the Santals. It is cultivated on high land, ripens in Oct.—Nov., when it is cut or (if the straw is short) pulled out and thrashed. The straw is unfit for cattle-food, but is used for some purposes, thus by the potters as kiln fuel. The hạṇḍi manufactured from janhẹ is said to be very intoxicating.

The hen collected all these kinds of grain to brew from; a Santal, of course, only makes use of one kind at a time.

6 The jackal collects what he is in the habit of eating, to manufacture beer from that; according to Santal ideas it must have become a wonderful brew. The first-mentioned lizard (in Santali kakṛa) is a very common one, seen everywhere. There are several varieties, one with a red head. Arak̔ kakṛa bọhọk̔, lit. Red lizard head, is a veiled name for a police constable among them, a part of the uniform of these people being a red turban.

7 What has been called 'brown lizard' is another very common reptile, by the Santals called ghirṛi. They have some stories of having seen such a ghirṛi come out of the mouth of a sleeping person; when the sleeper awoke, he told he had had such and such a dream; when put to the test, it was found that the dream, which to a large extent corresponded with the movements of the lizard, was true. Consequently, the lizard was the soul of the person out on an expedition.

8 Brew according to jackal ideas.

9 See above note 3.

Khange ado̱ sim oṛak̓tekin calaoena, ado̱ uniak̓kin ńũyet̓a. Ado̱ ạḍi sebelkin ạikạuet̓a. Khange tho̱ ado̱ ńũkin ńũyet̓a se̱, be̱bạṛićkin ńũket̓a. Khange tho̱ ado̱ sim do̱e lahraok̓ kana, ado̱ uni toyo do̱ mo̱ne̱ mo̱ne̱teye kurmurạuk̓ kana, ado̱e me̱net̓a, Durre̱! nuiak̓ hạṇḍi do̱ ạḍi sebeltaea. Ho̱ṛte̱t̓ hõ jạnić khube sebel co̱ń cet̓ co̱ń. Hape nãhãk̓e bul gitićlen khan do̱ń jo̱mea.

Ado̱ kathae, uni sim do̱ bulente ko̱bo̱k̓ ko̱bo̱gok̓ kanae. Ado̱ kathae, un jo̱khe̱ć uni toyo do̱ rạskạteye sereń go̱t̓ket̓a (sereńako do̱ń rạṛte):

Baṛgere, sim, nalom nạtińa,
Nam ńe̱lte, sim, toyoe land kan,
Gạḍiạre, kõk̓, nalom nạtińa;
Ro̱ṭe̱ kaṭa me̱nte suṛạm sogak̓ket̓.
Hạṇḍi do̱, sim, nalom ńũia;
Nam ńe̱lte, sim, toyoe land kan.

Onka uni toyo do̱, kathaeye sereńjo̱ń kana.

Ado̱ uni sim do̱ ạḍite̱ṭe lahraoena. Ar onae sereń baṛayet̓ jo̱khe̱ćge uni sim eńgaren ho̱po̱nko do̱ko ńe̱ńe̱l kan tahẽkana. Ado̱e bul gitićen khan do̱e ho̱ho̱ae kana, E̱ phul, ma beret̓me; ma bana ho̱ṛlań sereńa.

Ado̱ uni sim do̱ cet̓ hõ bae ro̱ṛet̓a, gitić thirenae. Ado̱ un jo̱khe̱ćgeye jo̱m go̱t̓kedea. Ado̱ onko sim ho̱po̱nko do̱ko rak̓ baṛayet̓a.

. Ado̱e jo̱m biyen khan do̱e calaoena. Ado̱ ać oṛak̓re se̱nkateye gitić akana, ado̱e me̱net̓a, Durre̱! sim jel do̱ ạḍi sebeltakoa. Gapa do̱ onko ho̱po̱n hõ jo̱to̱ń jom cabakoa.

Ado onko sim ho̱po̱n do̱ko ṭuạren khanko bud baṛajoń kana, Cekakotebo ạsulok̓a, ar uni toyo do̱ cet̓ lekatebo go̱jea? Ado̱ un

---

[10] There is a do̱ń dance with a peculiar do̱ń drumming; there are do̱ń songs with do̱ń melodies.

[11] The paddy-bird is very common in the Santal country. There are several species. The Santal name for some of these, kõk̓ (with a prefixed word to

So they went to the hen's house and were drinking her beer. They both found it delicious, and consequently they drank and drank; they drank tremendously. The result was that the hen was becoming prostrate, and the jackal was becoming excited in his mind, and said: "Dear me, this beer of hers is very delicious. The person herself very likely also is very savoury, I reckon. Wait a bit, when she lies down drunk, I shall eat her."

Ultimately, people tell, the hen became drunk and was nodding with her head. When this came to pass, the jackal out of joy commenced to sing (here they sing at a d ǫ ṅ[10] melody):

"Do not feed, hen, in the house-field;
Seeing you, hen, the jackal is laughing;
Do not feed, paddy-bird[11], in the pond.
Thinking it is the leg of a frog you will
peck a sedge[12] culm.
Do not, hen, drink beer;
Seeing you, hen, the jackal is laughing."

In this way, it is told, the jackal was singing.

Ultimately the hen became entirely prostrated. Whilst the jackal was singing as told, the hen's chickens were watching what was happening. When the hen lay down drunk, the jackal called out to her: "O flower, do get up! let us both sing!"

But the hen did not say a single word; she was lying quiet. Then at that time the jackal ate her; and the chickens were crying.

When the jackal had had his fill, he went away. He went home and was lying down; then he said: "Oh dear me, the flesh of fowls is very delicious. To-morrow I shall eat all those chickens also."

Now when these chickens had become orphans, they were pondering: "How shall we maintain ourselves? and how shall we manage

distinguish the different kinds) is onomatopoetic, i. e., their call or cry sounds very much like the Santal name. The paddy-birds feed on insects, fish and frogs.

12 The sedge, in Santali s u ṛ ạ or s u ṛ e (Cyperus tegetum, Roxb.) is found in the more low-lying parts of the country, and is fairly common.

jo̱khe̱ćge, kathae, uni toyo do̱e he̱ć go̱ťena; ado̱e metako kana, Cedaǩ bha̱gna̱pe raǩjoṅ kana?

Ado̱ko metae kana, Hola mahn̩d̩erre, mamo̱, eṅgaṅe go̱ć ba̱giaťlea, onatele raǩ ba̱ṛajo̱ṅ kana.

Ado̱e kuliketǩoa, Okarepe gitića?

Ado̱ko la̱iadea, baṅma, Culha̱re ale do̱le gitić kana.

Ado̱e metaťkoa, Acha bogege. Ma e̱n̩d̩e̱khan dandha baṛajoṅpe.

Ado̱ kathae, uni toyo do̱e calaoena. Ado̱ onko sim ho̱po̱n do̱ ako mo̱to̱ko galmaraoketa, baṅma, Nui toyo do̱ dhorage nãhãǩ abo do̱e jo̱mbongea; onatege gitić reaǩ do̱e kuliyeťbona, okarepe gitića me̱nte. Holanoǩ aboren ayo hõ thó nui toyogeye jo̱mkedetabona. Ma nui toyo do̱ teheṅ do̱bo go̱jegea. Nõǩõe ṅe̱ltabonpe, ayo do̱e bele oṭokaťa. Ado̱ o̱ko̱e busa̱ga ona bele do̱? Ona beletegebo go̱ć ocoyea.

Ado̱ko me̱nkeťa, E̱ ya bele, am do̱ culha̱re tahe̱ntabonme; uni toyobo go̱jea; mẽť nãhãǩ so̱bo̱ǩ kãṛã go̱deme. Ar am do̱ ya tok, kocare tahe̱ntabonme; je̱mo̱n mẽť nãhãǩe so̱bo̱gea, ṅir od̩okoǩ jo̱khe̱ć nãhãǩ am do̱ dal gitić go̱deme. Ado̱ ukhuṛko metae kana, E̱ ya ukhuṛ, am do̱ dua̱r ṭhenaǩ sate ṭhen tãṛãǩtabonme; je̱mo̱n nãhãǩ oṛaǩ bhitri khone ṅir od̩ok go̱doǩa, un jo̱khe̱ć nãhãǩ am do̱ ota go̱deme. Nui toyo do̱ no̱n̩d̩e̱ gebo go̱ć uta̱rea.

Ado̱ko me̱nkeťa, Tise hijuǩa?

---

13 See p. 166, note 6.

14 A large wooden pestle.

15 The construction of the Santali language in this place is somewhat 'ungrammatical', but like what is often heard.

16 The ukhuṛ is a large wooden mortar found in practically every Santal household. It is made of a log, some 30 cm., more or less, in diameter, and some 40 to 60 cm. high, hollowed out at one end, generally with a little 'waist' to make it easier to handle and less heavy. It is used for husking rice and for other similar purposes. Many who cannot afford a d̩hiṅki have an ukhuṛ and a tok. The ukhuṛ is found all over the East; but the Santal form seems to be nicer to look at than what is generally seen with other races.

17 The eaves over the front side of the house are generally coming further out than at the other sides, in this way giving roof to a small front verandah. The entrance door is here.

to kill that jackal?" Just at that time the jackal suddenly came and said to them: "Why, nephews and nieces[13], are you crying?"

"A few days ago, uncle[13]," they replied, "our mother died and left us; therefore we are crying."

"Where do you sleep?" he asked them.

"We sleep in the fire-place," they answered.

"Very well," he said to them, "now then take care to maintain yourselves."

Thereupon the jackal went away, and the chickens had a talk together, saying: "This jackal will without doubt presently try to eat us; therefore he is asking us about the place where we sleep. Yesterday this jackal ate our mother also. Come, let us kill this jackal to-day. Here, look, mother has laid an egg that she has left behind. Who is going to hatch out this egg? By the aid of this egg we shall get him killed."

So they said: "Listen, you egg! you please stay in the fire-place for us; we are going to kill this jackal; you hit his eyes and make him blind! And you, you pestle[14], be standing there in the corner for us; just as it[15] hits him in his eyes, when he then runs out, you be quick and knock him down." Thereupon they said to the mortar[16]: "Listen, you mortar, you lie in wait for us on the eaves[17] above the door; he will presently run out from the house, at that moment you, please, press him down[18]. We shall kill this jackal here on this spot utterly."

"When[19] will he come?" they asked.

18 The egg, the pestle and the mortar are all addressed as living beings. This does not seem to be Santali imagination. There are also some other points that might point to something borrowed in this part of the story. When the jackal runs out, he seems to be doing so twice, i. e., possibly from one room to another; a Santal house has not more than one room.

19 The Santali language has two interrogatives for our 'when', one asking about the day, the other about the time of the day. The former is used here.

Adọ onko simko mẹnkeťa, Teheń ńindạge.

Adọ sanam hoṛko mẹnkeťa, Acha bogege, abo sanam hoṛe ṭuạr oco akaťbona, ać hõ nẹṇḍẹgebo mohor meṭaoea.

Khange adọ onka apan ạpinko tãṛãǩena. Ar sim dọ ṭẹṅgọćante pakhareko duṛuṗ thir akana, ar ona bele dọ lọlọ tọrọćteko topa akaťa.

Adọ ạyuṗen khange uni toyo dọe hẹć gọťena; adọko bọlọ ocoadea. Adọ ẹkkalte uni toyo dọ culhạ duạr ṭhen sẹnkateye paṭgaṇḍo ẹsẹť gọťketa, adọ banar laha jaṅgate culhạ tọrọće gạduć gọťketa. Khange ona bele dọ ṭhu gọťena, ẹkkalte mẽťrege paṛaoadea; adọe kãṛã gọťena. Adọe itkidoǩ kana are mẹneťa, Khạṛijoṅań! khạṛijoṅań! Adọe ńir oḍokoǩ kan tahẽkana.

Khange tok bindạṛ gọťadea; adọe mẹn gọťketa, Khạṛijoṅań, khạṛijoṅań! Adọ onka mẹn tulućgeye ńir oḍokoǩ kan tahẽkana. Adọ duạr piṇḍạí parọmleť khange sạṛim khon ukhuṛ ńũr gọťadea. Khange thọ ẹṇḍẹgeye ṭẹp ṭẹpẹ gọťena. Adọ onko sim họpọn ṭẹṅgọćanteko ńir hẹć gọťena, adọ bọhọǩko kuṭạm gọťkedea; ẹkkalte hataṅgeko kuṭạm toťkeťtaea. Adọ inạ hataṅko jọm baṛakeťtaea, adọko mẹnkeťa, Aḍoleťam! Ạḍi cọṅ aleren ayom jọmkede; am hõ bale jọm halakeťmea?

Ẹnẹ adọ cabayena katha dọ; in maraṅgea nịạ dọ.

---

20 See p. 166, note 7.

21 The word khạṛi refers to a peculiar practice of the ojhas for finding things out (such as character and cause of diseases) by magic, making marks on the ground or on a leaf. The idea is that the jackal is going to find out who is responsible, so that he may take revenge.

22 The Santali word used is aḍo, their most common word for urinating. It is extensively used as an expletive, and also in threatening language, or exultingly, like here. In cases like this it refers to the commonly observed happening that animals, and also human beings, when becoming suddenly frightened, unconsciously pass water. The word is not supposed to be used in this sense by women. As an expletive the women use atar, burn up, in stead.

23 To eat an animal in revenge is not unknown among the Santals. I remember what happened here many years ago now. The Santals managed to take the

"This very night," the chickens replied.

So all of them said: "All right; he has made all of us orphans; here in this very place we shall make an end to himself also."

Thereupon they all, each one as arranged, lay in wait; and the chickens were sitting quietly in the niche[20] with a small axe; and the egg they had buried with hot ashes.

When it became evening, the jackal suddenly came, and they let him come in. The jackal went straight up to the fire-place opening, and sitting down on his haunches he shut this up, whereupon he with both his forelegs vigorously scraped the ashes in the fire-place towards himself. Then the egg burst and got straight into his eyes, so he became blind. The jackal was rubbing his eyes and said: "I shall find out by magic[21], I shall find out by magic!" Hereupon he started running out.

The pestle then fell down over him, and he called out: "I shall find out by magic, I shall find out by magic!" As he was saying this, he ran out of the house. As soon as he had passed the verandah in front of the door, the mortar suddenly tumbled down on him. There was no help for it, he was at once felled down as long as he was, there, on that spot. Now the chickens at once came running, bringing their axe with them; they hammered his head; they hammered it with such force that the brains came out. Thereupon they ate his brain and said: "You managed it[22]! You did much, you ate our mother; now we have eaten you also in return![23]"

So there the story is finished; it is thus much this one.

life of an ugly-looking leopard, measuring seven feet. They brought the dead animal to me and gave me the skin; but, they said, he has eaten so much for us, now we are going to eat him in return, and they did so; no one enjoyed the feed, some even vomited; but it had to go down.

14. Toyo ar kǫ̃k̔ reaṅ.

Tis cọṅ sedae jọkhẹn, kathae, toyo ar kǫ̃k̔ phulkin pataoleťa, arkin mẹpẹnlena, Amak̔ ạt baṅ calak̔ hilok̔ dọ iń, ar ińak̔ ạt baṅ calak̔ hilok̔ dọ am ạsulińtalaṅme. Iń dọ setoṅ din am iń ạsulmea, ar am dọ jạput̔ din ạsulińtalaṅme. Adọ sạri ona katha dọ bana họṛkin khusiat̔ khan dọkin hẽ hũkeťa.

Khange tahẹn tahẹnte toyo dọe mẹnkeťa, Iạ kǫ̃k̔geń ạsulea, nui por jạt dọ! Eṅgateń ạsul baṛayea, jãhã lekateń bulạulege, ar mit̔ din dọń jọm gọťkaea. Noa katha dọ mọnẹregeye dọhọkaťa. Khange galmaraote dọ khubkin gateyena, mit̔ mạci mit gaṇḍoyenakin.

Khange mit̔ din dọ toyoe mẹnkeťa, Iạ phul, nẽotayeťmeaṅ, ma niạ phalna dinre dọ iń ṭhen hana ṭhãire sẹnok̔talaṅme, ọṇḍẹ miťtelaṅ jọm ńũlege.

Adọe mẹnkeťa, Achaṅ calak̔a.

Khange sạri din tiok̔en khan dọe calaoena. Ar uni toyo dọ aema utạr rọṭẹ ar sọsrọće jarwa akaťko tahẽkana. Adọ nui kǫ̃k̔e metadea, Ma phul, nǫ̃k̔ǫ̃e iń peṛayeťmea; ma khub leka jowanme ạurim bik̔ hạbić; ar bam bik̔ khan dọ lạime, arhǫ̃ ą̃ṛti juṭućama.

Adọe mẹnkeťa, Achaṅ jọmlekoge, ẹnkhanteń khọja.

---

[1] See p. 192, note 11.

[2] See p. 164, note 1.

[3] It does not appear from the Santali text who is to maintain the other during the hot season, and who during the rains. But as the paddy-bird during the rainy season has opportunities of finding food everywhere, it is likely meant it is for this time the bird undertakes the provisioning.

[4] The word used in the original is very commonly used, both as an abuse and as a term of 'benevolence'; it is really the name of a part of the male anatomy. It is usually cut short and i ạ (which means 'so and so' and is constantly used for any other word not at once remembered, or for some other reason not wanted to be expressly mentioned, also often for the word here suppressed) substituted. The Santali word is ẹṇḍ. It is not so many years ago that the use of this word as an abuse might be taken up before the Santal village council, and the offender was punished. Now-a-days the word seems to have lost every meaning and may be translated as done. Very frequently 'rascal' would seem to render it.

14. THE JACKAL AND THE PADDY-BIRD.

Some time or other, who knows when, in the old days, people tell, a jackal and a paddy-bird[1] had engaged themselves to flower-friendship[2] for life, and had said to each other: "The day you have no means of support, I shall, and the day I am unable to maintain myself, you support me for us. I shall support you during the hot season, and you support me during the rains[3]". And in very truth, as they both were pleased with this arrangement, they both grunted their assent.

As time passed by, the jackal one day said: "This unspeakable[4] paddy-bird! I am to support this fellow of another race[5]! Dash it, I shall support him somehow; in some way or other I shall trick him, and then some day I shall eat him." This matter he kept to himself. Talking together they were extremely companionable, they were quite inseparable[6].

Then one day the jackal said: "Listen, flower[7], I invite you; please come on such and such a day to me over at that place; there we shall eat and drink together."

"All right," he replied, "I shall come."

When the day came, the paddy-bird actually went and the jackal had collected an immense number of frogs and grass-hoppers. He said to the paddy-bird: "Please, flower, look here, you see what I am entertaining you with; please help yourself to your heart's content until you are satisfied; and if you do not get enough, let me know, and I shall give you a second helping."

"All right," he replied, "let me first eat these; then I shall ask for more."

5 The word is Hindi and generally has an admixture of contempt, one born by another, of another race or caste, an alien, outside the pale.

6 The Santali word cannot be rendered literally; it is said 'the two became one stool, one sitting-board'; it is a common expression for extreme intimacy.

7 See p. 164, note 1.

Adǫ kathae, enko jǫm jǫmtegeye alǫć palǫćena. Khangeye mẹnkeťa, Ią phul, inąk̓geń jǫma; jǫm bhagaoenąń.

Adǫe metadea, Acha, ẹnḍẹkhan dẹ laṅ joharjoṅa, ar ma laṅ apan ąpinok̓a. Adǫ sąri johar baṛakatekin apan ąpinena.

Adǫ tinąk̓ din tayǫm cǫṅ uni kǫ̃k̓ hǫ̃e metadea, Ią phul, maṅ nẽotayeťmea, nią din hilok̓ dǫ iń ṭhen hanḍẹ calak̓me, ǫnḍẹlaṅ jǫm ńũia.

Khange toyoe mẹnkeťa, Achań calak̓a.

Adǫ kathae, ẹn hilok̓ dǫ aema utąr cuṭią saṕkeťkote miťṭaṅ tumbąreye bhǫrao akaťko tahẽkana. Adǫ toyoe hẹćen khan dǫ, miťṭaṅ bunum ṭhene idikedea are metadea, Ma onko tumbąreń dǫhǫ akaťkoa, jǫmkom ąurim bik̓ dhąbić; arhǫ̃ bam bik̓ khan dǫń emama.

Khange, kathae, tumbąre ma moca baṅ bǫlǫk̓ kantae. Khange bae tawak̓ posak̓ gǫťkeťa? Khange adǫm dǫ jivẹťko tahẽkana; onko dǫko dąṛ gǫťkeťa. Khange cure mare lagayeťkoa. Adǫ un jǫkhẹn dǫ kǫ̃k̓ dǫ bogeteye landawadea. Khange toyo dǫe edreyena, mẹnkẹťae, Nui kǫ̃k̓ dǫ manǫtiń lągiť dǫ bae nẽota akadińa; mẹnkhan nui dǫ landawąń lągiťgeye nẽota akadińa. Uni toyo dǫ mǫn mǫnte nonkae edreyena. Adǫe mẹnkeťa, Hapẹ, neko chuṭiąń jǫmlekoge. Johar jǫkhẹnlaṅ ńammea. Adǫ enko dąṛ sarẹćko cuṭiąye jǫm cabakeťkoa.

Adǫ kǫ̃k̓e kulikedea, Cele phul, bilenam sẹm baṅ?

8 Salutation is a formal matter with the Santals and has, on 'official' occasions, to be gone through seriously. A full description of their customs in connexion with this is found in the writer's paper On the different kinds of Salutation used by the Santals, Journal, Asiatic Society of Bengal, Vol. LXVII, Part III, p. 35 ss. Two phul are supposed to use so johar, i. e., they both 'receive', or salute in the same way, not like a younger to an older one, or vice versa.

9 See p. 169, note 12. A tumbą is, as a rule, long and narrow with a narrow neck.

10 See p. 172, note 16.

11 See above, note 9.

Now he kept on eating these until he was crammed and over-filled, whereupon he said: "I say, flower, I shall not have any more, I have done eating."

"All right," the jackal said, "then let us salute each other[8] and say good-bye, and let us part each to our own place." Thereupon they, truth to tell, saluted each other and went each to his own.

Some time afterwards the paddy-bird also spoke to the jackal and said: "Listen, flower, I invite you; on such and such a day come to me over there; we shall eat and drink there."

"All right," the jackal replied, "I shall come."

Now, people tell, that day the paddy-bird had caught an immense number of mice and put them into a gourd[9]. When the jackal came, he took him near a white-ant hill[10] and said to him: "You see these I have put into the gourd; please eat of them until you are satisfied; if you do not get enough, I shall give you more."

Now the jackal could not get his snout into the gourd[11]. Then did he not dash the gourd down on the ground and break it? Now some mice were alive; these ran away at once, and the jackal chased them all he could. When this happened, the paddy-bird laughed heartily. Then the jackal became angry and said[12]: "This paddy-bird has not invited me to do me honour; but he has invited me to laugh at me." In this way the jackal was angry in his heart. So he said: "Wait a little, let me first eat these mice; when we salute each other-we two[13] shall find you." Thereupon he ate the mice that were left after the others had run away.

The paddy-bird then asked him: "How is it, flower, are you satisfied or not?"

---

12 The paddy-bird is not supposed to hear what the jackal says.

13 Here and below in several places the inclusive dual of threatening language.

Adoe menkeťa, Ho khub iń biyena, phul. Ado cigạri leka noa katha doe metadea; tãhã bae bilena. Ado toyoe menkeťa, Iạ phul, de laṅ johar hoťjoṅa. Jom biyente erseń torseń iń ạikạueťa; gitićge sanayediń kana. Adolaṅ apan ạpinokteń gitić jirạujoṅa.

Ado kōk̉e menkeťa, Acha, de eṇḍekhanlaṅ joharjoṅa.

Ado kathaekin joharjoṅ kan tahẽkan jokhengeye ota goťkedeteye ger goć goťkedea. Khange uni toyo do ạḍiye rạskạyena, are menkeťa, Am do enanem landa akawadiṅa. Ona bodol am hõ nit do landakatelaṅ jommea. Ado kathae, khub togoć ḍaṭa ńõk̉kate se thoṛa do isiṛ ńõk̉ateye jome kana. Khange uniak̉ do jotoe jom cabakeťtaea; cetteť hõ bae sarećleťtaea, jaṅ hõ jaṅ, rama hõ rama, miť miťteye jomkeťtaea. Ado khange khube biyena ar monre ạḍi rạskại ạikạukeťa. Ado rạskạte miťṭaṅ kathae roṛ goťkeťa, nonka leka: Tumbạ tumbạ cuṭiạ khaelom, bunum danaṅ kõk̉ khaelom tui here. Ado nonka roṛkate bar dhaoteye don don goťkeťa. Ado oṇḍe khone calak̉ kana, ar rạskạte oka leka coe taṛam idiyeť kan.

Ado calak̉ calak̉te miťṭaṅ sim ać lahareye ạtiń kane ńelkede khane hoho goťkeťa. Men sim, hor ocok̉aṅme, baṅkhan iń jom goťmea. Tumbạ tumbạ cuṭiạ khaelom, bunum danaṅ kõk̉ khaelom, tui here. Khange uni sim hõ hor bae ocok̉adete nuiye jom goťkedea.

Arhõ eṇḍe khone calak̉ kana. Ado calak̉ calak̉te ać lahare miťṭaṅ merome ńel ńamkedea. Adoe hoho goťkeťa, Men merom, hor ocok̉aṅme, baṅkhanlaṅ jom goťmea. Tumbạ tumbạ cuṭiạ khaelom, bunum danaṅ kõk̉ khaelom, tui here. Ado uni merom hõ bae ocok̉lente kathaeye jom goťkedea.

14 See p. 196, note 23.

15 The jackal's outburst is partly Santali, partly rustic Bengali. The Bengali words are translated in German. The last two words, t u i h e r e, are doubtful. T u i is a form of the pers. pron. used in addressing inferior persons; h e r e is an interjection, 'hey there'.

"O flower," he replied; "I am extremely well satisfied." It was sarcastically that he said, this to the other one; in reality he had not had his fill. The jackal then said: "I say, flower, come let us salute each other and say good-bye at once. I have eaten so much that I feel unable to sit or stand; I feel the need of lying down. Let us separate and lie down and rest."

"All right," the paddy bird said, "come then, let us salute each other."

Whilst they were saluting each other, it is told, the jackal suddenly pounced upon the paddy-bird and pressed him down, and at once bit him and killed him. The jackal then became very pleased and said: "A short while ago you were having a laugh at me; in return[14] for that we two shall now have a laugh at you also and eat you." Thereupon he ate the paddy-bird, gnashing his teeth somewhat or snarling a little. He ate up all there was of him; he did not leave the least bit of him; even his bones and his claws he ate, every bit. Ultimately he had his fill and more and felt very pleased in his mind. Out of sheer joy he called out as follows: "Gourdfuls of mice habe ich gefressen[15]; behind the white-ant hill habe ich the paddy-bird gefressen, du da!" And having spoken thus twice, he jumped and jumped. Thereupon he went away from that place, and out of joy he walked along in an indescribable way.

As he was walking along, he caught sight of a fowl in front of him, picking and feeding, and called out: "Take care, fowl, get out of my way; else I shall eat you in a trice. Gourdfuls of mice habe ich gefressen; behind the white-ant hill habe ich the paddy-bird gefressen, du da!" And as the fowl did not get out of his way, he ate it also.

From there he went further on. As he was passing along, he caught sight of a goat in front of him, and called out: "Take care, goat, get out of my way; else we two shall eat you in a trice. Gourdfuls of mice habe ich gefressen; behind the white-ant hill habe ich the paddy-bird gefressen, du da!" Then, as the goat did not get out of his way either, he ate it also.

Adǫ arhǫ̃ ǫṇḍẹ khon calaǩ calaǩte ać lahare miťṭan bhiḍiye ńẹlkedea. Khangeye hǫhǫ gǫťkeťa, Mẹn bhiḍi, hǫr ǫcǫǩanme, baṅkhanlaṅ jǫm gǫťmea. Tumbạ tumbạ cuṭiạ khaelǫm, bunum danaṅ kǫ̃ǩ khaelǫm, tui here. Adǫ kathae, uni hǫ̃ bae ǫcǫǩlenteye jǫmkedea.

Adǫ arhǫ̃ ǫṇḍẹ khone calaǩ kana. Calaǩ calaǩte ać lahare miťṭaṅ gạiye ńẹlkedea. Khange ini hǫ̃e hǫhǫadea, Mẹn gạI, ǫcǫǩme, baṅkhanlaṅ jǫmmea. Tumbạ tumbạ cuṭiạ khaelǫm, bunum danaṅ kǫ̃ǩ khaelǫm, tui here. Khange uni gạI hǫ̃ bae ǫcǫǩlen khane gẹr gǫćkedete im bǫrǫe jǫmkeťtaea.

Arhǫ̃ ǫṇḍẹ khone calaǩ kana. Adǫ calaǩ calaǩte ać lahare miťṭaṅ bitkile ńẹl ńamkedea. Adǫ khangeye hǫhǫ gǫťadea, Mẹn bitkil, hǫr ǫcǫǩańme, ar baṅkhanlaṅ jǫm gǫťmea. Tumbạ tumbạ cuṭiạ khaelǫm, bunum danaṅ kǫ̃ǩ khaelǫm, tui here. Adǫ kathae, uni bitkil hǫ̃ bae ǫcǫǩlente ńir sẹnkate uniye gẹr gitić gǫťkedea, ar uniaǩ im bǫrǫe jǫmkeťtaea. Khange bẹbạṛiće bi puṅ puṅena.

Adǫ arhǫ̃ ǫṇḍẹ khone calaǩ kana. Khange calaǩ calaǩte miťṭaṅ darha ać lahareye ńẹl ńamkeťa. Khangeye hǫhǫ gǫťkeťa, Mẹn darha, ǫcǫǩme, baṅkhanlaṅ ńũ aṅjẹť gǫťmea. Tumbạ tumbạ cuṭiạ khaelǫm, bunum danaṅ kǫǩ khaelǫm, tui here. Adǫ kathae, ona darha hǫ̃ baṅ ǫcǫǩlena; bhala ona dǫ okate ǫcǫgoǩa? Adǫ kathae, ńir sẹnkate ona hǫ̃ ńũye ńũkeťa sẹ, jǫtǫ daǩe ńũ cabakeťa. Khange artẹťe biyena.

Adǫ inạkate arhǫ̃ ǫṇḍẹ khone calaǩ kana. Adǫ calaǩ calaǩte ać lahare miťṭaṅ khunṭiye ńẹlkeťa. Adǫe hǫhǫ gǫťkeťa, Mẹn khunṭi, ǫcǫǩme, ar baṅkhanlaṅ dǫn parǫmmea. Adǫ kathae,

[16] When wild beasts kill other animals, it is with many of them the custom to start eating from behind (the genitals); the liver, lungs, heart and kidneys are apparently delicacies and taken before the flesh. The jackal follows this custom.

[17] The Santal khunṭi is a post of any form fixed at one end. It is not necessarily high.

As he was again passing along from that place, he caught sight of a sheep in front of him, and called out: "Take care, sheep, get out of my way; else I shall eat you in a trice. Gourdfuls of mice habe ich gefressen; behind the white-ant hill habe ich the paddy-bird gefressen, du da!" And as the sheep did not get out of his way either, he ate it also.

Then he went further from there also. As he was passing along, he saw a cow in front of him, and he called to this one also: "Take care, cow, get out of the way; else we two shall eat you. Gourdfuls of mice habe ich gefressen; behind the white-ant hill habe ich the paddy-bird gefressen, du da!" Then as the cow did not get out of the way, he bit her and killed her and ate her liver and lungs[16].

He went along from there also. Then as he passed along, he caught sight of a buffalo cow in front of him, and called out to her: "Take care, buffalo cow, get out of my way; else we two shall eat you in a trice. Gourdfuls of mice habe ich gefressen; behind the white-ant hill habe ich the paddy-bird gefressen, du da!" Then, people tell, as the buffalo cow did not get out of the way either, he ran up to her and bit her at once, so she fell down, whereupon he ate her liver and lungs. Then he was awfully crammed and distended.

Thereupon he went along from there also. As he was passing along, he caught sight of a water-pool in front of him, and called out: "Take care, water-pool, get out of the way; else we two shall drink you dry in a trice. Gourdfuls of mice habe ich gefressen; behind the white-ant hill habe ich the paddy-bird gefressen, du da!" Now, people tell, the water-pool did not get out of the way either; I wonder, where should it remove itself to? Then, people tell, the jackal ran down there and commenced to drink that also; he drank and drank; he drank all the water up. Consequently he became still fuller.

Thereupon he went along from that place also. As he was passing along, he saw a wooden post[17] in front of him, and called out: "Take care, post! get out of the way, else we two shall jump

khunṭi hõ baṅ o̱co̱k̕lena. Khangeye me̱n go̱t̕ket̕a, Tumbạ tumbạ cuṭiạ khaelo̱m, bunum danaṅ kõk̕ khaelo̱m, tui here. Onka me̱nkateye do̱n paro̱met̕ tahẽkan do̱, khunṭirege lac̕e bhosa go̱t̕enteye so̱bo̱k̕ go̱c̕ena.

Ado̱ e̱ne̱ṅ purạuket̕a niạ katha do̱.

15. Toyo ar kulại reaṅ.

Kulại ar toyokin galmaraaona, Alaṅ do̱ phullaṅ pataoa. Phulkin pataoket̕aa, do̱kin me̱njoṅ kana, Iạ, phul, laṅ toa dakaea. Khan ado̱ e̱n hilok̕ do̱ haṭ din tahẽkana. Ado̱ oka ho̱rte ho̱ṛko haṭṭeko hijuk̕ se̱nok̕, ona ho̱r aṛere por latarre uni kalại do̱e burum hape akana, ar toyo do̱ pharak ṅõk̕reye tãṛãk̕ akan tahẽkana.

Ado̱ khange ona ho̱rte caole ạkriṅkoko calak̕ kana, ado̱ uni kulạiko ṅe̱l ṅamkedea. Khan caole do̱ho̱kate haṇḍe̱ ota nhaṇḍe̱ otako ota baṛayedea. Un jo̱khe̱c̕ toyo do̱ caoleye ạtkir go̱t̕ket̕a, ado̱ tayo̱mtekin ṅapamena. Ṅapamkate kulại do̱ toyoe kulikedea, Cele, ạtkirket̕talaṅam?

Ado̱e me̱nket̕a, Hẽ̱ṅ ạtkir akat̕a.

[1] This story has many points in common with the two previously recorded ones, about a jackal and a hen and a jackal and some chickens. Here it is a hare who acts the other part. The narrator was a man named Kanhu Marndi, who died in Mesopotamia some years ago. Kanhu was, for a Santal, a very well educated man; he belonged to village Chondorpura in Jubdi (or Damin-i-koh, as this part of the Santal Parganas district is called, a Government estate), and all his environments were fairly different from those of Sagram Murmu, who has taken down so many of these stories. This may to a certain extent explain the difference in their stories; originally identical, the stories may in the course of time have been clothed in different garb in different parts of the country. The language of this narrator is very different from that of Sagram. The latter is a born story-teller; he has a beautiful, easy-flowing language, just as it is spoken in the villages. He apparently enjoys telling, recording many details, and now and then also recording his own ideas and speculations. Kanhu's language is of a more dignified character and a good deal more staccato than that of the

right over you!" Now, people tell, the post did not get out of the way either. The jackal then called out: "Gourdfuls of mice habe ich gefressen; behind the white-ant hill habe ich the paddy bird gefressen, du da!" Saying this he tried to jump over; the wooden post ran into his stomach, and he was stabbed to death.

So there I have finished this story.

15. THE JACKAL AND THE HARE[1].

A hare and a jackal had a talk together: "Let us two engage ourselves to flower-friendship[2] for life." They did so, and they said among themselves: "I say, flower[3], let us prepare rice porridge[4]." Now it was market-day that day, and close to the road by which people were going to and coming from the market the hare crouched under a bush and kept quiet, whilst the jackal was lying in wait a little distance off.

Presently people who were going to sell rice[5] came along this road, and they caught sight of the hare, whereupon they put their rice down and chased the hare, trying to pounce on him, now here, now there. Meanwhile the jackal made haste and carried the rice off; afterwards the two met; then the hare asked the jackal: "Well, did you carry anything off for us?"

"Yes," the jackal said, "I did."

other one. He is not so unconscious. His language may perhaps show traces of his having been to school.

2 See p. 164, note 1.

3 See p. 165, note 3.

4 What in Santali is called toa daka, lit. milk boiled-rice, is prepared by boiling sundried rice (adwa caole) in milk. It is not a common dish with the Santals, and is considered somewhat better than the ordinary. It is a dish more common among the Hindus than among the Santals.

5 Here and in the following things are mentioned that are supposed to be brought to every market-place every market-day, necessaries of the daily life of the villagers. Rice is the staple food of all classes of people in these parts.

Inạ tayom arhõ onkage toyo doe tãṛãk̕ akana ar kulại doe obor akana. Khan ado toa ik̕diyić hoṛẹ ńelkedea. Uni hõ onkage toa dohokate haṇḍẹ nhaṇḍeye ota baṛayedea. Enkate ạḍi sạṅgiṅe khudạu idikedea. Ado oṇa takre toyo do toae ạtkirket̕a. Khudạu mokoṅkate uni hoṛ doe heć ruạṛena are calaoena ekenak̕ge. Tayomte unkin dokin ńapamena. Ado kulại doe kukli kana, Cele, phulem ạtkirket̕a?

Menket̕ae, Hẽń ạtkir akat̕a.

Inạ tayom sahan ạk̕kriṅkoko calak̕ kana, ar uni kulại hõ pạhil leka galasaṅe obor hape akana. Sen tiok̕kede khanko ńelkede, kulạiye burum akan. Ado onko hõ sahan dohokateko lagayede kana. Laga laga ạḍi sạṅgiṅko lagakedea, ota ota bako ota ńamledea, ar sahan pataṛak̕kote hõ bhageteko lebda baṛakedea. Note inạk̕tege toyo do sahane ạtkirket̕a. Khan ado mit̕ ṭhenkin ńapamena. Adoe kuliyedea, Cele, phulem ạtkirket̕a?

Adoe menket̕a, Hẽń ạtkirket̕a.

Ona ror baṛakate arhõ pạhil lekagekin tãṛãk̕ena. Khange mit̕ ghạri tayom kuṅkạl bhajanko idiyet̕ kana. Ado uni kulại do horre menaea se baṅ? Ńel ńamkedeako, ado bhajan dohokateko otaye lạgit̕. Haṇḍe nhaṇḍe ota baṛa ota baṛa ạḍi sạṅgiṅko lagakedea. Inạk̕tege uni toyo hõe ńir hećena, ar mit̕ṭạṅ bhajane ạtkir got̕ket̕a. Ado toyotekin arhõkin ńapamena. Adoe kuliyedea, Cele, phulem ạtkirket̕a.

---

6 Milk is not much used by the Santals for drinking; as for the Hindus, it is what they value very highly. Santals use milk for preparing ghi, for preparing food, like here, and for a few other purposes; Santal children get, of course, milk to drink; grown up Santals very seldom take milk 'neat'. They like to let it stand to become d a h e, sour milk, or kephir.

7 In these parts fire-wood is to be had on the market-places, thin branches or pieces of wood, cut to short lengths (40 to 50 cm. long) and split. In other parts dried cow-dung, in cakes or rolled round the peeled stalk of jute or the like, is the most common fuel. Fuel for cooking food is a great problem in India, and very little is done to get the problem solved.

8 Earthenware vessels, for all kinds of household purposes, and of great variety of shape, are manufactured by the local potters; these are not Santals, but a Hindu

After this the jackal was again lying in wait, whilst the hare was squatting. Then a man who was carrying milk[6] along saw him. This man also in the same way put the milk down and chased the hare hither and thither, trying to catch him. In this way he chased him to a great distance. At that moment the jackal carried the milk off. When he got tired of chasing the hare, the man returned and went away emptyhanded. Afterwards the two met, and the hare was asking: "Well, flower, how is it, did you carry anything off?"

"Yes," he said, "I did."

Afterwards people who sold fire-wood[7] were passing, and the hare then also as previously was crouching absolutely quiet. When they reached the place, they saw that a hare was crouching there. Then these people also put their fire-wood down and commenced to chase the hare. They chased and chased, until they chased him very far off; they tried again and again to seize him, but could not; they also flung a good many pieces of split fire-wood at him. Meanwhile the jackal made use of his opportunity at his end and carried the fire-wood off. Thereupon the two met, and the hare asked him: "Well, flower, how is it, did you carry anything off?"

"Yes, I did," the other one said.

After having talked this much, they again lay in wait as previously. A short while afterwards some potters came along, carrying earthenware vessels[8]. Now the hare was there on the road, was he not? They spotted him, and having put their pottery down, they started chasing to catch him. Chasing him and trying to catch him, now here, now there, they chased him a very great distance off. In the meantime the jackal also came running and carried a cooking-pot away. Thereupon the hare and the jackal again met, and he asked the jackal: "Well, flower, did you carry anything off?"

---

caste. It is a curious sight to see these people coming along, carrying their pots, tied together by the necks, hanging down from the ends of a carrying pole, several dozens at a time.

Adọe mẹnkeťa, Hẽń ạtkirkeťa.

Nokoko calaoen khan, adọ arhõ uni ḳulạ̣i dọe lambẹť hapeyena. Miť ghạṛi khange patṛa ạkriṅkoko calaḱ kana. Khangeko ńẹlkede, kulạiye burum akan. Adọ onko hõ uni kulạiko ota legakedea, ar ḍher sạṅgiṅko laga idikedea; bako gọć daṛeadea. Adọ toyo dọ patṛae ạtkirkeťa. Adọkin ńapamena. Kulikedeae, Cele, phulem ạtkirkeťa?

Hẽ, phuliṅ ạtkirkeťa.

Nonkate jọtọaḱkin ńam tearkeťa. Sẹṅgẹlge thọ okarekin ńama? Khange toyo dọ miťṭaṅ atote sẹnkate miťṭaṅ rạṇḍi buḍhi oṛaḱte sẹṅgẹl kọkọeye calaoena. Uni buḍhi dọ jạnum loboḱe huḱṛuṅ kan tahẽkana. Adọ uni toyo dọe mẹnkeťa. Dẹn buḍhi, sẹṅgẹl emańme.

Uni dọe mẹnkeťa, Ma ạgujoṅme. Iń dọ rẹṅgẹć jalateń huṛuṅjoṅ kana.

Khange toyo dọe mẹnkeťa, Do, amge ạguańme. Iń nãhãḱ iń huṛuṅ hatara.

Adọ buḍhi dọ sẹṅgẹl ạgui calaoena, ar uni toyo dọe huḱṛuṅ kana. Huṛuṅ baṛa huṛuṅ baṛa uni dọ miť ukhuṛem ić pẹrẹćkaťa, ar cetanre dọ jạnum loboḱteye ẹsẹťkaťa. Adọ buḍhi dọ sẹṅgẹle ạguadea. Adọ toyo dọe mẹnkeťa, Iạ, buḍhi, alom huṛuṅ hataṛa. Hapẹ, miť por danaṅ ocoańme.

Toyo miť poro danańen khan, buḍhi dọ huḱṛuṅe pọrtọnkeťa. Huṛuṅ huṛuṅ, adọ iće huṛuṅ toťkeťa jạnum baja jạnum baja. Adọe mẹnkeťa, Nui toyo dọe ić oṭoaťtińa.

---

9 Leaf-plates are always wanted; the brass thạri, or plate, is heavy, and no one has any large number of them. If one has to feed many people, as at a feast, or working people, leaf-plates are used. They are made from sal leaves, fastened together with stiff straw pins. They are used only once and then thrown away. There is one central leaf with three or four others fastened round it.

10 It is even now a very common thing with the Santals to go to some neighbour to ask for fire. Matches are a 'luxury' with many; to make fire by mechanical means takes some time and exertion, and to keep fire from one day to another is not always successfully done.

11 The woman uses a mortar and a pestle.

12 The fruit of the jạnum, Zizyphus Jujuba, Lam., is eaten, both ripe and raw, as an ordinary fruit, or pounded into a flour and cooked, as here. In certain

"Yes, I did," he said.

When these last ones had gone away, the hare again crouched and was lying quietly. A moment afterwards some people passed, who were going to sell leaf-plates[9]. They saw him, there was a hare squatting; and these also tried to seize the hare and chased him a great distance off; they were unable to kill him. And the jackal carried the leaf-plates off. Thereupon they met, and the hare asked him: "Well, flower, did you carry anything off?"

"Yes, flower, I did."

In this way they collected everything necessary. But fire now, where should they get that? The jackal then went to a village to the house of an old widowed woman to ask for fire[10]. Now this old woman was occupied pounding[11] thorn-plum[12] flour, and the jackal said: "Do, old woman, give me fire."

"Do fetch it yourself," she replied; "I am suffering from hunger[13] and am occupied pounding."

"Please, fetch it for me you," the jackal said; "I shall pound for you in the meanwhile."

The old woman then went to bring fire, and the jackal was pounding. He pounded and pounded, and whilst doing this he filled the mortar with his own dung, but on the top he covered it with thorn-plum flour. The old woman then brought him the fire, and the jackal said: "I say, old woman, don't pound just now; wait a little, let me get behind one bush[14]."

When the jackal had got behind one bush, the old woman commenced to pound. Pounding, pounding, she pounded the dung out, stringy plums, stringy plums, and she said: "This jackal has got away having stooled in my mortar."

---

respects the fruit reminds one of a plum, having a stone and flesh. The Santals enjoy eating the fruit, especially of the cultivated variety.

13 The Santal expression may have a double meaning, either as here translated, or, on account of, forced by poverty.

14 The expression is a common Santali one, hidden behind one (not a) bush; then no one knows what may happen, or no one will be able to find or find one out. It is more especially used in connexion with women. When a woman is out of sight there is no knowing what she may do!

Adǫ toyo ruạṛkate sẹṅgẹlkin jolkeťa arkin toa dakayeťa. Toa dakakate adǫ umoǩkin apaj kana. Toyo hõe mẹneťa, Do phul, am maṛaṅ um hijuǩme; ar kulại hõe mẹneťa, Do, amge um hẹć maṛaṅoǩme. Khange adǫ toyoge umoǩe calao maṛaṅena. Jãhã leka khẹṛẹ pẹṭẹye um gǫťena; adǫe hẹćena. Tayǫmte adǫ kulạiye kolkadea, Do phul, um hẹć hǫdoǩme. Adǫe calaoena kulại dǫ. Ạḍi saphae umoǩ kana ạḍi ghạṛić.

Nǫtẹ toyo dǫ celaṅregeye jǫm biyena. Jǫm bikate miť celaṅe ićkeťa, ar cetanre dǫ dakateye topakaťa. Adǫ kulạiye hẹćena. Duṛuṗ ṅapamenakin. Adǫ daka lolokin apaj kana. Toyo hõe mẹneťa, Ma phul, amge loetalaṅme; ar kulại hõe mẹneťa, Ma phul, amge loetalaṅme.

Khange adǫ kulại dǫe lolo kana. Adǫ ićgeye lo tioǩkeť khane ṅẹlkeť, ićge. Adǫ ḍạḍuteye capať baṛakedea, are mẹnkeťa, Noa khicṛi daka lạgiťge unạǩ hǫr hǫrteṅ ǫbǫr baṛae kana? Adǫe laga ṅirkedea.

Khange toyo dǫ miťṭaṅe tumdạǩkeťa, ar miťṭaṅ band latarre dinạm hiloǩge jẹḍẹrkateye ru baṛaea. Adǫ kulại dǫ miť dine

15 The Santali word is used about urging each other to do something first; it may be out of politeness, or it may be because one does not care to take the first step.

16 Here the use of a ladle is mentioned; the story has forgotten to tell where they had procured one.

17 The dancing-drum (tumdaǩ) has a slightly conical body of burnt clay; the body is covered with batches of strips of bullock hide wound tightly round it; both ends are covered with skin, the broad end generally with bullock hide, the narrow end with the skin of a goat or of the hanuman monkey. Both ends are laced with strips of bullock hide, stretched from end to end, close together; these strips make the whole so much stronger, and they are placed closely enough together to prevent the clay body from being easily touched. The ends are given a small layer of boiled rice spread over the surface in circular form, often, when new, painted black, with a red and a white ring outside. The tumdaǩ is carried over the shoulder in leather thongs, the broad end always to the left side. It is drummed with the hands, the broad end with the left, the narrow end with the right hand. The tumdaǩ is always made in pairs, tuned

When the jackal returned, he and the hare lighted a fire and started cooking rice porridge. When they had prepared this, they urged[15] each other to go and bathe. The jackal was saying: "Please, flower, you go and bathe first, do!" And the hare also was saying: "Please, you go first and have your bath." Ultimately the jackal went first to bathe. Floundering and plunging he had his bath quickly somehow, whereupon he came back. Afterwards he sent the hare off, saying: "Do, flower, be quick, have your bath and come back." The hare then went. He bathed so as to become thoroughly clean, it took a long time.

Here where he was the jackal ate his fill out of the cooking-pot. When he was satisfied, he filled the pot with his own dung, and on the top he covered it with rice. Then the hare came, and they sat down facing each other. Then they commenced to contend[15] who was first to take rice out of the pot. The jackal was saying: "Please, flower, you take first for us;" and the hare also was saying: "Please, flower, you take first for us."

The hare then commenced to ladle[16] out. When ladling out he came to the dung, he saw it, it was dung, whereupon he threw the contents about with the ladle and said: "Was it for the sake of this rice stew that I was crouching so many times along the road?" And he drove the jackal away.

Thereupon the jackal procured a dancing-drum[17], and he was in the habit of drumming every day whilst he was sunning

together; the sound of the broad end is of a deeper tone than that of the narrow end, the difference being about a fourth. It is not unmusical in sound. It is the dancing-drum of the Santals above all other drums; but it is not uncommon to hear the sound of it from a Santal house, somebody enjoying to play it, just to listen to the two notes. That is what the jackal is supposed to do here. The Hindus have some drums of a similar shape, but not exactly of the Santal model; they use it for play. It might be remarked that the Santal drum is brittle and easily smashed; the rainy season impoverishes the clay, so it will never last long.

aṅjo̱mket́a ruru. Khange uni do̱ band piṇḍhạ piṇḍhạteye calaoena, ar tumdạḱe ko̱ekedea, De̱ se̱ phul, iṅ ru legaetam. Adoe emadea. Ru baṛa ru baṛa uni do̱m tawaḱ posaḱ go̱t́kat́taea, are dạṛket́a.

Khange ado̱ lagae lagakedea se̱, uni kulạị do̱ mit́ṭaṅ bunum bhugạḱreye bo̱lo̱yena. Ado̱ toyo se̱nkateye duṛup̂ e̱se̱t́kedea. Ona bunum bhugạḱ do̱ tapap̂ge tahẽ̱kana. Uni kulạị do̱ ona bhugạḱ khone ṅir tot́ena. Bae disạledea, dạṛ tap̂ket́ae.

Toyo do̱ duṛup̂ akan duṛup̂ akan ḍe̱ke̱ do̱ tinre co̱ko ṅindirkedea. Khange do̱e beret́ena, are oyoṅ baṛayena. Ado̱ bạihạṛ se̱ne calaoena. Mit́ṭaṅ buḍhi do̱ hakoe sasap̂ kan tahẽ̱kana. Uni ṭhene calaoena, ado̱e metae kana, Dini buḍhi, mit́ṭaṅ puṭhi hako emaṅme.

Ado̱e metae kana, Ma bacha, sap̂joṅme.

Ado̱e sap̂joṅ kana. Mit́ṭaṅ puṭhi hakoe sap̂kedea are jo̱me kana. Ado̱e taboḱ kana mit́ talaoge. Ado̱e me̱net́a, E̱kṭi paelam, e̱kṭi paelam.

Ado̱ buḍhi do̱e me̱nket́a, Inige co̱m jo̱me kana, inigeye taboḱ kan.

Ado̱ khange ḍe̱ke̱ye oyoṅena, ado̱e ṅe̱lket́tae do̱, sạrige. Ado̱ puṭhi hako sap̂kate muci ṭhene calaoena. Ado̱ khange uni puṭhi do̱e uduḱ go̱de kana, arhõ̱e cuput́ oko go̱de kana. Ado̱e metae kana, Nõ̱ḱõ̱e ṭaka. Ma ḍe̱ke̱ dap̂katiṅme. Ado̱e dap̂katae kana. Dap̂ sạt́ket́taeae. Uni puṭhi hako do̱e capat́ giḍi go̱t́kadea, are dạṛket́a.

18 During the cold season people and animals may be seen every morning after sunrise in some sheltered place warming themselves in the rays of the sun.

19 In Santali bạihạṛ, see p. 174, notes 19 & 22.

20 See p. 175, note 24.

21 The word used (bacha) really means 'calf', and is very frequently used as a term of endearment in addressing young men and boys; it is especially used by old women.

22 The jackal gives went to his joy in Bengali.

23 See p. 176, note 26.

himself[18] below the embankment of a tank. One day the hare heard him drumming; he went along the top of the embankment and asked him to lend him the drum: "Do give it to me, flower, let me try to play your drum." He gave it to him; he drummed and drummed, and then suddenly threw his drum down and smashed it for him, whereupon he ran away.

The jackal then chased the hare, chased and chased; and the hare ran into a hole in a white-ant hill. The jackal came and sat down blocking the way for him. Now this white-ant hill had a hole right through it, and the hare ran out at the other end of that hole. The jackal was not aware of it; the hare ran right away.

The jackal was sitting and sitting, and meanwhile the white ants, who knows when, attacked his hind-quarters. Ultimately he got up and peered down; thereupon he went towards some low-lying land[19]. Here an old woman was catching fish. He went up to her and said to her: "Give here, old woman, give me a carp[20] fish.

"Please, dear youngster[21], catch some yourself," she said to him.

He commenced to try to catch. He caught one carp, and was eating this over and over again; it passed through incessantly. And he was saying: "Einen[22] habe ich gefangen, einen habe ich gefangen!"

Then the old woman called out: "Why, it is the same one you are eating; this same one is passing through."

Then the jackal, truth to tell, looked at his hind-quarters, and he saw it was really so. So he took the carp and went to the shoemaker[23]. Here he showed him the carp a moment, and then again he quickly closed his paw over the fish and hid it. He said to him: "Here, you see, is a rupee. Please cover my hind-quarters for me with skin." The shoemaker covered it for him with skin. He finished his work, whereupon the jackal just threw that carp down there, and ran away.

Khange adǫ buḍhi ṭhene calak̓ kana kaskǫm goḍa goḍate. Adǫ ona kaskǫm darete phẹdok̓. Khange saḍetaea. Adǫ ona pẹṭẹćkateye ru baṛaea. Ar uni buḍhi ṭhẽn dinąmge sim kǫkǫeye calak̓a. Uni buḍhi dǫ hǫpǫntẹt̓koe lạiako kana, Din hilok̓ge mit̓ṭan toyo sime kǫeyeńa.

Adǫ khange sitạt̓ren buḍhiko benaokedea, ar chaṭkareko dǫhǫkadea. Adǫ toyo dǫ ru ruteye hijuk̓ kana. Hẹćen khane adǫe mẹnket̓a, Teheń dǫ ią buḍhiye landa daramań kana. Adǫ khange ona ruru ḍaṇḍǫmtegeye capat̓ gǫlkedea. Khange adǫe loka gǫt̓ket̓a. Ona dǫ bań laṭkaoena? Adǫe mẹnet̓a, Nui ią buḍhi yae lokaket̓tińa. Adǫ ńir sẹnkateye thąyą gǫt̓kedea. Adǫ ona jańga hõ laṭkaoena.

Adǫ khange hǫpǫntẹt̓ koṛakoko chaḍaokedea. Chaḍaokede khanko, gitilte bhageteko gadaokedea arko aṛak̓ kadea.

Tayǫmte mit̓ṭań puṭhi hako saṗkate kamar ṭhene calaoena. Adǫe metae kana, Ḍẹkẹ balkatińme. Adǫe balkatae kana. Ḍẹkẹ dǫe oyoń akat̓a. Adǫ khangeye ṭuṇṭi gǫladea goṭa mẽt̓ãhã sẹnte. Adǫ toyo dǫe dạṛket̓a, ar kamar dǫ saṇḍasikoteye capat̓ baṛakedea.

24 The Santali word (p h ẹ t̓) is used as in this place about a branch or the like striking when suddenly released from having been turned aside; it is also used about playing with the fingers or a small bit of wood on a stringed instrument.

25 The Santali word c h a ṭ k a means the ground just outside the front entrance to the court-yard. In some houses there is a mud-wall with an entrance door between the c h a ṭ k a and the r a c a, the court-yard proper. It is, however, more seen in Hindu houses than with the Santals.

After this he was returning to the old woman through a cotton-field, and the cotton bushes were striking against[24] him, and it was sounding. So he broke off a twig and commenced to drum. And he went every day to that old woman to ask her for fowls. The old woman told her sons: "Every day a jackal asks me for fowls."

So they prepared an old woman of wax, and put her down in the street outside the court-yard[25]. Now the jackal was coming along drumming. When he reached there he said: "To-day this unspeakable old woman is meeting me with a laugh," whereupon he threw that drum-stick at her; then he took the stick in his mouth. Then did not that stick? So he said: "This unspeakable old woman has caught it in her hands." Then he ran up to her and kicked her, and so that leg of his also stuck.

Thereupon the old woman's sons disentangled him. When they had extricated him, they crammed[26] him in good style with sand, and so they let him off.

Afterwards he caught a carp and went to the blacksmith, and said to him: "Pierce[27] a hole for me in my hind-quarters." He was doing this; the blacksmith was looking at the place, and he suddenly spurted at him over his face. Thereupon the jackal ran away, whilst the blacksmith flung his thongs at him.

---

26 The word gadao is mostly used about filling and stuffing tightly; it is the word used about loading a muzzle-loading gun.

27 See p. 176, note 28.

STORIES ABOUT WOMEN

INTRODUCTORY REMARKS.

A few remarks on the position of women in the Santal world will make it easier to appreciate some of the points of the stories here collected.

The original and still often theoretically accepted idea about women among the Santals seems to be that she is a kind of irresponsible and untrustworthy being, a necessary and useful, but somewhat inferior member of human society.

Some proverbs show how women are often considered to be morally irresponsible; they are not supposed to be able to resist a man. That this does not correspond with reality, it is unnecessary to point out. At the same time it might be mentioned that, whilst the Indian Penal Code makes adultery a criminal offence, it is only the man who is punished, not the woman. It is not the Santals alone who deem women irresponsible.

Stories are told about the foolishness of women, about their lack of sense and of understanding life and life's demands. They are supposed to be unable to see the consequences of their actions and words. In a quarrel, they will always try to carry the day by resorting to lies and whatever may be thought effective in order to vanquish the other part. They will act on the spur of the moment, heedlessly. And so on.

Further, every woman may be suspected of being a witch, and a witch is, according to their ideas, a demoniacal being, capable of the greatest atrocities and entirely devoid of mercy and human feelings.

These and similar ideas are found among the Santals with regard to women in general. The practical result of such ideas is that the Santal women are to a certain extent disqualified religiously and as regards civic rights.

A Santal woman may have movable property, money, cattle, clothes, &c., but she cannot properly possess real estate, i. e. land (landed property entails certain civic and religious duties upon the owner, which a woman cannot discharge). She has no direct influence on anything concerning the village, nor, legally, on the affairs of her own household. She is only to a certain extent responsible. She is not independent or her own mistress; she is always somebody's "property", first her father's (or her brothers' or nearest male relative's), later on her husband's or his family's, and as a widow she belongs to her sons; if there should not be anyone to represent the right of ownership, she will revert to her first "owners", or practially become a derelict.

It should be remembered that every woman is supposed to be married. Marriage is the goal of every Santal girl, and if a girl is not married, people will think that there is something physically, mentally or otherwise wrong with her. It should not be forgotten, either, that every Santal woman expects to be married. It is unnecessary to point out that such ideas cannot fail to influence the mental attitude, both of the women and also of the men.

If a Santal woman commits an offence against the laws of Santal communal life (we leave out here any consideration of the state of affairs brought about by the Indian Penal Code having been introduced), the matter is brought before the village "Five" and adjudicated, and sentence is passed. It is, however, always the husband or father or brothers, etc., who will have to pay. The punishment is always a fine, when the misdemeanour is not so heinous (according to Santal rules or ideas) that the woman is driven away. Until this happens, the responsible male relative has to pay.

It is not of very frequent occurrence, but it happens, that a man complains to the village "Five" against his wife. The matter is taken up; the wife is found guilty and sentenced to a fine. But the husband has to pay.

This impunity of the Santal women cannot fail to react upon the women themselves; many will, just on account of this freedom from direct punishment, permit themselves to do what they would not likely do in other circumstances; they are perhaps specially liable to let their tongue run without restriction.

The, not very high-classed, remedy that a man will resort to, when nothing else will avail, is the stick. Wife-beaters are not held in great respect by the people. On the other hand, I have heard a story of a termagant, who did not appreciate the qualities of her good and longsuffering husband. One day he could not stand it any longer, but found a stick and gave his wife a thrashing. "Now I can feel that you are a man," was what the woman said. She acknowledged the authority of the man.

Besides being so heavily disqualified as to civic rights, a Santal woman is also in very much the same position as regards religious rights. A woman may salute the Sun, i. e. the Supreme Being, and she may be made to take an oath, or may herself call on the Supreme Being; but she is not permitted to participate in worship. If she feels the need of invoking the **boṅgas**, she has to do it through her male "owners". She is, as is natural, incapacitated from officiating at sacrifices and also from participating in the act; she may partake of the flesh of most sacrificed animals, although never of the head. In the case of certain sacrifices, women are not permitted to eat anything of the sacrificed animals, and, with regard to certain **boṅgas**, the Santals are very particular that not even their names shall be known to women, the reason for this precautionary measure being said to be that if a woman should get to know such a name, she might be able to get into communication with the **boṅga** in question and seduce him to do her will.

Certain "holy" things are polluted by the presence of women. That certain old women, especially the wife of the village priest, may get a little nearer to the "holies" than ordinary women does not alter the general state. It should be remarked that the women are supposed to prepare some of the ingredients, such as flour, used at sacrifices.

As I have remarked elsewhere, I am inclined to think that the practice of witchcraft by Santal women is, to a certain extent, really secret worship, resorted to by women because they are not permitted to take part with the men directly and personally in ordinary public worship.

In spite of all the disqualifications mentioned above, the position of the Santal woman is much better than with many other primitive races. Human feelings assert themselves, and nature itself makes up for much.

In spite of all the men may talk and possibly also think, they love and respect their women-folk. They are always and at once ready to stand up for sisters, daughters, mothers and wives.

With regard to the last mentioned ones, there are some reservations to be made. Regular marriage is among the Santals not the result of young people falling in love with each other. It is a family arrangement, a union between two families, arranged through a go-between; the two persons most concerned have very little choice, are not, before marriage, permitted to speak to each other, only just to see one another from a safe distance; they may now-a-days refuse to marry the party selected, but will otherwise leave everything to the older ones. A wife is bought (this is the legal base, but the bride-price should perhaps be considered more as a symbol than as an actual payment) and becomes the property of the husband's family. It does not always work well; the young ones are sometimes divorced after all accounts have been squared, and a new union is arranged. When it goes well, it will in any case take some time for the two to learn to know each other; but when they do so, their relations may become very good.

So far as natural abilities are concerned, the Santal woman does not seem to be inferior to the man; in many cases and with regard to certain matters she may give the impression of being better than the man, quicker and more sharpwitted. Otherwise the same differences in quality, found with other peoples between the male and the female, may also be observed among the Santals. The woman is generally livelier than the man and also more industrious. While the men may have long periods off work, the women have always something to do in the house or the family.

The Santal woman is a woman and knows her powers as such and how to use them. She manages the house and keeps it clean (as well as she may know), she prepares the food, &c., and as a matter of fact does everything necessary to make the man free to pursue his special work. She is what in Santali is called oṛak'hoṛ, i. e., the house-person (a term which may also, however, be used about a husband). She will frequently be found to be the one who rules in the house; frequently it is not so long a step from this to something more, if the woman is endowed with the desire for power and is ambitious. *Mutatis mutandis*, there is, so far as the writer has been able to observe, no great natural difference between the Santal woman and those of more civilized races, although, as could not be otherwise expected, there is a tremendous difference in practical life.

The Santal woman is not kept shut up in a zenana, more or less secluded from the outside world. She is free and may go wherever she likes, provided she has accepted or proper company. It might be said to be symbolic that she, unlike so many oriental women, goes about with an uncovered head and face.

In a good Santal household the state of matters will generally be as follows: the woman acknowleges the superiority of the position of the man. She depends on him; she is subordinate to him, but it depends to a large extent on herself how subordinate or co-ordinate her position will be. Husband and wife will consult each other in most matters. It is frequently the case that the

wife keeps the purse. It will never contain much, but still it will be enough for the man to show his confidence in his wife.

It must not, however, be lost sight of that the civic and religious disqualifications of the Santal women cannot but create a barrier between the two sexes, and it may happen that the female 'society' may be quite untouched, barring a few exceptions, when the men are much excited by some thing or other.

The following, which was told the writer by an English gentleman who played a rôle in it, will go some way to show what qualities may be found with Santal women. It happened during the war; the Englishman in question had been to a Santal village and was taking a number of men along with him to send them to the Front as members of a Labour Corps. They were walking along, the women following to say good-bye. So long as the men were there, there was nothing else than high spirits, nobody saying or doing anything to lower the spirits of those who were going away. Then a halt was called, the men were sent on, and the women had to return to their village. As soon as the men were out of sight and hearing, the scene suddenly altered entirely: all these light-spirited women crowded round the Englishman, commenced to cry, fell at his feet and gave vent to what was in their hearts, imploring him to do everything he could to bring their men back to their homes. He had only admiration for the spirit shown by these uncivilized women.

It should not be omitted that there is a kind of movement on foot among the Santal men to give their women a more secure position. They have long had a way of circumventing the law prohibiting women from inheriting land. In case of a man having only daughters and no sons, he may, with the knowledge and sanction of the village people, get a man to marry his daughter on the understanding that he is to remain in the house and take over the whole when the father is no more. No bride-price is paid, this being settled by the young man working for his wife (just like Jacob of old), and as far as marriage ceremonies are

concerned, everything is reversed. The girl's father acts as otherwise the bridegroom's father would have done. Only, of course, the bridegroom does what only the man can do, puts sindur on the girl's forehead.

The present day Santals have, at several times, given formal expression to a desire of theirs that the position of their women should be bettered, in as much as, on the one side, widows should have a right of sustenance from their late husbands' estate, and, on the other hand, that daughters should have the right of inheritance in preference to remote male relatives.

With reference to the folktales here translated, the points of which are various supposed qualities of women, whilst some of them are undoubtedly true to nature, others have to be marked as 'man-made'. Whilst the foolishness of women may be the subject of some, there are other stories showing quite the opposite. It is quite frequent to hear allusions to the cunning and guiles of women. In a story about the origin of witchchraft among the Santals it is told how the women outwitted not only their husbands, but even Marań Buru, the Santal devil, himself.

16. Dundhi maejiu reaṅ.

Sedae jo̱khe̱n Ho̱ṛ ho̱po̱n do̱, kathae, dundhạ dundhigeko tahẽkana. Ona reak̓ mit̓ṭaṅ kạhni menak̓a.

Mit̓ṭaṅ atore, kathae, ato sudhạ ho̱ṛte kuṭạm ḍaṅgrak̓ko neṇḍaket̓a; ado̱ oṛak̓ oṛak̓ mimit̓ goṭaṅ hạṇḍiko ḍo̱ho̱ket̓a. Ado̱ ona neṇḍa din do̱ mit̓ din baṅ tiok̓ akan tahẽkanrege, kathae, he̱re̱l ho̱po̱n do̱ mit̓ mit̓te jo̱to̱ raj biṭhiko sap̓ idiket̓koa, arko metat̓koa, Ape do̱ mõṛẽ mãhã din o̱ṇḍe̱ge tahe̱n hoyok̓tapea. Ado̱ sipạhi bo̱to̱rte o̱ko̱e hõ cet̓ hõ bako ro̱ṛ daṛeat̓a. Ado̱ko idiket̓kogea.

1 When the men also are here styled foolish, this likely refers to what is told about their permitting themselves to be carried away without the least show of protest or opposition.

2 Kuṭạm ḍaṅgra, lit. 'felled bullock', is a sacrifice to the Ancestors. It is performed either as the result of a vow, or in connexion with the so-called jo̱m sim, a large family festival with sacrifices in honour of the jo̱m sim boṅga, originally, it is told in the Traditions, a sacrifice to Siń boṅga, the Sun, representing the Supreme Being. At kuṭạm ḍaṅgra three oxen are sacrificed, one to the Ancestors, one to the oṛak̓ boṅga, i. e. the house or family boṅga, and one to Maraṅ Buru, the chief national godling of the Santals. There is one notable difference between sacrifices to the Ancestors and to the boṅgas. A sacrifice of an animal or a fowl to a boṅga is performed by decapitation, whilst to the Ancestors it is done by striking the neck or back of the head of the animal with the head of an axe. This operation gives name to the performance, kuṭạm in Santali meaning to strike with a hammer or the like. The kuṭạm ḍaṅgra festival is the business of one man, the head of a family, and not, as might be supposed from what is told in this story, something undertaken by the village community as such.

16. THE SILLY WOMEN.

In the olden times, people tell, the Santals, both men and women, were foolish and witless[1]. There is a tale about this.

In a certain village, it is told, the whole village population had fixed a day for feasting with a sacrifice of a bullock to the Ancestors[2]; in every house they had consequently commenced brewing a pot of rice-beer[3]. Then just one day before the day appointed, it is told, people came and carried the men, every single one of them, away to do forced labour for the zemindar[4]; they told them: "You will have to remain there for five days." Out of fear for the zemindar's messengers[5] no one was able to say anything, and they took the men away with them.

Where the whole village, as sometimes happens, belongs to the same family, they will naturally all participate.

3 See end of last note. If all do not belong to the same family, it is irregular that they brew beer in every house for this festival. Haṇḍi is beer brewed from rice or some other cereal. The process of fermenting takes five days; when it is ready, water is poured on, and the stuff drunk. The fermenting is done in earthen-ware pots. Haṇḍi cannot be kept for any length of time. See p. 186, note 3.

4 Forced labour is, I believe, at the present day illegal in India. In spite of this, it is even now very commonly practised especially by petty landlords and others who have some kind of power over tenants and subordinates. When people are taken for such service, they will generally get their food and sometimes a little more, the last to screen the illegality of the matter.

Adǫ khange onko ąimąi dǫko as chuṭąuena; mǫnkeťako, Ǫkǫ baḍae, aboren hǫrǫl dǫko aṛaǩko cǫṅ baṅ cǫṅ; pasǫ nāhāǩko maǩ gǫćkotabona.

Adǫ ona atoren ąimąiko jarwayenteko rǫṛ ṭhikkeťa, Ma teheṅ dǫ hare pharebon teke sǫbǫť hǫdoǩa arbon um naṛkaǩa; adǫ ąyuṗ jǫkhǫn hǫrǫl hǫpǫn leka nẽo dhǫrǫm lągiťbon naekeǩa. Ma teheṅ ṅindą dǫ ǫtregebon gitića, ar gapa dǫ aboge gąibon kuṭąmkoa hana birre idikate.

Adǫ sanam hǫṛko mǫnkeťa, Acha, ma ǫṇḍǫkhanbo onkaea.

Adǫ sąriko teke sǫbǫťenteko nẽo dhǫrǫmkeťa. Adǫ aṅgayen khan, boṅga reaǩ jǫtǫ sǫrǫmjamko sajaokeťa, ar gąiko tǫlkedea. Adǫ birre idikate, kathae, miťṭan sarjǫm dare buṭą ṭhenko hǫṛheť ṭąṇḍikeťa arko gurićkeťa. Adǫ khõṇḍ baṛakate caoleko curuć-

5 The word here translated 'messenger' is the word commonly used for native soldiers (sipąhi, sepoy, the same orig. Persian word which, with a somewhat different meaning, has come into French via Algeria as spahi). Every native 'king' or landlord and similar persons have, according to their importance and power, more or less of those. They are used for every possible purpose, as messengers, as private guards and to enforce commands. They very frequently do not seem to have any feeling of conscience. Their employer has the responsibility. The incident here reported is very much like what has often taken place.

6 When they think it is time to wash their clothes, the Santal women do the washing themselves. The clothes are first boiled with ashes at home, whereupon the woman puts them on the ends of a stick, and balancing this on her head she takes the clothes down to water and washes them there. The washing is done by dumping each piece of cloth on a stone, or by beating it against it. It is finally rinsed in water and spread on the grass or on a rock or anywhere to dry, a very short process in the Indian climate.

7 To wash their hair the Santals, both men and women, make use of a kind of alkaline earth that gives some lather.

8 Nẽo dhǫrǫm, here translated with 'sanctifying oneself', is something deemed necessary previously to the performance of a sacrifice. The male members of a household, especially the sacrificer, have during the night before the sacrifice to be abstinent. They are not to eat or drink, they do not sleep on a bedstead,

The women now lost hope and said: "Who knows whether they will set our men free or not; perhaps they will presently kill them for us."

The women-folk of that village then came together, and talked and decided: "Let us to-day boil and wash our clothes[6], bathe and wash our hair[7]; then we shall this evening sanctify ourselves[8], like the men do, and become priests[9]. This coming night we shall sleep on the floor, and to-morrow we shall ourselves take the cows[10] over to that forest and fell them there."

"That is good," they all of them said, "let us then do so."

So they verily boiled and washed their clothes and sanctified themselves, sleeping on the floor. As soon as it became dawn, they made the things necessary for the sacrifice[11] ready and tied a cow up. Having taken the cow nd everything to the forest, they weeded a small spot clean at the foot of a sal

but on a mat on the floor, and they must not go near to women. With some of the septs it is demanded of the sacrificer that he is not even to sit down on a stool until after he has performed the sacrifice; otherwise the whole will be vitiated. In some cases the wife of the priest has also to sleep on the floor, perhaps because she, in such cases, may have to come a little nearer to the performance than women are otherwise permitted to. Otherwise this nẽo dhọrọm does not apply to the women of a household.

9 It is entirely against all Santal ideas that a woman should officiate as a priest, i. e., as a sacrificer. As already remarked, they are disqualified from participating in sacrificing. All religious ceremonies have to be performed for them through their nearest male relative.

10 The sacrificial animal should be an uncastrated male. It happens, however, now-a-days that female fowls, goats and sheep are used, but only when they are so young that sex has not commenced to manifest itself. A cow would be an impossibility for sacrificial purposes.

11 I. e., an implement for beheading (ordinarily the old battle-axe, now-a-days used exclusively for this purpose, here an ordinary axe), some rice, sindur (the red lead used for applying religious marks), a little flour (not always) and a little cow-dung.

keťa arko sindur baṛawaťa. Adǫ uni gąi daǩko chiṭkąuadete ona khǫ̃ṇḍ ṭhenko samaṅkedea; adǫko mẹneťa, Dẹ nabon bakhẹ̃ṛa, dẹ guruǩtabonpe, ǫkǫepe baḍae khan dǫ.

Adǫ ǫkǫe hǫ̃ bako baḍaete sanam hǫṛko apaj kana. Adǫ ǫkǫe hǫ̃ bako rẹbẹn kana.

Adǫ uni mąṅjhi erage, kathae, baǩkhẹ̃ṛe ẹhǫp̌keťa, Nǫ̃ǩǫ̃e kuṭąm ḍaṅgra boṅga, gąile kuṭąmam kana; ma aleren hẹrẹl jẹmǫnko ruąṛ hijuǩ ma; raj aloe boṅgakotale ma, hẹć ruąṛ gǫdoǩ mako.

Adǫ enka rǫṛkatege mąṅjhi erae mẹnkeťa, Dẹ ho, ceťkobo bakhẹ̃ṛa? Ma rǫṛtabonpe, jǫtǫkotebon bakhẹ̃ṛa.

Adǫko mẹnkeťa, Baṅa, besgem bakhẹ̃ṛkeťtabona. Adǫ ceť babon bakhẹ̃ṛ? Ma cabayena, adǫbon kuṭąmea.

Adǫ kathae, sanam hǫṛko tẹhẹ̃ mẹhẹ̃ baṛae kana. Adǫ mąṅjhi erae ẹgẹr gǫťkeťkoa, Ma hako pako ṭaṅga sap̌kate kuṭąmepe.

Adǫko mẹnkeťa, Oka ṭhenle kuṭąmea? Ba cǫle baḍae kan.

12 When a sacrifice is to be performed, they first make a so-called khǫ̃ṇḍ, a small magic circle. A small spot is cleaned, plastered with cow-dung and sometimes with flour. Here they put a handful of rice, and a small streak of sindur is put there. The animal to be sacrificed is then made to feed on the rice; whilst this goes on, the sacrificial invocation (called bakhẹ̃ṛ) is offered, always a stereotype rigmarole, with now and then some words not understood by the present day Santals.

This khǫ̃ṇḍ is, when made at the foot of a tree, generally made at the foot of a sal (Shorea robusta, Gaertn.) tree, the only exception being that a matkǫm (Bassia latifolia, Roxb.) tree is used when sacrificing to Gosãe era; when sacrificing kuṭąm ḍaṅgra, as here, no khǫ̃ṇḍ is made, but the bullock is made to feed on rice from a leaf-plate put before it. There is consequently a double mistake here.

13 See preceding note.

14 This is customary. Just previous to sacrificing, a handful of water is sprinkled on the animal.

15 See note 12. It should be remarked that the animal is made to face towards the East when feeding on the rice.

tree[12] and plastered it with cowdung. Having prepared the magic circle in this way, they put a handful of rice there and applied sindur[13]. Thereupon they sprinkled water on the cow[14] and made her face the magic circle. "Now, girls," they said, "we shall offer an invocation[15]; do lead us, please, whoever of you knows how to do it."

But as no one knew how to do it, they all of them excused themselves and asked the other ones to act. No one was willing.

Then the wife of the headman of the village, it is told, commenced to offer an invocation[16], as follows: "Look here, thou bonga of the felled bullock, we are felling a cow for thee; may our men come back; may the king not sacrifice them for us; may they come quickly back."

Having spoken in this way the wife[17] of the village headman said: "Now then you, what are we to make invocation for? Do say something; we shall all of us make invocation."

"No," they said, "you offered a very good invocation for us. What need for any more invocation? That's finished; let us now fell the cow."

But all of them were hanging back. Then the wife of the village headman commenced to scold them: "Now be quick, please, take the axe and strike her."

"Where are we to strike her?" they asked. "Surely we don't know that."

16 The women knowing nothing of the regular invocations, against all practice give utterance to what at the moment is uppermost in their hearts. Ordinarily the smallest deviation from the stereotype form of the bakhẽṛ is supposed to give occasion for revenge from the side of the boṅga invoked. The idea of invoking a boṅga to get help is foreign to the Santals, the underlying idea always being to induce the boṅgas in question to abstain from hurting or harassing. This also holds good with regard to the Ancestors.

17 The wife of the village headman will naturally be expected to take the lead, if she is at all fit. The maṅjhi era has a reputation for wishing to rule the village.

Adǫ uniye mẹnkeťa, Oka ṭhen jivi menaǩtaea, ǫṇḍẹ dǫ bape kuṭạmea?

Adǫko mẹnkeťa, Okor ẹnte, oka ṭhen´menaǩtaea?

Adǫe metaťkoa, Jāhā̃ ṭhenge laṛaoǩpe ńẹla, ǫṇḍẹ baṛẹ kuṭạmepe.

Adǫ khange sạriko bẹṅgẹť baṛawae kana, adǫ caṇḍbǫlge sạri laṛaoǩ kanko ńẹlefa; adǫko mẹnkeťa, Ǫṇḍẹge jivi dǫ menaǩtaea, ma kuṭạm hǫde ma.

Adǫ sạri hǫṭǫǩreko tǫlkedete pẹ pon hǫṛteko saṕ akadea, ar mitťaṅ ạimại dǫe kuǩṭạm kana. Adǫ ona phẹḍ caṇḍbǫl ṭhenaǩ jaṅregeye kuṭạm gǫťkedea bar dhaote. Adǫ uni gai dǫ, kathae, hasokede khane aḍo gǫťkeťa. Adǫko mẹnkeťa, Ma na, ma na, mā̃yā̃mtẹť ạtuǩ kana, ma bạṭire ataṅ hǫdpe. Adǫ sạriko ataṅkeťa, kathae.

Arhǫ̃ko kuṭạmkede khan, uni gạị dǫ hasokede khan bogeteye dǫnkeťa; adǫe paskaoenteye dạṛkeťa. Adǫ kaskǫm gọḍa talateye dạṛkeťa, adǫ bogeteko khudạukedea; adǫ kaskǫm ǫṭẹć dǫ bogeteye kolsa ńū̃r idikeťa. Adǫko mẹnkeťa, Nǫ̃ǩǫ̃e na, itil dǫ nonkate bogete jǫrǫ idiyentaea."

Adǫ uni gạị dǫe dạṛkeťa, bako laga saṕ daṛeadea. Adǫ ona kaskǫmge itil mẹnteko jǫmkeťa.

Adǫ cabayena katha dǫ, in maraṅgea. Sedae jugren ạimại do, kathae, ǫnẹ onka lilhi sẹ dundhiko tahẽkana.

18 The Santal idea of what the soul is, is difficult to determine. The soul, jivi, as it is called, is the principle of life or what is the condition of life in all beings that can move. A plant has life, but has not a soul. The body is the 'hut', as it is freqently called, of the soul. When the soul departs, death takes place. They may speculate on where the soul is, but do not, as is natural, come to any result, further than putting questions.

19 Movement in a body is a sign of life, and so they draw their own conslusions. It might be noted that, while they do not locate the soul, they make use of the expression jivi hǫr, soul-way, for parts of the body from which the soul may

"Where the soul[18] is," she answered, "won't you strike her there?"

"Where is that then?" they said; "in which place has she got her soul?"

"In any place where you see anything moving[19]," she replied, "strike her there."

So they looked at the cow, it may be, and in very truth they saw the tail moving; then they said: "There she has got her soul; do be quick and strike her."

Then, to tell the truth, they tied the cow[20] by her neck, and three or four of them caught hold of her, whilst one woman was giving her blow after blow with the head of an axe. She twice hit her on the bone close to the tail, and when the cow felt the pain of this, she urinated. "Look girls," they cried, "look girls, the blood is flowing; be quick, receive it in a cup." And so they did, it is told.

As they again hit the cow with the axe-head and she felt the pain of it, she jumped and kicked; then she got loose and ran away. She ran off through a cotton field, and they gave chase all they could. Running along the cow kicked down a good deal of burst cotton pods. "Look here, girls," they said, "all along here her fat has fallen down."

The cow ran away; they were not able to catch hold of her. So they ate that cotton, thinking it was fat.

There the story is ended; it is thus much. In olden times, people tell, the women were silly or witless in this way.

depart, especially where a hurt may cause instantaneous death. The genitals are also included in this.

20 An animal to be sacrificed is led along by a rope or the like to the place of sacrifice; but there it is unchained.

17. Maejiukǫ reak̕ katha.

Sedae jǫkhẹn, kathae, mit̕ṭen atore` dǫ ẹkẹn akoge bhạiạdi hǫpǫnko tahẽkana; mit̕ oṛak̕ gan hõ eṭak̕ hǫṛ dǫ bạnuk̕koa. Khange onko bhạiạdi dǫko mẹnket̕a, Ẹ ya, ḍher din khon babon kuṭạm ḍaṅgra akana; ma nẹs dǫbon kuṭạm ḍaṅgrak̕a, hapṛamkobon kuṭạmakoa.

Adǫ adǫm hǫṛko mẹnket̕a, Onabon kaj khan dǫ, ma ẹṇḍẹkhan nią batarre, ar baṅkhan dǫ ạḍi dinte calak̕a.

Khange sạri adǫko neṇḍa gǫt̕ket̕a, Ma hạṇḍiko dǫhǫ baṛa ocoko ma, nin din in dinre dǫbon kaj gǫda. Adǫ, kathae, oṛak̕re dǫ onkako lại saḍe baṛaket̕a. Ar ako hẹrẹl hǫpǫn dǫ bạnij beparko calak̕ kana; adǫ onko maejiuko dǫko mẹnet̕a, Noa kạmi mape batlao oṭokak̕ kan, ar ape mape calak̕ kan; adǫ ǫkǫe nãhãk̕ noa dǫ cekaea ar ǫkǫe ba gẹt̕ kuṭiale?

[1] This story is a variant of the preceding one. It omits something found in the first tale and has something not found there. Both stories are written by the same man, Sagram Murmu, the first about 1896, the second some twelve years later.

[2] See p. 228, note 2. Formerly it was fairly common that the inhabitants of a village belonged to the same stock, were descendants from a known, not remote ancestor. Even now there are villages where the majority of the people are related in this way. It might be mentioned in this connexion that the inhabitants of the same village will always, if they are not related, make up an artificial relationship. The reason given for this is that related people do not need to restrain themselves so much in their daily intercourse; they feel an absolute need, they say, of having such an arrangement and to feel themselves as belonging to one family. Another reason is that related people will naturally make use of the terms of relationship when calling to or addressing each other. To use names in adressing is not considered good and is avoided as much as possible. We possibly find something of a similar nature among ourselves, when children are taught to address family friends as uncles or aunts, etc.

[3] See p. 228, note 2.

[4] See p. 229, note 3. Beer brewing is ordinarily the work of women.

[5] This is the regular way of letting the women know of anything of a public nature. The head of the family tells it so that all may hear. The Santali expression lại saḍe, lit. 'telling make a sound', speaks for itself.

17. THE STORY OF SOME WOMEN[1].

In the old days, people tell, in a certain village there once upon a time only lived people of the same stock, sons of brothers[2]; there was not even one family of others. One day these brothers and cousins said among themselves: "Look here, you, it is a very long time that we have not felled an ox in honour of our Ancestors[3]. Let us have the feast now this year; let us make a sacrifice to our Ancestors."

"If we are to have that," some of them said, "let us have it now at this time; otherwise it may be postponed for any length of time."

So they, truth to tell, at once fixed a day: "Well, get them to start brewing beer[4]; on such and such a day we shall have the thing done." Hereupon they mentioned the matter in their respective families[5]. The men were going away to trade[6], and the women were saying: "Now you are giving instructions concerning this work, and you are going away; then who will presently do this, and who will cut the flesh into pieces for us[7]?"

6 It is not common for Santals to trade. No Santal keeps a shop; they may take anything they want to sell to a market-place and dispose of it there, otherwise there is little trading. The writer has heard of Santals who have gone away to sell cattle, or who have bought up clothes and the like at home and have gone away for shorter or longer periods to sell the goods. One man known to the writer was in the habit of going with cloth from his village in the Santal Parganas and up to the Assam districts to sell it to other Santals in tea-gardens. A variant states that the men went off to sell charcoal. In former days, when they were living in the forests, they cut down trees, prepared charcoal and went and sold this to the Hindus.

7 The remark is intended to show the women up. Their thoughts are only for the material side of the whole. Incidentally it may be noted that, when Santals prepare flesh of any kind for eating, the whole is, before being cooked, cut into small pieces. They have only their fingers to eat with, so all the pieces must be so small that there will be no need of cutting at the time of eating.

Adọko mẹnkeťa, Ma sẹ ape dọ tear hataṛpe, nią iną dinre dọle ruąṛ hijuǩgea, ar nią dinre dọbon kajgea.

Adọ onkako neṇḍawaťko khanko thirena. Ar ako hẹrẹl họpọn dọko calaoengea, ar noko maejiuko dọ hąṇḍikoko dọhọ tearkeťa. Adọ ona neṇḍa din tioǩenre hō̱ hẹrẹl họpọnko dọ bako sẹṭẹroǩ kan. Adọ onko ąimąi dọko mẹneťa, Okor nako hijuǩ kana, na, noko hẹrẹl dọ? Nō̱ǩō̱e gapa dinge kaj reaǩko neṇḍa oṭoaťbona, adọ okorko sẹṭẹrlena?

Adọ iną bąrsiṅ dinko ṅẹl họrkeťkoa; adọ bako sẹṭẹrlen khanko mẹnkeťa, Noko hẹrẹl dọ, na, ọhọko hẹćlena; ma gapa dọbon teke sọbọdoǩte ar gẹć gurijoǩte abogebo pujhąroǩtebo kuṭąmkoa.

Adọko mẹpẹn kana, Henda na, ọkọeko boṅga ṅutumtebon kuṭąmkoa?

Adọ uni maraṅ họṛren oṛaǩ họṛko mukhiąkedea, ẹn kathae, Dẹ dąi, amge mukhiąǩtabonme; am dọ boṅga hō̱m baḍaea ar ọkọeko dāṛẽ̱, ona hō̱ jąnić am dọm baḍaegea, arem ṅẹl ceť ągu akaťgea.

Adọ uniye mẹnkeťa, Hẽ̱, dāṛẽ̱ko dọe ląi ceť oṭoadiṅgea, baṅma, oṛaǩ oṛaǩ mimiť goṭaṅbon oḍokkoa; ar boṅga dọ neko gọć họṛkoge tinąǩ haṛam buḍhiko gọć akan, enkokogebon bakhẽ̱ṛakoa.

8 See p. 230, note 6.

9 The smearing with cow-dung makes the place 'clean'; it is especially done before a sacrifice is to be performed. The floor and part of the court-yard is treated in this way.

10 See p. 231, note 9.

11 Women will know the names of the common, national godlings, or the names used for these in common parlance; but they are not supposed to know any form of worship. In some cases the names of the boṅgas are kept secret with great care, to prevent the women from knowing them. The supposition that any woman should know anything is likely meant to show how utterly foolish they can be.

12 The wife of the senior brother cannot resist this appeal. She has heard something, and she draws her own conclusions. 'One bullock for every house' is an idea that will appeal to the Santal sense of humour; it would mean a great feed and capacity for such.

"Do, please," they said, "you make everything ready; after so and so many days we shall return, and on that day we shall do the thing."

As they appointed a day for them in this way, the women did not say anything more. So the men went away, and the women commenced brewing beer. But the appointed day came; still the men did not arrive. The women then said among themselves: "How is it, girls, that they do not come, these men? See now, it was for to-morrow that they appointed the day for this matter for us when they went away; how is it that they have not come?"

They then waited for them for two days; still they did not come, so they said: "These men will never come, girls; let us therefore boil and wash our clothes[8] and clean everything with cow-dung, ready for the sacrifice[9]; then let us ourselves become priests and perform the sacrifice[10]."

"Look here, girls," they said to each other, "in the name of which **boṅgas**[11] are we going to sacrifice the animals?"

They thereupon constituted the wife of the eldest brother their leader, saying: "Please, elder sister, you please be our leader; you know the **boṅgas** also; and what animals are to be sacrificed, that you also likely know; you have seen and learnt from time to time."

"Well, yes," she replied, "the animals to be sacrificed he has told me before he went away, namely, that we are to take out one for every house[12], and the **boṅgas**, they are these dead people[13], as many men and women as are dead, to them we are to offer our invocation."

[13] The dead ones are looked upon as having become **boṅgas**. It is not only the dead males but also the dead women to whom sacrifices are made. Otherwise those in the other world are thought to live in somewhat the same way as they do here; after death, at certain ceremonies, the first human pair are invoked to take care of the departed one.

Adǫ sanam hǫṛko mẹnkeťa, Dẹ dại, ẹṇḍẹkhan amge purkhạǩtabonme.

Adǫe mẹnkeťa, Acha, ma ẹṇḍẹkhan iṅgeń purkhạǩtabona; ạikạ kuṭạm dǫ apege kuṭạmkotabonpe.

Adǫko mẹnkeťa, Acha, inạ dǫ jǫtǫkotele kạmia.

Adǫ kathae, onka sanam hǫṛ rǫṛ ṭhikkateko teke sǫbǫťena, ar gẹć gurićente hǫlǫṅkoko huṛuṅkeťa; adǫ kuṭạmko ṭhen gạiko laga idikeťkoa. Adǫko gurić ṭạṇḍikeťte hǫlǫṅteye khǭṇḍkeťa, caolekoe curućkeťa; adǫ gạiko ạgu sorkedete daǩko chiṭkạuadea. Adǫ khǭṇḍ ṭhen samaṅkedeteko ạtiṅkedea arko bakhẹ̃ṛkeťa.

Adǫ uni purkhạ erae mẹnkeťa, Dẹ, adǫ nui gại kuṭạmetabonpe.

Adǫ jǫtǫgeko apaj kana; nui hǭe mẹneťa, Dẹ na, amge kuṭạmem, ar huni hǭe mẹneťa, De na, amge kuṭạmem. Adǫ onkako apaj kana. Adǫ miť hǫṛe jhũk 'gǫťenteye mẹnkeťa, Dẹn thǫ, ṭaṅga emaṅpe, kuǩṭạmko apaj baṛae kana! Dẹn emaṅpe.

Adǫ ṭaṅgae saṕkeťa are metako kana, Ma ape dǫ saṕaṅpe.

Adǫ hǫṭǫǩre baber akawadeteko saṕ akadea. Adǫe metako kana, Ma lạiaṅpe oka ṭhen iṅ kuṭạmea

Adǫko mẹn gǫťkeťa, Oka ṭheniṅ kuṭạmea? Jivi hǫrre dǫ bam kuṭạmea?

Adǫ, kathae, phẹḍ caṇḍbǫlreye kuṭạm gǫťkedea. Adǫe khẹṇṭẹ pẹṛẹ gǫťen khan dǫ, kathae, ḍẹkẹreye kuṭạm gǫťkedea. Adǫ kathae, andhe pạthạuṛiye kuṭạmedea, ghanẹ ḍẹkẹre, ghanẹ caṇḍbǫlre. Khange uni gại dǫe ạḍo gǫť keťa. Adǫko mẹn gǫťkeťa,

[14] She draws the line here; it is otherwise the work of the sacrificer to kill the animal.

[15] Cf. p. 238, note 9 and the notes to the preceding tale.

[16] It does not seem that they have more than one cow. The plural is in Santali often used for expressing something indefinite, some one or other, about one only.

[17] Note the different pronouns.

[18] See p. 235, note 20.

"Do, elder sister," they all of them said, "you then please be our leader."

"All right,," she replied, "then I shall be our leader; but mind you, the felling[14] — you must do that for us."

"Very well," they said, "so far as that is concerned, we shall, all of us, see to that being done."

Thereupon they all talked together and came to a decision, boiled and washed their clothes, and cleaned the ground with cow-dung and prepared flour[15]; when this was done they took a cow[16] to the place where they were going to sacrifice her. There they cleaned a place and plastered it with cow-dung, and she[17] made a magic circle with rice-flour and put a handful of rice there. Thereupon they brought the cow near and sprinkled water on her; then they made her face the magic circle and offered the invocation.

"Now then," the leading wife said, "fell the cow for us."

But all of them were telling somebody else than themselves to do it. This one said: "Do, my girl, you fell her," and that one said: "Do, my girl, you fell her." In this way they were hanging back and trying to make somebody else than themselves do it. At last one of them plucked up courage and said: "Come then, give me the axe; they are all of them backing out of the felling; here, give it to me."

So she caught hold of the axe and was saying to the others: 'You please, hold her for me."

Now they had put a rope round the cow's neck[18] and were holding her. She then says to them: "Please tell me, where am I going to strike her."

"Where am I to strike her?" they replied; "are you not to strike her where the soul's way is?[19]"

Then, people tell, she gave her a blow at the foot of the tail, and when the cow was jumping and struggling to get free, she hit her a blow on the hind-quarters; and then she hit her wherever she could, over and over again, now on the hind-quarters, now on the tail. The cow then urinated, and they called out:

Dẹ na, dẹ na, bạṭiko ạguipe na, māyāmbon ataṅa, māyām jọrọ giḍiḱ kana.

Adọ kathae, bạṭikore celaṅkoreko ataṅketa; adọ ona māyāmko ataṅketre hō̱ bae gujuḱ kan. Khange arhō̱e kuṭạm dohṛakedea. Khange arhō̱e aḍo gọtket khanko mẹn gọtketa, Ma na, ma na, māyāmtẹt jọrọ giḍiḱ kana. Khan dọ inạ hō̱ko ataṅketa, adọ ẹnre hō̱ bae gujuḱ kan.

Khanko metae kana, Okor nam gọć daṛeae kana?

Adọe mẹnketa, Iń dọń kuṭạm laṅgayena, adọ dẹ ape kuṭạmletabonpe.

Khange sạri onko hō̱ko kuṭạm laṅgayena, ẹn hō̱ bae gujuḱ kan. Khanko aṛaḱ dapoṛkadea. Khange uni gạị dọe dạṛketa, adọ bogeteko landaketa, adọ māyāḱ mōyōḱko ruạṛ baṛayena. Adọ ẹn hiloḱ khon hot husitko bạgi utạrketa. Ar boṅga hō̱ bako khusilena, arko mẹnketa, Ạimại tite dọ baṅtẹtgebon ataṅa. Un khon, kathae, ạimại dọ dāṛẽ bako samaṅetkoa.

Adọ, kathae, inạ dosar tesar hẹrẹl hopọn dọko sẹṭẹrena; adọ onko ạimạiko cepetena, mẹpẹnenako, Ọkọe hō̱ apnar hẹrẹl ṭhen noa katha dọ babon lạia.

Adọ, kathae, apan ạpin oṛaḱreko kuliyetkoa, Hạṇḍiko dọpe dọhọ akata sẹ baṅa?

Adọko mẹneta, Dọhọ akatgeale; hẹćge bape hẹć hodoḱ kan, ńẹl hortele bhagaoena. Nō̱ḱō̱e neṇḍa din hō̱ parọmena.

Adọ jọtọgeko mẹnketa, Ma gapa dọ teke sọbọtkalepe, arbon um naṛkana, meaṅ dọbon boṅgana.

Adọ onakoko kạmikette dosar hiloḱko kuṭạm ḍaṅgrayena. Adọ unreko ńẹlketkoa, baṅma, totkareko kuṭạmkoa. Khange onko

19 See p. 234, note 19. It may here be something else than the moving tail which is in the narrator's mind. A variant states that they took a bullock and tried to kill it by hammering where the 'soul moved', viz. the tail.

20 The Santals have a strong sense of humour and are quite capable of enjoying a joke against themselves, women just as much as men.

"Do, girls, do, girls, bring a cup, girls; let us catch the blood; the blood is running out and away!"

So they received it in cups and in pots; but even though they did so with this blood, the cow was not dying. She then hit her again. As the cow again urinated, they called out: "Look, girls, look, girls, the blood is flowing out and away!" So they received this also in cups; but still the cow did not die.

They then said to the woman using the axe: "How is it you are not able to kill her?"

"I have been battering so that I am tired," she replied; "so now you have a try, do, and fell her."

Then these also hit and hit, until they became tired; still the cow was not dying. So they let the cow loose in disgust, and she ran off, whilst they had a good laugh[20]. But thereafter they dolefully went back. From that day the women left this kind off utterly. The boṅgas, also, were not pleased, and said: "At the hands of women we are utterly unwilling to receive anything." From that time, people tell, women do not offer sacrifices[21].

Well, two or three days afterwards the men returned home. The women then took counsel together and said to each other: "None of us must tell our men about this matter."

The men asked them in their respective houses: "Have you brewed beer or how?"

The women replied: "We have brewed; but you did not put in an appearance; we lost all patience in waiting. Now see, the day fixed has also passed."

Then they all said: "Please then, boil and wash our clothes to-morrow; then we shall all of us bathe and wash, and the day after to-morrow we shall have the sacrifice."

They consequently did so, and the day after they sacrificed a bullock to the Ancestors. At that time the women saw how they

21 It is scarcely necessary to say that this is 'willkürlich eingetragen', to use a common expression in German commentaries.

ạimại dọ muluć mulućko landajọń kana. Khange hẹrẹl họpọn dọko mẹneťa, Ceťpe landayeť kana?

Adọ un jọkhẹn dọko mẹna, Ceť hõ bale landayeťa. Khange ạyup̣ jọkhẹn dọ hạṇḍiko ńũńũ kana, un jọkhẹn arhõko landa gọťketa. Adọ khub lekako kulikeťkoa; adọ unreko lạikeťa, bańma, Ape ńẹl họrtele, mọkọńente alegele kuṭạmeťko tahẽkana; adọ bhala ḍẹkẹrele kukṭạm kana, adọ caǩ bhalam gọjea? Adọ onale landayeť kana. Adọ kathae, sanam họṛge bogeteko landakeťa.

Adọ ẹnẹ cabayena, ẹṇḍẹge mucạťena.

18. Ạimại ṭhẹn alo lại reań.

Sedae pạṛiạ jọkhẹćrege, kathae, miť họṛe tahẽkana; adọ ceť dọrbar cọe calaǩ kan tahẽkana; adọ baṛge simạ sẹnteye calaǩ kana, adọ baṛgere aćren kạmṛĩ kuṛi dọ ona takre gurić dọe giḍi gọťkaťa. Adọ ona gurić dọ pạsirente uni họṛaǩ ḍeṅgan kicrićre laṭkaoena, Adọ uni họṛe ńẹlkeť khane ˌmẹnkeťa, Durrẹ! noa dọ bań jut ńẹloǩ kana, noa dọ bạń idia; họṛ nãhãǩko landawańa; ọkọe tora ruạṛkate noa dọń dọhọkaǩa, eṭagaǩtegeń ḍeṅga calaǩa."

Adọ onka mẹnkateye ruạṛena, adọ eṭaǩ kicrićteye ḍeṅgayena. Ar ọnẹ gurićen kicrić dọ miťṭań celańreye bhoraokeťa; adọ

---

22 This would presuppose that the women were permitted to be present. This belongs to the story; it is against the common rule. See p. 231, note 9.

23 When an animal is sacrificed in this way, it is hit at the back of the head, just where neck and head join.

18[1] The idea underlying this story is that women are incapable of keeping a secret. That is an axiom with a great many Santals.

2 Meant is a village council called together to adjudicate some matter. The word used in Santali (dọrbar) presupposes something grander than the ordinary village councils; hence the man feels the necessity of changing his soiled clothes.

3 The baṛge, home-field, is the plot of land on which a Santal builds his houses. The houses generally lie at the end of the field running up to the village street. It is used for Indian corn and cold weather crops. It is the only farm-land which the Santals ordinarily manure.

did it[22], that they struck the animal on the neck[23]; and they were smiling and tittering among themselves. So the men asked them: "What are you laughing at?"

Just then they were replying: "We are not laughing at anything." But when they were drinking beer in the evening, the women again burst out laughing. So they asked them persistingly, and then they told them: "We got tired of waiting for you, and so we ourselves tried to sacrifice the animal. "Why, we gave blow after blow on the hind-quarters; in such a way, why, how should you kill it? That is what we are laughing at." And then all of them had a good laugh.

Now this is finished, there is the end.

18. NOTHING MUST BE TOLD TO WOMEN[1].

At a certain time long ago, people tell, there lived a man. One day he was going to some meeting or other[2]; whilst he was walking along towards the boundary of his home-field[3], it so happened that a servant girl of his just at that moment threw some cow-dung out on that field. Some of the cow-dung was spattered about and stuck to the loin-cloth of the man. When he saw this, he said: "Fie, fie! this does not look nice; I can't go with this, presently people will laugh at me. Let me go back at once and take this off and leave it and take some other loin-cloth on to go in."

With this intention he returned and changed his loin-cloth. The cloth that had been bespattered with cow-dung he put into a pot[4], and having covered the mouth with a leaf-plate, he hung

[4] The Santali celañ, here translated 'pot', is an earthen-ware vessel of a peculiar shape, round with a very wide mouth. It is never very large, and is used by the Santals especially for cooking their utu, i. e., curry, but also for other purposes.

patṛateye bẹt́kett́e 'ona ạkin haṛam buḍhikin gitić mohṇḍare cọṭreye akakat́a; adọ ać dọ dọrbare calaoena.

Adọ inạ dosar tesar hilok̓ khange uńi hoṛren oṛak̓ hoṛtẹt́ doe kuliyede kana, Henda, bhala ona celańre dọ cet́em aka akat́a?

Adoe metaea, Cet́ hõ bań kana, ar am lạiamre hõ cet́ bań hoyok̓?

Adọ kathae, ẹn hilok̓ dọ bae lạiadea. Adọ arhõ inạ dosar tesar hilok̓ khange gitić akan jọkhẹn uni ạimại doe ńẹl ńamket́a; adọ arhõe kuliyede kana, Ona dọ bhala cet́ bam akaket́? Masẹ lạiạńme.

Adọ uni hoṛe mẹnket́a, Bań, ọhọń lạilema. Ạimại dọ lạiape khan dọpe lại baṛaea, laćre dọ bape sea daṛeak̓a; ọhọge am dọń lạilema.

Adoe mẹnket́a, Ọhọń lại baṛaea, mage lạiańme. Ań ṭhenge ẹnte bam lại khan dọ ọkọe ṭhenem lạia? Ma lạime, iń dọ ọkọe ṭhen hõ ọhọń lại baṛaea.

Adoe metadea, Mẹn ẹnḍẹkhan iń lạiam kana, ạikạ ọkọe ṭhen hõ alom lạia.

Adoe mẹnket́a, Cedak̓ iń lạia? Lạile khan apnar bhọrọmge bạń bhańgaoa? Apnar apnar reak̓ katha dọ cedak̓ iń lạia? Ọhọń lạilea.

Adoe metadea, Iạ, ona celańre dọ —, mit́ hoṛ iń mak̓ akadea, adọ nisạn aloko ńama mẹnte uni hoṛ reak̓ bọhọk̓ ạgukate ona celańre dọń bhorao akat́a.

Adọ uni ạimạiye mẹnket́a, Sạrigem bhorao akat́a sẹm ẹṛẹyedíń kana?

Adoe metadea, Sạrige; mẹn noa katha dọ jivi calak̓re hõ alom lạia. Arem lạiket́a mẹnkhan, ạikạ amgelań gọćmea. Adọ enka rọṛ baṛakategekin thir baṛayena.

---

5 A literal translation of the Santali expression, which is very commonly used, the meaning being that any information received must not be divulged to others; everything must be forgotten. About equivalent to: silent like the grave.

6 The woman is not startled at this horrible 'confession'; she seems only to be concerned with the question whether it is true or not.

7 A common Santal expression.

the pot high up somewhere near the place where he and his wife were in the habit of sleeping. Thereupon he went to the meeting.

A couple of days afterwards his wife was asking him: "I say, what is it you have hung up in that pot?"

"It is nothing," he said to her; "and even if you were told, what use would it be?"

That day he did not tell her. A couple of days afterwards it so happened, whilst she was lying down, that she caught sight of the pot and plied her husband with questions: "What in the world is it you have hung up there? Do tell me, please."

"No," the man said, "I shall certainly not tell you. If you women-folk are told anything, you tell it to others; you don't let a matter rot in your stomach[5]. I shall certainly never tell you."

"I shall surely not tell it to anybody," the woman replied. "Do, tell me, please! You see, if you don't tell me, then whom should you tell? Do tell, I shall never tell it to anybody."

"Take care then," the man said; "I am telling you; be sure you must not tell anybody."

"Why should I tell?" she replied; "if I told, should I not put myself to shame? Anything concerning ourselves, why should I tell that? Be sure, I shall never tell."

"The matter is this," he said; "in that pot, — I have killed a man, and to prevent them from getting any proof, I have brought the head of the man and put it into that pot."

"Have you really put that into the pot?" the woman asked, "or are you only fooling me[6]?"

"Really and truly," the man replied; "beware, even if your soul should depart[7], you must not tell. And if you tell, be sure, we two[8] shall kill you." After they had talked together in this way, they became quiet.

[8] The inclusive dual (alaṅ), you and I, is very frequently used for the first person singular in threatening language. It is to be a matter between the speaker and the person adressed, which the speaker will see through to the finish.

Adǫ tin din bad̉re cǫṅ, kathae, mit́ din dǫ ạkin ạkingekin kạphạriạuente bogetekin dapalena. Khạnge uni ạimại dǫe mẹnketa, Ạḍim daleṅ kana. Am dǫ hǫrem̈ gǫć akadea, onalaṅ lại napoṛkama.

Adǫ khange sạriye lạiketa. Adǫ ǫṇḍẹnić mạṅjhi ato hǫṛe jarwaket́kote uni hǫṛko tǫlkedea ar thanareko ijhạrketa. Adǫ thana khon pulis dǫrǫga hẹćkate ona celaṅ raṛa ạgukateko ṅẹlket́ dǫ, kicrić kan. Adǫ ǫṇḍẹnić mạṅjhiko ruhet́kedea arko dạṇḍǫmkedea, adǫko ruạṛ calaoena.

Adǫ unre uni hǫṛe mẹnketa, Ẹ yoi, metape kanaṅ, teheṅ khon jãhãn ǫntǫr katha ạimại ṭhen dǫ tis hõ alope lại baṛaea sẹ alope lạiakoa, baṅkhan dǫ jãhã hilok̉ daoko ṅamle khan, ona kathako utlạuge cạhiye. Ona iạte sǫntǫrkate ạimai tuluć dǫ galmaraope, baṅkhan mit́ din kalre dǫ ạimạige aperen bạdiko hoyok̉a.

Adǫ un khon noa katha dǫle cet́ akat́te goṭa ṭạṇḍi pasnao akana; ar noa katha dǫ sạri kangea; jãhãn oko katha judi ạimại ṭhenem lạiketa mẹnkhan, ona dǫ sǫdǫrǫk̉ge cạhiye.

Adǫ ẹnẹ nià katha dǫ cabayena, in maraṅgea.

---

9 What is here described is a trait of fairly recent origin. It does not necessarily mean that the whole story is of recent date, only that this feature has been painted in recently. If a serious crime has been committed and they think they have founded suspicion against a person, they will act as here told. Note that the headman takes the lead, but acts in conjunction with the village people.

10 The regulated districts and also the so-called non-regulation districts (the latter not to such an extent as the former ones) have police stations spread over the country, with resident subordinate police officers, who are supposed to be guardians of law within their sphere. Such a police station is called **thana**, a word in common use in the British administration, originally Skr. **sthāna**, and at first, it seems, used about fortified posts with a garrison. Being a convenient word

Then some time afterwards husband and wife one day had a quarrel and walloped each other in grand style. Then the woman said: "You are thrashing me. You have killed a man; we two[8] shall give information about you and have done with you."

And this she really did; she gave information. The village headman there then called the village people together, and they bound the man[9], took him to the police station[10] and made a statement. Thereupon police officers came from the t h a n a; they took that pot down and brought it out and had a look inside, — it is clothes. So they gave the headman of that village a good scolding and fined[11] him, whereupon they went away.

Then this man spoke: "Look here, you, I tell you, any secret or matter of importance[12] — from to-day never tell such to the women-folk, or so that they can hear; otherwise, some day or other, when they get an opportunity, they must necessarily divulge that matter. Therefore, be careful what you talk with women; otherwise, women will at some time or other in days to come become your accusers."

From that time we have learnt this story, and it has been spread abroad everywhere; and it is a true thing; if you tell any secret to a woman, it is sure to be made public.

There this story is ended; it is this much.

it was adopted by the Portuguese, and has from them been taken over by the present rulers, only, however, about the civil police.

11 Quite a common thing, if one is to believe what is told. The police have naturally no right to such fining.

12 The Santali word, ọntọr katha, literally means 'inner word'; ọntọr has been adopted from Bengali and means in Santali 'mind', 'heart', 'the inner man', if one likes. It is used in a double sense as here translated.

19. Mahra reak̕ katha.

Sedae jo̱khe̱n mit̕t̤aṅ kisa̱ṛe tahẽ̱kana, ar uniren do̱ a̱ḍi uta̱r ga̱iko tahẽ̱kantaea. Ado̱ onko ga̱i gupiko la̱git̕ mit̕t̤aṅ mahrako do̱ho̱kedea. Ado̱ uni mahrage onko ga̱i do̱e gupi kan tahẽ̱kana; ado̱ urni birkoreye gupi kan tahẽ̱kana.

Ado̱ kathae, gupi gupite mit̕ din do̱ mit̕t̤aṅ ga̱i tinre co̱ṅ ona urni birregeye busa̱k̕ at̕ ocokede, bae disa̱ledea. Ado̱ a̱yup̕ ber oṛak̕teye laga a̱guyet̕koa, un jo̱khe̱ne lekha baṛayet̕ko do̱, mit̕t̤aṅ ga̱i do̱ ba̱nugić. Ado̱ tayo̱m se̱ne be̱ṅge̱t̕ rua̱ṛket̕ khane ṅe̱lkede do̱, ga̱i eskargeye ṅir hijuk̕ kan, mīhũ do̱ bae a̱gu daralede. Khange mo̱ne̱reye he̱le̱t̕at̕a, are me̱nket̕a, Kisa̱ṛ nãhãk̕ cet̕ co̱e metaṅ.

Ado̱ oṛak̕teye laga idiket̕ko khan, uni gupiyić do̱ bae la̱iyet̕a, busa̱k̕ at̕ ocokedeaṅ me̱nte. Khange uni ga̱i do̱, kathae, be̱ba̱ṛiće bhokraoet̕a. Khange kisa̱ṛ do̱ mahrae kulikedea, Henda ya, o̱ko̱e-t̤ak̕ ga̱i bejãeye bhokraoet̕ do̱? Cedak̕e bhokraoet̕a? Mīhũ do̱ menaea se̱ baṅ?

Ado̱ uni mahrae me̱nket̕a, Nuiren mīhũ do̱ okare co̱ṅ busa̱k̕ at̕ ocokedea; ba̱ṅ disa̱ledea; onate uni ga̱i dõ̱e bhokraoet̕ kana.

[1] The moral of this story is very much the same as that of the preceding one: it is impossible to trust the discretion of women. This story may have been originally taken over from Hindu narrators.

[2] Mahra is the name used by the Santals for a Hindu cowherd caste, generally known as goala. The word is of Skr.-Hindi origin, but is in Hindi mostly used about 'a man who appears in the habit of a woman', or 'an effeminate person', also about some palanquin bearers. Although the dictionaries do not mention the use of the word about goalas, Sir H. Risley is undoubtedly correctly informed when he mentions (in his Tribes and Castes of Bengal) that mahra is used as 'a title of Chamárs and men employed to herd cattle'. The Santal use of the word is a proof of this, as they have not invented the word. It may be noted that well-to-do people, also Santals, may make use of the mahra to herd cattle, sometimes only to milk their cows. They are also often called in for advice and assistance in the case of cattle disease.

19. THE STORY OF A MAHRA MAN[1].

ONCE upon a time long ago there lived a rich man, who had a great many cows. To herd these cows, he engaged a mahra[2], a man of the cowherd caste. So this mahra was herding the cows mentioned, and he was grazing them in the primeval[3] forest.

Whilst he was occupied herding, people tell, it one day happened that he, some time during the day, lost sight of a cow while she was giving birth to a calf; he was not aware of it and did not remember her. Then, when he, at evening time, was driving the cows home, he was counting them, and lo, one cow is missing. When he looked towards the rear, he caught sight of the cow, she was coming running alone; she was not bringing her calf along. This gave him a fright in his mind, and he said to himself: "What will my master now say to me?"

Therefore, when he had driven the cows home, the cowherd did not tell that he had lost sight of a cow giving birth to a calf. The cow was lowing incessantly; the master, therefore, asked the mahra: "Look here, which cow is it that is lowing so incessantly? Why is she lowing? Has she got her calf with her or not[4]?"

The mahra then answered: "This cow's calf I have allowed to be lost, after she had given birth to it; I was not aware of it; that is why this cow is lowing."

[3] The description of the forest would point to the scene of the story being far away from the habitations of the ordinary villagers.

[4] What is here told of the behaviour of the cow is, excepting one detail, what may be seen every day in the Santal country. The cow is very anxious for the calf, and runs to it when she can. When a cow is being milked, the calf must always stand in front of the cow, which otherwise refuses to give any milk! With such anxiousness in the cow, it seems unlikely that she would leave her calf in the forest. As a matter of fact, they do not.

Khange uni kisạṛ' doe edreyente uni mahra do bogeteye ruhetkedea hirkhạge. Khange onkae ruhetkede khan, uni mahra do aćak ṭheṅga ar siliye sapketa, ar ona ńindạge uni mĩhũ ńańame calaoena. Ado biro boloyen khange thoe eskarok kana; are meneta, Nit ńindạ do cekateń ńamea? Ńel hõ ohoń ńel ńam daṛelea, ar uni mĩhũ do ohoe bhokrao saḍelea. Nahakgeń haronoka, mĩhũ do ohoń ńam daṛelea.

Ado onka hudis baṛakateye menketa, Noa ńindạ do neteregeń tahẽ aṅgalenge, gapa doń ńam baṛayea. Ado goṭe sahane ńamketa, ar ona khon seṅgele gharṛa totketteye jolketa. Adoe jorok akana are bhabnajoṅ kana. Arhõe hudisketa, Durre! iń eskarge noa bir bhitrire menańa; seṅgel do bạń jola, baṅkhan nãhãk jãhãnkoko ńameńa.

Ado onka hudiskate, kathae, ona ṭheṅgate seṅgel doe sobok ĩṛĩćkette ać doe menketa, Nonḍe do bạń tahena. Onka menkate ać do dareteye dećena onḍe gitić lạgit; ar ṭheṅga ar sili do onḍe otregeye bạgiata.

Ado kathae, inạ mit ghạri khange kul do manwa basteye hec gotenteye duṛup gotena, ado uni mahrae jome lạgit. Ado unre ṭheṅga ar silikin galmaraojoṅ kana; menetakin, De bhala, nit do alańren kisạṛren bạiri doe hećena. De unilań bańcaoea.

Unre ṭhẽṅga doe menketa, Hẽ ma hege, menkhan iṅge tho mẽte kạṛãkettiń; cekate iń doń lạṛhại daṛeaka? Iń do asol daṛege rạputentińa. Ma amge bańcaoetalańme.

---

5 The hair-string (sili) is made of the tail-hairs of a cow generally; it is four to five feet long or even more, and of thickness like a thin cord. It is kept round the neck, but is not of a distinctive nature that might be compared with the brahminical poeta. Fakirs are in the habit of using it. It is supposed to be effective in driving evil spirits away. Very seldom seen with the Santals.

6 The Croton oblongifolius, Roxb., fairly common in the Santal forests. The wood is soft and dry, and is used for the purpose here described.

7 When out in the forests and without other means of lighting a fire the Santals may do so by taking a flat piece of wood like the one here mentioned, and another one like a thin stick, some 30 cm. long. The stick is given a blunt point at one end. Kept between the hands, the point is pressed down on the flat piece,

The owner then became angry and scolded the mahra badly and reviled him in a disgusting way. As he railed him in this manner, the mahra took his stick and his string of hair[5] and went that very night to search for the calf. But when he came into the forest, he was naturally feeling lonely and said: "How shall I find it now at night? I shall not even be able to catch sight of it, and the calf will certainly not low loudly enough to be heard. I am quite uselessly giving myself trouble; I shall certainly not be able to find the calf."

Having reflected in this way he said: "To-night I shall remain somewhere here until dawn; then I shall search for the calf to-morrow." So he found some croton[6] firewood, and having drilled fire[7] out of this he lighted a fire. And there he was sitting and warming himself and thinking sorrowful thoughts. Then again he thought by himself: "Oh dear me, here I am alone in the middle of this forest; I must not light a fire; otherwise somebody or other[8] will find me presently."

Reflecting in this way, he poked the fire with his stick and extinguished it; then he said to himself: "I shall not stay here." Having said this, he climbed a tree to pass the night there; but his stick and his hair-string he left on the ground.

In a short while, people tell, a tiger came, smelling man, and sat down there; he intended to eat the mahra. At that time the stick and the hair-string were talking together, saying: "See there, now our master's enemy has come. Look, we two must save him."

The stick then said: "Yes, that is quite so; but, you see, he has blinded my eyes[9]; how shall I then be able to fight? As for me, my real strength has been broken. You, please, do save him for us."

---

whilst the stick is being turned round by the flat hands being moved backwards and forwards against each other. With the proper kind of wood it does not take a man with experience any long time to produce fire. Now-a-days this method is very seldom resorted to; but the writer has seen it done.

8 Meant are wild animals of sorts, and also spirits.

9 By using it to put out the fire.

Adǫ siliye mǫnketá, Acha, ǫṇḍǫkhan iń lạṛhạí gelaḱa.

Adǫ kathae, unre ona sili dǫ hurlạ ṛcuroḱ kana, ać kathae, ǫkǫe ghiriạyeť lekage; ar kathae, bhan bhan saḍe kana. Ar uni kul dǫ, kathae, ona ańjǫmteye bhaṛoyena are mǫnetá, Ayo! hǫṛtǫť ma bae ńǫloḱ kan, adǫ ceť ṭhen onka dǫ saḍe kana, sǫ celeye bheonayediń kana?

Adǫ kathae, onka saḍe kante uni kul bae sor daṛeatá. Adǫ ǫṇḍǫ duṛuṕkategeye aṅgakeť khane calao dapoṛena. Adǫ ona sili hǫ̃ thirena.

Adǫ setaḱ khange, kathae, uni gạí dǫ bhokraoateye ńir calaḱ kana. Khange uni mahra dǫ hako pako dare khone ā̃ṛgoyente ona theṅga ar siliye saṕkeťte uni gạí tayǫm tayǫmteye calaoena.

Adǫ uni gạí aćren mĩhũi kuliyede kana, metae kanae, Am dǫ, bacha, teheń ńindạ dǫ ạḍi harkhettem aṅgayena; tinạḱ cǫń jạnić rabaṅkeťmea.

Adǫ unre uni mĩhũi rǫṛ ruạṛadea, Baṅa, ayo, iń dǫ bạń harkhetlena. Noa ponea jaṅgań lǫbǫť akan, noa dǫ pon ghaṛa ṭaka cetanreń lǫbǫť akana; ar noa ṭaka cetanregeń burumlente latar khon lǫlǫge rakaṕadińte bạń harkhetlena. Adǫkin thir baṛayena.

Ar uni mahra dǫ noako jǫtǫ kathae ańjǫmketá. Ar uni gạiye calaoen khan, uni mahra dǫe mǫnketá, Sạri sǫ nase kana, bhalań laea.

---

10 In Santali lit: 'the man is not to be seen', i. e. he who produces the sound.

11 The Santali word has reference to happenings like what is here told: fright caused by something not understood and supposed to be supernatural.

12 Animals are commonly supposed to be able to make themselves understood to each other. How the mahra understands their talk is not explained.

13 A very common term of endearment used, perhaps, especially by women to their sons or to young boys. Lit. 'calf'.

14 The ghaṛa here mentioned is found among the Santals, but only with more well-to-do people. It is very common in Hindu households. It is of brass, round with a narrow neck and a fairly broad brim. It is used especially to fetch water. It has a capacity of several litres. As is well known, it is common with Indians

"All right," the hair-string answered, "then I shall try to fight."

Then, people tell, the hair-string commenced to swing round and round, just as if somebody were whirling it round, and it was making a high buzzing sound. When the tiger heard this, he became astonished and said: "Oh mother! no man[10] is seen; where then is such a sound produced? or is some one trying to frighten me[11]?"

Now as it was sounding in that way, the tiger was not able to go near, and when he had been sitting there until dawn of day, he went away disappointed. Then the hair-string also stopped whirling.

As soon as it was morning, the cow came running along lowing. The mahra then quickly climbed down from the tree, and, picking up his stick and hair-string, he followed after the cow.

The cow asked her calf[12], saying: "You, my darling[13], you have spent this whole night until dawn in great misery; who knows how much you have suffered from cold!"

"Not at all, mother," the calf answered, "I did not suffer any hardship. I was standing on these four legs, and with these four I was treading on four brass-pots[14] full of money; and when I lay down on the top of this money, warmth came up from below, and I did not suffer any hardship." Thereupon they ceased talking.

Now the mahra heard all this, and when the cow had gone away, he said: "I wonder, whether this is true or not; well, let me dig."

---

to hoard their money; they bury it in the ground or where they think it safe, with the result that the whole is lying there unused, and it very frequently happens that the owner dies without having told any one of his hiding-place. So the money is lost, until somebody some day happens to find the treasure. When hiding away in this manner, the money is generally put into some metal vessel, sometimes, if not a large amount, in a ṭoṭa otherwise in a ghaṛa like here.

Adǫ kathae, ǫnẹ mĩhũi burum aṅgalen ṭhen uni dǫe laket́ khan, sạri ponea ghaṛa reak̀ kankhaġeye la ńamket́a. Khane mẹnket́a, Baṅa, sạrige uni mĩhũ dǫ ṭhikgeye mẹnlet́a. Adǫ uni mahrae mẹnket́a, Noa ṭaka dǫń idia; adǫ oṛak̀re iń bạhuń biḍạulege, bhala noa ṭakań idile khan dǫe lại baṛakea sẹye okokea.

Adǫ onka mẹnkate ẹn hilok̀ dǫ bae idilet́te oṛak̀re sẹnkate ać bạhui metae kana, Iạ, ma hare phare teheń dǫ daka hǫt́aṅpe. Iń dǫ peṛa hǫṛǫk̀ iń calak̀ lạgit́.

Adǫe metadea, Okatem calak̀a?

Adǫe metadea, Raj linḍhire hǫṛǫe bǫlǫk̀ kana, uni ńẹńẹl iń calak̀ lạgit́.

Khange bạhuttẹt́ dǫe landaket́teye mẹnket́a, Dak̀ bạnuk̀anẹć; cet́teń dakaea? Hapẹ, ẹnḍẹkhan dak̀ iń lo ạgulege.

Adǫ kathae, kanḍae hẹrmẹt́ gǫt́ket́te dak̀ lo ạḍi ãṭe taṛam idiyet́ kana. Khange atoren maejiuko dǫko ńẹlkede, ạḍi ãṭe taṛamet́ kan; adǫ bako kulikedea, Henda hǫ, setak̀rege teheń dǫ bejãe ãṭ dak̀pe loyet́ dǫ?

Khange uni dǫe rǫṛ gǫt́ket́a, Hẽ hǫ, teheń dǫ setak̀regele loyet́a, baṅma, kathae, raj linḍhire hǫṛǫe bǫlǫk̀ kana. Uni ńẹńẹle calak̀tale lạgit́. Unile daka hǫt́ae lạgit́, onate setak̀regele lo idiyet́a.

Adǫ ǫnẹko mẹnge, Jãhã mit́ lutur khon bar luturena mẹnkhan, katha dǫ baṅ okona. Uni mahra ạimại dǫe lại ket́ khan, ona katha dǫ mit́ ghạṛite goṭa ato ḍamḍahe gǫt́ena. Adǫ kathae, onka lại

15 The word used in Santali is about equal to rectum. It is not very elevated.

16 The Indian word **r a j** or **r a j a** means a king, but is frequently and commonly used about a landlord or zemindar.

17 Hindu women very frequently carry their waterpots under the arm; when empty, they are easily carried thus with the arm round the neck of the vessel; when full and heavy, the bottom rests on the hip, the arm being kept round the neck.

18 Ordinarily they move 'mit Anstand und Würde'; the unusual speed and also the early hour attract attention.

And, so people tell, when he dug where the calf had been lying down until morning, he really came upon the rims of four brass-pots. Then he said: "To be sure, the calf really spoke the truth." Whereupon he said: "I shall take this money away; but at home I must first test my wife, and find out whether she, if I take this money home, will tell of it, or whether she will keep it secret."

Having come to this conclusion, he did not take the money away that day, but went home and said to his wife: "I say, please make haste to-day and give me food quickly. I am on the point of going on a visit."

"Where are you going?" she asked him.

"A tortoise," he replied, "has entered the back[15] of the king[16]; I am going to see to that."

His wife laughed and said: "There is no water; what shall I prepare food with? Wait a little then, let me first go and fetch water."

She thereupon took a water-pot under her arm[17] and went along all she could to fetch water. When the village women now saw her, that she was walking along in such a hurry, they naturally asked her: "Listen you, you are awfully hard at[18] it fetching water this morning?"

"That is so," she replied; "to-day we are fetching water in the early morning; it is this: a tortoise enters the back of the king. Our one[19] is starting to see this. We are in a hurry to prepare food for him; therefore we are fetching water so early in the morning."

Now, as people say, "If anything from one ear becomes that of two ears, it is not to be hidden[20]." When the mahra woman had told this, the matter was immediately spread over the whole

---

[19] A very common way of referring to a husband. Husband and wife will not mention each other's names, fearing that in such case their children would become deaf. The best is to be as vague as possible in reference.

[20] The same as in Norwegian: 'Hvad tvende vet, vet hele verden'.

lạitege raj ṭhen hạbić baṅ seṭerena? Khange uni raj do̱ mo̱ne̱ mo̱ne̱te ạḍiye edreyena are me̱nketa, Ạyo! noa katha do̱ o̱ko̱e unạnketa ạuṛiakte? Iṅko lajaokidiṅ do̱. Disom sudhạ hoṛ noako baḍaeketa, baṅma, raj linḍhire ho̱ro̱e bo̱lo̱k kana. Baṅ, noa katha do̱ń sabgea.

Khange, kathae, raj do̱ sukṭike po̱rto̱nketa. O̱ko̱e noa khatae ro̱ṛ akata, uni ho̱ṛ do̱bo sabea, ar sapkatebo kuliyea, Tisem ńe̱lkedea, raj linḍhire ho̱ro̱ bo̱lo̱k do̱? Ma ona lạime, to̱be̱m chuṭika, ar baṅkhan do̱le go̱ćmea. Cedak am do̱ un maraṅ ho̱ṛem bibho̱ro̱mkedea? Onka raje me̱nkette o̱nte̱ no̱te̱ peadakoe kolketkoa.

Khange bhại, onko do̱ suṭik suṭikteko calaoena. Ado̱ kathae, mitṭaṅ peada do̱e suṭik ńamkedea uni mahra ạimạige, ado̱ uni khon hereltetge. Khange uni mahra hõe aṅgo̱cketa, Hẽ, sạrigeń ro̱ṛ akata me̱nte.

Ado̱ peadako me̱nketa, Acha, bogegem ro̱ṛ akata; me̱nkhan raje me̱n akawatlea, delabonle idimea me̱nte. Raj nãhãk boksise emama.

Khange uni mahra do̱ ạḍi rạskạkate oṛakteye bo̱lo̱ go̱tente daka jo̱mkateye ḍeṅga pherao baṛa go̱tente peadae metadea, Delaṅ raj ṭhen idiṅme.

Ado̱ kathae, raj ṭhene idi seṭerkede khan do̱, rajko ko̱bhe̱radea, baṅma, Uni ho̱ṛ do̱le ạgu akadea.

Khange raje me̱nketa, Ma uni ho̱ṛ do̱ barahite to̱lepe. Khange sạri barahiteko to̱lkedea. Ado̱ raje kuliyede kana, Ma lạime, tisem ńe̱lkedea raj linḍhite ho̱ro̱ bo̱lo̱k do̱? De̱ ona sạbudme, ar baṅkhan am do̱le go̱ćmea. Am do̱ raj lekan ho̱ṛem lajaokede do̱. De̱ ona sạbud puraume, se̱ cetem me̱neta?

---

21 Here the word peada, lit. one on foot, a footman, very much of the same importance as sipạhi, see p. 230, note 5.

22 The audience is addressed by the narrator. Lit. 'brother', the word is in common use like here with the Santals; but they ordinarily use another word for a real brother.

village. And then, passing in this way from mouth to mouth, did it not ultimately reach the king also? The king now became very angry in his mind and said: "Oh mother! who has started this lying report? They have disgraced me! Every soul in the country have now got to know that a tortoise enters the back of the king. No, this won't do! I shall follow this matter up."

The king thereupon commenced to make enquiries. "Any one who has told this we shall catch, and having caught him we shall ask him: When did you see the tortoise enter the king's back? Please tell that, then you will be let free; otherwise we shall kill you. Why have you dishonoured so big a man?" Having spoken in this way, the king sent his messengers[21] out in all directions.

Thereupon, my dear fellow[22], these went off making enquiries everywhere as they came along. In due course one of the messengers, at the end of his enquiries, came to this mahra woman, and from her he reached the man himself. The mahra also confessed: "It is quite true, I have said so," he said.

The messengers then said: "Very well, you have spoken quite right; but the king has ordered us, so come along, we shall take you there. The king will give you a prize presently."

The mahra thereupon, highly rejoicing, went in and had his food; so he changed his loin-cloth quickly and said to the messenger: "Come along, take me to the king."

Now, when they had brought him to the palace, they sent word in to the king, saying: "We have brought the man."

The king then said: "Bind the man with a rope." And so they did, they tied him with a rope. Thereupon the king asked him: "Please tell, when did you see a tortoise enter the king's back? Do, prove that, otherwise we shall kill you. You have disgraced a man like a king. Do prove it entirely, or what have you to say?"

Adọ unre uni mahrae mẹnkeťa, Ią, raja saheb, hoṛọ bọlọǩ dọ baṅ ńẹl akadea. Mẹnkhan miť ṭhen ṭạkaṅ ńẹl akaťa, adọ ona iạte iṅ bạhu dọṅ biḍạuede tahẽkana, bhala ona ṭakaṅ ạgule khan dọe lạikea sẹ ọhọ. Onka hudiskateṅ mẹnkeťa, Bhala nonka iṅ bạhu dọṅ metaea, bhala noa katha dọ ceťe metaǩa, lạia sẹye baṅ. Judiye lại baṛae khan, ona ṭaka dọ bạṅ ạguia, ar bae lại khan dọṅ ạguia. Adọ ọnẹ ẹnte jẹmọn iṅ metadea, tẹmọngeye lại gọť-keťa. Khan iṅ mẹnkeťa, nui dọ ạgulere hõ ọhọe okolea mẹnte. Adọ ona iạte ṭaka hõ baṅ ạguleťa.

Adọ raje mẹnkeťa, Okarem ńẹl akaťa?

Adọ uni mahrae mẹnkeťa, Tọl raraṅpe, tọbẹ khan iṅ lạiapea.

Adọ kathae, tọlko raṛakedea. Adọ raje mẹnkeťa, Ma lạime, tinạǩ menaǩa ar okare.

Adọ uni mahrae mẹnkeťa, Ponea ghaṛare menaǩa, adọṅ uduǩ-apea, tinạǩ iṅ dọpe emaṅa?

Adọ raje mẹnkeťa, Ona dọ bara bạritebon hạṭiṅa.

Khange ẹnẹye ạyur idiketkoteko lakeťa. Uni bar ghaṛako emadea, ar raj bar ghaṛae idikeťa. Ẹnẹko ikạkadea. Adọ uni mahra hõe kisạṛ utạrena.

Ạdọ cabayena, in maraṅgea.

Ar noa katha reaǩ bhẹd dọ nonka kana: Jãhãe hoṛ tuluć gateǩ khub gate menamre hõ, apnar ọntọr katha dọ alom lạia, sẹ apnar haṛam buḍhi ṭhen hõ asọl katha dọ tisre hõ alogem lạia. Arem lạikeťa mẹnkhan, oka hiloǩ cọṅ unim edre ocole khan, ẹn hiloǩ dọ ona kathae sọdọr gọda, ar mõṛẽ hoṛ amko tọl ulṭạu gọťmea. Inạ kangea katha dọ.

23 See p. 249, note 12.

24 The advice is here given a much wider application than in the previous story. It is the narrator who gives vent to his own opinions. It may not be the opinion of all; but there is no doubt that distrust of others is a very common trait of the people. It takes a very long time before they will open themselves up to anybody, and they will not do so, unless they have convinced themselves that they can do it with safety and confidence. The story itself does not go so far as the narrator. The story preaches mistrust to women.

Then the mahra answered: "Listen, my Lord king, I have not seen any tortoise entering; but at a certain place I have seen money, and for that reason I was testing my wife, whether, if I brought the money home, she would blab or not. With this intention I said to myself: Well, let me tell my wife so and so; I wonder what she will say to that, whether she will tell it or not. If she tells, I shall not bring the money home; if she does not tell, I shall fetch it. Then see, no sooner had I told her than she told it to others. So I said: Even if I bring it here, she will certainly not keep it secret. Therefore I did not take the money home either."

"Where did you see it?" the king asked.

"Unbind me," the mahra said, "then I shall tell you."

So they released him from his bonds, whereupon the king said: "Please tell how much there is and where it is."

"It is in four brass-pots," the mahra replied; "if I show it to you, how much are you going to give me?"

"We shall divide it equally between us," the king said.

Thereupon the man guided them to the spot, and they dug. To the mahra they gave two brass-pots, and the king took two away with him. Therewith they let the man alone. So the mahra also became a very wealthy man.

So it is finished; it is this much.

And the meaning of this story is this: If you are on friendly terms, even very friendly terms with somebody, don't let your innermost thoughts[23] out, or, never tell the real thing to even your own husband or wife[24]. If you tell, then if you some time in the future causes him or her to become angry, that day he will make that matter public, and the 'Five' will bind you and turn you over on your back. That's what it is.

20. Mohajon ar khatok.

Sedae jokhen, kathae, mitṭaṅ horren'maejiui tahẽkana, ar uni hoṛ do mohajon reak tinak coe dharao akat tahẽkana. Ado hala rakap hala ãṛgoetege ḍher idiyena, ado nawa hõe agu bolo idigea; ado sesre bae hala caba daṛeak kante mohajon adiye ruheda. Ado ona ruhet botorte uni hoṛ do mohajon ac oṛak sen calake

[1] The original title of this story, given by the Santal narrator, was Dundhi lilhi aimaiak katha, the story of a silly foolish woman Possibly two stories have been mixed up together, one about a woman who does not understand and cannot speak Bengali or Hindi, and another about a man who tricked a money-lender. It might be noted that the Santals look upon persons who cannot use any other language than their own as foolish. Living as the Santals do, among other races, speaking languages of their own, entirely different from Santali, it is an absolute necessity with them to be able to understand and speak at least one of these languages, seeing that very often they have to go to these other people for their daily needs. A man who cannot have intercourse with outsiders is handicapped in life and is naturally looked upon as one of inferior parts. As a matter of fact, there are very few grown-up Santals who cannot, to some extent, make use of Bengali or Hindi or some other language used by others who would never think of learning Santali. Their knowledge of the foreign language is naturally very limited and will not, except in a very few cases, go beyond the ordinary language of everyday village life. This story is one which the Santals enjoy very much.

[2] There are very few Santals who do not need money and therefore do not have transactions with money-lenders. At certain times of the year, they need some little capital to carry them through, and to get this they go to those who lend money out or give foodstuffs on credit. The interest paid is generally 25 per cent, often, however, much more, as, e. g., 37 1/2 per cent per annum, or even 6 1/4 to 12 1/2 per cent compound interest per month. This money-lending question is one of the big problems of the people, and it is beset with so much difficulty that the older one becomes among the people, the more wary and cautious one becomes. The ordinary Santal has few scruples against running into debt, as long as any one will lend; he thinks of his immediate needs and very little of how he will be able to repay. To his excuse must be said that his economic conditions are so straitened that it is difficult for us to grasp the possibility of such poverty. Further, that the average Santal has not got far in the way of understanding the value of money, especially sums of money. The writer has again and again seen things that have made him say to himself that they have learnt

20. A MONEY-LENDER AND HIS DEBTOR[1].

ONCE upon a time, people tell, there was a woman, the wife of a man who was owing money to a money-lender[2], who knows how much. In spite of his paying a little now and a little then, the old debt increased, he was also taking fresh loans; at last he was unable to pay it off[3], and the money-lender was scolding him much. The man was afraid of this scolding; therefore as

---

to understand the value of a pice, but not of a rupee. It must also be added that they are not as yet far enough away from their old forest-life to have properly realized the value of property, as the result or fruit of their own work. It might be remarked that Government have enacted several laws to protect the Santals (and other aborigines) from the money-lenders, and from themselves. It is unnecessary to point out that the missionaries have done all they have been able to do to assist and guide in this respect, and some of the enactments of the early seventies were, I believe, the result of investigations started in the first instance at the earnest request of missionaries. Some of the money-lenders are reasonable, but many are quite the opposite, usurers of the very worst type, whose one object is to get the debtor and his possessions into their hands.

Santals are not, somehow, fit to become money-lenders; they are either too credulous or too grabbing and will, in a comparatively short time, run through their means. There may be a few exceptions, but they are not many; besides, as a general rule, they have no capital and must borrow themselves. The money-lenders are mostly Hindus, who at the same time do business as traders and shopkeepers. During later years Mohammedan weavers and others have commenced to get a rather large share in this business.

2 The common name for a money-lender is m o h a j o n or m a h a j o n, lit. a great man, in these parts, the first form being the common one (by the Santals pronounced with stress on the first and last syllables). The word is in common use over northern India. Another name, not quite so commonly used, is s ạ u, probably also of Aryan origin (perhaps the same word as s a d h u). I am under the impression that this last name was more commonly used formerly. In the Santali text both words occur. In the translation s ạ u is rendered by banker. Both are used about the same man.

3 What is here told is of everyday occurrence. The original loan is permitted to run up with compound interest to several times its original amount. It may have been actually paid off and more; but as the Santal has no means of controlling this (at least he does not do so, barring a few exceptional cases) the debt remains. Then a little is added, and finally the result becomes like what is here stated.

ńe̱lle khan, uni ho̱ṛ do̱e oko baṛaea. Ado̱ uni mohajo̱n do̱ onka bar pe̱ dhaoe calaoena, ado̱ bae ńam daṛeae khan, uni bạhutte̱t́e kuli baṛakedege, okayenae me̱nte; ado̱ uni ạimạị hõ bae lại.

Ado̱ arhõ onkage mit́ dhao Pus cando jo̱khe̱ne calaoena; ado̱ oṛak̇reye ho̱ho̱ baṛayet́a, Okayenam, phalna, menama se̱ baṅ? Ado̱ uni ho̱ṛ ma setak̇ akan se̱, oṛak̇re ma bae tahe̱n. Ado̱ uni ạimạige arhõe kulikedea, Phalna do̱e okayena?

Ado̱e metadea, Uni do̱ ạglạ pạclạ e̱ne̱će se̱n akana.

Ado̱ uni dekoe me̱nket́a, Henda mạńjhạn, dinge bạń ńame do̱?

Ado̱ uniye me̱nket́a, Dinạmge e̱ne̱će calak̇ kana. Tãhã uni do̱ rabaṅte se̱ṅge̱le jolkak̇a, ado̱ o̱ṇḍe̱geye jorok̇kok̇a.

---

4 Also a very common device to avoid listening to the upbraidings of the great man, and perhaps also to avoid saying or doing things one might repent of later on.

Of daily occurrence. The money-lender will come himself or send his servants, when he has reached the psychological moment. Up to this time, everything is fair and friendly; from now on commences the pulling of the net. Not finding the man, he speaks to the wife.

6 Pus, a name received from Bengali or Hindi, is a month corresponding to the last half of December and the first half of January. The heavy paddy ist harvested at this time, and it is the time when everybody has a little foodstuff, on the threshing-floor or in the house. It is therefore also the time when the money-lenders or people who have given others anything on credit try to be repaid. In the latter half of Pus the Santals have their s o̱ h r a e, a kind of harvest festival, generally a debauchery of a very low kind. Up to this time the Santals eat as much as they like of their new harvest of rice. One of the last days of the s o̱ h r a e, a man walks through the village street beating a branch with dry leaves, to drive the d ạ r d ạ h a, the 'glutton' away, a symbolic action to tell people that from now on they have to eat measuring the quantity of rice. The money-lenders or their servants come to the threshing-floors and make them 'measure out to them' the largest possible amount of paddy, in repayment of advances and debts.

7 The Hindu is standing in the court-yard; it would be against propriety for the man to knock; so he calls out.

8 The Santali text implies that the Hindu calls out the name; this is against the rules of good behaviour, the name being used only in addressing persons much

soon as he saw the money-lender coming towards his house, he would hide himself[4]. The money-lender in this way came two or three times, and as he did not find the man at home, he asked his wife where he had gone; but the woman did not tell either[5].

Then it happened once in the month of Pus[6] that he again went there on the same errand, and he was calling out[7] there in the house: "Where are you, so and so[8]? Are you here or not?" Now the man, as soon at it was morning, did not stay at home[9]. So the money-lender again asked the woman: "What has become of so and so?"

"He has gone," she replied, "to play Back and Forward[10]."

"Look here, madam[11]," the Hindu[12] said, "how is it I never find him?"

"Every day," she replied, "he goes to play." What really was happening was that he, because it was cold, lighted a fire and was warming himself[13] there.

---

younger than or inferior to oneself. The name may be used, provided an honorific title is added; but so is not done here.

9 See above note 4. To avoid the unpleasant meeting, if they cannot hide, they may go away somewhere, generally on some pretext or other.

10 Agla pacla, lit. 'foremost backwards' (both words are of Hindi extraction), on account of this and similar stories being told among the Santals, is sometimes heard as a jocular name for moving backwards and forwards. They have no play so called.

11 Mańjhi is a title used by 'foreigners' addressing a Santal; mańjhan is the same, to a Santal woman.

12 The word of the Santali text, deko, is a name used to signify a person of another race than the Santals, i. e., Hindus and Mohammedans. Other aboriginals and the so-called semi-hinduized races (Paharias, Bhuiyas and Doms) are not called so, and Mohammedans are now mostly styled either musla or jolha, the latter being a Mohammedan weaver-'caste', to which very many of the Mohammedans living in these parts belong.

13 It is a very common sight in the early mornings of the cold season to see people sitting, alone or together, over or near to a fire to warm themselves. They do not, like us, attempt to keep themselves warm by exercise.

Adọ uni deko dọ' malhan jọ akane ṅẹlkeťtako, jhaṭare bẹbạṛić jọ akana. Adọ uni dekoe mẹnkeťa, O mạṅjhạn, mọrọd tọ nại, sim amake dẹ.

Adọ uni ạimạiye mẹneťa, Ki bọlchi, hẹrẹl? Amra nại bujchi.

Adọ uni dekoe mẹnkeťa, Sim, mạṅjhạn, sim dẹ.

Adọ uni ạimạiye mẹnkeťa, Ọh! sim simok̕ kanae! Am lạgiť baṅdọle sim akaťko? Bareak̕getaleakin, unkin hõ eṅga mẹntele dọhọ akaťkina, are sim simok̕ kana! Cele sim bhalale emama? Bale emam lạgiť.

Jạnić adọ deko hõ bae bujhạueťa uni ạimạiak̕ rọṛ dọ, ar uni ạimại hõ dekoak̕ rọṛ dọ bae bujhạueťa.

Khange uni deko dọ malhan jhaṭareye dẹjok̕ kana; adọ uni ạimạiye mẹnkeťa, Ayọ gọ! nui deko ya simteṅ bhagaokede khan dọ ya jhaṭarem dẹjok̕ kan. Khub leka kạṛạiye ma thọ!

---

14 The bean here mentioned, malhan (Dolichos Lablab, L.), is a runner bean with large broad pods, very commonly found planted in the court-yards or near the houses of the Santals. The pods and beans are much relished as curry.

15 To support climbers of the kind here mentioned, the Santals simply take one or more bushes or small trees and fix in the ground. The climbers run all over the branches.

16 Where in the following German has been used, it is to translate sentences given in what is meant to be a kind of rustic Bengali. The Santal woman does not understand Bengali; she has picked up a few words, but is in ignorance as to their proper use and speaks in a way delightful to the Santals. That happenings like what is here told are quite possible, the writer is able to testify. Some years ago it happened that a 'deko' came through the village street just outside our compound. There he saw a small goat and offered a Santal woman he saw twelve annas for it (it happened so long ago that a price like this would not be out of the ordinary at that time). The word he used was barọ; the woman did not know that this meant twelve, but likely thinking that it had something to do with the Santal bar (also barea), which means two, she replied that he might have it for gẹl, ten, annas. Another time a Santal couple came to a market-place, wishing to sell a goat. A 'deko' offered pã̄c sikạ, five four-annas (Re. 1—4—0); hearing this the woman at once protested and said that if the man would give miť ṭaka, one rupee, he should have the goat. Her husband tried to persuade her that five 4-anna pieces were more than one rupee; but she would not have anything of this 'deko' nonsense; would he give one rupee, well and good, otherwise others might get

The Hindu now saw that their malhan beans[14] were bearing fruit; there was an immense amount of fruit on the bean supports[15]. So he said: "Frau, der Mann ist nicht hier; gieb mir einige Bohnen[16]."

"Was sage er[17], you man[18]? Wir verstehen es nicht," the woman replied.

"Bohnen, Frau," the Hindu said, "gieb einige Bohnen."

"Oh," the woman said, "he is 'hen-hen'ning[19]. Is it for you, do you think, that we are keeping hens? Two are all we have, and those two we have kept to have them for laying eggs, and he is 'hen-hen'ning! What kind of hen, I wonder, are we going to give you?"

Now, likely, the Hindu did not understand what the woman was saying, nor was the woman understanding the Hindu's language.

The Hindu thereupon tried to climb the supporting poles; but the woman called out: "O ma, O mother[20]! this Hindu fellow — I worsted him so far as the hens were concerned; then you are now, you fellow, climbing the bean poles. He should have a sound buffeting[21], that fellow!"

---

the goat. The man felt so ashamed that he gave in to his wife. At the present time most women have learnt enough not to commit such blunders. Still, of course, as they have to depend on what they can pick up whilst they are not supposed to have any conversation with 'deko' men, it is only natural that they are not very proficient.

17 The woman uses a wrong form of the verb, but tries to speak Bengali.

18 Here she does not know what word to use and says hẹrẹl, a Santali word meaning 'male' or 'man' (corresponding to Norwegian 'mandfolk'), never used in addressing in Santali.

19 The Hindu says sim, which is his name for this particular bean (in Santali malhan); now in Santali sim means the domestic cock or hen, and the woman thinks the 'deko' wants to take these and scolds accordingly.

20 Ayọ gọ, a very common interjection or exclamation used to express wonder or astonishment or pain, lit. means 'mother, mother', both words being in use in Santali.

21 The Santali word kạṛại means to beat with a club or heavy stick. To get alliteration to show the misunderstanding of the 'deko' 'buffet' is used in the translation. Hearing kạṛại the Hindu is reminded of kaṛa (in Santali kaḍa), which means a buffalo, and follows the idea up.

Ado uni dekoe ṁen goťkeťa, Hã mạṅjhạn, kaṛa dibi to kise abad kurbe?

Ado arhõ uni ạimạiye menkeťa, Ayo go! nui deko do bae bataoeť do. De se na, tok ṅawaṅpe, nãhãk khub iṅ kạṛạiyea.

Ado arhõ uni dekoe menkeťa, Kaṛa dibi to, mạṅjhạn, bhalo hobe, sob khalạs hũyạ̃ jabek.

Ado, kathae, uni ạimại doe chuṭạulen, tok saṗkate dale lạgiťe epel idi goťkeťa. Khange ado uni deko mohajon do botorteye dạṛ taṗkeťa, ado ạḍiye edre calaoena.

Ado dosar hiloḱ khange sim raḱreye heće̱nte oṛaḱreye sen esetkedea. Adoe ṅamkede khane metae kana, Henda phalna, je dharaoaḱ do cedaḱ bam emkạtiṅ kana? Adom emaṅa se baṅ? Ma ona roṛme. Dinge iṅ do am ṭhen iṅ hijuḱ kana, oṛaḱrege baṅ heć ṅameťmea. Ado am bạhuṅ kuliye khan doe mena, baṅma, Ạglạ pạclạ eneće sen akante oṛaḱre do bam heć ṅame kana. Ar hola do malhan iṅ goťeť tahẽkanre tokanteye lagakidiṅa. Ado ceť lekam eneć kante am do din hiloḱ onḍegem calaḱ kana?

Ado uni hoṛe menkeťa, Ceť baṅ se, sạu, ạḍi mõṅj eneć kana, onate iṅ do dingeṅ calaḱ kana?

Ado uni dekoe menkeťa, Henda mạṅjhi, iṅ doṅ ceť daṛekea se oho?

Ado uni hoṛe menkeťa, Deko hopon ma arhõ ạḍi algateko ceťkea.

Ado uni dekoe menkeťa, Iạ mạṅjhi, enḍekhan iṅ hõ ceťaṅme.

Ado uni hoṛe menkeťa, Hẽ entem ced khan doṅ ceťama; ạikạ okoe ṭhen hõ alom lại baṛaea.

Adoe menkeťa, Acha, okoe ṭhen hõ baṅ lạia.

Adoe metadea, Acha bogege, enḍekhan ma gapa nonka ạḍire hijuḱme; teheṅ do nonḍege marsalena, onate oho jutlena. Ona ceceť do ạḍire calaḱ hoyoḱa. Ma gapa nonka ạḍire hijuḱme, adoṅ ceťama.

---

22 The tok is an implement found in every Santal household. It is a heavy wooden pestle, some four to five feet long, with an iron ring in the one (thinner) end, primarily intended for use in husking rice or other cereals in the ukhuṛ, the wooden mortar.

"Ja, Frau," the Hindu said, "wenn man aber die Büffel giebt, womit wird man dann arbeiten können?"

The woman then again spoke: "Oh ma, Oh mother! this Hindu will not give in. Here, my girls, bring me the pestle[22]; I shall buffet him and give him a good beating."

The Hindu then again said: "Falls Sie die Büffel geben, Frau, wird es gut sein; alles wird getilgt werden."

Then the woman made a start; she took the pestle, raised it high in the air and went towards the man to strike him. The money-lender then was frightened and ran straight off; he was very angry, as he went.

The following morning he came at cock-crow, before the man could get away. When he met him, he said to him: "Look here, you so and so, why don't you pay me what you are owing? Are you going to pay me or not? Please tell that. Day after day I am coming here to you; I don't find you at home. And when I ask your wife, she says: He has gone to play Back and Forward; therefore you do not find him at home. And yesterday, whilst I was plucking a few beans, she came with the pestle and chased me away. Now what kind of play is it you are occupied with, since you are going there day after day?"

"You have no idea, banker," the Santal replied, "what a beautiful play it is; that is the reason that I go day after day."

"Look here, governor," the Hindu said, "would it be possible for me to learn or not?"

"Of course," the Santal replied, "Hindus would learn it much more easily even."

"I say, governor," the Hindu said, "then teach me also."

"Well yes," the Santal replied, "if you will learn, I shall teach you; but mind you, don't tell anybody."

"All right," he said, "I shall not tell anybody."

The man then said: "Very well; come then to-morrow, early like this; to-day it has become full day already, so it will not be possible to-day. To learn, it is necessary, to be out early. Please, come to-morrow early like you did to-day, then I shall teach you."

Adoe menkeṭa, Acha, endekhan gapa do adireń hijuka.

Ado uni hore menkeṭa, Hẽ, ma hijukme, aika okoe ṭhen hõ alom laia, ar bańkhan do ohom cet dareleа.

Adoe menkeṭa, Acha, ohoń laia. Ado onka men baṛakatekin apan apinena.

Ado khange sari uni deko do dosar hilok adireye heć goṭena, adoe hoho goṭketa, Cele ho, oṛakre menama se bań?

Adoe gońkedea, menańgea mente; ado enka roṛ sãotegeye odokena. Adoe menkeṭa, Raca sen iń senlenge. Ado kulhi sen odok senkate mit hore hoho agukedea. Ado uni dekoe metae kana, Agla pacla eneć iń ceṭam khan do nãhãk ceṭem emoka?

Ado uni dekoe menkeṭa, Ṭakam ńam khan, ṭakage, ar jomakem ńam khan do, jomak iń emama.

Ado uni hore menkeṭa, Iń do ṭaka hõ bań ar jomak hõ bań; iń do tinak korja menaktiń, inage khalaskańme, endekhan iń ceṭama, ar bańkhan do ohoń cetlema.

Ado uni mohajon hõe menkeṭa, Acha, endekhan iń khalasmea, aika cet utarańme.

Ado uni hore menkeṭa, Acha, bhed bhoń sanam iń lai utarama. Mã endekhan korja ńutumte careć hulejme, ar delabon nitgeń cet utar goṭama; ar bań ceṭatmea menkhan, nui hoṛ sakhi menaea.

Khange sari ado bujhau baṛakate uni deko do uni goha hoṛ samańrege careće hulećketa ona rin pan ńutumte, are menkeṭa, Nẽkẽ iń chuṭiketmea. Ado delabon ceṭańme.

23 In Santali lit. 'I must first go towards the court-yard', the last words being constantly used as a veiled expression for passing water.

24 The Santals like to make use of symbolic acts to testify to the reality of actions. In connexion with the sale of moveable property, e. g. of a bullock, they may finish the transaction by giving a bit of dhubi ghãs (Cynodon dactylon, Pers.). The seller takes a piece of cloth over his head, takes a little of the grass mentioned and rubs it between his flat hands and gives it to the buyer with both hands. The buyer gives a little back. When no dhubi ghãs

"All right", the other replied, "then I shall come early tomorrow."

"Yes, please, come," the man said; "but remember, don't tell anybody; otherwise you will not be able to learn."

"All right," the other replied, "I shall certainly not tell." After having had this talk they separated.

Then really and truly the following morning very early the Hindu put in an appearance and called out: "Hallo, so and so, are you at home or not?"

The man answered him, saying that he was there, and as he said this, he came out. "Let me first go a little aside[23]," the man said. He thereupon went out into the village street and called another man; then he said to the Hindu: "If I teach you the Back and Forward play, how much will you give then?"

"If you want money, I shall give money," the Hindu answered; "and if you want foodstuffs, I shall give you that."

"Neither money nor foodstuffs do I want," the Santal said; "whatever debt I have with you, let me off that; then I shall teach you; otherwise I am not going to do so."

"All right," the money-lender said, "then I shall let you off; but mind, teach me all there is."

"All right," the Santal replied; "I shall tell you all there is about it, meaning and signification. Please then break the straw[24] to show you have let me off my debt, and come along and I shall now at once teach you all and everything; and if I don't teach you, here is this man as a witness."

After having thought the matter over, the Hindu thereupon really broke the straw in the presence of the witness, to wipe off all debts and obligations, and said: "There you are, I have let you off. Now please teach me."

is available, they may each take a bit of straw, break it into two, whereupon they give one another one bit and keep one bit for themselves. This is what is done in the story.

Ado̱ sạri uni ho̱ṛ do̱ oṛaḱteye bo̱lo̱yente ṭhuṭkuṫ seṅge̱le oḍok-keṫa, ar uni deko ar goha ho̱ṛ banargeye riạu idikeṫkina. Ado̱ bir se̱nre se̱nkate janhe̱ khạṛạ̣i ṭhenko durup̃ena. Ado̱ uni ho̱ṛe me̱nkeṫa, Ma no̱ṇḍe̱ge kicrić do̱ sanam ho̱ṛbo do̱ho̱ea; ar nui goha ho̱ṛ do̱e do̱ho̱ere hõ baṅre hõ, me̱nkhan alaṅ do̱ bana ho̱ṛ laṅ do̱ho̱le ane̱ć jutoḱa.

Ado̱ sạri bana ho̱ṛkin do̱ho̱keṫa, ar uni goha ho̱ṛ do̱ ona kicrić ṭhengekin duṛup̃ ocokedea, ar ạkin do̱ ona janhe̱ busup̃ sorrekin calaoena. Ar e̱n hiloḱ do̱ rabaṅ hõ ạḍi ãṭ rabaṅ kan tahẽ̱kana. Ado̱ uni ho̱ṛ do̱ janhe̱ busup̃te se̱ṅge̱le jolkeṫa, ado̱e metae kana; Iạ sạu, ma thoṛalaṅ joroḱ ńõḱlenge, ado̱ nãhãḱ iń ceṫama.

Ado̱ sạri bana ho̱ṛkin joroḱ akana; ado̱ ḍher ńõḱe ṭhekaole khan do̱ ạḍi tạpis ḍạu ḍạu jol go̱doḱ kantekin pạc go̱doḱ kana; arhõ hạrsuṛ idiḱ khankin sor idiḱ kana. Ado̱ uni dekoe me̱nkeṫa, Ma ceṫ ho̱ṫańme, inạḱgelaṅ joroḱa.

Ado̱ uni ho̱ṛe me̱nkeṫa, Nõḱõe co̱laṅ e̱ne̱ć kange, bam bujhạueṫa? Ńe̱lme, laha se̱n hõlaṅ calaḱ kana, tayo̱m se̱n hõlaṅ pạcoḱ kana. Niạ kangea ạglạ pạclạ e̱ne̱ć do̱. Ma ado̱ kurumuṭute ceṫ do̱ho̱kam.

Ado̱ khange uni deko do̱ ạḍi bạṛiće kastaoena; ado̱e me̱nkeṫa, Baṅ, noa e̱ne̱ć babo̱tte nunạḱ rin do̱ o̱ho̱ń cabaletama. Am do̱ ạḍiń e̱ṛe̱kidińa.

Ado̱ uni goha ho̱ṛe metadea, Ma ho, katha ańjo̱m ṭhikkataliṅme. Nui deko enaṅ ceṫe me̱nleṫa, ar nitoḱ ceṫe me̱neṫa? Ma ańjo̱mkam.

Ado̱e me̱nkeṫa, Hẽ̱, ańjo̱mkeṫtabenaṅ. Khange ado̱ko apan ạpinena.

---

25 Janhe̱ (Paspalum scrobiculatum, L.) is very commonly cultivated on outlying high lands. It is freely eaten by the Santals, is reported to give a rather intoxicating beer, but is not considered sufficiently valuable to be seized by the money-lenders. The straw is valueless as fodder, but is used during the cold season as here described. It is suitable for stuffing mattresses, and is much used by potters as fuel in their kilns.

26 For threshing jungle corn of sorts, they will plaster a small bit of ground anywhere near the field, not, however, in such a solid and careful way as when making their ordinary threshing-floors.

The Santal then, truth to tell, entered his house and brought out a small piece of burning firewood, whereupon he invited both the Hindu and the witness to come along. Having gone towards the forest, they sat down on a jungle-corn[25] threshing-floor[26]. The Santal now said: "Let all of us put our clothes down here; it does not matter whether the witness will take off his clothes or not; but we two must take them off; then only it will do."

Thereupon both of them took off their clothes, and he made the witness sit down at the clothes, whilst the two went close to the jungle-corn straw. Now it also was very cold that day. The Santal then set fire to the straw and said to the other: "I say, banker, let us warm ourselves a little first; then I shall teach you presently."

Both of them were warming themselves at the fire, and as the man put quite a lot of straw into the fire, it suddenly blazed up into great flames, and they had to be quick and draw back. Again, when it burned low, they drew near to the fire. The Hindu then said: "Please, be quick and teach me; let this be enough warming ourselves."

"Look, here we are playing, don't you understand?" the Santal replied; "see, we are moving forwards, and we are also drawing back. This is the Back and Forward play. Please be diligent and learn so that you know it."

The Hindu then felt exceedingly regretful and said: "No, on account of this play I am certainly not going to wipe off so much debt of yours. You have played a trick on me."

The Santal then said to the witness: "Please, sir, hear and mark exactly what we two are saying. This Hindu — what did he say a while ago, and what is he saying now? Please hear and mark what he says."

"Yes," he said, "I have heard what you have said." Thereupon they went, each their way.

Khange adǫ uni deko dǫe lạlisketa ona rin babǫtte. Adǫ din tioken khan, uni goha hǫ̃e idi torakedea. Khange adǫ hạkim ṭhen uni hǫṛ hǫ̃ ǫnẹko galmaraoleť lekae sọalketa. Ar uni goha hǫ̃ onkageye rǫṛkeť khan, mambla dǫ ḍhismisentakoa, ar uni dekoge ạḍi bạṛićko ruhetkedea.

Adǫ cabayena katha dǫ, onkate uni hǫṛ dǫe paskaoena.

21. Mitṭaṅ kạki eṅgat reaṅ.

Mitṭaṅ hǫṛ, kathaeye bạhuan tahẹ̃kana; adǫ uni eratae dǫ khub khạṭoya erae tahẹ̃kana, adǫ onate khubkin arjao gǫtketa. Ar gidrạ dǫ mitṭaṅ koṛa gidrạye tahẹ̃kan tạkina. Adǫ bana hǫṛ onka rǫd bǫdǫlkin kạmia; jãhãn kạmi unkin dǫ hạlạregekin kạmi caba gǫda. Adǫ ona hiskạte baṅ dǫ cette ṭạṭakge uni bạhutae dǫe gǫćentaea. Pẹ pon mãhãge bǫhǫk haso ńǫ̃kledea; inạtegeye gǫćentaea.

Khange uni hǫṛ dǫ ạḍi bhabnae ńamketa; adǫ ẹn serma dǫ enkategeye tahẹ̃yena. Adǫ eskar iạte kạmi baṅ calak kante, dosar serma dǫ chuṭkiye ńawana. Adǫ tahẹn tahẹntẹ cetko daete cǫṅ ạḍikin jhogṛakgea; adǫ enka rẹgẹń tẹgẹńtegeko tahẹ̃yena; oka dǫe usạť gǫdǫkgea.

27 The conclusion is, perhaps, not impossible according to Santal, or even Indian, ideas.

21[1] Stepmothers have no good reputation among the Santals.

2 The Santali word would show that whatever they may have earned is the result of industrious agricultural work.

3 According to Santal ideas death is not natural; especially when young people die, they are always ready to believe that death in such cases is due to the malevolence of evil spirits and of witches. One of the causes inducing those beings to attack people, is envy. It is, it is thought, too much for them to see the happiness of people.

4 A very common description of how a person may come to die. It is the symptom observed, and deemed insufficient to cause death.

5 It would be quite out of the common for a Santal widower, still in his best years, to remain single. It would not, generally, be understood. A Santal man

The Hindu thereupon brought a suit on account of this debt. When the day fixed came, he also took along with him the witness. Before the judge the Santal pleaded in accordance with what they had talked together; and when the witness also deposed the same, the case was dismissed, and they gave the Hindu a good rating[27].

So the story is ended; in this way this man slipped through.

21. A STEPMOTHER[1].

THERE once lived, people tell, a man who had taken to himself a wife; and this wife of his was a very industrious person, so they quickly earned some competence[2]. As for children, they had one son. Both of them were equally industrious; whatever work they applied themselves to, they got through with it in an incredibly short time. Then, whether it was from envy[3], or whatever the cause was, this wife of his suddenly died. She suffered a little, three or four days, from head-ache[4]; from this she died.

It was a great grief to this man, and that year he remained as he was. Then, as his work did not go well, because he was alone, he married again[5] the year following. As time passed, for some cause or other they were always having a good deal of quarrelling, and they lived in this way squabbling; sometimes the woman had sulky fits.

---

needs a wife. When his wife has died, the widower will generally wait until the crops of one season have been harvested. Then friends will commence to offer to arrange a marriage with a widow (so generally; it seldom happens that a spinster will agree to marry a widower), and a marriage takes place, with, however, much less ceremony than what is used when previously unmarried persons are joined together, one reason for this being that a second marriage is only for this world. Bachelor and spinster, once properly married, will be husband and wife also in the next world, whether they have been separated by death or divorce or not, whether they have remarried or not. To remarry too quickly is

Ado̠ mit́ din do̠e kulikedea uni ba̠hutae do̠, Cet́ ia̠te am do̠ siń sa̠ṭupge mit́ raṅgaogeń a̠ika̠umea?

Ado̠ unre uniye me̠nket́a, Iń do̠ cet́ ia̠te co̠ṅ nui gidra̠ do̠ a̠ḍi sikiṛ iń ńe̠le kana.

Ado̠ unre uni ho̠ṛe me̠nket́a, Cekate sikiṛ do̠m ńe̠le kana? Nui ma ać daṛetegeye a̠sulok̀ kan. Cet́ hõ̠ tho̠ bae sakeaṛet́mea, ado̠ cekatem a̠ṛisae kana?

Ado̠ uniye me̠nket́a, Cekate co̠ṅ! Nui do̠ edregeń ńe̠le kana; nui gidra̠ no̠ṇḍe̠ye tahe̠n khan, e̠ṇḍe̠khan iń do̠ bań tahe̠na.

Ado̠ uni ho̠ṛe me̠nket́a, E̠ṇḍe̠khan nui gidra̠ do̠ lań ceka lekayea?

Ado̠ uniye me̠nket́a, Ma nui gidra̠ do̠ go̠jeme, ar bańkhan jāhãtege idi giḍikaeme.

Ado̠ uni ho̠ṛe me̠nket́a, Okateń idikaea? Janamkedeań; ado̠ unire hõ̠ co̠ṅ māyā menak̀tiń, ar go̠go̠ćem metań kana. Cet́ lekate nui do̠ń go̠jea?

Ado̠ uni a̠ima̠iye me̠nket́a, Nui gidra̠ go̠je reak̀ do̠ algagea; ińren gidra̠ khan do̠ń go̠ć go̠t́kea.

Ado̠ uni ho̠ṛe me̠nket́a, Ma e̠ṇḍe̠khan amge go̠jeme.

Ado̠ uni a̠ima̠iye me̠nket́a, Iń do̠ o̠ho̠ń go̠ćlea amren do̠. Ińrene tahe̠n khan do̠ń go̠ć go̠t́kea. Amren kanae, ma amtege go̠jeme.

Ado̠ uni ho̠ṛe me̠nket́a, Cet́ lekateń go̠jea? Magete ma ińge a̠ḍi bo̠to̠ṛ iń a̠ika̠uet́.

Ado̠ uni a̠ima̠iye me̠nket́a, Acha, uni go̠je reak̀ bhe̠d do̠ń la̠iam kana. Siok̀ jo̠khe̠n uni do̠ lahakaeme, ar am do̠ tayo̠mre siok̀me, ar am siok̀ isi do̠ khub sagak̀ leka lak̀ coelokak̀me, ar siok̀

not thought quite proper; but a man must have somebody to cook his food and to do a woman's part of the agricultural work. If a man has children who can work, it is not infrequent that a widower will remain as he is, for the sake of the children. They dread a stepmother.

6 The Santal ploughing is something very superficial. Their plough is an instrument of very ancient model, entirely of wood, except for an iron ploughshare (a bit of iron, some 25 to 30 cm. long, some 3 cm. broad and some 7 to 9 mm. thick, placed in a space cut for it on the upper side of the plough, and kept in position by an iron staple). Except for the small iron part, the Santals make their own ploughs. It is easily understood that, with such an instrument, no

Then, one day, he asked his wife: "Why is it that, all day long, I feel that you are continually angry?"

She replied: "For some reason or other it always irritates me to see this boy."

"How can it irritate you to see him?" the man said. "Why, he is supporting himself by his own ability. He is certainly not giving you trouble of any kind whatever; how then can you be annoyed with him?"

"How?" she replied; "it makes me feel angry to see him; if this boy is to remain here, in that case I shall not remain."

"What are we then to do with the boy?" the man asked.

"Well," the woman replied, "kill the boy, or else take him somewhere and get him out of the way."

"Where am I to take him?" the man asked; "I am his father; I have affection for him also, you must understand, and you tell me to take his life. How could I possibly kill him?"

"It is easy enough to kill this boy," the woman said; "if he were my child, I should soon kill him."

"Well then," the man said, "then you kill him."

"No," the woman answered, "I shall certainly not kill any one who belongs to you. If he were mine, I should soon kill him. He is yours; do kill him yourself."

"In what way can I kill him?" the man asked. "To cut him down, — — I am feeling very much afraid at the thought."

"All right," the woman said, "I shall tell you how you are to go about killing him. When you are ploughing, make him lead, and you follow[6] ploughing; cut the beam of the plough you use

---

deep ploughing is possible. The earth is just scratched a little. Ploughing can be done only when the earth is soft from rain. This method explains how it is possible for a boy to handle a plough. It is not hard work, demanding the strength of a full-grown man. Generally several ploughs are worked at the same time, one following the other, with an experienced man in charge of the front plough. When stating the age of a Santal boy, it is often done by telling that he is 'fit to plough', or, 'he can plough following after people'. Such a boy is anything from 10 years and upwards.

jo̜khe̜n khub laga lagakinme. Ado̜ ona isi coelote so̜bo̜k̕ harar̥ ocoyem.

Ado̜ sa̜ri uni ho̜r̥ do̜ a̜ima̜iak̕ kathageye se̜nat̕te ać siok̕ nahel isiye lak̕ coeloket̕a. Ado̜ sa̜rikin siok̕a; ado̜ ać do̜ a̜d̥i taeno̜m-reye tahe̜na, ar uni gidra̜ do̜ a̜d̥i sa̜ṅgiń laga jita̜uka̜kina. Ado̜ din hilok̕ onkage bae laga bhir̥a̜ukina. Ado̜ uni a̜ima̜iye me̜na, Okor, tisem go̜je kana? Am do̜ e̜ke̜n iṅgem andha bar̥ayediń kana.

Ado̜ unre uni ho̜r̥e me̜nket̕a, Acha, gapa do̜ń go̜jea, a̜ika̜, setak̕re lo̜lo̜ daka bar̥e̜ e̜m go̜t̕aeme.

Ado̜e me̜nket̕a, Acha bogege e̜n̥d̥e̜khan.

Ado̜ sa̜ri dosar hilok̕ khange setak̕rege lo̜lo̜ lo̜lo̜e daka utu go̜t̕ket̕a; ado̜e metadea, Ma a̜uriye bik̕ dha̜bić emaeme; a̜khir iń go̜jegea, lo̜lo̜ dakae jo̜m torawange.

Ado̜ uni he̜re̜l ho̜r̥e me̜nket̕a, Okareliń siok̕a? Siok̕teak̕ ma jo̜to̜liń sï cabaket̕; ado̜ okareliń siok̕a.

Ado̜ uni a̜ima̜iye me̜nket̕a, Hana t̥a̜n̥d̥ire gundlibo e̜r akat̕, ona gundlige si gid̥iben; ado̜ nãhãk̕ ona gundlire d̥aṅgrako a̜tiṅte o̜ho̜ko se̜n se̜nok̕a. Am do̜ nahak̕ tayo̜m ka̜kinme; ado̜ ona a̜tiń jo̜khe̜n khub leka laga bhir̥a̜u go̜t̕kinme, ado̜ ona isite nãhãk̕e so̜bo̜k̕ hãrar̥ go̜dok̕a.

Ado̜ sa̜ri onka ro̜r̥ mit̕kate e̜n hilok̕ do̜ setak̕rege lo̜lo̜ dakae emadea; ado̜ jo̜m bar̥akate nahelkin jor̥aoket̕a. Ado̜ uni gidra̜i me̜nket̕a, Henda baba, okare tehen̕ do̜lań siok̕a?

[7] Her Santali word is s a g a k̕, the awn of s a̜ u r̥ i (Heteropogon contortus, R. & S.), sharp and piercing.

[8] There are many analogies to such an attitude, even if we do not count what is reported to be done in the way of food for persons about to pay the last penalty. The writer remembers what happened some years ago to a young man, who insisted on becoming a Christian. When the day for his baptism came, he was given by his own mother the best food she could prepare, whereupon he was told that after baptism he would not be their son any longer, but a stranger, who might go wherever he liked, but not think of coming back to his old home. He was henceforth dead to them.

and give it a point sharp as a needle[7]; then whilst ploughing you drive the plough bullocks all you can. In that way stab him and transfix him on the pointed plough-beam[6]."

Then the man really listened to what the woman said and cut the end of his plough-beam into a fine point. So they were ploughing; he himself remained far behind, and the boy was driving the bullocks far away in front, always gaining on his father. In this way, his father never any day drove his bullocks close up. And the woman was constantly saying: "How is it? when are you going to kill him? You are only trying to hoodwink me."

"All right," the man then said, "I shall kill him to-morrow; mind, be sure to give him some nice warm food[8] in the morning".

"All right, that is well then," she said.

Then really, next morning she made haste to prepare some very nice and warm rice and curry; the man said to her: "Now give him until he is satisfied; now I shall kill him; let him first have some nice warm food, as he goes away."

The man again spoke: "Where are we to plough? We have finished all there was to plough; where are we to plough?"

"In that field over there," the woman said, "we have sown millet[9]; plough that millet down; the bullocks will feed on that millet and will consequently not move quickly. You keep your bullocks behind, and whilst his ones are feeding, be quick and drive yours at once close up; then he will certainly be stabbed and transfixed on the pointed plough-beam."

So really that morning, after they had talked together and agreed as mentioned, she gave the boy some nice warm food; after they had eaten, they yoked the ploughs; then the boy said: "Look here, father, where are we to plough to-day?"

---

9. The millet here mentioned, gundli (Panicum miliare), is fairly commonly cultivated on the outlying high lands by the Santals.

Adọ uni apattẹte menkẹta, Hanẹ hana ṭaṇḍirelaṅ siok̕a.

Khange nahelkin sọk̕ idiket̕a ona ṭaṇḍite; adọe metae kana, Ią bąbu, noa gundlilaṅ si giḍia, adọ surgująlaṅ ẹra.

Adọ uni gidrąye mẹnket̕a, Henda baba, noa gundli dọ ąḍi cọṅ hoe akan, gapa meaṅ khange nāhāk̕ belek̕a. Cedak̕laṅ si giḍia? Adọ ma ńẹlme, noa dọ hoe cas kana, nahaklaṅ bąṛić giḍia, ar tayọmtelaṅ ẹra. Ona dọ ọkọe ńẹl akat̕a, hoeyok̕ cọṅ baṅ cọṅ. Nahak niągelaṅ kharapkak̕a.

Adọ sąri ona kathage apattẹt̕ dọe bujhąuket̕a, Baṅa, nui gidrą dọ ṭhikgeye metaṅ kana, baṅma, pąhil cas dọ pąhil gidrą tuluć jurik̕ kana; nui gidrą dọ kąmi leke hoeyena. Adọ nui gidrą hō̱ń gọćle khan ọkọe ąsuliṅa? Ar sąrige tayọm cas leka, tayọm era dọe gidrąko cọṅ baṅ cọṅ, ọkọe ńẹl akat̕a? Baṅa, nui gidrą dọ ọhọń gọćlea, nią kąhīste dọe tahẹnre hō̱ baṅre hō̱.

Adọ onka mẹnkatekin aṛak̕ baṛakat̕koteye ruąṛ hẹćena; adọe metadea, Gọgọćem metadiṅa, adọ baṅ gọćledea, ar ọhọń gọćlea, nią kąhīstem tahẹnre hō̱ baṅre hō̱. Ni eskargetiṅae, arhō̱m gọć ocoyediṅa? Adọ hapẹn tayọmte dọm janamko cọṅ baṅ cọṅ, ona dọ ọkọe ńẹl akat̕a?

10 The plough-cattle work in pairs. A yoke is put across the necks of the two bullocks or buffaloes, and the plough-beam is fastened to the yoke with a leather-thong. When going to or coming back from the field, the whole plough is hoisted up and carried on the yoke between the bullocks, the beam standing high up into the air.

11 Surgują (Guizotia abyssynica, Cass.) is one of the most commonly cultivated oil-yielding plants. The seed (called Niger seed) yields the oil. Whilst gundli is cultivated during the rainy season, surgują is a cold-weather crop, often sown where gundli or some other crop has grown earlier in the year.

12 Support in old age is a problem with the Santals as with other people. It is solved by giving the son with whom the old people stay some small advantage (in case there are more sons than one). If there are no sons, they will arrange with some one else (a son-in-law or an adopted son) to take care of them, on the understanding that the care-taker will get the land when the old man dies. It would not be possible to enter on details here; I only wish to say that

"You see that field over there," his father replied, "there we shall plough."

Thereupon they let the bullocks carry the ploughs suspended on the yoke[10] over to the field; then the father said to him: "I say, my boy, we shall plough this millet down, and then we shall saw sunflower[11]."

"Look here, father," the boy replied, "this millet, why, it is a heavy crop; in a few days it will ripen. Why shall we plough this down? And remember, this is a ready grown crop; to no purpose we shall destroy this, and then afterwards sow. Who has seen that, whether it will come to anything or not? To no purpose we shall ruin and destroy this."

Then the father in very truth realized the meaning of these words: "No, this boy is quite right in what he says to me; the first crop and the first children tally; this boy has become fit to work. And if I should now kill this one, who will support me[12]? Truly, like a second[13] crop, who can tell whether a second wife will bear children or not? who has seen it? No, I shall certainly not kill this boy, whether she, being annoyed at it, will stay or not."

After having spoken in this way, they unyoked the bullocks and returned home; then he said to her: "You told me to kill; I did not kill him, and I shall certainly not kill him, whether you, being annoyed at it, will remain here or not. He is my only child; in spite of that you try to make me kill him? And whether in days to come you will bear me children or not, who has seen that?"

---

when it has been said that the Santals do not practise adoption, it is a mistake. The idea underlying adoption is not, however, to secure a successor, but to secure support in old age.

13 Meant is the cold weather crop cultivated on the same ground as the first crop, estimated as the more essential or real one. With the Santals, the second crop is practically always cultivated on their high lands, not on the lower lying rice-fields.

Adǫ onka mẹn baṛakate bhageteye ruhet́ baṛakedea; ar onka rọṛ rọṛteye raṅgaoen khane humạḱ gọt́kedea. Adǫ uni ạimại usạt́e dạṛket́a; adǫ pańja hõ bae pańjalĕdea.

Adǫ tin din cǫe tahẽyen; adǫ apat baretko ạgu oṭokadea; adǫ unre noa kathae lạiket́a onko samańre; adǫ apat baret hõ bogeteko ruhet́kedea, adǫe tahẽyena.

Adǫ cabayena katha dǫ.

22. Bạḍohi sẹ chutạr hǫṛ reaṅ.

Sedae jǫkhẹn, kathae, mit́ṭaṅ atore mit́ṭaṅ kaṭ bạḍohi sẹ chutạr hǫṛe tahẽkana. Ar unkinren gidrạ dǫ mit́ṭaṅ koṛa hǫpǫne tahẽkantạkina, ar uni chaḍa dosra gidrạ dǫ bạnuḱko'ṭạkina, janamreye ini eskargea. Adǫ sadher hǫpǫn iạte uni dǫ ạḍikin jǫtǫn ar ạḍikin dulạṛea, ar hạṭiạ bạṭiạ khon lạḍu miṭhai sẹ uni dǫ bes besaḱ jǫmkin emaea sẹkin ạguaea. Arkin cẹrẹjea, Ma bạbu, hara hǫdoḱme, ạsulliṅam, kạmi gǫṛǫaliṅam. Adǫ onkakin landawaea.

---

14 To run away, home or to near relatives, is a very common expedient with newly married women, when they are in the sulks, or are dissatisfied. If there is nothing really serious at the bottom, the husband is expected soon to follow after his wife and bring her back again, he thereby showing that he wants to live in peace. If the woman is guilty of any serious offence, or rather has given her husband real cause for complaint, the husband will often not follow his wife; others may try to make peace; this may succeed, or it may end in a divorce. Sometimes, when the relatives of the woman understand that she is at fault, they may, as here, take her back to her husband themselves. It is an acknowledgement that the husband is not to be blamed.

22[1] The title given by the Santal to the following story is Bạḍohi sẹ chutạr reaḱ katha, the story of a worker in wood or carpenter. The first part is the story of a spoilt child; the latter part may to some degree remind one of the Askelad of the Norwegian folk-tales. Except for the last portion the whole background of the story is genuine Santal.

2 The present day Santals have become agriculturists. As clearers of jungle they have few to equal them in India; as agriculturists they have not as yet advanced

Having said this, he roundly rated her, and as he continued in this way, he flew into a passion and gave her a licking, whereupon the woman ran away in the sulks; but he did not even once go to look after her[14].

The woman stayed away for some time; then her father and brothers brought her back[14]. On that occasion the man told this story to their face; then her father and brothers also scolded her roundly, whereupon she remained there.

So it is finished, this story.

22. THE STORY OF A CARPENTER[1].

ONCE upon a time long long ago, people tell, there lived in a village a man who was a worker in wood, i. e., a carpenter[2]. He and his wife had one child, a boy; besides this one they had no other children; this was the only one born to them. And as he was their only child, the parents were taking great care of him and loved him very much; from every market-place they were in the habit of bringing him cakes and sweetmeats, and they were giving him the best kind of food. They were fondling him, saying: "Please, young man, be quick to grow big; you will support us two; you will help us in our work." In this way they were playing with him.

---

very far; but it may be said that it is a goal with every Santal to have, or to acquire, some land to cultivate. Whilst this is so, the Santals are not, like the Hindus, bound by caste rules to occupy themselves with any special work. A Santal man is expected to be able to make all his own implements (except at the present day what is of iron and bamboo); they have formerly generally woven their own clothes; now this is not so often done. It seems as if they have more than ordinary ability in using their hands. A good deal might be said on this point. Here I shall only mention that it is not uncommon to come across Santals who are quite good carpenters. Although the names used for people engaged in such work are of Hindi or Bengali origin, this is no reason for supposing that people so called should not be Santals.

Adǫ sạriye harayena, kạmi reaḱe lek manena. Khange apat hǫṛ dǫ kạmiye ạcuyea sẹye riạuea, Ma ya, noa ona kạmime; sẹ, hona noa dẹn ạguitalaṅme; sẹ, dela teheń dǫ kạmi kisạṛe metadiń tahẽkana, dela ǫṇḍẹlaṅ calaḱa.

Adǫ onkae ạcu baṛaye khange eṅgat hǫṛ dǫe dhomkao gǫdea, sẹye mẹn gǫda, Alo sẹm ạcuyea, haralengeye. Haralen khan dinẹće kạmigea. Alaṅ daṛe bhor dǫ alaṅtegelaṅ kạmia. Daṛe baṅ calaḱtalaṅ hiloḱ dǫ hapẹn bae ạsullaṅgete? Ạsullaṅgeae dinẹć. Ar gidrạ hõe ni eskargetalaṅa. Adǫ kichu bae mãyãḱgete? Mãyãḱgeae dinẹć.

Adǫ apat hǫṛe mẹna, Nit khon kạmilaṅ ceťae nạhĩ thǫe ạsullaṅa. Nit khone kạmi hewalen anẹć, ạṛis hõ bhaṅgaoḱtaea ar kạmi hõe ceda, ar baṅkhan bǫe bǫeye harayenge. Kạmi hõ bae ceda, tǫbẹ khan cekateye ạsullaṅa? Kạmi daṛele nạhĩye ạsulmea, ar baṅkhan boser ṭãke ạsulmea. Onateń ạcuyede kana sẹń delawae kana, jãhã lekate jẹmǫn iṅaḱ kạmiye ced. Nit khon ạṛis bhaṅgao akan tahẹntae khan, sẹye ńẹl ceť idile khan, inạ dǫ algategeye kạmi gǫda. Ona mẹnkateń ạcuyede kana. Ar am sẹ eṭaḱgem metań kana. Am dǫ iṅgem hantao ruạṛediń kana.

Adǫ eṅgattẹťe mẹnkeťa, Koṛa hǫpǫn kanae, baṅ dinẹće cedgete? Bae ạsullaṅ khan, hapẹn khublaṅ dalea.

Adǫe metadea, Harakate dǫm dal daṛekea? Ǫhǫm dal daṛelea, am khon uni ma khube daṛeyen. Adǫ uni tuluć dǫm daṛekoḱa? Ǫhǫm daṛelena. Ar hara hǫpǫn dalko dǫ lajao paṛagea. Hǫṛko rǫṛǫṛgea. Ạuri haraḱ khon tinạḱem sikhạu paṛhaoea sẹ tinạḱem

[3] The father takes it for granted that any one at first will feel dislike for work. The Santali word is generally used about becoming 'tired of', 'disgusted at', and the like. The talk between the father, who wants to make something out of his son, and the doting mother, may to some extent be typical. The training of children is one of the weak points with the Santals. When the young ones so often become nothing, the fault is very commonly to seek in circumstances like those here described. On the other hand, when Santal children turn out well, according to their circumstances, as often as not the mothers are to have the credit.

So he really grew up and became fit to work. His father then tried to make use of him or requested him to help, saying: "Come, my boy, do this or that," or, "Please fetch that thing or this," or, "Come along, the rich man told me to work for him to-day; come, we shall go there."

When he tried to make him work in this way, the boy's mother would at once rebuke him, or say to him: "Don't, please, make him work; let him grow up first. When he grows up, he will be sure to work some day. We two shall ourselves work as much as we can. When the day comes that we cannot work any longer, will not he support us, or how? He will be sure to support us some time in future. He is also our only child; will he not feel pity for us, or how? Of course, he will have pity for us."

The father would then reply: "Only when we teach him from now on to work, he will support us. Only if he, from now on, becomes accustomed to work, he will not feel the dislike of work[3], and he will also learn to work; and if he does not now, he will only grow up into a lazy sluggard. Work he will not learn either; then how will he support us? Only when he is able to work, he will be able to support you. That is the reason why I try to make him work, or why I ask him to come along, in order that he may somehow learn my work. If from now on he learns to get over the dislike of working, or if he, by looking on, gradually learns, he will in that way easily and quickly become competent. It is for this purpose that I am trying to employ him. Whilst you, see now you are telling me to do something else. You are putting me down."

"He is a boy," the mother said, "will he not learn some day? If he will not support us two, we shall give him a good beating by and by."

"When he grows up," the man replied, "will you then be able to beat him? You will certainly not be able to do that; he will be much stronger than yourself. Would you then be able to be a match for him? No, you will certainly not. And to thrash grown-up children is disgraceful. People will talk. As much as

cet̕aea, onageye guna ar onage kajre lagaok̕a. Ar harakate do̱ muskilgea. Cet̕ leka gidrạko do̱ hako bạ̃ṛsiko lagat̕ khicạrege jạnum do̱ko liveda, ar joaokate ma rạp̕udok̕ge, onkage gidrạ hõ̱ kạṭić khon tinạk̕em ạcu hewayea, uni gidrạge kaje e̱ma. Ar onkan gidrạgeko mãyãk̕a arko ạk̕sula arko guna. Ar bam ạcu hewale khan, uni ma amren bạiriye hoeyok̕tam. Jãhãnak̕ ãṭ ṅo̱k̕ kạmim ạcuye khan, amgeye tardham ruạṛmea. Ado̱ cekate uni do̱m ạcu daṛeaea? E̱ne̱ ado̱ amge bae bhagaoket̕mea? Onate koṛa ho̱po̱n se̱ kuṛi ho̱po̱n gidrạ khongem ạcu hewayede kana, ar gidrạ khonge kạmi se̱nem ạyur idiyede kana.

Ado̱ onka eṅgattet̕e dulạṛkedete gidrạ hõ̱ dho̱mo̱ke cet̕ket̕a; apatak̕ ro̱ṛ do̱ baṅgeye bạsutak̕a. Ado̱ bana ho̱ṛtekin galmarao baṛawade khan, oka do̱ apat sãote kạmiye calak̕a ar oka do̱ baṅ.

Ado̱ onka tahe̱n tahe̱nte uni do̱e hara juạnen khan, ato koṛako tulućе gate hewayena. Kuṛi sendrako e̱ho̱p̕ket̕a, do̱ṅ lagṛe̱ e̱ne̱ć se̱nge se̱ kuṛiko se̱nge mo̱n calaoentaete kạmi do̱e ḍhilạuket̕a. Jãhãnak̕kin ạcuyea, ona se̱n do̱ luturge bae luturak̕a. Apat kạmiye riạuyea, o̱nte̱ hõ̱ baṅataea.

---

4 Such relations between child and parents as here hinted at may seem strange to us; but I am afraid it is often what is met with.

5 Formerly, perhaps not so frequently now-a-days, Santals made their own fishing hooks as described. I have seen it done with the long sharp thorns or spikes of the bael tree (Ægle Marmelos, Correa). When the thorns are young, they are quite supple and flexible. At this time the thorn is bent to the required shape, the point being fixed in the bark and thus kept in position until the thorn matures, when it is removed and is strong enough to be used for catching small fish.

6 Do̱ṅ is the name of a Santal dance, one of their most common. It is danced in daylight and at night, by all people, male and female, small and big. Do̱ṅ is danced at marriages and at chạṭiạr (the festival when a young Santal is given tribal rights), now-a-days also at any other time. The music is furnished by drums, flutes, &c., and by songs. They have a special kind of drumming for this dance, also special songs and melodies.

7 Lagṛe̱ is the most common Santal dance. When any dancing is going on, they will nearly always also have lagṛe̱. At lagṛe̱ they may use drums, flutes, cymbals and other musical instruments. They also have certain melodies sung. Mostly young people make use of this dance. The girls make a row (or two rows, if necessary) with arms linked together and move slowly backwards and

you instruct and tutor a boy, or as much as you can teach him, before he grows up, so much will have an effect, and that will be of any worth. But when he is grown up, it is difficult[4]. Just like children when they are going to fish, they bend the thorn while it is immature[5]; if it is matured, it will break; in the same way, as much as you can make children accustomed to be employed from they are small, just as much that child will be of worth. And such children have affection and support their parents and are of value. And if you don't make him accustomed to be employed, he will surely become your enemy. If you put him to any kind of heavy work, he will snarl back at you. And then, how will you be able to make him work? There then, did he not gain the upper hand with you? Therefore you make both boys and girls accustomed to work from childhood on, and from childhood on you gradually lead him to work."

As his mother idolized him in this way, the boy also learnt to be arrogant; he did not at all like his father's talking to him. When both his parents spoke to him, he sometimes went with his father to work and sometimes not.

The time passed in this way, and when the boy had grown up, he became accustomed to keep company with the village boys. They commenced to run after the girls; his mind was drawn towards dancing doṅ[6] and lagṛẽ[7], or towards the girls, and he neglected work. When they attempted to put him to something or other, he would not give ear to that at all. When his father asked him to come along and work, he was absolutely unwilling.

forwards, with their bodies swaying, the whole row at the same time circling round, so the dancers gradually face from one direction to another. Whilst the girls move in this way, they sing, and a couple of boys are jumping in front of the girls, beating the drum or whatever instrument they may have. It should be noted that Santal boys and girls in dancing never take hold of each other; this would be thought an absolute indication that there was something wrong. Except for a couple of dances that are downright obscene (danced by men alone) the Santal dances look decent and quiet; but especially the lagṛẽ gives the two sexes an opportunity of meeting at night time, with inevitable consequences.

Khange apattet́ 'doe acu arisen khan doe endreyena. Ado engattete metadea, Ńelketam? Iń do pahil khon iń metam kangea, alo se onka dom dularea. Am do iṅak rorge bam aṅjomlet́ khan doń cekamea? Un jokhen ma iṅgem dhomkaoediń tahẽkan. Ado cet́ cekayena, ma ńelme. Okor nit do alaṅak ror doe aṅjometa?

Khange uni eṅgattet́ doe kekleset́ hapeyena, cet́ hõ bae ror ruar dareata. Khangeye metadea, Teheń iń laiam kana; judi iṅak katham aṅjomtiń khan, nuilaṅ koboj dareaea; ar bam aṅjom khan, nui do oholaṅ kobojlea.

Adoe metadea, Acha, ma rorme.

Adoe metadea, Katha do noa kana: judi iń sãote kamiye calak khan, daka utu emaeme, ar bae calak khan, alom emaea.

Adoe menketa, Achaṅ batlao gelawaea, ar bae aṅjom khan, endekhan dakage baṅ emaea.

Ado sari batlao barakate pe pon mãhãe ńelketa seye batlao barawadea. Ado bae aṅjomlettae khan, sarige pe pon mãhã do bae emadea. Ado atore okoeko then coṅ gate korako orakregeye jom baraketa. Ar oka do mãyãte eṅgtatet́ hõ apat baṅ tahen ghuriye em okowaegea. Are metaea, Kami bam calak kante, babu, apume edren kana. Apum soṅgete kami do calakme bare. Am karonte apum do iṅge bogeteye dhuṅgrauediń kana. Kami do calakme bare.

Ado un jokhen uni kora do cet́ hõ bae ror ruara, hape akangeye tahena, enhõ kami sen do baṅataea. Khange mit́ din do dakae em akawade, are jojom kane heć ńam gotkedea. Khangeye ruhet́ gotkedea, Kurhia heṅgla mara, okoe arjaoak yam jojom

[8] The whole might be taken out of life; but it is evident that the narrator does not approve of such behaviour.

[9] The Santals have not the kind of swearing and cursing used by Europeans; the only expression coming near to it, which the writer for the moment can call to mind, is one used by women, viz., tenae (or with another pronoun, tenam, or tenape, &c.) gaṇḍke herel, lit. man on which a log should be pressed down; the expression implies a wish that the person in question might be on the funeral pyre when logs are put across the body. The language is, however, full of expletives. Women may use a few of these; but it is not considered

His father ultimately became tired of asking him to work, and got angry; he said to his wife: "Do you see? I have from the very first been telling you, please don't love him in this way. As you have not listened to what I have said, what can I do with you? When I spoke, you rebuked me. Now see what it has resulted in. Whenever does he now listen when we speak to him?"

The boy's mother then became frightened and silent; she could not answer a single word. Her husband then said to her: "I am telling you to-day; if you listen to what I say, we shall be able to subdue him; but if you don't, we shall never be able to bring him into subjection."

"Very well," she replied, "speak then."

"What I have to say is this," the man said, "if he goes with me to work, give him curry and rice, and if he won't go, don't give him."

"Very well," she replied, "I shall try to make him understand, and if he will not listen, then I shall give him no food."

She thereupon really tried to make him understand, and looked for results for three or four days, that is to say, she tried; and as he would not listen to her, she really did not give him food for three or four days. He had food somewhere in the village, in the house of some or other of his chums. And sometimes his mother also, when his father was not there, would out of pity secretly give him food. She would then say to him: "As you do not go to work, my boy, your father is angry. Do go with your father to work. On account of you your father is speaking very harshly to me[8]. Do go and work, please."

At such time the boy would not answer anything; he would remain silent; still go and work, that he was quite unwilling to do. Then one day when she had given him food and he was eating, his father came and found him. "You lazy sluggard," he scolded him, "whose earnings are you eating now, you scamp? If there is any work, then he stares like a dead cat, and if there is food to be had, if he can get a lot of food, then, dash it[9], he

kańa ya? Kạmi sẹk khan, gọć pusiye bẹṅgẹda, ar ḍaka jọm sẹn khan dọ khub ḍaka jọm khan eṅgate bẹgẹ bẹgẹye cahaḿ ạguia. Iạ gidrạ, dallaṅ dalmea sẹ, gạí dallaṅ ḍalmea.

Adọ onkae ruheťede kanre hõ uni koṛa dọ ceť hõ bae rọṛ ruạṛleťa, tumbuťkate dakae jọmjoṅ kana. Adọ uni apat họṛ dọ, eṅgattẹť sẹn kathae ucạṛkeťa. Eṅgattẹťe ruheťede kana, Am hõ iṅak kathage bam aṅjọma. Nõkõe nonka iṅ bạṅ tahẹnre dakam emaea. Oko okotem ẹm okowae kana. Nonkate dọ chạiae iṅak katha dọe aṅjọma. Amge eṅgate nui dọm barmaṇḍkedea, tọbẹrege iṅak katha dọ bae aṅjọmeťa. Iṅak katha dọ ićak jọťak. Ạsulok sẹn iṅ budiyeť khan, iṅak katha ma tahẽge baṅ tahẹn kan, adọ boser ṭãkem batlaoa. Kạmi ạgu sẹṅ nalha ạguaben kana, ar aben dọ eṅga họn bẹgẹ bẹgẹben jọmjoṅ kana eṅgate. Nonkate aben dọ iṅgeben andak ṅamkidiṅa. Aben eṅga họn dọben miť mọnena, adọ iṅ eskarte dọ ceť iṅ cekaea?

Adọ unạke rọṛ idikeťre hõ unkin dọ miť katha hõ bakin rọṛleťa, bana họṛ thirgekin tahẽyena. Adọ enka rọṛ baṛakate khange nui hõe thirena.

Khange dosar hilok uni koṛa dọ ać eṅgattẹťe metae kana, Iạ ayo, iṅ dọ oṛakrege bạṅ tahẹna. Bogete babae ruheťediṅ kana, ar iṅ karọnte am hõ bogeteye ruheťeťmea. Iṅ karọnte cakben kạphạriạuka?. Iṅge bạṅ tahẹna, inạ dọ jhogṛage caba dapoṛoka.

Adọe metadea, Okate, beṭam calaka? Alom calaka. Ạpum dọ rọṛ ocoae.

---

nice and comme-il-faut. Many men seem unable to speak without filling up with this kind of words, feeling, as they express it, that their language is 'tailless', if they leave those words out. It should, however, be noted, that the use of all these expletives is not considered fully proper. At the present day some of them, perhaps most of them, have worn down to mean very little, especially not what they have originally meant. But it is not more than a generation ago that people were brought before the village Five and fined, if they had used certain improper words. Some of the expletives have lost every meaning; the one used in the Santal text here (e ṅ g a t e, pronounced sometimes with stress on the initial vowel, sometimes with stress on the much lengthened a)

comes with his mouth wide open. You unspeakable child, we two[10] shall give you a beating, be sure; as they beat a cow, we two shall beat you."

Although he was scolding him in this way, the boy did not answer anything; with his head bent he continued eating his food. His father then turned towards his mother, and commenced to scold her: "You don't listen to what I say either. Here you see, in this way you give him food, when I am away. Secretly you give him on the sly. In this way he will be sure to heed my words! You, dash it[9], you have indulged and spoiled the boy; that is the reason he does not heed what I say. What I say is like dirt, at once wiped off. When I am having in mind how we shall be supported, what I say does not count at all; and you instruct him to no purpose whatever. I am working at home or working for wages and bring you what you need, and you, both mother and son, are eating as much as you can gape over, dash it. In this way you two have made me sick. You two, mother and son, have become of one mind; then what can I do alone?"

Although he talked on in this way, the two other ones did not answer a single word; both of them remained silent. And when the man had spoken in this manner, he also stopped.

The following morning the boy said to his mother: "I say, mother, I shall not stay at home. Father is scolding me exceedingly much, and for my sake he is scolding you also exceedingly. Why should you two quarrel on my account? I shall not stay at home; then there will be an end to the squabble at least."

"Where will you go, my son?" she asked. "Don't go away. Let your father talk."

I have not heard a Santal able to explain. It likely originally means 'by the female principle', 'by mother', or something similar. It might be noted that most of the expletives used by men seem to have reference to the sexual organs or to natural functions.

10 Dual in threatening langnage.

Ḅaṅa, ayo, calak̕geaṅ. Am hǫ̃m edreạṅ kangea. Am hǫ̃ pe̩ pon din ma daka hǫ̃ bam emadiṅa, onate iṅak̕ mǫn dǫ ạḍi utạr lǫk̕ kantiṅa. Abengeben janamkidiṅa, abengeben ạsul harakidiṅa, adǫ nǫ̃k̕ǫ̃e nitkate dǫ abengeben kǫsṭǫyediṅ kana. Abenge baben emaṅ khan, iṅ dǫ okareṅ ṅama? Boge dǫ atore gate koṛako tahẽ̩kan te̩ṛǫṅ, ar baṅkhan iṅ dǫ re̩ṅge̩ćteben gǫćlidiṅ tahẽ̩kana.

Adǫe metadea, Ạpumge thǫ onkae metadiṅa, onatege bạṅ emat̕mea. Henda beṭa, tǫbe̩ iṅgeṅ bạṛićket̕a? Acha, adǫ ǫhǫṅ onkamea. Uni dǫ rǫṛ ocoae ma. Rǫṛ dǫ sahaokak̕me.

Adǫe me̩nket̕a, E̩ ayo, harayenaṅ, nit dǫ onkan rǫṛ bạṅ sahao daṛeak̕ kana, ar okare bạṅ tahe̩n? Siṅ sạṭup̕ nãhãk̕ onkageye rǫṛeṅa. Ar am hǫ̃ tinre bam emaṅ? E̩ne̩ thǫ hola hǫ̃ dakaṅ jǫjǫm kan jǫkhe̩ngeye he̩ć ṅamkidiṅa. Daka hǫ̃ sukte dǫ bạṅ jǫmlet̕a. Adǫ inạ karǫnte am hǫ̃ tinạk̕e ruhet̕ket̕mea. Adǫ, ayo, jivire baṅ sahǫp̕ lekageṅ ạikạuet̕a. Adǫ nẽ̩k̕ẽ̩ṅ lại ọṭoam kana, jãhãteṅ oḍok calak̕a.

Adǫe metadea, Jãhãte dǫ, beṭa? Okatem calak̕a? Alom calak̕a. Baṅ jut nãhãk̕ iṅ ạikạua.

Adǫe metadea, Jãhãtege mẽ̩t̕ lutur calak̕tiṅ, ǫnte̩geṅ calak̕a.

Khange eṅgatte̩t̕ak̕ mẽ̩t̕ dak̕ dǫ hiḍir hiḍir jǫrǫ gǫt̕entaea. Adǫ jãhãnak̕ bae rǫṛ daṛeat̕a, e̩kkalte linkede lekae ạikạuket̕a. Adǫ e̩n hilok̕ ṅindạge tinkore cǫṅ kicrićkoe ṅamket̕taea, ar mit̕ṭaṅ bạslạ ar mit̕ṭaṅ rukại okoket̕a. Adǫ kedok̕ko jǫm baṛaket̕ khan, uni

11 In Santali lit. 'burning'.

12 A very common Santali expression, lit. 'anywhere eyes ears go'!

13 The adze (in Santali bạslạ) is a tool like an axe, but with the edge crossing the direction of the handle. It is used for cutting away surface of wood, the end of the handle being kept in the armpit or near there, while the worker catches hold of the handle near to the adze itself. It is slow work, but a skilled man may do very nice work with it. The Santal uses the adze in many cases where others would make use of a plane. There are several forms of the bạslạ, but the principle is the same with all.

"No, mother, I shall go. You also are angry with me. You also did not give me any food for three to four days; therefore, my heart is feeling exceedingly sore[11]. You two have given birth to me; you two have maintained me and brought me up; and then, see now, now you two are making it hard for me. If you two don't give me, where am I to get anything? It was fortunate there were some chums of mine in the village, otherwise you two would have made me die from hunger."

"It was your father," she replied, "he told me this; therefore I did not give you. I say, my son, have I then done wrong? Very well, I shall not treat you so any more. Let him talk as much as he likes. Stand the talk."

"Mother," the boy said, "I am grown up; I cannot stand such talk now any more, and where should I stay? All day long he will be sure to give me a talking to of this kind. And when would you find an opportunity of giving me anything? Remember, yesterday also, whilst I was having my food, he came and caught me unawares. I could not have my food in peace even. And then, on this account, how much did he not scold you also? Therefore, mother, I feel as if I cannot stand it any longer. So there now, I am telling you beforehand; I am going away to some place or other."

"To some place or other, my son?" she asked. "Where are you going? Don't go away. I shall feel heart-sick."

"Wherever my eyes and ears will lead me[12]," the boy replied, "there I shall go."

Then the tears commenced to flow down from his mother's eyes, and she was unable to speak; she felt just as if some one was throttling her. That same night, some time or other, the boy collected his clothes and hid an adze[13] and a chisel[14]. When

14 The chisel (in Santali ruką) used by carpenters does not in form diverge much from the plain bevelled-edge chisel of others. It varies in size. Both this and the bąslą are manufactured by the local blacksmiths.

eṅgattet́ do̠ koṛawak̕ katha apattet́e lạiae kana, baṅma, Bạbu do̠ nonka onkae me̠net́ kana.

Khange apattet́ do̠e raṅgao go̠t́enteye me̠n go̠t́keta, Bese calaoen khange, kuṛhiạ mara. Se̠n ocoae.

Khange rinićte̠t́ hõe thir dorok̕ena. Arhõ uni koṛa do̠ ona kathae aṅjo̠man khan, arte̠t́ge mo̠n do̠ khaṭo̠ cabayentaea. Ado̠ tin ṅindạre co̠ṅ oṛak̕ khone oḍok calaoena, disạ hõ bakin disạ go̠t́ledea. Ar ho̠rte jo̠m ṅũi lagat́ do̠ cet́ge bae idiana; inạ bạslạ ar rukạgeye idi toraket́a. Ado̠ kadraote ulṭi baṭe oḍok calaoena.

Ado̠ calak̕ calak̕te ạḍi sạṅgiṅe calaoena. Mo̠n kadrao akantaete tin sạṅgiṅ co̠e calaoen, ona do̠ bae disạ hudisleta, ar un jo̠khe̠n do̠ re̠ṅge̠ć hõ bae ạikạuleta. Ado̠ tara siṅ jo̠khe̠n se̠ huḍiṅ dak̕ lo ber khange re̠ṅge̠ćkedea, ar jaegak̕ reak̕e hudis baṛayeta. Ado̠ onka hudis baṛakate mit́ṭaṅ dare buṭạreye duṛup̔ena. Mit́ṭaṅ ato sor dare buṭạreye duṛup̔ akan tahe̠kana. Ar ona dare buṭạrege ona atoren ho̠ṛ do̠ go̠ć ḍaṅgrako khal jo̠m baṛakoa. Ado̠ o̠ne̠ye duṛup̔ akan ṭhenge ḍaṅgra jaṅko do̠ bogete me̠nak̕a. Ado̠ cet́ co̠e hudiskette ona ḍaṅgra jaṅ do̠e sap̔kette bạslạteye lak̕ e̠ne̠ć kana, ar kạṭić kạṭiće lak̕ chaḍaoeta. Ar mo̠n do̠ okaretae co̠ṅ, ạuṛige ona do̠e lak̕ baṛayeta. Ado̠ cekate co̠ṅ onae po̠ho̠mket́ khan do̠e ṅe̠lket́ do̠ caole leka ṅe̠lok̕ kan. Khangeye me̠nketa,

---

15 It seems strange that the story does not reflect on the boy being himself the cause of his father's attitude.

16 If a Santal takes himself off, having, or imagining he has, a grudge, he will generally start without saying good-bye. If there are any formalities imposed by custom and usage, they have ceremonial leave-taking; but otherwise there is the least possible. It has been a pitiful trait in Santal history that they take themselves off, instead of standing up.

17 The Santals having no clocks, divide the twenty four hours according to what is done at certain times, according to the position of sun or stars, or according to light, cock-crow, etc. They are never far out of the true reckoning. In the afternoon they have maraṅ dak̕ lo ber (big water drawing time) and huḍiṅ dak̕ lo ber (lit. small water drawing time), the former referring to a time when the sun is high up, and the latter to a time about one hour later.

they had had their supper, the boy's mother told the father what the boy had said, viz. "the boy is saying so and so."

The boy's father then flew into a passion and said: "Excellent if he goes away, the lazy sluggard. Let him go."

His wife then did not say anything more, what would be the use? The boy also, when he heard what was said, became still more down-hearted[15], and some time during the night he went away from home; they were not aware of his going[16]. He did not take anything with him to eat and drink on the way; only his adze and chisel he took with him, and in high dudgeon he went off, not knowing whereto.

Walking along he went far away. He was so upset in his mind, he was not aware of and did not think how far he had gone, and all this time he felt no hunger either. Then, in the middle of the afternoon, or at the time when the women fetch water[17], he became hungry; he also commenced to think of where he should spend the night. Whilst his thoughts were occupied in this way, he sat down at the foot of a tree. He was sitting under a tree that was near to a village. At the foot of that tree the inhabitants of the village were in the habit of flaying and eating dead bullocks[18]. In the place where he was sitting there was consequently a lot of bones of bullocks. Who knows what was in his mind, as he picked up a bullock-bone and commenced to amuse himself chipping it with his adze; he was chipping off tiny bits. His mind was wandering, who knows where; he was chipping and chipping, without giving it a thought. Then, as he somehow became aware of what he was doing, he saw it was looking like rice. So he said to himself: "Oh, I have no rice;

At these times women go to fetch the water they need for cooking the evening meal, &c. They approximately correspond to our 4 p. m. and 5 p. m.

18 This can scarcely be said to be Santal. The writer has never heard of anything of this kind among them. They will, of course, slaughter and eat bullocks, but it is of necessity of such rare occurrence that there would not be time for any collection of bones.

Ho, caole hō bạnuḱtiṅa. Noage bes hikmọtkateń laḱ caolea, ar jãhãe iń daka ocokoa. Adọ onka mẹnkate sạriye laḱ caoleket khan, amdaj mit́ lọṭ tala gan hoeyena. Adọe mẹnket́a, Ho, niạge jãhãegiń daka ocokoa. Adọ onka mẹnkate kicrićreye ghẽṭket́a.

Adọ ọṇḍẹ khon calaḱ calaḱte mit́ṭaṅ atoe ńamket́a. Ar bela hõe jhọl phọlaoḱ kanteye mẹnket́a, Teheń dọ niạ atoregeń gitić aṅgalenge. Gapa dọ arhõ jãhã sẹn iń calaḱa. Adọ onka mẹnkate ona atoteye rakapena. Adọ mit́ṭaṅ oṛaḱre bes piṇḍạko menaḱtakoa. Adọe mẹnket́a, Neko ṭhengeń bọlọḱa, neko ṭhen iń tahẽ aṅgalenge. Judi raca senaḱ piṇḍạre bako gitić ocoạń khan, niạ kuḍạm senaḱ piṇḍạre dọ jạnićko gitić ocoạṅgea. Mọnre onka hudis baṛaket́te ona oṛaḱ raca sẹne bọlọyena, adọe họhọ saḍeket́a, Cele, baba peṛa, menaḱpea sẹ baṅ?

Adọ ona họhọ ańjọmte mit́ṭaṅ kuṛiye oḍokena. Adọ peṛae mẹnet́te parkọme beladea. Adọe kulikedea, Oka sẹn khon peṛa dọ? Ba cọń ńẹl oromet́me.

Adọe mẹnket́a, Peṛa dọń baṅ kana, ayo, iń dọń gitić rẹṅgẹć họṛ kana. Adọ noa piṇḍạko ạḍi sapha ar uḍi sahtaṅ ńẹlket́tapeteń

---

19 An approximate Santal way of giving a measure. When they are to state the size of, or to give the measure of something, they do it by showing how much or how little, how big or how small, with any suitable part of their body, especially hands and fingers. Their standards of measure are consequently in accordance with this. For comparison they also use well-known natural objects of a fairly uniform size. At the present time they have, as a matter of course, had to learn to make use of standardized weights and measures.

20 Santal houses are built round a court-yard, to which the doors lead. On the same side as the door the dwelling houses generally have more or less of a verandah, according to circumstances, the eaves being more or less lengthened.

21 Now and then, but not as a general custom, the eaves on the back side of the house are also lengthened, so as to form the roof of a small verandah. This is, however, seen more frequently with other races.

22 In Santali baba peṛa, lit. father friend. Baba is used in respectfully addressing men older than oneself; peṛa means a relation, or a friend, and may originally have been used about a person known to be, or supposed to be related, in any case belonging to the Santal race. Now the word may be used also like our

I shall use my skill and chip this into rice; and then I shall get somebody to prepare food with it." He was thinking this, and when he had chipped the bone into bits like rice, he had about as much as will go on the open hand[19]; and he said: "Oh, this I shall get somebody to prepare food of." With this intention he tied it up in his cloth.

As he was walking along from this place, he reached a village. As the sun was just setting, he said: "I shall sleep to-night in this village. To-morrow I shall go somewhere else." Thinking so, he went into the village. In one house they had good verandahs, and he said: "I shall go in to these people; let me stay the night with these. If they will not let me sleep in the verandah facing the court-yard[20], they will likely let me lie down in the verandah here on the backside of the house[21]." Having thought so by himself, he entered the court-yard of this house and called out: "I say, good friends[22], are you here or not?"

Hearing this shout, a girl came out, and as he used the word 'friend', she placed a bedstead for him to sit on, whereupon she asked him: "From what side is the friend? Why, I cannot recognize you."

"I am not a related friend, mother[23]," the boy answered, "I am a person in need of a place to pass the night, and as I saw

---

'friend'. It may be noted that, when a Santal meets a stranger at night, and he thinks it is another Santal, he will address him (or her) by peṛa hoṛ, somewhat corresponding to 'kinsman'. When known to each other, they will use the special term, or, e. g., 'father of so and so', 'aunt of so and so', and so on.

Santals may be heard to address girls, even children, as 'mother'. It is intended to show respect and to reassure the person addressed that the speaker may be trusted. People of the so-called kharwar movement among the Santals have at times insisted on their followers always using this term in addressing females. I believe also people of other races may do the same. I have heard Bengalis do so. When we do the same, the 'sentimental' background is somewhat different.

bo̱lo̱ẏena. Ado̱ń me̱nkeťa, Oṛaǩre baṅkhan nią piṇḍąkore do̱ jąnićko gitić ocoaǩgea. Ado̱ onka me̱nkate, ayo, ape ṭhen do̱ń bo̱lo̱yena, ar baṅkhan peṛa do̱ń baṅ kana.

Ado̱e metadea, Hẽ, nõǩõe piṇḍąko do̱ uḍi sahta menaǩtalea. Noakore do̱le araggea. Nonkage ąḍi ho̱ṛko gitićale kangea. Ma nõǩõe, ąiką piṇḍąkorege tho̱.

Ado̱e me̱nkeťa, Acha, iń bidisią ho̱ṛ do̱ piṇḍąkore hõń besoǩgea.

Arhõ uni kuṛiye me̱nkeťa, Ale do̱ bąḍohi ho̱ṛ kanale. Iń baba ąḍiye bąḍohia, onate ale oṛaǩre do̱ siń sąṭuṗ ho̱ṛ reaǩ hel kana. Setaǩ ąyuṗ miť lagharge ho̱ṛko tahe̱na, onate sahta do̱le piṇḍą akaťa, je̱mo̱n noakore ho̱ṛko duṛuṗ. Teheń do̱ iń baba ar iń go̱ bąnuǩkinte ho̱ṛ hõ bako he̱ć baṛaǩ kana.

Ado̱e kulikedea, Am go̱ ar am baba do̱ okatekin se̱n akana?

Ado̱e metadea, Nhatere phalna ato menaǩa, o̱ṇḍe̱ peṛa ho̱ṛo̱ǩkin se̱n akana. Teheńge ruąṛa me̱ntekin se̱n akana. Ado̱ nõǩõe, nit hõ bakin ńe̱loǩ kana. Baṅdo̱kin hijuǩ kan baṅdo̱ baṅ.

Ado̱ uni koṛae me̱nkeťa, Ią, ayo, miť kathań metam kana. Katha do̱ ceť hõ baṅ. Caole do̱ menaǩtińa, ado̱ dayakatem dakaletiń khan, ąḍi boge hoekoǩa.

Ado̱e metadea, Hẽ, daka daṛeaǩań. De̱n e̱nte caole emańme.

Ado̱ haṭaǩe ągukeťa, onareye raṛawadea. Ado̱ idikate uni kuṛi do̱ ona caole do̱ ńe̱le ńe̱leťa se̱, khub leka ąri bąndhiye ńe̱leťa. Are me̱neťa, Caole ma saphage ńe̱loǩ kan, ado̱ cekate ke̱ṭe̱ćge ąikąuǩ kana? Ado̱e me̱nkeťa, Noa caole do̱ bąń dakaea; aleaǩ dakagele emaea. Ado̱ onka me̱nkate ona caole do̱e do̱ho̱kaťa, akoaǩgeye isinadea.

24 See above note 20 & 21. To build for a purpose like that here mentioned is not common, but may be met with also among the Santals. It presupposes some kind of position which involves visits of strangers.

25 A standing formula, used to introduce even the most momentous matter. It is possibly intended to imply that the person addressed may do as he likes, to take notice of it or not.

these very clean and spacious verandahs of yours, I entered. And I said to myself: 'They will likely let me lie down, if not in the house then somewhere here in the verandah'. With such thoughts, mother, I have come in here to you; else I am not a related friend."

"Yes," the girl replied, "as you see, we have very spacious verandahs. Hereabouts we permit people to find a place. In this way lots of people lie down with us. Please, find a place; but, mind, somewhere in the verandahs."

"All right," he said to her, "a man from another country like myself will do very well in the verandah also."

Then the girl spoke again: "We are carpenters. My father is much occupied working in wood; therefore there is all day long lively with people. Morning and evening we have constantly people here; therefore we have provided spacious verandahs, in order that people may sit in these[24]. To-day my father and my mother are not at home; therefore people do not come."

"Your mother and your father", he asked her, "where have they gone?"

"Over in that direction," she replied, "there is such and such a village; they have gone there on a visit to friends. They have gone with the intention of returning to-day. But you see, even now they are not to be seen. A question whether they will come or not."

"I say, mother," the boy said, "I have something to say to you. It is not worth mentioning[25]. I have some rice, and if you would be so very kind and cook it for me, it would be very well."

"Yes, I am able to do that," she said to him. "Please, then, give me the rice."

She brought a winnowing fan, and he untied and let it run out on this for her. When she had taken it in, the girl commenced staring at this rice; she looked carefully at it and examined it, and she was saying to herself: "The rice is looking clean enough; how is it that it is so hard to feel at?" Again she said: "I shall not cook this rice; I shall give him of our food." With this thought she put that rice aside and cooked some of their own for him.

Adọ daka ạuriye emaerege eṅgat apatkin sẹṭẹr gọt́ena. Adọ ọntẹnak̕ duk suke kuli baṛaket́kina. Adọ onakate uni koṛa dakakatae lạgit́ caoleye ẹm akawade, ona caoleye uduk̕akin kana. Metakin kanae, Masẹ, ayo, noa caole ńẹlben; cet́ leka ńẹlok̕ kana?

Adọ sạri bana hoṛ saṗkatekin ńẹl baṛayet́a. Adokin metadea, Henda mạ̃i, noa caole dọ okarem ńamket́a? Nonkan caole ma bạnuk̕tabon cọń. Okarem ńamket́a?

Adọe mẹnket́a, Mase ẹnte ńẹlben, caole kana sẹ bań.

Adọ arhõ divhe marsalkate khub leka ạri bạndhikin ńẹlket́ khan dọkin metadea, Noa dọ, mạ̃i, caole dọ bań kana. Noa dọ jań leka ńẹlok̕ kana. Okarem ńam akat́a?

Adọe mẹnket́a, Nui abo ṭhene heć akan, nui koṛage daka ocok̕ lagat́e ẹm akawadińa. Metadińae, Nẹ, ayo, nia caole dakakatińpe! Adọ caole leka bań ạikạulet́te bạń dakalet́taea, aboak̕geń khadle bạṛti akat́a, ar ẹm dọ bạń ẹm akawadea.

Adọkin kulikedea, Henda mạ̃i, bam kuliledea okaren kanae mẹnte?

Adọe mẹnket́a, Onako dọ bạń kuliledea, Ẹkẹn gitić ṭhãoye kulikidińa, Aṛagape sẹ bań? Adọń metadea, Nõk̕õe, noa piṇḍạkore dọle aṛak̕kegea. Adọ onka mẹnkateye duṛuṗena. Are mẹnket́a, Teheń dọ nọṇḍẹ ape ṭhengeń gitić rẹṅgẹćapea. Nẹ ayo, nią caole dakakatińpe. Onkae mẹnket́te iń dọ caoleń atańket́teń ạguket́a. Adọ okaren gitić rẹṅgẹć hoṛ kan cọe, ona dọ bạń kuliledea.

Adọkin mẹnket́a, Achalíń kuliyea. ar uni lagat́ hõm daka akat́ khan, ma emaeme. Arkin mẹnket́a, Nui dọ khub bạḍohi hoṛ kanae. Nõk̕õe jọkhọn jańe caole oco akat́a, nui kiye kọm bạḍohi kana? Kọm bạḍohi hoṛ dọ nonka bako tear daṛeak̕a. Bạḍohi dõ sọrọsgea.

Arhõkin mẹnket́a, Henda mạ̃i, cet́ lekan hoṛ kanae, haṛama sẹye koṛagea?

[26] This part of the story is not much in accordance with what is usual. But it is not impossible.

Before she gave him his food, her parents arrived. She asked them how people were faring where they had been. After this she showed them the rice that the boy had given her to cook for him, and said to them: "Look here, mother, look both of you at this rice; how does it look?"

Then both of them took a little and had a look at it, whereupon they asked her: "Look here, my girl, where have you got this rice? Why, we have no rice of this kind. Where did you get it?"

"Do look well at it," the girl said, "is it rice or not?"

And when they with lamp light had again looked very carefully at it, they said to her: "This, my girl, is not rice. It looks like bone. Where have you got it?"

"He who has come to us," she replied, "that boy has given it to me to get food cooked. He said to me: Here, mother, please cook this rice for me. But as I did not feel it like rice, I did not cook his; I put in some more of our own; but I have not given him anything."

"Look here, my girl," they asked her, "did you not ask him from where he is?"

"No," she replied, "I did not ask him about those matters. He only asked me for a place to lie down in, saying: Do you allow people a place here or not? Then I said to him: Here, somewhere on the verandah, we might let people have a space. And after having talked in this way, he sat down. Then he said: To-day I shall pass the night with you. Here, mother, please cook this rice for me. When he had said this, I received the rice and brought it in. But from where he is, this man in need of a place to sleep in, that I did not ask him."

"All right," they said, "we shall ask him, and as you have prepared food also for him, give it to him." They said: "He must be an excellent carpenter. Look at this, since he has been able to make bone into rice, would you think he is an inferior kind of carpenter? An inferior kind of carpenter would never be able to make anything like this. As a carpenter he is first rate."

Again they said: "Look here, my girl, what kind of a man is he? is he old or is he a young man?"

Aḍo̱e me̱nket́a, Ba̱e haṛama, baba, khub koṛa kanae, ar dekte sunte hõ khub mõńje ńe̱lok̓ kana.

Ado̱kin me̱nket́a, Henda ma̱i, nuige gha̱rdi jãwãelin̓ do̱ho̱am khan do̱m tahẽkok̓a se̱ o̱ho̱? Am hõm am eskargea, babon saṅgea. Ado̱ do̱ho̱le khan do̱m khusikok̓a se̱ o̱ho̱?

Ado̱ uni k̓uṛiye me̱nket́a, O̱ko̱ baḍae e̱nte, ona do̱ abengeben baḍaea. Abenge cet́ lekanko ṭhen co̱ben ṭhãoen̓, ona do abengeben baḍaea. Abenge ńe̱l khusik̓ben e̱nte. Nigeben do̱ho̱an̓ khan do̱n̓ tahe̱ngea, ar abenben baṅle khan, ina̱ hõ bogege. Inten̓ me̱na, nui do̱ho̱aṅben me̱nte, ado̱ tayo̱mre hape̱n in̓ co̱ben nisṛa̱uin̓. Ona ia̱te in̓ do̱ cet́ hõ o̱ho̱n̓ me̱nlea. Ado̱ abenak̓ khusi.

Ado̱kin me̱nket́a, Acha, gapa setak̓lin̓ ńe̱llege, e̱ṇḍe̱ ena jãhãṭak̓ do̱lin̓ me̱na. Ma daka loepe, ar bes lekage daka do̱ emaepe. Oka do̱ dakate hõko lo̱bhaok̓gea.

Ado̱ daka lo baṛaket́te, dak̓ko taṅkette oṛak̓teko ho̱ho̱ aderkedea, ado̱ rokoṛok̓ lekageko emadea. Ado̱ ona dakae jo̱jo̱m kan jo̱khe̱nkin ńe̱le kana. Ado̱ nakhe mukhe do̱ besgekin ńe̱lkedea. Khange un jo̱khe̱nkin kuliyede kana, Henda ba̱bu, am dom okaren kana, ar okatem calak̓ kana?

Ado̱ uniye me̱nket́a, Phalna disom phalna atoren kanan̓, ar in̓ baba do̱ phalnawaea. Aṛ in̓ do̱ disom ńe̱lgen̓ oḍok akana. Jãhã se̱nge calak̓ sanan̓, o̱nṭe̱gen̓ calak̓a. Jãhãre kisa̱ṛ in̓ ńamleko khan, enko ṭhengen̓ tahe̱kok̓a.

Ado̱kin metadea, Henda ba̱bu, ale ṭhenle do̱ho̱mea; tahe̱kok̓am se̱ o̱ho̱a?

Ado̱e menket́a, Hape̱ e̱nte, aṅgalenge, iṅak̓ mo̱nren̓ bujha̱u baṛalege. Nit do̱ cet́ hõ o̱ho̱n̓ me̱n daṛelea. Noa katha gapa kuliṅpe, ado̱ unre jo̱to̱ katha do̱bon galmaraoa.

---

27 Ba̱bu, the common word of address to a man younger than oneself, has possibly no connexion with the Bengali title of 'babu'. The word is in Santali used also about membrum virile.

28 A genuine Santal trait. There are very few Santals who do not enjoy disom ńe̱l, to see country, as it is called. They do not object to hardship and real difficulties, if they can satisfy their wishes in this respect.

"He is not old, father," she replied; "he is a strapping young man, and as to appearances, he is very nice-looking."

"Look here, my girl," they said, "if we give you this one for your husband, would you stay with him or not? You are also an only one; we are not many. If we kept this one, would you be pleased or not?

"Who knows?" the girl replied; "you two will know about that. What kind of people you will settle me with, that you two must know. You two see that you are satisfied, therefore. If you give me this one, I shall stay; but if you two are unwilling, then that is also good. If I myself should say that you should give me this one for a husband, you would without doubt afterwards some day upbraid me. Therefore I shall say nothing at all. It is as you like."

"Very well," they said, "we shall first have a look at him to-morrow morning; then only we shall decide one way or the other. Now take the rice out of the pot, and give him a good portion. Sometimes food will also make a person desirous[26]."

So they took the food out of the pot, poured out water and called the boy in; and they gave him so that it was a feast to his eyes. Whilst he was now eating his food, they were looking at him. They saw he was of good appearance and comely. At this time they commenced asking him: "Look here, young man[27], where do you come from, and where are you going?"

"I am from such and such a country and such and such a village," he replied, "and my father's name is so and so. I have come out to see foreign countries[28]. In whatever direction my mind takes me, there I shall go. If I find a good master anywhere, I might stay with him."

"Look here, young man," they said to him, "we shall keep you here with us; would you be willing to stay or not?"

"Wait a while then," he answered; "let morning come first; I must think the matter over. Just now I am unable to say anything. Ask me about this to-morrow morning; then we shall talk together about it all."

Ado enka men barakatege en hilok doko thir barayena. Ar uni do dakae jom odoken khan, arhõ pindategeye calaoente otre bin atettege otreye kundlan akana. Ado ako hõ dakako jom baraket khan, parkomko ader baraketa, adoko galmaraojon kana. Menetako, Jãwãe lek do bhagegeye ñelok kana, ar ror hõ aran do besge añjomok kantaea, bae gungrawa. Ar nui ar abo maitikin do khubkin jurikoka. Cet ban se, boeha lekakin ñelkoka. Ia, ti janga nakhe mukhe ma besgeye ñelok kan. Ado kamige cet lekantaea, inage ohobon men darelea, ar bankhan hor doe besgea.

Ado uni maejiu hore menketa, Horte do khub iñ khusiyena; hor dobon enkangea. Ar kami bae badae khan, babon cetaea? Jan jokhone caoleketa, ona do begor badaetegeye caole akata? Badaegeae. Ado pariskoge cet leka jutoka se ban, inage mittan katha do.

Ado uni herel hore menketa, Hẽ sari, ina do thikgem meneta. Onako auribo kuliyetege jãwãeye reakbon galmarao kan, noa do adi lelha reak katha kana. Adoe men gotketa, Do tho notege hohoae ma. Tinak ontere ać eskare tahena? Notege hohoae ma, ar onakobon kuliyea.

Ado sari uni budhige uni then calaoenteye hoho sadeketa, Japitketam, babu pera hor?

Ado uniye menketa, Ban japit akata, kundel akangean. Ado cedakem hohoan kana?

Ado uni budhiye menketa, Dela note orak senregele jaegamea. Am eskar notere tinakem tahena? Ale hirlam heć akana. Dela note orakregele jaegamea. Oneko menge, Horte ror hor do

29 The bedsteads are light and easily moved from one place to another by one person. During day-time they are frequently used to sit on; when not in use, they are put somewhere out of the way, generally on end, or rather on side.

30 The appearances play a considerable part in choosing a mate.

31 The Santals are endogamous with regard to tribe, but exogamous with regard to sept. A Santal must marry a Santal, or be outcasted; but he must not marry within his own sept or sub-tribe; if he does this, he is also outcasted.

32 See above notes 22 & 27.

After they had had this talk, they did not mention this any more that day. When he had done eating, he again went out to the verandah and was lying on the floor, having thrown himself down without anything underneath. When they themselves were ready with their food, they took their bedsteads in[29] and commenced talking together. They were saying: "He looks very well, suitable as a son-in-law, and his talk and voice are nice to hear; he is not tongue-tied. And he and our girl would be splendidly matched. What would it not be? they would look like brother and sister. I say, his hands and feet, his countenance are looking nice; but then, what he is as a worker we are unable to say; otherwise the man is good enough[30]."

The mother then said: "I am very well pleased with the man; we Santals are such. And if he does not know to work, can we not teach him? As he was able to make bone into rice, has he done that without knowing how to work? Of course, he knows. But then the septs[31], how will they fit in? that is one matter."

The man then said: "Yes, that is true; it is right what you say. Before we ask him about these matters, we are talking about making him our son-in-law; that is very foolish." Then he quickly added: "Do let him be called in here. How long is he to remain alone out there? Let him be called in here, and we shall ask him about these matters."

Then, truth to tell, the old woman went out to him and called out: "Are you asleep, young friend[32]?"

"No," he replied, "I am not sleeping; I am lying down. Why are you calling me?"

"Come over here," the woman said, "we shall give you a place for the night inside. Why should you remain alone out here? You have come and taken shelter with us. Please come over here, we shall give you a place for the night in the house. It is a common saying: People speaking to each other on the road are all related[33].

33 When you have entered into conversation with somebody, you are not strangers any longer.

jotoge peṛa. Eka haṇḍi salpat manwa dobon mitgea. Gai do gai palge, ar hoṛ do hoṛ palge. Jāhāre mit hoṛ eskar do babon tahē̃ daṛeaka. Ar okoe hoṛ murukkate eskarko tahē̃ aṅgak kangea, menkhan uḍi nacarte. Ar gai hō̃ jāhāerenko atlen khan, ar jāhāeren gaiko ńamleko khan, enko sāotegeko tahē̃ aṅgaka. Ar bako ńamleko khan, tahē̃ doko tahē̃ aṅgak kangea, menkhan uḍi jivi koṭopkate. Ar am dom manwa kana, ale hirlam boloyena. Tobe khanem peṛa kangea. Dela bes okoćtele jagakama. Ina do jāhā hilokem lai baṛalea, baṅma, Phalna atore, phalna hoṛ then iń bololena. Uḍi bhale sabit peṛa kanako. Jom hō̃ko emadińa ar apnar hoṛ leka oṛakreko jaegakidińa. Nonka hapen senlen khan, bam lai baṛaea? Ar noa dhartire do, babu, bar lekan hoṛgeko ńutumok kana. Mit do khub bhage hoṛ se khub māyāk hoṛ; ar mit do aḍitet kharap hoṛ se bodmas hoṛ. Neko bar lekan hoṛge noa dhartire do man menaktakoa, ar baṅkhan celeak hō̃ man do banukan. Arhō̃ mucatre do ultaugea kathatet do. Metakme cet leka ultau? Ona do nonka kana: metakme bes hoṛ do baṛić sene lekhayena, ar baṛić hoṛ do bes sene lekhayena. Ona do metakme nonkare roṛogok kana. Bes hoṛ judi jāhān kaire, se hajotreye paṛaolen khan, seye goćlen khan, unre hoṛko mena, Uh! phalna do aḍi bhage hoṛe tahē̃kana, goć giḍiyenae. Ado ene unre uni bes hoṛ dom giḍiyena. Ar jāhāe baṛić hoṛ onkan ghoṭnareye paṛaolen khan, seye goćlen khan, unre hoṛko mena, Bhageyenae, goćenae. Uni do nonka se onkae tahē̃kana. Ado ene un jokhen uni baṛić hoṛ doe bhageyena. Ado mase oka lekan katha aṛaṅok kana?

Ado inak khange haṛame hoho gotketa, Onteregeben leher maraoet do! Note do baben hijuka? Ina do ale hōle aṅjom cet baṛajońa. Notege aguyem; noteregebon galmaraoa.

34 She Santali expression may also be translated 'he has become good, or well'; it is a play on words.

35 The Santali expression lit. means make soft, semi-liquid, viz. in order to make fit for use.

We people who drink beer with sal-leaf cups of the same, pot are one and the same. Cows go to the flock of cows, and people to the flock of people. Nowhere are we able to remain by ourselves alone. Some people make an effort and remain alone over night, but it is out of helplessness. Also if somebody's cows get lost, and they meet with somebody else's cows, they will stay the night with those. And if they do not meet with any, they will naturally have to stay over night, but only with straining of every nerve. And you are a human being; you have taken shelter with us. Therefore you are a friend. Come, we shall give you a good sleeping-place. Then you will also some day speak of us, saying: In such and such a village I once entered the house of so and so. They are excellent splendid friends. Food they also gave me, and they gave me a place to sleep in, as if I were their near relative. If you should go away afterwards, will you not speak in this way? And in this world, my young friend, two kinds of people are given a name. On the one hand very good or very compassionate people, and on the other hand utterly wicked people or scoundrels. These two kinds of people are famed here in this world; and otherwise no one has any fame. And further, when the end comes, the word is reversed. In which way reversed? It is this way: good people are counted with what is bad, and bad people are counted with what is good. In cases as these it is said: if a good man finds himself in some fault, or in prison, or if he dies, then people say: What a pity! so and so was a splendid man; he is dead and thrown away. There you see, then, that good man was thrown away. And if some wicked one finds himself in such a case, or if he dies, then people say: Excellent, served him right[34]; he is dead. He was such a one or such a one. There you see, then that wicked man was called good. And see, what kind of word is being voiced."

When she had got thus far, the old man called out: "What are you two soaking[35] out there? Will you not come in here? Then we shall also hear what it is about. Bring him in here; we shall talk together here."

Adọ buḍhiye mẹnkeṫa, Dela bạbu, tọbẹ nọtẹ oṛaḱregele jagamea.

Adọ ẹnẹye ạgukedea. Miṫ sẹćre miṫṭañ parkọmreko jagakedea. Adọ unre jạt pạris reaḱko kulikedea, ar uni hõe lạikeṫa, adọ bań miṫlena. Adọ ako mọtọreko amdajkeṫa, jutoḱgea mẹnte. Khange adọko thir baṛayena.

Adọ tinre unkin buḍhi haṛamkin jạpiṫkeṫa, khọr khọrkin udureṫ kana, un jọkhẹn uni kuṛi dọ koṛa ṭhen hẹćkate uni tuluće gitić miṫena. Adọ khange koṛa hõ bae bataoleṫa. Mẹnkeṫae, Jọkhọn bakhra dakae hartawań kana, cedaḱ bań jọma? Jāhāe hoṛ aćaḱ bakhra dakae emam khan sẹye metam khan, Nẹ, iń khusitege ińaḱ dakań emam kana, adọ rẹṅgẹć akame ghuṛi dọ, cekate hale bam jọma? Adọ onka uni koṛa dọ mọnreye gaṇḍọn baṛakeṫ khan dọ lọṭghuṭiye lagaokeṫa. Khange uni kuṛi dọ ạḍiye khusiyena. Ar uni kuṛi dọ ać mọnre nonkae hudis pạhilkeṫa, Jẹmọn nui koṛa dọ jāhā lekate ale ṭhene tahẹn ar nuireko jāwāekạń. Adọ marsalrege ạkin ạkin dọkin ńẹpẹl akana sẹ bań? Unrege uni kuṛiaḱ mọn dọ gaḍao akan tahẽkantaea. Mọnẹ mọnẹte dọe mẹnjoń kan tahẽkangea, Nenkan koṛareko jāwāelin khan dọń tahẽ gọṫkoḱa. Adọ bạhuanić koṛa kanae sẹye ḍạṅguạgea, onako dọ bae ọnmanleṫa. Jāhā mọn dọ gaḍaoen dọe hoegea.

Ar nitre hõ kuṛi họpọn dọko onkangea. Jāhā ać mọnẹteye mẹnkeṫ dọ, ona dọe hoegea cạhiye, ẹṇḍẹ ena mọn dọ tirpitoḱtakoa. Adọ onka leka nui kuṛi hõ pạhilkin ńẹpẹlenrege mọn dọ gaḍao akan tahẽkantaea. Adọ ona iạte ọnẹye jaegayen khan, uni kuṛi dọ luṭuḱ luṭuḱe ạikạueṫ tahẽkana. Mọnẹ mọnẹteye mẹneṫ tahẽkana, Tinre bako jạpiṫ? Nui tulući dọń lọṭghuṭigea. Adọ onate ọnẹ aćaḱ sana dọe puṛạukeṫgea.

Ar noa katha dọ sạri kangea. Nitre hõ kuṛi jọkhẹn dọ jāhāe koṛa bes, ńõke ńẹloḱ khan, kuṛi dọ akotege uni tuluć dọko leao gọdoḱa, arko jọṭ baṛaḱa, ar uni sọṅgẹko ṛọṛ sinḍạṅa. Kuli

36 There is accordingly no hindrance to marriage, as far as septs are concerned.

"Come along, young man," the old woman said, "we shall give you a place to sleep in inside in the house."

Thereupon she brought him in. They gave him a bedstead to sleep on at one side. At that time they asked him about his tribe and sept, and he also told them; their septs were not the same[36]. So they calculated between themselves that it would be suitable. Thereupon they all became quiet.

When the old people had fallen asleep and were loudly snoring, at that time the girl went over to the boy and lay down with him. And the boy did not restrain himself. He said to himself: 'When any one puts a share of his food before me, why should I not eat? If any one gives you a share of his rice, or he says to you: Here please, I am of my own accord and pleasure giving you my food, then, when you are feeling hungry, why should you not eat? When the boy had been pondering in this way, he had illicit intercourse with her, and the girl was very pleased. The girl had from the beginning thought in her heart: O, that this boy might somehow or other stay with us and be married to me! Now these two had seen each other whilst it was daylight, you see. At that time the girl's heart had become attached to the boy. She was thinking and saying to herself: If they would only marry me to such a boy, I should at once stay with him. Whether he already had a wife, or he was a bachelor, these matters she did not give a thought to. Whatever the mind fixes itself on, it will carry through.

Now-a-days also girls are of the same kind. Whatever a girl may decide in her mind, that she is sure to carry out; then only they are satisfied in their mind. In this way, when they first saw each other, the girl had got a strong impression. Therefore, when he had gone to bed, the girl was feeling excited. She was thinking in her mind When will they fall asleep? I shall enjoy myself with him. Thus she did what she wanted to.

Now this is a true thing. Also now-a-days, in the time of girl-hood, if some boy is looking fairly nice, the girls will on their account mate themselves with such a one and pair themselves

goṭkoako, Henda peṛa, okaren kanam am do̱? Okatem calaḱ kana? Se̱, Okatem calaḱ kan la̱ialeme, peṛa. Nui ma bhala ro̱ṛ hõ bae ro̱ṛa; baṅdo̱ pane ko̱pe̱ṭ akaṭ baṅdo̱ ceṭ, baṅdo̱e guṅga̱ge. Nonka emanteaḱko ro̱ṛ siṇḍa̱ṅa. Ado̱ ina̱tege koṛa do̱ko baḍae go̱da, nui kuṛi do̱ mo̱ṇ hećae kana me̱nte. Ar judi koṛa hõ ona menaḱtae khan, onka lekageye ro̱ṛ idia, onko tuluće be̱ce̱roḱa. Ar bae mo̱ne̱aḱ khan, sojhe sojheye ro̱ṛ rua̱ṛaṭkoge. Kuṛikoaḱ mo̱n do̱ o̱ne̱ onkana. Ar tire juge bhuṅja̱u lagaṭ mo̱n un jo̱khe̱n do̱ baṅ tahe̱ntakoa. E̱ke̱n onko do̱ ina̱ aṭkar baṛajoṅ lagaṭgetako mo̱n do̱.

Ado̱ onate nui kuṛi hõ uni koṛa reaḱ aṭkar sanakedete o̱ne̱ye pura̱ukeṭgea. Ado̱ enka lo̱ṭghuṭi baṛakate uni kuṛi do̱ arhõ aćaḱ parko̱mteye calaoena. Ado̱ ǰe̱ne̱ko gitić aṅgayen khan, buḍhi haṛam do̱ khub lekakin be̱ṅge̱ṭ baṛawae kana. Ado̱ sanam ho̱ṛge ina̱ hara go̱doḱ se̱ jua̱noḱ takre do̱ mõṅjgebo ṅe̱loḱa. Kuṛi se̱ koṛa ina̱ jo̱khe̱n do̱ cehra begaroḱgea. Ba̱ṛić ho̱ṛ hõ ina̱ umerre do̱ jutgeko ṅe̱loḱa. Ado̱ onkage nui koṛa hõ ina̱ takre do̱ khub ḍho̱be ṅe̱loḱ kana.

Khange jo̱to̱ ho̱ṛko khusi uta̱rena. Ado̱ko me̱nkeṭa, Ma nui gidṛa̱ gha̱rdi jãwãelaṅ do̱ho̱aea. Ado̱ onako niṭkeṭte uni koṛa

---

[37] The story as told is perhaps not impossible; but I could not think that such behaviour should be common. The comments of the narrator may be taken for what they are worth. Nature is undoubtedly strong with them; on the other hand it is nature.

[38] To understand the following it is necessary to bear in mind one particular Santal custom in connexion with marriage. To put it bluntly, a Santal buys a wife and brings her home as his property; she belongs from marriage on to his family. When a Santal has only girls, he would ordinarily lose all his children when they are married, and would remain behind alone. To obviate this, and especially also to make it possible for girls to inherit land, they have introduced the system of gha̱rdi jãwãe, house-son-in-law, as it might be translated. There are two varieties of such. One is that a man pays for his wife by working five years with his father-in-law, with liberty after that time to go elsewhere with his wife. Another is that the son-in-law pays for his wife in the same way (by putting in work), but with the understanding that he is to remain with his parents-in-law, inheriting their property, as if he were their son. This kind of gha̱rdi jãwãe is now generally called ghar jãwãe,

with him, and they will speak to him to find some pretext. They will ask the boy something like this: "I say, friend, wherefrom are you? Where are you off to?", or, "Tell us where you are going, friend. This fellow, well, he does not even speak; perhaps he has his mouth full of betel-nut or whatever it may be, or perhaps he is dumb." In this way they speak this, that, and the other to provoke him. By this a boy will at once know that the mind of this girl comes out to him; and if the boy also is of the same mind, he will answer in similar way and keep the talk going with the girls. But if he does not care, he will give them a straightforward answer. Girls' mind is of such a nature. To get a mate with whom to spend life for ever and always, for such they have no mind at such times. They want experience[37].

This was what was in the mind of the girl, and when she had had her wish, she went back to her own bed. When they had passed the night and got up, the old man and woman were looking hard at the boy. Just when we reach maturity or are in our prime, at that time all of us look fine. Whether it is a girl or a boy, at that age the whole look is different. Even evil-favoured persons look well at that age. In this way this boy also was looking very comely at this time.

All of them became absolutely pleased, and they said: "Well, let us give our girl this boy for a husband[38]." When they had decided this, they spoke to the young man that he should

---

an expression framed, I believe, by Settlement officials, and now commonly adopted by the Santals. It is in very common use, but must be done with the approval of the village community. In such cases the father of the bride pays all expenses in connexion with the marriage, and the bride is, as far as possible, acting as if she were the principal.

For further particulars the reader is referred to the writer's paper 'Some remarks on the Position of Women among the Santals', *Journal of the Bihar & Orissa Research Society*, Sept. 1916. See also the introductory remarks pp. 221—227.

The young man of the story is to become a g h ạ r d i j ã w ã e (or, if one prefers, a g h a r j ã w ã e). The Santal text has all along this (former) word.

jãhãte aloe calaka menteko metadea, Ią bąbu, sen botećkokam. Alom calaka; alegele dohomea. Arem calakre hõ besge, menkhan daka jom barakatem calaka.

Adọ uni kọrae menketa, Dọhọ ma dọhọńgepe menet kan, adọ cet leka dọhọ ar cet leka dọrmaha, onakope ląiańa, tọbẹ thọ jut dọń ąikąua, ar bańkhan jut dọ ọhọ cọń ąikąule.

Adọkin metadea, Guti leka dọ bań, ghąrdi jãwãe lekalin meneta. Gidrą hõe ni eskargetąlińa, onate amge nui kuṛire ghąrdi jãwãe dọhọmelin nit akata.

Adọ uni kọrae menketa, Acha besge. Dẹn bar pẹ họr ągukope, galmaraoabo. Ar ona reak cet leka lẹg dustur kana, onakobo rąpuda, enko hoṛko ańjọmkaka. Iną dọ jãhã hilok gohako purąua.

Adọ uni haṛame menketa, Onkoko ąguko lagat iątege thọ am dọń hapẹam kana, ẹn kathae, hapẹ dakako jọm baṛakatem calaka mente.

Adọe menketa, Acha, nit dọń bujketa, adọ ọhọń calaka; do ągukom.

Adọ hoṛ ągu uni haṛam dọe calaoen khan, uni kuṛi dọ koṛawak rukạ ar bąslą dọ oṛakteye aderkettaea. Adọ uni haṛam dọ ontẹrege hoṛko tuluć cetko cọko galmarao kan ineaktege tikinen khan, dakako isinkette uni kọṛa dọ dakako emadea. Adọe jọm jirąu akan jọkhẹnge uni haṛam dọ turui hoṛe ąguketkoa. Adọ goṛare parkọm idikateko belketa, onareko duṛuṗena. Khange buḍhi dọ uni kọṛae metadea, Do onko goṛareko duṛuṗ akan hoṛ am dọ ḍọbọk baṛawakome.

39 A marriage is, of course, a public affair in which Society or the community is concerned and must take part. The young man is cautious and thinks it necessary to have witnesses to the proposed settlement. A Santal will ordinarily act in this way.

40 It is very common to let visitors sit down in the cow-shed, which is empty during day-time. Their cow-sheds are generally open to one or more sides, often all round. Here is shelter and air, and the state of the ground will not affect them; as a rule it is fairly dry. Bedsteads are taken here to sit down on.

not go anywhere: "I say, young man, you might perhaps go away. Don't go; we shall keep you here. Even if you go away, it is all right; but only when you have had food, you may go."

"Well," the boy replied, "you talk about keeping me; then how am I to be kept and at what wages, that you must tell me; then only I shall feel well; otherwise I shall not feel well at all."

The old couple then said to him: "Not as a servant, but as a husband for our girl we intend to keep you. This girl is the only child we have; we have therefore decided to keep you as a husband for this girl of ours."

"Very well," the boy replied, "that is all right. Please fetch two or three people: we shall talk the matter over. Then we shall settle what is usual and customary on such an occasion, and those people will hear it. Then they will some time, if necessary, be able to bear witness[39] to it."

The old man then said: "Why, it is just to be able to bring those people that I am telling you to wait, as I said, wait, when you have had food, you may go!"

"All right," the boy replied, "now I have understood it, and I shall certainly not go away. Please, fetch the people."

When the old man had gone to fetch people, the girl took the boy's chisel and adze and brought them into the house. Now it became noon, whilst the old man was talking about something or other with the people he had gone to, and they prepared food and gave it to the boy. Whilst he was resting after food, the old man came with six people. They took some bedsteads out and placed them in the cow-shed[40], and they sat down there. The old woman then said to the boy: "You go and salute those who are sitting in the cow-shed."

and the conversation may go on without disturbing, or being disturbed by, the routine of the household.

Adǫ sạri sẹnkateye ḍǫbǫk̕at̕koa. Inạkateko metadea, Ma bạbu, thamakur benaoletabonme, jǫmabo.

Adǫ uni koṛae mẹnket̕a, Thamakur cuṅge thǫ, baba, bạnuk̕tiń.

Adǫ mit̕ hǫṛe mẹnket̕a, Nẹń ẹmok̕ kana, benaokate emabonme.

Adǫ sạriye ataṅket̕teye benaoket̕a, adǫe ẹm baṛawat̕koa. Adǫ unreko bẹṅget̕ baṛawade khan, mit̕ hǫṛ dǫe rǫṛ gǫt̕ket̕a, Nũk̕ũi cọṅ khub koṛa kanae. Nui kuṛi gidrạtikin dǫ khubkin jurik̕a; boeha lekako metakina.

Adǫ mit̕ hǫṛe mẹnket̕a, Henda bạbu, am dǫ celeama ar amren baba dǫ celeaea?

Adǫ uni koṛa onako tinạk̕ kathae kulikedea, ṭhik ṭhik onako jǫtǫ katha reak̕ rǫṛ ruạṛe emadea. Arhǫ̃e kulikedea, Henda bạbu, bạhu akawat̕meako sẹ bań? Ar cekate nun sạṅgiń dǫm hẹć akana?

Adǫ koṛae mẹnket̕a, Bako bạhu akawadińa, ḍạṅguạgeań. Ar oṛak̕regele rǫpǫṛ baṛalena, ona karǫntege iń dǫ usạt̕ iń oḍok calak̕ kana. Onatege nun sạṅgiń disom dǫń hẹć akana.

Henda bạbu, adǫ usạt̕ raṛẹćlentam khan, oṛak̕te dǫm ruạṛa sẹ bań?

Adǫe mẹnket̕a, Jãhãre kisạ̃ṛ iń ńam ṭhikleko khan, oṛak̕te dǫ bań ruạṛa, ar bań ńamleko khan dǫń ruạṛge cǫń, purạ dǫ ǫhǫń mẹn daṛelea.

Adǫ bạbu, noakore kisạ̃ṛle sap̕am khan dǫm tahẹ̃kok̕a sẹ ǫhǫ?

Adǫe mẹnket̕a, Suk iń ńamle khan, ẹkkalte jǫnǫm kal iń tahẹ̃ utạrkok̕a.

[41] Santals do not ordinarily smoke tobacco; those who do so have learnt it from the Hiṇdus. (Cf. p. 50, note 11.)

[42] They ask for tobacco to get an opportunity of having a good look at the young man. It is customary to make use of dodges of this nature when they want to 'inspect' a person without making him (or her) embarrassed. Of course, all know what is going on.

[43] It might be noted that here and in the following the village people called in act on behalf of the old man. The responsibility is put on others, who cannot be called to account.

He then really went and saluted them. When this had been done, they said to him: "Please, young man, prepare some tobacco[41] for us; let us take a pinch."

The boy replied: "Tobacco and lime, sirs, I have none."

Then one of them said: "Here, I am giving tobacco; prepare it and give to us all."

The boy then received the leaf, prepared it and gave them. Whilst he was doing this, they were looking well[42] at him, whereupon one of them said[43]: "This one is a strapping young man. The girl and this boy will be exceedingly well matched; people will say they are like brother and sister."

Then another said: "Look here, young man, what is your name and what is the name of your father?"

The boy gave correct answers to everything he asked him about. Then again the man asked him: "Look here, young man, have they given you[44] a wife or not? And how is it that you have come so far away from home?"

"They have not given me a wife," the boy answered, "I am a bachelor. We had some altercation at home, therefore I am out of temper and am going away. That is the reason why I have come to a country so far away."

"Look here, young man, when your temper cools down, will you go home again or not?"

"If I can find a master to serve somewhere," the boy replied, "I shall not return home; but if I do not find such a one, I may perhaps go home again; I cannot say that for certain."

"Then, young man, if we get you a master to serve hereabouts, would you stay or would you not?"

"If I find happiness and ease," the boy replied, "I should immediately stay on for all time."

44 The form of the question is due to the way in which a regular Santal marriage is brought about. Ordinarily the father, or somebody representing a father, procures a wife for a son; it is not his choice.

Adọ inạk̓kate khạnge uni khạmid haṛamko kulikedea, Cele baba phalna, dẹsẹ bhala lạiletam, cet̓ko lagat̓ ale dọm dela ạguket̓le dọ. Adọ am ṭhen khon aṛaṅ bale aṅjọmle khan, jāhānak̓ dọ cekatele mẹn oco daṛeak̓a?

Adọ uniye mẹnket̓a, Katha dọ noa kana. Nui peṛa koṛage okateye calak̓a ar tinạk̓e dāṛā baṛaea? Adọ jāwāe gomkeye lekaṅ mẹnet̓a. Gidrạ hõe mit̓ gọṭẹn eskargetiṅa, adọ uni gidrạge ghạrdi jāwāe dọhọae iṅ mẹnet̓a. Nui koṛageṅ ṅẹl ṭhike kana.

Khange onko ato hoṛko mẹnket̓a, Ọtẹ, bạbu, amge, kathae ghạrdi jāwāe dọhọmeko mẹnet̓a. Khusikok̓am sẹ ọhọa? Masẹ ona katha khulạsate lạialeme. Ar ale bujre dọ besgele metak̓ kana. Am hõ kisạṛgeyem ṅam baṛayet̓koa. Adọ cak̓ guti lekam tahẹna? Ẹkkalte amgele tala[45] oṛak̓kam kana.

Adọ uni koṛae mẹnket̓a, Tọbẹ baba ape mõṛẽ hoṛ,[46] bogepe metak̓ kan khan, iṅ hõ khusige. Adọ jāhā hilok̓ agoṛ digoṛok̓ khan, ape ato hoṛtege bape ṅẹlkatiṅa? Ar iṅren engaṅ ạpuṅ dọ tin jọjọnre cọṅ. Adọ un jọkhẹn ọṇḍẹ thọ ọhọṅ sẹnlena. Ape ato hoṛgeṅ rak̓apea nit oka kathak̓ kana. Adọ tayọm hilok̓ ona baṅ purạuk̓ khange thọ rọṛ dọ janamok̓a, ar baṅkhan kisạṛ reak̓ bam rọṛ baṛae.

Adọ onko mõṛẽ hoṛko mẹnket̓a, Albọt un jọkhẹn dọ ṅẹṅẹltege hoeyok̓talea. Amren eṅga apa dọle ale kangea.

Adọ uni koṛae mẹnket̓a, Tọbẹ baba, iṅren oaris dọpe ape kangea. Adọ ẹṇḍẹkhan ghạrdi jāwāe reak̓ cet̓ko lẹg dustur kana,

---

[45] Tala is in Santali in expressions similar to the one here made use of employed to signify, 'belonging to'.

[46] Note the way of addressing. 'The Five' represent the community-in-Council, if such an expression can be used. Mõṛẽ hoṛ (lit. the five men, or, Santals) corresponds to what in Hindi is called panchayat, a village council, or a court of arbiters, as the name would show, properly of five members. Whether the institution has been originally borrowed by the Santals or not, it is working on Santal lines. The headman is the natural president and must be present, or represented. Any male Santal, belonging to the village, may be present and speak. There is no voting properly speaking; but they will generally do what they consider to be the sense of those assembled. The headman, if he is any-

When they had got thus far they asked the old master of the household: "Well, sir, now please tell us what is the matter that you have brought us here for. If we do not hear anything from you, how shall we be able to get anything said?"

"The thing is this," the man said; "this young friend — where is he to go, and how much is he to wander about? I am thinking something about making him my son-in-law. I have only one child, and I am thinking of giving this child of mine a husband. This boy seems to me to be exactly suitable."

"Listen, young man," the village people then said; "they are thinking of keeping you, as you hear, as a son-in-law. Would you be pleased at that or not? Please tell us freely what you think of it. In our opinion we say it is excellent. You are seeking a master to serve. Why should you remain as a servant? We are placing you at once in the middle of the house[45]."

The boy then said: "Then, my fathers village-Five[46], when you say it is good, I am also satisfied. Then if, some future day, there should come any hitch, will not you village people look into the matter for me? My parents are so very far away; at such a time I should not be able to go there, you see. I shall put my case before you village people in connexion with what we are now arranging. If some time or other in the future it should not go well, then the matter will come up; otherwise you will not speak about your master."

The village Five then said: "Of course, on such an occasion it will be our duty to look into the matter. Your father and mother are we."

The boy then said: "Consequently, my fathers, you are my helpers to stand up for me. Then let us see what is usual and

thing of a personality, will generally make his will prevail. On the whole it is a very well-working institution, that might with advantage be much more used than it is at present. A Santal will, as a rule, not think of defying the council of his own village. He would, if he did so, not be able to stay there long.

onabo̱ ńe̱la. Ar un, jo̱khe̱n sedae mare hapr̥amko cet́ lekako katha akat́a, inạkobo galmaraokak̇a. Ar cet́ko un jo̱khe̱nko kạmia, inạkobon kạmikak̇a. Do, ado̱ be̱gege. Nit do̱ iń hõ̱ń go̱k̇et́ khan do̱ nukin buḍhi har̥am ạuriń ạsul go̱ćkin dhạbić do̱ ińak̇ chuṭi do̱ bạnuk̇an.

Ado̱ko me̱ńket́a, Hẽ̱ge, bạbu, acha katha bachaokatem ro̱r̥ket́a. Onako do̱ katha kangea, bańa me̱nte do̱ bań. Katha kangea. Nui kor̥awak̇ katha do̱ mucạt́ena, ar in hạbićgeko kathaea. O̱ne̱ co̱ń, aćtege gujuk̇ gurok̇ hạbić reak̇e kathaket́. Ado̱ de̱se̱ bhala, am khạmid ho̱r̥ le kuliyet́mea, se̱ aben har̥am buḍhigelc kuliyet́bena, noa jo̱khe̱n cet́ko lagaok̇a, ona do̱ben e̱mok̇a se̱ bań?

Ado̱kin me̱nket́a, Jo̱khon eṭak̇ ho̱po̱nliń apnarede kana, ado̱ cedak̇ baliń e̱mok̇a? Nit do̱ e̱mok̇tege hoeok̇a.

Ado̱ uni buḍhiye me̱nket́a, Cet́koliń e̱mok̇a? O̱ne̱ co̱ń jo̱to̱ or̥ak̇ duạr, gho̱r korna, cij bạsut, jo̱to̱liń jimạwae kan. Ado̱ cet́liń emaea? Ạliń do̱ mit́ lapet́ daka ar mit́ bitạ bo̱sto̱r, inạ khạjukkin emaliń. Inạte khạjuk alokin ko̱sṭo̱liń. Inạge tho̱ ạlińak̇ re̱ńge̱ć do̱, je̱mo̱n jive̱t́ bhor suktekin do̱ho̱liń, ar go̱ćlen gurlen hilok̇kin gaya gańgakaliń, inạge. Ar noako cij bạsut do̱ ạkinak̇ge. Nõ̱k̇õ̱e co̱ń jo̱to̱liń soprotạkin kan. Ado̱ cet́liń emaea?

---

47 It might be noted that the idea of the Santals when taking a man as a son-in-law, as here described, is to make sure of support, when they cannot work any longer The idea of succession does not come in, properly speaking.

48 The Santali expression *gaya gaṅga* (also *gaṅga gaya*) most probably has reference to the Ganges and to Gaya (Hindu *śraddha* performed here sends the soul of the departed to the paradise of Vishnu, it is said, and the ashes of the dead bodies are thrown into the Ganges); but it must not here be taken to mean anything more than what is translated. The Santals take the bones of their dead ones to the Damuda river, and the funeral ceremonies are, except for this, all performed at home. The expression may likely be taken as a testimony that the Santals have adopted much in connexion with their rites and ceremonies from the Hindus. As a matter of fact, the Santal traditions explicitly mention that their ancestors, at a certain specified time, decided to give up certain old customs and adopt new ones. Among the customs given up.

customary when one becomes the son-in-law and comes to live with his wife's father. Let us discuss what our ancestors of old have ordained for such occasions. What people do at such a time, let us do exactly that. Please do so, and it is well. As I have now taken this upon myself, there will be no release for me, until I shall have supported[47] this old couple as long as life lasts."

"Yes, that's it, young man," they said; "you have chosen your words well in speaking. That is the real thing, there is no gainsaying that. That is what there is to it. Now the matter of this boy has come to an end; it is as much as people have to say. We have heard it, he has himself mentioned everything, right up to death and decease. Then now, you master of the house, we are asking you, or rather, we are asking you both, husband and wife, whether you two will give the things that are due on this occasion, or not?"

They answered: "When we are making somebody else's son our own, why should we not give? Now we are bound to give."

"What shall we have to give?" the old woman asked; "you see, the whole house and possessions, household chattels, goods and property, everything we are giving into his charge. What more are we to give him? Provided those two will give us a mouthful of food and a span of clothes, only this much. Provided they will not let us suffer hardships in connexion with this. That is what we two are in need of. That these two, so long as life lasts, will keep us comfortable and happy, and, when we shall die and fall away, that they will then perform the last rites with our bodies[48], that is all. And all these goods and chattels belong to these two. You see, here we are giving everything over to them. Then what more are we to give?"

---

was the burial of the dead, in stead of which they adopted cremation, following the Hindus.

Adǫ ato hǫṛko mẹnkeťa, Noako tinạk̕ katham rọṛ ạguketa, noako dǫ asǫl katha kangea, ạuṛi dǫ baṅ kana, ar dusạu lek hõ baṅ kana. Ar abo eṅga apa ma kạmĩ baṅ calak̕te, sẹ hǫṛte khaṭǫ ịate, sẹ gidrạkoren peṛa bako lagaok̕ karǫnte ghạrdi jãwãe dǫko dǫhǫkoa. Abo dǫ aosanok̕a mẹntebon mẹna. Adǫ pasẹć aboren kuṛi gidrạ bae khusik̕, ar pasẹć nui tuluć bae rọṛ, bakin bǫnǫtok̕, tǫbẹ khan cekate nui jãwãe dǫe tahẽ daṛeak̕a? Ẹnẹye dạṛkeťge. Adǫ nahakge thǫ aboren gidrạ kuṛi dǫe khǫṭkadea, bhalǫ name durkadea. Ona ịate uniak̕ mǫn ropha dǫ ẹmok̕tege hoeok̕a. Adǫ kuṛi nui tuluć bae tulujok̕ khan, ẹn hilok̕ dǫ inạ saṕkateye sẹnjoṅa.

Adǫ buḍhiye mẹnkeťa, Tǫbẹ baba ape mõṛẽ hǫṛ, iń dǫ bạń baḍae kana. Ape ṭhen iń kulijoṅ kana, noa kuli jugreń kulijoṅ kana, ceťko lagaok̕a lạiạńpe. Iń dǫń mẹneťa, ạliń eṅga apateliń rǫhǫekae kana. Ạlińak̕ katha dǫ jạnić ǫhǫe nẹhǫttạlińa.

Adǫ onko mõṛẽ hǫṛko mẹnkeťa, Ona ma hẽ kangea. Abo ma besok̕a mẹntegebon mẹneťa. Pasẹ bakin jutok̕. Nãhãk̕ dǫ disom huti cayayena, eṅga apawak̕ rọṛ baṅ tahẹna. Ǫnẹ lagṛẽ sereń sikte ma: Lok hoelo cạtur, muluk hoelo phạtur, dekho he raja Dasarat; ghǫre ghǫre ṭikis joma lạgilo, dekho he raja Dasarat. Aćǫ ona sik katha nitkate dǫ abo khon gidrạge bạṛti

49 People with girls are not supposed to seek husbands for them; they are to be sought by other people, who have sons. The initiative must come from the male side. This does not preclude hints from the party with girls.

50 It is customary what is here demanded. When a man becomes a ghạrdi jãwãe, a calf is shown to him, i. e., is given him at the time of marriage; the reason for this act is as here stated, whatever it may have originally been. It is a fact that the parties generally know very little of each other, and the possibility of their not being able to hit it off with one another is always to be taken into account.

51 The Santali expression kuli jug (asking age) is likely meant as a play on kali jug (the Kali age, the fourth age of the Hindus), often heard mentioned.

52 Lit. translated.

53 A rather drastic description. The weevils (in Santali huti) are larvæ of sorts that eat and destroy timber and foodstuffs, always present in the country and causing much damage. The caya is an unpleasantly stinking bug, also very common.

The village people then said: "All that you have mentioned is to the point; there is nothing irrelevant. There is nothing to blame either. And when work does not go any longer for us who are parents, or when we are short-handed, or when no friends come for the children[49], then for such reasons people take in sons-in-law to live in their homes. We think we are going to get relief. Then perhaps our girl is not pleased, and perhaps she will not talk with him, perhaps they will not pull together, then how will this son-in-law be able to remain? You see, he would run away. Then without cause our girl would cast a slur on the man; she would take his good name away from him. Therefore you will have to give him something to make his mind content and quiet[50]. If the girl should not hit it off with her husband, that day he may take this and go his way."

The old woman then said: "Then, sirs, you Five, I do not know. I am asking you, in this asking[51] age I am asking, tell me what are the dues? I myself mean that we, the mother and father of the girl, are planting[52] him. Likely he will not transgress our word."

The Five then answered: "That is quite so. We of course mean that all will be well. But perhaps they will not hit it off. Now-a-days the land has been damaged by weevils and made stinking by bugs[53]; the word of parents is disregarded. Just as it is in a lagṛẽ song: The village people have become clever, the country has become upset: look out, O king Dasarat! In every house rent notice is fixed: look out, O king Dasarat![54] And corresponding to this, now-a-days the children are sharper than we are. If they bring you to silence on one

[54] The lagṛẽ verse is in a kind of Bengali. It might be remarked that, whilst phatur in Bengali means weak, infirm, &c., the word is here used in a meaning found in Hindi. Dasarat is the father of Rama. I have been told by Santals that this verse dates from a time shortly after the Santal rebellion (1855). If that is so, one might think that somebody has assisted in producing this verse. The last words refer to the agricultural land being assessed. It seems strange

dǫkǒ calaǩa. Okaṭaǩ cǫṅ miť kathae ęsęťlem khan, ǫhǫm rǫṛ ruạṛ daṛelea. Onate nitre katha dǫ chiṇḍạu idikaǩge bogea. Inạ dǫ tayǫmre bako rǫṛ daṛeaǩa. Katha reaǩ ḍǫg dǫ huleć idikaǩge ṭhika.

Adǫ buḍhiye mẹnkeťa, Acha besge. Ma tǫbẹ uni gidrạ kuṛibo kulikaea ninạǩ hǫṛ samaṅre, khusiǩ kana sẹye baṅ, ar nui jãwãeye khusiae kana sẹ baṅ. Ma ape mõṛẽ hǫṛge kuliyetabonpe.

Adǫko mẹnkeťa, Ṭhik, nią dǫle pạtiạuena. Ma uni kuṛi gidrạ hǫhǫaepe.

Adǫ sạriko hǫhǫ ạgukedea. Hẹćenae. Adǫko metadea, Ma mại, duṛuṕme, miť kathale kulime lagať.

Adǫ duṛuṕenteye mẹnkeťa, Ceť katha kana, baba? Ma kuliṅpe.

Adǫ mõṛẽ hǫṛko mẹnkeťa, Katha dǫ noa kana, mại. Amren ayo babate, sẹ ale mõṛẽ hǫṛte, ghạrdi jãwãele dǫhǫam kana, nui koṛage. Adǫm khusiǩ kana sẹ baṅ, ar nui koṛam khusiae kana sẹ baṅ? Adǫ amaǩ mǫnre khub leka bujhạu kandhaokate lạialeme. Nitrege jǫtǫ lại cabawaleme, jẹmǫn tayǫmte alo ḍiḍhi bạḍhiǩtabon.

Adǫe mẹnkeťa, Ǫhǫ jạnić ḍiḍhi bạḍhiǩa, baba. Iṅren eṅgaṅ ạpuṅ sẹ ape mõṛẽ hǫṛte ṅẹl ṭhikkatege jạnićpe dǫhǫaṅ kana. Adǫ apepe khusiyen khan, iṅ hǫ̃ jạnić khusige. Adǫ apasula mẹntegẹ jạnićpe juri pạrikạliṅ kana; adǫ iṅ hǫ̃ṅ khusigea. Adǫ miť katha, baba, ape inõṛẽ hǫṛ samaṅre ar iṅren eṅgaṅ ạpuṅ samaṅre miť kathaṅ rǫṛkaǩ kana.

Adǫko mẹnkeťa, Mõṛẽ gǫṭẹn rǫṛme.

Adǫ baba, katha dǫ noa kana. Dǫhǫ mape dǫhǫaṅ kange, ar iṅ hǫ̃ nui ṭhen tahẹnteliṅ miť mǫnoǩgea. Adǫ kǫtǫ nạhĩ kam kaj menaǩtabona, rụạ haso menaǩtabona, nẹao jhǫgǫṛ menaǩ-

---

that a foreign language should be used to express such thoughts. On the other hand it is of a very common occurrence that Santals, both men and women, make verses, sung to tunes of their own, describing or criticizing contemporary and local events. It apparently causes them no trouble to produce them.

55 The responsibility is to be with others.

56 A common way of saying that one is at liberty to speak. It is especially made use of by people in authority, just like here.

point, whatever it may be, you will not be able to answer. Therefore it is better to settle everything now at present. Then they will not be able to say anything about that afterwards. It is good to break off the buds of words as they come out."

The old woman then said: "All right, that is good. Let us then, please, ask the girl in the presence of so many people whether she is pleased or not, and whether she is pleased with this man for a husband or not. You Five please ask her for us."

"Excellent," they said; "we believe in that. Please call the girl."

So they called the girl out. She came, and they said to her: "Please, my girl, sit down. We are going to ask you one question."

She then sat down and said: "What matter is it, my fathers? Please ask me."

The Five then said: "The matter is this, my girl: Your father and mother, or we village people are arranging to give you a husband to remain with your parents, namely this young man. Are you pleased or not at this? and are you pleased with this young man or not? Think it over and consider it well in your mind and tell us. Tell us everything there may be now at the present time, that the matter may not afterwards get out of order and be spoilt for us."

"Oh no, likely not," the girl replied; "it is not likely to get out of gear, my fathers. My father and mother, or you Five have likely seen to it that all is right, as you are giving him to me for a husband. When you are pleased, then, likely, I am also pleased[55]. Likely it is in order that we shall live together and support each other, that you mate us as husband and wife. Then I am also pleased. Then there is one word, my fathers. In the presence of you Five and in the presence of my father and mother there is one word I have to speak."

"Speak five[56]," they said.

"This is what I have to say, my fathers. To be sure, you are giving me a husband, and we are of one mind as to my staying with him. Now all of us have our work to do, we suffer from fever and pain, we have quarrels and disputes. Now perhaps, on

tabonạ. Adọ kam kaj karọnte, sẹ daka utu karọnte, sẹ ceť karọnte cọṅ, pasẹćliṅ rọpọṛenge, ar pasẹne usạťenge are oḍok calaoenge. Adọ baba, un jọkhẹn dọ okareṅ paṅjayea? Oṛaǩ duạr ma bạṅ ṅẹl akaťtae, adọ okareṅ paṅja sẹṭẹrea? Onage muskiltẹť iṅ metaǩ kana. Adọ ceť leka abo hõ jãhã khon bạhukobon ạguyeťkoa, adọ usạťkateko dạṛle khan, eṅgat apat oṛaǩrebon paṅja sẹṭẹrkako kana — adọ baba, nui dọ okareṅ paṅja sẹṭẹrea? Ona reaǩ họr uduǩaṅpe.

Adọ jọtọ họṛko mẹnkeťa, Nui gidrạ ṭhikgeye mẹneťa. Inạ dọ sạrige, aboaǩ bhul kạmi kantabona.

Adọ miť họṛe mẹn gọťkeťa, Acha, onate hõ baṅ cekaǩa. Ạikạ lại gọdme tinre usạťe calaǩa. Un jọkhẹn am dọ ruạṛem, ar judi bae ruạṛ khan, saṭ mẹnte lại gọťaleme. Un jọkhẹn koṛakole dhurạukoa, khubbon thạyạ ocoyea. Ar inạte bae ruạṛ khan, onkogebon metakoa, Do paṅja sẹṭẹrkaepe.

Adọ kuṛiye mẹnkeťa, Tọbẹ katha dọṅ mucạťkeťa.

Adọ mõṛẽ họṛko mẹnkeťa, Jọtọ katha dọbon khudạu mucạťkeťa, ar jọtọ ghọr kornabon jimạwakin kana. Judi arhõ koṛa gidrạko tahẹn khan dọ, miť bighạ jumibon uduǩkea sẹbon lẹbẹť ạcurkea. Se leka ma kathage bạnuǩtabon. Tọbẹ khan mọn ropha dẹn miťṭaṅ gại uduǩaeben. Uni hõ nit dọ aperengeye tahẹna. Adọ judi nit sẹ jãhã hiloǩ nui jãwãe bape khusiaea sẹpe laga todea, adọ ẹn hiloǩ mõṛẽ họṛe raǩalea. Adọ unre galmaraokate ape

---

57 She speaks as if she were a man. A Santal wife is not expected to trace her husband.

58 The village community promises to assist, while she is exhorted to do all she can herself, before applying to them. All talk about kicking, &c., is not here to be taken at its face-value. Santals do not resort to such drastic measures in cases like the one here supposed. When a man has forcibly applied sindur to the forehead of an unmarried girl (thereby making her his wife), they will use violence, otherwise not.

59 If there is a son, he is the proper heir. Santals arrange with ghạrdi jãwãe, also when there are sons, but only when the girls are grown up and the sons very small, the object being to get help to work. In such cases they may give the son-in-law a small plot of land. It is often done, but is not obligatory. The bighạ is the common unit for land-measure, in these parts 80 cubits (120 ft.) square, about one third of an acre.

account of the work, or on account of the food, or for some cause or other, whatever it may be, perhaps we two may some day have words together, and perhaps he may become sulky and dissatisfied and then walk away. If such things should happen, my fathers, where shall I then try to find him[57]? I have not seen his house and home, so where shall I be able to follow him? That is what I call the difficulty. You see, when we bring a bride from somewhere or other, and she runs away in the sulks, then we follow after her to her parents' house, — but this one, my fathers, where am I to follow him home? Show me the way there."

"This child is speaking right," they all of them said. "That is true; that is our mistake."

Then one man said: "All right, it does not matter. But mind, tell at once when he becomes sulky and takes himself off. At such a time bring him back yourself, and if he will not come back, tell us immediately[58]. Then we shall call out the boys; we shall let him get a good kicking. And if he will not return with this, we shall order them: do, follow after him to his home."

"Then I have nothing more to say," the girl said.

Thereupon the Five said: "We have followed everything up to the end, and we are giving these two charge of all the household goods. Now if there had been sons also, we should have pointed out[59] one *bigha* of rice-land, or we should have walked round it[60]. We have nothing to do with anything like this here. Therefore you two old people show him a cow, please, to keep his mind at ease[61]. He also will now be yours. But if now or some day in the future you should not be pleased with your son-in-law, or you should drive him away, then he will apply to us, the Five. If we, on such an occasion, after having talked the matter over, should find fault with you, he will drive this cow

60 The Santal way of pointing out land. They walk round the boundaries, noting any natural objects that may serve as landmarks.

61 See above note 50. At such a marriage a 'calf' is also 'shown' to the bride, as a general rule.

sengẹ dosle ńamle kḥan, ini gại sotoḱkateye senjoṅa. Ar bestepe dohoye khan mae aperen kange. Ado ma ceťben meneťa? Ar baṅkhan den uduḱaeben, ale mõṛẽ hoṛle ńelkaḱa.

Ado haṛame menkeťa, Acha, mon ropha doliń emaegea, ape mõṛẽ hoṛ lagaete bon ńela. Ado inạ chaḍa ar ceťkó katha menaḱtabona? Nịạ duṛuṕrege joto katha dobon macoṭ utạrkaḱa.

Ado mõṛẽ hoṛko menkeťa, Katha do noa kana. Judi kulạn menaḱ khan, mabon bapla utạrkakina; ar kulạn bạnuḱ khan, neṇḍa goṇḍakama. Ona hõ bochor din se mạhnạ din do baṅ jutoḱa, nịạ dos baro din se hapta din, in dinge jutoḱa.

Khange haṛam buḍhikin cepeť baṛayentekin menkeťa, Ma nịạ sat dinliń neṇḍayeťa. Ma inre nịạ phalna din hiloḱ bon baplakakina. Ape hõ en hiloḱ do alope okakoteḱtabona.

Ado mõṛẽ hoṛko menkeťa, Bạhu kicrić, sara dạhṛi, sindur, dạuṛạ, tetre kuṛi — noako do amge lagaoama. Ar maraṅ baplam ńam khan do, Ḍomko hõ jạruṛgea.

Ado banar haṛam buḍhitekin menkeťa, Hẽ, unạḱ dobon ikạkaḱa.

62 As remarked above, at a ghạrdi-jãwãe-marriage all expenses are borne by the bride's father. All dues and customary outlays, ordinarily paid, or paid for, by the bridegroom, are met by the bride's father. The things here mentioned are not all the dues. Bạhu kicrić (also, and commonly, called sindur kicrić) is a plain piece of cloth, ten to eleven cubits (about 5 m.) long. For use at the present occasion it is steeped in a solution of turmeric and made yellow. The bride is clothed in this just before the sindrạdan, the binding act, when the bridegroom applies sindur, the red-lead, to the forehead of the bride. Hence the name sindur kicrić.

63 The sara dạhṛi (dạhṛi means head-cloth or turban, sara is another form for salạ, wife's brother, found in some Hindi dialects and adopted by the Santals for use in this term; it is one of the words that may be of help in showing where the Santals' ancestors have been) is a plain piece of cloth, five cubits long (2,5 m.), also coloured yellow for the occasion. Just before the sindrạdan the bridegroom puts this cloth on the head of the bride's younger brother. Both are during the act riding on the shoulder (not on the neck) of the husband of an elder sister (or some corresponding relation, if there are none such).

in front of him and go his way. And if you keep him well, he is, of course, yours. Well then, what have you to say? Otherwise, please point her out to him; we Five shall see it done."

"All right," the old man said, "we shall give him heart-content; we shall together with you Five look to that. Besides this, is there then anything else for us to do? We shall finish and settle everything whilst we are sitting here now."

The Five then said: "The matter is this: if you are sufficiently prepared, let us marry the two and have done with it; and if you are not prepared, a time shall be fixed for you. But as to that, in a year's time or in a month's time, that will not do; ten or twelve days, or a week's time, such a time will do."

The old man and woman consulted together and thereupon said: "We fix the day for to-day seven days. Then on such and such a day we shall marry them. You also please do not go anywhere on that day."

The Five then said: "The bridal cloth[62], the brother-in-law's head-cloth[63], sindur, the flat bottomed basket[64], the anointing girls[65] — all this you will have to provide. And if you want a big marriage festival, Ḍoms[66] will also be necessary."

Then the old man and the old woman both of them said: "O well, that much we shall leave out".

---

64 Among the many kinds of baskets found with the Santals, there is one called bạhu tul dạuṛạ, bride-lifting basket. It is a wide, flat-bottomed bamboo basket with low sides. Sitting in this, the bride is lifted shoulder high by the bridegroom's followers and is carried opposite to the bridegroom, who is riding on the shoulder of the babṛẽ koṛa (lit. brahmin boy, his elder sister's husband; see preceding note). While they are both up in the air, the bridegroom, with his right-hand little-finger, five times puts sindur on the top of the girl's forehead.

65 The anointing girls are girls from the village of the bride. called tetre kuṛi, because their special work is to anoint, or rather rub in (from tere), especially bride and bridegroom, with oil and turmeric.

66 See p. 128, note 12.

Adọ mõṛẽ hoṛko menkeťa, Cele adọ ceťko katha menaǩtabona sẹ bań? Menaǩ khan, ma nią takre rọṛ gọdpe, ar bańkhan delabon.

Adọ miť họṛe mẹn gọťkeťa, Iń miťṭań huḍiń huḍiń kathań disą. akaťa, adọ onage bańdọń rọṛ bańdọ bań.

Adọko metadea, Disąkeť khanem, ma rọṛme.

Adọe mẹnkeťa, Acha, tọbẹ ańjọmkatińpe. Katha dọ noa kana. Enanrebo hẹć akana; kam kajbon bągiaťte nuiaǩge jọtọkotebon kąmikeťa. Adọ nią mańjan mąṇḍi dọ bae emabona? Setaǩreye ągukeťbonte iń dọ baske mocage menańa.

Adọko mẹnkeťa, Jọtọ họṛ enkage. Ọnẹ cọń miť dhaotege jọtọ họṛe ągu akaťbon.

Khange uni kuṛi dọ daǩ ar dątąunikoe ąguaťkoa. Adọ ąbuk bọlọyente dakako emaťkoa. Daka jọm oḍokkate thamakurko beǩnao kan jọkhẹnge mõṛẽ siką poesae emaťkoa, adọ ẹnẹko bereť baṛayena. Adọ ọnẹko batlao baṛa oṭoade, onakoe juṛąukeťa, ar bhọjko lagať hõe tearkeťa.

Adọ ona neṇḍa din tioǩen khan, setaǩre jọg mąńjhi ṭhene calaoena; uni ar mąńjhi paranik ar atoren miť bar họṛe họhọ

---

67 The matter now mentioned is not, of course, something suddenly remembered; some one has to mention the matter, and it is done in this way. When the Five work as arbiters, they generally demand five siką (Re. 1—4—0) from each side, or the double. This money was formerly spent in buying a goat, a pig or something that was divided and taken home for consumption. Now-a-days they mostly go to a liquor shop and spend it there. In cases like the present, when only comparatively few have met and the people are fairly well-to-do, they are often invited to take a meal.

68 Before sitting down to eat they always wash their hands and rinse their mouths. When there are guests, a loṭa (or a cup) with water is given to them successively; they take this, go to the border of the court-yard or to the nearest vicinity and wash. This is an intimation that they are to sit down to eat. As they always eat with the (right) hand, this ablution is necessary. If needed, the feet are also washed. Besides with water, the guests are here also provided with tooth-brushes. The Santals are very careful with their teeth. They brush them with a twig of the sal (Shorea robusta, Gaertn.). The twig is chewed at one end, until it becomes like a brush; this is then used, and the mouth is

The Five then said: "Well then, what else have we to talk about, or how? If there is anything, then please say it at once now at this time; otherwise, come, let us be off."

One of them then said: "There is one very small matter that has occurred to me[67]; but then, whether I shall mention it or not, I am not sure."

"If you have come to think of something," they said to him, "out with it."

"All right," he said, "then listen to me. It is this: we came some little while ago; we left our own work and have all of us attended to the business of this man. Will he not then give us this mid-day meal? He brought us here in the morning, and I for my part have a mouth for breakfast."

"It is the same with all of us," they said. "As we know, he brought us all here at the same time."

The girl then brought them water and tooth-brush-twigs[68]. They washed their hands and mouth and went in, whereupon they gave them food. After they had finished eating and had come out, while they were preparing tobacco for chewing, the old man gave them five four-annas in cash[69], whereupon they rose and went their several ways. What they instructed him about before they went, all that he provided; he also made preparations for a feast.

When the fixed day arrived, he went in the morning to the headman of the village morals[70]; he called on him, on the village

finally rinsed with water. The sal contains some resin that may be of assistance in cleaning. The Santals get accustomed to this tooth-brush from childhood on; they all look upon the use of it as a necessity; one might say it has become an instinct with them. This tooth-brush (dạtạuni as it is called) is used the first thing in the morning, many refusing even to drink water until they have cleaned their teeth and mouth in this way. If thought necessary, the cleaning may be repeated before a meal.

69 See above note 67.

70 A Santal village has five officials, viz., (1) headman (mạńjhi), (2) his deputy (called paranik), (3) headman of morals (called jọg mạńjhi), (4) his deputy

ạguketḱkoa. Adọ hạṇḍiye emaťkoteye galmaraoaťkoa, baṅma, Teheṅ dọ alope okateḱa; nukin gidrạbo baplakakina. Atoren jọtọ guni guribge lạiakotabonpe, nią tiḱin ọktẹ jẹmọn jọtọ hoṛ nọṇḍẹ iṅ ṭhenbo jarwaḱ.

Adọ jọg mạṅjhiko dhurạukadea, Ma ya, jọg mạṅjhi, tọbẹ inạ ọktẹ dọ jọtọ hoṛ lại baṛawabonme. Ar tetre kuṛi dọ nitrege ṅam ạgukakome, jẹmọnko kạmi gọṛọ hataṛako.

Adọ uniye mẹnkeťa, Acha besge, katha bajaoen khan, onako dọṅ kạmia.

Adọ kuṛikoe ṅam ạgukeťkoa. Ar uni mạṅjhi dọ bako hẹć ocoadea, ọṇḍẹgeye tahẽyena, bud batlao baṛawako kanae; ar daka hõ ọṇḍẹgeko emadea. Adọ tikin khange jọg mạṅjhi dọ atoren hoṛe raḱ jarwakeťkoa. Adọ sunum sasaṅ ọjọḱ baṛakate ar hạṇḍiko ṅũ baṛakate adọko ituť sindurkaťkina. Ar bạdhiạko gurlede tahẽkaṅa. Bhọjkeťako. Miť ṅindạko ẹnẹćkeťa, ar bhọj hõko jọmkeťa. Ar setaḱ jọkhẹn uni jãwãe koṛa miťṭaṅ gạiko uduḱadea. Adọ ẹnẹko apan ạpinena. Cabayena.

Adọ tahẹn tahẹnte uni jãwãe koṛa dọ ceť hõ bae kạmia; ọntẹ nọtẹye taṕ baṛaegea; huni nui ṭhen ẹkẹne ajare baṛajoṅgea, ar daka jọm ghuṛi dọe hẹćenge. Adọ miť cando din onkageye ayaḱ baṛaea.

Khange uni kuṛiren apat haṛam dọ bẹbạrića edrena. Mẹnae, Cele kuṛhiạ jãwãe cọṅ jãwãe gomkekede? Kạmi usạsoḱa mẹnteṅ mẹnleť khan, okor eṅgateye usạsediṅ kana? Uh! nahakge eṅgate bon dọhọkedea. Adọ oṛaḱre sẹ hoṛko ṭhen hõ onkae roṛ baṛaea.

(called jọg paranik), (5) the headman's messenger (called gọḍet). Besides these there are the naeke, the village priest, and the kuḍạm naeke, who worships certain bongas, when the naeke sacrifices to the national bongas or spirits. The 'headman of morals' here mentioned is the village custos morum, supposed to be responsible for the good behaviour of the young people of the village, and the one to take action if anything has happened. The jọg mạṅjhi is the ceremonial leader at the name-giving festival (janam chạṭiạr), at the festival when a Santal is given full tribal rights (caco chạṭiạr) and at marriages. He is also the leader at certain other festivals, when young people come together. The traditions tell that, in former days, the jọg mạṅjhi was looking

headman and his deputy and on a couple of the village people and brought them along. He then gave them some beer and spoke to them: "Do not go anywhere to-day; we shall marry these two children. Tell all we have in the village, poor and indigent, that to-day at noon we shall all come together here with me."

Thereupon they set the headman of morals to work: "Please, you headman of morals, tell all of us at that time. But fetch, now at once, the anointing girls, that they may help here in the work."

"All right," he replied; "as the matter has been told, I shall do this."

He then brought those girls. The headman they would not let come away; he stayed on there, giving them advice and instruction; they gave him his food also there. When it became noon, the headman of morals called the village people together. Having got through the anointing with oil and turmeric and having had some beer to drink, they had them perform the ceremony of applying sindur. They had killed a hog and had a feast. They danced the whole night and feasted. And in the morning they showed the bridegroom a cow. Thereupon they dispersed to their several homes. The whole was over.

Now as the time passed, this son-in-law did not do any work; he was always slipping through hither and thither; he did nothing else than to go to some one or other to gossip; but when the time for food came, he was always coming. About one whole month he was skulking in this way.

Then the old man, the father of the girl, became awfully angry and was saying: "What kind of a lazy fellow is it I have made my son-in-law? Whilst I thought I should get some relief in my work, how is he, dash it, giving me any relief? Oh dear, it is to no purpose, dash it, that we have taken this one to be with us." In this way he was talking at home and also before other people.

---

after his work in a proper way; now-a-days he is perhaps often the opposite of what he ought to be. He is generally fully aware of all intrigues going on, the young people keeping him informed.

Adǫ atoren erveltẹt́ koṛako dǫko metaea, Henda ho, am dǫ cet́ hǫ̃ bam kạmi baṛae dǫ? Nahakgele dǫhǫ akat́mea.

Adǫe metakoa, Noa ulphạ dinre dǫ ẹñte cet́ iń kạmia? Dak̕ din tiok̕len nạhĩ thǫń siok̕a. Nẹtar dǫko sia? Nẹtar ma bako siok̕.

Adǫko metaea, Jãhãkore kaṭka koṭko hasako dǫ bam laea?

Adǫe metak̕oa, Okakore cǫń khẹt hǫ̃ menak̕, bạń ńẹl akat́ khan okareń laea?

Adǫko metadea, Kạmi bae ńẹl orometa, oṇḍeot́! Dela gapanok̕ ale sãote, birtebon calak̕a.

Adǫe mẹnketa, Birre dǫ cet́bon cekaea?

Adǫko metadea, Durrẹ! bam baḍaea? Nẹtarrege cǫń kạmi din lagat́ko jogaṛjoń, isi arãṛ, nahẹl, kãṛba, ãṛgǫm, kuṭhẹ, pareaṛe — noako se kạmi din sukok̕ lạgit́. Sahan hǫ̃ nẹtarregeko ạgu rańjkak̕a. Inạ dǫ ona din ńańam bań hoyok̕a.

Adǫe mẹnketa, Acha ho, ẹṇḍẹkhan gapa dǫń calak̕a. Riạuińpe, iń dǫń ạnạṛigea; eskar dǫ oka sẹn iń calak̕a?

Adǫko metadea, Acha besge, ẹṇḍẹkhan alele riạu idimea.

Adǫ ẹnẹ dosar hilok̕ khange, kathae ko riạu idikedea. Adǫ ṭẹńgǫće ńamketa, adǫ noko sǫńgẹte birteye calaoena. Birre onko dǫ sojhe sojheak̕ kaṭko mak̕eta, ar adǫm hǫṛ dǫ cur mar sahanko ńam jaṛwayeta. Ar nui dǫ cet́ hǫ̃ bań. Ona birre hǫ̃ nui dǫ ǫntẹ nǫtẹ ạuṛigeye dãṛã baṛae kana. Adǫ dãṛã dãṛãte eskarge mit́ṭań dhasna sẹn eskargeye calaoena, ar kaṭkogeye nolao baṛa

---

71 The girl is an only child; the younger brothers here referred to are either cousins (called brothers) or others standing in artificial relationship to the girl. See p. 236, note 2. It might be remarked that the relationship between a man and his wife's younger brothers is called landa sạgạl, lit. laughing relationship, i. e., people standing in such relationship to one another are permitted to laugh and jest with each other and to be intimate. They need not observe the forms otherwise considered necessary.

72 It is customary with the Santals to use the off-season for preparing implements and household goods.

73 The Santals have different sizes of axes. The one here mentioned (ṭẹńgǫć) is small, fit only for cutting branches and small trees. All axes used by the Santals are manufactured by the local blacksmiths.

The younger brothers[71] of his wife in the village were constantly saying to him: "Look here you, you are doing absolutely no work? It is to no purpose that we have taken you in."

He would answer them: "What shall I do then in this dull time, when there is nothing on? Only when the rainy season comes, I shall have to plough. Do people plough at present? Of course, they don't."

Then they say to him: "Could you not use the spade here and there where the ground is rough and uneven?"

"Where should I dig," he would answer, "as I have not seen whereabouts the ricefields are?"

"He does not recognize what work is, the imbecile scamp," they said to him. "Come along with us to-morrow to the forest."

"What are we going to do in the forest?" he asked.

"Oh dear!" they said to him, "don't you know? Why, at the present time people make the necessary preparations for the working season: plough-beams and yokes, plough-handles, clod-crushers, legs and frames of bedsteads[72], these things are all needed to be comfortable in the working season. Firewood also people collect and pile up at the present time; then it will not be necessary to fetch it at that time."

"All right," he replied; "then I shall go to-morrow. Call me to come along; I am a stranger here; where should I go alone?"

"Very well," they said; "then we shall call you to come along."

So the next day they called and took him along. He found a small axe[73] and went together with the other boys to the forest. In the forest the other ones were cutting straight and good timber, and some were busily engaged collecting firewood. But this one was doing absolutely nothing. There in the forest also this fellow was walking about hither and thither at random. As he was rambling about apart from the others, he quite alone reached the slope of a hill; during this he was looking at the timber, what it might be good for. Then there on that hill-slope

idiyeṭa. Adọ ona dhasnare mitṭaṅ kaṭ dọe rọreṭ kane aṅjọmkeṭa. Ona dọ nonka leka aṛaṅok̓ kana, baṅma, Iṅ dọ jãhãeko idiliṅ khan, ar parkọm kuṭhẹko benaoliṅ kham, uni hoṛ dọ ẹkkalte rajgeye hoyok̓a.

Adọ onkae aṅjọmket̓ khan dọe sẹn sorena. Adọ arhõ mit̓ dhaoe rọṛketa. Khange nui dọe mẹnketa, Noa kaṭgeṅ maga ar kuṭhẹṅ benaoa. Ar kaṭṭeṭ dọ baṅ sojhea, ạḍiteṭ kaṛbaṅ kuṛbạṅgea. Adọ ona aṅjọmtegeye mak̓keṭa. Mẹnketae, Bhalaṅ biḍạugea, sạri sẹ nase kana.

Adọ onko atoren koṛa dọ mak̓ baṛakateko duṛup̓ akan tahẹ̃kana. Ọṇḍẹge nui koṛa hõe gọk̓ ạguketṭaea, adọ bogeteko landa dhut̓-adea. Metae kanako, Nui iạ hoṛ ya, un maraṅ birre kaṭge eṅgate baṅ juṭạuade. Noa dọ cet̓ yae mak̓keṭa ya? Hoṛ dọ sojhe sojhe-ak̓ko bachao baṛayet̓ khan, nui dọ eṅgate koṇḍeawak̓geye ńam baṛayeṭa.

Onkako metae kana, arko lẹbẹt̓ ulṭạu baṛayet̓taea. Ar nui dọ cet̓ hõ bae rọr baṛayeṭa, thir akangeae. Adọ enko sọṅgẹte inạ kaṭge oṛak̓teye gọk̓ ạgukeṭte haḍ baḍe giḍi gọt̓kaṭa. Adọ atoren koṛa dọ ako oṛak̓reko lạiyeṭa, adọ bogeteko landawae kana. Adọ hẹćkateko ńẹl baṛayet̓ dọ, sạrige koṇḍeage. Adọko mẹn baṛajoṅ kana, Nui jãwãe dọe lelhagea. Ako oṛak̓re dọko ạculede baṅdọ baṅ, ạḍitẹt̓e lelhage dọ. Uni hoṅhartẹt̓ haṛam hõe mẹneṭa, Cele lelha jãwãe cọṅ eṅgateṅ jãwãe gomkekede? Nui dọ hapẹn batlao bhorsae kạmia, aćte dọ ọhọe ńẹl oromlea. Adọko mẹn baṛaketa, Cekaeam? Abo gọrọjbon dọhọkedea, batlaotege hoyok̓tabona.

Dosar hilok̓ khange, kathae, jokhaket̓teye giriketa, adọ parkọm kuṭhẹye benaoketa. Ar ona kuṭhẹ dọ ạisạ hikmọtkateye benaoketa dọ, ẹkkalte hoṛak̓ mẽt̓ lagao utạrena; ńẹl torage ẹkkalteko mạluṅ

74 A Santal bedstead consists of eight pieces of wood, the four legs and four pieces for the frame, two short and two long ones, fixed in holes cut in the legs. The bottom consists of string, quite artistically woven on the frame. A properly made Santal bedstead is quite good and might be used as a model for camp bedsteads.

he heard a log speaking. It was sounding like this: "If any one would take me away and make me into the legs of a bedstead, then that man would at once become a king."

As he heard this he went near to it. Then it spoke once more in the same manner. He then said to himself: "I shall cut this tree-log and make bedstead-legs out of it." Now this log was not straight, it was very twisted and crooked. But having heard this, he cut it, saying: "Well, I shall test it, whether it is true or not."

Now the other village boys had cut what they needed and were sitting down. There to that place this boy also carried what he had on his shoulder, and the other ones laughed him to scorn. They were saying to him: "This unspeakable humbug! in such a big forest there was not, dash it, any timber found to suit him! What is this that he has cut, boys? Whilst other people are in the habit of choosing what is straight and good, this fellow, dash it, is searching for what is crooked."

They spoke to him in this way, whilst they were kicking at and turning his wood over. And he was not saying a single word; he kept quiet. So together with those others he carried this same bit of timber home and threw it with a clash down on the ground. The other village boys told of it in their several homes, and they were laughing a good deal at him. And people were coming to have a look at it; it was quite true, it was crooked. Then they were saying: "This son-in-law is a fool. We wonder whether people in his own home ever put him to work or not; he is extremely foolish." And the old man, his father-in-law, was also saying: "What a fool of a son-in-law is it that I, dash it, have brought in? In days to come this fellow will have to rely on what other people show him to work; he himself will not be able to see what is proper." Then they said: "What will you do? It is at our own desire that we have taken him in; we shall have to instruct him."

The next day, it is told, he cut the wood up in measured lengths, whereupon he made bedstead-legs. And these legs he made so deftly that people's eyes were at once taken in; as soon as they

uṭạrèna. Un uṭạrko' mẹnkeťa, Durrẹ! kạmi dọ khubgeye baḍaea, lelha dọe baṅ kana; ona dọe sean kan. tahẹ̃kana. Adọ onako kuṭhẹ benao sạtkeťteye pareaṛe baṛawať khan, khub sọjọntọr ṅẹlena. Khange uni jā̃wāe koṛa dọe mẹnkeťa, Noa parkọm dọṅ ạkriṅa. Jāhā̃ege miť ṭakako emaṅ, onkogeṅ emakoa.

Adọ jọtọ họṛko metaea, Miť ṭaka dọ ọhọ damlentama, ar unạǩ dam dọ ọkọe hõ ọhọko ẹmlema.

Adọe metakoa, Bako emaṅ khan, ọhọṅ ẹmlekoa.

Adọ sạri benao sạtkate miť cando gan hoeyena. Adọ cekakote cọṅ raj dọe aṅjọm ṅamkeťa, phalna atore khub mõ̃ṅj parkọmko benao akaťa mẹnte. Adọ sipạhiye kolkaťkoa, Do ona parkọm dọ kiriṅ ạguạṅpe baṛẹ. Jāhā̃ tinạǩgeko damaǩ, unạǩge emakote ona parkọm dọpe ạguạṅgea.

Adọ dame emaťkote sạri onko sipạhi dọko hẹćena. Adọ ona parkọmko ṅẹlkeť khan, onko hõ ẹkkalteko mạluṅ uṭạrena. Adọ bẹgọr dam kulitege bar ṭakako raṛa gọťkeťte uni koṛako emadea. Khange onko atoren họṛ dọko hahaṛayena. Mẹnkeťako, Durrẹ! abo dọ baṅ ạkriṅoǩbon metaťtaea, oṛaǩ khonge ạkriṅentaea. Adọ ṭakae ataṅkeť khan, uni họṅharṭẹť hạram dọ khube rạskạyena. Ar ona ṭaka dọ ataṅkate uni họṅharṭẹť haṛamgeye caladea. Adọ un khon dọ ceť hõ bako mẹn daṛeaea, ar landa hõ bako landawaea.

Ar ona parkọm dọ onko sipạhiko idikeťa. Adọ kuṭhẹko pareaṛeko nunạǩ husnạk, ar ạisạ mĩhĩ baberteye teṅ akať tahẹ̃kana, ọṇḍẹko sẹṭẹrkeť khan dọ, kathae, raj hõ ṅẹl torageye mạluṅ

75 The story refers to a time when money had another value than it has at present among the Santals. As an example it may be mentioned that I have heard it said that formerly cows were paid at the rate of one rupee per half *seer* (one *seer* about one litre) of milk they gave per day. A Santal cow very seldom gives so much as half a *seer* per day. I think I have seen a small bedstead sold for eight annas (8 d.).

76 They have no pockets in their clothes, which are ordinarily draped round the body. Money and small articles are tied up in the cloth at an end-corner.

77 He had not even to take the bedstead to a market-place to get it sold; people came for it.

saw them, people were at once utterly bewitched. Then only people said: "Oh dear me! as for work, he knows that excellently well; he is no fool; that other thing only meant that he was cunning." When he had made those legs ready and he had provided a rame for them[74], it was all looking exceedingly beautiful. The son-in-law then said: "I shall sell this bedstead. Any one who is willing to give me one rupee I shall give it to."

All people then said: "It will certainly not be priced at one rupee[75]; so much certainly no one will be willing to give you."

"If they don't give me," he said to them, "I shall certainly not let them have it."

After he had made this ready, about one month had passed. Then somehow or other the king heard about it, that in such and such a village they had made an exceedingly beautiful bedstead. He sent his messengers, saying: "Do buy and bring that bedstead to me. Whatever price they put on it, pay them that and bring the bedstead to me."

He gave them money to pay with, and the messengers came. When they saw the bedstead, they also at once became utterly bewitched, and without asking about the price they untied their cloth[76], took out two rupees and gave to the boy. Then the village people became astonished. They said: "Oh dear! we were saying that it would not be sold; and it has been sold from his home[77]."

When he had received the money, his father-in-law became very pleased. When he had received that money, he handed it over to the old man, his father-in-law. From that time on they could not say anything to him, nor did they laugh at him.

The king's messengers now took the bedstead away. The legs and the frame of the bedstead were so delightful to look at, and he had woven the bottom[78] with such fine cord, — so when they reached there, the king also, it is told, was charmed as soon as he

---

78 See above note 74. The string used is twined very carefully and otherwise stretched and worked, so as to be strong and even. The Santals weave the bottom in a way peculiar to themselves, commencing with a string stretched

goťena. Landakate oṛaǩteye ader ocoketkoa, ado onḍe miť pohor ganko ńelketa. Ado onko sipahiye kuliketkoa, Noa reaǩ dam do tinaǩpe emketa?

Adoko menketa, Raja saheb, cetle menkea, bańdom edreale bańdo ceť. Parkom ńel toragele maluń goťente bar ṭakale emadea. Ar uni tuluć dor dam reaǩ do jāhān katha bale roṛleta, ale khusitege unaǩle em goťena.

Ado raje menketa, Baṅa, besgepe emadea. Arhō bickom pon ana gan haṇḍi ńū hōpe emae khan jutkoǩgea. Boge jinis hataote do baṛti dam emoǩre hō bań haǩsoa. Baṅa, besgepe emadea.

Ado ńinda khange raj do ona parkomre gitiǩkateye japitketa. Ado onako ponea kuṭhe do, kathae, parkom khon boćena. Miťṭań kuṭhe do purubte calaoena, miť do pachimte, ar miť do utorte ar miť do dakhinte. Ado purub reaǩ kuṭhete do uni raj uparte laṛhai lagiť phadko hijuǩ kan tahẽkana, onkoe daram akaťkoa. Ar pachim senaǩ kuṭhete do raj cetanre dolan bhit bindaṛoǩ kan tahẽkana, onae oṭkao daram akata. Ar utor senaǩ kuṭhete do bińc eseť akadea; uni raj jome lagať rajaǩ panahireye bolo akan tahẽkana; uniye horho akadea. Ar ona dakhin senaǩ kuṭhete do cete cekaketa? Miťṭań rakas uni raj jome lagate cahaṕ aguyeť tahẽkana. Ado ona kuṭhete mocae ṭibhi daram akadea, bae sor ocoadea. Nonka uni raj doe kukmū kana.

Ado sari setaǩ jokhen bereťenteye ńeleť kan do ponon kuṭhege banuǩ, otreye gitić akan. Adoe meneta, Ayo! noa kukmū do sari kangea se? Bhala odokkateń ńellege. Ado onka menkate panahi horog lagate ńam barayeť khan, kuṭheye roṛ goťketa, Hā hā! alom horoga. Onare do amren bairiń eseť akadea; iń

diagonally over the frame from one end-corner to where a rope is fixed right across the frame, near the foot end. This contrivance makes it easy to stretch and tighten the bottom when it is sagging.

79 A pourboir is not common, but it is occasionally given. A bakshish is very frequently spent as here indicated.

saw it. Laughing he ordered it to be taken into his house, and there they looked at it for quite a while. He then asked the messengers: "What price did you pay for this?"

"Raja Saheb," they replied, "what should we say? We don't know whether you will be angry with us or not. As soon as we saw the bedstead, we were quite bewitched and gave him two rupees; but we did not speak anything with him concerning the price; we gave him so much of our own accord with pleasure."

"That is nothing," the king said; "it was quite in order what you gave him. Rather if you had given him some four annas more to drink beer with[79], it would have been nice. When you receive a good thing, it does not give pain, even if you pay too much. It is nothing; it was quite in order what you gave him."

That night the king lay on this bedstead and fell asleep. Now the four legs slipped off from the frame, it is told. One bedstead-leg went towards the East, one towards the West, one towards the North and one towards the South. The leg that went towards the East — armies were coming to fight against this king, and it was meeting them. As for the leg gone towards the West, — a wall of the palace was going to fall over the king, and the leg was hindering this. And the leg in the North had shut up a snake; this one had entered the shoes of the king with the intention of killing him; the leg was keeping a watch on the snake. And what was the leg that had gone towards the South doing? An ogre was coming with his mouth wide open to eat the king. And this leg met him and put itself as a prop into his mouth; it did not permit him to come near. This was what the king was dreaming.

Then when he got up in the morning, he in very truth sees: the four bedstead-legs are not there; he is lying on the floor. Then he says: "Oh mother! should this be a true dream, or how? Well, I shall go out and see, before doing anything else." When he, thinking this, was searching for his shoes, the bedstead-leg called out: "Stop, have a care! don't take them on. I have shut your enemy up in them; if I had not been there, he would have

baṅkhan hutẹne jọmkema. Khange raj dọe họhọketa, adọ ṭheṅgako ạguketa, arko dal gọćkedea.

Inạkate pạchim senak duạrteye ọḍokȯk kan tahẽkana. Adọ ọntẹnak kuṭhẹye mẹnketa, Hã hã! nọtẹ dọ alom hijuka. Nọtẹre dọ amren bạiriṅ ẹsẹt akadea. Adọ sạriye ṅẹlket dọ, dolan bhit laḍe akan, ar ona kuṭhẹte ṭesa daram akan. Khangeye họhọkette ona bhitko ṭesaketteko ḍhaka ruạṛkata.

Adọ bahrẹ sẹn oḍokkateye ṅẹle kan dọ, mitṭaṅ rakase cahap akat nui jọme lagat. Adọ kuṭhẹye mẹnketa, Dẹn bạnduk ạguime, gọjeme. Nui dọ amren bạiriṅ daram akadea. Iṅ baṅkhan hutẹn teheṅgeye jọmkema. Adọ iniko ṭhu gọćkede khan, kuṭhẹ dọ tinre cọṅ hẹć gọten.

Adọ ini gọćkate raj dọ oṛakteye hẹćente kuṭhẹye todarotet kana. Pea dọ tinre cọṅ hẹćente pareaṛere gotao akan, ar mit dọ bạnuk. Khangeye mẹnketa, Noako kuṭhẹ jọkhọn iṅren bạiriko ẹsẹt daram akatko tahẽkana, nui hõ onkage jạnić bạirigeye ẹsẹt akatkoa, onatege baṅ hijuk kana.

Adọ sọntọri phạde juṭạuketkoa. Adọ purub nakha sẹ cando rakap sẹnko calaoen khan, aema utạr phạde ẹsẹt akatkoko ṅẹlkedea. Adọ nokoko calaoen khan, kathae, ona kuṭhẹ dọ tinre cọṅ hẹćente parkọm pareaṛere dọ gotao gọten. Ar raj dọ onko phạd tuluć laṛhạiyente, onkoe bhagaoketkoa. Adọ ruạṛ hẹćkateye ṅẹlket dọ, ponon kuṭhẹge pareaṛere pạhrạu akan menakgeye ṅẹlketa.

Khange ạḍi bạṛiće rạskạyena, are mẹnketa, Noa parkọm iạte iṅak baṅcao hoeyentiṅa, ar baṅkhan iṅ dọ hutẹn teheṅreṅ mọhọr meṭao koka. Adọe mẹnketa, Ọkọe họṛe benao akata noa parkọm, uni dọṅ ạguyegea.

80 On special occasions the principals are expected to give a feast of some kind, to show their satisfaction and joy and to make others merry. We are here fairly near to primitive customs.

81 Curds (in Santali d a h e, Hindi d a h i, from Skr. d a d h i), sour milk, something like kefir, a very common article of food, also much appreciated as a remedy in certain complaints. As the name shows, the stuff belongs originally to the Hindus, and is much more in use with them than with the Santals.

eaten you." The king then called out; they brought a stick and killed the snake.

Thereafter the king was on the point of going out through the western door. Then the leg that was there called out: "Stop! have a care! don't come this way. Over here I have shut your enemy up." Then in very truth he sees: the wall of the palace is slanting and the leg is standing as a prop to prevent it from falling. He then called out, and people came, put props against the wall and pushed it back into position.

When he came outside, he saw: an ogre has opened his mouth wide up to eat him. The bedstead-leg then said: "Do bring a gun; kill him! This enemy of yours I have opposed. If I had not been here, he would have devoured you to-day." When they had shot the ogre dead, the bedstead-leg came back some time or other.

When this one had been killed, the king went inside his house and commenced to investigate concerning the bedstead-legs. Three had some time or other come back and fastened themselves on to the frame-pieces; but one is missing. Then he said: "As these bedstead-legs have been opposing and keeping my enemies back, this one also has likely shut my enemies up; therefore it is not coming."

He thereupon collected the soldiers of his guard regiment. When they reached the eastern part of the country, or towards the rising of the sun, they saw he had stopped an immense army. And when these came there, this bedstead-leg some time or other came back and fastened itself again to the frame-pieces of the bed. The king fought with that army and vanquished it. And when he returned home, he looked and saw, all four legs are there, fastened to the bedstead-frame.

Then he became very glad and said: "On account of this bedstead I have been saved; otherwise I should have been utterly annihilated to-day." Then he said: "He who has made this bedstead, him I shall surely fetch."

Ado̱ sạri ho̱ṛe koḷketkote unkin do̱ haṛam buḍhiko idiketkina. Ar raj do̱ disom ho̱ṛe jarwaketkoa, are lại pasnaoketa, baṅma, Nui ho̱ṛ ho̱te̱te iṅak jivi do̱ rukhiạ akantiṅa. Onate nui ho̱ṛ do̱ teheṅ iṅak rajo̱sṭi mit khap iṅ hạṭiṅae kana. Ado̱ teheṅ khon baḍae orome lagat iạte ape disom ho̱ṛ do̱ṅ dela akawatpea.

Ado̱ disom ho̱ṛko me̱nketa, Nawa rajem bohalkedea. De̱ to̱be̱ bho̱j emalem. Inạge ale do̱, ar jãhãn do̱ baṅ.

Ado̱ sạri dahe taben disom ho̱ṛe ematkoa, ado̱ e̱ne̱ko apan ạpin baṛayena. Ar nui koṛa do̱e rajena.

Ado̱ dosar tesar serma khange uni koṛa do̱ aćren eṅgat apate ạguketkina. Ar dosar serma do̱ unkin hanhar ho̱ṅharte̱te idiketkina. Ado̱ e̱ne̱ jo̱to̱ ho̱ṛ raj naṅgraharegeko tahe̱yena.

Ado̱ e̱ne̱ niạ katha do̱ṅ caba hataṛ akata. Inạk hạbićkak kangeaṅ.

23. Mitṭaṅ mahra koṛa reaṅ.

Sedae jo̱khe̱n, kathae, mitṭaṅ mahra koṛae tahe̱kana; ado̱ uni koṛa do̱ gại gupi gupitegeye harayena. Ado̱e harayen khan do̱ bạhuko ṅamkedea uni koṛako bạhuae lạgit. Ado̱ko neṇḍa goṇḍaketa, Niạ phalna dinre do̱ bạriạtokbon calaka. Ado̱ sạri neṇḍa din hilok do̱ bạriạtokko calak kana; ar uni koṛa do̱e jãwãe beṭa akana, pạlkireko tul akadea.

---

82 Taben is parched rice, pounded flat in a ḍhiṅki, a husking 'machine', especially set up for this purpose. The sun-dried paddy is first soaked, then roasted and finally pounded. It is generally eaten with dahe. It is not much of a feast they get; but as there was no time for preparing, it was what they could do.

83 The end here given would seem to presuppose that there should be a continuation. I have not heard any.

23[1] Inspite of the Santali garb this story seems to be borrowed from Hindu sources.

2 Mahra is the name used by the Santals for the Hindu caste commonly called goala or gowala. The caste occupation is more especially to herd cattle.

He then sent people and they took both of them, husband and wife, away with them. The king called the people of his country together and announced: "Through this man my life has been saved. Therefore I am to-day giving this man a share of my kingdom. And in order that you may recognize him from to-day, I have invited you, the people of my country, to come."

The people then said: "You have appointed a new king. Please, then, give us a feast[80]. That is what we want, and otherwise nothing."

The king then, in very truth, gave his people curds[81] and flat rice[82]. Thereupon they dispersed, every one to his own home, and this young man became king.

After a couple of years, the young man fetched his father and mother; and the next year he took his parents-in-law away there. So all of them lived in the king's city.

So now there I have for the present ended this story[83]. I am telling as much as up to this.

23. THE STORY OF A MAHRA BOY[1].

ONCE upon a time, long ago, people tell, there was a *mahra*[2] boy; this boy grew up herding cows. When he had grown up, they sought and found a girl to marry her to the boy; and they fixed a time: "on such and such a day we shall start for the marriage ceremony". On the day fixed they really started; the boy was now the bridegroom, they were carrying him in a palanquin[3].

In the Santal country mahras are fairly common; most of them have some land to cultivate; all of them have cattle, some living on the produce of these. By more well-to-do people they are employed as cow-herds. They also have some experience in veterinary matters. When the cattle is suffering from some disease or other, the Santals will often call a *mahra* in to help them.

3 Cp. p. 32, note 1. What is here told, refers to the Hindu custom.

Khange calak̕ calak̕te adǫ mit̕ṭaṅ gạị dǫ hǫr aṛerege mit̕ṭaṅ lẹḍreye thạli ak̕ana. Khange uni koṛako tul idiyede khane metadea, Ẹ jãwãe beṭa, bạhu ạgum cak̕ak̕ kana, ạḍi rạskạm ạikạuet̕a. Dẹ noa thạli khon ǫr oḍokkaṅme.

Adǫ uni koṛa dǫ ona rǫṛe aṅjǫm ṭhikket̕teye rǫṛ ruạṛket̕a, Ọhǫṅ oḍoklenia, lǫsǫḍok̕aṅ nãhãk̕.

Adǫ gạị dǫ, kathae, uni koṛae sarap gǫt̕adea, mẹnket̕ae, Cet̕, iṅ bam beret̕lidiṅte ṅẹlme nãhãk̕ am dǫ bạhum jọṭẹt̕le khangem gadhak̕a.

Adǫ uni koṛa dǫ onae aṅjǫmket̕ khane metat̕koa, Masẹ kahaṛ, dǫhǫlepe, ṭạṇḍiteṅ sẹnlenge.

Adǫ sạriko dǫhǫkedea; adǫe ãṛgoyente uni koṛa dǫ uni gạị ṭhene calaoenteye ǫr beret̕kedea. Adǫ uni koṛae mẹnket̕a, Henda gạị, cedak̕ onka dǫm ạsisadiṅa? Ma ona ạsis dǫ ạgu ruạṛtam, baṅkhan dǫ nãhãk̕ hǫṛ ạḍi bạṛić̕ko landawaṅa.

Adǫ uni gạiye mẹnket̕a, Nitok̕ dǫṅ rǫṛket̕a, ona dǫ amre paṛaok̕gea; ar nitok̕ dǫ cekate ona dǫṅ ạgu ruạṛa? Ona dǫ ǫhǫ jutlena, nitok̕ dǫ ẹnteṅ rǫṛ cabaket̕ dǫ. Pạhilre baṛẹm beret̕liṅ khan hutẹć̕, bes hoekok̕a.

Adǫ uni koṛae mẹnket̕a, Ẹṇḍẹkhan iṅ dǫ cekate bạhu tuluć̕ dǫṅ rǫṛ landaea? Iṅ dǫ ạḍim moskilkidiṅa.

4 A thing like this would not happen in the Santal country proper, where the country is a little hilly. In the low-lying, flat and muddy Bengal country such incidents are of common occurrence. The writer has a vivid recollection of a journey at night in a bullock-cart across country in one of the eastern Bengal districts. The driver kept him awake by his talk, generally to the bullocks, but sometimes also to the occupant of the cart, telling stories of what had happened here and there, as we were passing along. At one place he called out that at that particular spot in the month of July-August two years previously a cow belonging to a certain person had sunk in the mud and had died, as they had been unable to get the animal out in time.

5 To the Hindus the cow is a sacred animal, in which divinity is residing. Not to help a cow is therefore to them a more serious matter than it would be to a Santal. To the Santals the cow is a useful animal. The idea of a cow cursing is not Santali.

6 Cf. p. 42, note 4.

Whilst they were travelling along, they happened to pass a cow, which had sunk and stuck in a miry hole by the side of the road[4]. As they were carrying the young man along, the cow said to him: "O bridegroom, you are going to fetch your wife, you are feeling very happy. Please pull me out of this mud in which I have stuck."

The boy heard and clearly understood what the cow said, but answered: "I cannot pull you out, I should only be bespattered with mud."

The cow[5] then cursed the boy and said: "What! as you did not raise me up, behold, as soon as you touch your wife, you will be turned into a donkey."

When the boy heard this, he said to the carriers: "Please, bearers[6], put the palanquin down a moment; I have to go somewhere[7] at once."

They consequently put him down, and the boy got out, went to the cow and pulled her up on her legs. Then he said: "I say, cow, why did you curse me in such a way? Do take that curse of yours back again; otherwise people will laugh very much at me."

The cow replied: "Now I have spoken, and what I have spoken must come to pass with you; how can I then take that back again? That would never do, as I have completed the whole utterance[8]. If you had only put me on my legs at once, everything would have been well."

"How then," the boy said, "shall I be able to talk and laugh[9] with my wife? You have put me in an awful difficulty."

---

7 Lit. go to the field, one of several Santali veiled expressions about going to respond to the call of nature. He prefers not to tell at once why he wants to get down.

8 The word already spoken cannot be taken back; the only remedy is to give a blessing which will counteract or remedy the curse. The same idea is, as is well known, met with among other peoples.

9 'To talk' or 'to talk and laugh with', when used about persons of different sex, is often a veiled expression for sexual intercourse. It has not, of course, always this meaning. It is significant for what they think of the mutual relations especially of young people.

Adọ uni gạiye mẹnkeťa, Acha, alom raga; thoṛań bhọram kana: uni ań bạhuge hapẹńe hoṛ ruạṛ ocomea, ar bańkhan dọ ọkọe hõ ọhọko hoṛ daṛelema.

Adọ sạri enkae metade khan, uni koṛa dọ ạḍi bhabnakate uni gại ṭhen khone calaoente pạlkireye dẹćena. Ar uni gạiye rọṛkeť katha dọ uni koṛa chaḍa ọkọe hõ bako bujhạuleťa. Adọ uni koṛako kulikedea, ceťkoben galmarao kana mẹnte. Adọ unre uni koṛae lạikeťa, Ińak dọ nonka onka hal hoyoktińa nãhãk, ona katha uni gại dọe metadińa.

Khange adọ ona katha ańjọmte sanam hoṛko bhabnayena, arko mẹnkeťa, Acha delabon sẹ, bhalabon biḍạua, sạri kana sẹ nase.

Khange adọ sạriko tul idikedeteko calao tiokkeťa. Adọ sạrige baplak jọkhẹn sindurade torage, kathae, ẹnḍẹge uni koṛa dọe gadha gọťena. Adọ sanam hoṛko ńẹlkede khan dọ, ạḍi bạrićko bhabnayena arko hahaṛayena. Adọ kuṛiren eńgat apatko mẹnkeťa, Bańa, nui dọe gadhayena; họpọnera dọ ọhọle kollepea.

Adọ ona katha uni kuṛiye ańjọmkeť khane mẹnkeťa, Bańa, iń dọ uni jãwãe ṭhengeń tahẹna. Adọ Ṭhạkurge ceť iạte cọń nonka likhọn dọe emadiń. Jãhãnić akangeye, iń dọ ini jãwãe ṭhengeń tahẹna.

Adọ sạri onkae mẹnkeť khan dọ, eńgat apat hõ ceťko mẹna? Khangeko biḍạ gọťkadea, adọe calaoena koṛa reak oṛakte, sẹ koṛaren eńgat apat oṛakteko idikedea. Adọ bapla nimbhạuen khan,

---

10 Red-lead, applied to the bride at marriage.

11 Ṭhạkur is the name commonly used by the Santal gurus for the Supreme Being. It is known to all Santals, but except on special solemn occasions, such as when taking certain oaths, this name is not commonly used now-a-days. Some attempts have been made to prove that this word is the original Santal name for God, and that it is a non-Aryan, or non-Sanscritic word, introduced into Sanscrit at a very late period. The present writer has not been convinced by the arguments adduced, but is inclined to think that the word is of Aryan origin and to be derived from the root sthā (so prof. dr. Sten Konow). It might be remarked that the word is a fairly common brahminical family-name in certain parts of northern India. It might be noted that the well known Indian name written Tagore is the same name, pronounced like the Santali word.

"Well, well," the cow replied, "don't cry; I am giving you a small blessing: your wife, she will some time in future make you turn into a human being again; otherwise no one will be able to do that."

As the cow spoke to him in this way, the boy went away from her much grieved and mounted the palanquin. Now no one except the boy had understood what the cow said, and the other ones asked the boy what they had been talking together. The boy then told them: "Such and such my fate will be presently, that's what the cow told me."

When they heard this, all of them became much grieved and said: "Well, come along, let us put it to the test, whether it is true or false."

So they carried him along, until they reached their destination. Then in very truth, people tell, as soon as he during the marriage ceremonies applied the sindur[10] to the bride, then and there the boy at once became a donkey. All those who were present there saw this and became awfully grieved and astonished. The parents of the girl said: "This won't do; the boy has become a donkey; we are utterly unwilling to send our daughter with you."

But when the girl heard this, she said: "Not so, I shall remain with my husband. It is Ṭhạkur[11] who, for some reason or other, has given me such a fate. Let him be turned into whatever he may, I shall remain with this husband of mine."

As she spoke in this way, what could her parents say? They thereupon bade her farewell, and she went away to the boy's home, that is to say, they took her off to the home of the boy's parents. When everything in connexion with the marriage had been finished, the girl said: "I say, father, we two[12] shall go on

---

12 It might be noted that parents-in-law and children-in-law always in Santali address one another in the dual number and also use the exclusive dual form of the personal pronoun when speaking of themselves, even if only one person is meant. The husband or wife, as the case may be, is always mentally included when these relatives talk together. It should be borne in mind that the dual

uni kuṛiye mẹnkeť'a, Ią baba, balamtekoliń hiri ạgukoa. Adọ tãhã énkate ọṇḍẹ khon uni koṛa sẹ jãwãetẹťe ạṇḍije lạgiť. Adọ onkae rọṛ saḍekeť khan dọ, sạriko sapṛaoketkina, adọ nạihạrtekin calaoena.

Adọ ọṇḍẹ hõ uni kuṛi dọ ạḍiko landawaea, adọ ona lajaote uni kuṛiye mẹnkeťa, uni gadhae metadea, Nọṇḍẹ dọ balań tahẹna, delań jãhã disomteń idimea; nọṇḍẹ dọ ạḍi bạṛić hoṛko landawań kana. Adọ onka mẹnkate hoṛte jọm lạgiťe sajaoketa, adọ uni gadha sotokkatege, kathaekin oḍokena.

Adọ calak calakte, kathae, mitṭań raj disomkin tiokketa. Adọ uni rajakge pukhri menaktaea, ar ona pukri aṛerege mitṭań indạra kũi menaka, adọ uni gadha dọ ona pukhri aṛe aṛeteye ạtiń baṛayede kana. Ar ona atoren hoṛ dọ ona kũi reak dakko

---

number does not properly denote two separate individuals but marks them, or one of them, as belonging to a pair. In a similar way people whose children have married use the inclusive personal pronoun of the plural when speaking together, even when actually only one person is meant. Only when absolutely necessary, they may use the exclusive form of the plural to one another. Cf. next note.

13 **Bala** (the word is in Santali never used without the abridged personal pronoun suffixed, thus **balań, balam, balat**, my, thy, his or her **bala**) means what has been called a 'co-parent-in-law' i. e., a man or woman whose child has been married to a child of the other person. The writer is inclined to think, that **bala** is derived from Sanscrit, where the word means strength. **Balań hoṛ** would thus in Santali really mean 'the man of my strength', or 'who is my strength'. The common word in Santali for marriage is **bapla**, which is a reciprocal form of **bala**, and consequently really means 'mutual strengthening', if the original meaning is as supposed. In support of this view the following may be mentioned: a marriage among the Santals is, when regular, always arranged, not by the young people, but by the heads of the families concerned; the bride is bought by the family of the bridegroom and is the property of this family, legally speaking. It is a family arrangement. **Balaya**, i. e., two whose children have been married, are considered special friends, who are always supposed to honour one another and behave towards each other in a special, polite way. Cf. what is mentioned in the note above about the way in which these relatives address one another. The Santals have a proverb: **hako leka utu, seńgel leka pạurạ, balam leka peṛa, okarem ńamkoa?**

a visit to the family of your bala[13]." What she really wanted to do, was in this way to get a pretext for taking the boy, i. e., her husband, away from there; and when she had spoken in this way, they made them ready for the journey, and they started for the girl's parents' home.

There also they laughed very much at the girl, and as she felt ashamed at this, she said, i. e., she said to the donkey: "We shall not remain here; come along, I shall take you to some country or other; here people are laughing at me immoderately." Having said this, she prepared what was needed for the road, whereupon she took the donkey with her, and they went away.

As they were walking along, they reached the country of a certain king. Now there was a tank[14] belonging to the king, and by the side of this tank there was a masonry[15] well, and the girl let the donkey graze on the sides of the tank. The people of that village

Curry like fish(-curry), liquor like fire, friends like your bala, where will you find them? It might further be mentioned that most of the names for relationship brought about by, or founded on marriage, are of Aryan, or Sanscritic origin. — So much has been said about this matter, because it is of some ethnological interest. It tends towards showing, not that the Santals or their ancestors received the idea of marriage from the Aryan peoples, but that marriage in its present form among the Santals owes much to Aryan influence. Their traditions mention that their ancestors at the time when they were leaving Champa (probably a part of the present Chota Nagpur plateau) deliberately decided to give up some of their old customs and to adopt new ones. It is not unlikely that the marriage forms and customs were among the things altered.

14 See p. 34, note 5. It might be mentioned that agricultural lands lying lower than a tank are always considered very good for rice cultivation, because they will generally have a sufficiency of moisture, a prime necessity for the rice plant.

15 The common Santal wells are narrow pits, where a man can go down and come up by putting his feet into small hollows made for the purpose on opposite sides of the well. Larger wells with masonry walls, as the one here mentioned, are generally the property of well-to-do Hindus or Mohammedans; in outlying places like that here described they are frequently dug and built by some person who wants in this way to make himself a name or to acquire merit by a good act. Now-a-days the local authorities build such wells at roadsides or in public places.

lo idiyeťa. Ar uni ķuṛi hǫ̃ ona kũi ṭhenge jǫl pane jǫmkeťa. Ar ona pukhri latarre dǫ rajren siokko menakkoa, kuṛi pocis nahelko joṛao akaťa. Ar uni kuṛi dǫ onko šiok sor macha sǫnreye duṛup akana.

Adǫ tikinok kan hǫ̃ onko siokko dǫ baskeakge bako idiako kana. Adǫ oňko siokko dǫ ạḍi bạṛićko kadraok kana, mǫneťako, Henda ya, teheń dǫ ceť iạte bako ạguabon kana? Noakoren sanam hǫṛko ạguaťkoa; abo bhala ceť iạte teheń dǫ bako ạguabon kana? Nitok nãhãk jãhãeko ạgukeťa mǫnkhan, dalbo dalkoa sǫ, khub lekabon dalkoa. Ceť iạte nun marań berenre hǫ̃ bako ạguyeťa?

Adǫ kathae, enka hǫ̃ko rǫṛ sãotegeko bǫṅgǫťleť dǫko ńǫlkeťa, rajren kạmṛĩ kuṛi aćren gidrạ sotokkate baskeake dipil ạguako kan. Adǫko mǫnkeťa, Hạni ya darae kana; nit ǫnǫć eṅgate baskeake berae kana? Adǫ enka rǫṛ baṛakategeko thirena. Adǫ uni kạmṛĩ kuṛi dǫ onko siokko phǫḍre baskeake dǫhǫkaťte ać dǫ ona kũite dak lo ạgui lạgiť kanḍa hǫrmǫťkateye calaoena. Ar uni aćren gidrạ hǫ̃ tayǫm tayǫmteye pańja idikedea.

Adǫ ona takrege okaren bạriạtko cǫń ạḍi bạrić rajan bhajanateko ru idiyeťa. Adǫ uni kạmṛĩ kuṛi dǫ onko bạriạtko sǫngeye bǫṅgǫť akạťa; ar uni aćren gidrạ dǫ ać samańregeye teṅgo akan dǫ bae disạyede kana. Adǫ kanḍa pạsia mǫnte uni gidrạ hǫṭǫk-

---

16 When not carried on the hip, children are generally kept walking in front, so as to make it easy to keep an eye on them.

17 A very common way of carrying an empty water-pot, the arm being kept round the neck of the pot. A full water-pot is generally carried on the head, but may occasionally be seen carried on the hip, with the arm round the pot-neck, very much like the way in which children are carried on the hip. Hindu women frequently carry the filled water-pot in this way.

18 A marriage-procession generally has a number of musicians in attendance. The musicians are mostly of the ḍǫm casṭe (see p. 128, note 12), the instruments used being drums of sorts, clarinets, pipes, triangles, cymbals and several kinds of horn. The number varies according to the importance of the party. Every time the marriage-procession passes a village, they start drumming, tinkling and blowing and make a tremendous noise, easily heard even at a great distance.

were in the habit of drawing water from this well. The girl herself also took some refreshments at that well. Below the tank the king's ploughmen were at work, they had twenty to twenty-five ploughs going. The girl was sitting somewhere fairly near to where they were ploughing.

Now it was becoming nearly noon, they were not even then bringing the forenoon meal out to those who were ploughing, and the ploughmen were grumbling, saying: "Look here, why are they not bringing us anything to-day? They have brought food to all the rest round here; what can possibly be the cause that they do not bring anything to us? Now if anybody should bring anything, we shall beat them, we shall give them a good thrashing. Why don't they bring, even when the day is so far advanced?"

Even whilst they were talking in this way, they looked up and saw that a servant-girl of the king's was coming towards them, having her child walking in front of her[16] and carrying their forenoon meal on her head. "Look," they said, "over there she is coming; now only, dash it, she is finding time to bring the forenoon meal." Having spoken in this way, they did not say anything more. The servant-girl put the food down near the ploughmen, whereupon she, with a water-pot under her arm[17], went to the well to draw water, and her child also followed after her there.

Just at that moment some marriage-procession or other was passing with great pomp and music, drumming[18] as they went past. The servant-girl was looking at the marriage-procession and was not aware that her child was standing there just in front of her. Thinking that she was putting a noose round the neck of the water-pot she put it round the neck of her child and let it

The idea seems to be to make people take notice, but also to scare ghostly enemies away. It is a non-Santal custom, but now frequently adopted by them.

' The number of ḍoms hired by Santals varies according to their means, but is never very large.

geye pąsikeťte kũiteyẹ ãṛgokedea. Adǫ ǫr rakab jǫkhẹće ńẹlkede dǫ, giḋrąi pąsi akadẹ. Adǫ uni gidrą dǫe gǫćentaea; adǫ ąḍiye bhabnayena. Adǫ phǫrphundi joṛaoa mẹńte uni gidrą dǫ onko siokko ṭhene hǫbǫr idi hǫťkedea, ar onako baskeaḱ dǫ jǫťǫe chitiąu giḍikaťa. Adǫ gidrą hǫbǫrkate kąumąu bogeteye rakketa. Adǫ gidrą hǫbǫrkate uni kąmṛī dǫ raj ṭhene ląliskeťa je, Amren siokkoge ińren gidrą dǫko dal gǫćkedetińa.

Adǫ raje mẹnkeťa, Ceḋaḱ, ceť iąteko dal gǫćkedetama?

Adǫe mẹnkeťa, Apege berenre hõ baskeaḱ bape ẹm hǫťadińa; rẹṅgẹćteko kadraoente baskeaḱ hõ jǫtǫko chitiąu giḍikeťte ińko daleń kan tahẽkana, adǫ nui gidrągeko dal gǫćkedetińa. Ar bam pąṭiąuḱ khan, miťṭań okaren maejiu cǫń ǫṇḍẹ gadhae ąṭińede kana, uniye ńẹlleťlea.

Adǫe raje mẹnkeťa, Durrẹ! noa dǫ bhąri moskil hoeyena. Adǫ sipąhikoe kolkeťkote onko jǫtǫ siokkoko hǫhǫ ąguketkoa. Adǫ onkoe kuliketkoa, Henda ya siok koṛa, sąri nui kąmṛī kuṛiren gidrą dǫ apegepe dal gǫćkedetaea? Ar kathae, baskeaḱ hõ bape jǫmleťa, jǫtǫ, kathaepe chitiąu giḍikaťa. Mase bhala dhǫrǫm dhǫrǫm rǫṛpe, noa katha dǫ sąri kana sẹ nase. Ma sińbǫṅga sewakąte dhǫrǫm rǫṛpe. Noa dǫ bhąri ińgepe modoikidiń dǫ.

Adǫ oṇko siok hoṛ Sin cando sẹn sewakate dhǫrǫm phukąrkateko mẹnkeťa, Ale dǫ dhǫrǫm dhǫrǫmle rǫṛeťa, ma ańjǫmtaleme. Nui kąmṛī kuṛi dǫ baskeaḱe idikeťte onale siok kan aṛere-

19 The way in which the woman here acts is not impossible; the writer has seen Indian women trying to get out of a scrape in similar absurd ways.

20 Shop-keepers, people who have any kind of business of some importance, not to mention 'kings', i. e., zemindars, always have a smaller or larger number of persons round their offices and elsewhere, doing service as watchmen, messengers, &c. These people are a kind of private soldiers. The greatness and importance of a potentate is calculated according to the number of these attendants. Santals have no such servants, except very exceptionally.

21 What is here described is very much what may be witnessed in a village-council, before 'the Five'. The person exhorted to swear salutes the sun, as one bows to some superior person. It is remarkable that, if the council sits in

down into the well. When she drew it up, she saw that she had snared her child. Her child was dead, and she was very much grieved. To concoct a false story and put the blame on other people she quickly carried her child in her arms to where the ploughmen were, and scattered the whole forenoon meal over the place and threw it away. Thereupon she commenced to make an awful noise crying, whilst she had her child in her arms[19]. Carrying her child in her arms the servant-girl went to the king and complained: "Your ploughmen have beaten my child to death."

"Why," the king said, "what was the cause that they beat your child to death?"

"You," she replied, "even when the day was far advanced, you did not give me the forenoon meal quickly; out of hunger they were grumbling and angry, scattered and threw away all the food and beat me, and this child of mine they beat to death. If you don't believe it, a strange woman is grazing a donkey there, she saw us."

"Dear me," the king said, "this has become an awfully difficult matter." He thereupon sent some peons[20], who summoned and brought all the ploughmen, and asked them: "Look here, you ploughboys, did you really beat the child of this servant-girl to death? You did not even eat your forenoon meal, it is said, you scattered the food over the place and threw all of it away. Now, please, speak what is right and true, is this true or false? Make your obeisance to the day-god and speak the truth[21]. You have put me in an awfully difficult position with this."

The ploughmen then made their obeisance towards the sun, swore and said: "We are speaking what is the truth, listen to us. This servant-girl brought our forenoon meal and put it down close to where we were ploughing; she also had this child with

the afternoon, the person in question salutes the sun and also towards the east, the region of the rising sun. As a rule the oath taken is a promise to speak the truth, adding that Chando is seeing; the speaker is to be responsible

geye dọhọkeťa, ar nụi gidrạ hõe idi toraledegea. Adọe dọhọkatte ać dọ kaṇḍae hẹrmẹťkette kũi sẹne calaḱ kana, ar nui gidrạ hõ ać tayọm tayọmtegeye calaoena, bana ňọṛge. Ona indạra kũi ṭhenkin sẹn akan jọkhẹnge okaren bạriạtko cọṅ ạḍi bạṛić rajaṅ bhajanate ọṇa phalna ḍaharteko calaḱ kana, adọ onko sẹngeye, bẹṅgẹť akaťa. Adọ ọntẹ kọyọḱkatege kaṇḍa pạsia mẹnteye mẹnleťa cele, adọ aćren gidrạ samaṅreye teṅgo akan dọ bae ňẹle kana. Adọ uni gidrạge hoṭọḱreye pạsikedete ọna indạra kũireye ãṛgokedea. Adọ ọr rakaṕkateye ňẹle kan dọ, aćren gidrạgeye pạsi gọćkede. Adọe raṛakedete ale ṭhen hare phare ọnẹle sioḱ kan ṭhene họbọr ạgu gọťkedete ona baskeaḱ dọ jọṭọe chitiạu giḍikaťa, adọ cur mar kạumạu bogeteye garjaoketa. Adọ ale hõle ňir hẹćentele ňẹlkede dọe gọćentae. Adọ alege cur mar bogeteye ẹgẹrkeťlea are metale kana, Apege iň hõpe dalkidiňa, ar iňren gidrạ hõ apegepe dal gọćkedetiňa. Adọ enka mẹnkatege nui dọ aćren gidrạ họbọrkate raḱ raḱte nọtẹge oṛaḱteye họbọr ạgukedea. Ar ale dọle metae kangea, Iạ ạimại, aćtegeye gọćkedetaea, adọ ahak nahakte aboe bọdnameťbona. Adọ ọnẹ onka aćtegeye gọćkedetaea; adọ ạuṛiaḱte ale dọe bọhọḱ akaťlea. Ma ẹnẹ anaṅ katha dọ. Ale dọ dhọrọm dhọrọmle rọṛeťa. Họṛren họpọn dọ ceť iạtele gọćkoa? Ale dọ kichu bọtọr dọ bạnuḱtalea?

Adọ raje mẹnkeťa, Dhọrọm dhọrọmgepe rọṛeťa, sẹ ẹṛẹpe rọṛeťa? Judi ẹṛẹpe rọṛeť khan dọ, apetegepe sẹn hamaloḱa.

Adọko mẹnkeťa, Ale dọ dhọrọmgele rọṛeťa; judi ẹṛẹle rọṛeť khan dọ, aletegele sẹn hamaloḱa.

Adọ arhõ raje mẹnkeťa, Ona sioḱ aṛekore dọ ọkọekoko tahẽkanu bhala? Baskeaḱe chitiạu giḍikaťa, ona dọko ňẹlledea sẹ baňa?

before him. This kind of oath is, in its present form, likely something introduced from the local law-courts. The Santals have a number of additional forms of oaths, the swearer calling some specific curse down on himself. In such cases they always have something symbolic to visualize the consequences of perjury.

her. When she had put the food down, she took a water-pot under her arm and went towards the well, and this child also followed after her; they went there both of them. Just as they had gone to the masonry well, some marriage-procession or other was passing along that particular road with great pomp and music, and she was looking towards them. Whilst she was looking away towards them, she apparently intended to put a noose round the neck of the water-pot, and she did not see her child, which was standing in front of her. So she put a noose round the neck of her child and let it down into the well. When she had drawn it up, she saw that she had strangled her own child. Then she loosed it and in a hurry brought the child in her arms near to where we were ploughing and scattered and threw all our forenoon meal away; then she started to make all the noise she could and howled. Then we also came running up to her and saw that her child was dead. She at once commenced to abuse us something awful and said to us: You, me you have beaten, and this child of mine you have beaten to death. Speaking in this way she took her child in her arms, and carrying it thus she went crying away in this direction towards your house. We were saying to her: This unspeakable woman, she has herself killed her child, and without any cause at all she puts the blame on us. As we have stated, she herself killed her child, and she has falsely accused us. Well, that is what there is to it. We are speaking the truth. Why should we kill anybody's child? Do you think there is no fear in us?"

"Do you speak the truth?" the king asked them, "or are you telling lies? If you are telling lies, you will yourselves bear the consequences."

"We are speaking the truth," they replied; "if we are telling lies, we shall ourselves take the consequences."

Again the king said: "Close to where you are ploughing, I wonder who happened to be there? She scattered and threw the food away, did anybody see that or not?"

Adǫ onkoko mǫnkeťa, Noa atokoren dǫ ǫkǫe hǫ̃ bako tahẹ̃kana, mǫnkhan okaren cǫ̃ṅ miťṭaṅ maejiuye ńǫlleťlea. Uni dǫ ona pukhri aṛe aṛete miťṭaṅ gadhae ạtiń baṛaye̠de kana. Uni dǫ khub khạṭiye ńǫl akaťlea.

Adǫ khange raje mǫnkeťa, Do sǫ bhala uni maejiu hǫhǫ ạguyepe. Adǫ sạri bar' hǫṛ, dosrakingeko kolkeťkina, adǫ raje mǫnkeťa, Do aben phalna phalna sipạhi calaǩte hǫhǫ ạguyeben bes ǫkǫće; aloben huṛum dhuṛumea, arben huṛum dhuṛumkedea mǫnkhan, nãhãǩ abengeń sạjạibena.

Adǫ enkae metaťkinte sạri unkin sipạhi dǫkin calaoena; adǫkin metae kana, Ią mạ̃i, delaliń idimea, raj ceť lạgiť cǫe khǫj akaťme.

Adǫ uniye mǫnkeťa, Iń bidisią hǫṛ dǫ ceť lạgiťe khǫjeń kana?

Adǫkin mǫnkeťa, Baṅa, ceť lạgiť cǫṅ ạḍi jạruṛgeye khǫj akaťmea. Delabon hare phareliń idi hǫťmea; am hǫǩhǫge ạliń dǫe kol akaťliṅa.

Adǫe mǫnkeťa, Acha bogege, delabon ẹṇḍẹkhan.

Adǫkin mǫnkeťa, Baṅa, sǫngẹteliń idi toramea, ạliń eskar dǫ ǫhǫliń lahalena. Adǫ uni gadha ṭhene sẹnenteye laga torayede kana. Adǫ unkinkin mǫnkeťa, Baṅa, mạ̃i, gadha dǫ nǫṇḍẹ baṛẹ ạtiń hataṛ ocoaeme; arhǫ̃ nãhãǩem hẹć gǫdoǩa.

Adǫ uni kuṛiye mǫnkeťa, Baṅa, nui gadha dǫ ǫhǫń bạgilea, iń dǫ sǫṅgẹteń idi torayea. Adǫ sạri uni gadha hǫ̃e sotoǩ torakedea.

Adǫ raj samaṅ ṭhenkin teṅgoyena; adǫ raje mǫnkeťa, Nui gadha dǫ, mạ̃i, cedaǩem ạgu darakedea? Nǫṇḍẹ dǫ ceťe jǫma? Ǫṇḍẹ khan dǫ hutẹće ạtiń hataṛkea.

Adǫ uni kuṛiye mǫnkeťa, Baṅa, raj, nui gadha dǫ ǫhǫgeń bạgilea.

22 The Santali word shows that the two were called by their names.

23 The text does not seem to justify this rejoinder. The woman has agreed to go with them. The meaning may possibly be that the two peons object to the girl taking the lead.

"No one from any of the villages about here was there," they answered; "but a woman from we don't know where saw us. She was grazing a donkey there by the side of the tank. She has certainly seen us."

The king then said: "Well then, fetch that woman." So they sent two men, others than the ploughmen, and the king said: "You two, so and so, and so and so[22], peons go and fetch this woman in a nice way; don't hustle or illtreat her; if you do that, I shall punish you presently."

When he had spoken to them in this way, the two peons went and said to the woman: "I say, my girl, please come along with us, the king has for some reason or other asked for your presence."

"I am from another country," the girl replied, "what can he possibly want to see me for?"

"Don't say so," they said, "for some purpose or other he has demanded your presence very urgently. Come along, we shall take you there in a hurry; he has sent us two to fetch you."

"Very well," the girl replied, "let us go then."

"Not so," they said, "we shall take you along with us[23]; we two cannot go ahead alone." The girl then went to the donkey and commenced to drive him along with her. "No; my girl," they said, "let the donkey graze here in the meantime; you will presently be back here again."

"No," the girl replied, "I am not going to leave the donkey here; I am taking him along with me." And this she actually also did.

Presently they were standing before the king, and the king said: "My girl, why have you brought this donkey along with you here? What can he eat here? If he had been left there, he might have been feeding in the meantime."

"No, king," the girl replied, "I am not going to leave this donkey behind."

Adoe menkeťa, Acha bogege eṇḍekhan. Adǫ amgeń kuliyeťmea, okam ńel akať, onage ṭhik ṭhik lạiańme.

Adǫ uni kuṛiye menkeťa, Ceť katha kańa, raj? Adǫń ańjǫmle nạhīń rǫṛ daṛeaǩa.

Adǫ raje menkeťa, Acha, ona reaṅ bhǫṅṭeť dǫń lạiam kana. Bhala ona pukhrirege gadham ạtiń baṛayede kan tahẽkana. Ona pukhri latarrege ińren siokkoko tahẽkana; onko dǫm ńelleťkoa se baṅ?

Adoe menkeťa. Ńelleťkogeań; nõǩõe nokogeko siok· kan tahẽ-kana.

Acha, ar nui kuṛi baskeaǩe idileť dǫm ńelledea se baṅ?

Adoe menkeťa, Ńelledegeań.

Acha, eṇḍekhan thiroǩme; nitoǩ dǫ bhedem ńamkeťa. Adǫ ańjǫm mucạťlem, enkhantem rǫṛa.

Adoe menkeťa, Acha bogege, ma eṇḍekhan do rǫṛlem.

Adǫ raje rǫṛ idiyeťa, Noko ińren siokko dǫ pukhri latarreko siok kan tahẽkana, ar nui kạmṛī kuṛi dǫ gidrạ sotoǩkate baskeak idile kolledea. Adǫ bhala am dǫ onakoregem tahẽkana. Adǫ sạrige nuiren gidrạ dǫ noko siokkogeko dal gǫćkedea, se aćtegeye gǫćkedea? Ma adǫ amge ǫnte nǫtenren goha kanam. Ale mõṛẽ hǫṛ dǫ alom bǫtǫralea; cǫṭren Siń boṅga bǫtǫraeme, uni dǫ sanam hoṛe ńeleťbongea, ar ǫṇḍe khetrepe tahẽkanre hõe ńel akaťpegea. Adǫ dhǫrǫm dhǫrǫm rǫṛme; okam ńel akať ona baṛe rǫṛme; nit turtạkate dǫ alom rǫṛa, ar baṅkhan amtegem sen hamaloǩa. Adǫ ma inạǩgeń kuliyeťmea, dhǫrǫm dhǫrǫm rǫṛme.

Adoe menkeťa, Acha, raj, eṇḍekhan iń rǫṛeťa, ańjǫmtińpe, dhǫrǫm iń rǫṛeťa. Siń boṅga pukạrkate nui ińren gadhareń dibok kana; judi dhǫrǫm iń rǫṛ khan eṇḍekhan nui gadhae hǫṛoǩtińa, ar judi bedhǫrǫm iń rǫṛ khan, eṇḍekhan gadhageye tahentińa. Inạ baṛe bạḍaetińpe.

24 She has been cited as a witness by both parties.

25 See above note 21. These words are commonly heard, when a witness is warned to speak the truth.

"Very well then," the king said. "Now I am asking you a question: tell truly and correctly what you have seen."

"What is the matter, king?" the girl replied. "When I hear that, then only I shall be able to speak."

"Well," the king said, "I shall tell you the gist of it. As a matter of fact, you were grazing your donkey near the tank. Below that tank my ploughmen were; did you see them or not?"

"Yes, I saw them," she replied; "those here present were there ploughing."

"Very well, and did you see this girl carrying food there or not?"

"Yes, I saw her," she replied.

"Very well then, be quiet; now you have caught the purport of it. Hear the whole to the end; thereafter you shall speak."

"Very well," the girl said, "please then first tell everything."

The king then continued speaking: "These ploughmen of mine were ploughing below the tank, and we sent this servant-girl, who had her child with her, to carry the forenoon meal out there. You were there in the vicinity. Now did these ploughmen really beat this woman's child to death, or did she kill it herself? You are a witness for both parties[24]. Don't fear us Five; fear the day-god[25] above; he is seeing us all, and whilst you were there at the rice-fields he also saw all of you. Now speak what is the truth; please tell what you have seen. Don't speak anything you concoct now here, otherwise you will yourself bear the consequences. Now this is what I am asking you. Speak what is the truth."

"Very well, king," she said, "then I am speaking, listen to me; I am speaking the truth. Making my obeisance towards the day-god[26] I swear by my donkey: if I speak the truth, this donkey of mine shall become a man, and if I speak what is false, he shall remain a donkey. Please know this."

Adǫ raje mẹnkeťa, Acha bogege, má ẹṇḍẹkhan rọṛme; amaḱ kathatege bicạr dǫ pȟaṇḍaoḱa.

Adǫe mẹnkeťa, Sạrige iń dǫ ona pukhrire gadhań ạtińede kan tahẽkana, ar noko siokko dǫ ona latarregeko siok kan tahẽkana. Adǫ sanam hǫṛ lạgiť baskeaḱko idikeťa arko jǫmkeťa, ar noko lạgiť dǫ baskeaḱge bań sẹṭẹroḱ kan. Adǫ ạḍi bạṛićko edren kana, mẹneťako, Nun marań beren hõ abo dǫ bako ạguabon kana; nit nãhãḱko ạgukeťa mẹnkhan, dalbo dalkoa sẹ, khubbo dalkoa ar baskeaḱ hõ babon jǫmtakoa. Adǫ enkako rǫṛ baṛae jǫkhẹngeko ńẹlkede, nui kạmṛī kuṛi dǫ gidrạ sotoḱkate baskeaḱe dipil idiyeť kan. Khange adǫko thir baṛayena. Adǫ nui kuṛi dǫ baskeaḱ onko phẹḍregeye dǫhǫkaťte ać dǫ kaṇḍa hẹrmẹťkate kũite daḱ loe calaḱ kana, ar uni aćren gidrạ dǫ ać tayǫm tayǫmteye pańja idikedea. Adǫ ona kũi ṭhenkin tioḱ akať jǫkhẹnge okaren bạriạtko cǫń ạḍi rajan bhajanate ona hǫrtegeko calaḱ kana. Adǫ nui kạmṛī kuṛi dǫ onko sẹn kǫyǫḱkategе kaṇḍa pạsia mẹnteye mẹnleťa, aćren gidrạge hǫṭǫḱreye pạsikedete kũireye caḍokedea. Adǫ ǫr rakaṕkateye ńẹle kan dǫ, gidrạge hǫṭǫḱreye pạsi akade are gǫćentae. Adǫ hako phare noko sioḱko ṭhene hǫbǫr ạgu gǫťkedete baskeaḱ dǫ jǫṭǫe chitiạu giḍikaťte ać dǫ gidrạ hǫbǫrkatege cur mare raraḱ kana, ar noko sioḱkogeye metako kana, Apege ińren gidrạ dǫpe dal gǫćkedetińa. Adǫ noko hõ ńir jarwakateko ńẹlkede dǫ, sạrigeye gǫćentae, arhõko ruheťkedea, Aćtegeye gǫć akadea, adǫ ahak nahakte abo dǫe bǫdnameťbona. Adǫ onkako rǫṛ baṛakede khan, nui dǫ gidrạ hǫbǫrkatege nǫṭẹye hǫbǫr ạgukedea. Adǫ nǫṭẹre dǫe ceť lekakede cǫń, ona dǫ ǫhǫń mẹnlea. Adǫ ẹnẹ iń

---

26 See above note 21. In addition to the ordinary oath she refers to her donkey. In a village-council a thing like this will of course not happen; it belongs to the fairy-tale and has numerous parallels in Hindu tradition. In real life it is always a curse which is called down on the person in question. He may, e. g., be made to stand on a leopard skin and to say that if he does not speak the truth then may a leopard take him, or, as in boundary disputes, he may be made to take some earth from the land in question and keep this on his head whilst swearing, the idea being that if he speaks falsely, the land will become a curse to him, and so on.

"Very well," the king said, "that is good; please speak then; by your statement the case will be settled."

She then said: "It is true, I was grazing the donkey at the tank, and these ploughmen were ploughing below the tank. For all the other ones people brought their forenoon meal, so they had their food; but for these their forenoon meal did not arrive. They were very angry and said: The day is so far advanced, still they are not bringing us anything; if they should bring food now, we shall beat them, we shall give them a sound thrashing, and we shall not eat their food either. Whilst they were speaking in this way, they caught sight of her; this servant-girl was coming having her child in front of her and carrying the food on her head. Then they became quiet. This girl put the food down there close to these people and herself went with a water-pot under her arm to the well to draw water, and her child followed after her. Just at the moment when they had reached the well, a marriage-procession from somewhere or other was passing along that road with much pomp and music. Whilst this servant-girl was looking away towards it, she intended to put a noose round the neck of her water-pot, but putting the noose round the neck of her child she let it down into the well. When she had drawn it up, she saw she had put the noose round the neck of her child, so it had died. Then she in a hurry carried her child to where the ploughmen were, and having scattered and thrown away over the place all the food she commenced, whilst holding her child in her arms, to cry violently and said to the ploughmen: You, you have beaten my child to death. Then these also came running together and saw that the child was really dead; so they again scolded her, saying: She has herself killed her child, and now she is without any cause whatever putting the blame on us. When they had rebuked her in this way, she took the child in her arms and carried it away in this direction. What she did to it here in these parts, I am unable to say. That is what I have seen, please understand that. If I have spoken falsely, Chando is seeing, and if I

ńe̱lak̉ katha do̱, ma bujhąutabonpe. E̱ṛe̱ń ro̱ṛ akat́ khan Candoe ńe̱ńe̱l kana; ar dho̱ro̱mgeń ro̱ṛ akat́ khan, nui gadhae ho̱ṛ go̱dok̉ ma. — Ado̱ onka ro̱ṛ sãotege uni aćren gadha deareye ceṭak̉ go̱t́kedea. Ado̱ khange sąriye ho̱ṛ go̱t́entaea.

Khange ado̱ sanam ho̱ṛko pątiąuena. Ar raj hõe me̱nket́a, Baṅa, sąri kangea. Ńe̱lpe, pąhilreye me̱nket́a, Dho̱ro̱m iń ro̱ṛ khan do̱ gadhae ho̱ṛoktiṅa, ar baṅkhan do̱ o̱ho̱e ho̱ṛlena. Ado̱ o̱ne̱ tho̱bo ńe̱lket́a biswąs do̱. Ado̱ uni kąmṛī kuṛi raje metadea, O̱te̱ mą̃i, amtege co̱m go̱ćkedetam, ado̱ cedak̉ noko ḍo̱m dohmotet́koa?

Ado̱ uni kąmṛī kuṛi do̱ cet́ hõ bae ro̱ṛlet́a; gidrą ho̱bo̱rkate hape hapeteye sayena. Ado̱ uni raje me̱nket́a, Do aben do̱ se̱njoṅben, ado̱ cabayena katha do̱. Ado̱ onkae metat́kin khan nukin do̱kin he̱ćena, ado̱ ako akoge cet́ko co̱ko galmaraoket́.

Ado̱ nukin mahra kuṛi koṛa do̱ nąihą̃rte hõ bakin he̱ćlena, ar koṛawak̉ eṅgat apat oṛak̉te hõ bakin he̱ćlena. Ado̱ o̱nte̱rege kisąṛkin sap̉ante o̱ṇḍe̱gekin guti kąmṛīyena. Ado̱kin oṛak̉ duąrket́te tayo̱mte do̱ casakin hoeyena. Ado̱ un khonge, kathae, mahra jąt do̱ gąi do̱ ąḍi bąṛićko jo̱to̱nkoa.

Ado̱ e̱ne̱ anaṅ katha do̱, in maraṅgea, cabayentakina.

24. Ṭąkate baṅ ńamok̉a.

Mit́ṭaṅ mahra kisąṛe tahẽkana. Unkin do̱ mit́ṭaṅ kuṛi gidrąi hoelentąkina, ado̱ inąkategekin teṅgoyena; ado̱ bakin gidrąlet́koa.

1 The following story touches one side of the inner life of Santal women, and also of Santal men. To be childless is considered a great calamity, often a curse. The Santal traditions tell that, in the old days, when a wife remained barren, she would herself bring a second wife into the house, that there might be children. This is explained to be the first, originally the only cause for a man having more than one wife among the Santals. The story of Abraham and Sarai might fit a Santal family in many points. As to 'cattle-owner', in Santali mahra, see p. 342, note 2.

have spoken the truth, may this donkey become a man." As she was speaking in this way, she suddenly gave her donkey a slap on the back with her hand. And in very truth, her donkey at once became a man.

Then they all believed it, and the king also said: "Undoubtedly, that is the truth. Observe, she said beforehand: 'If I speak the truth, my donkey shall become a man; otherwise he would certainly not have become a man. So there we have seen visible proof of the truth." The king thereupon spoke to the servant-girl: "Listen, girl, do you hear? you yourself killed your child. Then why do you falsely accuse these?"

The servant-girl did not say anything; carrying her child in her arms she quietly went aside without saying a word. The king then said: "Now you two, please, may go away; the case is finished." When he had said this to them, they came away, and those other ones had some talk, who knows what, among themselves.

Now the mahra boy and girl did not go to the home of her parents, nor did they come to the house of the boy's father and mother. They found a master in those parts and took service there. So they made themselves house and home, and afterwards they became farmers. From this time, people tell, the mahra caste people take such intense care of cows.

Now that is the story, it is thus much; the story of those two is finished.

24. NOT TO BE HAD FOR MONEY.

THERE was once a rich cattle-owner[1]. One child was born to them, a girl, whereupon they ceased[2] getting children; they did not get any more.

---

2 The Santal word is teṅgo, stand, come to a standstill, their term. tech., so to say, for what is here referred to.

Adọ uni gidrại hárayenre hõ pẹragẹ bako lagaoḱ kan. Adọ kathae, ghạrdi jãwãeḱin dọhọadea. Adọ unkin hõ baplakate ạḍi din hoeyena, pasẹ isi bọchọr gan, ẹnre hũ bakin gidrạjoṅ kan. Khange uni kuṛi dọ gidrạjoṅ reaḱ ńẹl họrteye mọkọńen khàn dọ, dingeye raga; adọ ona bhabnate uni kuṛi dọe osoḱena. Adọ eṅgat apatkin metaea, Henda mãi, cekate bẹbạṛićem osoḱen dọ? Ceť bhabna menaḱtama?

Adọe metaťkina, Iń dọ, baba, ạḍi maraṅ bhabna menaḱtińa. Aben lạiabenre hõ ona bhabna dọ ọhọben cabaletińa.

Adọkin mẹnkeťa, Masẹ ẹnte lạịlem, bhala ceť lekan katha kana.

Adọ unreye metaťkina, Iń dọ, baba, dhulạ muṭi kicrićge bạń bandeleť dọ, onate iń dọń bhabnaḱ kana.

Adọkin mẹnkeťa, Họ, ona lạgiť am dọm bhabnaḱ kana? Ona dọbon kiriń ạguia. Adọ ṭaka emaťkote họṛkin kolkeťkoa. Metaťkoakin, Do ape dọ dhulạ muṭi kicrić kiriń ạguipe.

Adọ sạri calaoente goṭa bajarko kuli baṛayeťkore hõ, onkan kicrićge bako ńam daṛeaḱ kan. Adọ kathae, jẹmọn tẹmọnaḱ miťṭaṅ kicrićko kiriṅkeťa. Adọ ạgukate onako emadea. Adọ ona hõ bae khusilena. Adọ arhõko mẹnkeťa, Do eṭagaḱ kiriń ạguipe.

Adọ uni kuṛiye mẹnkeťa, Ẹ baba, ạuṛiaḱte ṭaka alope khọrọca. Iń dọ Candoge dhulạ muṭi kicrić dọ bae emadiń khan iń cekaea? Ape dọ dhulạ muṭi reaḱ bhẹd dọ bape bujhạueťa. Dhulạ muṭi reaḱ bhẹd dọ noa kana: gidrạko tahẹntiń khan, dhuṛite kicrićko

3 The same fate follows the child. No one wanted to ask for the girl; they had to arrange for a husband for her themselves.

4 Cf. above p. 310, note 38.

5 The two words translated 'dusty' are not Santali, but Hindi. The first word dhulạ means dust; the other word muṭi may have several meanings; it may in Santali pronunciation be the same as mạṭi, earth, or dirt. It may mean a handful, and also other things. The girl's parents and the others think it is the name of a special kind of cloth.

6 The word bajar, the same as our bazar, is a town with shops, not necessarily only shops, in Santali.

When this child grew up, no one asked for the girl in marriage either[3]. Ultimately, it is told, they procured a husband[4] for her, who was to stay with them. Now these two also lived together for a very long time after their marriage, perhaps for twenty years or so; still they were not getting any children. When the girl at last understood that she could not any longer hope to get children, she cried every day; and because she was grieving over this, she wasted away. Her parents often said to her: "Look here, our girl, how is it you have become so awfully lean? What is preying on your mind?"

"Father," she replied, "I have a very great sorrow. But even if I tell both of you, you will not be able to end my sorrow."

"Do tell us, so we may know it anyhow," they said, "we wonder what kind of matter it is."

"Father," she replied, "I have never dressed in dusty[5] cloth; that is what I am grieving over."

"Oh," they said, "is that what you are grieving over? We shall buy and bring you that. So they gave some people money and sent them off to buy. They said to them: "Do buy some dusty cloth and bring it here."

These people really went, but although they asked people all over the town[6], they were unable to get any such cloth. So they bought a cloth such as they could find[7], and brought it and gave it to the girl. But she was not pleased at that either. They then said to them: "Go, buy some other and bring it."

The girl then said: "Father, don't spend money to no purpose. When Chando[8] has not given me the dusty cloth, what is there for me to do? You have not grasped the meaning of dusty. The meaning of dusty is this: if I had children, they would make

7 The word used in Santali generally connotes that the thing so described is what may just pass, but what is not quite up to the mark or satisfactory.

8 See p. 68, note 11.

mạilạketiṅa. Ona kaṇa dhulạ muṭi kicrić dọ. Adọ gidrạge bạnuḱkotiṅ ḱhan, okortiṅaṅ ona kicrić dọ?

Khaṅge eṅgat apatkin raḱ gọt́keťa, arkiṅ mẹnkeťa, Cekaealiṅ, biṭi? Họṛ họtẹte hoyoḱ khan, jãhãeko ạcukatebon benao ocokekoa. Adọ ona lekaṇ kathage baṅ kan. Adọkin raḱketa: —

(Sereṅ. Lagṛẽ rạṛ.)
Pọrẹr putạ hoeto kiba yayo jala, kiba bẹdọn kọrẹ;
Apọn putạ hoeto ạiso putạ kole libạ he.

Metaḱme, Eṭaḱ họṛren họpọnko tahẹn khan, ceť hõ jala joṅjal bhabna bạnuḱ; ar apnarren họpọn tahẹn khan, dhuṛi akanre hõm hẹo gọt́kea.

Adọ kuṛiye mẹnkeťa, Ọnẹ onatege, ayo, iṅaḱ jivi dọ sarage patale lọḱ kantiṅa. Onateṅ metaben kana, ṭaka aloben khọrọca. Iṅ dọ Candoge bae emadiṅ khan, ceť iṅ mẹna? Ona bhabnate iṅ dọṅ osogoḱ kana. Nit daṛe calaḱ bhor ma hẽge. Adọ jãhã hiloḱ ạliṅliṅ buḍhi haṛamlen khan, cele ạsulliṅa ar cele jọtọnliṅa? Onako bhabnate iṅ dọṅ raḱeť kanteṅ osogoḱ kana.

Adọkin metadea, Nit dọliṅ baḍaekeťtama. Adọbon cekaea? Ma jivi dọ tẹntam. Bhabnakate hõ ọhọbon ṅamlekoa. Daṛe calaḱ

---

9 Grief is very commonly given vent to in song; the Santals have a special melody, always used in their lamentations over dead ones. Such 'songs' as a rule consist of only a couple of lines, quite exceptionally there is more.

10 The melody here used, according to the narrator, is lagṛẽ, a dance melody par excellence.

11 The song is in a rustic form of Bengali.

12 The narrator has, for the benefit of his audience, given a free translation of the 'song'.

13 In Santali also the soul or heart 'burns'; the way in which it burns is here described as sarage patale, lit. heavenwards, hadeswards; there is nothing left to live for.

14 A common expression for resignation.

15 The thoughts here given expression to are those of a Santal. It is not succession that is uppermost in their minds, but to have somebody to look after them when

my cloth dirty with dust. That is the dusty cloth. I have no children, then where can I have that cloth?"

When they heard this, her parents commenced to cry and said: "What shall we do, daughter? If such a cloth were made by man, we should hire some one or other and let them make it. But it is not anything of that kind."

Thereupon they cried[9]: (here is the song, sung at lagṛẽ melody[10]).

"If it is a son of other people, what gives anxiety,
mother, what gives pain?
If it is your own son, come, my son, I shall take
you in my arms[11]."

That is to say[12]: If it is other people's children, there is no anxiety, trouble, sorrow; and if it is one's own child, you will at once take him on your hip, even if he is dirty from dust.

Then the girl said: "That's the reason, mother, that my soul burns within me and I am grieving unto death[13]. Therefore I am saying to you both, don't spend any money. When Chando has not given me a child, what can I say[14]? That is my grief, therefore I am wasting away. It may go so long as my strength lasts. But some day in the future, when my husband and I become old, who will support us, who will take care of us[15]? It is on account of these anxieties that I am crying and wasting away."

"Now we[16] know what is the matter with you," they said to her. "But what can we[17] do? Be patient, control yourself. Even

they become old and cannot work any longer. To a childless Santal it is a real, often grave and vital problem.

16 The pronoun used is the exclusive dual.

17 The pronoun used is the inclusive plural; it may, besides the one addressed, include the whole world, or only the family.

bhor dǫ apnartegeboṇ laṛaok̉a, ar baṅ hilok̉ dǫ jãhãe peṛako mãyãk̉ṛe ma hẽge. Ar baṅkhan nią cij bąsut ńẹlte jãhãeko ąsulbongea. Noa cij jimąwako khan dǫ, jąnić albǫtko ąk̉sulgea. Ar rak̉ ar bhabnakate hõ cet̉bo cekaea?

Adǫ ẹnẹ cabayena katha dǫ.

---

18 See above note 15. Above were the feelings of a woman, here are given the reflexions of an elderly, resigned man.

if we grieve, we shall not get any. As long as our strength lasts, we shall move about ourselves; when we cannot do that any longer, if some relative or other will feel compassion, well and good. If not, then some one or other will support us, seeing all this property. If this property is given into their charge, they will likely be sure to support us[18]. And even crying and grieving, what can we do?"

So there, the story is ended.

SANTAL FOLK TALES

SANTAL FOLK TALES

(IN THREE VOLUMES)

P.O. Bodding

VOL. II

GYAN PUBLISHING HOUSE
NEW DELHI

Santal Folk Tales
(Anthropology Culture, Literature)

ISBN : 9788121203449(Set)

ISBN : 9788121203463(Vol-2)

Published in **2007** in India by
Gyan Publishing House
5, Ansari Road,
New Delhi-110 002

Printed at Goyal Offset Printers Delhi

CONTENTS

HUMOROUS TALES

25. Jhōr̥ē ar Bạjun reak̕ katha.

Sedae jugre, kathae, Jhōr̥ē Bạjun ńutumakin bar boehakin tahẽkana; Bạjun doe marańa, ar Jhōr̥ē doe huḍińić kana, ar unkinren eṅgat apat do Bạjun bạhuade sermagekin gođena. Khange ado Bạjun doe siok̕a are kạmi baṛaetạkina.

Tahen tahente ado mit̕ din do uni Bạjun bạhu do rụa ehop̕kedea; khange ado dāṛā sōr̥ẽ rụa rụategeye kạhil idiyena. Khange ado Bạjune menket̕tạkina, E ya Jhōr̥ē, hilim ạḍiye ruạk̕ kana, bae duṛup̕ daṛeak̕ kana, ar iń hō siok̕ iń calak̕ kana. Teheń do amge nāhāk̕ daka hataṛtabonme; kạmi khon hećkate do nāhāk̕ ạḍi reṅgeća, tinre iń doń dakaea? Onate amiń lại oṭoam kana, daka hataṛme, pe pại nāhāk̕ khadleme. Khange sạri onkaye batlao baṛa oṭoadete ać do nahele sokket̕te siok̕e calaoena.

Ado khange sạri Jhōr̥ē do seṅgele jolket̕a, ar ṭukućre dak̕e dulket̕te culhạreye condaket̕a; ado bhagete sahane ṭhekaoet̕teye

---

[1] All tales are as told by Sagram Murmu of Mohulpahari, when no other name is given.

[2] The Santal custom is that the parents, or the responsible head of the family, procure a wife for a son, first for the oldest one, then for the next one, and so on. The young people concerned are just asked for their consent.

[3] The way of adressing and mentioning relatives and, for that sake, also other people, may be noted. They avoid using the proper names, as much as possible. To persons younger than the speaker the proper name may be used; its use implies familiarity or lack of respect.

[4] The Santali word pại is a measure equal to half a seer, varying in size according to locality. The standard seer is about equal to one kg. The Santals never weigh their rice, but measure it. When preparing their daily food they naturally estimate how much rice is needed, rice being their principal food. The average amount of rice consumed by an ordinary Santal, who is not obliged to stint himself, is about one pại per day. The amount here mentioned is consequently abundant.

25. THE STORY OF JHORE AND BAJUN[1].

In olden times, it is told, there lived two brothers named Jhore and Bajun. Bajun was the elder and Jhore the younger one. Their parents died the year they had brought a wife[2] for Bajun. So Bajun was ploughing and carrying on the work for them.

In the course of time it so happened one day that Bajun's wife fell ill, and as this kept on, one day a little better, another day somewhat worse, she gradually grew weaker and weaker with the fever. Bajun then said: "Look here, Jhore, your sister-in-law[3] is very ill; she is unable to sit up, and as for myself, I have to go and plough. Therefore you must prepare the food for us, while I am away to-day. When coming back from work, one feels very hungry; when shall I find time to prepare food? Therefore I am telling you before I go to prepare food, while I am away. Put in three pints[4]." And, truth to tell, when he had instructed him in this way, he himself fastened the plough to the yoke[5] and went to plough.

Now Jhore actually lighted a fire, poured water in the cooking pot and put it on the fire; he heaped a lot of wood on to the fire

---

The pạl is mentioned, because the pạl measure is the one commonly found in Santal households.

5 The Santal plough is light in weight, being, except for the ploughshare, entirely made of wood. When they take the plough to the field, it is suspended on the yoke and carried on this by the bullocks, the beam pointing straight up into the air. It is brought back in the same way, if they do not leave it in the field, only taking the iron ploughshare home; this is never left.

They commence ploughing at sunrise and work until nearly noon, the length of the working hours depending on the strength of the bullocks and the amount of work to be done. During the rice-planting season they may also work a little in the afternoon, but this is avoided, if possible.

jolaḱ kana; ado daḱ basaṅenkhan do ado paiye nam barayeta. Ado akoaḱ paiye ńamketa. Adoe menketa, Durre, aleaḱ pai ma miť goṭaṅge, ar seye men akawadiṅa, pe pai nãhãḱ khadleme; miťtaṅ eskar nãhãḱ iṅ khadlele khan doe ruhediṅa. Okoe tora arhõ barea paiyiṅ koe agukoa.

Ado khange onka hudis barakate atoren hor ṭhen khon barea paiye koe aguketa; ado onako pene paiye khadlekata. Khange adoe jolaḱ kana are ghanṭayeta. Khange ado onka baraetegeye tikinketa. Unre dadattet hõ si mokoṅente oraḱte nahele soḱ aguketa. Ado chaṭkareye araḱketkinte gorateye laga aderketkina. Ado khange oraḱ khon Jhõrẽ doe odok gotena.

Ado dadattet doe kulikedea, Cele ya, Jhõrẽ, dakaket tabonam?

Ado Jhõrẽye menketa, Khadle akataṅ. Khange dadattete menketa, Acha, isinoḱa nãhãḱ. Am do ma unkin ḍaṅgra busuṕ emakinme; ar hilim doe okayena?

Adoe menketa, Ona muṅga dare sećrege jederre parkom iṅ bel akawadea.

Khange ado dadattet doać bahu ṭhene calaoena; adoe kuli barayede kana: Cele, cet lekam aikaueta? Okakore hasoyetmea, laime; kami din ruaḱ do adi muskil iṅ aikaueta; cekatebo kamia? Iṅ hõ adi muskil iṅ aikaueta; nõkõe am hõm ruaḱ kana, ar kami hor banuḱkotabona — ma pharia hodokme.

Ado bahuttete menketa, Ma se, ti jaṅga peter barakatiṅme, adi laṅgaṅ aikauet kana. Khange ado ti jaṅgakoe iskir barayede kana. Adoe menketa, Sunum aguime, ekenaḱte do adim haso ocoyediṅ kana.

Khange ado uni Jhõrẽ do ḍaṅgra busuṕe emaṫkinte oraḱte bolokate tiṅgiye tiṅgiaḱ kana se, cur mare tiṅgiaḱ kana. Ado

6 The munga tree (Moringa pterygosperma, Gaertn.) is common in the Santal courtyards. The tree is planted, the leaves, flowers and fruit being used for food.

7 Every Santal is supposed to know how to give massage, and many are quite expert performers. Massage is very frequently resorted to. They have several ways of giving it. As a rule they do it kneading, twisting and stroking with their hands, sometimes applying a little oil.

and made it blaze; when the water had commenced to boil, he tried to find some pints. Ultimately he found their own pint. Then he said: "That's strange, we have only one pint, and he has told me to put in three pints; if I put in only one, he will certainly scold me. I shall at once ask somebody to lend me two more pints."

Consequently, having thought this out, he went and borrowed two pints from some of the village people, and put all three pints into the pot. Then he again kept the fire going and stirred and stirred. He worked with this until noon. By that time his brother had done ploughing for the day[5] and returned home with the plough suspended on the yoke. Having unyoked the bullocks at the entrance to the court-yard, he drove them into the cattle-shed. Just then Jhore came out of the house.

The elder brother then asked him: "Well, how is it, Jhore, have you prepared food for us?"

"I have put in," Jhore answered. The elder brother then said: "All right, it will be ready cooked presently. Now you give the two bullocks straw; but what has become of your sister-in-law?"

"Near that munga[6]-tree," he replied. "I have put her bedstead for her in the sun."

The elder brother then went to his wife and asked her: "Well, how do you feel? Tell whereabouts it is paining you; to be ill during the working season, that I feel to be a great difficulty; how shall we get the work done? Personally I feel it difficult; here now you also are ill, and we have no working people — get well soon, do."

His wife then said: "Please knead and rub[7] my arms and legs for me; I am feeling very tired." He then massaged her arms and legs. While he was doing this, she said: "Bring some oil; you are causing me a good deal of pain by doing it with a dry hand."

Now after having given the bullocks straw Jhore had gone into the house and was keeping the fire going; he was feeding the fire all he could. During this his elder brother came in to

khange sunum ạgui lạgiť dadattẹť dọ oṛaǩteye bọlọ gọťena; adọe metae kana, Cele ya, isinkeťam? Adọ uni dọ ceť hō̃ bae rọṛeťa. Khange uni dọe mẹnkeťa, Dẹ sẹń ghanṭa aṭkartama. Adọ khange sạri kā̃ṛchu saṗkateye ghanṭakeťte haḍ baḍe ạikạukeťa. Adọe metae kana, Ceť ya haḍ baḍaoǩ kana? Adọ kọcẹkateye ńẹlkeť dọ, pẹa pạiye khadle akať. Khange adọe ruheť baṛayede kana, Cedaǩ noa pại dọm khadle akaťa? Am dọ ạḍi bạṛić lelha hoṛ kanam, miť hō̃ bud dọ bạnuǩtama.

Adọ Jhō̃ṛẽye mẹnkeťa, Amge cọṅ, dada, pẹ pại khadleyem metadiń; onatẹ iń dọ pẹ pạigeń khadle akaťa, bạṛti thọ bań khadle akaťa.

Khange adọ dhur mare ruheť baṛakedea, adọe metae kana, Caole dọ bam khadlea? Pại dọ cedaǩem khadle akaťa?

Adọe mẹn ruạṛkeťa, Amge cọṅ, dada, pẹ pại khadleyem metadiń, caole khadle thọ bam metadińa; onate-iń dọ pạigeń khadlekeťa. Adọ khange pại dọ kin oarkaťa, adọ caole kin khadlekeťa, adọe metadea, Ma, nitoǩ dọ tiṅgiam; adọe tiṅgiaťa. Khange adọ isinena, adọ dadaťtẹťgeye ā̃ṛićkeťteye lokeťa, adọko jọm baṛakeťa.

Khange adọe metadea, Ma, ḍaṅgra aṛaǩ idikinme ar ạtiń baṛakinme. Alom aḍa ocoakina, baṅkhan nā̃hā̃ǩ ọhọkin bilena. Khange adọe aṛaǩ idikeťkina, ar ać dọ sunume ńamkeťte bạhuttẹťe iskir baṛakadea, adọ ać dọ kedoǩ reaǩe tana bhanayeť kana.

Adọ khange dosar hiloǩ dọe metae kana, Ẹya Jhō̃ṛẽ, ma teheń dọ amge sioǩtalaṅme; ar miťṭaṅ ṭẹṅgọć idi toraeme, ar rẹhẹť

8 The rice is cooked with a little water; when it is ready, the water is poured off and kept, being used for medicinal purposes or for cattle food.

9 At about mid-day grazing cattle are taken to some place generally near the village, where there is some shade, and permitted to lie down to rest and ruminate. This gives also the cattle-herds some liberty.

10 The axe mentioned is the smallest the Santals have.

11 It is not possible in English to render exactly the Santali expression. Maǩ akinme has in Santali a double meaning; it may be either 'cut at the two' or 'cut for the two,' to help them.

fetch the oil and said to him: "Well, how is it, have you cooked it?" The other one does not say a word. Then the elder brother said: "Give here, let me stir and feel what you have prepared." He then took the ladle, commenced to stir and felt something knocking, whereupon he said to his brother: "You fellow, what is rattling?" He tilted the pot and looked, and there he saw three pint measures put in. And he commenced to scold him: "Why have you thrown these pints in? You are an awful fool, you have not one bit of wits."

Then Jhore said: "Why, you yourself, brother, told me to put in three pints; therefore I have put in just three pints; more I have not, as you see, put in."

The elder brother rated him soundly and said to him: "Should you not put rice in? Why have you put pints in?"

The other replied: "Why, you yourself, brother, told me to put three pints in; you surely did not tell me to put rice in; therefore I put pints in." So they got the pints out and put in rice, whereupon the elder brother said: "Well, now make a good fire under it," and he did so. When it was ready cooked, the elder brother poured off the rice-water[8] and took the rice out with a ladle, and so all of them had their food.

Thereupon the elder brother said to the other: "Do take the bullocks out and graze them. Don't let them lie down[9] to rest; if you do so, they will certainly not get enough." So Jhore took them out, and the elder brother himself found the oil and gave his wife massage; thereupon he himself made the necessary preparations for the evening neal.

The next day he said to his brother: "Look here, Jhore, you plough for us to-day; take an axe[10] along with you, and if the plough should stick in some root or other, then use the axe.[11] You do not know even to cook food; yesterday on account of that you put into the pot only pints and made a rattle; therefore I tell you, to-day you yoke the bullocks and go and plough."

tanakre ḍhaṅlenkhan dọ nāhāk̔ mak̔akinme. Am dọ dak̔ka hõ bam baḍaea, hola onkate ẹkẹn pạige haḍ baḍem khadlelak̔a; onateṅ metam kana, ma teheṅ dọ amge joṛaokinte siok̔ calak̔me.

Adọ khange sạri adọe joṛaoket̔kinte siok̔e calaoena, ar ona ṭẹṅgọć hõe idi toraket̔a. Khange adọe siok̔ kana. Khange adọ siok̔ jọkhẹć ḍhaṅ gọt̔ena. Khange adọ unkin ḍaṅgra jaṅgage cur mare mak̔et̔kina. Adọ khange hasoket̔kinkhankin pạcena. Adọe ọr chaḍaoket̔a ona nahel dọ; khange adọ onka ḍhaṅ gọdọk̔ khangeye mak̔kina. Adọ khange banar ḍaṅgrae mak̔ leḍhaket̔kina.

Adọ tikin jọkhẹć oṛak̔te nahele sọk̔ ạguket̔a. Khange adọ dadattẹt̔e ṅẹlket̔kina, jẹ leḍhọk̔ leḍhọk̔kin taṛamet̔ kan; adọe mẹnket̔a, Henda ya, cekate lẹḍhọk̔ lẹḍhọk̔ dọkin taṛamet̔a?

Adọe mẹnket̔a, Mak̔ akawat̔kinaṅ.

Khange adọe mẹnket̔a, Cedak̔em mak̔ket̔kina?

Adọe mẹnket̔a, Amge cọṅ dadam metadiṅ, jẹ ḍhaṅlenkhan dọ nāhāk̔ mak̔akinme; onate iṅ dọṅ mak̔ akawat̔kina.

Adọ bogeteye ruhet̔ baṛakedea; adọe metae kana, Am dọ ạḍim orlogea; rẹhẹt̔ mamak̔ iṅ metat̔mekhan am dọ ḍaṅgra jaṅgagem mak̔ket̔kina. Am dọ ạḍim lelhagea; noa budte dọ am dọ cekatem ạsulok̔a? Onka bogete dhur mare ruhet̔ baṛakedẹa.

Adọe mẹnket̔a, Gapa dọ caolekoṅ oḍok otoama, āmge dak̔aeme; dak̔em basaṅlet̔ leka basaṅme, adọ basaṅkate caọle khadleme, ar ona caole dọ ghạṛi ghạṛi tunumme, adọ lạbit̔ena mẹnkhan dọ nāhāk̔ ạṛījme; adọ āṛgokate pẹa patṛare loeme. Nọ̃k̔ọ̃e iṅ lạiam kana, disạ dọhọkam, alom hiṛiṅa; ar nāhāk̔ ạyup̔ jọkhẹć iṅ uduk̔ cet̔ama. Adọ ạyup̔ jọkhẹć, kedok̔ko dakae jọkhẹće uduk̔ cet̔adea. Khange adọe uduk̔adekhane cet̔ket̔a; adọ dosar hilok̔ khon dọ unigeye dakaket̔ takoa.

---

12 Leaf-plates are very commonly used, if people have no brass-plates. They are made of sal-leaves, stitched together with straw.

Truth to tell, Jhore yoked the bullocks and went to plough; the axe he also took with him. So he commenced to plough. Then, while he was doing this, it suddenly stuck, and he again and again cut the legs of the bullocks. This natúrally pained them, so they backed. He then pulled the plough free. Whenever it stuck in this way, he cut at them, and the result was that he by his cutting lamed both bullocks.

At noon time he slung the plough on to the yoke and brought it home. Then the elder brother saw the two bullocks, that they were limping, and asked: "Look here, you, how is it that they are limping?"

"I have used the axe," Jhore answered.

"Why did you cut them"? he asked him.

Then he said: "Why, you yourself, brother, told me that, when it stuck, I should use the axe; therefore I have done so and cut at them."

The elder brother then scolded him soundly and said to him: "You are an awful booby; I told you to cut the roots, and you cut the legs of the bullocks. You are awfully foolish; with such wits, how will you be able to support yourself?" In this manner he rated him soundly.

Afterwards be said: "To-morrow I shall take out rice for you, before I go; then you prepare the food. Boil the water, as you did, and when it is boiling, put in the rice; again and again feel the rice with your hand, and as soon as it becomes soft, pour off the water; then take the pot off the fire, take the rice out and put it on three leaf-plates[12]. There now, I am telling you, remember it, don't forget it. Presently this evening I shall also show you, so you may learn." And in the evening, when food was prepared for their evening meal, he showed him and taught him how to do it. From the next day the younger brother prepared food for them.

Adọ khange tahẹn tahẹnte tin din badre cọṅ khange adọe metae kana mit' din dọ, Ẹ ya Jhõṛẽ, dak'ka uk'tu dọm cet'ket'a, adọ alom hiṛiń̇a. Adọ arhõ teheń mit' kathań lại̤am kana, daka baṛakate nãhãk' nią ṭukuće dak' dulkate culhạre condaeme, ar thoṛa urgum ṅõk'kate nãhãk' hilim dọ umkaeme. Enkae lại baṛawadea; adọ ać dọ siok'e joṛaoket'te kạmiye calaoena.

Khange adọ Jhõṛẽ dọe daka baṛaket'a; adọ onae batlao oṭoade leka dak'e condaket'a, adọ khub lekae tiṅgi basaṅket'a. Khange adọ uni hilittẹt' dọe gitić akan tahẽkana. Khange Jhõṛẽ dọ ṭukuć dak' uni hilittẹt' phẹḍ ṭhene kuṭuṇ idi gọt'ket'a. Khange adọ bạṭire taṅkate hilittẹt'e dul gọt'adea. Khange uni dọe lọk' kanteye metae kana, Alom dulań̇a, alom dulań̇a. Khange nui dọe landae landayet'a sẹ, are dulae kana.

Onka onkate sạriye dul gọćkedea ona basaṅ dak'tege. Adọe gọćenkhan dọe thirena. Khangeye thirenkhan dọ adọe iskir baṛayedea; adọe iskir baṛakedete adọ eṭak' kicrić ạgukateye oyo pọṭọmkadea. Adọ dakae loket'a, adọ sẹnkate hilittẹt'e metae kana, Ẹ hili, dakaṅ ạguama sẹ? Tãhã uni dọe gọćenkhan dọe rọṛa? bae rọṛlet'a. Adọ khange bae rọṛlet'khan ać dọe ruạṛente dakae jọmket'a, ar unkinak' dọe hạrupkat' takina.

Adọ ina mit' ghạṛi khange dadattẹt'e hẹćena; adọe kuli gọt'kedea, Cele ya, umkedeam? Adọe mẹnket'a, Hẽ, um baṛakateń oyo pọṭọm akadea. Adọ ḍaṅgra goṛate laga aderkate bạhuttẹt' ńẹńẹle calao gọt'ena. Kicrić oṭak'kateye ńẹlkede dọe gọćen; adọe mẹnket'a, Dhora basaṅ dak'tegeye dul gọćkedea. Khange adọe rak' gọt'ket'a.

Are mẹnket'a, Cedak' ya basaṅ dak'te dọm dul gọćkedea? Teheń dọ am hõ ạurilaṅ gọćme dhạbić dọ balaṅ bạgiama. Adọ khange kạpiye ńam baṛayet'a.

---

13 The relationship between a man and his elder brother's wife is very intimate; there are few restrictions theoretically. It all depends on what the persons are. This to explain that the younger brother could be asked to wash his sister-in-law.

14 Inclusive dual used in threatening language.

15 Found in many Santal houses, now used for sacrificial purposes.

As time passed, after some days, the elder brother one day said to the other: "Listen, Jhore, you have learnt to prepare food, so don't forget it. Now to-day I am telling you something more; when you have cooked the food, pour water into this pot and put it on the fire, and when it becomes a little warm, wash[13] your sister-in-law." In this manner he instructed him, whereupon he himself yoked the plough and went off to work.

So Jhore prepared the food; afterwards he put water on the fire, as his elder brother had instructed him, and making a good fire he made the water boil well. Now his sister-in-law was lying on her bed, and Jhore took the pot with water and carried it close to where his sister-in-law was lying. Having poured some water in a cup he poured it over her. She was burned and said to him: "Don't pour on me, don't pour on me." But he only laughed and laughed and continued to pour.

Going on in this way he, truth to tell, killed her pouring on the boiling water. When she died, he stopped pouring hot water on her and commenced to give her massage, and having done this he brought another piece of cloth and wrapped her up in this. Thereupon he ladled the rice out, and going to his sister-in-law he said to her: "Sister-in-law, shall I bring you food or how?" Now she was dead, so how could she speak? She did not say anything, and, as she did not speak, he went back and had his food himself, and the food for the two other ones he covered up.

A short while afterwards the elder brother came and at once asked him: "How is it, you, have you washed her?" "Yes," he replied, "I have washed her and afterwards covered her up." Having taken the bullocks into the cattle-shed the elder brother went to see his wife. Having removed the cloth he saw she was dead. Then he said: "There is no doubt, he has killed her by pouring hot water on her." And he commenced to cry.

"Why," he said, "did you kill her by pouring hot water on her? To-day we two[14] shall not leave you, until we have have killed you also." Whereupon he commenced to hunt for the battle-axe.[15]

Khange Jhõṛẽ doe daṛketa. Ado kapi ńamkate lagae lagayedea se, bebaṛiće lagayede kana. Khange ado mitṭań birreye laga atkedea. Khange ado uni Jhõṛẽ do ona birrege merom poṭae ńamketa. Khange ado uni Jhõṛẽ doe hoho gotketa, Okayenam, dada? Jelíń ńam akata.

Ado khange Bajune menketa, Aurilań goćme habić do balań bagiam kana.

Khange Jhõṛẽ do onkae ańjomketkhan do ona merom poṭa doe hobor gotketa are daṛketa. Khange thoe lagae lagayedea se; ado mitṭań dare ḍoḍhorreye laga aderkedea. Khange ado laṛga lakṭha makkate luṛgaue luṛgauedea se, bhageteye sobokede kana. Khange ado uni Jhõṛẽ do merom poṭae hobor akat tahẽkana, ado adi ãṭe sobokkedekhan ona merom poṭa doe paskao gotketa. Khange lijhṛak marte ńũr gotena. Khange Bajune menketa, Ho, nitok doń goć akadea; eṅgate lać iń sobok totkettaea, enre hõ bae gujuka? Goć adokae nãhãk.

Khange adoe bagiadete ać do oṛakteye ruaṛena; ado unkin ḍaṅgra busupkoe ematkinte ato hoṛe jarwaketkoa gok sahan lagit, ado uni bahuttetko gok onḍoṅkedeteko sahan seṅgeladea, ado har halań baṛakate oṛakteko ruaṛ heċena.

Ado khange tahen tahente tin din badre coń adoe bhanḍanetkina, kathae; ado oṛak duaṛ en hilok do kathaeye geć gurić onḍoṅketa; ado ayup jokheć unkin ńutumte meromko ar simkoe kuṭamketkoa. Ar uni Jhõṛẽ do tinre coń en hilok do hećkate, kathae, koalere

---

16 After cremation a couple of bones (now-a-days a bit of the skull, and the collar-bone, in all three pieces) are picked up, washed and put into an earthenware pot. These bones are later on carried to the Damuda river and immersed there.

17 It might be remarked that the description here given of the ceremonies gone through after death is not in full accordance with what is generally done. The ceremonies are several and are finished off with a festival, when the dead person is, so to say, removed from this world and given over to the authorities of the next world, the ancestors and Marang buru. The dead one is now a bonga, and sacrifices are performed to him or her, with this difference, however, that all

Now Jhore ran away. When the elder brother had found the battle-axe, he pursued him eagerly; he chased him all he could. Ultimately he chased him into a forest and lost sight of him there. Now Jhore in that forest happened to find the stomach of a goat and called out: "What has become of you, brother? I have found flesh."

But Bajun answered: "Until we[14] kill you, we are not going to leave you."

When Jhore heard this, he took the goat's stomach in his arms and ran off, and his brother chased him and chased him, until he at last chased him into the hole of a tree. Thereupon he cut a large pole and commenced to poke and poke him with this; he stabbed him again and again. Now Jhore had the stomach of the goat in his arms, and as the other stabbed him forcibly, he let the goat's stomach slip, so it fell down with a flop. Then Bajun said: "O, now I have killed him; dash it, I have stabbed him so his stomach came out; will he not die then? Surely he will die, the wretch."

Thereupon he left him and himself went back home, and having given the bullocks straw he called the village people together to assist at the cremation. They carried his wife out and cremated her, and, after having collected the bones[16], they returned to their respective houses.

The days passed, and after some time he made arrangements for the final ceremonies[17] of the two dead ones, it is told. That day, it is told, he cleaned the whole house and smeared it with cow-dung[18], and in the evening he killed goats and fowls in the names of these two. Now Jhore had some time during that

sacrifices to the dead ones are killed by a blow on the neck, whilst animals sacrificed to the ordinary bongas are killed by beheading. This last festival is, according to circumstances, often a big affair with many participating.

18 The Santals and many other races clean their houses, especially the floor and courtyard, with cow-dung mixed with water; this is the finishing touch after sweeping and plastering with earth wherever necessary. Strange enough, one learns to approve of this practice in Santal houses.

dẹćkateye duṛuṕ akana. Uni dadattẹt́ cetkoe cekayeta, onako tan man jọtọe ńẹle kana.

Adọ khange Bạjun dọ jọtọe rọ gẹtketkoa, adọe utu dakaketa, mit́ dạuṛạ hopọne dakaketa ar mit́ celańe utuketa, ar bohọkteṭko dọ mitṭań celańreye suṛe dakaketa, adọ ona suṛe dakae boṅgayet́ kana, adọe bakhẽṛeta, Nẹ ińren oṛak̕ hoṛ, um sãohã ńutumte sea daka sea mạṇḍiń emam calam kanań, inạgem cẹrẹćke marańkeam. Adọ enka bakhẽṛ baṛakate ọtre dakae curuć baṛakata.

Adọ Jhõṛẽye emae kana, adọe bakhẽṛeta, Nẹ Jhõṛẽ bọkọń, um sãohã ńutumteń emam calam kanań. Adọ un jọkhẹćge Jhõṛẽ dọe mẹn gọtketa, Dẹn, ẹntẹm emań khan dọń hataoa.

Khange adọ Bạjune mẹnketa, Durrẹ! ińren boṅga dọko rọṛeta? Eṅgate bhala hoṛiń kuli ạgulekoge, onkoren boṅga dọko rọṛeta sẹ bhala bańa. Onka bujhạu baṛakate Bạjun dọ hoṛ kuk̕liye calaoena. Adọe kuliyetkoa, Henda ho, aperen boṅga dọko rọṛa sẹ bańa? Ińren boṅga dọ eṅgateko rọṛet́ kana. Khange adọko metae kana, Aleren dọ bako rọṛtalea.

Adọ ọntẹ kuk̕liye sẹn akan jọkhẹćge Jhõṛẽ dọ dạuṛạ daka ar celań utui dipilketteye ạtkirketa; adọ ạḍi sạṅgińre idikateyẹ jọjọm kana. Adọe jọm biyenkhan dọe họhọyeta, Nẹ yoi hoṛtenko, birtenko, dạuṛạ daka celań utupe jọm khan. Onka adọ cur mare họhọyeta. Khange adọ kombṛo hoṛ kombṛoe lạgit́ ona sẹćteko calak̕ kan tahẽkana, adọko ańjọmketa uniak̕ họhọ. Adọ khange uni ṭhenko calaoena; adọko metae kana, Cetem họhọale kana?

[19] When Santals kill goats, sheep or pigs for eating, they do not flay them, but singe all hairs off, and then cut the flesh into small pieces.

[20] The heads of sacrificed animals are not eaten with the other flesh, but cooked with rice, as here, and eaten, sometimes by the sacrificer alone, sometimes by him and other men also, never, however, by women.

[21] The Santali oṛak̕ hoṛ, lit, house-person, house-Santal, is mostly used about the wife, as here; it may, however, also be used about the husband, by the wife, or by others in relation to the wife.

[22] The invocation here quoted is far from complete according to the usual ritual. The expression 'rotten rice, rotten food', is, however, always used in the invocation to the dead ones. It is meant to show humility and self-abasement.

particular day come, people tell, and, having mounted to the cross-beam, was sitting there, and was staring at his brother, seeing all he was doing.

When Bajun had singed[19] and cut all to pieces, he prepared curry and rice. One small basket full of rice he prepared, and one cooking-pot full of curry, and the heads of the animals he cooked together with rice[20] in a cooking-pot, whereupon he proceeded to offer that rice-hash and uttered the following invocation: "Here, my house-person[21], for the purpose of purification I am giving thee, handing thee rotten rice, rotten food; mayest thou like it, deem it excellent." Having offered this invocation[22] he put some handfuls of rice down on the ground here and there.

Thereupon he did the same to Jhore and uttered this invocation: "Here, Jhore, my younger brother, for the purpose of purification I am giving thee, handing thee —." At that moment Jhore called out: "Give here, then; as you are giving it to me, I shall take it."

Then Bajun said: "Strange, do my bongas[23] speak? Dash it, let me go and ask people whether their bongas speak or not." Having considered this with himself Bajun went out to ask people about it. He asked them: "Look here, do your bongas speak, or do they not? My bongas, dash it, do speak." But they said to him: "Our bongas do not speak."

While Bajun had gone out to inquire, Jhore took the basket with rice and the cooking-pot with curry, put it on his head and carried it off, and having taken it a good distance he commenced to eat. When he had had his fill, he commenced to call out: "Here, ye wayfarers, foresters, if you will eat basket-rice and pot-curry." In this way he called out again und again. Now thieves[24] were just passing in that direction, and they heard his calling. So they went up to him and said: "What are you calling out to us for?"

23 According to Santal belief a dead Santal becomes a bonga, a spirit.

24 India has professional thieves of sorts, operating in companies. So apparently here.

Adoe mẹnketa, Daka jọm lagit iń họhọyeta, adọ iń hõpe gateyiń khan iń emapea. Adọko mẹnketa, Acha, gatemeale. Khange adọe ematkoa; adọko jọmketa, adọ uni salakge kombṛoko calaoena.

Adọ mittạń kisạṛ họṛak oṛakko bhugạkketteko bolọyena; adọ onko kombṛo dọ thạri bạṭiko ar caolekoko ńam baṛayeta; ar nui Jhõṛẽ dọ tumdake ṭamḍao ńamketa; adọ onage cur mare ruru kan. Adọ khangeko disạ gọtketkoa, adọko lagaketkoa.

Adọ pharakre dọko ruhetede kana, adọko metae kana, Nui heṅglage thọe laga ocoyet bona, nui dọ babo gateyea. Adọe mẹnketa, Acha, bape gateyiń khan dọ dạuṛạ daka ẹmkatińpe. Adọko mẹnketa, Acha ya, gatemegeale.

Khange adọ mitṭen Ḍọm oṛakreko bolọyena, adọ khange noko dọ jọmakko ńam baṛayetkhan nui dọ ḍhọl ńamkate onae ruru kan. Adọ ọnḍẹ hõko disạketkoteko lagaketkoa. Adọ onkage arhõko ruhetede kana, Nui heṅglage thọe laga ocoyetbona; heṅglage, babo gateyea. Adọe metako kana, Dẹn ẹnḍẹkhan dạuṛạ daka ar celań utu ẹmkatińpe. Khange adọko mẹnketa, Acha ya, gatemegeale.

Khange adọ mittạn Deko kisạṛ oṛakreko calaoena, ar uni kisạṛren dọ mit gọṛa sadọm menakkotaea. Adọko mẹnketa, Sadọmgebo kombṛokoa, ẹnḍẹkhan dẹckate nãhãkbo calao gọdoka.

[25] The house walls, being generally mud-walls, are easily holed, the thieves having special implements made for the purpose.

[26] The drum here mentioned is the Santal dancing-drum.

[27] The Dom caste is one of the lowest Hindu castes; they support themselves in several ways. To a Santal a Dom is about equivalent to a 'musician', the Doms being hired to do what is wanted as regards drumming, playing the cymbals and the flute, especially at marriages. According to our ideas they do not produce music, only noise, the object often being only to make other people know that something grand is going on. A very common name for a Dom among the Santals is kukuć ṭheṅga, crooked stick, the name of their peculiarly shaped drumstick, with which the Doms belabour their drums.

"I am calling out, inviting people to eat, and if you will let me also be one of your company, I shall give you." "All right," they said, "we shall take you along with us." So he gave them, and they ate, and together with him they went to steal.

Having made a hole in the wall of a house[25] belonging to a wealthy man, they entered; now the thieves sought for brass plates and cups and rice, and Jhoře, groping with his hands in the dark, found a drum[26], and this he commenced to beat energetically. The people then became aware of them and drove them away,

When they had reached some distance, they scolded him and said to him: "This stupid rascal, it is due to him that we are driven away; we shall not take him with us any more." "All right," he said, "if you do not take me along with you, give me back my basket full of rice." "Very well then, you," they replied, "we shall take you along."

They thereupon entered the house of a Dom[27], and while the others were searching for food, Jhore found a big drum[28] and commenced to play this. Consequently the people there also became aware of them and drove them away. They again scolded him in the same way: "This stupid rascal, it is due to him that we are driven away; this stupid rascal, we shall not take him along with us." "Come then," he said to them, "give me back my basket full of rice and my pot full of curry." "Very well then, you," they replied, "we shall take you along."

Thereupon they entered the house of a wealthy Hindu, who had a cow-shed full of cows and a stable full of ponies. "Let us steal ponies," they said; "then we may mount these and get away quickly."

---

[28] The drum mentioned, called ḍhọl, is a large thing, made of wood, mostly of the Jack tree (Artocarpus integrifolia, L.), because this is said not to crack. The ends are covered with leather.

Khange sạri onka mẹn baṛakate adọ sadọm goṛa kuḍạm sẹnko calaoena. Khange noko dọ bhage bhage sadọmko bachaoketkoa, ar uni Jhõṛẽ dọ, kathae, sadọm jọmko lạgit mitṭaṅ kul ona goṛa kuḍạmregeye tãṛãk akan tahẽkana, adọ uni kulge, kathaeye tọl gọtkedea. Adọko kupuli baṛayena, Cele ya, ṅam baṛawanape?

Adọ sanam hoṛko mẹnketa, Hẽle ṅawana. Adọko mẹnketa, Delabo tiạk ondoṅkotebo dẹjoka.

Khan sạri adọko tiạk oḍokketkoa, adọko dẹć gọtena arko kãmsaoetkoa. Adọ Jhõṛẽ hõ uni dọ sadọm mẹnkategeye dẹć akana. Adọ khange kamsaoe jọkhẹć dọ birteye ạtkir aderkedea. Adọ un jọkheć uni Jhõṛẽ dọe mẹneta, Hoṛte, Deko sadọm, hoṛte, Deko sadọm. Khange birteye ạtkir aderkedea jạnum jhõṇḍ sẹćte, adọe ạtkir gọćkedea. Adọ cabayena katha dọ.

---

29 Lit. to the road, or along the road.

There are several variants of this story. There is a story of two brothers called Kãṛã and Gujạ, which may possibly contain some reminiscences of life in the forests. One of these stories (I have several variants) has got the last portion of the story of Jhore attached, from the point when Jhore had scalded his sister-in-law to death.

In another variant, where no names are given, we are told of two brothers and their mother. Here the younger brother is told to cook three pạ i and three pawa, that is to say, three pints and three half-pints, and to prepare egg-plant curry (the egg-plant is a very common Indian vegetable, a sister-plant to the tomato). He puts the measures in, and instead of the fruit he pulls the whole plant up and boils this. There is nothing told about the ploughing; but part of the story presupposes that he had cut the tendons of the leg of one bullock. Instead of the elder brother's wife it is here their mother that he washes with boiling water after having put her on a flat rock. In this way he kills her. The elder brother then pursues the other with a pitch-fork. The younger one had in the meantime been somewhere where they had slaughtered a bullock, and when he saw his brother coming after him,

Having spoken in this way they, truth to tell, went to the back of the stable. Now these other ones picked out the best ponies, while Jhore — now a tiger was lying in wait there at the back-side of the stable to eat a pony — he, so people tell, tied this tiger. Thereupon they conferred together: "How is it, fellows, have you procured any?"

All of them answered: "Yes, we have." "Come then," they said, "let us lead them out and mount."

Then, truth to tell, they led the ponies out, mounted quickly and galloped off. Now Jhore also had mounted his pony, or what he thought was a pony. But when he made him gallop, he took him off to the forest. At that moment Jhore called out: "The road[29], Hindu horse! The road, Hindu horse!" But his horse took him right into the forest towards a thorn-tree thicket. And in that way he killed him.

So the story is ended.

---

he ran away, taking the bullock's stomach along, and crept into a jackal's hole. The elder brother poked at him with the pitch-fork, and the younger one managed to get part of the bullock's stomach attached to the fork, and the other naturally believed that the had killed his brother. The elder brother thereupon calls the village people together, tells his story and cremates his mother's corpse. When they had returned, the elder brother proposed that they should have the b h a ṇ ḍ a n, the final funeral rites, at once, giving as his reason that the younger brother had damaged his bullock, and so they might kill this and perform the b h a ṇ ḍ a n for both mother and brother with this bullock. This was done, and while the elder brother uttered the invocation, the younger one called out to him to give him his portion. Very much as in the story told, only that the village people are present and all are dumbfounded by the speaking of the supposed dead man. He makes off with the rice and the curry, reaches the forest and calls out, as told. This variant ends here; it has nothing about the company of thieves and the rest.

26. Mitʼṭaṅ lelha kala hoṛ reaṅ.

Sedae do̠, kathae, Ho̠ṛ ho̠po̠n do̠ ạḍi lelhako tahẹ̃kana, ar Deko ho̠po̠n do̠ ạḍiko bo̠to̠rako kan tahẹ̃kana. Ona pạrịarege, kathae, uni lelha ho̠ṛ hõe tahẹ̃kana. Ado̠ mitʼṭaṅ goḍa ṭạṇḍireye siokʼ kan tahẹ̃kana, ar uni siokʼ ṭhen ho̠r do̠ docaṅgagea, o̠ṇḍe do̠ barea ho̠r hạṭiń akana. Ado̠ mitʼṭaṅ Deko ho̠r ho̠rteye hẹćena uni ho̠ṛe siokʼ kan ṭhen. Ado̠ khangeye kuliyede kana, Hã hõ, mạńjhi, ye rasta kidhạr jaega? aur ye rasta kidhar jaega?

Ado̠ khange uni ho̠ṛ do̠e haemoekaṭena, ado̠e mẹnketʼa, Nui Dekoge cetʼe mẹnetʼa? Nui ḍaṅgra ińren, nui ḍaṅgra ińren! Tis eṅgate amren ḍaṅgra do̠le ạgu akatʼkina, onate onka do̠m metań kana?

Khange ado̠ uni Deko do̠ o̠ṇḍẹgeye duṛupʼena, ar ona kathage ghạṛi ghạṛiye kuliyede kana, ado̠ bae bujhạuetʼ khan, ar baṅkhan tãhã ho̠re kuliyede kana, Henda mạńjhi, noa ho̠r do̠ okate calakʼa, ar noa ho̠r do̠ okate? Ado̠ ona katha do̠ bae bujhạuetʼa. Ado̠ ghạṛi hõ ghạṛiye mẹnetʼa, Tis amren ḍaṅgra do̠le ạgu akatʼkina? Nui ma jo̠m daka kane, ar nui ma jạituk kane. Tis amren do̠le ạgu akatʼkina?

Khange arhõe kuliyede kana, Hã hõ, mạńjhi, ye rasta kidhar jaega?

---

[1] Deko is a name for Hindus; sometimes Muhammedans may be included, but this is not the regular use. The word refers more to race than to religion.

[2] The Santals have three kinds of agricultural land, the rice-fields, the homestead fields and the class of land here mentioned, in Santali called goḍa. This kind of land is used for the cultivation of the so-called jungle corns. It is high-lying, generally some distance away from the village, and is never manured. The cereals here harvested serve to carry the less well-to-do people through a couple of months towards the end of the rainy season, when they have difficulty in getting food-stuffs from the money-lenders. These cereals have, according to what Santals tell, one special quality to recommend them: the money-lenders do not think it worth while to take them for debt.

[3] The Deko speaks Hindi.

26. THE STORY OF A STUPID DEAF MAN.

FORMERLY, people tell, the Santals were very stupid and were in great fear of the Dekos[1]. At that time, they say, this stupid man was also living. One day he was ploughing an outlying high-land[2] field; and where he was ploughing, there was a cross-road, the road bifurcated there. Just then a Deko came along the road to where the man was ploughing. He asked[3] him: "Höre mal, Hauptmann[4], wohin geht dieser Weg? und wohin geht dieser Weg?"

The Santal became utterly dumbfounded and said: "This Deko, what does he say? This bullock is mine, this bullock is mine. When have we, dash it, brought any bullocks of yours, since you are talking in such a way to me?"

The Deko then sat down there and asked him the same question over and over again, since he did not understand him; otherwise[5] he was asking him about the way, viz.: "Look here, headman, where does this road go, and where does this go?" Now the Santal did not understand it, wherefore he again and again repeated: "When did we bring your bullocks? This one is my wife's dowry from her father, and this one is his dowry to me[6]. When did we bring your bullocks?"

The Deko again asked him: "Höre mal, Hauptmann, wo geht dieser Weg hin?"

---

[4] The word used addressing the Santal, mạńjhi, is the appellative used by foreigners to Santals, also of them, as e. g. Dhunu Mạńjhi, Dhunu Santal. Among the Santals the word is used about a village headman, and about a couple of other persons in authority.

[5] The narrator goes out of his way to explain to those who may not understand Hindi what the Deko had said.

[6] The two words translated 'dowry' signify gifts from the bride's father given at the time of marriage, the first, jom daka, given to the bride, the other, jạituk, given to the bridegroom, always calfs.

Adǫ khange uni hoṛe mẹn gǫda, Nui ma jǫm daka kane, ar nui ma jạituk. Adǫ khange uni Deko hõ bae bujhạuetʼte ghạṛi ghạṛigeye kuliyede kana.

Khange adǫ uni hoṛ dǫ bẹbạṛiće bǫtǫrokʼ kana; adǫ ać mǫnẹreye mẹnjoṅ kana, Durrẹ! nią sorkore ǫkǫe hõ bạnukʼkoa. Nui Deko dǫ dhorage nãhãkʼ teheṅ dǫe dal gǫjeṅa. Mẹn iṅ ẹm dapoṛaea. Ar uni hoṛ dǫ kala hõe kala machagea. Ar noa hõe bujhạuketʼa: Pasẹtʼ nuiren ḍaṅgrage jǫm daka ar jạituk dǫko ẹm akawatʼle, pasẹne ṅẹl oromketʼkin.

Onka bujhạu baṛakate adǫ banar ḍaṅgrae aṛakʼketʼkina, ar ona joteteye joṛaketʼkina; adǫe laga gǫtʼadea are metae kana, Nukin idi dapoṛkinme. Enan khon eṅgateye ạris laṛaokidiṅa, ią Dekoge. Ma idi dapoṛkinme.

Adǫ khangeye laga idiade khan, uni Deko hõe bujhạu gǫtʼketʼa, baṅma, Nukin ḍaṅgra dǫ iṅgeye emaṅ kana. Khange adǫe berẹtʼ gǫtʼente unkin ḍaṅgra dǫe laga idiketʼkina. Thoṛa sạṅgiṅ hạbić dǫ bẹṅgẹtʼ ruạṛ bẹṅgẹtʼ ruạṛtegeye lagaketʼkina; adǫ bire danaṅ ṅõkʼen khan, ạḍi ãṭ adǫe khudạuketʼkina.

Ar uni hoṛ dǫ ǫnḍẹgeye duṛupʼ jạhpuṅ thirena. Adǫ ona jǫkhẹćge uniren eṅgat buḍhi baskeakʼ dakʼ mạnḍiye ạguadea. Ar uni buḍhi hõe kạligea. Adǫ dakʼko dạtạunikoe emadea; adǫ uni koṛa hõe dạtạuni hutum baṛayen khan, dakʼ mạnḍiye emadea. Adǫ un jǫkhẹć uni koṛa dǫ eṅgattẹtʼe lạiae kana, Ẹ gǫ, okaren

7 Strange as it may seem to others, this frightened attitude may be observed in Santals having suddenly to face a stranger of a superior race.

8 The story shows the estimation in which Santals may hold the Dekos.

9 When the Santals are out working in their fields some distance away from their home, some female or other of the household generally carries food out to the workers. The first meal in the morning is generally what is left over from the foregoing day's evening meal (therefore called baskeakʼ, cold and stale). The time is somewhere about 9 o'clock in the forenoon, this hour being called baskeakʼ ber, time for cold food. There is naturally nothing to prevent them from preparing warm food for this meal; but whatever is done, it is generally only rice or a kind of rice-soup that is served.

The Santal replied: "This one is my wife's dowry from her father, and this one is his dowry to me." As the Deko did not understand, he asked the same question over and over again.

The Santal then became awfully frightened[7] and said to himself: "O dear, here in the vicinity there are no people anywhere. This Deko will certainly beat me and kill me. Better give them to him and be done with him." Now this Santal was also somewhat deaf, and he also thought something like this: "Perhaps it is this one's bullocks they have given us as dowries, he has perhaps recognized them."

Having come to this conclusion he loosed both bullocks from the yoke and joined them together with the yoke-rope. Thereupon he drove them over to him and said: "Take these two away and be gone with you. The whole morning, dash it, he has been worrying and harrassing me, this unspeakable Deko. Take them away and be gone with you."

When he drove the bullocks over to him, the Deko on his side caught the meaning of what he did, viz., he is giving me these two bullocks. So he instantly got up and drove the two bullocks away. Until he reached some distance away, he was driving them, constantly looking back; but as soon as he was hidden by the forest, he commenced to drive them as quickly as he could[8].

Now the Santal sat down there, looking quietly in front of himself and doing nothing. At that time his mother came to him with his breakfast[9]. Now this woman was also deaf. She gave him water and a tooth-brush[10], and when the young man had brushed his teeth and rinsed his mouth, she gave him the food. At that time the young man told his mother, saying: "Mother, a Deko

[10] The Santals are very careful to rinse their mouths before eating; they always brush their teeth with a twig of the sal-tree at least once daily, and will not take any food before this is done.

Deko cọe hẹćlen; adọe mẹneťa, kathae, Nukin ḍaṅgra dọ, mạñjhi, iṅren kanakin. Cedaǩpe ạgu akaťkina? Nukin dọkin iṅren kana. Ar iṅ dọń metae kana, Amren dọkin baṅ kana, Deko, miť dọe jọm daka kana, ar miť dọe jạituk kana. Onkań metadea; adọ ẹnre hõ bae bataoeťa, nọṇḍẹgeye duṛup̌ena. Adọ ạḍiye jidkeť khan dọ raṛakateń joṛa gọťadea.

Khange adọ uni eṅgat buḍhi dọe mẹneťa, Ọkọe baḍae, bạbu, bạhuge ẹnteye sajao gọťadiṅa, baṅdọe buluṅať, baṅdo baṅ; ẹnte rẹťre dọ bae emadiṅa.

Tin dhao uni koṛae rọṛeťa, un dhaoge nui eṅgat buḍhi hõ ona kathageye rọṛeťa. Ghane hõ ghaneye mẹneťa, Ọkọe baḍae, bạbu, bạhuge ẹnteye sajaoadiṅa, baṅdọe buluṅať, baṅdọ baṅ. Ma enkate baṛẹ jọmkaǩme.

Khangeye jọm cabakeť khan dọ bạṭi celaṅkoe sajaokeťte oṛaǩteye hẹćena. Adọ uni buḍhiren haṛamtẹť dọ oṛaǩ mutul sẹnre toke lalaǩ kan tahẽkana. Adọ uni buḍhi dọ sẹṭẹr torage haṛamtẹťe lạiae kana, Bạbu teheń dọ bogeteye ruheťkidiṅa. Bạhuge ẹnte daǩ mạṇḍiye sajaoadiṅa, baṅdọe buluṅať baṅdọ baṅ, rẹt hõ bae rẹť gọťadiń khan. Onate bogeteye ruheťkidiṅa.

Khange uni haṛame rọṛ gọťkeťa, Ọkọe baḍae, toktam cọṅ ukhuṛtam cọṅ. Ar sẹ uni haṛam hõe kalagea. Adọ onka uni buḍhi dọ ạḍiye lại baṛayeťa. Khange adọ uni haṛam dọ ạḍi garteye rọṛ gọťkeťa, Họkọ baḍae, toktam cọṅ ukhuṛtam cọṅ. Iṅ dọ alom ạṛisiṅa.

---

11 Observe the way in which she speaks about her son and daughter-in-law. What is here translated 'my son' lit. means 'boy', or 'young man'.

12 Lit. daughter-in-law; it would be against custom to say 'your wife', or to use the name.

13 The old man is angry; it is no business of his wife's to make any remarks on what he is doing. The story states that he is making a tok, a large wooden pestle with an iron ring at one end. This pestle is used with what in Santali is called ukhuṛ, a large wooden mortar. These implements are found in every Santal household and are used to husk and clean paddy and rice and to make flour. Now-a-days the ḍhiṅki, a rice-husking machine, worked with the foot,

from somewhere came a while ago and was saying: "These two bullocks, headman, are mine." And I kept on saying to him: "they are not yours, Deko; one of them is my wife's dowry from her father, and one is his dowry to me." I told him this, but still he did not give in, and he sat down here. As he was so very persistent, I loosed the bullocks and joined them with the yoke-rope and gave them to him."

His mother then said: "How can I know, my son?[11] You see, my daughter-in-law[12] arranged everything and handed it to me, I don't know whether she has salted it or not; she did not give me any salt wrapped up."

Every time the young man spoke, the old woman always said the same. Again and again she said: "How can I know, my son, as my daughter-in-law arranged and handed it to me, whether she salted it or not? Do eat it as it is, please."

When he had finished eating, she put the cups and pots into the basket and came home. At that time her husband was occupied at the extremity of the house, paring a wooden pestle. As soon as the old woman arrived, she said to her husband: "Our boy scolded me a good deal to-day. You see, our daughter-in-law put the food into the basket and handed it to me, so I don't know whether she had salted it or not; anyhow she did not give me salt in a wrapper to take along. Therefore he scolded me so much."

Then the old man answered back: "Who knows, may be it is your pestle[13], may be it is your mortar." Now this old man was deaf also. The old woman tried several times to tell in this way. Then the old man called out in a loud voice: "Who knows, may be it is your pestle, may be it is your mortar. Don't worry me."

---

is generally introduced. The here mentioned pestle and mortar are, however, also often used. In some form or other these implements are found in many lands in the Tropics.

Khange adǫ uni budhi dǫ kimintęt́ ṭhene calaoena, ar uni kimintęt́ hõe kạligea; adǫ pinḍạreye takkoe kan tahẽkana. Adǫ uni ṭhen sęnkateye lạiae kana, Henda bạhu, dak mạṇḍi dǫben buluṅaťa sę baṅa? Teheń dǫ koṛa bogeteye ruheťkidiṅa; ręťre hõ baben kolatliń khan, sabakṭegeye jǫmkeťa. Ona kathage hęćkate ạpumliń lạiae kan khać dǫ uni hõ rukheťgeye chuṭạuk kana.

Adǫ uni kimintęt́ dǫe rǫṛ gǫťketa, Ǫkǫ baḍae, gǫ, cet́ leka cǫliń takoyet́, ḍambak cǫṅ ḍombok cǫliń cuṛạ dorokkak kana.

Onka lekate onko kạli kala hǫṛren ḍaṅgrakin calaoena, huni eṭagake rǫṛ khan, nhui dǫ eṭagak. Onka lekate onko hǫṛ dǫko ręṅgęćena.

Inạkgea katha dǫ.

27. Lelha jãwãe gomket reaṅ.

Sedae jugre, kathae, mitṭaṅ hǫṛren hǫpǫnerat jãwãe gomkete tahẽkana mitṭaṅ atore. Adǫ mit́ dhao, kathae, ać eskarge hǫṅhar hanhar oṛakte sę nạihạrte, peṛa hǫṛǫke sęnlen tahẽkana. Adǫ unre uni hanhartęt́ budhi dǫe daka utuyeťa, ar uni tuluć hõe galmarao kana. Adǫ enka baṛaetege ạyupena.

Adǫ unre uni budhi dǫ hạṇḍuạye utuleťa, adǫ daka utukate dake taṅadea daka jǫm lạgit́. Ar silpiń aṛe sęnrege gaṇḍo dǫe

[14] She is working the spinning-wheel. The Santal form of this is much heavier and more cumbersome than the spinning-wheel now famous in India.

[15] Parents-in-law and children-in-law always use the exclusive dual about themselves when talking together and also address one another in the dual. The other party, the husband or wife, as the case may be, of the speaker or the person addressed is always included.

27 [1] The Santali expression literally means 'to become a friend, or a relative,' consequently to be treated a such.

[2] The word translated 'home' has in Santali (and in Hindi from which the word is borrowed) the meaning of a man's father-in-law's home. There is no word for 'home' except 'house'.

The old woman then went to her daughter-in-law, who also was deaf. She was occupied in the verandah spinning[14]. To her she went and said: "Look here, daughter-in-law, did you[15] salt the food or not? The boy scolded me a good deal to-day; you did not send any salt along in a packet either; he had to eat it unsalted. When I after my return said the same to your father-in-law, he also started scolding."

The daughter-in-law then answered back: "How can I say, mother, how I am spinning, whether it be rough or rugged, I am making a heap of it as best I can."

In this way the bullocks of these deaf people were lost. When that one spoke of something, this one was talking of something else. In this way these people became impoverished.

That much is the story.

27. THE STUPID SON-IN-LAW.

Once in olden times, it is told, there lived in a certain village a certain man's son-in-law. One day, they say, he had gone alone to visit[1] his father-in-law and mother-in-law in their home[2]. While there his mother-in-law was engaged in cooking curry and rice, and at the same time she kept up a conversation with him. In this way the evening fell.

Now the old woman had prepared some bamboo shoots[3] as curry; when she had done cooking, she poured out some water for him to wash his hands ere sitting down to eat, and placed a stool[4]

[3] The very young bamboo shoots are considered very savoury food, but are scarcely ever used in this way now-a-days, the bamboo being too valuable. The dish here mentioned, the h a ṇ ḍ u a, is prepared in a special way. The shoots are collected, cut up and pounded in a ḍ h i ṅ k i. The flour resulting is put into a pot, covered carefully up for three days, and then spread on something hard, to dry. It may then be kept, and is used for curry.

[4] The 'stool' is here a piece of wood, cut flat, anything from some six to eight inches up to some fifteen inches long, some six inches broad and three to four inches high. It suits the Santals, who do not like to sit on anything high.

beladea. Adǫ ạbuk bǫlǫkate ona gaṇḍoreye duṛup̕en khan dǫ daka utui ạguadea. Adǫ jǫm jǫkhẹn uni jãwãe gomket dǫ jel utu lekae ạikạuet̕a, ar kuṭi sẹ bae ńamet̕a.

Khange adǫe kulikedea, Henda gǫ, cet̕ben utu akat̕a? Baliń ạtkar ṭhik daṛeak̕ kana. Adǫ uni jãwãe gomket dea sẹnre dǫ mat̕ silpińge tahẽkana.

Adǫ buḍhi dǫe mẹnket̕a, Ǫnẹ jãwãe, aben dea sẹnre menak̕, onageliń utu akat̕a.

Adǫ uni jãwãe gomket dǫ bẹṅgẹt̕ ạcurkateye ńẹlket̕ dǫ, mat̕ silpiń kan. Adǫe ńẹl hapekat̕gea, cet̕ hõ bae rǫṛlet̕a, ar uni buḍhi hõe inạk̕kat̕gea.

Khange uni jãwãe gomket dǫ ać mǫnẹ mǫnẹteye mẹnjoṅ kana, Noa utu dǫ ạḍi sebelkidińa; sanam hǫṛ nãhãk̕ko jạpit̕le khan, noa silpiń dǫń ạtkirgea. Onka ać mǫnẹreye hudis dǫhǫkat̕a.

Adǫ sạri jǫm baṛakateko jagayena. Adǫ sanam hǫṛko jạpit̕ket̕ khan dǫ, hape hapete beret̕ente ona silpiń dǫe raṛaket̕takoa, ar ona ńindạrege ona silpiń dǫe gugu ạtkirket̕takoa. Adǫ un jǫkhẹn dǫ bako disạledea.

Adǫ setak̕ sim rak̕ jǫkhẹnko ẹbhẹnen dǫko ńẹl baṛayet̕, silpiń dǫ bạnuk̕. Ar uni jãwãe gomketko hǫhǫae kan dǫ bae gǫṅet̕ kan. Adǫko mẹnket̕a, Masẹ ńẹlepe, bhala menaea sẹ baṅ; bae gǫṅet̕ dǫ. Adǫ sạriko ńẹl baṛakede khan dǫ bạnugićan.

Khange adǫ uni buḍhi hǫṛ dǫ ạḍi garteye landa gǫt̕ket̕a. Adǫ onko hǫpǫntẹt̕ kuṛi dǫko kulikedea, Henda gǫ, cet̕ un garte dǫm landaket̕a?

---

[5] The dual is used; see p. 26, note 15.

[6] It is quite in accordance with Santal custom to avoid giving the proper name to anything mentioned. They prefer a veiled hint.

[7] The door of a Santal house is generally a very simple thing, anything tied together, large enough to fill the door-opening. Sometimes it is made of straw, tied to saplings, sometimes it may be plastered over with mud. The door is fastened at the top and bottom to a pole fixed in the ground, just sufficient to keep it in position. It is easily removed; it cannot be closed securely. Now-a-days

for him near the door. When he had washed his hands and come in again, he sat down on the stool, and she brought him the curry and rice. Whilst eating the son-in-law thought it was meat curry he had; but he did not find any lumps.

So he asked his mother-in-law, "I say, mother, what kind of curry have you[5] prepared? I cannot make out exactly what it is." Now there was the bamboo door at the back of the son-in-law.

So the old woman said, "Look there what is at the back of you, my son-in-law, that is what I have made into curry[6] for you."

So the son-in-law turned round and saw it was a bamboo door; but looking he kept quiet and said nothing; and the old woman too said thus much and nothing more.

The son-in-law, however, thought in his mind: "I find this curry perfectly delicious; when every one is asleep presently, I shall walk off with this door." This he made up his mind to do.

True enough, when all had done eating, they retired for the night, and when every one had fallen asleep, he got up quietly and loosened the door[7], and that very night he took their door on his back and walked off with it, nobody being aware of it at the time the deed was done.

When they awoke at cockcrow in the morning and looked about, there was no door to be seen; and when they called out for the son-in-law, there was no answer. So they said: "Look and see if he is there or not; he doesn't answer." They looked about for him, but he was not there.

Then the old woman suddenly burst out into a loud laugh, whereupon her daughters said to her: "Why, mother, what are you laughing so heartily at?"

---

more well-to-do Santals have introduced more substantial doors. It is a curious fact that many have very elaborate doors made for them, with carvings, panels and so on. This is for show, taking the place of elaborate furniture. Such doors are one of the first things a creditor will seize in default of payment of debts.

Adọ unre uni buḍhiye lạiako kana, Noa silpiń dọ na, teńamge dhorae ạtkir akaťa. Holanoḱ hạṇḍuạń utuadea; adọ unreye mẹnleťa, Henda gọ, ceťben utu akaťa? Baliń aṭkar ṭhik daṛeaḱ kana. Adọ unreń metadea, Ọnẹ jāwāe, aben dea sẹnre menaḱ, onaliń utu akaťa. Adọ pasẹn onate silpiń dọ pasẹn teńamgeye ạtkirkeť.

Adọ onae lạiaťko khan dọ, sanam họṛ adọ ạḍi bạṛićko landakeťa, arko mẹnkeťa, Nui teńań dọ ạḍiye lelhagea.

Adọ sạri uni lelha họṛ dọ idikate ona silpiń dọe raṛa dhiṅgạl saṅgalkeťte miť miťte jọtọe samaḱ kuṭrạkeťa; adọ ać bạhui metae kana, Ma noage teheń dọ utuime.

Adọ uniye mẹnkeťa, Noa dọ ceť lekań utuia? Noa rọhọṛ mať dọ sebela? Noa do bań sebela. Am dọ ạḍim lelhagea.

Adọ unre uni dọe mẹn ruạṛkeťa, Bańa, ạḍi mõ̱ńj sebela. Holanoḱ ayoteko ṭheniń sẹnlena, unre noageko utuadiń dọ bań? Ceť bań sẹ, jel utu lekań ạikạukeťa. Onate noa dọń ạtkir akaťtakoa, bako ẹmoḱ kan iạte.

Adọ bạhutṭẹťe mẹnkeťa, Noa rọhọṛ dọ ẹnte ọkọe jọmtem utu ocoyedińa?

Adọe mẹnkeťa, Acha, apa bape jọm khan, ińge utuańpe.

Adọ sạri nokoaḱ katha bae sẹn ocoaťtako khanko utuadea, arko emadea daka sāote. Adọ sạri raseye dul gọťkeťa, adọ sipikateye lapeť gọťkeťa, ar uni bạhutṭẹť dọ tan mane ńẹle kana. Adọ ona rase tuluć bań sebelede khan dọ, kuṭi halańkateye gẹr gọťkeťa. Adọ ona hõ bae gẹr chaḍao daṛeať khan, uni bạhutṭẹť dọ landa bae sambṛaoleťte ạḍi garteye landa gọťkeťa. Adọ ać hõe landakeťa.

Then the old woman said to them: "Your elder sister's husband, girls, has most assuredly decamped with this door. Yesterday I made him a curry of bamboo shoots, and he asked me: 'I say, mother, what kind of curry have you prepared? I cannot make out exactly what it is.' Whereupon I said to him: 'Look there what is to the back of you, my son-in-law, that is what I have made into curry for you.' Perhaps that is why your elder sister's husband has carried off the door."

When she told them this, every one laughed very much and said: "This brother-in-law is dreadfully stupid."

True enough, when the stupid fellow had walked off with the door, he took the whole thing to pieces and chopped all of it into small bits. Then he told his wife: "Make this into curry to-day, please."

She replied: "How am I to make a curry of this? Will this dry bamboo taste well? Not a bit of it. You are very stupid."

He replied: "Not so, it is simply delicious. Yesterday I went to see your mother and the others there; then she made me some curry of this; you may not believe it, but I tell you, it tasted to me just like meat curry; and that is why I made off with this door of theirs, for they would not give it to me."

His wife said: "Who is then going to eat this dry stuff, that you want me to make curry of it?"

To which he replied: "All right, if you other people won't eat it, make some curry of it for me."

So, as he would not listen to her, she true enough made him some curry of it and gave it to him along with some boiled rice. Then he poured some of the gravy on it, and mixing it together with his hand he took a mouthfull, and all the while his wife was watching him closely. But as the rice and gravy did not taste particularly nice, he laid hold of a lump of the curry and gave it a bite; when he was unable even to bite a piece off, his wife, no longer able to restrain her mirth, burst into a loud laugh, in which he himself also joined.

Adoe meṅketa, Cet́ leka com utuket́? Bam batraoleta, onatege baṅ sebel kana. Cekate noa kuṭi do bam le ocoleta? Ayoe utuadiṅa, sanam kuṭiye le caba ocoleta; kuṭi do mit́ goṭen hõ baṅ ṅamleta. Am ma eken kuṭigem em akawadiṅa, ar cet́ lekaṅ kuṭilet́, enkagem dohokata; thoṛa hõ bam le ocoleta.

Ado bahuttete meṅketa, Iṅ do baṅ baḍaea noa utu do; amte baṛe utujoṅme.

Ado sari aćteye utuketre hõ baṅ lelen. Ado khange bogeteko landawadea; ado en hilok khon Lelhageko bahnakedea, ar ṅame picheko arisea, onageko metaea.

Ado cabayena katha do; in maraṅgea.

28. Kalu ar Laltekinak pagla galmarao.

Kalu do hoṛo rakab lagit́ kharaiye lalak kan tahẽkana. Un jokhenge Lalteko pe pon hoṛ birte kaṭ mag lagitko calak kana. Ado Kalui kharaiyet́ sentege hoṛ do sen akana; ado ona hoṛtege onko doko calak kana. Ar Kalu ar Lal do ḍhaulia sompok kantakina.

---

[1] The following is not, as will be seen, a folktale proper. It has, however, been recorded, because it gives a good example of how the Santals enjoy chaff and banter. Many years ago now, when I was one day pushing my bicycle along a very sandy road, I was accosted by a Santal, who was not quite sober. He was as eager to get into conversation with me, as I was to avoid a talk with a person in his state. The following was spoken. He: okaren kanam? (wherefrom are you?) Answer: you can see that; I am from Bilat (Europe). He: Hẽ do hẽge, meṅkhan nitok do okare menama? (Quite so, but where are you now?) Answer: You can see that also; I am here on the road. He: oka khonem hijuk kana? (where are you coming from?) I am coming from my home, he was told. Just then we had passed the heavy sand, and I mounted my bicycle; but the man came running after me all he could, he wanted to have more of this kind of talk.

Then he said: "What kind of a curry have you turned out? You have not succeeded, and therefore it is not savoury. How is it you have not dissolved this piece? Mother dissolved altogether every piece in the curry she gave me; I could not find a single lump in it, whereas you have given me nothing but lumps; you have got it in lumps just the same as when I cut them up; you have not dissolved them one bit."

Then his wife said: "I am not acquainted with this curry; you had better cook some for yourself."

And true enough, when he had cooked some for himself too, he could not get it to dissolve. Whereupon they had a good laugh at him. From that day forward he got the surname of 'Stupid', and by adressing him thus every time they met him they teased him well.

That is the end of the tale; it is so much.

28. KALU AND LAL'S QUIBBLING[1].

KALU was occupied paring a bit of ground for a threshing-floor[2], to have it to bring his paddy up there. Just then Lal and a couple of companions were on their way to the forest[3], to cut trees. The road was passing where Kalu was preparing the threshing-floor, and those mentioned were coming along this road. Now Kalu and Lal stood in the relationship to each other of brothers-in-law[4]. When

[2] A threshing-floor has to be prepared every year, and this is done in good time before the harvest commences. After some ceremonies the surface is pared, the soil is stamped hard and ultimately given a 'paint' with cow-dung.

[3] Formerly the Santal country was more or less covered with forest; now-a-days small patches are found here and there. The forest being the property of the zemindars, the villagers have no right without permission to cut trees that may be used for building or similar purposes. However, a Santal considers it his birthright to fell trees, in consequence of which there is very frequent trouble between the villagers and the representatives of the owners.

[4] These and some other relatives stand to each other in what is called l a n d a s a ̣ g a ̣ i, laughing relationship, that is to say, these relatives may jest and talk and be as free as they like; there is no formality and little restraint between them.

Khange uniko tiokkede khan Kạlu doe rọṛ goťkeťa, Okatepe helaoena ho, ṭạmbuć ṭạmbuć?

Khange Lal doe mẹn goťkeťa, Samaṅ sẹć.

Adọ Kạlui mẹnkeťa, Nuiak rọṛ ma eṅgate eṛṅga eṛṅgage.

Lale mẹnkeťa, Cekate eṛṅgagea? Samaṅ sẹn baṅkhan dea sẹnteko calaka? Ma bhala am dọ oka sẹntem calak kana, samaṅ sẹnte sẹ dea sẹnte?

Kạlui mẹnkeťa, Hẽ ma hẽge.

Lale mẹnkeťa, Sei bujhạume.

Khange Kạlui mẹnkeťa, Ceťpe mag lagiť?

Lal dọe rọṛ ruạṛadea, Kaṭle mag lạgiť.

Adọ Kạlui kulikedea, Okare?

Khange Lale ạcuradea, Phẹḍre.

Kạlu dọ rọṛkẹťa, Hẽ ya, hẽ, phẹḍ ma phẹḍregeko mag; adọ oka burure?

Khange Lal dọ ataṅ goťkeťa, Buru ma ẹnte bacọm kuliyediṅ kan, ẹkẹnem mẹneťa, Okarepe maga? Adọ ọnateṅ lạiam kana, phẹḍreko maga mẹnte.

Adọ inạko galmaraotege gạḍi sagaṛko laga ạgukeťa ona sẹntege, ar uni sagaṛ lakgaić dọ ọt ọttegeye calak kana. Adọ uni ṅẹlte Kạlu dọe mẹnkeťa, Henda ho, sagaṛre dẹćkate dọ cedak bam lagayeťkina? Ọt khon dọ ṅẹlme ọntẹ nọtẹ ạcurok hoyok kantama.

Khange Lale mẹn goťkeťa, Henda ya, am dọ ạḍi lelha họṛ kanam, am soman lelha dọ dhạrtire hõ bạnukkoa. Am dọ eṅgate ić hõ ić lelhage tama. Cekate orad dọ bạnuktama? Ṅẹl oradkate rọṛme sẹ. Am dọ ạḍi lelha họṛ kanam.

Adọ Kạlui mẹnkeťa, Henda ya, nunạk họṛ samaṅre bejãe rọṛ yam rọṛkidiṅ dọ. Ạḍitẹť lelhagem rikạkidiṅ dọ.

---

[5] The point cannot be fully rendered in English. One name of a wheel in Santali is sagaṛ, and the same word is also used about the common cart.

[6] The writer has often in village councils heard this not very elevated expression. There is nothing left out in the general estimation.

they reached him, Kalu asked: "Where are you bobbing off to in such a hurry?"

'Frontwards", Lal replied.

"The talk of this fellow, dash it," Kalu said, "is always perverse."

"How is it perverse?" asked Lal; "do people go backwards and not frontwards? You yourself, in which direction do you go, frontwards or backwards?"

"Yes, that is naturally so," Kalu said.

"Understand that then," Lal said.

"What are you going to cut?" Kala then asked.

"We are going to cut trees," replied Lal.

"Where?" asked Kalu.

"At the foot," Lal answered back.

"Yes, naturally," Kalu said; "people cut trees at the foot, I meant on which hill?"

"Why, you did not ask me anything about any hill," Lal retorted; "you only said: 'where are you going to cut?' Therefore I am telling you that they are going to cut at the foot."

Whilst they were talking together in this way, somebody was driving a bullock-cart in that direction, and the cart-driver was walking alongside. Seeing him Kalu said: "Look here, you, why don't you drive the bullocks sitting on the wheels?[5] You see, when-you drive walking, you have to come now to this side, now to that side."

Then Lal said: "Look here, you fellow, you are a very stupid person, in the whole world there is no stupid fellow compared with you. Dash it, even to your dirt you are a fool[6]. How is it that you have no judgment? Look and judge for yourself. You are an awfully stupid fellow."

"Look here, you," Kalu said, "you are rating me badly before so many people. You have made me out to be an awfully stupid person."

Adọ Lale mẹnketa. Hẽ, sạrige lelhaṅ mẹn daṛeama; ẹnte am dọ dare mamak̕ hõ nit dhạbić bam bạḍaea. Arhõ nui ma sagaṛre dẹjok̕em metae kana.

Adọ Kạlui mẹnketa, Sagaṛre baṅkhan okare ya dẹjok̕ iń metaea?

Adọ Lale mẹnketa, Sagaṛ ma ya guḍrạuk̕ kan, bam ńẹl ṭhiketa? Onare dọe dẹć ṭarhao daṛeak̕a? Ar dẹćlenre hõ ẹnte bae tẹn gujuk̕a? Masẹ bhala ńẹlme, guḍrạuk̕ kana sẹ baṅ?

Khange thọ Kạlu dọ bitkil lekae thirena, cet̕ hõ bae rọṛ daṛeata, mọnẹ mọnẹte ẹkẹn mulući mulućе landaketa ar uni sãotenko hõ jọtọgeko landaketa.

Adọ mit̕ họṛe mẹnketa, Nẹtar dọ candoe sesaoena, oka hilok̕kote cọṅ hapẹne dạṛa.

Adọ Kạlui mẹnketa, Henda ya, bhala nẹtar dọ okakore aṅgawae kana?

Khange Lal dọe mẹn gọtketa, Sermare ya aṅgawae kana. Am dọ inạ hõ ya bam bạḍae dọ? Tọbẹtege lelha dọlaṅ metam kana.

Khange adọ mit họṛe mẹnketa. Ẹ ho, ạḍi hạbijok̕ kana, delabon sẹn họdok̕a; galmarao dọ ọhọ cabalentabona. Ọnẹko mẹnge, Bọsle kọtha sutle sapọn. Jãhãm ńapamena mẹnkhan, baṅgem bhagao họdok̕a; mit̕ họṛe ẹhọb khan, mit̕ họṛe mucạt̕ idiyeta; arhõ mit̕ họṛe ẹhọp̕ idiyeta — nonkage galmarao dọ calao idik̕ kana. Delabo, arhõ nãhãk̕ tayọmte ruạṛ jọkhẹnbo galmaraoa.

Adọ sạri birteko calaoena. Adọ ọntẹrege okare cọṅ, kathae, mit̕ṭaṅ jambṛoko gọćkedẹa, ar uni jambṛo dọ jọmea mẹnte Lal

7 The Santal enjoys it; he does not take offence, knowing what the whole is meant to be.

8 The Santali expression literally means 'where does it dawn for her?' In Santali the sun is male and the moon female, and the stars are their children. Now-a-days the Santals are using either our months or, more commonly, the Bengali months. But the moon months play a great rôle. The phases of the moon are much more easily observed in India than in our northern latitudes and are reckoned with. They have several ways of showing the phases. During the last quarter the phase is generally described as here, by stating where the

"Yes," Lal replied, "in very truth I may call you stupid; why, even now you do not know how to cut trees, moreover you tell this man to mount the wheels."

"If I should not tell him to mount the wheels," Kalu asked, "where should I tell him to mount, you fellow?"

"The wheels turn round, you-fellow," Lal said, "can't you see that? Can he mount them and stay there? And if he mounted, would he not be crushed and killed? Why, look, they turn round, or don't they?"

Then Kalu became silent like a buffalo cow, he was unable to say a single word; he was only quietly smiling[7] to himself, and his companions also laughed, all of them.

Then one of them said: "The moon is now in its last phase, it will not be many days before we shall have a new moon."

"Listen, you," Lalu said, "I wonder whereabouts the sun finds her[8] in the morning?"

Lal at once replied: "In the sky, you fellow. You don't know even this? Therefore we naturally call you stupid."

Then one of them said: "Hallo, it is getting late, come along, let us go at once, otherwise we shall never have done with this kind of talk. As people say[9], 'Lass dich nieder: dann Gespräch; schlafe: dann Träume.' If you by any chance meet with somebody, you will not get away in a hurry; if some one commences, another will take it up and tell the end; then somebody else will commence something else, and in this way talk goes on. Come along; when we presently return, we may have more talk."

So truth to tell, they went to the forest. Somewhere there, they tell, they killed a jambro[10] snake, and Lal was bringing

moon was just before sunrise. They make use of the expression 'run', 'run off', about the change to new moon.

9 The speaker quotes a Bengali proverb.

10 Jambṛo is the Santali name for the Zamenis mucosus snake. It is non-poisonous. There are several kinds distinguished by the Santals. This snake may grow to a considerable size, two metres being very common; often it is more.

doe agu darayede kangea. Ado arhõ uni Kalu horteko tuluć ona kharai thengeko ńapamena, arhõ onka phukti kathagekin ehopketa. Khange Kalui men gotketa, Cele biń ya lawar lawarem kutuń akadea?

Ado Lale menketa, Oko badae ente, mase ńel oromem.

Adoe menketa, Iń do jambro lekań ńele kana. Am do cele biń com metae kan?

Ado uniye menketa, Jambro doe bań kana ya. Nui do buru ayańko metae kana; ente hatak lekae saroka.

Ado Kalui menketa, Okarepe goćledea?

Ado Lale men gotketa, Hotokrele dalledea.

Ado Kalui menketa, Okarepe ńamledea?

Ado Lale menketa, Aćak nij orakre.

Ado Kalui menketa, Ape do iako siń satup pharia baj kathagetape.

Ado Lale menketa, Bańa ho, ale do thikgele laiam kana, ma honeć bujtam; okam kuliyetlea, ona reakgele lai ruaram kana.

Ado Kalui menketa, Bań, apeak do thik katha do bań kana, enteń kuliyetpea, Nui biń do okarepe goćledea? Adom meneta, Hotokrele dalledea. Arhõń kuliyetpea, okarepe ńamledea mente, adope meneta, Aćak nij orakre. Ado noako ki katha kantapea? Biń do kokhono ki orak doko benaoeta? Onate thik katha do bań metak kantapea.

Ado Lale menketa, Thik bańkhan cet? Ńelme, hotokrele dalledetele goćkedea, ar bhugakrele ńamledea, ondegele goćkedea. Ona do kichu uniak orak do bań kana? Ma tobe amge lai bujhaualeme.

Khange Kalu do cet hõ bae ror dareata, thir utarenae; eken muluć muluće landawana, inage, ar bańkhan katha do bae ror

[11] This snake is, like the python, eaten by the Santals.

[12] A jambro may in jest be called so. There is some resemblance to a cobra in a jambro, and the one may be mistaken for the other, when seen at a distance. It is a common belief among the Santals that the jambro, or rather

this snake along with him in order to eat it[11]. Again they met with Kalu and his companions at that same threshing-floor, and the two again commenced the same kind of joking and bantering. Kalu said: "What kind of a snake, you fellow, are you carrying there bobbing up and down?"

"Who knows," Lal replied, "look and see yourself which it is."

The other said: "To me it looks like a jambro. What kind of a snake do you call it?"

"It is not a jambro, you fellow," Lal replied, "this they call hill-cobra[12]; you see, it raises its hood, big as a winnowing fan."

"Where did you kill it?" Kalu asked.

"We struck it in the neck," Lal replied.

"Where did you find it?" Kalu asked.

"In its own house," Lal replied.

"You unspeakable ones," Kalu said, "always you are twisting one's words and nothing else."

"Not at all," Lal replied, "it is absolutely correct what we are telling you; only understand what you say; we are answering what you are asking us, just that."

"No," Kalu said, "it is not correct what you say. I ask you: 'Where did you kill this snake?' Then you say: 'We struck it in the neck.' Again I ask you: 'Where did you find it?' and you say: 'In its own house.' Now what kind of talk is this of yours? Have you ever heard that snakes build houses? Therefore I do not say that your talk is right."

"It's right, else what is it?" Lal replied. "Look here, we struck it in the neck and killed it in that way; we found it in a hole; there we killed it. Is not that perhaps its house? So then you please explain it to us."

Then Kalu was unable to say anything; he was absolutely quiet; he was only laughing quietly to himself, that was all;

one special kind, breeds with the cobra. That a jambṛo should raise its hood like an angry cobra is a joke.

ruạṛ daṛeaťa. Adọ Lale mẹnkeťa, Oka hõ bam rọṛ ruạṛ daṛeaťa. Ma tọbẹ cun thamakur ẹmoǩtabonme.

Adọe mẹnkeťa, Achaṅ ẹmoǩa. Adọ thamakure ẹmente miť họṛ dọe beǩnao kantakoa. Adọ inạǩtege miťṭaṅ gupi koṛa dọ kaḍae laga ạguketǩoa; adọ onko kaḍa mọtọre barea dọ khub moṭakin ṅẹloǩ kana. Adọ unkin kaḍa ṅẹlte Kạlu dọe mẹn gọťkeťa, Nukin kaḍa dọ khubkin moṭa akana.

Adọ Lale mẹn gọťkeťa, Ẹnte ho moṭa baṅkhankin cekaǩa? Ente nukin dọ goṭa ṭạṇḍikin daṛan kana, onatekin moṭa akana. Am hõ goṭa ṭạṇḍi daṛanme thọ, nukin lekage nāhāǩem moṭaǩa.

Adọ inạre hõ Kạlu dọ baṅgeye rọṛ ruạṛ daṛeaťa; adọko thir baṛayena. Adọ ẹnẹ oṛaǩteko calao baṛayena, apan ạpinenako.

Adọ ẹnẹ noa katha dọ ẹṇḍẹgeṅ mucạťkaťa.

29. Miťṭaṅ raj ar guṅgạ họṛaǩ katha.

Sedae jugre, kathae, oka ọktẹ cọṅ miťṭaṅ khub maraṅ kisạṛ raje tahẽkana, ar uni eskarge goṭa disom kathaeye dọkhọl akať tahẽkana. Ar uniren dọ ạḍi utạr gại kaḍa, mẹrọm bhiḍi, hạti, sadọm, ũṭ, gadhako tahẽkantaea; ar sor sipạhi hõ, ạḍi utạr laskarko tahẽkantaea, ar amla kapla, dewan mosodi, bẹtọṅ bẹtọṅre jọtọge menaǩ idikoa. Ar dhọnte hõ purun menaete uni raj dọ ać mọnre ạḍi

13 The Santals use tobacco, mostly chewing it. A bit of a dried leaf is crushed in the hand with the right thumb or the end of a stick and mixed with unslaked lime prepared from mussels. When all is properly mixed, the 'preparant' puts a pinch of it into the right hand of every one present. The stuff is popped into the mouth and chewed, being ultimately spat out. When Santal men meet and they want to get into a talk, the first thing they do is to ask for tobacco, even if they have some themselves. This company-chewing of tobacco is enjoyed; it is one of their social amenities. They have no peace-pipe, but a peace-quid.

29 1 Kings mentioned in these tales are landlords, ordinarily called zemindars. They own the land and generally make use of their position as feudatory chiefs to their utmost ability. Very often the property is shared by several; this naturally

otherwise he was unable to utter a single word. "You are not able to answer anything," Lal said. "So please give lime and tobacco to us[13] all."

"All right," he said, "I shall give." Consequently he gave the tobacco, and one of them prepared it. While they were occupied with this, a herding boy came, driving some buffaloes along; among the buffaloes two were looking very fat and plump. Seeing those two buffaloes Kalu said: "Those two buffaloes are very fat and plump."

"Yes," said Lal, "what else should they be, if not fat? They are wandering about everywhere; therefore they have become fat. You also, wander about everywhere; then you also will become like these two presently."

To this also Kalu had nothing to answer, and so they left off talking, whereupon they went home, every one to their own.

So there I have brought this story to an end.

29. THE STORY OF A KING AND A DUMB MAN.

In olden times, who knows when, people tell, there was living an exceedingly wealthy king; he was alone in possession of the whole country[1], it is said. He had a multitude of cows and buffaloes, goats, sheep, elephants, horses, camels and donkeys[2]; a body-guard he also had, very numerous, and writers and peons, ministers and personal attendants, each in their several capacities, all were there[3]. And as he had enough wealth to satisfy him,

---

gives less power and less income. In the case here mentioned it is expressly stated that the 'king' owns the whole land.

2 All kinds of domesticated animals are mentioned. It gives the Santal idea of wealth.

3 The description given is intended to show how great the 'king' was. Such a king must naturally have a body-guard, if these servants may be so styled. He further has a number of more or less necessary or unnecessary men round him, to do some work and to show his importance. The 'officials' mentioned are such as are known to the Santals and met with round the offices of a zemindar.

rạskạị ạikạua, ar mo̱ne̱ mo̱ne̱teye me̱na, Dhạrtire do̱ iń khon marań do̱ cele hõ̱ bạnuk̕koa. Ado̱ noa kathage uni raj do̱ dinge mo̱nreye me̱njońa, ar phuṭạu do̱ o̱ko̱e ṭhen hõ̱ bae phuṭạua, are me̱na, Noa katha do̱ bhala o̱ko̱eko buj daṛeketińa se̱ bań?

Ado̱ ho̱ṛak̕ mo̱ne aṭkara me̱nte mit́ din do̱ aćren jo̱to̱ no̱ko̱r cako̱r jo̱n munise metat́koa, Gapa do̱ nịạ bela nịạ o̱kte̱ jo̱to̱ge mit́ mit́te no̱ṇḍe̱ he̱ć jarwak̕pe, mit́ṭań kathań kulipea.

Ado̱ sạri sanam ho̱ṛko lạpạiyente ona o̱kte̱ do̱ jo̱to̱ge uni raj ṭhenko hạjirena. Ado̱ raje oḍokenteye kuliket́koa, e̱n kathae, Jo̱to̱kogepe he̱ć akana se̱ bań?

Ado̱ko me̱nket́a, Am oṛak̕re ạcurok̕ kan ho̱ṛ do̱ jo̱to̱gele he̱ćena, o̱ko̱e hõ̱ bale tayo̱m akana, ar disomren perjako do̱ bale ạgulet́koa, e̱ke̱n amren gutikogele he̱ć akana.

Ado̱ raje me̱nket́a, Bań, ape mo̱to̱geń kho̱jet́pea, disom perja do̱ bań ńam kana.

Ado̱ko me̱nket́a, To̱be̱ khan jo̱to̱gele hạjirena. Ado̱ ma cet́ko katha lạgit́em to̱lo̱pket́lea, ona do̱ phuṭaleme, to̱be̱ bale buja.

Ado̱ unre raje me̱nket́a, To̱be̱ khan ma ańjo̱mtińpe. Oka katha iń iń metapea, ona reak̕ jobab emańpe.

Ado̱ko me̱nket́a, Ma ro̱ṛme.

Ado̱ unre raj do̱ jo̱to̱ ho̱ṛ samańreye me̱nket́a, Mase̱ lạiańpe bhala ińak̕ mo̱nre do̱ cet́ bhabna menak̕tińa se̱ bańa; ińak̕ mo̱nre cet́ iń me̱net́a, ona lạị ruạṛańpe. Ma inạge katha do̱; ona lạgit́ge ape do̱ń to̱lo̱p akat́pea. Ado̱ inạ katha ro̱ṛkatege uni raj do̱e thirena.

Ado̱ sanam ho̱ṛge ako akoak̕ mo̱nre cet́ lekako bujket́a, onka lekako lạị idiket́takoa. Ado̱ e̱ke̱ e̱ke̱te jo̱to̱geye ńum idiket́koa; o̱ko̱e do̱ko lạiket́a, o̱ko̱e do̱ cet́ hõ̱ bako lạilet́a. Ado̱ uni raj okae me̱n akawana, ona tuluć do̱ o̱ko̱eak̕ katha hõ̱ bań ńapamlentakoa.

---

[4] It is the same idea as that underlying what is told about kings who dreamed and demanded both the dream and its interpretation from the interpreters. The best known example of this is what is told of Nebukadnezar. Cf. Heller, Das Traumerraten im Buche Daniel, Z. A. W. 1925, p. 243 ss., where examples are mentioned.

[5] Lit. 'is turning round'.

this king was very happy and glad and was thinking in his mind: "In the whole world there is no one bigger than myself." The king was daily saying so to himself[4], but he did not reveal it to anybody. He was thinking: "I wonder, whether anybody will be able to understand this matter of mine, or not."

To test the mind of people he one day said to all his servants, dependants and hired workers: "Every one of you come here to-morrow at this time, I have something to ask you."

Then, truth to tell, all of them talked together and presented themselves before the king at the time fixed. The king came out and asked them: "Have you all come or not?"

"Every one who moves about[5] in your house," they replied, "we have all come; none among us has remained behind, but the people, your tenants, we have not brought; only we, your servants, have come."

"Quite so," the king said, "it is you alone that I want, I do not wish for the country people."

"In that case we are all here," they said. "What is the matter in connexion with which you have summoned us? Explain that to us, then only we shall understand what it is."

"Hear then what I have to say," the king said. "Give me an answer to what I say to you."

"Please speak," they said.

Thereupon the king spoke before them all: "Please tell me whether in my heart I have any care or not; answer me what I am thinking of in my own mind[4]. That is the matter. It is for this sake that I have summoned you." When the king had spoken this, he said no more.

So all, one after the other, told what each of them thought. The king called on them all by name successively; some of them said something or other, and some of them said nothing at all. But what the king was thinking in his heart, — there was not one of them whose word agreed therewith.

Khange raje męnkeťa, Apeaǩ katha dǫ iňaǩ mǫn reaǩ katha tuluć baň ňapamlena. Tǫbę ceť iň męna? Khange raj dǫ dewąne hukumadea, baňma, Iňaǩ mǫnęr mǫtǫn hǫṛem ňam ąguaňa. Nonkan hǫṛem ňamea, ǫkǫe iňaǩ mǫnę reaǩ katha jęmǫne lại daṛeaň. Onkan hǫṛ nią miť cando mǫtǫrem ňam ąguaňa. Ma inạge katha dǫ. Ma adǫ apan ąpin kąmi ňęltape. Adǫ ęnęko uṭhąu baṛayena, adǫ apan ąpin kąmiteko calao baṛayena.

Khange uni dewan sę mǫntri dǫ bhar paṛaoade khan, mǫnre ạḍi bhabnae ąikąukeťa, męnkeťae, Durrę! nonkan hǫṛ dǫ okareň ňamkoa? Adǫ ęn hǫ̃ rajaǩ katha leka hǫṛ ňaňame calaoena.

Adǫ okakore cǫe ňam baṛa gelaťkoa, adǫ bae ňam daṛeaťkote, kathae, miť din dǫ ać oṛaǩrege kirdhume duṛuṗ thirena, ar cele tuluć hǫ̃ bae rǫṛ baṛayeťa, hape akangeae, ar belayenre hǫ̃ bae um hijuǩ kana. Adǫ onka momoyoť ňęlte hǫpǫnerat dǫ sęn sorenteye kulikedea, Henda baba, caǩ onka bąpuṛić dǫm duṛuṗ akana? Ceťem bhabnaǩ kana? Enan khon mulinge duṛuṗ akan iň ňęleťmea; belayena, do um hijuǩte jǫmme.

Adǫ ęnre hǫ̃ apatteť dǫ ceť hǫ̃ bae rǫṛleťa, hape akangeye tahẽyena. Adǫ enka męn baṛakatege uni kuṛi dǫ oṛaǩ sęne calaoena. Adǫ ona tayǫm arhǫ̃e ňęle kan dǫe duṛuṗ akange. Adǫ uni kuṛi ar eňgatteť jǫtǫ hǫṛge uni ṭhen hęć sorenteko kuliyede kana, uni kuṛigeye kukli kana, metae kanae, Henda baba, cedaǩ bam um hijuǩ kana? Ceť bhabna menaǩtama? ma lại me.

Adǫ unre uni mǫntri dewane menkeťa, Ią, biṭi, am dǫ ceťem baḍaekea, am gidrą hǫṛ dǫ?

Adǫ erateťe męnkeťa, Masę ęnte lạialeme, pasę dǫle bujhąukeťge.

---

[6] The person referred to, in Santali d e w a n, a word borrowed from Hindi, is the chief of the servants, the one who has entrance to the presence, and through whom all matters are managed. He is the 'prime minister'.

[7] In hot climates a bath is a necessity and not a luxury. It is not, however, a Santal custom to have a bath regularly before one's food. They take it when it suits them. The people here referred to are likely not Santals.

The king then said: "What you say does not agree with my thought. What can I then say?" So the king gave his minister[6] the following order: "Bring me a man who is privy to my mind. You have to find a man who will be able to tell me what is in my mind. You must find and bring me such a man within one month. So is my order. Now go all of you and attend to your respective work." Thereupon they got up and went every one to his work.

When this task fell upon the minister or chief secretary, he became very anxious and said: "Dear me, where shall I find such a person?" Still in accordance with the king's order he went to seek such a man.

He made inquiries here and there, but he was unable to find any such person; so one day, people tell, he was sitting at home absolutely quiet and hanging his head; he did not talk to anybody, he was sitting silent, and in spite of its becoming late he did not have his bath[7]. Seeing him so down in the mouth his daughter went to him and asked him: "Look here, father, why are you sitting so miserable? What are you anxious about? Since morning I have seen you sitting out of spirits; it is late, do have your bath and come and have food."

Still her father did not say anything, he was sitting there silent. Having spoken in this way the girl went inside. But afterwards she again saw him sitting there. So the girl and her mother and all of them went near to him and asked him, that is to say, the girl asked and said to him: "Look here, father, why do you not have your bath and come? What grief is it that you have? please tell."

Then the chief minister said: "I say, my daughter, what should you know, you child?"

"In any case please let us know," his wife said, "perhaps we might understand."

Adǫ unre uni dewane mẹnketa, Rajiń dǫ nonkae mẹn akawadińa, bańma, Nią miť cando mǫtǫrege nonkan miťtạń hǫṛ ńawańme, ińaḱ mǫn reaḱ katha jẹmǫne lại daṛeań; inaḱ mǫnre ceť iń mẹneťa ar ceť iń hudiseťa, ona katha reaḱ jẹmǫne rǫṛ ruạṛań, onkan hǫṛ iń dǫ ńam ạguańme. Adǫ biṭi, onkan hǫṛ dǫ okareń ńamkoa? Dāṛākeťań, nią dhara dhạriren hǫṛ dǫ jǫtǫń kuli baṛakeťkoa, adǫ onkan hǫṛge bạń ńam daṛeaťkoa. Ar sẹ din hō̃ tiogoḱ kana, adǫ raj ceť iń rǫṛ ruạṛaea, onań bhabnaḱ kana.

Adǫ ona katha ańjǫmkate uni hǫpǫnerat dǫe mẹn gǫťkeťa, Noa dǫ, baba, ceťem bhabnaḱ kana? Ma um hijuḱte daka jǫmme. Ma onkan hǫṛ dǫ ińiń ńawama. Adǫ oka hiloḱ raj ṭhen dǫ calaḱ hoyoḱa?

Adǫe metadea, Nẹ̄ḱẹ̄ tioḱena, gapa meań khange.

Adǫ kuṛiye mẹnkeťa, Acha, calaḱ hiloḱ dǫ lạiańme, ińiń ńam ạguama.

Adǫ kathae, mǫnre thoṛae bhorsa ńǭḱena, arhǭ thoṛa dǫe dhokaḱ kangea. Adǫe mẹneťa, Ǫkǫ baḍae, pasẹ noa dǫ bạń jǫmeťte, daka jǫm ocoń reaḱko rikạyeťte pasẹ onka dǫe mẹneť. Arhǭe mẹnkeťa, Achań ńẹlletaege. Adǫ enka mẹn baṛawanteye thirena.

Adǫ gapa leka calaḱ din adǫ teheń lekareye kuliyede kana, metae kanae, Ią biṭi, okor hǫṛ dǫm ńawań kana? Gapage cǫń calaḱ din dǫ.

Adǫ kuṛiye mẹnkeťa, Ią baba, ẹṇḍẹkhan gapa setaḱge uni hǫṛ iń hạjirama.

Adǫ kathae, luṭuḱ luṭuḱe gitić ańgayena. Adǫ setaḱ khange uni kuṛiye mẹn gǫťkeťa, Ma baba, umoḱte jǫm daṛeḱme, uni hǫṛ iń ạguam kana.

Adǫ kathae, uni dewan hǭe umenteye jǫm daṛeyena. Adǫe mẹnkeťa, Dini mại, uni hǫṛ ạguańme.

Then the minister said: "The king has given me such an order, viz., 'Within one month bring me a man who is able to tell me what is in my mind; find and bring me a person who is able to answer me what I say to myself and what I think in my mind.' So my daughter, where shall I find such a person? I have wandered about, here in the neighbourhood I have asked every one; but such a person I have been unable to find. And now, the day is drawing near, then what shall I answer the king? that is what I am anxious about."

When she heard this, his daughter at once said: "Why are you anxious about this, father? Do have your bath and come and take food. I shall find you such a person. Which day will you have to go to the king?"

"It is just coming," he replied, "to-morrow or the day after, then."

"All right," the girl said, "tell me the day when you have to go; I shall bring you the man."

The father then felt a little confident and encouraged; on the other hand he was also in doubt and said: "Who knows, perhaps it is because I do not eat, perhaps she is speaking in this way, because they are trying to make me take food." Again he said: "Very well, I shall see what she can do." Thinking this he did not say any more.

Now the day to go was like to-morrow, then like to-day he asked her and said to her: "I say, my daughter, how is it, where is the man you are to bring me? To-morrow is the day to go."

"Well, father," the girl replied, "then to-morrow morning I shall bring the man before you."

He spent the night anxious and watchful. In the morning the girl said: "Now father, have your bath, and take food, so you may have some strength; I am bringing you the man."

So, people tell, the minister had his bath, had food and strengthened himself, whereupon he said: "Bring him here, my girl, bring me the man."

Adọ kathae, akorenge bhiḍi gupi guti koṛae tahẽkantakoa; ar uni koṛa dọe guṅgạgea, rọṛ hõ bae rọṛ daṛeak̕a, ar aṅjọm hõ bae aṅjọm daṛeak̕a — onkan họṛe tahẽkana. Ar koṛaren hõ judạge bhiḍi mẹrọm dọ menak̕kotaea, ar uni dewanren hõ bhiḍi mẹrọm menak̕kotaea, ar gupi dọ uni guṅgạ họṛgeye gupi kantakoa. Ar uni guṅgạren hõ pẹa bheḍa menak̕kotaea.

Adọ uni guṅgạ koṛage uni kuṛi dọe họhọ ạgukedete dakako emadea are bhẹdadea, baṅma, Iń baba sãote raj ṭhen ben calak̕a. Adọ uni guṅgạ koṛa dọ cet̕ hõ bae mẹnlet̕a. Adọ daka jọm baṛakate uni kuṛi dọe mẹnket̕a, Ma baba, sapṛaok̕me.

Adọ dewane mẹnket̕a, Ukuric̕, mạ̃i, uni họṛ dọ?

Adọ uni kuṛiye mẹnket̕a, Uni baba, aboren bhiḍi gupiyic̕ge, idiyem thọ.

Adọ apate mẹnket̕a, Henda mạ̃i, uni mae guṅgạ cọṅ, uni dọe rọṛ daṛeak̕a?

Adọ kuṛiye mẹnket̕a, Am dọ uni baṛẹ idiyem thọ, rajak̕ mọnẹ reak̕ katha dọ unigeye lạị daṛeak̕a, ar baṅkhan dọ ọkọe hõ ọhọko lạị daṛelea.

Adọ ona katha aṅjọmte dewan hõe mẹnket̕a, Sạrige cọṅ cet̕ cọṅ; unre unạk̕ họṛle jarwalena, okorle lạị daṛeat̕a? Sạri thọ bhalaṅ idi gelalege. Adọ onka mẹnkate dewan dọe mẹnket̕a, Delan ya guṅgạ, raj ṭhenlaṅ calak̕a. Adọ ẹnẹkin calaoena.

Adọ ona katha aṅjọm lạgit̕ uni raj ṭhen dọ aema họṛko jarwa hataṛ akana; ẹnteko baḍae akat̕ tahẽkana sẹ baṅa, mọnẹ reak̕ katha lạlạị họṛ dewan dọ nãhãk̕ niạ din hilok̕ onkan họṛe ạguyea mẹnte, ona iạte họṛ dọko jarwa tear akana. Ar ghạṛi ghạṛiko kọyọk̕et̕a, okor bae hijuk̕ kan? Adọ sạṅgiṅreko ńẹl ńamkede khan dọ rajko lạị gọt̕adea, dewan dọ mit̕ họṛe ạguyede kana mẹnte.

Khange raj dọ ona kathae aṅjọmket̕ khan dọe oḍok hẹc̕ gọt̕ena; adọ ac̕ak̕ duṛup̕ak̕reye duṛup̕ akana. Khange adọ unkinkin sẹṭẹren khankin ḍọṇḍbot̕adea, adọ ọṇḍẹge uni samaṅrekin teṅgo akana,

[8] A raised small platform outside, where the king sits cross-legged.

Now they had a shepherd boy, and this boy was deaf and dumb; he could neither speak nor hear; such a one he was. This boy had also some sheep and goats of his own; the minister had also sheep and goats, and this dumb boy was their shepherd. This dumb boy had three rams.

So the girl called this dumb boy and gave him food and made him understand that he should go with her father to the king. The dumb boy did not say anything, but when they had had their food, the girl said: "Now, father, make yourself ready."

"Where is that man, my girl, I don't see him," the minister said.

"This is the one, father," the girl replied, "our shepherd, take him along."

"Look here, my girl," the father said, "why, he is dumb, will he be able to speak?"

The girl replied: "You take him along with you. What the king has in his mind, this one will be able to tell, or else certainly no one."

When he heard this, the minister also said: "So it may possibly be; on that occasion we were so many people assembled, and we were unable to tell. Verily, I shall have a try and take him along." Thinking this the minister said: "Come along, you dumb fellow, we shall go to the king." Whereupon the two went.

Now a large crowd of people had collected at the king's place to hear this matter; they knew, you see, or didn't they, that on this particular day the minister was to bring a man who would tell what the king had in his mind; therefore people had assembled there and were ready to listen. Every moment they were looking up, wondering, why, is he not coming? When they saw him far off, they at once sent word to the king, that the minister was in sight, bringing a man along with him.

When the king heard this, he came out at once and sat down on his seat[8]. When these two arrived, they made their bow and were standing there before the king, and the dumb boy was looking

ar uni guṅgạ do̠ raj se̠ngeye be̠ṅge̠t́ akat́a. Khange tho̠ raj do̠ uni koṛa mit́ kạṭuṕe uduḱ go̠t́adea. Khange tho̠ uni guṅgạ do̠ barea kạṭuṕe uduḱ go̠t́ket́a. Khange raj do̠ pe̠a kạṭuṕe uduḱ go̠t́ket́a. Khange tho̠ guṅgạ do̠ ona pe̠a kạṭuṕe ńe̠lket́ khan do, ạḍi ā̃ṭteye hutmạ go̠t́ena ar o̠ṇḍe̠ khone calao utạrena.

Khange raj do̠ mo̠ne̠reye rạskạyente muluć mulućе landaket́a. Ar onko jarwa akan ho̠ṛ do̠ ńe̠ltegeko hahaṛayena, ṭo̠ro̠ḍaṅ lekako cahap̃ hapeket́a, ar cet́te̠t́ge bako bujlet́a. Khange raj do̠ landawateye me̠nket́a, Do do do ruạṛepe.

Khange uni ruạṛe lạgit́ bar ho̠ṛkin ńir calaoena; ado̠kin metae kana, Dela ruạṛlenme; raje me̠net́a, Do ruạṛ ạguyepe.

Ado̠ kathae, baṅte hõ baṅgeye ruạṛlena. Khangekin ikạ dapo̠ṛkedete ruạṛkate rajkin metadea, e̠n kathae, Baṅgeye ruạṛ kana.

Ado̠ raje me̠nket́a, Acha ikạkaepe; oka mo̠nre tahẽkantiń, ona do̠e lạiadińa. Ado̠ raje me̠nket́a, Baṅa, dewan, khub bhage ho̠ṛem ńam ạguadińa. Acha ṭhike utạr ruạṛadińa, bes iń khusi utạrena. Ape do̠ nunạḱ ho̠ṛ, inạ hõ bape buj daṛeadińa.

Khange sạri o̠ko̠e hõ cet́ hõ bako ro̠ṛ ruạṛ daṛeadea. Ar uni dewan do̠ mo̠ne̠ mo̠ne̠teye me̠net́a, Noa kạṭuṕkin uduḱ baṛawana, ona reaḱ do̠ cet́ bhe̠d kana? Ạkin makin bujket́, iń tho̠ baṅ bujlet́a. Acha, noa katha do̠ raj iń kuliyegea. Ado̠ kathae, dewan do̠ bae jivilet́te raje kulikedea, Henda raja, aben ma bhalaben bujket́ge, ale ńe̠ńe̠l ho̠ṛ tho̠ bale bujlet́a; e̠ke̠n kạṭuṕge uduḱ baṛawanle ńe̠lket́bena. Ado̠ onate do̠ cet́ben bujket́a, onageń kulijoṅ kana. Lạiańme, se̠ lạialeme.

Ado̠ uniye me̠nket́a, Bape bujlet́a? Achaṅ bhe̠dapea. Ona do̠ nonka kana; iń do̠ mit́ kạṭuṕ iń uduḱadea — ona do̠ń kulikedea,

[9] The fish-trap referred to, in Santali ṭo̠ro̠ḍaṅ, is one found in every Santal house. It is made from split bamboo, generally with a large opening at one end and closed up at the other. It is put where water runs in such a way that all water has to pass through this trap. The ṭo̠ro̠ḍaṅ is used especially at the close of the rainy season. Some water is permitted to run out from the rice-fields through a small opening made for the purpose in the lower ridge of the field.

towards the king. The king then suddenly showed the boy one finger, and the dumb boy at once put up two fingers, whereupon the king showed three. But as soon as the dumb boy saw three fingers, he jerked his head violently and went straight away from there.

Then the king felt very glad and smiled to himself. But the people assembled, seeing this, wondered; they were standing gaping with their mouths open like a fish-trap[9], and were utterly without understanding. Then the king said: "Do, bring him back, do."

Two men ran to turn him back and were saying to him: "Come along, come back at once; the king says, Do bring him back."

But he was absolutely unwilling to go back, and so they let the fellow alone, returned to the king and reported: "He is not returning."

"Very well," the king said, "let him alone; he told me what was in my mind," whereupon he continued: "To be sure, minister, you brought me an excellent person. He answered me exactly right; I am absolutely pleased. You, so many people, you were unable to let me understand even this."

Then, truth to tell, no one was able to say anything, and the minister was saying to himself: "They showed fingers to each other, what can be the meaning of that? They apparently understood each other; I could not make anything out of it. Well, I shall ask the king about it." And as the minister was unable to restrain himself any longer, he asked the king: "Listen, O king, you two apparently understood what it was, but we onlookers understood nothing; we only saw that you two showed fingers to each other. Therefore I am asking, what did you two understand by it? Tell me, or rather tell us."

"Did you not understand?" the king replied; "very well, I shall explain it to you. It is this way: I showed him one finger, thereby

---

Somehow or other some small fry are found in the rice-fields, and these are caught. The figure of speech is not inept.

Raj doń iń eskargea seko tinąka? Uni do bareae udukketa—ona doe menketa, bańma, Bar horaben, mit do am ar mit do Ṭhąkurge —onae metadińa. Ado arhõń kulikedea, bańma, Pea raj menakkoa? Ado unrege ạdi ãṭteye hutmạ gotena. Menketae, bańma, Bareage menakkina, mit do amge ar mit do Ṭhạkurge. Ado sạri utạrgeń pạtiạuengea, ente noa kathage din hilok monreń bhabnak kan tahẽkana, raj doń iń eskargea mente. Menkhan nui hore bujadińa, bańma, bar horaben. Ado sạri utạr bar horge. Ado sạri uni dewan hõe pạtiạuena; ado enekin thir barayena.

Ado ạyup jokhen dewan do orakre hećkate uni guńgạ korae kulikedea, Henda ya, en kathae, enanok raj ṭhen iń idiletmea, ado unre raj do cete metatmea, menkhan ale do bale bujleta. Pea kạṭupe udukatme khange am do huń martem hec utạrena. Ruạr ruạrkatmeako, ado bam ruạrlena. Ado mase bhedaleme, bale bujleta.

Ado kathae, uni dewanak katha ma bae bujhạuet; ado dosra horko lại bujhạuadea. Khange uni guńgạ doe menketa, Raj do bheḍae koeyeń kana. Judi am bareye koelem khan hutec, bam sap idikea? Ado ińe koeyeń kana. Raje menketa, Mitṭań bheḍa emańme. Adoń metadea, Raj kanam, mitṭań do cak? Bareań emama. Ado bareań gokket khan, raj do peae ńam kana. Ado endokań emokań. Ado endekhan itạm maraokotińa? Tobe ạkhirge ba ạkhir mit goten hõ balań emama! Unre iń do edreteń hećena, onate ruạr idińre hõ bań ruạrlena.

Ado ene cabayena. Ar uni dewan do tinạk gan coń boskise ere daporana. Ado ene cabayena.

---

[10] Thakur is the name used by the Santal gurus for the Supreme Being. It is probably a word of Aryan derivation.

[11] Lit. seed. The possibility of getting others.

[12] Dual in threatening or defiant language.

I asked him: "Am I alone king, or how many are there?" He showed me two fingers, thereby he said: "You are two; you are one and Thakur[10] is the other," this he told me. Then I again asked him: "Are there not three kings?" Then he jerked his head very violently. He said: 'There are two, you are one and Thakur is the other.' And I really and truly believed, because it was this matter about which I was anxiously thinking every day, whether I am the only king or not. But this man made me understand that we are two. And really and truly we are two." So the minister also believed, and they did not say anything more.

In the evening, when he came home, the minister asked the dumb boy: "Look here, you fellow, in the morning I took you to the king; then the king said something to you, but we other ones did not understand what it was. When he showed you three fingers, you came away and straight here without any warning. They tried to turn you back, but you did not go back. Now explain this to us; we did not understand it."

Now the boy did not understand what the minister said, so some other people explained it to him. Then the dumb boy said: "The king was asking me for a ram. Now if he had asked you for one, would you not have taken it to him? But he asked me to give him one. The king said: 'Give me a ram.' Then I said: 'You are the king, why only one? I shall give you two.' But when I promised him two, the king wanted three. 'I'll be blowed if I give. Then will you exterminate all I have root and branch?[11] So happen what may, we two[12] shall not give you even one single one.' Then I came away in anger; therefore also I did not turn back, when they tried to make me."

There it is ended. But the minister tricked the king into giving him who knows how big a present.[13] So it is ended.

---

[13] Without this touch, true to Indian thought, the narrator will not feel the story complete.

30. Mit́ṭaṅ pạpi kuṛi reaḱ katha.

Mit́ṭaṅ họṛren, kathae, họpọnerate tahẽkana; adọ uni kuṛi dọ mit́ṭaṅ dosra atoreye ṭhão akadea; adọ pẹ pon gọṭẹnkin gidạr pidạrana. Adọ mit́ dhao uni apat họṛe mẹnket́a, Ọkọń tora teheń dọ phalna mạĩtekoń hiri ạgukoa, ḍher din khon onko dọ babon hiri akat́koa.

Adọ sạri onka mẹn oṭokate ẹn hiloḱ dọ setaḱrege bin jọmtegeye mohṇḍayena. Adọe mẹnket́a, Tioḱ gọdań nãhãḱ, ọṇḍẹgeń jọma. Adọ calaḱ calaḱte mit́ ṭhen mọrọn aṛaḱe ńẹllet́a, ona hõ bae jọmlet́a. Khange adọe calao sẹṭẹrena; adọ parkọmko beladete daḱko tańadea, adọ boge judạye kuli baṛakedea.

Adọ ẹn hiloḱge uni apattẹt́ dọ ruạṛe mẹnet́a; adọe mẹnket́a, Iạ mạĩ, iń dọ ạḍi hạbić dọ bań peṛa họṛọḱape kana, iń dọ teheńgeń ruạṛa.

Khange adọe metadea, Iạ baba, ạkhirem calaḱgea, lọlọaḱ tạṅgi toraeme. Ar uni jãwãe gomket dọ ạḍiye sendrawa, adọ ẹn hiloḱ hõ mit́ṭaṅ maraḱe gọć ạgu akadea, adọ rọ gẹt́ akadete uni dọ oka sẹn cọe calaoen. Adọ uni họpọnerat dọ apat haṛam menae iạte bae utu dakayet́a. Adọ khub setońen khan, racae lẹbẹt́ ạikạuket́a, setońte ạḍi baṛić dhipạuen. Un jọkhẹn adọe metae kana, Ma baba, lọlọaḱ nitoḱ dọ tioḱena, ma calaḱme.

---

1 The Santali word lit. means 'place'; it is the common expression for giving a daughter away in marriage. It might be remarked that the original abounds in idiomatic expressions.

2 The commom custom with the ordinary Santal is to wait taking food up to the middle of the forenoon, many waiting even till noon before breaking fast.

3 The herb referred to, mọrọn aṛaḱ, lit. death-vegetable, Gymnema hirsutus, W. & A., var. Decaisneanum, Wight, is used in Santal medicine, and the leaves are eaten as curry.

4 This is the common way of treating visitors. The bedstead is during day-time used to sit on, when it is not put aside somewhere. Water is partly given for drinking, partly for washing the feet of the visitor.

5 The Santal expression means 'what is hot', and the father naturally takes it to mean food.

30. THE STORY OF A STINGY GIRL.

A certain man, people tell, had a daughter, and this girl he had settled[1] in another village, and with her husband she had got three or four children. One day the father said: "Now at once to-day I shall go and see our daughter and her husband and children, how they are; it is a long time since we have visited them."

And really and truly, after having said this he started that very morning without having had any food[2]. He said: "I shall reach there presently, and shall get food there." Walking along he saw at a place a certain eatable herb[3], but did not take it. So he reached the place, and they put a bedstead for him to sit on and poured out water for him[4], whereupon he asked the girl how they were.

Now the girl's father intended to return home the same day and said: "I say, my girl, I am not paying you a long visit, I shall return home to-day."

The girl then said to him: "Well, father, certainly you will go, but wait for the hot[5]." His son-in-law was an eager hunter; that day he had also killed and brought a peacock[6], and after having singed[7] and cut this up he had gone off somewhere. But because her father was there, the daughter did not prepare food. When the sun had become intensely hot, she stepped out into the court-yard and felt that the ground was burning hot from the sun, and then she said to her father: "Please, father, now the hot has come, now you may go."

---

[6] Peafowls were formerly fairly common in the Santal country; even now they are often seen and hunted in the forest-covered hills. The tail feathers of the peacock are used by the disciples of the Santal ojha or medicine-man at their ceremonial dances.

[7] Except the larger animals (cattle) the Santals will not ordinarily flay an animal killed to be eaten. They put them on a smouldering fire and in this way singe off all hair, whereupon they cut the whole into small bits. They use their natural implements when eating, consequently everything must be so small that the need of a knife is obviated. A peafowl may be treated in the same way.

Adọ uni họpọnerat onkae mẹnket́ khan, uni haṛam dọ mọnẹreye bujhạuket́a, daka dọ ọhọko ẹmliṅa mẹnte; Ọkọṅ toraṅ beret́ calak̃a. Khange ṭheṅgae sap̃ket́taea, adọ beret́ calak̃ jọkhẹn uni haṛam dọe rọṛ oṭoako kana, Iạ mạ̃i, mit́ kathaṅ lại oṭoam kana, jẹ jāwāe do ạḍiye sendrawa; adọ jāhā leka marak̃ tanak̃e gọćleko khan dọ, kūiṇḍi kaṛete lẹṭọkope thọ, ạḍiko sebela.

Adọe mẹnket́a, Acha ẹnḍẹkhanle lẹṭọkoa.

Adọ enka mẹn baṛakatege uni haṛam dọe calaoena; cet́ hō̱ bako emadea, upạstegeye calaoena.

Adọ uniye calaoen tayọm khange uni họpọnerat dọ ona marak̃ jel dọe utuket́a, ar uni haṛame mẹnlet́ lekage sạri kūiṇḍi kaṛeteye lẹṭọket́a. Adọ jāwāetẹt́ ar onko gidrạkoe ẹm lahawat́koa. Adọko jọm gelat́ dọ bogete haṛhat́. Adọ jāwāetẹt́e mẹnket́a, Cet́ leka ba teheṅ dọm utuket́? Bogete haṛhat́ kan dọ.

Adọ uniye mẹnket́a, Baṅa, teheṅ dọ ạḍi sebel iṅ utu akat́a. Adọ onka mẹnkateye mẹnket́a, Hape sẹṅ jọm gelalege. Adọ sạriye jọm gelaket́ dọ, bogete haṛhat́ge. Adọe mẹnket́a, Babage thọe metadiṅa, Kūiṇḍi kaṛete lẹṭọeme thọ, ạḍi sebela. Onate teheṅ dọ kūiṇḍi kaṛeteṅ lẹṭọket́a. Baba dọ ạḍiye ẹk̃rẹa, sanam jele bạṛić ocokidiṅa.

Adọ jāwāetẹt́e mẹnket́a, Baba dọ daka utu dọpe emadea sẹ baṅ?

Adọe mẹnket́a, Bale emadea.

Ẹnḍẹkhan rẹṅgẹćtegeye calaoena?

Adọe mẹnket́a, Hẽk̃, rẹṅgẹćtegeye calaoena.

Adọe mẹnket́a, Tọbẹrege ẹnḍẹkhan nonka dọe lại oṭoat́mea. Cedak̃ bam emadea? Ạpum lekan họṛge bam emae khan, ẹnḍẹkhan dọ celekom peṛakoa? Unim isinaea mẹnte cọṅ hare phareṅ gẹt́ kuṭi oṭoat́me. Adọ bam emadete noa dọe batlao oṭoat́mea. Ṅẹlme, uni bam emadete abo hō̱ okorbo jọm daṛeat́a? Jọtọ baṅ kharapena?

8 The mahua, as the Bassia latifolia, Roxb., is generally called in India, is an extremely useful tree. The dried flowers are eaten, so also the fruit, from the kernel of which an oil is expressed. The oil-cake is quite unfit for food.

9 According to custom, women get their food after the males have been served. Even when the family is alone, the husband will be served first, small children generally getting their food at the same time. The wife serves and cooks.

When his daughter spoke in that way, the old man understood that they would not give him food. "I shall at once rise and go," saying so he took his stick, and as he was rising to go, the old man said to them: "I say, my girl, I tell you one thing, before I go; my son-in-law is an eager hunter. Now if he should happen to kill a peacock or the like, be sure to prepare the flesh with mahua oil-cake[8]; it is very savoury."

"Very well," the girl said, "then we shall prepare it in that way."

Having said this the old man went off; they had not given him anything, he went away without having tasted food.

After he had gone, his daughter made curry of that peacock flesh, and as the old man had said, she really prepared it with mahua oil-cake. She gave her husband and children[9] first to eat. They tried to eat, but it was so bitter. The husband then said: "How have you prepared curry to-day? It is awfully bitter."

"Not at all," she replied, "to-day I have prepared some very savoury curry." Thereupon she said: "Wait, let me have a taste." And when she tasted it, it really was very bitter. Then she said: "Why, my father told me, be sure to prepare the curry with mahua oil-cake, it is very savoury. Therefore I have done so to-day. Father is a great hoaxer, he has made me spoil all the flesh."

"Did you give father any food?" her husband then asked.

"We did not give him any," she replied.

"Then he went away hungry?"

"Yes," she replied, "he went hungry."

"In that case," he said, "that is the reason why he told you this, when he went away. Why did you not give him anything? If you do not give a man like your own father, whom should you show hospitality to? Why, it was to enable you to prepare food for him that I so quickly cut the flesh up into bits for you, before I went. Then as you did not give him anything, he instructed you in this way: See, because you did not give him, why, we have not been able to eat either. Was not all spoilt?"

Adǫ uni bąhuttẹt́ dǫ cet́ hō̃ bae rǫṛleťa, hapegeye tahẽyena. Adǫ jǫtǫ jelko giḍikaťa.

Cabayena katha dǫ.

31. Nạihạrte calak̕ kạnić koṛa ar mǫrǫn aṛak̕.

Mit́ṭaṅ koṛa dǫ ạḍi sạṅgiṅreye nạihạran tahẽkana. Khange bạhui dạṛket́tae khan uni koṛa dǫ bạhu paṅjage nạihạrteye mohṇḍayena; mẹnkhan bir hǫrteye calak̕ kan tahẽkana. Adǫ hǫr aṛerege, kathae, mǫrǫn aṛak̕ nãṛīye ṅẹl ṅamketa. Adǫ mǫnẹ mǫnẹteye mẹnoana, Noa mǫrǫn aṛak̕ dǫ baṅ jǫma; ẹnte noaṅ jǫmle khan dǫ, nạihạrteṅ calak̕ kana, adǫ nãhãk̕ ǫṇḍẹ oka laćre daka dǫṅ jǫma. Onae niṭoante mǫrǫn aṛak̕ dǫ bae jǫmleťa.

Adǫ ǫṇḍẹ khonge nạihạrte dǫe mohṇḍa idiyena; adǫe sẹn tiok̕keťa nạihạr dǫ. Adǫ parkǫmko beladea; adǫe duṛup̕ena. Adǫ thoṛa ghạṛi tayǫm khange daka utuko tearketa, adǫ uni ar uniren bahǫṅhartẹt́ adǫ dak̕ko taṅat́kina, adǫkin ạbuk bǫlǫyena. Ạḍi sebel sebel utu dakako ẹm akawat́kina. Adǫ uni sẹn akan koṛa dǫ daka utu ṅẹlte ạḍige cele mǫnẹre rạskạ hẹćadea, ạḍi garteye landaketa. Ẹnte mǫrǫn aṛak̕geye disạ maṛaṅketa.

---

[10] The moral of the story is given towards the end, but I do not think one is mistaken in taking it that what impresses the Santal mind most is the thought of those who had to eat the stuff prepared. The nature of the Santal does not need any lecturing of the kind here given.

A variant of the story related above tells of a man with several children, all married. The father goes on a visit to one of his married daughters, stays over one night and intends to go home the next morning, when his daughter asks him to await what is hot. The story thereupon runs very much as here told. When they have tasted the spoiled food, the husband becomes very angry, the more so, as he thinks that his father-in-law must believe that it was out of fear of him (the husband) that the woman had not given him food. "Whereupon he commenced to thrash her, and she cried: Alas! alas! my father has caused me to be beaten! Alas! O dear! it was my father who instructed me to do this! Her crying brought the village people together; they asked what was the matter and why they were fighting. The story was told, and in this way this story became known and is being told even now."

His wife did not speak, she remained silent. And they threw all the flesh away[10].

The story is ended.

31. THE YOUNG MAN WHO PASSED THE VEGETABLE ON HIS WAY TO HIS FATHER-IN-LAW[1].

A young man had very far to his father-in-law's home. Once his wife had run away[2], the young man set off for her father's house to bring her back. He was walking through a forest; here on one side of the way he caught sight of a 'death-vegetable' climber, but he said to himself: "I shall not eat this vegetable, because if I eat this, — I am on my way to my wife's father's home, — then how shall I have room[3] for the food I get there?" Having made up his mind in this way he did not eat it.

Now he continued his way from here to his father-in-law's house and reached there. They put a bedstead for him to sit on, and he sat down, and after a short while they prepared curry and rice, whereupon they poured water out for him and his wife's elder brother; they washed their hands and mouth and went inside. They gave them excellent savoury curry and rice. When the young man who had come here saw this curry and rice he felt naturally very glad and burst out laughing. You see, he remembered the 'death-vegetable.'

---

31 [1] This story, as told by Bhuju Murmu of Dhopahar, is related here as an appendix to the proceding one, where this vegetable is mentioned and plays a part similar to what is here told. See note 3 pag. 54.

[2] It is very common with recently married people that the young wife, for some reason or other, runs away home. With the way in which Santal marriages are arranged, this is not strange. The husband is expected to follow after her and take her back. Only in very exceptional cases the girl's relatives will take her back; this would mean that the girl was in the wrong, when running away. Alone, she could not go.

[3] Lit. in which stomach shall I eat.

Adọ uni bahọṅhartẹt́ landa aṅjọmkate ạḍiye edreyena. Ẹnteye mẹnketa, Nui hoṛ dọ dakale ẹm akawadea, adọ okaṭaḱe rạskạyente nonka dọe landaketa? Uni sẹn akan koṛa dọ ona daka thoṛa hõ bae jọmleta. Adọ bhageteye thapakedea, are-metadea, Am sala dọ, jivi baṅcao lạgit́ cọṅ dakale ẹm akawat́mea, adọ cedaḱem landaketa? Adọ bae jọm ocoadea, thapa ṅirkedeae.

Adọ ruạṛ jọkhẹn inạ mọrọn aṛaḱgeye joharata, are mẹnketa, Lahare noaṅ jọmle khan pasẹ nonka dọ ọhọ hoelena. Onate, kathaeko mẹna, jãhãtegem calaḱ judi họrre mọrọn aṛaḱem ṅamle khan dọm jọmet́gea; ẹnteko mẹna, Candoe edrena baṅ jọmle khan; adọe mẹna, Am dọ tin maraṅ hoṛ kanam? cedaḱ mọrọn aṛaḱ dọ bam jọmlaḱa? Onate mọrọn aṛaḱ dọko jọmgea.

32. Kuṛhni kuri reaṅ.

Mit́ṭaṅ koṛa kathaeko bạhuade tahẹ̃kana. Adọ tahẹn tahẹnte ạkin haṛam buḍhi dọ bhage sulukgekin tahẹ̃kana, mẹnkhan uni bạhuttẹt́ dọ ạḍi kuṛhnigeye tahẹ̃kana. Kạmi ãṭ hiloḱ khangeye ruạḱa; Asaṛ San cando dọ ạḍitẹt́geye kuhrạ kuhri baṛaea, ar sanam hoṛ kạmiko sẹn caba baṛayena mẹnkhan, kusiạ̃ daka dọ gẹćkateye jọange, ar baṅ tahẹn khan dọe dakawange.

Adọ uni hoṅhartẹt́ haṛam dọe mẹnketa, Ọkọe tora bhala ojhakoṅ ạgukoa, tikoṅ tunum baṛa ocokoa, bạhu dọ cet́ leka bae ruạḱ kan;

[4] Sala, sister's husband, is a very common low abuse. The speaker implies that the sister of the one addressed is no better than to have been dishonoured by the speaker. The word is borrowed from Hindi and is only seldom used by Santals; their abuse generally takes some other, more concrete form.

[5] The sun representing the Supreme Being.

32 [1] Cases like the one here described may be met with; but it should be noted that the Santal women as a rule are much more energetic and work more than the men.

[2] The two months Asaṛ and San correspond to the time from the middle of our June to the middle of August. They are the first two months of the rainy season in north-eastern India and are the busiest time the agriculturists have

[3] The ojha or medicine-man is supposed to know medicine and especially also to be able to do what is needed to counteract the evil influence of the spirits and the

When his brother-in-law heard him laughing, he became very angry. He thought: "We have given this man food; what joy did it give him, since he laughed in this way?" But the young man who had come there had not even tasted the food. The other thereupon slapped him again and again and said to him: "You brother-in-law[4], to save you alive we have given you food; why then did you laugh?" And he did not let him get any food; he slapped him and drove him away.

On his way back, when he passed that 'death-vegetable', he bowed to it and said: "If I had taken and eaten this previously, perhaps I should not have had this experience."

For this reason, people say, if you on your way anywhere happen to find this 'death-vegetable', you must eat it; for people say, Cando[5] is angry, if it is not eaten; he will say: 'How big a man art thou? why didst thou not eat the 'death-vegetable'? That is the reason why people eat this vegetable.

32. ABOUT A LAZY GIRL.

SOMEWHERE, people tell, they had brought a wife for a young man. As time passed, these two, husband and wife, were living well and in peace together, but the wife was very lazy[1]. Whenever there was any heavy work, that day she became ill; especially during the months af Asar and San[2] she was groaning, but when all people had gone away to work, she set to, scraped out any rice there was and had food, and if there was nothing left, she prepared food for herself.

One day her father-in-law said: "I shall without delay bring some medicine-men[3] and let them feel her pulse[4]; it is a strange

witches. A full description of these people and their doings will be found in the writer's work The Santals and Disease in the Memoirs of the Asiatic Society of Bengal.

4 Lit. 'feel the hands with one's hand.' This is the first thing an ojha does after having been called in, and he is expected to be able to know from the pulse what is the matter with the patient, especially also what is at the back of the suffering.

rankobon kotẹć baṛa ocoaea, ar judi bae besoḱ khan dọ, nạihạrtegebon idi oṭokaea.

Adọ sạri ojhakoe ńam ạguketḱoa; adọe metaḱkoa, Ma sẹ bạhutale tiko tunum baṛaetaepe cet́ lekae ruạḱ kana. Ale dọ bujge bale ńam daṛeaḱ kana, ar baṅkhan balańtekoko mẹn bọtẹćkea, Nõḱõe ape dọ oka hõ bape utjogadea.

Adọ sạri onko ojha dọ tiko tunumkedea, ar thoṛa mulući machae landaketa. Khan dosra ojha hõe tunumkedea, adọ uni họe landa machaketa. Adọko duṛuṕ thir baṛayena.

Adọ unre uni khạmid họṛe mẹnketa, Cele baba, cet́ lekaben buj baṛaketa? Adọ ma lạiben. Adọ ona reaḱ jãhãṭaḱ babon utjoga?

Adọ unkin ojhakin mẹnketa, Ruạ dọ uḍi gạhṛigetaea; ma kurumuṭute ran rẹhẹt́ dọ kọṭẹć ocoaeme.

Adọ uni khạmid họṛe mẹnketa, Ran rẹhẹtko ma baṅ baḍae; dẹ adọ abengeń saṕetbena; cet́ lekateye bhạlạioḱ, onako ran ńam ạguiben, sẹ kiriń ran lagaoḱ khan, ona hõ lạiben sẹ; ẹnte cet́ lekate jutoḱa, ona dọ sanam lại cabaeben, tọbẹ nạhĩ onakole juṛạua.

Ar noako katha dọ uni ruạḱ kan bạhu kuṛi samaṅregeko galmarao kana, uni hõe aḱńjọm kangea. Adọ unkin ojhakin mẹnketa, Hẽ dọ hẽge, baba, adọ ạlińem saṕketliń khan dọliń lagaogea;

[5] The expression has reference to the way in which an ojha ordinarily prepares his medicines. The ingredients are generally brought directly from the forest, washed and then crushed on a flat stone with a spice-crusher, whereupon the ojha sprinkles on a little water and squeezes the juice out with his hand into a leaf-cup. It is all done coram publico; any one may look at it.

[6] Lit. 'my co-parent-in-law and those (there).' The reason given for action is a not uncommon one. In cases of real disease the Santals will do all they can, as a rule; they have to reckon with what the blood relations of a recently brought daughter-in-law may say, and they feel very keenly any remarks made as to lack of care, &c.

[7] The plural might be noted. From the context it is seen that two only are called in. The plural may in Santali be used about the indefinite, the class, and the like, when only one or as here two of a class are meant. Above it is said in Santali that the ojha should feel the hands, hands being plural.

kind of disease our daughter-in-law is suffering from. We shall let them crush[5] some medicines for her, and if she does not recover, we shall send her to her father's and leave her there."

He then really got hold of some medicine-men, brought them and said to them: "Please, feel the pulse of our daughter-in-law and find out what she if suffering from. We are unable to understand what it is. Otherwise her parents and people[6] might say: 'Here you see, you have not tried to help her a bit'.'

So the medicine-men[7] felt her pulse, and the one who had done this just smiled a little. Thereupon the other medicine-man also felt her pulse, and he also laughed a little. So they sat down and kept quiet.

Then the head of the house said: "How is it, sirs, what have you two made it out to be? Please tell. Then shall we not try to use some remedy or other?"

"Her complaint is very difficult and chronic," the two medicine-men replied; "please exert yourself, find medicinal roots and let them be crushed and given to her."

"I do not know anything of medicinal roots," the head of the house replied; "so I am engaging[8] both of you; bring such medicines as may make her well again, or, if medicine is to be bought and applied, let me know that also. Whatever will suit, let me know all; then only shall we be able to procure it."

This they were talking before the sick girl; she was also hearing it. The two medicine-men then said: "That is quite so, sir, and as you have engaged us two, we shall apply medicine; but we have a small request to make; only after some exorcism[9] has been

8 Lit. 'catch hold of'. The proceedings described are true to nature. The ojha likes to be persuaded and does not himself offer his service, at the same tim urging the need of professional help.

9 The first thing an ojha is expected to do is to counteract the influence of malevolent spirits; so long as such are at work, medicine is deemed to be inefficacious Generally his action takes the form of a promise of a sacrifice; but it may als take other forms, such as exorcism.

mẹnkhan thoṛaliń babape kana, ẹnte husiť ńõḱle ẹnẹć ran dọ lagaoḱa, ar bańkhan ọhọ lagaolena.

Adọ uniye mẹnkeťa, Acha, jathete jutoḱa, onka baṛẹ kạmiben, aloben tar antara.

Adọ unkin ojhakin mẹnkeťa, Ma ẹnḍẹkhan rọṛ dọ inạḱgea; adọ ranliń ńam ạgulege, adọ onako ńam johṛaokatebon husidea ar ran hõbon lagao utạr gọda.

Adọ uniye metaťkina, Ma ẹnḍẹkhan nią teheń gapate baṛẹ ńam ạgu gọdben. Nẹtar dọ ạḍi ṭana ṭạni ạikạuḱ kana: ruạḱ hoṛ eskarre bạgiae hõ bań jut, ar miť hoṛe hoṛhoete ma jutkoḱge, mẹnkhan hoṛtege bańle kulạuḱ kan. Ma ran dọ hare phare baṛẹ ạgu gọdben.

Adọkin mẹnkeťa, Acha ẹnḍẹkhan teheńgeliń ńam ạgu gọda, gapa dọ ranbon lagaoa.

Adọ sạri unkin dọ enka mẹn baṛakatekin bereťena; adọ kulhi sẹnre teṅgokate uni khạmid hoṛkin lạiadea, nui dọ kuṛhni ruạ kantaea mẹnte. Adọ uniye mẹnkeťa, Tọbẹ ceť lekatebon bạgi ocoyea?

Adọ unkinkin mẹnkeťa, Hape, alom rọṛ baṛaea, ona reaḱ ran dọ ạlińliń baḍaea, am dọ thir hataṛoḱme.

Adọ sạri unkin dọ birte sẹnkate tiṛṛạ da khub hapṛaḱ hapṛaḱa, kohṇḍa un tititaḱ, barea dakin la ạgukeťa. Adọ ạyuṕ khange uni ruạḱ kan hoṛ oṛaḱte sẹnkatekin mẹnkeťa, Ran dọliń ńam ạgukeťa, teheń dọ baliń lagaoeťa, mẹnkhan gapa dọ ạḍi setaḱ piạń payańreliń lagaoa, ạikhạ hana kulhi mucạťre dọbạṭią then ape sanam hoṛ ar uni dukhạlite ọnḍẹliń bulạu baṛalepege; adọ ọnḍẹge nãhãḱ ran dọliń lagaoa. Adọ gapa setaḱ ọkọe hõ alope jãhãkoteḱa mẹnte teheńreliń lại sạḍeape kana.

Adọko mẹnkeťa, Acha, besge ẹnḍẹkhan.

---

[10] In Santali also called patal kohṇḍa, lit. netherworld pumpkin, the tuber of Pueraria tuberosa, DC., a large climber growing wild in the forests. The tubers may grow to an enormous size and are sometimes used by the people for food.

[11] The Santali expression may mean both a special kind of exorcism and to persuade, seduce, deceive. Both meanings are possible.

performed, will the medicine take effect, otherwise it will certainly not be of any use."

"All right," the man replied, "work in any way whatever that will bring a cure, don't take half measures."

The two medicine-men then said: "Very well then, it is quite sufficient what has been said; we shall at once bring the medicine, and having procured that, we shall exorcize her, and we shall also at once apply the medicine."

"Please then," the man said to them, "be quick and find and bring the medicine to-day or to-morrow. At the present time great difficulty is felt; it is not well to leave a sick person alone either. It might do, if one kept watch; but we have not enough working people. Please bring the medicine quickly without delay."

"Very well then," they said, "we shall find and bring it to-day, to-morrow we shall apply the medicine."

Having spoken this the two medicine-men started, and when they were out in the village street, they stopped and told the head of the house that the girl suffered from lazy-fever. "How then shall we be able to cure her?" the man asked.

"Wait", they replied, "don't say anything; we two know the proper medicine for this; you keep quiet in the meantime."

So, truth to tell, the two medicine-men went to the forest and found some very big tirra[10] tubers, as big as pumpkins, dug out two and brought them. As soon as it became evening, they went to the patient's house and said: "We have found and brought the medicine, but we shall not apply it to-day; to-morrow very early at the break of dawn we shall apply it; but mind you, at that far-away end of the village street at the cross-road, there we must before anything else exorcize all of you[11], also the patient; there we shall apply the medicine. We are making this known to you to-day, in order that none of you go anywhere to-morrow morning."

"All right," they said, "then that is good."

Adokin menketa, Ma endekhan ror do niage, alin hõ gapa do adirelin heć godoka. Ado kedok dak mandiko ematkina, ado jom barakatekin calaoena.

Ado dosar hilok do sim rakrekin heć gotena, ar ona tirra da do kulhi mucatrekin idi maran otokata, ado onko thenkin hećentekin beretketkoa. Ado lota dak ar sindur ar dhadra hatakkin khojketkoa. Ado onako ńamkate joto hor ona kulhi mucat dobatiarekin idiketkoa. Ado uni ruak hor ona dhadra hatakre cando rakap sen samankatekin durup ocokedea, ar ona hatakkin sindur barawata, ar sukri dhumbakkotekin bulau barakedea. Ado ona tirra agukate banarge uni kurhni kuri hotokrekin akawadea, arkin metadea, Am do, bahu, pe dhao noa kulhi do dãrã rakap dãrã ãrgoeme, ale do nendegele tahẽ hatarokа. Pe dhaoem dãrãle eneć ber kataoka, ar ende aneć ale hõ nonde khonle uthau dareaka. Ma hako pako pe dhaote dãrã rakap hodben.

Ado sari uni bahu kuri do setakrege kulhi kulhiteye calak kana; ado bogeteko landawae kana, ar gidrako do uni tayom tayomete bogeteko pańja barayedea, arko tayoyeta ar deke cetak cetakte raskate ućateko kikiau idiyeta. Ar onko kulhi mucatrenko bogeteko landawae kana. Ar unkin ojha dokin metae kana, Aikha aurim bogek dhabić noa tol ran do tahẽ ocoam; tisem besoka

[12] The Santals are early risers, generally awake from cock-crow, even if they do not move about, until it becomes light.

[13] The things mentioned are constantly used by the ojhas. Sindur is the red lead used ceremonially.

[14] A full description of this kind of exorcism is found in the work referred to above, The Santals and Disease. The ojha stands before the patient and, taking a fowl in his hand, he makes a sweep over the patient, carrying the hand with the fowl under his thigh from behind; with his other hand he then takes the fowl and makes the same sweep, only finishing under his other thigh. The whole is repeated thrice. Instead of a fowl the ojha has here some balls of pigs' excrement. This is not according to custom, but naturally an ojha is supposed to know his business.

"So then that is enough said," the two medicine-men replied, "we two shall also come very early to-morrow." Thereupon they gave them supper, and having eaten they went away.

The next day they came at cock-crow; before anything else they carried the tirra tubers to the end of the village street and left them there. Thereupon they went to the people concerned and got them up[12]. They asked them for a brass-cup with water, some sindur and a worn- out winnowing-fan[13]. Having got these things they took them all along to the end of the village street to the cross-ways. Here they made the patient sit down on the winnowing-fan, and they excorcized[14] the girl with pigs' excrement. Thereupon they brought the tirra tubers and hang them both on the neck of the lazy girl and said to her: "You, daughter-in-law[15], walk three times up and three times down this village street; we shall stay here in the meantime. Only when you have walked three times, the adverse occult hindrance will be removed, and then only we shall also be able to go away from this spot. Please be quick and walk three times up and down."

So, truth to tell, this daughter-in-law of theirs commenced to walk along the street in the morning, and people laughed very much at her, and the village children followed after her in crowds and were clapping their hands[16], and slapping their buttocks they were skipping with joy and screaming. And those standing at the end of the village street were laughing at her boisterously. The two medicine-men said to her: "Mind you, let this medicine remain on you, until you are cured; when you recover entirely, loosen it and throw it away." Now the girl

---

15 One of the ojhas addresses the girl as stated, using the dual. If there is no real known relationship, they will always make an artificial one to allow an easier and more familiar intercourse.

16 Clapping of hands does not convey applause in our sense among the genuine Santals; it conveys the idea of mockery, 'skadefryd', as it is called in Norwegian. Now-a-days Santals have learnt to clap their hands in applauding from foreigners.

rarạ gidikaben. Adọ uni bạhu kuri dọ bar dhaogeye dāṛāleťa, adọ ạḍiko landawae kan lajaote ona tọl ran dọe capať giḍikeťte oṛaǩteye dạṛkeťa; adọ artẹťge bogeteko landawadea

Khangeye dạṛkeť khan, adọ sanam hoṛ oṛaǩteko calaoena. Adọ ojhakin metae kana, Henda bạhu, boge gọťente ran dọben rarạ giḍikaťa sẹ ceť leka?

Adọ uni hō̃ muluć muluće landajoṅ kana. Adọ unkin ojhakin mẹnkeťa, Mẹn adọ tis hō̃ nonkan ruạ dọ aloben ruạǩa, baṅkhan ona rangeliṅ lagaoabena. Sanam ruạge ạliṅ dọliṅ pachnao daṛeaǩa.

Adọ ẹn hiloǩ khon uni kuṛi dọe phạriạ utạrena, adọ tis hō̃ bae ruạlena, adọ kurumuṭuteye kạmijoṅa. Adọ ọnẹ onkate uni kuṛhni dọe besena arko bạgi ocokedea.

Adọ cabayena katha dọ, in maraṅgea.

33. Kuiri ar nạ̃u reaǩ.

Sedae jugre, kathae, miťṭaṅ atore miťṭaṅ kuiri ar miťṭaṅ nạ̃u unkin dọ oḍok duạr oṛaǩ tahẽkantạkina. Uni kuiri dọ khub kisạ̃ṛe tahẽkana, ar uni nạ̃u dọ rẹṅgẹćgeye tahẽkana. Khange

---

17 She does not deny her Santal nature, but is able to see the ludicrousness of the whole.

I have several variants of this story. In one of them the proceedings are referred to a Sunday, a day considered favourable for medical treatment in many cases. The patient is here ordered to carry a large earthen pot full of water to the end of the village street; here the ojha ties two tirra tubers to her neck and pours the water over her. She is then ordered to go straight home without looking back. The scene is thereupon the same, and as she cannot stand the shame of it, she throws the tubers away and runs home to her own parents in another village. From there she is afterwards brought back cured.

In another variant a husband of the sister of the husband's father is called in; he happens to be a professional ojha. This may perhaps explain the dual used by one of the ojhas in the above story. After having found out the nature of the complaint this ojha the next morning brings his remedy, which he ties

walked twice up and down, but as they were laughing so much at her, she for very shame threw this tied-on medicine away and ran home; then they laughed still more at her.

When she had run away, all of them went to their house, and the two medicine-men said to her: "Look here, daughter-in-law, was it because you got well so quickly that you loosened and threw the medicine away or how?"

And she also was smiling and laughing[17] to herself, whereupon the medicine-men said: "Be careful, never any more become ill in the same way, otherwise we shall apply the same medicine. We are able to distinguish all kinds of disease."

From that day the girl became entirely well again; she never was ill again, and she was diligently working. In this way this lazy girl became well, and they made her leave off being lazy.

So the story is ended, it is so much.

33. THE FARMER AND THE BARBER.

ONCE upon a time long ago, people tell, in a certain village a farmer[1] and a barber[2] were living, their houses lying opposite to one another in the village street. The farmer was very wealthy,

in a bundle round the neck of the girl, telling her that she must have this on so long as she is ill, but may throw it away, as soon as she recovers. His medicine is faeces tied up in some rags. The horrid smell affects the girl; she tries to arrange it so that she may not be inconvenienced, but does not succeed and finally throws the whole away, finds a hoe and goes straight off and commences to hoe Indian corn. The others praise the old man for his efficiency as a doctor, whereupon they have a feast with rice-beer, and talking they make the girl so ashamed that her lazy-fever is cured once for all.

33 [1] What is translated farmer, in Santali kuiṛi, is a Hindu caste, the members of which have as their special occupation to cultivate vegetables.

[2] The barber, in Santali nãu or napit or lapit, is another low Hindu caste. It might be noted that all castes may take to agriculture and often support themselves in this way, leaving their caste-occupation alone. It is not strange; they have the soil to fall back on, it is felt as a kind of life-insurance.

adọ uni nạ̃u dọ ać mọnẹ mọnẹteye mẹnjoṅa, Durrẹ, nui kuiri dọ cekate baṅ nonka dọe kisạ̃r akan, ar ale dọ cekatele rẹṅgẹć akana? Ale dọ cele, noko leka dọ bale kạmi kan cọṅ cet́ cọṅ, onate nonka dọle rẹṅgẹjok̇ kana.

Adọ onka leka uni nạ̃u dọ mọnẹreye hudis baṛajoṅa. Adọe mẹnket́a, Nẹs dọ bhala ale hõ noko lekagele kạmi gelaea; bhala hoyok̇a sẹ baṅa; bhala ona reak̇ tak iṅ biḍạua.

Adọ mit́ din dọ ako oṛak̇ren sanam hoṛ ạyup̍ jọkhẹće galmaraoat́koa: Nẹs dọ ọkọe hõ alope kuṛhiạk̇tabona! Kurumuṭutebon kạmia. Nõk̇õe kạmibo ḍhil idiyet́tebo rẹṅgẹjok̇ kana. Adọṅ metabon kana, nẹs dọ jidạ jidbo kạmia. Bhalabon ṅẹla, hoyok̇tabona sẹ baṅ.

Khange adọ sanam hoṛko mẹnket́a, Acha bogege.

Adọ sạri khange uni nạ̃u dọ ẹn hilok̇ khon dọ cun thamakur jọm lasaṛhẽte onko kuiri oṛak̇te dọ dinạmgeye calak̇a; cun thamakur ać ṭhen tahẹnre hõ, ẹnre hõe calak̇gea. Oka ma ako oṛak̇re sẹṅgẹl tahẹnre hõ, ẹnre hõ hukạ ṅũi lạgit́ sẹṅgẹl kọe onko oṛak̇teye calak̇a, ar oka dọ ẹkẹn ajaregeye calak̇a. Mẹnkhan uni dọ ẹkẹn ajare sẹ cun thamakur jọm dọ bae calak̇a, tãhã uni dọ katha cecet́e calak̇a. Uni dọ ać mọnẹreye mẹna, Bhala teheṅ dọ oka kạmi reak̇e batlaoakoa.

Adọ okakoe batlaoako, onkage ać hõ adọ oṛak̇re hẹćkate akorenkoe batlaoakoa. Ar ạyup̍ jọkhẹć hõ onkogeye atẹn baṛakoa; bae gitić họdok̇a; onkoe aṅjọm jagakoa, ẹṇḍẹ anẹć ać dọe jagak̇a. Ar tinre kạḍa ḍaṅgrako aṛak̇koa, unrege ać hõe aṛak̇koa, ar tin jọkhẹć siok̇ko joṛaoa, unrege ako hõko joṛaoa, ar oka berko aṛaga, inạ berge noko hõ siok̇ko aṛaga.

---

[3] See Vol. I., page 50, note 11. This way of using tobacco is Santal.

[4] The hookah, or hubble-bubble, as it is also called, on account of the sound produced when the smoke passes through the water bowl, is now coming into use among the Santals also, but is by no means common.

but the barber was very poor. The barber was saying to himself: "Dear me, how is it that this farmer has become so wealthy, and how have we become poor? Very likely, somehow or other we do not work like those people, therefore we are becoming poor."

The barber was thinking such thoughts; so he said: "Well, this year we also shall try to carry on the work in the same way as those, then we shall see whether it will come to anything or not; I shall have a try at their mode of working."

So in the evening one day he spoke to all those with him: "This year none of you must be lazy. We shall work diligently. You see, we have been negligent in our work, and therefore we are becoming poor. So I say to all of us: 'This year we shall work all we can. We shall have a try and see whether we shall succeed or not'."

"All right, that is good," they all of them said.

Truth to tell, from that very day the barber went every day to the farmer's house on the pretext of chewing[3] tobacco and lime; even if he had lime and tobacco himself, he was in the habit of going. Sometimes, although they had a fire in their own house, he would go to the other ones to ask for fire to light his hookah[4], and now and then he would go simply to have a chat. But this was not his reason, he did not go only to chat or to chew lime and tobacco, he went to learn what to do. He was saying to himself: "I wonder what work he is giving orders about to-day."

And what the farmer was telling his people to do, the same the barber also, when he came back home again, instructed his people to do. In the evenings also he was listening for those other ones; he did not go early to bed; he heard that the other ones retired for the night; then only he himself also went to bed. And at what hour those other ones let out their buffaloes and bullocks, at the same time he also let out his cattle, and when they yoked the ploughs, at the same time he also did the same, and at what hour they unyoked their ploughs, at the same hour these also stopped ploughing.

Adọ din hiloḱ onkage uni dọ onkogeye atẹn baṛakoa. Uni kuiri kisạṛ okakore sioḱe metako, ona aṅjọmkate ać hõ akoreṅkoe metakoa, ar oka hiloḱ okako itạko ẹr, adọ ako hõ onako itạgeko ẹra sẹko aphọra; ar onko kuiri dọ bako baḍae akadea, baṅma, nui nạu dọ aboaḱ batlao ceťte ać hõe kạmi kana mẹnte. Mẹnkhan ḍher din tayọmko baḍaekedea, baṅma, aboaḱ batlaoaḱ kạmi aṅjọmtege nui nạu dọe kạmi kana; adọ ẹnre hõ ceť hõ bako metadea.

Khange sạri adọ ẹn serma dọ uni nạuaḱ cas hõ khubge hoeyentaea, joṇḍra, bajṛa sẹ jẹ kichuye casleť, jọtọge hoeyentaea. Adọ ạḍi rạskạkate rihṛạḱ rihṛạḱe bạndiketa. Adọe mẹnketa, Nõḱõe katha ar bud iṅ ceťkeťte abo hõbo arjaoketa; mẹnkhan iṅ dọ katha ced. dọ ọhọṅ bạgilea. Adọe arjaoketre hõ, ẹnre hõ onko oṛaḱte calaḱ dọ bae bạgileta.

Adọ Mag boṅga tioḱen khan, uni kuiri dọe metaťkoa, Ma nẹtar dọ ạkbo rọhọea. Khange uni nạu hõe aṅjọmkeť khan dọ, ako oṛaḱte sẹnkateye metako kana, Ẹ ya, ma abo hõ ạk rọhọe lạgiť si lạhudtabonpe.

Khange sạri si lạhuťkeťteko rọhọeketa. Adọ uni nạu ma cas kạmi reaḱ mọrọm bae baḍae, ar cas mae caskeť; adọ onko kuiri kisạṛren ceť lekako kạmi, adọ noko hõ onkageko kạmia.

Khange sạri tahẹn tahẹnte adọ ona ạk dọ harayena, onkoaḱ hõ ar nuiaḱ hõ. Khange adọ uni kuiriye mẹnketa, Nui nạu dọ ya abo aṅjọm aṅjọmtegeye kạmi kan dọ; eṅgate bhala teheṅ

5 The Santals have two names for sowing, one for sowing in general and another for sowing in beds or, especially, in rice-fields, to get seedlings, that are pulled up and transplanted. Nearly all the paddy is treated in this way, anyhow in the more hilly Santal country.

6 What is translated grain is what in Santali is called bajṛa, Sorghum vulgare, Pers.

7 The Santals store their paddy, or for that sake, any kind of grain in bundles made of straw-rope. It is said to be a very effective way of storing. These bundles are not easily attacked by rats and keep the grain dry. Such a bundle may contain anything from say 50 up to 600 kg., a very common size being one containing about 400 kg.

Every day he in this way listened to those other ones. When the farmer told his people to plough somewhere, having heard this he himself also instructed his people to plough in similar places, and when those other ones some day sowed some kind of seed or other, they also sowed the same kind of seed broadcast or for transplantation[5], and the farmer's people had not understood that this barber also was working according to what he learnt by their instruction. However, after a long time they understood that the barber was working in accordance with what he heard with them; still they did not say anything to him.

Truth to tell, that year the cultivation of the barber also gave splendid results: maize, grain[6], or whatever he cultivated, all succeeded for him, and with great joy he stoved it away in a number of straw-bundles[7]. He said: "Here we see, because I learnt what to do and got understanding, we also have earned good crops; but I shall certainly not give up learning." So although he had good crops, he did not give up going to the house of those other ones.

When the month of Mag[8] came, the farmer said to his people: "Now at the present time we shall plant sugar-cane." When he heard this, the barber went home and also said to his people: "You here, we also shall plant sugar-cane, so plough and prepare the soil for that."

Truth to tell, they ploughed and prepared the soil and planted. Now the barber did not know the proper method of cultivation, still he was having cultivation, and just as the people of the wealthy farmer were working, so these also worked.

As time went, the sugar-cane crop, truth to tell, grew up both that of the farmer and that of this barber. One day the farmer said: "This barber fellow is working all along hearing what we

---

8 The month of Mag corresponds to the latter half of our January and the first half of February.

dǫbo biḍạuea. Khange adǫ ạyuṗen khan, uni kuiri dǫe metaťkoa, Eya guti kạmiạ, gapa dǫ ạk ãṛgǫmkatabonpe.

Khange adǫ uni nạ̃u hǫ̃e aṅjǫmkeť khan, aćren hǫ̃e metako kana, E ya, abo hǫ̃ gapa dǫ ạk ãṛgǫmkatabonpe. Khange aṅgayen khan dǫ, ãṛgǫmko joṛao gǫťkeťa; adǫ ona hoe ạkge curmarko ãṛgǫmkeťa, sanamko ãrgǫm gitićketa. Ar uni kuiri dǫ bae ãṛgǫmleťa.

Khange adǫ ạḍiko landawadea. Adǫ inạ ťayǫm khange uni nạ̃uaǩ ạk dǫ mõṛã mõṛãyena sẹ, ạḍi bạṛić candheṛ oḍokentaea; adǫ ạḍi bạṛić hoeyentaea. Uni kuiriaǩ khon dǫ nuiaǩge sǫrǫsentaea.

Adǫ inạkate miť din dǫ uni kuiriye galmarao kantakoa, baṅma, Gapa dǫ buṭbon ẹra; ma ona buṭ bạndi bǫgǫjte teheṅre baṛẹ ata dǫhǫkape; atale khan dǫ, miť dhaote nãhãǩ janam gǫdoǩa, ar bin atawaǩ dǫ baṅ batraoǩa. Gapa dǫ tinrepe ataea? Bilǫmoǩale nãhãǩ; ma teheṅre baṛẹ ata dǫhǫkape. Adǫ onka uni kuiri dǫ ạuṛiaǩgeye rǫṛkeťa, adǫe thirena.

Khange adǫ uni nạ̃u hǫ̃ onae aṅjǫmkeť khan, oṛaǩre sẹnkate ać hǫ̃ buṭ ḇạṅḍiye bǫgǫćkeťa, are ata oçokeťkoa. Khange adǫ dosar hiloǩko ẹṛkeťa. Adǫ uni kuiriaǩ dǫ miť sãote jǫtǫ janam gǫťentaea, ar uni nạ̃uaǩ dǫ jãhã kãhã miť bar janamena. Khange adǫ uni nạ̃ue mẹneťa, Henda ho, amaǩ dǫ miť dhaote jǫtǫ ǫmǫn gǫťentama, iṅaǩ dǫ cekate baṅ ǫmǫn cabalena?

Adǫ uni kuiriye mẹnkeťa, E ho, ale dǫ atakatele ẹr akaťa, onate janam gǫťentalea.

Adǫ uni nạ̃ue mẹn gǫťkeťa, Ale hǫ̃le ataleťgea.

---

9 What is called a harrow is a kind of clod-crusher, a piece of wood some five to seven feet long and about five to four inches thick, in the middle of which is fastened a pole, to which the yoke is attached. It is used to crush clods after ploughing and to make the surface smooth, but naturally not for a purpose like that one here described.

10 The gram is the Cicer arietinum, L. commonly cultivated in many parts of Bengal, but not commonly by the Santals.

are doing; dash it, to-day we shall try him." So when evening came, the farmer said to his people: "Listen, servants and workers, to-morrow you shall harrow[9] down our sugar-cane."

Hearing this the barber also said to his people: "Listen you, to-morrow we also shall harrow our sugar-cane." And as soon as day dawned, they yoked the harrows and harrowed the grown sugar-cane energetically down, they harrowed all of it and laid it down; but the farmer naturally did not harrow his sugar-cane.

They had a good laugh at the barber; but after this the barber's sugar-cane commenced to send out any amount of shoots from the joints, an awful number of clumps came out, and he got a very rich crop. The barber's was better than that of the farmer.

After this the farmer one day was speaking to his people: "To-morrow we shall sow gram[10]; so open that straw-bundle with gram to-day and roast it ready for to-morrow; when it is roasted, it will all come up at the same time and quickly; what is not roasted, will not germinate well. When will you find time to roast it to-morrow? We should be delayed; so roast and have it ready to-day." The farmer in this manner talked rubbish, and then he stopped. When the barber heard this, he went home and himself also opened a gram-bundle and made his people roast the gram, and the next day they sowed it. Now the farmer's gram all came up evenly and quickly, but that of the barber came up here and there just one or two. The barber then asked: "Look here, your gram came all up quickly and at the same time, how is it that mine has not all germinated?"

"You see," the farmer replied, "we have sown after having roasted the gram; that is the reason why it has all germinated quickly."

"We also roasted it," the barber said.

Adọ kuiriye mẹnketa, Pasẹć ape dọ atare bape batraolet? Khub leka bape ata rọṅgọea? Ẹnẹ ńẹlme, okako rọṅgọlentape, inạge janamena, ar oka baṅ rọṅgọlen, ona dọ baṅ janamlentapea.

Adọ uni nạue mẹnketa, Hẽ ho, cele atarege ale dọ bale ṭhikleta. Adọ oṛakre hẹćkate ạḍi bạṛić kạhur mạhure ruhet baṛaketkoa. Adọ inạ mit barakgeye tahẽ ocoata. Adọ inạ buṭge, cet baṅ sẹ, uniak khọn bạṛti hoeyentaea, ar ẹn jaṅkate hõ nuiakge ḍherentaea.

Khange adọ pẹ pon sermatege uni kuiri khon dọ nuige bạṛtiye kisạṛena, ar uni kuiri dọe hẽṭena. Onka lekate uni nạu dọe kisạṛlen tahẽkana.

Inạkgea katha dọ, cabayena.

34. Tili ar uniren guti reaṅ.

Sedae jugre kathae nonka hoelena, baṅma, mitṭaṅ tili haṛam dạuṛạre sunum jạluạ sajaokate atote ạkriṅ lạgite calak kana. Adọ calak jọkhẹćge mitṭaṅ họṛe ńamkedea, adọe metae kanạ, Henda ho, iṅ ṭhen gutim tahẽkoka?

Adọe mẹnketa, Hẽ ẹntẹm dọhọń khan dọń tahẹna.

Adọe mẹnketa, Ẹṇḍẹkhan ḍẹ, noa sunum dạuṛạ dipiltiṅme; noa dipil reak dọ nãhãk bar ana poesaṅ emama.

---

11 It might be remarked that the point of the story is not to give some up-to-date instruction in agriculture. The idea is on the one hand to show the ignorance of the barber and the practical joking of the kuiri, on the other hand how the barber in spite of all gained.

34 1 This is the Sạntal form of an old story, found in a very similar shape in the Pancatantra and obviously borrowed from Hindu sources, but in its entirety adapted to Santal ideas and what a Santal may see every day. One of the actors is also especially stated to be a Santal.

2 A common sight in the Santal villages. People belonging to the Hindu tili caste, whose work is to press oil (hence their name teli or tili from tel, oil), are fairly numerous also in the Santal country. Like many other castes they may earn their livelihood by agriculture or by trading, but those who stick to their ancestral work may be met with in the villages, as they walk about

"Perhaps," the farmer said, "perhaps you did not succeed in roasting it properly? Should you not roast it thoroughly, even to burning point? Look at it, what was properly burnt of yours, that has come up, and what was not burnt, that has not germinated."

"Yes, yes," the barber replied, "likely we did not do the roasting properly." And when he came home again, he abused and scolded his people no end. But he let the gram be just as it was. And this same gram, you have never seen the like of it, it became very much more than that of the farmer, and when they had threshed it, it also was more than the other one's.

It the course of three to four years the barber became better off than the farmer; the farmer lagged behind. In this way this barber became rich[11].

The story is that much, it is ended.

34. THE OILMAN AND HIS SERVANT[1].

Once upon a time long ago, people tell, it so happened that an old oilman had put an earthenware pot with oil in a flat basket[2] and was on his way to a village to sell oil. As he was walking along, he met with a Santal[3] and said to him: "Look here, would you be willing to become my servant?"

"Yes," he replied, "if you take me on, I shall stay with you."

"In that case," the oilman said, "carry this flat basket with the oil for me; for doing this I shall presently give you two annas[4] in copper."

---

with their oil (mostly mustard-oil, used for culinary purposes in every household) in an earthenware pot placed like here told in a bamboo basket.

[3] The word used means in Santali either a human being or a Santal. The story presupposes that it is a Santal. Cf. note 10 below.

[4] When mentioning any amount of annas ($^1/_{16}$ of a rupee) it is very common to make use of this expression, so and so many annas in pice, the pice being a copper-coin, one quarter-anna. It is likely a proof that the money ordinarily used by the Santals has been copper-pice, as it is, even now-a-days.

Adoe menkeťa, Acha bogege, endekhan iń dipiltama.

Khange sari adoe dipilkeťtaea; ado calak̔ tuluć uni hoṛ do hoṛ horteye hudis idiyeťa, je bar ana poesa nāhāk̔e emańa; miť anate do khorcań kirińa; iną do nāhāk̔ iń joma ar miť ana sarejok̔a; inąte do sim iń kirińkoa; ado eṅga iń dohokoa, adoko belea arko busąk̔koa; adoko haralenkhan kaloṭ do eṅga iń doho idikoa ar sąṇḍi doń gayakoa, ado onko gaya do harakate cącąr anateń ąkrińkoa; ona poesate ado merom iń kirińkoa, khange meromko busąk̔lenkhan do pąṭhi do eṅga iń dohokoa ar boda doń kąsikoa, ado onko kąsi ąkrińkate ona ṭakate do gąi iń kirińkoa; ado gąiko busąk̔lenkhan bąchi mīhū do puńjigeń dohokoa, ar ḍaṅgra doń koṭećkoa; ar adom ḍaṅgra doń ąkrińkoteń ṭakaea, ar adom ḍaṅgrate do bitkil iń kirińkoa; ado onko bitkilko busąk̔lenkhan kąḍi hopon do bąḍgeń dohokoa, ar kaḍa hopon do harakateń koṭećkoa, ar jumi bąṛi kirińkateń siok̔a; ado cas bas hoeyena menkhan doń bąhujońa, ado gidąr pidąrko hoyok̔tińa; adoko haralenkhan ghuṭ ghuṭko ńir baṛaea; ado khange iń do kąmi khon iń hoć godok̔a, ado hećkate parkomreń duṛup̔ godok̔a, ado iń bąhu do dak̔ko dątąunikoe ąguańa, adoń dątąuni baṛa godok̔a; ado dątąuni baṛakate doń duṛup̔ thirkok̔a, ado gidrąkoko metańa, Ma baba, daka jom lągiť ąbukok̔me; ado un jokhoć bohok̔ iń ruku goda ariń mena, Ũhũk̔, ũhũk̔, bań joma ya.

Onka hudis baṛakate ado ũhũk̔ ũhũk̔e men jokhećge sunum dąuṛą do bohok̔ khon ńũr goťena, sunum ṭhili hõ posak̔ gejer

---

5 A Santal man may, when absolutely necessary, carry things on his head; otherwise a man ordinarily carries them on his shoulder, while the women carry on their heads. This is so much the custom that, when the sex of a new-born babe is announced, it is almost invariably done by stating bhąrią or dipil, the former, meaning 'carrying on the shoulder', about a boy, and the latter, 'carrying on the head', about a girl.

6 An operation very commonly performed by the Santals.

7 The price refers to the time when this story was written down, some thirty years ago. At that time a capon was generally bought for four annas, i. e. four pence. Now the price is at least thrice that.

"Very well," the other replied, "then I shall carry it for you."

So, truth to tell, he took it on his head[5] and carried it along. While he was walking along, the Santal was thinking in this way: He will presently give me two annas in coppers; for one anna I shall buy food; this I shall eat, and then there will be one anna left; for this I shall buy fowls and keep hens, and they will lay eggs and hatch chickens; when these grow up, I shall keep the pullets as laying hens, and the cocks I shall caponize[6], and when the capons grow up, I shall sell them for four annas[7] a piece; for that money I shall buy goats, and when the goats kid, I shall keep the she-kids for breeding, and the he-kids I shall castrate, and selling these I shall for that money buy cows; when the cows calve, I shall retain the female ones as my stock, and the bull calfs I shall geld[8]; some bullocks I shall sell and get money for, and for some bullocks I shall buy buffalo-cows; then when these buffalo-cows calve, I shall keep the female ones for breeding, and the male calves I shall let grow up and then geld them, and I shall buy rice-land and fields and plough; then when my cultivation gets on, I shall marry, and so I shall get children; and when they grow up, they will run about capering; then I shall come in from my work and sit down on my bed, and my wife will bring me water and tooth-brushes; then I shall just brush my teeth, and having done this I shall sit down quietly; then my children will say to me: "Please, father, wash your hands and come and have food;" then at that moment I shall shake my head and say: "No, no![9] I shall not eat."

While he was thinking in this way, just as he was saying "No, no", the basket with the oil tumbled down, the pot with the

8 In the case of cattle Santals as a rule do not castrate, but destroy the seminal ducts by beating, the final result being the same. They have some special implements made for the purpose.

9 The Santali interjection ũ h ũ k̓, signifying strong remonstrance, is always accompanied by a vigorous shaking of the head.

goťena. Khange adǫ uni tili haṛame ruheť gǫťkedea, Durrẹ, ceť leka mạńjhim dipil akaťa? Sanam sunumem loksankeťtińa miť poesa reak̓ hõ ạurilań ạkrińrege. Am dǫ jǫtǫ sunumem hirićkeťa, miť poesa hõ ǫhǫlań ẹmlema, arhõ bickom nawa sunum reak̓ dam nitgelań ạgumea.

Adǫ khange uni hǫṛe mẹnkeťa, Nawa sunum reak̓ dam dǫ ǫhǫlań ẹmlema. Am dǫm mẹneťa, je ạḍi utạr sunumem loksankeťtińa, mẹnkhan amak̓ khon dǫ ińak̓ge bạṛti loksan akantińa. Khange adǫ uni tili haṛam dǫe hạriạ̃ busiạyena. Adǫ khange bogetekin jhogṛayena. Khange adǫ uni hǫṛe mẹnkeťa, Alom ruheda onka dǫ, bana hǫṛak̓lań hisạblegi. Judi amak̓ ḍherok̓ khan, ẹnḍẹkhan ona reak̓ dam ińiń emama; ar judi ińak̓ ḍherok̓ khan, ẹnḍẹkhan ona reak̓ dam ạikhạ emańme.

Adǫ khange sạri uni tiliye mẹnkeťa, Acha bogege, malań hisạba. Ar uni tili thǫ bae baḍaelak̓a, je nui hǫṛ dǫ nonka onkae hudis akaťa mẹnte. Ać dǫe bujhạueťa, je nui hǫṛ ma ẹkẹnak̓geń ạgulede, ceť hõ thǫ bań ńẹlleťtaea, adǫ ceťe hisạb ocok̓ lạgit? Adǫ uni tiliye mẹnkeťa, je, Ińak̓ dǫ bar ṭaka reak̓ sunum tahẽ-kantińa, ar miť ana reak̓ jạluạtẹť; noam loksankeťa; dẹn, bar ṭaka miť ana ẹmok̓me.

Adǫ uni hǫṛe mẹnkeťa, Acha, adǫ ińak̓ iń lạiama, ona hisạb-tińme. Khange adǫ uni hǫṛ dǫ poesa ńam khone ẹhǫṗkeťa, poesa khon dǫ sim, sim khon dǫ mẹrǫm, adǫ ǫnẹ ceť lekae hudis ạguleť, ar ceť lekateye baḍhao ocokeť, ar ceť leka rǫṛkate ona sunum dạuṛạị ńurhạ posak̓ ocokeťtae.

Onako jǫtǫe lại cabawade khan, uni tili haṛam dǫe landa gǫťkeťa; adǫ ghạṛi ghạṛige mulućmuluće landayeť kana.

Adǫ onka lekate jǫtǫ kathae lại cabakeť khan dǫe mẹnkeťa, Ma sẹ bhala, ǫkǫeak̓ ḍher loksanentalańa?

---

10 Mạńjhi, see above p. 21, note 4.

11 Inclusive dual in threatening language.

oil also went to pieces. The old oilman scolded him and said: "O dear, how are you carrying it, headman?[10] You have caused all my oil to be lost, even before we have sold for a farthing. You have spilt all the oil; we[11] shall not give you a single farthing, on the contrary we[11] shall this instant trouble you for the price of the fresh-made oil."

"We[11] shall certainly not give you the price of the fresh-made oil," the Santal replied. "You are saying that I have made you lose very much oil, but I have lost much more than you have."

The old oilman then became sullen and angry, and they had a big quarrel. At last the Santal said: "Don't scold in this way, let us first make up our accounts. If your claims exceed mine, I shall pay you what it amounts to, and if my claims exceed yours, then you shall pay me the amount, mind you."

Truth to tell, the oilman replied: "Very well, let us make up our accounts." Now the oilman naturally did not know that the Santal had been thinking as related. So far as he understood it, he thought: "I took this man along empty-handed; I saw absolutely nothing with him, what is it then that he has to be made an account of?" Thereupon the oilman said: "I had oil worth two rupees, and the cost of the pot is one anna; this you have caused me to lose; please, out with two rupees and one anna."

The Santal thereupon replied: "Very well, now I shall tell you my claim; make up my account for me." The Santal then commenced to state his claim from the money he was to get, from the money he came to the fowls, from the fowls to the goats, and so on, how he had been thinking and how he had got everything to increase, and how he, by speaking, had caused the basket with the oil to fall down and go to pieces.

When he had told him all this, the oilman laughed; again and again he laughed and smiled.

When the Santal had in this way told the whole story, he said: "Now, how is it, of us two whose loss is the greater?"

Khange adǫ uni tili haṛame mẹnketa, Iń dǫń hisạbkettalaṅa, je bana hǫṛak somangea, bana hǫṛak bara bạrige loksanentalaṅa. Cetlaṅ cekaea? Amge adǫ bana hǫṛakem loksanket khan, cekaealaṅ nitok dǫ? Ma bogeyentalaṅa. Adǫ muluć muluć landakatekin apan ạpinena.

Cabayena katha dǫ. Adǫ onate nit hạbić Hǫṛ hǫpǫnko mẹna, Tili jǫṛ leka alom aodaea, ǫhǫm lẹṭẹćlea.

35. Mẹrǫmko jǫmlede reak katha.

Sedae jǫkhẹn ǫkǫeren mẹrǫm cǫṅ, kathae, dosra hǫṛ oṛakteye bǫlǫlen tahẽkana. Adǫ uni hǫṛ dǫ bǫlǫ torage uni dosra hǫṛren mẹrǫm dǫe gǫć gǫtkedete oṛakteye ader gǫtkedea.

Adǫ ńuhum khangeonko mẹrǫm kisạṛ dǫ ńaṅamko hẹćena. Adǫko kuliketkoa, Henda ho, pasẹ nǫtẹ mẹrǫmko hẹć jãhãn akawatpe?

Adǫko mẹnketa, Ǫkǫ baḍae ho ẹnte, baṅdǫko hẹć akan baṅ dǫ baṅ, ale dǫ bale ńẹlledea. Adǫ masẹ bhala aleren mẹrǫm gudṛire ńẹlkom, pasẹye bǫlǫ akange. Adǫ divhe oḍokkate mẹrǫm gudṛireko arsal baṛaketkoa; adǫ bạnugićkhan dǫ onko ńaṅam hǫṛ dǫko ruạṛ calaoena.

Adǫ tala ńindạ hoeyen khan, uni mẹrǫm dǫko khalkedeteko gẹt kuṭikedea, adǫko kokṛo jǫmketa, ar adǫm jel dǫko dǫhǫkata.

---

[1] According to what is told — and there does not seem to be any doubt as to the truth —, the Santals were formerly quite honest, except in connexion with goats and sheep. The old Santal guru Kolean says: "Formerly the Santals did not steal; now-a-days they have learnt this also from the Dekos. From a former time only one kind of theft is remembered, to steal and eat sheep and goats. When these went astray and were lost, then on being found by others the whole village would kill and eat these, and the village headman they used to give a double part, twice of what the others got. If such a theft were proved, they would make them give back head for head and fine them five four-anna pieces for each. Now-a-days people bring all to the smooth verandah." The last expression means, that such matters are brought to the court, 'smooth verandah' being a veiled expression for a court-of-law, or, sometimes, for a prison. It should further be noted that, when it is said that they make the thief give back the head, it means that he is to give a living animal of the same kind in restitution.

The oilman then replied: "According to the account I have made up for us, our losses are equal; we have both of us lost equally much. What shall we do? You caused us both to lose, what can we do now? Let it be well as it is." So they parted laughing.

The story is ended. On account of this story it is even now said among the Santals: Don't be overconfident like an oilpress bullock; you will not be able to manage.

35. A STORY ABOUT A GOAT THAT WAS EATEN.

Once upon a time long ago, people tell, somebody's goat had entered the house of another man. As soon as the goat came in there, the man at once killed it, although it belonged to somebody else, and took it inside into his house[1].

When the sun had set and it was twilight, the people that owned this goat came searching for it and asked: "Look here, has perhaps by any chance a goat come here to you?"

"Who knows," they replied, "whether any has come or not? We have not seen any. Please have a look into our goat-shed[2]; it might possibly have come in there." So they got a lamp[3] out, and with this light they looked over the goats in the goat-shed; but as the goat was not there, the searchers went away.

At midnight's time they flayed the goat and cut it into small bits[4], and huddled together and in secret they ate it, but a part

Another kind of theft they had was to take another man's wife. Even now a man who has misbehaved with a woman is technically called a kombṛo, a thief.

[2] Santals have separate sheds for goats and for sheep; especially the goats have to be kept separate. To have these with other animals is believed to be detrimental to the other ones.

[3] In any case a most primitive contrivance, the most common 'lamp' being a small earthenware bowl with some vegetable oil, into which a primitive wick is put.

[4] All meat is, before being cooked, cut into small pieces; this is necessitated by the absence of all implements when eating. The fingers are used.

Adọ uni apat hoṛ dọ aćren gidrạkoe metako kana, E yọi ape gidrạ dọ, nõk̕õe mẹrọm jelbon jọmeta̕, adọ gupi ṭhen hoṛren gidrạ ṭhen dọ alope sorok̕a, ẹnte mẹrọm jel dọ ạḍi bogea, baṅkhanko bas ṭhik bọtẹćkepea. Adọ un jọkhẹn onko gidrạ dọ cet̕ hõ bako roṛleta̕.

Adọ dosar hilok̕ uni akoren gại gupi gidrạ dọ setak̕ jọkhẹn gại, mẹrọm bhiḍikoe aṛak̕ idiket̕koa, adọ atoren gidrạ ṭhene laga mit̕ket̕koa. Adọ onko atoren gidrạ ać ṭhenko sorok̕ khange ać dọe pharak idik̕ kana, adọ arhõ uni sẹngeko sẹn idik̕ kana. Adọ unreye metako kana, Mẹn ya, iṅ sẹn dọ alope sorok̕a, baṅkhan sọpea nãhãk̕.

Adọko mẹnketa̕, Cet̕ ya sọlea?

Adọe metat̕koa, Mẹrọm jel ya, hola ạyup̕ iṅ jọm akata̕ ẹnte, arhõ adọm jel dọ menak̕gea.

Khange onko aṅjọmlet̕ gidrạ dọ oṛak̕reko lại keta̕; adọ uni hoṛko sap̕kedete oṛak̕ko todarotket̕ khan jelko ńamketa̕; adọ mõṛẽ sikạko ḍanḍọmkedea; adọ bọhọk̕ko ạcur ocokedea.

Adọ cabayena katha dọ.

---

5 The Santals are rather negligent in herding their cattle. So long as the rice is standing, they have to see that the cattle does not eat the crop; when the rice is harvested, the cattle is permitted to roam about very much as they like, young children, boys and girls, being supposed to look after them. As a rule all cattle belonging to one village graze together, the herding boys and girls amusing themselves as best they can, now and then paying a little attention to the cattle in their charge. The herding business is one of the great difficulties of the Santal villages. It is bad for the cattle; it is bad for the people, because any one wanting to have any kind of cultivation after the rice is harvested is prevented from doing so, on account of the roaming cattle, if he cannot go to the expense of putting up fences or keep a watch. It is also damaging to the young people who act as herds; they learn nothing that has any worth and much that is downright bad.

of the flesh they put aside. The father then said to his children: "Listen, you children; as you are aware, here we are eating goat's flesh; now when you are out herding, don't go near to the children of other people; you see, goat's flesh is excellent, and they might smell it in you." At that time these children did not say a word.

The next day this man's cowherd boy[5] let their cows, goats and sheep out in the morning and took them off; he drove them off to the same place as where the village children were herding[6]. Now when these village children came near to the boy, he himself always went off some distance; but they were constantly coming near to him. Then he called out to them: "Be careful, you fellows, don't come near to me, otherwise you will smell."

"What shall we smell, you fellow?" they asked.

"Goat's flesh, you fellows," he replied; "yesterday evening I have eaten goat's flesh, you see; even now there is some flesh left."

The children who heard this told it at their homes, and when they had caught hold of the man and searched his house, they found the flesh, whereupon they fined him five four-anna pieces[7] and made him give in restitution another goat.

So there this story is ended.

---

6 See preceding note. They all go together.

7 The sikạ, a four-anna piece, is a common unit of money. Five such, i. e. one rupee and four annas, is the amount very generally imposed as a fine. Formerly this amount was very seldom surpassed in ordinary cases. Now-a-days they may charge much more. When anybody brings a case in the village council, the same amount is charged against both sides 'for food', or if one likes as 'court-fees'. In petty 'criminal' cases the man who gains his case is often not charged more than half, i. e. ten annas. These 'fees' are paid after the case has been heard.

It will be seen that the story adheres to the oral law of the ancestors quoted above.

36. Pea lelha koṛako reaḱ katha.

Tis jọkhẹnre cọṅ, kathae, pea koṛa miťṭaṅ jọjọ dare buṭạreko duṛuṕ akan tahẽkana, ar onkatege miťṭaṅ họr sẹn paṛọm akana. Adọ onko koṛa dọ ceťko cọṅ emanteaḱko galmarao kaṅ tahẽkana. Adọ un jọkhẹnge, kathae, okaren cọṅ miťṭaṅ họṛ dọ kaerae gọḱ ạguyeť tahẽkana. Adọ onkoe ńẹlkeťko khan, uni họṛ dọ onko samaṅre ona kaera dọe dọhọ gọťkaťa, ar miť dhaoe ḍọbọḱ oṭokaťa, adọe calaoena; ar ona kaera dọ ọnḍẹgeye bạgiaťa.

Adọ onko koṛa dọko kạphạriạu kana — huni hõe mẹneťa, Noa kaera dọ iṅgeń hataoa, ẹnte iṅgeye ḍọbọḱ oṭoadiṅa; ar huni hõe mẹneťa, Baṅa ya, iṅgeye ḍọbọḱ akawadiṅa. Adọ onka cur marko kạphạriạu kana, arko mẹneťa, Am dọ ya, ạḍim lelhagea; ar huni hõe mẹneťa, Am hõm lelhagea. Adọ onka jọtọge lelha lelhako rupuhedoḱ kana. Adọ miť họṛ dọe mẹn gọťkeťa, Henda ya, am dọ lelham metaṅ kana; ceť yaṅ lelhawa? Adọ uni hõe rọṛ ruạṛ gọda, Henda ya, iṅ dọ ceť iṅ lelhawa? Adọ onkage ạḍi tekhra tikhriko kạphạriạu kana, ar kaera dọ ọkọe hõ bako idiyeťa.

Adọ onka kạphạriạu kạphạriạute miť họṛ dọe mẹnkeťa, Sạrige ya, eṅgate iṅ dọ ạḍiṅ lelhagea.

Adọ unkin bar họṛkin mẹnkeťa, Henda ya, cekatem lelhawa? Masẹ ona lạilem.

Adọ uni koṛae mẹnkeťa, Ẹ ya, iṅko bạhuadiṅa; adọliṅ gidrạwana. Adọ miť din dọ iṅ ṭhen gidrạ dọe dọhọ oṭokadete aċ dọ birte atorenko sãote sahan ạgui calaoena. Adọ nunu gidrạye bạgiadea sẹ baṅ? Adọe ạdo baṛakeť khange rẹṅgẹċkedea, adọ bogeteye raḱeť kana, ar sẹ bako ruạṛ họdoḱ kana. Adọe raḱeť khan dọń asẹn baṛayede kana, adọ hapege bae hapeḱ kana.

[1] The man bows to the plantains, not to the three young men.

[2] Among the Santals it is customary that the women go to the forest to fetch fire-wood (fire-wood and leaves, as it is called); for protection, also against Mrs. Grundy (or in their case perhaps rather the male representatives), they never go alone. Very frequently every house in the village is represented.

36. THE THREE FOOLS.

ONCE upon a time, who knows when, three young men, it is told, were sitting at the foot of a tamarind tree, where a road was passing. The young men were talking of something or other, when a man, a stranger, was coming along, carrying a bunch of plantains. When he caught sight of these young men, he put the bunch of plantains down in front of them, bowed once[1] and went away, leaving the plantains there.

The young men then commenced to quarrel; this one was saying: "I shall take these plantains; it was I to whom he bowed;" and that one also was saying: "No, you fellows, it was I; he put them down before me." In this way they were quarrelling hotly and were saying to each other: "You fellow, you are a great fool." And they all said the same. In this way they were scolding each other and called each other names. Then one of them said: "Look here, you fellow, you are calling me a fool; in what respect am I a fool, you fellow?" The other then answered in the same way. They were quarrelling and wrangling, and none of them carried the plaintains away.

While they were keeping it going in this way, one of them said: "It is quite true, you fellows, dash it, I am a great fool."

The other two then said: "Look here, you, how is it that you are a fool? Please tell at once."

The young man then said: "Well you, they had me married, and we got a child. Then one day she left the child with me and went with the village women to the forest to fetch fire-wood[2]. Now the child she left was a sucking babe, you see. First it passed water; then it became hungry and was crying a good deal; and those women did not come back quickly. As it was crying, I carried it about; but it would not stop crying. I gave it rice and rice-water and molasses and cow's milk also; no use; it would not take any thing and would not be quiet; and I

Dakako, dak' mạṇḍiko, guṛkoṅ emae kana, ar gại toakoṅ emae kana; adọ onako hõ bae jọmet', ar hape hõ bae hapek' kan; adọ ạḍi bạṛić iṅ ạṛisok' kana. Adọ inạ mit' ghạri khange eṅgatteṭe heċena; adọ uniye heokedea. Adọ nunureye lagaokede khan, uni gidrạ dọe hape gọt'ena. Adọ uni gidrại hapeyen khan iṅ dọ ạḍi hahaṛaṅ ạikạuket'a; adọṅ mẹn utạrket'a, Durrẹ! nui gidrạ bhala nitok' dọe hape gọt'ena; enan dọ guṛ iṅ emae kana, ona hõ bae jọm; toaṅ emae kana, ona hõ bae jọm; taben khạjạṛi, daka dak' mạṇḍiṅ emae, ayọgọ, ona hõ bae jọm ar bae hapek' kan. Adọ nõk'õeyem nunuade khane hape gọt'ena. Adọ iṅ bạhuṅ metae kana, Henda, bhala jọtọ khonak' họṛ toa dọ ạḍi sebela sẹ? Adọ uni hõe mẹnket'a, Ọkọe baḍae ẹnte, sebel baṅdọ baṅ, ona dọ cekateṅ mẹnkea? Jọtọ họṛ thọ gidrạregebon nunu akat'a, harakate thọ baṅ; cekatebo mẹn daṛekea? Adọ unreṅ mẹnket'a, Dẹ sẹ bhalaṅ nunu gelaea, cet' leka ạikạuk'a, adọṅ lạiama. Adọ onka mẹnkate sạriṅ nunu gelaket' dọ; ạḍi sebelkidiṅa, gại toa khon hõ bạṛti sebelkidiṅa. Adọ khangeṅ pạrkạu ut'ạrena, adọ dingeṅ nunuyea. Onka onkate iṅge jọtọ toaṅ nunu cabaket'a, khange gidrạ dọliṅ gọćkedea. Adọ ọnẹ onka iṅ dọ ạḍi bạṛić iṅ lelhagea.

Adọ inạkate arhõ mit' họṛe mẹnket'a, Iṅ hõ ya, sạri ạḍiṅ lelhagea.

Adọ uni pạri arhõkin kulikedea, Henda ya, bhala am dọ cet' lekam lelhawa? Masẹ adọ lạialiṅme.

Adọ uniye mẹnket'a, Sạri utạrge ya, iṅ dọ nui leka ạḍi lelha họṛ kanaṅ. Eṅgateko bạhuadiṅa; adọ besgeliṅ tahẽyena, besgeliṅ hijuk' sẹnok'a. Adọ onkage mit' dhao dọ bạhu ạguṅ sẹnlena;

---

[3] Taben and khajari are rice, the former pounded flat, the latter roasted, like what is called Japanese rice in Scandinavia. Both forms of rice are used for eating outside the ordinary meals, especially also on journeys. With molasses this form of food is estimated something like cakes with children.

[4] As a curiosity it might be mentioned that Santal mothers often suckle two children at one time. I have heard of a case where a mother was in the habit of daily taking food out to a son who was their cattle-herd, at the same time as a kind of dessert giving him the breast.

was awfully worried. Then a short while afterwards its mother came, and she took it up on her hip, and as soon as she gave it the breast, the child at once became quiet. When the child stopped crying, I was absolutely amazed and said: 'O dear, now this child suddenly stopped crying, I wonder why; a while ago I was giving it molasses; it would not have it. I gave it milk; it would not take that either. I tried to give it taben and khajari[3], rice and rice-water; O mother, it would not have any of it and would not be quiet. And now, look, as soon as you nursed it, it stopped crying at once.' So I said to my wife: 'Look here, how is it, is human milk very much sweeter than anything else?' Then she replied: 'Who can say whether it is sweet or not; how should I be able to say? When we were children, we have naturally all of us sucked, but not after we have grown up[4]; how should we then be able to say?' Then I said: 'Please let me, I should like to have a try how it tastes; then I shall tell you.' After having said this I really had a try at sucking; it tasted very sweet, I thought it much sweeter than cow's milk[5] even. Then I got into a constant habit and sucked her every day. In this way I sucked all her milk, and we let the child die. And that is how I am such an awful fool."

After this another of them also said: "I also am, in very truth, a great fool."

So in their turn they asked him also: "Look here, you fellow, how is it, in which way are you a fool? Please tell us that."

"It is absolutely true, you fellows," he replied; "like this one I am an utter fool. Dash it, they gave me a wife, and we were living well together; we were going and coming[6] in the best way.

[5] The Santals do not care much for cow's milk; they keep cows as many as they can, but the calf as a rule takes the milk.

[6] It is customary that new-married people pay frequent visits to the bride's home. The young wife naturally longs for her old home, and it is good policy with the husband to take her there.

adọko kol gọṫkaṫliń, ar iń bạhu dọ khub rọt nạkićkateko sindur gọṫkadea, ar jaṅgare hõ̱ko arta gọṫkadea. Khange adọ hijuḱ hijuḱte daḱ ńamkeṫliń; adọ miṫṭaṅ atoreliń umulena. Adọe asoṛkeṫ khan dọ, ọṇḍẹ khonliń hijuḱ kana; adọ khange miṫṭaṅ gaḍa dọliń ẹsẹṫen, bes ḍaṇḍa hatlaḱte daḱ dọ̀ calaḱ kana. Khange adọń hudis baṛakeṫa, Durrẹ! nui hoṛ dọ cekateń parọmea? Tiạḱ parọme khan ma nãhãḱ jaṅga reaḱ arta lọhọdoḱtae; eṅgateń gọḱ parọmea. Adọ khange ona gaḍareń gọḱ parọmede kana, jaṅga dọń cọṭkeṫtaea arta lọhọdoḱ bọtọrte, ar bọhọḱ dọń phẹḍkeṫtaea. Adọ onkakateń parọmkede khan, iń ńẹlkede dọe gọćen! Adọń mẹnkeṫa, Oh re! bọhọḱ iń phẹḍkeṫtaetegeń gọć ocokedea, ar baṅkhan hutẹć ọhọe gọćlena. Adọ ọnẹ onkate iń bạhu dọń gọć ocokedea, ar ọnẹ onka iń dọ ạḍi bạṛić iń lelhagea.

Adọ unkinkin mẹnkeṫa, Hẽ̱ ya, sạrim lelhagea.

Adọ arhõ̱ miṫ hoṛe mẹnkeṫa, Iń hõ̱ ya, sạri ạḍiń lelhagea.

Adọ unkinkin mẹnkeṫa, Henda ya, ceṫ lekam lelhawa? Masẹ lạilem.

Adọ uniye mẹnkeṫa, Hẽ̱ ya, ạḍiń lelhagea. Bạhuadińako, ar iń dọ hukạ ạḍiń ńũńũ kan tahẽ̱kana. Adọko bạhuadiń khan,

7 The red lead applied to the forehead of the bride at the marriage. At the ceremony it is the bridegroom who does it. Afterwards the woman will herself apply it, especially on festive occasions. It shows that she is a married woman.

8 The red pigment, in Santali a r t a, is used for dying the feet (sides) of the bride red at the time of marriage and also at other times. It is cotton impregnated with lac-dye that is used for the operation. It is common with the Hindus, but only rarely resorted to by the Santals. It is the same as Hindi (and Bengali) a l t a. A r t a in Hindi refers to a marriage ceremony in connexion with the bridegroom.

9 It is not the young pair that cannot hit it off together, but the wife and the relatives of the husband. Nothing is said about where the fault is to be sought. Among the Santals, as elsewhere, it happens that the women cannot work together; very frequently the old mother is blamed. The Santals have a significant proverb; they say: h a n h a r e r a h a ṛ h a ṫ h ọ t ọ ṫ, b a ń s e b e l a, a mother-in-law, a bitter pumpkin, do not taste well. But here, as elsewhere, the proverb may take the wrong part or be false.

So it happened once I had gone to fetch my wife home; they bade farewell to us and let us go; they dressed my wife's hair nicely and painted sindur[7] on her forehead; to her feet they also applied the red pigment[8]. Then, as we were coming along, we were overtaken by rain and took shelter in a village. When the rain ceased, we started on our way home from that place; then we were stopped by a river, the water was running well up to the waist and the armpits. I then was saying to myself: 'O dear, how shall I get this lady across? If I lead her across, the pigment on her feet will become wet; dash it, I shall carry her across.' So I was carrying her on my shoulder across that river; I kept her feet up in the air out of fear that the pigment should otherwise become wet, and her head I kept downwards. When I had in this way carried her across, I saw she was dead! I said: 'Oh! O dear! I have killed her by keeping her head down; otherwise she would certainly not have died.' In this way I caused my wife to die, and that is how it is that I am an awful fool."

The two other ones then said: "Yes, you fellow, surely you are a fool."

Also the third young man then said: "I also, you fellows, am in very truth a great fool."

"Look here, you," the two other ones then said, "how are you a fool? Please tell at once."

"Yes," he said, "I am a great fool. They gave me a wife; now I was greatly addicted to smoking the hubble-bubble. When they had given me a wife, somehow or other we did not hit it off together[9] in our family; so they separated[10] me from the

[10] When all sons have married, they may set up separate households; the land is then portioned out in equal parts between them (and the parents, if they are alive; in which case they very frequently stay with the youngest son). Sometimes, but only for special reasons, one son may be given some land, from which he is to support himself and his family. So here.

cetkore cọṅ bale jutlena; adọko begarkadiṅa, ar un dọ baliṅ gidrạ akawan tahẽkana. Adọ begarkate kulhi mucạt́ sẹćre mit́taṅ baṛge tahẽkantalea; adọko metadiṅa, Ma hana phalna baṛge am dọle emat́mea, onare oṛagok̕ben. Adọ sạri ona baṛgere oṛak̕ iṅ benaoket́a; adọ ọṇḍẹliṅ tahẹna. Adọ mit́ din dọ hukạṅ ṅũi lạgit́ sẹṅgẹl iṅ họṭọr baṛayet́ dọ bạnuk̕, ar sẹ ạḍi bạṛić ṅũṅũ sanayediṅ kana. Adọ sẹngẹl kọe iṅ calak̕ kan; khan dọṅ hudiset́a, nọṇḍẹ nãhãk̕ ać eskar iṅ bạgiae kana, ar sẹṅgẹl kọe iṅ kolere ma arhõṅ hudiset́ kan, ać eskar nãhãk̕e calak̕a, ar sẹ ạḍi ṅindạge menak̕a. Adọ onka bujhạu baṛakate iṅ dọ hukạṅ teweṅket́a ar iṅ bạhuṅ ghoṛakedea. Adọ uni ghoṛakate oṛak̕ oṛak̕ sẹṅgẹl kọeliṅ dãṛã baṛae kana. Adọ atoren họṛ dọ bogeteko landawat́liṅa. Adọ ọnẹ onka iṅ dọ ạḍiṅ lelhagea.

Adọ jọtọ hoṛko mẹpẹnena, Sạrigea, eṅgate jọtọ hoṛbon lelhagea; nahakgebon rupuhedok̕ kana. Adọ ma ẹṇḍẹkhan noa kaerabon hạṭiṅjoṅa, ar delabon apan ạpin oṛak̕tebon sẹnjoṅa. Adọ sạri inạ kaerako hạṭiṅana; adọ oṛak̕teko calao baṛayena.

Adọ ẹnẹ cabayena katha dọ, in maraṅgea.

---

11 What is here translated 'homestead-land', in Santali baṛge, is the land on which the houses are built. It is land unfit for rice cultivation on account of its high situation, but otherwise it is the best land they have and the only land that the Santals have hitherto learnt to manure. Here they have their maize, and when that is harvested, some other crop, and, during the cold season, generally some kind of oil-seed (mostly mustard). What is here given to the young man, is naturally land of this class, but hitherto not used for houses.

12 The huka or hubble-bubble has an earthenware bowl, in which the tobacco is put; to light the pipe a bit of live coal is put on the tobacco. The 'bowl' alone (without the water-holder) is also very often used. The huka is not common with the Santals; it is only quite lately that some have commenced to use it. It is the common pipe of the Hindus and Muhammedans. The word huka is Arabic, so judging from the name it has its origin to the West of India.

family. At that time we had not as yet got any children. After we had been separated, — we had some homestead-land[11] towards the end of the village street, — they said to me: "Well, we have given you that particular homestead-land; make your home there.' So, truth to tell, I built a house on that plot of land, and we are living there. One day when I was going to smoke the hubble-bubble, and I was trying to pick out some live coal[12], there was none, and I had an awful desire for a smoke. So I was starting to go and ask for fire; then I was thinking that I was leaving her alone there; then, on the other hand, if I sent her to ask for fire, I was thinking, she would go quite alone[13]; you see, it was already late night. Having considered all this I took the hubble-bubble in my hand and carried my wife along sitting astride on my shoulder[14]. As I was carrying her astride on my shoulder, we went from house to house to ask for fire; and the village people burst out laughing at us. And that is how I am a great fool."

Then all of them said to each other: "It is absolutely true; dash it, we are all of us fools; it is quite without reason that we are scolding each other. Therefore, let us divide these plantains between us and let us go home to our houses. And, truth to tell, they divided the plantains and went off to their respective homes.

So there the story is ended; it is thus much.

---

13 A woman must not be left alone; she must have protection; she is deemed unable to protect herself. Theoretically she is not trusted.

14 A man carries another on his shoulder by letting him sit astride. With a boy it would not have been considered strange; it is not done with women.

37. Ḍoho koṛa reaṇ.

Sedae jokhen mitṭaṅ atore molonre ḍoho koṛae tahẽkana. Ar uni koṛaren bahu do khub mõṅj kuṛi kanae. Ado one molonreye ḍohogete jãhãkote dãṛã baṛae uni songete do bae khusiḱa. Apan apingekin daṛana. Metaḱme haṭia baṭia, peṛa horoḱ, ṅel buru ṅel karam, uni jãwãeteṭ songe do bae khusiḱa. Jãhãte calaḱ jokhen uni jãwãeteṭ hõe calaḱ khan, bahutteṭ doe usaṭ godoḱa. Are metaea, Aćge laha lahae camdaṛaḱ baṛaea. Am songete do okoe ba tuloḱ lagaṭ?

Onkae metae khan, uni doe siṭi siṭi baṛaea. Khange arhõe eger godea. Siṭkoć cudi! Egerede khane isiṛ isiṛ baṛae kana. Ado onkae egere khan, uni do arteṭgeye bartao kana. Ado onkakin phukṭi baṛajoṅa. Ar oka doe haso ocoyegea; ado enre hõ bae usaṭa, sahaokaḱgeae. Monereye bujjoṅa, Iṅ do nonḍeṅ ḍohoyentegeye dusauediṅ kana. Ado onkae dusauea, arhõe mãyãwaegea.

---

[1] The word ḍoho, translated 'growth', signifies an excrescence or outgrowth, generally a protuberance like a bowl. Often seen on tree trunks.

[2] To understand the story it should be remembered that marriages among the Santals are not regularly the result of two people 'falling in love' with each other, but are arranged by the parents or others in authority. The young people are only just questioned. They are very sensitive as to their looks.

[3] Most of the shopping, in any case by women, is done in the market-places; such markets are held on fixed days, once or twice weekly, in many places easily accessible to the people of the locality. These market-places are much resorted to, not only for buying and selling but also for meeting people, after previous agreement, or just for the pleasure of it. People go there 'to see the people of the land and be seen by them', as one of their expressions may be translated. The wife objects to being seen in company with a man with such a deformity.

[4] The expression refers to the public gatherings, always connected with some religious performance; on such occasions hundreds and thousands of Santals come together in the afternoon and stay late, often until break of day. The majority of the visitors are the youths of the villages of the country-side; they generally go together village by village. The young people spend the night

37. THE MAN WITH A GROWTH IN THE FOREHEAD.

Once upon a time long ago there was living in a certain village a man with a growth[1] in his forehead, and the wife of this man was an exceedingly good-looking girl; therefore, because he had this growth in his forehead, she did not like[2] to go anywhere in his company. When going out they were in the habit of going their several ways. That is to say, when going to the market or the bazar[3], to visit relatives, to festivals and public dances[4], she did not like to go with her husband. When going anywhere, if her husband also wanted to go, the wife at once got a sulky fit, and would say: "He is giving himself airs and is putting himself forward. Whoever is to have a move in your company?"

When she spoke to him in this way, he would laugh shrilly, whereupon she would again abuse him, You horrible-looking beast! When she was scolding, he grinned and laughed. And when she abused him in this way, he would only become still more vivacious. In this way they were poking jokes[5] at each other. Now and then she would cause him pain; still he would not sulk; he would put up with it and bear it. He would think something like this: "I have got a growth here; therefore she is finding fault with me." In this way she was finding fault with him, but then again she would be kind to him[6].

---

amusing themselves in many ways, especially dancing. Many young men take the dancing-drum or other noise-producing apparatus along; the girls sing and beat the cymbals. Other music is not used. To visit such places is called by the Santals 'to go ńẹńẹl, seeing'. Incidentally it may be mentioned that these gatherings give occasion to much immorality. The first half of the expression (ńẹl buru) refers to such general gatherings; the last half (ńẹl karam) to the karam festival especially.

5 The narrator evidently thinks that this quarrelling is not so bad as it seems.

6 The word māyā, generally translated 'mercy', signifies considerably more than mercy; it is often used where we should say 'affection' or 'love'.

Adọ kathae, miṭ́ dhao dọ atoren kuṛi koṛa pata ńẹlko calaḱ kana. Adọ uni ḍoho koṛaren bạhu hõe mẹnketa, Iń hõ pata ńẹl dọń calaḱgea.

Adọ uni koṛae mẹnketa, Iń hõ tọbẹń calaḱgea.

Adọ bạhutaeye mẹnketa, Am dọ alom calaḱa. Nui soṭa cudi iń calaḱ iń mẹn khange aćhõe ruhu ṭuhu baṛaea.

Adọ koṛae mẹnketa, Am eskarge eṅgate ńẹńẹl sad dọ, hoṛ dọ alo sẹnlen khange.

Adọ bạhutaeye mẹnketa, Sad dọ ẹnte sanam hoṛge. Adọ ọṇḍẹm ḍohoyenteń manayetmea. Hoṛ nãhãḱ bako landawańa? Mẹnako, Durrẹ! kuṛi ma napae ọkọć, jãwãege thọe ḍohogetaea. Bejãe nonkan kuṛi unireye khusiyen dọ! Iń khan, ọhọń rẹbẹn atarlena. Onkako landawań iạte am dọń manayetmea.

Khange uni koṛa hõe bataoketa. Metadeae, Acha, ma ẹnḍẹkhan am eskar baṛẹ calaḱme, kahelae iń salaḱre dọm khẹndọḱ kana. Ma, bań calaḱ kana.

Ado kathae, uni dọe calaoena. Adọ atoren sọṅgẹte uniye ńẹl gọtkadea. Adọ ać hõ dosra oṛaḱ reaḱ kicrińe kọeketkoa, ar onate khube dhuti dạhṛi sajena. Ńẹl hoṛ hõko ńẹl erkaḱ kana. Ạdi hạbićem bẹṅgẹtae ena, kathaeyem orom daṛeaea. Ẹnte ti jaṅga bọhọḱ, goṭae pọṭọm ẹsẹt́ akana; inạ ḍoho ar mẽt́ge ńẹlọḱ kantaea, baṅkhan goṭae ẹsẹt́ caba akana. Adọ kathae, pata ṭạṇḍire ać eskargeye dãṛã baṛae kana, ako atoren hoṛ tuluć dọ bae mesao họdọḱ kana.

---

7 The pata festival is a remnant of the hook-swinging Hindu festival (to obtain the favour of Mahadeo or Shiva). It should occur on the last day of the month of Chaitra (last day of the Bengali year, about the middle of April). Locally it is held any day during the following month or even later. Those who arrange the festival here are generally Hindus of some low caste or other, but also Santals. The hook is not used any more, but persons may be swung comfortably lifted up in cloth and cords tied round their chest. The pata festival has a bad reputation for dissipation.

8 The following utterance is taken out of life. Such thoughts are the first that will occur to a Santal woman's mind, for that sake, to that of a man also.

So once it happened, it is told, that the boys and girls of that village were going to a pata[7] festival, and the wife of this man with the growth in his forehead said: "I shall go to the pata festival, I also."

"Then I also shall go," the young man said.

But his wife said: "Don't go, you. This horned beast, as soon as I say I shall go, then he also becomes very eager to go."

"Naturally you alone, dash it, have a desire to go and amuse yourself," the man replied; "if only no one else would go."

"Of course, all people desire to go," his wife said; "but as you have that growth there, I warn you not to go. Would not people laugh at me? They would say[8]: 'O dear, dear! the girl is quite all right, the husband, you see, is one with a growth. She must have been very hard hit, being such a girl, to agree to him. If it had been myself, I should certainly never have acquiesced.' They will laugh at me in this way; therefore I tell you not to go."

Then the man also gave in and said to her: "All right, so go yourself alone; why in the world should you have your amusement impaired by being in my company? Well, I am not going."

The girl then went, people tell, and her husband saw her off with the others from the village. Then he himself went to some other house and asked the people there for the loan of clothes, and with these he decked himself out fine[9] with loincloth and turban. Even people who knew him would take him for somebody else. Only if you looked long and carefully at him, you would be able to recognize him, they say. You see, hands and legs and head he had all covered up; that growth in his forehead and his eyes were all that could be seen; otherwise he was entirely wrapped up. So, they tell, he was walking about, he himself alone, in the pata place; he was in no hurry to mix with the people of his own village.

[9] The proceedings described are quite thinkable with the Santals. Among relatives it is quite frequent that clothes are out on loan.

Adọ setak̕ jọkhẹn, kathaeye ńẹlkede dọ, ać bạhu ẹnẹće saṗ akan. Khange adọ bae metat̕koa, Dẹ sẹ ya, tumdak̕ emańpe, mit̕ akhọṛ gan iń rulege.

Adọ sạriko emade khan, kathae, ać bạhu samańrege ḍher dọe ruyet̕a are dọnet̕ kana. Ar oka ghuṛi dọ uni samań sẹngeye lạṭić calao gọdok̕ kana. Adọ onka dọn baṛae ńẹlte ạḍiye bẹṅgẹt̕ae kangea. Mọlọṅre ḍoho hō̃e ńẹlet̕getaea, mẹnkhan bae orom daṛeadea.

Adọ kathae, bạhutae ẹnẹće aṛak̕en khan, nui hō̃ tumdak̕ dọe emat̕koa. Adọ okako sẹn uniye dā̃ṛā̃ baṛae kana, adọ uni ṭhen ńẹl ocok̕ leka ghạṛi hō̃ ghạṛi uni laha lahageye tahẹna, ar rọṛ dọ cet̕ hō̃ bakin rọṛana. Adọ uni hijuk̕ lekae ạikạulede khan, aćge hako pako lahateye hẹć gọt̕ente onako kicrić dọ jọtọe bhạnduṛ baṛakat̕teye idi baṛakat̕takoa; adọ gupiye calaoena. Adọ ńẹńẹl khon bạhuttẹt̕e hẹć laha ocoadea, tọbẹ ena ać hō̃ gupi khone hijuk̕ kana, mẹn baṛẹ gupigeye sẹnlena mẹnte.

Adọ hẹćkate bạhuttẹt̕e kuli baṛayede kana, Cele cet̕ lekam ńẹl ạguket̕koa? Bam sẹn ocoadińa, ma lại baṛawańme.

Adọ unreye mẹnket̕a, Cedak̕ cọń am hō̃ bam sẹnlen? Ńẹl ạgukekoam hutẹć.

Adọ uniye mẹnket̕a, Amge thọm manakidińa, bańkhan iń dọ calak̕geń mẹnlet̕a. Bam calao ocoadińte ạḍi mọn khaṭọń ạikạuket̕a.

Adọ bạhuttẹt̕e mẹnket̕a, Ḍoho iạte ẹnte bań sẹn ocoat̕mea. Adọ pata ṭạṇḍireń ńẹlket̕ko dọ, bogete am lekan ḍohoko. Mit̕ṭań onkan

---

10 See above note 4. People returning from the pata festival may be seen passing late in the forenoon

11 Santal dancers do not dance in pairs. If both sexes dance together, the women keep together, the men acting in front. In their most common dance, the socalled *lagṛẽ*, the women stand in one or more rows, keeping hold of each other, linking their arms, while the young men, generally only a few, are in front of the women, each with a drum (two with a *tumdak̕* or dancing-drum, one with a *ṭamak* or kettle-drum, or if there are many women, the double number of each), capering, jumping, beating the drum and exhibiting themselves. Among the spectators a number of young boys stand blowing the flute.

Towards morning[10], people tell, he saw his wife, she was joining[11] the dancers. Then did he not speak to those there, saying: "Come, you fellows, give me the drum, and let me drum one turn[12] or so."

As they really let him have it, he was drumming and frisking about mostly in front of his wife, they tell; now and then he made a dash towards her and capered[13] before her. When she saw him jumping about in this way, she looked at him again and again; she also saw the growth in his forehead, but she was not able to recognize him.

As soon as his wife left off dancing, he also, people tell, gave them back their drum. And wherever she was walking about, he again and again took care to be in front of her, as if he wanted to be seen by her; but they did not have any talk with each other. When he unterstood that she would start for home, he himself hurried off beforehand, and having reached home he got out of all his clothes and took them back to those from whom he had borrowed them, whereupon he went off to herd the cattle. He let his wife get back from the dancing; then only he himself also came home from herding the cattle, just let it be understood that he had been away herding cattle.

Having reached home he asked his wife: "Well, how did you find the people? You did not let me go, so tell me about it."

Then she replied: "Why could not you have gone also? You might in that case have seen how they fared."

"Why, you yourself," he said, "warned me not to go; otherwise I had made up my mind to go. I felt very downhearted, because you would not let me go."

"It was on account of that growth, you know," his wife replied, "that I would not let you go. But on the pata plain I saw people,

12 The word used, akhṛa or akhọṛ, means both the place where the dancing goes on, and one dance or dancing turn.

13 The boys caper about as they best can; the word here used (lạṭić) signifies bending backwards. They try to show themselves off.

ḍohoićge bhala abo akhṛare bogete tumdaḱe ruru kan are ḍoneť kana. Adọ uni ńẹlteń mẹnkeťa, Noko cọṅ goṭa disomrenko ḍohoge. Ọhọ hutẹćko dusạuliṅa. Cedaḱ cọṅ aleyić hõń manakede? Rạskạ hoṛ hutẹće ńẹl idikekoa. Adọń ńẹlkeťko goṭa disom ḍoho. Amge hale ḍoho, goṭa disom ḍoho.

Adọ ẹnẹ in khonaḱ miťtekin daṛana ar ńẹńẹl eman hõ miťge. Un khon dusạu rọṛ dọ cabayentaea. Adọ ẹnẹkin bhuṅjạukeťgea, baṅkhan hutẹć ḍoho iạte dosrareye ucạṛkoḱ cọṅ ceť cọṅ. Adọ ẹnẹ onkate uni dọe mạluṅkedea are andhaledea.

Adọ ẹnẹ niạ katha dọń purạukeťa.

38. Rẹṅgẹć hoṛaḱ katha.

Sedae jọkhẹn, kathae, miťṭẹn rẹṅgẹć hoṛe tahẽkana. Uni hoṛ dọ ghọrkornajoṅ sad ạḍi tahẽkantaea. Kisạ̃ṛ hoṛ ńẹlte ạḍiye kastaoḱa. Mẹnae, Noko hoṛ leka cekate baṅ kisạ̃ṛlen khan, ạḍiń khusikoḱa. Nenka kạmitege thọko kisạ̃ṛoḱ kana. Iń hõ tiriť leka khub kạmiń kạmia, ar jãhãnaḱko baṅ ublạ ḍublạ giḍia. Ar noako katha ać bạhuttẹť hõe galmaraoaea; adọ nonka bana hoṛ miť murukkatekin kạmia.

Adọ khange pạhil pọrthọm dọ simkin juṛạukeťkoa, adọ beleko họpọnko ạḍikin jọtọnkeťkoa. Ar dingekin lekhawako lekhawakoa, ar miťṭaṅ gan kuṛiť tanaḱe ạtkirle khan dọ ạḍikin haecọḱ haecọḱ gọda. Adọ họpọnkoko hara baṛalen khan dọkin ạkriṅkoa. Adọ ona poesate sukriko, mẹrọm bhiḍikokin juṛạukeťkoa, ar gidrạko dọ onkoko kạsni bhẹdrekin dọhọkakoa. Adọ onkoko hõko busạḱ

14 Note the inclusive plural. Although not present the husband belongs to the 'we'.

15 The statement is in accordance with what often takes place. Divorce is very common, but is believed to be valid only for this world. In the next those who have married for the first time (i. e., a bachelor and a spinster) will be joined together again.

38 1 The man aided by his wife follows the pattern given in the story about the oilman and his Santal servant (no. 34).

a good many, with a growth like you. One man with just such a growth you should have seen, he was beating the drum and jumping about all he could, where we from here were dancing[14]. Seeing him I thought: 'Why, these from all over the country, these are people with growths. They would surely not blame me. Why in the world did I also warn our man not to come. He might have seen all these glad people.' I saw them, the whole country has growths. You have a growth, the whole country has growths."

From that moment on they went about together, together also to dances and festivals. From that time her fault-finding also ceased. So they lived well together: otherwise she might on account of that growth very likely have left him and gone[15] to some one else. In the way told he fascinated her and misled her.

So there I have finished that story.

38. THE STORY OF A POOR MAN.

ONCE upon a time, people tell, long ago there was a poor man. He was very desirous of acquiring property. Seeing people being wealthy he felt very badly and would say: "If somehow I became rich like these people, I should be very pleased. It is by working in the same way as myself that they are getting rich. I myself am also working untiringly, all I can, and I do not squander anything away." In a like manner he also was in the habit of talking to his wife; and in this way both of them were working with one mind, all they could.

So, to make a beginning, they first got hold of fowls, and they took very great care of the eggs and the chickens[1]; every day they counted and counted them, and if it happened that a hawk[2] or the like carried one off, they wailed loudly over the loss. When the chickens grew up, they sold them, and for this money they

[2] It is a matter of daily occurrence that hawks (or other birds of prey) carry off chickens.

baṛayen khan, mīhũkokin kiriṅketkoa. Adọ enko hõko busạk baṛak khan, ạḍikin khusika.

Mẹnakin, Ho, nitok dọ arjao idi sẹnlaṅ mohṇḍak kana. Alaṅak duk harkhet ar noakolaṅ galmaraojoṅ, ona dọ Candoe aṅjọmkettalaṅa. Bạl bạiteye sepeṅ rakap idiyetlaṅa. Adọ jãhãnak balaṅ kạia, saporelaṅ tahẹna. Am hõ moca alom aṛak giḍia. Ar dak lo emankore ape maejiu hoṛpe ṅapama, jãhãnak alom lại agaea. Ar hoṛ oṛakte hõ ajare alom sẹn kạioka. Hoṛ oṛakte calak dọ ẹkẹn hoṛakgeko galmaraoa, hoṛakgeko oktawa. Adọ ẹnẹye gohaketmege, baṅma, Noko onkoko ninạk hoṛle tahẽkana. Adọ ẹnẹm leṭhayenge. Adọ ẹnẹ ọkọe cọm ḍaṇḍọmkedege cọṅ amge cọe ḍaṇḍọmketmege, adọ ẹnẹ apnarak ghọrkorna akat jinis hoṛem khawaokadege. Adọ onateṅ metam kana, ajare jạtge alom daṛana.

Adọ erataeye mẹnketa, Am hõ alom ḍaṇḍọm ocolaṅa. Hoṛren hopọnera misera ṅẹlte ikil sikil bae bogea; sasapako, ṭakkawako. Ar ṅũ hạṇḍi ṅũ pạurạ moca alom aṛak giḍia. Edre dọ ọr ruạṛtam. Jãhãeko nīhạtme khan, rọṛ ocoako, sahao dorokkatakom; ẹnḍẹ ena bara bạrire takhẽa. Ar baṅkhan niạ oṛak reak dhọngem ublạ

3 Chando, the sun, the Supreme Being.

4 Women are supposed to let their tongue run much more freely than the men. I have heard Santals explain it in this way: a woman will always try to carry off the palm in any controversy, and to do this she will talk without paying any attention to facts. Santal men agree not to pay much heed to women's talk; they are according to their theories naturally inferior and not quite responsible. This should not, however, be understood, as if the Santal women were mediocre. As a matter of fact it is frequently the women who rule. It will be seen a little further down how the woman turns the matter against her husband.

5 The Santal word signifies going to anyone without having any errand, only to have a talk. It is only applied to women and is generally an opprobrium. The husband follows up the idea and describes the possible results. His talk shows that he has nothing to upbraid his wife for.

6 The wife pays him back in current coin. A Santal flirting will generally not be innocent.

acquired pigs, goats and sheep, and they saw to it that their children kept a careful watch on these. And when these in their turn had young ones, they bought cattle; and when these also calved, they were very pleased indeed.

They would say: "O well, now we two are on the way to earn something. What we two have been talking together, about our misery and troubles and about these matters, that Chando[3] has heard. Gradually and slowly he is lifting us up on his hands. Now we shall not commit any kind of offence; we shall live in amity with all people. You on your side, don't let your tongue run[4]. And when you women meet, when fetching water or anywhere, don't tell and exaggerate, and don't make the mistake to go to the house of other people to gossip[5]. When you go to the house of others, it is only about other people that they talk; they slander other people. Then there you are, they call you as a witness, saying, we were these and these, so many people; and there you are fixed in trouble. And then somebody or other is fined, or who knows, perhaps they fine you yourself, and so there you will have to feed that person with the goods you have yourself had trouble to acquire. Therefore I tell you, never go about to have anything to do with gossiping."

His wife then said: "You on your side must not get us fined either. To commence flirting[6] when you see somebody's daughter or sister is not good; they take such matters up; they make money come out of it[7]. And don't let your mouth get away with you, when drinking beer or drinking liquor[8]. If angry, keep a check on yourself. If any one should slight you, let them talk; put

[7] The meaning is not that the other party will try to gain money; but the offender will have to pay out money; the offence becomes a financial affair.

[8] The meaning is not to exhort the man to leave drink alone, but to take care that he does not bring himself into trouble when affected. Now-a-days Santal women will also drink, although they will not go to a beer-shoop; formerly mostly only men indulged in beer.

ḍublạị khan, cedak̕ tọbẹ nonka ramọ ramọ babae dọm metaň kana? Ma adọ nią teheň rọṛtege jẹmọn bana hoṛlaň dalok̕ ma.

Adọ nonka thoṛa din dọ ạḍi sulukte kam kaj calak̕tạkina. Hẹrẹl hõ ạimạiye bọtọr lajaowaea, ar ạimạị hõ hẹrẹle bọtọr lajaowaea. Bana hoṛ mọnre onkakin hudisjoňa, jãhãnak̕ eskarte dọ bakin karbara. Ạimạị hõe mẹna, Noaň nonkale khan, pasẹć hẹrẹliň cet̕e metaň. Ar uni hẹrẹl hõe mẹna, Noaň nonkale khan, pasẹ era cet̕e metaň.

Adọ onka bana hoṛak̕ mọnre onkakin hudisjoňte ạḍikin ghọrkornaket̕a. Kisạ̃ṛenakin, bọchọr salko jọm purạuena. Ar unạk̕ko sim sukri mẹrọm bhiḍiket̕koa, mẹnkhan oṛak̕re jọmko lagat̕ dọ mit̕ din gan hõ baňko gọć jọmlet̕koa. Sẹ jãhã sẹn khon peṛa tanko hẹćakore hõ, baňgeko jelat̕koa; iną dạl daka aṛak̕ sakamkotege peṛa hõko bodhaokoa.

Khange uni era hoṛ dọe mẹna, Jọtọgem ạkriň horayet̕ko dọ. Nẹtar dọlaň ghọrkornaket̕a. Masẹ abo oṛak̕re eňga hopọn jọmko lagat̕ gọćabonme.

Adọ uni hẹrẹl hoṛe mẹna, Hẽ, sạrige baň gọć baṛa akawat̕bona. Cet̕ bam mẹnte? Lạgtige baň cabak̕ kan dọ. Ona iạtẹge gọgọć

---

9 Lit. 'in order that we may both be struck by this talk.'

10 The fortune should not be measured with a western measure. They are now according to Santal standards well-to-do. How much it amounts to, the story partly shows.

11 A Santal, who has enough out of his land to be able to live on it the whole year round, is considered to be very well off. As a rule they have to go to the shopkeepers, to borrow victuals to keep them going part of the year. This means being always in debt and becoming always more impoverished on account of the very heavy, often exorbitant interest charged.

12 It is with the Santals as with others, when friends come on a visit, they like to give them the best they can.

13 The food of a Santal consists of rice (or some other cereal) with a curry prepared of some kind of pulse, or of some kind of vegetable (grown by themselves), or of some kind of jungle produce, that they know the use of. Meat is very rare with them, once or twice monthly or even much more rarely, if they do not

up with their nonsense; then only we shall have peace. Otherwise, if you squander the property of this house, why are you talking to me about being careful and frugal to save up? Well, let this talk we have had to-day be a warning[9] to both of us."

Hereupon their work and business went along in great peace for some time. The husband had respect for the woman and was ashamed to do anything against her, and the wife on her side acted in the same way towards the man. Both of them were thinking in their minds that none of them should engage in any business alone without the other. The woman would say: "If I should do this in such and such a way, what will my man perhaps have to say to me?" And the man also would say: "If I do this in such and such a way, perhaps the wife will say something or other to me?"

As both of them were having such thoughts, they made a great fortune[10]. They became wealthy; their crops were sufficient to keep them in food the whole year round[11]. And they got so many fowls, goats and sheep; but in spite of this they did not even once kill and eat any in their own house. Or when friends from anywhere came on a visit[12] to them, even then they never gave them meat to eat; what they had themselves, curry of split peas, or vegetables or leaves[13], with that same they also tried to satisfy their visitors.

Then the wife would say: "You are selling away all, as we get them. Now-a-days we have made our fortune. Please kill something for us to let your family have to eat here at home."

The man would then answer: "Yes, it is quite so, I have not killed any for ourselves. What can you say: Expenses[14]

happen to kill some wild animal or bird. Sacrificed animals are eaten. Cattle having died from rinderpest are eaten, apparently with impunity. When friends or relatives come on a visit, they will as a rule give them a cock, at least, to partake of.

14 The description of the character is taken from life; it is not a psychological study.

hõ baṅ sanaṅ kana. Acha, adọm mẹnkeť khan, noko sẽṛāko dọń ạkriṅkogea. Ma hapẹn neko kạṭićkoko haralen khan, miťṭẹn gan dọń gọćabongea. Adọ unre adọm dọbon utuia, adọm dọbon kọhraea, lаćtẹťko dọbon lẹṭọea, ar itiltẹť dọbon piṭhạia. Ar ẹn hilok̓ dọ khub mĩhĩ caole reak̓ dakawabonme.

Adọ uni eratae dọe mẹnkeťa, Ọkọ baḍae, pasẹ rọṛtegem piṭhạ lẹṭọ ocokeťbon.

Adọ uniye mẹnkeťa, Ọhọ jạnić. Hapẹ sẹko haralenge. Nit dọ ceť iń mẹnkea? Adọ ẹnẹkin thir baṛayena.

Adọ enko hõko hara horayena. Eratae dọe cẹrẹćakoa. Mẹnae, Oka hilok̓ cọṅ nãhãk̓e jelalegea. Ar uni hẹrẹl họṛ sẹ jel sẹn dọ bae mọnẹak̓a. Khange miť din dọe metadea, Masẹ jelabonme.

Adọ unre hõe metadea, Noko dọ poesaren mal, babon jọm giḍikoa. Hona noakoń ẹm dogok̓a. Ạḍi lạgti lagaok̓ kana. Ma hẹnkoko haralen khan, unre dọń jelabongea. Adọ onka bar pẹ dhaoe ẹrẹ baṛakede khan, tayọmte dọ ceť hõ bae mẹn baṛawaea.

Adọ onakate ḍher dinge hoeyena. Uni hẹrẹl họṛ dọ ona rọṛ dọe hiṛiṅkeťa, ar uni ạimại dọe disạ akaťgea. Khange miť din dọ okate cọṅ uni hẹrẹl họṛ dọ peṛak̓e calak̓ kan. Adọe batlao baṛa oṭoako kana, Ma niạko hinạko kạmi hataṛpe, ar neko mĩhũko mẹrọmko disạ baṛa hataṛkope. Iń dọ hanko phalnaren peṛako khọj akadiṅa; ọṇḍẹń sẹnlenge. Gapa dọ baṅ, meaṅ dọ nãhãk̓ khạṭigeń ruạṛgea. Adọ enka batlao baṛa oṭoadete peṛa horok̓e calaoena.

---

[15] Except the stomach all the entrails are eaten after having been 'milked' and prepared.

[16] Not pastry. What is in Santali piṭhạ is unfermented dough or the like, formed into a small flat piece with the hands and baked in several ways, often by being put into boiling mustard-oil.

[17] The rice eaten by the Santals is generally fairly coarse. They have a large variety of rice, the small fine grain being considered the best, as it also is.

[18] Lit. 'giving be rescued', i. e. pay off obligations so as to get out of the power of the creditors.

are never coming to an end. That is the reason why I don't like to kill any. Very well, as you have mentioned it, I shall sell these big ones. When later on these small ones grow up, I shall kill one or so for ourselves. And then we shall prepare some of it as curry, some we shall fry, the entrails[15] we shall boil with flour, and the fat we shall make into cakes[16]. And that day remember to use the finest rice[17] for us."

"Well, who knows?" his wife said, "perhaps it is only with talk that you let us make cakes and prepare the tripe."

"Likely not," he replied. "Wait, just let them grow up. What can I say now?" There the talk ended.

So these also all of them grew up. His wife was petting them, and would say: "Some day or other he will presently give us meat to eat." But the man had no thought for meat. Then one day she said to him: "Please, give us meat."

Then also he said to her: "These are worth money, we shall not eat them and throw that away. There is this, that and the other that I have to pay to be free[18]. There are very heavy expenses. Well, let those there grow up; then I shall give us meat to eat." He tricked her twice or thrice in this way, and when he had done this, she did not afterwards mention this matter to him.

In this way a long time passed. The man forgot all about it; but the woman was remembering it. So one day it happened that the man was going somewhere or other on a visit. He left instructions with them, saing: "Please, do this and do that during my absence, and keep these cattle and these goats in your minds. The friends of such and such a place want me, and I have to go there at once. I shall not return to-morrow[19], the day after I shall be sure to come back." Having instructed her in this way he went to visit those mentioned.

---

19 The meaning is that he will leave the next morning and not return the same day. They will not leave home in the afternoon or evening, if it is not absolutely necessary.

Adọ iniye calaoen ạyup̃ khange uni ạimại dọe jhũkente mit̕ṭẹn sim gaya dọe gọćkedeteye rọ gẹt̕kedea are utu dakakedea. Ar laćtẹt̕ dọe lẹṭọkedea, ar cet̕tẹt̕ko cọṅ gidrại rapak̕ baṛawat̕koa. Inạ dọ gidrạ aloko jạpida mẹnteye anmanao hataṛ akat̕koa. Adọ daka utu jọtọe isin sạtket̕ khan, lo hạṭiṅ baṛakate jọtọ gidrạ mit̕ dhaoteye ạbukket̕koa, ar mit̕ dhaote jọtọ gidrại emat̕kotaea.

Adọ un jọkhẹne bintiako kana, Iạ, boi bạburaeko dọ, ạpuṃe hẹćlen khan nãhãk̕, ape dọ lạṭić baṛaepe. Teheṅ maraṅ gayabon jọme kana. Ạpum dọ jaoge sim gọgọć iṅ metaea, adọ tisre hõ bae gọćkoa. Adọ ona edrete teheṅ dọ maraṅ gayaṅ gọćat̕bona. Ma bes leka jọmkok̕pe. Alope lại baṛaea, ar baṅkhan nãhãk̕ ape dọ ạpume hẹćlen khan dọ lạṭić baṛaepe. Onkae bintiako kana arko jọmet̕a. Ar onko gidrạ dọ cur marko lapet̕ dorok̕joṅ kana. Cet̕ hõ bako mẹn ruạṛae kana, hape hapete cur marko jọmjoṅ kana. Adọ jọm baṛakateko jaega baṛayena.

Adọ dosar hilok̕ khange onko kạṭić gidrạ dọ oka mohṇḍate apattẹt̕ko ṅẹl gọt̕ akade, ọntẹ ghạṛi ghạṛiko kọyọk̕et̕ kana. Adọ tin ọktẹre cọṅ apattẹt̕ hijuk̕ kanko ṅẹl ṅam gọt̕kedea. Khange gidrạko dọ atra họrregeko ṅir daram gọt̕kedea, adọ uni samaṅre cur mar bogeteko lạṭijok̕ kana. Khangeye metako kana, Henda ya, sẹ henda na, cedak̕ onka dọpe lạṭijok̕ kana? Rạput̕ bọtẹćkok̕ape.

---

[20] A special way of preparing meat or anything. The meat is put in an earthenware pot and put over the fire and fried dry.

[21] Always done before eating. The hands are washed and the mouth rinsed. The mother naturally performs the ablution with the children.

[22] The expressions used are playful. B o i is used to small girls and means something like a 'hussy'. B ạ b u r a e is used about boys, 'young lord'. Newly married girls may use the latter word about their husbands.

[23] The Santali word l ạ ṭ i ć is used about being bent or twisted the wrong way, recoiling, bending backwards. A child will naturally take this to be the meaning, remembering their own antics. The word is, however, also used in the meaning of telling, tale-bearing. What the mother here tells her children to do, they understand in their own way, that they should show their father what they can

The same evening that he went away, the woman plucked up courage and killed a capon, singed and cut it up and made it into curry. The entrails she boiled with flour, and part of it she fried[20] and gave to the children. This last she gave to the children in the meanwhile to prevent them from falling asleep. When she had prepared the rice and curry and all of it was ready, she ladled it out in portions, washed the hands and faces[21] of all the children together at the same time, and finally gave all her children their food together.

Just then she gave the children some instructions: "I say, you girls and young lords[22], when your father presently comes, be sure to make a clean breast[23]. To-day we are eating the big capon. I have over and over again told your father to kill a fowl for us, but he is never doing so. So being angry on that account I have to-day killed the big capon for us. Eat well. Don't tell it to anybody, or else when your father presently comes, be sure to make a clean breast. In this way she was giving them a talking-to, and they were eating. The children were filling their mouth all they could. They did not answer her anything; without a word they were quietly eating all they could. And when they had had their food, they went to sleep.

The next day the little children were again and again out to look in the direction in which they had seen their father go away. And when their father eventually came, they at once saw him, and the children at once ran off to meet him half-way and commenced to bend backwards again and again in front of him. He naturally asked them: "Look here, you boys, or look here, you girls, why are you bending backwards in this way? You might break your backs."

---

do in the way of antics. The translation is only an attempt to find a word that might be misunderstood like the Santali expression.

Adǫ unre gidrạko mẹnkeťa, Gọgọge ẹnte onkae mẹn akawaťle. Metaťleae, Ape boi bạburaeko dọ ạpum nāhāk̕e hẹćlen khan, ape dọ lạṭić baṛaepe. Onatele lạṭić baṛae kana.

Adọe metaťkoa, Cedak̕ yae metaťpea?

Adọko mẹnkeťa, Marań gayale jọmkedea, adọ un jọkhẹngeye metaťlea.

Khangeye bujhạuketteye metaťkoa, Acha alope lạṭijok̕a; bujhạukeťań. Delabon oṛak̕te.

Adọ oṛak̕re hẹć sẹṭẹrkate parkọmreye duṛup̕ena. Adọ ọṇḍẹ hõ onko gidrạ dọ cur marko lạṭijok̕ kana. Ar uni eṅgattẹť dọ ọrak̕ bhitri khon sẹ duạr khonge gidrạ dọe hap̕ ikṛum baṛawako kana. Adọ ẹnre hõ onko gidrạ dọ baṅgeko bujhạueťa. Ar apat họṛ dọ muluć muluće landajoń kana. Are metae kana, Gidrạko dọ ceť lekam sikhạu akaťkoa? Ma ńẹlkom. Ceka baṛae kanako?

Arhõe mẹnketa, Acha, beṭa, bujhạukedań, ma thirkok̕pe. Ạḍi din khonge jelabone metań kana. Adọ sim tanak̕ hõ nun din bań gọćaťbona, ona iạte nonka dọe mẹn akawaťpea. Acha besge, teheń dọń jel dakawabongea.

Adọ enka mẹnkatege bāṛā khon sukriye ọr toťkedeteye kuṭạm gọćkedea. Are mẹnkeťa, Ma teheń dọ bes leka caole sọgme ar họlọńme; bes lekabon jọwange.

Adọ sạri ọnẹye metade lekageye kạmikeťa. Adọ rọ gẹťkedete adọm dọko kọhrakeťa, adọm dọko utukeťa, itiltẹťko dọko piṭhạkeťa, lać dọko lẹṭọkeťa ar bọhọk̕ jel dọko suṛekeťa; arko jọmkeťa. Adọ

24 The father understands; he is not wholly spoilt by his endeavours to acquire wealth and takes the whole from the comical side, in true Santal fashion.

25 One of a Santal woman's ways of silently showing resentment.

26 The head of an animal is prepared and eaten in this way, especially also when the animal has been sacrificed.

A variant of the story omits the first part. The man is wealthy from the commencement of the tale, but is stingy and grudges an occasional feed to his wife and family. Then one day when her husband goes on a visit, the wife kills the big capon, and they all partake of it. They eat it at night, even those children that had gone to rest for the day and had to be awakened. Again at

The children then replied: "Mother has told us to do it, therefore. She said to us: 'You girls and young lords, when your father presently comes, be sure to make a clean breast.' Therefore we are making clean breasts."

"Why did she say this to you, you boys?" he asked them.

"We have eaten the big capon," they replied; "just at that time she said this to us."

So he understood the matter[24] and said to them: "Very well, don't make clean breasts any more; I see what it is. Come along home."

Having reached home he sat down on a bedstead; there also the children were bending backwards incessantly. From inside the house, that is to say from the door, the mother was biting her underlip[25] and making signs to them; still the children did not understand the meaning of that. The father was smiling quietly to himself. So he said to his wife: "How is it you have taught the children? Look at them. What has come to them?"

Again he said: "All right, boys, I see it all; please stop. For a long time she has been saying to me that I should give us meat to eat. So long a time I have not even killed a fowl or the like to give us for food; therefore she has told you this. Very well, to-day I shall give us rice and meat-curry."

Having said so he fetched a pig out of the sty and felled it, and said: "Please, clean the rice well to-day and make flour; we shall have a good feed now."

So in very truth she did as he had told her. And after he had singed and cut up the pig, they fried part of it; some of it they prepared as curry; the fat they made into cakes, the entrails they boiled with flour, and the flesh of the head they cooked with rice to a hash[26], whereupon they ate. During this

---

cock-crow she kills a young hen and gives them. At the time of eating she explicitly instructs her children not to tell of this, naturally meaning to other people; as regards their father, she uses the same expression as in the tale

un jokhen noako kathakin roreťa arkin landayeťa. Ado unre eneye binti barawadea.

Ado cabayena; nia katha doń mucaťketa.

39. Miťtań kombro, kul, bana ar toyo.

Miť goteć kisarren gaiko ar marań utar miťten sande tahẽkana; bir seć idileko khać kul doe mena, Uni sanḍ iń jomle khan, adi bariće itil akana, adi din iń tahẽkoka.

Ar miť goten kombroe menjoṅa, Nui sanḍ iń kombrole khan adi utar ṭakateń akrińkea. Bhador din jokheć tahẽkana; kul hõ ona dine nenda thikoana, ar kombro hõ.

Ado kul tinre coṅ jondra gajarreye bolo thir akan tahẽkana, are menjoṅ kana, Japiťlegeko hor, ado nãhãk iń kombro odokea. Khange uni kombro doe ńelkedea uni kul, adoe menkeťa, Tinre coṅ sande odok akan, kombro reań jarur do bań hoelentińa, aćtegeye hećadińa. Adoe tolkedea. Tolkede khan ado cur mare pitau idiyedea; khange setak dela dili mundu sećgeye tanaok kana; khange bohok cur mare pitau and mandaokedea.

---

translated. When the father returns, they run out to meet him; he takes the youngest one on his hip and carries him home, while the others act as described in this tale. The father does not understand the meaning of it all. In the house he asks them again, and they tell that it is according to their mother's order. And when he asks them why she has told them to do so, they let it out that they had taken a fowl and eaten it. Whereupon husband and wife look at the children and look at each other and finally burst out laughing. The story ends in the same way: the husband kills a pig and they have a grand feed. "And the husband and wife were laughing, as they remembered what the children had done. Also they patted and fondled their children and called out to them: 'Give us one more treat of backwards bending, you little folk!' They continued in this way for two or three days and had much fun and laughing."

39 [1] The story was told to the writer by an old Santal guru in 1891. It is of the kind that is especially enjoyed by Santal children.

husband and wife talked over the matter and had a laugh. Then she gave him a talking-to.

So it is ended. I have finished this story.

39. A THIEF, A TIGER, A BEAR AND A JACKAL[1].

THERE was a rich man, who had a number of cows and a very big bull. When they took the cattle towards the forest to graze them, the tiger would say: "If I ate this bull — he is awfully fat —, I should remain satisfied for many days."

There was also a thief, who was in the habit of saying: "If I could steal this bull, I might sell him and get a lot of money. It was the time of August and September[2]; the tiger fixed on that time to take the bull, and so did the thief also.

Some time or other during the day the tiger had entered the maize-field thicket[3] and stayed quietly there; he was saying to himself: "Let the people go to sleep; then I shall presently steal the bull and bring him out." And the thief caught sight of the tiger and said: "Some time or other the bull has come out; there is no longer any need for me to steal; he came to me of his own accord." Whereupon he tied him[4]. When he had done this, he beat him vigorously and drove him along; towards morning he was being dragged along in the direction of the jungle, and he beat him vigorously in the head and made him quite confused.

---

[2] The month of bhadọr corresponds to the time from about the middle of August to the middle of September.

[3] At this time of the year the maize has grown high and, standing dense, gives a thicket, that cannot be seen through. Jackals and sometimes other animals may hide here, especially to catch fowls. In the field on which the Santals have their houses standing, they have always maize; this is sown about the beginning of June and harvested some three months later.

[4] They have apparently no difficulty in imagining a tiger being tied up; several stories have the same.

Khange marsalena; ayoge, kul kanae! rara gotkedeae; ać mit sećе darketa, kul do bir sećе darketa ahap cahap.

Khange toyo do kule metae kana, Okate, mamo, nunak āt do ahap cahapem dareta?

Kule menketa, Bhagna, cet iń mena? teheń do mit ńinda mod thotkae saplidińa, mit ńindai mod thotkakidińa.

Cet lekanae, mamo, mod thotka do? Delań se udukańme.

Ado kule menketa, Ohoge babuń senlena, mod thotka then do. Hani ńeleme, do calakme.

Bhala, mamoń ńelegea. Adoe calaoena.

Nui kombro adoe durup akana, bhabnak kanae, Jomkińae honeć kul do, cet iate coń bae jomledińa? Khange toyoe ńel ocoyen khan doe gitićena uni kombro do oyo potomkate.

Toyo do berhaeteye acurok kana, are menjoń kana, Cet lekan mod thotka kanae, bhalań ńelea. Adoe acur idik kana bohok seć.

Khange bai baite kombro do tiye husiarettaea; khange phed candbolre sapkate cun lekae acurkedea; acur acurteye lańgayen khane capat gotkadea.

Adi barićе botorena toyo do, are darketa leńget sopot; kule tiokkede khane menketa, Bań kanae, mamo, mod thotka do, ghur pāk 'kanae, ińgem erekidińa.

---

5 The forest 'inhabitants' are supposed to establish a certain relationship between themselves, that of maternal uncle (or aunt) and nephew (or niece); the bigger or more dangerous animal is the uncle or aunt. According to the rules of Santal society these relations have to honour each other, as one honours the sun, as they express themselves.

6 The names given here and further on to the man is in a kind of rustic Bengali and not proper Santali. I remember the narrator emphasized these names, they were so funny. Incidentally it might be mentioned that the majority of the names used by the Santals for themselves are of Aryan origin. Second names are sometimes Santali. As a rule the meaning of the names used is more or less clear.

Then it became light; O mother, it is a tiger! the man loosed him at once; he himself ran off in one direction; the tiger ran off towards the forest in haste and hurry.

The jackal then asked the tiger: "Whereto, uncle[5], are you running in such haste and hurry?"

"O nephew," the tiger replied, "what shall I say? to-day the head-thumper[6] had hold of me for the whole night; he was thumping my head a whole night."

"What kind is he, uncle, the head-thumper? Come along and show him to me."

The tiger replied: "You may be sure, boy, I shall not go to the head-thumper. Look over there, there he is; go to him."

"I wonder, uncle, I shall have a look at him;" whereupon the jackal went.

Now this thief was sitting there, saying to himself in anxiety: "He might have eaten me, the tiger; I wonder why he did not eat me." When the jackal came into sight, the thief lay down covering himself up with his clothes.

The jackal walked round the man and was saying: "How does he look the head-thumper? I should like to see him;" whereupon he turned towards his head.

Then the thief very slowly and with great caution got his hand out, and catching hold of the jackal by the root of his tail he swung him round like they swing shells round[7] when burning lime; when he had swung him until he got tired, he threw him away.

The jackal became awfully afraid and ran away in fear and trembling; when he reached the tiger, he said: "He is no head-thumper, uncle; he is a turn-twister[6]; you lied to me."

---

7 The Santals use lime burnt from mussels to chew with their tobacco leaves. The shells are, with chips of wood, wrapped up in a bundle, the outer covering being a straw-rope (of the same kind as that used for making their paddy-bundles), the whole looking like a miniature paddy-bundle. This is tied to the

Khange daṛ daṛte banatikinkin ńapamena; adoe metae kana, Okate, bhagna, nunak̕ ãṭ dom daṛeta?

Toyoe roṛ ruaṛketa, Cet̕ baṅ, mamom mente, mit̕ goṭen ghur pãke ghur pãkkidińa se, gujuk̕ lekaṅ aikau akata.

Ado banae menketa, Cet̕ lekan bae, bhagna? onkanko do kotoń jom akat̕koa.

Oho mamom jomlea ho, ińiń baḍaeyeta; do entem jome khać. Khangeye calak̕ kana. Uni hoṛ do adoe duruṕ akana, banae ńelkedea, hijuk̕ kanae iń sećte. Khangeye menketa, Jomeńae, dareren dejoka, baṅkhan khaṭigeye jomeńa. Adoe dećena, uni tayomte bana hõe dećena. Khange lenget̕ sopot̕ coṭṭeye deć idiyena hoṛ do, bana hõe deć idiyena; ḍher laphaṅen khan nanha ḍaṛte khange hamalte raputena, ńũr gotenakin; bana doe latarena ar hoṛ do bana cetanre; oṛgo poṛgo chaḍaoenteye daṛketa bana do.

Khange toyotikinkin ńapamena, adoe meneta, Am do, bhagna, aḍim pagola, iń dom erekidińa, baṅma, ghur pãk kanae. Baṅ kanae ghur pãk do, upor cap kanae.

40. Merom, kul, bana, ar toyo.

Mit̕ṭaṅ khub maraṅ merom bodae tahẽkana, khube gocoana, ar deren do khub titit̕ hapṛak̕ hapṛak̕ tahẽkantaea. Khange gupiyić do bir sеće idiket̕koa; aḍi maraṅ urni bir bhitri talateye idiket̕koa.

end of a rope, and it is set fire to. If the bundle is fairly large, it is hung in a tree and swung to and fro; the common way is, however, for a man to take hold of the other end of the rope and swing the bundle round and round, until the contents are properly burnt. This swinging or turning is necessary in order to give the necessary draft to keep the fire going. It is a curious sight to see in the evening after dark has set in, the time often chosen for this operation. Cun ḷeka laṅ acurmea nãhãk, we two shall swing you round like lime, is a very common threat.

So running along he met with a bear, who asked him: "Whereto, nephew, are you running in such hurry?"

"What would you say, uncle?" the jackal replied: "a turn-twister turn-twisted me something awful, I felt as if I should die."

"Indeed, what kind, nephew?" the bear said; "of such ones I have eaten quite a number."

"Surely not, uncle, you will never be able to eat him; I know that; well, have a try, if you will eat him."

The bear then went. The man was sitting there and caught sight of the bear: "he is coming towards me." So he said: "He will eat me, I shall climb a tree, otherwise he will be sure to eat me." So he climbed, and the bear climbed after him. The man continued to climb in fear and trembling, higher and higher, and the bear followed after; when he got very high up to the thin branches, it broke and they both tumbled down; the bear fell underneath and the man on the top of the bear. Somehow or other, having disengaged himself, the bear ran away.

When the bear and the jackal met, the bear said: "You nephew, you are a great wag; you lied to me, saying it was a turn-twister. He is no turn-twister he is a top-tumbler[6].

40. A HE-GOAT, A TIGER, A BEAR AND A JACKAL[1].

THERE once was an extraordinarily big he-goat; he had a long beard, and he had also exceedingly large horns. One day the herd took the cattle towards the forest; he took them into an immense primeval forest.

---

40 [1] The story was told by the same man who told the preceding one, and was taken down at about the same time.

Adọ ona bir talare mit́ gọṭẹć cạṭạni dhiri menak̕a; ona dọ ạḍi usula, gẹl mõṛẽ moka; ona dhiri latarre kul dander menak̕a. Ona danderren kul dọ okate cọṅ ạk̕tiṅe dukạna, ona takrege uni mẹrọm dọ ona usul dhirire dọn ẹnẹć baṛae lạgit́e dẹćlena.

Khange adọ bae ãṛgo daṛeak̕ kana, gupiyić hõ bae disạledea; adọ gupiyić ạyup̕en khan gạiko, mẹrọmko oṛak̕teye ạguyet́koa; kulhi mucạt́reye lekhayet́koa; adọ maraṅ boda dọ okare cọe at́kede.

Khange oṛak̕te laga idi họt́kate adọ oṛak̕renkoe lạiako kana, baṅma, Maraṅ boda dọ okare cọń paskaokedea.

Apatt́ẹt́e metae kana, Oka sẹć bạbum idilet́koa? Pasẹt́ tạrup̕ tanak̕rem jọm ocokede.

Mẹn ruạṛket́ae, Jọmle khan iń disạkea; ona maraṅ urni bir talatege ạtiń iń idilet́koa.

Ona maraṅ dhiri ṭheć ọṇḍẹ ma, bạbu, kul cọe tahẹn. Adọe metat́koa, Oka sẹćtem idilet́koa, onkate ńam baṛayepe.

Khangeko calaoena.

Adọ ńũten khan kul dọ bir khon danderteye oḍok hẹćena, cạṭạni kọyọk̕ket́ae, ayoge, cele kanae, un maraṅ dọ? Mẹrọm dọ bọtọrteye kiṭ miṭạuk̕ kana dhiri cọṭre, ar kul hõ bọtọrteye kuc kucạuena.

Kule mẹnet́a, Henda, maharaja, cet́ nọṇḍẹ dọm ńam kana? mẹn, oṛak̕ aṛak̕kạtińme.

Mẹrọme mẹnket́a, Noa birren mit́ mit́te kul bana bạń jọm cabaleko khan bań bạgina.

---

2 According to the habit of goats, always trying to get higher and higher.

3 The narrator had nothing more to tell about the goat's owners. They have no interest for the story any longer.

4 In uninhabited parts I believe tigers and other animals may be met during day-time; in these parts these animals sleep in their dens during day-time and start prowling at or just after sunset.

5 The Santali word is used about the trembling of excitement, whether it be due to fear or anything else.

In the middle of this forest there is a rock; it is very high, fifteen cubits, and below this rock there is a tiger's den. The tiger living in this den had gone away somewhere to find food; just at that time the he-goat had mounted that high rock to caper and gambol there[2].

Afterwards he was unable to get down, and the herd also forgot all about him; when it became evening, the herd was driving the cows and goats home; at the entrance to the village he was counting his flock and saw that he had lost the big he-goat somewhere.

Thereupon he drove the animals home in a hurry and told them at home: "Somewhere or other I have let the big he-goat slip away."

"Where did you take them, my boy?" his father asked him; "perhaps you have let a leopard or such an animal eat him."

The boy answered: "If any animal had eaten him, I should have become aware of that; I took them through the large primeval forest to graze."

"At that big rock, why, a tiger is living there, my boy." Thereupon he said to them: "Where you took them, go all of you and search for him thereabouts."

So they went[3].

When it became dark[4], the tiger came out of the forest to his den; he looked up to the rock; O mother! who is that, so big? Now the goat was trembling with fear[5] there on the top of the rock, and the tiger also out of fear felt uncomfortable inside[6].

"Listen, maharaja," the tiger said, "what do you want here? beware, leave my house."

The he-goat said: "Until I have eaten every tiger and bear found in this forest, I am not going to stop."

---

6 When put in great fear animals will unconsciously pass water or even watery stools. This is what is hinted at here. There are many instances of human beings acting in the same way. A very common Santali expression about frightening is 'to cause to pass water.'

Onkae aṅjomket' khan uni kul doe daṛ tapketa; daṛ daṛte se phõe sahetketa.

Khange banae metadea, Okate nunak' ăt do, mamom daṛeta?

Cet' baṅ, babu, inak' oṛak're cele kan coe, godor godor gocoanae, bohok're barci leka menak'taea.

Ente mamom cekayea? tahẽ ocoae.

Ona ma, babu, hẽge, iṅiṅ metadea, Henda, maharaja, oka khonem heć akana nonḍe do, cetem ṅam kana? Ayupen coṅ, bam eskarok' kana? Unre, babu, noa kathaṅ roṛ kailak'a. Adoe menketa, Noa birren kul bana mit' mit'te baṅ jom cabaleko khan boroṅ upasteṅ tahena, enre hõ cabakogeaṅ; baṅ bagina. Khange, babu, kiṭ miṭau baṛae kanae, ona botorteṅ daṛeta; dela am hõm daṛ khać.

Khange banae menketa, Delaṅ, mamo, bar hoṛalaṅ, oho janić mit' dhaote doe jom laṅa. Adokin hijuk' kana. Horre toyotekoko dapramena, Henda mamo, teheṅ do bar hoṛ cekateben gateyena? Ona katha laiaṅben.

Adokin laiae kana, Cet baṅ se, babu, iṅ oṛak're mit' goṭen rakase heć akana.

Cet' lekanae? toyoe meneta.

Aḍi maraṅae, babu, kule meneta.

Tobe khan, mamo, iṅ hõṅ calak'a; jotokotebo lagayea; khange joṛak'abo, mamo, jãhãebon laṅgalen khan, daṛe hoṛe atkirbona; paset' iṅ coṅ laṅgak', paset' am com laṅgak'; joṛa mit'kate khan jotoge jom khane jombona; baclao khan jotogebon baclaok'a. Delabo ṅelea.

---

[7] The jackal is naturrally curious, as can often and easily be ascertained; he is believed to be crafty and cunning, more so than the other animals here mentioned. To be able to follow he proposes that they should tie themselves together. The word used presupposes that they are to be joined together with the help of something round their necks.

When the tiger heard this speech, he ran off; he ran and ran, so that he commenced to pant and gasp.

The bear then said to him: "Whereto are you running in such hurry, uncle?"

"You can't imagine, master, there is some one, who knows who, in my house; he has a long flowing beard, and on his head he has something like a spear."

"What then can you do with him, uncle? let him stay."

"That is quite so, master; I said to him: 'Listen, maharaja, wherefrom have you come here? what do you want? Why, it is night now; are you not getting lonely?' At that time I made the mistake of saying this. Then he replied: 'If I do not eat every single tiger and bear found in this forest, I shall rather remain fasting; anyhow I shall finish them; I am not going to stop.' And, master, he was trembling with anger; this frightened me, and I am running away; come along you also, if you will run."

The bear then said: "Come along, uncle, we are two; he will surely not be able to eat both of us at the same time." So they were coming along. As they went, they met a jackal, who asked: "Look here uncle, how is it that you two have become companions to-day? Tell me this."

They told him: "You can't imagine, young man, an ogre has come to my house?"

"How does he look?" the jackal asked.

"He is awfully big, young man," the tiger said.

"Then, uncle, I shall also go along with you; we shall all of us together drive him away. Then we shall tie ourselves up together[7], uncle; if any of us should be tired, the strong one among us will get us off; perhaps I may be tired, perhaps you may become tired; if we are joined together, then if he eats any one, he will eat us all; if we are saved, we shall all be saved. Come along, let us have a look at him."

Joṛa miťenako. Joṛa miťkateko calaoena ona dander ṭhen. Nui mẹrọm dọ onkoe disạleťko khan phurkate ạḍi ãṭe dọn ạcurkeťa dhiri cọṭre; kaṭaṕ kaṭaṕ saḍeyena.

Khange onko bana, kul, toyo dọ ona añjọmte birạm paṭko dạreťa. Khange bana dọe bindạrena; bindạren khane ọr rad radao idiye kanakin; adọe mẹneťa, Alo mamọben ọreńa, mare mare mạilạ, mamọ, chaḍaoǩ kan tińa.

Khange toyo hõe gurena; ar onkayeťakin, Alo, mamọ, am dọm marań hoṛ kana, mare mare mạilạ, mamọm toraokeťṭạlińa. Khangeye gẹr gọćkeťkina.

41. Bar boeha reaǩ.

Bar boehakin tahẽkana; unkinaǩ dọ miťṭańge pichạuṛi tahẽkana. Miť hoṛ dọ sin ar miť hoṛ dọ ńindạ oyona. Sińe oyoǩ hoṛ dọ khub leka sagaǩkoreye oyo baṛaea; adọ ńindạ oyoǩić dọ bogeteye pạṭiǩa.

Unkinrenge miťṭań gạiye tahẹn tạkina; uni gạ dọ banar horgekin hạṭińkedea, miť hoṛ dọ tala khon ạṇḍuạr sẹć, ar miť hoṛ dọ bọhoǩ sẹć. Adọ uni gạ dọ gupi gupitekin busạǩ ocokedea. Khange uni ọkoe ạṇḍuạr sẹće ńam akade uni renge busạǩ mĩhũ dọe hoeyena; adọ unige duhạue lạgiť dọe calaoena. Uni bọhoǩ senić hõe calaoena; khange ạṇḍuạr senić dọe duhạuede kana. Adọ uni bọhoǩ senić dọ un jọkhene mẹnkeťa, Ẹṇḍaǩge, iń senić

[8] 'Old, old dirt' is here used instead of 'skin'.

41 [1] As told by Bhuju Murmu of Dhopahar.

[2] The pichạuṛi is an overcloth consisting of generally two widths of cotton cloth sown together, the size of the overcloth being ordinarily five cubits (two and a half yard) long and three cubits (one and a half yard) broad.

[3] During the cold season, when such an overcloth is used, a number of grasses with pricking awns ripen; these awns may be very troublesome indeed, if they prick the skin. The worst are probably the awns of the most commonly used

They tied themselves up together, and in this way they went to the den. When the goat became aware of them, he commenced to jump about snorting on the top of that rock; it gave a clattering sound.

When the bear and the tiger and the jackal heard this, they ran away head over heels. Then the bear fell to the ground; when he went down, the two other ones dragged him along, and the bear called out: "Don't, uncle, don't drag me along; my old, old dirt[8], uncle, is being torn off!"

Thereupon the jackal also fell down, and the two of them were calling out: "Don't uncle, don't! you are a big man, you have helped to get our old, old dirt off, uncle." Thereupon he bit and killed them both.

41. TWO BROTHERS[1].

THERE were two brothers; they had together only one over-cloth[2]. One of them used it to cover himself during daytime and the other had it at night. The brother who used it during the day espezially had it on where there was much of pricking awns[3]; consequently the other, who had it at night, was pricked all over.

These two also had a cow; this cow they divided between themselves, one owned the part from the middle towards the udder, and the other the front part with the head. As they tended this cow, she in time calved. The calf naturally became the property of him who had the hinder part, and he went to milk the cow. The one who had the head-part also went; now the owner of the hinder part was milking; at that time the owner of the head-part said: "Confound it! I am driving the cow belonging to me away." Whereupon he commenced to beat her vigorously

thatching grass (Heteropogon contortus, R. & S.), found everywhere. They are like tiny needles and stick to the clothes in an amazing way.

gại doń lagayetińa. Adọ bhagete bọhọk̓ sẹne dale kana; khange gại dọe laṛaok̓ kana ar bae duhạu daṛeae kana.

Adọe metae kana, Henda ya, cedak̓ gại dọm dale kana?

Uniye mẹnket̓a, Amren ma bạń dale kan, ińrengeń dale kana. Onkate bana họṛge toa dọ bakin jọma.

42. Ạrjun ar uniren bạhu reak̓.

Sedae jugre, kathae, mit̓tań Ạrjun ńutuman họṛe tahẽkana, ar uniren bạhu dọ ạdi gesṭahigeye tahẽkana, oṛak̓ko sẹ racako hõ bae jọk̓ ṭạṇḍia. Ar oka dọ inạ duạr aṛe sẹ piṇḍạ aṛekoregeye ṭạṇḍite aṛe racatea; ạdi asketia, ar gesṭahigeye tahẽkana, ar daka dak̓ mạṇḍikate hõ bae jọk̓ ṭạṇḍia, katwar cetanrege aćren hẹrẹltẹt̓ hõ dakae emaea.

Adọ uni hẹrẹl họṛ dọe ruhet̓ baṛakedege, ẹnre hõ uni ạimại dọ bae jọga. Khange uni họṛ dọe oṅ ṭạṇḍiket̓ge; adọ ọṇḍẹye duṛupenge. Adọ uni ạimại dọ dak̓ ghaṭkoreye lại baṛaea, Bhala họ, ale bạbu apat ma bhala mantar chaḍa bae jọma. Adọe mẹna, Ọkọe baḍae, ẹnte simko dọ bae jọm baṛakoa.

---

[1] Name of narrator forgotten; taken down by the writer in 1892.

[2] The veiled names ordinarily used for the natural functions referred to are 'to the field' and 'to the court-yard', 'go to' being implied; the construction may also be used as a verb. The Santals are generally careful, especially in connexion with the first named, going often long distances to find a suitable place. Conduct like what is here described is not that of an ordinary Santal.

[3] Here and nearly everywhere in the following the wife is referred to as ạimại. The word may be used about women in general, but as a rule it conveys an idea of disparagement. The Norwegian kvindfolk is used very much like the Santal word.

[4] The place from where the women fetch water is the place of gossip, where all happenings are reported and discussed, that is to say, by the women of the village. Men will in certain circumstances help their women to bring water; but they are careful not to go at the time when the women collect to fetch

over the front part. The cow then was moving, and the other was unable to milk her.

So he said to his brother: "Look here, you fellow, why are you beating the cow?"

"Why," the other replied, "I am not beating your cow; it is my own I am beating." In this way none of them could get any milk.

42. ARJUN AND HIS WIFE[1].

ONCE upon a time long ago, people tell, there was a man named Arjun; his wife was very sluttish, she did not even sweep the house and the court-yard clean. And sometimes she would stool and pass water[2] just beside the door or just below the veranda; she was very lazy and sluttish, and even when she had prepared food, she would not sweep the place clean; she gave her husband his food on the top of the rubbish.

Her husband would scold her; still that woman[3] would not sweep. Then her husband would blow the place clean and sit down there. And the woman would tell others at the place[4] where they go to fetch water: "What will you say to this, our boy's father does not eat without having uttered an incantation." She would, however, add: "Who knows what it may be; you see he does not eat the fowls[5]."

---

water. It is especially in the afternoon that they meet to get what is needed for preparing the evening-meal. The time about 4 p. m. is called maraṅ dak lo ber, i. e., the big water-drawing hour; about one hour later is called huḍiṅ dak lo ber, the small water-drawing hour, 'big' and 'small' having reference to the position of the sun, high or low in the sky.

5 The woman is a mischief-maker; she feels she has said too much, so she tries to qualify her tale by this statement. A mantar or invocation is generally accompanied by a sacrifice; her husband does not perform such. Fowls are commonly used for certain kinds of sacrifice.

Inạ tayom khange mitṭan disomre ạḍi bagahi hoeyena, rakas reak; sanam hoṛe jom khankaretkoa. Ado ona disomren raje hukumketa, banma, Ma ojhak hoṛ ńamkope; okoe ojha nui rakase goćle khan uni hoṛ do mit ghaṛa takań emaea.

Khange onte note ojha ńamko lagit sipạhikoe kolketkoa; ado ojha hoṛko sap idiyetkoa; menkhan okoe ojha hõ uni goje reak bako dillaka; ado sesre nui idiye lạgitko hećena.

Adoko kuliyetkoa, Noa atore okoeko ojha hoṛ menakkoa? lạipe.

Ado uniren ạimại doe menketa, Aleić hõe ojhakgetalea.

Ado uni herel doe menketa, Dhut, alom lạiyeńa.

Maejiu doe menketa, Baṅa se, calakme baṛe; ṭaka ńamoka nãhãk.

Adoe menketa, Dhut, iń do bạń baḍaea, ohoń senlena.

Khange sipạhikin ańjom ńamket khan kin bolo gotena; adokin metae kana, Nitge delalin idimea.

Adoe menketa, Ohoń senlena.

Ado uni ạimạiye metadea, Ma se am do calakme, inge bań baḍaea, am do ma calakme baṛe; mitṭan jote ar mitṭan ṭengoć idi toraeme. Khange ado jormoṭgekin indikedea, jote ar ṭengoć songeteye idi toraketa Khange ado raj ṭhenko idi seṭerkedea.

Ado raje kulikedea, Rakasem goć daṛekea?

Adoe menketa, Okoe baḍae, paetarle eneć iń daṛeaka.

Adoe metadea, Acha ma paetarlem.

---

6 The word is ordinarily used about a locality having been infested with tigers or leopards.

7 The king calls for anybody who knows the business of an ojha. In Santali this word is especially used about medicine-men who, besides giving medical treatment, profess to be able to pacify or obviate the malevolent spirits believed to be at the bottom of illness. Here it is this side that is reflected on; he wants a man who knows magic.

8 In cases like this a sum is not mentioned; it would not be good form to count, and a fixed sum would perhaps not be appreciated. A ghaṛa is a brass-pot, seldom seen with the Santals, but very common in Hindu households, used

Some time after this it so happened that a certain country became very dangerous[6] to live in, on account of an ogre; eating all he was making the country a waste. The king of that country then sent out an order: "Find and bring people who know how to exorcize[7]; if any exorcist kills this ogre, that man I shall give a pot[8] full of money."

Thereupon he sent his soldiers in all directions to find such exorcists; but there was no exorcist, who dared to attempt to kill this ogre; at last they came to take this man along with them.

They asked the people of this village: "Are there any exorcists to be found in this village? tell who they are."

Then this man's woman said: "Our one also engages in exorcism."

Her husband then said: "Nonsense, don't mention me."

But the woman replied: "Don't say so, please go; there is money to be had."

"Nonsense," he said: "I do not know; I shall certainly not go."

When the two soldiers heard this, they at once entered the court-yard and said to the man: "Come now at once, we shall take you along."

"I shall certainly not go," he said.

The woman then said to him: "Do, you go; I do not know anything; you go, please; take a yoke-rope and an axe along with you." Thereupon they took the man away with force. He had the yoke-rope and an axe with him. So they took him before the king.

The king asked him: "Might you be able to kill the ogre?"

The man replied: "Who knows? only after having performed some divination[9] I shall be able to do it."

"Very well then," the king said, "make the divination at once."

---

especially for fetching water. It is round with a narrow neck and may take up to about ten quarts or even more.

[9] The word paetar translated divination is used about getting some idea of coming events, by performing some juggling tricks or, especially, through dreams.

Adoe menketa, Noṇḍe do ohoń paetarlea; hana kulhi mucaṭreń paetara. Khange ado ona kulhi mucaṭteko calaoena, ar un jokheć do aḍi baṛić phaḍ oṇḍeko jarwa akan tahẽkana; ado onko salakge tala ńinda jokheć kulhi mucaṭteko calaoena.

Adoe menketa, Thoṛabo gitić ńoklenge; tobe nãhĩń paetartabona. Ar uniak motlob do oṇḍe khon daṛe bundis akawana. Khange tho sanam hoṛko japitket khan do bai baiteye beretena; jote ar teṅgoće sapkettaea, ado oṇḍe khon phuc menteye daṛ hoṭketa. Khange tho jemon note khone daṛ idiyet tahẽkan, un jokhećge onte khon rakas hõ hoṛ jomko lagite hijuk kan tahẽkana; khankin ńapam goṭena.

Khange uni hoṛe roṛ goṭketa. Henda ho, okatem calak kana?

Adoe menketa, Hoṛ jom iń calak kana; am do okatem calak kana?

Khane men goṭketa, Am ńamgeń hijuk kana.

Cedakem ńameń kana?

Kathae, Am lekanko aḍi hoṛ iń do guniń cet akawatkoa; ado ar hõ cetako menteń heć akana.

Adoe menketa, De, eṇḍe khan iń hõ cetańme.

Adoe menketa, Cedam eṇḍe khan?

Hẽ, iń ceda.

Adoe metadea, Eṇḍekhan cet hõ alom roṛa, eṇḍe enećem cet daṛeaka.

Acha, eṇḍekhan ohoń roṛa.

Acha, eṇḍekhan thirokme.

Adoe metadea, Ma eṇḍekhan do gitićme, ar cet hõ alom roṛa; arem roṛlekhan do ohom cet daṛelea.

Khangeye gitićena, ar aćak pichauṛite bohoke ṭoparkedea, ar joto ti jaṅgae tolkedea ona jotete, ar ona teṅgoćte bohoke kuṭame kuṭamkedea se, adoe kuṭam goćkedea.

The man then replied: "I shall not possibly be able to perform the divination here; I shall do it over there at the end of the village street." So they went to the end of the village street; at that time a tremendous crowd of people had assembled, and with this crowd following they went at midnight time to the end of the street.

The man then said: "Let us lie down a little; then only I shall be able to perform the divination for us." Now his wish was to run away from there; so he had figured it out to himself. Consequently, when all had fallen asleep, he rose very quietly; taking his yoke-rope and his axe he started running like an arrow shot out. Then, just as he was running along from this side, at the same time the ogre also was coming from the opposite direction to eat people, and they suddenly met.

"Look here," the man said, "where are you going?"

"I am going to eat people," the other replied; "where are you going?"

"I am coming to find you," the man said.

"Why are you wanting to find me?"

He said, people tell: "I have taught magic to many a one like you; and I have come to teach still more."

"Do, teach me also then," the ogre said.

"Then you will really learn?" the man asked.

"Yes, I will."

"In that case," the man said, "don't say a word; only so you will be able to learn."

"All right, in that case I shall not say a single word."

"All right, keep quiet then."

Thereupon the man said to him: "So lie down then, and don't speak; if you speak, you will be absolutely unable to learn."

So the ogre lay down, and the man covered his head up with his overcloth, and with the yoke-rope he tied his arms and legs up, whereupon he hammered him incessantly with the axe; finally he hammered him to death.

Adọ onko gitić akan hoṛ ṭhẹn ńir sẹnkateye metako kana, Ẹnḍ hoṛge, bhage ona dọko pahra kana, eṅgate pusuć pusućko gitić akana. Delabo, rakas gọk ạguyepe.

Khange adọko hahaṛayena, arko mẹnkeťa, Sạri sẹya nase ya? pasẹťe ẹṛẹyeťbon.

Adọ ạḍi ãṭte ruheťkateye metaťkoa, Bereť gọdọkpe tọ, heṛan iń ẹṛẹyeťpe.

Khange adọ calaoenteko ńẹlkede dọ sạrigeye gọć akade. Khanko gọk ạgukedea, ẹkkalte raj oṛakteko idikedea. Adọ miť ghaṛa ṭakae emadea; adọ apan ạpin oṛakteko calao baṛayena.

Adọ oṛakte sẹnkate ạimạitẹť dọe metae kana, Ńẹlkeťam, ińiń kolkeťmẹte nẽkẽ bam arjao ạguaťbona? Am dọ bań calakem mẹneť tahẽkana.

Adọ ceť hõ bae mẹnlaka; thir dorokenae.

43. Miťṭań kul ar kulại.

Hoṛko mẹna, kathae, Sedae jugre dọ kul dọ kulạ[1] ṭhenko jọm ocok kan tahẽkana.

Miťṭań kamar, kathae, birte huruť kuṭạm kuilại lạgiťẹ sẹn akan tahẽkana; un jọkhẹćge, kathae, kulạị dọ kule lagaye lagayedea sẹ. Khange uni hoṛ ṭhen sẹ uni aṛete kul dọe ńir calaoena. Khangeye okoyena, uni kul dọ; adọ dhãoṛa dhạuṛi uni kulạị dọ kule ńam baṛayede kana.

Khange adọ uni kule mẹnkeťa, uni kamare metae kana, Ẹ ho, dẹ bańcaokańme.

Uni kamar dọe mẹnkeťa, Ọhọń okolema, jọmeńam nãhãk.

---

1 Taken down in 1891; narrator a schoolboy of about 17. This and the two preceding ones are good examples of what Santal children are told in the way of stories by grandmothers and such people.

2 It is not easy to understand how they have imagined that hares should chase tigers; the next story tells that hares have been eating human beings also. It may possibly have been suggested by the names in Santali, kul being their name for a tiger and kulạị for a hare.

Thereupon he ran off to the people who where lying down and said to them: "You unspeakable people! these are keeping a nice watch! dash it, they are sleeping quietly and comfortably. Come along, carry the ogre here!"

They were naturally astonished and said: "Is it true, you fellow, or is it false? Perhaps he is hoaxing us?"

The man scolded them right and left and said to them: "Get up in a hurry, you may be sure I am hoaxing you."

So they went and saw the ogre, he had really killed him. Thereupon they carried him on their shoulders and took him straight to the king. And he gave the man one brass-pot full of money, whereupon they all went away every one to their own homes.

When the man came home, the woman said to him again and again: "Do you see now? Because I sent you, have you not earned this here for us? You were saying you were not going."

He did not answer a word; he kept quiet, poor fellow.

43. A TIGER AND A HARE[1].

THE Santals tell that in a former age the tigers[2] were eaten by the hares.

A blacksmith had once, they tell, gone to the forest to cut tree stumps to make charcoal[3] from; just at that time, they tell, a hare was chasing a tiger most vigorously. The tiger then ran to this man or close to where he was. The tiger hid himself, and the hare was hunting for him all over the place.

Then the tiger said, that is to say, he said to the blacksmith: "Listen you; do save me!"

"No, certainly not," the blacksmith replied, "I am not going to hide you; you will eat me presently."

---

[3] The local blacksmiths always use charcoal, prepared by themselves or, now-a-days, often bought.

Adǫ uni kule mẹnkeťa, Ǫhǫń jǫmmea.

Adǫ khangeye okokedea. Adǫ taenǫmte khange tǫe metae kana, Ǫkǫe ṭhen hõ alom lạị baṛaea, arem lạile khan dǫ dhorageń jǫmmea.

Adǫe cekaea bẹcara, pạhil mae okokede, taenǫmte ma onkae metae kan. Khange adǫ ghań ghuń bạị bạiteye mẹnkeťa, Ǫhǫń lạia. Inạkin rǫṛ baṛae jǫkhẹćge kulạị dǫe ńir hijuḱ kan tahẽkana. Khange uni kamar dǫ ṭẹńgǫćte kulạiye capaťledea sẹyẹ capať gǫć gǫťkedea. Ar kul dǫe rǫṛ oṭokaťa, Am dǫ ǫkǫe ṭhen hõ alom lạia, are dạṛkeťa.

Adǫ uni kamar dǫ kuilạ baṛakate tarasiń[5] ber jǫkhẹć kuilạko ar uni kulạị hõe gǫḱkeťte oṛaḱteye hẹćena. Khange adǫ rǫ gẹťkate uni kamar ạimạị dǫe utu dakakeťa; adǫ khankin jǫm baṛakeťa.

Adǫe kuliyede kana, Okare nui kulạị dǫm gǫćledea?

Adǫ uni kamar dǫ ceť hõ bae rǫreťa. Khane mẹnkeťa, Ma sẹ lạime, okarem gǫćledea? Ạḍiye sebela, gapa dǫ iń hõ am sǫńgẹteń calaḱa; am dǫ sendra baṛakom, ar iń dǫ inạkoře huruťkoń kuṭạm baṛaea.

Adǫe mẹnkeťa, Iạń lạiam kana, ạikạ ǫkǫe ṭhen hõ alom lạị baṛaea.

Adǫe mẹnkeťa, Ǫhǫń lạia.

Adǫ khangeye lạiae kana, je, Miťṭań kul dǫ kulạị ṭhene laga ocoḱ kan tahẽkana, un jǫkhẹćge ṭẹńgǫćte iń dǫ kulạị iń capaťledea sẹń gǫć utạr gǫťkedea. Adǫ unre kule metadińa, Ǫkǫe ṭhen hõ alom lạia, bańkhanlań jǫmmea. Onate am hõń metam kana, ǫkǫe ṭhen hõ alom lạia.

Khange uni kul dǫ tinre cǫń kuḍạmre hẹćkateye aḱten kan tahẽkana; khankin jạpiťkeť khan uni kul dǫ bǫlǫyente uni kạmar hẹrẹl dǫe jhuṭịạu oḍokkedea. Adǫ khange ṭạṇḍiteye oḍok idikedea; mẹnkhan ceť lekate cǫe idikede, okare hõ bae ghaoledea. Khange adǫ idikateye dǫhǫ akadea; khange adǫ bǫtǫrte uni kamar reaḱ liṇḍhi dǫ luyuť luyuḍoḱ kantaea.

---

[4] The Santali word especially means indistinct speaking through the nose.

[5] The Santali tarasiń lit. means 'half-day' and is used about the middle of the afternoon, i. e., about 3 o'clock, midway between noon and sunset.

The tiger said: "I shall surely not eat you."

So the blacksmith hid him. Afterwards the tiger said to him: "Don't tell it to anybody; if you do, you may be sure I shall eat you."

Now what should he do the poor fellow? First he hid him; afterwards the tiger spoke to him in this way. So he very slowly and gruntingly[4] said: "I shall certainly not tell." While they were talking in this way, the hare came running along, whereupon the blacksmith threw his axe at the hare, and he just hit him and killed him. Before leaving, the tiger again said: "Don't tell anybody," whereupon he ran away.

When the blacksmith had made his charcoal, he took this and also the hare on his shoulder and carried it home some time in the middle of the afternoon[5]. After he had singed and cut the meat into small pieces, the blacksmith's wife prepared rice and curry, whereupon they both had their food.

At that time she asked him: "Where did you kill this hare?"

But the blacksmith did not answer anything. Then she said: "Do tell, where did you kill him? He is so very savoury; to-morrow I will also go out with you; then you shall hunt hares, and I shall cut tree-stumps in the meanwhile in the vicinity."

Then the man said: "I am going to tell you something; but beware, don't tell it to anybody."

"Certainly not, I shall not tell," she replied.

So he told her, viz.: "A tiger was being chased by a hare; just at that time I threw my axe at the hare and killed him at once. At that time the tiger said to me: 'Don't tell anybody, otherwise we two shall eat thee.' Therefore I warn you also, don't tell anybody."

Now the tiger had some time or other during the evening come there at the back of the house and was listening, and when they had fallen asleep, the tiger went in, seized the blacksmith and carried him out; then he carried him away outside the village; who knows how he managed to carry him, he did not hurt him anywhere.

Khange ona ńe̱lte uni kul do̱e me̱nketa, Henda ho, lịṇḍhi do̱ cedak lukut lukudok kantama.

Ado̱ uni kamar do̱e me̱nketa, Enań kulạige laćreń bhorao akade tahẽ̱kana, nuige oḍokoke me̱net kana.

Khange kule me̱nketa, Hape ho, alom aṛagea, sạṅgiń ńõ̱k iń dạṛlege.

Ado̱e me̱nketa, Acha o̱ho̱ń aṛagea, ma dạṛ ho̱dme.

Khange ado̱ kule̱ dạṛketa; ado̱ uni kamar bańcaoenteye ruạṛ he̱ćena.

44. Ho̱ṛ ar kulại reak katha.

Sedae jugre do̱, kathae, ho̱ṛ hõ̱ kulại ṭhenko jo̱m ocok kan tahẽ̱kana. Ado̱ onka tahe̱n tahe̱nte, kathae, mit din do̱ mitṭań ho̱ṛ do̱ Ṭhạkur ṭhen aro̱joke calaoena. Ado̱e metae kana, E̱ Ṭhạkur baba, am ṭhenge mitṭań aro̱jok lạgit iń he̱ć akana.

Ado̱e metadea, Cet ạrji kantama? Lạime.

Ado̱e me̱nketa, Noko kulại jạtge ạḍi bạṛićko noksanetlea. Huḍiń janwarko hoeyena, sakam latarre hõ̱ko okokok kana, ado̱ bale ńe̱l ńam ho̱tetkoa. Acka mạrko jo̱m go̱tetlea. Lạṭu janwar khan do̱, ńe̱l daram go̱tkotele ńir sajoṅa. Noko kạṭić janwar do̱ bale ńe̱l daram hoṭ daṛeako kana, onate am ṭhen aro̱jok iń he̱ć akana. Jãhã lekate noko janwar do̱ ale khonem haraokako khan do̱ ạḍi bes hoekoka. Niạ ạrji lạgitge am ṭhen iń do̱ń he̱ć akana. Ma dayakate ańjo̱mkatińme.

Ado̱ Ṭhạkure me̱nketa, Acha bogege. E̱ṇḍe̱khan phalna din hilok setakre he̱ć go̱dokme, ar kulạiren so̱rdar hõ̱ e̱n hilok do̱ń maṅgaoea. Am hõ̱ inạ din hilok do̱ ạikhạ hijukme.

---

[6] The word translated 'hindquarters' lit. means rectum and perineum.

44 [1] Ho̱ṛ in Santali may mean both a human being and a Santal. The last seems to be the meaning here, because a Santal custom is explained.

[2] One of their names for the Supreme Being.

When he had taken him far away, he put him down, and the hindquarters[6] of the blacksmith were trembling from fear. Seeing this the tiger said: "Look here you, your hindquarters are trembling exceedingly; why is that?"

"A while ago," the blacksmith replied, "I put the hare into my stomach; he wants to get out."

"Wait, wait," the tiger said, "don't let him loose, let me first get away some distance."

"All right," he said, "I shall not let him out; please be quick and run off."

The tiger then ran away, and the blacksmith was saved and returned home.

44. SANTALS AND THE HARES.

In a former age, people tell, Santals[1] also were eaten by the hares. As this went on for a long time, people tell, one day a Santal went to Thakur[2] to make an appeal. He said to him: "O Father Thakur, I have come to make an appeal to thee."

"What is thy complaint," he replied, "tell."

"These hare beings," the man said, "are causing us awful injuries and loss. They are small animals, they hide even under leaves, so we are unable to see them at once. Suddenly and without any warning they come over us and eat us. If they had been big animals, we should be able to see them coming and run aside. We are unable to see at once these tiny animals coming; therefore I have come to thee to appeal. If somehow or other thou wouldst put these down and make them to be under us, it would be very well. It is to make this appeal that I have come to thee. In mercy and pity listen to me."

Thakur then answered: "Very well. Come here then on such and such a day in the morning; I shall let also the foreman of the hares be called here that day. Have a care that thou also comest that day."

Adoe menkeťa, Acha bogege.

Khange ona din tioǩen khan sari setaǩreye calaoena, ar kulai hõ tinre coe sen akan. Khange ado bana horkin sen ńapamena. Ado Thakure kuliyeťkina, Henda ya kulai, ańjomeť kanań, bańma, adi barić am dom jomeťkoa; sari se nase?

Ado kulaiye menkeťa, Okor ba? Iń do bań jomeťkoa; akoge aleko jomeťlea.

Tobe bam jomeťkoa?

Adoe menkeťa, Bańa.

Ado uni hore kulikedea, Henda ya manwa, sari, kathae, ape do kulaipe jomeťkoa?

Adoe menkeťa, Okor ba? Ale do bale jomeťkoa. Akoge bogete ale manwa jatko jomeťlea.

Ado Thakure menkeťa, Kulai ar manwa, bana hor iń kuliyeťbena. Bana horgeben hunda hesaǩ hunda bareǩ kana. Okoe hõ baben kabuleťa. Miťtań bicar hoyoǩtabena; aikha ona kamiben, onarege abenaǩ do phandaoǩtabena.

Ado bana horkin menkeťa, Acha, ma hukumalińme.

Ado kulaiye metadea, E ya kulai, am do kita horho iń metam kana. Judi noa bochor dinte kita sakamem horho ńũrkeťa menkhan, endekhan manwam jom dareakoa; ar bam horho ńũrkeťa menkhan, amgeko jommea. Onkae metadea.

Ar uni hor hõe metae kana, E ya manwa, am iń metam kana.

Adoe menkeťa, Ma rorme.

Am do korkot sakam horhoeme. Judi onam horho ńũrkeťa menkhan, kulaiyem jom dareakoa; ar bam horho ńũrle khan,

---

[3] Kita, Phoenix acaulis, Roxb., is fairly common in the Santal country. It has no stem besides what the leaves are growing out from.

[4] Korkot, Dillenia indica, L., also fairly common, is quite a large tree, with large leaves. It is an evergreen, i. e., it does not shed its leaves once yearly, standing leafless for some time. Fresh leaves come out periodically, and the old leaves fall down from time to time. The man had a much better chance than the hare.

"Very well," the man said.

When that day came, he, truth to tell, went in the morning; the hare had also arrived some time or other. They both of them met; then Thakur asked them: "Look here, thou hare, I am hearing that thou art eating these very badly; is this true or not?"

"Why, not at all," the hare replied, "I do not eat them; they themselves are eating us."

"Then thou doest not eat them?"

"No," he said.

Then he asked the man: "Look here, thou man, is it a fact, as people say, that you eat hares?"

"Why, not at all," he replied, "we do not eat them. But they themselves eat us human beings very frequently."

Then Thakur said: "Hare and man, I am asking both of you. Both of you are blaming each other. None of you will confess. Your case will have to be taken up for judgement; beware, do what you are ordered to do; thereby your case will be settled."

Both of them then said: "Well, give us thy command."

He then said to the hare: "Hare, I am ordering thee to watch the dwarf date palm[3]. If within the space of this year thou watchest and seest a leaf of this palm fall down, thou shalt be free to eat human beings; and if not, then they shall eat thee." This he said to him.

He also spoke to the man: "Thou man, I am ordering thee."

"Speak," he said.

"Watch thou the leaves of the korkot[4] tree. If thou watching seest these fall down, thou shalt be free to eat the hares; and if not, then ye human beings shall be liable to be eaten by the hares. Within this year both of you watch and see the leaves fall down. Next year in this month and on this very day bring me the leaves of those trees, and I shall have a look at your leaves. Now thou watch this tree, and this one that tree over there; watch both from noon to-day. When a leaf falls down, bring it at once. Any day it falls, bring it at once that day.

eṇḍekhan ape manwa do kulạị ṭhenpe jom ocoḱa. Niạ bochor motorege bana hoṛ horho ńūrben. Kalom niạ cando niạ din hiloḱ ona reaḱ sakam ạguạńben, ar ona sakam iń ńeltabena; sạrigeben horho ńūr akaťa se bań, onań ńeltabena. Ma am do inạ dare, ar nui do hane hana dare, ma tikin khonge horhoeben. Ona sakam ńūr tora baṛe ạgu godben. Jãhã hiloḱge ńūroḱ, unrege ạgu godben. Ar bicạr do noa cando noa din hiloḱ iń bicạrtabena. Inạge katha do; ma calaḱben. Adokin calao baṛayena, apan ạpin horhokin dhurạuena.

Khange ado horho horhote ḍeke sanam cedeyentakina, enre hõ bańge ńūroḱ. Enre hõ, kathae, bạgi do bakin bạgiaḱ kana. Kulạị hõ jãhãe hoṛe ńamleko khan doe metakoa. Dose ya, uni manwa ńel ạgulepe, bhalae horho ńūrkeťa se bań. Khanko ńel ạgukedege, adoko heć ruạṛenge, adoe kulikoa, Cele ya, horho ńūrketae?

Adoko metaea, Bańa ya, bae leṭeć daṛeaḱ kana.

Adoe metakoa, Okoe baḍae, nãhãḱe horho ńūrkeťa menkhan, abo doko jombongea. Ar judi iń nãhãḱ iń horho ńūrkeťa menkhan, onkobo jomkoa. Ado ako jạt onkae galmaraoakoa.

Ar uni hoṛ hõ jãhãeko ać ṭhenko senlen khan doe metakoa, Dose ya, uni kulạị ńel ạguyepe, bhalae horho ńūrkeťa se bań. Adoko ńel ạgukedege, adoe kulikoa, Cele ya, horho ńūrketae se bań?

Adoko metaea, Bae leṭeć daṛeaḱ kana.

Adoe metakoa, Okoe baḍae, judi uniye horho ńūrkeťa menkhan do abo manwa doko jombongea; ar iń baṛeń horho ńūrle khan, eṇḍekhan onkobo jomkoa. Ado sạri onka jidạ jid horhotegekin tahẽyena.

Ado sari bochor din tiogoḱ dela dili khange korkoṭ sakam do ńūr goťena. Khange ado uni hoṛe rạskạ goťena; ado halańkate ona sakam do Ṭhạkur ṭhene idi goťkeťa. Ado uni kulạị hõe horho bhagaoen khan, mocateye geṛ topaḱkeťa are idikeťa. Ado Ṭhạkurkin metae kana, Nõḱõe baba, lih horho ńūr ạgukeťa; ńeltalińme.

And in this month on this same day I shall pass judgement in your case. That is what I have to say; now go both of you." So they went away and commenced to watch each his own tree.

They were watching and watching, so ultimately their buttocks became bald and hairless; still no leaf fell down. Even so, people tell, they did not leave off watching. When the hare met with anybody, he would ask them: "Please you, be good enough and see how that man is faring, and let me know whether he has seen a leaf fall down during his watch or not." So they would go and have a look at him, and come back, when he would ask them: "Well, how is it, has he, during his watching, seen it fall?"

Then they would answer him: "No, you; he is unable to manage."

"Who knows," he would say to them; "if he presently should watch it fall down, then they would eat us. And if I should watch a leaf fall down now, then we shall eat them." It was his own kind, other hares, he was speaking to in this way.

The man also, when some one went to him, he would say to them: "Please you, be good enough and see how the hare is faring, and let me know whether he has seen a leaf fall down during his watching or not." So they would go and have a look, and he would ask them: "Well, how is it, has he, during his watching, seen it fall or not?"

And they would say to him: "He is unable to manage."

Then he would say to them: "Who knows? If he should watch it fall down, then they will eat us human beings; and if I should be fortunate enough to watch it fall down, then we shall eat them." So really and truly they both remained watching assidously.

Then, truth to tell, when the day fixed was drawing near, a korkot leaf fell down, and the man became glad; and picking the leaf up he took it at once to Thakur. The hare also, when he became tired of watching bit off a leaf and brought it. Both of them said to Thakur: "Here, Father, we have watched it fall down and have brought it; look at our leaves."

Khange adọ bana hoṛak̕ sakame ńẹlket̕tạkina. Adọ kulạiye metae kana, Am dọ bam hoṛhọ ńũrlet̕a; amak̕ dọ baṅ sạbudok̕ kana.

Adọ kulạiye mẹnket̕a, Baṅa, baba, hoṛhọ ńũr akat̕geaṅ.

Adọ Ṭhạkure mẹnket̕a, Baṅa, bam hoṛhọ ńũr akat̕a. Am dọ bhiṭuạk̕ ṭhen mundhi dọ okor ńẹlok̕ kana? Ar nuiak̕ sakam bhiṭuạk̕, ńẹlme cet̕ leka ńẹlok̕ kana. Amak̕ dọ okor onka dọ ńẹlok̕ kana? Am dọm gẹr topak̕ akat̕a; ṭhik sẹ baṅ?

Adọ uni kulạị dọ cet̕ hõ bae mẹn daṛeat̕a, tirup̕ hapeyenae. Adọ paha tulạmte jaṅgae malaoket̕taea are bhoṛadea, are metadea, Am dọń bhọram kana; teheṅ khon dọ sakam oṭaṅok̕ lekam dạṛa, hako pako dọ ọhọko tiok̕ daṛelema. Ar am dọm haraoente manwa ṭhenem jọm ocok̕a, jãhãregeko ńamme sẹ ape jạtko, laga lagateko gọćpea, ar gọćkate apeak̕ dọ moela hõ moelako jọmtapea, ẹnte am dọ apnartegem bạṛićket̕a. Cedak̕em gẹr topak̕ket̕a? Ona iạte am dọ onkaṅ sarapam kana.

Cabayena katha dọ. Ona iạte ale hoṛ họpọn dọ kulạị reak̕ dọ nit dhạbić moela hõ moelale jọmet̕takoa; onkoak̕ dọ bale giḍiyet̕a, jọtọle suṛe jọmet̕takoa.

---

[5] The feet of the Indian hare are light coloured.

[6] Hares are fairly common in the country and are much liked as food. Hares are caught in several ways (nets &c.); to let dogs chase them is common.

This is according to custom. The hairs are singed off, otherwise the whole is eaten, even the intestines and stomach with all contents.

A variant has several details. It starts with stating that there was once a great quarrel between man and the hares, both threatening to eat each other. When Cando (the same as Thakur) heard about the quarrel, he went near to them and asked them what they were quarrelling about. The hare then at once spoke and asked Cando to bless him and give him permission to eat human beings from that day. The man on his side made the same petition. Cando bonga then commenced to think: these hares are such small beings; they are able to get in under any shrub and lie quietly in wait there, and would be able to utterly eradicate man. It would never do to let these become the 'big ones'; I shall let man become the superior one, so when the hares see human beings come, they shall run away. Cando thereupon said to them that he could not give them any blessing just then, but he would give them a work to perform, and the one who succeeded, him he would make the superior one. Then he ordered

He then had a look at the leaves of both and said to the hare: "Thou hast not watched it fall down; thy statement is not to be proved."

"No, Father," the hare said, "I have watched it falling."

"No," Thakur said, "thou hast not watched it falling. As for thee, the lower end of the leaf-stalk, why, where is that to be seen? And the leaf-stalk of the leaf that he has, look at it how it looks. Why, where has thy leaf the same look? Thou hast bitten it off; is it so or not?"

The hare was unable to say anything; he hung his head and was quiet. Thereupon Thakur rubbed his feet with cotton balls[5], blessed him and said: "I am giving thee this blessing: from to-day thou shalt run like a leaf that is carried away by the wind; they shall surely not be able to reach thee quickly[6]. As thou wert beaten, thou shalt be eaten by man; wherever they find thee, or any of thy kind, they shall chase you and kill you, and when they have killed you, they shall eat even your excrements[7], because thou thyself spoilt thy case. Why didst thou bite it off? Therefore I am laying such a curse on thee."

The story is ended. This is the reason why we Santals eat even the excrements of the hares to this day; theirs we do not throw away; we cook all to a hash and eat it.

---

them to watch the two trees, as is told in the story translated. They were not too far from each other to be able to see each other. They watched for nearly a whole year, when in March or April some korkot leaves fell down. The man at once took the leaf to Cando, and when the hare saw this, he bit a leaf off and also brought it to Cando.

The end of the story is as in the other one. Cando said: From to-day you human beings are the superior ones and the hares the inferior ones. The hare tried to deceive and brought the leaf to me; because he acted in this deceitful way, I am laying a greater curse on him; therefore you shall eat even their excrements. Whereupon he added to the hare: now if your leaf did not fall down, should you not have implored me? Why did you act in a deceitful way?

This variant is possibly an attempted improvement on the story translated. Another variant follows in the text.

45. Kulại ar hoṛ reak̉.

Ạḍi sedaere, kathae, kulại ar hoṛkin akhajilena; unre kulại bae daṛelente uni hoṛe mẹnketa, Amak̉ do ić hõ ić iń jom aḍoetama; un khon teheń hạbić hoṛko do kulạiak̉ ićko jometa.

Ona do nonka kana. Mit̉ṭań hoṛ okate coṅ peṛak̉e sẹnjoṅ kan tahẽkana; hoṛ aṛerege mit̉ṭań ćinḍkạ munḍu tahẽkana; onare mit̉ṭań kulạiye tahẽkana. Uni kulại do calak̉ kan hoṛ reak̉ ti laṛaok̉ ńẹlteye hudisana, Okare coṅ nãhãk̉ ti do topak̉ ńũruk̉tae. Khạṭige ona ịate uni kulại do uni hoṛe pańjakedea; tinạk̉ sạṅgińe pańjakedere hõ uni hoṛak̉ ti do baṅge ńũrok̉ kantae. Uni hoṛ do cekakate coṅ tayom sẹne bẹṅgẹt̉ ruạṛketa, ado kulạiye ńẹl ńamkedea. Uni horten hoṛ do kulại kuliye lạgit̉e teṅgoyena; ado thoṛa gan kulại haṛam hõe sẹn sorena. Uni horten hoṛ do kulại kuliyege portonketa, nonkae kulikedea, Henda kulại haṛam, am do bhala iń tayomte do cedak̉em hijuk̉ kana?

Unre kulại aćań katha lạlạiye ẹhop̉ena, mẹnket̉ae, Iń do amgiń pańjayet̉mea.

Horten hoṛe mẹnketa, Cedak̉em pańjayediń kana?

Kulạiye mẹnketa, Iń do nonkań mẹnoan tahẽkana, Amak̉ ti nãhãk̉ topak̉ ńũruk̉a, ariń joma, noa mẹnkate nõk̉õe ạḍi sạṅgiń iń pańja ạguket̉mea, baṅge ńũrok̉ kantama, pańja pańjateń laṅgayenre hõ.

Khange uni horten hoṛe mẹnketa, Am do ya, kulại, ạḍitẹt̉gem lelhagea; do calak̉me khijur ḍạr horho ńũr ạguime; onam horho ńũr ạgule khan ińak ti hõ nãhãk̉ ńũruk̉tińa, adom joma.

Khange uni haṛam kulại do khijur dare buṭạre tinạk̉ din coe duṛup̉ bhagaoena, ẹnre hõ khijur ḍạr do baṅge ńũrlena. Uni kulại do uni hoṛ ṭhene hẹć ruạṛena, are metae kana, Bań ńũrok̉ kana khijur ḍạr do. Unrege uni hoṛ kulạiye metadea, Baḍaeme, khijur ḍạr cet̉ leka tisre hõ bań ńũrok̉a onka leka ińak̉ ti hõ tisrege bań ńũrok̉a; tisiń gujuk̉a unrege ińak̉ ti do sea lambaok̉a.

45. THE HARE AND THE SANTAL.

LONG long ago, people tell, a hare and a Santal had fallen out; as the hare did not prevail, the Santal said to him: "We shall eat you, even your excrements." From that time even until to-day the Santals eat the excrements of the hares.

It happened thus: A Santal was going somewhere or other on a visit; at one place there was a small bit of jungle along one side of the road; a hare was there. This hare saw the man's hand move, as he went along, and thought: somewhere or other his hand will come off and fall down.

Surely this was the reason that the hare followed after the man; still, however far he followed, the man's hand would not come off. For some reason or other the man happened to look behind himself and caught sight of the hare. The wayfaring man stopped to ask the hare; the old hare also came a little nearer. The wayfarer then commenced to question the hare; he asked him as follows: "Look here, you old hare, say, why are you coming after me?"

The hare then commenced to tell his story and said: "I am following after you."

"Why do you follow after me?" the wayfaring man asked.

The hare replied: "I was saying thus to myself: Your hand will presently come off and fall down; then I shall eat it; with this in mind I have, as you see, followed you here a very long way; it does not come off, although I have become tired out, following you."

Then the wayfaring man said: "You fellow of a hare, you are an utter fool; now go and watch a date tree, and see whether its leaves fall down; if you can watch and see those fall down and bring them, then my hand will also fall down, and you may eat it."

Then the old hare went and sat down at the foot of a date palm, who knows for how long a time, until he could not any

Adọ teheń khon iń ạsisam kana, Am dọ hapẹnko gọćlem khan ić hõ ićko jọmtama, ar noa sarap dọ ape sanamkorege tahẽyen tapea.

Sạrige hoṛ dọ kulạiko gọćkore, lać ar kulạiić sanamko sipi mida arko lẹṭọea, haṛhat́ machage sebela.

46. Kul ar Banakin jhogṛalen reak̀.

Mit́ṭań birre mit́ṭań kul ar mit́ṭań bana rabań din jọkhẹć dãṛã baṛaerekin ńapamena, ar ẹn hilok̀ dọ ạdi ãṭ rabań kan tahẽkana. Khange adọ kule mẹnket́a, Cele ho, teheń dọ cet́ leka ạikạuk̀ kana?

Adọ banae mẹnket́a, Iń dọ bogegeń ạikạuet́a.

Adọ kule mẹnket́a, Henda ho, bhala, oka din bạṛti dọ rabańa?

Adọ banae mẹnket́a, Jạput́ dinge bạṛti dọ rabańa.

Adọ kule mẹnket́a, Bańa ho, Pus Magge bạṛti dọ rabańa.

---

45 [1] The date palm mentioned in this story is the Phoenix sylvestris, Roxb., fairly commonly planted in the country.

One detail might point to this story being rather old. The man refers to his body decaying after death. Now-a-days the Santals ordinarily cremate the dead body, generally the same day when the person dies. Their traditions expressly state that this is a custom adopted from the Hindus at a special time (likely some four hundred years ago); before that time they buried their dead.

46 [1] Some fifty years ago tigers and bears were common in the country; they are even now well known to every Santal, but are not so commonly met with.

[2] Pus is the Santali form of Bengali p a u s h a, corresponding to the later half of December and the first half of January. Mag (in Bengali Magha or Magh) is the month following, up to about the middle of February. The Santals are adopting the Bengali names for the months of the year, side by side with our months and years, which latter are generally mostly used by people who have been to school. It is noteworthy that the people, for their practical purposes, generally follow the lunar months, and when giving these a name, they will always use the Santalized form of the Bengali names, and not our European names. As the Bengali almanack has twelve months in the solar year (unlike

more; still no date leave would fall down. The hare then came back to the man and said to him: "They do not fall down, the date-palm leaves." Then the man said to the hare: "Know this, just as a date-palm leaf never falls down, in the same way my hand also will never fall down; when I die some day, then my hand will decay and rot. So from to-day I lay this curse on you: When people some day kill you, they will eat even your excrements, and this curse shall remain on all of you."

It is really so, when the Santals kill hares, they knead the intestines and hare excrements into one mass and cook it; it has a somewhat bitter, but pleasant taste[1].

46. WHEN THE TIGER AND THE BEAR QUARRELLED.

One day during the cold season, whilst out strolling, a tiger and a bear[1] met in a forest; it was intensely cold that day. The tiger said: "Well, how does it feel to-day?"

"Quite well," the bear replied.

"Look here," the tiger said, "say, which season it the coldest?"

"The rainy season," the bear replied, "that is the coldest."

"No, not at all," the tiger answered, "the months of Pus and Mag[2] are the coldest."

the Muhammedan year, that consists of twelve lunar months, and consequently is some fourteen days shorter than our year), it is only occasionally that a lunar month and an almanack-month will practically correspond to each other. This often results in some confusion and may be the cause of two lunar months getting the same name. These remarks refer to the village life. If anything has to be written, in documents and so on, the Bengali or Christian dates are always used.

Adọ banae mẹnketa, Baṅa ho, San Bhadọrge bạṛti dọ rabaṅa. Adọ noa kathage ạḍi bạṛić jhunạ jhunkin rọpọṛ kana. Bana mae gadlegete Pus Mag jọkhẹć ma baṅ rabaṅe; onate kulak katha dọ bae sẹn ocoak kana; ar jạput din ma mit lọhọtgeye tahẹna; onate ona din dọ ạḍi rabaṅea.

Khange adọ onka rọpọṛ rọpọṛtekin aṅga ńamena, ẹnre hō ona rọpọṛ dọ baṅkin cabayeta. Khange adọ ona takre mitṭaṅ họṛ ona mohṇḍategeye calak kan tahẽkana. Adọ uni kin ńẹl ńamkede khankin họhọadea; adọ uni họṛ dọ bọtọrteye dạret tahẽkana. Kkaṅgekin khudạu ẹsẹtkedea; adọkin metae kana, Ẹ ho, mitṭaṅ phaṇḍaokataliṅme; ẹnte ạliṅ dọ enaṅ khon ạḍiliṅ jhogṛak kana.

Adọ uni họṛe mẹnketa, Masẹ ẹnte rọṛleben, adọń aṅjọmle nạhĩń rọṛa.

Khange adọ kul dọe mẹnketa, Enaṅre bana tuluć iń ńapamena, adọ banaṅ kulikedea, Cele ho, teheń dọ cet leka ạikạuk kana? Adọe metadiṅa, Iń dọ bogegeń ạikạueta. Adọń metadea, Henda ho, bhala, oka din bạṛti dọ rabaṅa? Adọe ạcuradiṅa, Jạput dinge bạṛti do rabaṅa. Adọ iṅiń mẹnketa, Baṅa ho, Pus Magge bạṛti dọ rabaṅa. Mẹnkhan banae mẹnketa, Baṅa ho, San Bhadọrge bạṛti dọ rabaṅa. Ọnẹ anaṅ ạliṅak jhogṛa dọ; onage phaṇḍaokataliṅme.

Ar bana hõe mẹnketa, Onagetaliṅ jhogṛa dọ. Dẹ bicạrkataliṅme.

Adọ kule mẹnketa, Judi bana sẹn lekam rọṛ khan dọlaṅ jọmmea; inạ hō sọntọrokme.

---

3 San (from Bengali shravana or shraban) is the time from the middle of July to the middle of August. San is followed by Bhadọr (from Bengali bhadra), which lasts to the middle of September. Pus and Mag are the coldest months, especially Mag. According to a Santal saying, in Mag it may be so cold that even the horns of a buffalo become loose. San and Bhador form the middle of the rainy season and may be steaming hot. The Santals generally agree that the temperature of the rainy season is the most comfortable one; with their very scanty clothing it seems to them that this season is neither hot nor cold.

"No, certainly not," the bear said, "the months of San and Bhador[3] are the coldest."

So they had a violent quarrel over this matter. You see, the bear has a heavy coat, so he does not feel it cold in Pus and Mag; therefore he would not agree to what the tiger said; and during the rainy season he remains always soaked through, from first to last; therefore he feels so cold during that season.

They quarrelled in this way, until day dawned on them; even so they did not end their quarrel. Just then it so happened that a man was walking along in that direction. When they caught sight of him they called out to him; but the man commenced to run from fear, whereupon they chased him and blocked the way for him. They said to him: "Hey you, settle a dispute for us two; we have been having a violent quarrel since we met a while ago."

The man then said: "You must first tell; only when I hear what it is, shall I be able to say anything."

The tiger then said: "A while ago I met the bear; then I asked him: 'Well, how does it feel to-day?' He then said to me: 'Quite well'. So I said to him: 'Look here, say which season is the coldest?' Then he answered me: 'The rainy season is the coldest.' And as for me, I said: 'No, not at all, the months of Pus and Mag are the coldest.' But the bear said: 'No, certainly not, the months of San and Bhador are the coldest.' There, that is what we quarrel about; decide this matter for us."

The bear also said: "That is just what we quarrel about. Do, judge in our case."

The tiger then said: "If you say anything in favour of the bear, we two shall eat thee; be careful to remember this also."

Europeans living in the mufassil will generally agree with the bear that the rainy season is the most uncomfortable; the rain and mud make it difficult to get about. The Indian cold season is glorious; there is no finer climate anywhere.

Bana hõe metadea, Judi kul sen lekam ror khan do, tobe iń hõń jommea.

Ado khange uni hor doe luyuť luyudok kana; ado ać monereye hudiseťa, bańma, Kul sen lekań rorre ma banae jomeń, ar bana sen lekań rorre ma kule jomeń. Bana horkin jojom janwar kana; oka lekań bicartakina?

Ado onakate mitťen kathae hudis ńamkeťa; ado enre hõ bae ror phutau dareak kana. Ado unkin kin rorkeťa, Ma ho, bicar hoťkatalińme, okorem roreťa?

Ado uni hore menkeťa, Bicar doń bicargea; paseben jomeń?

Adokin menkeťa, Oholiń jommea.

Arhõe menkeťa, Acha, tobe oka katha ińiń metaben, ona doben bataotińa se bań?

Adokin menkeťa, Hẽ, ona kathaliń dohoetama; ado põcliń badao akaťmea, cekate baliń dohoea? Katha doliń dohoegetama; menkhan aika! Thik bicarkatalińme; khusi ocolińme, bańkhan do dhorageliń jommea.

Adoe menkeťa, Acha, endekhan iń roreťa; aika bujhauben, thika se baňa.

Adokin menkeťa, Ma rorme.

Khange adoe menkeťa, Pus Mag hõ bań rabańa, ar San Bhador hõ bań rabańa, menkhan hoe khange rabańa. Ma honeć bujhauben, teheń hõ miť ńinda halae halaeye hoekeťte nonka do rabań kana, ar bańkhan huteć rabań do oho aikaulena. Ar japuť din hõ eken dak

4 Lit. the Five, an expression commonly used about the village-council, assembled to administer justice.

5 This represents the Santal idea on which the story is built. It is fairly common to hear them express themselves as here. Naturally they agree that not every wind is cold.

6 The Santals have an idea that the rain of the rainy season does not hurt. No one will catch a cold or get a chill from being exposed to the rain of this season. This belief is possibly due to the fact that, when they expose themselves to the rains, they are very scantily clothed and vigorously working. The expression

The bear also said: "If you say anything in favour of the tiger, then I also shall eat thee."

Now the man was all in a tremble from fear; he was saying to himself like this: "If I speak in favour of the tiger, the bear will eat me, and if I speak in favour of the bear, the tiger will eat me. They are both of them dangerous animals; how shall I settle their dispute?"

Thereupon an idea came to him; still he was unable to get a word out. Then those two said: "Now, be quick and decide our matter; why, you do not speak!"

The man then said: "Naturally I shall settle your dispute; but perhaps you will eat me?"

"We shall certainly not eat you," both of them assured him.

Then he again said: "Very well, then, whatever I say to you, will you heed that or not?"

"Yes," they replied; "we shall comply with what you say; we have appointed you to be our court of justice[4]; why should we not comply? We shall comply with your word; but beware! judge right between us; make us pleased, otherwise we shall eat you without fail."

"Very well," he said, "so I am speaking; be careful, understand whether it is right or not."

"Please speak," they both said.

The man then said: "It is not cold in Pus and Mag; neither is it cold in San and Bhador: only when there is a wind, it is cold[5]. Understand how it is, to-day a strong breeze has been blowing the whole night; therefore it is so cold; otherwise it would not have felt cold. So also during the rainy season it is not on account of the rain[6] alone that it is cold; but any day

---

should not be taken in support of a very common misunderstanding in our countries, that the rainy season is one continual drizzle of rain. It is mostly what we should call showery weather; but the showers may be heavy, last long and come frequently. There may be breaks with clear days and sunshine in between.

eskarte dọ baṅ rabaṅa, mẹnkhan họe hilok̕ge bạṛti rabaṅ dọ ạikạuk̕a. Masẹ bhala, bujhạuben. Bana dọ jạput̕ din mit̕ lọhọt̕geye tahẹn kana, onate ona din dọ rabaṅea; ar nẹtar ma up̕ menak̕taete golop̕ golop̕e ạikạuet̕te baṅ rabaṅede kana. Ar am ma up̕ bạnuk̕tamte rabaṅet̕me, mẹnkhan asọl dọ họege rabaṅ kana. Nahakte aben dọben jhogṛak̕ kana. Masẹ bujhạuben, ṭhikiṅ rọṛet̕a sẹ baṅa?

Khange adọ sạri bana họṛkin bujhạu baṛaket̕ khankin mẹnket̕a, Sạriak̕ge, họe khange rabaṅ kana, ar baṅkhan dọ baṅ rabaṅa. Nịạ kathage balaṅ hudis ńam daṛeak̕ kan tahẽkana; nahakte alaṅ dọ enaṅ khonlaṅ jhogṛak̕ kana. Adọ ma nẽk̕ẽ jhogṛa dọ cabayena; mabo apan ạpinok̕a.

Adọ ẹnḍẹ khonge apan ạpinko calao baṛayena. Adọ kul ar bana reak̕ katha uni họṛe phanḍaokat̕takina.

47. Bitnạ ńutuman koṛa reaṅ.

Sedae jọkhẹn, kathae, nui Bitnạ koṛa dọ eṅgat hoṛmọreye tahẽkanre apattẹt̕ dọe gọćena. Khange eṅgattẹt̕ dọ apa bare oṛak̕teye hẹćena. Adọ ọnḍẹ tahẹnrege, kathae, uni Bitnạ koṛa dọe janamena. Uni koṛa dọ mit̕ bitạgeye usullena, inạk̕ khon dọ baṅgeye haralena; onatege uni dọ Bitnạko ńutumkadea. Adọ ạḍi serma hoeyenre hõ bae haralente uni dọ ọkọe kuṛi hõ bako khusiadete enka ḍạnguạtegeye hara juạnena. Ar gocoe dọhọket̕te ona dọ mit̕ bitạ pon kạṭup̕ harayentaea.

---

1 When the husband dies and there are no children, the widow often returns to her parental home. Her father, and if he is not living, her brothers are her natural protectors. If she has sons, or if any of her husband's younger brothers will take her for his wife, she will stay; otherwise she is considered to be ownerless.

2 Most Santal measures of length refer to the body. A fathom (a r p a) is the space between the finger-tips when both hands are stretched out; a m o k a is the space from the elbow to the point of the middle finger; a m u ṇ ḍ r ạ is the distance between the elbow joint and the knuckle of the little finger when the fist

there is a wind, it is felt to be colder. Well then, understand this. During the rainy season the bear is always soaked through from first to last; therefore it feels cold to him, and now at this time, because he has such hair, he feels comfortable and no cold. And as for you, you have no such hair, therefore it feels cold to you; but as a matter of fact, it is the wind that is cold. It is quite without reason that you two are quarrelling. Understand this, am I right or not?"

So, truth to tell, when both of them had thought the matter over, they said: "It is quite true; when there is a wind, it feels cold; otherwise it is not cold. This we were unable to understand; it has been quite without any cause that we two have had this quarrel all this while. So now there, there is an end to our quarrel; let us go each to our own."

So they separated there and went each his own way. In this way the man settled the dispute between the tiger and the bear.

47. THE BOY WHO WAS CALLED SPAN.

LONG long ago, people tell, whilst Span was still unborn, his father died, whereupon his mother went to her father and brothers[1]; and while she was there, they tell, Span was born. The boy grew to a hight of one span[2], more than this he did not grow; therefore they called him Span. As he, in spite of his years, did not grow, no girl took any fancy to him, and he grew into maturity without getting a wife. He let his beard grow, and it became one span and four fingers[2] long.

is closed; next comes **bitạ**, the span, the distance between the tips of the thumb and the little finger when stretched out; **mūṭ** is what is covered by the closed hand, but with the thumb stretched out; **kạṭuṗ** is the breadth of one finger, and so on. They have naturally no standards others than what they carry about in their own bodies, and these are sufficient for their ordinary wants. In the larger bazars the traders of course use a measure of length (the yard, **gọj**); but in the villages people buy e. g. cloth, using their natural **moka**.

Khange adọ onko mamọtteko ṭhen khon dọkin begarente judạrekin oṛakketa. Ar uni Bitnạ dọ kathakore dọ khub calaki hoṛe hoeyena. Jāhān kathare uni leka dọ ọkọe hō bako rọṛ daṛeaka.

Adọ tahẹn tahẹnte uni Bitnạ dọ mitṭaṅ bitkile kiriṅkedea. Ar uni dọ khube jọtọn moṭakede khan dọ siṅ marsal dọ ạtiṅge bae ạtiṅa, onate uni dọ gọtọm bitkile ṅumkedea. Adọ unire dẹckate mit ṅindại ạtiṅea, ar siṅ marsal dọ oṛakregeye aderkaea.

Adọ tahẹn tahẹnte onka mit din dọ ṭaṇḍite ạtiṅe idi akade tahẽkan jọkhẹnge, kathae, cet lạgit cọe ãṛgolen tahẽkana. Adọ kathae, jaṅga sẹnteye dẹjọk kan tahẽkan jọkhẹnge, kathae, uni bitkil dọe ic gọtkette uni Bitnạ koṛa dọe ic topa ocoyena. Adọ kathae, ọṇḍẹgeye topayena; adọ bae uṭkạu daṛeata, ọṇḍẹgeye laṭha ṭarhaoena. Ar uni bitkil dọe ạtiṅ mọkọṅen khan, setak dọ oṛakteye calaoena. Adọ uni koṛa bae ṅẹl ṅame kante eṅgattẹt dọ ạḍi bạṛice rak baṛayeta. Mẹnetae, Tạrup cọṅ cele janwar cọko jọmkedea. Onka bogete ṅum ṅumteye rak halaṅeta.

Adọ kathae, tikin jọkhẹn dosra atoren kuṛiko dọ gọeṭha guric halaṅko sẹnlena. Adọ kathae, mitṭaṅ kuri dọ ona bitkil gurice uṭkạu gọtket khan, kathae, uni Bitnạ koṛae uṭkạu ṅam gọtkedea. Ar uni koṛa hõe beret gọtena. Adọ darhateye calaoenteye um saphayena, adọ oṛakteye calaoena. Eṅgattẹt dọe rạskạyena. Ar uni Bitnạ koṛa dọ ṭaṅgae ṅamkette uni bitkil dọe kuṭạm gọc

---

3 The mother's brothers are referred to as the boy's uncles, according to custom; it would not be best form to speak of them as the mother's brothers.

4 The word (c a l a k i, borrowed from Hindi) has in Santali always a side-meaning. A man so described is energetic and vigorous, but he will try to gain his ends through trickery and highhandednes, if necessary.

5 Especially during the hot season buffaloes are grazed at night. They apparently cannot well stand the sun, when it is very hot. What is told, is not anything out of the ordinary.

6 G ọ t ọ m means clarified butter, unsalted, used for a number of culinary purposes. The name given is possibly due to gọtọm melting in the head.

7 It is a fairly common sight to see the buffalo-herds riding on the back of the animal.

Afterwards he and his mother were separated from his maternal uncles[3] and built a house for themselves in another place. And this Span became a headstrong[4] man with a very glib tongue. No one was able to speak like him in connexion with any matter whatsoever.

As time passed, Span bought a buffalo-cow, and when he had fed and looked after her, so that she became fat, she would not graze at all during day-time[5], wherefore he called her butter-buffalo-cow[6]. And, sitting on her back[7], he was in the habit of taking her out to graze the whole night, and during day-light he kept her inside.

As time passed in this way, it once happened, when he had taken her out somewhere to graze, that he for some purpose or other had got down. Then, people tell, just as he was climbing up by her hind-legs, the buffalo-cow suddenly dropped something, and Span was buried beneath the dung. He was buried there; he was unable to get away and remained stuck fast there. When the buffalo-cow had done grazing, she went home in the morning, and when his mother did not see the boy, she commenced to cry awfully. She was saying: "A leopard or some other animal has eaten him." In this way she wailed and cried, mentioning his many qualities[8].

Now, people tell, at about noon some girls from another village had gone to pick up cow-dung[9]. Then just as one of the girls picked up that buffalo-cow-dung, she suddenly caught hold of and picked Span up. The boy stood on his legs, whereupon he went to a pool in the river, bathed and cleaned himself, and so he went home. His mother rejoiced. But Span took an axe and

[8] When women wail over their dead ones, it is customary to mention the different qualities remembered in connexion with the dead person, and also whatever may come to their mind.

[9] Fuel is one of the great problems of large tracts in India. Where they have no forests and no coals, cow- or buffalo-dung is collected and dried to be used as fuel. People go round hunting for dung and pick it up, even if it is quite fresh.

uṭạrkedea. Adọ atoren hoṛe lạiatkoteko jọmkedea. Adọ ona bitkil harta dọe rọhọṛkette mit din dọ eṅgattẹte metadea, Iạ, ayo, sạtu sambarạṅme, iṅ dọ hartaṅ ạkriṅ ạguia. Adọ kathae, juṛạuadete uni dọ harta ạkriṅe calaoena.

Adọ calak calakte tin sạṅgiṅ hoṛ cọe calaoen. Adọ ayupena. Adọe mẹneta, Noa ṅindạ dọ okareṅ giticá? Deko oṛakre ma nãhãk ọhọko gitić ocoliṅa. Adọ onkae hudiskette ṅuhum jọkhẹn mitṭaṅ dare buṭạreye ḍerayena. Adọe mẹnketa, Dare cọṭre dẹćkateṅ giticá; ọtre dọ jãhãeko ẹṛẹ bọṭẹćkiṅa. Onka mẹnkate, kathae, dareteye dẹćena, ar ona harta hõe ọr rakapketa; adọ luṭuk luṭuke dẹć thir akangea.

Adọ kathae, tala ṅindạ khange kombṛo dọ oka khon cọṅ aema ṭakako kombṛo idikette ona dare buṭạregeko dọhọketteko hạṭiṅet kana. Un jọkhẹnge Bitnạ dọ, kathae, ona harta dọ haḍ baḍe ṅurhạ gọtkata. Khange kombṛo dọ, kathae, bọtọrte jọṭọko daṛ gọtketa. Un jọkhẹn Bitnạ dọe ãṛgo gọtente, kathae, onako ṭaka dọ bẹbake idiketa, ar harta dọ ọnḍẹgeye bạgi dapoṛata, ar ona ṭaka dọ oṛakteye ạgu sẹṭẹrketa.

Adọ eṅgattẹte metadea, Iạ, ayo, do sẹ mamateko ṭhen khon pại kọe ạgukom. Adọ kathae, sẹnente pạiye kọe ạguketkote ọnẹye ạgulet ṭakakin sọṅketa. Adọ kathae, tinạk gan ṭaka cọṅ pại paṛakkoreye sọgẹ baṛakata. Are metadea, Do, ayo, idikatakom.

---

[10] The Santali word means hammering with any suitable instrument, especially, as here, the head of an axe.

[11] Food for the road is any kind of food that may be eaten without cooking, something dry, often made into balls.

[12] Manufactured measures are rather rare with the Santals and are certainly not found in every house. Now-a-days metal measures may be seen, manufactured (cast) by a local Hindu caste. A piece of a bamboo-joint is also used, especially by people living where large-sized bamboo grows. The most common is, however, a measure made of turned wood, often with mounts of iron and brass. It is such a one that is borrowed here. The wood used should not crack. A pại is half a seer, a little less than one pint. The size, however, varies; the standard seer is 80 tolas (1.750 pint); but several other sizes are in common use. The village

hammered[10] the buffalo-cow, so he at last killed her. And when he had told the village people, they ate her. Then, having dried the buffalo-cow's hide, he one day said to his mother: "I say, mother, make up some food for the road[11] for me; I am going to sell the hide." So, people tell, she prepared this for him, and he started to go and sell the hide.

He walked along and had got who knows how far; then evening fell, and he said: "Where am I going to sleep to-night? In a Hindu's house they will surely not let me lie down." While he was thinking over this, it became dusk, and he settled for the night at the foot of a tree. He said: "I shall climb high up in the tree and sleep there; here on the ground somebody or other might trick me." Thinking this he climbed the tree; he also pulled the hide up with him; so he stayed up there quiet and uneasy in his mind.

About midnight, people tell, it so happened that thieves, who had somewhere or other stolen a large sum of money, came, and, having put the money down there at the foot of the tree, they were dividing all between themselves. Just at that time Span let the hide fall down, and it fell with a rattling sound. Then, people tell, the thieves all of them ran away from fear. At that moment Span got down in a hurry and took all that money away; he left the hide there, and the money he brought home.

He then said to his mother: "I say, mother, please ask my uncle's people to lend us a pint-measure[12] and bring it." Thereupon she went, asked them for the loan of a pint-measure and brought it, whereupon they together measured the money he had brought. And, people tell, he pushed some rupees into some fissures in the measure, and said to his mother: "Now, mother, please, take their measure back to them."

---

trader frequently buys using a measure considerably larger than standard, and sells using a much smaller one, reserving the standard for those who know.

Adọ sạriye idikaťtako khan, pạị paṛaǩre ṭaka sọgẹ akanko ńẹlkeť khan dọko mẹnkeťa, Durrẹ! nui dọ abo khone sọrọsoǩ kan dọ, abo khon sọrọse kisạ̃ṛoǩa. Adọ onkako hiskạkeťteko mẹnkeťa, Ma nui dọ nenkarebo jẹrẹdea. Reṅgẹć ocoyeabon; baṅkhan hapẹne dạbṛuć cababona.

Adọ onkako hiskạkeťte miť din dọ jẹrẹdeko mẹnkeťa. Arhõ miť họṛ dọe mẹnkeťa, Hapẹ babon jẹrẹdea; uniaǩ bhẹdbon ńamlege, bhala ceť lekate unạǩ ṭaka dọe ńamleťa mẹnte. Khange sạriko kulikedea, Henda bạbu, okare harta dọm ạkriṅkeťa, ar tinạǩ dam hoelentama?

Adọ unreye mẹnkeťa, Ạḍi sạṅgiń, hana bajarre, mamọ. Iń ma, mamọ, miť gọṭaṅgeye tahẽkantińa, onate thoṛage hoelentińa. Ape ma, mama, aema kaḍa bitkil menaǩkotapea. Ape dọ ceť baṅ sẹ, bar pẹ khạclạǩ ṭakape ạgukea, ar baṅkhan aperen kaḍa bitkil kiriṅte emaṅpe thọ, iṅgeṅ hataokotapea.

Adọko mẹnkeťa, Baṅ, aletegele ạkriń ạguia.

Adọ sạri uniaǩ kathateko mạluṅente jọtọ kaḍa bitkilko kuṭạm gọćkeťkoa, ar harta ạkriṅko calaoena. Mẹnkhan cele hõ bako hataoleťtakoa. Adọ aṇḍhọṅ maṇḍhọṅ miť bar ṭakateko dhasao giḍi baṛakaťte ạḍi bạṛić karać kurućko edre hẹćena. Arko mẹnkeťa, Iạ yae ẹṛẹkeťbon dọ! Nahakge kaḍa bitkile gọć ocokeťbon dọ.

Adọ oṛaǩteko ruạṛ hẹćen khane kuli baṛayeťkoa. Adọ edrete uni tuluć dọ bako rọṛ baṛayeťa. Arko mẹnjoṅ kana, Nui dọbo jẹrẹdea; baṅkhan hapẹn abo dọe latarbona.

Adọ onako niṭkeťte sạri miť din dọko jẹrẹťkedea. Adọ unre bogeteye họhọkeťa, mẹnkhan onko mamọtteko dọ ọkọe hõ bako hẹćlena. Adọ ạḍi tayọm enako hẹćena. Adọ unre uni dọ ọhmateye

---

[13] Lit. set fire to him. Such an act of revenge as here described is not uncommon. I believe it is very seldom that Santals will commit a crime of this kind; but the hill-people living in these parts have a bad reputation in this respect.

[14] It is not so very long ago that no one bought or sold hides in these parts. Now-a-days agents for buying hides are found in many places. The story presupposes that hides were not locally salable.

Truth to tell, when she had brought back their pint-measure, they saw the rupees stuck in the fissures and said: "O dear, this one is getting ahead of us; he is becoming wealthier than we." And feeling such envy they said: "Come, we shall set fire to his house[13], since he is so situated. We shall cause him to become poor; otherwise he will some day utterly reduce us to bondage."

As they felt such envy, they one day said they would set fire to his house. Then one of them said: "Wait, we shall not set fire to him; let us first find out how he may have got hold of so much money." So they actually asked him: "Look here, young man, where did you sell that hide, and how much did you get for it?"

He replied then: "Very far away, in that market-town over there, uncle. You see, uncle, I had only one hide; therefore I got only a little. You, uncle, you have a large number of buffaloes and buffalo-cows. You, well, what might not happen? you might bring home two three baskets full of rupees; otherwise sell me your buffaloes and buffalo-cows; I shall take them."

"No," they said, "we shall ourselves go and sell."

Then, truth to tell, being quite fascinated by what he had said, they felled all their buffaloes and buffalo-cows and went off to sell the hides[14]. But no one would buy what they had. So they had to dispose of them very much below their value, and having let them go for a couple of rupees, they returned home, grumbling and very angry, and they said: "That unspeakable fellow, he has fooled us. For no reason he made us kill our buffaloes and buffalo-cows."

When they had returned home, he asked them about the matter; but because they were so angry, they would not speak to him; and they were saying among themselves: "We shall set fire to his house, otherwise he will some day make us be below him."

Having decided on this, they actually one day set fire to his house. During the fire he called out all he could, but none of his uncle's family came to help. Only a long while afterwards they came. Then he from this drew his conclusion and knew, viz.,

baḍaeketa, banma, Iń dọ nokogeko jẹrẹt́kidiña. Adọe cekaea, bẹcara? Ać ma huḍiń huḍiń họṛ, cete ceka daṛeaḱa?

Khange jọtọ oṛaḱ lọ cabayentaea, bako īṛīć daṛeata. Adọ jọtọ oṛaḱ lọ tọrọćentaea. Adọ sẹṅgẹl īṛīćen khan ona tọrọćko dọ jọtọe hạr samṭaoketa. Adọ onko mamọttekoge bostae kọeket́kote ona tọrọć dọ bostareye bhoraoket́te bepare idiketa. Adọ mit́ṭaṅ bajare tioḱketa. Adọ ạyupen khan mit́ṭaṅ baṛe buṭạreye ḍerayena. Adọ ńindạyen khan uni dọe mẹnketa, Iń eskar nọṇḍẹ tahẹn dọ baṅ jutoḱa. Jāhāeko kombṛo bọtẹćkiña. Adọ ona aṛerege bepariko ḍera akan tahẽkana. Adọ onko ṭhen sẹnkate mit́ aṛere nui hõe ḍerayena. Adọe jạpit́ ocoat́koa.

Adọ tala ńindạ jọkhẹn nui dọe beret́ente aćaḱ tọrọć bosta dọ onkoaḱ gạḍireye bhạrikata, ar onkoaḱ bosta dọ aćaḱ gạḍireye bhạriketa. Ar onko bepari dọ bako disạledea. Adọko tahẽ aṅgayen khan onko hõko lagaketa, nui hõe joṛaoket́teye lagaketa. Nui dọ ẹkkalte oṛaḱteye laga ạguketa. Adọ ạgukateye ńẹlket́ dọ, ẹkẹn ṭaka kan. Adọ eṅgattẹte metadea, Do ayo, mamateko ṭhen khon pạī ạguime. Ṭakalaṅ sọṅa.

Adọ sạriye kọe ạguket́te ṭakakin sọṅketa. Ar ona pạī paṛaḱkore dọ mõṛẽ turui gọṭẹn ṭakakin rẹbẹt́ baṛakat́te pạī dọkin idi oṭokat́takoa.

Adọko ńẹlket́ khan dọko hahaṛayena. Mẹnketako, Durrẹ! noa tọrọć khon hõ aema ṭaka hoeyentaea. Bhalabon kuliyea, okareye ạkriṅketa mẹnte.

Khanko kulikede khane mẹn gọt́keta, Iń ma, mamọ, oṛaḱ hõ huḍiṅge tahẽkantiń, onarege nõḱõe nunạḱ ṭaka hoeyentiña. Ar ape ma napṛaḱ napṛaḱ oṛaḱ menaḱtape, ape dọ aemape ṭakakea.

---

15 The banyan-tree (Ficus bengalensis, L.), is likely the largest spreading tree, anyhow in India. It is very common.

16 The Santali expression may mean both that they might carry himself off, and that they might steal from him. The latter is the general meaning.

It is these who have set fire to my house. Now, what could he do, poor fellow? He himself was a tiny, tiny man, what could he do?

All his houses burnt down; they were unable to put out the fire. All his houses were burnt to ashes. When the fire was extinguished, he gathered all the ashes. Thereupon he borrowed a number of bags from his uncle's people, and filling them with the ashes he started off to sell. On his way he reached a market-town, and as it became evening, he settled down for the night at the foot of a banyan-tree[15]. When it became night, he said to himself: "It will not do for me to stay here alone. Somebody might carry off[16] what I have." Now some traders were camping there on the side where he was; so he went over to them and himself also settled down on one side of them; whereupon he let them fall asleep.

About the time of midnight he got up and loaded his own bags with ashes on their carts, and their bags he loaded on his own cart. And the traders were not aware of what he did. They remained until dawn, when they drove their carts off, and Span also yoked his cart and drove off. He drove straight home. When be had brought it home he saw, it was all rupees and nothing else. So he said to his mother: "Please, mother, go and borrow a pint measure from my uncle's. We shall measure money."

So, truth to tell, she went and asked them for the loan of a measure, and they measured the money together. And, after having stuck five six rupees into the fissures of the pint-measure, they brought the measure back to the owners.

When these saw it, they were astonished and said: "O dear, out of those ashes also he has got so much money. Let us ask him where he sold them."

When they asked him, he replied at once: "You know, uncle, my house was only a small one; from that I got so much money, as you see. Now you have big big houses; you might make an enormous amount of money."

Khangeko mẹnkeṭa, Sạrige thọ ya, abo dọ aemabo ṭakakea. Adọ onkako hudisketteko mẹnketa, Ṭakale khan oṛak beknao dọ algagea. Ma noa oṛak dọbon jẹrẹtakte tọrọć ạkriń ạgukate arhõ oṛak dọbon benaoa.

Khange kathaeko jẹrẹtattakoa; adọ tọrọć sajaokette ạkriń dọko idiketa. Adọ kathae, cele hõ bako hataolettakoa. Adọ ạrisente gaḍa dakreko up̣ giḍi dapoṛkata. Adọ siṭhạl miṭhạl karać kurućko ruạṛ hẹć dapoṛena. Adọ hẹćkate Bitnạ dọ bogeteko ruhetkedea.

Adọ inạ dosar tesar khange Bitnạ dọe mẹnketa, Ḍạku bọtẹćkińako. Adọ ona bọtọrte ọnḍẹ khon dọe dạṛketa.

Adọ ẹnẹ cabayena; katha dọ in marańgea.

---

[17] The inclusive plural is used, showing that it is not an answer to Bitna.

[18] The word refers to what is known in India as dacoity, robbery by an armed gang, often combined with murder.

A variant, where the hero is calleed Bitkạ, has a number of different details. Bitka is the youngest of seven brothers; when born he was only a span big. He was lazy and refused to work, so his brothers decided to seclude him and his mother. They built a small house, and when Bitka asked them for whom that was, they told him that it was for him and his mother.

Bitka was very grieved at this; he would not eat; his mother just prevailed upon him to take food once daily. He did not know what to do, as he was unable to work. When they separated him and his mother from the others, they gave him an old buffalo-cow with a calf. Bitka herded this buffalo, milked her and sold the milk, and bought rice for the money. In this way he and his mother lived. When out herding the buffalo, he would take hold of the cow's tail; he was often buried beneath her dung; but when his mother came out to pick up cow-dung, she would find him. In this way they lived for many years.

His brothers were in the habit of going to do earth-work and earn money; but Bitka never did so, and they wondered how he could live, and were very angry with him. So one day they set fire to his house. Bitka felt great grief; his brothers came and asked him who had set fire to his house; but he declared that he did not know and asked his brothers to help him to rebuild his house; but they refused, saying they had to go and work. Thereupon Bitka put the ashes in a bag and went away to sell this. He called out that he had ashes to sell, but no one would buy. In this way he was benighted; then he somewhere came across some traders, who asked him what he had. He answered: What

"That is quite true," they said among themselves, "we[17] might make an enormous amount of money." And, having thought over this, they said: "If one makes money, it is easy to build houses. Come, let us set fire to this house, and let us sell the ashes; then we shall build a new house."

Thereupon, people tell, they set fire to their house, and, having packed the ashes, they took them away to sell; but there was no one who would buy. So they became disgusted and threw the ashes out into a running river. Disheartened and grumbling they came back, poor fellows; and having returned, they abused Span all they could.

A few days afterwards Span said: "They might rob[18] and kill me." Fearing this he ran away from there.

So there it is ended: the story is thus much.

I have, is white gold. On their asking him what he would do with that, he replied that he would sell it.

Among the traders there was a very wealthy man; the traders had a talk together and decided to rob Bitka of what he had and put their own money instead. They did so, when he was sound asleep. He had his bag with ashes as a pillow under his head; they took this away and put their bag with money there instead, whereupon they started. When it became day and Bitka found the money, he became exceedingly glad, and, carrying it, he returned home. There his mother asked him where he had got the money. He replied that he had sold the white gold and brought the money for it.

When his brothers heard about this, they wondered greatly and asked how such a tiny tiny fellow could have so much sense. Whereupon they said: Come, let us put him into a bag and throw him into the Ganges. They did so; they tied him, put him into a bag and went to the Ganges. When they reached the bank of the river, all of them, under some pretext or other, went off and left him there alone on the edge of the water. Just at that moment a man of the cattle-herding caste was grazing his buffaloes on the banks of the river. This man went up to Bitka and asked him where he was going. To this Bitka answered that he was the son of a king on his way to be married. Hearing this the mahra (so this caste is called by the Santals) man became very much astonished and also filled with desire; he said: Perhaps I also might marry a princess.

The mahra man thereupon said to Bitka: Look here, well, might not I also marry? Whereto Bitka replied: All right, then you do it first. So the mahra

48. Kāṛā ar Gujạ reaṅ.

Sedae jǫkhẹn, kathae, Hāsdak̕ khũṭren bar boehakin tahẽkana, unkin dǫ Kāṛā ar Gujạwạkina. Unkin dǫ khub dhinkiạ hǫṛkin tahẽkana. Ona jǫkhẹn, kathae, disomre kuṛit̕ reak̕ ạḍi bagahi hoelena, baṅma, mit̕ṭaṅ darere kuṛit̕kin hǫpǫnlet̕ko tahẽkana, ar unkin kuṛit̕ dǫ hǫṛ gidrạ ạḍi bạṛićkin ạtkiret̕ko tahẽkana, disom sudhạkin khaṅkaret̕ tahẽkana.

Adǫ unre disom hǫṛko mẹnket̕a, Bhala nukin kuṛit̕ dǫ cekatebon gǫćkina? Adǫ disom sudhạ hǫṛ riạuente raj ṭhenko calaoena, adǫ rajko metadea, Dẹ bhala unkin kuṛit dǫ cekatebo gǫćkina?

---

being very eager untied Bitka and got him out of the bag, whereupon he himself crept into the bag. Bitka tied the mahra hands and feet and pushed him into the river. Afterwards he collected all the cows and buffaloes that the mahra had, and drove them all to his home.

When they saw him, his brothers became very angry and said to him: Look here, you, where did you get all these cows and buffaloes? Bitka answered: You see, my elder brothers, it was a little to one side that you set me adrift; if you had set me adrift about the middle of the river, who knows how many I might have been able to bring; it is impossible to say. They then asked him: Very well, Bitka, might we also be able to bring some or how? Bitka replied: All right, I shall tie you up in bags.

Thereupon he took them to the banks of the Ganges. Now an immense number of cattle, cows and buffaloes, were grazing on the bank. Bitka pointed to the reflections of them in the water and said to them: Look, look there, how many you will be able to bring. Being very eager, they said: Please tie us up and put us in the bags, in order that we may bring many. Thereupon he put all of them in bags and pushed them into the water, and all of them were drowned. In this way he got the better of all his brothers.

48 [1] The Saṇtals are divided into twelve septs; one of these is called Hãsdak̕, lit. 'swan-water', but possibly some other meaning may be hidden in the name. According to the Santal traditions all mankind is descended from one pair, by the Santals called Pilcu haṛam and Pilcu buḍhi. The meaning of pilcu is uncertain; it is very seldom used except as here; it is heard in an expression pilcu kạpi, about a small-sized battle-axe. The meaning 'small' does not seem to fit in here. Haṛam and buḍhi mean respectively 'old man' and 'old woman', or husband and wife. The eldest son of this pair was called Hãsdak̕, and the

48. KARA AND GUJA.

LONG long ago, people tell, there were two brothers belonging to the Hãsdak̕ sept[1]; their names were Kara and Guja[2]. They were crack shots with bow and arrow. In their time, it is told, the country had become dangerous to live in on account of a pair of kites[3]; they had got young ones in a tree, and these two kites were constantly carrying off Santal children; they were making the country[4] desolate.

The inhabitants of the country then said: "Well, how shall we kill these two kites?" All the people then went to the king in a body and said to him: "Please, how shall we get these two kites killed? They are making the whole country desolate. Now,

tribe descending from him (or rather from the eldest son of the righteous pair that alone escaped from the great flood; they called their sons with the names of the sons of the first original pair) are called so. Each of the twelve Santal septs is divided into a number of sub-septs; tradition says twelve but, as a matter of fact, they are many more. One of the Hãsdak̕ sub-septs is called Cil bindhạ, kite-piercing; whether this is the original meaning or not (the words are Hindi), the Santals take them to mean this, and the story here told is their account of the way in which this particular sub-sept got its name. There may possibly be some actual facts to which reference is found in the story; the whole may also be a pure invention to explain the name.

2 Kãṛã in Santali means blind. It is very common that people are called Halt, Deaf, or even Mad, without any insult being intended. The Santals have generally two names, an esoteric, real name, very seldom used, and a second one in daily use. They are named after some relative (they have certain rules they follow), and if this particular relative, or his namesake, had any special quality, this might result in his being so called; the name resulting from this will be attached to all succeding namesakes, for common use.

3 The kuṛit̕, Falco ceela, is a very common bird of prey. They may carry off snakes and the like; they do a good deal of mischief by carrying off chickens, &c.; but I have never heard of their being able to take anything big.

4 It should be remembered that when these stories mention countries or lands, the words refer to something much smaller than what we combine with these words. In the same way a 'king' is a landlord, the owner of an estate, sometimes very large, sometimes quite small.

Disom sudhạkin khaṅkarket́ dọ. Ma noa reak̓ cet́em mẹnet́tabona? Ar baṅkhan ale dọ noa disomre ọhọle tahẽ daṛelena; jọtọ hoṛ mit́ mit́te noa disom khonle dạṛa.

Adọ khange raje mẹnket́a, Hapẹ, alope dạṛa, adọbo gọć gelakina; judi babon gọć daṛeakin khan, adọpe dạṛa. Adọ raje mẹnket́a, Masẹ bhala, unkin kuṛit́ jãhãepe gọć daṛeakin khan dọ, mit́ nakha disom iń emapea.

Adọ sạri raj onkae hukumket́ khan, unkin kuṛit́ gọćkin lạgit́ hoṛko dhurạuena. Ar kathae, unkin kuṛit́ dọ hoṛak̓ ãṛgọm ar nahẹlkokin tukạ akat́ tahẽkana, onate tuńkinre hõ, unkin dọ bako tuń ńam daṛeakin kan tahẽkana. Adọ kathae, sanam hoṛko tuń bhagaoen khan, sẹsre Kãṛã ar Gujạkin mẹnket́a, Bhala sanam hoṛpe tuń bhagaoen khan, ạliń aṛak̓ạliṅpe. Adọ unre, kathae, Kãṛã ar Gujạko aṛak̓at́kina.

Adọ unkin dọ aṭakin bạisạuket́a; adọ unkin kuṛit́ dọ hopọnkin ajọako jọkhẹn tukạ ṭhenkin hẹćena. Un jọkhẹn, kathae, ãṛgọm bhugạk̓ khonkin tuńlet́kina, — sạri banar kuṛit́kin tuń ńũr gọt́ket́kina. Adọ unkin kuṛit́ dọ Gạṅgi jạmin jharnarekin ńurhạyena, ar onakin ńurhạlen ṭhen dọ ạḍi maraṅ ṭhạikin paska gaḍaket́a.

Adọkin gọćen khan dọ raj ṭhenkin gọk̓ ạguket́kina. Adọ uni raj dọ disom hoṛe maṅgaoket́koa, adọ unre mit́ nakha sẹn disome emat́kina. Ar ọnẹ kuṛit́kin paskã gaḍalet́ ṭhen dọ maraṅ uṭạr

---

5 This is an essentially Santal trait; when dissatisfied or when feeling the difficulties of getting along in accordance with their wants, they may easily try the expedient of going somewhere else. They have been wandering always, according to their traditions; either because they could not find the means of living where they were, or because they were driven away by others. One reason for this attitude has certainly been their lack of civilization, more especially proper agriculture. One gets the impression that they are altering now in this respect.

6 The word aṭa (probably borrowed from Hindi) is in Santali used about an ambush. If it is on the ground, it is generally a little raised and furnished with branches and leaves so as to hide it. It may also be made among the branches of a tree.

7 The kites must have been of an enormous size to be able to lift up and make use of these heavy agricultural implements. The clod-crusher (ãṛgọm) consists

what have you to say for us in this matter? And if you have not, we shall not be able to stay in this land; we shall every one of us leave[5] this country."

The king then replied: "Wait, don't run away; we shall try to kill them; if we should not be able to kill them, then you may leave." Further the king said: "Listen, if any of you are able to kill these two kites, I shall give you a tract of land."

When the king had given this order, people commenced to try to kill the kites. Now these two kites had, people tell, built their nest of people's clod-crushers and ploughs, so that even when people shot at them, they were unable to hit the kites. When all had been shooting until they could not any more, then, people tell, at last Kara and Guja said: "Well, now since you all of you have abandoned shooting any more, let us two have a try." Then they let them come to.

So those two brothers made an ambush[6] in a tree. Now when the two kites should feed their young, they came to the nest; just at that time, people tell, the brothers shot them through a hole[7] in the clod-crusher; really and truly they shot the two kites with arrows, so that they fell down. The two kites fell down in the Gangi Jamin[8] spring, and where they fell down, they clawed and scratched, so that they made a big hole in the ground.

When they were dead, the two brothers carried them to the king, and the king sent for the people, and on that occasion he gave the two brothers a tract of the land. Where the kites had

---

of a piece of wood, some 2 to 3 m. long, some 10 to 15 cm. square, with a plough-beam fixed in a hole made in the middle of the ạṛgọm. It is used for levelling the surface of agricultural land. The plough is always of wood and fairly heavy. The plough-beam of the aṛgọm has apparently been removed, and it is through this hole that they shoot their arrows.

The Gạṅgi Jạmin spring is by present-day Santals said to be the fountain-head of the Damuda river, which plays a great part in the religious life of the people The bones of the dead are carried to the Damuda and immersed there.

mitṭan ḍhabko benaoketa, ar ona ḍhab do̱ unkinge mạnko emat-kina. Ado̱ unkin Kãṛã Gujạ do̱ onakokin ńawan khan do̱, ạḍikin ṛąskạyena.

Ado̱ unkin Kãṛã Gujạ do̱ ona birkoregekin tahe̱na, emanteak bir reak paṛahuṛikokin dukhmạ baṛajońa. Ar mittań dhiri dan-derrekin jaegak kan tahe̱kana, ar ạyup jo̱khe̱n do̱ o̱ṇḍe̱gekin daka mạṇḍijońa, ar at aser hõ o̱ṇḍe̱gekin rapak baṛajońa.

Ado̱ tahe̱n tahe̱nte, kathae, kul do̱e ciạketkina. Ado̱ mit din do̱ at aserkin rakpak kan jo̱khe̱nge uni kul do̱e calao go̱tena, ado̱e metakin kana, Henda ya, cetben rakpak kana? De̱n iń hõ emańben, ar bańkhan iń jo̱mbena.

Ado̱ at aser do̱ rapakkate ạkingekin jo̱ma ar ona kuilạko do̱ uni kulkin capat oḍok go̱taea, khange ado̱ khạyur khạyure jo̱m go̱da. Arhõ oka do̱ besakkin capat tot go̱taea. Ado̱ uni hõe jo̱m pạrkạuen khan do̱, uṭhạuge bae uṭhạuk kan.

Khange ado̱kin me̱nketa, Durre̱! bae calak kan do̱, pase̱ye jo̱mlań. Cekate nui do̱lań lagayea? Khange Gujạ do̱e chuṭạu go̱tenteye ńir calao go̱tente caṇḍbo̱lreye sap go̱tkedete cure mareye pe̱ṭe̱rkettaea. Khange bhạiye pe̱ṭe̱r topakkettae khange uni kul do̱e aḍrao go̱tketteye dạrketa.

Khange unkin Kãṛã Gujạ do̱ ona caṇḍbol do̱ rapakkatekin jo̱mketa; ado̱ cet bań se̱, ạḍi bạrić sebelketkina. Ado̱kin me̱nketa, Durre̱! ạḍi sebel kana; delalań sendra go̱jea.

---

9 Mạn, here translated rent-free, is ordinarily used to signify agricultural land set aside for the various village officials; this land is not personal tenure, but belongs to the office, and is meant to be a kind of honorarium for the work done for the village. Formerly this land was rent-free; now mạn has been partly abolished, rent has partly to be paid. What is here told as done out of gratitude, is in accordance with Santal thought and is not without a parallel.

10 Even now-a-days the Santals increase their supply of food-stuffs by making use of wild vegetables, fruits, leaves, roots and tubers, of many kinds. Here two kinds of tubers are mentioned, one is that of the Zehneria umbellata, Thw. (in Santali at). Some of these vegetables are eaten after having been roasted on the fire or on live coals, naturally not in a pan or the like.

made that hole in the ground, they made a tremendously big low-lying rice-field and gave this to the two brothers rent-free[9]. And when Kara and Guja got this, they were very glad.

Now Kara and Guja were staying here and there in the forest, striving to sustain themselves on whatever they could find of eatables in the forest. They were spending the night in a rock-cave; in the evening they were in the habit of preparing their food there; and different kinds of jungle tubers[10] they also used to roast there.

As time passed, people tell, a tiger spied them out; and one day, while they were roasting jungle tubers, the tiger suddenly went up to them and said: "Look here, you fellows, what are you roasting? Come, give me also, otherwise I shall eat you."

Now as they roasted the jungle tubers, they themselves ate these, and the burnt out coals they threw out to the tiger, and he would at once crunch and eat them. Now and then they would also throw something good out to him. When the tiger in this way became accustomed to eat, he would not move from the place.

The two brothers then said: "O dear, he is not going away; perhaps he will eat us. How shall we get him driven away?" Guja then fell to, and running quickly out he caught hold of the tiger's tail and commenced to twist it all he could. And, friends[11], he twisted it right off, whereupon the tiger roared and ran off.

Kara and Guja roasted that tail[12] and ate it; you have no idea, it tasted awfully nice, and they said: "O dear, it is very savoury; come, let us chase him and kill him."

---

11 Lit. brother. The narrator gets a little excited over his story and wants to assure his audience that he is telling a true, but marvellous story. Hence he uses this word.

12 The writer has known Santals to eat leopards; they will also eat tiger flesh, if they can get it. In the case of these animals it is perhaps not so much that they like the flesh, as the belief that the eating of such animals may confer to

Khange, bhai, bana horkin jhũkente sesendrakin portonketa. Khangekin sendra ńamkedete lagakin lagakedea se, digla digkin khudaukedea, adokin goćkedea. Ado sengel jolkatekin rokedea, ado ondegekin rapak jomkedea. Ado ina jelkotegekin jom biyen khan, laćtet do bakin jomleta. Kãrã doe meneta, Laćtet hõlań joma, ar Guja doe meneta, Bań. Khange tho Kãrã doe gokket-takina; ado onde khonkin calaoena.

Ado hor arere mittań bare dare umulrekin durup akan tahekana. Ado ona sentege okaren raj bariatko coko calak kan. Ado onkokin ńelketko khan, ona bare daretekin dećena, ar ona kul lać hõkin rakap toraketa. Khange onko bariatko hõ ona dare butaregeko durup jarwayena, ar adomko doko gitićena. Ado raj hõ khurkhuri khon odokente uni hõ ona dare umulregeye gitićena. Ado uni Kãrã doe meneta, Henda ya Guja, laćtet doń ńũr gotkak se?

Ado Gujai meneta, Alo ya, bańkhan nãhãkko saplańa.

Ado Kãrãe meneta, E ya, hobor hoborteń lańgayen do. Arhõe metae kana, Alo ya, sapkelańako.

Adoe hobor lańgayen khan do, kathaeye ńũr gotkata; ado ona kul lać do ekkalte uni rajak laćrege ńurha gotena. Ado joto bariatkoko botorente adi garteko kikiauketa, Rajar pet bhoskaelo re, rajar pet bhoskaelo re! Onka menkate joto bariatko ar Dom

the eater some of the qualities of the consumed animal, especially strength and invincibility. They once killed a very large leopard close to the writer's bungalow. They came to me with the skin, and said that this leopard had eaten so much for them, now they were going to have their revenge and would eat him. And so they did.

13 The Ficus bengalensis, L. is often found as a roadside tree.

14 The Santal word shows that it is the bridegroom's party on their way to the bride's home, to celebrate the wedding there. Such parties may be small or quite large, according to the importance of the bridegroom. Some guns may be carried for saluting purposes; some of the Dom caste are taken along to furnish the music, or rather noise, needed. Whenever they pass a village or inhabited place, they belabour their big drums, strike their cymbals, and so on, to let people know what is passing.

15 When well-to-do people are being married, the bridegroom and the bride are carried or are riding. The palanquin here mentioned is in Santali called khurkhuri,

And so, friends, both of them set to with a will and started hunting. When they had tracked him, they chased and chased him, they pursued him, so that they raised a cloud of dust, and ultimately they killed him. Thereupon they made a fire and singed him; and there they also roasted the flesh. When they had had their fill from the flesh, they did not eat the stomach. Kara said: "Let us eat the stomach also." But Guja said: "No." Whereupon Kara took it up on his shoulder and carried it; so they went away from there.

Afterwards they were sitting down by the side of the road in the shade of a banyan[13] tree. Just then the wedding-party[14] of a king from somewhere or other was passing that way. As soon as they saw those, they climbed into the banyan tree; they took also the tiger's stomach up with them. Presently the wedding-party also sat down together at the foot of that tree; some of them also lay down. The king came out of his palanquin[15], and he also lay down in the shade of that three. Then Kara said: "Look here, Guja, shall I let the stomach fall down or how?"

"Don't, you fellow," Guja replied, "otherwise they will catch us presently."

"O you," Kara said, "I am tired of keeping this in my arms."

Again Guja says to him: "Don't, you fellow; they might catch us."

But when he became so tired that he could not hold the stomach any more, he let it fall down; and the tiger's stomach fell straight down on the king's stomach. Then the whole wedding-party became frightened and screamed at the top of their voice and said: "Des König's Magen[16] ist geborsten, oh! Des König's Magen ist

---

a name that possibly has something to do with the form of the conveyance. The contrivance in which the traveller reclines is fixed to a pole of a peculiar shape; it has a curve in the middle, i. e., above the seat, being bent something like the back of a camel. A cloth hanging down on both sides from this pole screens the traveller. Instead of a cloth they may also use thin boards.

16 They call out in Bengali.

Kahaṛko miť miťteko dạṛkeťa; jo̱to̱ asbabko ńir bạgiaťa. Arhõ̱ thoṛa sạṅgiń se̱n ńõ̱ḱkate do̱ko me̱nkeťa, Durre̱! jo̱to̱ asbabbon ńir bạgiať do̱; nonkate do̱ cekate bạriạt do̱bon calaḱa? Delabon ruạṛgea; bhalabon ńe̱lea, cekate lać do̱ oḍokentaea se̱ celeye nonkaketbona. Delabon ruạṛkatebon ńe̱llege. Onka mo̱ne̱teko hudiseťa arko galmarao kana.

Ar nukin Kãṛã Gujạ do̱ dare khon ãṛgoyente kicrićko se̱ bhale bhale jinis do̱ jo̱to̱kin hame̱ṭana, ar daretekin rakaṕkeťa. Ar uni Kãṛã do̱ ona ḍho̱l hõe rakaṕkeťa, ar ona ḍho̱l do̱ miť se̱ne bhugạḱkeťa ho̱po̱n ho̱po̱n. Ar ona darerege, kathae, ńe̱le̱ko tahẽ̱kana; ado̱ onko ńe̱le̱ do̱ miť miťte jo̱to̱ ona ḍho̱lreye bhoraoketkoa.

Ado̱ onko bạriạtko phạdko he̱ćena, ado̱ko ńe̱lkeťkin do̱kin ho̱ṛ kan. Ado̱ unkinko metakin kana, Aleren raj cedaḱben be̱mano̱tkedea? Aben do̱le go̱ćbena.

Ado̱kin me̱nkeťa, Ma e̱ntepe go̱ć daṛealiń khan; e̱k do̱ ạlińpe go̱ćliń, e̱k do̱ apeliń go̱ćpe.

Ado̱ onkakin me̱nkeť khan, lạṛhạiko e̱ho̱pkeťa. Khange bạndukteko ṭhuyeťkina, me̱nkhan baṅgeko ṭhu ńam daṛeakin kana. Ado̱ ṭhu ṭhuteko laṅgayena, baṅgeko ṭhu jo̱s daṛeakin kana; sanam guli dạru cabayentakoa. Ado̱ khange unkin kin me̱nkeťa, Cele nitoḱ do̱ ạliń bape aṛaḱaliṅa?

Ado̱ko be̱ṅge̱ť baṛawakin kan do̱, miťṭań ḍho̱l chaḍa ceť hõ̱ bạnuḱtakin. Khangeko me̱nkeťa, Male aṛaḱaben kana.

17 Kahar is the name of a low Hindu caste; they are, among other matters, also professional palanquin-carriers.

18 Ḍho̱l is a very big drum; its body is of wood hollowed out (generally of the Jack tree, Artocarpus integrifolia, L., the wood of which is said not to crack). It is covered at both ends with skin; it is belaboured with the hand or with a small stick bent in one end; this peculiarly shaped stick is the origin of the nickname by which the Santals very frequently call the Doms, kukuć ṭheṅga, bent stick.

19 The ńe̱le̱ (Megachile rufiventris) are fairly common wild bees: if irritated, they become very agressive.

geborsten, oh!" Calling out in this way the whole wedding-party and the Dom musicians and the palanquin-carriers[17] ran away every one of them; as they ran off, they left all things there. But when they had gone some little distance, they said: "O dear, we have run away and left all the things; how shall we in this manner be able to proceed as a wedding-party? Come, we must go back; let us have a look at him, how his stomach burst, or who has done this to us. Come along, let us go and have a look at him, before doing anything else." In such manner they were thinking and speaking.

Kara and Guja meanwhile came down from the tree and helped themselves to all the clothes and fine and nice things and took it all up into the tree. Kara took also the big drum[18] up with him; he made a tiny hole in the drum, at one end. Now there were wild bees[19] in that tree, people tell; and these bees he all put into the drum, every one of them.

When the marriage-party crowd returned, they saw the two brothers, that they were Santals[20], and they said to them: "Why did you dishonour our king? We shall kill both of you."

The brothers replied: "Do so, if you are able to kill us two; either you kill us two or we shall kill you."

When the brothers had spoken in this way, the other ones commenced to fight; they fired guns at the brothers, but were unable to hit them. They fired and fired, until they became tired; they were utterly unable to touch them with their guns; and all their powder and shot were used up. So the two brothers said: "Well, now then will you let us have our chance?"

The others were looking at them; besides the drum they had nothing. So they said: "Well, we are giving you your chance now."

---

20 The word may signify both a human being and a Santal. People out here will generally at once see whether a man is a Muhammedan, a man of any Hindu caste, a Santal, &c., so there is nothing from this side to object against translating it a 'Santal'.

Khange adọ ḍhọlkin ru gọt́keta arkin mẹneta, Laṛo bacha, laṛo bacha. Adọ khange onko ńẹlẹ dọ ona ḍhọl khonko uḍạu tot́ gọt́ente onko bạriạtko dọ toṛko toṛket́koa sẹ. Khange thọ onko bạriạtko dọko dạṛ tap̣keta. Khange cet́ baṅ sẹ, laga lagateko toṛket́koa, adọ ghuriạ̃ onko bạriạtko dọ bako ruạṛlena.

Adọ jẹ kichu asbab tahẽkantako, onako dọ nukinaḱge hoeyentakina. Adọ onako asbabkin ńawan khan, maraṅ rajko ńutumket́kina, adọ ạkin oṛaḱrekin tahẽyena.

Adọ cabayena katha dọ. Ar noa kạhni reaḱ sereń hõ menaḱa, mẹnkhan iń dọń hiṛiṅketa.

---

21 The brothers speak to the bees in Hindi.

22 I have heard of this song, but have never been able to meet any Santal who knew it.

A variant of the above story, written down by Kạnhu Mạrṇḍi (see Vol. I, no. 9, note 1), is of some interest. It has nothing about Kãṛã and Gujạ killing the kites, but starts with telling that these two brothers daily were in the forest digging for saṅ, a kind of wild potatoes. One day they were very much belated and Kara sent his brother to look at the sun to see how high up it was. Guja returned saying (in Bengali) that one sun was setting and another rising. They were benighted in the forest and went to a female leopard, whom they addressed as aunt (father's sister). When they heard that she was at home, they asked her to roast the saṅ tubers for them. She did so, but herself ate the saṅ and gave the two brothers the outburnt coals. They then said: Saṅ tastes very nice and is soft to chew; she is giving us coals. Whereupon they twisted her tail off, roasted and ate this. But the leopard ran away in anger.

The brothers then said: If she goes to the river, we shall not follow her, but if she goes through the open fields, we shall follow. The leopard heard this and said: Listen there, they say that if I go along the river-bed, they will not follow me, but if I go over the open field, they will follow. Whereupon the leopard went along the river-bed.

When the two brothers had eaten the tail, they followed after the leopard in her tracks and found her. The leopard then said: What are you following me for? Now in a moment I shall fetch my friends like a whirlwind.

Hearing this they became afraid and climbed a palmyra palm-tree. A moment afterwards the leopard brought her friends like a whirlwind. When she had brought them, they saw that the two brothers had climbed into the palm-tree.

The two brothers then beat the big drum and said: "Heraus zum Kampf[21], Kinder! Heraus zum Kampf, Kinder!" And the wild bees at once came flying out of the big drum and stung the wedding-party to good purpose. The wedding-party then ran away in a panic; you have never seen anything like it, they chased them and stung them; and the members of the wedding-party never came back there any more.

Whatever goods they had with them, that henceforth belonged to the two brothers. And when they had acquired all these goods, people called them great kings, and they stayed in their own home.

So the story is ended. There is also a song[22] about this story, but I have forgotten it.

Now they were up there, very high up, and seeing their shadows, the leopards jumped and jumped, whereupon Kara said: I shall pull them, poor fellows. But Guja warned him: Don't; they might eat us.

When they were tired of jumping, they laid themselves into a pile, one on the top of the other, at the foot of the palm-tree. In this way they reached up to the two brothers. Then Kara said: Give me, elder brother, the swallow-tail axe. When he had given him this, Kara hammered the topmost one on the head, with the result that they all tumbled down in a heap. Some of them were killed, and the rest ran away in a panic. The two brothers then came down and looked at the leopards lying there; some of them were not quite dead, there was just a faint sign of life in them, and these they finished off with blows from the small axe. When they had killed them all, they commenced to feast on them. Some they finished, the rest they had to leave there. But Kara said he would take the stomach along with him, and so he did.

On their way they camped at the foot of a banyan-tree. Then the marriage party came, as told in the above story. The two brothers were up in the tree and in great fear, moving from one branch to another. When Kara let the stomach fall down, the same thing happened as told in the other story; only here it is added that the king removed the stomach and himself also ran away.

Thereupon the two brothers came down; Kara took a couple of big drums, and Guja as much clothes as he could carry on his back, whereupon they went to the primeval forest. But the others fixed a day for killing these two brothers. But the brothers made a hole in the ḍhọl and filled it with bees and wasps. The day fixed for the fight came. The king's soldiers fired guns at them, any

49. Kuṛhia̯ ho̱ṛ reaṅ.

Sedae jo̱khe̱n, kathae, mit́ṭaṅ atore mit́ ho̱ṛe tahẽkana, ar uni ho̱rren do̱ pe̱a kuṛi ho̱po̱n ar pe̱a do̱ koṛa ho̱po̱nko tahẽkantaea. Ado̱ bareae ba̯huat́kin tayo̱mge uni ho̱ṛ do̱e beṇḍaoena.

Ar nukin ba̯huat́kin koṛa do̱ khubkin ka̯mia, ar uni ḍa̯ṅgua̯ menae koṛa do̱ a̯ḍiye kuṛhia̯gea. Jãhãnak̓ko a̯cuyea, baṅgeye re̱be̱na. lutur hõ bae ṭhe̱pe̱a, ar jo̱jo̱m ghuṛi khan, unige laha lahae chuṭa̯uk̓a. Onate unkin napṛak̓kin dadattekin do̱ a̯ḍi ba̯ṛić̓kin ruhedea, metaeakin, Henda ya, am do̱ cetat aṅgra hõ bam chuṭa̯uk̓ do̱, cekate nonkate do̱m a̯sulok̓a? Ar nonkate do̱ cekate ba̯hu hõko tahe̱na? Am do̱ nun maraṅem harayena, cet́ge bam laṛaok̓ kan do̱. Begar giḍi dapo̱ṛkamaliṅ.

---

number of times, until they were tired, and they were unable to hit them, whereupon they said: Now we shall let you two have a chance.

As in the other story they let the bees loose, and they stung them so that they swelled up and their bodies became like ḍho̱ls. They asked them to call the bees back, and they did so. Afterwards the king gave them half of his land, and they stayed there.

From here this variant has added part of the story told about Bajun and Jhore (no. 25). Guja, who is the elder brother, stays at home, while Guja goes and ploughs; with the axe he cuts the plough-bullocks, as told there. Kara is then ordered to stay at home. Now his sister-in-law was with child, and as Kara had never seen anything of that kind, he said: What has possibly happened to her? He found a spindle-rod, heated this and was going to puncture her with the red-hot iron. But she drove him away.

Now it so happened that some people were feasting on a bullock just below their homestead land. Passing there Kara took the stomach and carried it off; he ran and hid himself in the hollow of a tree. They prodded him with a stick; the bullock's stomach was hit and part of it came out, whereupon they deduced that he was dead.

Then comes the same as in the other story about the brother performing the last ceremonies for his dead brother; Kara ran off with the basket full of rice and a pot with curry and got into the company of thieves. When they were out to steal one night they came into a house, where Kara found some milk boiling in a fire-place. A man was lying there asleep with one hand stretched

49. ABOUT A LAZY MAN.

ONCE upon a time long ago, people tell, there lived a man in a certain village; this man had three daughters and three sons; and after he had married[1] two of his sons, he departed this life.

The two married young men were industrious workers; but the unmarried one was very lazy. Whatever they set him to do, he was utterly unwilling to work; he did not even move his ears[2]; but when the time for food came, he set to before any one else. Therefore the two big ones, his elder brothers, constantly scolded him and would say to him: "Look here, you, you are utterly useless, you don't bother to do anything, how will you support yourself in this way? And in such circumstances how would you expect a wife to remain with you? You have grown so big; you don't move a bit. We shall separate you from us and let you support yourself, and serve you right."

---

out. Kara then found a leaf, made a leaf-spoon, and with this he poured some boiling milk into the hand of the sleeping man. The sleeping man got up in a hurry, and the thieves had to run away.

The thieves then said they would not have Kara's company any longer, with the same result as told in the other story. The same happened another time, when Kara stole a drum and commenced to beat it.

The story ends in the same way as the other, only that it is here the house of a Saheb (with Santals now generally understood as meaning a European, but also sometimes used about the better class of Indians). He got hold of a 'horse', who ran off to the forest with him, while he called out: Along the road, Saheb horse! In the forest he was caught in the branches of a tree and was unseated. He came down from the tree, and did not understand that it was a leopard he had been riding on.

This story does not tell that Kara was killed.

[1] The father, or when he is dead, others occupying the authority of a father, will arrange the marriage of a son or a younger male relative.

[2] The translation is literal; it is an expression used by the Santals to indicate that a person is absolutely unwilling to listen and to work. The Santals are not able to move their ears more than other people.

Adọ onkako ruhedere hõ, ẹn hõ uni dọ bae mọnẹaḱa; luturge bae ṭhẹpẹa. Adọ onka hēsa hīsite kạmi hõko ḍhil idiket́a; adọ pạhil khon dọko hạrsuṛenteko rẹṅgẹćena, ar uni koṛa dọ edrete bạhu hõ bako bạhuae kana.

Adọ khange mit́ din dọe usạt́ente bidese oḍok calaḱ kana; adọ kicrićko hõ bạnuḱtaea, inạ ḍeṅganaḱ eskarge menaḱtaea, adọ koṭotegeye oḍok calaḱ kana. Adọ bhại, calaḱ calaḱte tin sạṅgiń cọe calaoen; adọe ạyup̣en khan, mit́ṭań atoe ńẹl ńamket́a, adọe mẹnket́a, Ọkọe tora ona atoteń rakap̣a, teheń ńindạ dọ ona atoreń gitić aṅgaḱa. Ar ona jọkhẹn dọ Pus cando tahẹ̃kante rabań hõ ạḍi ãṭ rabań kan tahẹ̃kana, ar uni koṛa dọ kicrić bạnuḱtaete ạḍi ãṭ rabańede kana.

Adọ ona atoe tiogtegeye ńuhumena. Adọ ona atoren gạigupi koṛa dọ kulhi mucạt́re sẹṅgẹl jolkate goḍoko lat́ jọmet́koe ńẹlket́koa. Adọ rabańede kanteye mẹnket́a, Ọkọe tora ona sẹṅgẹlreń joroḱ ńõḱlenge. Adọ onka mẹnkate onko gupi koṛako jol akat́ ṭhene calaoena.

Adọe metako kana, Dẹ bạbu, mit́ sẹn joroḱ ocoańpe, ạḍi bạṛić rabańediń kana. Adọ onkae metat́kote mit́ sẹćreye duṛup̣ena, adọe metako kana, Henda bạbu, noa dọ cet́ ato kantapea? Khange adọko lạiadea. Adọ goḍoko lat́ rapaḱ baṛaket́koa, adọ hạṭiń baṛaket́kote uni hõko emadea; ar ako hõko jọmket́ khan, apan ạpin akoaḱ oṛaḱkoteko dạṛ idiket́a; uni dọ ọnḍẹgeko bạgiadea.

---

[3] The Santali word koṭo, generally translated 'naked', does not mean that the person has no clothes on; it conveys the idea of being without any outer garments, or any clothes except what is needed to cover the private parts.

[4] Pus is the month from the middle of December to the middle of January.

[5] Santali lat́, here translated 'roast in leaves', denotes a peculiar Santal way of preparing food. It is used in connexion with certain small animals, such as rats, small birds, small fish, crabs and the like. The parts not eaten are removed, the whole is cut into small pieces and put into leaves fastened together with pins of straw, thorns or the like. The leaves used are mostly those of the sal (Shorea robusta, Gaertn.) or of the mahua (Bassia latifolia, Roxb.). When this is ready, it is placed on the live coals or in hot ashes and buried in them. When roasted, it is taken from the coals and eaten with a little salt and even oil and spices, if such are available.

But although they constantly scolded him in this manner, he would not pay any heed; he did not move his ears. As they were scolding and abusing each other in this way, they also gradually neglected their work; they were reduced from their former state and became poor; and because they were angry, they did not take any steps to get him married.

So one day he went away in the sulks and was on his way abroad; he had no clothes even, only just his loin-cloth, so he was going away nearly naked[3]. Well, friends, as he walked along, he went who knows how far; and when it became evening, he sighted a village and said: "I shall at once go up to this village; I shall spend the night in this village." This happened in the month of Pus[4], so it was very cold, and as the young man had no clothes, he felt it intensely.

While he was on his way up to this village, it became dusk. Then he saw some of the village cowherds, who had made a fire at the entrance to the village and were roasting rats in leaves[5] and eating them. As he was feeling the cold, he said: "Let me, before anything else, at once warm myself a little at that fire." Saying this he went up to where the cowherds had made a fire.

He said to them: "Please, youngsters, let me warm myself here at your side; I feel the cold intensely." Saying this to them he sat down at one side, and again said to them: "Look here, youngsters, what village is this of yours?" They told him; and as they were roasting the rats in the fire, and were dividing them between themselves, they also gave him some; and when they had themselves eaten, they separated and gradually started off to their respective houses; him they left there.

This method is used at home also; it is especially resorted to by the cowherd boys when out with the cattle. They naturally often find or catch and kill small animals; instead of taking these home to get them prepared for eating there, they make up a fire out in the field. They never have any abundance of food, rather the opposite, so that they are glad to get anything available

Adọ uni koṛa dọ ọṇḍẹgeye jorok̓ akangea. Adọ onko gidrạko idilet̓ sahankogeye tiṅgiyet̓ kana; adọe duṛup̓ akangea. Adọ duṛup̓ duṛup̓teye laṅgayen khane mẹnket̓a, Nit dọ hoṛ hõko jạpit̓ket̓a, ạuri dọ ọkọe oṛak̓teṅ calak̓a? Pasẹ piṇḍạko hõ bạnuk̓tako khan, okareṅ gitić̓a? Ar oṛak̓ oṛak̓ tinạk̓ iṅ kuli baṛakoa? Ọhọṅ sẹnlena; nẹṇḍẹge nia sẹṅgẹl aṛeregeṅ gitić aṅgak̓a.

Adọ onka mẹn baṛakate ona sẹṅgẹl aṛe aṛeteye kuṇḍlaṅena. Adọ oyon lạgit̓ bhagwae raṛayet̓ tahẽkana. Adọ tisre cọṅ, kathae, nạri sutạme gocha akat̓ tahẽkane ṅamket̓, adọe mẹnket̓a, Kicrić hõ thọ sutạm reak̓geko benaoet̓a; tọbẹ noa hõ kicrić kangea, iṅ dọ noategeṅ oyona. Adọ onka hudis baṛakate uni koṛa dọe gitićente ona nạri sutạm dọ jaṅga kạṭup̓reye pạsiket̓te luturreye bak̓ket̓a; adọ ona sutạm ạuri cabak̓ dhạbić onkage banar luturreye bak̓ket̓a, ar sojheteye telṅjo akat̓a. Adọ tinre cọṅ sẹṅgẹl dọ iṛićen, bae disạlet̓a. Adọ ona tọrọć cetanre okaren seta cọṅ hẹćkateye burum akan, ar uni seta hõ ạnạrigeye ṅẹlok̓ kana.

Adọ ona atoren mạṅjhi dọ, kathae, khub kisạ̃ṛ hoṛe tahẽkana, ar guti kạmṛi hõ aema menak̓kotaea. Adọ setak̓ jọkhẹn hoṛo ẹn lạgit̓ ẹn hilok̓ dọ aćtẹt̓tege kaḍa ḍaṅgrae laga idiyet̓koa. Adọ kulhi mucạt̓re uni koṛa ar seta gitić akan ṅẹlte kaḍa ḍaṅgrako dọ mit̓ sẹnko sahaṛ idik̓ kana. Adọe mẹnet̓a, Ayo, cele ṅẹlte bako bhiṛkạuk̓ kan? Adọko paṛọm cabayen khane ṅẹle kan dọ, mit̓ hoṛ ar setakin gitić akan. Khange adọ mạṅjhi haṛame họhọket̓a, Henda ho, ọkọe nọṇḍẹ dọpe gitić akana?

Khange adọ uni koṛa dọ ãs ũse beret̓ gọt̓ena; adọe mẹn gọt̓ket̓a, Durrẹ! tinre eṅgate aṅga gọt̓ena? Disạ hõ baṅ disạlet̓a.

[6] The piece of clothing referred to is a strip of cloth fastened in front and behind in the ḍora, or string, worn round the waist by all Santal males. The cloth is passed between the thighs; a little may hang down in front and also behind. It just hides the privy parts. Especially when out working in the fields during the rainy season, this piece of cloth (bhagwa, as it is called) is often their only clothing. A man with a bhagwa is koṭo (see above note 3), but not laṅṭa, stark naked.

[7] Here thread spooled, really intended for use in a weaving-shuttle.

The young man was warming himself at the fire; he was feeding the fire with the wood the cowherds had brought there; he was sitting there. When he got tired of sitting, he said: "Now the people have gone to bed also; not having any definite business, to whose house shall I go? Perhaps they have not even a veranda, and if so, where should I lie down? And how can I go from house to house and ask them? No, I shall not go; I shall lie down and pass the night until dawn here beside this fire."

Having said this to himself he rolled over and stretched himself beside the fire. To cover himself he was just going to take off his loin-cloth strip[6]. Now some time or other he had tied up in a corner of his cloth a thréad-bobbin[7]; this he found and then said: "Well, it is of thread that they make cloth; consequently this is also cloth; I shall cover myself up with this." Having hit upon this thought, the young man lay down, and fastening the thread by a noose to his toe he hooked it on his ear; and he ran this thread from his toes to both his ears, until no more tread was left, and he himself was lying stretched straight out at full length. The fire went out some time during the night, but he did not become aware of it. A dog from somewhere or other came during the night and was lying coiled up on the ashes; this dog was also a stranger to look at.

Now, people tell, the headman of this village was an exceedingly wealthy man; he had also a large number of servants and servant-girls. In the early morning that very day he was himself driving his buffaloes and bullocks over to thresh paddy. Seeing the young man and the dog lying asleep at the end of the village-street the buffaloes and bullocks moved to one side, and the man said: "O mother! what do they see to be scared at?" When they had all passed, he sees them, a man and a dog are lying there asleep. The old headman then called out: "Hey there, who are you lying here!"

The young man then reluctantly got up and said: "O dear, dash it, when has it become dawn so quickly? I never was aware of it."

Ona katha aṅjọmte uni mạṅjhi haṛam dọ ạḍiye hahaṛayena. Adọe kulikedea, Henda bạbu, baṅ rabaṅetmea?

Adọe mẹnketa, Baṅ, baba, rabaṅediṅ kana, nọ̃kọ̃e cọṅ oyo akange. Ar sẹye ṅẹlkedea koṭoge, ẹkẹn sutạmtegeye ganak baṛa akan.

Adọ mạṅjhi haṛame mẹnketa, Iṅ ma, bạbu, ạḍi bạṛić rabaṅediṅ kana ar am ma koṭoge, onateṅ kuliyetmea, Bhala am dọ rabaṅetmea sẹ baṅ?

Adọ uni koṛae mẹnketa, Iṅak rabaṅ dọ, baba, nui setageye jọm horayettiṅa. Nui seta dọ, lak poṅcas rabaṅe jọmet kana; onate iṅ dọ baṅ rabaṅediṅ kana.

Adọ ona katha aṅjọmte họ̃ uni mạṅjhi haṛam dọe hahaṛayena. Adọ mọnẹ mọnẹte uni haṛam dọe hudis baṛaketa, Iṅ dọ bọchọr bọchọr guti kạmṛi kicrićko lạgit ạḍi bạṛić ṭakaṅ khọrọcet kana; adọ ẹnre họ̃ rabaṅge bale aṭkao daṛeak kana, bogete rabaṅetlea. Adọ ạkhirge baṅ ạkhir iṅ dọ nui setageṅ kiriṅea; inạ dọ jọtọ rabaṅe jọm horaetalea. Adọ onka bujhạu baṛakate sạri khange uni koṛae metadea, Iạ bạbu, dini nui seta dọ ẹmokme.

Khange koṛae mẹnketa, Ọhọ babaṅ ẹmlema; nui seta iạte rabaṅiṅ baṅcaok kana.

Adọ uni haṛame mẹnketa, Onkate bam ẹmok kan khać, dam iṅ emama; ẹnre họ̃ nui seta dọm ẹmokgea. Adọ ma nui seta reak dam lạime tinạkem hataoa.

Adọ uni koṛae mẹnketa, Iạ baba, nui setam hataole khan, ạḍi bạṛićem dusko ocoṅa. Dam lạlại họ̃ sanayediṅa, ar baṅ họ̃ baṅ. Pasẹ dam iṅ rọṛle khan, unạk dọ pasẹ ọhọm ẹmlen.

Adọ uni haṛame mẹnketa, Ma ẹnte rọṛme; tinạkem mẹna, unạkgeṅ emama.

Adọ uni koṛae mẹnketa, Iṅ dọ ạikhạ mit dhaoge nui seta reak dam dọṅ rọṛa. Adọ unạk ṭakam emaṅ khan dọṅ emama, ar baṅkhan dọ baṅ ẹmoka.

---

8 What is likely meant is that the dog is able to take the cold away from fifty lakhs of people.

Hearing this the old headman became very much astonished and asked him: "Look here, young man, are you not feeling cold."

"No, sir," he replied, "I am not feeling it cold; why, look here. I am covered up." The other sees that he is without clothes, he has only some threads stretched over himself.

The old headman then said: "Well, young man, I myself am feeling exceedingly cold, and you have no clothes; therefore I am asking you whether you are feeling the cold or not."

The young man replied: "Whatever cold I may feel, sir, this dog is eating it all up for me, as it comes. This dog eats up fifty lakhs[8] cold; that is the reason why I do not feel cold."

Hearing this the old headman was still more astonished, and he turned this over in his mind, saying to himself: "Every year I am spending an enormous amount of money in keeping my male and female servants in clothes; still we are unable to keep the cold away; we are feeling the cold intensely. So, happen what may, I shall buy this dog; in that case he will eat up all cold for us, as it comes." Having come to this conclusion he, truth to tell, said to the young man: "I say, young man, give me this dog."

"No, sir," the young man replied, "I am certainly not giving the dog away; because of this dog I am rescued from the cold."

"If you are not giving it for the pleasure of giving", the old man said, "I shall pay for him; anyhow, you must give this dog. So please, tell the price of this dog, how much you will take."

"I say, sir," the young man replied, "if you were to take this dog, you would put me to no end of trouble. I feel both like telling you the price and also like not telling it. Perhaps if I state the price, perhaps you will not give so much."

"Well, tell it in any case," the old man said, "any amount you say, that much I shall give."

The young man then replied: "As for me, have a care, I shall once for all tell the price of this dog. If you give me so much money, I shall give him to you, and if not, I shall not give him."

Adoe metadea, Ma rorme. Ceťteń kom akante bań emama? Endekhan nui seta reak damge ohoń em darelea. Mase bhala rorme.

Ado uni korae menketa, Nui seta reak dam do, baba, lak pońcas rabańe jometa. Ado lak pońcas ṭakam emok khan doń emama, ar bańkhan do ohoń emlema. Ina khusire khusi, bańre bań. Ado judi nui setam hataoe khan, ma inak ṭaka emańme ar nui setań emama; ar bańkhan emtetge bań emama. Ma ado ceťem meneta? Ar bańkhan iń doń calak kana.

Ado uni harame menketa, Acha, hataoegeań. Delań orakreń emama, ar nui seta hõ idi torayem.

Ado sari uni kora do setae tolkedete uni haram tayom tayomteye idikedea, ado uni haram orakreye tolkedea. Ado lak pońcas ṭakako lekhawadea. Ado ona ṭaka moṭeamkate orakteye ruarena.

Ado orakre senkate dadattikine metakin kana, Ma iń lagiť bahubon ńamkoa.

Adokin metadea, Am kurhia hor do okoe rebenama? Ar alíń do ṭaka poesa hõ banuktalińa. Ma amte bare ńamkom ar bahujońme.

Ado uni kurhia korae menketa, Henda ya, aben do unakben kami kanre hõ, okor tinakben arjao akata, ar okor tinakben ṭaka akata? Sedae khon tho miť tálaoge kurhia kurhiageben ruheťedíń

[9] It is scarcely necessary to remark that the narrator or, for that matter, any Santal has no idea of what the sum mentioned really amounts to. A lakh is one hundred thousand; the sum consequently amounts to five millions, and would in silver rupees weigh more than 60 tons. It would take us too far to say anything here about the ordinary Santal's understanding of numbers. He has names for the numbers up to twenty in his own language, and higher numbers he counts by scores. The Bengali or Hindi numerals are now being gradually adopted. The numerals here used are Bengali, and what has been in the mind of the narrator has possibly been the last word pońcas, that means fifty. With the risk of being misunderstood I should say that the present-day Santal (the educated ones always excepted) know the value of a pice (one farthing), but not of a rupee. I have seen a whole village quite agitated over one pice; I have heard the highest

"Please tell," he said to him: "in what respect have I become lacking, so that I should not give you? In such case I should certainly not be able to pay the price of this dog. Please then, tell."

The young man then said: "The price of this dog, sir, — he eats up fifty lakhs cold —, so if you will give fifty lakhs of rupees[9], I shall give him to you, and if not, I shall certainly not give him. If you are pleased with this, well and good; if not, there is nothing more to be said. So if you will take this dog, please give me so much money, and I shall give you the dog; and if not, you may rest assured I shall never let you have him. Well then, what have you to say? Otherwise I am off."

The old man then said: "All right, I shall take him; come along, I shall pay you at home; and take the dog along with you also."

Then, truth to tell, the young man tied the dog and took him along after the old man; and he tied him up in the house of the old man. Thereupon they counted out fifty lakhs of rupees to him, and having taken charge of the money he returned home.

When he reached his home, he said to his two elder brothers: "Now please, we shall get me a wife."

But they said to him: "You lazy fellow, who will consent to marry you? And as for us two, we have no money either. So please, you yourself find a girl and marry her."

The lazy young man then said: "Look here, you fellows, so much you are working, still how much is it you have earned, and how much money have you made? Nothing! Since time out of mind you two have, without intermission, scolded me and called me a lazy fellow. Now please, you two stand as leaders; whatever

council of the Santals (the people assembled at their annual hunt, sitting in council during the night) spending the whole night to adjudicate the question of the real ownership of a hare killed and eaten the previous year; but no large amount will make any impression on them, because they have not reached the stage of grasping what it really means. Up to a few generations ago they did not much need money; all their business was more or less a kind of barter.

kana. Ma aben dọ mukhiạ leka teṅgonben; jẹ kichu baplare khọrọcok̕, ona dọ iṅtegeṅ ẹma, aben dọ ọhọṅ ẹm ocolebena.

Adọkin mẹnket̕a, Henda ya, ṭaka dọ menak̕tama?

Adọe mẹnket̕a, Hẽ ya; nõk̕õe ṅẹltiṅben; tinạk̕ khọrọcok̕, unạk̕geṅ ẹma.

Adọ khange dadattikin ạḍikin hahaṛayena; adọkin gatekedea ona ṭaka ṅẹlket̕te; ar baṅkhan pạhil dọ ạḍikin ruhet̕ede kan tahẽkana. Adọ tayọmte dọ ruhet̕tẹt̕ge bakin ruhet̕ledea. Adọ bạhuko ṅamkedeteko bạhuadea; adọ mit̕regeko tahẽyena.

Ar uni setae kiriṅlede haṛam dọ ạḍiye rạskạk̕ kana, ar uni seta hõ khub dakae emae kana. Adọ kathae, ạyuṗen khan, guti koṛae metako kana, Ẹ yoi phalna, ma nui seta dọ khạṛạite idi torayepe ar kumbạ duạr ṭhen tọlkaepe, ar setak̕ jọkhẹn manḍape lak̕gaoa; unre dọ nui seta hõ tiạk̕ ạcurepe, ar un jọkhẹn dọ oyon kicric̕ko dọ jọtọ dọhọkape, nui setage nãhãk̕ apeak̕ rabaṅ dọe jọma. Uni seta kisạ̃ṛe metadiṅa, baṅma, nui seta dọ lak poṅcas rabaṅe jọma. Ona iạte iṅ dọ nui setaṅ kiriṅ akadea; adọ onate apeṅ metape kana, kicric̕ dọhọkate manḍa dọ lak̕gape; onka biḍạuepe, bhalae jọma sẹ baṅ.

Adọ sạri kisạ̃ṛ onkae hukumket̕ khan dọ khạṛạiteko idi torakedea uni seta dọ. Ar ọnẹye metat̕ko lekage uni seta dọ kumbạ duạrreko tọlkadea; adọ ẹnre hõ bogete rabaṅko. Adọko mẹnet̕a, Henḍa ya,

10 The expression used is very commonly heard in connexion with children. Gate means companion; here lit. 'they companioned him', made him a companion, let him join in all matters.

11 The threshing-floor is very frequently rather far away from the village houses, and a watch is necessary. The watchers have a kind of hut set up in one corner of the floor; generally it is some poles or sticks put up tent fashion, with straw thrown over to cover it up. The entrance or door is always very small and low; one has mostly to creep in. Incidentally it may be mentioned that the threshing-floor is the place where the folk-tales are especially heard. They help to keep the watchers awake.

12 The Santals thresh paddy in several ways; the most common one is to open out the sheaves and spread the paddy over the threshing-floor. Some bullocks (or other cattle) are tied together by their necks and made to walk round and round

will have to be spent for the marriage, that I shall myself give, I shall certainly not let you spend any of yours."

"Look here, you," they said, "have you any money?"

"Yes, you fellows," he replied; "look here, what I have; whatever will have to be spent, I shall give it all."

His two elder brothers became very much astonished, and seeing all this money, they were friendly with him[10]; otherwise they had at first been scolding him very much. Now afterwards they did not scold him any more. And having procured a bride for him, they had him married, and afterwards they were all staying together.

Now the old man who had bought the dog, he was very pleased; he also fed the dog plentifully. Then, when it became evening, people tell, he spoke to his servants: "Listen, you so and so, take this dog along with you to the threshing-floor, and tie him up at the entrance to the watch-hut[11], and to-morrow morning you will drive the bullocks over the paddy to be threshed[12]; then take this dog and lead him round[13], and meanwhile take off all your outer garments[14]; this dog will eat all the cold you feel. The owner of this dog told me that this dog eats fifty lakhs of cold. Therefore I have bought this dog; and therefore I am telling you, take off your clothes and drive the threshing bullocks round; test him in this way, whether he will eat the cold or not."

Then, truth to tell, when the master had given such an order, they took this dog along with them to the threshing-floor, and as he had instructed them, they tied the dog up at the entrance to the watch-hut; but in spite of this they felt it intensely cold. They said: "Look here, you, where is he eating the cold up and

in the straw. In this way the grain is made to fall down on the floor. The driver generally has a pitchfork, with which he lifts the straw and arranges it as may be needed. Ultimately the cattle is sent away; the straw is thereupon carefully shaken, to let all grain come out. When the straw has been removed, the grain is cleaned with the help of a winnowing-fan; all impurities and empty grains are winnowed away.

13 The idea is that the dog is led round by a string.

14 See above notes 3 and 6.

okore jom darameťa? Pahil leka rabaň kan do. Ado adom horko meneťa, Oko badae; ia setage, bhagete humage ma tho! Arhõ adom hor doko meneťa, Baňa ya, kisãre ruheťbona, babo dalea.

Ado sim rak̔en khan, mandako lak̔ga kana; ado miť hore menkeťa, Kisãre men akaťa, Manda lak̔ga jokhen kicrić dohokate nui seta tiak̔kate manda do lagaepe, bhala adoń bidautabona, joma seye baň.

Ado sari kicrić dohokate setae tiak̔ akadea ar mandae lak̔ga kana, ado kathae, bogete rabaňkede khane menkeťa, E ya, iń doń tiak̔ bhagaoena; ado ni se ape pari tiak̔letabonpe. Ado sari dosra gutiye tiak̔kedea, ado uni hõe bhagaoena. Ado arhõ dosra gutiye tiak̔kedea, ado uni hõe bhagaoena, adoe menkeťa, Ia setageń tiak̔ barayea! Bogete eňgate rabaňediń kana. Ni ya, jãhãepe tiage khan, ar baňkhan iń tol iakaea.

Adoko metadea, Ma tol iakaeme; rabaň hõ eňgate bae jomeťa, ceť auri dobon tiak̔ barayea?

Adoe menkeťa, Endekhan iń tolkae kana.

Adoko menkeťa, Oko badae ente, tiak̔ sanayeťme khan, ma tiagem, ar baň sanayeťme khan do tolkaeme; menkhan ale do ohole tiak̔ baralea.

Ado onkako menkeť khan, arhõ ona kumba duarregeye tol daporkadea.

Ado setak̔ khange, kathae, uni setae kiriń akade kisãr hor doe heć goťena; adoe metako kana, Henda ya, ape do ceť lekan hor kanape? Seta tiak̔ iń metaťpe khan, ape dope tol akadea. Cedak̔ bape tiak̔ede kana?

Adoko menkeťa, Ia setage, ale do ohole tiak̔ baralea. Rabaň hõ eňgate bae jomeťa, ceť ajwari dole tiak̔aea? Ma amgem kiriń

keeping it away? It is just as cold as it has been from the first." Then some of them said: "Who can say? this unspeakable dog, thrash him well some one!" But still some other ones said: "Not so, you; the master will scold us; we shall not beat him."

When it became cock-crow time, they commenced treshing; then one man said: "The master has said, When you are treshing, take off your clothes, and drive the treshing cattle round, having this dog led after you; I wish to try whether he will eat the cold or not."

So, truth to tell, the man took off his clothes and led the dog along, driving the treshing bullocks round and round. As he felt it intensely cold, he said: "Hey there, I am tired of dragging this dog round; so you or any of you take a turn and lead him for us." Truth to tell, another servant then took and led him round; but he also got tired of it. Again another servant led him round, but he also got tired of it and said: "Shall I drag this unspeakable dog! Dash it, I am feeling intensely cold. Here he is, you fellows, if any of you will lead him; otherwise I shall tie him up, the wretch."

So they said to him: "Tie the wretch up; dash it, he does not eat up the cold either, so why shall we drag him round to no purpose."

"Then I am tying him up," he said.

"Who knows," they said, "if you want to lead him round, do so by all means; but if you do not want to, tie him up; but as for us, we shall certainly not lead him round."

When they had spoken in this manner, he tied the wretch again at the door of the watch-hut.

When it became morning, the rich man who had bought the dog came along quite suddenly and says to them: "Look here, what manner of men are you? I ordered you to lead the dog round, and you have tied him up. Why are you not leading him round?"

"This unspeakable dog," they said; "we are certainly not going do drag him round. Dash it, he does not eat the cold either; for what needless purpose shall we lead him? Here, you bought him

akadea, am baṛe̱ tiạk̕ dapoṛem. Ale do̱ enan sim rak̕ khonle tiạk̕ bhagao akana, ale do̱ o̱ho̱le tiạk̕ baṛalea.

Ado̱e me̱nkeťa, Dini se̱, raṛa ạguạnpe. Lak poṅcas ṭakate eṅgateṅ kiriṅ akadea; nahakge e̱ṇḍe̱khan unạk̕ ṭakaṅ e̱mkeť do̱.

Ado̱ sạriko raṛa ạguadea; ado̱ bhạị, kicriće̱koe do̱ho̱ baṛa go̱ťkeťa, ado̱ seta tiạk̕kate manḍae lak̕ga kana. Ado̱ bar pe̱ dhaoe laga ạcurleťko khange rabaṅteye thar tharaoena. Ado̱e metako kana, Ni se̱ ya, tiạk̕ gelalepe.

Ado̱ko me̱nkeťa, Ale do̱ enanrele tiạk̕ bhagao akana, o̱ho̱le tiạk̕lea. Ma amge tiạk̕ sanayeťme khan, tiạgem, ar baṅkhan do̱ aṛak̕kaeme.

Ado̱ uni kisạṛ ho̱ṛ hõe tiạk̕ baṛakedea; ado̱ rabaṅ hõ bae jo̱meť khan do̱ edreyente ona manḍa talarege humạk̕e humạk̕kedea se̱, andhe pathạuṛiye dalkedea. Khange uni seta do̱ kao kaoe garjaoeťa are ciḍireťa. Khange ado̱ dal dalteye dal go̱ć utạrkedea. Ado̱ onko guti koṛa do̱ bogeteko landawadea. Ar ona seta rak̕ aṅjo̱mte atoren ho̱ṛ hõko he̱ćena; ado̱ onko guti koṛa do̱ ona kathako lạiako kan khać, onko ato ho̱ṛ hõ bogete uni kisạṛko landawadea. Ado̱ e̱ne̱ cabayena.

Ado̱ onko guti koṛako me̱neťa, Noa manḍare do̱m dal ić akadea; ale do̱ busup̕ hõ o̱ho̱le giḍilea; ma am baṛe̱ giḍi iạkam.

Ado̱ uni kisạṛ do̱ ceť hõ bae ro̱ṛleťa. Ado̱ enkageko ro̱ṛkaťa, giḍi do̱ bako giḍi ocoledea, akogeko giḍikeťa.

Ado̱ mucạť utạrena katha do̱; in maraṅgea.

---

15 The effect of fear, often observed in animals.

16 Naturally not at the man's cruelty to the poor dog, but at his wisdom. It is a pity they are not always so kind to their animals as they ought to be.

yourself, you take and lead him round, the wretch. We have been dragging him round from cock-crow to-day and are tired of doing so; we shall certainly not lead him."

"Bring him here," he said, "loose him and bring him to me. I have, dash it, bought him for fifty lakhs of rupees; it was for nothing then that I gave so much money."

So, truth to tell, they loosed the dog and brought him to the man, and he, friends, at once took off his clothes, and, leading the dog along, he commenced to drive the threshing bullocks. But when he had driven them twice or three times round, he was trembling with cold. Then he said to them: "Take him, you, try to lead him round."

But they said: "We have got tired of dragging him long ago; we are not going to drag him any more. If you wish to drag him round, do so please; and if not, let him loose."

So the master again led the dog round; but as he was not eating any cold, he became angry and there, in the middle of the paddy spread out on the threshing-floor, he commenced to beat the dog without ceasing; he beat him mercilessly, not heeding where he struck. The dog was howling and crying and purging[15]. And in this way, beating and beating, he ultimately killed the dog, and the servants laughed[16] well at him. Now, hearing the cries of the dog, the village people also came there, and when the servants told them this story, these village people also laughed well at him. So there it is ended.

The servants said: "You beat the dog so that he purged here in the paddy on the threshing-floor; we are not going to throw this straw away; do it you yourself."

The master did not say a single word. Now the others spoke in this way; but they did not let him throw the straw away; they did it themselves.

So there is the story absolutely finished; it is thus much.

50. Dhõk rog hoṛ reaḱ katha.

Sedae jokhen, kathae, mitṭaṅ hoṛ dhõk rog ńamledea; ado uḍi baṛiće ran baṛa ocoyena, seye ojha baṛaketḱoa, merom simko bogeteye em baṛawaṭkoa, bogekae mente uḍi baṛiće khorocena. Ado okoe hõ bako ran boge daṛeadea, pe pon serma hoeyenre hõ bae bogelena.

Khange ran ocoḱ hõye thirena, ar osoḱ hõ ḍhere osoḱena; ar sẽṛãko koṛa hopon hõ baṇuḱkotaea, ar se kami din se cas bas din tioḱena, ar se oroḱko ma menaḱkotaege, do cele siaea? Ado aćtegeye sioḱa; bar pāk gane laga acura, are duṛupa, laṅgate bae si daṛeaḱ kana, ado enkakategeye aphor baṛaketa.

Khange Asaṛ tioḱena, ado khete paṛaḱ baṛayeta, miť ghaṛiye sioḱa, adoe aṛaḱketge. Ado mitṭaṅ teńa era hoṛ ona aṛereye sioḱ kan tahẽkana; ado uni ṭhen cun thamakur jome calaoena; ado thamakure koekede khan uni hõ nahele teṅgokette tamakure emadea, are duṛupena. Adokin galmarao kana, ar uni hoṛ do bogeteye khoḱeť kan gea.

Adoe metae kana, Bam bogelena?

---

1 Dhõk, here translated 'cough', may be anything with chronic coughing. Most commonly it is tuberculosis of the lungs.

2 s. above p. 60, note 3.

3 The expression refers to the animals, &c., given for sacrificial purposes. Malevolent spirits are supposed to be behind most diseases, and they have to be satisfied or placated, before any medicine can be expected to take effect.

4 The very primitive ploughing of the Santals always works round and round, although the fashion of their plough does not make such a proceeding necessary.

5 With the exception of a kind of highland rice and rice sown in places that later on are turned into pools with fairly deep standing water (only found in the flat low country) all rice is sown in fields very thickly; when the seedlings are grown to a proper size, they are pulled up and transplanted. This sowing is called aphor, as distinguished from er, to sow broadcast.

6 Asaṛ corresponds to the period from the middle of June to the middle of July and is the first month of the rainy season proper, when all agricultural work is in full swing.

50. THE STORY OF A MAN WITH A COUGH.

Once upon a time, people tell, long ago it so happened that a man became ill with a cough[1]; he tried all kinds of medicine, that is to say, he engaged medicine-men[2], he gave them goats and fowls any number[3]; he spent an awful amount, that they should make him well. But no one was able to give him a medicine that would cure him; three to four years passed, still he did not get well.

So he gave up taking medicines; he also became very emaciated; and he had no grown-up sons either, and then the working season, that is to say, the agricultural season came; ploughing cattle he had; but who should plough? So he was ploughing himself; he would plough about two turns[4] round and then sit down; he was so tired that he could not plough more, and in this way he managed to sow[5] the rice.

Then the month of Asar[6] came, and he broke the ground[7]; he ploughed a short while, then he stopped. Now a brother-in-law[8] of his was ploughing near to him, and he went over to him to ask him for tobacco to chew; and when he asked him for tobacco, this man also let his plough stand and gave him tobacco, and he sat down, and they were talking together, but he was coughing a great deal.

The other man then said to him: "Have you not got well?"

---

[7] Lit. split. The Santals have different names for ploughing a field, the first ploughing being called paṛaḱ, to split; the next is dẹć, lit. to mount, plough across the first; the third is jabọḍ, the fourth and last ploughing is called lọsọt́, lit. make mud. This refers to the cultivation of their paddy fields. Lands for other crops not standing in water is ploughed twice or sometimes thrice; if so, the third time is called uṭhạu.

[8] The term is used only in addressing a man who may be one's elder sister's husband or wife's younger brother. It might be noted that Santals living in the same village will always make up an artificial relationship, if they are not actually related, to make the daily intercourse easier. Somewhat the same as that underlying the custom of letting European children call grown up people uncle and aunt.

Adọ uniye mẹnketa, Hẽ ho, saṅgat, bạń bogelena, ar goć hõ bạń gujuk kana, ạdi bạṛić, saṅgat, iń harkhetok kana, baṅ geń gujuk kana, baṅ geń besok kana; okage baṅ, sanam rarankoń bhagaoketkoa. Adọ jọtọ lekan ran hõń hajamketa, ẹnre hõ bạń beslenteń thir dapoṛena, adọ dẹ, amem baḍae khan ranạńtalańme.

Adọ uniye mẹnketa, Ẹ ho saṅgat, baḍae dọń baḍae gea, pasẹć baṅ lagaok; mẹnetam, ḍher ḍher ranem ńũ jọm hajamketa, pasẹ noa hõ baṅ lagaok.

Adọ uniye mẹnketa, Acha ho, saṅgat, lagaok sẹ baṅ lagaok, mit dhao gan ran legawạńmẹ, inạtege nãhãk ạṭkarokа.

Adọ uniye mẹnketa, Iạ ho, saṅgat, tọbẹ khan rangeń lạiama, amtege lagaojoṅme; judi onate bam thirok khan mit din dọ bhala iń titeń lagao gelawama; pạhil dọ amtege lagaolem.

Adọe mẹnketa, Acha tọbẹ khan ma range lạiạńme.

Adọe metadea, Iạ ho, saṅgat, ran dọ noa kana; am dọ bẹrẹl sọsọte linḍhi sọsọkme thọ, ẹkkaltem boge utạroka.

Khange uniye mẹnketa, Dur ho, saṅgat, am dọ ạḍi pagla họṛ kanam, khok khokte eṅgateń aḍoyeta, am dọ ẹnḍić landa sẹnge.

Adọ uniye mẹnketa: Baṅa ho, landa katha dọ baṅ kana, noa dọ biḍạu ran kana ho; lagao gelaemẹ sẹ ho, ẹkkalte bam nikạṛ khaṛ utạr akana mẹnkhan range alom metaktińa. Am dọm mẹnetа, Landa sạgại iạteye landawạń kana, landa dọ baṅ kana ho; ọnẹ bako

---

9 Every grown-up Santal may be supposed to 'know' one or more medicines or remedies.

10 The pericarp of the fruit of the marking-nut tree (Semecarpus Anacardium L., var. cuneifolia) is extensively used by the Santals as a counter-irritant. The juice is applied, and in a couple of days a blister develops. If not taken properly care of, it may develop into ugly sores. Children eat the hypocarp of the fruit, and if not all of the pericarp has been removed, they develop horrible sores round the mouth and on the face generally.

11 A 'proved medicine' is a very common expression; it has been tested and proved effective, according to their opinion.

"O no, brother-in-law," he replied; "I have not got well, and I am not dying either; I am suffering awfully, brother-in-law; I am not dying, I am not getting better, neither the one nor the other; I have put all the medicine-men to rout; I have also drunk and eaten and digested all kinds of medicine; in spite of this I have not got well, so I have stopped taking any more such stuff; so then now, if you know[9] any medicine, please give it me."

"Well, brother-in-law," the other one said, "I certainly know something; but perhaps it will have no effect; you say you have drunk and eaten and digested very much medicine, so perhaps this will have no effect either."

"All right, brother-in-law," he replied, "whether it will have any effect or not, try and give it me once anyhow; by that it will be seen."

The other one then said: "I say, brother-in-law, then I shall tell you the medicine; you must apply it yourself; if it does not stop by that, I shall some day have a try and apply it with my own hand; but first apply the remedy yourself."

"Very well then," he replied, "tell me the medicine."

The other then said: "I say, brother-in-law, the medicine is this; apply fresh marking-nut[10] to your hind-quarters; you will at once be absolutely cured."

He then replied: "O dear me, brother-in-law, you are a great wag; I am coughing and coughing so that I cannot restrain myself, dash it; you scamp, you are making fun of it."

The other one then said: "No, not at all; it is not a joke; this is a proved[11] medicine; just try and apply it; if you do not at once get entirely well, don't call my remedy a medicine. You are thinking: on account of the joking relationship[12] between us he

[12] Certain people stand to each other in what is called landa sągąi, joking or laughing relationship. Such relatives (real or artificial) are permitted to talk very freely on all matters; there is no restraint. These brothers-in-law stand in such relationship to each other; other brothers-in-law have to be very careful in their behaviour towards each other. See the writer's paper on Taboo and connected customs among the Santals (J. A. S. B., vol. LXVII, Part III, note 22).

men, Landa kathage sạrika, rosom ruạge gogoća. Ona sik katha ho; ma se am do mit́ dom laga gelalem, adolaṅ ńela se laṅ biḍạua.

Ado uniye menket́a, Dhut ho, noa do bạń pạtiạulena; eṭakre karon, eṭakre ranem lagao ocoń kana; noate ki bebesa? onate bạń pạtiạuatam kana.

Ado uniye menket́a, Acha bam pạtiạuḱ kan khan iń cekamea; baṅkhan besaḱ mentegeń batlaoam kana. Ado enka men bạṛakatege kin apan ạpin bạṛayena.

Ado en hiloḱ ńindạ khange ạḍiye khoḱet́ kana; ado mone moneteye hudiset́ kana, Baṅ do uni hoṛaḱ ran iń lagaotae baṅ do baṅ. Nonkae hudis baṛajoṅ kana. Ado setaḱ khangeye muruk gotket́te linḍhiye soso aḍoyena. Ado dosar tesar khange phokayente lagaḱ lagaḱ ghao aḍoyentaea, ar bogete hasoye, ṭạnḍite jokhen hõ cirạ aḍoḱ kantae; khog jokhen hõ cirạ aḍoḱ kantae. Ado bogeteye garjaoa, are mena, Enḍ hoṛ, okare baṅ ńame, eṅgateye ghao oco akadina, khub lekań humạḱkea.

Ado noa katha uni hoṛ doko lại tioḱade khan uni ṭhen do bae soroḱa; uniye ńelle khan pharakteye gusạu calaḱa. Ar uni hoṛ do soso ghaote linḍhi cagaṛoḱ kantaete khoḱ do kurumuṭuteye sambṛaoa, khoḱ sanayere hõ bae khoga, kurumuṭuteye sambṛaotaea.

Ado sạri onkaye sambṛaoket́ khan khoḱ do cabayentaea, ar ona soso ghao hõ bogeyentaea; ado khoḱ cabayentae khan si hõ khubgeye si daṛeaḱ kan, ar thoṛa thoṛateye lomo idiḱ kana.

Adoe menket́a, Durre, bhage ran kangetaea, pạhil do ereń metat́taea, ado nõkõe eṅgateń boge aḍoyena; acha besge mit́ din uni hoṛ doń mankaea.

---

13 The Santali word signifies the anus and perineum.

is poking fun at me; it is not a joke, my friend; don't they say: 'a joke comes true, low fever kills.' It is the same with this; well, you have a try and apply this once; then we shall see or we shall prove its worth."

The man replied: "O fie, I don't believe this; the complaint is in one place, and you are making me apply the medicine in another place; should that bring a cure, do you think? So I do not believe in your remedy."

The other then said: "Very well, if you will not believe, what can I do for you? otherwise it is because I believe it is good that I am instructing you to make use of it." After they had had this talk, they separated.

That very night the man had a very bad bout of cough, and he was considering with himself: "Shall I apply his medicine or shall I not?" He was thinking over the matter. When it became morning, he made up his mind and applied the marking-nut to his hind-quarters[13]. After two or three days the blisters burst and became horrible sores, causing him much pain; when he had to go out, the parts were torn; also when he coughed, the same happened. He shrieked and howled and would say: "This unspeakable fellow, wherever I meet him — dash it, he has given me these sores — I shall give him a good trashing."

As people reported this word to the other man, he took care not to come near to him; when he saw him, he would slip away to a distance. Now as his hind-quarters were being torn by the marking-nut sores, he exerted himself all he could to repress his cough; even when he felt the necessity of coughing, he did not do so; he exerted himself to keep it back.

Then, truth to tell, as he in this way repressed the coughing, it ceased, and the marking-nut sores were also healed; and when his cough ceased, he was very well able to plough, and little by little he gained strength.

And he said: "O dear, his medicine is good; at first I thought it was all rot; but now, dash it, here I am cured; all right, some day I shall honour this man."

Adọ sạri hạṇḍiye dọhọ ocokeťkote isinen khan dọe họhọ idikedea. Khange pạhil dọe bọtọroḱ kan tahẽkana; ać mọnreye mẹnjoṅ kan tahẽkana, nui hoṛ dọ eṅgateń ghao ocoledea, dal aḍoń cọe ceť cọṅ. Uni oṛaḱte calaḱ tuluć nonkaye hudis baṛa idijoṅ kana.

Adọ uni oṛaḱe tioḱkeť khan parkọmko beladea duṛuṕ lạgit; adọ miť ghạṛi khange oṛaḱteko họhọ aderkedete hạṇḍiko ạguadea.

Adọ bar dọme ńũkeť khan dọe kulikeťkoa, Henda ho, saṅgat, ceťko reaḱpe hạṇḍiketa? ńũ mabo ńũyeť kange, sebelge thọ baṅ ạikạuḱ kana, ar mera hõ baṅ ńamoḱ kana. Adọ ọnẹ bako mẹn, jẹ, Dakale, utule, buluṅge sebela, jãhãtinạḱ rọṅ chọṅme buluṅ bam lagaole khan sebel dọ bạnuḱan. Ar hạṇḍile, pạuṛạle, kathage sebela, jãhãtinạḱ sebel hạṇḍi ńũime, bam galmaraoaḱ khan sebel dọ bạnuḱan. Adọ ona sik katha kana, sebelge baṅ ńameťa.

Adọ uni hoṛe mẹnkeťa, Noa hạṇḍi dọ ho, saṅgat, amgeń hạṇḍi akawaťmea, uḍi bạṛić ojhakoṅ jọm ńũ ocoleťkoa, bạṅ beslena. Adọ amem batlaoạdiṅ ona rantegeń bogeyena, adọ onateń mẹnkeťa, Miť phũṛũḱ ganteń man dapoṛkaea.

Adọ tọbẹyena uni hoṛ dọ phu manteye sahẹťkeťa; baṅkhane bọtọroḱ kan tahẽkana, daleń cọe ceť cọṅ; adọe khulạsayente uḍikin phukṭijoṅ kana. Adọ ọnẹye ghaolen jọkhẹć reaḱkoe lạiae kana, ar kin landayeťa; adọ ona landa aṅjọmte, arhõ miť hoṛe bọlọyena; adọ oṛ khon uni hoṛkin lạiae kana. Adọ ona aṅjọmte uni hõ khaḱ khaḱe landakeťa, sẹ sanam hoṛgeko landakeťa, arko mẹnkeťa, Nịạ dọ uḍitẹť hahaṛa ran kana.

Adọ cabayena katha dọ.

---

14 When there is only a small party, they are generally called into the house, to partake of what is offered. They like to be unobserved by strangers, and inside there is never much light.

15 Rice-beer may be served in brass-cups; very frequently, however, a leaf-cup is made for the occasion. They have a special form of leaf-cup called hạṇḍi phũṛũḱ, lit. rice-beer leaf-cup.

16 Mera is the grain on which the beer is brewed, or, especially, has been brewed.

17 The words here quoted and somewhat amplified are a saying frequently heard. It is customary, when beer is served at any ceremony or festival, for some one to ask 'what beer is this?', whereupon the occasion of it is stated in some form or other. Every social act of theirs is, one might say, ratified in beer.

So, truth to tell, he told them to brew beer, and when it was ready, he sent for the man. At first this one was afraid, he was saying to himself: "Dash it, I gave him sores, now he will give me a thrashing as likely as not." On the way to the other man's house he was having such thoughts.

When he reached his house, they put a bedstead for him to sit on; a moment afterwards they called him in [14] and brought him beer.

When he had emptied his cup [15] twice, he asked them: "Look here, brother-in-law, what is the occasion that you have brewed beer? here we are drinking, but the sweetness of it is not to be felt, any of the grain [16] is not to be found either. Is it not so that people speak: 'preparing rice and curry, it is the salt that makes it sweet' [17]; you may season it with spices as much as you like, if no salt is added, there is no sweetness. And when beer and liquor are served, the spoken word makes it sweet; drink as delicious a beer as you like, if you do not add any talk to it, there is no sweetness. And this is what is the matter here, I do not find the sweetness of it."

The man then said: "This beer, brother-in-law, I have had brewed for you; I gave any number of medicine-men to eat and drink, but did not get well. Then I got well by applying the medicine you instructed me to use; so I said: I shall in a small way honour him by giving him one leaf-cup or so."

Then only the other man breathed freely; otherwise he had been afraid that he would perhaps beat him; and when his anxiety was relieved, they talked and joked together for a long while. He told him how it was with him the time he had the sores, and they were having a good laugh. Hearing this laughter, another man came in, and they told him the whole from the very beginning. When this one heard it, he also laughed boisterously [18], or rather all of them laughed and said: "This is a most marvelous medicine."

So the story is ended.

---

[18] They all obviously have understood that the whole was a practical joke and enjoy it.

51. Eṭak dhō̱k ho̱ṛaḱ katha.

Ar hō̱ dhō̱k ho̱ṛaḱ kathageń lạiyeť kana. Ona do̱ nonka kana. Miť ho̱ṛ kathaeye dhō̱klena, pe̱ pon sermae hoeyena, e̱n hō̱ bae bogeḱ kana, ar go̱ć hō̱ bae gujuḱ kana. Ado̱ ran ranteko bhagaoen khan bako ran ocoledea; ado̱ ạdite̱ťe mora cabayena.

Ado̱ kathae, miť din do̱ o̱ko̱e co̱ṅ miťṭaṅ ayaṅ biń do̱ko go̱ć akadeye ńamkedea; ado̱e me̱nkeťa, Boge hō̱ bạń bogeḱ kana, ar baṅgeń gujuḱ kana, nui bińạḱ bis iń jo̱m ạdoetaea, inạ do̱ń go̱ć ho̱doḱa; harkhet tinạḱ iń sahaoa?

Ado̱ kathae, onka me̱nkate dhirite ho̱ṭo̱ḱe ko̱ṭe̱ć kuṭrạkeťtaea, ar ona bo̱ho̱ḱte̱ť do̱ idikateye rapaḱ jo̱mkeťa, ar aćaḱ joto̱ kicrióe ńam toťkeťte ado̱m do̱e aṭe̱ťkeťa, ar ado̱mte do̱e oyo po̱ṭo̱mena. Me̱nkeťae, Bis iń jo̱mkeťa, dhorage teheń do̱ń gujuḱgea nāhāḱ. Ayoge, goṭa ńindại gitić aṅgayenre hō̱ bae go̱ćlen; ado̱ ać ho̱ṛmo̱reye ạikạueť kan do̱, khoḱ hō̱ normao ńō̱ḱentaea. Ado̱ kathae, bại bạite khoḱ hō̱ okayen co̱ṅ; tayo̱mte do̱ khube moṭa ạdoyena. Ado̱ ho̱ṛko kuli baṛayea, Henda ya, o̱ko̱e ranaťmea me̱nte?

Ado̱e me̱na, O̱ko̱e hō̱ baṅ, aćtege thirentińa.

Ado̱ khub lekae daṛeyen khan bo̱cho̱r din purạukate noako katha do̱e lạiaťkoa, baṅma, Iń do̱ nonka lekate noa ro̱g khon do̱ń boge akana.

Ado̱ ho̱ṛko me̱nkeťa, Gujuḱem me̱noana, onatege am do̱ Candoe dayawaťmetem bogeyena.

Ado̱ e̱ne̱ niạ katha hō̱ cabayena, in marań gea.

---

[1] There is no joke in this story, which may have been taken out of life; it is given here as a kind of appendix to the previous one.

51. THE STORY OF ANOTHER MAN WITH A COUGH.

I am telling another story[1] of a man with a cough. It is this: A certain man, people tell, had acquired a cough; three four years passed; still he was getting no better, and he did not die either. When they had without success done all they could giving him medicine, they stopped this; afterwards he became very lean and weak.

Now, people tell, one day it so happened that he found a cobra[2], which somebody had killed, and he said: "I am not getting well, and I do not die either; I shall eat the poison of this snake; thereby I shall get a quick death; how much suffering shall I stand?"

With this in his mind, people tell, he took a stone and smashed off the head, and taking this along with him, he roasted and ate it; thereupon he took all his clothes out; some he spread out to lie on, and with some he covered himself up. He said: "I have taken poison; without doubt I shall die shortly to-day." O mother, he lay the whole night until dawn, still he did not die; then he was feeling the condition of his body, his cough also was somewhat less. Thereupon, people tell, little by little his cough disappeared and afterwards he grew very fat. And people would ask him: "Look here, who has given you medicine?"

He would reply: "No one, it has stopped spontaneously."

When he had gained full strength a full year afterwards, he told people this story, saying: "In such and such a way I have been cured of this disease."

And people said: "You intended to die; therefore Cando took pity on you, and you were cured."

So there this story is also ended; it is thus much.

---

[2] The cobra de capello (lit. hooded snake, in Portuguese), Naja tripudians, is one of the most common snakes in many parts of India. Not only is it a deadly snake, but it is very aggressive, attacking people without being in any way molested.

52. Gune baḍae haṛam reak̕.

Sedaere, kathae, mit̕ atore bar haṛam buḍhikin tahẽkana; uni haṛam dọ jaejugge kicriće teṅa. Mit̕ din dọ uni buḍhi piṭhạwạkin lạgit̕e hǫlǫṅket̕a; adọ un jọkhẹn uni haṛam hõ kicriće teṅok̕ kan tahẽkana. Buḍhi dọe piṭhạyet̕a oṛak̕ bhitrire, mẹnkhan tinạk̕ dhaoe dulet̕a piṭhạ, unạk̕ dhaoge saḍe dọ haṛame aṅjọmet̕gea, uni haṛam hõ ọtre mạkuteye daget̕ kana.

Khange uni buḍhi dọe piṭhạ bhagaoena, adọe gaṇḍaket̕a pẹ gaṇḍa pẹa piṭhạ hoeyena. Adọ buḍhi haṛame lạiae kana, metae kanae, Piṭhạ dọ pẹ gaṇḍa ge hoelena, adọ turui gọṭẹn kate hạṭiṅ dọ hoyok̕talaṅa. Khange uni haṛame mẹnket̕a, Baṅ, piṭhạ dọ ar hõ pẹa bạṛtigea.

Adọ uni buḍhiye mẹnket̕a, Iṅren haṛam dọe jan guruk̕a nãhãk̕. Adọ ạimạị ạimạiko galmaraore uni buḍhiye lạiakoa, Ale hẹrẹl ma bhalae janok̕ge! sanamak̕ge bin ṅẹlteye lạị daṛeak̕ kana.

Khange tahẹn tahẹnte ḍher din hoeyena. Khange mit̕ṭaṅ raj eṭak̕ raj sãote lạṛhạị sanakedea; khange uni raj dọ lạṛhạikogeye ṅam baṛayet̕koa. Khangeko lạiadea, Phalna jaegare lạṛhai lek họṛ menaea.

---

[1] The story was taken down by Bhuju Murmu of Dhopahaṛ village.

Cloth weaving was very common among the Santals formerly; now-a-days very few engage in this; the mill-made cloth is finer to look at and is always to be had, if one has the money. Besides the Muhammedan Jolhas, now very plentiful in the country, weave and sell cloth, something like what the Santals themselves used to weave. It is a pity that this home industry is being abandoned. To explain one detail in the story, it might be mentioned that the weaver sits on the ground with his legs in a hole dug for the purpose. The loom, if it can be so called, is of the most primitive character.

[2] The Santals make a few different kinds of 'cakes'. The 'cake' here mentioned is what is called dul piṭhạ, lit. poured out cake. A kind of paste or batter is made of flour with sugar and some other ingredients, and this is poured into

52. THE MAN WHO KNEW MAGIC.

ONCE upon a time long ago, people tell, there lived in a certain village a pair, a man and his wife; the man was always weaving cloth[1]. One day the wife prepared flour to make cakes; at that time also the man was weaving cloth. The woman was making cakes[2] inside, but every time she let the batter fall into the oil to be cooked, the husband heard the sound, and every time he made a mark in the ground with his shuttle.

When the woman had finished making cakes, she counted them, they were fifteen[3] cakes. The wife then told her husband, saying: "It became twelve cakes, so we shall both of us get six each." "No," the man said, "there are three more cakes."

The woman then said: "My old man will become a witch-finder[4] presently." And when the women were talking together, the wife used to say to them: "Our man will likely some day become a witch-finder; he is able to tell everything without seeing it."

Now as they were living, a long time passed. Then there was a king who wanted to fight another king, and this king was endeavouring to get hold of people who could fight; and they told him: "In such and such a place there is a man who will be capable of fighting."

---

boiling mustard-oil, enough for one cake at a time. When the batter touches the boiling oil, it naturally sets up a fizzing sound.

[3] Lit. three sets of four and three. It is very common to use gaṇḍa, a set of four, as a unit in counting.

[4] Jan, a word borrowed from Hindi, is the Santal name for a witch-finder; they are supposed to receive revelations from supernatural beings and to be able to name the witches and also to reveal things hidden. They are unmitigated scoundrels and responsible for a good deal of suffering and cruelty. The Santals of the present day acknowledge that they are humbugs; still they make use of them.

Khange raj do sipahi hore kolketkoa, metatkoae, Do calakpe, hani hor sap aguyepe. Khange uni sasap sipahiko calaoena, arko metae kana, Dela se, raj cet lagit cone khoj akatmea.

Khange uni hore menketa, Raj do cet lagite khojen kana? Akil hõ banuktina, lelha utargean. Khange onko sipahiko menketa, Ban, am do calaktege hoyoktama.

Khange uni hor rajak hukum lekate adoe calaoena; khange raje metae kana, Am do khub gunan hor kanam?

Khangeye menketa, Ban, raja, adi do ban badaea, thora thuri don badaegea.

Ado raje menketa, Ende khan am do larhai calak hoyoktama; am moto do ban, am sãote aema sipahiko tahena, ar sadom cetanten kolpea.

Khange aema sipahi ar uni hõ sadomreye dećkedea; khange dećkede khan uni do adi botorgeye aikauketa; ente uni do tisre hõ sadomre do bae dećlena; ene utargeye deć legak kana. Khangeko mohndayena.

Khange aswariako do khub leka sadomko kamsaoketkoa, ar nui hõ onko sãote aćren sadome kamsaokedea; ado kathae, uni do botorte ekkalteye keklesetena, ar mittan darereye harupena; uni sadom mae ńir paromen, ar hor ma ona dareregeye harup tahẽyen. Ado ona ńelte uni raj do adiye haharayena, menketae, Nonka do ban ńel akawana. Onate uni raj do thorage boksis takae emadea, are kol ruarkadea ać orakte. Khange orakre hećkate aćren erae metae kana, Ńelme, iń do thora dintege aema utar takań rojgar aguket talańa.

Eratet doe menketa, Jorãeyiń kolletmete.

---

5 The word lelha means foolish; it is, however, also often used about people who do not know any other language than their own Santali. Most male Santals are bi- or tri-lingual; they need in their daily life to use both Bengali and Hindi,

The king then sent some soldiers, saying to them: "Do go; get hold of that man and bring him." The soldiers that should fetch this man went and said to him: "Come along, the king wants your presence for some purpose or other."

The man replied: "For what purpose does the king want my presence? I have no wisdom; I am utterly ignorant and foolish[5]." But the soldiers said: "It does not matter, you will have to come."

So the man went in accordance with the king's command; and the king said to him: "You are a man much skilled in magic?"

"No, king," he replied, "I do not know much, just a little I know."

The king then said: "Then you will have to go and fight; not you alone; a large number of soldiers shall go with you, and I shall send you on horseback."

Thereupon he let a large number of soldiers and this man also mount horses; and when they had put him on a horse, he became very much afraid; he had never previously mounted a horse; this was the very first time that he had attempted to ride. So they started.

Now the riders made their horses gallop along; this man also had to let his horse gallop together with the others; and he, people tell, became absolutely frightened out of his wits, and he caught hold of and clung to a tree; the horse continued to run, and the man remained clinging to the tree. Seeing this the king became very much astonished and said: "I have never seen anything like this." So the king gave him a few rupees as a present and sent him back home. When he reached home, he said to his wife: "Look, in a few days I have earned and brought us a large sum of money."

His wife replied: "Because I forced you to go."

---

and a person who has not been able to learn a little of one of these is considered a fool, perhaps with some reason.

53. Bul hoṛak̕ katha.

Sedae jokhen, kathae, sohraere mit̕ṭen hoṛ do hanḍi ńũ bulkate kulhi se chaṭka duar macha sen jhanṭi phedreye bul bindaṛ akana, ar cele hõ banuk̕koa. Ado kathae, ghaṭao ńinda jokhen raj do hatire dećkate ona kulhi talatege okate coe calak̕ kan. Khange uni bul hoṛ doe disa got̕kedea, ar se beret̕ do bae beret̕ daṛeak̕ kana. Ado kathae gitić kategeye adop got̕ket̕a, men got̕ket̕ae, Kiska hati hae, becega to ham lega. Ketna rupaiya dam hoga, ham hati lega, ar jaruṛ ham hati lene sakega.

Onkaye roṛket̕ khange tho raj doe bharo utarena, menket̕ae, Okoe perja nonka kisaṛ do menak̕kotińa? Bhala thoń ńelegea.

Ado oka tin sangiń coń calak̕ motlob tahẽkantaea, ado ona roṛ ańjomteye hahaṛayente mahute kulikedea, en kathae, Noa atore okoe nonkan hoṛ menaea, je hatiye hatao daṛeaetińa?

Ado mahute menket̕a, Oko badae coń.

Ado raje menket̕a, Balań calak̕a, kulhi mucatrelań ḍerak̕a; judi nui hatiye hataole khan bogege, ar hõ iń do ina damtege eṭak̕koń kirińjońa. Onka menkatekin ḍerayena.

Ar uni hoṛ do bae badaelet̕a, je nui doe raj kana, ar rajren hati kanae mente do, ar one raj ar mahut cet̕kokin roṛ idiket̕, ona roṛ hõ uni hoṛ do bae ańjomlet̕a; menkhan dosra oṛak̕ren doko ańjomlet̕gea, ar nui hoṛak̕ roṛ hõko ańjom ṭhiklet̕taegea.

Ado setak̕ko ńelkede do, kulhi mucatre hatiye ḍera akan; ado khanko bujhau got ket̕te uni hoṛko laiadea, bańma, nonka onka raje

[1] It is not much of a story, but it is recorded, because it throws some light on the attitude of the Santals to the subject. When a Santal drinks, it is to become drunk; the quicker a man becomes drunk, the better is the beer or the liquor.

[2] Sohrae is a kind of harvest festival, now annually taking place during the first half of January. It is the great festival of the Santals, lasting for generally five days; it is an absolute orgy; all get drunk and all restraint is done away with.

[3] The king, raj, is the landlord or zemindar.

[4] The man speaks in Urdu (Hindustani), not quite faultlessly and pronounced according to Santal phonetic rules.

53. THE STORY OF AN INTOXICATED MAN[1].

LONG ago, people tell, it so happened during the Sohrae[2] festival that a man, who had become drunk from drinking beer, had fallen down in the village street somewhere near the entrance to his court-yard close to a fence, and there were no people there. Then, people tell, shortly after midnight a king[3] was passing through the street, riding on an elephant, on his way somewhere. The intoxicated man then became aware of him; but he was unable to stand up; and lying there he commenced to brag[4] and said: "Wessen Elefant ist es? Falls er feil ist, ich werde ihn nehmen. Wie viel Geld der Preis auch betragen wird, ich werde den Elefant nehmen; ich muss notwendig den Elefant haben."

When he spoke in this way, the king became utterly amazed and said: "Whom have I got as tenants of mine here, who are so wealthy? I shall have a look at him."

Now the king had been intending to proceed somewhere, who knows how far; but hearing this speech, he became so astonished that he asked his elephant-driver: "Who is there in this village so well off that he is able to buy my elephant?"

"Who knows?" the elephant-driver replied.

"We shall not go further," the king said: "we shall camp at the end of the village street; if he will buy this elephant, well and good; I shall for the price of this buy other ones." After these words they camped there.

Now this man did not know that the man was the king, and that it was the king's elephant; neither did he hear what the king and his elephant-driver talked together; but some people living in a neighbouring house heard it; they had also heard quite plainly what this man had said.

The next morning people saw that an elephant was camped at the end of the village street; and when they understood what it

ror idiketa mente. Khange uni hor do ać monreye hudis gotketa. Ado jeder ketećkate khange raj doe heć gotenteye kulikedea, Henda ho, en kathae, hola ńinda jokhen ińren hati hataoeye menlet hor doe okayena? Delabon dor damea.

Khangeye metadea, Uni hor do celeaea?

Ado raje menketa, Ńutum do bań kulildea, menkhan noa orakren kangeae; nia chatka then khongeye metadińa.

Adoe metadea, Hẽ ho, noa orakrege okaren coń mit hore hećlengea; ar amren hati hataoegeye menleta, ado uni hor ma enan sim rakrege oka sen coe calaoen, banugićan; ado holanak tho nui hati akrińe reak katha do bacom metade, onate enan ńindarege oka sen coe calaoen. Khange raj doe bhagawenteye ruar calaoena.

Ado noa reak bhed do noa kana, Bulkate do adi lekako bhakaea, ńelme, lindhire bhagwa hõ banuktaea ar uni hõ ya hati kirińeye menleta, ar ńelme thik kathageye acuradea; ente uni hormore nisa tahẽkana; ado uni nisageye ror ocoledea; ado nisa mae odok calaoen, seye cetaoena, ado kajege uni hor do bae calaoengea? Ado ona iate handi ńũan horak mambla adi utar do bako saba; cedak? ente bin disage rorogoka, ona ghuri do cetko com rorketge, ar tayomte do bam disa dareaka; ma ńelme nui hor bul jhũkte hati hõ hatiye kirin adoyede tahẽkana. Ado nia golpo hõń purauketa.

[5] The tail added is the reflections of the narrator; but they represent Santal ideas on the subject.

meant, they told the man that the king had been saying this and this. The man then considered this matter with himself. When the sun was well up, the king came and asked him: "Look here, what has become of the man who said last night that he would buy my elephant. Come, let us fix a price for him."

"What is the name of the man?" he asked.

The king replied: "I did not ask him his name; but he belongs to this house; he spoke to me here from this court-yard entrance."

"O yes," the man said; "there was a man from somewhere, who came here, and he spoke about buying your elephant; but this man went away, who knows where, this morning at cock-crow; he is not here; you did not say anything to him yesterday about selling this elephant; therefore he went off this night some while ago." In this way the king was outwitted and went away.

The meaning[5] of the story is this: Tipsy people brag in many ways; observe, he has not even a strip of cloth to cover his nakedness, and this fellow said he would buy an elephant; and see, he answered him correctly, because he had a spirit in his body, and this spirit made him speak; afterwards the spirit went out, that is to say, the man became sober again; then did not that man actually go away? For this reason they do not enter seriously into the cases of people who were intoxicated by beer. Why? because any word spoken is spoken without consciousness; at such a time you may speak who knows what, and afterwards you are unable to remember. Remember, this man was buying even an elephant, when he was made bold by being intoxicated. There now I have finished this talk also.

54. Ghus jọmkateko gohak̔ họṛ reak̔.

Deko ar họṛ reak̔ katha. Mit̔ṭaṅ deko mahajọn dọ họṛ khatọk dena babọtteye ḷalisadea, ar uni họṛ dọ thoṛae lelha machagea, ar dena tinạk̔e dharaolet̔a, onako dọ jọtoye hala caba akat̔getaea. Adọ onae emae jọkheć goha bae dọhọ idilet̔koa; inạgetae uniak̔ lelha dọ. Adọe ẹm cabaket̔re hõ bạkigeye metaea, baṅma, Nunạk̔ unạk̔ am ṭhen iń ńama, dẹn ẹmọk̔me, baṅkhan laṅ ḷalisama. Adọ ona karọnte ḍherkin rọpọṛ baṛayena.

Adọ mahajọne mẹna, Acham ẹm akawadiń khan okorkotam goha dọ? Ọkọeko samaṅre tin titit̔em ẹm ạgu akawadińa, dẹnko goha ạgukotam; am samaṅreń kulikoa. Adọ goha bạnuk̔kotaete uni họṛ dọe bhagao ocok̔ kangea, bae ṛọṛ daṛeak̔ kana; ẹnte eskarregeye ẹm ạgu akawadea.

Khange uni họṛ dọ murukket̔teye mẹnket̔a, Acha besge, nunạk̔ iń emadere hõ bạkigeye metań kana; lanḍe ḷalisket̔ khange, ḷalis ocoae, inạ dọ ẹkkalte caba dapoṛok̔a. Ar uni họṛ dọ jumi jaega dọ khubge menak̔taea, ar mõṛẽ nahel jotdar họṛ kanae; adọ onka ać mọnre uni họṛ dọ onkae niṭket̔te mahajọn tuluć khub jhunạ jhunkin rọpọṛena.

---

[1] The following story is perhaps not a folktale proper, although by the Santals themselves treated as such. Whatever else may be said, it gives in certain respects an excellent description of how a court-case may be handled by the litigants.

[2] What is here told is a matter of very common occurrence. The Santals will borrow as much as they can get, and pay back when they can. This borrowing is one of their great faults. A money-lender wil try to get his money back, if not from the one then from the other; an exorbitant interest is always charged, which in other countries would come under the law of usury. When a Santal pays back a loan or part of it, he will not get any receipt for it. If the Santal or one of his friends can write, the money-lender will let him enter the loan in his account-books, and when it is paid back, he will also himself enter the sum in the accounts. It is further customary when a man pays back to have a number of witnesses present. If this precaution is not taken, the matter may develop as here mentioned. It would take us far away from the story, if these matters

54. A STORY OF PERSONS WHO BEAR WITNESS AFTER HAVING TAKEN BRIBES.

THIS is a story[1] of a deko and a Santal. A deko money-lender had brought a suit against a Santal debtor of his on account of some debts. Now the Santal was something of a fool; the debts he had been owing to him he had all paid back in full. But on the several occasions when he had paid his debts to him[2], he had not taken any witnesses along; this was his foolishness.

Although he had paid back in full, the money-lender constantly said[3] to him: "I shall have so and so much from you; pay, otherwise we two shall bring a suit against you." On account of this many words passed between them.

The money-lender would then say: "Very well, if you have paid me, where are your witnesses? In whose presence have you from time to time given me so and so much? now bring your witnesses; I shall ask them in your presence." But as he had no witnesses, the Santal was being defeated; he was unable to say anything, because he had paid him while alone with him.

The Santal then took courage and said: "All right, he says I am in his debt, although I have given him so much; confound it, if he brings a suit, let him do so; that will once for all make an end to this wretched matter." Now this man had very extensive agricultural lands; he was a man needing five ploughs[4] to cultivate his lands; having made up his mind as told, he had a violent quarrel with the money-lender.

---

should be treated as they really deserve. Many a tragedy has been caused by actions like what is here described, the end has been otherwise.

[3] A money-lender will try to get all he can out of a Santal by worry and bluff, and many will be taken in.

[4] Now-a-days a Santal's land is measured and recorded; but even now it is very common to hear them estimating their agricultural land by saying that so-and-so has one or more ploughs' land; he needs so many ploughs to get his land cultivated. They style it 'ploughs turning round' or 'being joined', i.e., yoked.

Khange uni mahajon do nui hoṛ upạrteye lạlisketa; ado parwanako jạriadete tạrik din hilok doe hạjirena, ar goha eman do bạnukkotaea. Ar uni deko do ṭaka emkate se ghus emkate pe hoṛe goha akatkoa, are lại ṭhik akawatkoa, baṅma, Ape do nonka onka nãhãk lạipe mente, baṅma, Ale salakrege nui hõ nunạk unạke em akawadea mente, ape do niạ kathage lạipe.

Ar onko pe hoṛ motore mit hoṛ doe lelha machagea; ado ona iạte calak jokhen hor horte onko goha do mit talaoe sikhạu idiyetkoa, baṅma, Ape do niạ kathage roṛtabonpe, niạ khon do alope eṭagtabona. Ar nãhãk dahe taben khub iṅ jom ocopea, ar hạṇḍi ñũ lạgit hõñ emapea. Nonka horreye kạbulako kana. Ar uni hoṛ do bạnukkotaete eskargeye calaoena, ar oṇḍe hõ eskarge mayak moyoke teṅgo baṛae kana.

Ado ona takrege mit hoṛ uni ṭhene sen sorenteye kulikedea, Henda baba, cet mokordoma kantama mente?

Ado uni hoṛe menketa, Mahajone lạlis akawadiṅa dena karonte, jotoṅ em cabakattaea, enre hõye lạlis akawadiṅa.

Ado uni hoṛe menketa, Goha menakkotama?

Adoe metadea, Goha do bạnukkotiṅa.

Ado uni hoṛe menketa, Den tobe khan barea ṭaka emaṅme, ar joto katha oṛe oṛpat lại cabawạṅme, ar iṅge gohaṅme, bebak nãhãk iṅ khalas ocokatama.

Ado uni hoṛe menketa, Achaṅ emama, ạikạ khalaskaṅme. Ado joto katha oṛ phede lạiadea, ar mõṛẽ nahelko joraoa, ona hõye lạiadea.

---

5 All know that such things are being practised. Witnesses are to be had for a few pence. There are more lies told and sworn to around the law-courts than elsewhere. Witnesses are tutored; to make it possible for them to stand cross-examination a scene may be acted before their eyes, so that they are able to tell what they have seen! Here the money-lender refers them simply to what they may have observed any day in his shop.

6 Apparently a Santal. It is not often, but examples are known of Santals having come so far down as to act as touts. A Santal may try to make use of such

This one consequently brought a suit against the Santal; a summons was served upon him, and he appeared at the court on the date and day fixed; but he had no witnesses. Now the deko had given money, that is to say bribes, and got three witnesses[5]; he had instructed them exactly what to say: "You shall say the following, viz., 'while we were present, he gave also this man so and so much'; you say just this."

Among these three men one was somewhat dull-witted; for this reason the money-lender was incessantly tutoring these witnesses, as they were passing along the road, saying: "You speak just this; do not say anything different from this. And presently I shall give you a full treatment with curds and flat rice, and I shall also give you beer to drink." In this manner he was giving promises, while on the road. As the Santal had no one to take along, he went himself alone, and there at the court he was also standing alone, looking quite lost.

Just then a man[6] came up to him: "I say, sir, what kind of a case have you?"

The Santal replied: "A money-lender has brought a suit against me on account of some debt; I have paid him all in full, still he has brought a suit against me."

"Have you any witnesses?" the man asked.

"No, I have none," the Santal replied.

The man then said: "In that case give me two rupees, and tell me everything from the beginning in detail, and make me your witness; I shall get you entirely acquitted presently."

The Santal then said: "All right, I shall give you; but have a care, get me acquitted." So he told him everything from the very beginning; he also told him that he worked five ploughs.

---

persons; he is not accustomed to the law-courts and will cling to any one who may promise help.

Adọ onakoye añjọm cabakeťtae khan barea ṭakaye kọekedea, are metadea, Ọkọeṭak̕ kantamae mahajọn, ar uniren goha, onko am dọ uduk̕ ṭhikạńme. Adọ sạriye uduk̕adea.

Adọ khange uni họṛ dọ goha akan họṛ ṭhene calao gọťenteye kuli baṛayeťkoa, ar ceťko cọye kuli mõñjeťkoa, enkate onkoak̕ mọne ńameťtakoa. Adọ uni lelha gohage ḍher dọe kuli baṛayede kana; khange mahajọn dọ uni ṭhen ạḍi họṛ sorok̕ kane ńẹlkeťko khan dọe mẹnkeťa, Nui goha dọ nãhãk̕ dhorageko bhañṭaoetińa.

Adọ onkaye bujhạukeť khan sẹn sorkateye metadea, Am dọń lạiam kana, họṛ dọ jãhãnạk̕geko metam onkoak̕ dọ añjọmtẹťge alom añjọmtakoa. Am dọ saheb okaye metama, inạ reak̕ rọṛ ruạṛaeme, ar am ṭhen họṛko hijuk̕ khan onko tuluć dọ alom galmaraoa, am dọ saheb okaye metama, inạge rọṛ ruạṛaeme; adọ onka uni lelha goha dọe sikhạu baṛakadea.

Adọ inạ miť ghuṛi tayọm khange phukạr hoe gọťentạkina; adọ hạkim dọ mahajọn ar uni họṛe kuli baṛakeťkina; adọ ona tayọm uni họṛren gohako phukạrkedea.

Adọ họlọp baṛakateko kulikedea, Tum in donaka keya hal janta hai, dhọrọm dhọrọm bọlọ, keya hal janta hai?

Adọ uni họṛe mẹnkeťa, Hạjur, ham tọ hal nãhī jante hai, keya jan, sal ka hal banaya hai, ki asọn ka banaya hai, ki dhao ka banaya hai, lekin pãc ṭhọ hal joṛta hai; so ham jante hai, kon kaṭ ka hal banaya hai, so ham nãhī jante hai.

---

7 Saheb used by a Santal practically always means a European. The judge here described is very likely a European; an experienced man will very soon know what kind of a case he has before him.

8 The language used is a not too good Hindi; the peculiarities of what is quoted may be due to the Santal narrator or may be a reproduction of something heard in court. Hindi is the court-language in the narrator's district, although Bengali may be permitted in certain courts.

9 Hindi has two words, both pronounced hal in the eastern parts of North India. The one is derived from the Arabic and conveys the meaning of state, condition, circumstance, case, &c. The other is derived from Sanskrit and means a plough. The word has been adopted in Santali in the former meaning; for the plough

When the man had heard all this to the end, he asked him for the two rupees and said to him: "Now show me plainly who is your money-lender and his witnesses." And, truth to tell, he did so.

Thereupon this man went up to those who were brought as witnesses and began to question them; he was asking them all kinds of funny things, and in this way he was getting at what was in their minds. He was asking especially the dull-witted witness a great many questions; when the money-lender saw that a great many people were assembling round him, he said: "This witness they will surely spoil for me presently."

With this in his mind he went up to him and said: "I am telling you this, whatsoever people say to you, don't listen to them at all. What the saheb[7] says to you, answer just that, and when people come to you, don't have any talk with them; just answer what the saheb will say to you." In this way he tutored this dull-witted witness.

A short while afterwards the case of these two was called on; the judge first examined the money-lender and the Santal; thereupon the Santal's witness was called.

After having administered the oath to him they asked him: "Was weisst du von der Sache[8] dieser zwei Leute? Sage die Wahrheit, was weisst du von der Sache."

The man then answered: "Ew. Hoheit, ich weiss nichts von den Pflügen[9]; wer weiss, ob die Pflüge von Sal[10] gemacht sind, oder von Ason[11] gemacht, oder von Dhao[12] gemacht; er spannt aber an fünf Pflügen Ochsen[13]; dass weiss ich; aus welchem Holz die Pflüge gemacht sind, dass weiss ich nicht."

the Santals have another word (n a h e l). Although the man is a Santal, or perhaps just therefore, he takes the second meaning to be meant.

10 S a l is the Hindi or Bengali word for what the Santals call s a r j o m, Shorea robusta, Gaertn., one of the most common and best timbers they have.

11 A s o n, in Santali called a t n a k', Terminalia tomentosa, W. & A.

12 D h a o, in Santali called h e s e l, Anogeissus latifolia, Wall., a tree with a very hard wood.

Adọ kathae, onkaye rọṛket́ khan uni dọko ḍhaka oḍokkedea; adọko kulikedea, Ar hõ goha menak̕kotama sẹ baṅ?

Adọe mẹnket́a, Bạnuk̕koa, ini eskargeae.

Adọ khange uni mahajọnren gohako phukạrena, pạhilkin dọ cet́ leka cọko kuli baṛaket́kintekin thirena.

Adọ uni lelha gohako phukạrkedea, adọ bọlọyente hạkim samaṅreye teṅgoyena; adọ capṛasiko họlọpede kana, metae kanako, Dhọrọm dhọrọm bọlọ. Khange uni họṛ dọ kathae, cet́ hõ bae rọṛet́a, thir akangeae. Adọ onka bar pe dhaoko metae kana, Dhọrọm dhọrọm bọlọ.

Adọ bae rọṛlet́ khan dọ hạkime mẹn gọt́ket́a, Keya, tum pagla hai?

Adọ kathae, uni họṛ hõye rọṛ gọt́ket́a, Keya, tum pagla hai?

Arhõ hạkime mẹn gọt́ket́a, Are ardali, isko nikal do.

Adọ kathae, uni họṛ hõ ti tulkate, sẹ uduk̕ateye mẹn gọt́ket́a, Are ardali, isko nikal do. Adọ khange inạk̕e mẹnlet́ khange ọṇḍẹn họṛ dọ bogeteko landaket́a, ar hạkim sudhạge khak̕ khak̕e landaket́a; adọ ẹnẹko ḍhaka oḍokket́koa, ar mọkọrdoma dọ ḍhismisena.

Adọ uni họṛ oḍokkate gohataeye metae kana, Oka lekam rọṛket́a? Bạṅ bujhạulet́a.

Adọ uni gohalen họṛe mẹnket́a, Durrẹ, eṭak̕re rọṛ iṅ mẹnlet́a ho, adọ hạkim eṭak̕reye kuli gọt́kidiṅa, nahelge lahareye kuli gọt́kidiṅa, Keya hal jante hai? Adọ am hõ thọ nahel dọ bam lạiạdiṅa, noa kaṭ sẹ ona jạt reak̕ nahelko dọṅ benao akat́a mẹnte.

---

13 See above note 4.

14 A judge has always a clerk; also others may be present; here a *caprasi*, a peon or messenger, is mentioned.

15 Generally the first words when administering the oath to people of this class. There are many stories about how the oath has been administered among the Santals. Many ways have been tried to find something that will impress their minds. In olden times, that is to say, now some two generations ago, before the magistrates had learnt Santali so as to understand it, they had got somebody to translate into the language an oath that ran like this *dọrọm dhọrọm*

When he had spoken in this way, they pushed him out; thereupon they asked the Santal: "Have you any other witnesses or not?"

He replied: "No, no others; he is the only one."

Thereupon the money-lender's witnesses were called; the two first ones were asked something or other, whereupon they had nothing more to say.

So they called the dull-witted witness; he came in and stood before the judge, and the court-servants[14] were administering the oath to him, saying: "Sage die Wahrheit"[15]. But the man, it is told, did not say a single word; he kept quiet. Again they spoke to him in the same way: "Sage die Warheit."

As he did not speak, the judge called out: "Was, bist du verrückt?"

Then, people tell, he answered at once: "Was, bist du verrückt?"

Again the judge called out: "Ordonanz[16], jage diesen hinaus."

Then this man also, lifting his hand up or pointing his finger said: "Ordonanz, jage diesen hinaus." And when he said this, all people present burst into laughter; the judge himself laughed boisterously. So they pushed them out, and the case was dismissed.

When he came out, the Santal asked his witness: "How did you speak? I did not understand it."

The man who had acted as a witness then said: "O dear, I intended to speak on something else; then the judge suddenly asked me about another matter; he asked me about the ploughs, viz., 'Was weisst du von den Pflügen?' Now you did not tell me anything about ploughs, that you had made the ploughs of this

---

rọṛme; ẹṛẹñ rọṛlekhan kul boṅgage jọmmea, translated: speak the truth; if I speak false, a tiger bonga will eat thee. This the witness was made to repeat exactly word for word. The Santals have had many a laugh over this; it was something to fear!

16 The Hindi word ardali is a corruption of the English 'orderly'.

Ado ona iąteń metadea, Sarjom reak̕ kan, bań do atnak̕, bań do hesel reak̕e benao akat̕; ona do bąń badaea, menkhan mõrẽ nahelte doye siok̕ kan gea, nią do hąkim samańre hõń lai akat̕gea. Ado am hõ ente ma se bujme, oka leka lań galmaraolet̕a, ar uni hąkim hor okareye eset̕ got̕kidińa, ado onde khonge note lai agu iń menlet̕a, ado inąk̕ khangeko thelao odok got̕kidińa. Ado ene bar ṭakae hajam daporana.

Ar uni mahajon hõ, kathae, aćren lelha gohae metae kana, Henda ho, kuliyet̕meako, cedak̕ bam rorlet̕a?

Ado uniye menket̕a, Amge com metadiń, hąkim okae metama, seye kulimea, inąge rorme. Ado hąkim okae rorlet̕, inąge thoń ror akat̕a. Caprasiye metań kana, Dhorom dhorom bolo; ado uniak̕ ror do landiń rora, se cak̕ iń ańjoma. Ado enanem metadińte uniak̕ ror do bąń hetaoat̕taea; ado hąkim okae rorket̕a, inage tho iń hõń ror akat̕a. Ado mahajongeye bhagao ocoyena. Ado rąiko ańjomadea, bańma, Mokordoma do dhismisentama.

Ado one onkate uni hor doe khalasena.

Oneyan ghus jom reak̕ katha doń mokońket̕a.

55. Jolha jątak̕ gam.

Mit̕tań jolha do ato atote sadom kirińe dãrã barae kan tahẽkana; orak̕ orak̕e kuliyet̕koa, Henda ho, sadom hoponpe ąkrińkoa?

Din hilok̕ onkageye kulikoa. Ado mit̕ṭeć orak̕reko metadea, Sadom hopon do bąnuk̕kotalea, sadom bele menak̕a. Ado koeko lągit̕e boloyena, metako kanae, Den ona sadom belege imąńpe.

---

[1] The following story was written down by Bhuju Murmu of Dhopahar.

[2] Jolha is the name of Muhammedan weavers, found in Bengal and Bihar; they have a reputation of being stupid. They are fairly common in this district and it may be questioned whether there is much foundation for the estimate in which they are held. The story as here told is probably borrowed; the details are, however, generally genuine Santal ones. The story has a few traits similar to what is told in the tale of Bajun and Jhore.

or that kind of wood. Therefore I answered him: 'Whether they are of sarjom[10] or of atnak[11] or of hesel[12], this I do not know; but he is ploughing with five ploughs'; this I have stated also before the judge. Now also understand how we two talked together, and then how the judge suddenly stopped me; I had intended to tell everything from that point; but when this much had been said, they suddenly pushed me out." But he had digested two rupees the wretch.

The money-lender also, it is told, spoke to his dull-witted witness: "Look here, I am asking you, why did you not speak?"

He replied: "Why, you yourself said to me, 'What the judge says to you or asks you, speak just that'. So what the judge said, I said just the same. The court-servant said to me: 'Sage die Wahrheit'; so I'll be blowed if I should say anything; why should I listen to that? Because you told me so in the morning, I did not pay any attention to him; then what the judge said, just that I also said. So the money-lender was defeated; and they let him hear the court's order: "Your case has been dismissed."

In this way the Santal was acquitted.

So there I have finished the story about taking bribes.

55. THE STORY OF A JOLHA[1].

A Jolha[2] was going about from village to village to buy a horse[3]; he was enquiring in every house: "I say, have you colts to sell?"

Every day he asked people the same question. Then he came to a house, where they said to him: "We have no colts; but we have a pony-egg." So he went in to them and said: "Please, give me that pony-egg."

---

[3] The Muhammedans are generally horsedealers.

Adǫ onko hoṛ dǫ mitṭaṅ bora bora kohṇḍako tiok̕ akat̕ tahẽkana; ona kohṇḍako oḍoṅadea, arko metae kana, Nẹ, noa bele dǫ sadǫmak̕ kana, pichạuṛire ghẽṭme khub kajakte, baṅkhanem paskaoa; gaṛhao bele kana, ar okare hõ alom dǫhǫ baṛaea; baṅkhan sadǫm hǫpǫn busạk̕kateye dạṛa.

Tǫbẹ inạ katha aṅjǫmkate uni jǫlha dǫ kohṇḍa jǫ gǫk̕kateye mohṇḍayena; ać dǫe mẹnket̕a, Sadǫm bele kangea jạnić. Ạḍi ãṭẹ rạskạyena, hǫrre jãhãekoko kuliyede kana, Cet̕em moṭraket̕a hǫ? Adǫe metako kana, Sadǫm bele kana.

Adǫko metae kana, Henda hǫ, sadǫm dǫko belea? Unreye metako kana, Bako beleyet̕tegeko hǫpǫnok̕ kan khan, cekateko bạḍok̕ kana tǫbẹ? Inạko rǫṛ baṛakategeye parǫmok̕ kana, ar onko hǫṛ dǫko landawae kana.

Calak̕ calak̕te mit̕ṭẹć birteye bǫlǫyena; ona moṭra dǫhǫkate racate lạgit̕e duṛuṗ akana; oka sẹn khon cǫṅ mit̕ṭaṅ toyo dǫ hẹćente ona moṭra dǫe ji baṛayet̕ tahẽkana; ona kohṇḍa dǫ dǫhǫe jǫkhẹnrege posak̕ akana; adǫ racate khon beret̕kateye ṅẹlket̕ posak̕ akan, ar ǫṇḍẹ khonge mit̕ṭaṅ toyoe dạṛket̕a. Adǫ uni jǫlha dǫe mẹnkẹt̕a, Pasẹć sadǫm hǫpǫngeye dạṛket̕tiṅ. Ạḍi ãṭẹ uh uhket̕a are hahawae kana teṅgo ocoye lạgit̕; onka mẹnkateye lagakedea, mẹnkhan baṅgeye tiok̕ daṛeae kana, sara dine khudạukedere hõ; ṅindạk̕ kanre hõ bae bataolet̕a, ḍher ṅindạ hạbiće khudạukedere hõ bae saṗ daṛeadea.

Oṛak̕te ruạṛ jǫkhẹn dǫ khube ṅindạyena; hǫrre kombṛoko ṅamkedea, adǫko metae kana, Ǫkǫe kanam hǫ?

Unre uni hǫṛ dǫe mẹnket̕a, Iṅge hǫ, peṛa hǫṛ. Adǫko metae kana, Okatem sẹnlena hǫ? Unre ar hõe mẹnket̕a, Ẹho, mit̕ṭẹć sadǫm hǫpǫniṅ khudạuede ṭahẽkana. Adǫko metae kana, Okarem ṅamledea? Adǫe lạiat̕koa. Belegeṅ kiriṅlet̕a. Adǫko metadea, Cele

[4] The word used conveys the meaning of a fruit, that is withering, turning bad and falling off, before it is ripe. Pumpkins are grown everywhere; very frequently the climber is found running over the roof of the small houses.

Now these people had taken down a pumpkin, that was turning bad[4]; they brought this out to him and said: "Here, take this; this egg is a pony-egg; pack it very carefully up in your outer garment, otherwise you will let it slip; it is an egg in which the young has already been developed, do not put it down anywhere; otherwise the foal will be hatched and run off."

Having heard this the Jolha took the pumpkin up on his shoulder and started; himself he thought: It is likely a pony-egg. He was full of joy, and when anybody meeting him on the road asked him: "What is it you have packed up there?" he would say to them: "It is a pony-egg."

When they asked him: "Look here, do ponies lay eggs?" he answered: "If they do not lay eggs and get youngs, how do they multiply then?" When they had talked that much, he was passing and left them behind, and the people were laughing at him.

As he walked along, he came into a forest. Having put his bundle down, he was sitting down to pass water; just then a jackal came there from somewhere or other and was nosing at the bundle; now the pumpkin had been split open, when it was put down. When the Jolha stood up, he saw that the pumpkin was split open, and that a jackal was running away. He then said: "Perhaps it is my young colt that has run away." He cried oh! oh! and shouted stop! stop! to him all he could, to make him stand; calling out in this way he chased him, but was utterly unable to overtake him, although he pursued him the whole day; even when it was becoming night, he did not heed it; but although he pursued him until late night, he was unable to catch him.

As he was returning home, it became very late night, and some thieves met him on the road; they said. "Who are you?"

He answered: "It is I, friend." So they asked him: "Where have you been?" Then he told these also: "O you, I was chasing a young colt." They asked him: "Where did you get it?" He told them: "I bought an egg." They asked him: "What kind

belem kiriṅleta? Adoe metatkoa, Sadom bele kiriṅkateṅ aguyet tahẽkana, racate mente noa birreṅ doholeta, unrege busakenteye darketa.

Ado unreko metadea, arko dhomkaokedea, Dhur boka, sadom doko belea? Uni jolhae ror ruarketa, Bele baṅ khanko cekaea. Adoko bujhauadea, Sadom do baṅko belea, ereketmeako; dela alele idimea. Adoe menketa, Okatepe idiṅa? Metadeako, Sadom kombro. Menkhan bae patiauk kana; metako kanae, Okarepe ṅawaṅa? Adoko metae kana, Dela se, ale tuluć gatekme, tinak sadomem cekakoa.

Ado uni hore menketa, Acha, delabon. Adoko calaoena mittaṅ kisar orakre kombroe lagit; dealko mak bhugakketa, arko metadea, Do, bolokme ar bhage bhage jinis aguime.

Adoe boloyen khan uni jolha do mitteć hatake ṅam odokketa are metako kana, Nõkõe. Ado onko do bai baiteko khae khoeae kana, Noa do bhage jinis kana? Do, arhõ bolokme, khub bhari jinis aguime. Uni jolha do sen ruarkate janteye aguketa, are metako kana, Nõkõe. Ado onkoko metae kana, Dhut lelha, toberege enan doko ereletmea. Noa do bhari jinis kana? Noa ma jante kan; do arhõ bolokme ar khub sapha jinis aguime. Uni doe boloyente tukućre dakae ṅamketa, ar ona daka do had bade aguketa. Unre ona orakren horko disakedea, arko laga odokkedea. Onko kombro ma jotoko darketa, uni doko ṅir bagiadea; tayom tayomte, Hape ho, hape ho, menkateye dar idiyeta; laga tiokketkoae. Adoko metae kana, Am do bale gatemea, bhage bhage jinis bam odoketa. Adoe metako kana, Acha nit doṅ odok adoea. Ado onae menketkhan doko gatekedea.

Ado mitteć raj orakteko calaoena kombro; onde hõ dealko la bhugakketa, ado unigeko bolo ocokedea, khange bolokate janteye

[5] The word used actually means 'heavy', but may also be used in the meaning of heavily priced, valuable. The Jolha naturally takes the common meaning.

[6] A hand-mill is found in many houses; the nether millstone is fixed in the ground; the upper one is always easily removable.

of an egg did you buy?" He replied: "I bought a pony-egg and was bringing it along; I wanted to pass water, so I put it down here in this forest; just then it was hatched and ran away."

So they spoke to him and rebuked him: "Shut up, you idiot! Do ponies lay eggs?" The Jolha replied: "If they do not lay eggs, what do they do?" So they explained it to him: "Ponies do not lay eggs; they have cheated you; come with us, we shall take you along." "Where will you take me?" he asked. "To steal ponies," they replied. But he did not believe it and said to them: "Where will you find me any?" They said: "Come along with us; be our companion; what will you do with ponies?"

The man then said: "All right, come along." So they went to steal in the house of a rich man; they cut an opening in the wall and said to the man: "Do, go inside and bring precious things out."

When he had got inside, the Jolha found a winnowing-fan and brought that out, saying to them: "Here, look at this." The others whispered softly to him: "Is this a precious thing? Do, get in again; bring out some very weighty[5] things." The Jolha went inside again and brought a millstone[6], saying: "Here, look at this." But the others said to him: "Tut! you fool; so we can understand that they cheated you a while ago. Do you call this a weighty thing? Why, this is a millstone; now, get in again and bring some very clean things out." He went inside and discovered some cooked rice in a pot, and he brought this out with a rattle. Then the inmates of the house became aware of him and drove him out. The thieves fled all of them, and the Jolha they left behind; he was running after them calling out to them: Wait, you! wait, you! He followed, until he overtook them; but they said to him: "We shall not let you come in company with us; you do not bring precious things out." He answered them: "All right, now I shall do so, dash it." As he said so, they again took him with them.

Thereupon they went to a king's house to steal; there also they dug a hole in the wall and made the Jolha go inside. He entered

oḍokḱkeťa are metako kana, Nõk̇õe ho. Adoko ńelketa, bhari jinis do baṅ kana. Adoko metae kana, Huṭ, am do baṅle gatemea; enan hõ jantegem oḍoṅaťlea ar nit hõ, men daṛme ale ṭhen khon do. Adoe metaťkoa, Acha nit do bhage jinisgeń aguia.

Bolokate miťṭaṅ ḍhulkiye ńamketa, ar ona ru ruteye oḍokena onko ṭhen; ado onkoko manayede kana, metae kanako, Alom ruia, baṅkhanko disaia. Adoko metae kana, Noa do cedaḱem agukeťa? noa dobo joma? Ado uni hoṛe menketa, Tobe khan ceť iń aguia? Dela bon joto hoṛgebon boloḱa. Ado uni doe lahayen takoa, ayur aderkeťkoae; ać do miťṭaṅ kandhare tumdaḱe ńamketa ar rurui dhurauena are hohoako kana, Nõk̇õe ho, bhage jinisiń ńamketa.

Enre hõ uni rajaḱ oṛaḱren hoṛ do bako disayeťa; onko kombroko modren miť hoṛ senkate uni hoṛe manaye kana, khae khoekateye metae kana, Alom ruia, baṅkhanko sap̣bona.

Khange uni lamoṭ hoṛ do adi ńinda hoeyenkhan reṅgećkedea. Rajren miťṭaṅ mahrae tahẽkana; uni mahra do toa duhaukate ać ṭhengeye basaṅ dohọ akať tahẽkana; uni hoṛ do mahrae gitić oṛaḱteye boloyena; ńelkeťae, miť kara toa culhareko conda akaťa; caole ńamketťe ona toareye khadleketa, dakae isinketa, jomkeťae.

Mahra tikin do haṛam budhi parkomrekin gitić akan tahẽkana; ado uni maejiu do aćaḱ tire bohoḱe lade akaťtaea balis leka, ar ti talka do ataṅ akan leka ńeloḱ kana; uni lamoṭ hoṛ doe hudisketa, pase nui aimai do iṅge dakae koeyeń kan. Khange ona tiregeye loadea lolo daka. Uni aimai doe loyen khane ńir bereťena, are kaumauketa; khange joto kombroko daṛketa, ar ać do, pacri bhitrire busup̣ cake tahẽkana, ona coṭreye dećena; kombro do ceť hõ bako idileta.

---

[7] The small drum called ḍhulki is made of earthenware, having a slightly tapering body covered with skin at both ends. It is played with the hands. It resembles the tumdaḱ (see below), but is much smaller.

[8] The tumdaḱ is the Santal dancing-drum; see Vol. I, p. 212, note 17.

[9] The word used, mahra, is the name of a low Hindu caste, otherwise generally called goala; one of their special caste employements is the herding of cattle.

[10] It is customary just to boil the milk after milking; it is really a kind of sterilizing. They have a special word for this, basaṅ.

and brought a millstone out saying to them: "Here, look at this you!" They saw that it was no precious thing and said to him: "Tut! we shall not take you along with us; a while ago you brought a millstone out to us and now also the same; get off, run away from us." He replied: "All right, now then I shall bring out some excellent things."

Having entered again he found a small drum[7], and drumming on this he came out to them; they remonstrated with him and said: "Don't drum, otherwise they will become aware of us." "Why have you brought this?" they asked; "shall we eat this?" The man then said: "What shall I bring out then? Come, let all of us go inside." So he entered first and guided them in. He himself discovered a dancing-drum[8] in a room and commenced to drum and call out to them: "Here, you, hear this; I have found an excellent thing."

In spite of all the inmates of the king's house did not become aware of them; one of the thieves went and remonstrated with the Jolha and said to him in a whisper: "Don't drum, otherwise they will catch us."

Now as it had become very late, far into the night, this madcap felt hungry. The king had a cowherd[9], and this cowherd had milked the cows and, having boiled[10] the milk, he had kept it with himself; the Jolha entered the house where the cowherd was sleeping, and saw that they had put a large iron-pan full of milk on the fireplace. So he found some rice and put this into the milk, boiled it and ate it.

The cowherd and his wife were sleeping on a bedstead; the woman lay with her head on her arm as on a pillow, and her hand looked as if she had put it out to receive something; it struck the madcap: "Perhaps this woman is asking me for rice." So he ladled some hot rice into that hand. The woman was burnt, got up in a hurry and raised the alarm. All the thieves fled, and this man — there was a rick of straw inside the enclosure — himself mounted this; the thieves did not take anything away.

Uni hoṛ do busup coṭrege luṭuk̓ luṭuk̓e gitić aṅgak̓ kana; setak̓ jokhen oḍokok̓ lagit̓e asbasaoena; khangeko ńamkedea arko hohoket̓a, Nũk̓ũi ho kombṛo. Uni hoṛ doe menket̓a, Baṅ ho, kombṛo doń baṅ kana. Onko hoṛ doko menket̓a, Ma ho tole ma ar dale ma!

Uni hoṛ doe roṛ ruaṛket̓a, Alope daleńa, alope toleńa, in do kombṛo doń baṅ kana; kombṛo boroṅko hećlen tahẽkana, onkogeko aguledińa. Adoko metae kana, Kombṛom baṅ kan khan cekatem gatelena? Menket̓ae, Iń do sadom kirińiń hećlena, unre kombṛoko ńamkidińa, arko metadińa, Delale gatemea. Khange eskarenteń hec aḍoyena onko sãote; adoko metaṅ kana, De kombṛole idimea, bogeń hećen, baṅkhan ape oṛak̓ reak̓ jinis do sanamko idi cabaketapea.

Raj hõko paṭiauena, metae kanako, Sarige, bhage am reṅgećtem dakaket̓te kombṛom lagaket̓koa. Unreye menket̓a, Hẽ ente tire lolo dakaṅ loadea disa ocoyea mente; hohole khan ma onko kombṛoko ruhet̓kiń. Mit̓ jaegare nonkagele bololena, unreń gulmallet̓a, unreko ruhet̓lidińa, onate nia dhao do baṅ hoholet̓a.

Khange onko rajko menket̓a, Acha uḍim bogeket̓a, baṅkhan aḍi utar jinisko idiketalea, thari baṭi, loṭa emanteak̓ko, aema jinisko sajaolet̓ tahẽkana. Adoko hohoadea, Acha dela notege hijuk̓me. Mit̓ṭen pacri bhitri senko hoho aderkedea, onḍeye ńelket̓koa, aema utar sadomko tol akat̓koa; adoe metako kana, Noko sadom dope akrińkoa se baṅ? Baṅkhan dini mit̓ṭeć imaṅpe, tinak̓pe damaea? Adoko kulikedea, Tinak̓ ṭaka menak̓tama? Uni hoṛ doe menket̓a, Pea ṭaka menak̓tińa. Adoko metae kana,

[11] The word for 'king' is in this story always put in the plural; this may be to give an indefinite sense, or to show that there were several shareholders.

[12] The sum of money is naturally fanciful. I have, however, seen miniature nags sold for Rs. 10; a couple of generations ago, I have been told, cows were priced one rupee per half seer (about one pint) of milk they gave, and as they very seldom gave more than a couple of pints, if so much, the price was on a par with that.

Now he spent the night in anxiety on the top of the straw-rick until dawn. He was greatly perplexed how he should get out in the morning; ultimately they discovered him and called out: "Here he is, here is the thief!" The man said: "No, good people, I am not a thief." The people called out: "Set to, let him be tied and get a thrashing!"

The man answered: "Don't beat me, don't tie me; I am not a thief; rather some thieves were here, and they brought me here." They then asked him: "If you are not a thief, how is it that they took you along with them?" He replied: "I had come to buy a pony; just then the thieves met me and said to me: 'Come along, we shall take you along with us.' And as I was absolutely alone, I came with them, how could I help it; they said to me: 'Come, we shall take you with us to steal'; it was good I came, otherwise they would have taken away whatever is found in your house, all of it."

The king[11] and his people also believed this and said to him: "Verily, it was fortunate that you were hungry and cooked food and drove the thieves away." "Quite so," he said; "I ladled hot rice into her hand to make her aware of them; if I had called out, the thieves might have scolded me. In one place we entered in the same way as here; then I made a noise, and they scolded me; therefore I did not call out this time."

The king then said: "All right, you have acted exceedingly well; otherwise they might have got away with any amount of goods belonging to us, brass-plates and brass-cups, brass-pots and such things; they had arranged to take a large number of things away." Thereupon they called him: "All right, come here." They called him inside an enclosure, and there he saw an immense number of horses tied up. So he asked them: "Will you sell these horses or how? Else let me have one; how much will you take for one?" They asked him: "How much money have you?" He replied: "I have three rupees[12]." "Is that all you have?"

Inąk̕getama? Adoe metako kana, Hẽ, raj, inąk̕getiń; reṅgeć hoṛ kąnąń, okareń ńama? Unre raj do bujhąukateko metadea, Acha, baṅle damam kana, ma enkatege idiyem, jāhāeṭak̕geyem khusiae kan bin damtege idiyem; am ịate ente ạḍi utạr jinis baṅcaoentalea. Khange uni jolha do ạḍi khusiyente sadome tolkedea are tiạk oḍoṅkedea.

56. Rajren sipạhi.

Miťṭaṅ raje tahẽkana ar uniren miťṭaṅ sipạhi. Uni sipạhi do pạcri duạr ṭhene pahraea; ado jāhāe hoṛ jāhānak̕ ạkriń lạgiť raj ṭhenko ạgui khan doe metakoa, Noa jinis tinạk̕ damok̕tapea, ona reak̕ adha dampe emaṅ khan, enḍekhan raj ṭhen bhitri moholteń bolo ocoapea; ar bape emaṅ khan do ohoń bolo ocolepea. Ado cekaeako becara? Reṅgeć hoṛ bako ạkriṅle khan ma din gujrạn baṅ calak̕tako. Ado khange adha damko gok̕aea, tobeko bolok̕a. Nonkage uni sipạhi do je kichu onḍe calak̕ hoṛ do, sanam hoṛgeye onkakoa.

Ado khange miť dhao do miťṭaṅ kẽoṭa maraṅ utạr hakoe jhạlikedea; adoe menkeťa, Nui hako do raj ṭhen iń ạkriṅea, ḍher dam nāhāk̕ hoyok̕tiṅa. Onka bundis baṛakate uni kẽoṭa doe idikedea. Ado ona pạcri duạr ṭhećren sipạhi doe metae kana, Okatem bolok̕ kana bin hukumte do? Hape teṅgonme.

Ado uni kẽoṭa doe menkeťa, Raj ṭhen nui hako ạkriṅe lạgiť iń bolok̕ kana.

---

1 The well-to-do people, naturally also the 'kings' or landlords, do not live so as to let people have immediate access to them. One has to enter through an outer entrance, where watch is kept. Here the situation is a 'palace' or large houses surrounded by a wall. But the 'king' does not seem to be so very important, since he apparently has only one sentry and admits people with food-stuffs to his presence.

2 Kẽoṭa, is the name, as pronounced by the Santals, of a Hindu fisherman caste.

they asked. "Yes, raja," he replied; "that is all I have; I am a poor man, where shall I get money?" The king's people understood how it was and said to him: "All right, we shall not take anything from you; please, take one for nothing, whichever you like take him free of charge; you see, because of you a very large number of goods has been saved for us." The Jolha was utterly pleased and binding a pony he led him out and away.

56. THE KING'S SENTRY.

THERE once lived a king, and he had a sentry. This man was keeping watch at the outer wall[1] entrance; and when anybody brought anything to the king to sell, he used to say to them: "If you give me half of what this may fetch, I shall let you enter the inner quarters to the king, and if you will not give me, I shall certainly not let you in." Then what could they do, the poor people? If poor people did not sell, they would have no means of supporting themselves; so they promised to give him half the price; thereupon they would pass in. In this way this sentry acted towards every one who came there.

So it one day happened that a fisherman[2] caught in his net[3] a very large fish, and he said: "This fish I shall sell to the king; I shall get a good price for it." With such thoughts the fisherman took the fish there. But the sentry at the outer wall entrance said to him: "Where are you entering without permission? Wait, stop there."

The fisherman replied? "I am going in to sell this fish to the king."

[3] These fishermen mostly use nets of sorts to catch the fish; a cast net is most commonly used in these parts.

Adoe metadea, Nui hako tinąke damoktam, ona reak adha dam emańme. Cet kichu am do bam badaea? Nun din khonem ąguyetkore hõ bam badaea? Ąnąrik kangeam?

Khange adoe menketa, E baba, badae doń badaegea, menkhan, baba, am then iń nehõrok kana, nią dhao do ikąkańme. Nui hako reak purą dam iṅge hatao ocoańme; alo onka dom pajhetińa; ikąkańme bare. Jähã hilok iń ąguleko khan do unre doń emamgea, ohoń eremea; menkhan nią dhao do ikąkańme. Menkhan sipąhi do bae ańjomlettaea; unąke nehõrenre hõ bae ikąledea.

Ado khange uni kẽoṭa ać monereye bujhąu barakéta, Judi nui hako bąń ąkriṅle khan do nãhãke seaktińa. Nonka hudis barakate ado bąpuṛićkate adha dame gokadea.

Khange ado bhitri moholte raj ṭhene boloyena. Ado raje kulikedea, Cele ho, okatem heć akana?

Adoe menketa, Hakoń ągu akadea; nui hako reak dam emańme.

Adoe metadea, Nui hako do tinąkem damea?

Ado uni kẽoṭae menketa, Ią, raja saheb, nui hako reak dam do mit sae ṭheṅga dal.

Ado khange raje menketa, Henda kẽoṭa, cedak onka dom dame kana? Nonkan dam do nun jug iń hoyok kana, menkhan bań ańjom akata. Onate ądi hahaṛań ańjomet kana. Mase noa reak bhed bhaṅgaoańme. Noa do cet lekan dam kana?

Adoe ląiae kana, Noa reak bhed do noa kana: jãhãe horge jãhãnak ąkriń lągit am ṭhenle hijuk khan, uni pącri duąrren sipąhi do bae bolo ocoalea. Adoe metalea, Noa jinis tinąk damoktape, ona reak adha dam emańpe, endekhan iń bolo ocoapea. Onkae metalea, ado adha damle gokaea, tobe enec am ṭhenle bolo daṛeak kana. Ar teheń hõ adha dam ąuriń gokae habić do bae bolo ocoań kan tahẽkana, onate onka doń dam akadea; mit sae

[4] As is well known, behaviour like that of the sentry is of common occurrence, one of the very real hindrances to get sound administration introduced. Often this behaviour is winked at by the superior employers, or even counted on in lieu of pay. The 'king' of our story is possibly of another stamp.

The sentry then said: "Whatever will be the price given for this fish, half of it you give to me[4]. Don't you know anything at all? For so long a time you have brought fish, still don't you know this? Are you posing as a stranger?"

The other one replied: "O sir, of course I know it, but, sir, I am imploring you, let me off this time. Let me get the full price of this fish; don't worry me in this way; let me alone. Some other day when I bring fish, I shall give you; but let me off this time. But the sentry would not listen to him; although he implored him so much, he did not let him off.

The fisherman turned this matter over in his mind and said to himself: "If I do not sell this fish, it will presently turn bad for me." Having thought thus the poor fellow promised to give him half the price.

Thereupon he entered the inner quarters to the king, who asked him: "Well, what is your destination?"

He replied: "I have brought a fish; give me the price of this fish."

"How much will you take for this fish?" he asked him.

"Well, raja saheb," the fisherman replied, "the price of this fish is one hundred blows with a stick."

"Look here, fisherman," the king said, "why do you put such a price on it? I have been living so long a time, but such a price I have never heard mentioned. Therefore it sounds so strange in my ears. Please explain this to me. What manner of a price is this?"

So he told him: "The meaning of it is this: if any of us come to you to sell anything, the sentry at the outer entrance will not let us come in. He says to us: 'Give me half of what this will fetch, then I shall let you go in.' That is the way he speaks to us; so we promise him half the price; then only may we have access to you. And to-day also he would not let me pass in, until I had promised to give half the price; therefore I have put

ṭheṅgam dalliń khan, ẹnḍẹkhan ona reak̕ adha, bar isi gẹl ṭheṅga dọ unim dalea.

Khange adọ noa kathae ańjọm cabaket̕ khan, raj dọe raṅgaoente uni sipạhige mit̕ sae bẽte dalkedea, ar cạkri khon hõe barkhas utạrkedea.

Inạk̕gea katha dọ.

57. Koṛa dọ ać budhiteye bạhuana.

Mit̕ṭaṅ atore bar boeha menak̕kina; mẹnkhan maraṅić dọ bạhu menaetae, ar huḍińić dọ bako bạhu akawadea. Adọ unkin maraṅićtikin dọ haṛam buḍhikin galmaraojoṅa. Rinićtẹt̕e mẹna, Huḍińić dọe harayena, malaṅ bạhuaea.

Adọe rọṛ ruạṛaea, Aćren hopọnge hapẹne bạhuaea.

Adọ uni rinićtẹt̕ dọe mẹnjoṅa, Durrẹ! Cet̕e mẹnet̕a? Aćren hopọnge hapẹne bạhuaea. Ać ạuriye bạhujoṅa, are mẹnet̕a, Aćren hopọngeye bạhuaea. Adọe guni bhạbik̕a rinićtẹt̕ dọ, Dingeń metaea, Huḍińić dọlaṅ bạhuaea, mẹnkhan dinge inạgeyẹ mẹn ruạṛańa.

Khange mit̕ din dọ arhõ onkagekin rọpọṛ kana huḍińić ńutumte. Adọ uni hẹrẹltẹt̕ dọ inạko rọṛ baṛakate peṛa horọk̕e calaoena. Adọ khange huḍińić dọ gạiye gupia. Khange tikinena, adọ gạiye aḍaket̕koa. Adọ dak̕e taṅadea ini hilittẹt̕ge. Adọ jaṅgakoe ạbuk bọlọyena, adọ mańjane emadea. Jọm baṛakate uni koṛa dọe jirạu

[1] This story was written down by Sạṅkhi Hãsdak̕, the wife of the local postmaster. She is dead now long ago. With its several peculiarities it has a special interest as being told by a woman.

[2] According to Santal custom it is the duty of the elder brother, if the father is dead, to make the necessary arrangements for the marriage of his younger brothers. The woman, as is often the case, here takes the initiative.

[3] The cattle here naturally graze the whole year round. At about noon the cattle is always taken to a place where they can lie down and chew the cud for a couple of hours. This gives the cowherds an opportunity of getting food and

such a price on the fish; if you give me one hundred blows with a stick, then you will have to give him half, two scores and ten blows."

When he had heard this matter to the end, the king became angry and let the sentry get one hundred blows with a cane and dismissed him once for all from his service.

The story is thus much.

57. THE YOUNG MAN WHO GOT A WIFE THROUGH HIS WITS[1].

In a certain village two brothers were living; the elder one was married, but for the younger one they had not got a wife. The elder brother and his wife[2] were talking together; the wife was saying: "The little one has grown up, let us get a wife for him."

The husband answered: "His own child will some day procure him a wife."

Then his wife said: "O dear! what is he talking? His own child will some day procure him a wife! He has not as yet got a wife, and he says: 'His own child will procure him a wife'." The wife was turning this over in her mind with anxiety: "Every day I am saying to him: 'Let us get a wife for the little one'; but day after day he answers me back just that."

Then it one day happened that they again had some words over the younger brother; and after having said the same thing the man went somewhere on a visit to friends. Now the younger brother was herding their cows, and when it became midday, he gave the cattle their midday rest[3]. At home his sister-in-law poured out some water for him, whereupon he washed his feet and went inside, and she gave him his midday meal. After he

also a little rest. Sometimes food is taken out to them, sometimes they will go home to eat.

akan tahẽkanre hilitteť dọ seye gọsẹć baṛayede kana. Adọ gọsẹć baṛa gọsẹć baṛa hilitteť dọ hiḍir hiḍir mẽť daǩ jọrọǩ kantaea, koṛawaǩ dearege jọrọǩ kana. Adọ uni koṛa dọe ạikạu gọťkeťa. Adọ khangeye mẹnkeťa, Ạiyo! ceť iạtem raǩeťa, ma lạiaṅme. Noa reaǩ bhẹd baṅ tahẹn khan, ọhọm raǩlea. Ma lạiaṅme. Enaṅ hõṅ ṅẹlkeťmea, maṅjanem emadiṅa arem raǩeťa. Enaṅ bạṅ kulileťmea. Ma nitoǩ dọ lạiaṅme, ceť iạtem raǩeťa?

Adọ hilitteť dọe mẹnkeťa, Iạ, ceť iạteṅ raǩeťa? Iṅ dọ dadam iṅ metae kana, Huḍiṅić dọe harayena, malaṅ họṛaea. Adọe metadiṅa, Aćren họpọnge hapẹne bạhuaea.

Uni koṛa dọ ona kathae aṅjọman khan, hape hapete aćaǩ sapaṗe ṅamkeťtaea, are moṭrakeťteye oḍoṅ calaoena disomte. Khange ạḍi sạṅgiṅ disomteye calaoena. Adọ calaǩ calaǩte miťṭaṅ haṛam tuluće dapramena. Adọe họhọae kana, Ẹ baba, Ẹ baba, tạṅgiṅtalaṅme. Uni haṛam dọe sẹn idiǩ kangea. Khange ạḍiye dạṛ idikeťa are khudạu tioǩkedegea. Adọe metae kana, Henda baba, unạǩ iṅ họhọam kana, cedaǩ bam tạṅgiṅ kana?

Adọ haṛame mẹnkeťa, Iạ bạbu, iṅ dọṅ mẹnkeťa, Nui dọ nãhãǩ koṛa họṛ ar iṅ dọ haṛam họṛ; nui tuluć dọ nãhãǩ iṅ daṛeaǩa? Iṅ dọṅ sẹn jarwaǩa. Onka mẹnkate baṅ tạṅgiyeťmea.

Khange uni koṛae rọṛ ruạṛkeťa, Hẽ baba, amem rọṛkeť dọ sạri ma sạrige, iṅ tuluć ma daṛe ma ọhọm daṛelen. Mẹnkhan, baba, ọnẹko mẹnge, Miťṭaṅ haṛam họṛ tahẹn ar buḍi era tahẹn dọ ạḍi subitạ. Nẽkẽ họrtelaṅ calaǩ kana, am dọ hutkạm emanteaǩ jạṛem uṭhạutalaṅa.

Ẹnẹ adọ emanteaǩkin kupuli kana. Haṛam hõe kuli gọťkedea, Am dọ, bạbu, tin sạṅgiṅem calaǩa?

---

[4] A not very uncommon operation, often gone through coram publico. The Santals are certainly not worse than other Indians in this respect; but the process is now and then quite a necessary one.

[5] Lit. 'give or procure a person', used about procuring a wife for

had had his food, the young man was lying down to rest, while his sister-in-law was picking vermin[4] out of his head. While she was occupied with this, her tears were trickling down and falling on the back of the young man. The young man suddently felt this and said: "O dear dear! why are you crying? Do tell me. If there were not some cause for this, you would surely not cry. Do tell me. A while ago also I saw you; you gave me my midday meal and were crying. At that time I did not ask you; but tell me now, why are you crying?"

His sister-in-law then said: "You so-and-so, why am I crying? I am constantly saying to your brother: 'The little one has grown up; let us get him a mate[5]'. But he said to me: His own child will some day procure him a wife'."

When the young man heard this, he quietly, without saying a word, collected his things and, having made it into a bundle, went out and away; he went to a country very far away. As he was walking along, he met with an elderly man and called out to him: "I say, father, father! wait for me!" But the old man walked along, whereupon the young man commenced to run and chased him, until he overtook him. Then he said to him: "I say, father, I am calling out to you so loudly; why don't you wait for me?"

The old man replied: "Well, young man, I thought, this one is a young man and I am old; shall I be able to be a match for him? I shall go along ahead. This is the reason why I have not been waiting for you."

The young man answered: "Yes, father, what you said is quite true; you would certainly not be a match for me. But father, as people say: 'There being an old man and a venerable lady is very satisfactory.' Here we two are walking along the road; you will in the circumstances be able to start talk on sundry matters."

Consequently they commenced to ask each other questions; the old man also asked: "You, my young fellow, how far are you going?"

Uni do̱e me̱nketá, Iń do̱, baba, a̱ḍi sa̱ṅgińgeń se̱noḱa.

Ar haṛam hõe kulikedea, uni hõe me̱nketá, Nia̱ buru paro̱m iń calaḱa.

Ado̱e me̱nketá, E̱ṇḍe̱khan, baba, miťtegelaṅ se̱n idiḱa.

Uniye me̱nketá, Hẽ e̱ṇḍe̱khan.

Khange uni koṛa do̱ miťṭaṅ kathae ro̱ṛkeťtakina, me̱nketáe, Ia̱ baba, miť dhao am ghõṛãńtalaṅme, miť dhao ińiń ghõṛãmea, e̱ṇḍe̱khan, baba, calaḱ leka hõ o̱ho̱laṅ a̱ika̱ulea.

Ado̱ uni haṛam do̱ noa kathae ańjo̱man khane guni bha̱biḱ kana, Durre̱! ać do̱ na ho̱e koṛa ho̱ṛ kanae, nãhãḱe ghõṛã daṛeańa; ar iń do̱ haṛam ho̱ṛ una̱ḱ daṛe hõ ba̱nuḱtińa. O̱ho̱ co̱ń ghõṛã daṛele. Ado̱ onka galmarao galmaraotekin calaoena. Noa reaḱ man do̱ noa kana: E̱ baba, miť dhao am galmarao e̱ho̱btalaṅme, ar miť dhao ińiń e̱ho̱btalaṅa. Uni haṛam do̱ noa reaḱ man bae bujlaḱa.

Ar ho̱rtekin calaḱ kana. Uni koṛa do̱ panahi do̱e teweńkaḱ kana, ar daḱre do̱e panahiḱ kana. Ar cato̱m hõ ho̱rte calaḱre do̱ bae cato̱moḱ kana, dare buṭa̱rekin umullen khane cato̱mkoḱ kana. Ado̱ uni haṛam do̱ mo̱ne̱ mo̱ne̱teye me̱netá, Nui koṛa do̱ a̱ḍite̱ťe lelhagea.

Ado̱ khange calaḱ calaḱte daḱ tetaṅkeťkina. Ado̱ miťṭaṅ pukhrikin ńe̱l ńamkeťte o̱ṇḍe̱ daḱ ńũkin calaoena. Ado̱ uni koṛa do̱ ona pukhri ńe̱lteye me̱nketa, Uh! baba, nui kisa̱ṛ do̱ pukhri mae pukhri akať bhagege, me̱nkhan, baba, cok khuṇṭige tho̱ ba̱nuḱtaea. Ina̱ bogeyena.

---

[6] In India 'tank' means an excavated water-reservoir.

[7] Cok (also ca̱k) khuṇṭi is here used about a pole fixed in the middle of a tank. When a man has dug a tank, the neighbourhood will assemble for a feast, the so-called tank-marriage. A post is fixed in the middle of the water, and an old man is hired to fix a thin iron-pin in the pole. Having done this he applies sindur to the iron-pin, and the people call out Horibol, just as they do, when the bridegroom has applied the sindur to the forehead of his bride at the marriage-ceremony. Afterwards the people dance (the do̱ṅ dance)

"O father," he replied, "I am going very far."

The old man again asked him, saying about himself: "I am going past this hill."

"Then, father," he said, "we may go along together."

"All right then," the old man replied.

The young man then said one thing: "I say, father, you carry me a while on your shoulder, and I shall carry you a while in my turn; then, father, we shall not feel like walking along."

When the old man heard this, he commenced to turn this over in his mind: "Dear me, he himself is a young fellow; he may be able to carry me on his shoulder; but I am an old man and have no such strength; I shall surely not be able to carry him." Talking together in this way they went along; but the meaning of what he said is this: "Father, commence you once to talk about something, then I also shall commence in my turn." But the old man did not understand that this was the meaning.

So they were walking along. The young man carried his shoes in his hand, but when crossing any water he put them on. And when he was walking along the road, he did not use his umbrella; but when they were in the shadow of a tree, he kept it up. And the old man was saying to himself: "This young fellow is a dunce out and out."

As they passed along, they became thirsty, and when they sighted a tank[6], they went there to drink. When the young man saw the tank, he said: "What a pity! the owner of this has dug a tank quite good, but you see, father he has no marriage-pole[7]." So much in connexion with this. The old man was drinking water

---

until morning, when they are treated to molasses and roasted rice before going away. This water-marriage is very rare among the Santals. The idea underlying is to secure for the owner water in the next world. For a similar purpose they also may 'marry' trees of sorts.

Ar uni haṛam dọ ghaṭre dak̕e ńũketa; nui koṛa dọ bin ghaṭreye ńũketa, arkin calaoena.

Uni haṛam dọ arhõe mẹnjoṅ kana, Durrẹ! nui koṛa dọe cet̕ lekan hoṛ kan cọṅ? Sanamgeye ulṭạutaea. Dak̕ ńũ hõ iń ńũ ghaṭre dọ bae ńũleta. Ar talare menak̕a cok khuṇṭi ńẹlok̕ kana, are mẹneta, Henda baba, nui hoṛ dọ pukhri mae pukhri akat̕ge, mẹnkhan, baba, cok khuṇṭige thọ bạnuk̕taea. Sanam reaṅge bhagegetaea, mẹnkhan nianko dọ ulṭạugeń ạikạuede kana.

Khan arhõkin calao idiyena. Adọ calak̕ calak̕te uni haṛam reak̕ atokin tiok̕keta. Adọ uni haṛame mẹnketa, Dela goṭa hoṛ mit̕telaṅ hẹćena, delà iń oṛak̕re dak̕ko ńũ torawanme. Ạkhirem calak̕gea. Ma dela dak̕ko ńũ jirạuanme, adọm calak̕gea. Nonka mẹnkate haṛam reak̕ oṛak̕tekin calaoena. Khange sẹṭẹrkate uni haṛam dọ hopọnerate họhọadea, Ẹ mại, dẹ nọtẹ parkọm aderaeme peṛa hoṛ. Adọ uni kuṛi dọ parkọm ẹkkalte oṛak̕teye aderadea, ar dak̕ko taṅ baṛawadeteye ḍọbọk̕ baṛawadea.

Khange oṛak̕re uni haṛamtikinkin duṛup̕ akan tahẽkanre unre hõe metae kana, Hẽ, baba, oṛak̕ maben oṛak̕ akat̕ge, oṛak̕te mań khusiyenge. Mẹnkhan, baba, kham khuṇṭige thọ bạnuk̕anaṅ. Uni haṛam dọ arhõ ạḍitẹt̕ lelhae bujhạuede kana, tãhã kham khuṇṭi phẹḍrege parkọmko bel akawadea.

Adọ uni haṛam dọ ọṇḍẹ khon oḍoṅ sẹnkate hopọnerate kuliyede kana, Henda biṭi, nui dọbon jãwãe gomkekea; mẹnkhan, biṭi, ạḍitẹt̕ lelhae galmarao kana. Ńẹlme, nit hõe mẹneta, Oṛak̕ ma, babam oṛak̕ akat̕ bhagege, mẹnkhan, baba, kham khuṇṭige thọ bạnuk̕anaṅ; ar sẹ kham khuṇṭi ṭhengem bel akawadea.

---

8 Ghaṭ (borrowed from Hindi) is in Santali especially used about the way down to water, the place where water may be fetched or crossed. It is, however, also used figuratively.

9 The Santal bedstead is during daytime constantly used to sit on, more especially by visitors.

10 The kham khuṇṭi is the central post supporting the roof of one type of Santal houses.

at the common water-fetching place[8], and the young man drank where there was no such place, whereupon they went along.

Again the old man said to himself: "O dear, what kind of a man is this young fellow? He turns everything upside down; even when drinking water he did not do so at the water-fetching place where I drank. And the marriage-pole that is in the middle of the tank is to be seen; still he says: 'Look here, father, this man has certainly dug a tank; but, father, why, he has no marriage-pole. He is otherwise quite all right; but with regard to these matters I feel him to be out of his right mind."

So they again walked on; as they went, they reached the old man's village, and he said: "Come in; we have come together all the way; come in to me and get some water to drink in my house before going further. Later on you may go; please come now and have a drink of water and rest a while; afterwards you may go." As he was saying this, they went to the old man's house. When they reached there, the old man called his daughter: "My girl, do take a bedstead[9] in for this friend." The girl did so at once and took a bedstead into the house for him, and after having poured out water for him she saluted him.

Now while they, the old and the young man, were sitting there in the house, then also the young man said to him: "Well, father, you have built a house and I am well pleased with it; but why, father, there is no central post[10]." The old man again got the impression that he was an egregious fool; you see, they had put the bedstead for him just close to the central post of the house.

The old man went out from there and was asking his daughter: "I say, my girl, how would it be to have this one for our son-in-law? But, my daughter, he is an awful fool in his talk. Observe, even now he says: 'Well, father, you have built a house, very good, but father, there is no central post; and there, just at the central post you put the bedstead down for him."

Khange kuṛi dọe rọṛ ruạṛ gọt́keṭa, Ọtẹ cọṅ, baba, ṭhikgeye mẹnet́; ẹnte oṛak̕ mabon oṛak̕ akat́, piṇḍạ ma ba cọbon piṇḍạ akat́, ẹkkalte cọṅ oṛak̕te parkọmbon aderade. Onage cọṅ kham khuṇṭi ma hoeyen, piṇḍạge. Ọtẹ cọṅ besgeye mẹn akat́.

Adọ khange hanẹ ẹtọhọp̕ khonak̕e lại ạguae kana, Arhõ ńẹlme, biṭi, họrteliń hijuk̕ kana, adọe metań kana, Iạ baba, mit́ dhao aṁ ghõṛãńtalańme, mit́ dhao ińiń ghõṛãmea, ẹṇḍẹkhan, baba, calak̕ leka hõ balań ạikạua.

Khange kuṛiye mẹn gọt́keṭa, Ọtẹ cọṅ, baba, b'esgeye mẹn akat́. Ona dọe mẹneṭa, Mit́ dhao am ẹhọbtalańme galmarao, mit́ dhao ińiń ẹhọbtalańa, ẹṇḍẹkhan calak̕ leka hõ balań ạikạua.

Ar mại, họṛ dọ họrte calak̕re panahiko họrọk̕kak̕a arko catọmkok̕a; nui dọ, mại, bańa, panahi mae teweńkak̕ ar dak̕re mae panahikok̕.

Uni kuṛiye mẹnkeṭa, Ọtẹ cọṅ, baba, besge; ẹnte họrte calak̕re dọ emanteak̕e ńẹl ńameṭa, dak̕re dọ cet́ko cọṅ menak̕, bacọbon ńẹl ńamet́, onate dak̕re dọe họrọk̕eṭa. Ar họrte calak̕re hõ bae catọmok̕ kana, ar dare umulreye umulok̕ kana. Noa reak̕ bhẹd dọ noa kana: ẹnte, baba, dare cọṭre emantenko cẽṛẽ ciprut́ko ićeṭa ar ńũrok̕ kana, onate dare umulre dọe catọmkok̕a.

Acha, mại, mit́ṭań bandliń ńamkeṭa. Khange dak̕ ńũ bana họṛliń ãṛgoyena. Iń dọ ghaṭreń ńũkeṭa, nui dọ bin ghaṭreye ńũkeṭa. Ar talare cok khuṇṭiko bit́ akaṭa; nui dọe mẹneṭa, Ẹ baba, nui họṛ dọ pukhri mae pukhri akat́ge, mẹnkhan, baba, cok khuṇṭige thọ bạnuk̕taea.

---

11 To take a visitor straight into the house is not ordinarily done, for obvious reasons. It is dark inside, and a visitor might religiously defile the inner part.

12 As a rule every house has a small veranda, the eaves being prolonged on one side, so as to give shelter. Here there is nothing of the kind, with consequences as stated.

The girl answered back at once: "Why, father, he is speaking quite right, because we have built a house, but we have not added any veranda; we took the bedstead to sit on for him straight into the house[11]. Why, the central post has become the veranda[12]. There you see, he has spoken quite correctly."

So he commenced to tell her from the very beginning: "Listen now again, my daughter, we were coming along; then he said to me: "I say, father, you carry me a while on your shoulder, and I shall carry you a while in my turn; then, father, we shall not even feel like walking along."

The girl at once replied: "See there, father, why, he has spoken well. He was saying to you: 'Commence to talk you once, and I shall commence something in my turn, in that case we shall not feel like walking along'."

"And my girl, when people walk along a road, do they not take their shoes on and keep their umbrella up for a shade? not so this one, my girl; he carries his shoes in his hand and takes them on when passing through water."

The girl said: "Well, there you hear, father, quite good; when he walks along the road, he catches sight of this, that and the other; when we cross water, we cannot see what there may be in the water; therefore he takes them on, when going through water. And when he walks along a road, he does not keep his umbrella up, and when in the shade of a tree, he shelters himself. The meaning of this is this: you see, father, up in a tree various birds stay and they void excrements and these fall down; therefore he shelters himself, when in the shade of a tree."

"Very well, my girl, we came to a tank, and both of us went down to have a drink of water. I drank at the common water-fetching place; but as for him, he drank away from that place. In the middle of the tank they had put a marriage-pole, and this fellow says: 'Father, the man has certainly dug a tank; but, father, why, he has no marriage-pole'."

Henda baba, dak̕ ńũben ãṛgoyena, am do̱ ghaṭrem ńũket̕a ar uni do̱ bin ghaṭre. E̱ baba, amge co̱ṅ mạilạ dak̕em ńũket̕, uni ma sapha dak̕e ńũket̕. E̱nte, baba, ghaṭre do̱ emanten Deko pusiko ap̕ ạbukok̕ kana, tho kharak̕et̕ako, ạḍitẹt̕ co̱ṅ ghaṭ reak̕ do̱ mạilạ dak̕ kan. Ar henda baba, ona pukhri piṇḍhạre do̱ jãhãn dareko do̱ menak̕a se̱ baṅa?

Ado̱e me̱nket̕a, Dare do̱ bạnuk̕anaṅ.

Ho̱, onage co̱ṅ, baba, cok khuṇṭi do̱. Hutkạm dak̕ ńũ baṛakate dare umulreben duṛup̕ jirạukok̕a mit̕ ghạṛi. O̱te̱ co̱ṅ, baba, bae lelhawa.

Ado̱ uni koṛa do̱e aṅjo̱met̕kingea. Are kulikedea, To̱be̱, biṭim khusiyena?

Hẽ̱, baba, iń do̱ń khusigea; ado̱ unige kuliyepe.

Khange uni koṛa ṭhene calaoena haṛam do̱, are kuliyede kana, Cele, bạbu, cet̕em me̱net̕a? Alegele me̱net̕a, jãwãe gomkeme. Ado̱m re̱be̱nkok̕a se̱ baṅa?

Uniye me̱nket̕a, Hẽ̱ e̱nte, baba, ado̱ kuṛiye khusiań khan do̱ń khusigea iń hõ̱.

Ado̱ bana ho̱ṛ ado̱ samna sạmniko kuliket̕kina, banargekin khupusiena, kuṛi hõ̱e hẽ̱k̕ket̕a ar koṛa hõ̱. Khangeko baha sãohãket̕kina. Ar kuṛi do̱ bogeteye daka utu baṛa go̱t̕ket̕a are emat̕kina.

Ado̱ e̱ne̱ uni koṛa do̱e bạhuana. Uni koṛaren ho̱po̱ntẹt̕ do̱ aćak̕ budhi hoeyena, metak̕me aćak̕ budgeye bạhuadea. E̱ne̱ ado̱ e̱ṇḍe̱gekin tahẽ̱yena, ar dadat ṭhen ar do̱ bae ruarlena. Mucạt̕ena.

---

[13] It is quite astonishing how careless people may be and what they may drink other races perhaps more so than the Santals.

[14] Deko pusi, a Deko cat, is a contemptuous name, commonly used about the Hindus living round the Santals, the Santals apparently feeling themselves something like mice, hunted by the others.

"Listen, father, you went both down to drink water; you drank at the common fetching-place and he elsewhere. Why, father, you drank dirty[13] water, and he naturally drank clean water. For you know, father, at the common fetching-place various sorts of deko cats[14] wash themselves, they spit and clear their throat; why, at the common fetching-place the water is awfully dirty. And how, father, were there any trees on the embankment of the tank?"

"There were no trees," he replied.

"O, then, father, that was what he meant with marriage-pole. If there had been any such, you might have sat down a while and rested in the shade of some tree, after having drunk water. Why, you see, father, he is no fool."

The young man was hearing what they were talking. The father then asked her: "Then you are pleased, my daughter?"

"Yes, father, I am pleased; so ask him."

The old man then went to the young man and asked him: "Well, young friend, what do you say? As for us, we say we will have you for our son-in-law. Would you agree or how?"

He replied: "Why, yes, father; if the girl is pleased with me, I am pleased, I also."

Thereupon they confronted them both and asked them, and they were both pleased with each other. The girl said yes and the boy also. So they married them, and the girl in a hurry prepared a fine lot of curry and rice and gave it to the young man and her father.

So in this way the young man got a wife. The young man's wit was his child, that is to say, his wit procured him a wife. And there they both remained, and the young man did not return to his elder brother.

It is ended.

58. Ho̱ńharea reaḱ katha.

Sedae jugre, kathae, mit́ṭaṅ ho̱ṛ so̱hhrae boṅga jo̱khe̱ć aćren jãwãe gomket ṭhen peṛa ho̱ṛo̱ḱe se̱nlena. Ado̱ khange tahẽ̱ aṅgakate dosar hiloḱ do̱ khe̱t se̱ne ạyur idikedea, ado̱e metae kana, Delaṅ baba, khe̱tḳolaṅ hiri baṛa ạgulege; nit khonaḱ oṛaḱrege tinạḱlaṅ duṛuṕkoḱa? Delaṅ eṅgate dãṛã hõ̱laṅ dãṛã pharnao hijuḱa. Ado̱ sunumko dạṭạunikoe ńamkeťa, ar ać bạhu do̱e. me̱n oṭoadea, Am do̱ hạṇḍi nãhãḱ daḱ hataṛaḱme. Enka me̱nkate ạkin do̱ khe̱t ńe̱lkin calaoena.

Ado̱ khe̱tkoe uduḱ baṛawae kana, Nẽ̱ḱẽ̱, baba, niạkotabon khe̱t do̱. Ado̱ onka sanam ṭạṇḍi reaḱe uduḱ idiae kana. Ado̱ uni ho̱ńharte̱ť haṛam do̱e me̱neťa, Cas ma besge, jãwãe, me̱nkhan pãeṛẽ̱ge tho̱ baben e̱se̱ť akaťa.

Ado̱ uni jãwãe gomket do̱e me̱neťa, Baṅa, baba, e̱se̱ť akaťgealiń. Ado̱ tinạḱ ṭhen khe̱te uduḱae kan, un ṭhenge uni do̱ onkageye me̱n ruạṛae kana, Cas ma hẽ̱ge, jãwãe, pãeṛẽ̱ge tho̱ baben ese̱ṭeťa. Ado̱ e̱nre hõ̱ uni jãwãe gomket do̱ bae bujhạulaḱa.

Khange ado̱ ńe̱l caba baṛakatekin um baṛayena, ado̱ oṛaḱtekin he̱ćena. Ado̱ he̱ćkate hạṇḍiḱin ńũjoṅ kana.

---

1 Part of this story might be called a variant of the preceding one. In essential features, however, it is entirely different. It has been given here, especially on account of the description of the formal talk between visitors and their hosts. See further reference to this below notes 7 ss.

2 The Sohrae festival referred to is now-a-days held just after our new year (second half of the month of Pus); formerly it was held in the month of Kartik (second half of our October and first half of November); this month is even now by the Santals very commonly called Sohrae. It has been suggested that the festival has been moved to January, because then they have just harvested their fields, while they formerly harvested their principal crops in October and November. The festival is undoubtedly a kind of harvest festival. The name is possibly to be connected with Hindi d a s a h r ā. The time here referred to must be the original time of the festival; the fields in the story are not yet ripe for harvesting

58. THE STORY OF A MAN AND HIS SON-IN-LAW[1].

ONCE upon a time long long ago, people tell, a man had gone on a visit to his son-in-law at the time of the harvest festival[2]. When he had passed the night there, his son-in-law the next morning took him round to his rice-fields; he said to him: "Come along, father, let us go and have a look at the rice-fields; should we sit from now on so long a time here in the house? Come along, dash it, we shall take a walk and also get over our drowsiness." Thereupon he brought oil and toot-brush twigs[3], and he also said to his wife: "While we are away, add some water to the rice-beer." When he had said this, the two of them went to have a look at the rice-fields.

So he was showing his father-in-law their rice-fields, saying: "Here you see, father, these are our rice-fields." In this manner he showed him everywhere what they had. Then the old man, his father-in-law, said: "Well, your crops are quite good, my son-in-law; but you have not closed the outlets[4]."

His son-in-law replied: "Surely, father, I have closed them up." Everywhere where he showed him a rice-field, his father-in-law answered him in this manner: "Well, your crops are quite good, my son-in-law; but you have not closed the outlets." But in spite of this his son-in-law did not understand what he meant.

When they had seen everything, they had a bath and came home; and here the two of them were drinking beer.

---

[3] After bathing a little oil is applied, to keep the skin soft; all Santals every morning make use of the tooth-brush (a twig of the Sal tree) before taking any food.

[4] The rice needs much water; the rice-fields are consequently made level and supplied with ridges to keep the water standing. In the Santal country the land is not flat (like in the lower parts of Bengal); the rice-fields lie one above the other, like huge stairs. To regulate the amount of water, a small outlet is made in the outside ridge. These tiny channels may be closed up whenever wanted; a couple of spadefuls of earth is all that is required.

Adọ inạ dosar hiloḱ dọ uni haṛame mẹnkeťa, Iạ, jãwãe, dela nọtẹ peṛako khọj akadińa, delalaṅ hiri baṛa ạgukoa. Khange adọ bana hoṛkin panahiyena arkin calaḱ kana. Adọ khange uni jãwãe gomket dọ chatare ạsiť akaťgetaea, ar panahi hõ bọćkateye teweń akaťgetaea. Adọ miťṭaṅ gaḍakin ńamkeťa, ar ona gaḍare dọ ṭhĩṭṛạḱte daḱ ạtuḱ kana. Adọ uni jãwãe gomket dọ onare paṛọmoḱ jọkhẹć dọe panahiyena; arhõ paṛọmkate dọe bọćkeťtaea. Ar uni haṛam dọ paṛọmoḱ jọkhẹće toťkeťa, ar paṛọmkate dọe horọḱkeťa.

Adọ calaḱ calaḱte setońen khan dọ miťṭan dare buṭạrekin jirạuḱ kana. Adọ un jọkhẹć uni jãwãe gomket dọe ńẹle kana, ona chatar dọe pasarkeťtaea, ar uni haṛam dọe sikup̍keťtaea. Adọ ọṇḍẹ khonkin bereť calaḱ kan khać dọe sikup̍keťtaea. Adọ onkage goṭa hoṛ daḱrekin paṛọmoḱ khan dọe panahiḱ kana, arkin paṛọmena mẹnkhan dọe bọja; ar dare buṭạrekin umuloḱ khan dọe chataroḱ kana, ar setońre dọ bae chataroḱa.

Adọ uni haṛam dọ uni jãwãe gomket ńẹlte ạḍi bạṛiće hahaṛaḱ kana, adọe mẹnjoṅ kana, Durrẹ! nui hoṛ dọ ạḍi bạṛiće lelhagea. Adọ ẹnre hõ ceť hõ bae metadea.

Adọ peṛa oṛaḱkin tioḱkeťa. Khange adọ parkọmko belaťkina, adọ onarekin duṛup̍ena. Adọ daḱ taṅkateko ḍọbọḱ baṛawaťkina; adọko kuli baṛayeťkina, Cele baba, aben dọ oka sẹć khonben hijuḱ kana?

Adọkin mẹnkeťa, Oṛaḱ sẹn khonge, ape hiḱrigeliń hẹć akana; adọliń mẹnkeťa, Delaṅ, nọkolaṅ hiri baṛa ạgukakoa; ḍher din khon noko dọ babon hiri akaťkoa. Adọ onka mẹnkate teheń dọliń taṛam gọť akaťa.

Adọko mẹnkeťa, Bogege ẹṇḍẹkhan, ale hõ jaogele khọjpea; mẹnale, Phalnaren babateko dọ nẹs dọ bako hẹć baṛawabon kana. Adọ nõḱõeben hẹćente ale hõ ạḍile rạskạyena; baṅkhan noko

[5] It is rather a roundabout way of mentioning people; but it is in accordance with what is considered good form among the Santals. It is against their nature

The next day the old man spoke to his son-in-law: "I say, my son-in-law, come along, some friends in these parts have wanted me; come, let us pay them a visit." Thereupon both of them fetched their shoes and started. Now the son-in-law had closed his umbrella and had taken his shoes off also and was carrying them in his hand. Then they came to a river, and here the water was running up to the calf of one's leg. When crossing here, the son-in-law put his shoes on, and when they had crossed, he took them off again. But the old man took his ones off, when he crossed, and took them on again on the other side.

As they walked along and the sun became hot, they rested under a tree. There the old man saw his son-in-law: he opened his umbrella, while he himself closed his; but when they got up and went along, his son-in-law closed his umbrella. In this manner it was all the way; when they crossed water, he took them off; and when they found shade under a tree, he shaded himself with his umbrella; but out in the sun he did not do so.

Seeing the bahaviour of his son-in-law, the old man was very much astonished and was saying to himself: "O dear, this fellow is awfully stupid." Still he did not say anything to him.

So they reached the house they were to visit. They placed a bedstead before them, and they sat down on it. After having poured out water for them, they saluted them, whereupon they asked them: "Well, sirs, from which direction are you two coming?"

They replied: "From home; we have come to pay you a visit; we said: 'Come, let us two go and look these friends up; it is a long time since we paid them a visit.' When we had decided on this, we started and have come."

"That is very good then," they said; "we are constantly wanting to see you; we say: 'The family of the father of so-and-so[5] have not come to us this year'. And now, here you have come, so we are

to mention the name of other people, when these represent a position in the village or Santal society.

gidrạko dọliń metakoa, Nẹs dọ ya nui phalna gọrọm baba dọe hiṛińkeťbona. Abo dọ okorko hiriyeťbona? Onkaliń metakoa.

Adọ unkinkin mẹn ruạṛa, Hẽ, jaoge hijuk̕ dọle mẹna, mẹnkhan ọpsọrge bale ńam: hinạ khon hinạ kạmitege hinạ khon hinạ kạmitege, teheń hijuk̕ gapa hijuk̕, enkategele tahẽyena, bale hẹć daṛeaťa. Oka ma hijuk̕ lạgiť sapṛao baṛakatege arhõle thirenge. Adọ noko jãwãeteko ṭhen iń hẹćlena, adọ nokoń hiri baṛakeťkoa; adọ nui jãwãegeń ḍoḍekede, ẹnkathae, Oḍok akan sik delań noko peṛa hõlań hiri baṛa ạgukakoa. Oṛak̕ khon sapṛao hijuk̕te dọ, ẹnkathae, muskilgea. Onka mẹnkate adọ nõk̕õe ape sẹn dhạbić geliń hẹć idi akana.

Adọ arhõ onkoko rọṛ ruạṛa, Ẹ baba, adọ eṭak̕ eṭak̕ak̕gebon galmarao kana. Adọ ceť leka jivi jạti dọ, boge baṛageape?

Adọ unkinkin mẹn ruạṛa, Hẽ, adọ niạ ghạṛi dọ Cando baba dayate ar apeko dohaete gọć sarẹćko dọ sanam. họṛ besge nẹs dọ menak̕lea. Ini phalṭak̕ thoṛa dine ruạ ńõk̕len tahẽkana; adọ ini hõ ran baṛa ocoade khan dọ,adọ ṭamak ṭumuke phạriạyengea. Adọ Cando dohaete nẹs dọle bes baṛagea. — Adọ apege ceť leka menak̕-petabona? Adọ dẹnẹ banar bupujhạulen khan, ạḍi beskok̕tabona.

6 The Santal equivalent to the Norwegian 'dørstokkmilen er altid den lengste', 'the step over the door-stone in always the longest'.

7 It is a mistake to believe that uncivilized people are without forms and ceremonies; it is quite the opposite; they are more bound by such considerations than we are, and faults and mistakes or omissions are deemed serious and may have consequences. Even when coming on an occasional visit, more or less elaborate formal conversation is gone through. What is here recorded, is not in any way more than what is ordinary among friends living at some distance from one another. Note, the pronoum used is plural; the questions and answers refer to the families on both sides.

8 It might be noted that the terms here mentioned are used by the ordinary uneducated Santal, non-Christians. It is strange how this has got into the heads of people, and how it is observed by e. g. people writing a letter. I have myself received many such, where more than one page has been filled with these formalities, while the real object of the letter has been stated at the end in perhaps one line, generally preceded by the words 'the matter is this'.

exceedingly glad; otherwise we have been saying to these children: 'This year, children, so-and-so's grandfather has forgotten us. Why, they are not paying us any visit.' In this way we have been speaking to them."

The two visitors then answered back: "Quite so; we have constantly been talking about coming; but we never find the leisure: from this work to that, from that work to this, start to-day, start to-morrow, so it has always been; we have been unable to come. Sometimes it has happened that even after we had made us ready to come, we again had to give it up. But now I came to the family of my son-in-law here and have been paying them a visit; so I asked him to come with me, saying: 'Since I have got away from home, come, let us two pay these friends also a visit.' As they say[6], the difficulty is to get ready and come away. Having come to this conclusion, here you see, we have come along even unto you."

Then the others said again: "Father, we are talking of all other kinds of things. How are you[7] faring with regard to mind and body? Are you well?"

The two of them then answered back: "Yes, at present by the grace of Chando the Father and your goodwill[8] all we who are left after the death of the others[9] are well this year. So-and-so was just a little ill for a few days; but as he got some medicine, he also recovered and got well. So by the grace of Chando we are well this year. Then you, how are you faring? When we come to understand how we are faring on both sides, then only it will be well with us."

Cando baba, Sun father, is the Supreme Being. Ape dohaete, by your mercy or goodwill, is commonly used, but likely not much understood; it is a formula conveying the meaning of goodwill. The word dohae is borrowed from Hindi, but constantly used in Santali. It is really a cry for mercy, but is in the present Santali language used often also about showing mercy (as e. g. Ṭhạkur dohaete, by the mercy or grace of Thakur).

9 Lit. dying left, i. e. left alive; the more common expression is perhaps lo̱ sarẹć, left after burning.

Ádo̱ onka peṛako ro̱ṛ ruạṛa, Hẽ̱, ado̱ nią ursiń bạrsiń do̱ ape dohaete ar Cando dayate, o̱ne̱ko me̱n leka, e̱r sare̱ć itạ ar go̱ć sare̱ć jivi, ado̱ je sare̱ć ho̱ṛ do̱, baba, ape dohaete nin din do̱ jivi jạti, ho̱rmo̱ harta bes baṛageale.

Ado̱ onkoko me̱n ruạṛa, Cando dayate besgebon ńam kana, je jive̱t́ tahe̱n khan do̱ nẽ̱k̕ẽ̱ nenkabo ńe̱pe̱l kana; ar go̱ćlen khan tho̱ sanam cabayena; ado̱ ghuriạ̃ babo ne̱pe̱l kana.

Ado̱ko me̱na, Hẽ̱ sạriak̕ge, ona do̱ katha kangea.

Ado̱ onkoko me̱n go̱da, Ale se̱n do̱, baba, teṅgo ruạge tho̱ ạḍiye jạbun akat̕lea.

Ado̱ unkinkin me̱n ruạṛket̕a, Ona ruạ do ale se̱n hõ̱ onkage ạḍiye jạbun akat̕legea.

Khange ado̱ko landa baṛawana. Ado̱ jaṅga dak̕ko o̱ḍokk̕et̕a, ado̱ jangako ạbukket̕kina. Ado̱ inạkate thamakurko benaoket̕a, ado̱ko jo̱m baṛaket̕a. Ado̱ unkin peṛa ho̱ṭ do̱ bạrsiń din o̱ṇḍe̱gekin tahẽ̱yena.

Ado arhõ̱ o̱ṇḍe̱ khonkin ruạṛ kańa. Arhõ̱ onkage uni jãwãe gomket do̱ dak̕re do̱e panahik̕a ar ghuṭure do̱e bo̱ja; ar dare buṭạre do̱e chatarok̕a ar setońre do̱e ạsit̕kataea.

Ado̱ onka onkatege oṛak̕tekin he̱ć se̱ṭe̱rena. Ado̱ uni ho̱po̱nerat do̱e lạiae kana, E̱ mãi̱, uni jãwãe do̱ eṅgate, cet̕ bań se̱, ạḍi bạṛiće lelhagea.

Ado̱ uni ho̱po̱nerat do̱e me̱net̕a, Cekate, baba? Lelha leka ma ba co̱e ạikạuk̕.

---

10 Lit, 'one day two days', a couple of days.

11 Jivi jạti, lit. soul nature, used to signify the general state of health and well-being, especially so far as the mind is concerned; ho̱ṛmo̱ harta, lit. body skin, in this connexion refers to the bodily well-being. Both words, or harta alone, are very frequently used where we use 'bodily' as opposed to 'spiritual'.

12 The expression refers to this world. The Santals believe in a continued existence in the other world.

Then the friends said: "Yes, these few days[10] by your goodwill and the grace of Chando, as people say: the seed left after sowing and the souls left from death, so many people as are left, father, by your goodwill, so many days up to now we are well as to soul and race, as to body and skin[11]."

So the others answer back: "By the grace of Chando we are faring well, when we, being alive, may see each other just like this; and when one dies, all is over; then we are not meeting[12] any more."

"Yes, that is the truth," they say; "that is what there is to it."

Thereupon the friends fall in: "Here in our parts, father, the standing illness[13] has quite overpowered us."

The two visitors then answered: "That illness has also in our parts in the same way quite overpowered us."

Thereupon they talked and joked. So they brought foot-water out and washed their feet. Afterwards they prepared tobacco, and they chewed it together. And the two visitors remained there for two days.

After that they returned, and again the son-in-law took his shoes on when passing through water and took them off when reaching the bank; and under a tree he shaded himself with his umbrella, and in the sun he took it down.

In this way they reached home. And the old man said to his daughter. "My girl, this son-in-law, dash it, you have no idea, he is awfully stupid."

His daughter asked him: "How so, father? Why, he does not give the impression of being stupid."

---

[13] Teṅgo ruạ, lit. standing illness, is a very common veiled expression for hunger or starvation, or scarcity of means of subsistence. As the Santals live, this is a constant and real complaint with very, very many. I wonder what many people would think of supporting themselves and a family on ten shillings a month. In spite of this they are cheerful.

Adọ uni haṛame mẹnkeťa, Baṅa, mại, ạḍi lelhaṅ ạikạukedea. Ẹnte nọṇḍẹ khon peṛa họṛọk̕liṅ calak̕ kana, unreṅ ṅẹle kana, baṅma, dak̕reliṅ parọmok̕ jọkhẹćgeye panahik̕ kana ar ghuṭure dọe teweṅkak̕ kana; ar dare buṭạreliṅ umulok̕ jọkhẹćgeye chatarok̕ kana, arhọ̃ ọṇḍẹ khonliṅ bereť calak̕ khan dọe ạsiťkataea. Onate uni dọ ạḍi lelha iṅ dọṅ metae kana.

Adọ uni họpọnerate mẹnkeťa, Baṅa, baba, bae lelhawa, amgem lelhagea. Adọ ona kathage ạkin apa họngekin ẹpẹsẹť kana. Adọ họpọnerate mẹnkeťa, Baṅa, baba, ṅẹlme, ona reak̕ bhẹd nãhãk̕ iṅ lạiama. Ṭạṇḍire dọ cedak̕ bae panahik̕ kana? Ẹnte ṭạṇḍire ma ṅẹlkateye taṛameť kan, onate bae panahik̕ kana; ar dak̕re thọ bam ṅẹleťa, dak̕ bhitrire ceť cọṅ menak̕ — jaṅ cọṅ, jạnum cọṅ, dhiri cọṅ — ona iạte uni dọ dak̕re dọe panahik̕ kana. Ar dare dare buṭạre dọ cak̕e chatarok̕ kana? Ẹnte ḍạr alo ṅũraea mẹnte, sẹ darere dọ cẽṛẽ emanko tahẹna, onko dọ aloko moelawaea mẹnteye chatarok̕ kana, ar phãkre mae ṅẹl daramge; onate phãkre dọ bae chatarlena.

Khange adọ uni haṛame mẹnkeťa, Baṅa, mại, sạrige thọ ṭhikgem rọṛkeťa! iṅge ẹṇḍẹkhan iṅ lelhayena.

Adọ uni kuṛiye mẹnkeťa, Hẽ baba, amgem lelhagea. Adọko inạk̕ hạbićkaťgea, adọko thir baṛayena.

Adọ uni haṛam dọ dosar hilok̕ ako oṛak̕teye calaoena. Adọ arhọ̃ hana Mag cando jọkhẹć unkin họpọnerat jãwãe gomket ṭhenge peṛa họṛọk̕e calaoena. Adọ unre bạndikoe ṅẹl baṛayeťtakoa, are metako kana, Okorko, tinạk̕pe ader akaťa?

Adọ uni jãwãe gomkete mẹneťa, Nẽk̕ẽko baba, ninạk̕gele aderleťa.

---

[14] Our January-February.

[15] The Santals store their rice and other cereals in straw-bundles, taking anything up to 4—500 kg. each and sometimes more. They are kept inside their houses on a kind of scaffolding (called ḍhulạ), erected for the purpose.

The old man replied: "Not so, my girl; he gave me the impression of being very stupid. You see, we were going from here to visit friends. Then I observed him; whenever we passed through water, he put his shoes on; and when we reached the bank, he took his shoes off and carried them in his hand; and whenever we sat in the shade of a tree, he shaded himself with his umbrella, and when we rose and again went away, he took it down. For this reason I think him very stupid."

His daughter then said: "No, father, he is not stupid; it is you who are the stupid one." And the father and daughter continued arguing this matter. The daughter said: "Now, look here, father; I shall tell you what this means. Why does he not put shoes on when walking on dry ground? Because there he can see while walking; therefore he does not put his shoes on; and when you pass through water, why, you cannot see what there may be in the water, may be a bone or a thorn or a sharp stone; therefore he puts his shoes on when passing through water. And why does he shade himself at the foot of every tree? You see, a branch might fall down on him, and in trees birds and sundry beings are found; so he shades himself to prevent these from dirtying him; in the open he can see and guard himself; therefore he did not shade himself in the open."

The old man then answered: "Quite so, my girl; really it is quite right what you said; so it was myself who became the stupid one."

"Yes, father," the girl said, "you are the stupid one." They argued up to this point and then ceased.

The following day the old man went home. About the time of the month of Mag[14] he again went on a visit to his daughter and son-in-law. On this occasion he looked for their paddy-bundles[15] and asked them: "Why, where are they? How many did you bring in?"

His son-in-law replied: "What you see here, father; that is as many as we brought in."

Adọ uni haṛame mẹnkeťa, Henda jãwãe, ninạk̕ge hoelena? Khẹtre ma ạḍi utạrliń ńẹlleť.

Adọ uni jãwãe gomkete mẹnkeťa, Hoe dọ ḍherge hoelena, baba, adọ laharegeliń kại akať khan, adọ onkogeliń ẹm baṛawaťkoa, arliń khajna baṛakeťa; onkate jọtọ cabayena.

Adọ unrege uni haṛame mẹnkeťa, Ọnẹ jãwãe, ẹn betarrege cọń ạliń dọliń metaben kan tahẽkan, Henda jãwãe, pãeṛẽ dọben ẹsẹť akaťa sẹ bań? Adọben mẹnkeťa, Ẹsẹť akaťgealiń. Mẹnkhan pãeṛẽ reak̕ bhẹd dọ noa kana: pãeṛẽte dak̕ ạtu calak̕ leka noa dhọn calaoentabena. Adọ masẹ bujhạuben, ṭhik kana sẹ bań.

Adọ uni jãwãe gomkete mẹnkeťa, Bańa, baba ṭhikgeben metaťlińa; mẹnkhan dọ ạlińge baliń bujhạuleťa, pãeṛẽte dak̕ ạtu calak̕ leka ạlinak̕ dhọn cabayena.

Adọ in marangea katha dọ; cabayena.

59. Haṛam buḍhi reak̕ jhogṛa.

Sedae jọkhẹn, kathae, miťṭẹn uḍi khańcẹṛ hoṛe tahẽkana, siń sạṭup̕ge ạimại dọe dik dikạu cabakoa. Jãhã khongeye hijuk̕, sẹ kạmi ṭhen khongeye hijuk̕, ẹkkalte dakageye khọjkoa. Mẹnae, Dẹn daka dak̕ mạṇḍi ẹm gọťańpe. Adọ khọjkeť torako ẹm gọťaere ma bogege, ar bańkhan ẹkkalteye dhum utạrkoa. Mẹnae, Nit hõ ạuripe isina? Ceťpe kạmi kana nun hạbić? Ceťpe cekayeť tahẽkana? Bela dọ bape ńẹle kana, sẹ rẹńgẹć bela dọ bape baḍaea?

Adọko metaea, Ẹ sẹ, onka dọ alo sẹm rọṛlea. Kạmi kangeale, adọ kạmi kạmitege belak̕ kan khan, ceťle mẹna? Ar bańkhan enan sim rak̕ khongele kạmi kana.

---

[16] Lit. 'have sinned', here about borrowing from others, especially the money-lenders and shopkeepers, one of the great difficulties of the people.

[17] As often remarked the Santals like to express themselves figuratively; they prefer to use a veiled name or a hint to the real name. This has become something like second nature with them; my impression is that a veiled and vague reference is more effective than downright statement of fact.

The old man then said: "Look here, son-in-law, was this all it came to? I saw a great quantity in the fields."

His son-in-law replied: "We certainly had a good crop, father; but as we previously had committed a fault[16], we gave it to those people; and we sold it to pay the rent; in this way all was finished?"

Then the old man said: "There you see, my son-in-law, why, on my visit some time ago, I was talking to you several times, saying: 'Look here, my son-in-law, have you closed the outlets[17] or how?' Then you answered: 'I have done so.' But the meaning of outlet is this: just as the water runs out through the oulet, so this substance ran out. Please, understand it, is it so or not?"

His son-in-law then answered: "Certainly, father, it was quite right what you said to me; but I did not understand it, that just as water runs out through an outlet, so our substance was finished."

The story is thus much; it is ended.

59. A QUARREL BETWEEN HUSBAND AND WIFE.

ONCE upon a time long long ago, people tell, there lived an extremely hot-tempered man; all day long he was worrying[1] his women-folk. When he came home from somewhere or other or he came in from work, he straightway demanded food. He would say: "Here, give me rice and food at once." When they gave him as soon as he demanded, well and good; but if not, he at once made a row and abused them. He would say: "Have you not cooked as yet? What have you been doing up to now? What were you occupied with? Can't you see the time of the day, or don't you know when people become hungry?"

They would answer him: "Please, don't talk in that way. We are working; and what can we say, when through constant work it becomes a little late? Else know that we have been at work right since cock-crow."

59 [1] The type of man here described is met with, but cannot be said to be the common one among the Santals.

Adoe men gotketa, Cetkope kamiketa? Den se bhala hisab udukanpe, ar iń cetkoń kami akata dela hisab iń udukapea.

Ado aimaitaeye menketa, Onka hisab tisab dom alo rora. Ohom darelena, ente amak kami do mit gotengete ńel ńamok kana, onate hisab hõm uduk dareaka. Ar aleak do aemaka ar khucra kami kantalea. Ar aleak kami dobon jom horayeta. Oka khon hisab dole lai dareama? Acha besge, gapalaň bidautalaňa. Am hõ gapa setak sim rak khonak tinakem kamia, ona ret jarwaeme, ar iń hõ tinak iń kamia, onań ret jarwakaka. Ado daka jomem hijuka, unre onako hisab ret do agu daraeme.

Adoe menketa, Acha besge, gapa ocoak. Den tehentet em hotanpe. Netar do Aghãr din, oka hõ baň thikanok kana. Mit gharitege ayubok kana. Enege jeder akan lekam aikaua, ayogo! tikin gotenge.

Ado erataeye menketa, Ina bare menme se. Ado cedak hisab dom khoj kana? Menetam, Cetpe cekayet tahẽkana? Cetkope kami kana? Den ona reak hisab batlaoanpe ar iňak kami ńelpe. Ado amge thom tokrar kana.

Adoe menketa, Acha besge, gapanok hisabbo milautabona.

Ado sari dosar hilok uni herel hor do sim rakre kadae arak idiketkote enoke joraoketkoa. Ado mandae lahutkette busupe gidiketa, te tandiketae, har samtaoketae. Ado tikinen khan, orakte daka jome hecena. Ado pahil leka onkageye ruhetetkoa. Ado

---

2 It is only a few among the latter-day Santals who attempt to write down an account. When they need keeping a count of anything, it is done in several ways. One is to tie knots on a string, each knot representing a day or e. g. one rupee. Another way is to put down a small heap, e. g. when they measure cereals. Here it is to be done in the following way: for each unit a small stone is wrapped up in a leaf and kept as a counter.

3 Lit. Aghar time, Aghar being the month corresponding to the second half of November and the first of December. This is the principal harvest-month; the days are comparatively short also here.

"What did you do?" he said at once; "well then, show me an account of it, and let me also show you an account of what I have been occupied with."

His woman then replied: "Don't speak in this way about account. You will never gain on us; your work is only one and may be seen; therefore you are also able to show an account. And our work is of many kinds and divided into small bits; and it is what we do that we eat as soon as it is ready. Wherefrom should we be able to give you an account? Very well then, let us test each other's work to-morrow. Now whatever you do from to-morrow at cock-crow, collect it and wrap it all up[2], and I shall also do the same. Then, when you come in to have food, bring along with you what you may have made up."

"All right," he said; "let it be to-morrow. Here, give me to-day now quickly. At present it is harvest[3]-time; there is no certainty with anything; it becomes evening in a moment. You feel it, when it has just become a little warm, o mother, then it is noon."

"Say just that," his wife answered; "why then are you asking for an account? You say: 'What have you been occupied with? What are you doing? Here, render me an account of that and look at my work.' Why, it is you who are asking again and again."

"Very well," he said; "to-morrow we shall compare our accounts."

So, truth to tell, the next day the man let the buffaloes out at cock-crow[4] and started treshing with them. When he had threshed the grain out, he threw the straw off, winnowed the chaff off and collected the grain. When it became noon, he went home to have his food, and he commenced to scold them just as before. His

---

[4] The Santals are very early risers; although they may lie down a little afterwards, they generally start their day's work at the time of first cock-crow. What is here further told, is a fair description of what a Santal man will do just at this time of the year.

erataeye mẹnkeťa, Hapẹ, ạuriń dakaea. Ar holam mẹn akaťa, Gapa dọ hisạbbon uduga. Adọ dẹn udugme ar iń hō̱ń udukama.

Adọe metadea, Ma hisạbtińme. Sim raḱ kaḍań aṛaḱ idiketkoa. Adọ inạ reaḱ miť gọṭẹne rẹťketa. Adọ hoṛo chiṭạukateń ẹnketa. Adọ inạ reaḱ miť gọṭẹne rẹťketa. Adọ busuṕ iń giḍi giḍiketa. Adọ inạ reaḱ miť gọṭẹne rẹťketa. Adọ hoṛoń teketa. Adọ inạ reaḱ miť gọṭẹne rẹťketa. Adọ hoṛoń hạr puńjiketa, adọ oṛaḱteń hẹćena. Inạ reaḱ miť gọṭẹne rẹťketa. Adọe metadea, Ma lekhaetińme, tinạḱ rẹť hoeyena mẹnte. Adọe lekha baṛakettae dọ turui gọṭẹnge. Adọe mẹn gọťketa, Ma ńẹlme, samani utạr iń kạmiketa.

Adọe metadea, Ona ma ẹkẹn miť lekan kạmi kange, judạ thọ bam kạmi akata. Ona ma ẹkẹn hoṛo reaḱ kange.

Adọ uni hẹrẹl hoṛ ạḍi garteye rọṛ gọťketa, Am dọ okor cetko judạm kạmiketa. Dẹn sẹ bhala hisạb udukańme.

Adọe rẹť jarwa akat tahẽkana. Onako rẹť uni samańre ạgukateye giḍi gọťkata. Are metadea, Ma lekhaetińme.

Adọ hẹrẹl hoṛe mẹnketa, Bańa, ẹkẹ ẹkẹte hisạb lại pạhilańme, ẹnkhanteń lekhaetama.

Adọe mẹnketa, Acha besge; ma nãhãḱ mimiť gọṭẹn pharak horaeme. Sim raḱ hoṛoń huṛuńketa — miť. Racań jọḱketa — miť. Gurić iń giḍiketa — miť. Daḱ iń ạguketa — miť. Thạri bạṭikoń mańjao sapha ạguketa — miť. Gidrạko daḱ mạṇḍiteń bodhaoketkoa — miť. Gupiko ar sẽṛã hoṛko baskeaḱ iń ẹm baṛawatkoa — miť. Culhạń chō̱cketa — miť. Sẹńgẹl iń jolketa — miť. Daḱ iń basańketa — miť. Dakań ạ̃ṛić ãṛgoketa — miť. Tuṛi aṛaḱ iń siť ạguketa — miť. Utuketań — miť. Daka utukoń hạṭińketa — miť. Adọ nẽḱẽń

[5] One counter has not been explained.

[6] The fire-place is cleaned by daubing superficially, not with the hand, but with a tiny broom or a piece of cloth.

wife then said: "Wait, I have not prepared food as yet. And you said yesterday that we shall show our accounts to-day. So come with it, show what you have, and I also shall show you."

So he said: "Well, count what I have. At cock-crow I let the buffaloes out." Whereupon he put one piece aside for that. "Then I spread the paddy out and threshed." Whereupon he put one piece aside for this. "Then I threw the straw away." And he put one piece aside for this. "Thereupon I winnowed the paddy grain." And he put one aside for this. "Thereupon I collected the paddy into a heap, and came home." And he put one piece aside for this, and said to his wife: "Now count what I have, how many pieces has it come to." She counted them, they were six[5]. Whereupon he said: "Now see then, I have done an awful lot."

She answered: "Well, that is only one kind of work; you have not done anything else. That is all only in connexion with paddy."

The man then called out in a loud voice: "You, why, what have you done, what different kinds? Come with it, show me your account."

Now she had collected her pieces, and bringing these she threw them down in front of the man and said: "Now count what I have."

The man then answered: "Not so, first give me an account of every single piece; thereafter I shall count yours."

"All right," she said; "so put aside one by one as I tell. At cock-crow I husked, paddy — one. I swept the court-yard, — one. I threw the cow-dung out, — one. I fetched water, — one. I scoured and cleaned the brass-plates and cups and brought them, — one. I gave the children food and quieted them, — one. I gave the cow-herds and the grown up people the morning's cold food, — one. I cleaned the fire-place, daubing it[6], — one. I made fire, — one. I boiled water, — one. I poured the water off the rice and took the pot down, — one. I went and plucked mustard leaves and brought them, — one. I prepared curry, — one. I portioned out

ẹm baṛawako kana — mit̕. Adọ ma bujme, mit̕ lekan kạmi kantiń sẹ judạ judạgea? Arhõ rel gumko renak̕ ma bań lạiet̕ kan. Adọ ma lekhaeme. Am dọ onkatem metań kana, cet̕kom kạmi kana mẹnte. Ẹnte bhala ạimạiak̕ kạmi dọ khọrọc horak̕ kana sẹ jọm horak̕ kana. Adọ oka ṭhen hisạb dọm uduk̕ daṛeak̕a? Dak̕em lo ạguket̕ge, inạ hõ mit̕ ghạṛitege caba baṛayenge. Dakam hạṭiń baṛaket̕a, adọ ona hõm ẹm baṛawade, khange cabayena. Muńjrạ thọ bạnuk̕an. Ma adọ lekhaeme.

Adọe lekhaket̕ dọ pẹ [7]gaṇḍa pea hoeyen. Khange cet̕ hõ bae rọṛlet̕a, tirup̕ hapeyenae. Adọ ẹn hilok̕ khon ạimạı dhomkaoko dọe bạgi utạrket̕a. Adọ erataeye mẹnket̕a, Alo sẹ ẹkkalte saegat katha dọ ạimạı hũyạte alope metalea. Ale hõ jọtọak̕gele kạmi kana. Adọ sedaere oka lekate cọń niạ siok̕ ar oṛak̕ dap̕ ar rumok̕, niạ dọe barọnkat̕lete bale jọṭẹtet̕a, ar bańkhan jọtọge thọle kạmi gọṛọape kangea. Adọ ẹnre hõ oka lekate cọń siń sạṭup̕ge iạ ạimạı, iạ ạimạipe ruhet̕ akale tahẹna. Adọ masẹ bhala aleak̕ kạmige ńẹltalepe. Ar bańkhan ẹnte niạ siok̕ chaḍakate kạmik̕ak̕re dọbon pherao hataṛok̕a sẹ cet̕a?

Adọ eratae unạk̕ hạbiće rọṛ idiket̕re hõ nui hẹrẹl họṛ dọ cet̕ge bae rọṛlet̕a. Adọ ọnẹ onkate uni khacaṛ hẹrẹl họṛ dọe bhagao ocoyena, adọ ẹkkalteye seta baragena. Seta ọnẹbon lẹhakoa, tọbẹko jọma. Adọ onkage abo hẹrẹl họṛ dọ ạimạiren seta kanabo. Tinre ạbukok̕ko metabona, un utạrbon jọmet̕a.

Adọ ẹnẹ niạ katha hõń mọkọńket̕a.

---

[7] Four is a very common unit for counting, called gaṇḍa, borrowed, however, from the Aryan peoples.

the rice and curry, — one. And now here I am giving it out. Now please, understand, have I only one kind of work or different kinds? Then again the sifting and cleaning of the rice in the winnowing-fan I have not mentioned. Now please count. You spoke to me and said, what are you doing? Well, see, women's work is always done away with as soon as it is done, or what they do, is consumed; then where can you show an account of it? One fetched water; that is used up in a moment. One portioned out the food; that also, as soon as it is done, is finished. There is nothing left to be counted. Now then count."

So he counted and it came to three times four[7] and three. The man did not say a single word; he hung his head and was quiet. And from that day he left utterly off to rebuke his women-folk. So his wife said: "Do not at once use harsh words to us, because we are women. We are also doing all kinds of work. In olden times they have for some reason or other forbidden us to plough and to thatch a house and to be possessed by a spirit, just these things, and therefore we do not touch these, but otherwise we are helping you to do all kinds of work. And still, somehow or other, you are all day long abusing us, calling us unspeakable women, unspeakable women. And then please look at what we do. Otherwise, shall we, except for the work in connexion with ploughing, change work for some time or how?"

Although his wife spoke so much as this, the man did not say a single word. In this way this hot-tempered man was brought to his bearings; he became quite like a dog. You see, we call a dog: then only he will get food. In such manner we men are the women's dogs. When they tell us to wash our hands, then only we get food.

So there, I have finished also this story.

60. Barea phạsiạrakin reaṅ.

Miťṭaṅ sat phạsiạra ar miťṭaṅ eka phạsiạra ạḍi gatekin tahẽkana. Adọ miť din uni sat phạsiạra dọ hoṛko metadea, Am dọ uni eka phạsiạra sọṅgẹ dọ ọhọm daṛelena. Khange uni sat phạsiạra dọ mọnẹ mọnẹteye mẹnkeťa, Ayọgọ! noko hoṛ dọ ceťko mẹneťa? Iṅ dọṅ sat phạsiạra kana, ar uni eka phạsiạra sọṅgẹ baṅ daṛeǩa? Bhalaṅ biḍạuea sạri sẹ naseko lạị baṛayeťa.

Nonkae bundisante miť din dọ uni eka phạsiạra oṛaǩte peṛaǩe calaoena. Khange uni eka phạsiạra dọ miťṭaṅ khub bhage kuṛi ạgukate aćaǩ bhitạrreye dọhọkadea. Ar aćren bạhu dọe metadea, Ma daka condaeme. Khangeye condakeťa. Adọe metae kana, Ẹ ho, sat phạsiạra, hape, maṅjan tạṅgi toraeme. Khangeye tạṅgi ocokedea.

Adọ uni eka phạsiạraren bạhu dọ daǩe taṅaťkina, adọkin ạbuk bọlọyena. Adọ uni eka phạsiạra sorre miťṭan muṅgạr tahẽkana. Adọ dakakin jọjọm kana. Khange uni eka phạsiạra dọ aćren bạhui ruheť gọťkedea, Dundhi, buluṅ hõ bam adaleťa. Noa muṅgạrtelaṅ dal kuṛi gọťkema. Khange uni eka phạsiạra dọ aćren bạhu ona muṅgạrte miť dhao ḍẹkẹreye dal gọťkedea. Ar bhitạr sẹne ḍhaka ader gọťkadea, ar uni bhage kuṛiye ọr toť darakedea.

---

[1] This story was written down by Lothro Murmu, at the time (1902) Branch post-master at Mohulpahari.

[2] The word phạsiạra is generally used about hypocrites, dishonest persons. Sat means seven and is here to be taken in the meaning of sevenfold, not one who knows seven tricks. The story makes him out to be rather sevenfold the other way. The story does not say anything explicitly, but the reference is possibly to persons who know juggling-tricks.

[3] Inside every Santal house there is in one corner a small place divided off from the rest of the (one-roomed) house by a small wall. This is a place especially sacred to the Ancestors. Food is placed here for these, beer is also libated. Outsiders are not permitted to go in here, as they might make the place religiously

60. THE STORY OF TWO TRICKSTERS[1].

A seven-trickster[2] and a single-trickster were great friends. Then one day some people told the seven-trickster: "You are no match for the single-trickster." Then the seven-trickster turned this over in his mind, saying: "O mother, what is it that these people say? I am a seven-trickster, and I should be no match for the single-trickster? Well, I shall put it to the test and see whether they tell the truth or not."

With this in his mind he one day went to the single-trickster's house on a visit. The single-trickster then brought a fine-looking girl and put her into the inner compartment[3], reserved for the ancestors. He said to his wife: "Put the rice on the fire to boil." And she did so. Thereupon he said to his friend: "I say, seven-trickster; wait a bit, stay for the midday meal, before you go." And he made him wait.

Thereupon the wife of the single-trickster poured out water for them, and they washed their hands and went inside. Now there was a mallet[4] close to where the single-trickster was sitting. The two friends were having their food, when the single-trickster suddenly commenced to scold his wife: "You dunderhead, you have not salted the food. We two might like to beat you into a young girl with this mallet," whereupon he quickly trust her into the inner compartment and dragged the nice-looking girl out with him.

unclean; up to the time of marriage, daughters of the house may go inside; afterwards several of the Santal subsepts do not permit married daughters, when on a visit to their old home, to enter the bhitạr, as this room is called. They are supposed to have come under the influence of other spirits. The separating wall mentioned is sometimes quite low, but may be so high as to hide a Santal. It might perhaps be called a stall, what it really is.

[4] The Santal muṅgạr is made entirely of wood, generally it is a short thick piece of wood with one end pared down so as to be a kind of handle.

Khange uni sat phạsiạra uni kuṛiye ńẹlkede khan, mọnẹ mọnẹteye mẹnkeťa, Iń hõ noa muṅgạr iń idia ar iń bạhuń dal kuṛiyea. Adọ khange ona muṅgạr okoteye idikeťa.

Khange adọ ać hõ onkage daka jọjọm jọkhẹć ona muṅgạr dọ ać sorreye dọhọ akaťa. Khange daka jọmkateye ruheť gọťkedea, Dundhi, buluṅ hõ bam adaleťa. Noa muṅgạrtelaṅ dal kuṛi gọťkema. Khangeye bereť gọťena ar ać bạhui dal gọťkedea ar bhitạr sẹne ḍhaka ader gọťkadea. Arhõe ọr toť gọťkadea are ńẹlkede dọ, ini buḍhi kangeae.

Khange mọnẹ mọnẹteye mẹnkeťa, Cekate bhại bae kuṛilena? Pasẹć baṅ jutleť. Arhõ bhala miť din iń onka legaea. Pasẹ ẹn hilok̕ dọ bạị bạị ńõk̕tegeń dalkeťa, onate pasẹ bae batraolen. Bhala teheń ãṭ ńõk̕teń dalea, pasẹń kuṛikadege. Ona mẹnkate ẹn hilok̕ dọ ãṭteye dalkedea, ar miť dalregeye ṭhẹs gọťkedea.

Adọ khange ar miť din dọ uni eka phạsiạra oṛak̕teye calaoena. Khange uni eka phạsiạrae mẹnkeťa, E ho sat phạsiạra, dela teheń dọ birte sendralaṅ sẹnlenge. Adọkin calaoena. Ar oṛak̕re aćren ạimại dọe mẹn oṭoadea. Am dọ nãhãk̕ miťṭaṅ kulại kiriṅkate oṛak̕re dọhọ hataṛem. Khange uni ạimại dọ sạrige miťṭaṅ kulạiye kiriṅkedea, ar oṛak̕reye dọhọ hataṛ akadea.

Ar unkin dọ sendra sendrate miťṭaṅ kulạikin ńam gọťkedea. Khange 'uni eka phạsiạraren miťṭaṅ setae tahẹ̃kantaea, ar uni seta dọ ạḍi pocrae tahẹ̃kana. Ar uni seta hõ sendrakin idi tora akade tahẹ̃kana. Khange uni eka phạsiạra dọ kulại ńam torae mẹn gọťkeťa, Libhạć! libhạć! ẹk bar ki ghọrer aṅnake nia jao; metak̕me, ẹkkal racate idiyem. Ar uni setae aṛak̕ gọťkadea. Khange uni pocra mara seta dọ kulại bạgiate bọtọrte ḍhumbạk̕kate oṛak̕teye dạṛkeťa. Ar uni eka phạsiạra dọ ać bạhui họhọae kana, Mẹn noi! oṛak̕ jhijme, seta kulạiye idiyedea.

---

5 Hares are fairly common even now after so much of the forest has been cut down.

6 The first two words are the interjections used by Santals to egg dogs on; the rest is in Bengali, but afterwards rendered in Santali by the narrator.

7 A common way of hunting the hare with the Santals is to let the dog chase and catch the hare. This is what the dog is supposed to do here.

When the seven-trickster saw this girl, he said to himself: "I shall take this mallet with me and also beat my wife into a girl again." So he secretly took the mallet away.

While having his food he also had put the mallet down close to himself; and having taken his rice, he started scolding his wife: "You dunderhead, you have not salted the food. We two should like to beat you into a girl again with this mallet." So he rose and gave his wife a blow and thrust her inside the inner compartment. Again he dragged her out and looked at her, she was the same old woman.

He then asked himself: "How is it, my friend, that she did not become a girl again? Perhaps I did not hit her properly. I shall try to do it over again some day. Perhaps it was because I this day beat her somewhat lightly that it did not take any effect on her. Well, I shall try to give her a fairly hard blow; then perhaps I may make her into a girl again." Having come to this decision, he that day gave her a hard blow; with one single blow he cracked her.

Afterwards he again one day went to the single-trickster's house. This one said: "I say, seven-trickster, come along, let us to-day go to the forest to hunt, before doing anything else." So they went. Before they went, he instructed his wife: "You buy a hare and keep it in the house." And, truth to tell, his wife bought a hare and kept it in the house until their return.

Now these two as they were hunting caught sight of a hare[5]. The single-trickster had a dog, and this dog was an awful poltroon. This dog they had also taken along with them for the hunt. As soon as the single-trickster saw the hare, he called out: "At him! at him! nimm[6] ihn augenblichlich nach dem Hofe des Hauses!" that is to say, take him at once to the court-yard. So he set his dog free; but this poltroon of a dog let the hare alone[7] and, crouching from fear, ran straight home. And the single-trickster was calling out to his wife: "Have a care, you! open the door; the dog is taking a hare home!"

Adǫ khange uni eka phąsiąrae mẹneťa, Ẹ ho sat phąsiąra, delaṅ nitoḱ dǫ oṛaḱtelaṅ calaḱa, ẹnte ąḍi bhage seta nitoḱ dǫ jąnić oṛaḱteye idi sẹṭẹrkedea. Khange oṛaḱtekin calaoena. Ar oṛaḱ sẹṭẹr tora uni eka phąsiąra dǫ aćren bąhui kuli gǫťkedea, Nǫtẹge seta kuląiye ągukede? Adǫe metadea, Uni oṛaḱreń dǫhǫ akadea.

Khange adǫ uni sat phąsiąrą dǫ mǫnẹ mǫnẹteye mẹnkeťa, Durrẹ! nui dǫ bejãe bhage seta kantaeyae. Adǫe mǫnẹana, Iń dǫń hijuḱa ar iń ątkirea.

Khange sąri miť din dǫ ńindą hẹćkateye ątkirkedea. Ar dosar hiloḱ dǫ ać hõ sendrae idikedea. Ar bir bǫlǫ torage miťṭaṅ kuląiye ńam gǫťkedea. Ar ać hõ onkae libhąć libhąćkeťa, are mẹnkeťa, Ẹk bar ki ghǫrer aṅnake nia jao, are aṛaḱ gǫťkadea. Khange uni seta dǫ bǫtǫrte ẹkkal oṛaḱteye dąṛkeťa. Are hǫhǫ gǫťkeťa, Mẹn noi, oṛaḱte seta kuląiye idiyedea. Adǫ tayǫm tayǫmte ać hõ oṛaḱteye hẹćena, ar aćren hąhui kuli gǫťkedea, Nẹtẹge seta kuląiye ągukede?

Khange bąhuttẹťe rǫṛ ruąṛadea, Ukurić baṅ? Cele kuląi? Uni cǫṅ seta dǫ ẹkẹnaḱgeye ńir hẹćen.

Adǫ uni sat phąsiąrae mẹnkeťa, Tǫbẹ pasẹ jǫmkede cǫe ceť cǫṅ.

Adǫ arhõ miť dine idikedea, ar bire bǫlǫyente sendrae ẹkǫṕkeťa. Ar miť ghąṛi tayǫmte arhõ sąri miťṭaṅ kuląiye ńam gǫťkedea. Arhõ onkage libhąć gǫť ar ǫnẹ pąhil lekae hǫhǫ gǫťkeťa. Khange ẹn hiloḱ dǫ sǫṅgẹ sǫṅgẹteye khudąu idikedea, ar kuląi bągiate ąkinge ẹkkal oṛaḱtekin dąṛkeťa.

Adǫ atoren hǫṛko metae kana, Am lekan lelha dǫ bąnuḱkoa. Kuląi bągiate seta dǫ cedaḱem lagayedea? Khange adǫ ẹn hiloḱ khon adǫ sendra dǫe bągikeťa.

Adǫ arhõ uni eka phąsiąra oṛaḱte peṛaḱe calaoena. Adǫ uni eka phąsiąrae mẹnkeťa, Ẹ ho sat phąsiąra, delaṅ teheń dǫ hakolaṅ bąṛsi ągukoa. Ar bąhutae dǫe mẹn oṭoadea, Am dǫ nãhãḱ cǫḍgǫć

Thereupon the single-trickster said: "I say, seven-trickster, come along now, let us go home; because by now this excellent dog has likely reached home with the hare." So they returned home. Having arrived there, the single-trickster asked his wife: "Has the dog brought the hare here?" She replied: "I have put the hare inside."

The seven-trickster then said to himself: "Strange, this dog of his must be an extraordinary dog." And he made up his mind: "I shall come back and carry it off."

And, truth to tell, one night he came and stole the dog. The next day he also took the dog out hunting; and just as he entered the forest, he caught sight of a hare, and he also egged the dog on in the same way and said: "Nimm ihn augenblichlich nach dem Hofe des Hauses!" and set him free. But the dog from fear ran straight away home. He also called out: "Have a care, you! the dog is taking a hare home!" Some time afterwards he himself also reached home and at once asked his wife: "Did the dog bring the hare here?"

His wife answered: "Why, where is it? which hare? There is the dog, he came running back without anything."

The seven-trickster then said: "Then he has eaten him, very likely."

Again one day he took the dog out, and entering the forest, he commenced to hunt. A moment afterwards, truth to tell, he again caught sight of a hare. Again he egged him on like previously and called out like he did the first time. But that day he followed after the dog running, and leaving the hare alone they both ran straight home.

The village people then said to him: "There is no fellow stupid like you. Leaving the hare, why do you chase your dog home?" And from that day he left off hunting.

Again he went on a visit to the house of the single-trickster. This one said: "I say, seven-trickster, come along, let us catch fish to-day." But to his wife he said, before they started: "You

hako kiriṅkate dọhọ hataṛkom jivẹtge. Adọ ạkin dọ hako bạ̃ṛsikin calaoena.

Ar sẹn torae caḍo gọtketa darhare. Khange mitṭaṅ cọḍgọć hakoe gẹr gọtena, ar uni dọ ona daṅ sudhạ oṛak sẹne capat gọtketa. Are mẹnketa, Ẹ ho sat phạsiạra, delaṅ nitok dọ oṛaktelaṅ calaka. Jạnić nitok dọ jọtọko calaoena.

Adọ oṛaktekin hẹćena. Adọ hẹć sẹṭẹr tora uni eka phạsiạra dọ aćren oṛak họṛe kuli gọtkedea, Nọtẹ hakoṅ capat gọtkatko, baṅko hẹćlena?

Adọe rọṛ ruạṛadea, Hẹć akangeako. Onko phạtiạkreṅ dọhọ akatkoa. Adọ uni eka phạsiạra dọ bọlọkateye tul oḍoṅ gọtketkoa, mit phạtiạkge.

Khange onko hako ṅẹlkate uni sat phạsiạra dọ mọnẹ mọnẹteye mẹnketa, Noa dọ bejãe bhage bạ̃ṛsi kantaea. Din hilokge jạnić noṅkae gọćkoa. Adọe mẹnketa, Dhinạṅ nãhãk iṅ ạtkirtaea.

Adọ ạyup jọkhẹć hẹćkate ona bạ̃ṛsiye ạtkirkettaea. Adọ dosar hilok setakre bạ̃ṛsiye calaoena, ar sẹn tora darhareye caḍo gọtketa. Khange mitṭaṅ cọḍgọć hakoe gẹr gọtena, ar ać hõ onkage oṛak sẹne capat gọtkata. Are mẹnoana, Jạnićko calaoena. Adọe hẹć gọtena are kuliketkoa, Nọtẹge hakoṅ capat gọtkatko hẹćenako sẹko baṅa?

Adọko metae kana, Ẹkẹnake hẹćena ar hakoe khọj kana oṛakre, lelha cudi dọ!

---

8 We have no name for the fish mentioned; I believe the scientific name is Ophiocephalus gachua. It is considered one of the best fishes for food by the Santals.

9 The woman uses the third person, as they sometimes do, to express contempt; the person is, so to say, not there to be spoken to.

A variant of the above story, written by Sagram Murmu, tells of seven brothers, who are called s a t p a g ọ l, the last word being used somewhat like the p h ạ s i ạ r a of the story rendered above. It is told that these brothers were able to fool anybody in connexion with anything whatsoever; they could speak so smoothly and nice; they would persuade anybody to do their will and come out with things hidden. No one in their neighbourhood was able to speak like these.

buy some cọḍgọć fish[8] and keep them alive in the meantime." Thereupon the two of them went to fish.

As soon as they reached the pool, he at once let his line down, and a cọḍgọć fish rose to the bait at once; he then threw the fishing-rod and all in the direction of his home and said: "I say, seven-trickster, come let us go home now; they have likely all gone there now."

They reached home, and as soon as they arrived, the single-trickster asked his wife: "I threw the fish in this direction; did they not come here?"

She answered: "They have come. Look there, I have put them into the basket." The single-trickster then went in and brought the fish out, one basketful.

Seeing the fish, the seven-trickster said to himself: "It must be an exceedingly good fishing-rod that he has. Very likely he catches fish in this way every day." And he said: "Some time later to-day I shall carry his rod off."

In the evening he returned and carried the fishing-rod off. Next morning he went to fish, and as soon as he reached the pool, he let the line down. A cọḍgọć fish rose to the bait at once; then he also threw the whole tackle in the direction of his home, and said: "They have gone there likely". He returned home and asked them: "I threw the fish in this direction, have they come or how?"

His people said to him: "He[9] came empty-handed and demands fish here at home, the stupid wretch!"

For this reason other people were in the habit of taking these with them to speak for them in the village-councils, and so on.

Now there was a son of a sister of theirs; as he grew up, he learnt all the tricks of his uncles and a good deal more, the result being that they got angry and wanted to harm their nephew. When he learnt this, he invited his uncles, that their power might be tested. They came, he killed a castrated goat and

Khange mone moneteye menketa, Sarige uni eka phasiara songe do ohoń darelena. Ado en hiiok khone bagiketa uni songe gatek do. Ado mucatena.

61. Mittań lelha tuar kora reań.

Sedaere, kathae, mittań tuar korae tahẽkana. Ado bai baite uni gidra doe hara idiyena; menkhan jãhãnak kami eman sente do dhere lelhagea.

Mit dhao eṅgate kulikedea, Henda go, ińak bapla do hoe akana se bań? Eṅgat doe metadea, Amak bapla do, babu, gidrare hoe akantama phalna atore. Ado uni kora doe menketa, Den go, satu sambarańme, pańja aguyeań.

Ado uni eṅgattet doe satu sambaradea. Adoe calaoena; calak calakteye pańja ńamketa bahu orak, ar onko do jãwãe gomke menteko atań daramkedea, arko pera barakedea khub leka. Ar tayomteye pera bhagaoen khan doe metatkoa, Calakaliń, bidakaliṅpe. Adoko bidakatkina. Uni kora do lahateye odokena, ar uni kuri do adi tayom.

---

feasted them; they slept there, and early in the morning the nephew went out and arranged with some fisherman to bring six large fishes to his home. He arranged with his mother that she should receive and keep these fishes. Thereupon he took his uncles to a tank to bathe.

He started fishing, and as soon as he had a bite, he pulled his fishing-line out and called out in Bengali to the fish, that it should go home. When he had done so six times, he said he expected they now had enough for the day's need and asked his uncles to come home with him. They did not see any fish and asked where these were; to this the nephew answered: "Did you not hear me? Why, they have gone home." And there they found the fish.

Now these naturally would do the same; they invited their nephew, feasted him on fowls and kept him for the night. Next morning they all went to fish, and the uncles did exactly as the nephew had done, calling out in the same way in Bengali; but they had not made any previous arrangements, so when they came home and called for the fish, they were met with a flat denial. None there had even seen a fish.

Then he said to himself: "In very truth, I am no match for the single-trickster." And from that day he left off associating with him. So it is ended.

61. THE STORY OF AN IDIOTIC FATHERLESS BOY[1].

Once upon a time long ago, people tell, there lived a fatherless boy. The boy grew slowly into maturity; as regards work of any kind, he was utterly stupid.

One day he asked his mother: "I say, mother, has my marriage taken place or not?" His mother answered: "Your marriage, my boy, took place while you were a child[2] in such and such a village." And the young man said: "Do, mother, give me food for the journey; I shall go after her and bring her."

His mother made up some food for him for the journey, and he went. Going along, he found his wife's house, and they received him as their son-in-law and entertained him lavishly. Afterwards, when he thought he had been there long enough, he said to them: "We shall go; bid us farewell[3]." They did so. The man went out ahead, and the girl came a long while afterwards.

The uncles then understood that they had been taken in and commenced to seek some means of taking revenge. They thereupon killed a buffalo-cow belonging to their nephew. The story then goes on to tell the same as is told in the story of Span, the end being that his uncles first killed all their cattle and finally burnt down their own houses and became utterly poor.

61 [1] This story was told by the late Suna Hãsdak̔ Sirdar, of Benagaria. It is partly horrible, and it should not be understood as representing the standards of Santal feeling. The idea is to show how utterly stupid or downright mad people may be. It is recorded here to show what people may be able to tell. It is possibly a story current among the lowest castes of people found in the neighbourhood. Certain details are not in accordance with Santal customs.

[2] Since the Santal 'rebellion' (1855) a few Santals have been marrying their children early, generally to show themselves as 'civilized'; but I do not think it has been practised with quite small children. The Santal custom is to marry grown up youths; child marriage is a Hindu custom.

[3] Always a ceremonial affair when relatives leave after a visit.

Adọ uni kọṛa dọ mitṭaṅ dare buṭạre duṛupḱkateye tạṅgi akadea, are ṅẹl daramedea. Ar uni kuṛi dọ dustur lekako sindur gọṭadea. Ar cạndire jọrọṅ jọrọṅ sindur ṅẹlkeṭte uni kọṛa dọe mẹnkeṭa, Bạhu mẹnte maṅ idiyede, mẹnkhan bọhọḱ paṛaḱentae dọ; nui dọe gujuḱa, bae baṅcaoḱa; bạṅ dọhọyea, nui dọṅ bọdọlea.

Ona takrege mitṭaṅ họṛ ona họrte mitṭaṅ ḍaṅgrae idiye kan tahẽkana. Khangeye metadea, Dini ho, nui ḍaṅgra dọ imạṅme, nui iṅ dọṅ emama. Uni họṛ hõe kusiyena. Adọ uni ḍaṅgrae hataokedea. Adọ calaḱ calaḱte mitṭaṅ ḍạḍi lekae ṅamkeṭa, ar ọṇḍẹye jirạu ṅõḱena; khange uni ḍaṅgra dọ dustur lekae ạḍoyeṭ kana. Adọ uni kọṛa dọ uni ḍaṅgrae bẹṅgẹṭae kana are mẹnkeṭa, Iṅ bạhu hõ bọhọḱ paṛaḱentaea, onateṅ bọdọlkedea, ar nui hõ nitoḱ dọ laċ bọgọċentaea, ọhọe baṅcaolena; nui hõe gujuḱgea, bạṅ dọhọyea nui hõ.

Onakoe mọnẹjoṅ tak khange miṭ họṛ ona họrteye hijuḱ kana, mitṭaṅ mẹrọme idiye kana. Khangeye metae kana, Henda ho, nui mẹrọmem ẹmkoḱa? Nui ḍaṅgraṅ emama. Uni họṛ dọ ạḍiye kusiyena. Khange uni mẹrọme hataokedea, ar ḍaṅgrae emadea. Adọ calaḱ calaḱte mitṭaṅ gaḍae ṅamkeṭa, ar ọṇḍẹ dọ jọm lạgiṭe duṛupḗna, ceṭko cọṅko kol akawade nạihạr khon, adọe jojọm kana, ar mẹrọm dọe tọl akadea. Adọe jọjọm kan tuluċ uni mẹrọme bẹṅgẹṭae kana, aċ ceṭ leka mocae laṛaoeṭa, mẹrọm hõ akoaḱ dustur lekae pạḱgur kana. Khane mẹnkeṭa, Nui mẹrọm dọ ya iṅe besaoediṅ kana; ũh, nui dọ bae bhagea, iṅe besaoiṅ kan dọ, baṅ dọhọyea. Adọe jọm baṛakeṭteye jirạu akana.

Inạḱ khange mitṭaṅ họṛ mitṭaṅ kohṇḍae idiyeṭa. Khangeye metadea, E ho, ona kohṇḍa imạṅme, iṅ dọ mẹrọm iṅ emama. Khange uni họṛ dọ kohṇḍa bọdọl mẹrọme ṅamkedete ạḍiye rạskạyena. Khange adọe calao idiyena ar oṛaḱe tioḱkeṭa. Adọ

[4] Sindur is the vermilion or red lead applied to the bride's forehead, and otherwise extensively used for religious purposes.

The young man sat down at the foot of a tree and was waiting for her, and he saw her, as she was coming. Now they had according to custom applied sindur[4] to her. When he saw the bright red sindur on her forehead, the young man said: "I am taking her along to be my wife; but her head has cracked, she will die, she will not live; I shall not keep her, I shall exchange her."

Just then a man was driving a bullock along that road. He spoke to him: "Here you, give me this bullock, I shall give you this one." The man was pleased, so he got the bullock. As the young man passed along he came to a spring and rested there for a while; the bullock then, as is their custom, passed water. The young man was looking at the bullock and said: "My wife's head was cracked, so I exchanged her; now this one's stomach has been split open; he will certainly not live; this one also will die; I shall not keep this one either."

While he was turning this over in his mind, a man was coming along the road, leading a goat. So he says to him: "I say, you, would you give me your goat? I shall let you have this bullock." The man was very pleased. So he took the goat and gave the bullock to the man.

As he went along, he came to a river and sat down there to eat something or other that they had given him to take with him from his wife's home; he was eating, and the goat he had tied up. While he was eating, he was looking at the goat; now as he himself was moving his mouth chewing, similarly the goat also, according to the custom of goats, was chewing the cud. He then said: "This wretched goat is mimicking me; dear me, she is no good; she is mimicking me; I shall not keep her." After having had his food, he was resting.

Just then a man passed, carrying a pumpkin, and he said to him: "O you, give me that pumpkin; I shall give you this goat." As he got the goat in exchange for the pumpkin, the man was very glad. The young man then went along and reached home.

ạḍi rạskạte ona kohṇḍae gẹt́keta, ar aćgeye utui lạgit́ karahere bhoraokate khange khube jolak̓ kana; tayọmte ona dọ lẹyen khan ona dọ sẹṅgẹl tạpiste khub khad khad hẹḍẹjok̓ kana. Adọ uni koṛae mẹneta, Ạijo, iń dọ mẹrọm sẹ celeye mitạń kana, onateye bọd bodaoạń kana. Arhõe jol jolak̓ kana, ar onka khad khadge hẹḍẹjok̓ kana. Khane mẹnketa, Alom bọd bodaoka, baṅkhan iń tawak̓ gẹjermea. Mẹnkhan tinạk̓e jolak̓ kan, unạk̓ge onka saḍe kana. Adọ edrete racateye kuṭuṅ oḍokketa, are tawak̓ gẹjẹrketa, are mẹnketa, Ma nitok̓ dọ bọd bodaok̓me.

Adọ uni koṛaren eṅgat jọtọ uniak̓ katha añjọmte ar ona kạmi ńẹlte ạḍiye mọn dukena, are metae kana, Cekate, bạbu, unạk̓ dọm lelhawa? cet́ lekatem ạsuloka?

Adọ tahẹn tahẹnte hoṛo irok̓ din tiokena. Ar uni koṛa dọ cet́ kạmi hõ bae baḍaea, cekate hoṛo hõko ira ona hõ bae baḍaea. Adọ uniren engat dọe metadea, Do bạbu, datrọm idite hoṛo irok̓ calak̓me.

Khange uni koṛa dọ datrọm sap̓kate hoṛo khẹtteye calaoena, ar datrọm dọ hoṛo budạ ṭhene dọhọketa, are mẹnketa, Ma khub irok̓talaṅme; iń dọ dakań ạguia oṛak̓ khon.

Ona mẹnkateye calaoena oṛak̓te. Adọ eṅgat dọe kulikedea, Tinạk̓ ẹm irketa, bạbu? Uni dọe mẹnketa, Datrọmgeń mẹn oṭo akawadea, khub leka irok̓talaṅme, dakań ạguitalaṅa; dẹn bar bakhra daka imạńme, datrọm jạnić rẹṅgẹćedea, calao gọdok̓ạń.

Khange uniak̓ katha leka eṅgat dọ bar bakhrae emadeteye calaoena. Adọ sẹnkateye ńẹlketa, baṅ ir akana, enkage menaka. Adọe menketa, baṅ dọ teheń dọe ruạk̓ kan, ona iạte baṅ irok̓ kan.

---

[5] The karahe is a flattish, wide-mouthed dish, as a rule earthenware.

[6] The Santal word is ordinarily used about the sound emitted by he-goats in heat, it is also used about the babbling of drunk people.

With great joy he cut the pumpkin, and having put it in an earthenware dish[5] to make curry of it, he himself made a fire and kept this burning vigorously. Afterwards, when the pumpkin had dissolved, it was boiling and bubbling on account of the fire. The young man then said: "Strange, does it take me to be a goat or what, since it is babbling[6] at me?" He put more fuel to the fire, and it was boiling and bubbling in the same way. So he said: "Don't babble, else I shall dash you to pieces." But the more he added fuel to the fire, the more it was making the same sound. So he became angry, and carrying the dish out into the courtyard, he dashed it to pieces there and said: "Well, now babble away!"

Hearing what the young man said and seeing what he did, his mother became very grieved and said to him: "How is it, my boy, that you are so stupid? How will you be able to support yourself?"

Gradually the harvest-time came. The young man knew absolutely no work; he did not even know how people reap paddy. His mother said to him: "Now, my boy, take the sickle with you and go and reap paddy."

The young man then took a sickle and went to the paddy field; he put the sickle down at the foot of the paddy-straw and said: "Do work assidously and reap paddy for both of us; I am going to fetch food from home."

Saying this, he went home. His mother asked him: "How much have you reaped, my boy?" "I spoke to the sickle, before I left," he replied, "saying, 'work assidously and reap for both of us; I am going to fetch our food'; so now give me two portions of food; the sickle is likely hungry; I shall go at once."

In accordance with what he said, his mother gave him two portions of food, and he went. Having reached there, he saw that nothing had been reaped; all was as when he left. So he said: "I wonder whether it should be ill to-day; for this reason

Khange datrǫm sap̓kateye tunumket̓ dǫ lǫlǫ kan, adǫe mẹnket̓a, Uh, ruạk̓ kantege bae irlak̓a. Adǫe mẹnket̓a, Cekateye bogek̓a? Adǫ mit̓ṭaṅe hudisket̓a, Baberte pạsikate kũireń ãṛgoea, pasẹye bogeyenge. Sạrige datrǫm baberte pạsikate kũireye ãṛgoket̓a; adǫ dak̓re topoyen khan dǫ reaṛena; adǫe mẹnket̓a, Nit dǫe bogeyena; ẹnte lǫlǫ dǫ cabayena, reaṛ kanae.

Ona thoṛa din t̓ayǫmte eṅgattẹt̓e ruạyena, khange adǫ disạ hẹćadea, baṅma, Mit̓ dhao datrǫme ruạyenre iń dǫ kũireń ãṛgoket̓a are bogeyena, tǫbẹ nitok̓ nui hõń onkale khan dǫ pasẹ dhorageye bogek̓a. Ona mẹnkate eṅgattẹt̓ hǫṭǫk̓re pạsikedete kũireye ãṛgokedea. Khange uni eṅgat dǫe pạsikedeteye gǫćena; are ǫr rakap̓edere uni dǫe isiṛ akat̓a. Khangeye mẹn gǫt̓ket̓a, Nitok̓ iń gǫ dǫe bogeyenteye landawạń kana. Adǫ ǫr rakap̓kateye ńẹlkede dǫe gǫć akan.

Khane mẹnket̓a, Hǫṛko ma akoren gǫć hǫṛ gaḍateko idikoa, iń dǫ okateń idiyea? Ho, iń dǫ buruteń idiyea. Adǫ mit̓ṭań pạṭiạteye pǫṭǫmkedea, are hẹrmẹt̓kedea, ar buruteye mohṇḍayena. Adǫe calao idik̓ kana; calak̓ calak̓te hǫrre tinre cǫń eṅgattẹt̓ dǫe bujurena, ar uni dǫ ẹkẹn pạṭiạtẹt̓ge buruṛeye giḍi oṭokat̓a. Khane ruạṛ hijuk̓ kana, ar hǫrre eṅgattẹt̓e ńẹlkedea, adǫe mẹnket̓a, Ǫkǫe ren buḍhi hǫṛ cǫe gǫćente nǫṇḍẹko giḍi akade, jạnić toyo eman nãhãk̓ko jǫmea; cedak̓ cǫń nǫṇḍẹ dǫko giḍi akade? Iń gǫ ma hana buruteń idi oṭokade. Adǫ bạgiadeteye ruạṛena oṛak̓te. Uni koṛa reak̓ dǫ inạk̓tege cabayena.

[7] The 'feverish' sickle is a standing joke with the Santals, mostly applied to lazy people.

[8] What is referred to does not agree with any kind of disposal of a dead body. Santals burn their dead ones, generally and preferably near water; the Hindus do the same, and so far as possible on the banks of a stream. It is unnecessary to point out that the details have no reality behind them.

perhaps it does not reap." He took the sickle up and felt it, it was hot; so he said: "Dear me, it has fever[7]; therefore it did not reap." So he said: "How will it get well?" He then hit upon a remedy: "I shall fix a string-noose to it and let it down into the well." Truth to tell, he fixed the noose and let it down into the well, and when it had been immersed in the water, it became cool; and he said: "Now it is well again; it is not hot any longer, it is cold."

A short while afterwards his mother became ill, and the young man happened to remember this: "Once when the sickle had fever, I let it down into the well, and it was cured; so if I now do the same to her, she will perhaps get well undoubtedly." Having this in his mind, he put a noose round his mother's neck and let her down into the well. But he strangled his mother, so that she died. When he was pulling her up, she was grinning, and he said: "Now mother has got well again and is smiling to me." But when he had pulled her out, he saw that she was dead.

Then he said: "People take their dead ones to the river[8]; where shall I take her? O, I shall take her to the mountain." He wrapped her up in a mat, and taking her under his arm, he started for the mountain. He was going along; as he was walking, some time or other his mother fell out, and he carried the empty mat, threw this down somewhere on the mountain and left it there. As he was returning, he saw his mother lying on the road, and he said: "Somebody's old woman has died, and they have thrown her away here; likely jackals or the like will eat her presently; why have they thrown her away here? I took my mother to the mountain over there and left her there." So he let her lie there and returned home.

The story of this young man is finished with this.

STORIES REFERRING TO OGRES

SANTAL IDEAS ABOUT RAKAS.

SEVERAL Santal folktales contain some reference to a class of fabulous beings, which are called rakas or rakhas. The name itself is not originally Santali, but derived from Sanskrit rākshasa through Hindi.

We have no right to infer from this fact that all such stories or the ideas underlying them have been borrowed from Indo-Aryan peoples. The name may have been found convenient for application to fabulous beings believed by the Santals to inhabit forests and hills. Analogous cases might easily be adduced. And the stories themselves have throughout been modified so as to fall in with Santal ideas and imagination.

Some of the tales contain direct references to the Rāmāyaṇa, the well-known Sanskrit epos of the poet Vālmīki, which itself seems to be founded on some historical event.

The hero of the Rāmāyaṇa is Rāma, the eldest son of an ancient king of Ayodhyā, the present Oudh, who was banished by his father, at the instigation of one of his queens, and spent fourteen years in exile, accompanied by his wife Sītā and his brother Lakshmaṇa. They wandered about in the woods, and were much harassed by rākshasas and other beings, but found a faithful friend in the monkey king Hanuman, whose services were of special value when Rāvaṇa, the king of the rākshasas, robbed the faithful Sītā and brought her across the sea to Laṅkā or Ceylon.

Now it is a curious fact that Santal traditions state that their ancestors assisted Ram against Rabon raj, i. e. king Rāvaṇa, though a certain school of traditionalists deny that such was the case. Both statements taken together might be constructed to imply that part of the ancestors of the present-day Santals had something to do with the events underlying the confabulation of the Rāmāyaṇa, and that their settlements were, in those remote times, situated not far from the present Oudh, and in this connexion it is perhaps worth mentioning that one of the folktales in my possession makes the forests of Ayodhyā the scene of a Santal hunt.

In such circumstances it would become intelligible why Hanuman, Rāma's helper, and his hosts are described as monkeys. The word hanuman itself is in Hindi and Bengali the name of the common black-faced monkey. The assistance was actually rendered by aboriginal tribes. Brahmin pride would not permit the author to mention these helpers as human beings, but hit upon the idea of praising them as monkeys, endowed with supernatural powers. It might be mentioned that Hindus (especially formerly, it is now perhaps getting out of use) very frequently have referred to the Santals as hanumans or monkeys. One class of human beings is consequently called animals.

Now if this theory is correct, it would not be difficult to suppose that Rāma's different enemies of non-Aryan race were referred to as demons or evil spirits, having taken material shape, and consequently that the monsters referred to as rākshasa really were barbarous tribes fighting with king Rāma.

We may perhaps go one step further. Supposing that the story of the Rāmāyaṇa is not pure invention and imagination, but in some way or other refers to what may in the end be reality (however distorted), we should be justified in thinking that what is told of rākshasas and other monsters may be connected with superstitions current previous to or at the time of Vālmīki or his possible later 'editors'; they are not pure children of his own imagination.

Whatever the origin of the idea of rakas may be among the Santals, the present-day people have an indefinite belief that some fabulous beings, now so called, are found somewhere or, anyhow, have been found in a former age. None of the present age has ever seen them, and they are not believed to be found in this country at the present time.

Their ideas as to the shape or body of these monsters vary. Some say that they are bigger than any animal; some tell that they are able to open their mouth so wide as to fill the space between heaven and earth. They, or some of them, are also supposed to be able to alter their shape. They will devour all kinds of animals and also men. They may eat all they find, but are never satisfied. For this reason the present day Santals use rakas as a term of opprobrium for a voracious eater, something like glutton.

Some of the rakas beings are said to have bodies like that of man, the head only, or especially the mouth, being like that of a horse. This class consequently greatly resembles the beings called ekaguḍiạ or ghoṛmũhą̃, who are reported to have only one leg and a head (or only the mouth) like that of a horse. These ekagudias are (or were up to some fifty years ago) believed by the Santals to be living somewhere in the East; they eat human beings, which they buy for silver money, that they themselves cast. It is within the writer's knowledge that Santals have been fearing that persons who were taken to tea-gardens as coolies were exported to be sold to the ekagudias.

If we now turn to the stories, we find the qualities mentioned represented. They all refer to a former age, and some of them seem to be directly or indirectly connected with the story of the Rāmāyaṇa. The heroes Ram and Lokhon (acc. to Santal traditions twins), i. e., Rāma and Lakshmaṇa, are stated to have hunted these monsters and to have eradicated them.

Hearing the stories we should sometimes think that they referred to wild animals, such as tigers. Other rakas are described as practically human beings in shape; only they have some supernatural powers, and they eat people. They live in pairs, are males and females. Sons are never mentioned; but they have daughters, although these seem to be human girls, adopted and in some way kept for service. Marriage between such a daughter and a man is presupposed as possible. They have one characteristic in common: with all their supposed power they are all stupid and easily duped and outwitted.

We have in Norway, that is to say, in Norwegian folktales, a class of beings called 'troll', which in many characteristics seem to resemble the rakas. It has been suggested that some of these 'troll' find their explanation in the phenomena of nature, seen in dim light or indistinctly, not understood, but feared, and given life and shape by imagination.

Some of the qualities of the rakas might possibly be explained as referring to nature powers; but it does not seem easily possible to take the beings themselves as having such an origin. Perhaps an Indian Kittelsen (see the illustrations in his 'Folk og Trold') might here be able to find something hidden to others.

Besides animals, epidemic disease might be thought of in explanation of certain stories. But, as hinted at above, the most likely theory seems to the writer to be, that the rakas, both of the Rāmāyaṇa and of Hindu and Santal folktales, really represent some race or other, with which the people has been in some inimical contact, people with strange and not understood habits, looked upon as savages in comparison with the narrator's race, and consequently held in fear. Analogous misunderstandings are numerous; we may mention the origin of the centaur and the unicorn and other similar beings.

I shall confine myself to these remarks. To sum up: the name of these beings, rakas, is borrowed; many of the stories are probably also borrowed, although adapted to suit the Santals. The rakas possibly or even probably are ultimately to be connected with barbarous unrecognized races, dressed up by imagination, superstition and fear.

For the sake of non-Indian readers rakas has been rendered 'ogre'.

62. Rakas ar ḍom reak̕.

Ram Lokhon do sendrakin daṛan kan tahẽkana, ạḍi lạṭu lạṭu janwarkin goćet̕ko tahẽkana, ar rakas hõkin goćet̕ko tahẽkana. Sedae jugre nonka saṅge rakasko tahẽkana, onko do ekkalte disomko ujạṛet̕ kan tahẽkana; boge Ram Lokhonkin janamente disom khon rakaskin goć maraoket̕koa.

Mit̕ jaegare maraṅ utạr rakaskin goćkede khan ạkinak̕ khaṇḍate rakas reaṅ ramakin get̕ chaḍaoket̕taetekin calaoena oka sen coṅ. Khen leka mit̕ṭaṅ ḍom do loṭa dak̕ teveṅkate ṭạṇḍi sene calak̕ kana, ar ekkalte okare rakase goć akan ṭhenge baḍae akat̕ lekae calao got̕ena. Khangeye ńelkede do maraṅ utạre gitić akan. Uni ḍom ma bae baḍaejoṅ kan nui rakas do Ram Lokhon tikinkin goć akadea mente; ać doe menjoṅ kana, nui doe gitić akana mente. Ona loṭa dak̕e dohoket̕a bại bạite, ar maraṅ utạr dhiriye kuṭuṅ ạguket̕a, ar rakas hoṛmoreye giḍi got̕kat̕a. Uni rakas do nasenak̕ hõ bae laṛaolena. Uni ḍom ar hõ mit̕ṭaṅ dhiriye hobor ạguket̕a; unre hõ ạḍi ãṭteye giḍiadea, enre hõ thoṛa hõ bae laṛaolena.

---

[1] As told by Bhuju Murmu of Dhopahar. This story shows how the names of old heroes, Rama and Lakshmana, live among the Santals. With regard to Ram and Lokhon, as the Santals call them, the following may be noted. They tell that they were twins, sons of the bạṭki (first wife) of Dasarat, who is reported to have had three wives and to have had twins with each of them, all boys. When twins are born among the Santals, it is a general custom, if they are boys, to give the first pair the names of Ram and Lokhon, and succeeding pairs the names of the other twin sons of Dasarat; girl twins are named in the same way Chitạ and Kạprạ, Chitạ being the same as Sita, king Rama's wife.

62. THE OGRE AND THE DOM[1].

RAM and Lokhon were going about hunting; they were killing very big big animals; they were also killing ogres. In olden times there was such a multitude of ogres, they were absolutely devastating the country; it was fortunate that Ram and Lokhon were born, so that they killed and annihilated the ogres from the land.

Once when they in a certain place had killed an immensely big ogre, they cut off with their weapons[2] the claws of the ogre and went away somewhere. Accidentally a Dom was passing there with a lota[3] full of water on his way to the fields[4]; he came suddenly to the place where the ogre had been killed, just as if he knew of it. He suddenly caught sight of the ogre, lying there so immensely large. Now the Dom did not know that Ram and Lokhon had killed the ogre; he thought he was lying down there. So he very quietly put the lota with water down, and lifting up a very big stone[5] he carried this to the spot and threw it down on the ogre's body. The ogre did not move the least; so the Dom again brought a stone in his arms; this time also he threw it at the ogre with great force; still he did not move at all.

2 The word used generally implies weapon, such as arrow-head, spear or sword.

3 We have no word to translate loṭa, a small brass pot, found in every household.

4 A common veiled expression about going out to pay a call of nature, when water is carried along.

5 The words used about carrying here and immediately below imply that the stones were so big that the man just managed to carry them along, keeping them in his arms against his body.

Adoe bujhạuketa, goć akanae mente. Uni ḍom do ạḍi rạskạkate oṛakteye ńir calaoena, ar mitṭań marań utạr churiye ạguketa, ar Ram Lokhon tikinkin get saredlet rama, uni ḍom hõe get ạguketa.

Pạhil khone baḍae akat tahẽkana, Jãhãege rakasko goćle khan ar ramako ạgule khan, raj do hoponerae goṅakoa, ar mit hĩs disom hạtińe emakoa; onate uni ḍom do ạḍi kurumuṭu kate onako ramae chaḍaoketa, ar oṛakte senkate aćren era ar sanam gidrạkoe dal ńirketkoa, ar ḍhol hõ baṛge sene capat giḍikata.

Ado rakas reań rama raj ṭhene idiketa. Raj do ńelketre hõ bae pạtiạulena; menketae, Noa do amem goć akade rakas reań rama do bań kana, ente purạu rama do bań kana, noa rama reań coṭ sen do okoe coko get chaḍao idiketa.

Ado ona katha ańjomkate ḍom doe menketa, Bań, raja saheb, ińgeń goć akadea, ado den hoponera ar mit hạṭiń disom imạńme. Khange uni raj ona katha ańjomkateye menketa, Hẽ, hoponerań emokgea, ar disom hõń emokgea, hapeń suṭik baṛalege.

Raj do sukṭike ehopena, suṭik suṭikte ạḍi sạṅgińre barea koṛa Ram Lokhon ńutumanko ńamketkina, unkin ona rama dokin ạgu daraketa ar rajkin udukadea, ona ńelkate raj do ạḍiye rạskạyena; uni ḍom doe laga ńirkedea.

Ḍom do aćak oṛakteye heć ruạṛena ar aćren pạhil era ar hoponkoe hoho ạguketkoa, ar inạ ḍholge ar hõe ạgu ruạṛketa. Pạhil ma raj hoponera hatao sana tahẽkantaea, menkhan raj bae pạtiạulente hoponera hõ bae emadea, borcoń oṇḍe khone laga ńirkedea.

Uni raj do Ram Lokhone kuliketkina, Henda, rakas gogoćkin, cetben hataoa, mase lạiạńben? Adokin menketa, Ạliń do cet hõ bańliń hataoa, eken am udukam lạgitgeliń heć akana. Khange raj do rạskạ monteye bidạ gotkatkina; adokin calaoena.

[6] The Santali expression might mean that some of the claws had been left and not cut; the following shows that it is to be understood that Ram and Lokhon had cut off only the tips of tbe claws.

He then understood that he was dead. The Dom then in great joy ran home and brought a tremendously large knife, and with this he also cut off the claws that Ram and Lokhon had left part of[6].

He knew before that if anybody killed the ogre and brought his claws, the king would give such a person his daughter in marriage and give him a part of his kingdom; for this reason the Dom very eagerly cut off the claws, and coming to his house he beat his wife and all his children and drove them out; his drums he also threw out and away on the field.

Thereupon he took the ogre's claws to the king; but although he saw these, the king did not believe his story; he said: "These are not the claws of an ogre that you have killed, because the claws are not entire; somebody, whoever it may be, has cut off and taken away the tips of the claws."

When he heard this, the Dom said: "No, raja saheb, I myself have killed him; so give me your daughther and a part of your kingdom." Hearing this the king said: "Yes, quite so; I shall give my daughter, and I shall also give part of my kingdom; but wait; I must first investigate the matter."

The king commenced to make enquiries; as they carried these on for him, they found very far away two young men called Ram and Lokhon; these two brought the claws with them and showed them to the king, and seeing these the king became very glad; but the Dom he drove away.

The Dom returned to his own house and called his wife and children to him, and the same drums of his he also brought back. Formerly, you know, he wanted to have the princess; but as the king did not believe his story, he did not give him his daughter either; on the contrary, he drove him away from his place.

The king asked Ram and Lokhon: "Look here, you two ogre-killers, what will you have? let me know this." They answered: "We shall not have anything; we have come only to show you these." The king thereupon with joy in his heart sent them away, and they went.

63. Bar boeha reaṅ.

Sedae jọkhẹn, kathae, mitṭaṅ atore bar boehakin tahẽkana. Maraṅ họṛ dọe bạhuana ar huḍiń họṛ dọe ḍạṅguạgea. Ar unkinren eṅgat apat dọ bạnuḱko tạkina, huḍińkin tahẽkanrege eṅgat apat dọkin gọćena. Adọ mitṭẹn ạjittẹte tahẽkana, unige nukin dọ nalha tumạlteye ạsul hara nõḱketkina.

Khange ạjittẹt hõe jãwãeyena. Khange nukin gidrạ dọkin awa ṭapayena. Adọ mamọttekoko aṅjọmket khan, unkin gidrạ iḱdiko họćena. Adọko metakin kana, Iạ bạbu, aben dọben bẹhirlạyena, delale idibena. Okareben tahẹna, ar ọkọe isin aro baṛawabena? Ar ruạḱ hasoḱ ghuṛi hõ aben dọ cele bako jọtọnben. Nit dọle ńẹlettabena abenaḱ dọ ạḍi kọstọ. Onate ale dọ aben iḱdile hẹć akana. Ọnẹko mẹna, Gidrạko dọko tuạrlen khan, kaka khuṛạ ṭhenko haraḱa, ar baṅkhan mamkuṛreko haraḱa. Onate aben iḱdile hẹć akana.

Adọ onka unkin gidrạko galmarao baṛawatkina. Adọ inạ atorege unkin gidrạren kakattekoko tahẽkana. Onkokoko họhọ ạguketkoa. Adọ onko samaṅre hõ onka lekako lại saḍeketa. Khange unkin gidrạren huḍiń utạrić kakattẹt dọe mẹnketa, Ẹ ho, onka dọ baṅ. Mitṭaṅ dọ idiyepe ar banar dọ ọhọle idi ocolepea. Ini maraṅ gidrạ dọ iṅgeń dọhọyea, ar baṅkhanpe nisṛạulea. Ar nukin gidrạ hõ hapẹn jãhã hiloḱ dọpe nisṛạukina. Metakinape, Dẹ nẹć

[1] The first part of the story, referring to the fate of the two brothers when they were too small to take care of themselves, is true to life among the Santals. A sister may try to keep younger brothers like here, supporting them and herself by working for wages. But when she marries, everything will depend on what kind of a family she gets into; after marriage she belongs to her husband's family and cannot by right do anything for her blood relatives. It should, however, be noted that the relationship between a married girl and her old home is generally very good.

[2] When the father dies, his brothers, or cousins who are counted like brothers, are expected to take charge of the children, if they are too small to look after themselves. According to Santal law and custom (women having no right to inherit real estate, i. e., land, a law that many Santals are now trying to get

63. THE STORY OF TWO BROTHERS.

ONCE upon a time long ago, people tell, there lived two brothers. The elder one was married, the younger brother was a bachelor. They had no parents; their father and mother had died, when they were quite small[1]. They had a sister, older than themselves, and this sister had supported them for a time by working with others and by gleaning.

Then this elder sister was married, and these two children became homeless and destitute. When the maternal uncles of these two boys heard this, they came to take them away. They were saying to them: "Listen, boys, you have become homeless and without shelter; come with us, we shall take you on. Where will you live? Who will cook food for you? And when you get fever and are in pain, who will take care of you? We now see how both of you are in great distress. For this reason we have come to take you two home to us. Just as people say: 'When children become orphans, they live until they grow up with their paternal uncles[2]; and if not, then with their mother's relatives.' Therefore we have come to take you away."

In this way they spoke to the two children. Now the families of some paternal uncles of these two boys were living in that same village. So they called these; and also in their presence they spoke as told. The youngest of the two children's paternal uncles then said: "I say, that is not as it should be. Take one home with you, but both we shall not let you take away. I shall keep the elder one with me; otherwise you will blame us, and some future day you would also blame these two children. You would say to them: 'Well, there you see how it is, boys,

altered) the brothers of a man are his prospective heirs, if there is no male issue; it is therefore natural that these relatives should take an interest in orphaned nephews and nieces. They often, perhaps generally, do so. The story gives a very fair impression of what is sometimes actually happening.

ọnẹ cọṅ, bạbu, ato pẹrẹć peṛa pạrbhạ kaka khuṛạko tahẽkantaben. Adọ okorko suṭućleťbena? Boge dọ alele tahẽkan tẹrọṅ nẽkẽle hạr sãohãkeťbena, ar baṅkhan hutẹn aben dọ okakore cọṅ jarmaǩ tormaǩben tahẽkoǩa hutẹn. Adọ abenre alele dayayente nõǩõele ạguketbentele mạnus mankaťbena. Un jọkhẹn kaka khuṛạ dọ okorko suṭućleťbena? Nonka hapẹn tayọm hiloǩ dọ ape hoṛgepe rọṛa. Adọ onateń mẹneťa, banar gidrạ dọ ọhọle idi ocolepea. Miť hoṛ dọle dọhọyegea.

Adọ enka mẹn baṛakatege ini huḍiṅić dọko idikedea, ar maraṅić dọ onko kakattekogeko dọhọkedea. Onkako galmaraoketa. Adọ arhõ miť hoṛe mẹnketa, E ho, onka dọ baṅ ṭhikoǩ kana. Abo mabon mẹneťge, adọ nukin gidrạ thọ babon kuliyeťkina, okarekin tahẹna mẹnte.

Adọ sanam hoṛko mẹnketa, Baṅa ho, noa dọ ṭhik kathagem mẹneťa. Acha, onate dọ baṅ ceka akana. Ma nukin gidrạ nitgebon kuli gọťkina.

Adọ sạri inạ ghạṛitegeko kuli gọťkeťkina, Cele bạbu, ceť lekaben mẹneťa? Masẹ lạileben, ar baṅkhan ale ma ọnẹ onkale mẹn ocoyeť kan.

Adọ ini sẽṛã gidrạgeye rọṛketa, ar uni dosarić ma ḍhertẹte huḍiṅge; adọ uni huḍiṅ gidrạ dọ ceť hõ bae rọṛleťa. Ini maraṅ gidrạgeye mẹnketa, Baṅa, mama, besgepe mẹneťa. Iṅ hõ mọnẹ mọnẹte dọ onkageń mẹneť tahẽkana. Bana hoṛ hutẹnpe mẹnle khan, iṅ dọ ọhọṅ sẹnlena. Cedaǩ? Ente nọṇḍẹ dọ jumi bạṛi menaǩtạliṅa, onate calaǩ dọ bạṅ mẹneť tahẽkana. Adọ ona lekage ape hõpe galmaraoket khan dọ ạdiṅ khusiyena. Adọ mama, ma nui bọkọṅge idiyepe. Iṅ dọ nẹṇḍẹgeń tahẽ hataṛoǩa. Judi nọṇḍẹ suk baṅ ṅamle khan, unre dọṅ calaǩgea.

Adọ onkako galmaraokette ini huḍiṅ gidrạ dọko idikedea, ar uni maraṅ gidrạ dọ kakattẹť ṭhene tahẽyena.

[3] The Santali word implies taking personal interest in.

you had friends and relatives, paternal uncles, the village full of them. How much did they search[3] for you? Fortunately we were in existence, so we, as you see, took you in and gave you a home; if we had not done so, you two would now have been wandering about like vagabonds, who knows where. We had compassion on you and brought you here, as you now see, and have made you into respectable people. At that time, why, your father's relatives did not search for you.' In such a way you people will talk some day hereafter. Therefore I say, we shall certainly not let you take both children away with you. One of them we shall keep here."

After having talked matters over in this way they were taking the younger one away, while the paternal uncle was keeping the elder one. They had talked in this way; then one of them again said: "Listen, this is not right. We say so, but we have not asked these children themselves where they will stay."

Then all of them said: "That is quite right what you say. Very well, nothing has happened so far. Let us then ask these two children now at once."

So they then and there at once asked the two children: "Well, boys, what have you to say? Let us hear this; otherwise we think as you have heard."

The bigger one then spoke; the other one was quite small, so he did not say anything. The big child said: "Quite so, uncle, it is good what you say. I was also saying so to myself. If you had said that we should both go, I should certainly have refused to go. Why? We have, you know, our land here; therefore I did not intend to go. Now as you also have spoken to the same effect, I am very pleased. Therefore, uncle, take this younger brother of mine with you. I shall remain here in the meantime. If I do not feel happy here, then I shall also go."

After they had talked in this way, they took the little one away with them, and the elder one stayed with his paternal uncle.

Adọ ọṇḍẹge tahẹn tahẹnte uni maraṅ gidrạ dọe harayente kakat kạkitgekin bạhuadea. Ar kam kajre hõ beskin kạmi gạkhuṛkadea. Casa kạmi reaḱ dọ jọtọge khube kạmi hewa akangea. Adọ bạhuko ạguade khange thọ bako jutoḱ. Ać ma kam kajre khubgeko khusiae kan, adọ uni bạhuttẹt́ge thọ bako khusiae kana. Cet́ko cọko rọṛ baṛale khangeye dạṛket́ge. Adọ nui hõ jao hiloḱ bạhugeye paṅja baṛayea, kạmi dọe ḍhilạuket́a. Adọ onate kạkit kakat hõkin rọṛ baṛakedea. Adọ enkategé huri hurite mit́ serma dọ jãhã lekateye purạukat́gea.

Dosar serma khange unkin ṭhen khon dọe oḍokente nạihạrteye sẹn mit́ena. Adọ ọṇḍẹ hõ bae tahẽ daṛeat́te nọṇḍẹgeye hẹćente ạkinaḱ baṛgerege oṛaḱe beret́ket́a; adọ bạhui ạgukedetekin tahẽyena.

Ar uni bọkọttẹt́ dọ mamọtteko ṭhen ạḍi dulạṛteko dọhọkedea. Cet́ kạmi hõ bako ạcu hewaledea, onate oka kạmi hõ bae cet́let́a. Ar ona katha nui maraṅ koṛa dọ bae baḍae kana, nui dọe kuṛhiạgea mẹnte. Adọ begarrekin oṛaḱket́ khan dọkin mẹnket́a, Ḍaṅgrako dọ ọkọe ẹsẹt́ baṛawalaṅa, ar guti hõ okarelaṅ ṅamkoa? Uni huḍiṅićgelaṅ ạguyea. Ẹsẹt́ baṛawalaṅae.

Adọ onka mẹnkate sạrikin ạgukedea. Khange thọ ạgu makin ạgukede, adọ cet́ kạmi hõ bae ganoḱ. Gupi hõ calao khane

[4] The same as elsewhere; among the Santals it is generally the women who cannot hit it off with each other. It always ends in their setting up separate households.

[5] Another very common trait. A newly married girl, who is not pleased, believes herself aggrieved, and feels herself out of touch with her new surroundings, and so on, is very apt to run back to her old home, where her affections are, and where she may have left some particular friend. It must be borne in mind that regular Santal marriages are family arrangements and are founded, not on mutual love (at first anyhow), but on the basis of mutual need.

[6] The husband is always supposed to follow after his run-away wife to bring her back, provided that she has not misbehaved in such a way that a formal settling of the matter is required.

[7] The expression used implies that the man had undertaken servant's work; this is, when not for any special work, for the year. Santals engage servants generally in Mag (Jan.—Febr.), and they stay on until next Mag.

The elder brother lived there and grew into maturity, and his uncle and aunt procured a wife for him. They also taught him well and made him proficient in all work. He had by constant work become very efficient in farmwork. Bu' when they had brought a wife for him, they did not hit if off[4]. They were very pleased with himself in all work, but they did not like his wife. When they said something or other to her, she would run away[5]; and the young man had also day after day to go after her to bring her back[6]; he neglected his work. For this reason his uncle and aunt also rebuked him. In this way somehow or other he completed[7] one year.

Next year he left his uncle and aunt and went to stay with his father-in-law's[8]. But as he could not stay there either, he came back to his village and built a house on their own land, and having brought his wife he remained there.

Now the younger brother lived with his maternal uncles, and they treated him with much fondness. They did not put him or accustom him to any kind of work, and so he did not learn anything. The elder brother did not know this, that the younger one was lazy. When they had set up a separate house for themselves, they said: "Whom shall we get to look after[9] our bullocks, and where shall we get a servant? Let us bring the little one; he will look after them for us."

Having come to this decision they actually brought him. Now they had brought him, that is quite so, but he was unfit for any kind of work. As for herding the cattle, if he went, he went,

---

[8] To go and settle with one's wife's parents is sometimes done; but except in special circumstances it is not considered very praiseworthy. There is possibly a feeling that this man is lost to his own people.

[9] The Santali word used (ẹsẹt) means to block the way for, shut up, hinder. It is significant for what a Santal expects the duties of a cattle-herd to be, viz., to keep the cattle off the standing crops.

calaoenge, baṅkhan do̱ baṅ. Nukingeye laṅga utạrketkina. Ado̱ bogete kuṛhiạ kuṛhiạkin ruhedea. Ar uni do̱ unạkkin ruhedere hõ, ona do̱ baṅgeye luturaktạkina. Ar oka do̱ onko mamo̱tteko ṭhengeye dạṛa. Ado̱ kuṛhiạ iạte tayo̱mte do̱ onko hõ bako sebelaea, daka hõ bako emaea. Ado̱ arhõ siṭhạl miṭhạle ruạr he̱ćkenge. Ar atoren jo̱to̱ ho̱ṛko bad̦ae cabakedea, nui do̱ ạd̦itet-geye kuṛhiạgea me̱nte. Ona iạte uni tuluć do̱ o̱ko̱e hõ bako gateka. Ado̱ cet kana, kạmi se̱ bae kạmi daka dak mạṇd̦i do̱kin emaegea. Onate do̱ bakin go̱jea.

Ado̱ enkakotege tahe̱n tahe̱ntegeye juạnena. Ar ona kuṛhiạ iạte bạhuae reak do̱ cetge bakin ro̱ṛ baṛaea. Khange uni hõ tayo̱mte do̱e bujhạu ńamketa. Me̱nketae. Nukin do̱ o̱ho̱kin bạhuliṅa. O̱ko̱e tora jãhã disomteṅ od̦ok calaka. Ado̱ onka hudis baṛakate gateye riạu baṛakoa. Metakoae, Delabon ya, jãhã disomte cạkribon calaka. Ado̱ ona kuṛhiạ iạte o̱ko̱e hõ uniak katha do̱ bako bạsutataea.

Ado̱ onka tahe̱n tahe̱ntege, kathae, mit din do̱ ãṭ ńõkgekin ro̱ṛadea. Khange ạd̦i ãṭ hasokedea, ado̱ usạte od̦ok calak kana.

Ado̱ atoren gupi koṛae ńe̱lketko khan do̱e metako kana, Dela ya phalna, nhate peṛa ho̱ro̱k go̱ṛo̱aṅpe.

Ado̱ko me̱nketa, Okate?

Ado̱ uniye me̱nketa, Jãhãtege mẽt lutur calaktiṅ, o̱nte̱geṅ calaka.

Ado̱ onko koṛako me̱nketa, Am kuṛhiạ ho̱ṛ tuluć do̱ o̱ko̱e gateka? Ale do̱ am sãote do̱ o̱ho̱le se̱nlena.

---

10 This cannot be said to be a common Santal trait. As a rule they will not object to laziness, if they can get some fun.

11 A young married wife will run home, when in the sulks; a Santal man will run off to 'foreign' parts. She seeks what she knows; the young man is drawn towards the unknown, by his optimism. With civilization and education the tendency is lessened; it is unnecessary to point out that a lack of valuation of their own home is at the bottom, coupled with hopelessnes and a feeling that they do not care to take up a fight for existence, when they are not forced to do so. This tendency to stampede is likely connected with their traditional

otherwise not. He made his brother and wife utterly tired of himself, and they scolded him and called him Lazy, lazy! Now although they abused him so much, he did not listen to them in the least. Now and then he would run away to his mother's brothers; but on account of his laziness these did not like him either and would not give him food. So he had to return, as best he could, disappointed. And all the villagers learnt to know him, what an awfully lazy fellow he was. For this reason no one[10] would keep company with him; be that as it may, whether he worked or not, his brother gave him food. They would not let him die.

Living in this way he grew into maturity; but on account of this laziness his brother and sister-in-law did not say a word about getting him a wife. Afterwards he himself also began to understand this and said: "These two will certainly not procure a wife for me. Let me at once start for some other country[11]." With this in his mind he urged others to accompany him; he would say to them: "Come along, you fellows, let us go to some country or other to take service." But on account of his laziness no one heeded what he said.

As time passed, people tell, one day his brother and sister-in-law used somewhat hard words to him; this pained him much, so that he went away in the sulks.

He saw the village cattle-herds, as he went off, and said to them: "Come along you so-and-so, help me to go on a visit over there."

"Whereto?" they asked him.

"Wherever eyes and ears will take me, there I shall go," he replied.

But the young men said: "Who will keep company with you, you lazy fellow? We shall certainly not go with you."

wanderings; so far as their traditions take them back, they have always been receding and moving off from their old parts to new fields.

Ar onka atoren ma ọkọe hõ bako gọṛọae kan, onate adọ eskargeye calak̕ kana. Adọ tin sạṅgiń hor cọe sẹn akan; adọe disạket̕a, Atoren ma ọkọe hõ bako gọṛọadiń, adọ iń gọṛọań lạgit̕ ọkọe bań idi torako? Mahań muskilena. Adọ onkae hudis idiyet̕a ar tumbut̕ tumbut̕e calak̕ kana.

Adọ calak̕ calak̕te mit̕ ṭhen dhiri kaṭkọm gẹlẹć akat̕e ńẹlket̕a. Adọe mẹnket̕a, Atoren ma ọkọe hõ bako gọṛọadiń, nui kaṭkọmgeń la todea, ar nige iń sọṅgẹteń idi tora joṅa. Adọ onka mẹnkate kaṭkọm lalae dhurạuena. Adọ bhại, laye lakedea sẹ, ẹkkalte la tiok̕kateye sap̕kedea. Ar unregeye mẹnket̕a, Am dọ, kaṭkọm, iṅren gate kanam. Am dọ iṅren sọṅ bhại kanam. Jāhãtege iṅiń calak̕, ọntẹgeń idimea. Am dọ ọhọgeń bạgilema. Am dọ iń sãorem tahẹna. Adọ ać mọtọre rọṛ baṛakateye gochakedea.

Adọe calak̕ kana. Ar rẹṅgẹćle khan jãhã atoteye bọlọk̕ kana are kọe baṛayet̕a.

Adọ onka calak̕ calak̕te bar pẹ disome parọm calaoena. Khange mit̕ṭań disom dọ rakas reak̕ ạḍi udạu ak̕ana. Ona disome tiok̕ket̕a, ar ạyup̕ hõ ạyubok̕ kana. Ar ona disomren raj dọ ḍoṅkae piṭạu akat̕a. Mẹn akat̕ae, Nui rakas dọ iṅak̕ disome ujạṛet̕tiṅa. Judi nui rakas jãhãepe gọćkedea mẹnkhan, mit̕ṭań miserańiń ẹmọka, ar siki ọṅsọ disom hõń ẹmkea. Nonkae ḍamḍahe akat̕a.

Adọ ona disomge nui koṛa hõ ona ạyubok̕ kan ọktẹ jọkhẹne bọlọyena. Ar mit̕ṭań atoe ńamket̕a. Adọ ona ato kulhi mucạt̕re mit̕ṭań ul dare menak̕a. Ona ul dare buṭạreye ḍerayena. Ato

12 The crab here mentioned is found in the country; it is called dhiri kaṭkọm, lit. stone-crab; it is fairly large, dark in colour, and lives on the edge of rivers and water, where it burrows among the stones.

13 It should be noted that the Santals (except modernized ones) use pieces or lengths of cloth in which they drape themselves; no trousers, no coats. They have no pockets, but may easily tie anything up in a corner of their cloth.

14 The countries are naturally small, each representing the property of a landlord, a raja or king, as they are called.

15 Here only one quarter of the land is promised; later in the story the young man gets half the 'kingdom', as usual in these stories.

In this way none of the villagers would help him, and so he went along alone. When he had proceeded some distance, he commenced to think: "None of the villagers have helped me; should I not take somebody along to help me? This has put me in great difficulties." He was turning this over in his mind, as he was walking along, his head bent.

On his way he at a place saw that a crab[12] had burrowed there; then he said: "None of the villagers would help me; I shall dig out this crab and take it along with me." Having decided this he commenced to dig; and, my friend, he dug and dug, straightway he dug, until he reached the crab and took it. Then he said: "You crab, you are my companion; you are my intimate friend and companion. Wherever I go, I shall take you along. I shall never leave you behind. You shall stay with me." Having talked to himself in this way he tied the crab up in his cloth[13].

So he continued on his way. When he felt hungry, he entered some village or other and begged.

Walking along in this way he passed two or three countries[14]. Then there was a country where there were rumours of an ogre. He reached that country, just as it was becoming evening. The king of this country had made public proclamation and said: "This ogre is devastating my country. If anybody kills this ogre, I shall give him a sister of mine, I shall also give one quarter part[15] of my country." Such a proclamation[16] he had published.

As told, the young man entered this country just as it was becoming evening; he reached a village, and at the entrance to the street of this village there was a mango-tree. He camped at the foot of this mango-tree. He went to the village and asked

[16] The expression used above shows that the proclamation was made by beat of drum in public places, as is often done even now.

khon seṅgel koe ạgukeťte oṇḍeye jolkeťa, ar oṇḍegeye mạṇḍiạuena. Ado ona atoren hoṛ doko metae kana, Iạ bạbu, am dom am eskargea, noṇḍe do alom tahena. Dela note hoṛ gasenrege ḍerak̓me. Noa disom do rakas reak̓ ạḍi udạ̄u akana, bogete hoṛe jomeťkoa. Am eskar do nãhãk̓ khạṭigeye jommegea. Onatele metam kana, dela note hoṛ talarege ḍerak̓me.

Ado uni koṛae menkeťa. Baṅa, baba, bar hoṛaliṅ, iṅ eskar doṅ baṅ·kana.

Adoko menkeťa, Miť hoṛ do, bạbu, okorić? Am eskarge cole ńeleťme. Tayomre menaea se ceťa?

Adoe menkeťa, Baṅa, baba, bar hoṛge menak̓liṅa. Oho nãhãk̓liṅ eskarok̓a, neṇḍegeliṅ besok̓a.

Ado enteye jomme khan dom cekaea?

Pase do in dinrege gujuk̓ reak̓ likhạ menak̓ khan dom cekaea?

Ado onko hoṛko menkeťa, Henda bạbu, am eskarge cole ńeleťme, ar miť hoṛ do ukurić okare? Ale do bale ńel ńame kan do?

Adoe menkeťa, Baṅ, baba, sạrige bar hoṛ menak̓liṅa; menkhan ape do bape ńel ńame kana.

Ado onkae menkeť khan doko thirena. Ar ako monereko hudisketa, Ać ar Candoge jạnić bar hoṛ doe lạiok̓ kana. Adoko menkeťa, Acha eṇḍe khan baben calak̓ khan dole cekabena? Ado enka men baṛakatege onko atoren hoṛ do apan ạpin akoak̓ oṛak̓teko sen baṛayena; ado unkin do oṇḍegeko bạgiaťkina.

Ado uni hoṛ seṅgel jol baṛakate oṇḍe doe gitićena ona dare buṭạrege, ar uni kaṭkom doe aṛak̓ akadea. Tin ṭhen, kathae, ńindạ gitić hećen, un ṭhenge uni kaṭkom doe aṛak̓kaegea.

Ado tala ńindạ khange uni rakas do hoṛ jomko lạgiť atoteye hijuk̓ kan tahẽkana. Ado kulhi mucạťre uni hoṛe ńelkede khan

17 The Santals have a kind of belief in fate, taken over from the Hindus. At the time of birth Bidhi Bidhanta come and write the fate of the newborn babe on its forehead. It is not, however, a belief that seems to have any practical influence on them. The matter is more fully mentioned in 'The Santals and Disease', Memoirs of the Asiatic Society of Bengal, Vol. X., p. 27—28.

people for fire, and having brought this he made a fire there, and there he stayed. The people of this village said to him: "Look here, young man, you are alone; don't remain here. Come along over here and stay for the night among people. This country has become very dangerous on account of an ogre, who is eating a good many people. When you are alone, he will be sure to eat you. Therefore we tell you, come along and camp for the night among people."

"No, sirs," the young man replied, "we are two of us; I am not alone."

"Why, where is one then, young man?" they said. "We see only you. Is the other one somewhere behind or how?"

"No, sirs," he replied, "we are two; we shall certainly not be alone; we shall do very well here."

"And then, if he eats you, what will you do?"

"Perhaps it is my fate to die after so many days[17]; if so, what can you do?"

"Look here, young man," the people then said, "we see only you alone; where then is one? We see him nowhere."

"No, sirs," he replied, "we are really and truly two, but you have not caught sight of the other one."

When he went on in this way, they ceased speaking; but they thought: "He probably means himself and Chando, when he speaks about two persons." So they said: "Very well then, if you two will not come, what can we do for you?" After this talk the village people went away to their several houses; and these two they left there.

After having made a fire the young man lay down there at the foot of the tree, and the crab he set free. In all places, people tell, where he had come and spent the night, everywhere he had been setting the crab free.

At midnight the ogre was coming to this village to eat people. When he at the end of the village street saw this man, he at

do̱ uni ṭhene calao go̱ťena. Ado̱e ho̱ho̱ go̱ťkeťa, Ke̱ sutạl ke̱ jagal, bhại? Ar uni koṛa do̱ aṅjo̱meť kanre hõe thir akangea. Khange uni rakas do̱e he̱ć sor go̱ťena. Ado̱ uni koṛa jo̱me lạgiť je̱mo̱nge mocae idiyeť tahẽkan, te̱mo̱nge nui kaṭko̱m do̱ e̱kkalte ho̱ṭo̱ḱrege ona ḍiṭomteye limboť daram go̱ťkedea. Ado̱ ạisạn ḍiṭome ḍiṭomkedea se̱, e̱kkalteye go̱ć utạrkedea. Oka se̱n hõ bae ukus pukus daṛeaťa. Setaḱ hạbić uni kaṭko̱m do̱ enka ḍiṭom akangeye tahẽyena. Ado̱ uni koṛa bereťenteye ńe̱lkede do̱, rakase ḍiṭom go̱ć akade. Ado̱ naharni tahẽkantaea, ado̱ ona naharnite rakas luture bucạkedea, ar jo̱to̱ ramae ge̱ťkeťtaea, ar co̱ṭ alaṅe ge̱ťkeťtaea. Ado̱ arhõe gitićena.

Ado̱ setaḱen khan uni kaṭko̱m do̱e baekedea, ar ać do̱e gitić akangea. Ado̱ ona atore do̱ Ḍo̱m cạukidare tahẽkana. Ado̱ setaḱre hare phare se̱nkateye ńe̱lkede do̱, rakase go̱ć akan. Ado̱e ruạṛ go̱ťente kạpiye idiketťe miť buluye lạhur chaḍao go̱ťkeťa; ado̱ oṛaḱre go̱ḱ ạgukate luṭhum marteye giḍi go̱ťkaťa, ar aćren era ho̱po̱n jo̱to̱e laga toťkeťkoa ar ḍho̱lko jo̱to̱e giḍikaťa, ado̱e me̱neťa, Raj miserań hataoea, ar disom iń ńama; ado̱ noako do̱ń cekaea? Ado̱ onkae me̱neťa, ar jo̱to̱e laga ńireťkoa.

Khange ado̱ atoren jo̱to̱ ho̱ṛko jarwayena; ado̱ se̱nkateko ńe̱lkede do̱, sạrige go̱ć akade. Ado̱ arhõ ako mo̱ne̱re do̱ dhokageko ạikạueťa, ado̱ko me̱neťa, Pase̱ ya, nui bidisiạ ho̱ṛgeye go̱ć akade. Ado̱ onka ako mo̱ne̱regeko ro̱ṛjoṅ kana. Ar uni ho̱ṛ do̱ ceť hõ bae ro̱ṛ

[18] The ogre naturally does not speak Santali; it makes use of a kind of low Bengali.

[19] A variant tells that the young man was awakened, got up and killed the ogre with a stone, that he hurled at the ogre's head.

[20] Naharni, here called nail-cutter, is an instrument, made of iron, containing tweezers, a sharp pointed pin and a chisel-like cutting implement. For people walking barefoot and with bare legs and arms a thing like this is a necessity, more especially to get out thorns and the like, to cut one's nails, &c. There are several forms; the one used by men is carried fixed to the ḍora, the waist-string.

once went up to him and called[18] out: "Wer liegt? wer schläft da, Freund?" Although the young man heard, he remained quiet, and the ogre at once came close up to him. But just as the ogre was coming near with his mouth, the same instant the crab rushed at him and throttled his throat with his claws. He throttled him to such an effect, he killed him then and there[19]. The ogre was utterly unable to move. The crab remained with its claws on the throat of the ogre until morning. Then the young man got up and saw that the crab had throttled the ogre to death. Now he had a nail-cutter[20], and with this he cut off the tip of the ogre's ears; all his claws he also cut off, and also the tip of his tongue. Thereupon he again lay down.

When it became morning, he hid the crab away, and he himself continued to sleep. Now there was a Dom[21] watchman in this village. Early in the morning he came in a hurry and saw that the ogre was dead. Running home he at once returned with a battle-axe and sliced off one thigh, and carrying this to his house he threw it down there with a thud, whereupon he drove his wife and children out, all of them, all his drums he also threw away, and said: "I shall take the king's sister, and I shall get a country; what then shall I do with these?" So he spoke and drove all of them away.

Thereupon all the villagers came together; they went and saw: some one had really killed the ogre. Still they had some doubts in their mind and were saying: "Perhaps it is this stranger who has killed him." They were saying so to themselves; but the

---

21 The ḍọm caste is one of the lowest of the Hindu social system. The idea of a cạukidar, a village watchman, must be recent; they were introduced in the Santal villages by Government only some years ago. They are a kind of local police, one of their duties being to walk through the village street at night, calling out as they walk along, awakening people and warning thieves. In other parts they have been in existence for a long time.

baṛayeťa, thir akangeae. Adǫko kulikedea, Henda bąbu, nui rakas dǫ ǫkǫe gǫć akadea? Am sẹ nui Ḍǫmben gǫć akadea?

Adǫ uni koṛae mẹnkeťa, Acha, jãhãegeliñ gǫć akade, mẹnkhan jąnić nisąn dǫliñ dǫhǫ akaťgea.

Adǫ ato hǫṛko mẹnkeťa, Uni ma miťṭañ phąṛiye idi akať, ona nisąnle ńẹlleťtaea; ar am dǫ okortam nisąn dǫ?

Adǫ uni koṛae mẹnkeťa, Acha, do raj ląiaetape; adǫ jãhãege nisąnliñ uduǩ daṛeaǩ, inigeliñ goṭaǩa.

Adǫko mẹnkeťa, Acha, besgem mẹneťa, onage ṭhik kana; adǫ nãhãǩ rajgeye phanḍaotabena.

Adǫ sąri raj ṭhen hǫṛko kolkeťkoa, ar onako jǫtǫ kathako ląiadea. Adǫ raje mẹnkeťa, Acha, sipąhi iñ koleťkoa, ńẹleako, sąri kana sẹ ẹṛẹ; adǫ ńẹl baṛakate nǫṇḍẹpe gǫǩ ąguyea; ar Ḍǫm dǫ aćtege ona phąṛi dǫe ąguitae ma; ar uni bidisią hǫṛ hõ ągu darayepe, alope bągiaea.

Khange sąri ǫṇḍẹ khon hǫṛko hẹćena, ar sipąhiko adǫko ńẹlkede dǫ, sąrige. Adǫ onko sipąhi uni bidisią koṛako metae kana, Henda ho, am dǫ okor ceť cinhą menaǩtama? Ma ona reaǩ nisąn udugme.

Adǫ uni koṛae mẹnkeťa, Nǫṇḍẹ dǫ ǫhǫñ uduǩlea; delabon raj ṭhenge nãhãǩ iñ uduga.

Adǫko mẹneťa, Okor ya, oka ṭhenaǩ ceť nisąne dǫhǫ akaťa? Masẹ ńẹl baṛaepe.

Adǫ goṭako ńẹl baṛayede kana, adǫ ẹnre hõ bako hudis ńameťa, noa nisąne dǫhǫ akaťa mẹnte. Adǫ bae ląileť khanko metadea, Delabon ẹnḍẹkhan raj ṭhenge. Adǫ rakasko gǫǩkedete uni hõko idi torakedea.

Adǫ uni rakas dǫ raj ṭhenko gǫǩ idikedea, adǫ raj hõe ńẹl baṛakedea. Adǫ uni Ḍǫm dǫ ądi laha laha aćgeye rǫṛeťa, Nui

---

22 The word used here and several places in the Santal text is phąṛi which ordinarily means 'the shoulder with foreleg attached (of on animal)'. It was expressly stated above that he cut off the thigh. The rakas of this story seems to be rather an animal than a being with arms and legs.

young man did not say anything; he kept quiet. So they asked him: "Look here, young man, who killed this ogre? Did you or did the Dom kill him?"

The young man replied: "Well, the one of us two who has killed him is likely to have kept some proofs."

The villagers said: "He has taken away a leg and thigh[22]; we have seen this proof of his; but where are your proofs?"

"All right," the young man replied, "go and tell your king; the one of us who is able to show his proofs, he will be proved to be the right one of us."

"Very well," they said, "it is quite good what you say; that is right; so presently the king will settle your case."

Thereupon they, truth to tell, sent people to the king and told him everything. The king then said: "Very well, I am sending some soldiers; they will see whether it is true or not; and when they have seen, bring the ogre here, and let the Dom himself bring that leg and thigh of his; bring also the stranger along with you; do not leave him behind."

Truth to tell, the people who went came back, and the soldiers saw the ogre, it was quite true. The soldiers then said to the stranger: "Look here, you, where have you any proof? Show the tokens of proof."

"I am not going to show anything here," the young man replied; "come along, I shall presently show what I have before the king."

"Why, where?" they said; "from where has he taken and kept any token? Do look."

They looked all over the ogre; still no one hit upon the thought that he had kept the things mentioned as proofs. As he did not tell, they said to him: "Come along then to the king." So they took the ogre on their shoulders and carried him along also.

When they had carried the ogre before the king, he also looked at him. And the Dom put himself forward and said: "I have

rakas do̱ iṅgeń go̱ć akadea mente. Ado̱ raje me̱nketa, Hape! ho̱ṛ iṅ kulilekoge. Pase̱ am do̱ bam go̱ć akade.

Khange sạri ona atoren ho̱ṛ ar onkoe kolletko sipạhiye kuliketkoa, Henda ho, bhala ape do̱pe kuli baṛa akatkoa, nui rakas do̱ o̱ko̱epe go̱ć akadea me̱nte? Ar nui Ḍo̱m ma nõko̱e phạṛiye ạgu akat. Ado̱ bhala nuigeye go̱ć akadea, se̱ o̱ko̱eko go̱ć akadea?

Ado̱ onkoko me̱nketa, O̱ko̱ badae, khạṭi do̱ o̱ho̱le me̱n daṛelea. Miṭṭaṅ bidisiạ ho̱ṛ o̱ṇḍe̱geye gitić kan tahẽkana, ar nui rakas hõ o̱ṇḍe̱geye go̱ć akan tahẽkana. Ado̱ baṅ do̱ uni ho̱ṛgeye go̱ć akade, baṅ do̱ nui Ḍo̱mge; ar ạikạ uni ho̱ṛ hõe me̱neta, baṅma, Iń hõ nisạn do̱ń do̱ho̱ akatgea. Ado̱le metae kana, Mase̱ cet nisạnem do̱ho̱ akata? Udukaleme. Adoe me̱nketa, Iń do̱ raj ṭhengeń uduga. Ado̱ ma kulikinme, ar bana ho̱ṛ nisạn uduk ocokinme.

Ado̱ sạri raje me̱nketa, Mase̱ bhala nisạn udugtaben; nisạn baben udukette bicạr baṅ phanḍao daṛeak kana.

Ado̱ khange, kathae, uni Ḍo̱m do̱ ona rakas phạṛige raj samaṅreye idi go̱tketa, Nõko̱etiń iṅak nisạn do̱.

Ado̱ raje me̱nketa, Noa phạṛi do̱ amtegem go̱k ạgu akata, se̱ pase̱ć o̱ko̱ekom go̱k ocoletko?

Ado̱ uni Ḍo̱me me̱nketa, Iṅtegeń go̱k ạgu akata; o̱ko̱e hõ noa do̱ bạń jo̱ṭe̱t oco akatkoa.

Ado̱e me̱nketa, Acha bogege. Ado̱ uni koṛae kulikedea, Henda ho, am do̱ okor cet nisạn menaktama? Udugme.

Ado̱ kathae, o̱ne̱ alaṅ ar lutur ar ramae chaḍaolet, ona do̱ ghẽṭkateye gocha akat tahẽkana. Ado̱ onae udukketteye raṛaketa; ado̱ raj sạmaṅreye do̱ho̱keta, are me̱nketa, Nõko̱etiń, baba, nisạn do̱.

Ado̱ sạri rakas jaṅga ar lutur ar moca cahapkate alaṅko ńe̱lket do̱, sạri bạnuk. Ar uni Ḍo̱me idilet, ona jaṅgare hõko ńe̱lket do̱,

killed this ogre." "Wait," the king said, "let me ask people first. Perhaps you have not killed him."

Thereupon he, truth to tell, asked the village people and the soldiers he had sent: "Listen you, well, have you asked who has killed this ogre? This Dom has, as we see, brought this leg and thigh here. I wonder, has he killed him, or who has?"

They replied: "Who knows? we can not say anything for certain. A stranger was lying there sleeping; this ogre also had died there; so whether this man killed him, or the Dom killed him, we do not know; but mind, this man also says: 'I also have kept some proofs.' We were saying to him: 'Well, what proofs have you kept? Show them to us.' But he said: 'I shall show them before the king.' Therefore ask them both and let both show their proofs."

The king then, truth to tell, said: "Well then, both of you show your proofs; I am unable to settle the case, because you do not show your proofs."

Then, people tell, the Dom brought the ogre's leg and thigh before the king, saying: "Look at this here, this is my token."

The king asked him: "Have you carried this leg and thigh yourself, or perhaps you made somebody else carry it for you?"

"I have carried it here myself," the Dom replied; "I have permitted no one to touch this."

"Very well," the king said, whereupon he asked the young man: "Look here, you, where have you any proof of yours? Show it."

Now, people tell, the tongue and the ears and the claws he had cut off, all these he had tied up in his clothes and carried them so. He showed this and untied it, whereupon he put the whole down before the king and said: "Look here at what I have of proof, father."

And in very truth when they looked at the ogre's feet and ears and at his tongue after having opened his mouth, there was really nothing there. So they also looked at the leg that the Dom

rama bạnuḱ. Khange sạri raj ar sanam hoṛko menketa, Nui bidisiạ hoṛge rakas doe goć akadea. Ḍom pạhile goćlede khan, enḍekhan noa rama do cekateye ạguia? Baṅ, nui hoṛge rakas doe goć akadea.

Khange uni Ḍom do ạḍiye phareb gelaṫa, menkhan uniaḱ katha do bako bạsutaṫtaea, bhageteko ruheṫkedea. Ado khange ceṫ hõ bae roṛ daṛeaṫa, ado lajaote oṛaḱteye ruạṛena. Ado era hoponkoe goras ạguyeṫkoa; ado onko hõ cigạrigeko metae kana, Ale do bale calaḱa; am do raj miseram bạhu akawana; am do maraṅ hoṛ ar ale do choṭa jạt kanale. Am ṭhen do ohole senlena; ale do niạkoregele nalha ạsuloḱa. Ado en hiloḱ do bako senlena. Inạ tesar hiloḱko calao ruạṛena; ar uni Ḍom do ạḍiko landawadea; ado tayomte do uni Ḍom do ceṫ hõ bae roṛ daṛeaṫa.

Ar uni koṛa do eneko jarwalen, inrege raj do miserate goṅ utạradea, ar tara nakha disom hõe emena, ar ekraṛnama paṭaye oladea. Ar onko jarwalen hoṛ bhoje emaṫkoa. Ar uni rakas gogoć koṛa do sajkoe emadete moholteye aderkedea.

Ar uni raj doe baḍae kan tahẽkana, Nui koṛa ma nãhãḱ niạ ṅindạ bhitriregeye gujuḱa; ar disom ma arhõ enka iṅaḱge tahentiṅa. Cedaḱ? Ente uni kuṛi do ạḍi dhaoteko jãwãeledea, ado joto jãwãegeko goć hora akantaea. Ado ona disạkate noa katha do ać monre hudiskateye menketa, Nui ma nãhãḱ teheṅ ṅindạgeye gujuḱa, ar disom tho iṅaḱge tahena. Ado onate miseraṫ emoḱ hõe khaṛa goṫena. Ado eneye jãwãe gomkekedete ekkalteye tala oṛaḱkedea.

Ado ayup khange miṫṭaṅ dolan oṛaḱte parkomko idikeṫte ona oṛaḱreko jaegakeṫkina. Ado ṅindạ jokhen miṫrekin gitić akana. Ar lalṭen jeraṫkate oṛaḱ do khubkin marsal akaṫgea. Ar uni koṛa

[23] The young man had nothing, so they had to give him all he needed. The palace is evidently a complex of buildings.

[24] Lit. 'made him at once of the middle house', treated him with cordiality and intimacy.

had taken away: no claws there. Then, truth to tell, the king and all the people said: "This stranger has killed the ogre. If the Dom had killed him, how would he be able to bring the claw of this? No, this man has killed the ogre."

The Dom tried to bring forward all kinds of false accusations; but they did not approve of what he said, but scolded him roundly. And as he was unable to say anything, he went back to his house in shame. He tried to coax his wife and children to come back; but these also scoffed at him and said: "We shall not return; you have got the king's sister for your wife; you are a big man, and we are only low-caste. We shall certainly not go to you; we shall work for wages here somewhere and support ourselves." And that day they did not return; on the third day they went back, and people laughed very much at the Dom; and afterwards the Dom was unable to say anything.

While they were gathered there, as told, the king there and then gave him his sister in marriage; he also gave half his country, and he wrote him a legal document with his promises. He gave a feast to the people gathered; and after they had decked the young man out in fine clothes, he took him into the palace[23].

Now the king knew this: during the night coming this young man will die; so the country will be mine again as before. Why? They had married this girl many times, and all her bridegrooms had died in this way, one after the other. Remembering this he said to himself: "He will die this night, and the country will remain my own." For this reason he at once was willing to give his sister. So he made him his sister's husband and took him at once inside and treated him as one of themselves[24].

In the evening they took bedsteads into one of the palaces and accomodated the couple there for the night. During the night they were sleeping there together. They had lighted a lantern[25] and

25 The introduction of this modern name is another proof of how these tales may be adapted to the environments of the narrator, so to say, be modernized.

do̱ gitić jo̱khe̱nrege uni kaṭko̱m do̱e oḍokkedete aćak̓ koṛamreye do̱ho̱kedea. Ar ać do̱e jạpitkeťa. Ar uni rạni kuṛi ma lahateye jạpitket̓.

Ado̱ uni koṛae jạpitket̓ khan, kathae, uni rạni kuṛiak̓ mũ bhugạk̓ kho̱n do̱ jurite barea biṅkin oḍokok̓ kana nui koṛa jo̱me lagat̓. Ado̱ uni kaṭko̱mkin ńe̱lkede khankin pạc ruạṛena. Arhõ̱ mit̓ ghạṛi khangekin oḍokok̓ kana; ar se̱ nukin kuṛi koṛa ma khubkin jạpit̓ akaťa, cet̓ge bakin disạyeťa. Ado̱ uni kaṭko̱me me̱nkeťa, Durre̱! nukin biń do̱ nãhãk̓ dhorage ińren gate do̱kin jo̱mea. Me̱n, nukin do̱ń go̱ć giḍikina.

Ado̱ onka hudis baṛakate uni kaṭko̱m do̱, kathae, uni rạni kuṛiak̓ ho̱ṭo̱k̓ se̱ moca aṛe ṭhene calaoenteye tãṛãk̓ akana, ar ona ḍiṭomtae do̱e ṭap ṭapa akaťa. Ado̱ unkin biń do̱kin oḍok ńõ̱gok̓ kana, arhõ̱kin bo̱lo̱ ruạṛok̓ kana. Ado̱ onka onkate mit̓ dhao do̱ bes jeleń ńõ̱k̓ oḍokkatekin ko̱yo̱k̓ baṛayeťa arkin melot̓ baṛayet̓ kana. Ado̱ ona jo̱khe̱nge, kathae, uni kaṭko̱m do̱ saṭ me̱nte unkin biń do̱ onakin banar ḍiṭomteye cimṭạ go̱t̓ket̓kina. Ado̱ baṅgekin pạc bo̱lo̱ daṛeaťa, ar ona ḍiṭom kho̱n do̱ aṛak̓ge bae aṛak̓let̓kina. Khange ạkintege phiṛiạ paṭekin le̱ń toťena, ado̱ caṇḍbo̱lte goṭakin bedhaokedea. Ar jo̱no̱mrege bae aṛak̓let̓kina, enka ḍiṭomkategeye go̱ć utạrket̓kina. Ado̱kin go̱ćen khan, parko̱m kho̱n do̱ o̱tteye ãṛgoket̓kina.

Ado̱ paha poho jo̱khe̱n uni koṛa do̱ lahageye e̱bhe̱n go̱ťena. Khange kaṭko̱me tunum baṛa go̱t̓kedea. Ado̱ aćak̓ koṛamre bae ạikạulede khan do̱e dhak maraoaťa, ado̱ ạḍi garteye ńir beret̓ go̱ťena. Ado̱e ńe̱lkede do̱, ạkinkin gitić akan talarege banar biṅtekin to̱l ḍhumbạk̓ akade. Ado̱ ạḍiye hae haekeťa. Ado̱e ńe̱lket̓ko do̱, biń do̱kin go̱ć akan ar uni kaṭko̱m do̱e jivet̓ge. Ado̱ kathae, kaṭko̱me kuliyede kana, Henda gate, nukin biń do̱ okarem ńamlet̓kina?

Ado̱e metae kana, Nukin biń do̱ ne̱ge amkin jo̱met̓me tahẽ̱kana, boge do̱ ińem ạgu darakidińte am do̱m bańcaoena, bańkhan dhorage

[26] Lit. 'eat', very commonly used about destruction brought about by inimical powers such as witches and bongas, and also by snakes.

made the house very bright. When he lay down to sleep, the young man took the crab out and put it on his breast; then he fell asleep, and the princess had fallen asleep before him.

When the young man had fallen asleep, people tell, two snakes were coming out together from the nostrils of the princess, to kill[26] the young man. When they saw the crab, they drew back again. A short while afterwards they again were coming out; now these two young people were heavily asleep; they were aware of nothing. The crab then said: "O dear, these two snakes will undoubtedly presently kill my companion. Wait, I shall kill and do for these two."

Having decided this the crab, people tell, went up to the neck of the princess, near to her mouth, and lay in wait there, and its claws it kept well spread out. Now these two snakes were coming out a little and then again drew back. As they were over and over again acting in this way, it happened that they once came fairly out and were looking about and were darting out their tongues. Just then, people tell, the crab instantly seized both of them with its claws. They were utterly unable to get in again, and it did not let them loose from its claws. Then both the snakes wriggled out twirling their tails, and they wound their tails all round the crab. But the crab never let them go; pinching them with its claws it killed both of them outright. When they were dead, it brought them down from the bed to the ground.

At early dawn the young man awoke first. He felt round for the crab, and as he did not feel it on his breast, he was startled and got up in a trice. Then he saw it, between the bedsteads on which they were lying, entirely tied up by the two snakes so that it could not move. He called out Alas! alas! many times. Then he saw that the two snakes were dead and the crab alive. And, people tell, he asked the crab: "I say, chum, where did you find these two snakes."

The crab replied: "These two snakes were just on the point of killing you; it was fortunate that you had brought me along

huteċkin jomkema. Uni rani kuriak mũ bhuk khonge nukin biń dokin odoklena.

Khange ona kathaeańjomket khan, uni kora do adiye bhabnayena, are menketa, Ia gate, am do adi mũhĩn khon iń dom bańcao aguyediń kana; am iate ińak jivi bańcaok kantińa, ar bańkhan do iń eskar khan, sedaereń mohor metao utarkoka.

Ado ona tayom uni rani doe ebhenena. Ado ebhenkatere hõ orak bhitrirege cetko coṅkin gal golpojoṅ kana arkin khildu khamda kana. Belae rakapenre hõ orak bhitrirege menakkinge. Ar uni raj do bahre raca senre Hadi doe hoho jarwa tear akatkoa. Ado pahile badae kana se bań, nui ma nia ńinda bhitarregeye gujuka. Ado ona menkate onko Hadi doe joh johao tear akatkoa.

Ado ina mit ghuri khange, kathae, bana horkin beret odokena. Khange raj doe menketa, Ayoge! ia hor ya, bae goċlena. Iń doń menoan tahẽkana, dhora nia ńindaregeye gujuka mente. Nui kuriren do aema jãwãeko goċ akantaea; nui hõ nãhãk dhorageye gujukgea. Ona menkate gok odokea mente Hadi doń hoho agu ocoketkoa. Ayogeń ńele kan doe jivetge! Ado khange onko Hadi then uni raj do adiye lajao ocoyena. Ado enre hõ ona reak tinak berhonko ńama, ona doko koekedegea. Ado eneko tahẽyena.

Ar uni rani kuri do aċ hormore unkin bińkin tahẽkante, bań do cette, motage, kathae, bae motak kan tahẽkana. Ado uni hormo khon unkin biń hõe goċketkintaea, ar bapla dak hõ bhijauadea. Ado kathae, tayomte do khube motayena.

Ado inakate arhõ dos baro din uni katkom do onka gitiċ jokhen aċ koramreye dohokedea. Adoe ńelketa, Nit do jãhãn mũhĩn do banuktińa, joto cele parom akana. Ado aċ monre onka hudis

27 The hadi is of about the same social status as the Dom; they are scavengers.

28 The sentence, which comes somewhat malapropos here, naturally refers to the young man and the king's family.

with you; thereby you were saved; otherwise they would doubtlessly have killed you. These two snakes came out of the queen's nostrils."

When he heard this, the young man became very sad and said: "I say, chum, you have been saving me all along from many dangers; because of you my life has been saved; otherwise, if I had been alone, I should have been utterly done for and killed long ago."

Afterwards the princess awoke; but although they were awake, they remained inside the house talking this that and the other and amusing themselves. The sun got high up, still they remained inside. And the king had called together a number of Hadis[27] and had them ready outside in the court-yard. He thought he knew from his former experience, you know, that this man would die in the course of the night. Thinking this he had brought these Hadis and kept them ready.

Then a moment afterwards both of them, people tell, got up and came out. "O mother!" the king exclaimed, "this rascal of a fellow, he is not dead. I was thinking that without fail he would die this night. A large number of bridegrooms have died for this girl; this one would also die without fail. Thinking this I had these Hadis called here to carry him out. O mother! I see him, he is alive!" The king was made utterly ashamed before these Hadis. In spite of all, they asked him for the wages that would be due to them for the work. After this they all[28] stayed on.

Because the princess had had these two snakes in her body, or for some other reason, she had, people tell, never been putting on flesh. Now these two snakes had got out of her body, she also conceived. And afterwards, people tell, she became very stout.

After the happenings mentioned the young man for some ten to twelve days kept the crab with him on his breast, while he was sleeping. Then he understood: "Now there is no more danger for me; likely all such has passed." And turning

gaṇḍọn baṛakateye mẹnkeťa, Nit dọ uni kaṭkọmgeye girạ bạsikidińa, bạhuạdińae are rajkidińa. Nui hō̱ miťṭaṅ bhage thạ̃i ńe̱l ṭhikkate ọṇḍẹń idikaea.

Adọ miť din dọe metadea, Iạ gate, adọ ḍher dinem gọṛọadińa ar ḍher mũhĩn khonem bańcaokidińa, adọ ona reaǩ iń dọ ceť hō̱ bạń ẹm daṛeam kana. Adọ ma rọṛme ceť iń emama?

Adọ uni kaṭkọme mẹnkeťa, Acha bogege, adọ am thọń bańcaoketmea.

Adọ uniye hẹ̃keťa, Sạrigem bańcaokidińa, baṅa mẹntẹ dọ baṅ.

Adọ uni kaṭkọme mẹnkeťa, Acha, am ṭhen dọ ceť hō̱ bạń ńam kana, adọ dayakateń metam kana, nui rajaǩ pukhri menaǩtaea, adọ okaṭaǩ pukhri tis hō̱ baṅ ańjẹdoǩ kan, khub daǩ tahẽ puṛạuǩ kan, adọ ona pukhrire delaṅ idi oṭokạńme, ar jãhãeko saṕ jãhãnlíń khan, unre am dọ chaḍaokạńme.

Adọ sạrige okaṭaǩ pukhri baṅ ańjẹdoǩ, ona pukhriteye idikadea are metadea, Ma adọ ạsuloǩme ar jãhã leka noa pukhri sẹn umoǩ iń hẹćlen khan, iń tuluć ńẹpẹloǩ dọ oḍokoǩme baṛẹ. Adọ uni koṛa dọe ruạṛ hẹćena.

Adọ inạkate mō̱ṛẽ̱ tuṛui caṇdo hoeyen khan, dadattekoko ańjọm ńamkeťa, nui koṛa dọe rajentabona mẹnte, ar disom hō̱e ńamkeťa mẹnte. Adọ miť din dọ hạti sadọmante dadatteko ṭhen hiǩriye calaoena. Adọ dadattekine metakin kana, Ńẹlben ya, kuṛhiạben metaṅ kana; cekate eṅgate hạti sadọmreń dẹćena, ar aben dọ unạǩben kạmi kanre hō̱ hạti sadọmre dọ okorben dẹjoǩ kana?

Ar unkin dadattekin dọ ceť hō̱ bakin rọṛ ruạṛleťa. Adọko peṛa baṛakedea. Adọ uni koṛae mẹnkeťa, Nọṇḍẹ dọ rẹṅgẹćte tinạǩpẹ kọsṭọǩa? Disom iń ńamketťabona, adọ delabon ọṇḍẹgeń idipea.

this over in his mind he said: "Now this crab has settled me down; it procured a wife for me and made me a king. I shall find out a fine place for it also and take it there."

So one day he said to the crab: "I say, chum, it is a long time you have been helping me and you have saved me from many dangers, and I am unable to give you anything for all this. Tell me, what shall I give you."

The crab then replied: "Very well, I have, as you know, saved you."

He agreed to this: "In very truth you have saved me; there is no denying this."

The crab then said: "Very well, I do not ask for anything from you; but I tell you, show me kindness; this king has tanks; any tank that never dries up and in which there is plenty of water at all seasons, do take me to such a tank and leave me there, and if anybody should happen to catch me, then rescue me."

So, truth to tell, he took the crab to a tank that never dried up and said to it: "So now support yourself, and when I happen to come to this tank to have a bath, come out to meet me, please." And the young man returned from there.

When some five or six months had elapsed, his elder brother and family heard that this young man of theirs had become a king and got a country. And one day he went with elephants and horses to pay his elder brother a visit. He then said to his elder brother and sister-in-law: "See now, both of you, you were calling me lazy; how then, dash it, have I been able to mount elephants and horses, while you, although you are working so much, never mount an elephant or a horse?"

They did not answer a single word to this. Afterwards they feasted him, and the young man said to them: "How much distress will you continue suffering here? I have got a countrv for us; come along, I shall take you there."

Adǫko metadea, Nẹs dǫ bale calaḱ kana; ma kalǫm hijuḱme. Adǫ ẹnẹ tara nakhareye rajena. Adǫ onakate turui eae serma hoeyen khan, sẹ goṭae ạidạri cabaket́ khan, aćren hilit dadattekine ạguket́kina. Adǫ ẹnẹ mit́ ṭhenko tahẽyena. Are metakoa, Pạhil dǫ kuṛhiạ kuṛhiạ bogetepe ruhet́edin̉ tahẽkana. Adǫ ma ńẹlpe, iń kuṛhiạ hǫṛge bạń rajentabona? Ape dǫ unạḱpe kạmitabona, ar okorpe rajlena?

Adǫ enkae rǫṛ baṛaket́a. Adǫ ẹnẹye thir baṛayena, ạḍi utạr dǫ bae rǫṛ idilet́a. Ać mǫnreye hudisket́a, Ạḍi utạr nãhãḱ iń rǫṛ idile khan, nukin hilin̉ dadan̉aḱ mǫnre ban̉ jutkin ạikaua. Mẹnakin, Noako rǫṛe an̉jǫmalan̉ lagat́ge alan̉ dǫe ạgu akat́lan̉a. Delalan̉ ruạṛ dapoṛoḱa. Adǫ onka mǫnreye hudis baṛaket́te bae rǫṛlet́a. Inạḱkategeye thir doroḱena.

Adǫ inạ tayom uni rajaḱ ḍinḍạ khon dǫko ucạṛena; dosra sẹnreko dǫn̉gǫlket́a. Adǫ ẹnẹ jugạ jugko rajena. Ar gidǫr pidǫrko hoeyenteko san̉ge idiyena.

Adǫ ẹnẹ niạ katha hõń khǫtǫmket́a, in maran̉gea.

There are some variants of this story. One has not the long introduction about the childhood of the young man and how he grew into such a lazy fellow. It starts with the young man's running away in the sulks, because his brother and his wife have scolded him for his laziness.

Another does not mention the incident of the Dom, a part that Santals will enjoy immensely, especially where it is told how the rascal thinks himself great and drives his wife and children out of his house.

One story mentions the unhappy fate of all who have been previously married to the princess (or queen, as she is also called, because her husband had become king of a part of the country), but says nothing about how the king counts on this happening.

But they said: "We are not leaving this year; come back next year."

So he became king of half the country. When six or seven years had passed, that is to say, when he had become the owner of the whole, he brought his elder brother and his sister-in-law. And thereafter they remained together. He said to them: "Formerly you were scolding me a good deal, calling me Lazy, lazy! Now see, have not I the lazy fellow become our king? You are working so much, why, you have not become kings."

He spoke in this way, but then he stopped; he did not talk much of this kind. He said to himself: "If I talk much of this kind, my sister-in-law and brother will be hurt; they may say: 'It is to let us two hear this kind of talk that he has brought us here. Come, let us return and have done with it.' Thinking thus he did not say any more. He stopped and had done with it.

Afterwards they moved away from the grounds of the other king and built a palace in another place. Thereupon they were kings for ever. They got children and multiplied, as time went.

So there I have made an end of this story also; it is so much.

One variant tells that the young man took the crab not to a tank, but to a river with pools of continuous water.

The motif, so well known from the tales of other races (e. g. the Askelad of the Norwegian folktales), is there, but has been more or less covered up by the Santal narrator's wish to take in many details. The tale is probably borrowed, but has been dressed up and adapted to Santal ideas.

64. Eṅgat ṭuạren koṛa.

Sedae jugre, kathae, mit́ṭaṅ raje tahẽkana. Uni raj do̠ mit́ gele̠ gidrạ eṅgatkatege uni oṛak̕ ho̠ṛte̠t́ do̠e go̠ćena, se̠ rạnitae do̠e go̠ćena, ar uni ho̠po̠nte̠t́ do̠ koṛa gidrại tahẽkana. Ado̠ kurumuṭute uni gidrạ do̠e ạsul harakadea. Ado̠ uni gidrại cacoyen khan do̠ rajren mit́ṭaṅ ạsul pusiye tahẽkana. Ado̠ uni gidrạ do̠ uni pusi tuluć e̠ne̠će latayena; siń sạṭup̕ uni pusigeye kho̠jea are ho̠bo̠r baṛayea.

Ado̠ atoren ho̠ṛ se̠ aćren peṛako, sanam ho̠ṛkoge rajko metaea, baṅma, Arhõ bạhujoṅme, noa nun marań bakho̠lre e̠ke̠n he̠re̠l ho̠po̠n tahe̠nte do̠ bań sajaok̕ kana, ạdite̠t́ bạpuṛićge haeta hoetole ńe̠letmea. Ado̠ uni raje metakoa, Baṅa, bań bạhujoṅa, iń do̠. Tayo̠m era do̠ bako bhagea; tayo̠m era tuluć do̠ katha hõ bań jurik̕a, ar onka lekate dho̠n hõ ase̠ć tase̠jte sanamko ublạ ḍublạia ar jo̠n kạmiạ hõ ṭhik bako do̠ho̠kote sanamko chir chạturok̕gea; ar tayo̠m era do̠ pạhil era ho̠po̠n gidrạ do̠ ạḍiko ạṛisakogea; ar tayo̠m erań ńamleko khan do̠ nui gidrạ hape̠n ạḍi bhabnae ńama; siń sạṭup̕ hape̠n te̠ge̠ć te̠ge̠će ro̠ṛaea, ar jãhãnak̕e huṛsole khan do̠ etrań etraṅe metaea. Onkate hape̠n nui gidrạ do̠ ạḍiye hado̠sok̕a. Ado̠ nui gidrạ ńe̠lte hape̠n iń hõ ạḍi bhabnań ńama. Baṅa, iń do̠ bań bạhujoṅa, nenkategeń tahe̠na.

Ado̠ unreko metaea, Baṅa, raj, jo̠to̠ ạimại do̠ baṅko onkana. Ado̠mko do̠ko bhagegea, adhanko do̠ pạhil era lekageko ạikạuk̕a, ar gidrạko hõ bako ạṛisakoa, pạhil era lekage apnar ho̠po̠n lekageko do̠ho̠koa.

---

1 The Santali title of the story is 'A stepmother'; to avoid confusion with other stories it has been altered as shown.

2 The 'king' is apparently a landlord, not much different from other villagers, except that he has wealth and is a landlord.

3 The stepmother-problem is the same everywhere; many widowers remain single on account of the experience of other people's children. It might be noted that the Santals have difficulty in understanding how anybody can live single; a man needs somebody to take care of his bodily wants and his household, to cook his

64. A BOY WHO LOST HIS MOTHER[1].

Once upon a time, long long ago, people tell, there was a king. When the wife of this king had become the mother of one child, she died, that is to say, his queen died; the child was a boy. The king did all he could to get the boy to live and grow up. When the child commenced to toddle, there was a cat that the king had, and the child became attached to playing with the cat; all day long he asked for this cat and was carrying her about in his arms.

Now the village people[2] or rather his friends, all of them, were speaking to the king, saying: "Marry again; it is not as it should be that only men should live in such a big palace as this is; we see how utterly miserable and lonely you are." The king would then answer them: "No, I shall not marry. A second wife is not good; your opinions do not agree with those of a second wife, and in this way second wives will scatter and squander your wealth, all of it, and as they do not take proper care of the work people and servants, these will all be dispersed, and a second wife will be sure to worry the children of the first wife; if I should get a second wife, this child of mine would later on get much trouble; all day long she would nag at and scold him; and if he should ask to get something or other, she would speak angrily to him. In this way this child would later on have much grief; and then, seeing how it would be with my child, I myself should have much pain. No, I shall not marry; I shall stay as I am."

Then they would say to him: "Not so, raja, all women are not of that kind. Some are good ones; some half of them are to be felt like the first wife[3]; they do not worry the children either; like the first wife they take care of them, as if they were their own children."

---

food, and so on. How should he otherwise be able to do his ordinary work? An unmarried woman is unthinkable; if such are found, the Santals have no doubt that it must be due to some mental or bodily defect, that makes marriage impossible This to explain the behaviour of the king's friends.

Adǫ unre raje mẹnkeťa, Baṅa, bạń pạtiạuaǩ kana; ạimại dǫ sanamko miť dharagea.

Adǫ jãhã leka sẹn ńapamlen khan ona bạhujoṅ reaǩ kathageko ẹhǫba. Adǫ uni raj dǫ ạḍi ạṛis ona katha dǫe ạikạua.

Adǫ onka onkate miť din dǫe mẹnkeťa, Hẽ, judi pạhil era leka nui gidrạ ǫkǫeko jǫtǫne khan, ẹnḍẹkhan dǫń bạhukekogea; ar baṅkhan dǫ ǫhǫń bạhulekoa.

Adǫko metadea, Baṅa, judi onka mạ̃hīrkoko ńamlen khan dǫm dǫhǫkekogea sẹ baṅ?

Adǫe mẹnkeťa, Hẽko ńamoǩ khan dǫń dǫhǫkoa, ar baṅkhan baṅ.

Adǫko mẹnkeťa, Baṅa, raj, ona katha dǫ pạhilregebo kuli maṛaṅkoa, baṅma, nui gidrạ apnar eṅgat leka ǫkǫepe dǫhǫye khan, ẹnḍẹkhan raj ṭhenle lại baṛapea, ar baṅkhan baṅ. Nonka kulikatebo ạgukoa.

Adǫ raje mẹnkeťa, Acha ẹnḍẹkhan, ma siṛikope.

Adǫ sikṛiko dhurạuena; adǫ ḍher ṭhen onkako siṛikeťkoa, mẹnkhan gidrạ dǫǩhǫge bako rẹbẹn. Hǫrṭẹť ma napae napae ar raj ṭhen jãwãeoǩko khusiaǩ kangea; mẹnkhan gidrạ dǫǩhǫge bharko metaǩ kana. Kuṛiko ma akotegeko jǫṭǫǩ kan, raj ṭhen dǫ iṅge raebaraṅpe mẹnte. Adǫ noa kathako kulileko khạngeko pạc gǫdǫǩ kana.

Adǫ tin din badre cǫṅ, kathae, miťṭaṅ atore miťṭaṅ kuṛiye rạnḍi akan tahẽkana. Adǫ uni kuṛiye mẹnkeťa, Henda bhala, raj lạgiť bạhuko ńam baṛayeťko tahẽkan dǫko ńamkeťkoa sẹ baṅ? Onka hǫṛkoe kuli baṛayeťkoa.

Adǫko metadea, Hẽ, ńam dǫko ńam baṛayeťkogea; mẹnkhan gidrạ dǫǩhǫge ǫkǫe hõ bako rẹbẹn kana, oṅate bako ńam akaťkoa.

---

[4] The contents of the story point to its origin being non-Santal; but most details are genuine Santal traits; the story has been adapted to Santal standards or ideas. A Hindu widow is not permitted to remarry. With the Santals remarriage is permitted and very common, with this understanding, however, that the remarriage is for this life only; in the next world all who were married together as bachelors and spinsters will be reunited, whatever has happened in this world.

Then the king replied: "No, I do not believe this; the women are all of one kind."

Whenever they happened to meet, they started this about marrying; and the king felt very annoyed at this talk.

But as time went in this way, he one day said: "Yes, if any woman would take care of this child like my first wife, then I might be willing to marry such a one; otherwise I shall certainly not marry."

"Quite so," they answered him, "but if such gentle ones should be found, would you marry such ones or not?"

"Yes," he said, "if such are found, I shall marry, otherwise not."

"Naturally," they said, "we shall first ask them about this, viz., 'if you will take care of this child as if you were his own mother, then we shall inform the king about you, otherwise not'. Only when we have ascertained this, we shall bring one."

"Very well then," the king said, "look out for one."

So they commenced to search for a bride; they found suitable ones at many places; but they were not willing to take care of the child. The girls were nice and fine, and they were pleased to marry the king; but to take care of the child they deemed a heavy responsibility. Girls were even offering themselves to be matched, saying, 'Arrange for me to be married to the king'. But when they asked them about this, they would at once draw back.

Then some time afterwards, people tell, it so happened that in a certain village there was a girl who had been widowed[4]. This girl said: "Look here, they were seeking for a wife for the king, I wonder whether they have found one or not." She was asking people in this way.

"Well," they said to her, "they are certainly seeking for a bride; but no one is willing to take care of the child; therefore they have not found any."

The ceremonies of a second marriage are therefore also different from those of a first one.

Adọ uni kuṛiye mẹnkeťa, Cekate cọṅ bako rẹbẹn kan? Iń khan dọ jạnić iń rẹbẹn gọťkoǩa.

Adọko metae kana, Henda na, ẹnḍẹkhanem rẹbẹnkoǩa?

Adọe mẹnkeťa, Hẽ ẹnte ko khusiań khan dọń gankoǩgea.

Arhõko mẹnkeťa, Henda na, gidrạ dọm jọtọnketaea?

Adọe mẹnkeťa, Hẽ, ać eṅgat khon bạṛtiń dulạṛkea. Ceť ẹnte, iń ma rạnić hoekoǩa, iń thọ kạmi dọ bạnuǩtińa, ini gidrạge kurumuṭute bań jọtọnea?

Adọko mẹnkeťa, Hẽ ma hẽge, uni ṭhen jãhãe rẹbẹnlen khan, ạḍi sukko jọmkea.

Adọ inạ tayọm khange uni kuṛiye rọṛleť ona kathage pasnaoena. Adọ khange miťṭań hoṛ raebare dhurạuena; adọ noa kathage rajko lạiadea, bańma, Miťṭań rạnḍi kuṛile siṛi akadea, adọm khusilen khan dọle raebarkea.

Adọ uni raje mẹnkeťa, Gidrạ dọǩhọge thọ ọkọe hõ bako rẹbẹn kana — inạge jaia dọń metaǩ kana.

Adọ uni raebar hoṛe mẹnkeťa, Bańa raj, onako katha dọ jọtọń sutrạu akaťa, sanamle ṭhik ṭhak akaťa, adọ amem khusilen khange nãhãǩ, katha dọ gulạṇḍ gọdọǩa.

Adọ raje mẹnkeťa, Acha ẹnḍẹkhan iń ńẹlea. Ma nịạ phalna dinre nọnḍẹ ạguyepe, ar iń khusilen khan dọ iń samańre nãhãǩ nui gidrạ jọtọne reaǩ katha kuliyem, sạri sẹ naseye mẹneťa mẹnte, onabo ańjọma, ar iń hõ apnar luturteń ańjọmjońa.

Adọ uni hoṛe mẹnkeťa, Acha bogege, ẹnḍẹkhan ma inạ dinre dọ khạṭigele hijuǩa.

Adọe mẹnkeťa, Ma hijuǩpe baṛẹ.

---

[5] The plural is used in an indefinite sense, meaning the person concerned without direct reference.

[6] To bring a prospective wife to the man is not according to custom; the only explanation must be the position of the man. With the Santals all preliminaries are arranged by the marriage-broker and the parents, the parties concerned being — now-a-days — just permitted to have a look at each other and then

"What can the reason possibly be," the girl replied, "that they are unwilling? If it were myself, I should likely be willing quickly enough."

"Look here, girl," they asked her, "then you would be willing?"

"Yes," she replied, "for if they[5] are pleased with me, I should be agreeable."

Again they asked her: "Look here, girl, would you take care of his child?"

"Yes," she replied, "I should love him more than his own mother. For what does it amount to? I should naturally become queen; I should have no work to do, so should I not be diligent and take care of this child?"

"That is quite true," they said, "any one who agrees to marry him will enjoy very easy circumstances."

After this it was rumoured abroad what the girl had said; thereupon a man took upon himself to act as a marriage-broker, and they told the king, saying: "We have found a widowed girl, so if you are pleased, we might arrange for a marriage."

The king then said: "As you know, no one is willing to take charge of my child, — that is what I call the difficulty."

The marriage-broker then said: "No difficulty, raja. These matters I have enquired into; we have arranged it all properly, so if you are pleased, the matter will be moving presently."

"Very well then, I shall have a look at her," the king said. "Please bring her here[6] on such and such a day; and if I am pleased, ask her in my presence this question about taking care of my child; we shall hear whether she really says so or not; I want to hear this myself with my own ears."

The man then replied: "All right, then I shall without fail bring her on that day."

"Please come," the king said.

to consent or refuse. A discussion like the one here reported would not be well possible.

Adọ sạri ona din tioḱen khanko hẹćena; adọ raje ńẹl baṛakedea. Adọ uni raebar hoṛe metadea, baṅma, Hoṛte dọń khusiyena, adọ aćge ceṫe mẹneṫa, khusia sẹye baṅa?

Adọ uni hoṛe kulikedea uni kuṛi, Cele, mãi, raj dọe khusiaṫmea, aćo amge ceṫ leka?

Adọ kuṛiye mẹnkeṫa, Iń hõ khusige.

Adọ mãi, rajren gidrạ dọm jọtọn daṛekea sẹ ọhọa?

Adọe mẹnketa, Hẽ, jọtọn baṅkhanin cekayea? Ać eṅgat khon bạṛtiń jọtọnea,

Adọ sạrigem jọtọnea, sẹ ẹṛẹge pasẹm rọṛeṫ?

Adọe mẹnkeṫa, Baṅ, sạrigeń mẹneṫa, ẹṛẹ dọ baṅ. Cedaḱ ạuṛi dọń rọṛa? Tayọmre cọṅ hapẹn arhõpe rọṛaṅ, jẹ pạhil dọ nonkae mẹnkeṫa, ar nẹtar dọe ạṛisoḱ kana. Onka hapẹn bape rọṛeṅa?

Adọko mẹnkeṫa, Mẹn ạikạ, nõḱõe am mocatege nonkam rọrkeṫa, bam jọtọne khan dọ ạikạ tayọmtele sapmea.

Adọe mẹnkeṫa, Acha bogege, sabeṅpe.

Adọ enka rọṛ baṛakatege inrege bapla reaḱko neṇḍakeṫa, niạ din hiloḱbo ạguyea mẹnte.

Adọ sạri ona neṇḍa din tioḱen khan dọko ạgukedea, adọ bapla hoeyena. Adọ tayọmte uni gidrạ dọ ạḍiye jọtọnea — umeae, sunume ọjọḱaea, ar miṫ hẹogeye dọhọyea, tin ghạṛire hõ ọtre dọ bae dọhọyea, ar jãhãnaḱgeye khọj sẹye huṛso, onageye emaea. Adọe harayenre hõe hẹoegea; uni gidrạ bae hẹo ocoḱre hõ jọrmọṭge laga sapkateye hẹoea. Adọ tahẹn tahẹnte tin din badre cọṅ,

[7] The Santals always carry their children on their (left) hip. Men may sometimes let young boys or men ride on their shoulder; but the ordinary proceeding is to carry on the hip, the arm of the carrier keeping the child in position.

And, truth to tell, when that day arrived, they came, and the king looked at her. Thereupon he said to the marriage-broker: "I am pleased with the girl; now what has she herself to say? is she pleased or not?"

The man then asked the girl: "How is it, girl? the king is pleased with you; how is it with you?"

"I also am pleased," the girl replied.

"Then, girl, will you be able to take care of the king's child, or will you be unable to do this?"

"Yes," she replied, "I shall take care of him, what should I do otherwise? I shall take better care of him than his own mother would."

"Is it really true this that you will take care of him, or perhaps you are lying?"

"No," she replied, "I am speaking the truth and no lies. Why should I speak dishonestly? Afterwards some future day you would again speak to me, saying that at first she spoke so and so, but now-a-days she is being worried. Would you not scold me in this way some future day?"

"Be careful then," they said; "see now with your own mouth you have said this; if you do not take care of him, beware, we shall hold you responsible."

"Very well," she replied, "hold me responsible."

After they had conversed in this way, they then and there fixed a day for the marriage, saying: on such and such a day we shall fetch her.

And, truth to tell, when the day fixed came, they brought her and celebrated the marriage. Afterwards she took very good care of the child, she washed him, rubbed him in with oil and always carried him on her hip[7]; she would not put him down on the ground for a moment, and whatever the child asked for or had a desire for, she gave it to him. Also when he had grown somewhat, she carried him on her hip; even when the child did not want to be carried, she would chase him and catch him and

kathaekin gidrạwana, koṛa gidrạge. Adọ banar gidrạge ạḍiye dulạṛkina.

Adọ onka onkate uni chuṭkiren gidrạ hõe harayen khan, uni pạhilić gidrạ dọ edregeye ńẹlea; adọ pạhilreye hara akan iạte mocate dọ bae rọṛ hoṭ́ daṛeak̓ kana; ar uni rajak̓ mọn ma jọtọe saṕ cabaket́taea, ar uni tuluć mọn hõ mit́entakina, ar jẹge uni chuṭki rạniye hukum, onage raj hõe añjọma, uniak̓ katha dọ bae nẹhõt daṛeak̓a.

Adọ tahẹn tahẹnte uni chuṭki rạni dọ ać mọnẹ mọnẹteye hudisa, bañma, nui pạhil gidrạ dọ cet́ lekateń laga tot́ ocoyea? Ona kathage din hilok̓ uni dọe hudisa.

Adọ uni koṛa gidrạ dọ uni pusi ạḍiye dulạṛea; jãhã sẹn dãṛã baṛaeye calak̓a, adọ ontẹ khon hẹć tora pusigeye khọj maṛañea, ar uni họbọr baṛalẹ ẹnẹć daka hõe jọma.

Adọ mit́ din dọ oka sẹn cọñ dãṛã baṛaeye sẹnlena. Adọ ontẹ khon hẹć torage uni gidrạ dọe mẹnket́a, Henda gọ, pusi dọe okayentińa?

Adọ uni kạkit eṅgat dọ ạḍi garte tẹrgẹń marteye rọṛ gọt́ket́a, Pusige jọme kantama, siń sạṭuṕe pusi pusik̓a!

Adọ uni gidrạ dọ onkae tẹrgẹńade khane tiruṕena, adọ mọnẹ mọnẹte cet́ko cọñ bujhạu baṛakateye rak̓ket́a. Ar un jọkhẹn uni raj dọ oṛak̓re dọ bae tahẽkana, oka sẹn cọñ dãṛã baṛaeye sẹn akan tahẽkana. Adọ uni kạkit eṅgat dọ gidrạ bae hapek̓ kan ńẹlte uni pusiye ńamkedeteye capat́ oḍok gọt́adea, adọe metae kana, Hunitam pusi; nui pusi lạgit́ jivi lọk̓ kantaea. Adọ onkae metade khan uni gidrạ dọ artẹt́geye rak̓ket́a. Adọ uni pusi saṕkate jọrmọṭgeye họbọrae kana. Adọ uni gidrạ mọn baṛićentaete artẹt́geye kikiạuket́a. Adọ bae hapek̓ kante uni kạkit eṅgat dọ phọrphundiye

[8] It might be noted that the Santals have separate names for a first and later wives. The first wife is bạṭki, the second is called chuṭki, provided there are only two. When speaking of these, the names mentioned are constantly employed, as throughout in this story.

[9] Angry language, no subject is mentioned.

forcibly take him on her hip. Then as time passed, who knows how long afterwards it happened, they had a child, a boy. And she showed both children much love.

While they were living in this way, the child of the second wife[8] also grew, and when this came to pass, she got angry at the sight of the first child; but because he was the older one, she was unable to use harsh language quickly; now she had also become intimate with all that was in the king's mind; he also had become of one mind with her, and whatever this second queen might order, the king would also assent to; he was unable to go against her word.

As time passed, the queen commenced to turn over in her mind: "How shall I manage to get this first child driven away?" Every day she was turning this over in her mind.

Now this child was very fond of the cat; when he had gone anywhere to amuse himself, he would as soon as he came back before anything else ask for the cat, and only when he had got the cat in his arms, he would take food.

One day it happened that he had been out somewhere walking. As soon as he came back from there, the child said: "Look here, mother, what has become of the cat?"

His step-mother at once spoke loudly and snappishly: "Is[9] eating your cat! All day long he calls out Cat! Cat!"

As she spoke thus snappishly, he bowed his head, and having come to who knows what understanding he commenced to cry. At that moment the king was not at home, he had gone out somewhere. When the stepmother saw that the child did not stop crying, she got hold of the cat and threw it out to him, and said to him: "There is your cat; his soul is on fire for this cat!" When she spoke to him in this way, the child cried still more. She then took the cat and put it forcibly into his arms; but as the child had become utterly upset, he only screamed still more. Then as the child did not become quiet, the step-mother she

lagaoketa, ado uni pusiak janga sapkate aćtege tikore jangakore goṭae rabor khal ocoyena. Ado siro soro māyām joroyen khan do, ado aćge bogeteye rakketa, ar gidrạ̣i egere kana ar kạumạue raketa.

Ado khange atoren hor doko anjomket khan doko meneta, Chuṭki rạni doe cekayente ban teheń do kạumạue raket kan? Delabon sebo ńel ạguyea. Ado sạriko calaoen khan adoe uduk baṛawakoa je, Nõkõe ńelpe, nui gidrạ pusi ṭhen teheń do bogeteye rabor khal ocokidiṅa. Ar cetko coṅ bogete hirkhạgeye rorketa, ar onko hor samanre uni gidrạ hõ hirkhạgeye egerkedea.

Ado onka hirkhạ ror anjomte onko ato hor doko calao baṛayena apan ạpin oṛakte. Ado onko horko ror idijoṅ kana, banma, Kạki gaṛhan do ban bogea. En betar doe menketa, apnar hopon lekan dohoyea. Okor adoe doho dareae kana? Inạ pusi rabor karontege hapen nui gidrạ doe lagayea. Ado enka ror baṛakateko thir baṛayena.

Ado tin ghuṛire coṅ, kathae, raje hećen khan uni samanre hõ, kathae, onka kạumạue raketa, uni chuṭki do. Ado uni raj doe kuli baṛayede kana, Teheń dom cekayente unạk ãṭte dom raketa? Cetko hasoyetmea? Ma lạime.

Adoe raketa are roṛeta; ado one gidrạ̣i tergeńade lekage nui hõe tergeń gotadea. Adoe men gotketa, Hẽ, jolok pusim ạsul akawadea, bogeteye rabor ocokidiń do ban? Nõkõe ńelme, goṭae rabor khal ocokidiṅa, nui gidrạ do. Unạk iń jotone reak nõkõeye gun akawadiṅa. Iń do bạń tahena am ṭhen do. Tahen khan hapen nonkage nui gidrạ doe santaoiṅa. Bam pạtiạuak kan khać, ato hor kulikom, onko hõko ńel idi akadiṅa.

played a low trick; she caught hold of the cat's leg and let herself be scratched and clawed on her hands and her feet all over. And when the blood commenced to run down, she herself commenced to cry loudly; she scolded the child and was crying and making a noise.

When the villagers heard this, they said: "What can have happened to the present queen, since she is crying and making such a noise to-day? Come, let us go and see what is the matter with her." They then actually went, and she was showing them, saying: "Here look at this, this child has to-day made the cat scratch and claw me something awful." And she used a good deal of disgusting language, and she also abused the child in a disgusting way in the presence of those people.

Hearing such disgusting language the villagers went away home to their respective houses. And these people were talking together, saying: "A step-mother jade is no good. Some time ago she said: 'I shall take care of him like my own child'. Why, how is she able to take care of him? On account of these cat scratches she will some day drive this child away." They spoke in this way and then ceased talking of this matter.

Now when the king some moments afterwards came back, she, this second wife, cried and made the same kind of noise in his presence also, people tell. The king asked her again and again: "What has happened to you to-day, since you are crying so badly? What is giving you pain? Please tell."

Then she was telling and crying at the same time; and as she had been snapping at the child, she also snapped at him, and said: "Yes, it is a fiery cat you have kept for him; he has made it scratch me something awful, naturally. Here look at this, he has made it scratch and claw me all over, this child. Such care I have taken of him, look here how he is thanking me. I shall not stay with you any longer. If I remain, this child will some day cause me to suffer. If you do not believe, ask the village people, they have also been here and seen me."

Adọ sạri atoren mit́ bar họṛe kuliketḱoa, Henda ho, iń kuliyet́pea, bhala, phalna eṅgat dọ sạrige pusi dọe raboṛ akadea, sẹ ạuṛigeye lạiań kana?

Adọko mẹnket́a, Sạri baṅdọ nase, ona dọ ọhọle mẹnlea; mẹnkhan sirọ sọrọ mā̃yā̃mok̓ dọle ńẹllet́gea.

Adọ enka kuli baṛakatege uni raj dọe ruạṛena. Adọ ać chuṭki bạhuye metae kana, Ma hapekok̓me, gidrạ leka dọ alom raga. Uni albudạha gidrạ dọ ẹnte cet́e bạḍaea? Gidrạ reak̓ dọ sak̓haotege hoyok̓a. Seṛa gidrạ khan dọń dhomkaokea; mẹnkhan nui albudạha dọń cekayea?

Adọ uniye mẹnket́a, Ińak̓ katham dọhọe khan iń tahẹna, ar baṅkhan dọ bạń tahẹna.

Adọ raje mẹnket́a, Dọhọ baṅkhan iń cekaetama? Nun din iń dọhọ ạguket́tama, nit bạń dọhọea?

Adọ uni chuṭkiye mẹnket́a, baṅma, Ińiń metam kana, ma nui gidrạ dọ gọjeme. Nit khonge nonkae santaoediń kana, arhō̃ thọ din menak̓gea. Nui gidrạ ki dọhọńae? Ọhọe dọhọliṅa. Am baṅ hilok̓ dọ hapẹne laga todeṅa. Nō̃k̓ō̃e ńẹlme, gidrạrege nuiak̓ cọlọn dọ judạk̓ kangea. Arhō̃ hapẹne haralen khan dọ cet́ leka cọń. Onateń metam kana, baṅma, Ińak̓ katham dọhọe khan, nenkare nui gidrạ dọ gọć giḍikaeme. Ni lekan gidrạ dọko ḍhera; nenkan gidrạ dọ hapẹn ḍher iń janamama.

Adọ onkae mẹnket́ khan uni raj dọe bhabnayena; adọ cet́ hō̃ bae rọṛlet́a, tirup̓ hapeyenae. Adọ chuṭkitaeye mẹnket́a, Okorem rọṛet́a? Cet́ hō̃ bam mẹnet́a. Adọ uni raj dọ baṅgeye rọṛlet́a.

Adọ khange chuṭkiye mẹnket́a, Baḍaeket́meań, am dọ ińak̓ katha dọ ọhọm dọhọlea. Adọ ma aben apa hoṅge tahẹnben, iń dọ ni gidrạ heọkate jā̃hā̃teń oḍok calak̓a. Am dọ hapẹn nui

Then, truth to tell, he asked a couple of the villagers: "Listen, I am asking you, has the cat really scratched the mother of so-and-so, or is she telling fibs?"

"Whether it is true or not," they replied, "that we cannot tell; but we saw that blood was trickling down."

Having made these inquiries, he went back and said to his wife: "Now please be quiet, don't cry like a babe. This simple-minded child, what does he know? One has to bear with children. If he had been a big boy, I should have rebuked him; but what can I do with this undeveloped child?"

She then said: "If you do as I say, I shall remain, otherwise not."

"What should I else do?" the king replied; "so long a time I have all along done what you have wanted; should I not do the same now?"

The second wife then said: "I am telling you, kill the child Even now he is making me suffer in this way, and you know, there is some time coming. This child, do you think he will take care of me? He will do nothing of the kind. When you some day are no more, he will drive me out. Here, look at this, while still a child this one's behaviour is becoming different from that of others. Then again, when he grows up, what may it not be? Therefore I am telling you: If you will do as I say, kill him and do away with him, while he is still what he is. There are many children like this one; I shall in time to come bear you many such children."

When she spoke in this way, the king became downhearted; he did not say anything, he remained with his head bowed down. Then his second wife said: "Why, you are not saying anything. Have you nothing to say?". But the king did not speak at all.

Then his wife said: "I have learnt to know you; you will surely not do what I say. So there, you stay here, you father and son; I shall take this child of mine on my hip and go somewhere or other. Some future day you will have me beaten to death by

gidrạ ṭhenge mit́ din kalre dọm dal goć ocoña, ar bańkhan hapẹn nui gidrạị haralen khan, oka lekate cọñ iń reak̕ kathae lạiama; adọ am hō̱ hapẹn uniak̕ kathagem añjọmte hapẹn iń dọm dal gọjeña; adọ bań ceka akana, ma nenkarelań apan ạpinok̕a. Adọ unạk̕e rọṛ idiket̕re hō̱, raj dọ cet̕ hō̱ bae rọṛlet̕a.

Khange uni chuṭki dọe kạhīs gọt̕ente aćak̕ jọtọ sapap̕e ńamket̕taea; adọ gidrạ hẹokate usạt̕e ọḍok gọt̕ena. are ẹgẹr oṭokat̕a, Ma aben apa họnge tahẽkok̕ben; ạliń dọliń calak̕ kana.

Adọ unre raje mẹnket̕a, Okateben calak̕ kana? Aloben calak̕a. Adọe sẹn ńõk̕ ocoat̕kingea. Adọ cet̕ko cọe bujhạu baṛaket̕ khan dọ rukạṛe calaoena. Adọ pańja tiok̕kateye metae kana, Dela ruạṛme, alom calak̕a. Nui gidrạ hapẹn ạḍim harkhetea.

Adọ unreye mẹnket̕a, Nui gidrạ reak̕ dọ cet̕ jalayet̕mea? Amren gidrạ mań bạgi oṭoadetam. Amren ma bań ạguyede kan. Nui ma iṅren kane.

Adọ raje mẹnet̕a, Bańa, dela ruạṛben. Nui gidrạ reak̕ mãyã hō̱ bań chaḍao daṛeak̕ kana. Ma ruạṛgeaben. Adọ onka mẹnkate laha sẹn khone ẹsẹt̕kina.

Adọ unre chuṭkiye mẹnket̕a, Ma cet̕em ẹsẹt̕ baṛayet̕lińa? Sẹn ocoalińme. Am dọ unạk̕ iń galmaraoat̕mere hō̱, ińak̕ katha dọ bam añjọma; adọ cet̕em ẹsẹt̕ baṛayet̕lińa?

Adọ unre raje mẹnket̕a, Acha, ma ruạṛme, adọ amak̕ kathageń añjọma.

Adọ unre chuṭkiye mẹnket̕a, Uni pạhil gidrạm gọje khan dọń ruạṛa, ar bańkhan dọ bań ruạṛa.

Adọ raje mẹnket̕a bại bạite, Ma ẹnte ruạṛben, adọ unigeye bạṛić kan khan dọń gọjea.

Ẹnḍẹkhan adọe mẹnket̕a, Nitgem gọje khan dọń ruạṛa, ar bańkhan dọ, mẹn, sẹn ocoalińme; cet̕em ẹsẹt̕ akat̕lińa?

this child; and if not, then when this child grows up, he will tell you who knows what about me; then you also some day will listen to his words and have me beaten to death some day; now nothing has happened, so let us part, while it is still, as it is." But although she continued to speak in this strain, the king did not say a single word.

Then the woman suddenly lost her temper and collected all her things, and carrying her child on her hip she went straight away in a sulky fit; and as she went, she gave this scolding: "Now please, remain you two, father and son; we two are off."

"Where are you going?" the king asked. "Don't go." He let them go a little distance; then having come to some understanding, whatever it was, he went to bring them back. When he reached them, he said to her: "Come along, come back, don't go. You will give your child much suffering hereafter."

But she replied: "Why are you distressing yourself about this child? Why, I have left your child with you; it is not your one that I am taking along. This one is mine, you know."

"Not so," the king said, "come along, come back. I am not able to free myself of my affection for this child either. Please, you must come back." And speaking in this way he stood in front of them and blocked the way.

Then the woman said: "Why are you blocking the way for us? Let us go. Although I have spoken so much to you, you will not listen to what I say; why then are you blocking the way for us?"

The king then said: "Very well, please come back, and I shall do as you say?"

The woman then said: "If you will kill your first child, I shall go back, otherwise not."

The king then very slowly said: "Please then come back, and if he is bad, I shall kill him."

But then she said: "If you will kill him now, I shall come back; otherwise, have a care, let us go; why have you blocked the way for us?"

Adọ raje mẹnkeṭa, Acha, delabon, ruạṛben, ẹṇḍẹkhan nitgeṅ gọjea.

Adọ khange onkae mẹnkeṭ khankin ruạṛena. Adọ ruạṛkate hõe metae kana, Ma gọć họdeme.

Adọ raje mẹnkeṭa, Ạkhir iṅ gọjegea. Ma ẹṇḍẹkhan dahe tuluć taben sipikate emaeme. Inại jọm torawange; mẹnkhan nọṇḍẹ dọ ọhọṅ gọćlea. Hana bir sẹn ạyur idikateṅ gọjea.

Khange sạri dahe tabene sipikeṭa, adọe um napaekedea, sunumkoe ọjọḱadea, dhutikedeae, aṅgrọpkadeae; adọ ti ạbukkate dahe tabene emadea. Adọ uni gidrại jọjọm kan jokhange rajaḱ mẽṭ daḱ dọ mọnẹ mọnẹte hiḍir hiḍir jọrọyentaea.

Adọ uni chuṭki dọe mẹneṭa, Ceṭem raḱeṭa? Iṅ bogeteye santar ediṅ kan dọ baṅ? Ạḍi māyā sanayeṭmea.

Adọe jọm jọmkaṭa, adọ bae cabaleṭ khane itạṭkaṭa. Adọ raje mẹnkeṭa, Nuiaḱ itạṭ dọ iṅgeṅ jọmkaḱa. Adọ hapẹn nuiaḱ itạṭ dọ ọhọṅ ṅamlea. Adọ raḱ raḱte uniaḱ itạṭe jọmkeṭtaea. Ar tinạḱ gan cọṅ tabene ghẽṭkeṭa ar kạpiye oyo pọṭọmkeṭa. Adọe metae kana, Delaṅ bạbu, mamomtekolaṅ hiri ạgukoa, arhõ gapa dọlaṅ hijuḱa.

Adọ apattẹṭ onkae metade khan, uni gidrạ dọ ạḍiye rạskạ gọṭena; adọe mẹnkeṭa, Baba, panahitiṅ dọ okare? Adọ panahi ar chatare ṅawadea. Adọ panahiye horọḱade khane mẹnkeṭa, Henda baba, teheṅ dọlaṅ tioga sẹ baṅ? Tin sạṅgiṅre mamateko dọ menaḱkoa?

Adọe metadea, Sorgea, ạyuṕkote dọ nãhãḱlaṅ tioga. Khub taṛam taṛamtalaṅme.

Adọ calaḱ calaḱte, bhại, miṭṭaṅ maraṅ utạr birkin tioḱkeṭa, ar okaren cọṅ miṭṭaṅ seta unkin tayọm tayọmteye ọtọṅ idiyeṭkina.

---

[10] Taben, rice boiled and flattened, much used as provision for a journey.

[11] To eat what has been left by anybody on the plate is a sign of love and absolute confidence. Parents may eat what has been left by their small children; a wife may eat what her husband has left, this being a sure sign of love and feeling of belonging to her husband. A man would not ordinarily eat what his wife has left.

"Very well," the king said; "come along, come back; then I shall kill him now."

So when he had said this, they went back; and when they were back, she again said to him: "Be quick and kill him."

The king said: "Afterwards I shall kill him; now then mix curds and flattened rice[10] and give him. Let him have that and eat before going; but I am not going to kill him here. I shall lead him over to that forest and kill him."

So, truth to tell, she mixed curds and flattened rice, whereupon she washed and cleaned him, rubbed him in with oil, put on his loin-cloth and gave him a coat; thereupon she washed his hands and gave him curds and flattened rice. When the child was eating, the tears were running from the king's eyes at his thoughts. The woman then said: "What are you crying for? He is giving me so much suffering, or how? You are feeling much compassion with me."

The child tried to eat; but as he did not finish it all, he left some. The king then said: "I shall eat what he has left[11]. In the future I shall never get anything left by him." And crying he ate what the child had left. So he tied some flattened rice up in his cloth and covered a battle-axe up in a piece of cloth, whereupon he said to the child: "Come along, my boy; we two shall go on a visit to your mother's brothers; we shall come back to-morrow."

When his father said this to him, the child became very glad and said: "Father, where are my shoes?" So he brought him his shoes and an umbrella. When he put on his shoes, he said: "I say, father, shall we reach there to-day or not? How far away are my uncles living?"

"It is quite near," he replied; "we shall reach there towards evening. Walk as well as you can."

As they went along, friends, they reached a very large forest, and a dog belonging somewhere or other was following after them.

are my uncles living?"

Adọ ona bir talate mit́ṭań suṛuć hoṛtekin mohṇḍayena. Adọ ona bir talate calak̓ tulućge hoṛ hõkin at́ket́a. Adọ bin hoṛkoteye ạyur baṛayede kana, ar ber hõe hạsurok̓ kana. Adọ mit́ṭań dare ṭhenkin teṅgoyena. Adọe metadea, Ią, bạbu, ma noṇḍẹ duṛup̓ hataṛok̓talańme, iń dọ notẹreń ićanrege.

Adọ ona taben ghẽṭko dọ uni ṭhengeye dọhọ oṭokat́a, ar ać dọ uni ṭhen khone pharakena, ar uni seta dọ ać tayọmtegeye calaoena. Adọ ọntẹre uni setage sap̓kedetegeye mak̓kedea ar uni mãyãmte ona kạpi dọe jọdbọdaoket́a. Adọ uni gidrą mage dọe mãyãyente bae mak̓ledea. Adọe mẹnket́a, Noa birregeń bạgiaea, adọ bir janwar hẹćkate nãhãk̓ nui gidrą dọko jọmea. Adọ onka mẹnkate ona birregeye bạgiadea, adọ ać dọ oṛak̓teye ruạṛ hẹćena.

Adọ khange uni gidrą dọ ńẹl hoṛteye mọkọńen khan dọe rak̓ket́a, adọ inạk̓tege ńũt idik̓ kana. Khange eskarok̓ kante artẹt́geye rak̓et́kana, adọ ńindạyenre hõ ona dare buṭą khon dọ oka sẹn hõ bae sẹnlena, ọṇḍẹge ạḍi bạṛić kikiạuateye rak̓et́ kana.

Khange adọ, kathae, Ṭhạkure ańjọmket́ khane ãṛgoyena; adọ bọtọrte daṛ ocoyea mẹnte tạrup̓ chinteye hẹćena. Adọ bae daṛlet́ khane ikạkadea; adọ bana chinteye hẹćena, ẹnre hõ bae dạṛlet́a. Adọ bih chinte, hạti chinte, sẹ ạḍi lekateye bheona baṛa ocokedere hõ bae bọtọrlen khane ikạ dapoṛkadea.

Adọ kathae, sẹsre dọ mit́ṭań buḍhi hoṛ chinte uni gidrą ṭhene hẹćena, adọe metae kana, Ẹ bạbu, ma hapẹk̓me, alom raga. Adọ onka mẹnkateye họbọrkedea, adọ ạḍi dulạṛ kathakoe galmarao baṛawade khane hapẹyena. Adọ ona moṭra ghẽṭe kulikedea cẹt́ kana mẹnte, adọ ona taben ghẽṭ raṛakateye jọm ocokedea. Adọe kuliyede kana, Henda bạbu, oka sẹnre oṛak̓tape dọ, disạyet́a sẹm

[12] Ṭhạkur, Santal name for the Supreme Being. They have many stories of his walking about in former times, visiting people and taking an interest in their doings.

They followed a path through the middle of the forest. But as they were walking along through the forest, they lost their way; and he was leading him along where there were no roads, and the sun was also setting. Then they stopped at a tree, and he said to the child: "I say, my boy, you remain sitting here the while; I have to go aside a little to go to stool."

Thereupon he left the bundle with flattened rice with the child and came some distance away from him, the dog following after him. So he caught the dog there and cut him down, and he smeared his battle-axe with the blood of the dog. He did not feel able to cut the child, so he did not do so. He said: "I shall leave him here in the forest; presently some animal of the forest will come and eat him." With this in his mind he left him there in the forest and himself returned home.

Now when the child became tired of waiting, he commenced to cry; and during this it became darker and darker. Then as he was feeling alone, he was crying more and more, and even when it became night, he did not go anywhere away from the foot of that tree; there he remained, crying and screaming all he could.

When Thakur[12] heard this, people tell, he came down; and to make him run away from fear he came in the shape of a leopard; but as he did not run away, he let him alone. Thereupon he came in the guise of a bear; still he did not run away. So he came in the guise of a snake, of an elephant, and although he tried to frighten him in many ways, he let the poor child alone, as he did not fear.

Then at last, people tell, he came to the child in the shape of an old woman and said to him: "My boy, please be quiet, don't cry." And having spoken in this way she took him in her arms, and when she had spoken very kind and loving words to him, he became quiet. Then she asked him about the bundle, what that was, and opening the bundle she gave him flattened rice to eat. Then she asked him: "I say, my boy, whereabouts is your

baṅ? Oka sentem hećlena? Ma laime. Dela iń idi oṭokama. Ado uni gidrạ do ceť hõ bae meneťa.

Ado khange onka dulạṛ baṛakateye heokedea, ar ona moṭrakoe sapkeťtaea. Ado ona bire idi paromkede khan ado marsalena, ado dakkoe ńũ baṛawadea, ado miťṭaṅ atokin tiokketa. Ado ona ato kulhi mucạť ṭhen idikateye dohokedea, adoe metadea, Iạ bạbu, neṇḍege duṛup hataṛokme. Iń do ićjoṅ iń senlenge. Ado onka menkate uni gidrạ doe bạgiadea, ado ać doe okayen coṅ, ghuriạ do bae heć ruạṛlena.

Ado uni gidrạ do onḍege duṛupkateye rakeť kana. Ado ona atoren miťṭaṅ babṛẽ kisạṛ setakrege uni hõ ona kulhi mucạť senge ṭaṇḍiteye senlena. Ado uni gidrạ rarak kan ńelte uni ṭhene calaoena. Adoe metae kana, Henda bạbu, cedakem rakeťa? Okoe sãote nonḍe dom heć akana? Ado uni gidrạ do ceť hõ bae menleťa.

Khange ado uni babṛẽ do onte noteye beṅgeť baṛayeťa, ado okoe hõ bae ńel ńamleťko khan doe hudis baṛakeťa, baṅma, Nui gidrạ do oka khon coe ať heć akana. Adoe dayayente uni gidrạ do ać oṛakteye idikedea. Ado ać monereye menkeťa, Nui gidrạren oaris bako oḍokok khan do iń ṭhenge merom gupi nui gidrạ doń dohoyea. Ado onka bujhạukate sạri uni gidrạ do uni babṛẽgeye idikedea. Ado uni ṭhen tahen tahenteye hara ńokken khan merom bhiḍi gupiko dhurạukedea, ado onkogeye gupia.

Ar uni babṛẽ hopon gidrạko do, kuṛi koṛa joto gidrạge, iskulte olokko calaka. Ar uni merom gupi gidrạ do Lela ko ńutumkedea. Ado merom bhiḍi ạuri aṛakkore onko gidrạ doko metaea, Iạ ya Lela, delabo iskulte, puthiko ar sileṭko idikatalem. Ado sạri onako idi uni Lela hõ ạḍiye chuṭạuka. Ado din hilok onako oko idi

[13] The idea of a school is not Santal; that girls should attend, is not a regular feature elsewhere either. Apparently what is known of a modern village school has been introduced.

home? do you remember it or not? From which direction did you come? Please tell. Come along, I shall take you there." But the child did not say anything.

Now having shown him such kindness she took him on her hip and took his bundle in her hand. When she had brought him through the forest, day dawned; then she gave him water to drink, and they reached a village. Having carried him to the entrance to this village she put him down, and said to him: "I say, my boy, sit here the while; I have to go aside at once." And having said this she left the child; then she went who knows where, she did not come back there any more.

Now the child was sitting there crying. Now it so happened that a wealthy brahmin belonging to that village had in the morning also gone out to the fields in the direction of that entrance of the village. Seeing the child crying he went up to him: "I say, my boy, why are you crying? With whom have you come here?" But the child did not say anything.

The brahmin then looked round in all directions, and as he did not catch sight of anybody, he thought it over, saying: "This child has come here from who knows where and is lost." And taking pity on the child he took him along to his home. He said to himself: "If no one should come to claim this child, I shall keep him with me as my goat-herd. Having come to this conclusion the brahmin actually took the child with him. And when he, living with him, had grown somewhat, they put him to herd their goats, and this he was doing.

Now the children of this brahmin, girls and boys, all the children were going to school[13] to learn to write. And this goat-herd boy they gave the name of Lela. Before the goats and sheep were let out, the children would say to him: "I say, Lela, come along to school; carry our books and slates there for us." And Lela also was quite eager to carry those for them. So they made him do

ocoyea, ar onkoren eṅgat apatkin hō̃ onakoe idite do̠ bar̤ić do̠ bakin metaea, ar onko sãotege daka hō̃ko emaea. Ado̠ o̠ṇḍe̠ khon ruar̤ hećkate me̠ro̠m bhiḍiye ar̤akkoa.

Ado̠ din hilok onka iskulte se̠n se̠ntege uni hō̃ mit bar akho̠re ńe̠l cetketa; ado̠ inạko akho̠rge me̠ro̠m gupi ṭhen dhur̤ikoreye o̠l bar̤aea. Ado̠ enka ńe̠l ńe̠ltege jo̠to̠ akho̠re cetketa. Ado̠ ńutumkoe o̠l bar̤a ocokoa. Ado̠ enkakatege ńutum o̠lo̠k hō̃e cetketa.

Ado̠e metatkoa onko iskul gidrạge, De̠n ya, iń hō̃ mitṭań puthi emańpe.

Ado̠ko metadea, Am do̠m cekaea puthi do̠?

Ado̠e me̠nketa, Iń do̠ e̠r̤e̠ e̠r̤e̠ iń par̤hao bar̤aea me̠ro̠m gupi ṭhen. Iń do̠ e̠ke̠n ho̠r̤ iń mạluṅ bar̤akoa, ar baṅkhan iń cekae baṅ e̠nte iń do̠?

Ado̠ sạri mitṭań mare puthi o̠r̤e̠ć o̠r̤e̠ćakko emade khan ạḍiye rạskạ go̠tena. Ado̠ ona puthi ńe̠l ńe̠ltege khube cetketa. Ar o̠l hō̃ ona puthi reak akho̠r ńe̠l ńe̠ltege khube o̠l hewayena. Ar onko iskul gidrạko samaṅre, se̠ onko eṅgat apat samaṅre do̠ bae par̤hao bar̤aea. Onko par̤hao jo̠khe̠n do̠ e̠ke̠ne ańjo̠m hapekakgea, ar ṭạṇḍire khan do̠ sereńateye par̤haoa.

Ado̠e hara idik kan khać do̠ bud hō̃ o̠ḍok idik kantaea, ado̠ tahe̠n tahe̠ntegeye hara juạnena. Ado̠ onko babr̤ẽ ho̠po̠n gidrạko hō̃ko hara juạnena. Khange ado̠ mit din do̠ sileṭ puthiko idi oṭoako jokhange kur̤i ko̠r̤a apaṅgirok reak cithiye ńamketa. Ado̠ ona par̤haokate jo̠to̠ kathae bujhạuketa, baṅma, nią din hilok hana phalna dare buṭạ ṭhenlaṅ se̠n ńapamoka; ona katha jo̠to̠e baḍaekettakina.

Ado̠ ona din hilok do̠ uni Lelage lahare se̠nkate ona darereye de̠ć akana. Ado̠ tala ńindạyen khan uni babr̤ẽ kur̤i hō̃ mit jho̠ṭ

[14] Not knowing what caste or race the boy belongs to, the attitude of the Brahmin parents is referred to as kind. Lela might have belonged to the untouchables. They show an unprejudiced mind.

[15] The writer has personal knowledge of Santals having learnt to read and write very much as here described.

this for them daily, and their parents did not think it bad[14] either that he should carry these for them; they gave him also food together with the children. When he came back from there, he took the goats and sheep out to graze.

As he in this way every day was going to the school house, he also learnt to recognize a few letters, and he used to write these letters in the dust, where he was herding the goats. And using his eyes in this way he gradually learnt to know all the letters. Then he would make them write down names; and in this way he learnt also to write words[15].

Then he said to them, to the school-children: "Please you, give me also a book."

"What will you do with a book?" they asked him.

He answered: "I shall pretend to read, while I am herding the goats. I only want to make people astonished; otherwise what should I do with it?"

So when they really gave him an old torn book, he became very glad. And making use of this book he learnt quite a lot. And looking at the letters of the book he also became very proficient in writing. But in the presence of the school-children, or in the presence of their parents he did not read. When they were reading, he kept quiet and only listened to them; but when he was out in the fields, he used to sing and read.

Now as he was growing, his intellect also developed, and as time passed, he grew into maturity. Now the brahmin children also grew up into maturity. So it one day happened, as he was carrying their books and slates out to them, that he found a letter about a boy and a girl arranging to elope. Having read this he understood it all, viz., on this particular day we two shall meet at the foot of such and such a tree. He got to know all there was between them.

That day Lela went on ahead and climbed up into that particular tree. When it became midnight, the brahmin girl also went to that tree carrying a bundle with nice food. She was looking round,

sandesante ona dare ṭhengeye calaoena. Adọ bẹṅgẹt́ baṛaket́ dọ cele hõ bae ńẹl ńamlet́ko khan dọe duṛuṕena; adọ ghạṛi ghạṛi ato sẹngeye bẹṅgẹt́et́ kana. Adọ ńẹl họrteye mọkọńok̀ kan khaće khãs khũsik̀ kana. Adọe mẹnet́a, Hape sẹ, hẹćlen khan dọ nãhãk̀ khub lekań ẹgẹrea. Adọ onka mẹn baṛakateye thirena. Arhõe mẹnket́a, Pasẹ lahate hẹćkate oka sẹnreye oko akan; pasẹ ińgeye ńẹl mọ̃ńjeń kan.

Adọ onka hudiskate bae họhọ gọt́ket́a? Adọ sạri uni Lelage dare cọṭ khon bae gọṅ gọt́ket́te adọe mẹnk̀et́a, Nọṇḍẹye dẹć akana, ińe ńẹl mọ̃ńjeń kana. Ma ãṛgo họdok̀me. Delaṅlaṅ calao họdok̀a. Marsallen khan dọ nãhãk̀ ạḍi lajao. Adọ sạri unikin neṇḍalet́ koṛa dọ bae hẹć họt́lena. Adọ nui Lelage uni kọṛa mẹnkatekin mohṇḍayena.

Adọ calak̀ calak̀te tin sạṅgińre cọṅ, kathae, adọ aṅgayen khane ńẹl oromkede dọe Lela kan. Adọe metae kana, Hape, Lela, laṅ duṛuṕlenge. Adọkin duṛuṕena. Adọ unreye metae kana, Ẹ Lela, ạḍi bhabna nitok̀ dọń ạikạuet́a. Cedak̀ nun sạṅgiń dọm ạgukidińa? Pạhilre baṛẹń ńẹl oromlem khan dọ ọhọń hẹćlena. Cedak̀ nonka dọm ẹṛẹkidińa? Eṭak̀ họṛ sọṅgẹ galmarao tahẽkana; uni dọ bae hẹćlena. Am dọ ọkọe lạiat́mẹtem hẹćena? Ṗạhilre hutkạm nonkań baḍaele khan oṛak̀ khonge ọhọń oḍoklena.

Adọ Lelae mẹnket́a, Nit dọm ńẹl oromkidińa. Cele, adọm sẹnok̀a sẹ baṅ? Oṛak̀ khon hõ thọ iń dọ bań riạu ạgu akat́mea. Apan ạpintegelaṅ hẹć ńapam akana. Adọ nit hõ baṅ ceka akana; ẹnte ruạṛem mẹnet́ khan dọ, ma ruạṛme.

Adọ kuṛiye mẹnket́a, Onage thọń bujhạu baṛayet́a, ḅaṅdọń ruạṛ baṅdọ bań. Adọ ato họṛ hõko baḍaeket́a nitok̀ dọ, phalna họpọn kuṛi dọ Lela tuluće ạṅgir calaoena mẹnte. Onkate goṭa ȧto pasnaoena nitok̀ dọ, ariń ruạṛlen khan họṛko landawańa.

but as she did not catch sight of anybody, she sat down; again and again she was looking towards the village. And as she was getting tired of waiting, she became sulky. She said: "Wait a bit, when he comes, I shall give him a good scolding presently." Having said this she sat quiet. Again she said: "Perhaps he came here earlier and is now hiding somewhere; perhaps he is seeing me and making fun."

Having thought this, did she not call out? And, truth to tell, did not Lela answer at once from the top of the tree, so she said: "He has climbed up here; he is seeing me and making fun. Now come down quickly; come, let us go at once. If it should become daylight now, it would be a great shame for us." And, truth to tell, the boy with whom she had fixed it up did not come in time, so as she took Lela to be this boy, they started.

As they walked along and had reached who knows how far, the day dawned and she recognized him that it was Lela. Then she said to him: "Wait a little, Lela, let us sit down a moment." So they sat down, and she said to him: "Lela, now I am feeling grief. Why have you brought me so far? If I had recognized you at first, I should certainly not have come. Why did you deceive me in this way? There was an understanding with another one; he did not come. Who told you, so that you came? If I had known anything like this beforehand, I should certainly not have come away from home."

Lela then said: "Now you have seen who I am; how then, will you go or not? It is not I who have made it up with you and asked you to come away from home. We both came separately and met. Now nothing has happened either, so if you wish to return, please do so."

"Well," the girl said, "that is what I am turning over in my mind, whether I shall return or not. The village-people will also know by this time that the daughter of so-and-so has eloped with Lela. In this way it has by this time been spread all over the village, and if I returned, people would laugh at me."

Adǫ Lelae mẹnkeťa, Ona katha ma sạrige; sanam hoṛko rǫṛgea nitoǩ dǫ. Arem ruạṛlen khan dǫ, am karǫnte amren ạpum barem hõko biṭolkotama.

Adǫ khange sạri onka rǫṛ baṛakate khange uni kuṛi dǫ bhabnate tumbuťkate ạḍi bạṛiće rakketa. Adǫ rak mǫkǫńkateye mẹnkeťa, Delaṅ nitoǩ dǫ, jãhãtegem idiń, ǫntẹgeń calaǩa. Adǫ eṅga apa khon hõń bạṛićena. Am satatege nitoǩ dǫń ja lekaǩge, cahẹm gǫjeń cahẹm dǫhǫń. Mẹnkhan niạkore dǫ balaṅ tahẹna; jãhã sẹnge, mẹnkhan sạṅgiń nõǩlaṅ calaǩa.

Adǫ onka mẹnkate sạrikin bereťena; adǫkin calaǩ kana. Adǫ calaǩ calaǩte, kathae, tin din badre cǫṅ miťṭaṅ maraṅ utạr naṅgraha bajarkin tioǩkeťa. Adǫe Lelae mẹnkeťa, Iń dǫ jǫmaǩ hõ baṅ ạguleťa, nõǩõe adǫ amaǩ jǫm jǫmtege nun sạṅgińlaṅ hẹć akana. Alaṅ ṭhen jǫmaǩ menaǩre jãhãn cạkriń siṛialaṅa.

Adǫe mẹnkeťa, Acha bogege, ma siṛime.

Adǫ sạri ona bajartekin bǫlǫyena, adǫ miťṭaṅ rạpuť rạpuť oṛaǩrekin ḍerayena. Adǫ ǫnḍẹgekin tahẽ aṅgayena. Adǫ dosar hiloǩ setaǩ jǫkhẹć kacahạri sẹn kuli baṛako lạgiťe calaoena. Adǫ khange muktiạr kạmireye bhurtiyena, adǫ phạriạdi hǫṛ hõ nuige ạḍiko khusiadea. Ar dǫrkhastǫko nuigeko ǫl ocokedea, ar ǫl ńẹlte ẹnḍẹnić hạkim hõ ạḍiko khusiadea. Adǫe saj baṛayen khan dǫ, hǫṛtẹť khub ḍhǫb koṛae ńẹlena; adǫ ạkinaǩ basateye calaoen khan dǫ, uni kuṛi hõ nui ńẹlteye khusi gǫťena.

---

[16] The expression conveys the idea that the girl has decided to be dependent on the man; she surrenders herself to him absolutely as her lord. The only other alternative would have been to go away. The woman has to acknowledge the proper position of the man. The elopement or perhaps rather the run-away match is more in accordance with what Santals might do than what might occur among Hindus.

[17] The idea underlying seems to be an Indian prince with separate jurisdiction. As I do not think that the Santals have, within memory, had to do with such princes, it seems natural to think that the description here given is an adaptation of the known conditions and circumstances of the British-Indian law-courts to the circumstances of the story. On the other hand every landholder has what

"That is the truth," Lela said; "all will by this time be talking. And if you went back, they would also outcaste your father and brothers for your sake."

Then, truth to tell, after they had talked in this way, the girl bowed her head down with grief and cried very much. When she stopped crying, she said: "Come along now; wherever you take me, there I shall go. Now I have become a disgrace to my parents also and cannot go to them. Now, under your protection[16], whatever may happen to me, so it must be, whether you will kill me or you will keep me. But here in these parts we shall not stay; let us go anywhere, only it must be somewhat far away."

Having talked in this way they really got up and started. And walking along they after who knows how many days reached an immensely large city. Then Lela said: "I did not even bring any food; look, eating what you had we have come so far. While we as yet have some food, I shall look out for some work to do for us."

"Very well," she replied, "please get some work."

So, truth to tell, they entered the town and took up their quarters in a dilapidated house. Here they stayed until dawn. The next morning he went to the court-house[17] to make enquiries. Here he took work as an attorney[18]; and the litigants also were very pleased with him. So they had him to write their applications, and seeing what he had written the judges there also became very pleased with him. And when he became properly dressed, he looked a fine young man; and when he came to their own lodgings, the girl also got very pleased seeing him.

---

is called a cutcherry (kacahaṛi), a kind of public office or even court, where all kinds of matters may be quasi-judicially decided.

18 Muktiaṛ, as the Santals pronounce the Hindi (Arabic) mukhtar, is really a chosen agent; but a Santal understands by the word only a man who acts as an attorney or a pleader in the courts. Quite a number is found round every magistrate's court.

Adọ thạri ma bạnuḱtạkin, adọ patṛarege dakae loadea. Adọ ạbuk baṛakate daka jọme duṛuṕena. Adọ jọm cabakate patṛa giḍiye mẹnleťa. Adọ ẹn hiloḱ dọ bae giḍi ocoadea. Giḍiyeť tahẽkanae; adọe rẹć ruạṛkedete ona patṛarege ać hõe loana are jọmkeťa. Ar baṅkhan nun din uniaḱ itạť dọ bae jọmeť tahẽkana; adọ ẹn hiloḱ dọe jọmkeťtaea.

Adọ tahẹn tahẹnte ona raj kacahạrire jọtọ muktiạr khon cekakote cọṅ nuigeye lãhãt idiyena, adọ thoṛa din khange maraṅ muktiạre hoeyena.

Adọ tahẹn tahẹnte miť din dọ raje metaťkoa, Nui dọ nunạḱ mõñje ńẹloḱ kana; bhala nuiren bạhu dọe ceť lekantaea? Adọ onka hudiskate miťṭaṅ buḍhi hoṛ uniren bạhu ńẹle lạgiťe kolkedea. Adọ uni buḍhi uniren bạhu ṭhen sẹnkate boge judạ duk suk kathae galmarao kana: oka khonkin hẹćlena, ona kathae kuli baṛakedea. Inạ lasãṛhẽte uniye ńẹl ạgukedea.

Adọ hẹćkate raje lạiae kana, baṅma, Amren dọ uni leka mõñj era dọ bạnuḱkotama. Uni dọ ceť baṅ se? Hoṛ hõ hoṛ, boṅga hõ boṅga, hanko deb lekae ńẹloḱ kana. Amren dọ okor onka dọko ńẹloḱ kantama?

Adọ raje mẹnkeťa, Sạrigem mẹneťa, sẹ nase?

Adọ buḍhiye mẹnkeťa, Judi bam pạtiạuḱ khan, amte ńẹletaeme. Ạikạ nonka sajkatem sẹnlen khan dọ, ọhọm ńẹl daṛelea. Nonkan sapha kicrićte oyo ḍeṅga hoṛ ńẹlte dọ bae oḍokoḱa, siṅ pọṭọmọḱgeae.

Adọ sạri uni ọṇḍẹnić raj dọe bhagwayena, adọ uni ńẹle lạgiť bhagwakate koṭotege daṛạ baṛaeye calaoena. Adọ sạri unreye ńẹlkedea, ceť leka buḍhiye lạiadea, ona katha tuluć juriyentaea. Adọ uni raje mẹnkeťa, Nui hoṛ dọ maraṅ cạkrirebon bohalkedea. Ceka lekate uniren bạhu dọṅ rẹjetaea? Ar nui gọje thọ nitoḱ

[19] Quite a common expression to describe unusual beauty, something superhuman.

They had no brass-plate, so she served his food on a leaf-plate. Having washed his hands and face he sat down to have his food. Having finished eating, he wanted to throw the leaf-plate away; but that day she did not let him do so. He was on the point of throwing it away; then she suddenly caught hold of it and on that very leaf-plate she served also for herself and ate. Otherwise she had not up to this been eating anything left by him; but this day she did so.

As time passed, Lela gradually somehow or other outdistanced all the attorneys working in the court of this king, and in the course of a short time he became the leading attorney.

As time passed, the king one day said: "This man is looking so handsome; I wonder what his wife is like." Having thought over this he sent an old woman to see his wife; and the old woman went to his wife and entered into a conversation with her concerning their health and general conditions, from where the two had come she also asked her. Using this as a pretext she went and saw the girl.

Having returned she told the king: "You have no wife so beautiful as this one. You have no idea, like a human being and like a spirit[19], like those goddesses over there, so she is looking. Your wives, is any one of them looking like that?"

"Are you speaking the truth or telling fibs?" the king asked.

"If you do not believe," the old woman replied, "have a look for yourself. Only beware, if you go dressed finely like you are now, you will certainly not get a sight of her. Seeing people dressed in such clean clothes she will not come out; she shuts herself in."

So, truth to tell, the king of that place put on a strip of loin-cloth, and to catch a sight of her he walked about there in his cloth-strip without outer garments. And then he really saw her, just as the old woman had described her to him; what he saw tallied exactly with that. The king then said: "We have appointed this man to an important position. How shall I manage to take

do̦ muskilgea. Ado̦e hudiskeťa, je̦ nui ho̦ṛ do̦ rakas ṭhen iń jo̦m ocoyea; to̦be̦ nuiren bạhu do̦ń hatao daṛeaea.

Ado̦ onka hudiskate miť din do̦ uni Lelae metadea, E̦ Lela bạbu, am do̦ ạḍi bhale ho̦ṛ kanam, ar am do̦ bud ạkil hō̃ bạṛtigem hudis daṛeaǩa. Amaǩ bud ạkil ńe̦lte in do̦ ạḍiń khusiyena; onate am do̦ sanam ho̦ṛ khon iń marańkeťmea. Ado̦ arhō̃ miťṭań katha ińiń babam kana; judi onam kạmiletiń khan do̦, miť nakha disom iń aṛaǩkema, ar miťṭań miserań go̦ńkema.

Ado̦ Lelae me̦nkeťa, Achań kạmikatama, hē̦ge. Ado̦ ceť lekan kạmi kan co̦ń, onań ańjo̦mletam bạń hē̦ga? Pase̦ lahareń hē̦keťge, ar pase̦ bạń kạmile khan do̦ tho̦re̦n lajao. Ado̦ onateń metam kana, ma ro̦ṛlem, ańjo̦mlegeń.

Ado̦ raje me̦nkeťa, Katha do̦ noa kana — miťṭań baha kana. Phalna burure menaǩa; ona do̦ candmuni kusum phulko metaǩa. Ona baha judim ạgule khan do̦, oka katha e̦mo̦ǩ iń go̦ǩam kan, ona do̦ khạṭigeń emama.

Ado̦ Lelae me̦nkeťa, Ma e̦ṇḍe̦khan mō̦̃rē̦ ho̦ṛ samańre ekraṛo̦ǩme. Ona baha judiń ạgule khan, pase̦ tayo̦mte bam emań. Ona reaǩ ekraṛnama ninạǩ ho̦ṛ talare ma o̦lańme.

Ado̦ raj mae baḍae kan tahē̦kana, bańma, nui ho̦ṛ ma ona buru ṭhene se̦nlen khange dhorage nãhãǩ rakase jo̦mea. Ona bujhạukate uni raj do̦ unạǩ ho̦ṛ talare ạḍi rạskạkate ekraṛnamae o̦ladea, ado̦ onko do̦s jo̦na sạkhikin o̦lkeťkoa. Ado̦ ona o̦l saṗkate aćaǩ ḍerateye calaoena.

Ado̦ o̦ṇḍe̦ se̦nkate ać bạhui metae kana, Ma hare phare daka ho̦ťańme. Iń do̦ adi sạṅgińte raje koleń kana. Bańdo̦ń calaǩ, bańdo̦ bań.

20 Whatever may actually happen, the idea of a potentate acting in this way is not unthinkable to a Santal. On account of the position of the man concerned direct action is unadvisable, and the king tries another way to gain his object.

21 Lit. one side land. The context shows that half his 'kingdom' is meant, like always in tales of this kind.

22 Candmuni is a common Hindu woman's name, meaning 'moonray-gem' and sometimes used by the the Santals also; kusum is the name of a common cultivated flower-plant. Something like 'the moonray-gem flower'.

her from him? And now it is difficult to get this man killed[20]." Thereupon he hit upon this: "I shall let this man be eaten by an ogre; then I shall be able to obtain possession of his wife."

Having decided on this he one day said to Lela: "Lela babu, you are an excellent man, and you have also much wisdom and intellect. I am very pleased at seeing your intellect and wisdom; therefore I have also put you above all others. Now there is one more matter that I am imposing on you; if you are able to perform this for me, I shall let you have half of my land[21], and I shall give you a sister of mine in marriage."

"Very well," Lela replied; "I shall do what I can for you, that is quite so; but what kind of work it is, I must first hear, before I say yes. Perhaps I might say yes in beforehand, and then perhaps I shall not be able to do it; that would be a tremendous shame. Therefore I say this. Please, tell, let me hear what it is."

The king then said: "The matter is this, — it concerns a flower. This grows on such and such a mountain; they call it the chandmuni kusum[22] flower. If you bring this flower, I shall certainly give you what I am promising you to give."

"Well then," Lela said, "make an agreement before the village council. If I bring this flower, perhaps you will later on not give me what you have promised. Write me an agreement in the presence of so and so many witnesses."

Now the king thought he knew that when this man went to that mountain, the ogre would undoubtedly eat him. With this in his thoughts the king very gladly wrote him this agreement in the presence of so many people; and they put down the council's ten[23] as witnesses. With this written agreement in his hand he went to his lodgings.

Having reached there he said to his wife: "Please, be quick and prepare some food for me. The king is sending me to a very distant part. I am uncertain whether I should go or not."

---

23 Instead of Five, 'Ten' (the ten, the ten people) is often used about the village council.

Adǫ bạhuttẹťe mẹnkeťa, Okateye koleťmea?

Adǫ Lelae mẹnkeťa, Hana phalna burure, kathae, candmuni kusum phul menaǩa; ona ạguye mẹn akawadińa.

Arhǒ bạhuttẹťe mẹnkeťa, Adǫ ona baham ạgule khan dǫ, ceťe emama?

Adǫe mẹnkeťa, Ona bahań ạgule khan dǫ, miť nakha disom ar miťṭań miserat ẹmǫǩ mǫ̃ṛẽ hǫṛ samańreye ekraṛ akana.

Adǫ uni bạhuttẹťe mẹnkeťa, Acha, bogegeye mẹn akawaťmea. Miťṭań bǫkǫń kuṛi hǒ ǫṇḍẹge menaea; uni dǫ Candmuniaea. Ona baha dǫ unigeye rǫhǫe akaťa. Am dǫ ǫṇḍẹ sẹṭẹrkate ẹkkalte ńutum ńumkate hǫhǫ saḍe gǫdme, adǫ nāhāǩ ona baha dǫ unigeye emama.

Adǫ Lelae mẹnkeťa, Acha bogege ẹṇḍẹkhan. Adǫ sạri dakako jǫm baṛakate khangeye mohṇḍayena.

Adǫ Lela ǫnṭẹye mohṇḍayen khange uni bạhuttẹť dǫe rogayena, gǫṭa hǫṛmǫ bogeteye ghaoena. Khange adǫ raj dǫ uni buḍhiye metadea, Do sẹ bhala, uni Lela dǫ ńẹl ạguyem calao akana sẹye bańa. Adǫ sạri uni dǫ sẹnkateye ńẹlkede dǫ, bogete gǫṭa hǫṛmǫ lagaǩ lagaǩe ghao akana. Adǫe kuli baṛakedea, Henda mą̃i, jāwāe dǫe okayena teheń dǫ? Kacahạrire hǒ bań ńẹle kana, onateń kuliyeťmea.

Adǫe mẹnkeťa, Raj, kathae, okate cǫe kolkede. Enańreye calaoena, lại hǒ bae lại oṭoadińa. Adǫ bhala teheńge nǒǩǫe ceť roga cǫń ńamkidiń. Ạḍiń harkhetoǩ kana. Adǫ ayo, amgeń metam kana, ạyuṕ jǫkhẹn dǫ nāhāǩ gitić gǫṛǫ hijuǩme.

Adǫ uni buḍhiye mẹnkeťa, Acha bogege ẹṇḍẹkhan. Ọkǫe tora sẹnkate raj iń lạiaea, teheń dǫ uni ṭhen iń dǫ gitić gǫṛǫae lạgiť iń calaǩa mẹnte. Adǫe mẹnkeťa, Acha bogege, do lại oṭoaeme.

Adǫ sạri sẹnkate uni buḍhi dǫ noako jǫtǫ kathae lạikeťa. Adǫ ona katha ańjǫmkate raj dǫ ạḍiye hahaṛayena. Adǫ uni buḍhiaǩ katha bae pạtiạulente hẹćkate aćteye ńẹlkede dǫ, sạrigeye rogayen.

[24] One is reminded of what happened to Sita, when she had been carried off to Lanka.

[25] We generally 'catch' a cold, &c.; here it is the other way about, the disease catches, finds, gets hold of, &c.

"Where is he sending you? his wife asked.

Lela replied: "On that so and so called mountain, it is said, the chandmuni kusum flower grows; he has told me to fetch that."

Again his wife asked him: "If you bring this flower, what will he give you?"

"If I bring that flower," he answered, "he has in the presence of the village council given an agreement that he will give me half of the land and a sister of his."

"Very well," his wife said, "it is good what he has said to you. A younger sister of mine is also there; her name is Chandmuni. She has planted that flower. When you reach there, at once call out, calling her by name; she will presently give you this flower."

"All right," Lela said; "that is good then." And so, truth to tell, when he had had his food, he started.

When Lela had started for that place, his wife became diseased[24], she got sores all over her body. The king now said to the old woman: "Do go and see whether Lela has gone or not." So she went and saw the wife, that she was full of running sores all over her body. She asked her: "I say, my girl, what has become of your husband to-day? I do not see him round the court; therefore I am asking you."

She replied: "The king, it is said, has sent him somewhere. He went away a long while ago; he did not even tell me, when he went. And now, I wonder, look here, what kind of disease has got[25] me to-day. I am suffering very much. And, mother, I ask you, please come to sleep here with me, when evening sets in."

"Very well," the old woman replied. "I shall at once go and tell the king that to-day I shall come and sleep with such and such." Lela's wife said: "Very well, do tell him, when you come."

The old woman then, truth to tell, went and told all this; and hearing it the king was very much astonished; and as he did not believe the old woman's tale, he came and saw for himself

Adọ uni buḍhigeye metadea, Nui dọ ma amge ạuriye bogeḱ dhạbić jọtọnem. Adọ khange ranko uni buḍhigeye ẹm gọťadea, adọe metadea, Ma noako ran din hiloḱ lagaoaeme, are besena mẹnkhan dọ lạiańme.

Adọ uni buḍhiye mẹnkeťa, Acha bogege ẹṇḍẹkhan, beslen khan dọń lạiama. Adọ uni buḍhi dọ uni kuṛi jọtọnregeye tahẽyena.

Adọ uni Lela dọ calaḱ calaḱte, kathae, tin din badre cọṅ, kathae, ona buruye tioḱkeťa, adọ ona dhiri dander ṭhene calaoen khan, uni kuṛiye ńẹl ńam gọťkedea. Adọ ńutum ńumkateye rọṛ saḍekeťa. Khange uni kuṛiye mẹn gọťkeťa, Nọtẹ hijuḱme, teńań; tinrem hẹć akana?

Adoe mẹnkeťa, Nẽḱẽ nitge. Adọ un jọkhẹn uni rakas dọ ọṇḍẹ dọ bae tahẽkana, oka sẹn cọṅ dãṛã baṛae họṛ jọme sẹn akan tahẽkana. Un jọkhẹć uni Lela dọ ọṇḍẹye sẹṭẹrena. Adọ khange kuṛiye mẹnkeťa, Iạ teńań, dela nọtẹreń okokama, ar bańkhan dọ nãhãḱ iṅgạńe hẹć ńamlem khane jọmmea. Onateń metam kana, do nọtẹreń okokama. Adọ uni kuṛi họ nui Lelareye khusiyente uni rakas gọje reaḱ upạiye lagaokeťa. Adọe metadea, Iạ teńań, iṅgạńe hẹćlen khan dọ, am dọ nãhãḱ thirkoḱme, ceť hõ alom rọṛ baṛaea. Ić dọ uni tuluć dọń galmaraoa. Adọ khange Lela dọe kẹklẹsẹť hapeyena.

Adọ inạ miť ghaṛi khange sạri uni rakas dọe hẹć gọťena, adọ uni kuṛigeye oḍok daram gọťkedea. Khange adọ uni rakase mẹnkeťa, Henda mạ̃i, okare bań manwa? manwa manwage sọyeń kan. Adọe bẹńgeť baṛayeťa. Adọ uni kuriye mẹnkeťa, Okor ba gọ, okare? Ińge bań oṛaḱre dọ menańa; ẹṇḍẹkhan iṅge sọyeťmea. Ma ẹṇḍẹkhan do iṅge jọmeńme.

Adọ rakase mẹnkeťa, Bańa, mạ̃i, am dọ ọhọń jọmlema. Am dọ oṛaḱkom họrhọań kana ar emanteaḱkom sapha hataṛań kana.

---

[26] There is nothing told to explain how this girl knows that Lela is her brother-in-law; the hearer has to draw on his imagination.

[27] The ogre is a female one, and the girl calls her i ṅ g ạ ń, a woman's pronunciation of e ṅ g a ń, my mother. Some kind of relationship has been established for the sake of intercourse.

that she had really become diseased. Thereupon he said to the old woman: "Now you nurse her, until she gets well." He gave the old woman medicines and told her: "Apply these medicines every day; and when she recovers, tell me."

"Very well then," the old woman replied; "when she recovers, I shall let you know." So the old woman remained nursing the girl.

Now Lela, people tell, as he travelled along, at last after who knows how many days, reached the mountain, and when he came up to the rock-cave, he caught sight of the girl and called out her name. The girl at once replied and said: "Come here, brother-in-law[26]; when have you arrived?"

"Just now this moment," he said. Just at that moment the ogre was not there; she had gone somewhere to have a walk and eat people; it was at this time that Lela arrived there. The girl then said: "I say, brother-in-law, come over here, I shall hide you; otherwise, when my mother[27] presently comes and finds you, she will eat you. Therefore I am saying to you, let me hide you over here." Now this girl also took a fancy to Lela and therefore endeavoured to find means of killing the ogre. So she said to him: "I say, brother-in-law, when mother comes, you remain quiet; do not speak at all. I shall talk with her." And Lela became dumb with fear and did not speak.

A moment afterwards the ogre really came, and the girl went out at once to meet her. The ogre then said: "Look here, girl, wherever can the man be? I smell man man." And she was looking round. The girl answered: "Why where, mother? Why, I naturally am here in the house; then it must be me that you smell. Please then eat me."

The ogre then said: "No, my girl, I shall surely not eat you. You are taking care of the household goods for me, and you are cleaning many different things for me. while I am away."

Ado uni kuṛiye mẹnketa, Henda gọ, am dọ họṛ jọmem sẹnlena; pasẹć onate amak liṇḍhige sọyetme?

Adọe mẹnkate, Hẽ mãi cele, iṅak liṇḍhige sọyeṅ kana.

Adọe uni kuṛiye mẹnketa, E gọ, iṅ metam kana, ma gọtọm sunumre liṇḍhi dọ dibtam, ẹṇḍẹkhan ona bas dọ maraoka; ar baṅkhan nãhãk ghạṛi ghạṛi onka sọmetem andhaka, adọ nãhãk iṅgem jọmeṅa.

Adọe mẹnketa, Baṅa mãi, ṭhikgem metaṅ kana. Ma gọtọm sunum oḍokte karare dulme, ar onare liṇḍhiṅ diba.

Adọ sạri uni kuṛi dọ gọtọm sunum ṅamkate karareye dulketa ar sẹṅgẹle jolata, ar khub basaṅena. Adọ bhakaṛ bhakaṛ hẹḍẹjok kana, un jọkhẹće metae kana, Ma gọ, nitok dọ noa ṭhen liṇḍhi sekaotam.

Adọ liṇḍhiye sekao jọkhẹnge uni kuṛi dọ Lela ṭhen sẹnkateye metae kana, Judi nọṇḍẹ khon baṅcaok sana menaktam khan, nitge sẹnkate ona kara sunumre ḍhaka caḍo gọtkaeme. Onare nãhãke lọ gujuka; ar bam onkale khan dọ, dhorageye jọmmea.

Adọ Lelae mẹnketa, Hẽ tọbẹ khaniṅ onkayegea.

Khange rakas dọ hẹḍẹjok kan sunumre liṇḍhiye sekao akata ar liṇḍhigeye oyoṅ akata. Adọ un jọkhẹć Lela dọ ṅir sẹnkate hẹḍẹjok kan kara sunumre uni rakas dọe ḍhaka caḍo gọtkedea. Adọ ona sunumtege uni rakas dọe lọ gọćena.

Adọ uni kuṛiye mẹnketa, Henda teṅaṅ, ẹnre hõ baṅ kuliletmea; cele, am dọ okakotem hẹć akana? Cetkom disạ ạgu akata? Ma lạime.

Adọ Lelae mẹnketa, Iṅ dọ rajren cạkrịạ họṛ kanaṅ, ar uni raje metadiṅa, Candmuni kusum phul uni ṭhen menaka — do ona ạguaṅme. Ar ạjim hõe metadiṅa. Ona baha dọ uni bọkọṅ kuṛi ṭhen menaka; unigeye rọhọe akata. Adọ ona idi lạgit iṅ dọṅ hẹć akana.

---

[28] Kara is the biggest pan (of iron) known to the Santals, generally seen used for boiling crushed sugar-cane.

The girl then said: "I say, mother, you went to eat human beings; perhaps for that reason it is the smell from your hindquarters that you feel?"

"Yes, quite likely, girl," the ogre replied, "it may be my hindquarters from which I feel the smell."

The girl then said: "Mother, I tell you, exorcize your hindquarters in clarified butter; then this smell will be eradicated: and if you don't do this, you will again feel this smell and be mistaken; and then you will eat me presently."

The ogre replied: "No, girl, it is quite right what you say. So get the clarified butter out and pour it into the big pan[28], and I shall exorcize my hindquarters there."

So, truth to tell, the girl found the clarified butter and poured it into the pan and made a fire, and it boiled well. Now as it was boiling and bubbling, she said to her: "Please, mother, now heat your hindquarters here."

While the ogre was doing this, the girl went to Lela and said to him: "If you have any wish to be rescued from here, go now and push her down into the pan with oil. There she will presently be burnt to death; and if you do not do this, she will without doubt eat you."

Lela then answered: "Yes, then I shall do so to her."

Now the ogre had been heating her hindquarters over that boiling oil, and she was looking down at these parts. At that moment Lela ran up to the ogre and suddenly pushed her down into the pan with the boiling oil. And the ogre was burnt to death in the oil.

The girl then said: "Look here, brother-in-law, with all this I have not asked you: Well, what is your destination? What has brought you here? Please tell."

"I am a servant of the king," Lela replied; "and the king ordered me, saying, 'The Chandmuni kusum flower grows at her place, do bring me that,' and your elder sister also said to me: 'That flower grows where my younger sister is; she has planted it.' So I have come to take that away."

Adọ uni kuṛiye mẹnkeťa, Ona baha dọ sạrigeń rọhọe akaťgea, ariń emamgea. Adọ nọ̄ǩọ̄e, iṅgạń hō̤m gọćkedea, adọ iń dọ okareń tahẹna? Nin dara dọ ni hirlạń tahẹ̄kana — ado ọkọe ṭhen iń tahẹna?

Adọ Lelae mẹnkeťa, Acha, ẹnḍẹkhan dọ iṅgeń dọhọmea, iń ṭhenge tahẹnme. Dẹn baha emańme, ar delańlań calaǩa.

Adọ uni kuṛiye mẹnkeťa, Ma ẹnḍẹkhan nui rakas reaǩ alań, lutur ar rama gẹť chaḍaome, adọ ona hō̤lań idi toraea.

Adọ sạri onakoe gẹť chaḍaokeťa, adọ ona baha darekin lakeťa, adọ ọnḍẹ khonkin hẹćena, adọ ạkin basarekin hẹć maṛańena.

Khange adọ uni bạhuttẹťe rogalen, ona dọ Lelae hẹćen khan dọe boge gọťena, bin rantege. Adọ Lela dọ ona baha raj ṭhene idikeťa, ar onko sạkhiko tahẹ̄kan, onko hō̤e idikeťkoa.

Khange uni raj dọe bujhạukeťa, bańma, nui hō̤ miťṭań dọe mun kangea, nui tuluć dọ ọhọń daṛelena. Adọ onka bujhạu baṛakate onko goha samańre onae ạguleť bahae atańkeťa. Adọ inrege uni miserat gọńae reaǩko neṇḍakeťa, ar inrege ona disom hō̤bo emaea. Adọ enka galmarao kategeko apan ạpinena.

Adọ uni raje mẹnkeťa, Nui dọ rakas ṭhen jọm ocoyeń mẹnleťte noa baha ạgu dọń kolledea; mẹnkhan nọ̄ǩọ̄e, ọnḍẹ khon hō̤e jitạuena. Nui hoṛ dọ boṅga hara bạri hoṛ kanae. Adọ ẹn hiloǩ khon dọ raj hō̤ nui Lela dọ ạḍiye bọtọraea.

Adọ ona neṇḍa din tioǩen khanko baplayena, ar tara nakha disom hō̤ko ẹm utạradea; ar hạti sadọm, gại kaḍa, thạri bạṭi — jọtọge onka thoṛa thuṛiko emadea. Adọ onkate uni Lela dọ ona disomren raj ṭhene tala oṛaǩena. Adọ sanamaǩre nuigeye marańena, ar hoṛ hō̤ nuigeko khusiadea. Nui dọ khanḍare cawārre sanam

The girl then said: "It is quite true, I have planted that flower plant, and I shall give it to you. But now, look here, you have killed my mother also, so where shall I stay now? Up to this I have been under her protection; with whom shall I now stay?"

"All right," Lela said, "then I shall keep you; stay with me. Give me the flower and come along, let us go."

The girl then said: "Well then, cut off the tongue, ears and claws of this ogre, and we shall take these along also."

So, truth to tell, he cut these off; thereupon they dug up the flower bush and came away from there; and first they went to his lodgings.

Now his wife had become diseased, but as soon as Lela returned, this was cured without any medicines. Thereupon Lela took the flower to the king; the witnesses who had been there he also took along with him.

Then it was borne in upon the king: "This man is also semi-divine; I shall certainly not be able to take it up with him." Having come to this decision he received the flower he had brought in the presence of those witnesses. At the same time they fixed everything in connexion with the king giving him his sister in marriage; then, they said, we shall also give him the land. After having talked over these matters they separated.

And the king said: "I thought I should let him be eaten by the ogre, therefore I sent him to fetch this flower; but see now, also from there he has returned with success. This man is on a par with the spirits." And from that day on the king had a great fear of Lela.

When the day fixed arrived, they celebrated the marriage, and they also gave him half the kingdom for good; elephants and horses, cows and buffaloes, brass plates and brass cups — all such things they gave him, a quantity of each kind. In this way Lela became utterly at home with the king of this country. And in all matters he became the leading one, and the people also liked

ghuṛige, nui baṅkhan kamge baṅ sen̠oḱa. Hąnąḱ nuiaḱ manot̠ hoeyentaea. Ar nui Lelaren do̠ pea r̥aniko hoeyentaea, ado̠ judą sen̠re nui hō̠ maraṅ bakho̠le benaoketa. Ado̠ tahen̠ tahen̠te o̠ṇḍe̠ge khubko kisāṛena. Ar jo̠to̠ r̥anigeko gido̠r pido̠rana.

Ado̠ tahen̠ tahen̠te tin din hoekate co̠ṅ uni Lela raj do̠ aćren r̥anikoe metaťkoa, Iń hō̠ miť disomren raj ho̠po̠n kangeaṅ. Eṅgaṅ do̠ bąnugića; uni do̠ kąṭićregeye go̠ć bągiadińa, ar ąpuṅ do̠e tahe̠kangea. Ado̠ uni ńe̠l ąguye reaḱ ądi sana menaḱtińa. Ado̠ṅ metape kana, delabo calaḱa, bhala jive̠ť menaea se̠ye go̠ćena.

Ado̠ko me̠nketa, Acha e̠ṇḍe̠khan, delabo calaḱa.

Ado̠ calaḱ reaḱko neṇḍaketa, ar o̠ṇḍe̠nić rajko ląiadea, baṅma, Nui Lela hō̠ phalna disomren raj ho̠po̠n kangeae. Ado̠ ona katha uni raje aṅjo̠mkeť khan do̠ ądiye khusiyena. Arhō̠ko metadea, Apat do̠ menaegea, ado̠ uni ńe̠l ąguye lągiť nią phalna dinrele oḍokoḱ lągiť. Ado̠ ona kathagele ląi oṭoam kana.

Ado̠ uni raje me̠nketa, Acha bogege.

Arhō̠ko metadea, Me̠n, sanamaḱ am bhorsagele bągiaḱ kana; ado̠ disą hataṛtaleme.

Ado̠ onako neṇḍaleť din tioḱen khan, je̠ kichu akoaḱ sapap ar akoren mal jal, guti dąsi, sanamko samṭaokeťkoa. Ado̠ko oḍokoḱ kana, hąti sado̠mko, ar gąḍi sagaṛko, rāt gąḍiko, aema tahe̠kantakoa. Ado̠ akoaḱ do̠ sanamko idikeťtakoa, ado̠ ho̠r ho̠rte jo̠khe̠n ądi utąr laskarko ńe̠lena.

Ado̠ ho̠r ho̠rte calaḱ tuluć ho̠ṛe kuli idiyeťkoa, Henda ho, noa phalna disom do̠ oka se̠nre ar oka ho̠rtele calaḱa? Ado̠ unre ho̠r ar mohṇḍate̠ťko ląi idiako kana.

Ado̠ calaḱ calaḱte, bhąi, tin din e̠neć co̠ṅ ado̠, kathae, ako disomko tioḱketa. Ado̠ko kuliketkoa, Noa disomren raj do̠ oka

him best. In all matters of any kind, ever and always, without him nothing would do. In those matters he became the honoured one. And Lela got three queens; and on a separate plot of land he also built a large family-mansion. And as time went, they became very wealthy there; and all the queens bore children.

Now as they lived there, after some time king Lela told his queens: "I also am the son of the king of a country. My mother does not live; she died leaving me, while I was a babe; but my father lived. I have a very great desire to see how he is; therefore I am saying to you, come let us go; I wonder whether he is alive or he is dead."

"Very well," they said, "then come, let us go."

So they fixed a day for starting, and people told the old king, viz., "Lela is the son of the king of such and such a country." When the king heard this, he was very pleased. Again they told him: "His father is alive; and to see how he is doing we are to leave on such and such a day. And we are telling you this now, before we start."

"Very good," the king said.

They further said to him: "Have a care, we are leaving everything here trusting in you; during our absence keep an eye on our things."

When the day fixed came, they collected whatever goods they had and all their living property, and their male and female servants, everything and everybody. And they were setting out and had elephants and horses and carriages and chariots in large numbers. What they had of goods, they took all along with them; and when they were passing along the road, they seemed a very large procession.

As they were travelling along the road, he asked people: "Listen you, where is such and such a country, and which road are we to follow?" As they passed along, people told them about the road and the direction.

Now as they travelled along, friends, for who knows how many days, at last, people tell, they reached their own country. They asked

sẹnre oṛak' dọ menak'taea? Adọko lạiade khan dọ, ona raj ato sẹć sẹn sor ńọk'kateko ḍerayena.

Ar uni Lelaren apat haṛam dọ, nui ọnẹ birreye idi giḍikade, adọ ọnḍẹ khon ruạṛkate mõṛẽ turui māhā khange kathaeye kāṛāyena, adọ inạ kāṛāge tahẽyentaea. Adọ nui Lela dọ ạḍi utạr phạde idi tora akat'kote onakoren hoṛ dọ ạḍi bạṛićko bọtọrok' kana, adọko mẹnjoṅ kana, Durrẹ, noa disom dọ luṭok' cọṅ, cet' cọṅ! Ạḍi utar laskarko hẹć akana.

Adọ ḍera thirkate bạrsiṅ pẹ māhā hoeyen khan dọ, onakoren hoṛ onko hạti sadọm ńẹńẹlko calaoena. Adọ uni Lela dọ onko hoṛe kuli baṛayet'koa, Henda ho, noa dọ cet' disompe metak'a?

Adọko lạiadea, Noa dọ phalna disom kana.

Arhõe kuliket'koa, Raj dọ okare menaetapea?

Adọko mẹnket'a, Hane hana atore.

Arhõe kuliket'koa, Mare raj kangeae, sẹ nawako raj akana?

Adọko mẹnket'a, Baṅa, uni haṛam rajge menaete eṭak'ko dọ bako raj akana. Mẹnkhanko mẹna, baṅma, nui raj dọ họpọnṭẹte mak'kede khan dọe kāṛā akana, adọ nit hạbić enka kāṛāge menaea. Ar karbar lạgit' dọ mit'ṭaṅ dewane dọhọ akadea, unige raj lekae kạmi kana.

Adọ enka galmaraotege ạyup'en khan, onko hoṛ dọko hẹć baṛayena oṛak'te. Adọ onako kathage hẹćkate rajko lạiae ḳana, baṅma, Okaren raj cọe hẹć akan; ạḍi utạr phạd menak'kotaea; noa disom dọ hapẹne luṭ cọṅ cet' cọṅ. Ạḍi bạṛić oṛe oṛe kuliket'lea, baṅma, Raj dọe cet' lekantapea? Ọkọe rajko calaoet'a? Oṅako saname kuliket'lea, ar ale hõ jọtọ kathale lạiadea.

---

29 The fear expressed might be very well founded. Armed raiders overrunning the country were not unknown in former days; even now the Santals have reminiscenses of such marauders.

them: "Whereabouts is the home of the king of this country?" When they had told them, they encamped fairly near the king's village.

Now Lela's old father, he who had taken him to the forest and cast him off there, had some five or six days after he returned from there become blind, people tell; and this blindness continued unchanged. As Lela had brought along with him a very large company, the people of these parts were awfully afraid and were saying: "O dear! the country is to be plundered[29], or who knows what will happen! An enormous company has arrived."

When they had stayed quietly in camp for two or three days without anything happening, the people of these parts went to have a look at the elephants and horses. Lela then asked these people: "I say, what do you call this country?"

They told him: "This is such and such a country."

Again he asked them: "Where does your king live?"

They replied: "In the village you see over there."

Again he asked them: "Is he the old king, or has a new man become king?"

"No," they replied, "the old king is living, so no other has become king. But people say, viz., when this king had cut his own son to death, he became blind, and he has remained blind until this day. And to transact his business for him he has appointed a minister; he acts for the king."

As they talked in this way, it became evening, and these people gradually came away to their homes. After having reached home they told the king all this, saying: "A king from who knows where has come; he has a very large host with him; some day he will plunder this country, or whatever else he may do. He put an awful amount of questions to us, going into details from the very beginning, saying, 'What kind of a king have you got? Who is managing the kingdom?' He asked us about all these matters, and we also told him everything."

Ar noako galmarao jọkhẹn dọ dewan ar uni chuṭki rạni hõ ọnḍẹgekin tahẽkana. Unkin hõ noako jọtọ kathakin añjọmkeťa. Adọ raje mẹnkeťa, Luṭ khan dọñ cekaea? Iñ ma daṛe bạnuk̕tiñ. Iñ dọko gọćliñ khangeñ besok̕a. Ạḍiñ harkhetok̕ kana.

Adọ inạ galmaraokategeko apan ạpinena. Adọ inạ ñindạ khange uni dewan dọ bọtọrteye dạṛ tap̕keťa.

Adọ arhõ onko hoṛ dọ dosar hilok̕ khange onko hạti sadọm ñẹñẹlgeko calaoena. Adọ uni Lela dọ onko hoṛe ñẹl oromkeťkote arhõe kulikeťkoa, Henda ho, adọ bhala raj oṛak̕ren dọ jọtọko boge baṛagea sẹ bañ?

Adọko mẹnkeťa, Boge baṛageako.

Arhõe metaťkoa, Do sẹ bhala, uni haṛam raj dọ nọnḍẹ iñ ṭhen ạguyepe; uni tuluć mitṭañ galmarao menak̕tiña.

Adọ bar hoṛ sẹnkate uni rajkin metadea, Uni okaren raj cọe hẹć akan, delañ calak̕me, unige khọjkeťmea, jẹye mẹneťa, Uni haṛam raj tuluć mitṭañ galmarao menak̕tiña; doye hijuk̕ ma.

Adọ nuiye mẹnkeťa Ọhọñ sẹnlena, ạḍi bọtọr iñ ạikạueťa.

Khange onko lạlại hoṛko sẹn ruạṛenteko lạiadea, Uni dọ bae hijuk̕a, kathae, ạḍi bọtọre ạikạueťa.

Adọ Lelae mẹnkeťa, Do arhõ bar pẹ hoṛ calak̕te metaepe, Amren marañić họpọn kangeae, alom bọtọrok̕a. Uni dọ am tuluć mẽť ñẹpẹl sanayede kana. Sedaere, kathae, birrem idi giḍilẹdea, uni họpọn kantamae. Am tuluć mẽť ñẹpẹl sanayede kana.

Adọ sạri pẹ pon hoṛ sẹnkate noako jọtọ kathako lạiade khan, ạḍiye rạskạ gọťena. Ṭheñga sap̕kateye bereť gọťena. Adọ chuṭki rạniye mẹnkeťa, Unre dọ uni gidrạ dọ bam gọćledea?

Adọ raje mẹnkeťa, Mãyãyente bañ gọćledea, ona birreñ bạgiadea.

[30] A not uncommon expedient to avoid difficulties.

When they were talking of these matters, the minister and the king's second wife were also present there. These two also heard all this. The king then said: "If there is to be plundering, what can I do? As you see, I have no strength. If they only would kill me, it would be well for me. I am suffering very much."

After this conversation they separated; and as soon as it became night, the minister fled[30] from fear.

The next day these same people again went to look at the elephants and horses. When Lela recognized these people, he again asked them: "Listen, how is it, are all well in the king's family or how?"

"They are well," they answered.

Again he spoke to them: "Do, please, bring the old king here to me; I have something to speak to him about."

Two men then went and said to the king: "The king from who knows where has come; come along, go to him, he asked for your presence, saying, 'I have something about which I have to speak to your old king; please, let him come'."

"I shall certainly not go," he said, "I feel very much afraid."

The messengers then returned and said to Lela: "He will not come, he says, he is very much afraid."

Then Lela said: "Do, please, go again two or three men and say to him, 'He is your eldest son, don't be afraid. He wants to meet with you face to face.' Long ago, it is told, you took him to the forest and cast him off there; he is this son of yours. He wishes to meet you face to face."

So, truth to tell, three four men went and told him this, and when they had told him, he at once became very glad. He took a stick and stood up at once. His second wife then asked him: "Did you not kill this child at that time then?"

The king replied: "I felt compassion, so that I did not kill him; I left him in that forest."

Adọ khange tharam thurume mohṇḍạ gọťena, adọ thoṛa sạṅgiṅe sẹnlen khange sạri palaḱ poloḱe ṅẹl marsalkeťa. Ar uni sãote aema hoṛko calaḱ kana. Adọ sạriye tioḱkede khan dọ, khub purṭhại bẹṅgẹť marsalkeťa. Adọ sẹṭẹr torage hapaṛuṕkate ạḍi bạṛiḱkin raḱkeťa. Ar unkin raḱ ṅelte ato hoṛ hõ ạḍi bạṛiḱko raḱkeťa.

Adọ raḱ mọkọṅkate Lelae mẹnkeťa, Ma, baba, adọ ạsuloḱme. Iṅ dọ nią am tuluć mẽť ṅẹpẹl lạgiťgeṅ hẹćlena. Inạge iṅaḱ ·dọ ḍher rẹṅgẹć tahẽkantiṅa. Ar teheṅ dọ jẹ nọṇḍẹpe hẹć akan* hoṛ dọ, sanamge nọṇḍẹ iṅ ṭhenko maṅjanlenge, adọbo apan ạpinoḱa. Ar teheṅ dọ am sãote miťre dakalaṅ jọma. Adọ sạri onkae mẹnkeť khan dọ arhõko raḱkeťa. Adọ caolekoe oḍokkeťa, adọe metaťkoa, Ma dakaetabonpe. Ar mẹrọm kạsikoe emaťkoa, — Ma maḱkate rọ gẹťkope ar bhọj lagaope.

Adọ ọṇḍẹgeko jaora akan jọkhẹnge rajren kạmṛī kuṛi ar miťṭaṅ buḍhi onko ṭhen sẹnkatekin lạikeťa, baṅma, Rạni dọ oṛaḱ bhitrireye akayena. Dela hako pako sẹn hodoḱpe.

Khange adọ ọnṭẹko calaoena; ṅẹlkede dọe gọćen; adọ raṛakateko rapaḱkedea.

Khange adọ sẹnkate uni Lela ṭhengeko jọm ṅũkeťa. Adọ uni apat haṛame mẹnkeťa, Iạ bạbu, am dọ adọ ọhọṅ sẹn ruạṛ ocolema. Ma noa disom hõ amgeṅ soprotaťmea, ar amaḱ kangea. Am dọ ọhọṅ ṅẹl gọťlema. Iṅ dọ am iạte nõḱõe kãṛã khon iṅ besena; ar baṅkhan iṅ dọ ạḍi bạṛić harkhet iṅ jọmeť tahẽkana. Amem hẹć ruạṛente iṅ dọṅ baṅcaoena. Ọhogeṅ ṅẹl gọťlema.

Ar onko ato hoṛ hõ ạḍiko nẹhõrena, mẹnkeťako, Ọhọge, baba, am dọle ṅẹl gọťlema. Aleren raj dọ am kangeam; ọhọgele sẹn ocolema. Delabo nitge.

31 An oriental trait, literally overflowing sentiments.

Thereupon he started tottering along, and when he had gone a little distance, he really and truly commenced dimly to see the light. A large number of people went along with him. Truth to tell, when he reached his son, he was seeing quite distinctly. As soon as he arrived, they at once embraced each other and wept; and seeing these two weeping the village people also commenced to weep[31] ever so much.

When they ceased crying, Lela said: "Now, father, live on as you do. I came just for this, to meet with you; just this was my great desire. And now to-day, as many of you as have come here, all of you have your midday meal here with me, and then we shall part. Now to-day we two shall take our food together with each other." Then, truth to tell, when he had said this, they wept again. Thereupon he brought out rice and said to the villagers: "Please, prepare the food for us." He gave them some castrated goats, saying: "Do kill them, singe them and cut the flesh into pieces, and arrange the feast."

While they were gathered there, the king's servant girl and an old woman came out to them and told them, saying: "The queen has hanged herself inside the house. Come along, come at once quickly."

So they went there; they saw her, she was dead; so they took her down and cremated her.

Thereupon they went and ate and drank with Lela. The old father then said: "I shall certainly not let you go away any more. See, I am giving this country also over into your hands, and it is yours. I shall certainly not say good-bye to you. Because of you, see here now, I have been cured of my blindness; otherwise I was suffering awfully. You have come back; thereby I have been rescued. No, I shall certainly not let you go away."

The village people also implored him very much, saying: "Never, sir, shall we let you go away from us. You are our king; we shall surely not let you go. Come along with us, now this moment."

Adǫ ạḍi bạṛićko jidket́ khan dǫ onkoak̓ katha bae nẹhõtleta. Adǫ inrege ẹkkalte raj oṛak̓teko idi sẹṭẹrkadea. Adǫ uni manǫte lạgit́ sẹ peṛaye lạgit́ khạsiko idiadea ar emanteak̓ bhale bhale jinisko idiadea. Ar ato ato poesako biuriketťe uni tuluć ńẹpẹl reak̓ sandesko ńutumketťeko idiadea. Ar uni Lela hǫ̃ tayǫmte goṭa ona akoak̓ disomren rayǫt jarwakateye jǫm ńũ ocoketkoa. Adǫ jǫtǫ rayǫt uni tuluć dǫ ạḍi suluk tahẽyentakoa, adǫ ǫnḍẹge uni Lela dǫe rajena.

Cabayena katha dǫ.

65. Rakas reak̓ katha.

Sedae jǫkhẹn mitťań raj disomre rakas ạḍi bạṛiće cankeyena, disom hǫṛ ạḍi bạṛiće jǫm ujạṛetkoa. Khange disom hǫṛ dǫ riạukate mit́ jomkaote raj ṭhenko calaoena. Adǫko metae kana, Iạ raj, ale dǫ amak̓ disomre sẹ noa disomre dǫ ǫhǫle tahẽ daṛelena. Ale dǫ noa disom khon eṭak̓ disomtele dạṛeta. Onate am ṭhen lai oṭoam lạgitle heć akana.

Khange raje mẹnketa, Cedak̓pe dạṛeta? Cettepe kǫsṭǫyena sẹ cet́ iń jǫr julumketpete dạṛ dǫpe mẹneta? Karǫntẹt́ bape lạile khan, cekate iń dǫń baḍaetapea?

Adǫ unreko mẹnketa, Am sẹnte sẹ amak̓ jãhãn bạṛić dǫ bạnuk̓anań. Mẹnkhan noa urni bir bagahiyena, rakas ạḍi bạṛiće jǫmetlea; adǫm adǫm ato dǫe jǫm ujạṛketa. Adǫ uni bǫtǫrte ale dǫle dạṛet́

---

[2] Mutatis mutandis the same as with us. It might, however, be noted that the petty landlords and their servants employ the idea in order to squeeze money out of people. They often attempt to get money from their tenants by imposing salamis of sorts on them.

65 [1] The Santali word lit. means 'run'; another word of the same significance (ńir) is their terminus technicus for leaving their home to settle in other parts. What is here referred to may, so far as the tendency to 'run' is concerned, fit the Santals: on the other hand they are courageous and rather enjoy the dangers of a hunt.

And as they were so very persistent, he did not stand out against their words. And then and there they took him at once to the king's house. To honour him or to entertain him they brought him castrated goats and all kinds of excellent things. And having made a public collection of money from all the villages they called this a present on the occasion of meeting with him[32] and brought it to him. Afterwards Lela also called the tenants of his whole country together and feasted them. And all the tenants were living on excellent peaceful terms with him. So Lela became king there.

The story is ended.

65. THE STORY OF AN OGRE.

ONCE upon a time long ago, people tell, an ogre had become very ravenous in a certain kingdom; he was eating the inhabitants in an awful way and was devastating the country. The inhabitants then took counsel together and went in a body to the king, and said to him: "Listen, raja, we are utterly unable to remain in your country or in these parts. We are going away[1] from this to another country. For this reason we have come to you to tell you this, before we go."

The king said: "Why are you going away? In what respect are you suffering, or in what way have I harrassed you, since you intend to go away? If you do not tell me the reason, how shall I know what is the matter with you?"

"It has nothing to do with you," they replied, there is nothing bad on your part. But this large forest[2] has become dangerous; an ogre is eating us very badly; some villages he has devastated. It is out of fear of him that we are going away. So we said: 'Why

[2] The reference is to what is generally called primeval forest. The older generations of Santals were mostly living on the borders of such jungle; they like to live in the vicinity of a forest.

kana. Adole menkeṭa, Cedak hape hapetebo dara? En kathae, delabo calakte rajbon lai oṭoaea. Ado ona kathage nõkõele lai oṭoam kana.

Khange raj do noa katha añjomkate adi bariće bhabnayena; mone monete adi bariće khondrondkeṭa. Menkeṭae, Noa disom khon rayotko darle khan, disom do okor sobhak kantiña, ar iñak hõ ñutum do okor hoyok kana? Arteṭ bodnamgeñ harjoñ kana. Horko mena, Nui raj do bae besa, toberege nuiak disomre rayot do bako berelok kana. Ar iñ hõ tho rayot niage, ar rayot hõ raj nia. Noa do banar somangea, banarge gopor̥o jarurgea. Rayotko tahẽlen bañ iñak lab do hoyoka, ar bañkhan oka khon bañ iñak lab hõ hoyoktiñ? Bañ, nonka do ṭhik bañ kana. Noko rayot do iñak ṭakateñ goroakoa.

Ado onka hudis ṭhikkate rayote metaṭkoa, Hape, en kathae, alope dara. Nui rakas goje reakbon upai gelalege. Judi babon goć dareae khan dope darkeṭge. Ado apeñ metape kana, ma jãhãege nui rakaspe goćkedea menkhan do miṭ nakha disom iñ emapea ar miṭṭañ miserañ emapea. Ar ape bape goć dareae khan do, ma jãhãe nui goje lagaṭ sirikope. Nui dobon gojegea. Alope dara; ontere tahenpe botorok kan khan, ma notere iñ sorrege hijukte berelokpe. Nondeye hijuk khan do iñiñ ṭhu gojea

Adoe onkae metaṭkote jiviye tenkeṭtakoa. Ar aćren sipahikoe metaṭkoa, Ma ape do onte note pasnaokte nui rakas goje lagaṭ hor siri ñamkote nonde agukope, ar one okaṭak iñ gok akawaṭko, ona doñ purauakogea. Ar ape hõ ona katha do laiakope bare.

Ado enko disom hor hõko ruarena, ar hor ñañam sipahi hõ onte noteko pasnaoena. Ado daran darante, bhai, oka kõrre coñ

---

3 Likely an addition by some late narrator. The word implies the use of a gun.

shall we go away in silence? Come, we said, let us go to the king and tell him, before we leave.' This is what we are now here telling you, before we leave."

When the king heard this, he was awfully grieved; he turned the matter over and over in his mind; he said: "If the tenants go away from the country, what will become of the splendour of my country, and what will happen to my name? I shall only give myself a still worse name. People will say: 'This king is no good; that is the reason why no tenants settle in his country.' And I also am what I am because of my tenants, and the tenants are what they are because of the king. Both are in the same position; mutual assistance is necessary for both. Only when the tenants remain, I shall have any profit; and otherwise, from where should I get any profit at all? No, such is not as it should be. I shall help these tenants with my own money."

Having come to this conclusion he said to his tenants: "Wait," he said, "don't run away. Let us first try to find some means of killing this ogre. If we should be unable to kill him, you will naturally go away. So now I am telling you, if any of you kills this ogre, I shall give him half my kingdom and a sister of mine in marriage. And if you are unable to kill him, do look out for some one to kill him. We must kill him. Do not go away; if you are afraid to stay over there, come over here in my vicinity and settle here. If he comes here, I shall shoot[3] him myself."

By speaking to them in this way he reassured them, whereupon he ordered his soldiers: "Go out in all directions and look out for and find somebody to kill this ogre and bring them here; and what I have promised these people, I shall make good to them. You also tell people of this."

The people who had come returned home; at the same time the soldiers who should find a man also went out in all directions. As they were wandering about, my friend, they in some corner

miť hoṛko khoro ńamkedea. Uni hoṛe menkeťa, Raj noa gokak khatiye emań khan, uni rakas do miť gharitege kabtegeń goćkea. Ado sipahiko menkeťa, Acha, ale kathate bam patiauk kan khan do, delabo nitge raj thenbo calaka, ar am do ekraṛnama ol ocoyem. Ona kagoj am hõ hatiau pahillem, enkhantem gojea.

Ado sari onka menkate songetegeko agu darakedea, ado rajko laiadea. Ado rajteť khub lekae kuli pustaukedea. Ado uni hoṛ hõ khatige gojeye menkeťa. Ar ceťe emok kana, ona reak ekraṛnamako olkeťa. Ado uni hoṛe menkeťa, Aikha goć tora ekkalte uni rakas do nonḍeń aguyea?

Ado raje menkeťa, Hẽ, ekkalte nonḍe aguyem, tobe bale patiauk kana.

Ado unre uni hoṛe menkeťa, Den tobe khan miťtań bosta, miťtań barahi, miťtań tengoć, ar miťtań marań utar arsi emańpe. Ar oka horte dhere hijuk senok kana, ona hoṛ then delabon mãṛõm otoańpe.

Ado sari one ceťkoe bableť, onako jotoko emadea. Ar mãṛõmae lagať hoṛe jutauketkoa; oneye hijuk senok horre miťtań baṛe dare tahẽkana, ar onḍege miťtań sodok gaḍa hõ tahẽkana. Ado uni hoṛe menkeťa, Nia baṛe dare thenge benaoańpe. Nenḍe do dak hõ sorre menaka; ina do tetańiń khan, nia gaḍare dak iń ńũia. Ado onḍegeko tearadea, ado onako sana phanawante onḍeye dećena. Ar noko hoṛ doko ruaṛ hećena.

Ado kathae, ayup khange sari uni rakas do ona horte hoṛ jomko lagiťe hijuk kana. Ado uni tãṛãk hoṛe tiokkede khange, kathae, manwa manwage so goťkedea. Ado onte noteye benget

[4] To be quite safe he must have more than a mere word; the king's servants advice not only a written agreement, but also the precaution of having the document in his own possession. There is not much trust in others.

[5] Not necessarily of glass.

[6] The word generally refers to scaffolding set up for watching crops. It is here used about what is called a machan, a kind of platform arranged up in a tree, where the hunter may sit in safety waiting for the animal he is to shoot.

or other heard of one man. This man said: "If the king will be sure to give me what he has promised, I shall kill this ogre in a moment by magic."

The soldiers said: "Very well, if you do not believe what we say, come along, now this instant, let us go to the king, and let him write you a document with his promise[4]. Get this paper first into your own hands; thereupon you may kill him."

Truth to tell, after having had this talk they brought the man along; and they told the king. The king himself asked him searching questions, to find out what he meant. The man on his side said he was sure he would kill the ogre. Then the king gave a written promise of what he was going to give, and the man said: "How is it, shall I bring the ogre here at once, as soon as I have killed him?

"Yes," the king replied, "bring him here at once; then only we shall believe it."

So the man said: "Give me then a bag, a rope, an axe and a very large mirror[5]; and come and make me a scaffolding[6] at the road where the ogre is in the habit of frequently passing."

Truth to tell, they gave him all that he had demanded; the king also collected people to make a scaffolding for him; now there was a banyan[7] tree on the road where the ogre used to go and come; there was also a small deep river there. The man said: "Build me the scaffolding here at this banyan tree. Here it is also near water; if I get thirsty, I shall drink water from this river." So they made it for him there, and he mounted it with those different implements. Thereupon these other people returned.

In the evening, people tell, the ogre was actually coming along that road to eat people. When he reached the place where the man was sitting in wait, he suddenly felt the smell of man. He at once looked round in all directions and, people tell, caught

[7] The Ficus bengalensis, L., India's most spreading tree.

baṛa gọt́ket́ khange, kathae, mãṛõm cọṭre dẹć akane ńẹl ńam gọt́kedea. Adọe mẹn gọt́adea, Cedak̕ am eskar nọṇḍẹ dọm duṛup̕ akana? Bhagem hẹć sor akana, ińak̕ adharem hoe akana.

Khange, kathae, uni hoṛ khub ṭahakateye rọṛ gọt́ket́a, Hẽ, teheń dọlań ńapam akangea. Ar iń hõ amgeń ńam baṛayet́me kana. Goṭa bir iń sendra baṛaket́mea. Adọ bań ńam daṛeat́mete nọṇḍẹ dọń duṛup̕ akana. Adọń mẹnket́a, Nia̦ họrtege bae hijuk̕ sẹnok̕ kana? Nọṇḍẹgeń tãṛãk̕ hataṛok̕a; nonkateye hijuk̕reliń ńapama. Adọ ṭhik sa̦ri nõk̕õelań ńapam gọt́ena.

Adọ khange sa̦ri rakas hõ, kathaeye dhak cakao uta̦rena. Mọnẹreye mẹnket́a, Ayo! cet́ la̦git́ bhalae ńameń kana? Kuli pa̦hillegeń, ẹnkhanteń jọmea. Adọ sa̦riye kuli gọt́kedea, Henda ho, kathae, cet́ la̦git́em ńameń kana?

Adọ uni họṛe mẹnket́a, Ńamet́meań gun iń cet́am la̦git́. Am lekanko turui gọṭẹn iń cet́ akawat́koa. Adọ onate am ṭhen iń hẹć akana cet́am la̦git́, adọ ina̦ khan eae họṛpe hoyok̕a, ar eae họṛrege ińak̕ puruchun hõ hoyok̕tińa. Onate am ṭhen dọ jidkateń hẹć aka̦na. Ar bam pa̦tia̦uk̕ kan khan, dela hijuk̕te noko ńẹlkom, nọṇḍẹń nọkọl jarwa akat́koa.

Adọ onkae metade khan, sa̦riye pa̦tia̦u gọt́enteye mẹnket́a, Masẹ bhalań ńẹlkoa.

Adọe sẹn sorente ona a̦rsireye uduk̕ae kana. Adọ aćak̕ umul ar uniak̕ umulge ona a̦rsire ńẹlok̕ kana. Khangeye metae kana, Ma hanko ńẹlkom.

Adọ onae ńẹlket́ khan dọe pa̦tia̦u uta̦rena. Adọe mẹn gọt́ket́a, Ma ẹṇḍẹkhan iń hõ cet́ańme.

Adọe kuli dohṛakedea, Tọbẹ kha̦ṭige cedem mẹnet́a?

Adọe mẹnket́a, Hẽń cedgea.

Arhõe metadea, Tọbẹm ced khan ar iń cet́am khan, un jọkhẹn dọ cet́ hõ a̦ikha̦ alom rọṛa. Arem rọṛket́a mẹnkhan dọ, a̦ikha̦ ohọm cet́ daṛelea.

[a] The idea underlying is the performing of acts of penance. This is not a genuine Santal custom.

sight of the man that had mounted the scaffolding. He at once said to him: "Why are you sitting here alone? It is good you have come so near; you have come as a meal for me."

The man then at once very distinctly said: "Yes, to-day we two have met. I am also looking for you. I have been hunting for you all over the forest; as I was unable to find you, I have sat down here. I said: 'Is he not going and coming along this road? I shall lie in wait here in the meantime; when he comes in this direction, we shall meet. And right enough, now here we have met."

Then the ogre, people tell, became really utterly fluttered. He said to himself: "O mother! for what purpose does he want me, I wonder? Let me first ask him, thereafter I shall eat him." So, truth to tell, he asked him: "Look here you, for what purpose are you wanting me?"

"I am searching for you," the man replied," to teach you magic. I have taught six others like you; therefore I have come to you to teach you, so in that case you will be seven, and with seven persons my vow[8] will also be finished. Therefore I have come to you very eagerly. If you do not believe me, come and have a look at these; here I have collected their pictures."

When he spoke to him in this way, the ogre in fact at once believed him and said: "Well then, I should like to see them."

He went near, and the man showed him in the mirror. Now his own reflection and that of the man were seen there; and the man said to him: "Look, see those there."

And when the ogre had looked, he was convinced and said: "Then teach me also."

The man asked him once more: "So it is quite certain that you want to learn?"

"Yes, I will learn," the ogre replied.

Again the man said: "Then when you learn and I am teaching you, at that time, beware, do not speak a single word. If you speak, mind, you will be utterly unable to learn."

Adoe mẹnketa, Ọhọñ rọṛa; ma cetañme baṛẹ.

Arhõe mẹnketa, Tọbẹm ced khan dọ, ma noa bostare bọlọkme. Adọ sạri ona bostareye bọlọyena. Adọe metadea, Nit dọ cetge alom rọṛa. Iñ dọ oka lekateñ cetama, ona do iñgeñ baḍaea, mẹnkhan nit dọ cetge alom rọṛa.

Adọ sạri bostareye bọlọyen khan, barahite khub lekae tọl uriċkedea, ontẹ nọtẹye ṭhelao ulṭạu baṛakedea. Adọe ñẹl baṛakede dọ, oka sẹn khon hõ paskaok reak ạt bạnuktae. Khange ṭẹñgọċe sapkette mar cure mare kuṭạm kuṭạmkedea sẹ, ẹkkalteye kuṭạm gọċ utạrkedea.

Khange khube khusiyena. Adọ kuṭạm gọċkedete raj ṭhene calaoente uniye lạiadea, bañma, Rakas dọñ gọċkedea. Ma hoṛ juṭạukom, rakasko gọk ạguyea.

Adọ ona katha ạñjọmte uni raj dọ pạhil dọ ẹṛẹ ẹṛẹgeye metata, adọ ẹnre hõ hoṛe juṭạuadea. Adọ ạyur idiketkote sạrige rakase udukatkote adọ ḍañteko gọk ạgukedea. Ẹkkalte raj racare ạgukate luṭhum manteko giḍi gọtkadea. Adọ bosta khon raṛa oḍokkateko ñẹlkede khan, sạri raj hõe pạtiạu utạrena. Adọ kathae, unreko ñẹle kan dọ, ti ar jañga dọ hoṛ lekangetaea, ar moca sẹn dọ ṭhik ṭhak sadọm muṭhạngetaea.

Adọ ọnẹko ekraṛlente uni raj hõ bicạrreye haraoente disom ẹmọk ar miserat ẹmọk dọe haraoente ẹmọktege hoeyentaea. Adọ ona ẹmọk reake neṇḍaketa, bañma, Ma niạ din hilok ona gọkak dọ nui hoṛ iñ emaea. Adọ ona neṇḍa katha sạri aċak gọṭa disomreye lại saḍeketa.

---

9 The description given is similar to that of some fabulous beings about whom stories are told among the Santals, the difference being that while the ogre here referred to apparently has two legs, these other ones are reputed to have only one. These ekaguḍiạ or otherwise ghọṛmũhã are believed to live somewhere in the east; they eat people and some stories tell how people were sold to these ekagudias. As is well known, the Santals are not alone in having stories of

"I shall surely not speak," he replied; "please teach me."

Once more the man said: "So, as you will learn, get into this bag." And, truth to tell, the ogre entered the bag, whereupon the man said: "Now don't say a single word. In what manner I shall teach you, that is a thing I know; but don't speak a single word now."

When the ogre, truth to tell, had entered the bag, the man tied him tightly up with the rope and pushed him in all directions and rolled him over and over. He looked at him and saw that the ogre could not possibly get free on any side. So he took the axe and hammered and hammered him all he could; he hammered him to death then and there.

Now he was very pleased. When he had hammered the ogre to death, he went to the king and told him, saying: "I have killled the ogre. Please, collect people, let them carry the ogre here."

On hearing this the king at first thought that it was all lies; but still he collected some people for him; and leading the way the man really and truly showed them the ogre, whereupon they carried him, slung to a pole. They carried him straight to the king's court-yard and threw him down there with a thud. And when they had untied him and got him out of the bag and people saw him, the king also believed. When they then looked at him, people tell, his hands and legs were like those of a human being, but round his mouth he was shaped exactly like a horse[9].

Now as they had made a written agreement and the king was judged to be the looser, he had to hand over the kingdom and also his sister. He fixed a day for giving this, saying: "On this particular day I shall give this man what I have promised." And he let the proclamation of the fixed day be announced in all his kingdom.

---

such beings; what may perhaps not be known is that Santals were believing in their existence and were living in fear of them up to a few years ago.

Adọ inạ neṇḍare goṭa disọmren họṛko jarwayena. Adọ ẹn hiloḱ uni họṛ dọ aćren miserat emadeteye bapla bhọjkeťa. Ar dosar hiloḱ tara nakha disome lẹbẹť ạcuradea. Adọ ẹnẹ goṭa disom họṛko ńẹlkedea arko baḍaekeťa, noa disom dọ nuiye emadea mẹnte, ar raj oka kathae gọḱleť, ona dọe purạukeťa mẹnte. Ar raj hõ onko jarwalen họṛ dọe binti bhạkti baṛawaťkoa. Adọ dosar hiloḱ bhọjko jọm baṛakateye bidạ gọťkaťkoa.

Adọ un khon disom họṛaḱ mọn khạtirentakoteko ropha ruạṛena, ar disomreko rophayena; ar baṅkhan hutẹć ona disom dọ ẹkkalteko ujạṛ utạrkea. Adọ ẹnẹ jọtọ bọtọr cabayentakoa ar raj hõe khusiyena.

Adọ ọnẹ onkate uni họṛ dọe rajente miserat hõe hataokedea, ar miť nakhare raj hõe raj utạrena. Adọ ọnẹ onka ńẹlpe Cando reaḱ lilạte un marań dusmạn uni họṛe gurkedete uni rajaḱ disome

[10] The expression used in Santali means lit. 'trample round', referring to their custom of walking up the boundaries of a piece of land, to settle all questions concerning the site and size of such property.

[11] The last sentences are an addition by the narrator to whom the story apparently has some reality. The word translated 'dispensation' is ordinarily used about some showy entertainment.

[12] The word (come from Persian through Hindi into Santali) is especially used in Santali about enemies whom it is impossible to placate. Poisonous snakes are often called so.

There are several variants to this story. One commences with telling about a king whose land was being devastated by an ogre and who was getting anxious how this would go. He quotes to himself (the story does not mention that any complaints had been brought, like in the one translated) some lines of the poet Kalidas: 'When the forest is destroyed, the deer without forest is in trouble; when the king is destroyed, the tenants without king are in trouble; when the house-mother is destroyed, the house being broken the luck takes wings'. He decided to get hold of some one who would kill the ogre, and sent people round everywhere to find such a man, at the same time promising half his kingdom and his daughter to the ogre-killer.

When this order came to a certain village, the headman called his people together and read it out to them. Then there was a mad-cap (the Santali word is generally used about a licentious young man) who called out that he would kill this ogre in a trice. When they heard this, they said to him: 'Do so, kill

At the fixed time the inhabitants of the whole kingdom assembled. That very day he gave his sister in marriage to the man and gave a marriage-feast. The following day he showed [10] him the boundaries of half the kingdom. And so all the people of the country saw him, and got to know that the king had given this land to him, and that the king had fulfilled what he had promised. The king also gave the assembled people a nice address; and after they had partaken of the feast, he sent them home the next day.

From that time on the people felt secure and settled down again and remained quietly in the land; otherwise they would have left the country utterly desolate. And all their fears ceased; the king also was pleased.

In this way this man became a king and also got the king's sister; in one half of the country he became the only king. So there, see, how by Chando's dispensation [11] this man felled such a big enemy of mankind [12], and this king's country he

---

him; then you will get the princess, and all of us shall salute you'. Hearing this he became very pleased, commenced to strut about and repeated his boast. The headman wrote to the king about this young man; when he understood it might be taken seriously, the young man commenced to protest. But the headmau said that he would have nothing to do with the case; they might do with him whatever they liked. 'Don't you understand that it is the king's word? I do not lie, my friend. Don't you know that people do not disobey a king's word and a bonga's word; such are equally important. All day long you are only making fun; you may make a jesting promise to the bongas; but they will not let you off.'

Some ten twelve days afterwards soldiers came to take the young man to the king. He tried with these also to excuse himself, that it was all only a joke; but they told him that he would have to tell the king so himself; they had orders to take him there. When he understood that he had to go, he asked to be permitted to have his food first. Thereupon he collected some implements and found a splendid battle-axe and took these things along. As he went, he asked his father to propitiate the bongas, that he might be able to kill the ogre. And his father libated water to the bongas and invoked them (i. e., he made what is called m a n a n, a vow with promise of a sacrifice after successful performance of the intended act).

rophakettaete disom hoṛe barjão ruạṛketkoa. Ar rajak hõ nutum dọ baṅ nihạtlentaea, artẹte sabasiyente inạ dhara dhạri sẹ gota disomrege namjọs hoeyentaea, baṅma, Nui raj nun maraṅ rakas gọckedete disome rophakettaea.

Adọ ẹnẹ nia katha nẹṇḍẹge cabayena, in maraṅgea.

When they came before the king, this one at once repeated his promises; the young man said that it was all false about him; he would not kill the ogre. But the king did not believe this and ordered him to kill the ogre, as he had formerly said he would do. The young man said to himself that Thakur should judge his case; he understood he had to go and he asked the king for two mirrors and a large box. He got these things; asking them where the ogre was to be found he was told that he was living on a mountain to the west; there a river was coming down from the east, and at this river, just where there was a ford close to a banyan tree, the ogre was in the habit of eating people Quite a crowd of people thereupon took the young man and his implements to the spot and left him there, all in doubt whether he would not here be eaten by the ogre.

The young man climbed the tree, taking one of the mirrors with him, leaving the other and the box on the ground. Sitting there aloft he was rather down in the mouth; the ogre had been eating all who passed that way; he would take him also without doubt. But 'all right, he said, before he eats me, I shall try to hit upon something or other.'

He waited there the whole evening and the whole night; finally, just as the sun was rising, the ogre came, and the young man was trembling from fear, so that even the branches were moving, as if he were shaking them. The ogre smelled man, but did not at first catch sight of the young man. When he saw him, he said: 'Yes, now I have caught sight of my food.' The young man said: 'Yes, now I have got one more like those others.' The following conversation thereupon took place: Ogre: 'Look here, man, what are you saying?' Man: 'We have met to-day.' Ogre: 'Look here, man, why are you speaking in this way and why are you trembling?' Man: 'I am trembling from anger; don't you see, I am making even the tree shake? The question is, whether you will eat me or we two shall eat you.' Ogre: 'All right, come then.' Man: 'Come here.' But neither did the young man go down nor the ogre climb up. The talk continued. Ogre: 'Who are you? I have seen one thousand times four like you.' Man: 'Who are you? I have seen one thousand times four like you.' Ogre: 'Well then, come here.' Man: 'Well then, come here.' By this time the

pacified and caused the inhabitants to return and inhabit the land. The king's reputation was not disparaged either; rather he was even more praised, and in those parts or in the whole country he became famous, people saying: "This king killed such a big ogre and quieted down his country."

So there, here this story is ended; it is this much.

---

anger of the ogre had somewhat subsided and he thought: 'Perhaps this one is a person as strong as myself;' whereupon he asked the man what kind of a box it was, to which the man replied: 'In this box I put in persons like you that I have caught.' Ogre: 'How many are here?' Man: 'There are two or three.' Ogre: 'Come then and show them to me.' Man: 'I might show you; but perhaps you will take me unawares and eat me.' Ogre: 'No, I shall not eat you.' And he swore strong oaths and said: 'Don't be afraid; I shall not eat you; but if you do not show me, mind, I shall eat you.' Man: 'All right, if I do not show you, we shall fight.' Ogre: 'All right, do come down and show me.' The man came down, turned the box over, and having taken the cover off he showed the ogre the mirror that was inside the box and said: 'Look at those there;' with the mirror he had with him he also on one side showed the ogre, saying: 'Look here on the side at these here.' The ogre was quite fascinated; now and then he turned a little to one side and sometimes he gaped; and the ogre in the mirror did the same. When the young man saw him so charmed and occupied, he slashed him with the battle-axe and felled him then and there.

Having cut off the ogre's ears, tongue and feet with the toes he went to the king, who collected people and had the ogre brought; they kept the young man there. So the king sent letters round in the kingdom and invited the people to come; and when they were assembled, the king in the presence of all the people gave the young man his daughter in marriage and gave the couple half his kingdom. He gave them also elephants and horses; the young man stayed like an in-brought son-in-law and he gave them half of his household goods. Thereupon they had a proper marriage with a great festival, and the people went home.

Another variant is in details more like the one given in the text; it has a few details that may be noted.

The king orders the people to get hold of a j a n g u r u (a witchfinder, or soothsayer) or an o j h a (a medicine man who knows exorcizing and magic) or any person who will be able to kill the ogre. The king apparently believes that magic or some supernatural power is needed. He gives the same promise, and at the request of the people gives it in writing, to make others believe. Having got this they

66. Raj hoṕon ar rakas reak̕.

Mit̕ṭan raj hoṕon do̱ ạḍi utạr phạdante baplak̕ lạgit̕e calak̕ kan tahẽkana. Ado̱ calak̕ calak̕te ho̱rre ạḍi ãṭ reṅgećket̕koa, ado̱ ona takrege, kathae, ho̱rrege mit̕ṭan bhiḍi bo̱ho̱k̕ko ńamket̕a. Ado̱ko kupulik̕ kana; khange raj do̱e me̱nket̕a, Mabon jo̱m bạṛalege, ado̱bon calak̕gea tho̱. Ado̱ ado̱m ho̱ṛ do̱ sahan ạgu, ado̱m ho̱ṛ do̱ sakam ạgu, ado̱m ho̱ṛ do̱ se̱ṅge̱l ạgu, ar raj do̱ dak̕ ạk̕gui se̱nena.

---

commenced to hunt for a man and they found a Bauri (the Bauris are a low caste of Western Bengal, probably of non-Aryan origin, counting themselves as Hindus); his name was Ras Behari Bauri. He professed to be the only one who would be able to kill the ogre. He demanded that they should build a scaffolding for him, where the ogre used to pass; from there he would shoot him with bow and arrow. Ras Behari was taken before the king, who asked him about particulars. Finally they took him to the place, built a scaffolding for him there and left him. He had bought and brought with him seven mirrors; he had also his bow and arrows and an axe.

When the ogre comes, we have a conversation very much the same as that reported in the text. He has come to teach the ogre magic and professes to have been sent by seven other ogres, whom he has taught. He tells, that he had said to these that he was quite willing to go; but perhaps this one might eat him. The others had answered that he only needed to show this one pictures of the others. 'We ogres are all looking exactly alike.' They were very anxious that this ogre also should learn magic, so that they might all be equal. The man said: 'If you do not believe, here, have a look at their pictures.'

The man came down and showed the ogre one mirror after the other and made the ogre fully believe, whereupon he asked to be taught. The ogre promised to be quiet (as in the text) and the man found some fibres of the cihũṭ climber (a large climber, Spatholobus Roxburghii, Benth., that gives strong bast). Making a rope of this he tied him hands and feet, kicking him well at the same time; finally he covered his head with his outer garment. Thereupon he brought stones and stoned him in the head with these, and with the axe he hammered him behind the ears; he smashed his head to pieces; and when the ogre was dead, he sent an arrow into his armpit. The Bauri then went straight to the king, called the king out and told him; whereupon the king ordered the ogre to be brought, that the children might see him.

66. THE STORY OF A PRINCE AND AN OGRE[1].

A king's son[2] was on his way to be married with a very large host of attendants. As they passed along, they became very hungry, and just then they found on the road the head of a sheep. They asked one another what to do, and the prince said: "Let us have some food and then go on." So some people went to fetch firewood, others to fetch leaves[3], still others to get fire, and the prince himself went to fetch water.

The king would not let the assembled people go, but wanted to finish the 'difficulty' at once, quoting a proverb (aṅgalenkhan laṅgak̔a, kalọmlenkhange talọmok̔a, when it has become dawn, one is tired; when it has become next year, it will be inundated). He took all the village people and all others present to bathe; when he had brought them back, he gave them curds and flattened rice and made them put up a marriage-shed. He entertained them with theatricals and music in grand style and married the Bauri to his daughter, gave them half his kingdom and much wealth; he gave them also a palace. And those of his people who had not been present and came the next and the following days he also feasted.

The story ends: 'In this way this Bauri killed the ogre and became a king. And he brought all his children to this royal palace and fort.'

It might be questioned whether there might not be some slight real foundation for a little of the story. The introduction of a name and of a very low caste is significant.

66 [1] This story has been written down by Bhuju Murmu of Dhopahar village. It is obviously a borrowed story; Santal imagination does not expand like in this tale. When it has been recorded here, it is for several reasons: to show how a story may be adopted and how ideas in vogue among other races may be brought in without being understood and given a quite new 'value'. The narrator was not conscious that this was a recently borrowed story.

[2] Except in the superscription and here it is all along raj, i. e. king. To avoid confusion with another 'king' acting in the story it has been translated prince, where needed.

[3] To be used as plates, a detail that is according to Santal custom.

Adọ sahan ạk̕guyić dọ ạḍi usạrateye hẹć gọt̕ena, are mẹnoana, Acha iń dọń poṭor baṛa hataṛa; onka mẹnkateye sorlen dọ, ayoge, ona bọhọk̕ dọ ẹkkalte ọt ar sermae cahaḱket̕a; ar uni dọe ut̕ ocoyena. Adọ inạkate uni sẹṅgẹl ạk̕guyiće hẹćena; adọ uni hõ̱ onkageye mẹnoana, Ẹṇḍak̕ge rọ hataṛ aḍoeań; onka mẹnkateye sorlen dọ uni hõ̱e ut̕kedea. Adọ inạkate sạkam ạk̕guyiće hẹćena, uni hõ̱ onkageye mẹnket̕a, Acha iń dọń gẹt̕ hataṛ aḍoea, inạk̕teko hijuk̕talea; ayoge, onka mẹnkateye sorlen dọ uni hõ̱e ut̕ ocoyena. Arhõ̱ inạkate ṭukuć ạk̕guyiće hẹćena, uni dọe mẹnket̕a, Iń dọń rapak̕ hataṛa; onka mẹnkateye soren dọ uni hõ̱e ut̕ ocoyena. Ar onkoren sadọm hõ̱e ut̕ cabaket̕koa.

Khange ạḍi tayọmte raj dọ dak̕ anteye hẹćena; ńẹlket̕ko dọe, ọkọe hõ̱ bạnuk̕ko, ẹkẹn bhiḍi bọhọk̕ mọtọge menak̕a. Adọ uni raj ona jọm lạgit̕ dọe mẹnlet̕gea, mẹnkhan sermaren dut uni ṭhen ãṛgokateye metadea, Am dọ, raj, ọṇḍẹ mạtkate alom sorok̕a; bań khan am hõ̱ khạṭigeye jọm mea. Ar ẹnte, raj, bujme, nui dọ bhiḍi dọe bań kana, rakas bheskate ape ṭhen dọe hẹć akana. Khange inạko galmarao baṛaetege uni dọ ạḍi marań cahaḱkate uni sẹne hẹć idik̕ kana, khange raj dọ dạṛtege hoeyentaea. Ar sạṅgiṅgeye laga idikedea, thoṛa gan ạuri tiogerege mit̕ṭań pukhri pinḍhạre sińjo dare tahẽkana. Khange raj dọe mẹnket̕a, Sinjo, am ińem bańcaolin khan iń dọ ạḍiń manọtkema; ẹnte iń dọ ạḍi marań mũhĩnreń paṛao akana. Ona katha ańjọmkate ona sińjo

[4] The operations mentioned are three stages in the preparation of meat for cooking. The first man proposes to pull out (the hairs, not generally done with animals), the second man proposes to singe (the general proceeding with animals) and the third one proposes to cut it into bits (the last act. before the flesh is put in the cooking pot).

[5] Ægle Marmelos, Correa, commonly known as bael, also as the wood-apple. Bael is a way of writing the Hindi name, derived from Skr. bilva. The leaves are used ceremoniously, also by the Santals, The Santal name s i ń j o lit. means 'day-fruit' or even 'sun-fruit'. The fruit may grow to a fairly large size; it is

The man who went to fetch firewood came back very quickly, and he said to himself: "Very well, I shall clean[4] it in the meantime." Intent on this he went near to the head; then, O mother! the head at once opened its mouth so as to stand between heaven and earth, and this man was swallowed. Next came the one who had gone to fetch fire; he also said the same: "Hang it, I shall singe[4] it in the meantime." Saying this he went near and he also was swallowed. Next the man came who had gone to fetch leaves; he also said the same: "Very well, I shall cut it into bits[4] in the meantime; when that is done, the others will come." O mother! when he intent on this went near, he also was swallowed. Again after him the man came who had gone to fetch a water-pot; he said: "I shall roast it in the meantime." Having said this he went near, and he also was swallowed. It also swallowed all their horses.

A long while afterwards the prince came with water; he looked for the others, there is no one there, only the sheep's head is there. The prince wanted to eat this, but a messenger from heaven came down to him and said: "You, prince, beware, do not go near at all; otherwise it will surely eat you also. For understand, prince, this it not a sheep's head; it is an ogre, that has come to you having assumed this form." While they were talking this, it opened its mouth wide and was coming towards the prince, and he had to run away. It chased him a long distance; now just before it was reaching him, there was a bael tree[5] on the bank of a tank; and the prince called out: "O bael, if you will save me, I shall honour you highly; I am in the greatest danger." Hearing this the bael tree suddenly split up into two

round and has a hard shell; to open a fruit it is necessary to beat it against something hard or to use a hammer or the like. The fruit is formed in June or thereabouts and hangs on the tree for nearly a whole year. The pulp makes an excellent sherbet, of especial value in stomach complaints, as e. g. dysentery.

dare dọ bara bạrite paṛak gọtena, adọ uni raj ona siṅjo darereye bọlọyena; khange bae ńam daṛeadea.

Khange uni rakas dọ miṭṭaṅ ạḍi mõńj kuṛi bhesenae; adọ onka bheskatege ạḍi din ona siṅjo daregeye họrhọketa; ar ạḍi ãṭe raga. Adọ onka onkate mit din dọ raje aṅjọmketa, baṅma, ona siṅjo buṭạre ạḍi mõńj kuṛi menaea mẹnte.

Adọ sipạhiye kolketkoa, metatkoae, Do uni kuṛi ạguyepe. Khangeko sẹnena ar uni kuṛiko ạgukedea, adọ rạniye hoeyentaea. Adọ uni rạni dọ naṅgọste ruạke pọrtọnketa. Adọ ạḍi dine ruạyen khan raje kulikedea, Henda, rạni, am dọ cekate baṅ bam phạriạk kantalaṅ? Unre uni kuṛi dọ lạlạiye pọrtọnketa, baṅma, Iń dọ, ona band ghuṭure siṅjo dare menak, ona bam mak bhindạṛle khan iń dọ ọhọń baṅcaolena, ona baḍaeme. Khange raj dọ hoṛe kolketkoa, ona siṅjo dare mak bhindạṛ lạgit. Adọko calaoena ṭẹṅgọć ante; ona dareko tiokketa; khange uni pạhile bọlọ akan raj uni dọe jọ bhesena. Adọ jọkate ona pukhri dakreye ńũrena. Adọ bako ńamledea, adọ raj ṭhenko ruạṛena, arko lạiadea, baṅma Cele hõ bae ńamlena.

Khange ar hõ raje kulikedea, Henda, rạni, cekate baṅ bam phạriạk kan talaṅ? Masẹ bhala lạiạńme, iń dọ ạḍi bhabnaṅ ạikạueda. Adọ uni rạniye mẹnketa, Ona band reaṅ piṇḍhạ bam mak phoṛle khan, iń dọ pasẹ ọhọgeń baṅcaolena.

Adọ raj hoṛe kolketkoa, Do sẹnokpe kuḍi, ṭạmni ante, ona band mak phoṛpe; ar nãhãk miṭṭaṅ siṅjo jọpe ńama, ona ạguipe. Adọ sạrige rajak hukum lekate onako kạmiketa, ar siṅjo jọko ńamketa. Adọ ona siṅjo raj ṭhenko ạguketa; adọ raj ona ataṅkate ạḍi rạskạ mọnte aćak basateye idiketa. Ar rạniye lạiadea, baṅma, Siṅjoko ạguketa.

Adọ khange ona siṅjo khonge miṭṭaṅ aṛaṅge aṅjọmena, baṅma, Alope tawaga siṅjo dọ, sẹ alope kuṭạm paṛaga; ẹnte iń dọ raj

[6] This is the king of the country where the bael tree stands.

[7] Hindu houses have inner apartments, where the family lives. The male members spend much of the day in an outer apartment or separate house, where they receive visitors, transact business, and so on.

parts along the middle, and the prince entered into the bael tree; and the ogre was unable to find him.

The ogre then took the form of a most beautiful girl, and in this disguise it watched the bael tree for many days; and it was crying vehemently. In this way the king[6] one day heard that a most beautiful girl was there at the foot of the bael tree.

The king sent soldiers, saying to them: "Do bring this girl." They went and brought her, and she became his queen. Then this queen commenced to sham being ill. When she had been ill for many days, the king asked her: "I say, queen, how is it that you do not get well?" The girl then commenced to tell, saying: "I — on the bank of that tank there is a bael tree; if you do not have this cut down, I shall certainly not get well." So the king sent people to cut the tree down. They went with axes; they reached the tree; then the prince who had formerly entered there, took the shape of a fruit. When he bad become a fruit, it fell down into the water of the tank. So they did not find him and returned to the king, saying to him: "No one was found there."

The king then again asked: "I say, queen, how is it that you do not get well? Please tell me; I am very much grieved." The queen then said: "If you do not cut the embankment of the tank and let the water out, I shall perhaps not be saved."

The king then sent people: "Do take spades and pickaxes with you and go and cut the embankment of the tank, so that the water runs out; presently you will find a bael fruit; bring that." Truth to tell, they did all in accordance with the king's order, and found the bael fruit. They brought it to the king, and having received it the king went in great joy to his living apartments[7], and told the queen: "They have brought the bael."

Then a voice was heard out from this bael, saying: "Do not throw the bael down, and do not hammer it open, because I, the

Adọ koṛae mẹnkeṭ́a, Henda, gọṛọm ayo, miru họpọn iḱdiye kol akadiṅa, adọm imạṅa sẹ baṅa? Adọ buḍhi rạskạ mọnteye mẹnkeṭ́a, Hẽ, gọṛọm, miru dọ do idikaetaeme; uniren kangeae. Adọ ona katha aṅjọmkate koṛa dọ ạḍiye rạskạyena, are mẹnkeṭ́a, Ho, nit dọṅ ẹrẹ aḍo akadea. Ona mẹnkate uni mirui saṕkedea, ar aćaḱ oṛaḱteye ạgukedea.

Adọ okare uni rakas bhes rạniye tahẽkan, uni koṛa dọ uni miru saṕkate ona oṛaḱteye bọlọyena. Khange uni kuṛi dọe rakas ruạṛena; adọ arhõ onkage ạḍi maraṅe cahaṕkeṭ́a. Adọkin ṅapamena, adọe metae kana, Ma bhala nitoḱ jọmeṅme! Adọ bae jọm daṛeae kana; ẹnte uni rakas reaṅ jivi ma rajgeye hatma akaṭ́a.

Adọ raje metae kana, Am dọ unre ọkọekom jọmleṭ́koa, onko dẹnko ulạkom, tọbẹ khan nui miruṅ ẹmkaetama. Khange uni dọ miru ṅam ruạṛeae mẹnte, onko họṛ ar sadọmkoe ulạkeṭ́koa. Adọ unre uni raj dọ bại bạite uni mirui pẹṭẹr topaḱkedea; khange uni rakas dọe gọćena.

Sedae dọ kathaeko lạia, baṅma, rakas dọ ạḍi saṅgeko tahẽkana. Ar miṭ́ dinrege amdaj miṭ́ sae gan janwarko jọmeṭ́ko tahẽkana. Adọ unkin Dasarat rajren barea họpọnkin tahẽkan, Ram ar Lọkhọn, unkinkin gọć maraokeṭ́koa; baṅ khan ạḍi bạṛić họṛko jọmkekoa. Nia kạhni dọ cabayena.

The young man then said: "I say, grandmother, she has sent me to bring her parrot; will you give it to me or not?" The old woman replied with great joy: "Yes, grandson, do take her parrot with you; it belongs to her." When he heard this, the young man became very glad and said: "Oh, now I have fooled her, the wretch." And saying this he took the parrot and brought it with him to his home.

The young man took the parrot and entered the house where the ogre disguised as a queen was. The girl then at once became an ogre again; now also she opened her mouth so immensely wide. They met and he said to her: "Now try to eat me!" But she was unable to do so, because the prince had her soul in his power.

The prince said to her: "Now out with those[10] you ate at that time; then only I shall let you have your parrot." So in order to get her parrot back she brought up and out those people and horses. Just then the prince quietly wrung the parrot's neck; then the ogre died.

Formerly, people tell, there were a multitude of ogres. Daily they were devouring something like one hundred animals. Then lived the two sons of king Dasarat, Ram and Lokhon, and these two killed the ogres and made an end to them; if they had not done so, they would have eaten any amount of human beings. This story is ended.

---

[10] The Santal word is used about bringing up what one has eaten in its entire state; in this way it is different from other words signifying to vomit. It is often used figuratively about being forced to give back what one has taken.

67. Pẹa phul ar Bidhi Bidhạnta.

Mit́ṭaṅ naṅgrahare pẹ hǫṛko tahẽkana, adǫ onko pẹnẹ hǫṛ mit́ dinko kumiṭiket́a, baṅma, Abo dǫ mit́ muṭhạngeabon, adǫ mabon phuloḱa. Adǫ onko mit́ jạt dǫ bako tahẽkana, mit́ dǫ sodagǫrren hǫpǫn, mit́ dǫ rajren hǫpǫn, ar mit́ dǫ madhaeren hǫpǫn. Adǫ phulko pataoket́a; adǫ tahẹn tahẹnte mit́ dinko bundisket́a. Delabon calaḱa bideste, ar disombon ńẹl ạguia. Adǫ tabẹn, khạjạṛiko sajaoket́a hǫrte jǫm lạgit́; adǫ pẹnẹ hǫṛge sadǫmre dẹćkate bidesko oḍokena.

Calaḱ calaḱte mit́ṭẹć urni birko ńamket́a, adǫ ạyuboḱ kan iạteko mẹnket́a, Ma phul, noa birregebon gitić aṅgaḱa; ẹnte nit dǫ bela hõ bạnugića, okatebon calaḱa? Adǫ onako niṭante sadǫm khon phẹḍente sadǫm dǫ akoaḱ jaṅgareko tǫlket́koa, arko gitićena. Japit́ket́akin bar hǫṛ dǫ, mẹnkhan sodagǫrren hǫpǫn dǫ bae jạpit́ akat́a, thir akanae, bae rǫṛ baṛayet́a. Adǫ oka khon cǫṅ Bidhi ar Bidhạnta ǫnḍẹkin hẹćena, arkin teṅgoyena.

Adǫ Bidhạntae mẹnket́a, Bidhiye metae kana, Henda Bidhi, noko dǫ bhala okaren hǫṛ kanako?

Unre Bidhiye mẹnket́a, Noko dǫ disom ńẹlko oḍok akana. Adǫ Bidhi ar hõe mẹnket́a, Noko mǫtǫren mit́ hǫṛ menaea, uni madhae

---

[1] This tale was written down by Bhuju Murmu of Dhopahar. It is evidently not of Santal origin, but contains several points of interest having reference to certain superstitions current among the Santals; these will be mentioned further down. Bidhi Bidhanta, Fate and Destiny, are Aryan words and notions. The rôle in which they appear here is not the common one; but those who have written the fate of every human being on their forehead at the time of birth must be supposed to know what will happen and also how to trick fate

[2] See vol. I, p. 164, note 1.

[3] Madhae or Madhai is the title of a hypergamous sub-group of Rarhi Brahmans, a very numerous caste, having their name from Raṛh, as the north-western parts of the Burdwan division of Bengal is called. The caste of the two other ones is not mentioned. Sodagor is the Santali pronunciation (with stress on the first and the last syllables) of the Pers. saudāgar, a merchant or trader.

67. THE THREE FRIENDS AND BIDHI BIDHANTA[1].

In a certain town there lived three men, and these three men one day had a talk and made the following agreement: "We are looking alike; let us become flower-friends[2]." Now these three were not of the same caste; one was the son of a merchant, another was the son of a king, and the third was the son of a Madhae[3]. They went through the ceremony. As time passed, they one day made a plan: "Come, let us go to foreign parts and see other countries." So they provided themselves with flattened and parched rice, to have something to eat on the road, whereupon they all three mounted horses and started for foreign parts.

As they passed along, they came to a primeval forest, and as it was becoming evening, they said: "Well, flower, let us spend the night here in this forest; there is not day any longer, so where should we go?" Having decided on this, they dismounted, tied the legs of the horses[4] and lay down to sleep. Two of them fell asleep, but the merchant's son was not sleeping; he was lying quiet and did not speak. Then Bidhi and Bidhanta[5] came there from somewhere or other and halted.

Bidhanta said, that is to say, he spoke to Bidhi: "I say, Bidhi, I wonder, wherefrom these persons are."

"These," Bidhi replied, "have started on a journey to see other countries." Again Bidhi said: "Among these there is one man,

[4] Refers to a very common way of letting ponies graze, at the same time making it impossible for them to get far away. The front legs are tied together below the knees, with just enough space between the legs to allow the pony to stand and move the front legs a little. They cannot walk properly; when they want to move, it has to be done by jumping in a way. A pony tied up in this way will never be able to get far away. It looks cruel and must be painful, it seems.

[5] See above note 1.

hopon do nāhāḱ ạḍi utạr mũhĩn menaḱtaea. Ado Bidhạntae mẹnkeṭa, Acha Bidhi, masẹ lạiạńme, ceṭ ceṭ mũhĩn menaḱtaea?

Unre Bidhi lạlạie pọrtọnkeṭa, madhae hopon reaṅ, Nui sadom jaṅgareye tọl akadea; nui sadom jāhā lekae dạṛle khan doe ạtkirea nāhāḱ, ẹnẹ miṭ mũhĩn; ar miṭ mũhĩn do noa kana, calaḱako nāhāḱ, ado okare jọl panko jọma, unre nāhāḱ nạṇḍrire suiteye pạṭiḱa, adoe gujuḱa.

Ado unre Bidhạntae kulikedea, Acha Bidhi, ceṭe cekalekhan ona mũhĩn khon doe baṅcaokoḱa?

Ado Bidhiye mẹnkeṭa, Uniaṅ jọl pan dosra hoṛkin jọmle khan ẹṇḍẹ khan doe baṅcaoḱgea. Ar miṭ mũhĩn do noa kana, Calaḱ calaḱte miṭ jaegare nāhāḱ miṭṭaṅ maraṅ utạr pulko ńama, ona latarteko parọmoḱa nāhāḱ, ado ona pul do dhasao gọdọḱa; adoe gọć utạroḱa. Ona hõ Bidhạntae kuli ruạṛkedea, Acha Bidhi, ceṭe cekale khan ona mũhĩn khon doe baṅcaokoḱa?

Ado Bidhiye mẹnkeṭa, Judi ać laha sadome kamsaole khan khub āṭ, tọbẹ khan doe baṅcaokoḱgea; ado inạ miṭ mũhĩn calaoena. Ar miṭ mũhĩn do noa kana. Miṭṭaṅ urni birre nāhāḱko ńir apaṭa, ado unre rakas nāhāḱe jọmea.

Unre hõ Bidhạntae mẹnkeṭa, Ado Bidhi, acha, ona mũhĩn khor do ceṭ lekateye baṅcaokoḱa, masẹ bhala lạiạńme.

Ado arhõ Bidhi lạlạiye pọrtọnkeṭa, baṅma, Uni rakasren hopon-era menaea; uni sãoteye gatelen khan unigeye okokea. Saname lại mucạṭkeṭa, arkin calaoena.

Khange sodagọrren hopon do unkin Bidhi ar Bidhạnta reaṅ sanam kathae aṅjọmkeṭa, ar unkin ma gitićge menaḱkina, baṅkin disạyeṭa; ado aṅga marsalena, adoko mohṇḍayena. Khange thoṛa sạṅgiṅko sẹnen khange ạḍi āṭ belayena; ado jọl pan jọm lạgiṭ apan ạpin tabẹnko, khạjạṛikoko raṛakeṭa. Ado sodagor ren hopon Bidhiaḱ katha lekateye mẹnkeṭa, E phul, dẹn amaḱ tabẹn ar

6 There is no difference in the use of the two words here given for bridge, pul having come through Hindi from Persian, sakho the same way from Sanskrit. As a rule the reference is to bridges with only one span.

the son of the Madhae, he will presently be exposed to a great many dangers." Bidhanta replied: "Well, Bidhi, please tell me what the different dangers are."

Bidhi then commenced to tell about the Madhae's son: "He has tied the legs of this horse; if this horse somehow or other should shy and run, he will carry him off; that is one danger, and another is this: they will presently start; where they next take some food, he will get a needle in his throat, and so he will die."

Bidhanta then asked: "Very well, Bidhi, what could he do to be saved from this danger?"

Bidhi answered: "If somebody else took his food, he would be saved. Another danger is this: as they pass along, they will at one place come to a very big bridge[6]; they will cross below this, and this bridge will all of a sudden collapse, and he will die." Bidhanta asked a fresh question about this also: "Well, Bidhi, what could he do to be saved from this danger?"

Bidhi replied: "If he made the horse gallop at full speed in front of him, then he would he saved; so this danger would pass. Another danger is this: in a primeval forest they will get away from each other; then an ogre will eat him."

Then also Bidhanta said: "Well then, Bidhi, how could he be saved from this danger? Please tell me."

Again Bidhi commenced to tell: "The ogre has a daughter; if he made friends with her, she would hide him." He told all there was to tell, and the two went away.

The merchant's son heard all that Bidhi and Bidhanta said; the other ones were lying asleep and were not aware of anything; it dawned of day and they started. When they had proceeded some distance, the sun was high up, and they opened up their several bundles with flattened and parched rice to take some food. The merchant's son then said in accordance with Bidhi's words: "Flower, give me your flattened and parched rice and let

khạjạṛi dọ iṅiṅ jọma, ar iṅak̕ tabẹn ar khạjạṛi dọ am jọm talaṅme. Adọ onako onkaketa, adọ sạrige inạ mũhĩn khon dọe parọmena.

Adọ arhõ jọm baṛa kateko calaoena, adọ mit̕ ṭhen maraṅ utạr sakhọko ṅamketa; adọ unre hõ sodagọrren họpọne mẹnketa, Ẹ phul, ma am dọ ạḍi ãṭ jọrkate sadọm kamsaoem, ar ma lahak̕me.

Adọ kathae onkage sadọme lahakedea; adọ ạḍi jọrkate sadọme kamsaokedea, adọko parọmena. Inạ mũhĩn khon dọe baṅcaoena.

Adọ arhõko calao idiyena; adọ mit̕ṭan maraṅ utạr urni birko ṅamketa, adọko ṅir apatena. Adọ madhae họpọn dọe mẹnoana, Ọkọe tora ato sẹniṅ calak̕a, ar jọmak̕koṅ kọe baṛakoa. Adọ calak̕ calak̕te ona urni birrege rakas reaṅ mundil ṭhengeye calaoena. Adọ rakas ar rakas ren rạni dọ baṅkin tahẽkana, sendrakin sẹnlena; adọ ona takrege uni hõe sẹn sẹṭẹrena. Adọ rakasren họpọnera dọe ọḍokena, madhae họpọn dọe mẹnketa, Dẹn gọ ayo, kọe imạṅme. Adọ uni rakas họpọnera dọe mẹnketa, Kọe dọ bạṅ əmam kana; ma duṛup̕lenme. Adọ madhae họpọne mẹnketa, Baṅ, bạṅ duṛup̕ kana ạḍi ghạṛi dọ, baṅkhan rakas nãhãk̕ hẹćkateye jọmeṅa. Adọe mẹnketa, Baṅ, rakas ṭhen dọ ọhọṅ jọm ocomea; ẹnte iṅ dọ am ghạrdi jãwãe dọhọmeṅ mẹneta. Adọ ona katha aṅjọm kate madhae họpọn ạḍiye landaketa; ẹnte uni kuri ạḍi mõṅj kuṛigeye tahẽkana, ar madhaeren họpọn hõ dusạn dọ bae tahẽkana, uni hõ bes mõṅjgeye tahẽkana.

Adọ madhae họpọne mẹnketa, Acha, ma am ṭhen dọṅ tahẹngea, mẹnkhan rakas ṭhen khon baṅcaoiṅme. Adọ uni rakas họpọn-ẹra dọ uni koṛa tulạmteye pọṭọmkedea, ar mundil reaṅ cetan kandhareye okokadea; adọ thoṛa ghạṛi tayọmte rakas dọ haṛam buḍhikin hẹćena, adọ bahre khongekin metadea, Henda mại, bhala, okare manwa manwage sọ kana? Adọ uni kuṛiye mẹnketa,

7 The word translated 'palace' is commonly used about a (Hindu) temple.

8 From what is told further on it appears that the girl is not really the daughter of the ogres, but a human being kept by them.

me eat that, and you take and eat what I have." They did so, and he was really saved from this danger.

After having eaten they started and reached a very large bridge; then also the merchant's son said: "Flower, do put your horse to full-speed gallop, and get on ahead of us."

He made his horse run ahead as said; he made him gallop at full speed; and so they got across. He was saved from this danger.

So they again went along and came to a tremendous primeval forest; here they lost sight of each other. The Madhae's son said: "I shall at once go to some village and ask for food." As he went along through this primeval forest, he came to the ogre's palace[7]. The ogre and the ogre queen were not there; they had gone hunting; just at this time he reached there. The ogre's daughter[8] came out, and the Madhae's son said: "Please, my mother[9], give me something." The ogre's daughter then said: "I am not giving you anything; please, sit down." The Madhae's son replied: "No, I am not sitting down for any length of time; otherwise the ogre will come presently and eat me." She then said: "No, I shall not let you be eaten by the ogre, because I intend to keep you as a brought-in husband." When he heard this, the Madhae's son burst into laughter; the girl was a very beautiful girl; the Madhae's son was not bad to look at either; he also was a fine fellow.

The Madhae's son then said: "All right, let me stay with you then; but save me from the ogre." The ogre's daughter thereupon wrapped the young man up in cotton and hid him in an upper room of the palace. A short while afterwards the ogres, husband and wife, came, and while still outside they called out: "Look here, girl, wherefrom, I wonder, comes this smell of man?" The girl

---

9 G ọ and a y o both mean mother; many people use 'mother' when addressing even small girls; it is thought to be respectful and honorable, perhaps especially to eliminate the possibility of ungentlemanly intentions.

Iṅ kange cọṅ manwa, maben jọmeṅ khan jọmeṅben. Adọkin mẹnkeťa, Am dọ, mại, cedaǩliṅ jọmmea? Onka mẹn baṛa kate arhȭkin calaoena. Unkinkin calaoen khan dọkin goṭakeťa rakas gọćkin reaṅ. Kuṛi ma mā̃yā̃geye ại̇kạueťa, adọ uni koṛageye lại ṭhikadea, Am dọ hana dare buṭạre nā̃hā̃ǩ okokoǩme; adọ rakaskin hijuǩa, ona dareregekin ṭeṇḍaroǩa; adọ nā̃hā̃ǩ kạpite maǩ gọćkinme; adọ phaelaotelaṅ tahẹna.

Sạrige uni koṛa dọ sẹnkateye okoyena kạpiante; adọ rakas jẹmọnkin hẹćlena, tẹmọnge uni koṛa dọ banar hoṛẹ maǩ sumạrkeťkina; adọ bin bọtọrkin tahẽyena.

Tahẹn tahẹnte uni kuṛiaǩ bọhọǩ uṕ dọ ạḍi jhạlentaea, uni kuṛi dọ oṛaǩregeye tahẹna, ar uni jā̃wā̃etẹť koṛa dọ sendrae daṛana; adọ miť din gaḍate umoǩe sẹnlena, ar miťṭaṅ uṕ dọ ṅurhạyentaea, uṕ dọ samṭaokeťte sakamre pọṭọmkateye ạtu gọťkaťa. Ona latar sẹnre miťṭaṅ kā̃ṛā̃ raje umoǩ kan tahẽkana, ona uṕ dọ ẹkkalte kā̃rā̃ raj ṭhenge ạtu calaoena; kā̃ṛā̃ raj dọ onae oarkeťa, ar raṛa kateye ṅẹlkeťa, are mokakeťa, gẹl bar moka hoeyena. Adọ mọnẹ mọnẹteye mẹnkeťa, Noa uṕren mạlik dọ okareṅ ṅamea?

Adọ miťṭaṅ mirui metadea, Henda miru, am dọ noa uṕren mạlikem ṅam daṛekea, sẹ baṅ?

Adọ uni miru ạḍi bes bes jọmko emadea, arko kolkadea. Uni miru dọ ṭẽć ṭõć, ṭẽć ṭõć raǩ raǩteye calaoena. Adọ uni kuṛi menae ṭhene sẹn sorena, adọ uni reaṅ bọhọǩ uṕe gẹťkeťa ṭhọṇṭate, adọ ẹkkalte ona uṕ dọ kā̃ṛā̃ raja reaǩ oṛaǩreye ṅurhạkeťa. Adọ kā̃ṛā̃ raja mirui kulikedea, Henda miru, adọ oka naṅgrahare uni dọ menaea? Adọe lại̇adea, Hana birre miťṭaṅ ạḍi maraṅ mundil menaǩa, ona mundil bhitrire menaea.

---

10 Kāṛā in Santali means blind; but as the king of the tale has the use of his eyes, it must be a name. It is customary among the Santals to give the children the names of grand-parents, uncles and so on; if the latter have any peculiar defect, they may have been called by a name denoting this, and the later bearer of the name will inherit this nickname also, the real name being kept in the background and practically never used. Many examples might be adduced.

11 The Santali text attempts to give the sound of the parrot's screeching.

replied: "I am a human being, as you know; if you two will eat me, please do so." "Why should we eat you, girl?" they said. When they had said this, they again went away, and when they were gone, these two decided to kill the ogres. The girl felt affection for the young man, and she instructed him, saying: "Go and hide yourself presently at the foot of the tree over there; the ogres will come and lean against the tree; then cut them both down with the battle-axe and kill them; then we two shall be free and without restraint."

Truth to tell, the young man went and hid himself, taking a battle-axe with him; and as soon as the ogres came, the young man cut both of them and destroyed them; so the two lived on there without fear.

As time went, the hair of the girl grew very long; now the girl was in the habit of staying at home, while the young man, her husband, was out hunting; one day she had gone to the river to bathe, and one of her hairs came off, she wound it up, wrapped it in a leaf and let it be carried away by the floating water. Far below King Blind[10] was bathing, and the hair floated straight to this King Blind. King Blind took it out of the water; opening the wrapper he saw what it was; he measured the hair, it was twelve cubits long. He thought and thought: "Where shall I find the owner of this hair?"

Then he spoke to a parrot: "Look here, parrot, would you be able to find the owner of this hair or not?"

So they gave the parrot some very good food and sent it off. The parrot flew off screeching[11]. It went close to where the girl was, and cutting off a hair of her head with its beak it straight away let this hair fall down in the king's house. King Blind asked the parrot: "I say, parrot, in which town is she living?" The parrot told: "In the forest over there there is a very large palace; she is living in this palace."

Khange kãṛã raj do̱ uni kuṛi ạtkire reaṅe bundisket̕a, mo̱ne̱ mo̱ne̱teye me̱nket̕a, Cekate uni kuṛi do̱ṅ ạtkirkea? Ado̱e hudis ṅamket̕a, baṅma, uḍạuk̕ parko̱m benao jạruṛa. Ado̱ ać̣ren porjakoe metat̕koa, Uḍạuk̕ parko̱m benaoaṅ lạgit̕, o̱ko̱eko mistiripe baḍae akat̕koa, ạguạṅpe, baṅkhan iṅ mak̕ go̱ćpea. Mistiriko do̱ bako benao daṛeat̕ bo̱to̱rte barea mistiri do̱kin dạṛjo̱ṅ kana; ạḍi sạṅgiṅkin calaoen khan mit̕ṭen dare buṭạrekin jirạuena; laṅgayente gitićen-akin. Ona darerege cẽ̱ṛẽ̱ko ho̱po̱n akan tahẽ̱kana, mit̕ ghạṛi tayo̱m khange cẽ̱ṛẽ̱ eṅga do̱ hako ge̱rkateye he̱ćena, are ajo̱ako kana. Khange cẽ̱ṛẽ̱ ho̱po̱nko me̱nket̕a, Baṅle jo̱ma, ale latarre barea manwa menak̕kina, unkinem emakin khan ale hõ̱le jo̱ma, baṅkhan do̱ baṅ. Cẽ̱ṛẽ̱ren eṅgat apat do̱kin me̱nket̕a, Henda ho̱po̱n, unkin manwa do̱ be̱re̱lte ma bakin jo̱m, se̱ṅge̱l do̱ okarekin ṅama? Ado̱ ho̱po̱nko me̱nket̕a, Se̱ṅge̱l do̱ noa abonak̕ tukạ thoṛabon ṅũr ạkina; ado̱ onakin ghasaole khange se̱ṅge̱l do oḍokok̕a, ado̱kin rapak̕ jo̱mea.

Ado̱ mit̕ṭaṅ hakoko ṅũrat̕kina, ar thoṛa tukạ, ado̱ onakin ghasaoket̕a ar se̱ṅge̱l oḍokena, ado̱kin rapak̕ jo̱mkedea, biyenakin; ado̱ ho̱po̱n hõ̱ko jo̱m biyena. Khange cẽ̱ṛẽ̱ eṅga do̱ unkin manwae kuliket̕kina, Henda ho, aben do̱ okaren kanaben?

Ado̱kin lạiket̕a, baṅma, Ạliṅ do̱ phalna naṅgraharen kanaliṅ, uni kãṛã raj menae, unige ale do̱e laga ṅirket̕lea.

Ado̱ cẽ̱ṛẽ̱kin me̱nket̕a, Cet̕ karo̱nte uni raj do̱e lagaket̕pea. Ado̱kin me̱nket̕a, Karo̱n do̱ noa kana, uni kãṛã raj do̱ uḍạuk̕ parko̱me ṅam kana; ado̱ baṅle benao daṛeak̕ kana; ona edrete ale do̱e laga ṅirket̕lea.

Cẽ̱ṛẽ̱ do̱kin me̱nket̕a, Acha noa reaṅ do̱ cet̕ bhabna hõ̱ baṅ kana. Ma aben do̱ noa ale menak̕le dare reaṅ mit̕ṭaṅ ḍạr magben,

[12] The Santals know how to produce fire by friction. They take a small piece of fairly soft wood and a small stick of some hard wood and put some dry inflammable stuff on the soft wood that is kept lying on the ground. The small stick is then taken between the palms of the hands and turned round, the one end being kept firmly on the piece of soft wood. It takes about ten minutes to get fire in this way, and as it is rather tiring, usually two persons take turns 'drilling'. The

King Blind then speculated on how he should carry off this girl; he was saying to himself: "How shall I manage to carry off this girl?" Then he hit upon an idea, viz., it will be necessary to get a flying bedstead made. So he ordered his tenants, saying: "Bring me the carpenters you know to make me a flying bedstead; if you do not, I shall cut you down and kill you." Fearing that they would not be able to make such a thing two carpenters were running away; when they had got far away, they rested at the foot of a tree; they were tired and lay down. In this tree some birds had their youngs, and a short while afterwards the birds' mother came with a fish in her beak and was going to feed her youngs; but these said: "We will not eat; here below us are two human beings; if you give them, we also shall eat, otherwise not." The bird parents then said: "Look here, children, these two human beings do not eat anything raw; where will they get a fire?" The young birds answered: "We shall let a little of this nest of ours fall down to them; when they rub this, fire will come out[12], and so they will fry and eat the fish."

So they let a fish fall down to them and a little of the nest; they rubbed this, and fire came out, whereupon the two men fried and ate the fish; they were satisfied both of them, and the young birds also ate and had enough. The bird mother then asked the two men: "I say, wherefrom are you?"

They told, saying: "We are from such and such a town, where King Blind lives; he has driven us away."

The two birds then asked: "What was the reason that he drove you away?" They replied: "The reason was this: King Blind wants a flying bedstead; and we are quite unable to make such a one; being angry for this he drove us away."

The birds said: "Very well, there is no need to be troubled over this. You two cut a branch of this tree in which we are

writer has seen it done by Santals; now it is scarcely ever done; matches are to be had everywhere.

ar ona reaṅ miṭṭaṅ uḍạuk̓ parkǫm benaoben, ar benaokate nonka rǫṛben, Uṛ khaṭlạ uṛ jao, adǫ nãhãk̓ uḍạuk̓a.

Adǫ unkinkin mẹnlet̓ lekakin banaoket̓a, ar cẽṛẽkin mẹnlet̓ lekage parkǫmre ḍẹćentekin rǫṛket̓a, Uṛ khaṭlạ uṛ jao, ẹkdǫm sẹ kãṛã rajakẹ gharmẹ bạiṭh jao. Adǫ sạrige uḍạuena, ẹkkalte kãṛã rajak̓ oṛak̓te, adǫ racare ńũrena. Kãṛã raj dǫ ona ńẹlkate ạḍiye rạskạyena; adǫ aćren mạli buḍhiye metadea, Am dǫ, mạli buḍhi, noa uḍạuk̓ parkǫmre dẹćkate hạni rakas hǫpǫnera ṭhen calak̓me, ar uni jãhã lekatem dẹć ạgule khan ạḍi boge hoekok̓a.

Adǫ uni mạli buḍhiye calaoena ẹkkalte uni rạni oṛak̓te, uniak̓ oṛak̓re dǫ bae dǫhǫlet̓a; oka darhare uni kuṛiye umok̓ ona darha bhitrireye unum oṭokat̓a, ar ać dǫ kuṛiak̓ oṛak̓teye calaoena. Adǫ uni kuṛiye metadea, Henda mại, am dǫ okarem umok̓ kana? Delaṅlaṅ um hijuk̓a.

Kuṛiye mẹnket̓a, Dela ẹnte gǫṛǫmlaṅ um hijuk̓a. Adǫ uni kuṛi ar uni buḍhi darhate umok̓kin calaoena.

Adǫ oka darhare uḍạuk̓ parkǫme dǫhǫlet̓a, ona darhategekin calaoena; adǫ umok̓kin bǫlǫyena. Buḍhi dǫ thoṛa bhitri ńǫ̃k̓e bǫlǫyena; oka ṭhen uḍạuk̓ parkǫme unum akat̓ bǫlǫkate onaregeye duṛup̓ena, kuṛi ma aće umok̓ ghaṭreye bǫlǫ akan. Adǫ buḍhiye mẹnet̓a, Henda mại, nǫtẹ dǫ bam bǫlǫk̓a? Nǫṇḍẹ cǫṅ ạḍi mǫ̃ńj duṛup̓ jaega menak̓. Adǫ uni kuṛiye mẹnket̓a, Sạrige, gǫṛǫm? Uni buḍhiye rǫṛ ruạṛket̓a, Hẽ, sạrige.

Adǫ uni kuṛi buḍhi menae ṭhene sẹnena. Buḍhi dǫe rǫṛ gǫt̓ket̓a, Noare gǫṛǫm duṛup̓katelaṅ iskirok̓a. Adǫ napae onare duṛup̓-

[13] The flying bedstead is naturally addressed in a Hindi dialect.

[14] It is not clear whether it is a female gardener or the wife of the gardener, probably the latter; anyhow it is an old woman that may be used as a go-between. These characters are not uncommon.

[15] The girl is called a queen; one living in such a grand palace could not be less.

[16] Gǫṛǫm is used about a namesake, mostly about grand-parents and grand-children having the same name. 'Namesakes' are permitted to joke with each other. The narrator does not explain the apparent intimacy between these two women.

and make from this a flying bedstead; when you have made it, speak in this way[13]: 'Flugbett, fliege fort'; then it will immediately fly."

So they made a bedstead, as they had told them, and in accordance with what the two birds had said they mounted the bedstead and said: "Flugbett, fliege fort; geh sogleich und setze uns in König Blinds Haus nieder." Truth to tell, it flew away straight to King Blind's house, where it settled down in the courtyard. Seeing this King Blind was very pleased; he spoke to his woman gardener[14]: "You woman gardener, mount this flying bedstead and go to the daughter of yonder ogre, and if you somehow or other could make her mount this and bring her here, it would be very well."

The gardener woman went away straight to the house of this queen[15]; she did not, however, put the bedstead down in her house; she sank it in the pool where the girl was in the habit of bathing, whereupon she herself went to the girl's house. Here she spoke to the girl: "I say, my girl, where do you bathe? Come along, let us go and have a bath."

"Come along then, granny," the girl replied, "let us go and have a bath." Whereupon the girl and the old woman went to the pool to bathe.

They went to the pool in which she had left the flying bedstead and entered the water to bathe. The old woman went into fairly deep water, and, having reached where she had put the flying bedstead, she sat down on this, while the girl had entered the water at the place where she was in the habit of bathing. The old woman then spoke: "I say, my girl, will you not come out here? Here is a splendid place to sit down." "Is it really so, granny?" the girl asked. "Yes, it is true," the old woman answered.

The girl then went to where the old woman was sitting, and the old woman said: "We shall sit down, namesake[16], and let us have some

katekin iskir barak̕ kana. Ado uni kuri bae badaejon̕ kana, je nui budhi do kãrã raj thene idiyin̕ lagit̕; ado uni budhi do bai baite nonkae rorket̕a, Ur khatla ur jao, ekdom se kãrã rajake pas jakar baith jao. Ado ina rortege ona parkom do dak̕ khon adi cot apir rakap̕ena. [17]Ado ekkalte kãrã raj rean̕ racare senkate phedena. Ado uni kuriak̕ up̕ do ekkalte racare taseyentaea. Kãrã raj odokenteye n̕elket̕a, up̕ do sarige adi jelen̕taea. Ado unre rani do kãrã raje metae kana, Henda raj, am do cedak̕em agu akadin̕a?

Unre kãrã raj doe ror ruarket̕a, Am dohome lagit̕in̕ agu akat̕mea; adom tahena se ban̕?

Ado uni kuriye menket̕a, Henda raja, nonka do cet̕ leka? Am do raja lekan hor, bapla katege bam aguyin̕a? In̕ do okate hõ con̕ ban̕ daret̕a; ruarkan̕me, ado nendakate calak̕me. Adoe ruarkadea.

Ina tayom khange uniren jãwãe do banteko goc̕kedea. Uni kuri do adi bhabnaye aikauket̕a, auriye gujuk̕reye laiadea, In̕ak̕ hormo reak̕ tinak̕ toroc̕ nãhãk̕ hoyok̕a, ona am do sanam har samtaokate nawa bhajanre dohokam. Ado sarige uniye metade lekae kamiket̕a.

Ado ona dinrege unkin pahilkin senlen Kamru disom khon adi lekan bidia cet̕katekin hec̕ena, ar uni rani thenkin boloyena arkin kulikedea, Henda, rani, nonde madhaeren hopone tahẽkana, adoe okayena?

Uni kuri doe ror ruarketa, Ogni bante kãrã rajae goc̕kedea. Adokin menket̕a, Acha, jãhãn nisan dom doho akat̕a se ban̕?

---

[17] Tase is mostly used about spreading out for drying.

[18] Ban, adopted in Santali from Hindi, originally means an arrow or a dart. In Santali it is used about the 'darts' that witches and bongas blow out to destroy people; the word is often equivalent to 'sorcery' or 'magic.' See the writer's The Santals and Disease (Memoirs, As. Soc. of Bengal, Vol. X) p. 101. Ogni ban is a special form of the magic dart, mentioned in folk tales. Ogni is the Bengali form of agni, fire.

massage." They sat nicely down on the bedstead and were giving each other massage. Now the girl did not know that the old woman was going to take her to King Blind; and the old woman spoke very low saying: "Flugbett, fliege fort, sogleich geh gerade nach König Blinds Haus und setze uns dort nieder." At this word the bedstead rose out of the water and flew off high into the air, and going straight to King Blind's courtyard went down there. And the girl's hair was at once spread out[17] on the courtyard. King Blind came out and saw that her hair was really very long. Then the queen said to King Blind: "I say, raja, why have you brought me here?"

King Blind answered: "I have brought you here to have you; will you stay or not?"

The girl then said: "Look here, raja, how is this? You are a kingly person; will you not bring me properly after having married me? I am not running away anywhere; send me back, and come after having fixed a day." So the king sent her back.

After this they killed her husband by magic[18]. The girl was feeling great grief; before he died, her husband had said to her: "Collect all the ashes that may be found of my body and put them in a new vessel." And she really actually did as he had instructed her.

Now that very day the two other ones who had formerly gone away came back from Kamru's country after having acquired many kinds of knowledge[19] there; they went in to the queen and asked her: "Listen, queen, the Madhae's son was here; where has he gone?"

The girl replied: "King Blind has killed him with the fiery arrow[18] of black magic." They said: "Well, have you kept any mark of him or not?"

19 The two lost friends are reintroduced; they are supposed to have been to Kamru's country, famed in Santal folklore as the country of occult wisdom, magic, witchcraft and medicine. See The Santals and Disease, pp. 128 ss.

Adọ uni kuṛiye mẹnketa, Mẹn oṭoadiṅae, nawa bhajanre tọrọć dọkhọ, adọṅ dọhọ akatgea. Adọkin metadea, Dẹn ẹnḍẹ khan ạguime. Adọ oṛakre bọlọkateye oḍok ạguatkina.

Adọ kathae, Kạmru disọm reak rankin lagaoata; adọ thoṛa ghạṛi khange hoṛẹ benaoena pạhil leka, cet leka muṭhạn tahẽkantaea onkage. Adọ pẹnẹ hoṛ mit muṭhạngeako, okọe hõ bae orom daṛeako kana, metakme nui doe iṅren jãwãe kanae mẹnte.

Adọ nẹnḍa din tioken khan kãṛã raj dọ ạdi utạr phạd ante uni kuṛi ṭhene calaoena; adọ un jọkhẹnge onkoko mẹnketa, Bhala kãṛã rajbon ńẹlea tin maraṅ hoṛ kanae, aboren erae baplaye lạgit. Adọ ghaṭa mạrko lạṛhạiyena ạdi ghạṛić; onko pẹ hoṛ sãote baṅko daṛelena, sanamko gọć ocoyena; kãṛã raj hõko gọćkedea.

---

20 What is here told may possibly be a reference to polyandry. Such may be said to be found among the Santals (as among numerous other races) in a form that permits or tolerates sexual intercourse between the wife of a man and his younger brothers. It is undoubtedly found; much depends on the parties, both the elder

The girl replied: "Before he died, he told me to keep his ashes in a new vessel, and I have done so." "Do bring this then," they said to her. Whereupon she went in and brought this out to them.

They then, people tell, applied the medicine of Kamru's country, and in a short while he became a man again like formerly, looking just like he formerly did. Now these three were all looking exactly alike; she was unable to distinguish one from the other, or to say, this one is my husband[20].

When the day fixed arrived, King Blind went with a tremendous host of attendants to the girl. At this time these three men said: "Well, we shall have a look at King Blind and see how big a man he is, since he is going to marry our wife." Hereupon they fought furiously for a long while; but they were no match for these three; they were all killed; they killed King Blind also

brother and the woman; the younger brothers have no rights. See the writer's paper On Taboo and Customs connected therewith among the Santals (Journal A. S. B., Vol. LXVII, Part III, pp. 8 and 9.